Lecture Notes in Computer Science 2992
Edited by G. Goos, J. Hartmanis, and J. van Leeuwen

AF614013

Dear MyCopy Customer,

This Springer book is a monochrome print version of the eBook to which your library gives you access via SpringerLink. It is available to you at a subsidized price since your library subscribes to at least one Springer eBook subject collection.

Please note that MyCopy books are only offered to library patrons with access to at least one Springer eBook subject collection. MyCopy books are strictly for individual use only.

You may cite this book by referencing the bibliographic data and/or the DOI (Digital Object Identifier) found in the front matter. This book is an exact but monochrome copy of the print version of the eBook on SpringerLink.

Springer-Verlag
Berlin Heidelberg GmbH

Elisa Bertino Stavros Christodoulakis
Dimitris Plexousakis Vassilis Christophides
Manolis Koubarakis Klemens Böhm
Elena Ferrari (Eds.)

Advances in Database Technology - EDBT 2004

9th International Conference on Extending Database Technology
Heraklion, Crete, Greece, March 14-18, 2004
Proceedings

Volume Editors

Elisa Bertino
Università degli Studi di Milano, Dipartimento di Informatica e Communicazione
E-mail: bertino@dico.unimi.it

Stavros Christodoulakis
Technical University of Crete, Department of Electronic and Computer Engineering
E-mail: stavros@ced.tuc.gr

Dimitris Plexousakis
Vassilis Christophides
Institute of Computer Science, Foundation for Research and Technology Hellas
E-mail: {dp,christoph}@ics.forth.gr

Manolis Koubarakis
Technical University of Crete, Department of Electronic and Computer Engineering
E-mail: manolis@intelligence.tuc.gr

Klemens Böhm
Universität Magdeburg, Institut für Technische und Betriebliche Informationssysteme
E-mail: klemens.boehm@iti.cs.uni-magdeburg.de

Elena Ferrari
Università dell'Insubria, Dipartimento di Scienze Chimiche, Fisiche e Matematiche
E-mail: elena.ferrari@uninsubria.it

Cataloging-in-Publication Data applied for

A catalog record for this book is available from the Library of Congress.

Bibliographic information published by Die Deutsche Bibliothek
Die Deutsche Bibliothek lists this publication in the Deutsche Nationalbibliografie; detailed bibliographic data is available in the Internet at <http://dnb.ddb.de>.

CR Subject Classification (1998): H.2, H.4, H.3, C.2.4, K.4.4

ISSN 0302-9743
DOI 10.1007/978-3-540-24741-8

This work is subject to copyright. All rights are reserved, whether the whole or part of the material is concerned, specifically the rights of translation, reprinting, re-use of illustrations, recitation, broadcasting, reproduction on microfilms or in any other way, and storage in data banks. Duplication of this publication or parts thereof is permitted only under the provisions of the German Copyright Law of September 9, 1965, in its current version, and permission for use must always be obtained from Springer-Verlag. Violations are liable for prosecution under the German Copyright Law.

Springer-Verlag is a part of Springer Science+Business Media

springeronline.com

© Springer-Verlag Berlin Heidelberg 2004

MyCopy version of the original edition 2004

Typesetting: Camera-ready by author, data conversion by PTP-Berlin, Protago-TeX-Production GmbH
Printed on acid-free paper SPIN: 10989685 06/3142 5 4 3 2 1 0
www.springer.com/mycopy

Preface

The 9th International Conference on Extending Database Technology, EDBT 2004, was held in Heraklion, Crete, Greece, during March 14–18, 2004. The EDBT series of conferences is an established and prestigious forum for the exchange of the latest research results in data management. Held every two years in an attractive European location, the conference provides unique opportunities for database researchers, practitioners, developers, and users to explore new ideas, techniques, and tools, and to exchange experiences. The previous events were held in Venice, Vienna, Cambridge, Avignon, Valencia, Konstanz, and Prague.

EDBT 2004 had the theme "new challenges for database technology," with the goal of encouraging researchers to take a greater interest in the current exciting technological and application advancements and to devise and address new research and development directions for database technology. From its early days, database technology has been challenged and advanced by new uses and applications, and it continues to evolve along with application requirements and hardware advances. Today's DBMS technology faces yet several new challenges. Technological trends and new computation paradigms, and applications such as pervasive and ubiquitous computing, grid computing, bioinformatics, trust management, virtual communities, and digital asset management, to name just a few, require database technology to be deployed in a variety of environments and for a number of different purposes. Such an extensive deployment will also require trustworthy, resilient database systems, as well as easy-to-manage and flexible ones, to which we can entrust our data in whatever form they are.

The call for papers attracted a very large number of submissions, including 294 research papers and 22 software demo proposals. The program committee selected 42 research papers, 2 industrial and application papers, and 15 software demos. The program was complemented by three keynote speeches, by Rick Hull, Keith Jeffery, and Bhavani Thuraisingham, and two panels.

This volume collects all papers and software demos presented at the conference, in addition to an invited paper. The research papers cover a broad variety of topics, ranging from well-established topics like data mining and indexing techniques to more innovative topics such as peer-to-peer systems and trustworthy systems. We hope that these proceedings will serve as a valuable reference for data management researchers and developers.

Many people contributed to EDBT 2004. Clearly, foremost thanks go to the authors of all submitted papers. The increased number of submissions, compared to the previous years, showed that the database area is nowadays a key technological area with many exciting research directions. We are grateful for the dedication and hard work of all program committee members who made the review process both thorough and effective. We also thank the external referees for their important contribution to the review process.

In addition to those who contributed to the review process, there are many others who helped to make the conference a success. Special thanks go to Lida Harami for maintaining the EDBT 2004 conference Web site, to Christiana Daskalaki for helping with the proceedings material, and to Triaena Tours and Congress for the logistics and organizational support. The financial and in-kind support by the conference sponsors is gratefully acknowledged.

December 2003

Elisa Bertino, Stavros Christodoulakis
Dimitris Plexousakis
Vassilis Christophides, Manolis Koubarakis
Klemens Böhm, Elena Ferrari

Organization

General Chair: Stavros Christodoulakis, Technical University of Crete, Greece
Program Committee Chair: Elisa Bertino, University of Milan, Italy
Executive Chair: Dimitris Plexousakis, University of Crete, and ICS-FORTH, Greece
Industrial and Applications Chair: Vassilis Christophides, University of Crete, and ICS-FORTH, Greece
Proceedings Chair: Manolis Koubarakis, Technical University of Crete, Greece
Panel and Tutorial Chair: Klemens Bohm, University of Magdeburg, Germany
Software Demonstration Chair: Elena Ferrari, University of Insubria-Como, Italy

Program Committee
Suad Alagic (University of Southern Maine, USA)
Walid Aref (Purdue University, USA)
Bernd Amann (CNAM and INRIA, France)
Paolo Atzeni (Università Roma Tre, Italy)
Alberto Belussi (University of Verona, Italy)
Boualem Benatallah (University of New South Wales, Australia)
Phil Bernstein (Microsoft Research, USA)
Michela Bertolotto (University College Dublin, Ireland)
Philippe Bonnet (University of Copenhagen, Denmark)
Athman Bouguettaya (Virginia Tech, USA)
Luca Cardelli (Microsoft Research, UK)
Barbara Catania (Università di Genova, Italy)
Wojciech Cellary (Technical University of Poznan, Poland)
Ming-Syan Chen (National Taiwan University, Taiwan)
Panos Chrysantis (University of Pittsburgh, USA)
Cristine Collet (University of Grenoble, France)
Sara Comai (Politecnico di Milano, Italy)
Theo Dimitrakos (Rutherford Appleton Laboratory, UK)
Klaus Dittrich (University of Zurich, Switzerland)
Max Egenhofer (University of Maine, USA)
Wei Fan (IBM Research, USA)
Fosca Giannotti (CNR Pisa, Italy)
Giovanna Guerrini (Università di Pisa, Italy)
Mohand-Said Hacid (Université Claude Bernard Lyon 1, France)
Cristian Jensen (Aalborg University, Denmark)
Leonid Kalinichenko (Russian Academy of Sciences, Russia)
Daniel A. Keim (University of Konstanz, Germany)

Masaru Kitsuregawa (University of Tokyo, Japan)
Vijay Kumar (University of Missouri-Kansas City, USA)
Alex Labrinidis (University of Pittsburgh, USA)
Alberto Laender (Universidade Federal de Minas Gerais, Brazil)
Ling Liu (Georgia Institute of Technology, USA)
Fred Lochovsky (HKUST, Hong Kong)
David Lomet (Microsoft Research, USA)
Guy Lohman (IBM Research, USA)
Yannis Manolopoulos (Aristotle University, Greece)
Tova Milo (Tel Aviv University, Israel)
Bernhard Mitschang (University of Stuttgart, Germany)
Danilo Montesi (University of Bologna, Italy)
John Mylopoulos (University of Toronto, Canada)
Erich Neuhold (Fraunhofer IPSI, Germany)
Beng Chin Ooi (National University of Singapore)
Dimitris Papadias (HKUST, Hong Kong)
Evi Pitoura (University of Ioannina, Greece)
Jaroslav Pokorny (Charles University, Czech Republic)
Indrakshi Ray (Colorado State University, USA)
Krithi Ramamritham (IIT Bombay, India)
Tore Risch (Uppsala University, Sweden)
Mark Roantree (Dublin City University, Ireland)
Yucel Saygin (Sabanci University, Turkey)
Timos Sellis (National Technical University of Athens, Greece)
Kian-Lee Tan (National University of Singapore, Singapore)
Evimaria Terzi (University of Helsinki, Finland)
Costantino Thanos (CNR Pisa, Italy)
Athena Vakali (Aristotle University, Greece)
Kyu-Young Whang (Korea Advanced Institute of Science and Technology, Korea)
Philip Yu (IBM Research, USA)
Donghui Zhang (Northeastern University, USA)

Additional Referees

Ashraf Aboulnaga
Debopam Acharya
Charu Aggarwal
Mohammad Salman Akram
Mohamed Hassan Ali
Mourad Alia
Toshiyuki Amagasa
Anastasia Analyti
Torben Bach Pedersen
Miriam Baglioni
Spyridon Bakiras
Miroslav Balik
Roger Barga
Terry Bearly
Jonathan Beaver
Khalid Belhajjame
Salima Benbernou
Omar Benjelloun
Djamal Benslimane
Christophe Bobineau
Klemens Bohem
Francesco Bonchi

Alexander Borgida
Burak Borhan
Daniele Braga
Marco Brambilla
David Briggs
Agne Brilingaite
Linas Bukauskas
Benjamin Bustos
Luca Cabibbo
Diego Calvanese
Elena Camossi
Alessandro Campi
James Carswell
Joyce Carvalho
James Caverlee
Ugur Cetintemel
Chee-Yong Chan
Surajit Chaudhuri
Keke Chen
Wan-Sup Cho
Eliseo Clementini
Gregory Cobena
Edith Cohen
Latha Colby
Carlo Combi
Antonio Corral
Bi-Ru Dai
Theodore Dalamagas
Daniela Damm
Clodoveu Augusto Davis, Jr.
Yang Du
Marlon Dumas
Mohamed Galal Elfeky
Mohamed Yassin Eltabakh
Mohamed Eltoweissy
Pin-Kwang Eng
Ozgur Ercetin
Peter Fankhauser
Marie-Christine Fauvet
Alfio Ferrara
Beatrice Finance
Piero Fraternali
Michael Fuchs
Irini Fundulaki
Andrea Fusiello
Venky Ganti
Nimisha Garg
Bugra Gedik
Floris Geerts
Thanaa Ghanem
Aristides Gionis
Francois Goasdoue
Kazuo Goda
Andy Gordon
Roop Goyal
Goetz Graefe
Sergio Greco
David Gross-Amblard
Anne H.H. Ngu
Moustafa Hammad
Wei Han
Takahiro Hara
Weiping He
Mauricio A. Hernandez
Thomas B. Hodel
Mintz Hsieh
Xuegang Harry Huang
Michael Hui
Ihab F. Ilyas
Francesco Isgrò
Yoshiharu Ishikawa
Tamer Kahveci
Seung-Shik Kang
Murat Kantarcioglu
Verena Kantere
Haim Kaplan
Norio Katayama
Dimitris Katsaros
Zoubida Kedad
Mehmet Keskinoz
Thomas Klement
Predrag Knezevic
Georgia Koloniari
Maria Kontaki
Manolis Koubarakis
Yannis Kouvaras
P. Krishna Reddy
Kari Laasonen
Cyril Labbé
Juliano Palmieri Lage

Paul Larson
Alexandre Lefebvre
Patrick Lehti
Ilya Leontiev
Hanyu Li
Dan Lin
Bin Liu
Kaiyang Liu
Ken-Hao Liu
Sofian Maabout
Paola Magillo
Matteo Magnani
Bendick Mahleko
Zaki Malik
Nikos Mamoulis
Ioana Manolescu
Manuk Manukyan
Marcello Mariucci
Volker Markl
Stefania Marrara
Dmitry Martynov
Alessio Mazzanti
Eoin McLoughlin
Brahim Medjahed
Michele Melchiori
Marco Mesiti
Jun Miyazaki
Irena Mlynkova
Mohamed F. Mokbel
Anirban Mondal
Kyriakos Mouratidis
Claudio Muscogiuri
Jussi Myllymaki
Miyuki Nakano
Mirco Nanni
Alexandros Nanopoulos
Benjamin Nguyen
Claudia Niederee
Andrea Nucita
Dympna O'Sullivan
Francesca Odone
Tadashi Ohmori
Barbara Oliboni
Mourad Ouzzani
Helen Hye-young Paik
George Pallis
Euthymios Panagos
HweeHwa Pang
Christian Panse
Dimitris Papadias
Apostolos Papadopoulos
Yannis Papakonstantinou
Henrique Paques
Kostas Patroubas
Vanessa de Paula Braganholo
Dino Pedreschi
Peter Peinl
Fragkiskos Pentaris
Olivier Perrin
Jean-Marc Petit
Simon Peyton Jones
Dieter Pfoser
Willy Picard
Pascal Poncelet
George Potamias
Nitin Prabhu
Iko Pramudiono
Vijayshankar Raman
Lakshmish Ramaswamy
Ralf Rantzau
Indrajit Ray
Chiara Renso
Abdelmounaam Rezgui
Salvatore Rinzivillo
Stefano Rizzi
Daniel Rocco
Claudia-Lucia Roncancio
Rosalba Rossato
Marie-Christine Rousset
Stefano Rovetta
Prasan Roy
Jarogniew Rykowski
Simonas Saltenis
Sunita Sarawagi
Albrecht Schmidt
Jörn Schneidewind
Michel Scholl
Tobias Schreck
Holger Schwarz
Shetal Shah

Mohamed A. Sharaf
Qiongmao Shen
Richard Sidle
Altigran Soares da Silva
Giuseppe Sindoni
Aameek Singh
Mike Sips
Hala Skaf-Molli
Spiros Skiadopoulos
Halvard Skogsrud
Nikolay Skvortsov
Vaclav Snasel
Mudhakar Srivatsa
Fariza Tahi
Takayuki Tamura
Wei Tang
Yufei Tao
Wei-Guang Teng
Manolis Terrovitis
Theodosios Theodosiou
Leonardo Tininini
Kamil Toman
Vojtech Toman
Kristian Torp
F. Toumani
Farouk Toumani
Masashi Toyoda
Alberto Trombetta
Vassilis Tsotras
Grigorios Tsoumakas
Anthony K.H. Tung
Gokhan Tur
Genoveva Vargas-Solar
Michael Vassilakopoulos
Panos Vassiliadis
Alessandro Verri
Victor Vianu
Dan Vodislav
Tuyet-Trinh Vu
Jurate Vysniauskaite
Brian Walenz
Botao Wang
Jiying Wang
Min Wang
Markus Wawryniuk
Fang Wei
Andreas Wombacher
Hao Chi Wong
Raymond Wong
Kun-lung Wu
Yuqing Wu
Chenyi Xia
Tian Xia
Li Xiong
Xiaopeng Xiong
Jie Xu
Xifeng Yan
Xu Yang
Quan Z. Sheng
Nikolay Zemtsov
Jianjun Zhang
Jun Zhang
Rui Zhang
Panfeng Zhou
Patrick Ziegler

Table of Contents

Invited Papers

Distributed, Mobile, and Peer-to-Peer Database Systems

Data Mining and Knowledge Discovery

Trustworthy Database Systems

Innovative Query Processing Techniques for XML Data

Data and Information Management on the Web

Innovative Modelling Concepts for Spatial and Temporal Databases

Query Processing Techniques for Spatial Databases

Foundations of Query Processing

Advanced Query Processing and Optimization

Query Processing Techniques for Stream Data

Analysis and Validation Techniques for Data and Schemas

Multimedia and Quality-Aware Systems

Indexing Techniques

Imprecise Information and Approximate Queries

Industrial Papers

Demo Papers

Converged Services: A Hidden Challenge for the Web Services Paradigm

Richard Hull

Bell Labs Research, Lucent Technologies, Murray Hill, NJ 07974

The web has brought a revolution in sharing information and in human-computer interaction. The web services paradigm (based initially on standards such as SOAP, WSDL, UDDI, BPEL) will bring the next revolution, enabling flexible, intricate, and largely automated interactions between web-resident services and applications. But the telecommunications world is also changing, from isolated, monolithic legacy stove-pipes, to a much more modular, internet-style framework that will enable rich flexibility in creating communication and collaboration services. This will be enabled by the existing Parlay/OSA standard and emerging standards for all-IP networks, (e.g., 3GPP IMS). We are evolving towards a world of "converged" services, not two parallel worlds of web services vs. telecom services.

Converged services will arise in a variety of contexts, e.g., e-commerce and mobile commerce, collaboration systems, interactive games, education, and entertainment. This talk begins by discussing standards for the web and telecom, identifying key aspects that may need to evolve as the two networks converge. We then highlight research challenges created by the emergence of converged services along three dimensions: (1) profile data management, (2) preferences management, and (3) services composition. For (1) we describe a proposal from the wireless telecom community for giving services the end-user profile data they need, while respecting end-user concerns re privacy and data sharing [SHLX03]. For (2) we describe an approach to supporting high-speed preferences management, whereby service providers can inexpensively cater to the needs of a broad variety of applications and categories of end-users [HKL+03b,HKL+04]. We also discuss the issue of "federated policy management", which arises because policies around end-user preferences will be distributed across multiple applications and network components [HKL03a]. For (3) we discuss an emerging technology for composing web services based on behavioral signatures [BFHS03,HBCS03] and a key contrast between web services and telecom services [CKH+01].

References

[BFHS03] T. Bultan, Z. Fu, R. Hull, and J. Su. Conversation specification: A new approach to design and analysis of e-service composition. In *Proc. 12th World Wide Web Conf. (WWW)*, May 2003.

[CKH+01] V. Christophides, G. Karvounarakis, R. Hull, A. Kumar, G. Tong, and M. Xiong. Beyond discrete e-services: Composing session-oriented services in telecommunications. In *Proc. of Workshop on Technologies for E-Services (TES); Springer LNCS volume 2193*, September 2001.

E. Bertino et al. (Eds.): EDBT 2004, LNCS 2992, pp. 1–2, 2004.
© Springer-Verlag Berlin Heidelberg 2004

[HBCS03] R. Hull, M. Benedikt, V. Christophides, and J. Su. E-Services: A look behind the curtain. In *Proc. ACM Symp. on Principles of Databases (PODS)*, San Diego, CA, June 2003.

[HKL03a] R. Hull, B. Kumar, and D. Lieuwen. Towards federated policy management. In *Proc. IEEE 4th Intl. Workshop on Policies for Distributed Systems and Networks (Policy2003)*, Lake Como, Italy, June 4-6 2003.

[HKL+03b] R. Hull, B. Kumar, D. Lieuwen, P. Patel-Schneider, A. Sahuguet, S. Varadarajan, and A. Vyas. Everything personal, not just business: Improving user experience through rule-based service customization. In *Proc. Intl. Conf. on Service Oriented Computing (ICSOC)*, 2003.

[HKL+04] R. Hull, B. Kumar, D. Lieuwen, P. Patel-Schneider, A. Sahuguet, S. Varadarajan, and A. Vyas. Enabling context-aware and privacy-conscious user data sharing. In *Proc. IEEE International Conference on Mobile Data Management*, Berkeley, CA, 2004.

[SHLX03] Arnaud Sahuguet, Richard Hull, Daniel Lieuwen, and Ming Xiong. Enter Once, Share Everywhere: User Profile Management in Converged Networks. In *Proc. Conf. on Innovative Database Research(CIDR)*, January 2003.

GRIDS, Databases, and Information Systems Engineering Research

Keith G. Jeffery

Director, IT and Head, Information Technology Department
CCLRC Rutherford Appleton Laboratory
Chilton, Di2ot, OXON OX11 0QX UK
k.g.jeffery@rl.ac.uk
http://www.itd.clrc.ac.uk/Person/K.G.Jeffery

Abstract. GRID technology, emerging in the late nineties, has evolved from a metacomputing architecture towards a pervasive computation and information utility. However, the architectural developments echo strongly the computational origins and information systems engineering aspects have received scant attention. The development within the GRID community of the W3C-inspired OGSA indicates a willingness to move in a direction more suited to the wider end user requirements. In particular the OGSA/DAI initiative provides a web-services level interface to databases. In contrast to this stream of development, early architectural ideas for a more general GRIDs environment articulated in UK in 1999 have recently been more widely accepted, modified, evolved and enhanced by a group of experts working under the auspices of the new EC DGINFSO F2 (GRIDs) Unit. The resulting report on 'Next Generation GRIDs' was published in June 2003 and is released by the EC as an adjunct to the FP6 Call for Proposals Documentation. The report proposes the need for a wealth of research in all aspects of information systems engineering, within which the topics of advanced distributed parallel multimedia heterogeneous database systems with greater representativity and expressivity have some prominence. Topics such as metadata, security, trust, persistence, performance, scalability are all included. This represents a huge opportunity for the database community, particularly in Europe.

1 Introduction

The concept of the GRID was initiated in the USA in the late 1990s. Its prime purpose was to couple supercomputers in order to provide greater computational power and to utilise otherwise wasted central processor cycles. Starting with computer-specialised closed systems that could not interoperate, the second generation consists essentially of middleware which schedules a computational task as batch jobs across multiple computers. However, the end-user interface is procedural rather than fully declarative and the aspects of resource discovery, data interfacing and process-process interconnection (as in workflow for a business process) are primitive compared with work on information systems engineering involving, for example, databases and web services.

E. Bertino et al. (Eds.): EDBT 2004, LNCS 2992, pp. 3–16, 2004.
© Springer-Verlag Berlin Heidelberg 2004

Through GGF (Global GRID Forum) a dialogue has evolved the original GRID architecture to include concepts from the web services environment. OGSA (Open Grid Services Architecture) with attendant interfaces (OGSI) is now accepted by the GRID community and OGSA/DAI (Data Access interface) provides an interface to databases at rather low level.

In parallel with this metacomputing GRID development, an initiative started in UK has developed an architecture for GRIDs that combines metacomputing (i.e. computation) with information systems. It is based on the argument that database R&D (research and development) – or more generally ISE (Information Systems Engineering) R&D - has not kept pace with the user expectations raised by WWW. Tim Berners-Lee threw down the challenge of the semantic web and the web of trust [1]. The EC (European Commission) has argued for the information society, the knowledge society and the ERA (European Research Area) – all of which are dependent on database R&D in the ISE sense. This requires an open architecture embracing both computation and information handling, with integrated detection systems using instruments and with an advanced user interface providing 'martini' (anytime, anyhow, anywhere) access to the facilities. The GRIDs concept [6] addresses this challenge, and further elaboration by a team of experts has produced the EC-sponsored document 'Next Generation GRID' [3].

It is time for the database community (in the widest sense, i.e. the information systems engineering community) to take stock of the research challenges and plan a campaign to meet them with excellent solutions, not only academically or theoretically correct but also well-engineered for end-user acceptance and use.

2 GRIDs

2.1 The Idea

In 1998-1999 the UK Research Council community was proposing future programmes for R&D. The author was asked to propose an integrating IT architecture [6]. The proposal was based on concepts including distributed computing, metacomputing, metadata, agent- and broker-based middleware, client-server migrating to three-layer and then peer-to-peer architectures and integrated knowledge-based assists. The novelty lay in the integration of various techniques into one architectural framework.

2.2 The Requirement

The UK Research Council community of researchers was facing several IT-based problems. Their ambitions for scientific discovery included post-genomic discoveries, climate change understanding, oceanographic studies, environmental pollution monitoring and modelling, precise materials science, studies of combustion processes, advanced engineering, pharmaceutical design, and particle physics data handling and simulation. They needed more processor power, more data storage capacity, better analysis and visualisation – all supported by easy-to-use tools controlled through an intuitive user interface.

On the other hand, much of commercial IT (Information Technology) including process plant control, management information and decision support systems, IT-assisted business processes and their re-engineering, entertainment and media systems and diagnosis support systems all require ever-increasing computational power and expedited information access, ideally through a uniform system providing a seamless information and computation landscape to the end-user. Thus there is a large potential market for GRIDs systems.

The original proposal based the academic development of the GRIDs architecture and facilities on scientific challenging applications, then involving IT companies as the middleware stabilised to produce products which in turn could be taken up by the commercial world. During 2000 the UK e-Science programme was elaborated with funding starting in April 2001.

2.3 Architecture Overview

The architecture proposed consists of three layers (Fig.1). The computation / data grid has supercomputers, large servers, massive data storage facilities and specialised devices and facilities (e.g. for VR (Virtual Reality)) all linked by high-speed networking and forms the lowest layer. The main functions include compute load sharing / algorithm partitioning, resolution of data source addresses, security, replication and message rerouting. This layer also provides connectivity to detectors and instruments. The information grid is superimposed on the computation / data grid and resolves homogeneous access to heterogeneous information sources mainly through the use of metadata and middleware. Finally, the uppermost layer is the knowledge grid which utilises knowledge discovery in database technology to generate knowledge and also allows for representation of knowledge through scholarly works, peer-reviewed (publications) and grey literature, the latter especially hyperlinked to information and data to sustain the assertions in the knowledge.

The concept is based on the idea of a uniform landscape within the GRIDs domain, the complexity of which is masked by easy-to-use interfaces.

2.4 The GRID

In 1998 – in parallel with the initial UK thinking on GRIDs - Ian Foster and Carl Kesselman published a collection of papers in a book generally known as 'The GRID Bible' [4]. The essential idea is to connect together supercomputers to provide more power – the metacomputing technique. However, the major contribution lies in the systems and protocols for compute resource scheduling. Additionally, the designers of the GRID realised that these linked supercomputers would need fast data feeds so developed GRIDFTP. Finally, basic systems for authentication and authorisation are described. The GRID has encompassed the use of SRB (Storage Request Broker)

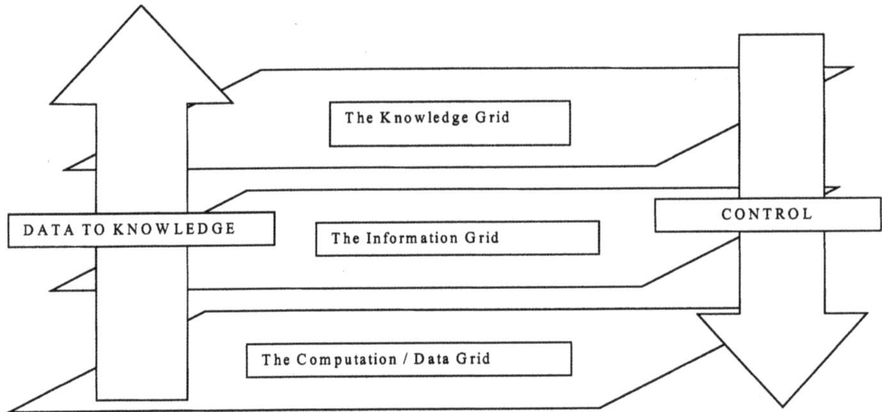

Fig. 1. Grids Architecture

from SDSC (San Diego Supercomputer Centre) for massive data handling. SRB has its proprietary metadata system to assist in locating relevant data resources. It also uses LDAP as its directory of resources. The GRID corresponds to the lowest grid layer (computation / data layer) of the GRIDs architecture.

3 The GRIDs Architecture

3.1 Introduction

The idea behind GRIDs is to provide an IT environment that interacts with the user to determine the user requirement for service and then, having obtained the user's agreement to 'the deal' satisfies that requirement across a heterogeneous environment of data stores, processing power, special facilities for display and data collection systems (including triggered automatic detection instruments) thus making the IT environment appear homogeneous to the end-user.

Referring to Fig. 2, the major components external to the GRIDs environment are:
a) users: each being a human or another system;
b) sources: data, information or software
c) resources: such as computers, sensors, detectors, visualisation or VR (virtual reality) facilities

Each of these three major components is represented continuously and actively within the GRIDs environment by:
1) metadata: which describes the external component and which is changed with changes in circumstances through events
2) an agent: which acts on behalf of the external resource representing it within the GRIDs environment.

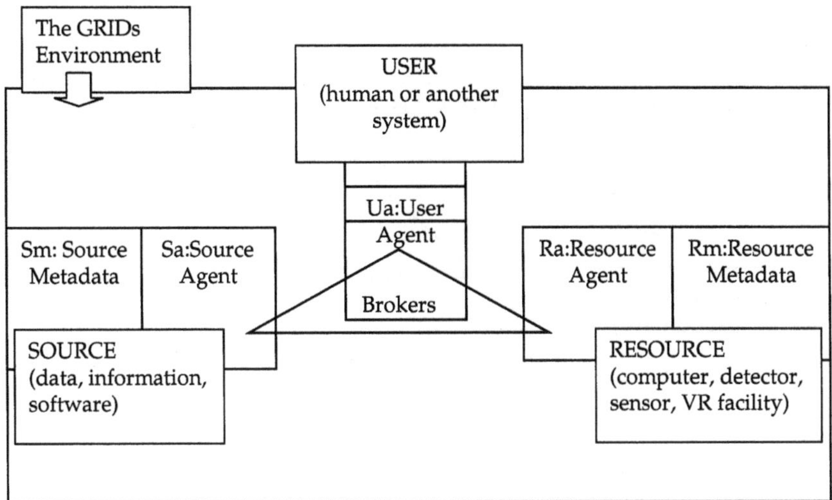

Fig. 2. The GRIDs Components

As a simple example, the agent could be regarded as the answering service of a person's mobile phone and the metadata as the instructions given to the service such as 'divert to service when busy' and / or 'divert to service if unanswered'.

Finally there is a component which acts as a 'go between' between the agents. These are brokers which, as software components, act much in the same way as human brokers by arranging agreements and deals between agents, by acting themselves (or using other agents) to locate sources and resources, to manage data integration, to ensure authentication of external components and authorisation of rights to use by an authenticated component and to monitor the overall system.
From this it is clear that they key components are the metadata, the agents and the brokers.

3.2 Metadata

Metadata is data about data [7]. An example might be a product tag attached to a product (e.g. a tag attached to a piece of clothing) that is available for sale. The metadata on the product tag tells the end-user (human considering purchasing the article of clothing) data about the article itself – such as the fibres from which it is made, the way it should be cleaned, its size (possibly in different classification schemes such as European, British, American) and maybe style, designer and other useful data. The metadata tag may be attached directly to the garment, or it may appear in a catalogue of clothing articles offered for sale (or, more usually, both). The metadata may be used to make a selection of potentially interesting articles of clothing before the actual articles are inspected, thus improving convenience. Today this concept is widely-used. Much e-commerce is based on B2C (Business to Customer) transactions based on an online catalogue (metadata) of goods offered. One well-known example is www.amazon.com.

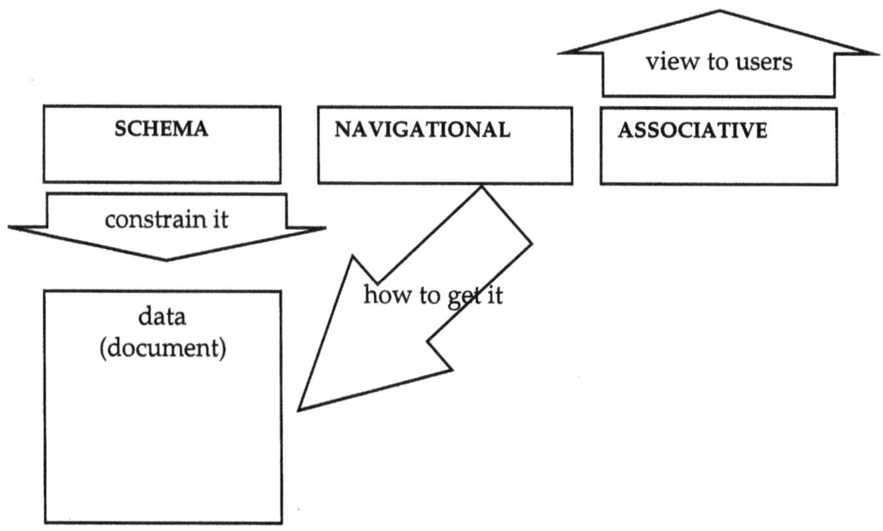

Fig. 3. Metadata Classification

What is metadata to one application may be data to another. For example, an electronic library catalogue card is metadata to a person searching for a book on a particular topic, but data to the catalogue system of the library which will be grouping books in various ways: by author, classification code, shelf position, title – depending on the purpose required.

It is increasingly accepted that there are several kinds of metadata. The classification proposed (Fig. 3) is gaining wide acceptance and is detailed below.

Schema Metadata. Schema metadata constrains the associated data. It defines the intension whereas instances of data are the extension. From the intension a theoretical universal extension can be created, constrained only by the intension. Conversely, any observed instance should be a subset of the theoretical extension and should obey the constraints defined in the intension (schema). One problem with existing schema metadata (e.g. schemas for relational DBMS) is that they lack certain intensional information that is required [8]. Systems for information retrieval based on, e.g. the SGML (Standard Generalised Markup Language) DTD (Document Type Definition) experience similar problems.

It is noticeable that many ad hoc systems for data exchange between systems send with the data instances a schema that is richer than that in conventional DBMS – to assist the software (and people) handling the exchange to utilise the exchanged data to best advantage.

Navigational Metadata. Navigational metadata provides the pathway or routing to the data described by the schema metadata or associative metadata. In the RDF model it is a URL (universal resource locator), or more accurately, a URI (Universal Resource Identifier). With increasing use of databases to store resources, the most common navigational metadata now is a URL with associated query parameters embedded in the string to be used by CGI (Common Gateway Interface) software or proprietary software for a particular DBMS product or DBMS-Webserver software pairing.

The navigational metadata describes only the physical access path. Naturally, associated with a particular URI are other properties such as:
a) security and privacy (e.g. a password required to access the target of the URI);
b) access rights and charges (e.g. does one have to pay to access the resource at the URI target);
c) constraints over traversing the hyperlink mapped by the URI (e.g. the target of the URI is only available if previously a field on a form has been input with a value between 10 and 20). Another example would be the hypermedia equivalent of referential integrity in a relational database;
d) semantics describing the hyperlink such as 'the target resource describes the son of the person described in the origin resource'
However, these properties are best described by associative metadata which then allows more convenient co-processing in context of metadata describing both resources and hyperlinks between them and – if appropriate - events.

Associative Metadata. In the data and information domain associative metadata can describe:
a) a set of data (e.g. a database, a relation (table) or a collection of documents or a retrieved subset). An example would be a description of a dataset collected as part of a scientific mission;
b) an individual instance (record, tuple, document). An example would be a library catalogue record describing a book ;
c) an attribute (column in a table, field in a set of records, named element in a set of documents). An example would be the accuracy / precision of instances of the attribute in a particular scientific experiment ;
d) domain information (e.g. value range) of an attribute. An example would be the range of acceptable values in a numeric field such as the capacity of a car engine or the list of valid values in an enumerated list such as the list of names of car manufacturers;
e) a record / field intersection unique value (i.e. value of one attribute in one instance) This would be used to explain an apparently anomalous value.

In the relationship domain, associative metadata can describe relationships between sets of data e.g. hyperlinks. Associative metadata can – with more flexibility and expressivity than available in e.g. relational database technology or hypermedia document system technology – describe the semantics of a relationship, the constraints, the roles of the entities (objects) involved and additional constraints.

In the process domain, associative metadata can describe (among other things) the functionality of the process, its external interface characteristics, restrictions on utilisation of the process and its performance requirements / characteristics.

In the event domain, associative metadata can describe the event, the temporal constraints associated with it, the other constraints associated with it and actions arising from the event occurring.

Associative metadata can also be personalised: given clear relationships between them that can be resolved automatically and unambiguously, different metadata describing the same base data may be used by different users.

Taking an orthogonal view over these different kinds of information system objects to be described, associative metadata may be classified as follows:
1) descriptive: provides additional information about the object to assist in understanding and using it;
2) restrictive: provides additional information about the object to restrict access to authorised users and is related to security, privacy, access rights, copyright and IPR (Intellectual Property Rights);
3) supportive: a separate and general information resource that can be cross-linked to an individual object to provide additional information e.g. translation to a different language, super- or sub-terms to improve a query – the kind of support provided by a thesaurus or domain ontology;
Most examples of metadata in use today include some components of most of these kinds but neither structured formally nor specified formally so that the metadata tends to be of limited use for automated operations – particularly interoperation – thus requiring additional human interpretation.

3.3 Agents

Agents operate continuously and autonomously and act on behalf of the external component they represent. They interact with other agents via brokers, whose task it is to locate suitable agents for the requested purpose. An agent's actions are controlled to a large extent by the associated metadata which should include either instructions, or constraints, such that the agent can act directly or deduce what action is to be taken. Each agent is waiting to be 'woken up' by some kind of event; on receipt of a message the agent interprets the message and – using the metadata as parametric control – executes the appropriate action, either communicating with the external component (user, source or resource) or with brokers as a conduit to other agents representing other external components.

An agent representing an end-user accepts a request from the end-user and interacts with the end-user to refine the request (clarification and precision), first based on the user metadata and then based on the results of a first attempt to locate (via brokers and other agents) appropriate sources and resources to satisfy the request. The proposed activity within GRIDs for that request is presented to the end-user as a 'deal' with any costs, restrictions on rights of use etc. Assuming the user accepts the offered deal, the GRIDs environment then satisfies it using appropriate resources and sources and finally sends the result back to the user agent where – again using metadata – end-user presentation is determined and executed.

An agent representing a source will – with the associated metadata – respond to requests (via brokers) from other agents concerning the data or information stored, or the properties of the software stored. Assuming the deal with the end-user is accepted, the agent performs the retrieval of data requested, or supply of software requested.

An agent representing a resource – with the associated metadata – responds to requests for utilisation of the resource with details of any costs, restrictions and relevant capabilities. Assuming the deal with the end-user is accepted the resource agent then schedules its contribution to providing the result to the end-user.

3.4 Brokers

Brokers act as 'go betweens' between agents. Their task is to accept messages from an agent which request some external component (source, resource or user), identify an external component that can satisfy the request by its agent working with its associated metadata and either put the two agents in direct contact or continue to act as an intermediary, possibly invoking other brokers (and possibly agents) to handle, for example, measurement unit conversion or textual word translation.

Other brokers perform system monitoring functions including overseeing performance (and if necessary requesting more resources to contribute to the overall system e.g. more networking bandwidth or more compute power). They may also monitor usage of external components both for statistical purposes and possibly for any charging scheme.

3.5 The Components Working Together

Now let us consider how the components interact. An agent representing a user may request a broker to find an agent representing another external component such as a source or a resource. The broker will usually consult a directory service (itself controlled by an agent) to locate potential agents representing suitable sources or resources. The information will be returned to the requesting (user) agent, probably with recommendations as to order of preference based on criteria concerning the offered services. The user agent matches these against preferences expressed in the metadata associated with the user and makes a choice. The user agent then makes the appropriate recommendation to the end-user who in turn decides to 'accept the deal' or not.

4 Ambient Computing

The concept of ambient computing implies that the computing environment is always present and available in an even manner. The concept of pervasive computing implies that the computing environment is available everywhere and is 'into everything'. The concept of mobile computing implies that the end-user device may be connected even when on the move. In general usage of the term, ambient computing implies both pervasive and mobile computing.

The idea, then, is that an end-user may find herself connected (or connectable – she may choose to be disconnected) to the computing environment all the time. The computing environment may involve information provision (access to database and web facilities), office functions (calendar, email, directory), desktop functions (word processing, spreadsheet, presentation editor), perhaps project management software and systems specialised for her application needs – accessed from her end-user device connected back to 'home base' so that her view of the world is as if at her desk. In addition entertainment subsystems (video, audio, games) should be available.

A typical configuration might comprise:
a) a headset with earphone(s) and microphone for audio communication, connected by bluetooth wireless local connection to
b) a PDA (personal digital assistant) with small screen, numeric/text keyboard (like a telephone), GSM/GPRS (mobile phone) connections for voice and data, wireless LAN connectivity and ports for connecting sensor devices (to measure anything close to the end-user) in turn connected by bluetooth to
c) an optional notebook computer carried in a backpack (but taken out for use in a suitable environment) with conventional screen, keyboard, large hard disk and connectivity through GSM/GPRS, wireless LAN, cable LAN and dial-up telephone;
The end-user would perhaps use only (a) and (b) (or maybe (b) alone using the built in speaker and microphone) in a social or professional context as mobile phone and 'filofax', and as entertainment centre, with or without connectivity to 'home base' servers and IT environment. For more traditional working requiring keyboard and screen the notebook computer would be used, probably without the PDA. The two might be used together with data collection validation / calibration software on the notebook computer and sensors attached to the PDA.

The balance between that (data, software) which is on servers accessed over the network and that which is on (one of) the end-user device(s) depends on the mode of work, speed of required response and likelihood of interrupted connections. Clearly the GRIDs environment is ideal for such a user to be connected.

Such a configuration is clearly useful for a 'road warrior' (travelling salesman), for emergency services such as firefighters or paramedics, for businessmen, for production industry managers, for the distribution / logistics industry (warehousing, transport, delivery), for scientists in the field... and also for leisure activities such as mountain walking, visiting an art gallery, locating a restaurant or visiting an archaeological site.

5 The Challenges

Such an IT architectural environment inevitably poses challenging research issues. The major ones are:

5.1 Metadata

Since metadata is critically important for interoperation and semantic understanding, there is a requirement for precise and formal representation of metadata to allow automated processing. Research is required into the metadata representation language expressivity in order to represent the entities user, source, resource. For example, the existing Dublin Core Metadata standard [2] is machine-readable but not machine-understandable, and furthermore mixes navigational, associative descriptive and associative restrictive metadata. A formal version has been proposed [Je99].

5.2 Agents

There is an interesting research area concerning the generality or specificity of agents. Agents could be specialised for a particular task or generalised and configured dynamically for the task by metadata. Furthermore, agents may well need to be reactive and dynamically reconfigured by events / messages. This would cause a designer to lean towards general agents with dynamic configuration, but there are performance, reliability and security issues. In addition there are research issues concerning the syntax and semantics of messages passed between agents and brokers to ensure optimal representation with appropriate performance and security.

5.3 Brokers

A similar research question is posed for brokers – are they generalised and dynamic or specific? However, brokers have not just representational functions, they have also to negotiate. The degree of autonomy becomes the key research issue: can the broker decide by itself or does it solicit input from the external entity (user, source, resource) via its agent and metadata? The broker will need general strategic knowledge (negotiation techniques) but the way a broker uses the additional information supplied by the agents representing the entities could be a differentiating factor and therefore a potential business benefit. In addition there are research issues concerning the syntax and semantics of messages passed between brokers to ensure optimal representation with appropriate performance and security.

5.4 Security

Security is an issue in any system, and particularly in a distributed system. It becomes even more important if the system is a common marketplace with great heterogeneity of purpose and intent. The security takes the forms:

a) prevention of unauthorised access: this requires authentication of the user, authorisation of the user to access or use a source or resource and provision or denial of that access. The current heterogeneity of authentication and authorisation mechanisms provides many opportunities for deliberate or unwitting security exposure;
b) ensuring availability of the source or resource: this requires techniques such as replication, mirroring and hot or warm failover. There are deep research issues in transactions and rollback/recovery and optimisation;
c) ensuring continuity of service: this relates to (b) but includes additional fallback procedures and facilities and there are research issues concerning the optimal (cost-effective) assurance of continuity.

In the case of interrupted communication there is a requirement for synchronisation of the end-user's view of the system between that which is required on the PDA and / or laptop and the servers.

There are particular problems with wireless communications because of interception. Encryption of sensitive transmissions is available but there remain research issues concerning security assurance.

5.5 Privacy

The privacy issues concern essentially the tradeoff of personal information provision for intelligent system reaction. There are research issues on the optimal balance for particular end-user requirements. Furthermore, data protection legislation in countries varies and there are research issues concerning the requirement to provide data or to conceal data.

5.6 Trust

When any end-user purchases online (e.g. a book from www.amazon.com) there is a trust that the supplier will deliver the goods and that the purchaser's credit card information is valid. This concept requires much extension in the case of contracts for supply of engineered components for assembly into e.g. a car. The provision of an e-marketplace brings with it the need for e-tendering, e-contracts, e-payments, e-guarantees as well as opportunities to re-engineer the business process for effectiveness and efficiency. This is currently a very hot research topic since it requires the representation in an IT system of artefacts (documents) associated with business transactions.

5.7 Interoperability

There is a clear need to provide the end-user with homogeneous access to heterogeneous information sources. His involves schema reconciliation / mapping and associated transformations. Associated with this topic are requirements for languages that are more representative (of the entities / objects in the real world) and more expressive (in expressing the transformations or operations). Recent R&D [10],[9] has indicated that graphs provide a neutral basis for the syntax with added value in graph properties such that structural properties may be used.

5.8 Data Quality

The purpose of data, especially when structured in context as information, is to represent the world of interest. There are real research issues in ensuring this is true – especially when the data is incomplete or uncertain, when the data is subject to certain precision, accuracy and associated calibration constraints or when only by knowing its provenance can a user utilise it confidently.

5.9 Performance

The architecture opens the possibility of, knowing the characteristics of data / information, software and processing power on each node , generating optimal execution plans. Refinements involve data movement (expensive if the volumes are large) or program code movement (security implications) to appropriate nodes.

6 Conclusion

The GRIDs architecture will provide an IT infrastructure to revolutionise and expedite the way in which we do business and achieve leisure. The Ambient Computing architecture will revolutionise the way in which the IT infrastructure intersects with our lives, both professional and social. The two architectures in combination will provide the springboard for the greatest advances yet in Information Technology. This can only be achieved by excellent R&D leading to commercial take-up and development of suitable products, to agreed standards, ideally within an environment such as W3C (the World Wide Web Consortium). The current efforts in GRID computing have moved some way away from metacomputing and towards the architecture described here with the adoption of OGSA (Open Grids Services Architecture). However, there is a general feeling that Next Generation GRID requires an architecture rather like that described here, as reported in the Report of the EC Expert Group on the subject [3].

Acknowledgements. Some of the material presented here has appeared in previous papers by the author. Although the author remains responsible for the content, many of the ideas have come from fruitful discussions not only with the author's own team at CCLRC-RAL but also with many members of the UK science community and the UK Computer Science / Information systems community. The author has also benefited from discussions in the contexts of ERCIM (www.ercim.org), W3C (www.w3.org) and the EC NGG Group.

References

[1] Berners-Lee, T; 'Weaving the Web' 256 pp Harper, San Francisco September 1999 ISBN 0062515861
[2] http://purl.oclc.org/2/
[3] www.cordis.lu/ist/grids/index.htm
[4] I Foster and C Kesselman (Eds). The Grid: Blueprint for a New Computing Infrastructure. Morgan-Kauffman 1998
[5] Jeffery, K G: 'An Architecture for Grey Literature in a R&D Context' Proceedings GL'99 (Grey Literature) Conference Washington 2 October 1999 http://www.konbib.nl/greynet/frame4.htm
[6] Original Paper on GRIDs, unpublished, available from the author
[7] K G Jeffery. 'Metadata': in Brinkkemper, J; Lindencrona, E; Solvberg, A: 'Information Systems Engineering' Springer Verlag, London 2000. ISBN 1-85233-317-0.
[8] K G Jeffery, E K Hutchinson, J R Kalmus, M D Wilson, W Behrendt, C A Macnee, 'A Model for Heterogeneous Distributed Databases' Proceedings BNCOD12 July 1994; LNCS 826 pp 221-234 Springer-Verlag 1994
[9] Kohoutkova, J; 'Structured Interfaces for Information Presentation' PhD Thesis, Masaryk University, Brno, Czech Republic
[10] Skoupy, K; Kohoutkova, J; Benesovsky, M; Jeffery, K G: 'Hypermedata Approach: A Way to Systems Integration' Proceedings Third East European Conference, ADBIS'99, Maribor, Slovenia, September 13-16, 1999, Published: Institute of Informatics, Faculty of Electrical Engineering and Computer Science, Smetanova 17, IS-2000 Maribor, Slovenia,1999, ISBN 86-435-0285-5, pp 9-15

Security and Privacy for Web Databases and Services

Elena Ferrari[1] and Bhavani Thuraisingham[2]

[1] Università dell'Insubria, 22100 Como, Italy
[2] The National Science Foundation, Arlington, VA, USA

Abstract. A semantic web can be thought of as a web that is highly intelligent and sophisticated and one needs little or no human intervention to carry out tasks such as scheduling appointments, coordinating activities, searching for complex documents as well as integrating disparate databases and information systems. While much progress has been made toward developing such an intelligent web, there is still a lot to be done. For example, there is little work on security and privacy for the semantic web. However, before we examine security for the semantic web we need to ensure that its key components, such as web databases and services, are secure. This paper will mainly focus on security and privacy issues for web databases and services. Finally, some directions toward developing a secure semantic web will be provided.

1 Introduction

Recent developments in information systems technologies have resulted in computerizing many applications in various business areas. Data has become a critical resource in many organizations, and, therefore, efficient access to data, sharing the data, extracting information from the data, and making use of the information has become an urgent need. As a result, there have been many efforts on not only integrating the various data sources scattered across several sites, but also on extracting information from these databases in the form of patterns and trends. These data sources may be databases managed by Database Management Systems (DBMSs), or they could be data warehoused in a repository from multiple data sources. The advent of the World Wide Web (WWW) in the mid 1990s has resulted in even greater demand for managing data, information, and knowledge effectively. There is now so much data on the web that managing them with conventional tools is becoming almost impossible. As a results, to provide interoperability as well as warehousing between multiple data sources and systems, and to extract information from the databases and warehouses on the web, various tools are being developed.

As the demand for data and information management increases, there is also a critical need for maintaining the security of the databases, applications, and information systems. Data and information have to be protected from unauthorized access as well as from malicious corruption. With the advent of the web

E. Bertino et al. (Eds.): EDBT 2004, LNCS 2992, pp. 17–28, 2004.
© Springer-Verlag Berlin Heidelberg 2004

it is even more important to protect the data and information as numerous individuals now have access to them. Therefore, we need effective mechanisms for securing data and applications. The web is now evolving into the semantic web. Semantic web is about ensuring that web pages can be read and understood by machines. The major components for the semantic web include web infrastructures, web databases and services, and ontology management and information integration. There has been a lot of work on each of these three areas. However, very little work has been devoted to security. If the semantic web is to be effective, we need to ensure that the information on the web is protected from unauthorized accesses and malicious modifications. We also need to ensure that individual's privacy is maintained. This paper focuses on security and privacy related to one of the component for the semantic web, that is, for web databases and services.

The organization of this paper is as follows. In Section 2 we give some background information on web databases and services. Security and privacy for web databases will be discussed in Section 3, whereas security and privacy for web services will be discussed in Section 4. Some issues on developing a secure semantic web will be discussed in Section 5. The paper is concluded in Section 6.

2 Background on Web Databases and Services

This paper focuses on security and privacy for web databases and services and therefore in this section we provide some background information about them.

2.1 Web Data Management

A major challenge for web data management is coming up with an appropriate data representation scheme. The question is: is there a need for a standard data model? Is it at all possible to develop such a standard? If so, what are the relationships between the standard model and the individual models used by the databases on the web? The significant development for web data modeling came in the latter part of 1996 when the World Wide Web Consortium (W3C) [15] was formed. This group felt that web data modeling was an important area and began addressing the data modeling aspects. Then, sometime around 1997 interest in XML (Extensible Markup Language) began. This was an effort of the W3C. XML is not a data model. It is a metalanguage for representing documents. The idea is that if documents are represented using XML then these documents can be uniformly represented and therefore exchanged on the web. Database management functions for the web include those such as query processing, metadata management, security, and integrity. Querying and browsing are two of the key functions. First of all, an appropriate query language is needed. Since SQL is a popular language, appropriate extensions to SQL may be desired. XML-QL and XQuery [15] are moving in this direction. Query processing involves developing a cost model. Are there special cost models for Internet database management? With respect to browsing operations, the query processing techniques have to be integrated with techniques for following links. That is, hypermedia technology has to be integrated with database management technology. Transaction management is essential for many applications. There may be new kinds of transactions for web data management. For example, various items may be sold through the Internet. In this case, the item should not be locked immediately when a potential buyer makes a bid. It has to be left open until several bids are received and the item is sold. That is, special transaction models are needed. Appropriate concurrency control and recovery techniques have to be developed for the transaction models. Metadata management is also a major concern. The question is, what is metadata? Metadata describes all of the information pertaining to a data source. This could include the various web sites, the types of users, access control issues, and policies enforced. Where should the metadata be located? Should each participating site maintain its own metadata? Should the metadata be replicated or should there be a centralized metadata repository? Storage management for Internet database access is a complex function. Appropriate index strategies and access methods for handling multimedia data are needed. In addition, due to the large volumes of data, techniques for integrating database management technology with mass storage technology are also needed. Maintaining the integrity of the data is critical. Since the data may originate from multiple sources around the world, it will be difficult to keep tabs on the accuracy of the data. Appropriate data quality maintenance techniques need thus be developed. Other data management functions include integrating heterogeneous databases, managing multimedia data, and mining. Security and privacy is a major challenge. This is one of the main focus areas for this paper and will be discussed in Section 3.

2.2 Web Services

Web services can be defined as an autonomous unit of application logic that provides either some business functionality features or information to other applications through an Internet connection. They are based on a set of XML standards, namely, the Simple Object Access Protocol (SOAP) [15] – to expose the service functionalities, the Web Services Description Language (WSDL) [15] – to provide an XML-based description of the service interface, and the Universal Description, Discovery and Integration (UDDI) [16] – to publish information regarding the web service and thus making this information available to potential clients. UDDI provides an XML-based structured and standard description of web service functionalities, as well as searching facilities to help in finding the provider(s) that better fit the client requirements. More precisely, an UDDI registry is a collection of entry, each of one providing information on a specific web service. Each entry is in turn composed by five main data structures `businessEntity`, `businessService`, `bindingTemplate`, `publisherAssertion`, and `tModel`, which provide different information on the web service. For instance, the `BusinessEntity` data structure provides overall information about the organization providing the web service, whereas the `BusinessService` data structure provides a technical description of the service.

Searching facilities provided by UDDI registries are of two different types, which result in two different types of inquiries that can be submitted to an UDDI registry: *drill-down pattern inquiries* (i.e., get_xxx API functions), which return a whole core data structure (e.g., `businessTemplate`, `businessEntity`), and *browse pattern inquiries* (i.e., find_xxx API functions), which return overview information about the registered data.

As far as architectural aspects are concerned, three are the main entities composing the Web Service Architecture (WSA): the *service provider*, which is the person or organization that provides the web service, the *service requestor*, which is a person or organization that wishes to make use of the services offered by a provider for achieving its business requirements, and the *discovery agency*, which manages UDDI registries. UDDI registries can be implemented according to either a third-party or a two-party architecture, with the main difference that in a two-party architecture there is no distinction between the service provider and the discovery agency, whereas in a third-party architecture the discovery agency and the service provider are two separate entities. It is important to note that today third-party architectures are becoming more and more widely used for any web-based system, due to their scalability and the ease with which they are able to manage large amount of data and large collections of users.

3 Security and Privacy for Web Databases

Security issues for web databases include secure management of structured databases as well as unstructured and semistructured databases, and privacy issues. In the following sections we discuss all these aspects.

3.1 Security for Structured Databases on the Web

A lot of research has been done for developing access control models for Relational and Object-oriented DBMSs [6]. For example, today most of the commercial DBMSs rely on the System R access control model. However, the web introduces new challenges. For instance, a key issue is related to the population accessing web databases which is greater and more dynamic than the one accessing conventional DBMSs. This implies that traditional identity-based mechanisms for performing access control are not enough. Rather a more flexible way of qualifying subjects is needed, for instance based on the notion of role or credential. Next we need to examine the security impact on all of the web data management functions. These include query processing, transaction management, index and storage management, and metadata management. For example, query processing algorithms may need to take into consideration the access control policies. We also need to examine the trust that must be placed in the modules of the query processor. Transaction management algorithms may also need to consider the security policies. For example, the transaction will have to ensure that the integrity as well as security constraints are satisfied. We need to examine the security impact in various indexing and storage strategies. For example, how do we store the databases on the web that will ease the enforcement of security policies? Metadata includes not only information about the resources, which includes databases and services, it also includes security policies. We need efficient metadata management techniques for the web as well as use metadata to enhance security.

3.2 Security for XML, RDF, and Ontology Databases

As we evolve the web into the semantic web, we need the capability to manage XML and RDF databases. This means that we need to ensure secure access to these databases.

Various research efforts have been reported for securing XML documents and XML databases [11]. Here, we briefly discuss some of the key points. XML documents have graph structures. The main challenge is thus to develop an access control model which exploits this graph structure in the specification of policies and which is able to support a wide spectrum of access granularity levels, ranging from sets of documents, to single documents, to specific portions within a document, as well as the possibility of specifying both content-dependent and content-independent access control policies. A proposal in this direction is the access control model developed in the framework of the Author-$\mathcal{X}$ project [5], which provides the support for both access control as well as dissemination policies. Policies are specified in XML and contain information about which subjects can access which portions of the documents. Subjects are qualified by means of credentials, specified using XML. In [5] algorithms for access control as well as computing views of the results are also presented. In addition, architectures for securing XML documents are also discussed. In [3] the authors go further and describe how XML documents may be securely published on the web. The idea is for owners to publish documents, subjects to request access to the documents, and untrusted publishers to give the subjects the views of the documents they are authorized to see, making at the same time the subjects able to verify the authenticity and completeness of the received answer.

The W3C [15] is also specifying standards for XML security. The XML security project is focusing on providing the implementation of security standards for XML. The focus is on XML-Signature Syntax and Processing, XML-Encryption Syntax and Processing, and XML Key Management. While the standards are focusing on what can be implemented in the near-term lot of research is needed on securing XML documents. The work reported in [5] is a good start.

Berners Lee who coined the term semantic web (see [2]) has stressed that the key to developing a semantic web is efficiently managing RDF documents. That is, RDF is fundamental to the semantic web. While XML is limited in providing machine understandable documents, RDF handles this limitation. As a result, RDF provides better support for interoperability as well as searching and cataloging. It also describes contents of documents as well as relationships between various entities in the document. While XML provides syntax and notations, RDF supplements this by providing semantic information in a standardized way. Now to make the semantic web secure, we need to ensure that RDF documents are secure. This would involve securing XML from a syntactic point of view. However with RDF we also need to ensure that security is preserved at the semantic level. The issues include the security implications of the concepts resource, properties and statements that are part of the RDF specification. That is, how is access control ensured? How can one provide access control at a fine granularity level? What are the security properties of the container model? How can bags, lists and alternatives be protected? Can we specify security policies in RDF? How can we solve semantic inconsistencies for the policies? How can we express security constraints in RDF? What are the security implications of statements about statements? How can we protect RDF schemas? These are difficult questions and we need to start research to provide answers. XML security is just the beginning. Securing RDF is much more challenging.

Another aspect of web data management is managing ontology databases. Now, ontologies may be expressed in RDF and related languages. Therefore, the issues for securing ontologies may be similar to securing RDF documents. That is, access to the ontologies may depend on the roles of the user, and/or on the credentials he or she may possess. On the other hand, one could use ontologies to specify security policies. That is, ontologies may help in securing the semantic web. We need more research in this area.

3.3 Privacy for Web Databases

Privacy is about protecting information about individuals. Privacy has been discussed a great deal in the past especially when it relates to protecting medical information about patients. Social scientists as well as technologists have been working on privacy issues. However, privacy has received enormous attention during the past year. This is mainly because of the advent of the web and now the semantic web, counter-terrorism and national security. For example, in order to extract information from databases about various individuals and perhaps prevent and/or detect potential terrorist attacks, data mining tools are being examined. We have heard a lot about national security vs. privacy in the media. This is mainly due to the fact that people are now realizing that to handle terrorism, the government may need to collect data about individuals and mine the data to extract information. This is causing a major concern with various civil liberties unions. In this section, we discuss privacy threats that arise due to data mining and the semantic web. We also discuss some solutions and provide directions for standards.

Data mining, national security, privacy and web databases. With the web there is now an abundance of data information about individuals that one can obtain within seconds. The data could be structured data or could be multimedia data. Information could be obtained through mining or just from information retrieval. Data mining is an important tool in making the web more intelligent. That is, data mining may be used to mine the data on the web so that the web can evolve into the semantic web. However, this also means that there may be threats to privacy (see [12]). Therefore, one needs to enforce privacy controls on databases and data mining tools on the semantic web. This is a very difficult problem. In summary, one needs to develop techniques to prevent users from mining and extracting information from data whether they are on the web or on networked servers. Note that data mining is a technology that is critical for say analysts so that they can extract patterns previously unknown. However, we do not want the information to be used in an incorrect manner. For example, based on information about a person, an insurance company could deny insurance or a loan agency could deny loans. In many cases these denials may not be legitimate. Therefore, information providers have to be very careful in what they release. Also, data mining researchers have to ensure that privacy aspects are addressed. While little work has been reported on privacy issues for web databases we are moving in the right direction. As research initiatives are started in this area, we can expect some progress to be made. Note that there are also social and political aspects to consider. That is, technologists, sociologists, policy experts, counter-terrorism experts, and legal experts have to work together to develop appropriate data mining techniques as well as ensure privacy. Privacy policies and standards are also urgently needed. That is, while the technologists develop privacy solutions, we need the policy makers to work with standards organizations (i.e., W3C) so that appropriate privacy standards are developed.

Solutions to the privacy problem for web databases. As we have mentioned, the challenge is to provide solutions to enhance national security as well as extract useful information but at the same time ensure privacy. There is now research at various laboratories on privacy enhanced/sensitive data mining (e.g., Agrawal at IBM Almaden, Gehrke at Cornell University and Clifton at Purdue University, see for example [1], [7], [8]). The idea here is to continue with mining but at the same time ensure privacy as much as possible. For example, Clifton has proposed the use of the multiparty security policy approach for carrying out privacy sensitive data mining. While there is some progress we still have a long way to go. Some useful references are provided in [7]. We give some more details on an approach we are proposing. Note that one mines the data and extracts patterns and trends. The idea is that *privacy constraints* determine which patterns are private and to what extent. For example, suppose one could extract the names and healthcare records. If we have a privacy constraint that states that names and healthcare records are private then this information is not released to the general public. If the information is semi-private, then it is released to those who have a need to know. Essentially, the inference controller approach we have proposed in [14] is one solution to achieve some level of privacy. It could be regarded to be a type of privacy sensitive data mining. In our research we have found many challenges to the inference controller approach. These challenges will have to be addressed when handling privacy constraints (see also [13]). For example, there are data mining tools on the web that mine web databases. The privacy controller should ensure privacy preserving data mining. Ontologies may be used by the privacy controllers. For example, there may be ontology specification for privacy constructs. Furthermore, XML may be extended to include privacy constraints. RDF may incorporate privacy semantics. We need to carry out more research on the role of ontologies for privacy control. Much of the work on privacy preserving data mining focuses on relational data. We need to carry out research on privacy preserving web data mining which contains unstructured data. We need to combine techniques for privacy preserving data mining with techniques for web data mining to obtain solutions for privacy preserving web data mining.

4 Security and Privacy for Web Services

Security and privacy concerns related to web services are receiving today growing attention from both the industry and research community [9]. Although most of the security and privacy concerns are similar to those of many web-based applications, one distinguishing feature of the Web Service Architecture is that it relies on a repository of information, i.e., the UDDI registry, which can be queried by service requestors and populated by service providers. Even if, at the beginning, UDDI has been mainly conceived as a public registry without specific facilities for security and privacy, today security and privacy issues are becoming more and more crucial, due to the fact that data published in UDDI registries may be highly strategic and sensitive. For instance, a service provider may not want that the information about its web services are accessible to everyone, or a service requestor may want to validate the privacy policy of the discovery agency before interacting with this entity. In the following, we thus mainly focus on security and privacy issues related to UDDI registries management. We start by considering security issues, then we deal with privacy.

4.1 Security for Web Services

When dealing with security, three are the main issues that need to be faced: *authenticity*, *integrity*, and *confidentiality*. In the framework of UDDI, the authenticity property mainly means that the service requestor is assured that the information it receives from the UDDI comes from the source it claims to be from. Ensuring integrity means ensuring that the information are not altered during its transmission from the source to the intended recipients and that data are modified according to the specified access control policies. Finally, confidentiality means that information in the UDDI registry can only be disclosed to requestors authorized according to some specified access control policies. If a two-party architecture is adopted, security properties can be ensured using the strategies adopted in conventional DBMSs [6], since the owner of the information (i.e., the service provider) is also responsible for managing the UDDI. By contrast, such standard mechanisms must be revised when a third-party architecture is adopted. The big issue there is how the provider of the services can ensure security properties to its data, even if the data are managed by a discovery agency. The most intuitive solution is that of requiring the discovery agency to be trusted with respect to the considered security properties. However, the main drawback of this solution is that large web-based systems cannot be easily verified to be trusted and can be easily penetrated. The challenge is then how such security properties can be ensured without requiring the discovery agency to be trusted.

In the following, we discuss each of the above-mentioned security properties in the context of both a two-party and a third-party architecture.

Integrity and confidentiality. If UDDI registries are managed according to a two-party architecture, integrity and confidentiality can be ensured using the standard mechanisms adopted by conventional DBMSs [6]. In particular, an *access control mechanism* can be used to ensure that UDDI entries are accessed and modified only according to the specified access control policies. Basically, an access control mechanism is a software module that filters data accesses on the basis of a set of access control policies. Only the accesses authorized by the specified policies are granted. Additionally, data can be protected during their transmission from the data server to the requestor using standard encryption techniques [10].

If a third-party architecture is adopted, the access control mechanism must reside at the discovery agency site. However, the drawback of this solution is that the discovery agency must be trusted. An alternative approach to relax this assumption is that of using a technique similar to the one proposed in [5] for the secure broadcasting of XML documents. Basically, the idea is that the service provider encrypts the entries to be published in an UDDI registry according to its access control policies: all the entry portions to which the same policies apply are encrypted with the same key. Then, it publishes the encrypted copy of the entries to the UDDI. Additionally, the service provider is responsible for distributing keys to the service requestors in such a way that each service requestor receives all and only the keys corresponding to the information it is entitled to access. However, exploiting such solution requires the ability of querying encrypted data.

Authenticity. The standard approach for ensuring authenticity is using digital signature techniques [10]. To cope with authenticity requirements, the latest UDDI specifications allow one to optionally sign some of the elements in a registry, according to the W3C XML Signature syntax [15]. This technique can be successfully employed in a two-party architecture. However, it does not fit well in the third-party model, if we do not want to require the discovery agency be trusted wrt authenticity. In such a scenario, it is not possible to directly apply standard digital signature techniques, since a service requestor may require only selected portions of an entry, depending on its needs, or a combination of information residing in different data structures. Additionally, some portions of the requested information could not be delivered to the requestor because of access constraints stated by the specified policies. A solution that can be exploited in this context (which has been proposed in [4]) is that of applying to UDDI entries the authentication mechanism provided by Merkle hash trees. The approach requires that the service provider sends the discovery agency a summary signature, generated using a technique based on Merkle hash trees, for each entry it is entitled to manage. When a service requestor queries the UDDI registry, the discovery agency sends it, besides the query result, also the signatures of the entries on which the enquiry is performed. In this way, the requestor can locally recompute the same hash value signed by the service provider, and by comparing the two values it can verify whether the discovery agency has altered the content of the query answer and can thus verify its authenticity. However, since a requestor may be returned only selected portions of an entry, it may not be able to recompute the summary signature, which is based on the whole entry. For this reason, the discovery agency sends the requestor a set of additional hash values, referring to the missing portions, that make it able to locally perform the computation of the summary signature. We refer the interested readers to [4] for the details of the approach.

4.2 Privacy for Web Services

To enable privacy protection for web services consumers across multiple domains and services, the World Wide Web Consortium working draft *Web Services Architecture Requirements* has already been defined some specific privacy requirements for web services [15]. In particular, the working draft specifies five privacy requirements for enabling privacy protection for the consumer of a web service across multiple domains and services:

- the WSA must enable privacy policy statements to be expressed about web services;
- advertised web service privacy policies must be expressed in P3P [15];
- the WSA must enable a consumer to access a web service's advertised privacy policy statement;
- the WSA must enable delegation and propagation of privacy policy;
- web services must not be precluded from supporting interactions where one or more parties of the interaction are anonymous.

Most of these requirements have been recently studied and investigated in the W3C P3P Beyond HTTP task force [15]. Further, this task force is working on the identification of the requirements for adopting P3P into a number of protocols and applications other than HTTP, such as XML applications, SOAP, and web services. As a first step to privacy protection, the W3C P3P Beyond HTTP task force recommends that discovery agencies have their own privacy policies that govern the use of data collected both from service providers and service requestors. In this respect, the main requirement stated in [15] is that collected personal information must not be used or disclosed for purposes other than performing the operations for which it was collected, except with the consent of the subject or as required by law. Additionally, such information must be retained only as long as necessary for performing the required operations.

5 Towards a Secure Semantic Web

For the semantic web to be secure all of its components have to be secure. These components include web databases and services, XML and RDF documents, and information integration services. As more progress is made on investigating the various security issues for these components, then we could envisage developing a secure semantic web. Note that logic, proof and trust are at the highest layers of the semantic web. Security cuts across all layers and this is a challenge. That is, we need security for each of the layer and we must also ensure secure interoperability. For example, consider the lowest layer. One needs secure TCP/IP, secure sockets, and secure HTTP. There are now security protocols for these various lower layer protocols. One needs end-to-end security. That is, one cannot just have secure TCP/IP built on untrusted communication layers. That is, we need network security. Next layer is XML. One needs secure XML. That is, access must be controlled to various portions of the document for reading, browsing and modifications. There is research on securing XML. The next step is securing RDF. Now with RDF not only do we need secure XML, we also need security for the interpretations and semantics. For example, under certain contexts, portions of the document may be Unclassified while under certain other context the document may be Classified. As an example, one could declassify an RDF document, once the war is over. Once XML and RDF have been secured the next step is to examine security for ontologies and interoperation. That is, ontologies may have security levels attached to them. The challenge is how does one use these ontologies for secure information integration. Researchers have done some work on the secure interoperability of databases. We need to revisit this research and then determine what else needs to be done so that the information on the web can be managed, integrated and exchanged securely. Closely related to security is privacy. That is, certain portions of the document may be private while certain other portions may be public or semi-private. Privacy has received a lot of attention recently partly due to national security concerns. Privacy for the semantic web may be a critical issue, That is, how does one take advantage of the semantic web and still maintain privacy and sometimes anonymity. We also need to examine the inference problem for the semantic web. Inference is the process of posing queries and deducing new information. It becomes a problem when the deduced information is something the user is unauthorized to know. With the semantic web, and especially with data mining tools, one can make all kinds of inferences. That is the semantic web exacerbates the inference problem. Security should not be an afterthought. We have often heard that one needs to insert security into the system right from the beginning. Similarly, security cannot be an after-thought for the semantic web. However, we cannot also make the system inefficient if we must guarantee one hundred percent security at all times. What is needed is a flexible security policy. During some situations we may need one hundred percent security while during some other situations say thirty percent security (whatever that means) may be sufficient.

6 Conclusions

In this paper we have focused on security and privacy issues for the semantic web. In particular, we have discussed these issues for two of the key components of semantic web, that is, web databases and services. Besides providing background information on web databases and services, we have discussed the main issues related to security and privacy: which are the main challenges, and which are the most promising solutions. Finally, we have discussed some of the issues in developing a secure semantic web.

References

1. Agrawal, R., Srikant, R.: Privacy-preserving Data Mining, Proceedings of the ACM SIGMOD Conference (2000), Dallas, TX, USA.
2. Berners Lee, T., et al.: The Semantic Web (2001), Scientific American.
3. Bertino, E., Carminati, B., Ferrari, E. Thuraisingham, B., Gupta, A.: Selective and Authentic Third-party Distribution of XML Documents. IEEE Transactions on Knowledge and Data Engineering, to appear.
4. Bertino, E., Carminati, B., Ferrari, E.: A Flexible Authentication Method for UDDI Registries, Proceedings of the ICWS Conference, (2003), Las Vegas, Nevada, USA.
5. Bertino, E., Ferrari, E.: Secure and Selective Dissemination of XML Documents. ACM Transactions on Information and System Security, **5(3)** (2002) 290-331.
6. Castano, S., Fugini, M.G., Martella, G., Samarati, P. : Database Security (1995), Addison-Wesley.
7. Clifton, C., Kantarcioglu, M., Vaidya, J.: Defining Privacy for Data Mining, Proceedings of the Next Generation Data Mining Workshop (2002), Baltimore, MD, USA.
8. Gehrke, J.: Research Problems in Data Stream Processing and Privacy-Preserving Data Mining, Proceedings of the Next Generation Data Mining Workshop (2002), Baltimore, MD, USA.
9. IBM Corporation: Security in a Web Services World: A Proposed Architecture and Roadmap, White Paper, Version 1.0, 2002. Available at: `www-106.ibm.com/developerworks/library/ws-secroad/`.
10. Stallings, W.: Network Security Essentials: Applications and Standards (2000), Prentice Hall.
11. Pollmann, C.G.: The XML Security Page. Available at: `http://www.nue.et-inf.uni-siegen.de/g̃euer-pollmann/xml_security.html`.
12. Thuraisingham, B.: Web Data Mining: Technologies and Their Applications to Business Intelligence and Counter-terrorism (2003), CRC Press.
13. Thuraisingham, B.: Privacy Constraint Processing in a Privacy Enhanced Database System, Data and Knowledge Engineering, to appear.
14. Thuraisingham B., Ford, W.: Security Constraint Processing in a Distributed Database Management System, IEEE Transactions on Knowledge and Data Engineering (1995).
15. World Wide Web Consortium: www.w3c.org.
16. Universal Description, Discovery and Integration (UDDI): UDDI Version 3.0, UDDI Spec Technical Committee Specification, July, 19th, 2002. Available at: `http://uddi.org/pubs/uddi-v3.00-published-20020719.htm`.

Content-Based Routing of Path Queries in Peer-to-Peer Systems*

Georgia Koloniari and Evaggelia Pitoura

Department of Computer Science, University of Ioannina, Greece
{kgeorgia,pitoura}@cs.uoi.gr

Abstract. Peer-to-peer (P2P) systems are gaining increasing popularity as a scalable means to share data among a large number of autonomous nodes. In this paper, we consider the case in which the nodes in a P2P system store XML documents. We propose a fully decentralized approach to the problem of routing path queries among the nodes of a P2P system based on maintaining specialized data structures, called filters that efficiently summarize the content, i.e., the documents, of one or more node. Our proposed filters, called multi-level Bloom filters, are based on extending Bloom filters so that they maintain information about the structure of the documents. In addition, we advocate building a hierarchical organization of nodes by clustering together nodes with similar content. Similarity between nodes is related to the similarity between the corresponding filters. We also present an efficient method for update propagation. Our experimental results show that multi-level Bloom filters outperform the classical Bloom filters in routing path queries. Furthermore, the content-based hierarchical grouping of nodes increases recall, that is, the number of documents that are retrieved.

1 Introduction

The popularity of file sharing systems such as Napster, Gnutella and Kazaa has spurred much current attention to peer-to-peer (P2P) computing. Peer-to-peer computing refers to a form of distributed computing that involves a large number of autonomous computing nodes (the peers) that cooperate to share resources and services [1]. As opposed to traditional client-server computing, nodes in a P2P system have equal roles and act as both data providers and data consumers. Furthermore, such systems are highly dynamic in that nodes join or leave the system and change their content constantly.

Motivated by the fact that XML has evolved as a standard for publishing and exchanging data in the Internet, we assume that the nodes in a P2P system store and share XML documents [23]. Such XML documents may correspond either to native XML documents or to XML-based descriptions of local services or datasets. Such datasets may be stored in local to each node databases supporting diverse data models and exported by the node as XML data.

* Work supported in part by the IST programme of the European Commission FET under the IST-2001-32645 DBGlobe project, IST-2001-32645

E. Bertino et al. (Eds.): EDBT 2004, LNCS 2992, pp. 29–47, 2004.
© Springer-Verlag Berlin Heidelberg 2004

A central issue in P2P computing is locating the appropriate data in these huge, massively distributed and highly dynamic data collections. Traditionally, search is based on keyword queries, that is, queries for documents whose name matches a given keyword or for documents that include a specific keyword. In this paper, we extend search to support path queries that exploit the structure of XML documents. Although data may exhibit some structure, in a P2P context, it is too varied, irregular or mutable to easily map to a fixed schema. Thus, our assumption is that XML documents are schema-less.

We propose a decentralized approach to routing path queries among highly distributed XML documents based on maintaining specialized data structures that summarize large collections of documents. We call such data structures *filters*. In particular, each node maintains two types of filters, a *local filter* summarizing the documents stored locally at the node and one or more *merged filters* summarizing the documents of its neighboring nodes. Each node uses its filters to route a query only to those nodes that may contain relevant documents. Filters should be small, scalable to a large number of nodes and documents and support frequent updates.

Bloom filters have been used as summaries in such a context [2]. Bloom filters are compact data structures used to support keyword queries. However, Bloom filters are not appropriate for summarizing hierarchical data, since they do not exploit the structure of data. To this end, we introduce two novel multi-level data structures, *Breadth* and *Depth* Bloom filters, that support efficient processing of path queries. Our experimental results show that both multi-level Bloom filters outperform a same size traditional Bloom filter in evaluating path queries. We show how multi-level Bloom filters can be used as summaries to support efficient query routing in a P2P system where the nodes are organized to form hierarchies. Furthermore, we propose an efficient mechanism for the propagation of filter updates. Our experimental results show that the proposed mechanism scales well to a large number of nodes.

In addition, we propose creating overlay networks of nodes by linking together nodes with similar content. The similarity of the content (i.e., the local documents) of two nodes is related to the similarity of their filters. This is cost effective, since a filter for a set of documents is much smaller than the documents themselves. Furthermore, the filter comparison operation is more efficient than a direct comparison between sets of documents. As our experimental results show, the content-based organization is very efficient in retrieving a large number of relevant documents, since it benefits from the content clusters that are created when forming the network.

In summary, the contribution of this paper is twofold: (i) it proposes using filters for routing path queries over distributed collections of schema-less XML documents and (ii) it introduces overlay networks over XML documents that cluster nodes with similar documents, where similarity between documents is related to the similarity between their filters.

The remainder of this paper is structured as follows. Section 2 introduces multi-level Bloom filters as XML routers in P2P systems. Section 3 describes a hierarchical distribution of filters and the mechanism for building content-based overlay networks based on filter similarity. Section 4 presents the algorithms for query routing and update propagation, while Section 5 our experimental results. Section 6 presents related research and Section 7 concludes the paper.

2 Routers for XML Documents

We consider a P2P system in which each participating node stores XML documents. Users specify queries using path expressions. Such queries may originate at any node. Since it is not reasonable to expect that users know which node hosts the requested documents, we propose using appropriately distributed data structures, called *filters*, to route the query to the appropriate nodes.

2.1 System Model

We consider a P2P system where each node n_i maintains a set of XML documents D_i (a particular document may be stored in more than one node). Each node is logically linked to a relatively small set of other nodes called its *neighbors*.

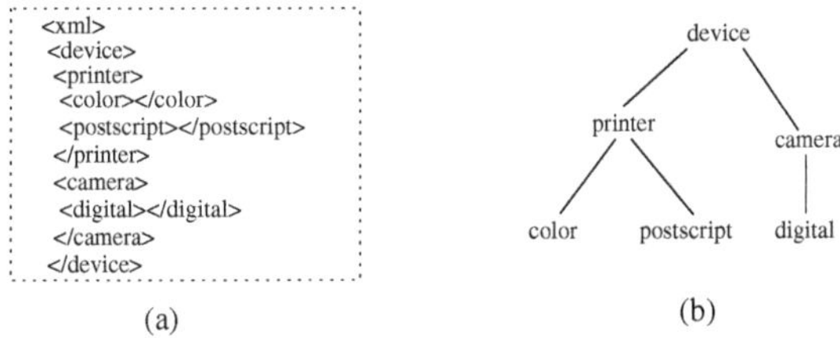

Fig. 1. Example of (a) an XML document and (b) the corresponding tree

In our data model, an XML document is represented by an unordered labeled tree, where tree nodes correspond to document elements, while edges represent direct element-subelement relationships. Figure 1 depicts an XML service description for a printer and a camera provided by a node and the corresponding XML tree. Although, most P2P systems support only queries for documents that contain one or more *keywords*, we want also to query the structure of documents. Thus, we consider *path queries* that are simple path expressions in an XPath-like query language.

Definition 1. (path query) *A path query of length p has the form 's_1 l_1 s_2 l_2 ... s_p l_p" where each l_i is an element name and each s_i is either / or // denoting respectively parent-child and ancestor-descendant traversal.*

A keyword query for documents containing keyword k is just the path query //k. For a query q and a document d, we say that q is satisfied by d, or *match(d, q)* is true, if the path expression forming the query exists in the document. Otherwise we have a *miss*. Nodes that include documents that match the query are called *matching nodes*.

2.2 Query Routing

A given query may be matched by documents at various nodes. Thus, central to a P2P system is a mechanism for locating nodes with matching documents. In this regard, there are two types of P2P systems. In *structured P2P* systems, documents (or indexes of documents) are placed at specific nodes usually based on distributed hashing (such as in CAN [21] and Chord [20]). With distributed hashing, each document is associated with a key and each node is assigned a range of keys and thus documents. Although, structured P2P systems provide very efficient searching, they compromise node autonomy and in addition require sophisticated load balancing procedures.

In *unstructured P2P* systems, resources are located at random points. Unstructured P2P systems can be further distinguished between systems that use indexes and those that are based on flooding and its variations. With flooding (such as in Gnutella [22]), a node searching for a document contacts its neighbor nodes which in turn contact their own neighbors until a matching node is reached. Flooding incurs large network overheads. In the case of indexes, these can be either centralized (as in Napster [8]), or distributed among the nodes (as in routing indexes [19]) providing for each node a partial view of the system.

Our approach is based on unstructured P2P systems with distributed indexes. We propose maintaining as indexes specialized data structures, called *filters*, to facilitate propagating the query only to those nodes that may contain relevant information. In particular, each node maintains one filter that summarizes all documents that exist locally in the node. This is called a *local filter*. Besides its local filter, each node also maintains one or more filter, called *merged filters*, summarizing the documents of a set of its neighbors. When a query reaches a node, the node first checks its local filter and uses the merged filters to direct the query only to those nodes whose filters match the query.

Filters should be much smaller than the data itself and should be lossless, that is if the data match the query, then the filter should match the query as well. In particular, each filter should support an efficient *filter-match* operation such that if a document matches a query q then filter-match should also be true. If the filter-match returns false, we say that we have a *miss*.

Definition 2. (filter match) *A filter F(D) for a set of documents D has the following property: For any query q, if filter-match(q, F(D)) = false, then match(q, d) = false,* $\forall\ d \in D$.

Note that, the reverse does not necessarily hold. That is, if filter-match(q, $F(D)$) = true, then there may or may not exist documents $d \in D$ such that match(q, d) is true. We call *false positive* the case in which, for a filter $F(D)$ for a set of documents D, filter-match(q, $F(D)$) = true but there is no document $d \in D$ that satisfies q, that is $\forall\ d \in D$, match(q, d) = false. We are interested in filters with small probability of false positives.

Bloom filters are appropriate as summarizing filters in this context in terms of scalability, extensibility and distribution. However, they do not support path queries. To this end, we propose an extension called multi-level Bloom filters.

Multi-level Bloom filters were first presented in [17] where preliminary results were reported for their centralized use. To distinguish traditional Bloom filters from the extended ones, we shall call the former *simple* Bloom filters. Other hash-based structures, such as signatures [13], have similar properties with Bloom filters and our approach could also be applied to extend them in a similar fashion.

2.3 Multi-level Bloom Filters

Bloom filters are compact data structures for probabilistic representation of a set that support membership queries ("Is element a in set A?"). Since their introduction [3], Bloom filters have seen many uses such as web caching [4] and query filtering and routing [2,5]. Consider a set $A = \{a_1, a_2,..., a_n\}$ of n elements. The idea is to allocate a vector v of m bits, initially all set to 0, and then choose k independent hash functions, h_1, h_2, ..., h_k, each with range 1 to m. For each element $a \in A$, the bits at positions $h_1(a)$, $h_2(a)$, ..., $h_k(a)$ in v are set to 1 (Fig. 2). A particular bit may be set to 1 many times. Given a query for b, the bits at positions $h_1(b)$, $h_2(b)$, ..., $h_k(b)$ are checked. If any of them is 0, then certainly $b \notin A$. Otherwise, we conjecture that b is in the set although there is a certain probability that we are wrong. This is a false positive. It has been shown [3] that the probability of a false positive is equal to $(1 - e^{-kn/m})^k$. To support updates of the set A we maintain for each location i in the bit vector a counter $c(i)$ of the number of times that the bit is set to 1 (the number of elements that hashed to i under any of the hash functions).

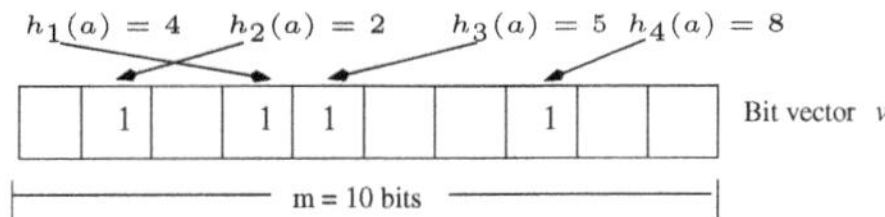

Fig. 2. A (simple) Bloom filter with $k = 4$ hash functions

Let T be an XML tree with j levels and let the level of the root be level 1. The *Breadth Bloom Filter* (BBF) for an XML tree T with j levels is a set of simple Bloom filters $\{\text{BBF}_1, \text{BBF}_2, \ldots \text{BBF}_i\}$, $i \leq j$. There is one simple Bloom filter, denoted BBF_i, for each level i of the tree. In each BBF_i, we insert the elements of all nodes at level i. To improve performance and decrease the false positive probability in the case of $i < j$, we may construct an additional Bloom filter denoted BBF_0, where we insert all elements that appear in any node of the tree. For example, the BBF for the XML tree in Fig. 1 is a set of 4 simple Bloom filters (Fig. 3(a)).

The *Depth Bloom Filter* (DBF) for an XML tree T with j levels is a set of simple Bloom filters $\{\text{DBF}_0, \text{DBF}_1, \text{DBF}_2, \ldots, \text{DBF}_{i-1}\}$, $i \leq j$. There is one Bloom filter, denoted DBF_i, for each path of the tree with length i, (i.e., a path of $i + 1$ nodes), where we insert all paths of length i. For example, the DBF for the XML tree in Fig. 1 is a set of 3 simple Bloom filters (Fig. 3(b)). Note that

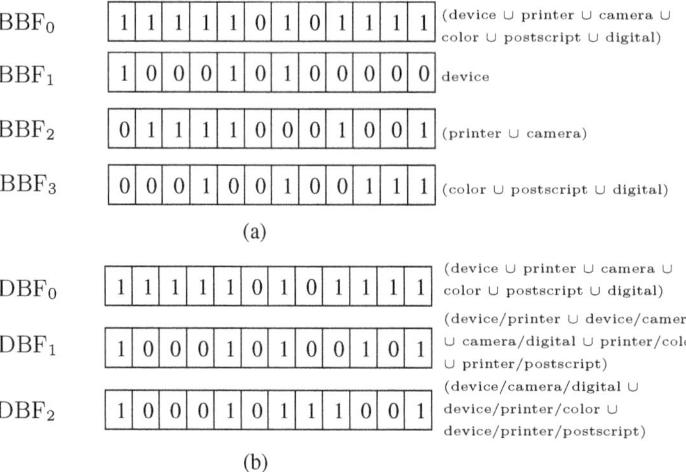

Fig. 3. The multi-level Bloom filters for the XML tree of Fig. 1: (a) the Breadth Bloom filter and (b) the Depth Bloom filter

we insert paths as a whole; we do not hash each element of the path separately. We use a different notation for paths starting from the root. This is not shown in Fig. 3(b) for ease of presentation.

The BBF filter-match operation (that checks whether a BBF matches a query) distinguishes between queries starting from the root and partial path queries. In both cases, if BBF_0 exists, the procedure checks whether it matches all elements of the query. If so, it proceeds to examine the structure of the path, else, it returns a miss. For a root query: $/a_1/a_2/.../a_p$, every level i from 1 to p of the filter is checked for the corresponding a_i. The procedure succeeds, if there is a match for all elements. For a partial path query, for every level i of the filter: the first element of the path is checked. If there is a match, the next level is checked for the next element and so on until either the whole path is matched or there is a miss. If there is a miss, the procedure repeats for level $i+1$. For paths with the ancestor-descendant axis //, the path is split at the // and the sub-paths are processed. The complexity of the BBF filter-match is $O(p^2)$ where p is the length (number of elements) of the query; in particular, for root queries the complexity is $O(p)$. The DBF filter-match operation checks whether all sub-paths of the query match the corresponding filters; its complexity is also $O(p^2)$. A detailed description of the filter match operations is given in [24].

3 Content-Based Linking

In this section, we describe how the nodes are organized and how the filters are built and distributed among them.

3.1 Hierarchical Organization

Nodes in a P2P system may be organized to form various topologies. In a *hierarchical organization* (Fig. 4), a set of nodes designated as *root nodes* are connected to a main channel that provides communication among them. The main channel acts as a broadcast mechanism and can be implemented in many different ways. A hierarchical organization is best suited when the participating nodes have different processing and storage capabilities as well as varying stability, that is, some nodes stay longer online, while others stay online for a limited time. With this organization, nodes belonging to the top levels receive more load and responsibilities, thus, the most stable and powerful nodes should be located to the top levels of the hierarchies.

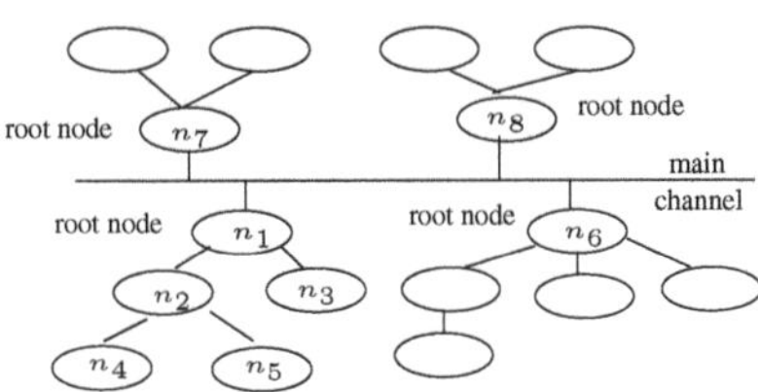

Fig. 4. Hierarchical organization

Each node maintains two filters: one summarizing its local documents, called *local filter* and, if it is a non-leaf node, one summarizing the documents of all nodes in its sub-tree, called *merged filter*. In addition, root nodes keep one merged filter for each of the other root nodes. The construction of filters follows a bottom-up procedure. A leaf node sends its local filter to its parent. A non-leaf node, after receiving the filters of all its children, merge them and produces its merged filter. Then, it merges the merged filter with its own local filter and sends the resulting filter to its parent. When a root computes its merged filter, it propagates it to all other root nodes.

Merging of two or more multi-level filters corresponds to computing a bitwise OR (BOR) of each of their levels. That is, the merged filter, D, of two Breadth Bloom filters B and C with i levels is a Breadth Bloom filter with i levels: $D = \{D_0, D_1, \ldots D_i\}$, where $D_j = B_j$ BOR C_j, $0 \leq j \leq i$. Similarly, we define merging for Depth Bloom filters.

Although we describe a hierarchical organization, our mechanism can be easily applied to other node organizations as well. Preliminary results of the filters deployment in a non-hierarchical peer-to-peer system are reported in [18].

3.2 Content-Based Clustering

Nodes may be organized in hierarchies based on their proximity at the underlying physical network to exploit physical locality and minimize query response time. The formation of hierarchies can also take into account other parameters such as administrative domains, stability and the different processing and storage capabilities of the nodes. Thus, hierarchies can be formed that better leverage the workload. However, such organizations ignore the content of nodes. We propose an organization of nodes based on the similarity of their content so that nodes with similar content are grouped together. The goal of such content-based clustering is to improve the efficiency of query routing by reducing the number of irrelevant nodes that process a query. In particular, we would like to optimize *recall*, that is the percentage of matching nodes that are visited during query routing. We expect that content-based clustering will increase recall since matching nodes will be only a few hops apart.

Instead of checking the similarity of the documents themselves, we rely on the similarity of their filters. This is more cost effective, since a filter for a set of documents is much smaller than the documents. Moreover, the filter comparison operation is more efficient than a comparison between two sets of documents. Documents with similar filters are expected to match similar queries.

Let B be a simple Bloom filter of size m. We shall use the notation $B[i]$, $1 \leq i \leq m$ to denote the ith bit of the filter. Let two simple Bloom filters B and C of size m, their Manhattan (or Hamming) distance, $d(B, C)$ is defined as $d(B, C) = |B[1] - C[1]| + |B[2] - C[2]| + \ldots + |B[m] - C[m]|$, that is the number of bits that they differ. We define the similarity, of B and C as $similarity(B, C) = m - d(B, C)$. The larger their similarity, the more similar the filters. In the case of multi-level Bloom filters, we take the sum of the similarities of each pair of the corresponding levels.

We use the following procedure to organize nodes based on content similarity. When a new node n wishes to join the P2P system, it sends a join request that contains its local filter to all root nodes. Upon receiving a join request, each root node compares the received local filter with its merged filter and responds to n with the measure of their filter similarity. The root node with the largest similarity is called the *winner* root. Node n compares its similarity with the winner root to a system-defined *threshold*. If the similarity is larger than the threshold, n joins the hierarchy of the winner root, else n becomes a root node itself. In the former case, node n replies to the winner root that propagates its reply to all nodes in its sub-tree. The node connects to the node in the winner root's subtree that has the most similar local filter.

The procedure for creating content-based hierarchies effectively clusters nodes based on their content, so that similar nodes belong to the same hierarchy (cluster). The value of threshold determines the number of hierarchies in the system and affects system performance. Statistical knowledge, such as the average similarity among nodes, may be used to define threshold. We leave the definition of threshold and the dynamic adaptation of its value as future work.

4 Querying and Updating

We describe next how a query is routed and how updates are processed.

4.1 Query Routing

Filters are used to facilitate query routing. In particular, when a query is issued at a node n, routing proceeds as follows. The local filter of node n is checked, and if there is a match, the local documents are searched. Next, the merged filter of n is checked, and if there is a match, the query is propagated to n's children. The query is also propagated to the parent of the node. The propagation of a query towards the bottom of the hierarchy continues, until either a leaf node is reached, or the filter match with the merged filter of an internal node indicates a miss. The propagation towards the top of the hierarchy continues until the root node is reached. When a query reaches a root node, the root, apart from checking the filter of its own sub-tree, it also checks the merged filters of the other root nodes and forwards the query only to these root nodes for which there is a match. When a root node receives a query from another root it only propagates the query to its own sub-tree.

4.2 Update Propagation

When a document is updated or a document is inserted or deleted at a node, its local filter must be updated. An update can be viewed as a delete followed by an insert. When an update occurs at a node, apart from the update of its local filter, all merged filters that use this local filter must be updated. We present two different approaches for the propagation of updates based on the way the counters of the merged filters are computed. Note that in both cases we propagate the levels of the multi-level filter that have changed and not the whole multi-level filter.

The straightforward way to use the counters at the merged filters is for every node to send to its parent, along with its filter, the associated counters. Then, the counters of the merged filter of each internal node are computed as the sum of the respective counters of its children's filters. We call this method *CountSum*. An example with simple Bloom Filters is show in Fig. 5(a). Now, when a node updates its local filter and its own merged filter to represent the update, it also sends the differences between its old and new counter values to its parent. After updating its own summary, the parent propagates in turn the difference to its parent until all affected nodes are informed. In the worst case, in which an update occurs at a leaf node, the number of messages that need to be sent is equal to the number of levels in the hierarchy, plus the number of roots in the main channel.

We can improve the complexity of update propagation by making the following observation: an update will only result in a change in the filter itself if the counter turns from 0 to 1 or vice versa. Taking this into consideration, each node just sends its merged filter to its parent (local filter for the leaf nodes) and not the counters. A node that has received all the filters from its children creates its merged filter as before but uses the following procedure to compute the counters: it increases each counter bit by one every time a filter of its children has a 1 in the corresponding position. Thus, each bit of the counter of a merged filter represents the number of its children's filters that have set this bit to 1 (and not how many times the original filters had set the bit to 1). We call this method *BitSum*. An example with simple Bloom Filters is show in Fig. 5(c). When an update occurs, it is propagated only if it changes a bit from 1 to 0 or vice versa.

An example is depicted in Fig. 5. Assume that node n_4 performs an update; as a result, its new (local) filter becomes (1, 0, 0, 1) and the corresponding counters (1, 0, 0, 2). With CountSum (Fig. 5(a)), n_4 will send the difference (-1, 0, -1, -1) between its old and new counters to node n_2, whose (merged) filter will now become (1, 0, 1, 1) and the counters (2, 0, 1, 4). Node n_2 must also propagate the difference (-1, 0, -1, -1) to its parent n_1 (although no change was reflected at its filter). The final state is shown in Fig. 5(b). With BitSum (Fig. 5(c)), n_4 will send to n_2 only those bits that have changed from 1 to 0 and vice versa, that is (-, -, -1, -). The new filter of n_2 will be (1, 0, 1, 1) and the counters (2, 0, 1, 2). Node n_2 does not need to send the update to n_1. The final state is illustrated in Fig. 5(d). The BitSum approach sends fewer and smaller messages.

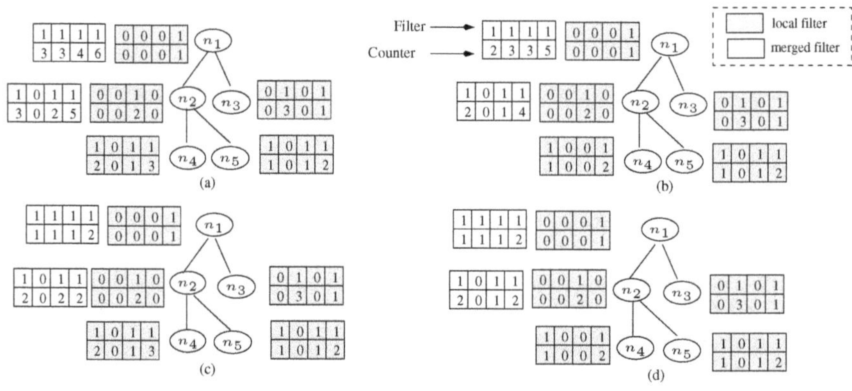

Fig. 5. An example of an update using CountSum and BitSum

5 Experimental Evaluation

We implemented the BBF (Breadth Bloom filter) and the DBF (Depth Bloom Filter) data structures, as well as a Simple Bloom filter (SBF) (that just hashes all elements of a document) for comparison. For the hash functions, we used MD5 [6]: a cryptographic message digest algorithm that hashes arbitrarily length strings to 128 bits. The k hash functions are built by first calculating the MD5 signature of the input string, which yields 128 bits, and then taking k groups of $128/k$ bits from it. We used the Niagara generator [7] to generate tree-structured XML documents of arbitrary complexity. Three types of experiments are performed. The goal of the *first set of experiments* is to demonstrate the appropriateness of multi-level Bloom filters as filters of hierarchical documents. To this end, we evaluate the false positive probability for both DBF and BBF and compare it with the false positive probability for a same size SBF for a variety of query workloads and document structures. The *second set of experiments* focuses on the performance of Bloom filters in a distributed setting using both a content-based and a non content-based organization. In the *third set of experiments*, we evaluate the update propagation procedures.

5.1 Simple versus Multi-level Bloom Filters

In this set of experiments, we evaluate the performance of multi-level Bloom filters. As our performance metric, we use the percentage of false positives, since the number of nodes that will process an irrelevant query depends on it directly. In all cases, the filters compared have the *same* total size. Our input parameters are summarized in Table 1. In the case of the Breadth Bloom filter, we excluded the optional Bloom filter BBF_0. The number of levels of the Breadth Bloom filters is equal to the number of levels of the XML trees, while for the Depth Bloom filters, we have at most three levels. There is no repetition of element names in a single document or among documents. Queries are generated by producing arbitrary path queries with 90% elements from the documents and 10% random ones. All queries are partial paths and the probability of the // axis at each query is set to 0.05.

Table 1. Input parameters

Parameter	Default Value	Range
# of XML documents	200	-
Total size of filters	78000 bits	30000-150000 bits
# of hash functions	4	-
# of queries	100	-
# of elements per document	50	10-150
# of levels per document	4/6	2-6
Length of query	3	2-6
Distribution of query elements	90% in documents 10% random	0%-10%

Influence of filter size. In this experiment, we vary the size of the filters from 30000 bits to 150000 bits. The lower limit is chosen from the formula $k = (m/n)ln2$ that gives the number of hash functions k that minimize the false positive probability for a given size m and n inserted elements for an SBF: we solved the equation for m keeping the other parameters fixed. As our results show (Fig. 6(left)), both BBFs and DBFs outperform SBFs. For SBFs, increasing their size does not improve their performance, since they recognize as misses only paths that contain elements that do not exist in the documents. BBFs perform very well even for 30000 bits with an almost constant 6% of false positives, while DBFs require more space since the number of elements inserted is much larger than that of BBFs and SBFs. However, when the size increases sufficiently, the DBFs outperform even the BBFs. Note than in DBFs the number of elements inserted in each level i of the filter is about: $2d^i + \Sigma_{j=i+1}^{l} d^j$, where d is the degree of the XML nodes and l the number of levels of the XML tree, while the corresponding number for BBFs is: d^{i-1}, which is much smaller.

Using the results of this experiment, we choose as the default size of the filters for the rest of the experiments in this set, a size of 78000 bits, for which both our structures showed reasonable results. For 200 documents of 50 elements, this represents 2% of the space that the documents themselves require. This makes Bloom filters a very attractive summary to be used in a P2P computing context.

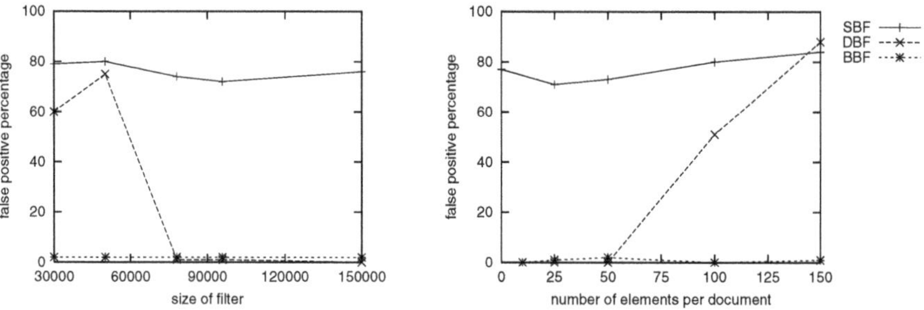

Fig. 6. Comparison of Bloom filters: (left) filter size and (right) number of elements per document

Influence of the number of elements per document. In this experiment, we vary the number of elements per document from 10 to 150 (Fig 6(right). Again, SBFs filter out only path expressions with elements that do not exist in the document. When the filter becomes denser as the elements inserted are increased to 150, SBFs fail to recognize even some of these expressions. BBFs show the best overall performance with an almost constant percentage of 1 to 2% of false positives. DBFs require more space and their performance rapidly decreases as the number of inserted elements increases, and for 150 elements, they become worse than the SBFs, because the filters become overloaded (most bits are set to 1).

Other Experiments. We performed a variety of experiments [24]. Our experiments show that, DBFs perform well, although we have limited the number of their levels to 3 (we do not insert sub-paths of length greater than 3). This is because for each path expression of length p, the filter-match procedure checks all its possible sub-paths of length 3 or less; in particular, it performs (p - i + 1) checks at every level i of the filter. In most cases, BBFs outperform DBFs for small sizes. However, DBFs perform better for a special type of queries. Assume an XML tree with the following paths: /a/b/c and /a/f/l, then a BBF would falsely match the following path: /a/b/l. However, DBFs would check all its possible sub-paths: /a/b/l, /a/b, /b/l and return a miss for the last one. This is confirmed by our experiments that show DBFs to outperform BBFs for such query workloads.

5.2 Content-Based Organization

In this set of experiments, we focus on filter distribution. Our performance metric is the number of hops for finding matching nodes. We simulated a network of nodes forming hierarchies and examined its performance with and without the deployment of filters and for both a content and a non content-based organization. First, we use simple Bloom filters and queries of length 1, for simplicity. In the last experiment, we use multi-level Bloom filters with path queries (queries with length larger than 1). We use small documents and accordingly small-sized filters. To scale to large documents, we just have to scale up the filter as well. There is one document at each node, since a large XML document corresponds to a set of small documents with respect to the elements and path expressions extracted. Each query is matched by about 10% of the nodes. For the content-based organization, the threshold is pre-set so that we can determine the number of hierarchies created. Table 2 summarizes our parameters.

Table 2. Distribution parameters

Parameter	Default Value	Range
# of XML documents per node	1	-
Total size of filter	200-800	-
# of queries	100	-
# of elements per document	10	-
# of levels per document	4	-
Length of query	1-2	-
Number of nodes	100-200	20-200
Maximum number of hops	First matching node found	20-200
Out-degree of a node	2-3	-
Repetition between documents	Every 10% of all docs 70% similar	-
Levels of hierarchy	3-4	-
Matching nodes for a query	10% of # of nodes	1-50%

Content vs. non content-based distribution. We vary the size of the network, that is, the number of participating nodes from 20 to 200. We measure the number of hops a query makes to find the first matching node. Figure 7(left) illustrates our results. The use of filters improves query response. Without using filters, the hierarchical distribution performs worse than organizing the nodes in a linear chain (where the worst case is equal to the number of nodes), because of backtracking. The content-based outperforms the non content-based organization, since due to clustering of nodes with similar content, it locates the correct cluster (hierarchy) that contains matching documents faster. The number of hops remains constant as the number of nodes increases, because the number of matching nodes increases analogously.

In the next experiment (Fig. 7(right)), we keep the size of the network fixed to 200 nodes and vary the maximum number of hops a query makes from 20 to

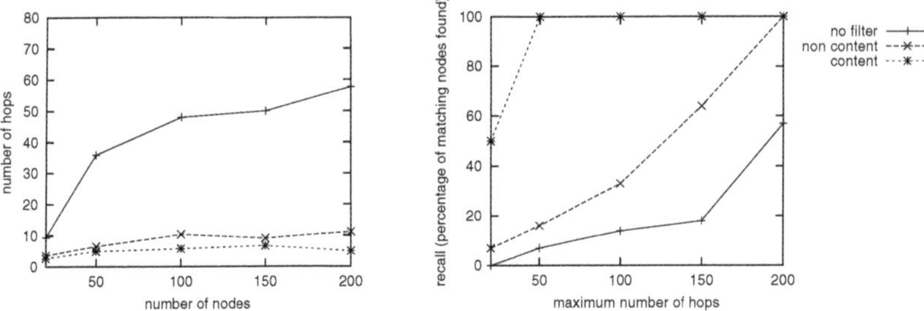

Fig. 7. Content vs non content-based organization: (left) finding the first matching node and (right) percentage of matching nodes found for a given number of hops (recall)

200. Note that in the number of hops, the hops made during backtracking are also included. We are interested in recall, that is, the percentage of matching nodes that are retrieved (over all matching nodes) for a given number of nodes visited. Again, the approach without filters has the worst performance since it finds only about 50% of the results for even 200 hops. The content-based organization outperforms the non content-based one. After 50 hops, that is, 25% of all the nodes, it is able to find all matching nodes. This is because when the first matching node is found, the other matching nodes are located very close, since nodes with similar content are clustered together.

We now vary the number of matching nodes from 1% to 50% of the total number of system nodes and measure the hops for finding the first matching node. The network size is fixed to 100 nodes. Our results (Fig. 8(left)) show that for a small number of matching nodes, the content-based organization outperforms further the other ones. The reason is that it is able to locate easier the cluster with the correct answers. As the number of results increases both the network proximity and the filter-less approaches work well as it becomes more probable that they will find a matching node closer to the query's origin since the documents are disseminated randomly.

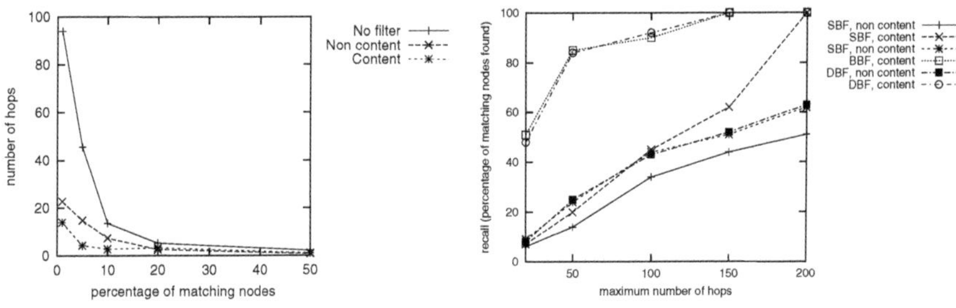

Fig. 8. (left) Number of hops to find the first result with varying number of matching nodes and (right) recall with multi-level filters

Using multi-level filters. We repeated the previous experiments using multi-level filters [24] and path queries of length 2. Our results confirm that multi-level Bloom filters perform better than simple Bloom filters in the case of path queries and for both a content and a non content-based organization. Figure 8(right) reports recall while varying the maximum number of hops.

5.3 Updates

In this set of experiments, we compare the performance of the CountSum and BitSum update propagation methods. We again simulated a network of nodes forming hierarchies and use Bloom filters for query routing. We used two metrics to compare the two algorithms: the number and size of messages. Each node stores 5 documents and an update operation consists of the deletion of a document and the insertion of a new document in its place. The deleted document is 0% similar to the inserted document to inflict the largest change possible to the filter. Again, we use small documents and correspondingly small sizes for the filters. The origin of the update is selected randomly among the nodes of the system. Table 3 summarizes the parameters used.

Table 3. Additional update propagation parameters

Parameter	Default Value	Range
# of XML documents per node	5	-
Total size of filter	4000	-
# of updates	100	-
Number of nodes	200	20-200
Repetition between deleted and inserted document	0%	-

Number and average size of messages. We vary the size of the network from 20 to 200 nodes. We use both a content-based and a non content-based organization and simple Bloom Filters. The BitSum method outperforms CountSum both in message complexity and average size of messages (Fig 9). The decrease in the number of messages is not very significant; however the size of the messages is reduced to half. In particular, CountSum creates messages with a constant size, while BitSum reduces the size of the message at every step of the algorithm. With a content-based organization, the number of messages increases with respect to the non content-based organization. This is because the content-based organization results in the creation of a larger number of more unbalanced hierarchies. However, both organizations are able to scale to a large number of nodes, since the hierarchical distribution of the filters enables performing updates locally. Thus, even for the content-based organization, less than 10% of the system nodes are affected by an update.

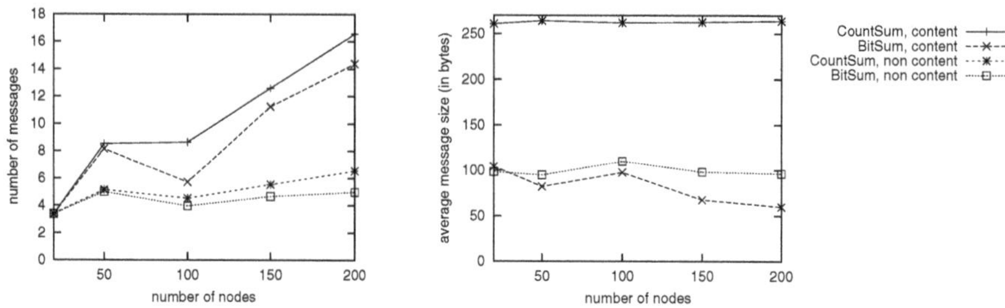

Fig. 9. BitSum vs CountSum update propagation: (left) number of messages (right) average message size

Using multi-level Bloom filters. We repeat the previous experiment using multi-level Bloom filters as summaries. We use only the BitSum method that outperforms the CountSum method as shown by the previous experiment. We used Breadth (BBFs) and Depth Bloom Filters (DBFs), both for a content and a non content-based organization. The nodes vary from 20 to 200. The results (Fig. 10) show that BitSum works also well with multi-level Bloom filters. The content-based organization requires a larger number of messages because of the larger number of hierarchies created. DBFs create larger messages as the bits affected by an update are more. However with the use of BitSum, DBFs scale and create update messages of about 300 bytes (while for CountSum, the size is 1K).

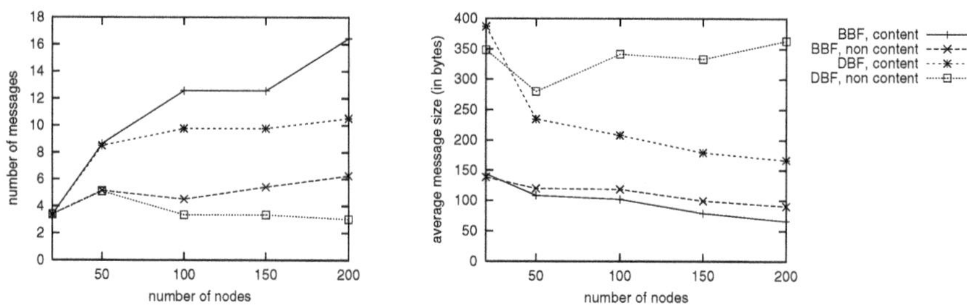

Fig. 10. BitSum update propagation with multi-level Bloom filters: (left) number of messages (right) average message size

6 Related Work

We compare briefly our work with related approaches regarding XML indexes and the use of Bloom filters for query routing. A more thorough comparison can be found in [24]. Various indexing methods for indexing XML documents (such as

DataGuides [9], Patricia trees [10], XSKETCH [11] and signatures [12]) provide efficient ways of summarizing XML data, support complex path queries and offer selectivity estimations. However, these structures are centralized and emphasis is given on space efficiency and I/O costs. In contrast, in a P2P context, we are interested in small-size summaries of large collections of XML documents that can be used to filter out irrelevant nodes fast with the additional requirements that such summaries can be distributed efficiently. Finally, when compared to Bloom filters, merging and updating of path indexes is more complicated.

Perhaps the resource discovery protocol most related to our approach is the one in [5] that uses simple Bloom filters as summaries. Servers are organized into a hierarchy modified according to the query workload to achieve load balance. Local and merged Bloom filters are used also in [14], but the nodes follow no particular structure. The merged filters include information about all nodes of the system and thus scalability issues arise. In both of the above cases, Bloom filters were used for keyword queries and not for XML data, whereas, our work supports path queries. Furthermore, the use of filters was limited to query routing, while we extend their use to built content-based overlay networks.

More recent research presents content-based distribution in P2P where nodes are "clustered" according to their content. With Semantic Overlay Networks (SONs) [15], nodes with semantically similar content are grouped based on a classification hierarchy of their documents. Queries are processed by identifying which SONs are better suited to answer it. However, there is no description of how queries are routed or how the clusters are created and no use of filter or indexes. An schema-based (RDF-based) peer-to-peer network is presented in [16]. The system can support heterogeneous metadata schemes and ontologies, but it requires a strict topology with hypercubes and the use of super-peers, limiting the dynamic nature of the network.

7 Conclusions and Future Work

In this paper, we study the problem of routing path queries in P2P systems of nodes that store XML documents. We introduce two new hash-based indexing structures, the Breadth and Depth Bloom Filters, which in contrast to traditional hash based indexes, have the ability to represent path expressions and thus exploit the structure of XML documents. Our experiments show that both structures outperform a same size simple Bloom Filter. In particular, for only 2% of the total size of the documents, multi-level Bloom filters can provide efficient evaluation of path queries for a false positives ratio below 3%. In general Breadth Bloom filters work better than Depth Bloom filters, however Depth Bloom filters recognize a special type of path queries. In addition, we introduce BitSum, an efficient update propagation method that significantly reduces the size of the update messages. Finally, we present a hierarchical organization that groups together nodes with similar content to improve search efficiency. Content similarity is related to similarity among filters. Our performance results confirm that an organization that performs a type of content clustering is much more efficient when we are interested in retrieving a large number of relevant documents.

An interesting issue for future work is deriving a method for self-organizing the nodes by adjusting the threshold of the hierarchies. Other important topics include alternative ways for distributing the filters besides the hierarchical organization and using other types of summaries instead of Bloom filters.

References

1. D. S. Milojicic, V. Kalogeraki, R. Lukose, K. Nagaraja, J. Pruyne, B. Richard, S. Rollins, Z. Xu. Peer-to-Peer Computing, HP Laboratories Palo Alto, HPL-2002-57.
2. S.D. Gribble, E.A. Brewer, J.M. Hellerstein, D. Culler. Scalable Distributed Data Structures for Internet Service Construction. In OSDI 2000.
3. B. Bloom. Space/Time Trade-offs in Hash Coding with Allowable Errors. CACM, 13(7), July 1970.
4. L. Fan, P. Cao, J. Almeida, A. Broder. Summary Cache: A Scalable Wide-Area Web Cache Sharing Protocol. In SIGCOMM 1998.
5. T.D. Hodes, S.E. Czerwinski, B.Y. Zhao, A.D. Joseph, R.H. Katz. Architecture for Secure Wide-Area Service Discovery. In Mobicom 1999.
6. The MD5 Message-Digest Algorithm. RFC1321.
7. The Niagara generator, http://www.cs.wisc.edu/niagara
8. Napster. http://www.napster.com/
9. R. Goldman, J. Widom. DataGuides: Enabling Query Formulation and Optimization in Semistructured Databases. In VLDB 1997.
10. B. F. Cooper, N. Sample, M. J. Franklin, G. R. Hjaltason, M. Shadmon. Fast Index for Semistructured Data. In VLDB 2001.
11. N. Polyzotis, M. Garofalakis. Structure and Value Synopses for XML Data Graphs. In VLDB 2002.
12. S. Park, H J. Kim. A New Query Processing Technique for XML Based on Signature. In DASFAA 2001.
13. C. Faloutsos, S. Christodoulakis. Signature Files: An Access Method for Documents and Its Analytical Performance Evaluation. ACM TOIS, 2(4), October 1984.
14. A. Mohan and V. Kalogeraki. Speculative Routing and Update Propagation: A Kundali Centric Approach. In ICC 2003.
15. A. Crespo, H. Garcia-Molina. Semantic Overlay Networks for P2P Systems. Submitted for publication.
16. W. Nejdl, M. Wolpers, W. Siberski, C. Schmitz, M. Schlosser, I. Brunkhorst, A. Loser. Super-Peer-Based Routing and Clustering Strategies for RDF-Based Peer-To-Peer Networks. In WWW 2003.
17. G. Koloniari, E. Pitoura. Bloom-Based Filters for Hierarchical Data. WDAS 2003.
18. G. Koloniari, Y. Petrakis, E. Pitoura. Content-Based Overlay Networks of XML Peers Based on Multi-Level Bloom Filters. VLDB International Workshop on Databases, Information Systems and Peer-to-Peer Computing, 2003.
19. A. Crespo, H. Garcia-Molina. Routing Indices for Peer-to-Peer Systems. In ICDCS 2002.
20. I. Stoica, R. Morris, D. Karger, M. F. Kaashoek, H. Balakrishnan. Chord: A Scalable Peer-to-Peer Lookup Service for Internet Applications, In SIGCOMM 2001.
21. S. Ratnasamy, P. Francis, M. Handley, R. Karp, S. Shenker. A Scalable Content-Addressable Network. In SIGCOMM, 2001.

22. Knowbuddy's Gnutella FAQ,
http://www.rixsoft.com/Knowbuddy/gnutellafaq.html
23. E. Pitoura, S. Abiteboul, D. Pfoser, G. Samaras, M. Vazirgiannis. DBGlobe: a Service-oriented P2P System for Global Computing. SIGMOD Record 32(3), 2003
24. G. Koloniari and E. Pitoura. Content-Based Routing of Path Queries in Peer-to-Peer Systems (extended version). Computer Science Dept, Univ. of Ioannina, TR-2003-12.

Energy-Conserving Air Indexes for Nearest Neighbor Search*

Baihua Zheng[1], Jianliang Xu[2], Wang-Chien Lee[3], and Dik Lun Lee[4]

[1] Singapore Management University, Singapore
bhzheng@smu.edu.sg
[2] Hong Kong Baptist University, Hong Kong
xujl@comp.hkbu.edu.hk
[3] Penn State University, University Park, PA 16802, USA
wlee@cse.psu.edu
[4] Hong Kong University of Science and Technology, Hong Kong
dlee@cs.ust.hk

Abstract. A location-based service (LBS) provides information based on the location information specified in a query. *Nearest-neighbor* (NN) search is an important class of queries supported in LBSs. This paper studies energy-conserving air indexes for NN search in a wireless broadcast environment. Linear access requirement of wireless broadcast weakens the performance of existing search algorithms designed for traditional spatial database. In this paper, we propose a new energy-conserving index, called *grid-partition index*, which enables a single linear scan of the index for any NN queries. The idea is to partition the search space for NN queries into grid cells and index all the objects that are potential nearest neighbors of a query point in each grid cell. Three grid partition schemes are proposed for the grid-partition index. Performance of the proposed grid-partition indexes and two representative traditional indexes (enhanced for wireless broadcast) is evaluated using both synthetic and real data. The result shows that the grid-partition index substantially outperforms the traditional indexes.

Keywords: mobile computing, location-based services, energy-conserving index, nearest-neighbor search, wireless broadcast

1 Introduction

Due to the popularity of personal digital devices and advances in wireless communication technologies, location-based services (LBSs) have received a lot of attention from both of the industrial and academic communities [9]. In its report "IT Roadmap to a Geospatial Future" [14], the Computer Science and Telecommunications Board (CSTB) predicted that LBS will usher in the era of pervasive computing and reshape mass media, marketing, and various aspects of our society in the decade to come. With the maturation of necessary technologies and

* Jianliang Xu's work was supported by the Hong Kong Baptist University under grant number FRG02-03II-34.

E. Bertino et al. (Eds.): EDBT 2004, LNCS 2992, pp. 48–66, 2004.
© Springer-Verlag Berlin Heidelberg 2004

the anticipated worldwide deployment of 3G wireless communication infrastructure, LBSs are expected to be one of the killer applications for wireless data industry.

In the wireless environments, there are basically two approaches for provision of LBSs to mobile users:[1]

- **On-Demand Access:** A mobile user submits a request, which consists of a query and its current location, to the server. The server locates the requested data and returns it to the mobile user.
- **Broadcast:** Data are periodically broadcast on a wireless channel open to the public. Instead of submitting a request to the server, a mobile user tunes into the broadcast channel and filters out the data based on the query and its current location.

On-demand access employs a basic client-server model where the server is responsible for processing a query and returning the result directly to the user via a dedicate point-to-point channel. On-demand access is particularly suitable for light-loaded systems when contention for wireless channels and server processing is not severe. However, as the number of users increases, the system performance deteriorates rapidly. On the other hand, wireless broadcast, which has long been used in the radio and TV industry, is a natural solution to solve the scalability and bandwidth problems in pervasive computing environments since broadcast data can be shared by many clients simultaneously. For many years, companies such as Hughes Network System have been using satellite-based broadcast to provide broadband services. The *smart personal objects technology* (SPOT), announced by Microsoft at the 2003 International Consumer Electronics Show, has further ascertained the industrial interest on and feasibility of utilizing wireless broadcast for pervasive data services. With a continuous broadcast network (called *DirectBand Network*) using FM radio subcarrier frequencies, SPOT-based devices such as watches, alarms, etc., can continuously receive timely, location-specific, personalized information [5]. Thus, in this paper, we focus on supporting LBSs in the wireless broadcast systems.

A very important class of problems in LBSs is *nearest-neighbor (NN) search.* An example of a NN search is: "Show me the nearest restaurant." A lot of research has been carried out on how to solve the NN search problem for spatial databases [13]. Most of the existing studies on NN search are based on indexes that store the locations of the data objects (e.g., the well-known R-tree [13]). We call them *object-based indexes.* Recently, Berchtold et. al. proposed a method for NN search based on indexing the pre-computed solution space [1]. Based on the similar design principle, a new index, called *D-tree*, was proposed by the authors [15]. We refer this category of indexes as *solution-based indexes.* Both of object-based indexes and solution-based indexes have some advantages and disadvantages. For example, object-based indexes have a small index size, but they sometimes require backtracking to obtain the result. This only works

[1] In this paper, mobile users, mobile clients, and mobile devices are used interchangeably.

for random data access media such as disks but, as shown later in this paper, does not perform well on broadcast data. Solution-based indexes overcome the backtracking problem and thus work well for both random and sequential data access media. However, they in general perform well in high-dimensional space but poorly in low-dimensional space, since the solution space generally consists of many irregular shapes to index.

The goal of this study is to design a new index tailored for supporting NN search on wireless broadcast channels. Thus, there are several basic requirements for such a design: 1) The index can facilitate energy saving at mobile clients; 2) The index is access and storage efficient (because the index will be broadcast along with the data); 3) The index is flexible (i.e., tunable based on a weight between energy saving and access latency; and 4) A query can be answered within one linear scan of the index. Based on the above design principles, we propose a new energy-conserving index called *Grid-Partition Index* which novelly combines the strengths of object-based indexes and solution-based indexes. Algorithms for constructing the grid-partition index and processing NN queries in wireless broadcast channel based on the proposed index are developed.

The rest of this paper is organized as follows. Section 2 introduces air indexing for a wireless broadcast environment and reviews existing index structures for NN search. Section 3 explains the proposed energy-conserving index, followed by description of three grid partition schemes in Section 4. Performance evaluation of the Grid-Partition index and two traditional indexes is presented in Section 5. Finally, we conclude the paper with a brief discussion on the future work in Section 6.

2 Background

This study focuses on supporting the NN search in wireless broadcast environments, in which the clients are responsible for retrieving data by listening to the wireless channel. In the following, we review the air indexing techniques for wireless data broadcast and the existing index structures for NN search. Throughout this paper, the Euclidean distance function is assumed.

2.1 Air Indexing Techniques for Wireless Data Broadcast

One critical issue for mobile devices is the consumption of battery power [3,8,11]. It is well known that transmitting a message consumes much more battery power than receiving a message. Thus, data access via broadcast channel is more energy efficient than on-demand access. However, by only broadcasting the data objects, a mobile device may have to receive a lot of redundant data objects on air before it finds the answer to its query. With increasing emphasis and rapid development on energy conserving functionality, mobile devices can switch between *doze mode* and *active mode* in order to conserve energy consumption. Thus, *air indexing* techniques, aiming at energy conservation, are developed by pre-computing and indexing certain auxiliary information (i.e., the arrival time of data objects)

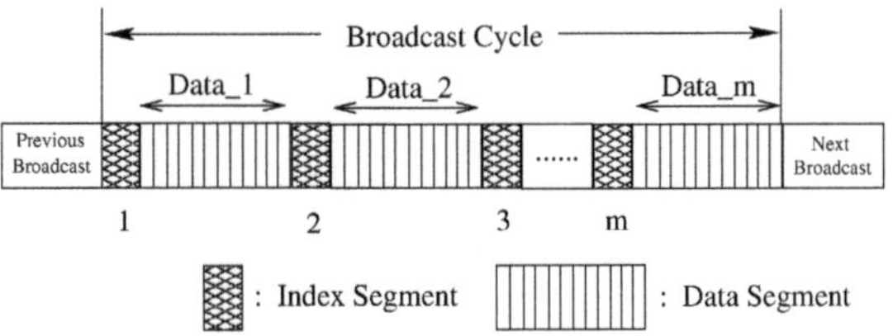

Fig. 1. Data and Index Organization Using the (1, m) Interleaving Technique

for broadcasting along with the data objects [8]. By first examining the index information on air, a mobile client is able to predict the arrival time of the desired data objects. Thus, it can stay in the doze mode to save energy most of the time and only wake up in time to tune into the broadcast channel when the requested data objects arrive.

A lot of existing research focuses on organizing the index information with data objects in order to improve the service efficiency. A well-known data and index organization for wireless data broadcast, called $(1, m)$ interleaving technique [8]. As shown in Figure 1, a complete index is broadcasted preceding every $\frac{1}{m}$ fraction of the broadcast cycle, the period of time when the complete set of data objects is broadcast. By replicating the index for m times, the waiting time for a mobile device to access the forthcoming index can be reduced. The readers should note that this interleaving technique can be applied to any index designed for wireless data broadcast. Thus, in this paper, we employ the $(1, m)$ interleaving scheme for our index.

Two performance metrics are typically used for evaluation of air indexing techniques: **tuning time** and **access latency**. The former means the period of time a client staying in the active mode, including the time used for searching the index and the time used for downloading the requested data. Since the downloading time of the requested data is the same for any indexing scheme, we only consider the tuning time used for searching the index. This metric roughly measures the power consumption by a mobile device. To provide a more precise evaluation, we also use **power consumption** as a metric in our evaluation. The latter represents the period of time from the moment a query is issued until the moment the query result is received by a mobile device.

2.2 Indexes for NN Search

There is a lot of existing work on answering NN search in the traditional spatial databases. As mentioned earlier, existing indexing techniques for NN search can be categorized into object-based index and solution-based index. Figure 2(a) depicts an example with four objects, o_1, o_2, o_3, and o_4, in a search space $\mathcal{A}$. This running example illustrates different indexing techniques discussed throughout this paper.

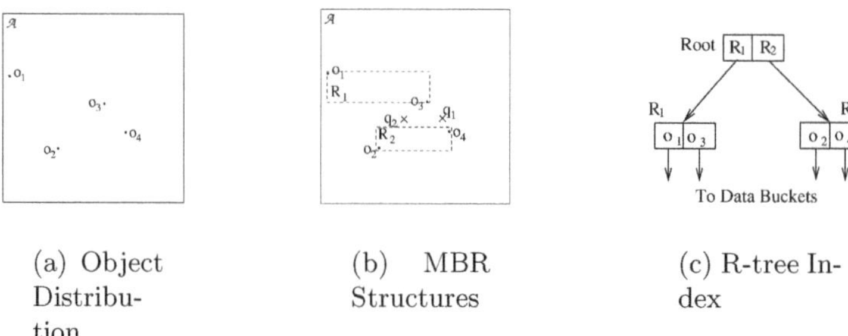

(a) Object Distribution (b) MBR Structures (c) R-tree Index

Fig. 2. A Running Example and R-tree Index

Object-Based Index. The indexes in this category are built upon the locations of data objects. R-tree is a representative [7]. Figure 2(c) shows R-tree for the running example. To perform NN search, a branch-and-bound approach is employed to traverse the index tree. At each step, heuristics are employed to choose the next branch for traversal. At the same time, information is collected to prune the future search space. Various search algorithms differ in the searching order and the metrics used to prune the branches [4,13].

Backtracking is commonly used in search algorithms proposed for traditional disk-access environment. However, this practice causes a problem for the linear-access broadcast channels. In wireless broadcast environments, index information is available to the mobile devices only when it is on the air. Hence, when an algorithm retrieves the index packets in an order different from their broadcast sequence, it has to wait for the next time the packet is broadcast (see the next paragraph for details). In contrast, the index for traditional databases is stored in resident storages, such as memories and disks. Consequently, it is available anytime.

Since the linear access requirement is not a design concern of traditional index structures, the existing algorithms do not meet the requirement of energy efficiency. For example, the index tree in Figure 2(c) is broadcast in the sequence of root, R_1, and R_2. Given a query point p_2, the visit sequence (first root, then R_2, finally R_1) results in a large access latency, as shown in Figure 3(a). Therefore, the branch-and-bound search approach is inefficient in access latency. Alternatively, we may just access the MBRs sequentially (see Figure 3(b)). However, this method is not the best in terms of index search performance since unnecessary MBR traversals may be incurred. For example, accessing R_1 for q_1 is a waste of energy.

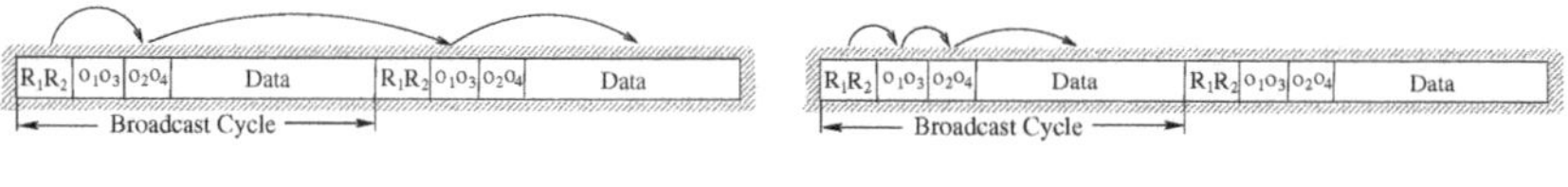

(a) Branch-and-Bound Search (b) Sequential Search

Fig. 3. Linear Access on a Wireless Broadcast Channel

Solution-Based Index. The indexes in this category are built on the pre-computed solution space, rather than on the objects [1]. For NN search, the solution space can be represented by *Voronoi Diagrams* (VDs) [2]. Let $O = \{o_1, o_2, \cdots, o_n\}$ be a set of points. $\mathcal{V}(o_i)$, the *Voronoi Cell* (VC) for o_i, is defined as the set of points q in the space such that $dist(q, o_i) < dist(q, o_j)$, $\forall\, j \neq i$. The VD for the running example is depicted in Figure 4(a), where P_1, P_2, P_3, and P_4 denote the VCs for the four objects, o_1, o_2, o_3, and o_4, respectively.

With a solution-based index, the NN search problem can be reduced to the problem of determining the VC in which a query point is located. Our previously proposed index, D-tree, has demonstrated a better performance for indexing solution-space than traditional indexes, and hence is employed as a representative of indexes in this category [15]. D-tree indexes VCs based on the divisions that form the boundaries of the VCs. For a space containing a set of VCs, D-tree recursively partitions it into two sub-spaces having similar number of VCs until each space only contains one VC[2]. D-tree for the running example is shown in Figure 4(b).

In summary, existing index techniques for NN search are not suitable for wireless data broadcast. An object-based index incurs a small index size, but the tuning time is poor because random data access is not allowed in a broadcast channel. On the other hand, a solution-based index, typically used for NN search in a high dimensional space, does not perform well in a low dimensional space due to the fact that efficient structures for indexing VCs are not available. In the following, we propose a new energy-conserving index that combines the strengths of both the object-based and the solution-based indexes.

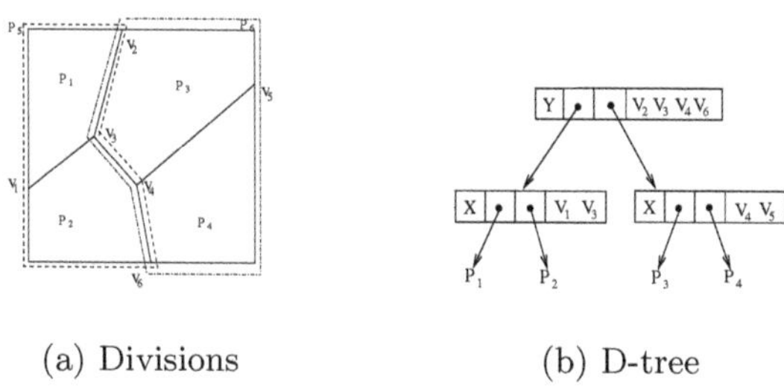

(a) Divisions (b) D-tree

Fig. 4. D-tree Index for the Running Example

3 A Grid-Partition Index

In this section, we first introduce the basic idea of our proposal and then describe the algorithm for processing NN search based on the Grid-Partition air index.

[2] D-tree was proposed to index any pre-computed solution space, not only for NN search.

3.1 The Basic Idea

In an object-based index such as R-tree, each NN search starts with the whole search space and gradually trims the space based on some knowledge collected during the search process. We observe that an essential problem leading to the poor search performance of object-based index is the large overall search space. Therefore, we attempt to reduce the search space for a query at the very beginning by partitioning the space into disjointed grid cells. To do so, we first construct the whole solution space for NN search using the VD method; then, divide the search space into disjointed grid cells using some grid partition algorithm (three partition schemes will be discussed in Section 4). For each grid cell, we index all the objects that are potential nearest neighbors of a query point inside the grid cell. Each object is the nearest neighbor only to those query points located inside the VC of the object. Hence, for any query point inside a grid cell, only the objects whose VCs overlap with the grid cell need to be checked.

Definition 1 *An object is* associated *with a grid cell if the VC of the object overlaps with the grid cell.*

Since each grid cell covers a part of the search space only, the number of objects associated with each grid cell is expected to be much smaller than the total number of objects in the original space. Thus, the initial search space for a NN query is reduced greatly if we can quickly locate the grid cell in which a query point lies. Hence, the overall performance is improved. Figure 5(a) shows a possible grid partition for our running example. The whole space is divided into four grid cells, i.e., G_1, G_2, G_3, and G_4. Grid cell G_1 is associated with objects o_1 and o_2 since their VCs, P_1 and P_2, overlap with G_1; likewise, grid cell G_2 is associated with objects o_1, o_2, and o_3, and so on and so forth.

The index structure for the proposed grid-partition index consists of two levels. The upper-level index is built upon the grid cells, and the lower-level index is upon the objects associated with each grid cell. The upper-level index maps a query point to a corresponding grid cell, while the lower-level index facilitates the access to the objects within each grid cell. The nice thing is that once the query point is located in a grid cell, its nearest neighbor is definitely among the objects associated with that grid cell, thereby preventing any rollback

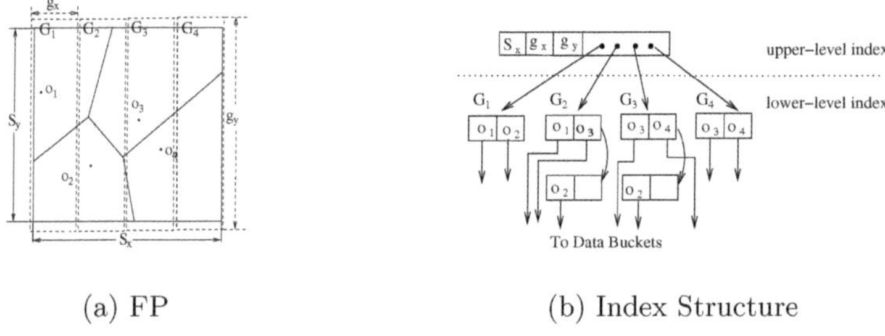

(a) FP (b) Index Structure

Fig. 5. Fixed Grid Partition for the Running Example

operations and enabling a single linear access of the upper-level index for any query point. In addition, to avoid rollback operations in the lower-level index, we try to maintain each grid cell in a size such that its associated objects can fit into one data packet, which is the smallest transmission unit in wireless broadcast. Thus, for each grid cell a simple index structure (i.e., a list of object and pointer pairs) is employed. In case that the index for a grid cell cannot fit into one packet, a number of packets are sequentially allocated. In each grid cell, the list of object and pointer pairs are sorted according to the dimension with the largest scale (hereafter called *sorting dimension*), i.e., the dimension in which the grid cell has the largest span. For example, in Figure 5(a), the associated objects for grid cell G_2 are sorted according to the y-dimension, i.e., o_1, o_3, and o_2. This arrangement is to speed up the nearest neighbor detecting procedure as we will see in the next subsection.

3.2 Nearest-Neighbor Search

With a grid-partition index, a NN query is answered by executing the following three steps: 1) *locating grid cell*, 2) *detecting nearest neighbor*, and 3) *retrieving data*. The first step locates the grid cell in which the query point lies. The second step obtains all the objects associated with that grid cell and detects the nearest neighbor by comparing their distances to the query point. The final step retrieves the data to answer the query. In the following, we describe an efficient algorithm for detecting the nearest neighbor in a grid cell. This algorithm works for all the proposed grid partition schemes. We leave the issue of locating grid cell to Section 4. This allows us to treat the problems of partitioning grid and locating grid cells more coherently.

In a grid cell, given a query point, the sorted objects are broken into two lists according to the query point in the sorting dimension: one list consists of the objects with coordinates smaller than the query point, and the rest form the other. To detect the nearest neighbor, the objects in those two lists are checked alternatively. Initially, the current shortest distance *min_dis* is set to infinite. At each checking step, *min_dis* is updated, if the distance between the object being checked and the query point, *cur_dis*, is shorter than *min_dis*. The checking process continues until the distance of the current object and the query point in the sorting dimension, *dis_sd*, is longer than *min_dis*. The correctness is justified as follows. For the current object, its *cur_dis* is longer than or equal to *dis_sd* and, hence, longer than *min_dis* if *dis_sd* is longer than *min_dis*. For the remaining objects in the list, their *dis_sd*'s are even longer and, thus, it is impossible for them to have a distance shorter than *min_dis*.

Figure 6(a) illustrates an example, where nine objects associated with the grid cell are sorted according to the x-dimension since the grid cell is flat. Given a query point shown in the figure, nine objects are broken into two lists, with one containing o_6 to o_1 and the other containing o_7 to o_9. The algorithm proceeds to check these two lists alternatively, i.e., in the order of o_6, o_7, o_5, o_8, $\cdots$, and so on. Figure 6(b) shows the intermediate results for each step. In the first list, the checking stops at o_4 since its *dis_sd* (i.e., 7.5) is already longer than *min_dis*

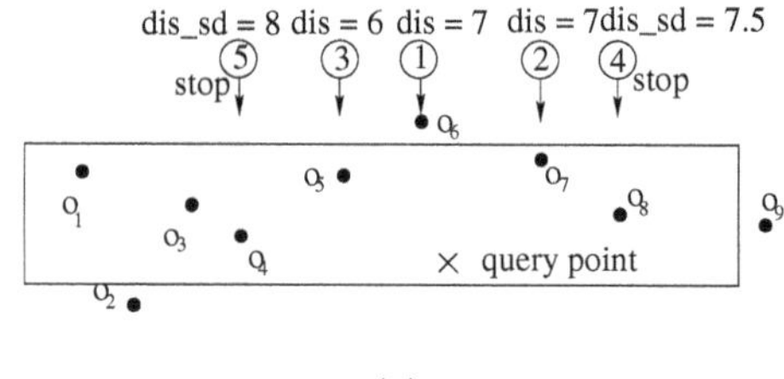

(a)

Step	Obj_{check}	dis_sd	cur_dis	min_dis
1	o_6	1	7	7
2	o_7	4	7	7
3	o_5	4	6	6
4	o_8	7.5	stop	
5	o_4	8	stop	

(b)

Fig. 6. An Example for Detecting Nearest Neighbor

(i.e., 6). Similarly, the checking stops at o_8 in the second list. As a result, only five objects rather than all nine objects are evaluated. Such improvement is expected to be significant when the scales of a grid cell in different dimensions differ greatly.

4 Grid Partitions

Thus far, the problem of NN search has been reduced to the problem of *grid partition*. How to divide the search space into grid cells, construct the upper-level grid index, and map a query point into a grid cell are crucial to the performance of the proposed index. In this section, three grid partition schemes, namely, *fixed partition*, *semi-adaptive partition*, and *adaptive partition*, are introduced. These schemes are illustrated in a two-dimensional space, since we focus on the geospatial world (2-D or 3-D space) in the real mobile environments.

Before presenting grid partition algorithms, we first introduce an important performance metric, *indexing efficiency* η, which is employed in some of the proposed grid partition schemes. It is defined as the ratio of the reduced tuning time to the enlarged index storage cost against a *naive* scheme, where the locations of objects are stored as a plain index that is exhaustively searched to answer a NN query. The indexing efficiency of a scheme i is defined as $\eta(i) = \Big((T_{naive} - T_i)/T_{naive}\Big)^{\alpha} / \Big((S_i - S_{naive})/S_{naive}\Big)$, where T is the average tuning time, S is the index storage cost, and α is a control parameter to weigh the importance of the saved tuning time and the index storage overhead. The setting of α could be adjusted for different application scenarios. The larger the α value, the more important the tuning time compared with the index storage cost. This metric will be used as a performance guideline to balance the tradeoff between the tuning time and the index overhead in constructing the grid-partition index.

4.1 Fixed Partition (FP)

A simple way for grid partition is to divide the search space into fixed-size grid cells. Let S_x and S_y be the scales of the x- and y-dimensions in the original space, g_x and g_y be the fixed width and height of a grid cell. The original space is thus divided into $\frac{S_x}{g_x} \cdot \frac{S_y}{g_y}$ grid cells. With this approach, the upper-level index for the grid cells (shown in Figure 5(b)) maintains some *header* information (i.e., S_x, g_x, and g_y) to assist in locating grid cells, along with a one-dimensional array that stores the pointers to the grid cells. In the data structure, if the header information and the pointer array cannot fit into one packet, they are allocated in a number of sequential packets.

The grid cell locating procedure works as follows. We first access the header information and get the parameters of S_x, g_x, and g_y. Then, given a query point (q_x, q_y), we use a mapping function, $adr(q_x, q_y) = \lfloor \frac{q_y}{g_y} \rfloor \cdot \lceil \frac{S_x}{g_x} \rceil + \lfloor \frac{q_x}{g_x} \rfloor$, to calculate the address of the pointer for the grid cell in which the query point lies. Hence, at most 2-packet accesses (one for the header information and maybe additional one for the pointer if it is not allocated in the same packet) in locating grid cells are needed, regardless of the number of grid cells and the packet size.

Aiming to maximize the packet utilization in the index, we employ a greedy algorithm to choose the best grid size. Let *num* be the number of expected grid cells. We continue to increase *num* from 1 until the average number of objects associated with the grid cells is smaller than the fan-out of a node. Further increasing *num* will decrease the packet occupancy and thus degrade the performance. For any *num*, every possible combination of g_x and g_y such that $\frac{S_x}{g_x} \cdot \frac{S_y}{g_y}$ equals *num*, is considered. The indexing efficiency for the resultant grid partition with width g_x and height g_y is calculated. The grid partition achieving the highest indexing efficiency is selected as the final solution.

While the fixed grid partition is simple, it does not take into account the distribution of objects and their VCs. Thus, it is not easy to utilize the index packets efficiently, especially under a skewed object distribution. Consequently, under the fixed grid partition, it is not unusual to have some packets with a low utilization rate, whereas some others overflow. This could lead to a poor average performance.

4.2 Semi-Adaptive Partition (SAP)

To adapt to skewed object distributions, the semi-adaptive partition only fixes the size of the grid cells in either width or height. In other words, the whole space is equally divided into stripes along one dimension. In the other dimension, each stripe is partitioned into grid cells in accordance with the object distribution.

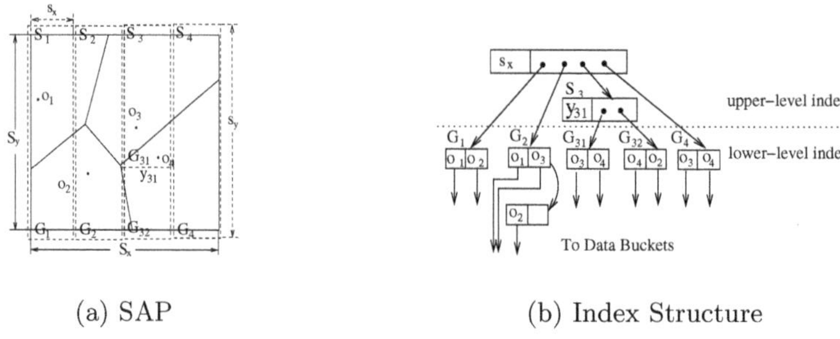

(a) SAP (b) Index Structure

Fig. 7. Semi-Adaptive Partition for the Running Example

The objective is to increase the utilization of a packet by having the number of objects associated with each grid cell close to the fan-out of the node. Thus, once the grid cell is identified for a query point, only one packet needs to be accessed in the step of detecting nearest neighbor.

Figure 7 illustrates the semi-adaptive grid partition for our running example, where the height of each stripe is fixed. Similar to the FP approach, the root records the width of a stripe (i.e., s_x) for the mapping function and an array of pointers pointing to the stripes. In each stripe, if the associated objects can fit into one packet, the objects are allocated directly in the lower-level index (e.g., the 1st and 4th pointers in the root). Otherwise, an extra index node for the grid cells within the corresponding stripe is allocated (e.g., the 3rd pointer in the root). The extra index node consists of a set of sorted discriminators followed by the pointers pointing to the grid cells. However, if there is no way to further partition a grid cell such that the objects in each grid cell can fit the packet capacity, more than one packet is allocated (e.g., the 2nd pointer in the root).

To locate the grid cell for a query point (q_x, q_y), the algorithm first locates the desired stripe using a mapping function, $adr(q_x, q_y) = \lfloor \frac{q_x}{s_x} \rfloor$. If the stripe points to an object packet (i.e., only contains one grid cell), it is finished. Otherwise, we traverse to the extra index node and use the discriminators to locate the appropriate grid cell. Compared with FP, this partition approach has a better packet occupancy, but takes more space to index the grid cells.

4.3 Adaptive Partition (AP)

The third scheme adaptively partition the grid using a kd-tree like partition method [12]. It recursively partitions the search space into two complementary subspaces such that the number of objects associated with the two subspaces is nearly the same. The partition does not stop until the number of objects associated with each subspace is smaller than the fan-out of the index node.

The partition algorithm works as follows. We partition the the space horizontally or vertically. Suppose that the vertical partition is employed. We sort the objects in an increasing order of the left-most x-coordinates (LXs) of their VCs. Then, we examine the LXs one by one beginning from the median ob-

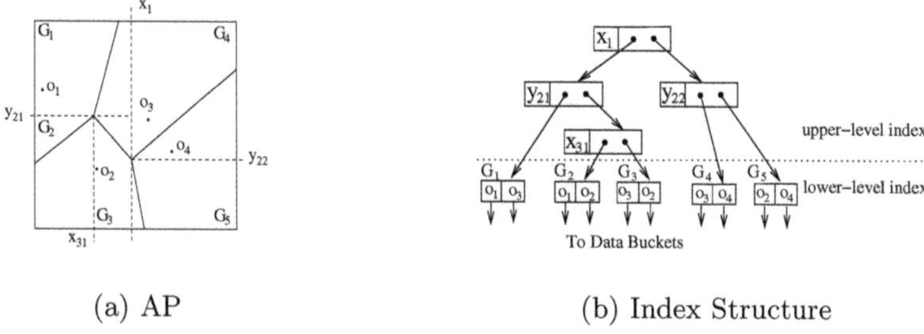

(a) AP (b) Index Structure

Fig. 8. Adaptive Partition for the Running Example

ject. Given a LX, the space is partitioned by the vertical line going through the LX. Let num_l and num_r be the numbers of associated objects for the left subspace and the right subspace, respectively. If num_l=num_r, the examination stops immediately. Otherwise, all the LXs are tried and the LX resulting in the smallest value of $|num_l\text{-}num_r|$ is selected as the discriminator. Similarly, when the horizontal partition is employed, the objects are sorted according to the lowest y-coordinates (LYs) of their VCs and the discriminator is selected much the same way in the vertical partition. In selecting the partition style between the vertical and horizontal partitions, we favor the one with a smaller value of $|num_l+num_r|$. Figure 8 shows the adaptive grid partition for the running example, where each node in the upper-level index stores the discriminator followed by two pointers pointing to two subspaces of the current space.

In this approach, the index for the grid cells is a kd-tree. Thus, the point query algorithm for the kd-tree is used to locate the grid cells. Given a query point, we start at the root. If it is to the left of the discriminator of the node, the left pointer is followed; otherwise, the right pointer is followed. This procedure is not stopped until a leaf node is met. However, as the kd-tree is binary, we need some paging method to store it in a way to fit the packet size. A top-down paging mechanism is employed. The binary kd-tree is traversed in a breadth-first order. For each new node, the packet containing its parent is checked. If that packet has enough free space to contain this node, the node is inserted into that packet. Otherwise, a new packet is allocated.

4.4 Discussion

For NN search, the VD changes when objects are inserted, deleted, or relocated. Thus, the index needs to be updated accordingly. Since updates are expected to happen infrequently regarding NN search in mobile LBS applications (such as finding nearest restaurant and nearest hotel), we only briefly discuss the update issue here.

When an object o_i is inserted or deleted, the VCs around o_i will be affected. The number of affected VCs is approximately the number of edges of the VC for o_i, which is normally very small. For example, in Figure 2(a) adding a new object in P_1 changes the VCs for o_1, o_2, and o_3. Assuming the server maintains adequate information about the VCs, the affected VCs can be detected easily.

For all the proposed grid partitions, we can identify the grid cells that overlap with the affected VCs and update the index for the objects associated with each of them. When updates are rare, the partition of the grid cells is not modified. On the other hand, partial or complete grid re-partition can be performed periodically.

5 Performance Evaluation

To evaluate the proposed grid-partition index, we compare it with D-tree [15] and R-tree, which represent the solution-based index and the object-based index for NN search respectively, in terms of tuning time, power consumption, and access latency. Two datasets (denoted as UNIFORM and REAL) are used in the evaluation (see Figure 9). In the UNIFORM dataset, 10,000 points are uniformly generated in a square Euclidean space. The REAL dataset contains 1102 parks in the Southern California area, which is extracted from the point dataset available from [6].

Since the data objects are available a priori, the STR packing scheme is employed to build R-tree [10]. As we discussed in Section 2.2, the original branch-and-bound NN search algorithm results in a poor access latency in wireless broadcast systems. In order to cater for the linear-access requirement on air, we revise it as follows. R-tree is broadcast in a width-first order. For query processing, no matter where the query point is located, the MBRs are accessed sequentially, while impossible branches are pruned similarly in the original algorithm [13].

The system model in the simulation consists of a base station, a number of clients, and a broadcast channel. The available bandwidth is set to $100K$ bps. The packet size is varied from 64 bytes to 2048 bytes. In each packet, two bytes are allocated for the packet id. Two bytes are used for one pointer and four bytes are for one coordinate. The size of a data object is set to 1K bytes. The results

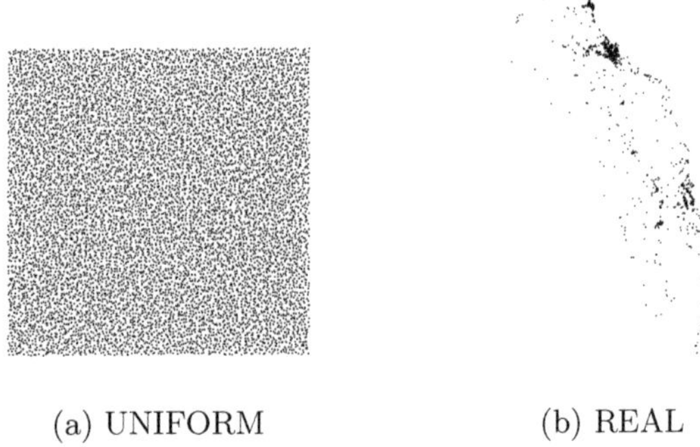

(a) UNIFORM (b) REAL

Fig. 9. Datasets for Performance Evaluation

presented in the following sections are the average performance of 10,000,000 random queries.

5.1 Sensitivity to Indexing Efficiency

Indexing efficiency has been used in the FP and SAP grid partition schemes as guidance for determining the best cell partition. The control parameter α of indexing efficiency, set to a non-negative number, weighs the importance of the saved packet accesses and the index overhead. We conduct experiments to test the sensitivity of tuning time and index size to α.

Figure 10 shows the performance of grid-partition index for the UNIFORM dataset when the FP partition scheme is employed. Similar results are obtained for the REAL dataset and/or other grid partitions and, thus, are omitted due to the space limitation. From the figure, we can observe that the value of α has a significant impact on the performance, especially for small packet capacities. In general, the larger the value of α, the better the tuning time and the worse the index storage cost since a larger α value assigns more weight to reducing tuning time. As expected, the best index overhead is achieved when α is set to 0, and the best tuning time is achieved when α is set to infinity. The setting of α can be adjusted based on requirements of the applications. The index overhead for air indexes is also critical as it directly affects the access latency. Thus, for the rest of experiments, the value of α is set to 1, giving equal weight to the index size and the tuning time.

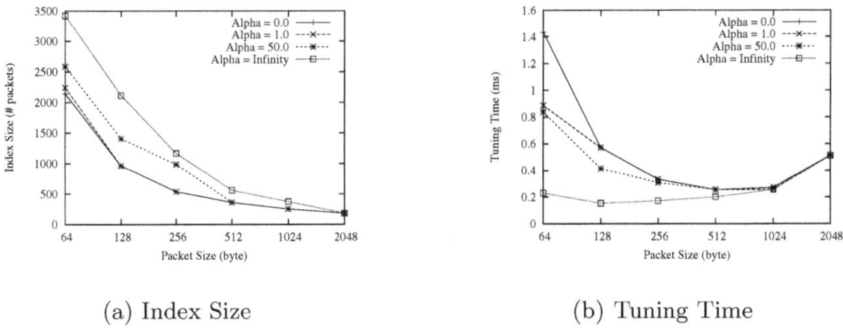

(a) Index Size (b) Tuning Time

Fig. 10. Performance under Different α Settings (UNIFORM, FP)

5.2 Tuning Time

This subsection compares the different indexes in terms of tuning time. In the wireless data broadcast environment, improving the tuning time generally saves power consumption. Figures 11(a) and (b) show the tuning time performance of compared indexes under UNIFORM and REAL datasets, respectively.

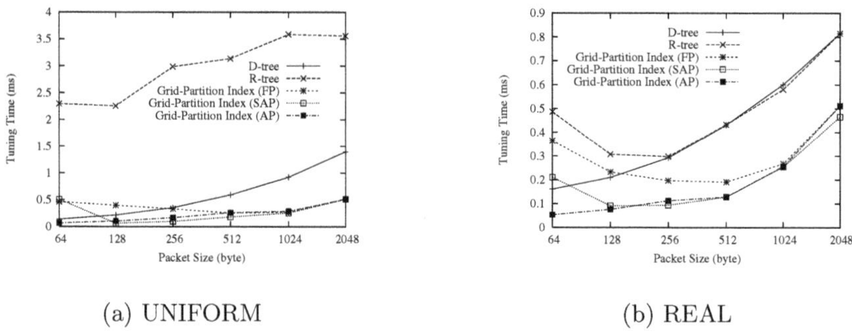

(a) UNIFORM (b) REAL

Fig. 11. Tuning Time vs. Packet Size

Two observations are obtained. First, the proposed grid-partition indexes outperform both D-tree and R-tree in most cases. As an example, let's look at the case when the packet size is 512 bytes. For D-tree, the tuning time is $0.59ms$ and $0.43ms$ for UNIFORM and REAL datasets, respectively. For R-tree, it needs $3.12ms$ and $0.43ms$, respectively. The grid-partition indexes have the best performance, i.e., no larger than $0.27ms$ for UNIFORM dataset and no larger than $0.19ms$ for REAL dataset.

Second, among the three proposed grid partition schemes, the SAP has the best overall performance and is the most stable one. The main reason is that the SAP scheme is more adaptive to the distribution of the objects and their VCs than the FP scheme, while its upper-level index (i.e., the index used for locating grid cells) is a simpler and more efficient data structure than that of the AP scheme. As a result, in most cases the SAP accesses only one or two packets to locate grid cells and another one to detect the nearest neighbor.

We notice that the grid-partition indexes with FP and SAP work worse than D-tree when the packet size is 64 bytes. This is caused by the small capacity of packet, which can fit in very limited objects information. Hence, the small size of the packet results in a large number of grid cells and causes duplications.

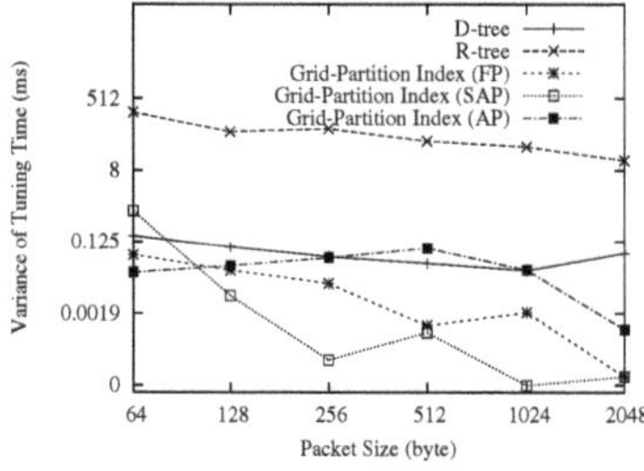

Fig. 12. Variance of Tuning Time (UNIFORM)

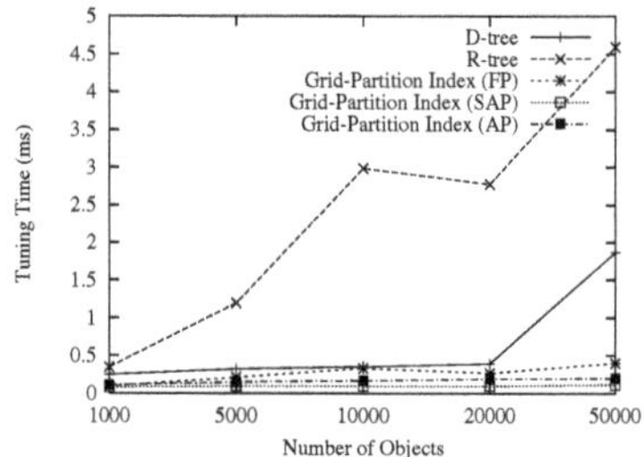

Fig. 13. Performance vs. Size of Datasets

We also measure the performance stableness of the compared indexes. Figure 12 shows the variance of their tuning time for the UNIFORM dataset. It can be observed again that the grid-partition indexes outperform both D-tree and R-tree in nearly all the cases. This means the power consumption of query processing based on grid-partition index is more predictable than that based on other indexes. This property is important for power management of mobile devices.

In order to evaluate the scalability of the compared indexes to the number of data objects, we measure the tuning time of indexes by fixing the packet size to 256 bytes and varying the number of objects from 1,000 to 50,000 (all uniformly distributed). As shown in Figure 13, the larger the population of the objects, the worse the performance as expected. The performance ratings among different indexes under various numbers of data objects are consistent. However, it is interesting to note that the performance degradation of the grid-partition indexes is much more gracefully than that of D-tree and R-tree, as the number of data objects increases. This indicates that the proposed grid-partition indexes are more pronounced for large databases.

5.3 Power Consumption

According to [8], a device equipped with the Hobbit chip (AT&T) consumes around $250mW$ power in the active mode, and consumes $50\mu W$ power in the doze mode. Hence, the period of time a mobile device staying in doze mode during query processing also has an impact on the power consumption. To have a more precise comparison of the power consumption based on various indexes, we calculate the power consumption of a mobile device based on the periods of active and doze modes obtained from our experiments. For simplicity, we neglect other components that consume power during query processing and assume that 250 mW constitutes the total power consumption. Figure 14 shows the power consumption of a mobile device under different air indexes, calculated based on the formula: $P = 250 \times Time_{active} + 0.05 \times Time_{doze}$.

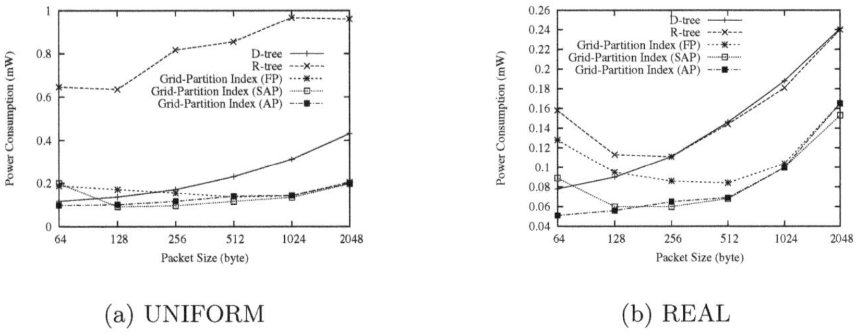

(a) UNIFORM (b) REAL

Fig. 14. Power Consumption vs. Packet Size

As shown in the figure, the grid-partition indexes significantly outperform other indexes. For UNIFORM dataset, the average power consumptions of D-tree are $0.23mW$, and that of R-tree is $0.69mW$. The power consumptions of grid-partition indexes are $0.17mW$, $0.14mW$, and $0.14mW$ for FP, SAP, and SP, respectively. For the REAL dataset, the improvement is also dramatic. The power consumptions of D-tree and R-tree are $0.13mW$ and $0.14mW$, while the grid-partition indexes consume $0.09mW$, $0.08mW$, and $0.06mW$. Although D-tree provides a better tuning time performance when the packet size is 64 bytes, that does not transform into less power consumption than the grid-partition index. This is caused by the large index overhead of D-tree, compared with that of grid-partition indexes (see Figure 15).

In summary, the grid-partition indexes can reduce the power consumption by the efficient search performance and small index overhead. Hence, it can achieve the design requirement of energy efficiency without any doubt and is extremely suitable for the wireless broadcast environments in which the population of users is supposed to be huge while the resources of mobile devices are very limited.

5.4 Access Latency

The access latency is affected by the storage cost of the index and the interleaving algorithm to organize data and index. Since index organization is beyond the scope of this paper, we count the access latency using the well-known $(1, m)$ scheme to interleave the index with data [8], as explained in Section 2.1. Figure 15 shows the access latency for all the index methods. In the figures, the latency is normalized to the expected access latency without any index (i.e., half of the time needed to broadcast the database).

We can see that the D-tree has the worst performance because of its large index size. The performance of those proposed grid-partition indexes is similar to that of the R-tree. They only introduce little latency overhead (within 30% in most cases) due to their small index sizes.

When different grid partition schemes are compared, the FP performs the best for a small packet capacity (< 256 bytes), whereas the SAP and the AP perform better for a large packet capacity (> 256 bytes). This can be explained as follows. When the packet capacity is small, the number of grid cells is large since we try to store the objects with a grid cell in one packet in all the three schemes. Thus, the index size is dominated by the overhead for storing the grid partition information (i.e., the upper-level index). As this overhead in the FP is the least (four parameters plus a pointer array), it achieves the smallest overall index size. However, with increasing packet capacity, the overhead for storing the upper-level index becomes insignificant. Moreover, with a large packet capacity the FP has a poorer packet occupancy than the other two. This is particularly true for the REAL dataset, where the objects are highly clustered. As a result, the index overhead of the FP becomes worse.

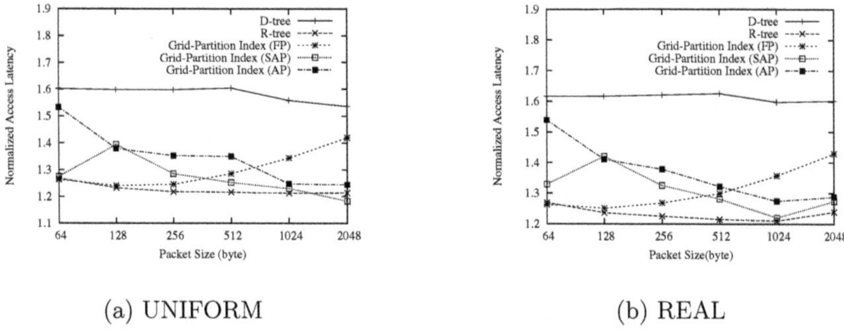

(a) UNIFORM (b) REAL

Fig. 15. Access Latency vs. Packet Capacity

6 Conclusion

Nearest-neighbor search is a very important and practical application in the emerging mobile computing era. In this paper, we analyze the problems associated with using object-based and solution-based indexes in wireless broadcast environments, where only linear access is allowed, and enhance the classical R-tree to make them suitable for the broadcast medium. We further propose the grid-partition index, a new energy-conserving air index for nearest neighbor search that combines the strengths of both the object-based and solution-based indexes. By studying the grid-partition index, we identify an interesting and fundamental research issue, i.e., grid partition, which affects the performance of the index. Three grid partition schemes, namely, fixed partition, semi-adaptive partition, and adaptive partition, are proposed in this study.

The performance of the grid-partition index (with three grid partition schemes) is compared with an enhanced object-based index (i.e., R-tree) and a solution-based index (i.e., D-tree) using both synthetic and real datasets. The results show that overall the grid-partition index substantially outperforms both the R-tree and D-tree. As the grid-partition index (SAP) achieves the best overall performance under workload settings, it is recommended for practical use.

Although the grid-partition index is proposed to efficiently solve NN search, it can also serve other queries, such as window queries and continuous nearest neighbor search. As for future work, we plan to extend the idea of the grid-partition index to answer multiple kinds of queries, including k-NN queries. As a first step, this paper only briefly addresses the update issue in a general discussion. We are investigating efficient algorithms to support updates. In addition, we are examining generalized NN search such as "show me the nearest hotel with room rate $< \$200$".

References

1. S. Berchtold, D. A. Keim, H. P. Kriegel, and T. Seidl. Indexing the solution space: A new technique for nearest neighbor search in high-dimensional space. *IEEE Transactions on Knowledge and Data Engineering (TKDE)*, 12(1):45–57, January/February 2000.
2. M. Berg, M. Kreveld, M. Overmars, and O. Schwarzkopf. *Computational Geometry: Algorithms and Applications*, chapter 7. Springer-Verlag, New York, NY, USA, 1996.
3. M-S. Chen, K-L. Wu, and S. Yu. Optimizing index allocation for sequential data broadcasting in wireless mobile computing. *IEEE Transactions on Knowledge and Data Engineering (TKDE)*, 15(1), 2003.
4. K. L. Cheung and W.-C. Fu. Enhanced nearest neighbour search on the r-tree. *SIGMOD Record*, 27(3):16–21, 1998.
5. Microsoft Corporation. What is the directband network? URL at http://www.microsoft.com/ resources/spot/direct.mspx, 2003.
6. Spatial Datasets. Website at http://dias.cti.gr/~ytheod/research/datasets/spatial.html.
7. A. Guttman. R-trees: A dynamic index structure for spatial searching. In *Proceedings of the ACM SIGMOD International Conference on Management of Data (SIGMOD'84)*, pages 47–54, 1984.
8. T. Imielinski, S. Viswanathan, and B. R. Badrinath. Data on air - organization and access. *IEEE Transactions on Knowledge and Data Engineering (TKDE)*, 9(3), May-June 1997.
9. D. L. Lee, W.-C. Lee, J. Xu, and B. Zheng. Data management in location-dependent information services. *IEEE Pervasive Computing*, 1(3):65–72, July-September 2002.
10. S. T. Leutenegger, J. M. Edgington, and M. A. Lopez. Str: A simple and efficient algorithm for r-tree packing. In *Proceedings of the 13th International Conference on Data Engineering (ICDE'97)*, pages 497–506, Birmingham, UK, April 1997.
11. S-C Lo and L.P. Chen. Optimal index and data allocation in multiple broadcast channels. In *Proceedings of the Sixteenth International Conference on Data Engineering (ICDE'00)*, February 2000.
12. B. C. Ooi, R. Sacks-Davis, and K. J. Mcdonell. Spatial indexing in binary decomposition and spatial bounding. *Information Systems*, 16(2):211–237, 1991.
13. N. Roussopoulos, S. Kelley, and F. Vincent. Nearest neighbor queries. In *Proceedings of the ACM SIGMOD International Conference on Management of Data (SIGMOD'95)*, pages 71–79, May 1995.
14. Computer Science and Telecommunications Board. *IT Roadmap to a Geospatial Future.* The National Academies Press, 2003.
15. J. Xu, B. Zheng, W.-C. Lee, and D. L. Lee. Energy efficient index for querying location-dependent data in mobile broadcast environments. In *Proceedings of the 19th IEEE International Conference on Data Engineering (ICDE'03)*, pages 239–250, Bangalore, India, March 2003.

MobiEyes: Distributed Processing of Continuously Moving Queries on Moving Objects in a Mobile System

Buğra Gedik and Ling Liu

College of Computing, Georgia Institute of Technology
{bgedik,lingliu}@cc.gatech.edu

Abstract. Location monitoring is an important issue for real time management of mobile object positions. Significant research efforts have been dedicated to techniques for efficient processing of spatial continuous queries on moving objects in a centralized location monitoring system. Surprisingly, very few have promoted a distributed approach to real-time location monitoring. In this paper we present a distributed and scalable solution to processing continuously moving queries on moving objects and describe the design of MobiEyes, a distributed real-time location monitoring system in a mobile environment. Mobieyes utilizes the computational power at mobile objects, leading to significant savings in terms of server load and messaging cost when compared to solutions relying on central processing of location information at the server. We introduce a set of optimization techniques, such as *Lazy Query Propagation*, *Query Grouping*, and *Safe Periods*, to constrict the amount of computations handled by the moving objects and to enhance the performance and system utilization of Mobieyes. We also provide a simulation model in a mobile setup to study the scalability of the MobiEyes distributed location monitoring approach with regard to server load, messaging cost, and amount of computation required on the mobile objects.

1 Introduction

With the growing market of positioning technologies like GPS [1] and the growing popularity and availability of mobile communications, location information management has become an important problem [17,10,14,5,15,13,16,9,2] in mobile computing systems. With continued upsurge of computational capabilities in mobile devices, ranging from navigational systems in cars to hand-held devices and cell phones, mobile devices are becoming increasingly accessible. We expect that future mobile applications will require a scalable architecture that is capable of handling large and rapidly growing number of mobile objects and processing complex queries over mobile object positions.

Location monitoring is an important issue for real time querying and management of mobile object positions. Significant research efforts have been dedicated to techniques for efficient processing of spatial continuous queries on moving objects in a centralized location monitoring system. Surprisingly, very few have promoted a distributed approach to real-time location monitoring over a large and growing number of mobile objects.

In this paper we present a distributed approach to real-time location monitoring over a large and growing number of mobile objects. Concretely, we describe the design of MobiEyes, a distributed real-time location monitoring system for processing *moving*

E. Bertino et al. (Eds.): EDBT 2004, LNCS 2992, pp. 67–87, 2004.
© Springer-Verlag Berlin Heidelberg 2004

queries over moving objects in a mobile environment. Before we describe the motivation of the MobiEyes system and the main contributions of the paper, we first give a brief overview of the concept of moving queries.

1.1 Moving Queries over Moving Objects

A moving query over moving objects (MQ for short) is a *spatial continuous moving query over locations of moving objects*. An MQ defines a spatial region bound to a specific moving object and a filter which is a boolean predicate on object properties. The result of an MQ consists of objects that are inside the area covered by the query's spatial region and satisfy the query filter.

MQs are continuous queries [11] in the sense that the results of queries continuously change as time progresses. We refer to the object to which an MQ is bounded, the *focal object* of that query. The set of objects that are subject to be included in a query's result are called *target objects* of the MQ. Note that the spatial region of an MQ also moves as the focal object of the MQ moves. There are many examples of moving queries over moving objects in real life. For instance, the query MQ_1: "Give me the number of friendly units within 5 miles radius around me during next 2 hours" can be submitted by a soldier equipped with mobile devices marching in the field, or a moving tank in a military setting. The query MQ_2: "Give me the positions of those customers who are looking for taxi and are within 5 miles (of my location at each instance of time or at an interval of every minute) during the next 20 minutes" can be posted by a taxi driver marching on the road. The focal object of MQ_1 is the solider marching in the field or a moving tank. The focal object of MQ_2 is the taxi driver on the road.

1.2 MobiEyes: Distributed Processing of MQs

Most of the existing approaches for processing spatial queries on moving objects are not scalable, due to their inherent assumption that location monitoring and communications of mobile objects are controlled by a central server. Namely, mobile objects report their position changes to the server whenever their position information changes, and the server determines which moving objects should be included in which moving queries at each instance of time or at a given time interval. For mobile applications that need to handle a large and growing number of moving objects, the centralized approaches can suffer from dramatic performance degradation in terms of server load and network bandwidth.

In this paper we present MobiEyes, a distributed solution for processing MQs in a mobile setup. Our solution ships some part of the query processing down to the moving objects, and the server mainly acts as a mediator between moving objects. This significantly reduces the load on the server side and also results in savings on the communication between moving objects and the server.

This paper has three unique contributions. First, we present a careful design of the distributed solution to real-time evaluation of continuously moving queries over moving objects. One of the main design principles is to develop efficient mechanisms that utilize the computational power at mobile objects, leading to significant savings in terms of server load and messaging cost when compared to solutions relying on central processing of location information at the server. Second, we develop a number of optimization techniques, including *Lazy Query Propagation*, and *Query Grouping*. We use the Query Grouping techniques to constrict the amount of computation to be performed by the moving objects in situations where a moving object is moving in an area that has many queries. We use Lazy Query Propagation to allow trade offs between query precision and network bandwidth cost and energy consumption on the moving objects. Third, but not least, we provide a simulation model in a mobile setup to study the scalability of the MobiEyes distributed location monitoring approach with regard to server load, messaging cost, and amount of computation required on the mobile objects.

2 System Model

2.1 System Assumptions

We below summarize four underlying assumptions used in the design of the MobiEyes system. All these assumptions are either widely agreed upon by many or have been seen as common practice in most existing mobile systems in the context of monitoring and tracking of moving objects.

– *Moving objects are able to locate their positions*: We assume that each moving object is equipped with a technology like GPS [1] to locate its position. This is a reasonable assumption as GPS devices are becoming inexpensive and are used widely in cars and other hand-held devices to provide navigational support.

– *Moving objects have synchronized clocks*: Again this assumption can be met if the moving objects are equipped with GPS. Another solution is to make NTP [12] (network time protocol) available to moving objects through base stations.

– *Moving objects are able to determine their velocity vector*: This assumption is easily met when the moving object is able to determine its location and has an internal timer.

– *Moving objects have computational capabilities to carry out computational tasks*: This assumption represents a fast growing trend in mobile and wireless technology. The number of mobile devices equiped with computational power escalates rapidly, even simple sensors [6] today are equipped with computational capabilities.

2.2 The Moving Object Model

MobiEyes system assumes that the geographical area of interest is covered by several base stations, which are connected to a central server. A three-tier architecture (mobile objects, base stations and the server) is used in the subsequent discussions. We can easily extend the three tier to a multi-tier communication hierarchy between the mobile objects and the server. In addition, the asymmetric communication is used to establish connections from the server to the moving objects. Concretely, a base station can communicate directly with the moving objects in its coverage area through a broadcast, and the moving objects can only communicate with the base station if they are located in the coverage area of this base station.

Let O be the set of moving objects. Formally we can describe a moving object $o \in O$ by a quadruple: $\langle oid, pos, \overline{vel}, \{props\} \rangle$. oid is the unique object identifier. pos is the current position of the object o. $\overline{vel} = (velx, vely)$ is the current velocity vector of the object, where $velx$ is its velocity in the x-dimension and $vely$ is its velocity in the y-dimension. $\{props\}$ is a set of properties about the moving object o, including spatial, temporal, or object-specific properties, such as color or manufacture of a mobile unit (or even the application specific attributes registered on the mobile unit by the user).

The basic notations used in the subsequent sections of the paper are formally defined below:

– *Rectangle shaped region and circle shaped region* : A rectangle shaped region is defined by $Rect(lx, ly, w, h) = \{(x, y) : x \in [lx, lx+w] \wedge y \in [ly, ly+h]\}$ and a circle shaped region is defined by $Circle(cx, cy, r) = \{(x, y) : (x - cx)^2 + (y - cx)^2 \leq r^2\}$.

– *Universe of Discourse (UoD)*: We refer to the geographical area of interest as the universe of discourse, which is defined by $U = Rect(X, Y, W, H)$. X, Y, W and H are system level parameters to be set at the system initialization time.

– *Grid and Grid cells*: In MobiEyes, we map the universe of discourse, $U = Rect(X, Y, W, H)$, onto a grid G of cells, where each grid cell is an $\alpha \times \alpha$ square area, and α is a system parameter that defines the cell size of the grid G. Formally, a grid corresponding to the universe of discourse U can be defined as $G(U, \alpha) = \{A_{i,j} : 1 \leq i \leq M, 1 \leq j \leq N, A_{i,j} = Rect(X+i*\alpha, Y+j*\alpha, \alpha, \alpha), M = \lceil H/\alpha \rceil, N = \lceil W/\alpha \rceil\}$. $A_{i,j}$ is an $\alpha \times \alpha$ square area representing the grid cell that is located on the ith row and jth column of the grid G.

– *Position to Grid Cell Mapping*: Let $pos = (x, y)$ be the position of a moving object in the universe of discourse $U = Rect(X, Y, W, H)$. Let $A_{i,j}$ denote a cell in the grid $G(U, \alpha)$. $Pmap(pos)$ is a position to grid cell mapping, defined as $Pmap(pos) = A_{\lceil \frac{pos.x - X}{\alpha} \rceil, \lceil \frac{pos.y - Y}{\alpha} \rceil}$.

– *Current Grid Cell of an Object*: Current grid cell of a moving object is the grid cell which contains the current position of the moving object. If $o \in O$ is an object whose current position, denoted as $o.pos$, is in the Universe of Discourse U, then the current grid cell of the object is formally defined by $curr\_cell(o) = Pmap(o.pos)$.

– *Base Stations*: Let $U = Rect(X, Y, W, H)$ be the universe of discourse and B be the set of base stations overlapping with U. Assume that each base station $b \in B$ is defined by a circle region $Circle(bsx, bsy, bsr)$. We say that the set B of base stations covers the universe of discourse U, i.e. $\left(\bigcup_{b \in B} b\right) \supseteq U$.

– *Grid Cell to Base Station Mapping*: Let $Bmap : \mathbb{N} \times \mathbb{N} \rightarrow 2^B$ define a mapping, which maps a grid cell index to a non-empty set of base stations. We define $Bmap(i, j) = \{b : b \in B \wedge b \cap A_{i,j} \neq \emptyset\}$. $Bmap(i, j)$ is the set of base stations that cover the grid cell $A_{i,j}$.

2.3 Moving Query Model

Let Q be the set of moving queries. Formally we can describe a moving query $q \in Q$ by a quadruple: $\langle qid, oid, region, filter \rangle$. qid is the unique query identifier. oid is the object identifier of the focal object of the query. $region$ defines the shape of the spatial query region bound to the focal object of the query. $region$ can be described by a closed shape description such as a rectangle, or a circle, or any other closed shape description which has a computationally cheap point containment check. This closed shape description also specifies a binding point, through which it is bound to the focal object of the query. Without loss of generality we use a circle, with its center serving as the binding point to represent the shape of the region of a moving query in the rest of the paper. $filter$ is a Boolean predicate defined over the properties $\{props\}$ of the target objects of a moving query q. For presentation convenience, in the rest of the paper we consider the result of an MQ as the set of object identifiers of the moving objects that locate within the area covered by the spatial region of the query and satisfy the filter condition.

A formal definition of basic notations regarding MQs is given below.

– *Bounding Box of a Moving Query*: Let $q \in Q$ be a query with focal object $fo \in O$ and spatial region $region$, let rc denote the current grid cell of fo, i.e. $rc = curr\_cell(fo)$. Let lx and ly denote the x-coordinate and the y-coordinate of the lower left corner point of the current grid cell rc. The *Bounding Box* of a query q is a rectangle shaped region, which covers all possible areas that the spatial region of the query q may move into when the focal object fo of the query travels within its current grid cell. For circle shaped spatial query region with radius r, the bounding box can be formally defined as $bound\_box(q) = Rect(rc.lx - r, rc.ly - r, \alpha + 2r, \alpha + 2r)$.

– *Monitoring Region of a Moving Query*: The grid region defined by the union of all grid cells that intersect with the bounding box of a query forms the monitoring region of the query. It is formally defined as, $mon\_region(q) = \bigcup_{(i,j) \in S} A_{i,j}$, where $S = \{(i,j) : A_{i,j} \cap bound\_box(q) \neq \emptyset\}$. The monitoring region of a moving query covers all the objects that are subject to be included in the result of the moving query when the focal object stays in its current grid cell.

– *Nearby Queries of an Object*: Given a moving object o, we refer to all MQs whose monitoring regions intersect with the current grid cell of the moving object o the *nearby queries* of the object o, i.e. $nearby\_queries(o) = \{q : mon\_region(q) \cap curr\_cell(o) \neq \emptyset \wedge q \in Q\}$. Every mobile object is either a target object of or is of potential interest to its nearby MQs.

3 Distributed Processing of Moving Queries

In this section we give an overview of our distributed approach to efficient processing of MQs, and then focus on the main building blocks of our solution and the important algorithms used. A comparison of our work with the related research in this area is provided in Section 6.

3.1 Algorithm Overview

In MobiEyes, distributed processing of moving queries consists of server side processing and mobile object side processing. The main idea is to provide mechanisms such that each mobile object can determine by itself whether or not it should be included in the result of a moving query close by, without requiring global knowledge regarding the moving queries and the object positions. A brief review is given below on the main components and key ideas used in MobiEyes for distributed processing of MQs. We will provide detailed technical discussion on each of these ideas in the subsequent sections.

Server Side Processing: The server side processing can be characterized as mediation between moving objects. It performs two main tasks. First, it keeps track of the significant position changes of all focal objects, namely the change in velocity vector and the position change that causes the focal object to move out of its current grid cell. Second, it broadcasts the significant position changes of the focal objects and the addition or deletion of the moving queries to the appropriate subset of moving objects in the system.

Monitoring Region of a MQ: To enable efficient processing at mobile object side, we introduce the monitoring region of a moving query to identify all moving objects that may get included in the query's result when the focal object of the query moves within its current cell. The main idea is to have those moving objects that reside in a moving query's monitoring region to be aware of the query and to be responsible for calculating if they should be included in the query result. Thus, the moving objects that are not in the neighborhood of a moving query do not need to be aware of the existence of the moving query, and the query result can be efficiently maintained by the objects in the query's monitoring region.

Registering MQs at Moving Object Side: In MobiEyes, the task of making sure that the moving objects in a query's monitoring region are aware of the query is accomplished through server broadcasts, which are triggered by either installations of new moving queries or notifications of changes in the monitoring regions of existing moving queries when their focal objects change their current grid cells. Upon receiving a broadcast message, for each MQ in the message, the mobile objects examine their local state and determine whether they should be responsible for processing this moving query. This decision is based on whether the mobile objects themselves are within the monitoring region of the query.

Moving Object Side Processing: Once a moving query is registered at the moving object side, the moving object will be responsible for periodically tracking if it is within the spatial region of the query, by predicting the position of the focal object of the query. Changes in the containment status of the moving object with respect to moving queries are differentially relayed to the server.

Handling Significant Position Changes: In case the position of the focal object of a moving query changes significantly (it moves out of its current grid cell or changes its velocity vector significantly), it will report to the server, and the server will relay such position change information to the appropriate subset of moving objects through broadcasts.

3.2 Data Structures

In this section we describe the design of the data structures used on the server side and on the moving object side, in order to support distributed processing of MQs.

Server-Side Data Structures

The server side stores four types of data structures: the focal object table FOT, the server side moving query table SQT, the reverse query index matrix RQI, and the static grid cell to base station mapping $Bmap$.

Focal Object Table, $FOT = (\underline{oid}, pos, \overline{vel}, tm)$, is used to store information about moving objects that are the focal objects of MQs. The table is indexed on the oid attribute, which is the unique object identifier. tm is the time at which the position, pos, and the velocity vector, $\overline{vel}$, of the focal object with identifier oid were recorded on the moving object side. When the focal object reports to the server its position and velocity change, it also includes this timestamp in the report.

Server-side Moving Query Table, $SQT = (\underline{qid}, oid, region, curr\_cell, mon\_region, filter, \{result\})$, is used to store information about all spatial queries hosted by the system. The table is indexed on the qid attribute, which represents the query identifier. oid is the identifier of the focal object of the query. $region$ is the query's spatial region. $curr\_cell$ is the grid cell in which the focal object of the query locates. mon_region is the monitoring region of the query. $\{result\}$ is the set of object identifiers representing the set of target objects of the query. These objects are located within the query's spatial region and satisfy the query filter.

Reverse Query Index, RQI, is an $M \times N$ matrix whose cells are a set of query identifiers. M and N denote the number of rows and the number of columns of the Grid corresponding to the Universe of Discourse of a MobiEyes system. $RQI(i, j)$ stores the identifiers of the queries whose monitoring regions intersect with the grid cell $A_{i,j}$. $RQI(i, j)$ represents the nearby queries of an object whose current grid cell is $A_{i,j}$, i.e. $\forall o \in O, nearby\_queries(o) = RQI(i, j)$, where $curr\_cell(o) = A_{i,j}$.

Moving Object-Side Data Structures
Each moving object o stores a local query table LQT and a Boolean variable $hasMQ$.

Local Query Table, $LQT = (qid, pos, \overline{vel}, tm, region, mon\_region, isTarget)$ is used to store information about moving queries whose monitoring regions intersect with the current grid cell in which the moving object o currently locates in. qid is the unique query identifier assigned at the time when the query is installed at the server. pos is the last known position, and $\overline{vel}$ is the last known velocity vector of the focal object of the query. tm is the time at which the position and the velocity vector of the focal object was recorded (by the focal object of the query itself, not by the object on which LQT resides). $isTarget$ is a Boolean variable describing whether the object was found to be inside the query's spatial region at the last evaluation of this query by the moving object o. The Boolean variable $hasMQ$ provides a flag showing whether the moving object o storing the LQT is a focal object of some query or not.

3.3 Installing Queries

Installation of a moving query into the MobiEyes system consists of two phases. First, the MQ is installed at the server side and the server state is updated to reflect the installation of the query. Second, the query is installed at the set of moving objects that are located inside the monitoring region of the query.

Updating the Server State
When the server receives a moving query, assuming it is in the form (oid, $region$, $filter$), it performs the following installation actions. (1) It first checks whether the

focal object with identifier oid is already contained in the FOT table. (2) If the focal object of the query already exists, it means that either someone else has installed the same query earlier or there exist multiple queries with different filters but the same focal object. Since the FOT table already contains velocity and position information regarding the focal object of this query, the installation simply creates a new entry for this new MQ and adds this entry to the sever-side query table SQT and then modifies the RQI entry that corresponds to the current grid cell of the focal object to include this new MQ in the reverse query index (detailed in step (4)). At this point the query is installed on the server side. (3) However, if the focal object of the query is not present in the FOT table, then the server-side installation manager needs to contact the focal object of this new query and request the position and velocity information. Then the server can directly insert the entry $(oid, pos, \overline{vel}, tm)$ into FOT, where tm is the timestamp when the object with identifier oid has recorded its pos and $\overline{vel}$ information. (4) The server then assigns a unique identifier qid to the query and calculates the current grid cell ($curr\_cell$) of the focal object and the monitoring region (mon_region) of the query. A new moving query entry (qid, oid, $region$, $curr\_cell$, mon_region, $filter$) will be created and added into the SQT table. The server also updates the RQI index by adding this query with identifier qid to $RQI(i, j)$ if $A_{i,j} \cap mon\_region(qid) \neq \emptyset$. At this point the query is installed on the server side.

Installing Queries on the Moving Objects

After installing queries on the server side, the server needs to complete the installation by triggering query installation on the moving object side. This job is done by performing two tasks. First, the server sends an installation notification to the focal object with identifier oid, which upon receiving the notification sets its $hasMQ$ variable to true. This makes sure that the moving object knows that it is now a focal object and is supposed to report velocity vector changes to the server. The second task is for the server to forward this query to all objects that reside in the query's monitoring region, so that they can install the query and monitor their position changes to determine if they become the target objects of this query. To perform this task, the server uses the mapping $Bmap$ to determine the minimal set of base stations (i.e., the smallest number of base stations) that covers the monitoring region. Then the query is sent to all objects that are covered by the base stations in this set through broadcast messages. When an object receives the broadcast message, it checks whether its current grid cell is covered by the query's monitoring region. If so, the object installs the query into its local query table LQT when the query's filter is also satisfied by the object. Otherwise the object discards the message.

3.4 Handling Velocity Vector Changes

Once a query is installed in the MobiEyes system, the focal object of the query needs to report to the server any significant change to its location information, including significant velocity changes or changes that move the focal object out of its current grid cell. We describe the mechanisms for handling velocity changes in this section and the mechanisms for handling objects that change their current grid cells in the next section.

A velocity vector change, once identified as significant, will need to be relayed to the objects that reside in the query's monitoring region through the server acting as a mediator. When the focal object of a query reports a velocity vector change, it sends its new velocity vector, its position and the timestamp at which this information was recorded, to the server. The server first updates the FOT table with the information received from the focal object. Then for each query associated with the focal object, the server communicates the newly received information to objects located in the monitoring region of the query by using minimum number of broadcasts (this can be done through the use of the grid cell to base station mapping $Bmap$).

A subtle point is that, the velocity vector of the focal object will almost always change at each time step in a real world setup, although the change might be insignificant. One way to handle this is to convey the new velocity vector information to the objects located in the monitoring region of the query, only if the change in the velocity vector is significant. In MobiEyes, we use a variation of dead reckoning to decide what constitutes a (significant) velocity vector change.

Dead Reckoning in MobiEyes

Concretely, at each time step the focal object of a query samples its current position and calculates the difference between its current position and the position that the other objects believe it to be at (based on the last velocity vector information relayed). In case this difference is larger than a threshold, say Δ, the new velocity vector information is relayed [1].

3.5 Handling Objects That Change Their Grid Cells

In a mobile system the fact that a moving object changes its current grid cell has an impact on the set of queries the object is responsible for monitoring. In case the object which has changed its current grid cell is a focal object, the change also has an impact on the set of objects which has to monitor the queries bounded to this focal object. In this section we describe how the MobiEyes system can effectively adapt to such changes and the mechanisms used for handling such changes.

When an object changes its current grid cell, it notifies the server of this change by sending its object identifier, its previous grid cell and its new current grid cell to the server. The object also removes those queries whose monitoring regions no longer cover its new current grid cell from its local query table LQT. Upon receipt of the notification, the server performs two sets of operations depending on whether the object is a focal object of some query or not. If the object is a non-focal object, the only thing that the server needs to do is to find what new queries should be installed on this object and then perform the query installation on this moving object. This step is performed because the new current grid cell that the object has moved into may intersect with the monitoring regions of a different set of queries than its previous set. The server uses the reverse query index RQI together with the previous and the new current grid cell of the object to determine the set of new queries that has to be installed on this moving object. Then the server sends the set of new queries to the moving object for installation.

[1] We do not consider the inaccuracy introduced by the motion modeling.

The focal object table FOT and the server query table SQT are used to create required installation information of the queries to be installed on the object. However, if the object that changes its current grid cell is a focal object of some query, additional set of operations are performed. For each query with this object as its focal object, the server performs the following operations. It updates the query's SQT table entry by resetting the current grid cell and the monitoring region to their new values. It also updates the RQI index to reflect the change. Then the server computes the union of the query's previous monitoring region and its new monitoring region, and sends a broadcast message to all objects that reside in this combined area. This message includes information about the new state of the query. Upon receipt of this message from the server, an object performs the following operations for installing/removing a query. It checks whether its current grid cell is covered by the query's monitoring region. If not, the object removes the query from its LQT table (if the entry already exists), since the object's position is no longer covered by the query's monitoring region. Otherwise, it installs the query if the query is not already installed and the query filter is satisfied, by adding a new query entry in the LQT table. In case that the query is already installed in LQT, it updates the monitoring region of the query's entry in LQT.

Optimization: Lazy Query Propagation

The procedure we presented above uses an eager query propagation approach for handling objects changing their current grid cells. It requires each object (focal or non-focal) to contact the server and transfer information whenever it changes its current grid cell. The only reason for a non-focal object to communicate with the server is to immediately obtain the list of new queries that it needs to install in response to changing its current grid cell. We refer to this scheme as the *Eager Query Propagation (EQP)*.

To reduce the amount of communication between moving objects and the server, in MobiEyes we also provide a lazy query propagation approach. Thus, the need for non-focal objects to contact the server to obtain the list of new MQs can be eliminated. Instead of obtaining the new queries from the server and installing them immediately on the object upon a grid cell change, the moving object can wait until the server broadcasts the next velocity vector changes regarding the focal objects of these queries, to the area in which the object locates. In this case the velocity vector change notifications are expanded to include the spatial region and the filter of the queries, so that the object can install the new queries upon receiving the broadcast message on the velocity vector changes of the focal objects of the moving queries. Using lazy propagation, the moving objects upon changing their current grid cells will be unaware of the new set of queries nearby until the focal objects of these queries change their velocity vectors or move out of their current grid cells. Obviously lazy propagation works well when the gird cell size α is large and the focal objects of queries change their velocity vectors frequently. The lazy query propagation may not prevail over the eager query propagation, when: (1) the focal objects do not have significant change on their velocity vectors, (2) the grid cell size α is too small, and (3) the non-focal moving objects change their current grid cells at a much faster rate than the focal objects. In such situations, non-focal objects may end up missing some moving queries. We evaluate the *Lazy Query Propagation (LQP)* approach and study its performance advantages as well as its impact on the query result accuracy in Section 5.

3.6 Moving Object Query Processing Logic

A moving object periodically processes all queries registered in its LQT table. For each query, it predicts the position of the focal object of the query using the velocity, time, and position information available in the LQT entry of the query. Then it compares its current position and the predicted position of the query's focal object to determine whether itself is covered by the query's spatial region or not. When the result is different from the last result computed in the previous time step, the object notifies the server of this change, which in turn differentially updates the query result.

4 Optimizations

In this section we present two additional optimization techniques aiming at controlling the amount of local processing at the mobile object side and further reducing the communication between the mobile objects and the server.

4.1 Query Grouping

It is widely recognized that a mobile user can pose many different queries and a query can be posed multiple times by different users. Thus, in a mobile system many moving queries may share the same focal object. Effective optimizations can be applied to handle multiple queries bound to the same moving object. These optimizations help decreasing both the computational load on the moving objects and the messaging cost of the MobiEyes approach, in situations where the query distribution over focal objects is skewed.

We define a set of moving queries as *groupable MQs* if they are bounded to the same focal object. In addition to being associated with the same focal object, some groupable queries may have the same monitoring region. We refer to MQs that have the same monitoring region as *MQs with matching monitoring regions*, where we refer to MQs that have different monitoring regions as *MQs with non-matching monitoring regions*. Based on these different patterns, different grouping techniques can be applied to groupable MQs.

Grouping MQs with Matching Monitoring Regions
MQs with matching monitoring regions can be grouped most efficiently to reduce the communication and processing costs of such queries. In MobiEyes, we introduce the concept of *query bitmap*, which is a bitmap containing one bit for each query in a query qroup, each bit can be set to 1 or 0 indicating whether the corresponding query should include the moving object in its result or not. We illustrate this with an example. Consider three MQs: $q_1 = (qid_1, oid_i, r_1, filter_1)$, $q_2 = (qid_2, oid_i, r_2, filter_2)$, and $q_3 = (qid_3, oid_i, r_3, filter_3)$ that share the same monitoring region. Note that these queries share their focal object, which is the object with identifier oid_i. Instead of shipping three separate queries to the mobile objects, the server can combine these queries into a single query as follows: $q_3 = (qid_3, oid_i, (r_1, r_2, r_3), (filter_1, filter_2, filter_3))$. With this grouping at hand, when a moving object is processing a set of groupable MQs with

matching monitoring regions, it needs to consider queries with smaller radiuses only if it finds out that its current position is inside the spatial region of a query with a larger radius. When a moving object reports to the server whether it is included in the results of queries that form the grouped query or not, it will attach the query bitmap to the notification. For each query, its query bitmap bit is set to 1 only if the moving object stays inside the spatial region of the query and the filter of the query is satisfied. With the query bitmap, the server is able to infer information about individual query results with respect to the reporting object.

Grouping MQs with Non-matching Monitoring Regions
A clean way to handle MQs with non-matching monitoring regions is to perform grouping on the moving object side only. We illustrate this with an example. Consider an object o_j that has two groupable MQs with non-matching monitoring regions, q_4 and q_5, installed in its LQT table. Since there is no global server side grouping performed for these queries, o_j can save some processing only by combining these two queries inside its LQT table. By this way it only needs to consider the query with smaller radius only if it finds out that its current position is inside the spatial region of the one with the larger radius.

4.2 Safe Period Optimization

In MobiEyes, each moving object that resides in the monitoring region of a query needs to evaluate the queries registered in its local query table LQT periodically. For each query the candidate object needs to determine if it should be included in the answer of the query. The interval for such periodic evaluation can be set either by the server or by the mobile object itself. A safe-period optimization can be applied to reduce the computation load on the mobile object side, which computes a safe period for each object in the monitoring region of a query, if an upper bound ($maxVel$) exists on the maximum velocities of the moving objects.

The safe periods for queries are calculated by an object o as follows: For each query q in its LQT table, the object o calculates a worst case lower bound on the amount of time that has to pass for it to locate inside the area covered by the query q's spatial region. We call this time, the *safe period*(sp) of the object o with respect to the query q, denoted as $sp(o, q)$. The safe period can be formally defined as follows. Let o_i be the object that has the query q_k with focal object o_j in its LQT table, and let $dist(o_i, o_j)$ denote the distance between these two objects, and let $q_k.region$ denote the circle shaped region with radius r. In the worst case, the two objects approach to each other with their maximum velocities in the direction of the shortest path between them. Then $sp(o_i, q_k) = \frac{dist(o_i, o_j) - r}{o_i.maxVel + o_j.maxVel}$.

Once the safe period sp of a moving object is calculated for a query, it is safe for the object to start the periodic evaluation of this query after the safe period has passed. In order to integrate this optimization with the base algorithm, we include a *processing time* (ptm) field into the LQT table, which is initialized to 0. When a query in LQT is to be processed, ptm is checked first. In case ptm is ahead of the current time ctm, the query is skipped. Otherwise, it is processed as usual. After processing of the query,

Table 1. Simulation Parameters

Parameter	Description	Value range	Default value
ts	Time step	30 seconds	
α	Grid cell side length	0.5-16 miles	5 miles
no	Number of objects	1,000-10,000	10,000
nmq	Number of moving queries	100-1,000	1,000
nmo	Number of objects changing velocity vector per time step	100-1,000	1,000
$area$	Area of consideration	100,000 square miles	
$alen$	Base station side length	5-80 miles	10 miles
$qradius$	Query radius	$\{3, 2, 1, 4, 5\}$ miles	
$qselect$	Query selectivity	0.75	
$mospeed$	Max. object speed	$\{100, 50, 150, 200, 250\}$ miles/hour	

if the object is found to be outside the area covered by the query's spatial region, the safe period sp is calculated for the query and processing time ptm of the query is set to current time plus the safe period, $ctm+sp$. When the query evaluation period is short, or the object speeds are low or the cell size α of the grid is large, this optimization can be very effective.

5 Experiments

In this section we describe three sets of simulation based experiments.The first set of experiments illustrates the scalability of the MobiEyes approach with respect to server load. The second set of experiments focuses on the messaging cost and studies the effects of several parameters on the messaging cost. The third set of experiments investigates the amount of computation a moving object has to perform, by measuring on average the number of queries a moving object needs to process during each local evaluation period.

5.1 Simulation Setup

We list the set of parameters used in the simulation in Table 1. In all of the experiments, the parameters take their default values if not specified otherwise. The area of interest is a square shaped region of 100,000 square miles. The number of objects we consider ranges from 1,000 to 10,000 where the number of queries range from 100 to 1,000.

We randomly select focal objects of the queries using a uniform distribution. The spatial region of a query is taken as a circular region whose radius is a random variable following a normal distribution. For a given query, the mean of the query radius is selected from the list $\{3, 2, 1, 4, 5\}$(miles) following a zipf distribution with parameter 0.8 and the std. deviation of the query radius is taken as 1/5th of its mean. The selectivity of the queries is taken as 0.75.

We model the movement of the objects as follows. We assign a maximum velocity to each object from the list $\{100, 50, 150, 200, 250\}$(miles/hour), using a zipf distribution with parameter 0.8. The simulation has a time step parameter of 30 seconds. In every time step we pick a number of objects at random and set their normalized velocity vectors to a random direction, while setting their velocity to a random value between zero and their maximum velocity. All other objects are assumed to continue their motion with

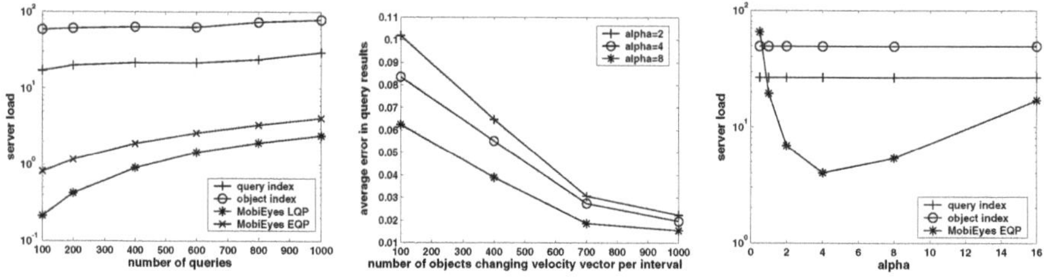

Fig. 1. Impact of distributed query processing on server load

Fig. 2. Error associated with lazy query propagation

Fig. 3. Effect of α on server load

their unchanged velocity vectors. The number of objects that change velocity vectors during each time step is a parameter whose value ranges from 100 to 1,000.

5.2 Server Load

In this section we compare our MobiEyes distributed query processing approach with two popular central query processing approaches, with regard to server load. The two centralized approaches we consider are indexing objects and indexing queries. Both are based on a central server on which the object locations are explicitly manipulated by the server logic as they arrive, for the purpose of answering queries. We can either assume that the objects are reporting their positions periodically or we can assume that periodically object locations are extracted from velocity vector and time information associated with moving objects, on the server side. We first describe these two approaches and later compare them with the distributed MobiEyes distributed approach with regard to server load.

Indexing Objects. The first centralized approach to processing spatial continuous queries on moving objects is by indexing objects. In this approach a spatial index is built over object locations. We use an R*-tree [3] for this purpose. As new object positions are received, the spatial index (the R*-tree) on object locations is updated with the new information. Periodically all queries are evaluated against the object index and the new results of the queries are determined. This is a straightforward approach and it is costly due to the frequent updates required on the spatial index over object locations.

Indexing Queries. The second centralized approach to processing spatial continuous queries on moving objects is by indexing queries. In this approach a spatial index, again an R*-tree indeed, is built over moving queries. As the new positions of the focal objects of the queries are received, the spatial index is updated. This approach has the advantage of being able to perform differential evaluation of query results. When a new object position is received, it is run through the query index to determine to which queries this object actually contributes. Then the object is added to the results of these queries, and is removed from the results of other queries that have included it as a target object before. We have implemented both the *object index* and the *query index* approaches for centralized processing of MQs. As a measure of server load, we took the time spent by the simulation for executing the server side logic per time step. Figure 1 and Figure 3 depict the results obtained. Note that the y-axises, which represent the sever load, are in log-scale. The x-axis represents the number of queries considered in Figure 1, and the different settings of α parameter in Figure 3.

It is observed from Figure 1 that the MobiEyes approach provides up to two orders of magnitude improvement on server load. In contrast, the object index approach has an almost constant cost, which slightly increases with the number of queries. This is due to the fact that the main cost of this approach is to update the spatial index when object positions change. Although the query index approach clearly outperforms the object index approach for small number of queries, its performance worsens as the number of queries increase. This is due to the fact that the main cost of this approach is to update the spatial index when focal objects of the queries change their positions. Our distributed approach also shows an increase in server load as the number of queries increase, but it preserves the relative gain against the query index.

Figure 1 also shows the improvement in server load using lazy query propagation (LQP) compared to the default eager query propagation (EQP). However as described in Section 3.5, lazy query propagation may have some inaccuracy associated with it. Figure 2 studies this inaccuracy and the parameters that influence it. For a given query, we define the *error* in the query result at a given time, as the number of missing object identifiers in the result (compared to the correct result) divided by the size of the correct query result. Figure 2 plots the average error in the query results when lazy query propagation is used as a function of number of objects changing velocity vectors per time step for different values of α. Frequent velocity vector changes are expected to increase the accuracy of the query results. This is observed from Figure 2 as it shows that the error in query results decreases with increasing number of objects changing velocity vectors per time step. Frequent grid cell crossings are expected to decrease the accuracy of the query results. This is observed from Figure 2 as it shows that the error in query results increases with decreasing α.

Figure 3 shows that the performance of the MobiEyes approach in terms of server load worsens for too small and too large values of the α parameter. However it still outperforms the object index and query index approaches. For small values of α, the frequent grid cell changes increase the server load. On the other hand, for large values of α, the large monitoring areas increase the server's job of mediating between focal objects and the objects that are lying in the monitoring regions of the focal objects' queries. Several factors may affect the selection of an appropriate α value. We further investigate selecting a good value for α in the next section.

5.3 Messaging Cost

In this section we discuss the effects of several parameters on the messaging cost of our solution. In most of the experiments presented in this section, we report the total number of messages sent on the wireless medium per second. The number of messages reported includes two types of messages. The first type of messages are the ones that are sent from a moving object to the server (uplink messages), and the second type of messages are the ones broadcasted by a base station to a certain area or sent to a moving object as a one-to-one message from the server (downlink messages). We evaluate and compare our

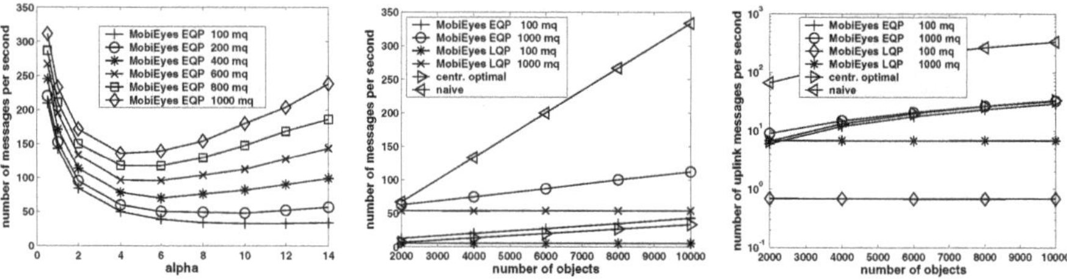

Fig. 4. Effect of α on messaging cost

Fig. 5. Effect of # of objects on messaging cost

Fig. 6. Effect of # of objs. on uplink messaging cost

results using two different scenarios. In the first scenario each object reports its position directly to the server at each time step, if its position has changed. We name this as the *naïve* approach. In the second scenario each object reports its velocity vector at each time step, if the velocity vector has changed (significantly) since the last time. We name this as the *central optimal* approach. As the name suggests, this is the minimum amount of information required for a centralized approach to evaluate queries unless there is an assumption about object trajectories. Both of the scenarios assume a central processing scheme.

One crucial concern is defining an optimal value for the parameter α, which is the length of a grid cell. The graph in Figure 4 plots the number of messages per second as a function of α for different number of queries. As seen from the figure, both too small and too large values of α have a negative effect on the messaging cost. For smaller values of α this is because objects change their current grid cell quite frequently. For larger values of α this is mainly because the monitoring regions of the queries become larger. As a result, more broadcasts are needed to notify objects in a larger area, of the changes related to focal objects of the queries they are subject to be considered against. Figure 4 shows that values in the range [4,6] are ideal for α with respect to the number of queries ranging from 100 to 1000. The optimal value of the α parameter can be derived analytically using a simple model. In this paper we omit the analytical model for space restrictions.

Figure 5 studies the effect of number of objects on the messaging cost. It plots the number of messages per second as a function of number of objects for different numbers of queries. While the number of objects is altered, the ratio of the number of objects changing their velocity vectors per time step to the total number of objects is kept constant and equal to its default value as obtained from Table 1. It is observed that, when the number of queries is large and the number of objects is small, all approaches come close to one another. However, the naïve approach has a high cost when the ratio of the number of objects to the number of queries is high. In the latter case, central optimal approach provides lower messaging cost, when compared to MobiEyes with EQP, but the gap between the two stays constant as number of objects are increased. On the other hand, MobiEyes with LQP scales better than all other approaches with increasing number of objects and shows improvement over central optimal approach for smaller number of

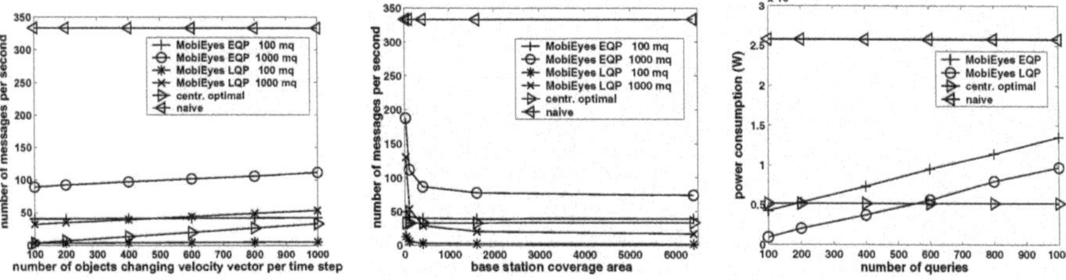

Fig. 7. Effect of number of objects changing velocity vector per time step on messaging cost

Fig. 8. Effect of base station coverage area on messaging cost

Fig. 9. Effect of # of queries on per object power consumption due to communication

queries. Figure 6 shows the uplink component of the messaging cost. The y-axis is plotted in logarithmic scale for convenience of the comparison. Figure 6 clearly shows that MobiEyes with LQP significantly cuts down the uplink messaging requirement, which is crucial for asymmetric communication environments where uplink communication bandwidth is considerably lower than downlink communication bandwidth.

Figure 7 studies the effect of number of objects changing velocity vector per time step on the messaging cost. It plots the number of messages per second as a function of the number of objects changing velocity vector per time step for different numbers of queries. An important observation from Figure 7 is that the messaging cost of MobiEyes with EQP scales well when compared to the central optimal approach as the gap between the two tends to decrease as the number of objects changing velocity vector per time step increases. Again MobiEyes with LQP scales better than all other approaches and shows improvement over central optimal approach for smaller number of queries.

Figure 8 studies the effect of base station coverage area on the messaging cost. It plots the number of messages per second as a function of the base station coverage area for different numbers of queries. It is observed from Figure 8 that increasing the base station coverage decreases the messaging cost up to some point after which the effect disappears. The reason for this is that, after the coverage areas of the base stations reach to a certain size, the monitoring regions associated with queries always lie in only one base station's coverage area. Although increasing base station size decreases the total number of messages sent on the wireless medium, it will increase the average number of messages received by a moving object due to the size difference between monitoring regions and base station coverage areas. In a hypothetical case where the universe of disclosure is covered by a single base station, any server broadcast will be received by any moving object. In such environments, indexing on the air [7] can be used as an effective mechanism to deal with this problem. In this paper we do not consider such extreme scenarios.

Per Object Power Consumption Due to Communication

So far we have considered the scalability of the MobiEyes in terms of the total number of messages exchanged in the system. However one crucial measure is the per object power

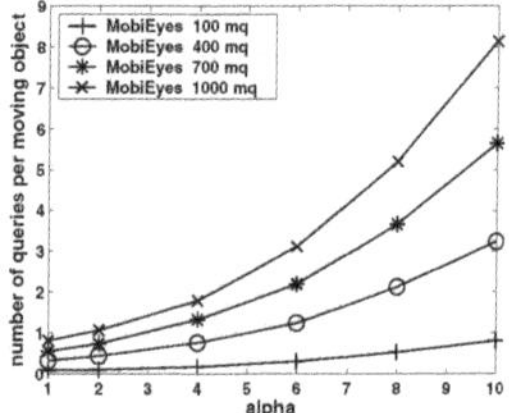

Fig. 10. Effect of α on the average number of queries evaluated per step on a moving object

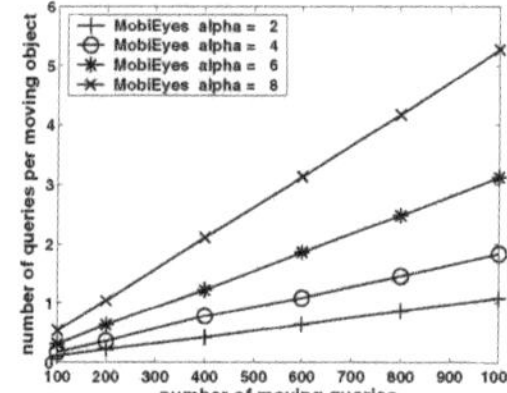

Fig. 11. Effect of the total # of queries on the avg. # of queries evaluated per step on a moving object

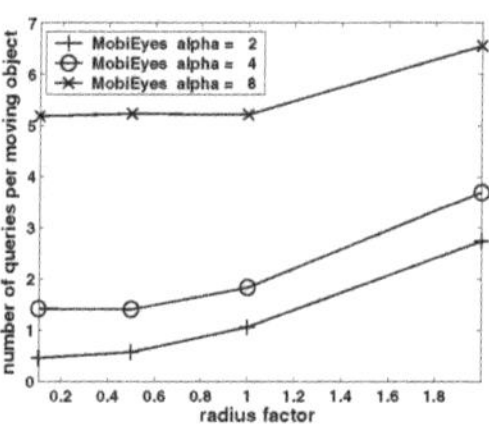

Fig. 12. Effect of the query radius on the average number of queries evaluated per step on a moving object

consumption due to communication. We measure the average communication related to power consumption using a simple radio model where the transmission path consists of transmitter electronics and transmit amplifier where the receiver path consists of receiver electronics. Considering a GSM/GPRS device, we take the power consumption of transmitter and receiver electronics as 150mW and 120mW respectively and we assume a 300mW transmit amplifier with 30% efficiency [8]. We consider 14kbps uplink and 28kbps downlink bandwidth (typical for current GPRS technology). Note that sending data is more power consuming than receiving data. [2]

We simulated the MobiEyes approach using message sizes instead of message counts for messages exchanged and compared its power consumption due to communication with the naive and central optimal approaches. The graph in Figure 9 plots the per object power consumption due to communication as a function of number of queries. Since the naive approach require every object to send its new position to the server, its per object power consumption is the worst. In MobiEyes, however, a non-focal object does not send its position or velocity vector to the server, but it receives query updates from the server. Although the cost of receiving data in terms of consumed energy is lower than transmitting, given a fixed number of objects, for larger number of queries the central optimal approach outperforms MobiEyes in terms of power consumption due to communication. An important factor that increases the per object power consumption in MobiEyes is the fact that an object also receives updates regarding queries that are irrelevant mainly due to the difference between the size of a broadcast area and the monitoring region of a query.

5.4 Computation on the Moving Object Side

In this section we study the amount of computation placed on the moving object side by the MobiEyes approach for processing MQs. One measure of this is the number of queries a moving object has to evaluate at each time step, which is the size of the LQT (Recall Section 3.2).

[2] In this setting transmitting costs $\sim 80\mu jules/bit$ and receiving costs $\sim 5\mu jules/bit$

Figure 10 and Figure 11 study the effect of α and the effect of the total number of queries on the average number of queries a moving object has to evaluate at each time step (average LQT table size). The graph in Figure 10 plots the average LQT table size as a function of α for different number of queries. The graph in Figure 11 plots the same measure, but this time as a function of number of queries for different values of α. The first observation from these two figures is that the size of the LQT table does not exceeds 10 for the simulation setup. The second observation is that the average size of the LQT table increases exponentially with α where it increases linearly with the number of queries.

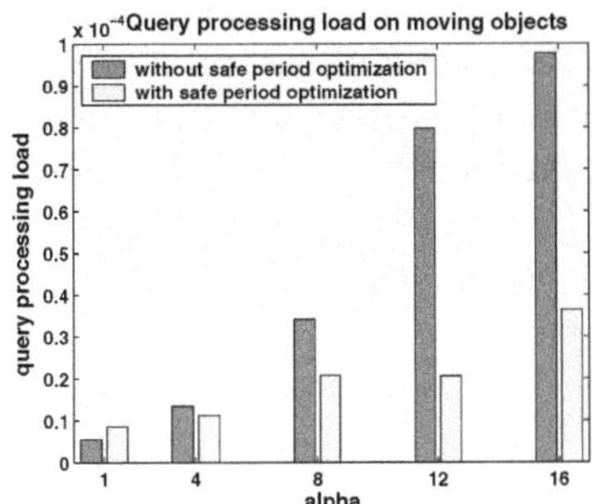

Fig. 13. Effect of the safe period optimization on the average query processing load of a moving object

Figure 12 studies the effect of the query radius on the number of average queries a moving object has to evaluate at each time step. The x-axis of the graph in Figure 12 represents the radius factor, whose value is used to multiply the original radius value of the queries. The y-axis represents the average LQT table size. It is observed from the figure that the larger query radius values increase the LQT table size. However this effect is only visible for radius values whose difference from each other is larger than the α. This is a direct result of the definition of the monitoring region from Section 2.

Figure 13 studies the effect of the safe period optimization on the average query processing load of a moving object. The x-axis of the graph in Figure 12 represents the α parameter, and the y-axis represents the average query processing load of a moving object. As a measure of query processing load, we took the average time spent by a moving object for processing its LQT table in the simulation. Figure 12 shows that for large values of α, the safe period optimization is very effective. This is because, as α gets larger, monitoring regions get larger, which increases the average distance between the focal object of a query and the objects in its monitoring region. This results in non-zero safe periods and decreases the cost of processing the LQT table. On the other hand, for very small values of α, like $\alpha = 1$ in Figure 13, the safe period optimization incurs a small overhead. This is because the safe period is almost always less than the query evaluation period for very small α values and as a result the extra processing done for safe period calculations does not pay off.

6 Related Work

Evaluation of static spatial queries on moving objects, at a centralized location, is a well studied topic. In [14], Velocity Constrained Indexing and Query Indexing are proposed for efficient evaluation of this kind of queries at a central location. Several other indexing structures and algorithms for handling moving object positions are suggested in the literature [17,15,9,2,4,18]. There are two main points where our work departs from this line of work.

First, most of the work done in this respect has focused on efficient indexing structures and has ignored the underlying mobile communication system and the mobile objects. To our knowledge, only the SQM system introduced in [5] has proposed a distributed solution for evaluation of static spatial queries on moving objects, that makes use of the computational capabilities present at the mobile objects.

Second, the concept of dynamic queries presented in [10] are to some extent similar to the concept of moving queries in MobiEyes. But there are two subtle differences. First, a dynamic query is defined as a temporally ordered set of snapshot queries in [10]. This is a low level definition. In contrast, our definition of moving queries is at end-user level, which includes the notion of a focal object. Second, the work done in [10] indexes the trajectories of the moving objects and describes how to efficiently evaluate dynamic queries that represent predictable or non-predictable movement of an observer. They also describe how new trajectories can be added when a dynamic query is actively running. Their assumptions are in line with their motivating scenario, which is to support rendering of objects in virtual tour-like applications. The MobiEyes solution discussed in this paper focuses on real-time evaluation of moving queries in real-world settings, where the trajectories of the moving objects are unpredictable and the queries are associated with moving objects inside the system.

7 Conclusion

We have described MobiEyes, a distributed scheme for processing moving queries on moving objects in a mobile setup. We demonstrated the effectiveness of our approach through a set of simulation based experiments. We showed that the distributed processing of MQs significantly decreases the server load and scales well in terms of messaging cost while placing only small amount of processing burden on moving objects.

References

[1] US Naval Observatory (USNO) GPS Operations. http://tycho.usno.navy.mil/gps.html, April 2003.

[2] P. K. Agarwal, L. Arge, and J. Erickson. Indexing moving points. In *PODS*, 2000.

[3] N. Beckmann, H.-P. Kriegel, R. Schneider, and B. Seeger. The R*-Tree: An efficient and robust access method for points and rectangles. In *SIGMOD*, 1990.

[4] R. Benetis, C. S. Jensen, G. Karciauskas, and S. Saltenis. Nearest neighbor and reverse nearest neighbor queries for moving objects. In *International Database Engineering and Applications Symposium*, 2002.

[5] Y. Cai and K. A. Hua. An adaptive query management technique for efficient real-time monitoring of spatial regions in mobile database systems. In *IEEE IPCCC*, 2002.

[6] J. Hill, R. Szewczyk, A. Woo, S. Hollar, D. E. Culler, and K. S. J. Pister. System architecture directions for networked sensors. In *ASPLOS*, 2000.

[7] T. Imielinski, S. Viswanathan, and B. Badrinath. Energy efficient indexing on air. In *SIGMOD*, 1994.

[8] J.Kucera and U. Lott. Single chip 1.9 ghz transceiver frontend mmic including Rx/Tx local oscillators and 300 mw power amplifier. *MTT Symposium Digest*, 4:1405–1408, June 1999.

[9] G. Kollios, D. Gunopulos, and V. J. Tsotras. On indexing mobile objects. In *PODS*, 1999.

[10] I. Lazaridis, K. Porkaew, and S. Mehrotra. Dynamic queries over mobile objects. In *EDBT*, 2002.
[11] L. Liu, C. Pu, and W. Tang. Continual queries for internet scale event-driven information delivery. *IEEE TKDE*, pages 610–628, 1999.
[12] D. L. Mills. Internet time synchronization: The network time protocol. *IEEE Transactions on Communications*, pages 1482–1493, 1991.
[13] D. Pfoser, C. S. Jensen, and Y. Theodoridis. Novel approaches in query processing for moving object trajectories. In *VLDB*, 2000.
[14] S. Prabhakar, Y. Xia, D. V. Kalashnikov, W. G. Aref, and S. E. Hambrusch. Query indexing and velocity constrained indexing: Scalable techniques for continuous queries on moving objects. *IEEE Transactions on Computers*, 51(10):1124–1140, 2002.
[15] S. Saltenis, C. S. Jensen, S. T. Leutenegger, and M. A. Lopez. Indexing the positions of continuously moving objects. In *SIGMOD*, 2000.
[16] A. P. Sistla, O. Wolfson, S. Chamberlain, and S. Dao. Modeling and querying moving objects. In *ICDE*, 1997.
[17] Y. Tao and D. Papadias. Time-parameterized queries in spatio-temporal databases. In *SIGMOD*, 2002.
[18] Y. Tao, D. Papadias, and Q. Shen. Continuous nearest neighbor search. In *VLDB*, 2002.

DBDC: Density Based Distributed Clustering

Eshref Januzaj, Hans-Peter Kriegel, and Martin Pfeifle

University of Munich, Institute for Computer Science
http://www.dbs.informatik.uni-muenchen.de
{januzaj,kriegel,pfeifle}@informatik.uni-muenchen.de

Abstract. Clustering has become an increasingly important task in modern application domains such as marketing and purchasing assistance, multimedia, molecular biology as well as many others. In most of these areas, the data are originally collected at different sites. In order to extract information from these data, they are merged at a central site and then clustered. In this paper, we propose a different approach. We cluster the data locally and extract suitable representatives from these clusters. These representatives are sent to a global server site where we restore the complete clustering based on the local representatives. This approach is very efficient, because the local clustering can be carried out quickly and independently from each other. Furthermore, we have low transmission cost, as the number of transmitted representatives is much smaller than the cardinality of the complete data set. Based on this small number of representatives, the global clustering can be done very efficiently. For both the local and the global clustering, we use a density based clustering algorithm. The combination of both the local and the global clustering forms our new DBDC (Density Based Distributed Clustering) algorithm. Furthermore, we discuss the complex problem of finding a suitable quality measure for evaluating distributed clusterings. We introduce two quality criteria which are compared to each other and which allow us to evaluate the quality of our DBDC algorithm. In our experimental evaluation, we will show that we do not have to sacrifice clustering quality in order to gain an efficiency advantage when using our distributed clustering approach.

1 Introduction

Knowledge Discovery in Databases (KDD) tries to identify valid, novel, potentially useful, and ultimately understandable patterns in data. Traditional KDD applications require full access to the data which is going to be analyzed. All data has to be located at that site where it is scrutinized. Nowadays, large amounts of heterogeneous, complex data reside on different, independently working computers which are connected to each other via local or wide area networks (LANs or WANs). Examples comprise distributed mobile networks, sensor networks or supermarket chains where check-out scanners, located at different stores, gather data unremittingly. Furthermore, international companies such as DaimlerChrysler have some data which is located in Europe and some data in the US. Those companies have various reasons why the data cannot be transmitted to a central site, e.g. limited bandwidth or security aspects.

The transmission of huge amounts of data from one site to another central site is in some application areas almost impossible. In astronomy, for instance, there exist several highly sophisticated space telescopes spread all over the world. These telescopes gather data un-

E. Bertino et al. (Eds.): EDBT 2004, LNCS 2992, pp. 88–105, 2004.
© Springer-Verlag Berlin Heidelberg 2004

ceasingly. Each of them is able to collect 1GB of data per hour [10] which can only, with great difficulty, be transmitted to a central site to be analyzed centrally there. On the other hand, it is possible to analyze the data locally where it has been generated and stored. Aggregated information of this locally analyzed data can then be sent to a central site where the information of different local sites are combined and analyzed. The result of the central analysis may be returned to the local sites, so that the local sites are able to put their data into a global context.

The requirement to extract knowledge from distributed data, without a prior unification of the data, created the rather new research area of Distributed Knowledge Discovery in Databases (DKDD). In this paper, we will present an approach where we first cluster the data locally. Then we extract aggregated information about the locally created clusters and send this information to a central site. The transmission costs are minimal as the representatives are only a fraction of the original data. On the central site we "reconstruct" a global clustering based on the representatives and send the result back to the local sites. The local sites update their clustering based on the global model, e.g. merge two local clusters to one or assign local noise to global clusters.

The paper is organized as follows, in Section 2, we shortly review related work in the area of clustering. In Section 3, we present a general overview of our distributed clustering algorithm, before we go into more detail in the following sections. In Section 4, we describe our local density based clustering algorithm. In Section 5, we discuss how we can represent a local clustering by relatively little information. In Section 6, we describe how we can restore a global clustering based on the information transmitted from the local sites. Section 7 covers the problem how the local sites update their clustering based on the global clustering information. In Section 8, we introduce two quality criteria which allow us to evaluate our new efficient *DBDC* (Density Based Distributed Clustering) approach. In Section 9, we present the experimental evaluation of the *DBDC* approach and show that its use does not suffer from a deterioration of quality. We conclude the paper in Section 10.

2 Related Work

In this section, we first review and classify the most common clustering algorithms. In Section 2.2, we shortly look at parallel clustering which has some affinity to distributed clustering.

2.1 Clustering

Given a set of objects with a distance function on them (i.e. a feature database), an interesting data mining question is, whether these objects naturally form groups (called clusters) and what these groups look like. Data mining algorithms that try to answer this question are called *clustering algorithms*. In this section, we classify well-known clustering algorithms according to different categorization schemes.

Clustering algorithms can be classified along different, independent dimensions. One well-known dimension categorizes clustering methods according to the *result* they produce. Here, we can distinguish between *hierarchical* and *partitioning clustering* algorithms [13, 15]. Partitioning algorithms construct a flat (single level) partition of a database D of n objects into a set of k clusters such that the objects in a cluster are more similar to each other

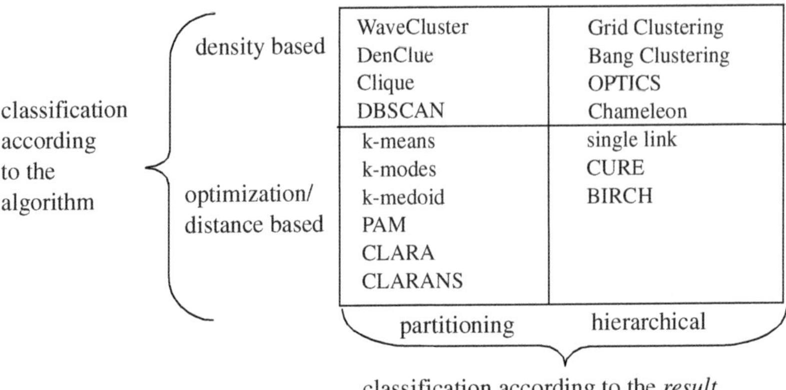

Fig. 1. Classification scheme for clustering algorithms

than to objects in different clusters. Hierarchical algorithms decompose the database into several levels of nested partitionings (clusterings), represented for example by a dendrogram, i.e. a tree that iteratively splits D into smaller subsets until each subset consists of only one object. In such a hierarchy, each node of the tree represents a cluster of D.

Another dimension according to which we can classify clustering algorithms is from an *algorithmic* point of view. Here we can distinguish between *optimization based or distance based* algorithms and *density based* algorithms. Distance based methods use the distances between the objects directly in order to optimize a global cluster criterion. In contrast, density based algorithms apply a local cluster criterion. Clusters are regarded as regions in the data space in which the objects are dense, and which are separated by regions of low object density (noise).

An overview of this classification scheme together with a number of important clustering algorithms is given in Figure 1. As we do not have the space to cover them here, we refer the interested reader to [15] were an excellent overview and further references can be found.

2.2 Parallel Clustering and Distributed Clustering

Distributed Data Mining (DDM) is a dynamically growing area within the broader field of KDD. Generally, many algorithms for distributed data mining are based on algorithms which were originally developed for parallel data mining. In [16] some state-of-the-art research results related to DDM are resumed.

Whereas there already exist algorithms for distributed and parallel classification and association rules [2, 12, 17, 18, 20, 22], there do not exist many algorithms for parallel and distributed clustering.

In [9] the authors sketched a technique for parallelizing a family of center-based data clustering algorithms. They indicated that it can be more cost effective to cluster the data in-place using an exact distributed algorithm than to collect the data in one central location for clustering. In [14] the "collective hierarchical clustering algorithm" for vertically distributed data sets was proposed which applies single link clustering. In contrast to this approach, we concentrate in this paper on horizontally distributed data sets and apply a partitioning clustering. In [19] the authors focus on the reduction of the communication cost by using traditional hierarchical clustering algorithms for massive distributed data sets. They developed a technique for centroid-based hierarchical clustering for high dimensional, horizontally distributed data sets by merging clustering hierarchies generated locally. In contrast, this paper concentrates on density based partitioning clustering.

In [21] a parallel version of DBSCAN [7] and in [5] a parallel version of k-means [11] were introduced. Both algorithms start with the complete data set residing on one central server and then distribute the data among the different clients.

The algorithm presented in [5] distributes N objects onto P processors. Furthermore, k initial centroids are determined which are distributed onto the P processors. Each processor assigns each of its objects to one of the k centroids. Afterwards, the global centroids are updated (reduction operation). This process is carried out repeatedly until the centroids do not change any more. Furthermore, this approach suffers from the general shortcoming of k-means, where the number of clusters has to be defined by the user and is not determined automatically.

The authors in [21] tackled these problems and presented a parallel version of DBDSAN. They used a 'shared nothing'-architecture, where several processors where connected to each other. The basic data-structure was the dR*-tree, a modification of the R*-tree [3]. The dR*-tree is a distributed index-structure where the objects reside on various machines. By using the information stored in the dR*-tree, each local site has access to the data residing on different computers. Similar, to parallel k-means, the different computers communicate via message-passing.

In this paper, we propose a different approach for distributed clustering assuming we cannot carry out a preprocessing step on the server site as the data is not centrally available. Furthermore, we abstain from an additional communication between the various client sites as we assume that they are independent from each other.

3 Density Based Distributed Clustering

Distributed Clustering assumes that the objects to be clustered reside on different sites. Instead of transmitting all objects to a central site (also denoted as server) where we can apply standard clustering algorithms to analyze the data, the data are clustered independently on the different local sites (also denoted as clients). In a subsequent step, the central site tries to establish a global clustering based on the local models, i.e. the representatives. This is a very difficult step as there might exist dependencies between objects located on different sites which are not taken into consideration by the creation of the local models. In contrast to a central clustering of the complete dataset, the central clustering of the local models can be carried out much faster.

Distributed Clustering is carried out on two different levels, i.e. the local level and the global level (cf. Figure 2). On the local level, all sites carry out a clustering independently from each other. After having completed the clustering, a local model is determined which should reflect an optimum trade-off between complexity and accuracy. Our proposed local models consist of a set of representatives for each locally found cluster. Each representative is a concrete object from the objects stored on the local site. Furthermore, we augment each representative with a suitable ε–range value. Thus, a representative is a good approximation

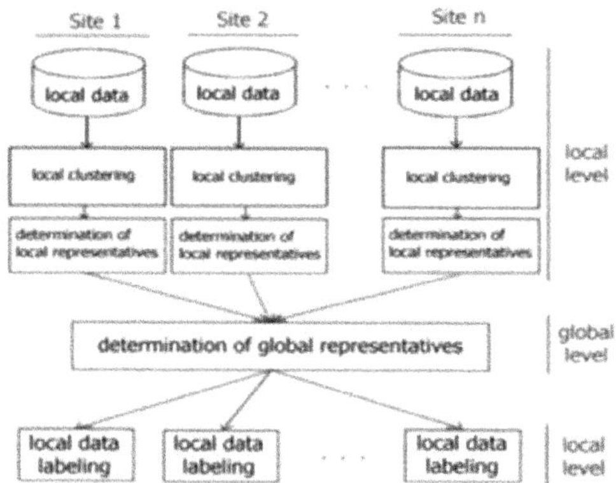

Fig. 2. Distributed Clustering

for all objects residing on the corresponding local site which are contained in the ε–range around this representative.

Next the local model is transferred to a central site, where the local models are merged in order to form a global model. The global model is created by analyzing the local representatives. This analysis is similar to a new clustering of the representatives with suitable global clustering parameters. To each local representative a global cluster-identifier is assigned. This resulting global clustering is sent to all local sites.

If a local object belongs to the ε-neighborhood of a global representative, the cluster-identifier from this representative is assigned to the local object. Thus, we can achieve that each site has the same information as if their data were clustered on a global site, together with the data of all the other sites.

To sum up, distributed clustering consists of four different steps (cf. Figure 2):

- Local clustering
- Determination of a local model
- Determination of a global model, which is based on all local models
- Updating of all local models

4 Local Clustering

As the data are created and located at local sites we cluster them there. The remaining question is "which clustering algorithm should we apply". K-means [11] is one of the most commonly used clustering algorithms, but it does not perform well on data with outliers or with clusters of different sizes or non-globular shapes [8]. The single link agglomerative clustering method is suitable for capturing clusters with non-globular shapes, but this approach is very sensitive to noise and cannot handle clusters of varying density [8]. We used the density-based clustering algorithm DBSCAN [7], because it yields the following advantages:

- DBSCAN is rather robust concerning outliers.
- DBSCAN can be used for all kinds of metric data spaces and is not confined to vector spaces.
- DBSCAN is a very efficient and effective clustering algorithm.

- There exists an efficient incremental version, which would allow incremental clusterings on the local sites. Thus, only if the local clustering changes "considerably", we have to transmit a new local model to the central site [6].

We slightly enhanced DBSCAN so that we can easily determine the local model after we have finished the local clustering. All information which is comprised within the local model, i.e. the representatives and their corresponding ε–ranges, is computed on-the-fly during the DBSCAN run.

In the following, we describe DBSCAN in a level of detail which is indispensable for understanding the process of extracting suitable representatives (cf. Section 5).

4.1 The Density-Based Partitioning Clustering-Algorithm DBSCAN

The key idea of density-based clustering is that for each object of a cluster the neighborhood of a given radius (*Eps*) has to contain at least a minimum number of objects (*MinPts*), i.e. the cardinality of the neighborhood has to exceed some threshold. Density-based clusters can also be significantly generalized to density-connected sets. Density-connected sets are defined along the same lines as density-based clusters.

We will first give a short introduction to DBSCAN. For a detailed presentation of DBSCAN see [7].

Definition 1 (directly density-reachable). An object p is *directly density-reachable* from an object q wrt. *Eps* and *MinPts* in the set of objects D if

- $p \in N_{Eps}(q)$ ($N_{Eps}(q)$ is the subset of D contained in the *Eps*-neighborhood of q)
- $| N_{Eps}(q) | \geq MinPts$ (core-object condition)

Definition 2 (density-reachable). An object p is *density-reachable* from an object q wrt. *Eps* and *MinPts* in the set of objects D, denoted as $p >_D q$, if there is a chain of objects $p_1, ..., p_n$, $p_1 = q$, $p_n = p$ such that $p_i \in D$ and p_{i+1} is directly density-reachable from p_i wrt. *Eps* and *MinPts*.

Density-reachability is a canonical extension of direct density-reachability. This relation is transitive, but it is not symmetric. Although not symmetric in general, it is obvious that density-reachability is symmetric for objects o with $|N_{Eps}(o)| \geq MinPts$. Two "border objects" of a cluster are possibly not density-reachable from each other because there are not enough objects in their *Eps*-neighborhoods. However, there must be a third object in the cluster from which both "border objects" are density-reachable. Therefore, we introduce the notion of density-connectivity.

Definition 3 (density-connected). An object p is *density-connected* to an object q wrt. *Eps* and *MinPts* in the set of objects D if there is an object $o \in D$ such that both, p and q are density-reachable from o wrt. *Eps* and *MinPts* in D.

Density-connectivity is a symmetric relation. A *cluster* is defined as a set of density-connected objects which is maximal wrt. density-reachability and the *noise* is the set of objects not contained in any cluster.

Definition 4 (cluster). Let D be a set of objects. A *cluster* C wrt. *Eps* and *MinPts* in D is a non-empty subset of D satisfying the following conditions:

- Maximality: $\forall p,q \in D$: if $p \in C$ and $q >_D p$ wrt. *Eps* and *MinPts*, then also $q \in C$.
- Connectivity: $\forall p,q \in C$: p is density-connected to q wrt. *Eps* and *MinPts* in D.

Definition 5 (noise). Let $C_1,..., C_k$ be the clusters wrt. *Eps* and *MinPts* in *D*. Then, we define the *noise* as the set of objects in the database *D* not belonging to any cluster C_i, i.e. $noise = \{p \in D \mid \forall \text{ i: p} \notin C_i\}$.

We omit the term "wrt. *Eps* and *MinPts*" in the following whenever it is clear from the context. There are different kinds of objects in a clustering: *core objects* (satisfying condition 2 of definition 1) or *non-core objects* otherwise. In the following, we will refer to this characteristic of an object as the *core object property* of the object. The non-core objects in turn are either *border objects* (no core object but density-reachable from another core object) or *noise objects* (no core object and not density-reachable from other objects).

The algorithm DBSCAN was designed to efficiently discover the clusters and the noise in a database according to the above definitions. The procedure for finding a cluster is based on the fact that a cluster as defined is uniquely determined by any of its core objects: first, given an arbitrary object *p* for which the core object condition holds, the set $\{o \mid o >_D p\}$ of all objects *o* density-reachable from *p* in *D* forms a complete cluster *C*. Second, given a cluster *C* and an arbitrary core object $p \in C$, *C* in turn equals the set $\{o \mid o >_D p\}$ (c.f. lemma 1 and 2 in [7]).

To find a cluster, DBSCAN starts with an arbitrary core object *p* which is not yet clustered and retrieves all objects density-reachable from *p*. The retrieval of density-reachable objects is performed by successive region queries which are supported efficiently by spatial access methods such as R*-trees [3] for data from a vector space or M-trees [4] for data from a metric space.

5 Determination of a Local Model

After having clustered the data locally, we need a small number of representatives which describe the local clustering result accurately. We have to find an optimum trade-off between the following two opposite requirements:

- We would like to have a small number of representatives.
- We would like to have an accurate description of a local cluster.

As the core points computed during the DBSCAN run contain in its *Eps*-neighborhood at least *MinPts* other objects, they might serve as good representatives. Unfortunately, their number can become very high, especially in very dense areas of clusters. In the following, we will introduce two different approaches for determining suitable representatives which are both based on the concept of *specific core-points*.

Definition 6 (specific core points). Let *D* be a set of objects and let $C \in 2^D$ be a cluster wrt. *Eps* and *MinPts*. Furthermore, let $Cor_C \subseteq C$ be the set of core-points belonging to this cluster. Then $Scor_C \subseteq C$ is called a *complete set of specific core points of C* iff the following conditions are true.

- $Scor_C \subseteq Cor_C$
- $\forall s_i, s_j \in Scor_C: s_i \neq s_i \Rightarrow s_i \notin N_{Eps}(s_j)$
- $\forall c \in Cor_C \; \exists s \in Scor_C: c \in N_{Eps}(s)$

There might exist several different sets $Scor_C$ which fulfil Definition 6. Each of these sets $Scor_C$ usually consists of several specific core points which can be used to describe the cluster *C*.

The small example in Figure 3a shows that if A is an element of the set of specific core-points *Scor*, object B can not be included in *Scor* as it is located within the *Eps*-neighborhood of A. C might be contained in *Scor* as it is not in the *Eps*-neighborhood of A. On the other hand, if B is within *Scor*, A and C are not contained in *Scor* as they are both in the *Eps*-neighborhood of B. The actual processing order of the objects during the DBSCAN run determines a concrete set of specific core points. For instance, if the core-point B is visited first during the DBSCAN run, the core-points A and C are not included in *Scor*.

In the following, we introduce two local models called, REP_{Scor} (cf. Section 5.1) and $REP_{k\text{-}Means}$ (cf. Section 5.2) which both create a local model based on the complete set of specific core points.

5.1 Local Model: REP_{Scor}

In this model, we represent each local cluster C_i by a complete set of specific core points $Scor_{C_i}$. If we assume that we have found n clusters $C_1,..,C_n$ on a local site k, the local model $LocalModel_k$ is formed by the union of the different sets $Scor_{C_i}$.

In the case of density-based clustering, very often several core points are in the *Eps*-neighborhood of another core point. This is especially true, if we have dense clusters and a large *Eps*-value. In Figure 3a, for instance, the two core points A and B are within the *Eps*-range of each other as $dist(A, B)$ is smaller than *Eps*.

Assuming core point A is a specific core point, i.e. $A \in Scor$, than $B \notin Scor$ because of condition 2 in Definition 6. In this case, object A should not only represent the objects in its own neighborhood, but also the objects in the neighborhood of B, i.e. A should represent all objects of $N_{Eps}(A) \cup N_{Eps}(B)$. In order for A to be a representative for the objects $N_{Eps}(A) \cup N_{Eps}(B)$, we have to assign a new specific ε_A–range to A with $\varepsilon_A = Eps + dist(A,B)$ (cf. Figure 3a). Of course we have to assign such a specific ε–range to all specific core points, which motivates the following definition:

Definition 7 (specific ε–ranges). Let $C \subseteq D$ be a cluster wrt. *Eps* and *MinPts*. Furthermore, let $Scor \subseteq C$ be a complete set of specific core-points. Then we assign to each $s \in Scor$ an ε_s–range indicating the represented area of s:

$$\varepsilon_s := Eps + max\{dist(s,s_i) | s_i \in Cor \wedge s_i \in N_{Eps}(s)\} .$$

This specific ε–range value is part of the local model and is evaluated on the server site to develop an accurate global model. Furthermore, it is very important for the updating process of the local objects. The specific ε–range value is integrated into the local model of site k as follows:

$$LocalModel_k := \bigcup_{i \in 1..n} \{(s,\varepsilon_s) | s \in Scor_{C_i}\}.$$

5.2 Local Model: $REP_{k\text{-}Means}$

This approach is also based on the complete set of specific core-points. In contrast to the previous approach, the specific core points are not directly used to describe a cluster. Instead, we use the number $|Scor_C|$ and the elements of $Scor_C$ as input parameters for a further "clustering step" with an adapted version of *k-means*. For each cluster C, found by *DBSCAN*, k-means yields $|Scor_C|$ centroids within C. These centroids are used as representatives. The small example in Figure 3b shows that if object A is a specific core point, and

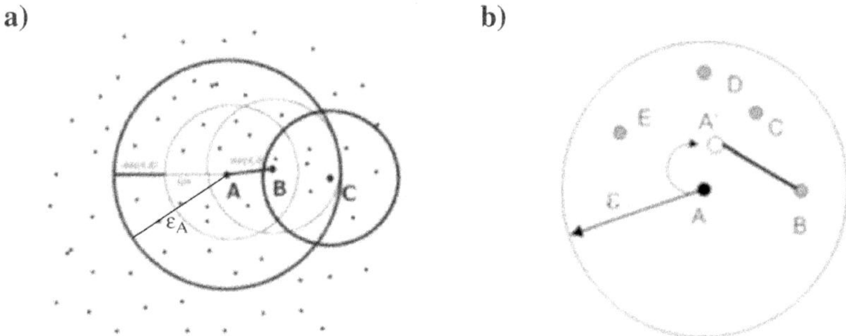

Fig. 3. Local models **a)** REP_{Scor}: specific core points and specific ε–range **b)** $REP_{k\text{-}Means}$: representatives by using k-means

we apply an additional clustering step by using k-means, we get a more appropriate representative A'.

K-means is a partitioning based clustering method which needs as input parameters the number m of clusters which should be detected within a set M of objects. Furthermore, we have to provide m starting points for this algorithm, if we want to find m clusters. We use k-means as follows:

- Each local cluster C which was found throughout the original DBSCAN run on the local site forms a set M of objects which is again clustered with k-means.
- We ask k-means to find $|Scor_C|$ (sub)clusters within C, as all specific core points together yield a suitable number of representatives. Each of the centroids found by k-means within cluster C is then used as a new representative. Thus the number of representatives for each cluster is the same as in the previous approach.
- As initial starting points for the clustering of C with k-means, we use the set of complete specific core points $Scor_C$.

Again, let us assume that there are n clusters $C_1,..,C_n$ on a local site k. Furthermore, let $c_{i,1}..c_{i,|Scor_{C_i}|}$ be the $|Scor_{C_i}|$ centroids found by the clustering of C_i with k-means. Let $O_{i,j} \subseteq C_i$ be the set of objects which are assigned to the centroid $c_{i,j}$. Then we assign to each *centroid* $c_{i,j}$ an $\varepsilon_{c_{i,j}}$–range, indicating the represented area by $c_{i,j}$, as follows:

$$\varepsilon_{c_{i,j}} := max\{dist(o, c_{i,j}) | o \in O_{i,j}\}.$$

Finally, the local model, describing the n clusters on site k, can be generated analogously to the previous section as follows:

$$LocalModel_k := \bigcup_{i \in 1..n} \bigcup_{j \in 1..|Scor_{C_i}|} (c_{i,j}, \varepsilon_{c_{i,j}}).$$

6 Determination of a Global Model

Each local model $LocalModel_k$ consists of a set of m_k pairs, consisting of a representative r and an ε–range value ε_r. The number m of pairs transmitted from each site k is determined by the number n of clusters C_i found on site k and the number $|Scor_{C_i}|$ of specific core-points for each cluster C_i as follows:

$$m = \sum_{i = 1..n} |Scor_{C_i}| .$$

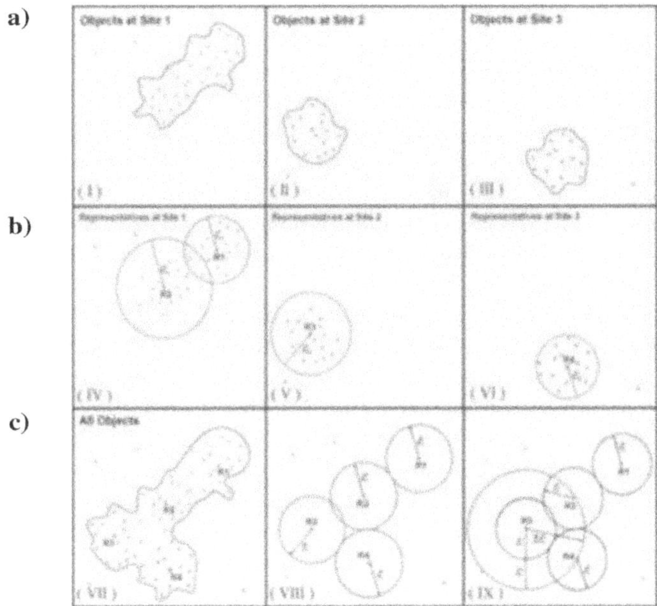

Fig. 4. Determination of a global model **a)** local clusters **b)** local representatives **c)** determination of a global model with $Eps_{global} = 2 \bullet Eps_{local}$

Each of these pairs (r, ε_r) represent several objects which are all located in $N_{\varepsilon_r}(r)$, i.e. the ε_r-neighborhood of r. All objects contained in $N_{\varepsilon_r}(r)$ belongs to the same cluster. To put it another way, each specific local representative forms a cluster on its own. Obviously, we have to check whether it is possible to merge two or more of these clusters. These merged local representatives together with the unmerged local representatives form the global model. Thus, the global model consist of clusters consisting of one or of several local representatives.

To find such a global model, we use the density based clustering algorithm DBSCAN again. We would like to create a clustering similar to the one produced by DBSCAN if applied to the complete dataset with the local parameter settings. As we have only access to the set of all local representatives, the global parameter setting has to be adapted to this aggregated local information.

As we assume that all local representatives form a cluster on their own it is enough to use a $Min\text{-}Pts_{global}$-parameter of 2. If 2 representatives, stemming from the same or different local sites, are density connected to each other wrt. $MinPts_{global}$ and Eps_{global}, then they belong to the same global cluster.

The question for a suitable Eps_{global} value, is much more difficult. Obviously, Eps_{global} should be greater than the Eps-parameter Eps_{local} used for the clustering on the local sites. For high Eps_{global} values, we run the risk of merging clusters together which do not belong together. On the other hand, if we use small Eps_{global} values, we might not be able to detect clusters belonging together. Therefore, we suggest that the Eps_{global} parameter should be tunable by the user dependent on the ε_R values of all local representatives R. If these ε_R values are generally high it is advisable to use a high Eps_{global} value. On the other hand, if the ε_R values are low, a small Eps_{global} value is better. The default value which we propose is equal to the maximum value of all ε_R values of all local representatives *R*. This default Eps_{global} value is generally close to $2 \cdot Eps_{local}$ (cf. Section 9).

In Figure 4, an example for $Eps_{global}=2 \cdot Eps_{local}$ is depicted. In Figure 4a the independently detected clusters on site 1,2 and 3 are depicted. The cluster on site 1 is characterized by two representatives *R1* and *R2*, whereas the clusters on site 2 and site 3 are only characterized by one representative as shown in Figure 4b. Figure 4c (VII) illustrates that all 4 clusters from the different sites belong to one large cluster. Figure 4c (VIII) illustrates that an Eps_{global} equal to Eps_{local} is insufficient to detect this global cluster. On the other hand, if we use an Eps_{global} parameter equal to $2 \cdot Eps_{local}$ the 4 representatives are merged together to one large cluster (cf. Figure 4c (IX)).

Instead of a user defined Eps_{global} parameter, we could also use a hierarchical density based clustering algorithm, e.g. OPTICS [1], for the creation of the global model. This approach would enable the user to visually analyze the hierarchical clustering structure for several Eps_{global}-parameters without running the clustering algorithm again and again. We refine from this approach because of several reasons. First, the relabeling process discussed in the next section would become very tedious. Second, a quantitative evaluation (cf. Section 9) of our DBDC algorithm is almost impossible. Third, the incremental version of DBSCAN allows us to start with the construction of the global model after the first representatives of any local model come in. Thus we do not have to wait for all clients to have transmitted their complete local models.

7 Updating of the Local Clustering Based on the Global Model

After having created a global clustering, we send the complete global model to all client sites. The client sites relabel all objects located on their site independently from each other. On the client site, two former independent clusters may be merged due to this new relabeling. Furthermore, objects which were formerly assigned to local noise are now part of a global cluster. If a local object *o* is in the ε_r–range of a representative *r*, *o* is assigned to the same global cluster as *r*.

Figure 5 depicts an example for this relabeling process. The objects *R1* and *R2* are the local representatives. Each of them forms a cluster on its own. Objects *A* and *B* have been classified as noise. Representative *R3* is a representative stemming from another site. As *R1*, *R2* and *R3* belong to the same global cluster all Objects from the local clusters *Cluster 1* and *Cluster 2* are assigned to this global cluster. Furthermore, the objects *A* and *B* are assigned to this global cluster as they are within the ε_{R3}–neighborhood of *R3*, i.e. $A, B \in N_{\varepsilon_{R3}}(R3)$. On the other hand, object *C* still belongs to noise as $C \notin N_{\varepsilon_{R3}}(R3)$.

These updated local client clusterings help the clients to answer server questions efficiently, e.g. questions such as "*give me all objects on your site which belong to the global cluster 4711*".

8 Quality of Distributed Clustering

There exist no general quality measure which helps to evaluate the quality of a distributed clustering. If we want to evaluate our new *DBDC* approach, we first have to tackle the problem of finding a suitable quality criterion. Such a suitable quality criterion should yield a high quality value if we compare a "good" distributed clustering to a central clustering,

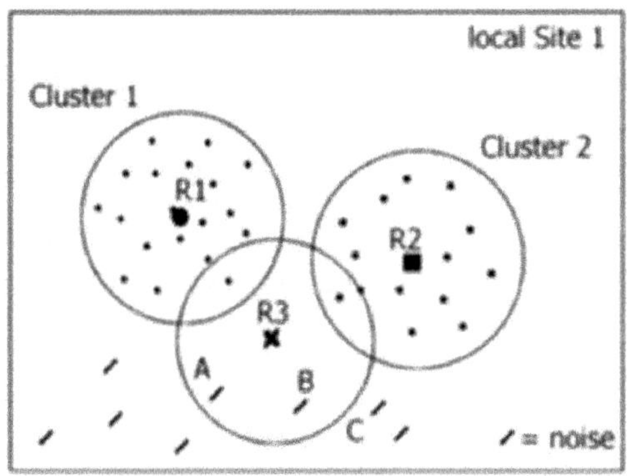

Fig. 5. Relabeling of the local clustering

i.e. reference clustering. On the other hand, it should yield a low value if we compare a "bad" distributed clustering to a central clustering. Needless to say, if we compare a reference clustering to itself, the quality should be 100%. Let us first formally introduce the notion of a clustering.

Definition 8 (clustering CL). Let $D = \{x_1, \ldots, x_n\}$ be a database consisting of n objects. Then, we call any set CL a clustering of D *w.r.t. MinPts,* if it fulfils the following properties:

- $CL \subseteq 2^D$
- $\forall C \in CL: (|C| \geq MinPts)$
- $\forall C_1, C_2 \in CL: C_1 \neq C_2 \Rightarrow C_1 \cap C_2 = \varnothing$

In the following we denote by CL_{distr} a clustering resulting from our distributed approach and by $CL_{central}$ our central reference clustering. We will define two different quality criterions which measure the similarity between CL_{distr} and $CL_{central}$. We compare the two introduced quality criterions to each other by discussing a small example.

Let us assume that we have n objects, distributed over k sites. Our *DBDC*-algorithm, assigns each object x_i either to a cluster or to noise. We compare the result of our *DBDC*-algorithm to a central clustering of the n objects using DBSCAN. Then we assign to each object x a numerical value $P(x)$ indicating the quality for this specific object. The overall quality of the distributed clustering is the mean of the qualities assigned to each object.

Definition 9 (distributed clustering quality Q_{DBDC}). Let $D = \{x_1, \ldots, x_n\}$ be a database consisting of n objects. Let P be an object quality function $P: D \to [0, 1]$. Then the quality Q_{DBDC} of our distributed clustering w.r.t. P is computed as follows:

$$Q_{DBDC} = \frac{\sum_{i=1\ldots n} P(x_i)}{n}$$

The crucial question is "what is a suitable object quality function?". In the following two subsections, we will discuss two different object functions P.

8.1 First Object Quality Function P^I

Obviously, $P(x)$ should yield a rather high value, if an object x together with many other objects is contained in a distributed cluster C_d and a central cluster C_c. In the case of density-based partitioning clustering, a cluster might consist of only *MinPts* elements. Therefore, the number of objects contained in two identical clusters might be not higher than *MinPts*. On the other hand, each cluster consists of at least *MinPts* elements. Therefore, asking for less than *MinPts* elements in both clusters would weakening the quality criterion unnecessarily.

If x is included in a distributed cluster C_d but is assigned to noise by the central clustering, the value of $P(x)$ should be 0. If x is not contained in any distributed cluster, i.e. it is assigned to noise, a high object quality value requires that it is also not contained in a central cluster. In the following, we will define a discrete object quality function P^I which assigns either 0 or 1 to an object x, i.e. $P^I(x) = 0$ or $P^I(x) = 1$.

Definition 10 (discrete object quality P^I). Let $x \in D$ and let C_d, C_c be two cluster. Then we can define an object quality function $P^I : D \rightarrow \{0, 1\}$ w.r.t. to a quality parameter qp as follows:

$$P^I(x) = \begin{cases} 0, & x \in Noise_{distr} \wedge x \notin Noise_{central} \\ 0, & x \notin Noise_{distr} \wedge x \in Noise_{central} \\ 1, & x \in Noise_{distr} \wedge x \in Noise_{central} \\ 1, & x \notin Noise_{distr} \wedge x \notin Noise_{central} \wedge (|C_d \cap C_c| \geq qp) \\ 0, & x \notin Noise_{distr} \wedge x \notin Noise_{central} \wedge (|C_d \cap C_c| < qp) \end{cases}$$

The main advantage of the object quality function P^I is that it is rather simple because it yields only a boolean return value, i.e. it tells whether an object was clustered correctly or falsely. Nevertheless, sometimes a more subtle quality measure is required which does not only assign a binary quality value to an object. In the following section, we will introduce a new object quality function which is not confined to the two binary quality values 0 and 1. This more sophisticated quality function can compute any value in between 0 and 1 which much better reflects the notion of "correctly clustered".

8.2 Second Object Quality Function P^{II}

The main idea of our new quality function is to take the number of elements which were clustered together with the object x during the distributed and the central clustering into consideration. Furthermore, we decrease the quality of x if there are objects which have been clustered together with x in only one of the two clusterings.

Definition 11 (continuous object quality P^{II}). Let $x \in D$ and let C_d, C_c be a central and a distributed cluster. Then we define an object quality function $P^{II} : D \rightarrow [0, 1]$ as follows:

$$P^{II}(x) = \begin{cases} 1, & x \in Noise_{distr} \wedge x \notin Noise_{central} \\ 0, & x \notin Noise_{distr} \wedge x \in Noise_{central} \\ 1, & x \in Noise_{distr} \wedge x \in Noise_{central} \\ \dfrac{|C_d \cap C_c|}{|C_d \cup C_c|}, & otherwise \end{cases}$$

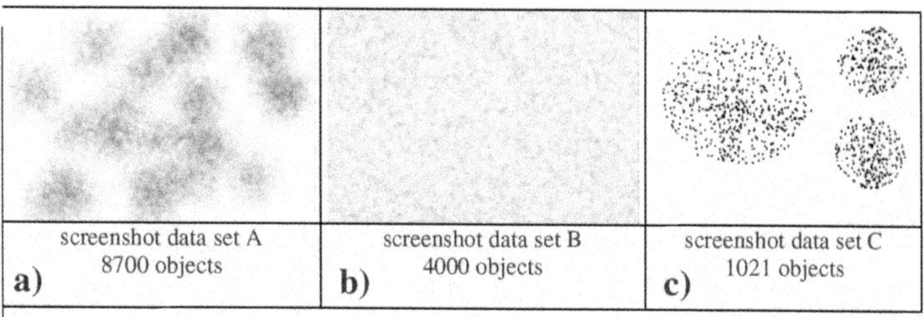

Fig. 6. Used test data sets **a)** test data set *A* **b)** test data set *B* **c)** test data set *C*

9 Experimental Evaluation

We evaluated our *DBDC*-approach based on three different 2-dimensional point sets where we varied both the number of points and the characteristics of the point sets. Figure 6 depicts the three used test data sets *A* (8700 objects, randomly generated data/cluster), *B* (4000 objects, very noisy data) and *C* (1021 objects, 3 clusters) on the central site. In order to evaluate our *DBDC*-approach, we equally distributed the data set onto the different client sites and then compared *DBDC* to a single run of *DBSCAN* on all data points. We carried out all local clusterings sequentially. Then, we collected all representatives of all local runs, and applied a global clustering on these representatives. For all these steps, we always used the same computer. The overall runtime was formed by adding the time needed for the global clustering to the maximum time needed for the local clusterings. All experiments were performed on a Pentium III/700 machine.

In a first set of experiments, we consider efficiency aspects, whereas in the following sections we concentrate on quality aspects.

9.1 Efficiency

In Figure 7, we used test data sets with varying cardinalities to compare the overall runtime of our *DBDC*-algorithm to the runtime of a central clustering. Furthermore, we compared our two local models w.r.t. efficiency to each other. Figure 7a shows that our *DBDC*-approach outperforms a central clustering by far for large data sets. For instance, for a point set consisting of 100,000 points, both DBDC approaches, i.e. $DBDC(Rep_{SCor})$ and $DBDC(Rep_{K\text{-}Means})$, outperform the central DBSCAN algorithm by more than one order of magnitude independent of the used local clustering. Furthermore, Figure 7a shows that the local model for REP_{Scor} can more efficiently be computed than the local model for $REP_{k\text{-}Means}$.

Figure 7b shows that for small data sets our *DBDC*-approach is slightly slower than the central clustering approach. Nevertheless, the additional overhead for distributed clustering is almost negligible even for small data sets.

In Figure 8 it is depicted in what way the overall runtime depends on the number of used sites. We compared DBDC based on REP_{Scor} to a central clustering with DBSCAN. Our experiments show that we obtain a speed-up factor which is somewhere between $O(n)$ and $O(n^2)$. This high speed-up factor is due to the fact that DBSCAN has a runtime complexity somewhere between $O(n\log n)$ and $O(n^2)$ when using a suitable index structure, e.g. an R*-tree [3].

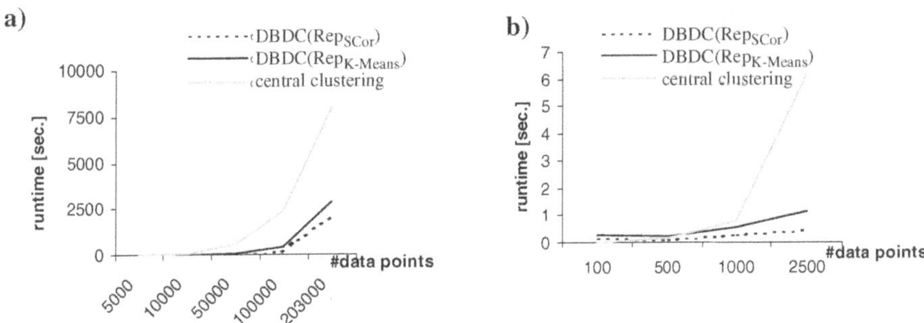

Fig. 7. Overall runtime for central and distributed clustering dependent on the cardinality of the data set A. **a)** high number of data objects **b)** small number of data objects.

9.2 Quality

In the next set of experiments we evaluated the quality of our two introduced object quality functions P^I and P^{II} together with the quality of our DBDC-approach. Figure 9a shows that the quality according to P^I of both local models is very high and does not change if we vary the Eps_{global} parameter during global clustering. On the other hand, if we look at Figure 9b, we can clearly see that for Eps_{global} parameters equal to $2{\cdot}Eps_{local}$, we get the best quality for both local models. This is equal to the default value for the server site clustering which we derived in Section 6. Furthermore, the quality worsens for very high and very small Eps_{global} parameters, which is in accordance to the quality which an experienced user would assign to those clusterings.

To sum up, these experiments yield two basic insights:

- The object quality function P^{II} is more suitable than P^I.
- A good Eps_{global} parameter is around $2{\cdot}Eps_{local}$

Furthermore, the experiments indicate that the local model $REP_{k\text{-}Means}$ yields slightly higher quality.

For the following experiments, we used an Eps_{global} parameter of $2{\cdot}Eps_{local}$.

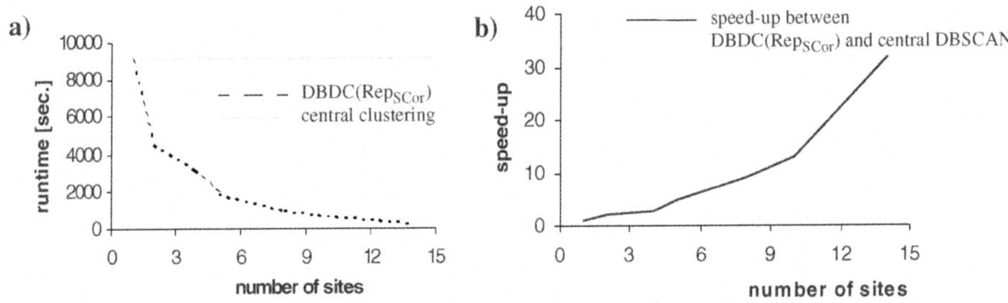

Fig. 8. Overall runtime for central and distributed clustering $DBDC(Rep_{SCor})$ for a data set of 203,000 points. **a)** dependent on the number of sites **b)** speed-up of $DBDC$ compared to central $DBSCAN$

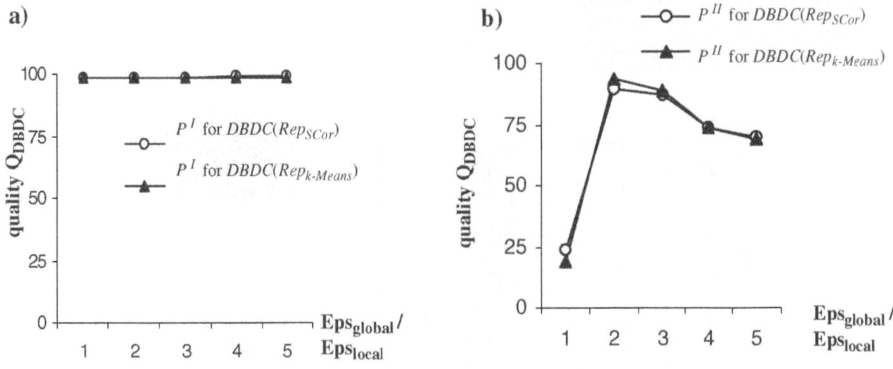

Fig. 9. Evaluation of object quality functions for varying Eps_{global} parameters for data set A on 4 local sites. **a)** object quality function P^I **b)** object quality function P^{II}

Figure 10 shows how the quality of our *DBDC*-approach depends on the number of client-sites. We can see that the quality according to P^I is independent of the number of client sites which indicates again that this quality measure is unsuitable. On the other hand, the quality computed by P^{II} is in accordance with the intuitive quality which an experienced user would assign to the distributed clusterings on the varying number of sites. Although, we have a slight decreasing quality for an increasing number of sites, the overall quality for both local models $REP_{k\text{-}Means}$ and REP_{Scor} is very high.

Figure 11 shows that for the three different data sets A, B and C our *DBDC*-approach yields good results for both local models. The more accurate quality measure P^{II} indicates that the *DBDC*-approach based on $REP_{k\text{-}Means}$ yields a quality which reflects more ade-

number of sites	number of local repr.[%]	$DBDC(REP_{k\text{-}Means})$		$DBDC(REP_{Scor})$	
		P^I	P^{II}	P^I	P^{II}
2	16	99	98	99	97
4	16	98	97	98	96
5	17	98	97	98	96
8	17	98	96	98	96
10	17	98	97	98	96
14	17	98	89	98	89
20	17	98	91	98	91

Fig. 10. Quality Q_{DBDC} dependent on the number of client sites, the local models $REP_{k\text{-}Means}$ and REP_{Scor}, and the object quality functions P^I and P^{II} for test data set A and $Eps_{global} = 2 \cdot Eps_{local}$

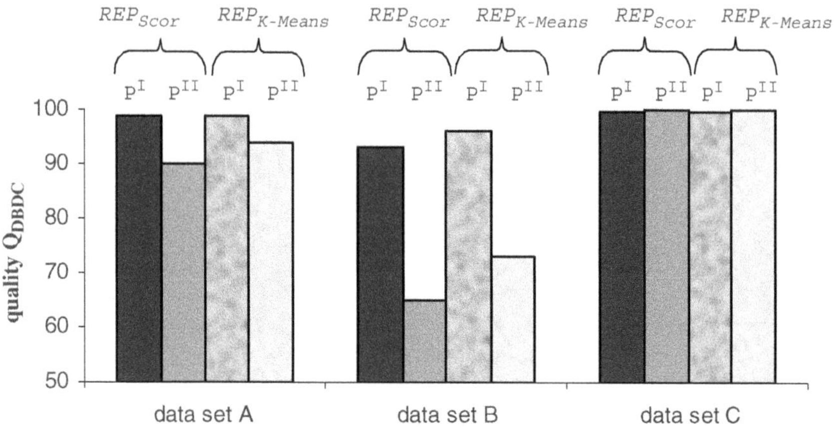

Fig. 11. Quality for data sets A, B and C

quately the user's expectations. This is especially true for the rather noisy data set B, where P^{II} yields the lower quality corresponding to the user's intuition.

To sum up, our new DBDC-approach based on $REP_{k\text{-}Means}$ efficiently yields a very high quality even for a rather high number of local sites and data sets of various cardinalities and characteristics.

10 Conclusions

In this paper, we first motivated the need of distributed clustering algorithms. Due to technical, economical or security reasons, it is often not possible to transmit all data from different local sites to one central server site and then cluster the data there. Therefore, we have to apply an efficient and effective distributed clustering algorithm from which a lot of application ranges will benefit. We developed a partitioning distributed clustering algorithm which is based on the density-based clustering algorithm DBSCAN. We clustered the data locally and independently from each other and transmitted only aggregated information about the local data to a central server. This aggregated information consists of a set of pairs, comprising a representative r and an ε–range value ε_r, indicating the validity area of the representative. Based on these local models, we reconstruct a global clustering. This global clustering was carried out by means of standard DBSCAN where the two input-parameters Eps_{global} and $MinPts_{global}$ were chosen such that the information contained in the local models are processed in the best possible way. The created global model is sent to all clients, which use this information to relable their own objects.

As there exists no general quality measures which helps to evaluate the quality of a distributed clustering, we introduced suitable quality criteria on our own. In the experimental evaluation, we discussed the suitability of our quality criteria and our density-based distributed clustering approach. Based on the quality criteria, we showed that our new distributed clustering approach yields almost the same clustering quality as a central clustering on all data. On the other hand, we showed that we have an enormous efficiency advantage compared to a central clustering carried out on all data.

References

1. Ankerst M., Breunig M. M., Kriegel H.-P., Sander J.: "OPTICS: Ordering Points To Identify the Clustering Structure", Proc. ACM SIGMOD, Philadelphia, PA, 1999, pp. 49-60.
2. Agrawal R., Shafer J. C.: "Parallel mining of association rules: Design, implementation, and experience" IEEE Trans. Knowledge and Data Eng. 8 (1996) 962-969
3. Beckmann N., Kriegel H.-P., Schneider R., Seeger B.: "The R*-tree: An Efficient and Robust Access Method for Points and Rectangles", Proc. ACM SIGMOD Int. Conf. on Management of Data (SIGMOD'90), Atlantic City, NJ, ACM Press, New York, 1990, pp. 322?331.
4. Ciaccia P., Patella M., Zezula P.: "*M-tree: An Efficient Access Method for Similarity Search in Metric Spaces*", Proc. 23rd Int. VLDB, Athens, Greece, 1997, pp. 426-435.
5. Dhillon I. S., Modh Dh. S.: "A Data-Clustering Algorithm On Distributed Memory Multiprocessors", SIGKDD 99
6. Ester M., Kriegel H.-P., Sander J., Wimmer M., Xu X.: "Incremental Clustering for Mining in a Data Warehousing Environment", VLDB 98
7. Ester M., Kriegel H.-P., Sander J., Xu X.: "A Density-Based Algorithm for Discovering Clusters in Large Spatial Databases with Noise", Proc. 2nd Int. Conf. on Knowledge Discovery and Data Mining (KDD'96), Portland, OR, AAAI Press, 1996, pp.226-231.
8. Ertöz L., Steinbach M., Kumar V.: "Finding Clusters of Different Sizes, Shapes, and Densities in Noisy, High Dimensional Data", SIAM International Conference on Data Mining (2003)
9. Forman G., Zhang B. : "Distributed Data Clustering Can Be Efficient and Exact". SIGKDD Explorations 2(2): 34-38 (2000)
10. Hanisch R. J.: "Distributed Data Systems and Services for Astronomy and the Space Sciences", in ASP Conf. Ser., Vol. 216, Astronomical Data Analysis Software and Systems IX, eds. N. Manset, C. Veillet, D. Crabtree (San Francisco: ASP) 2000
11. Hartigan J. A.: "Clustering Algorithms", Wiley, 1975
12. Han E. H., Karypis G., Kumar V.: "Scalable parallel data mining for association rules" In: SIGMOD Record: Proceedings of the 1997 ACM-SIGMOD Conference on Management of Data, Tucson, AZ, USA. (1997) 277-288
13. Jain A. K., Dubes R.C.: "Algorithms for Clustering Data", Prentice-Hall Inc., 1988.
14. Johnson E., Kargupta H.: "Hierarchical Clustering From Distributed, Heterogeneous Data." In Zaki M. and Ho C., editors, Large-Scale Parallel KDD Systems. Lecture Notes in Computer Science, colum 1759, 221-244. Springer-Verlag, 1999
15. Jain A. K., Murty M. N., Flynn P. J.:"Data Clustering: A Review", ACM Computing Surveys, Vol. 31, No. 3, Sep. 1999, pp. 265-323.
16. Kargupta H., Chan P. (editors) : "Advances in Distributed and Parallel Knowledge Discovery", AAAI/MIT Press, 2000
17. Shafer J., Agrawal R., Mehta M.: "A scalable parallel classifier for data mining" In: Proc. 22nd International Conference on VLDB, Mumbai, India. (1996)
18. Srivastava A., Han E. H., Kumar V., Singh V.: "Parallel formulations of decision-tree classification algorithms" In: Proc. 1998 International Conference on Parallel Processing. (1998)
19. Samatova N.F., Ostrouchov G., Geist A., Melechko A.V.: "RACHET: An Efficient Cover-Based Merging of Clustering Hierarchies from Distributed Datasets, Distributed and Parallel Databases, 11(2): 157-180; Mar 2002"
20. Sayal M., Scheuermann P.: "A Distributed Clustering Algorithm for Web-Based Access Patterns", in Proceedings of the 2nd ACM-SIGMOD Workshop on Distributed and Parallel Knowledge Discovery, Boston, August 2000"
21. Xu X., Jäger J., H.-P. Kriegel.: "A Fast Parallel Clustering Algorithm for Large Spatial Databases", Data Mining and Knowledge Discovery, 3, 263-290 (1999), Kluwer Academic Publisher
22. Zaki M. J.., Parthasarathy S., Ogihara M., Li W.: "New parallel algorithms for fast discovery of association rule" Data Mining and Knowledge Discovery, 1, 343-373 (1997)

Iterative Incremental Clustering of Time Series

Jessica Lin, Michail Vlachos, Eamonn Keogh, and Dimitrios Gunopulos

Computer Science & Engineering Department
University of California, Riverside
Riverside, CA 92521
{jessica,mvlachos,eamonn,dg}@cs.ucr.edu

Abstract. We present a novel anytime version of partitional clustering algorithm, such as k-Means and EM, for time series. The algorithm works by leveraging off the multi-resolution property of wavelets. The dilemma of choosing the initial centers is mitigated by initializing the centers at each approximation level, using the final centers returned by the coarser representations. In addition to casting the clustering algorithms as anytime algorithms, this approach has two other very desirable properties. By working at lower dimensionalities we can efficiently avoid local minima. Therefore, the quality of the clustering is usually better than the batch algorithm. In addition, even if the algorithm is run to completion, our approach is much faster than its batch counterpart. We explain, and empirically demonstrate these surprising and desirable properties with comprehensive experiments on several publicly available real data sets. We further demonstrate that our approach can be generalized to a framework of much broader range of algorithms or data mining problems.

1 Introduction

Clustering is a vital process for condensing and summarizing information, since it can provide a synopsis of the stored data. Although there has been much research on clustering in general, most classic machine learning and data mining algorithms do not work well for time series due to their unique structure. In particular, the high dimensionality, very high feature correlation, and the (typically) large amount of noise that characterize time series data present a difficult challenge. Although numerous clustering algorithms have been proposed, the majority of them work in a batch fashion, thus hindering interaction with the end users. Here we address the clustering problem by introducing a novel anytime version of partitional clustering algorithm based on wavelets. Anytime algorithms are valuable for large databases, since results are produced progressively and are refined over time [11]. Their utility for data mining has been documented at length elsewhere [2, 21]. While partitional clustering algorithms and wavelet decomposition have both been studied extensively in the past, the major novelty of our approach is that it mitigates the problem associated with the choice of initial centers, in addition to providing the functionality of user-interaction.

The algorithm works by leveraging off the multi-resolution property of wavelet decomposition [1, 6, 22]. In particular, an initial clustering is performed with a very coarse representation of the data. The results obtained from this "quick and dirty"

E. Bertino et al. (Eds.): EDBT 2004, LNCS 2992, pp. 106–122, 2004.
© Springer-Verlag Berlin Heidelberg 2004

clustering are used to initialize a clustering at a finer level of approximation. This process is repeated until the "approximation" is the original "raw" data. Our approach allows the user to interrupt and terminate the process at any level. In addition to casting the clustering algorithm as an anytime algorithm, our approach has two other very unintuitive properties. The quality of the clustering is often better than the batch algorithm, and even if the algorithm is run to completion, the time taken is typically much less than the time taken by the batch algorithm.

We initially focus our approach on the popular k-Means clustering algorithm [10, 18, 24] for time series. For simplicity we demonstrate how the algorithm works by utilizing the Haar wavelet decomposition. Then we extend the idea to another widely used clustering algorithm, EM, and another well-known decomposition method, DFT, towards the end of the paper. We demonstrate that our algorithm can be generalized as a framework for a much broader range of algorithms or data mining problems.

The rest of this paper is organized as follows. In Section 2 we review related work, and introduce the necessary background on the wavelet transform and k-Means clustering. In Section 3, we introduce our algorithm. Section 4 contains a comprehensive comparison of our algorithm to classic k-Means on real datasets. In Section 5 we study how our approach can be extended to other iterative refinement method (such as EM), and we also investigate the use of other multi-resolution decomposition such as DFT. In Section 6 we summarize our findings and offer suggestions for future work.

2 Background and Related Work

Since our work draws on the confluence of clustering, wavelets and anytime algorithms, we provide the necessary background on these areas in this section.

2.1 Background on Clustering

One of the most widely used clustering approaches is hierarchical clustering, due to the great visualization power it offers [12]. Hierarchical clustering produces a nested hierarchy of similar groups of objects, according to a pairwise distance matrix of the objects. One of the advantages of this method is its generality, since the user does not need to provide any parameters such as the number of clusters. However, its application is limited to only small datasets, due to its quadratic (or higher order) computational complexity.

A faster method to perform clustering is k-Means [2, 18]. The basic intuition behind k-Means (and in general, iterative refinement algorithms) is the continuous reassignment of objects into different clusters, so that the within-cluster distance is minimized. Therefore, if $\boldsymbol{x}$ are the objects and $\boldsymbol{c}$ are the cluster centers, k-Means attempts to minimize the following objective function:

$$F = \sum_{m=1}^{k}\sum_{i=1}^{N}\left\| x_i - c_m \right\| \tag{1}$$

The k-Means algorithm for N objects has a complexity of $O(kNrD)$ [18], where k is the number of clusters specified by the user, r is the number of iterations until convergence, and D is the dimensionality of the points. The shortcomings of the algorithm are its tendency to favor spherical clusters, and its requirement for prior knowledge on the number of clusters, k. The latter limitation can be mitigated by attempting all values of k within a large range. Various statistical tests can then be used to determine which value of k is most parsimonious. However, this approach only worsens k-Means' already considerable time complexity. Since k-Means is essentiality a hill-climbing algorithm, it is guaranteed to converge on a local but not necessarily global optimum. In other words, the choices of the initial centers are critical to the quality of results. Nevertheless, in spite of these undesirable properties, for clustering large datasets of time-series, k-Means is preferable due to its faster running time.

Table 1. An outline of the k-Means algorithm

	Algorithm k-Means
1	Decide on a value for k.
2	Initialize the k cluster centers (randomly, if necessary).
3	Decide the class memberships of the N objects by assigning them to the nearest cluster center.
4	Re-estimate the k cluster centers, by assuming the memberships found above are correct.
5	If none of the N objects changed membership in the last iteration, exit. Otherwise goto 3.

In order to scale the various clustering methods to massive datasets, one can either reduce the number of objects, N, by sampling [2], or reduce the dimensionality of the objects [1, 3, 9, 12, 13, 16, 19, 25, 26]. For time-series, the objective is to find a representation at a lower dimensionality that preserves the original information and describes the original shape of the time-series data as closely as possible. Many approaches have been suggested in the literature, including the Discrete Fourier Transform (DFT) [1, 9], Singular Value Decomposition [16], Adaptive Piecewise Constant Approximation [13], Piecewise Aggregate Approximation (PAA) [4, 26], Piecewise Linear Approximation [12] and the Discrete Wavelet Transform (DWT) [3, 19]. While all these approaches have shared the ability to produce a high quality reduced-dimensionality approximation of time series, wavelets are unique in that their representation of data is intrinsically multi-resolution. This property is critical to our proposed algorithm and will be discussed in detail in the next section.

2.2 Background on Wavelets

Wavelets are mathematical functions that represent data or other functions in terms of the averages and differences of a prototype function, called the analyzing or mother wavelet [6].

In this sense, they are similar to the Fourier transform. One fundamental difference is that wavelets are localized in time. In other words, some of the wavelet coefficients represent small, local subsections of the data being studied, as opposed to Fourier coefficients, which always represent global contributions to the data. This property is very useful for multi-resolution analysis of data. The first few coefficients contain an overall, coarse approximation of the data; additional coefficients can be perceived as "zooming-in" to areas of high detail. Figs 1 and 2 illustrate this idea.

The Haar Wavelet decomposition is achieved by averaging two adjacent values on the time series function at a given resolution to form a smoothed, lower-dimensional signal, and the resulting coefficients at this given resolution are simply the differences between the values and their averages [3]. As a result, the Haar wavelet decomposition is the combination of the coefficients at all resolutions, with the overall average for the time series being its first coefficient. The coefficients are crucial for reconstructing the original sequence, as they store the detailed information lost in the smoothed signal.

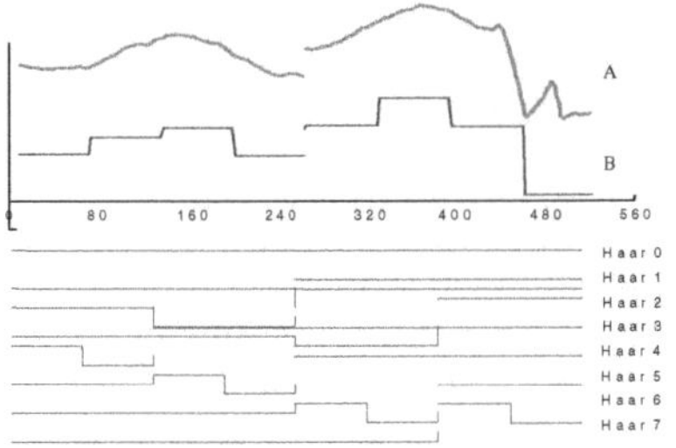

Fig. 1. The Haar Wavelet representation can be visualized as an attempt to approximate a time series with a linear combination of basis functions. In this case, time series A is transformed to B by Haar wavelet decomposition, and the dimensionality is reduced from 512 to 8.

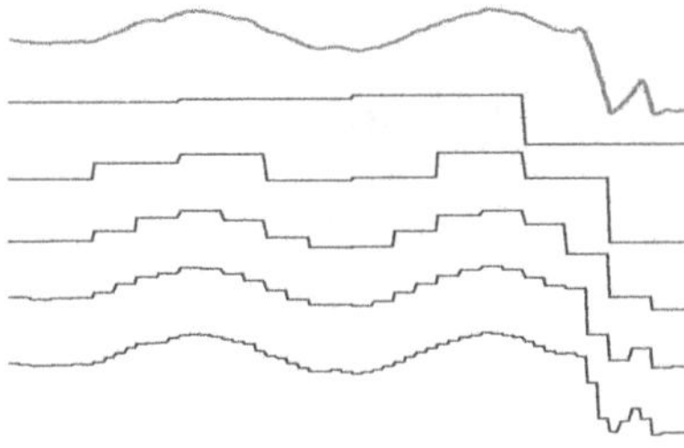

Fig. 2. The Haar Wavelet can represent data at different levels of resolution. Above we see a raw time series, with increasing faithful wavelet approximations below.

2.3 Background on Anytime Algorithms

Anytime algorithms are algorithms that trade execution time for quality of results [11]. In particular, an anytime algorithm always has a best-so-far answer available, and the quality of the answer improves with execution time. The user may examine this answer at any time, and choose to terminate the algorithm, temporarily suspend the algorithm, or allow the algorithm to run to completion.

The utility of anytime algorithms for data mining has been extensively documented [2, 21]. Suppose a batch version of an algorithm takes a week to run (not an implausible scenario in mining massive, disk-resident data sets). It would be highly desirable to implement the algorithm as an anytime algorithm. This would allow a user to examine the best current answer after an hour or so as a "sanity check" of all assumptions and parameters. As a simple example, suppose the user had accidentally set the value of k to 50 instead of the desired value of 5. Using a batch algorithm the mistake would not be noted for a week, whereas using an anytime algorithm the mistake could be noted early on and the algorithm restarted with little cost. This motivating example could have been eliminated by user diligence! More generally, however, data mining algorithms do require the user to make choices of several parameters, and an anytime implementation of k-Means would allow the user to interact with the entire data mining process in a more efficient way.

2.4 Related Work

Bradley et. al. [2] suggest a generic technique for scaling the k-Means clustering algorithms to large databases by attempting to identify regions of the data that are compressible, that must be retained in main memory, and regions that may be discarded. However, the generality of the method contrasts with our algorithm's explicit exploitation of the structure of the data type of interest.

Our work is more similar in spirit to the dynamic time warping similarity search technique introduced by Chu et. al. [4]. The authors speed up linear search by examining the time series at increasingly finer levels of approximation.

3 Our Approach – The I-kMeans Algorithm

As noted in Section 2.1, the complexity of the k-Means algorithm is $O(kNrD)$, where D is the dimensionality of data points (or the length of a sequence, as in the case of time-series). For a dataset consisting of long time-series, the D factor can burden the clustering task significantly. This overhead can be alleviated by reducing the data dimensionality.

Another major drawback of the k-Means algorithm is that the clustering quality is greatly dependant on the choice of initial centers (i.e., line 2 of Table 1). As mentioned earlier, the k-Means algorithm guarantees local, but not necessarily global optimization. Poor choices of the initial centers, therefore, can degrade the quality of clustering solution and result in longer execution time (See [10] for an excellent discussion of this issue). Our algorithm addresses these two problems of k-Means, in addition to offering the capability of an anytime algorithm, which allows the user to interrupt and terminate the program at any stage.

We propose using a wavelet decomposition to perform clustering at increasingly finer levels of the decomposition, while displaying the gradually refined clustering results periodically to the user. Note that any wavelet basis (or any other multi-resolution decomposition such as DFT) can be used, as will be demonstrated in Section 5. We opt for the Haar Wavelet here for its simplicity and its wide use in the time series community.

We compute the Haar Wavelet decomposition for all time-series data in the database. The complexity of this transformation is linear to the dimensionality of each object; therefore, the running time is reasonable even for large databases. The process of decomposition can be performed off-line, and needs to be done only once. The time series data can be stored in the Haar decomposition format, which takes the same amount of space as the original sequence. One important property of the decomposition is that it is a lossless transformation, since the original sequence can always be reconstructed from the decomposition.

Once we compute the Haar decomposition, we perform the k-Means clustering algorithm, starting at the second level (each object at level i has $2^{(i-1)}$ dimensions) and gradually progress to finer levels. Since the Haar decomposition is completely reversible, we can reconstruct the approximation data from the coefficients at any level and perform clustering on these data. We call the new clustering algorithm I-kMeans, where I stands for "interactive." Fig 3 illustrates this idea.

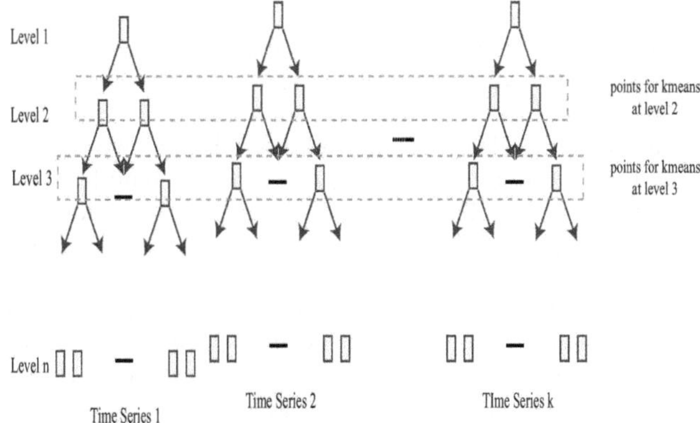

Fig. 3. k-Means is performed on each level on the reconstructed data from the Haar wavelet decomposition, starting with the second level

The intuition behind this algorithm originates from the observation that the general shape of a time series sequence can often be approximately captured at a lower resolution. As shown in Fig 2, the shape of the time series is well preserved, even at very coarse approximations. Because of this desirable feature of wavelets, clustering results typically stabilize at a low resolution, thus saving time by eliminating the need to run at full resolution (the raw data). The pseudo-code of the algorithm is provided in Table 2.

The algorithm achieves the speed-up by doing the vast majority of reassignments (Line 3 in Table 1) at the lower resolutions, where the costs of distance calculations are considerably lower. As we gradually progress to finer resolutions, we already start with good initial centers (the choices of initial centers will be discussed later in this section). Therefore, the number of iterations *r* until convergence will typically be much lower.

Table 2. An outline of the I-kMeans algorithm

	Algorithm I-kMeans
1	Decide on a value for k.
2	Initialize the k cluster centers (randomly, if necessary).
3	Run the k-Means algorithm on the $level_i$ representation of the data
4	Use final centers from $level_i$, as initial centers for $level_{i+1}$. This is achieved by projecting the k centers returned by k-Means algorithm for the 2^i space in the 2^{i+1} space.
5	If none of the N objects changed membership in the last iteration, exit. Otherwise goto 3.

The I-kMeans algorithm allows the user to monitor the quality of clustering results as the program executes. The user can interrupt the program at any level, or wait until the execution terminates once the clustering results stabilize. One surprising and highly desirable finding from the experimental results is that even if the program is run to completion (until the last level, with full resolution), the total execution time is generally less than that of clustering on raw data.

As mentioned earlier, on every level except for the starting level (i.e. level 2), which uses random initial centers, the initial centers are selected based on the final centers from the previous level. More specifically, the final centers computed at the end of level i will be used as the initial centers on level i+1. Since the length of the data reconstructed from the Haar decomposition doubles as we progress to the next level, we project the centers computed at the end of level i onto level i+1 by doubling each coordinate of the centers. This way, they match the dimensionality of the points on level i+1. For example, if one of the re-computed centers at the end of level 2 is (0.5, 1.2), then the initial center used for this cluster on level 3 is (0.5, 0.5, 1.2, 1.2). This approach resolves the dilemma associated with the choice of initial centers, which is crucial to the quality of clustering results [10]. It also contributes to the fact that our algorithm often produces better clustering results than the k-Means algorithm. More specifically, although our approach also uses random centers as initial centers, it's less likely to be trapped in local minima at such a low dimensionality. In addition, the results obtained from this initial level will be refined in subsequent levels. Note that while the performance of k-Means can be improved by providing "good" initial centers, the same argument applies to our approach as well[1].

The algorithm can be further sped up by *not* reconstructing the time series. Rather, clustering directly on the wavelet coefficients will produce identical results. However, the projection technique for the final centers mentioned above would not be appropriate here. Instead, we can still reuse the final centers by simply padding the additional dimensions for subsequent levels with zeros. For brevity, we defer further discussion on this version to future work.

4 Experimental Evaluation

To show that our approach is superior to the k-Means algorithm for clustering time series, we performed a series of experiments on publicly available real datasets. For completeness, we ran the I-kMeans algorithm for all levels of approximation, and recorded the cumulative execution time and clustering accuracy at each level. In reality, however, the algorithm stabilizes in early stages and can automatically terminate much sooner. We compare the results with that of k-Means on the original data. Since both algorithms start with random initial centers, we execute each algorithm 100 times with different centers. However, for consistency we ensure that for each execution, both algorithms are seeded with the same set of initial centers. After each execution, we compute the error (more details will be provided in Section 4.2) and the execution time on the clustering results. We compute and report the averages at the end of each experiment. By taking the average, we achieve better objectiveness than taking the best (minimum), since in reality, it's unlikely that we would have the knowledge of the correct clustering results, or the "oracle," to compare with (as was the case with one of our test datasets).

---

[1] As a matter of fact, our experiments (results not shown) with good initial centers show that this is true – while the performance of k-Means improves with good initial centers, the improvements on I-kMeans, in terms of both speed and accuracy, are even more drastic.

4.1 Datasets and Methodology

We tested on two publicly available, real datasets. The dataset cardinalities range from 1,000 to 8,000. The length of each time series has been set to 512 on one dataset, and 1024 on the other.

• **JPL**: This dataset consists of readings from various inertial sensors from Space Shuttle mission STS-57. The data is particularly appropriate for our experiments since the use of redundant backup sensors means that some of the data is very highly correlated. In addition, even sensors that measure orthogonal features (i.e. the X and Y axis) may become temporarily correlated during a particular maneuver; for example, a "roll reversal" [8]. Thus, the data has an interesting mixture of dense and sparse clusters. To generate data of increasingly larger cardinality, we extracted time series of length 512, at random starting points of each sequence from the original data pool.

• **Heterogeneous**: This dataset is generated from a mixture of 10 real time series data from the UCR Time Series Data Mining Archive [14] (see Fig 4). Using the 10 time-series as seeds, we produced variation of the original patterns by adding small time shifting (2-3% of the series length), and interpolated Gaussian noise. Gaussian noisy peaks are interpolated using splines to create smooth random variations. Fig 5 illustrates how the data is generated.

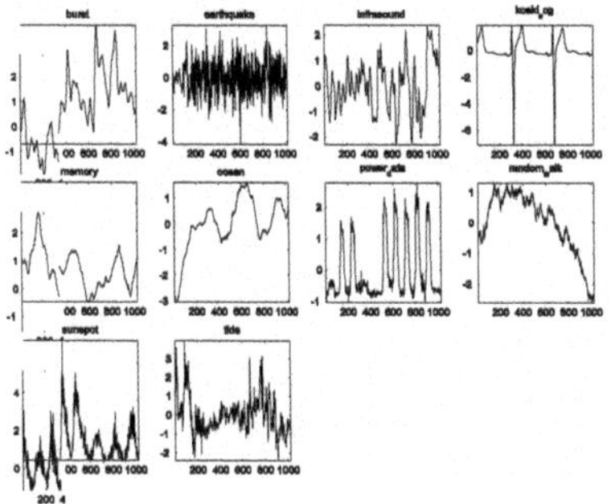

Fig. 4. Real time series data from UCR Time Series Data Mining Archive. We use these time series as seeds to create our Heterogeneous dataset.

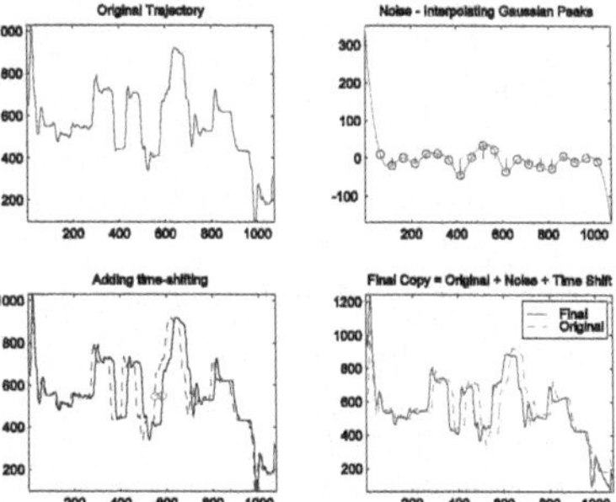

Fig. 5. Generation of variations on the heterogeneous data. We produced variation of the original patterns by adding small time shifting (2-3% of the series length), and interpolated Gaussian noise. Gaussian noisy peaks are interpolated using splines to create smooth random variations.

In the Heterogeneous dataset, we know that the number of clusters is 10. However, for the JPL dataset, we lack this information. Finding k is an open problem for the k-Means algorithm and is out of scope of this paper. To determine the optimal k for k-Means, we attempt different values of k, ranging from 2 to 8. Nonetheless, our algorithm out-performs the k-Means algorithm regardless of k. In this paper we only show the results with k equals to 5. Fig 6 shows that our algorithm produces the same results as the hierarchical clustering algorithm, which is in generally more costly.

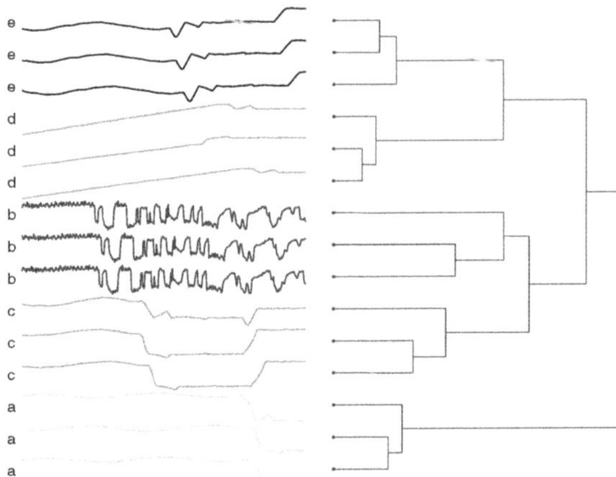

Fig. 6. On the left-hand side, we show three instances taken from each cluster of the JPL dataset discovered by the I-kMeans algorithm. We can visually verify that our algorithm produces intuitive results. On the right-hand side, we show that hierarchical clustering (using average linkage) discovers the exact same clusters. However, hierarchical clustering is more costly than our algorithm.

4.2 Error of Clustering Results

In this section we compare the clustering quality for the I-kMeans and the classic k-Means algorithm.

Since we generated the heterogeneous datasets from a set of given time series data, we have the knowledge of correct clustering results in advance. In this case, we can simply compute the clustering error by summing up the number of incorrectly classified objects for each cluster c and then dividing by the dataset cardinality. This is achieved by the use of a confusion matrix. Note the accuracy computed here is equivalent to "recall," and the error rate is simply (1-accuracy).

The error is computed at the end of each level. However, it's worth mentioning that in reality, the correct clustering results would not be available in advance. The incorporation of such known results in our error calculation merely serves the purpose of demonstrating the quality of both algorithms.

For the JPL dataset, we do not have prior knowledge of correct clustering results (which conforms more closely to real-life cases). Lacking this information, we cannot use the same evaluation to determine the error.

Since the k-Means algorithm seeks to optimize the objective function by minimizing the sum of squared intra-cluster error, we evaluate the quality of clustering by using the objective functions. However, since the I-kMeans algorithm involves data with smaller dimensionality except for the last level, we have to map the cluster membership information to the original space, and compute the objective functions using the raw data in order to compare with the k-Means algorithm. We show that the objective functions obtained from the I-kMeans algorithm are better than those from the k-Means algorithm. The results are consistent with the work of Ding et. Al. [5], in which the authors show that dimensionality reduction reduces the chances of the algorithm being trapped in a local minimum. Furthermore, even with the additional step of computing the objective functions from the original data, the I-kMeans algorithm still takes less time to execute than the k-Means algorithm.

In Figs 7-8, we show the errors/objective functions from the I-kMeans algorithm as a fraction of those obtained from the k-Means algorithm. As we can see from the plots, our algorithm stabilizes at early (i.e. 2nd or 3rd) stages and consistently results in smaller error than the classic k-Means algorithm.

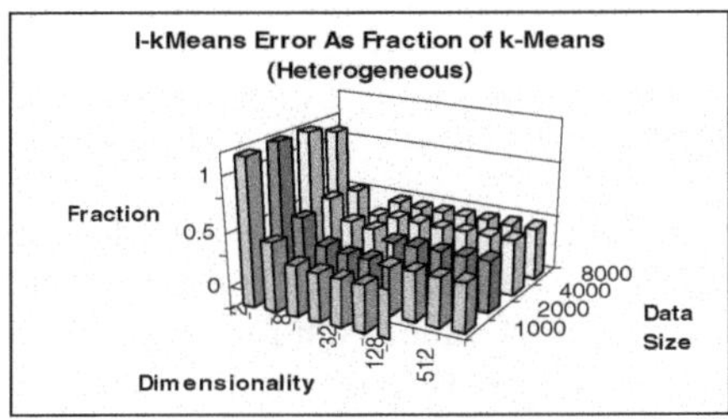

Fig. 7. Error of I-kMeans algorithm on the Heterogeneous dataset, presented as fraction of the error from the k-Means algorithm.

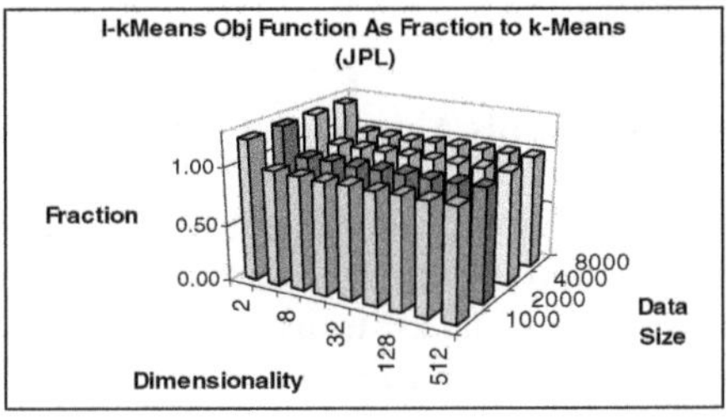

Fig. 8. Objective functions of I-kMeans algorithm on the JPL dataset, presented as fraction of error from the k-Means algorithm.

4.3 Running Time

In this section, we present the cumulative running time for each level on the I-kMeans algorithm as a fraction to the k-Means algorithm. The cumulative running time for any level i is the total running time from the starting level to level i. In most cases, even if the I-kMeans algorithm is run to completion, the total running time is still less than that of the k-Means algorithm. We attribute this improvement to the good choices of initial centers, since they result in very few iterations until convergence. Nevertheless, we have already shown in the previous section that the I-kMeans algorithm finds the best result in relatively early stage and does not need to run through all levels. The time required for I-kMeans is therefore less than 50% of time required for k-Means for the Heterogeneous datasets. For the JPL datasets, the running time is less than 20% of time for k-Means, and even if it is run to completion, the cumulative running time is still 50% less than that of the k-Means algorithm.

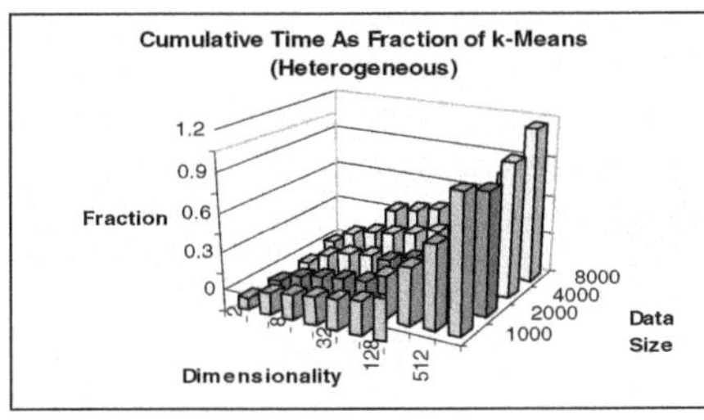

Fig. 9. Cumulative running time for the Heterogeneous dataset. Our algorithm cuts the running time by more than half.

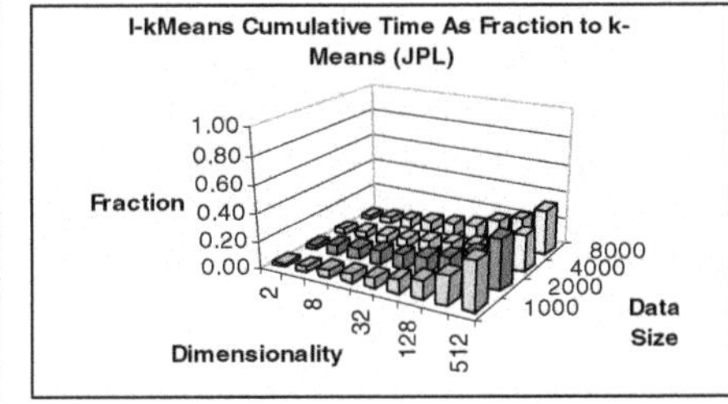

Fig. 10. Cumulative running time for the JPL dataset. Our algorithm typically takes only 20% of the time required for k-Means.

While the speedup achieved is quite impressive, we note that these results are only for the main memory case. We should expect a much greater speedup for more realistic data mining problems. The reason is that when performing k-Means on a massive dataset, every iteration requires a database scan [2]. The I/O time for the scans dwarfs the relatively inexpensive CPU time. In contrast, our multi-resolution approach is able to run its first few levels in main memory, building a good "approximate" model[2] before being forced to access the disk. We can therefore expect our approach to make far fewer data scans.

4.4 I-kMeans Algorithm vs. k-Means Algorithm

In this section, rather than showing the error/objective function on each level, we present only the error/objective function returned by the I-kMeans algorithm when it out-performs the k-Means algorithm. We also present the time taken for the I-kMeans algorithm to stabilize (i.e. when the result does not improve anymore). We compare the results to those of the k-Means algorithm. The running time for I-kMeans remains small regardless of data size because the algorithm out-performs k-Means at very early stages.

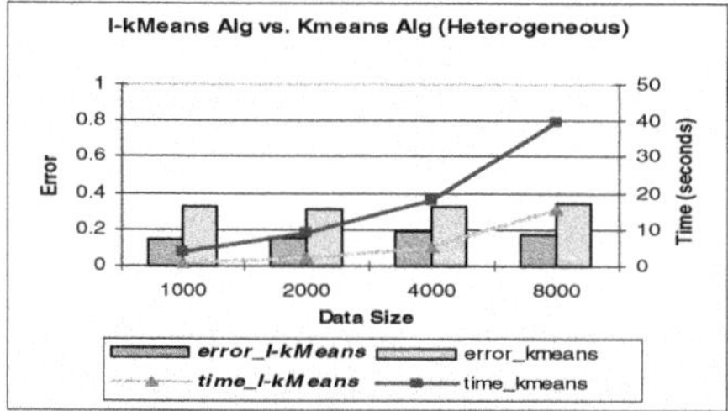

Fig. 11. The I-kMeans algorithm is highly competitive with the k-Means algorithm. The errors (bars) and execution time (lines) are significantly smaller.

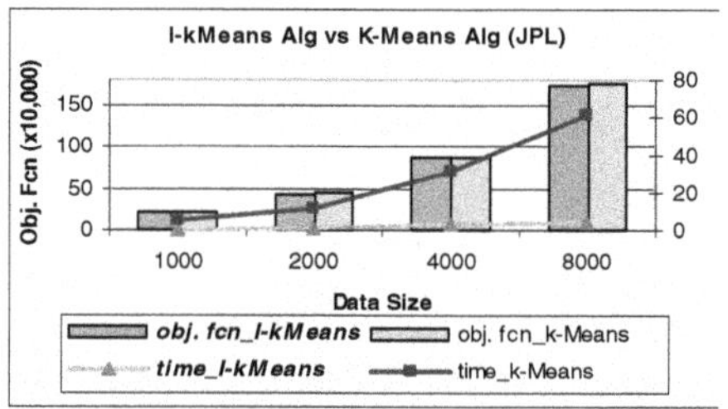

Fig. 12. I-kMeans vs. k-Means algorithms in terms of objective function (bars) and running time (lines) for JPL dataset.

Below we present additional results on a number of additional datasets from the UCR time-series archive. The running time recorded for I-kMeans is the time required to achieve the *best* result. Therefore, the speedup measured here is pessimistic, since I-kMeans typically outperforms k-Means in very early levels. We observe an average speedup of 3 times against the traditional k-Means and a general improvement in the objective function. Only in the *earthquake* dataset the cumulative time is more than k-Means. This happens because the algorithm has to traverse the majority of the levels in order to perform the *optimal* clustering. However, in this case the prolonged execution time can be balanced by the significant improvement in the objective function.

---

[2] As we have seen in Figs 7 and 8, the "approximate" models are typically better than the model built on the raw data.

Table 3. Performance of I-kMeans on additional datasets. Smaller numbers indicate better performance

Dataset	Obj. k-Means	Obj. I-kMeans	Time k-Means	Time I-kMeans	Speed Up
Ballbeam	6328.21	**6065.61**	5.83	**4.30**	1.36
earthquake	110159	**108887**	**12.9**	15.19	0.85
sunspot	4377E^{6}	**4361E^{6}**	7.45	**3.07**	3.36
spot_exRates	**2496.66**	2497.47	6.83	**2.71**	2.52
powerplant	9783E^{8}	**9584E^{8}**	10.33	**3.07**	3.36
evaporator	6303E^{3}	**6281E^{3}**	21.33	**6.59**	3.24
memory	1921E^{4}	**1916E^{4}**	19.48	**5.91**	3.29

5 Extension to a General Framework

We have seen that our anytime algorithm out-performs k-Means in terms of clustering quality and running time. We will now extend the approach and generalize it to a framework that can adapt to a much broader range of algorithms. More specifically, we apply prominent alternatives on the frame of our approach, the clustering algorithm, as well as its essence, the decomposition method.

We demonstrate the generality of the framework by two examples. Firstly, we use another widely-used iterative refinement algorithm – the EM algorithm, in place of the k-Means algorithm. We call this version of EM the I-EM algorithm. Next, instead of the Haar wavelet decomposition, we utilize an equally well-studied decomposition method, the Discrete Fourier Transform (DFT), on the I-kMeans algorithm. Both approaches have shown to outperform their k-Means or EM counterparts. In general, we can use any combination of iterative refining clustering algorithm and multi-resolution decomposition methods in our framework.

5.1 I-EM with Expectation Maximization (EM)

The EM algorithm with Gaussian Mixtures is very similar to k-Means algorithm introduced in Table 1. As with k-Means, the algorithm begins with an initial guess to the cluster centers (the "E" or Expectation step), and iteratively refines them (the "M" or maximization step). The major distinction is that k-Means attempts to model the data as a collection of k spherical regions, with every data object belonging to exactly one cluster. In contrast, EM models the data as a collection of k Gaussians, with every data object having some degree of membership in each cluster (in fact, although Gaussian models are most common, other distributions are possible). The major advantage of EM over k-Means is its ability to model a much richer set of cluster shapes. This generality has made EM (and its many variants and extensions) the clustering algorithm of choice in data mining [7] and bioinformatics [17].

5.2 Experimental Results for I-EM

Similar to the application of k-Means, we apply EM for different resolutions of data, and compare the clustering quality and running time with EM on the original data. We use the same datasets and parameters as in k-Means. However, we have to reduce the dimensionality of data to 256, since otherwise the dimensionality-cardinality ratio would be too small for EM to perform well (if at all!). The EM algorithm presents the error as the negative log likehood of data. We can compare the clustering results in a similar fashion as in k-Means, by projecting the results obtained at a lower dimension to the full dimension and computing the error on the original raw data. More specifically, this is achieved by re-computing the centers and the covariance matrix on the full dimension, given the posterior probabilities obtained at a lower dimension. The results are similar to those of k-Means. Fig 13 shows the errors for EM and I-EM algorithms on the JPL datasets. The errors for EM are shown as straight lines for easy visual comparison with I-EM at each level. The results show that I-EM outperforms EM at very early stages (4 or 8 dimensions).

Fig 14 shows the running time for EM and I-EM on JPL datasets. As with the error presentation, the running times for EM are shown as straight lines for easy visual comparison with I-EM. The vertical dashed line indicates where I-EM starts to out-perform EM (as illustrated in Fig 13, I-EM out-performs EM at every level forward, following the one indicated by the dashed line).

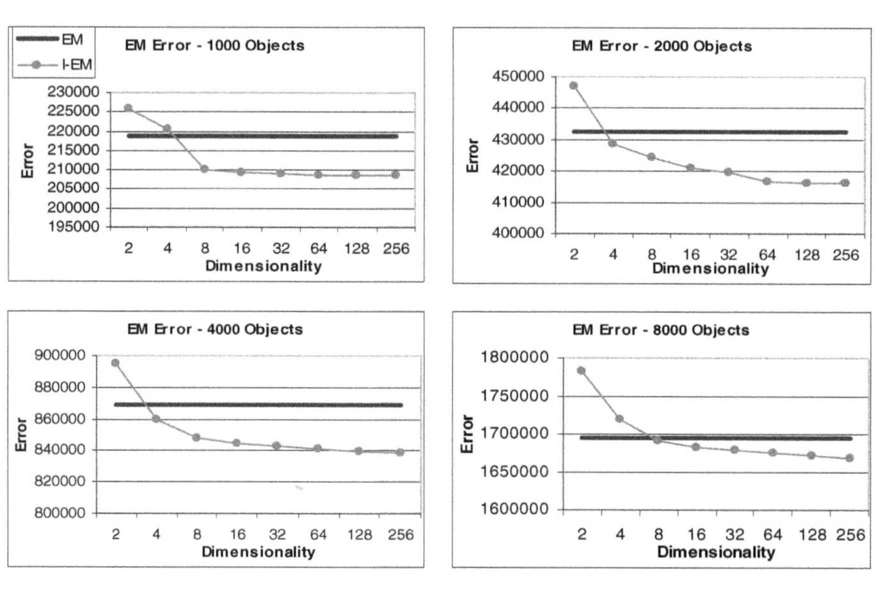

Fig. 13. We show the errors for different data cardinalities. The errors for EM are presented as constant lines for easy visual comparison with the I-EM at each level. I-EM out-performs EM at very early stages (4 or 8 dimensions)

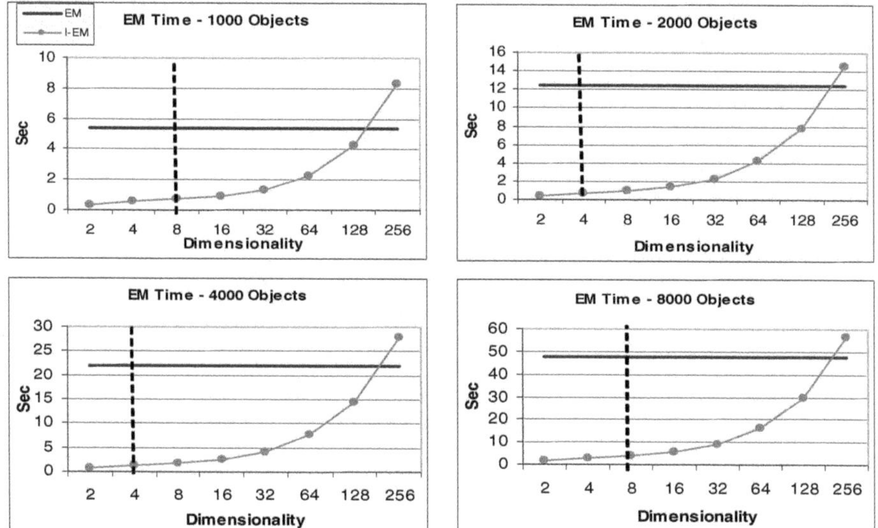

Fig. 14. Running times for different data cardinalities. The running times for EM are presented as constant lines for easy visual comparison with the I-EM at each level. The vertical dashed line indicates where I-EM starts to out-perform EM as illustrated in Fig 13

5.3 I-kMeans with Discrete Fourier Transform

As mentioned earlier, the choice of Haar Wavelet as the decomposition method is due to its efficiency and simplicity. In this section we extend the I-kMeans to utilize another equally well-known decomposition method, the Discrete Fourier Transform (DFT) [1, 20].

Similar to the wavelet decomposition, DFT approximates the signal with a linear combination of basis functions. The vital difference between the two decomposition methods is that the wavelets are localized in time, while DFT coefficients represent global contribution of the signal. Fig 15 provides a side-by-side visual comparison of the Haar wavelet and DFT.

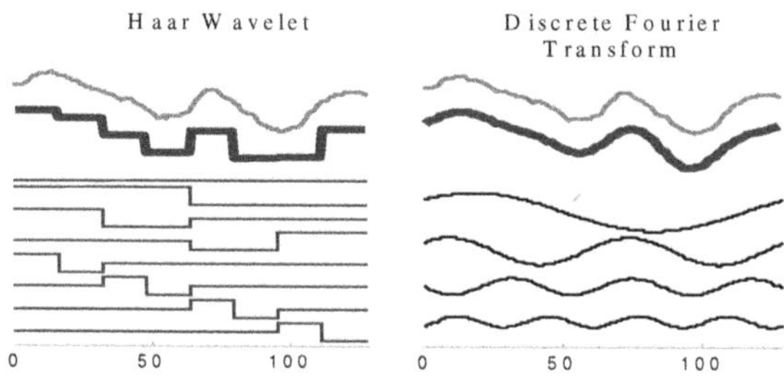

Fig. 15. Visual comparison of the Haar Wavelet and the Discrete Fourier Transform. Wavelet coefficients are localized in time, while DFT coefficients represent global contributions to the signal

Table 4. Objective functions for k-Means, I-kMeans with Haar Wavelet, and I-kMeans with DFT. Smaller numbers indicate tighter clusters.

Dataset	Obj. k-Means	Haar I-kMeans	DFT I-kMeans
ballbeam	6328.21	**6065.61**	6096.54
earthquake	110159	108887	**108867**
Sunspot	$4377E^6$	$\mathbf{4361E^6}$	$4388E^6$
spot_exRates	2496.66	2497.47	**2466.28**
powerplant	$9783E^8$	$\mathbf{9584E^8}$	$11254E^8$
evaporator	$6303E^3$	$\mathbf{6281E^3}$	$6290E^3$
Memory	$1921E^4$	$\mathbf{1916E^4}$	$1803E^4$

While the competitiveness of either method has been largely argued in the past, we apply DFT in the algorithm to demonstrate the generality of the framework. As a matter of fact, consistent with the results shown in [15], the superiority of either method is highly data-dependent. In general, however, DFT performs better for smooth signals or sequences that resemble random walks.

5.4 Experimental Results for I-kMeans with DFT

In this section we show the quality of the results of I-kMeans, using DFT as the decomposition method instead of the Haar wavelet. Although there is no clear evidence that one decomposition method is superior than the other, it's certain that using either one of these methods with I-kMeans outperforms the batch k-Means algorithm. Naturally it can be argued that instead of using our iterative method, one might be able to achieve equal-quality results by using a batch algorithm on higher resolution with either decomposition. While this is true to some extent, there is always a higher chance of the clustering being trapped in the local minima. By starting off at lower resolution and re-using the cluster centers each time, we minimize the dilemma with local minima, in addition to the choices of initial centers.

In datasets where the time-series is approximated more faithfully by using Fourier than wavelet decomposition, the quality of the DFT-based incremental approach is slightly better. This experiment suggests that our approach can be tailored to specific applications, by carefully choosing the decomposition that provides the least reconstruction error.

Table 4 shows the results of I-kMeans using DFT.

6 Conclusions and Future Work

We have presented an approach to perform incremental clustering of time-series at various resolutions using multi-resolution decomposition methods. We initially focus our approach on the k-Means clustering algorithm, and then extend the idea to EM. We reuse the final centers at the end of each resolution as the initial centers for the next level of resolution. This approach resolves the dilemma associated with the choices of initial centers and significantly improves the execution time and clustering quality. Our experimental results indicate that this approach yields faster execution time than the traditional k-Means (or EM) approach, in addition to improving the clustering quality of the algorithm. Since it conforms with the observation that time series data can be described with coarser resolutions while still preserving a general shape, the anytime algorithm stabilizes at very early stages, eliminating the needs to operate on high resolutions. In addition, the anytime algorithm allows the user to terminate the program at any stage.

Our extensions of the iterative anytime algorithm on EM and the multi-resolution decomposition on DFT show great promise for generalizing the approach at an even wider scale. More specifically, this anytime approach can be generalized to a framework with a much broader range of algorithms or data mining problem. For future work, we plan to investigate the following:

- Extending our algorithm to other data types. For example, image histograms can be successfully represented as wavelets [6, 23]. Our initial experiments on image histograms show great promise of applying the framework on image data.
- For k-Means, examining the possibility of re-using the results (i.e. objective functions that determine the quality of clustering results) from the previous stages to eliminate the need to re-compute all the distances.

References

1. Agrawal, R., Faloutsos, C. & Swami, A. (1993). Efficient Similarity Search in Sequence Databases. In *proceedings of the 4th Int'l Conference on Foundations of Data Organization and Algorithms*. Chicago, IL, Oct 13-15. pp 69-84.
2. Bradley, P., Fayyad, U., & Reina, C. (1998). Scaling Clustering Algorithms to Large Databases. In *proceedings of the 4th Int'l Conference on Knowledge Discovery and Data Mining*. New York, NY, Aug 27-31. pp 9-15.
3. Chan, K. & Fu, A. W. (1999). Efficient Time Series Matching by Wavelets. In *proceedings of the 15th IEEE Int'l Conference on Data Engineering*. Sydney, Australia, Mar 23-26. pp 126-133.
4. Chu, S., Keogh, E., Hart, D., Pazzani, M. (2002). Iterative Deepening Dynamic Time Warping for Time Series. In *proceedings of the 2002 IEEE International Conference on Data Mining*. Maebashi City, Japan. Dec 9-12.
5. Ding, C., He, X., Zha, H. & Simon, H. (2002). Adaptive Dimension Reduction for Clustering High Dimensional Data. In *proceedings of the 2002 IEEE Int'l Conference on Data Mining*. Dec 9-12. Maebashi, Japan. pp 147-154.
6. Daubechies, I. (1992). Ten Lectures on Wavelets. *Number 61, in CBMS-NSF Regional Conference Series in Applied Mathematics*, Society for Industrial and Applied Mathematics, Philadelphia.
7. Dempster, A., Laird, N., & Rubin, D. (1977). Maximum Likelihood from Incomplete Data via the EM Algorithm. Journal of the Royal Statistical Society, Series B. Vol. 39, No. 1, pp. 1-38.
8. Dumoulin, J. (1998). NSTS 1988 News Reference Manual. http://www.fas.org/spp/civil/sts/
9. Faloutsos, C., Ranganathan, M. & Manolopoulos, Y. (1994). Fast Subsequence Matching in Time-Series Databases. In *proceedings of the ACM SIGMOD Int'l Conference on Management of Data*. Minneapolis, MN, May 25-27. pp 419-429.
10. Fayyad, U., Reina, C. &. Bradley. P (1998). Initialization of Iterative Refinement Clustering Algorithms. In *proceedings of the 4th International Conference on Knowledge Discovery and Data Mining*. New York, NY, Aug 27-31. pp 194-198.

11. Grass, J. & Zilberstein, S. (1996). Anytime Algorithm Development Tools. Sigart Artificial Intelligence. Vol 7, No. 2, April. *ACM Press*.
12. Keogh, E. & Pazzani, M. (1998). An Enhanced Representation of Time Series Which Allows Fast and Accurate Classification, Clustering and Relevance Feedback. In *proceedings of the 4th Int'l Conference on Knowledge Discovery and Data Mining*. NewYork, NY, Aug 27-31. pp 239-241.
13. Keogh, E., Chakrabarti, K., Pazzani, M. & Mehrotra, S. (2001). Locally Adaptive Dimensionality Reduction for Indexing Large Time Series Databases. In *proceedings of ACM SIGMOD Conference on Management of Data*. Santa Barbara, CA. pp 151-162.
14. Keogh, E. & Folias, T. (2002). The UCR Time Series Data Mining Archive. [http://www.cs.ucr.edu/~eamonn/TSDMA/index.html].
15. Keogh, E. & Kasetty, S. (2002). On the Need for Time Series Data Mining Benchmarks: A Survey and Empirical Demonstration. In *proceedings of the 8th ACM SIGKDD International Conference on Knowledge Discovery and Data Mining*. July 23 - 26, 2002. Edmonton, Alberta, Canada. pp 102-111.
16. Korn, F., Jagadish, H. & Faloutsos, C. (1997). Efficiently Supporting Ad Hoc Queries in Large Datasets of Time Sequences. In *proceedings of the ACM SIGMOD Int'l Conference on Management of Data*. Tucson, AZ, May 13-15. pp 289-300.
17. Lawrence, C. & Reilly, A. (1990). An Expectation Maximization (EM) Algorithm for the Identification and Characterization of Common Sites in Unaligned Biopolymer Sequences. *Proteins*, Vol. 7, pp 41-51.
18. McQueen, J. (1967). Some Methods for Classification and Analysis of Multivariate Observation. L. Le Cam and J. Neyman (Eds.), In *proceedings of the 5th Berkeley Symposium on Mathematical Statistics and Probability*, Berkeley, CA. Vol. 1, pp 281-297.
19. Popivanov, I. & Miller, R. J. (2002). Similarity Search over Time Series Data Using Wavelets. *In proceedings of the 18th Int'l Conference on Data Engineering*. San Jose, CA, Feb 26-Mar 1. pp 212-221.
20. Rafiei, Davood & Mendelzon, Alberto. (1998). Efficient Retrieval of Similar Time Sequences Using DFT. In *proceedings of the FODO Conference*. Kobe, Japan, November 1998.
21. Smyth, P,. Wolpert, D. (1997). Anytime Exploratory Data Analysis for Massive Data Sets. In *proceedings of the 3rd Int'l Conference on Knowledge Discovery and Data Mining*. Newport Beach, CA. pp 54-60
22. Shahabi, C., Tian, X. & Zhao, W. (2000). TSA-tree: a Wavelet Based Approach to Improve the Efficiency of Multi-Level Surprise and Trend Queries. In *proceedings of the 12th Int'l Conference on Scientific and Statistical Database Management*. Berlin, Germany, Jul 26-28. pp 55-68.
23. Struzik, Z. & Siebes, A. (1999). The Haar Wavelet Transform in the Time Series Similarity Paradigm. In *proceedings of Principles of Data Mining and Knowledge Discovery*, 3rd European Conference. Prague, Czech Republic, Sept 15-18. pp 12-22.
24. Vlachos, M., Lin, J., Keogh, E. & Gunopulos, D. (2003). A Wavelet-Based Anytime Algorithm for K-Means Clustering of Time Series. In *Workshop on Clustering High Dimensionality Data and Its Applications, at the 3rd SIAM Int'l Conference on Data Mining*. San Francisco, CA. May 1-3.
25. Wu, Y., Agrawal, D. & El Abbadi, A. (2000). A Comparison of DFT and DWT Based Similarity Search in Time-Series Databases. In *proceedings of the 9th ACM Int'l Conference on Information and Knowledge Management*. McLean, VA, Nov 6-11. pp 488-495.
26. Yi, B. & Faloutsos, C. (2000). Fast Time Sequence Indexing for Arbitrary Lp Norms. In *proceedings of the 26th Int'l Conference on Very Large Databases*. Cairo, Egypt, Sept 10-14. pp 385-394.l Database Management. Berlin, Germany, Jul 26-28. pp 55-68.

LIMBO: Scalable Clustering of Categorical Data

Periklis Andritsos, Panayiotis Tsaparas, Renée J. Miller, and Kenneth C. Sevcik

University of Toronto, Department of Computer Science
{periklis,tsap,miller,kcs}@cs.toronto.edu

Abstract. Clustering is a problem of great practical importance in numerous applications. The problem of clustering becomes more challenging when the data is categorical, that is, when there is no inherent distance measure between data values. We introduce LIMBO, a scalable hierarchical categorical clustering algorithm that builds on the *Information Bottleneck (IB)* framework for quantifying the relevant information preserved when clustering. As a hierarchical algorithm, LIMBO has the advantage that it can produce clusterings of different sizes in a single execution. We use the IB framework to define a distance measure for categorical tuples and we also present a novel distance measure for categorical attribute values. We show how the LIMBO algorithm can be used to cluster both tuples and values. LIMBO handles large data sets by producing a memory bounded summary model for the data. We present an experimental evaluation of LIMBO, and we study how clustering quality compares to other categorical clustering algorithms. LIMBO supports a trade-off between efficiency (in terms of space and time) and quality. We quantify this trade-off and demonstrate that LIMBO allows for substantial improvements in efficiency with negligible decrease in quality.

1 Introduction

Clustering is a problem of great practical importance that has been the focus of substantial research in several domains for decades. It is defined as the problem of partitioning data objects into groups, such that objects in the same group are similar, while objects in different groups are dissimilar. This definition assumes that there is some well defined notion of *similarity*, or *distance*, between data objects. When the objects are defined by a set of numerical attributes, there are natural definitions of distance based on geometric analogies. These definitions rely on the semantics of the data values themselves (for example, the values $100K and $110K are more similar than $100K and $1). The definition of distance allows us to define a *quality measure* for a clustering (*e.g.*, the mean square distance between each point and the centroid of its cluster). Clustering then becomes the problem of grouping together points such that the quality measure is optimized. The problem of clustering becomes more challenging when the data is categorical, that is, when there is no inherent distance measure between data values. This is often the case in many domains, where data is described by a set of descriptive attributes, many of which are neither numerical nor inherently ordered in any way. As a concrete example, consider a relation that stores information about movies. For the purpose of exposition, a movie is a tuple characterized by the attributes "director", "actor/actress", and "genre". An instance of this relation is shown in Table 1. In this setting it is not immediately obvious

E. Bertino et al. (Eds.): EDBT 2004, LNCS 2992, pp. 123–146, 2004.
© Springer-Verlag Berlin Heidelberg 2004

what the distance, or similarity, is between the values "Coppola" and "Scorsese", or the tuples "Vertigo" and "Harvey".

Without a measure of distance between data values, it is unclear how to define a quality measure for categorical clustering. To do this, we employ *mutual information*, a measure from information theory. A good clustering is one where the clusters are *informative* about the data objects they contain. Since data objects are expressed in terms of attribute values, we require that the clusters convey information about the attribute values of the objects in the cluster. That is, given a cluster, we wish to predict the attribute values associated with objects of the cluster accurately. The quality measure of the clustering is then the mutual information of the clusters and the attribute values. Since a clustering is a summary of the data, some information is generally lost. Our objective will be to minimize this loss, or equivalently to minimize the increase in uncertainty as the objects are grouped into fewer and larger clusters.

Table 1. An instance of the movie database

	director	actor	genre	C	D
t_1 (Godfather II)	Scorsese	De Niro	Crime	c_1	d_1
t_2 (Good Fellas)	Coppola	De Niro	Crime	c_1	d_1
t_3 (Vertigo)	Hitchcock	Stewart	Thriller	c_2	d_1
t_4 (N by NW)	Hitchcock	Grant	Thriller	c_2	d_1
t_5 (Bishop's Wife)	Koster	Grant	Comedy	c_2	d_2
t_6 (Harvey)	Koster	Stewart	Comedy	c_2	d_2

Consider partitioning the tuples in Table 1 into two clusters. Clustering **C** groups the first two movies together into one cluster, c_1, and the remaining four into another, c_2. Note that cluster c_1 preserves all information about the actor and the genre of the movies it holds. For objects in c_1, we know with certainty that the genre is "Crime", the actor is "De Niro" and there are only two possible values for the director. Cluster c_2 involves only two different values for each attribute. Any other clustering will result in greater information loss. For example, in clustering **D**, d_2 is equally informative as c_1, but d_1 includes three different actors and three different directors. So, while in c_2 there are two equally likely values for each attribute, in d_1 the director is any of "Scorsese", "Coppola", or "Hitchcock" (with respective probabilities 0.25, 0.25, and 0.50), and similarly for the actor.

This intuitive idea was formalized by Tishby, Pereira and Bialek [20]. They recast clustering as the compression of one random variable into a compact representation that preserves as much information as possible about another random variable. Their approach was named the *Information Bottleneck (IB)* method, and it has been applied to a variety of different areas. In this paper, we consider the application of the IB method to the problem of clustering large data sets of categorical data.

We formulate the problem of clustering relations with categorical attributes within the Information Bottleneck framework, and define dissimilarity between categorical data objects based on the IB method. Our contributions are the following.

• We propose LIMBO, the first scalable hierarchical algorithm for clustering categorical data based on the IB method. As a result of its hierarchical approach, LIMBO allows us in a single execution to consider clusterings of various sizes. LIMBO can also control the size of the model it builds to summarize the data.

• We use LIMBO to cluster both tuples (in relational and market-basket data sets) and attribute values. We define a novel distance between attribute values that allows us to quantify the degree of interchangeability of attribute values within a single attribute.

• We empirically evaluate the quality of clusterings produced by LIMBO relative to other categorical clustering algorithms including the tuple clustering algorithms IB, ROCK [13], and COOLCAT [4]; as well as the attribute value clustering algorithm STIRR [12]. We compare the clusterings based on a comprehensive set of quality metrics.

The rest of the paper is structured as follows. In Section 2, we present the IB method, and we describe how to formulate the problem of clustering categorical data within the IB framework. In Section 3, we introduce LIMBO and show how it can be used to cluster tuples. In Section 4, we present a novel distance measure for categorical attribute values and discuss how it can be used within LIBMO to cluster attribute values. Section 5 presents the experimental evaluation of LIMBO and other algorithms for clustering categorical tuples and values. Section 6 describes related work on categorical clustering and Section 7 discusses additional applications of the LIMBO framework.

2 The Information Bottleneck Method

In this section, we review some of the concepts from information theory that will be used in the rest of the paper. We also introduce the Information Bottleneck method, and we formulate the problem of clustering categorical data within this framework.

2.1 Information Theory Basics

The following definitions can be found in any information theory textbook, e.g., [7]. Let T denote a discrete random variable that takes values over the set $\mathbf{T}$[1], and let $p(t)$ denote the probability mass function of T. The *entropy* $H(T)$ of variable T is defined by $H(T) = -\sum_{t\in\mathbf{T}} p(t)\log p(t)$. Intuitively, entropy captures the "uncertainty" of variable T; the higher the entropy, the lower the certainty with which we can predict its value.

Now, let T and A be two random variables that range over sets $\mathbf{T}$ and $\mathbf{A}$ respectively. The *conditional entropy* of A given T is defined as follows.

$$H(A|T) = \sum_{t\in\mathbf{T}} p(t) \sum_{a\in\mathbf{A}} p(a|t)\log p(a|t)$$

Conditional entropy captures the uncertainty of predicting the values of variable A given the values of variable T. The *mutual information*, $I(T;A)$, quantifies the amount of

[1] For the remainder of the paper, we use italic capital letters (e.g., T) to denote random variables, and boldface capital letters (e.g., $\mathbf{T}$) to denote the set from which the random variable takes values.

information that the variables convey about each other. Mutual information is symmetric, and non-negative, and it is related to entropy via the equation $I(T;A) = H(T) - H(T|A) = H(A) - H(A|T)$.

Relative Entropy, or *Kullback-Leibler (KL)* divergence, is an information-theoretic measure of the difference between two probability distributions. Given two distributions p and q over a set $\mathbf{T}$, the relative entropy is defined as follows.

$$D_{KL}[p\|q] = \sum_{t \in \mathbf{T}} p(t) \log \frac{p(t)}{q(t)}$$

2.2 Clustering Using the IB Method

In categorical data clustering, the input to our problem is a set $\mathbf{T}$ of n tuples on m attributes $A_1, A_2, \ldots, A_m$. The domain of attribute A_i is the set $\mathbf{A}_i = \{A_i.v_1, A_i.v_2, \ldots, A_i.v_{d_i}\}$, so that identical values from different attributes are treated as distinct values. A tuple $t \in \mathbf{T}$ takes exactly one value from the set $\mathbf{A}_i$ for the ith attribute. Let $\mathbf{A} = \mathbf{A}_1 \cup \cdots \cup \mathbf{A}_m$ denote the set of all possible attribute values. Let $d = d_1 + d_2 + \cdots + d_m$ denote the size of $\mathbf{A}$. The data can then be conceptualized as an $n \times d$ matrix M, where each tuple $t \in \mathbf{T}$ is a d-dimensional row vector in M. Matrix entry $M[t,a]$ is 1, if tuple t contains attribute value a, and zero otherwise. Each tuple contains one value for each attribute, so each tuple vector contains exactly m 1's.

Now let T, A be random variables that range over the sets $\mathbf{T}$ (the set of tuples) and $\mathbf{A}$ (the set of attribute values) respectively. We normalize matrix M so that the entries of each row sum up to 1. For some tuple $t \in \mathbf{T}$, the corresponding row of the normalized matrix holds the conditional probability distribution $p(A|t)$. Since each tuple contains exactly m attribute values, for some $a \in \mathbf{A}$, $p(a|t) = 1/m$ if a appears in tuple t, and zero otherwise. Table 2 shows the normalized matrix M for the movie database example.[2] A similar formulation can be applied in the case of *market-basket* data, where each tuple contains a set of values from a single attribute [1].

Table 2. The normalized movie table

	d.S	d.C	d.H	d.K	a.DN	a.S	a.G	g.Cr	g. T	g.C	p(t)
t_1	1/3	0	0	0	1/3	0	0	1/3	0	0	1/6
t_2	0	1/3	0	0	1/3	0	0	1/3	0	0	1/6
t_3	0	0	1/3	0	0	1/3	0	0	1/3	0	1/6
t_4	0	0	1/3	0	0	0	1/3	0	1/3	0	1/6
t_5	0	0	0	1/3	0	0	1/3	0	0	1/3	1/6
t_6	0	0	0	1/3	0	1/3	0	0	0	1/3	1/6

A *k-clustering* $\mathbf{C}_k$ of the tuples in $\mathbf{T}$ partitions them into k clusters $\mathbf{C}_k = \{c_1, c_2, c_3, ..., c_k\}$, where each cluster $c_i \in \mathbf{C}_k$ is a non-empty subset of $\mathbf{T}$ such that $c_i \cap c_j = \emptyset$ for all i, j, $i \neq j$, and $\cup_{i=1}^{k} c_i = \mathbf{T}$. Let C_k denote a random variable that

[2] We use abbreviations for the attribute values. For example d.H stands for director.Hitchcock.

ranges over the clusters in $\mathbf{C}_k$. We define k to be the *size* of the clustering. When k is fixed or when it is immaterial to the discussion, we will use $\mathbf{C}$ and C to denote the clustering and the corresponding random variable.

Now, let $\mathbf{C}$ be a specific clustering. Giving equal weight to each tuple $t \in \mathbf{T}$, we define $p(t) = \frac{1}{n}$. Then, for $c \in \mathbf{C}$, the elements of $\mathbf{T}$, $\mathbf{A}$, and $\mathbf{C}$ are related as follows.

$$p(c) = \sum_{t \in c} p(t) = \frac{|c|}{n} \quad \text{and} \quad p(a|c) = \frac{1}{p(c)} \sum_{t \in c} p(t)p(a|t)$$

We seek clusterings of the elements of $\mathbf{T}$ such that, for $t \in c$, knowledge of the cluster identity, c, provides essentially the same prediction of, or information about, the values in $\mathbf{A}$ as does the specific knowledge of t. The mutual information $I(A;C)$ measures the information about the values in $\mathbf{A}$ provided by the identity of a cluster in $\mathbf{C}$. The higher $I(A;C)$, the more informative the cluster identity is about the values in $\mathbf{A}$ contained in the cluster. Tishby, Pereira and Bialek [20], define clustering as an optimization problem, where, for a given number k of clusters, we wish to identify the k-clustering that maximizes $I(A;C_k)$. Intuitively, in this procedure, the information contained in T about A is "squeezed" through a compact "bottleneck" clustering C_k, which is forced to represent the "relevant" part in T with respect to A. Tishby et al. [20] prove that, for a fixed number k of clusters, the optimal clustering $\mathbf{C}_k$ partitions the objects in $\mathbf{T}$ so that the average relative entropy $\sum_{c \in \mathbf{C}_k, t \in \mathbf{X}} p(t,c) D_{KL}[p(a|t) \| p(a|c)]$ is minimized.

Finding the optimal clustering is an NP-complete problem [11]. Slonim and Tishby [18] propose a greedy agglomerative approach, the *Agglomerative Information Bottleneck (AIB)* algorithm, for finding an informative clustering. The algorithm starts with the clustering $\mathbf{C}_n$, in which each object $t \in \mathbf{T}$ is assigned to its own cluster. Due to the one-to-one mapping between $\mathbf{C}_n$ and $\mathbf{T}$, $I(A;C_n) = I(A;T)$. The algorithm then proceeds iteratively, for $n - k$ steps, reducing the number of clusters in the current clustering by one in each iteration. At step $n - \ell + 1$ of the AIB algorithm, two clusters c_i, c_j in the ℓ-clustering $\mathbf{C}_\ell$ are merged into a single component c^* to produce a new $(\ell - 1)$-clustering $\mathbf{C}_{\ell-1}$. As the algorithm forms clusterings of smaller size, the information that the clustering contains about the values in $\mathbf{A}$ decreases; that is, $I(A;C_{\ell-1}) \leq I(A;C_\ell)$. The clusters c_i and c_j to be merged are chosen to minimize the information loss in moving from clustering $\mathbf{C}_\ell$ to clustering $\mathbf{C}_{\ell-1}$. This information loss is given by $\delta I(c_i, c_j) = I(A;C_\ell) - I(A;C_{\ell-1})$. We can also view the information loss as the increase in the uncertainty. Recall that $I(A;C) = H(A) - H(A|C)$. Since $H(A)$ is independent of the clustering $\mathbf{C}$, maximizing the mutual information $I(A;C)$ is the same as minimizing the entropy of the clustering $H(A|C)$.

For the merged cluster $c^* = c_i \cup c_j$, we have the following.

$$p(c^*) = p(c_i) + p(c_j) \tag{1}$$

$$p(A|c^*) = \frac{p(c_i)}{p(c^*)} p(A|c_i) + \frac{p(c_j)}{p(c^*)} p(A|c_j) \tag{2}$$

Tishby et al. [20] show that

$$\delta I(c_i, c_j) = [p(c_i) + p(c_j)] D_{JS}[p(A|c_i), p(A|c_j)] \tag{3}$$

where D_{JS} is the *Jensen-Shannon (JS)* divergence, defined as follows. Let $p_i = p(A|c_i)$ and $p_j = p(A|c_j)$ and let $\bar{p} = \frac{p(c_i)}{p(c^*)}p_i + \frac{p(c_j)}{p(c^*)}p_j$. Then, the D_{JS} distance is defined as follows.

$$D_{JS}[p_i, p_j] = \frac{p(c_i)}{p(c^*)} D_{KL}[p_i||\bar{p}] + \frac{p(c_j)}{p(c^*)} D_{KL}[p_j||\bar{p}]$$

The D_{JS} distance defines a metric and it is bounded above by one. We note that the information loss for merging clusters c_i and c_j, depends only on the clusters c_i and c_j, and not on other parts of the clustering $\mathbf{C}_\ell$.

This approach considers all attribute values as a single variable, without taking into account the fact that the values come from different attributes. Alternatively, we could define a random variable for every attribute A_i. We can show that in applying the Information Bottleneck method to relational data, considering all attributes as a single random variable is equivalent to considering each attribute independently [1].

In the model of the data described so far, every tuple contains one value for each attribute. However, this is not the case when we consider market-basket data, which describes a database of transactions for a store, where every tuple consists of the items purchased by a single customer. It is also used as a term that collectively describes a data set where the tuples are sets of values of a single attribute, and each tuple may contain a different number of values. In the case of market-basket data, a tuple t_i contains d_i values. Setting $p(t_i) = 1/n$ and $p(a|t_i) = 1/d_i$, if a appears in t_i, we can define the mutual information I(T;A) and proceed with the Information Bottleneck method to clusters the tuples.

3 *LIMBO* Clustering

The Agglomerative Information Bottleneck algorithm suffers from high computational complexity, namely $\mathcal{O}(n^2 d^2 \log n)$, which is prohibitive for large data sets. We now introduce the *scaLable InforMation BOttleneck, LIMBO,* algorithm that uses distributional summaries in order to deal with large data sets. LIMBO is based on the idea that we do not need to keep whole tuples, or whole clusters in main memory, but instead, just sufficient statistics to describe them. LIMBO produces a compact summary model of the data, and then performs clustering on the summarized data. In our algorithm, we bound the sufficient statistics, that is the size of our summary model. This, together with an IB inspired notion of distance and a novel definition of summaries to produce the solution, makes our approach different from the one employed in the BIRCH clustering algorithm for clustering numerical data [21]. In BIRCH a heuristic threshold is used to control the accuracy of the summary created. In the experimental section of this paper, we study the effect of such a threshold in LIMBO.

3.1 Distributional Cluster Features

We summarize a cluster of tuples in a *Distributional Cluster Feature* (DCF). We will use the information in the relevant DCFs to compute the distance between two clusters or between a cluster and a tuple.

Let $\mathbf{T}$ denote a set of tuples over a set $\mathbf{A}$ of attributes, and let T and A be the corresponding random variables, as described earlier. Also let $\mathbf{C}$ denote a clustering of the tuples in $\mathbf{T}$ and let C be the corresponding random variable. For some cluster $c \in \mathbf{C}$, the *Distributional Cluster Feature* (DCF) of cluster c is defined by the pair

$$DCF(c) = \Big(p(c), p(A|c)\Big)$$

where $p(c)$ is the probability of cluster c, and $p(A|c)$ is the conditional probability distribution of the attribute values given the cluster c. We will often use $DCF(c)$ and c interchangeably.

If c consists of a single tuple $t \in \mathbf{T}$, $p(t) = 1/n$, and $p(A|t)$ is computed as described in Section 2. For example, in the movie database, for tuple t_i, $DCF(t_i)$ corresponds to the ith row of the normalized matrix M in Table 2. For larger clusters, the DCF is computed recursively as follows: let c^* denote the cluster we obtain by merging two clusters c_1 and c_2. The DCF of the cluster c^* is

$$DCF(c^*) = \Big(p(c^*), p(A|c^*)\Big)$$

where $p(c^*)$ and $p(A|c^*)$ are computed using Equations 1, and 2 respectively. We define the distance, $d(c_1, c_2)$, between $DCF(c_1)$ and $DCF(c_2)$ as the information loss $\delta I(c_1, c_2)$ incurred for merging the corresponding clusters c_1 and c_2. The distance $d(c_1, c_2)$ is computed using Equation 3. The information loss depends only on the clusters c_1 and c_2, and not on the clustering $\mathbf{C}$ in which they belong. Therefore, $d(c_1, c_2)$ is a well-defined distance measure.

The DCFs can be stored and updated incrementally. The probability vectors are stored as sparse vectors, reducing the amount of space considerably. Each DCF provides a summary of the corresponding cluster which is sufficient for computing the distance between two clusters.

3.2 The DCF Tree

The DCF tree is a height-balanced tree as depicted in Figure 1. Each node in the tree contains at most B entries, where B is the *branching factor* of the tree. All node entries store DCFs. At any point in the construction of the tree, the DCFs at the leaves define a clustering of the tuples seen so far. Each non-leaf node stores DCFs that are produced by merging the DCFs of its children. The DCF tree is built in a B-tree-like dynamic fashion. The insertion algorithm is described in detail below. After all tuples are inserted in the tree, the DCF tree embodies a compact representation where the data is summarized by the DCFs of the leaves.

3.3 The LIMBO Clustering Algorithm

The LIMBO algorithm proceeds in three phases. In the first phase, the DCF tree is constructed to summarize the data. In the second phase, the DCFs of the tree leaves are merged to produce a chosen number of clusters. In the third phase, we associate each tuple with the DCF to which the tuple is closest.

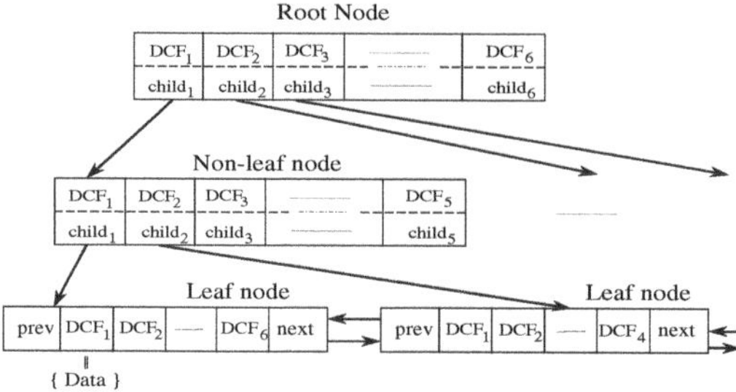

Fig. 1. A DCF tree with branching factor 6.

Phase 1: Insertion into the DCF tree. Tuples are read and inserted one by one. Tuple t is converted into $DCF(t)$, as described in Section 3.1. Then, starting from the root, we trace a path downward in the DCF tree. When at a non-leaf node, we compute the distance between $DCF(t)$ and each DCF entry of the node, finding the closest DCF entry to $DCF(t)$. We follow the child pointer of this entry to the next level of the tree. When at a leaf node, let $DCF(c)$ denote the DCF entry in the leaf node that is closest to $DCF(t)$. $DCF(c)$ is the summary of some cluster c. At this point, we need to decide whether t will be absorbed in the cluster c or not.

In our space-bounded algorithm, an input parameter S indicates the maximum space bound. Let E be the maximum size of a DCF entry (note that sparse DCFs may be smaller than E). We compute the maximum number of nodes ($N = S/(EB)$) and keep a counter of the number of used nodes as we build the tree. If there is an empty entry in the leaf node that contains $DCF(c)$, then $DCF(t)$ is placed in that entry. If there is no empty leaf entry and there is sufficient free space, then the leaf node is split into two leaves. We find the two DCFs in the leaf node that are farthest apart and we use them as seeds for the new leaves. The remaining DCFs, and $DCF(t)$ are placed in the leaf that contains the seed DCF to which they are closest. Finally, if the space bound has been reached, then we compare $d(c,t)$ with the minimum distance of any two DCF entries in the leaf. If $d(c,t)$ is smaller than this minimum, we merge $DCF(t)$ with $DCF(c)$; otherwise the two closest entries are merged and $DCF(t)$ occupies the freed entry.

When a leaf node is split, resulting in the creation of a new leaf node, the leaf's parent is updated, and a new entry is created at the parent node that describes the newly created leaf. If there is space in the non-leaf node, we add a new DCF entry, otherwise the non-leaf node must also be split. This process continues upward in the tree until the root is either updated or split itself. In the latter case, the height of the tree increases by one.

Phase 2: Clustering. After the construction of the DCF tree, the leaf nodes hold the DCFs of a clustering $\tilde{\mathbf{C}}$ of the tuples in $\mathbf{T}$. Each $DCF(c)$ corresponds to a cluster $c \in \tilde{\mathbf{C}}$, and contains sufficient statistics for computing $p(A|c)$, and probability $p(c)$. We employ the *Agglomerative Information Bottleneck (AIB)* algorithm to cluster the DCFs in the leaves and produce clusterings of the DCFs. We note that any clustering algorithm is applicable at this phase of the algorithm.

Phase 3: Associating tuples with clusters. For a chosen value of k, Phase 2 produces k DCFs that serve as *representatives* of k clusters. In the final phase, we perform a scan over the data set and assign each tuple to the cluster whose representative is closest to the tuple.

3.4 Analysis of LIMBO

We now present an analysis of the I/O and CPU costs for each phase of the LIMBO algorithm. In what follows, n is the number of tuples in the data set, d is the total number of attribute values, B is the branching factor of the DCF tree, and k is the chosen number of clusters.

Phase 1: The I/O cost of this stage is a scan that involves reading the data set from the disk. For the CPU cost, when a new tuple is inserted the algorithm considers a path of nodes in the tree, and for each node in the path, it performs at most B operations (distance computations, or updates), each taking time $\mathcal{O}(d)$. Thus, if h is the height of the DCF tree produced in Phase 1, locating the correct leaf node for a tuple takes time $\mathcal{O}(hdB)$. The time for a split is $\mathcal{O}(dB^2)$. If U is the number of non-leaf nodes, then all splits are performed in time $\mathcal{O}(dUB^2)$ in total. Hence, the CPU cost of creating the DCF tree is $\mathcal{O}(nhdB + dUB^2)$. We observed experimentally that LIMBO produces compact trees of small height (both h and U are bounded).

Phase 2: For values of S that produce clusterings of high quality the DCF tree is compact enough to fit in main memory. Hence, there is no I/O cost involved in this phase, since it involves only the clustering of the leaf node entries of the DCF tree. If L is the number of DCF entries at the leaves of the tree, then the AIB algorithm takes time $\mathcal{O}(L^2d^2 \log L)$. In our experiments, $L \ll n$, so the CPU cost is low.

Phase 3: The I/O cost of this phase is the reading of the data set from the disk again. The CPU complexity is $\mathcal{O}(kdn)$, since each tuple is compared against the k DCFs that represent the clusters.

4 Intra-attribute Value Distance

In this section, we propose a novel application that can be used within LIMBO to quantify the distance between attribute values of the same attribute. Categorical data is characterized by the fact that there is no inherent distance between attribute values. For example, in the movie database instance, given the values "Scorsese" and "Coppola", it is not apparent how to assess their similarity. Comparing the set of tuples in which they appear is not useful since every movie has a single director. In order to compare attribute values, we need to place them within a *context*. Then, two attribute values are similar if the contexts in which they appear are similar. We define the context as the distribution these attribute values induce on the remaining attributes. For example, for the attribute "director", two directors are considered similar if they induce a "similar" distribution over the attributes "actor" and "genre".

Table 3. The "director" attribute

director	a.DN	a.S	a.G	g.Cr	g.T	g.C	p(d)
Scorsese	1/2	0	0	0	1/2	0	1/6
Coppola	1/2	0	0	0	1/2	0	1/6
Hitchcock	0	1/3	1/3	0	2/3	0	2/6
Koster	0	1/3	1/3	0	0	2/3	2/6

Formally, let A' be the attribute of interest, and let $\mathbf{A}'$ denote the set of values of attribute A'. Also let $\tilde{\mathbf{A}} = \mathbf{A} \setminus \mathbf{A}'$ denote the set of attribute values for the remaining attributes. For the example of the movie database, if A' is the director attribute, with $\mathbf{A}' = \{d.S, d.C, d.H, d.K\}$, then $\tilde{\mathbf{A}} = \{a.DN, a.S, a.G, g.Cr, g.T, g.C\}$. Let A' and $\tilde{A}$ be random variables that range over $\mathbf{A}'$ and $\tilde{\mathbf{A}}$ respectively, and let $p(\tilde{A}|v)$ denote the distribution that value $v \in \mathbf{A}'$ induces on the values in $\tilde{\mathbf{A}}$. For some $a \in \tilde{\mathbf{A}}$, $p(a|v)$ is the fraction of the tuples in $\mathbf{T}$ that contain v, and also contain value a. Also, for some $v \in \mathbf{A}'$, $p(v)$ is the fraction of tuples in $\mathbf{T}$ that contain the value v. Table 3 shows an example of a table when A' is the director attribute.

For two values $v_1, v_2 \in \mathbf{A}'$, we define the distance between v_1 and v_2 to be the information loss $\delta I(v_1, v_2)$, incurred about the variable $\tilde{A}$ if we merge values v_1 and v_2. This is equal to the increase in the uncertainty of predicting the values of variable $\tilde{A}$, when we replace values v_1 and v_2 with $v_1 \vee v_2$. In the movie example, Scorsese and Coppola are the most similar directors.[3]

The definition of a distance measure for categorical attribute values is a contribution in itself, since it imposes some structure on an inherently unstructured problem. We can define a distance measure between tuples as the sum of the distances of the individual attributes. Another possible application is to cluster intra-attribute values. For example, in a movie database, we may be interested in discovering clusters of directors or actors, which in turn could help in improving the classification of movie tuples. Given the joint distribution of random variables A' and $\tilde{A}$ we can apply the LIMBO algorithm for clustering the values of attribute A'. Merging two $v_1, v_2 \in A'$, produces a new value $v_1 \vee v_2$, where $p(v_1 \vee v_2) = p(v_1) + p(v_2)$, since v_1 and v_2 never appear together. Also, $p(a|v_1 \vee v_2) = \frac{p(v_1)}{p(v_1 \vee v_2)} p(a|v_1) + \frac{p(v_2)}{p(v_1 \vee v_2)} p(a|v_2)$.

The problem of defining a context sensitive distance measure between attribute values is also considered by Das and Mannila [9]. They define an iterative algorithm for computing the *interchangeability* of two values. We believe that our approach gives a natural quantification of the concept of interchangeability. Furthermore, our approach has the advantage that it allows for the definition of distance between clusters of values, which can be used to perform intra-attribute value clustering. Gibson et al. [12] proposed STIRR, an algorithm that clusters attribute values. STIRR does not define a distance measure between attribute values and, furthermore, produces just two clusters of values.

[3] A conclusion that agrees with a well-informed cinematic opinion.

5 Experimental Evaluation

In this section, we perform a comparative evaluation of the LIMBO algorithm on both real and synthetic data sets. with other categorical clustering algorithms, including what we believe to be the only other scalable information-theoretic clustering algorithm COOLCAT [3,4].

5.1 Algorithms

We compare the clustering quality of LIMBO with the following algorithms.

ROCK Algorithm. ROCK [13] assumes a similarity measure between tuples, and defines a *link* between two tuples whose similarity exceeds a threshold θ. The aggregate interconnectivity between two clusters is defined as the sum of links between their tuples. ROCK is an agglomerative algorithm, so it is not applicable to large data sets. We use the *Jaccard Coefficient* for the similarity measure as suggested in the original paper. For data sets that appear in the original ROCK paper, we set the threshold θ to the value suggested there, otherwise we set θ to the value that gave us the best results in terms of quality. In our experiments, we use the implementation of Guha et al. [13].

COOLCAT Algorithm. The approach most similar to ours is the COOLCAT algorithm [3,4], by Barbará, Couto and Li. The COOLCAT algorithm is a scalable algorithm that optimizes the same objective function as our approach, namely the entropy of the clustering. It differs from our approach in that it relies on sampling, and it is non-hierarchical. COOLCAT starts with a sample of points and identifies a set of k initial tuples such that the minimum pairwise distance among them is maximized. These serve as representatives of the k clusters. All remaining tuples of the data set are placed in one of the clusters such that, at each step, the increase in the entropy of the resulting clustering is minimized. For the experiments, we implement COOLCAT based on the CIKM paper by Barbarà et al. [4].

STIRR Algorithm. STIRR [12] applies a *linear dynamical system* over multiple copies of a hypergraph of weighted attribute values, until a *fixed point* is reached. Each copy of the hypergraph contains two groups of attribute values, one with positive and another with negative weights, which define the two clusters. We compare this algorithm with our intra-attribute value clustering algorithm. In our experiments, we use our own implementation and report results for ten iterations.

LIMBO Algorithm. In addition to the space-bounded version of LIMBO as described in Section 3, we implemented LIMBO so that the accuracy of the summary model is controlled instead. If we wish to control the accuracy of the model, we use a threshold on the distance $d(c, t)$ to determine whether to merge $DCF(t)$ with $DCF(c)$, thus controlling directly the information loss for merging tuple t with cluster c. The selection of an appropriate threshold value will necessarily be data dependent and we require an intuitive way of allowing a user to set this threshold. Within a data set, every tuple contributes, on "average", $I(A; T)/n$ to the mutual information $I(A; T)$. We define the clustering threshold to be a multiple ϕ of this average and we denote the threshold by

$\tau(\phi)$. That is, $\tau(\phi) = \phi\frac{I(A;T)}{n}$. We can make a pass over the data, or use a sample of the data, to estimate $I(A;T)$. Given a value for ϕ ($0 \leq \phi \ll n$), if a merge incurs information loss more than ϕ times the "average" mutual information, then the new tuple is placed in a cluster by itself. In the extreme case $\phi = 0.0$, we prohibit any information loss in our summary (this is equivalent to setting $S = \infty$ in the space-bounded version of LIMBO). We discuss the effect of ϕ in Section 5.4.

To distinguish between the two versions of LIMBO, we shall refer to the space-bounded version as LIMBO_S and the accuracy-bounded as LIMBO_ϕ. Note that algorithmically only the merging decision in Phase 1 differs in the two versions, while all other phases remain the same for both LIMBO_S and LIMBO_ϕ.

5.2 Data Sets

We experimented with the following data sets. The first three have been previously used for the evaluation of the aforementioned algorithms [4,12,13]. The synthetic data sets are used both for quality comparison, and for our scalability evaluation.

Congressional Votes. This relational data set was taken from the *UCI Machine Learning Repository*.[4] It contains 435 tuples of votes from the U.S. Congressional Voting Record of 1984. Each tuple is a congress-person's vote on 16 issues and each vote is boolean, either YES or NO. Each congress-person is classified as either Republican or Democrat. There are a total of 168 Republicans and 267 Democrats. There are 288 missing values that we treat as separate values.

Mushroom. The Mushroom relational data set also comes from the UCI Repository. It contains 8,124 tuples, each representing a mushroom characterized by 22 attributes, such as color, shape, odor, etc. The total number of distinct attribute values is 117. Each mushroom is classified as either poisonous or edible. There are 4,208 edible and 3,916 poisonous mushrooms in total. There are 2,480 missing values.

Database and Theory Bibliography. This relational data set contains 8,000 tuples that represent research papers. About 3,000 of the tuples represent papers from database research and 5,000 tuples represent papers from theoretical computer science. Each tuple contains four attributes with values for the first Author, second Author, Conference/Journal and the Year of publication.[5] We use this data to test our intra-attribute clustering algorithm.

Synthetic Data Sets. We produce synthetic data sets using a data generator available on the Web.[6] This generator offers a wide variety of options, in terms of the number of tuples, attributes, and attribute domain sizes. We specify the number of classes in the data set by the use of conjunctive rules of the form $(Attr_1 = a_1 \wedge Attr_2 = a_2 \wedge \ldots) \Rightarrow Class = c1$. The rules may involve an arbitrary number of attributes and attribute values. We name

[4] `http://www.ics.uci.edu/~mlearn/MLRepository.html`

[5] Following the approach of Gibson et al. [12], if the second author does not exist, then the name of the first author is copied instead. We also filter the data so that each conference/journal appears at least 5 times.

[6] `http://www.datgen.com/`

these synthetic data sets by the prefix DS followed by the number of classes in the data set, *e*.g., DS5 or DS10. The data sets contain 5,000 tuples, and 10 attributes, with domain sizes between 20 and 40 for each attribute. Three attributes participate in the rules the data generator uses to produce the class labels. Finally, these data sets have up to 10% erroneously entered values. Additional larger synthetic data sets are described in Section 5.6.

Web Data. This is a market-basket data set that consists of a collection of web pages. The pages were collected as described by Kleinberg [14]. A query is made to a search engine, and an initial set of web pages is retrieved. This set is augmented by including pages that point to, or are pointed to by pages in the set. Then, the links between the pages are discovered, and the underlying graph is constructed. Following the terminology of Kleinberg [14] we define a *hub* to be a page with non-zero out-degree, and an *authority* to be a page with non-zero in-degree.

Our goal is to cluster the authorities in the graph. The set of tuples $\mathbf{T}$ is the set of authorities in the graph, while the set of attribute values $\mathbf{A}$ is the set of hubs. Each authority is expressed as a vector over the hubs that point to this authority. For our experiments, we use the data set used by Borodin et al. [5] for the "abortion" query. We applied a filtering step to assure that each hub points to more than 10 authorities and each authority is pointed by more than 10 hubs. The data set contains 93 authorities related to 102 hubs.

We have also applied LIMBO on Software Reverse Engineering data sets with considerable benefits compared to other algorithms [2].

5.3 Quality Measures for Clustering

Clustering quality lies in the eye of the beholder; determining the best clustering usually depends on subjective criteria. Consequently, we will use several quantitative measures of clustering performance.

Information Loss, (IL): We use the information loss, $I(A;T) - I(A;C)$ to compare clusterings. The lower the information loss, the better the clustering. For a clustering with low information loss, given a cluster, we can predict the attribute values of the tuples in the cluster with relatively high accuracy. We present IL as a percentage of the initial mutual information lost after producing the desired number of clusters using each algorithm.

Category Utility, (CU): Category utility [15], is defined as the difference between the expected number of attribute values that can be correctly guessed given a clustering, and the expected number of correct guesses with no such knowledge. CU depends only on the partitioning of the attributes values by the corresponding clustering algorithm and, thus, is a more objective measure. Let $\mathbf{C}$ be a clustering. If A_i is an attribute with values v_{ij}, then CU is given by the following expression:

$$CU = \sum_{c \in \mathbf{C}} \frac{|c|}{n} \sum_i \sum_j [P(A_i = v_{ij}|c)^2 - P(A_i = v_{ij})^2]$$

We present CU as an absolute value that should be compared to the CU values given by other algorithms, for the same number of clusters, in order to assess the quality of a specific algorithm.

Many data sets commonly used in testing clustering algorithms include a variable that is hidden from the algorithm, and specifies the class with which each tuple is associated. All data sets we consider include such a variable. This variable is *not* used by the clustering algorithms. While there is no guarantee that any given classification corresponds to an optimal clustering, it is nonetheless enlightening to compare clusterings with pre-specified classifications of tuples. To do this, we use the following quality measures.

Min Classification Error, (E_{min}): Assume that the tuples in $\mathbf{T}$ are already classified into k classes $\mathbf{G} = \{g_1, \ldots, g_k\}$, and let $\mathbf{C}$ denote a clustering of the tuples in $\mathbf{T}$ into k clusters $\{c_1, \ldots, c_k\}$ produced by a clustering algorithm. Consider a one-to-one mapping, f, from classes to clusters, such that each class g_i is mapped to the cluster $f(g_i)$. The *classification error* of the mapping is defined as

$$E = \sum_{i=1}^{k} \left| g_i \cap \overline{f(g_i)} \right|$$

where $\left| g_i \cap \overline{f(g_i)} \right|$ measures the number of tuples in class g_i that received the wrong label. The *optimal* mapping between clusters and classes, is the one that minimizes the classification error. We use E_{min} to denote the classification error of the optimal mapping.

Precision, (P), Recall, (R): Without loss of generality assume that the optimal mapping assigns class g_i to cluster c_i. We define precision, P_i, and recall, R_i, for a cluster c_i, $1 \leq i \leq k$ as follows.

$$P_i = \frac{|c_i \cap g_i|}{|c_i|} \quad and \quad R_i = \frac{|c_i \cap g_i|}{|g_i|}.$$

P_i and R_i take values between 0 and 1 and, intuitively, P_i measures the accuracy with which cluster c_i reproduces class g_i, while R_i measures the completeness with which c_i reproduces class g_i. We define the precision and recall of the clustering as the weighted average of the precision and recall of each cluster. More precisely

$$P = \sum_{i=1}^{k} \frac{|g_i|}{|T|} P_i \quad and \quad R = \sum_{i=1}^{k} \frac{|g_i|}{|T|} R_i .$$

We think of precision, recall, and classification error as indicative values (percentages) of the ability of the algorithm to reconstruct the existing classes in the data set.

In our experiments, we report values for all of the above measures. For LIMBO and COOLCAT, numbers are averages over 100 runs with different (random) orderings of the tuples.

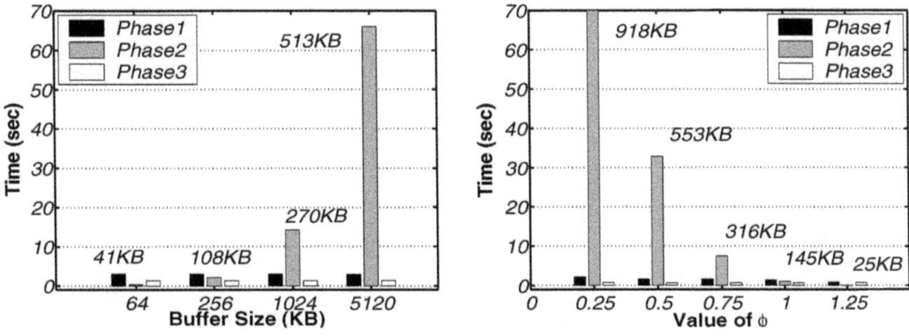

Fig. 2. LIMBO_S and LIMBO_ϕ execution times (DS5)

5.4 Quality-Efficiency Trade-Offs for LIMBO

In LIMBO, we can control the size of the model (using S) or the accuracy of the model (using ϕ). Both S and ϕ permit a trade-off between the expressiveness (information preservation) of the summarization and the compactness of the model (number of leaf entries in the tree) it produces. For large values of S and small values of ϕ, we obtain a fine grain representation of the data set at the end of Phase 1. However, this results in a tree with a large number of leaf entries, which leads to a higher computational cost for both Phase 1 and Phase 2 of the algorithm. For small values of S and large values of ϕ, we obtain a compact representation of the data set (small number of leaf entries), which results in faster execution time, at the expense of increased information loss.

We now investigate this trade-off for a range of values for S and ϕ. We observed experimentally that the branching factor B does not significantly affect the quality of the clustering. We set $B = 4$, which results in manageable execution time for Phase 1. Figure 2 presents the execution times for LIMBO_S and LIMBO_ϕ on the DS5 data set, as a function of S and ϕ, respectively. For $\phi = 0.25$ the Phase 2 time is 210 seconds (beyond the edge of the graph). The figures also include the size of the tree in KBytes. In this figure, we observe that for large S and small ϕ the computational bottleneck of the algorithm is Phase 2. As S decreases and ϕ increases the time for Phase 2 decreases in a quadratic fashion. This agrees with the plot in Figure 3, where we observe that the number of leaves decreases also in a quadratic fashion. Due to the decrease in the size (and height) of the tree, time for Phase 1 also decreases, however, at a much slower rate. Phase 3, as expected, remains unaffected, and it is equal to a few seconds for all values of S and ϕ. For $S \leq 256$KB and $\phi \geq 1.0$ the number of leaf entries becomes sufficiently small, so that the computational bottleneck of the algorithm becomes Phase 1. For these values the execution time is dominated by the linear scan of the data in Phase 1.

We now study the change in the quality measures for the same range of values for S and ϕ. In the extreme cases of $S = \infty$ and $\phi = 0.0$, we only merge identical tuples, and no information is lost in Phase 1. LIMBO then reduces to the AIB algorithm, and we obtain the same quality as AIB. Figures 4 and 5 show the quality measures for the different values of ϕ and S. The CU value (not plotted) is equal to 2.51 for $S \leq 256$KB, and 2.56 for $S \geq 256$KB. We observe that for $S \geq 256$KB and $\phi \leq 1.0$ we obtain clusterings of *exactly* the same quality as for $S = \infty$ and $\phi = 0.0$, that is, the AIB

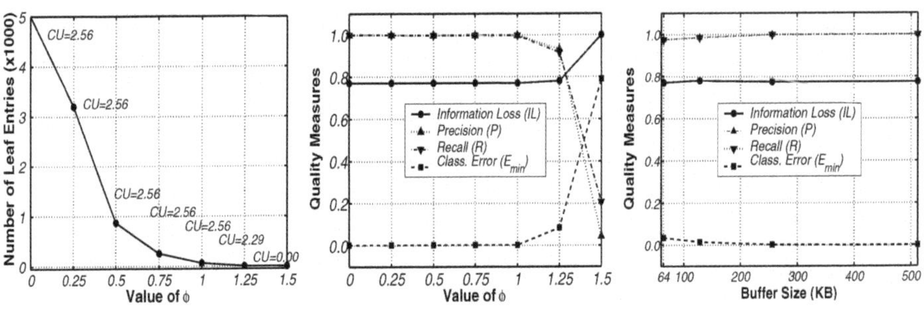

Fig. 3. LIMBO$_\phi$ Leaves (DS5) **Fig. 4.** LIMBO$_\phi$ Quality (DS5) **Fig. 5.** LIMBO$_S$ Quality (DS5)

algorithm. At the same time, for $S = 256$KB and $\phi = 1.0$ the execution time of the algorithm is only a small fraction of that of the AIB algorithm, which was a few minutes.

Similar trends were observed for all other data sets. There is a range of values for S, and ϕ, where the execution time of LIMBO is dominated by Phase 1, while at the same time, we observe essentially no change (up to the third decimal digit) in the quality of the clustering. Table 4 shows the reduction in the number of leaf entries for each data set for LIMBO$_S$ and LIMBO$_\phi$. The parameters S and ϕ are set so that the cluster quality is almost identical to that of AIB (as demonstrated in Table 6). These experiments demonstrate that in Phase 1 we can obtain significant compression of the data sets at no expense in the final quality. The consistency of LIMBO can be attributed in part to the effect of Phase 3, which assigns the tuples to cluster representatives, and hides some of the information loss incurred in the previous phases. Thus, it is sufficient for Phase 2 to discover k well separated representatives. As a result, even for large values of ϕ and small values of S, LIMBO obtains essentially the same clustering quality as AIB, but in linear time.

Table 4. Reduction in Leaf Entries

	Votes	Mushroom	DS5	DS10
LIMBO$_S$	85.94%	99.34%	95.36%	95.28%
LIMBO$_\phi$	94.01%	99.77%	98.68%	98.82%

5.5 Comparative Evaluations

In this section, we demonstrate that LIMBO produces clusterings of high quality, and we compare against other categorical clustering algorithms.

Tuple Clustering. Table 5 shows the results for all algorithms on all quality measures for the Votes and Mushroom data sets. For LIMBO$_S$, we present results for $S = 128K$

Table 5. Results for real data sets

Votes (2 clusters)							Mushroom (2 clusters)						
Algorithm	*size*	*IL(%)*	*P*	*R*	E_{min}	*CU*	**Algorithm**	*size*	*IL(%)*	*P*	*R*	E_{min}	*CU*
LIMBO ($\phi=0.0, S=\infty$)	384	**72.52**	**0.89**	**0.87**	**0.13**	**2.89**	LIMBO ($\phi=0.0, S=\infty$)	8124	**81.45**	**0.91**	**0.89**	**0.11**	**1.71**
$LIMBO_S(128KB)$	54	**72.54**	**0.89**	**0.87**	**0.13**	**2.89**	$LIMBO_S(128KB)$	54	**81.46**	**0.91**	**0.89**	**0.11**	**1.71**
$LIMBO_\phi(1.0)$	23	**72.55**	**0.89**	**0.87**	**0.13**	**2.89**	$LIMBO_\phi(1.0)$	18	**81.45**	**0.91**	**0.89**	**0.11**	**1.71**
COOLCAT ($s = 435$)	435	73.55	0.87	0.85	0.15	2.78	COOLCAT ($s = 1000$)	1,000	84.57	0.76	0.73	0.27	1.46
ROCK ($\theta = 0.7$)	-	74.00	0.87	0.86	0.16	2.63	ROCK ($\theta = 0.8$)	-	86.00	0.77	0.57	0.43	0.59

Table 6. Results for synthetic data sets

DS5 (n=5000, 10 attributes, 5 clusters)							DS10 (n=5000, 10 attributes, 10 clusters)						
Algorithm	*size*	*IL(%)*	*P*	*R*	E_{min}	*CU*	**Algorithm**	*size*	*IL(%)*	*P*	*R*	E_{min}	*CU*
LIMBO ($\phi=0.0, S=\infty$)	5000	**77.56**	**0.998**	**0.998**	**0.002**	**2.56**	LIMBO ($\phi=0.0, S=\infty$)	5000	**73.50**	**0.997**	**0.997**	**0.003**	**2.82**
$LIMBO_S(1024KB)$	232	**77.57**	**0.998**	**0.998**	**0.002**	**2.56**	$LIMBO_S(1024KB)$	236	**73.52**	**0.996**	**0.996**	**0.004**	**2.82**
$LIMBO_\phi(1.0)$	66	**77.56**	**0.998**	**0.998**	**0.002**	**2.56**	$LIMBO_\phi(1.0)$	59	**73.51**	**0.994**	**0.996**	**0.004**	**2.82**
COOLCAT ($s = 125$)	125	78.02	0.995	0.995	0.05	2.54	COOLCAT ($s = 125$)	125	74.32	0.979	0.973	0.026	2.74
ROCK ($\theta = 0.0$)	-	85.00	0.839	0.724	0.28	0.44	ROCK ($\theta = 0.0$)	-	78.00	0.830	0.818	0.182	2.13

while for $LIMBO_\phi$, we present results for $\phi = 1.0$. We can see that both version of LIMBO have results almost identical to the quality measures for $S = \infty$ and $\phi = 0.0$, *i.e.*, the AIB algorithm. The *size* entry in the table holds the number of leaf entries for LIMBO, and the sample size for COOLCAT. For the Votes data set, we use the whole data set as a sample, while for Mushroom we use 1,000 tuples. As Table 5 indicates, LIMBO's quality is superior to ROCK, and COOLCAT, in both data sets. In terms of IL, LIMBO created clusters which retained most of the initial information about the attribute values. With respect to the other measures, LIMBO outperforms all other algorithms, exhibiting the highest CU, P and R in all data sets tested, as well as the lowest E_{min}.

We also evaluate LIMBO's performance on two synthetic data sets, namely DS5 and DS10. These data sets allow us to evaluate our algorithm on data sets with more than two classes. The results are shown in Table 6. We observe again that LIMBO has the lowest information loss and produces nearly optimal results with respect to precision and recall.

For the ROCK algorithm, we observed that it is very sensitive to the threshold value θ and in many cases, the algorithm produces one giant cluster that includes tuples from most classes. This results in poor precision and recall.

Comparison with COOLCAT. COOLCAT exhibits average clustering quality that is close to that of LIMBO. It is interesting to examine how COOLCAT behaves when we consider other statistics. In Table 7, we present statistics for 100 runs of COOLCAT and LIMBO on different orderings of the Votes and Mushroom data sets. We present LIMBO's results for $S = 128$KB and $\phi = 1.0$, which are very similar to those for $S = \infty$. For the Votes data set, COOLCAT exhibits information loss as high as 95.31% with a variance of 12.25%. For all runs, we use the whole data set as the sample for COOLCAT. For the Mushroom data set, the situation is better, but still the variance is as high as 3.5%. The sample size was 1,000 for all runs. Table 7 indicates that LIMBO behaves in a more stable fashion over different runs (that is, different input orders).

Table 7. Statistics for IL(%) and CU

VOTES		Min	Max	Avg	Var	MUSHROOM		Min	Max	Avg	Var
LIMBO ($S = 128KB$)	IL	71.98	73.68	72.54	0.08	LIMBO ($S = 1024KB$)	IL	81.46	81.46	81.46	0.00
	CU	2.80	2.93	2.89	0.0007		CU	1.71	1.71	1.71	0.00
LIMBO ($\phi = 1.0$)	IL	71.98	73.29	72.55	0.083	LIMBO ($\phi = 1.0$)	IL	81.45	81.45	81.45	0.00
	CU	2.83	2.94	2.89	0.0006		CU	1.71	1.71	1.71	0.00
COOLCAT ($s = 435$)	IL	71.99	95.31	73.55	12.25	COOLCAT ($s = 1000$)	IL	81.60	87.07	84.57	3.50
	CU	0.19	2.94	2.78	0.15		CU	0.80	1.73	1.46	0.05

Notably, for the Mushroom data set, LIMBO's performance is exactly the same in all runs, while for Votes it exhibits a very low variance. This indicates that LIMBO is not particularly sensitive to the input order of data.

The performance of COOLCAT appears to be sensitive to the following factors: the choice of representatives, the sample size, and the ordering of the tuples. After detailed examination we found that the runs with maximum information loss for the Votes data set correspond to cases where an outlier was selected as the initial representative. The Votes data set contains three such tuples, which are far from all other tuples, and they are naturally picked as representatives. Reducing the sample size, decreases the probability of selecting outliers as representatives, however it increases the probability of missing one of the clusters. In this case, high information loss may occur if COOLCAT picks as representatives two tuples that are not maximally far apart. Finally, there are cases where the same representatives may produce different results. As tuples are inserted to the clusters, the representatives "move" closer to the inserted tuples, thus making the algorithm sensitive to the ordering of the data set.

In terms of computational complexity both LIMBO and COOLCAT include a stage that requires quadratic complexity. For LIMBO this is Phase 2. For COOLCAT, this is the step where all pairwise entropies between the tuples in the sample are computed. We experimented with both algorithms having the same input size for this phase, *i.e.*, we made the sample size of COOLCAT, equal to the number of leaves for LIMBO. Results for the Votes and Mushroom data sets are shown in Tables 8 and 9. LIMBO outperforms COOLCAT in all runs, for all quality measures even though execution time is essentially the same for both algorithms. The two algorithms are closest in quality for the Votes data set with input size 27, and farthest apart for the Mushroom data set with input size 275. COOLCAT appears to perform better with smaller sample size, while LIMBO remains essentially unaffected.

Web Data. Since this data set has no predetermined cluster labels, we use a different evaluation approach. We applied LIMBO with $\phi = 0.0$ and clustered the authorities into three clusters. (Due to lack of space the choice of k is discussed in detail in [1].) The total information loss was 61%. Figure 6 shows the authority to hub table, after permuting the rows so that we group together authorities in the same cluster, and the columns so that each hub is assigned to the cluster to which it has the most links.

LIMBO accurately characterize the structure of the web graph. Authorities are clustered in three distinct clusters. Authorities in the same cluster share many hubs, while the

Table 8. LIMBO vs COOLCAT on Votes

Sample Size = Leaf Entries = 384					
Algorithm	$IL(\%)$	P	R	E_{min}	CU
LIMBO	**72.52**	**0.89**	**0.87**	**0.13**	**2.89**
COOLCAT	74.15	0.86	0.84	0.15	2.63
Sample Size = Leaf Entries = 27					
Algorithm	$IL(\%)$	P	R	E_{min}	CU
LIMBO	**72.55**	**0.89**	**0.87**	**0.13**	**2.89**
COOLCAT	73.50	0.88	0.86	0.13	2.87

Table 9. LIMBO vs COOLCAT on Mushroom

Sample Size = Leaf Entries = 275					
Algorithm	$IL(\%)$	P	R	E_{min}	CU
LIMBO	**81.45**	**0.91**	**0.89**	**0.11**	**1.71**
COOLCAT	83.50	0.76	0.73	0.27	1.46
Sample Size = Leaf Entries = 18					
Algorithm	$IL(\%)$	P	R	E_{min}	CU
LIMBO	**81.45**	**0.91**	**0.89**	**0.11**	**1.71**
COOLCAT	82.10	0.82	0.81	0.19	1.60

those in different clusters have very few hubs in common. The three different clusters correspond to different viewpoints on the issue of abortion. The first cluster consists of "pro-choice" pages. The second cluster consists of "pro-life" pages. The third cluster contains a set of pages from `cincinnati.com` that were included in the data set by the algorithm that collects the web pages [5], despite having no apparent relation to the abortion query. A complete list of the results can be found in [1].[7]

Intra-Attribute Value Clustering. We now present results for the application of LIMBO to the problem of intra-attribute value clustering. For this experiment, we use the Bibliographic data set. We are interested in clustering the conferences and journals, as well as the first authors of the papers. We compare LIMBO with STIRR, an algorithm for clustering attribute values.

Following the description of Section 4, for the first experiment we set the random variable A' to range over the conferences/journals, while variable $\tilde{A}$ ranges over first and second authors, and the year of publication. There are 1,211 distinct venues in the data set; 815 are database venues, and 396 are theory venues.[8] Results for $S = $ 5MB and $\phi = 1.0$ are shown in Table 10. LIMBO's results are superior to those of STIRR with respect to all quality measures. The difference is especially pronounced in the P and R measures.

Table 10. Bib clustering using LIMBO & STIRR

Algorithm	$Leaves$	$IL(\%)$	P	R	E_{min}
LIMBO ($S = $ 5MB)	16	**94.02**	**0.90**	**0.89**	**0.12**
LIMBO ($\phi = 1.0$)	47	**94.01**	**0.90**	**0.90**	**0.11**
STIRR	-	98.01	0.56	0.55	0.45

We now turn to the problem of clustering the first authors. Variable A' ranges over the set of 1,416 distinct first authors in the data set, and variable $\tilde{A}$ ranges over the rest of the attributes. We produce two clusters, and we evaluate the results of LIMBO and STIRR

[7] Available at: http://www.cs.toronto.edu/~periklis/pubs/csrg467.pdf

[8] The data set is pre-classified, so class labels are known.

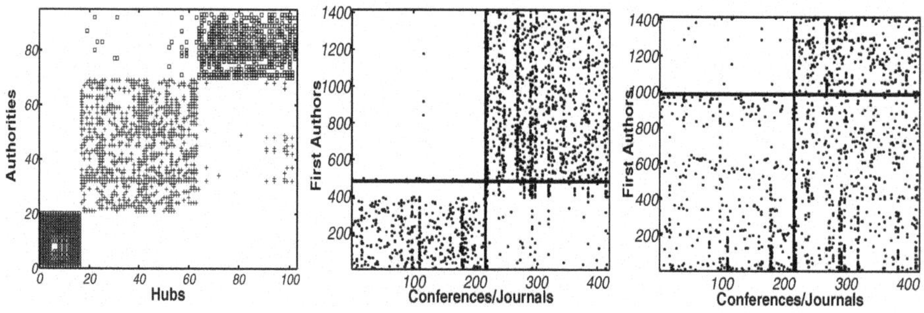

Fig. 6. Web data clusters **Fig. 7.** LIMBO clusters **Fig. 8.** STIRR clusters

based on the distribution of the papers that were written by first authors in each cluster. Figures 7 and 8 illustrate the clusters produced by LIMBO and STIRR, respectively. The x-axis in both figures represents publishing venues while the y-axis represents first authors. If an author has published a paper in a particular venue, this is represented by a point in each figure. The thick horizontal line separates the clusters of authors, and the thick vertical line distinguishes between theory and database venues. Database venues lie on the left of the line, while theory ones on the right of the line.

From these figures, it is apparent that LIMBO yields a better partition of the authors than STIRR. The upper half corresponds to a set of theory researchers with almost no publications in database venues. The bottom half, corresponds to a set of database researchers with very few publications in theory venues. Our clustering is slightly smudged by the authors between index 400 and 450 that appear to have a number of publications in theory. These are drawn in the database cluster due to their co-authors. STIRR, on the other hand, creates a well separated theory cluster (upper half), but the second cluster contains authors with publications almost equally distributed between theory and database venues.

5.6 Scalability Evaluation

In this section, we study the scalability of LIMBO, and we investigate how the parameters affect its execution time. We study the execution time of both LIMBO$_S$ and LIMBO$_\phi$. We consider four data sets of size $500K$, $1M$, $5M$, and $10M$, each containing 10 clusters and 10 attributes with 20 to 40 values each. The first three data sets are samples of the $10M$ data set.

For LIMBO$_S$, the size and the number of leaf entries of the DCF tree, at the end of Phase 1 is controlled by the parameter S. For LIMBO$_\phi$, we study Phase 1 in detail. As we vary ϕ, Figure 9 demonstrates that the execution time for Phase 1 decreases at a steady rate for values of ϕ up to 1.0. For $1.0 < \phi < 1.5$, execution time drops significantly. This decrease is due to the reduced number of splits and the decrease in the DCF tree size. In the same plot, we show some indicative sizes of the tree demonstrating that the vectors that we maintain remain relatively sparse. The average density of the DCF tree vectors, *i.e.*, the average fraction of non-zero entries remains between 41% and 87%.

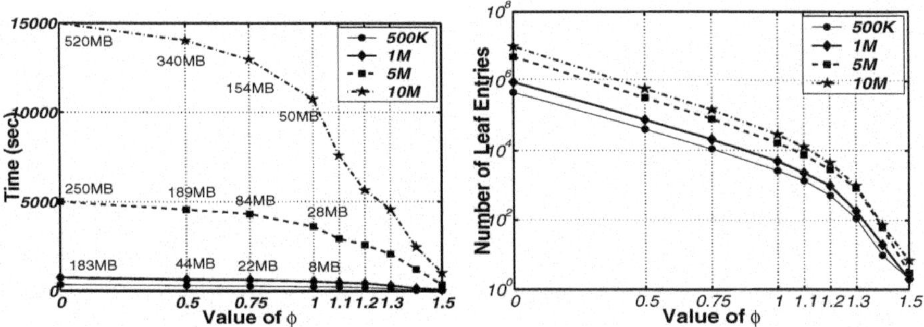

Fig. 9. Phase 1 execution times

Fig. 10. Phase 1 leaf entries

Figure 10 plots the number of leaves as a function of ϕ.[9] We observe that for the same range of values for ϕ ($1.0 < \phi < 1.5$), LIMBO produces a manageable DCF tree, with a small number of leaves, leading to fast execution time in Phase 2. Furthermore, in all our experiments the height of the tree was never more than 11, and the occupancy of the tree, *i.e.*, the number of occupied entries over the total possible number of entries, was always above 85.7%, indicating that the memory space was well used.

Thus, for $1.0 < \phi < 1.5$, we have a DCF tree with manageable size, and fast execution time for Phase 1 and 2. For our experiments, we set $\phi = 1.2$ and $\phi = 1.3$. For LIMBO$_S$, we use buffer sizes of $S = 1MB$ and $S = 5MB$. We now study the total execution time of the algorithm for these parameter values. The graph in Figure 11 shows the execution time for LIMBO$_S$ and LIMBO$_\phi$ on the data sets we consider. In this figure, we observe that execution time scales in a linear fashion with respect to the size of the data set for both versions of LIMBO. We also observed that the clustering quality remained unaffected for all values of S and ϕ, and it was the same *across* the data sets (except for IL in the $1M$ data set, which differed by 0.01%). Precision (P) and Recall (R) were 0.999, and the classification error (E_{min}) was 0.0013, indicating that LIMBO can produce clusterings of high quality, even for large data sets.

In our next experiment, we varied the number of attributes, m, in the $5M$ and $10M$ data sets and ran both LIMBO$_S$, with a buffer size of $5MB$, and LIMBO$_\phi$, with $\phi = 1.2$. Figure 12 shows the execution time as a function number of attributes, for different data set sizes. In all cases, execution time increased linearly. Table 11 presents the quality results for all values of m for both LIMBO algorithms. The quality measures are essentially the same for different sizes of the data set.

Finally, we varied the number of clusters from $k = 10$ up to $k = 50$ in the $10M$ data set, for $S = 5MB$ and $\phi = 1.2$. As expected from the analysis of LIMBO in Section 3.4, the number of clusters affected only Phase 3. Recall from Figure 2 in Section 5.4 that Phase 3 is a small fraction of the total execution time. Indeed, as we increase k from 10 to 50, we observed just 2.5% increase in the execution time for LIMBO$_S$ and just 1.1% for LIMBO$_\phi$.

[9] The y-axis of Figure 10 has a logarithmic scale.

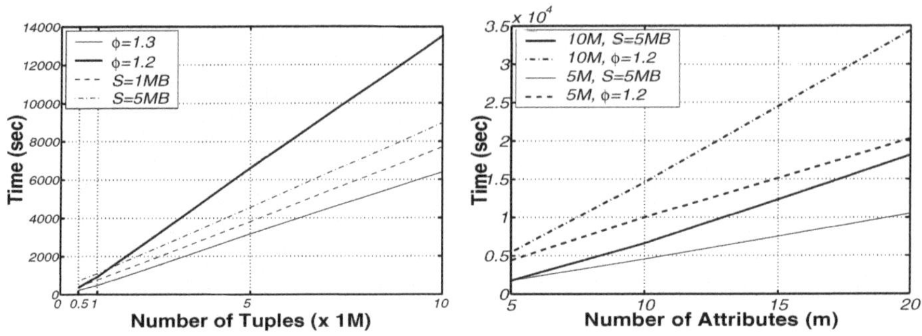

Fig. 11. Execution time (m=10)

Fig. 12. Execution time

Table 11. LIMBO_S and LIMBO_ϕ quality

$\textbf{LIMBO}_{\phi,S}$	*IL(%)*	P	R	E_{min}	CU
$m = 5$	49.12	0.991	0.991	0.0013	2.52
$m = 10$	60.79	0.999	0.999	0.0013	3.87
$m = 20$	52.01	0.997	0.994	0.0015	4.56

6 Other Related Work

CACTUS, [10], by Ghanti, Gehrke and Ramakrishnan, uses summaries of information constructed from the data set that are sufficient for discovering clusters. The algorithm defines attribute value clusters with overlapping cluster-projections on any attribute. This makes the assignment of tuples to clusters unclear.

Our approach is based on the *Information Bottleneck (IB) Method*, introduced by Tishby, Pereira and Bialek [20]. The Information Bottleneck method has been used in an agglomerative hierarchical clustering algorithm [18] and applied to the clustering of documents [19]. Recently, Slonim and Tishby [17] introduced the *sequential Information Bottleneck, (sIB)* algorithm, which reduces the running time relative to the agglomerative approach. However, it depends on an initial random partition and requires multiple passes over the data for different initial partitions. In the future, we plan to experiment with sIB in Phase 2 of LIMBO.

Finally, an algorithm that uses an extension to BIRCH [21] is given by Chiu, Fang, Chen, Wand and Jeris [6]. Their approach assumes that the data follows a multivariate normal distribution. The performance of the algorithm has not been tested on categorical data sets.

7 Conclusions and Future Directions

We have evaluated the effectiveness of LIMBO in trading off either quality for time or quality for space to achieve compact, yet accurate, models for small and large categorical data sets. We have shown LIMBO to have advantages over other information theoretic clustering algorithms including AIB (in terms of scalability) and COOLCAT (in terms of clustering quality and parameter stability). We have also shown advantages in quality over other scalable and non-scalable algorithms designed to cluster either categorical tuples or values. With our space-bounded version of LIMBO (LIMBO_S), we can build a model in one pass over the data in a fixed amount of memory while still effectively controlling information loss in the model. These properties make LIMBO_S amenable for use in clustering streaming categorical data [8] In addition, to the best of our knowledge, LIMBO is the only scalable categorical algorithm that is hierarchical. Using its compact summary model, LIMBO efficiently builds clusterings for not just a single value of k, but for a large range of values (typically hundreds). Furthermore, we are also able to produce statistics that let us directly compare clusterings. We are currently formalizing the use of such statistics in determining good values for k. Finally, we plan to apply LIMBO as a data mining technique to schema discovery [16].

References

[1] P. Andritsos, P. Tsaparas, R. J. Miller, and K. C. Sevcik. Limbo: A linear algorithm to cluster categorical data. Technical report, UofT, Dept of CS, CSRG-467, 2003.

[2] P. Andritsos and V. Tzerpos. Software Clustering based on Information Loss Minimization. In *WCRE*, Victoria, BC, Canada, 2003.

[3] D. Barbará, J. Couto, and Y. Li. An Information Theory Approach to Categorical Clustering. Submitted for Publication.

[4] D. Barbará, J. Couto, and Y. Li. COOLCAT: An entropy-based algorithm for categorical clustering. In *CIKM*, McLean, VA, 2002.

[5] A. Borodin, G. O. Roberts, J. S. Rosenthal, and P. Tsaparas. Finding authorities and hubs from link structures on the World Wide Web. In *WWW-10*, Hong Kong, 2001.

[6] T. Chiu, D. Fang, J. Chen, Y. Wang, and C. Jeris. A Robust and Scalable Clustering Algorithm for Mixed Type Attributes in Large Database Environment. In *KDD*, San Francisco, CA, 2001.

[7] T. M. Cover and J. A. Thomas. *Elements of Information Theory*. Wiley & Sons, 1991.

[8] D. Barbará. Requirements for Clustering Data Streams. *SIGKDD Explorations*, 3(2), Jan. 2002.

[9] G. Das and H. Mannila. Context-Based Similarity Measures for Categorical Databases. In *PKDD*, Lyon, France, 2000.

[10] V. Ganti, J. Gehrke, and R. Ramakrishnan. CACTUS: Clustering Categorical Data Using Summaries. In *KDD*, San Diego, CA, 1999.

[11] M. R. Garey and D. S. Johnson. *Computers and intractability; a guide to the theory of NP-completeness*. W.H. Freeman, 1979.

[12] D. Gibson, J. M. Kleinberg, and P. Raghavan. Clustering Categorical Data: An Approach Based on Dynamical Systems. In *VLDB*, New York, NY, 1998.

[13] S. Guha, R. Rastogi, and K. Shim. ROCK: A Robust Clustering Algorithm for Categorical Atributes. In *ICDE*, Sydney, Australia, 1999.

[14] J. M. Kleinberg. Authoritative Sources in a Hyperlinked Environment. In *SODA*, SF, CA, 1998.

[15] M. A. Gluck and J. E. Corter. Information, Uncertainty, and the Utility of Categories. In *COGSCI*, Irvine, CA, USA, 1985.

[16] R. J. Miller and P. Andritsos. On Schema Discovery. *IEEE Data Engineering Bulletin*, 26(3):39–44, 2003.

[17] N. Slonim, N. Friedman, and N. Tishby. Unsupervised Document Classification using Sequential Information Maximization. In *SIGIR*, Tampere, Finland, 2002.
[18] N. Slonim and N. Tishby. Agglomerative Information Bottleneck. In *NIPS*, Breckenridge, 1999.
[19] N. Slonim and N. Tishby. Document Clustering Using Word Clusters via the Information Bottleneck Method. In *SIGIR*, Athens, Greece, 2000.
[20] N. Tishby, F. C. Pereira, and W. Bialek. The Information Bottleneck Method. In *37th Annual Allerton Conference on Communication, Control and Computing*, Urban-Champaign, IL, 1999.
[21] T. Zhang, R. Ramakrishnan, and M. Livny. BIRCH: An efficient Data Clustering Method for Very Large Databases. In *SIGMOD*, Montreal, QB, 1996.

A Framework for Efficient Storage Security in RDBMS

Bala Iyer[1], Sharad Mehrotra[2], Einar Mykletun[2], Gene Tsudik[2], and Yonghua Wu[2]

[1] IBM Silicon Valley Lab
balaiyer@us.ibm.com
[2] University of California, Irvine, Irvine CA 92697, USA
{yonghuaw,mykletun,sharad,gts}@ics.uci.edu

Abstract. With the widespread use of e-business coupled with the public's awareness of data privacy issues and recent database security related legislations, incorporating security features into modern database products has become an increasingly important topic. Several database vendors already offer integrated solutions that provide data privacy within existing products. However, treating security and privacy issues as an afterthought often results in inefficient implementations. Some notable RDBMS storage models (such as the N-ary Storage Model) suffer from this problem. In this work, we analyze issues in storage security and discuss a number of trade-offs between security and efficiency. We then propose a new secure storage model and a key management architecture which enable efficient cryptographic operations while maintaining a very high level of security. We also assess the performance of our proposed model by experimenting with a prototype implementation based on the well-known TPC-H data set.

1 Introduction

Recently intensified concerns about security and privacy of data have prompted new legislation and fueled the development of new industry standards. These include the Gramm-Leach-Bliley Act (also known as the Financial Modernization Act) [3] that protects personal financial information, and the Health Insurance Portability and Accountability Act (HIPAA) [4] that regulates the privacy of personal health care information.

Basically, the new legislation requires anyone storing sensitive data to do so in encrypted fashion. As a result, database vendors are working towards offering security- and privacy-preserving solutions in their product offerings. Two prominent examples are Oracle [2] and IBM DB2 [5]. Despite its importance, little can be found on this topic in the research literature, with the exception of [6], [7] and [8].

Designing an effective security solution requires, among other things, understanding the points of vulnerability and the attack models. Important issues

E. Bertino et al. (Eds.): EDBT 2004, LNCS 2992, pp. 147–164, 2004.
© Springer-Verlag Berlin Heidelberg 2004

include: (1) selection of encryption function(s), (2) key management architecture, and (3) data encryption granularity. The main challenge is to introduce security functionality without incurring too much overhead, in terms of both performance and storage. The problem is further exacerbated since stored data may comprise both sensitive as well as non-sensitive components and access to the latter should not be degraded simply because the former must be protected.

In this paper, we argue that adding privacy as an afterthought results in suboptimal performance. Efficient privacy measures require fundamental changes to the underlying storage subsystem implementation. We propose such a storage model and develop appropriate key management techniques which minimize the possibility of key and data compromise. More concretely, our main contribution is a new secure DBMS storage model that facilitates efficient implementation. Our approach involves grouping sensitive data, in order to minimize the number of necessary encryption operations, thus lowering cryptographic overhead.

Model: We assume a client-server scenario. The client has a combination of sensitive and non-sensitive data stored in a database at the server, with the sensitive data stored in encrypted form. Whether or not the two parties are co-located does not make a difference in terms of security. The server's added responsibility is to protect the client's sensitive data, i.e., to ensure its confidentiality and prevent unauthorized access. (Note that maintaining availability and integrity of stored data is an entirely different requirement.) This is accomplished through the combination of encryption, authentication and access control.

Trust in Server: The level of trust in the database server can range from fully trusted to fully untrusted, with several intermediate points. In a fully untrusted model, the server is not trusted with the client's cleartext data which it stores. (It may still be trusted with data integrity and availability.) Whereas, in a fully trusted model, the server essentially acts as a remote (outsourced) database storage for its clients.

Our focus is on environments where server is partially trusted. We consider one extreme of fully trusted server neither general nor particularly challenging. The other extreme of fully untrusted server corresponds to the so-called "Database-as-a-Service" (DAS) model [9]. In this model, a client does not even trust the server with cleartext queries; hence, it involves the server performing encrypted queries over encrypted data. The DAS model is interesting in its own right and presents a number of challenges. However, it also significantly complicates query processing at both client and server sides.

1.1 Potential Vulnerabilities

Our model has two major points of vulnerability with respect to client's data:

- **Client-Server Communication:** Assuming that client and server are not co-located, it is vital to secure their communication since client queries can involve sensitive inputs and server's replies carry confidential information.

– **Stored Data:** Typically, DBMS-s protect stored data through access control mechanisms. However, as mentioned above, this is insufficient, since server's secondary storage might not be constantly trusted and, at the very least, sensitive data should be stored in encrypted form.

All client-server communication can be secured through standard means, e.g., an SSL connection, which is the current *de facto* standard for securing Internet communication. Therefore, communication security poses no real challenge and we ignore it in the remainder of this paper. With regard to the stored data security, although access control has proven to be very useful in today's databases, its goals should not be confused with those of data confidentiality. Our model assumes potentially circumvented access control measures, e.g., bulk copying of server's secondary storage. Somewhat surprisingly, there is a dearth of prior work on the subject of incorporating cryptographic techniques into databases, especially, with the emphasis on efficiency. For this reason, our goal is to come up with a database storage model that allows for efficient implementation of encryption techniques and, at the same time, protects against certain attacks described in the next section.

1.2 Security and Attack Models

In our security model, the server's memory is trusted, which means that an adversary can not gain access to data currently in memory, e.g., by performing a memory dump. Thus, we focus on protecting secondary storage which, in this model, can be compromised. In particular, we need to ensure that an adversary who can access (physically or otherwise) server's secondary storage is unable to learn anything about the actual sensitive data.

Although it seems that, mechanically, data confidentiality is fairly easy to obtain in this model, it turns out not be a trivial task. This is chiefly because incorporating encryption into existing databases (which are based on today's storage models) is difficult without significant degradation in the overall system performance.

Organization: The rest of the paper is organized as follows: section 2 overviews related work and discusses, in detail, the problem we are trying to solve. Section 3 deals with certain aspects of database encryption, currently offered solutions and their limitations. Section 4 outlines the new DBMS storage model. This section also discusses encryption of indexes and other database-related operations affected by the proposed model. Section 5 consists of experiments with our prototype implementation of the new model. The paper concludes with the summary and directions for future work in section 6.

2 Background

Incorporating encryption into databases seems to be a fairly recent development among industry database providers [2] [5], and not much research has been devoted to this subject in terms of efficient implementation models. A nice survey of techniques used by modern database providers can be found in [10].

Some recent research focused on providing database as a service (DAS) in an untrusted server model [7] [9]. Some of this work dealt with analyzing how data can be stored securely at the server so as to allow a client to execute SQL queries directly over encrypted tuples. As far as trusted server models, one approach that has been investigated involves the use of tamper resistant hardware (smart card technology) to perform encryption at the server side [8].

2.1 Problems

The incorporation of encryption within modern DBMS's has often been incomplete, as several important factors have been neglected. They are as follows:

Performance Penalty: Added security measures typically introduce significant computational overhead to the running time of general database operations. This performance penalty is due mainly to the underlying storage models. It seems difficult to find an efficient encryption scheme for current database products without modifying the way in which records are stored in blocks on disk. The effects of the performance overhead encountered by the addition of encryption has been demonstrated in [10], where a comparison is performed among queries performed on several pairs of identical data sets, one of which contains encrypted information while the other does not.

Inflexibility: Depending on the encryption granularity, it might not be feasible to separate sensitive from non-sensitive fields when encrypting. For example, if row level encryption is used and only one out of several attributes needs to be kept confidential, a considerable amount of computational overhead would be incurred due to un-necessary encryption and decryption of all other attributes. Obviously, the finer the encryption granularity, the more flexibility is gained in terms of selecting the specific attributes to encrypt. (See section 3.2 for a discussion of different levels of encryption granularity.)

Meta data files: Many vendors seem content with being able to claim the ability to offer "security" along with their database products. Some of these provide an incomplete solution by only allowing for the encryption of actual records, while ignoring meta-data and log files which can be used to reveal sensitive fields.

Unprotected Indexes: Some vendors do not permit encryption of indexes, while others allow users to build indexes based on encrypted values. The latter approach results in a loss of some of the most obvious characteristics of an index – range searches, since a typical encryption algorithm is not order-preserving. By not encrypting an index constructed upon a sensitive attribute, such as U.S. Social Security Number, record encryption becomes meaningless. (Index encryption is discussed in detail in section 4.6.)

3 Database Encryption

There are two well-known classes of encryption algorithms: *conventional* and *public-key*. Although both can be used to provide data confidentiality, their goals and performance differ widely. Conventional, (also known as symmetric-key) encryption algorithms require the encryptor and decryptor to share the same key. Such algorithms can achieve high bulk encryption speeds, as high as 100-s of Mbits/sec. However, they suffer from the problem of *secure key distribution*, i.e., the need to securely deliver the same key to all necessary entities.

Public-key cryptography solves the problem of key distribution by allowing an entity to create its own public/private key-pair. Anyone with the knowledge of an entity's public key can encrypt data for this entity, while only someone in possession of the corresponding private key can decrypt the respective data. While elegant and useful, public key cryptography typically suffers from slow encryption speeds (up to 3 orders of magnitude slower than conventional algorithms) as well as secure public key distribution and revocation issues.

To take advantage of their respective benefits and, at the same time, to avoid drawbacks, it it usual to bootstrap secure communication by having the parties use a public-key algorithm (e.g., RSA [11]) to agree upon a secret key, which is then used to secure all subsequent transmission via some efficient conventional encryption algorithm, such as AES [12].

Due to their clearly superior performance, we use symmetric-key algorithms for encryption of data stored at the server. We also note that our particular model does not warrant using public key encryption at all.

3.1 Encryption Modes and Their Side-Effects

A typical conventional encryption algorithm offers several modes of operation. They can be broadly classified as *block* or *stream* cipher modes.

Stream ciphers involve creating a key-stream based on a fixed key (and, optionally, counter, previous ciphertext, or previous plaintext) and combining it with the plaintext in some way (e.g, by xor-ing them) to obtain ciphertext. Decryption involves reversing the process: combining the key-stream with the ciphertext to obtain the original plaintext. Along with the initial encryption key, additional state information must be maintained (i.e., key-stream initialization parameters) so that the key-stream can be re-created for decryption at a later time.

Block ciphers take as input a sequence of fixed-size plaintext blocks (e.g., 128-bit blocks in AES) and output the corresponding ciphertext block sequence. It is usually necessary to pad the plaintext before encryption in order to have it align with the desired block size. This can cause certain overhead in terms of storage space, resulting in the some data *expansion*. A chained block cipher (CBC) mode is a blend of block and stream modes; in it, a sequence of input plaintext blocks is encrypted such that each ciphertext block is dependent on all preceding ciphertext blocks and, conversely, influences all subsequent ciphertext blocks.

We use a block cipher in the CBC mode. Reasons for choosing block (over stream) ciphers include the added complexity of implementing stream ciphers, specifically, avoiding re-use of key-streams. This complexity stems from the dynamic nature of the stored data: the contents of data pages may be updated frequently, requiring the use of a new key-stream. In order to remedy this problem, a certain amount of state would be needed to help create appropriate distinct key-streams whenever stored data is modified.

3.2 Encryption Granularity

Encryption can be performed at various levels of granularity. In general, finer encryption granularity affords more flexibility in allowing the server to choose what data to encrypt. This is important since stored data may include non-sensitive fields which, ideally, should not be encrypted (if for no other reason than to reduce overhead). The obvious encryption granularity choices are:

- **Attribute value:** smallest achievable granularity; each attribute value of a tuple is encrypted separately.
- **Record/row:** each row in a table is encrypted separately. This way, if only certain tuples need to be retrieved and their locations in storage are known, the entire table need not be decrypted.
- **Attribute/column:** a more selective approach whereby only certain sensitive attributes (e.g., credit card numbers) are encrypted.
- **Page/block:** this approach is geared for automating the encryption process. Whenever a page/block of sensitive data is stored on disk, the entire block is encrypted. One such block might contain one or multiple tuples, depending on the number of tuples fitting into a page (a typical page is 16 Kbytes).

As mentioned above, we need to avoid encrypting non-sensitive data. If a record contains only a few sensitive fields, it would be wasteful to use row- or page-level encryption. However, if the entire table must be encrypted, it would be advantageous to work at the page level. This is because encrypting fewer large pieces of data is always considerably more efficient than encrypting several smaller pieces. Indeed, this is supported by our experimental results in section 3.6.

3.3 Key Management

Key management is clearly a very important aspect of any secure storage model. We use a simple key management scheme based on a two-level hierarchy consisting of a single master key and multiple sub-keys. Sub-keys are associated with individual tables or pages and are used to encrypt the data therein. Generation of all keys is the responsibility of the database server. Each sub-key is encrypted under the master key. Certain precautions need to be taken in the event that the master key is (or is believed to be) compromised. In particular, re-keying strategies must be specified.

3.4 Re-keying and Re-encryption

There are two types of re-keying: periodic and emergency. The former is needed since it is generally considered good practice to periodically change data encryption keys, especially, for data stored over a long term. Folklore has it, that the benefit of periodic re-keying is to prevent potential key compromise. However, this is not the case in our setting, since an adversary can always copy the encrypted database from untrusted secondary storage and compromise keys at some (much) later point, via, e.g., a brute-force attack.

Emergency re-keying is done whenever key compromise is suspected or expected. For example, if a trusted employee (e.g., a DBA) who has access to encryption keys is about to be fired or re-assigned, the risk of this employee mis-using the keys must be considered. Consequently, to prevent potential compromise, all affected keys should be changed before (or at the time of) employee termination or re-assignment.

3.5 Key Storage

Clearly, where and how the master key is stored influences the overall security of the system. The master key needs to be in possession of the DBA, stored on a smart card or some other hardware device or token. Presumably, this device is somehow "connected" to the database server during normal operation. However, it is then possible for a DBA to abscond with the master key or somehow leak it. This should trigger emergency re-keying, whereby a new master key is created and all keys previously encrypted under the old master key are updated accordingly.

3.6 Encryption Costs

Advances in general processor and DSP design continuously yield faster encryption speeds. However, even though bulk encryption rates can be very high, there remains a constant start-up cost associated with each encryption operation. (This cost is especially noticeable when keys are changed between encryptions since many ciphers require computing a key schedule before actually performing encryption.) The start-up cost dominates overall processing time when small amounts of data are encrypted, e.g., individual records or attribute values.

Experiments: Recall our earlier claim that encrypting the same amount of data using few encryption operations with large data units is more efficient than many operations with small data units. Although this claim is quite intuitive, we still elected to run an experiment to support it. The experiment consisted of encrypting 10 Mbytes using both large and small unit sizes: blocks of 100-, 120-, and 16K-bytes. The two smaller data units represent average sizes for records in the TPC-H data set [13], while the last unit of 16-Kbytes was chosen as it is the default page size used in MySQL's InnoDB table type. We used MySQL to implement our proposed storage model; the details can be found in section 4.

Table 1. Many small vs. few large data blocks encrypted. All times in msec include initialization and encryption cost.

Encryption Alg	100 Bytes * 100,000	120 Bytes * 83,3333	16 KBytes * 625
AES	365	334	194
DES	372	354	229
Blowfish	5280	4409	170

We then performed the following operations: 100,000 encryptions of the 100-byte unit, 83,333 encryptions of the 120-byte unit, and 625 encryptions of the 16-Kbyte unit. Our hardware platform was a Linux box with a 2.8 Ghz PIV with 1-Gbyte of RAM. Cryptographic software support was derived from the well-known OpenSSL library [14]. We used the following three ciphers: DES [15], Blowfish [16], and AES [12], of which the first two operate on 8-byte data blocks, while AES uses 16-byte blocks. Measurements for encrypting 10-Mbytes, including the initialization cost associated with each invocation of the encryption algorithms, are are shown in Table 1.

As pointed out earlier, a constant start-up cost is associated with each algorithm. This cost becomes significant when invoking the cipher multiple times. Blowfish is the fastest of the three in terms of sheer encryption speed, however, it also incurs the highest start-up cost. This is clearly illustrated in the measurements of the encryption of the small data units. All algorithms display reduced encryption costs when 16-Kbyte blocks are used.

The main conclusion we draw from these results is that encrypting the same amount of data using fewer large blocks is clearly more efficient than using several smaller blocks. The cost difference is due mainly to the start-up cost associated with the initialization of the encryption algorithms. It is thus clearly advantageous to minimize the total number of encryption operations, while ensuring that input data matches up with the encryption algorithm's block size (in order to minimize padding). One obvious way is to cluster sensitive data which needs to be encrypted. This is, in fact, a feature of the new storage model described in section 4.2.

4 Partition Plaintext and Ciphertext (PPC) Model

The majority of today's database systems use the N-ary Storage Model (NSM) [17] which we now describe.

4.1 N-ary Storage Model (NSM)

NSM stores records from a database continuously starting at the beginning of each page. An offset table is used at the end of the page to locate the beginning of each record. NSM is optimized for transferring data to and from secondary storage and offers excellent performance when the query workload is highly selective

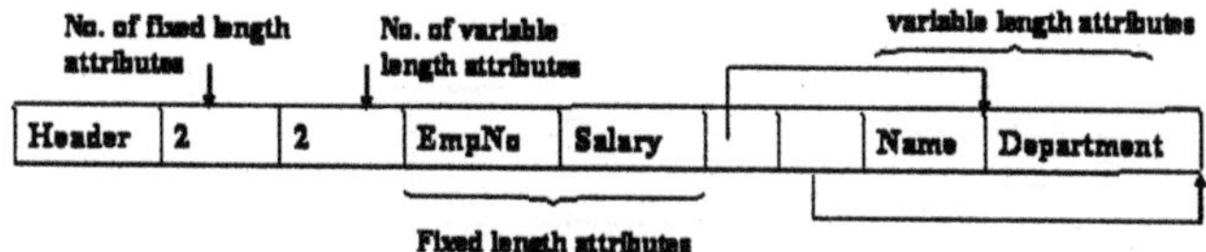

Fig. 1. NSM structure for our sample relation.

and involves most record attributes. It is also popular since it is well-suited for online transaction processing; more so than another prominent storage model, the Decomposed Storage Model (DSM) [1].

NSM and Encryption: Even though NSM has been a very successful RDBMS storage model, it is rather ill-suited for incorporating encryption. This is especially the case when a record has both sensitive and non-sensitive attributes. We will demonstrate, via an example scenario, exactly how the computation and storage overheads are severely increased when encryption is used within the NSM model. We assume a sample relation that has four attribute values: *EmpNo, Name, Department, and Salary.* Of these, only *Name* and *Salary* are sensitive and must be encrypted. Figure 1 shows the NSM record structure.

Since only two attributes are sensitive, we would encrypt at the attribute level so as to avoid unnecessary encryption of non-sensitive data (see section 3.2). Consequently, we need one encryption operation for each attribute-value.[1]

As described in section 3.1, using a symmetric-key algorithm in block cipher mode requires padding the input to match the block size. This can result in significant overhead when encrypting multiple values, each needing a certain amount of padding. For example, since AES [12] uses 16-byte input blocks, encryption of a 2-byte attribute value would require 14 bytes of padding.

To reduce thes costs outlined above, we must avoid small non-continuous sensitive plaintext values. Instead, we need to cluster them in some way, thereby reducing the number of encryption operations. Another potential benefit would be reduced amount of padding: per cluster, as opposed to per attribute value.

Optimized NSM: Since using encryption in NSM is quite costly, we suggest an obvious optimization. It involves storing all encrypted attribute values of one record sequentially (and, similarly, all plaintext values). With this optimization, a record ends up consisting of two parts: the ciphertext attributes followed by the plaintext (non-sensitive) attributes. The optimized version of NSM reduces padding overhead and eliminates multiple encryptions operations within a record. However, each record is still stored individually, meaning that, for each record, one encryption operation is needed. Moreover, each record is padded individually.

[1] If we instead encrypted at record or page level, non-sensitive attributes *EmpId* and *Department* would be also encrypted, thus requiring additional encryption operations. Even worse, for selection queries that only involve non-sensitive attributes, the cost of decrypting the data would still apply.

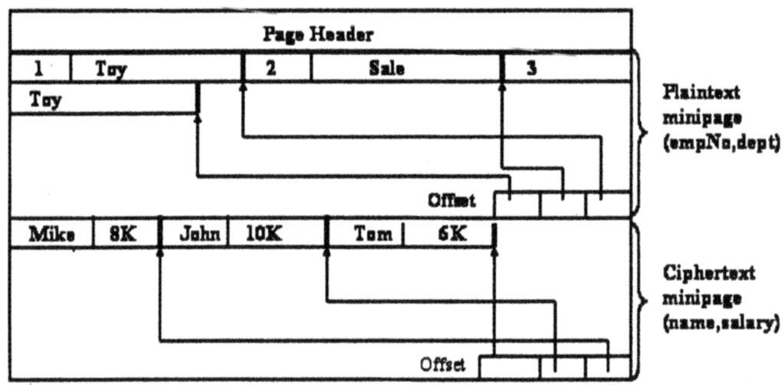

Fig. 2. Sample PPC page

4.2 Partition Plaintext Ciphertext Model (PPC)

Our approach is to cluster encrypted data while retaining NSM'a benefits. We note that, recently, Partition Attribute Across (PAX) model was proposed as an alternative to NSM. It involves partitioning a page into mini-pages to improve upon cache performance [18]. Each mini-page represents one attribute in the relation. It contains the value for this attribute of each record stored in the page. Our model, referred to as Partition Plaintext and Ciphertext (PPC), employs an idea similar to that of PAX, in that pages are split into two mini-pages, based on plaintext and ciphertext attributes, respectively. Each record is likewise split into two sub-records.

PPC Overview: The primary motivation for PPC is to reduce encryption costs, including computation and storage costs, while keeping the NSM storage schema. We thus take advantage of NSM while enabling efficient encryption. Implementing PPC on existing DBMS's that use NSM requires only a few modifications to page layout. PPC stores the same number of records on each page as does NSM.

Within a page, PPC vertically partitions a record into two sub-records, one of which contains the plaintext, while the other – ciphertext, attributes. Both sub-records are organized in the same manner as NSM records. PPC stores all plaintext sub-records in the first part of the page, which we call a *plaintext mini-page*. The second part of the page stores a *ciphertext mini-page*. Each mini-page has the same structure as a regular NSM page and records within two mini-pages are stored in the same relative order. At the end of each mini-page is an offset table pointing to the end of each sub-record. Thus, a PPC page can be viewed as two NSM mini-pages. Specifically, if a page does not contain any ciphertext, PPC layout is identical to NSM. Current database systems using NSM would only need to change the way they access pages in order to incorporate our PPC model.

Figure 2 shows an example of a PPC page. In it, three records are stored within a page. The plaintext mini-page contains non-sensitive attribute values EmpNo and Department and the ciphertext mini-page stores encrypted Name and Salary attributes. The advantage of encryption at the mini-page level can be seen by observing that only one encryption operation is needed *per page*, and, of course, only one decryption is required when the page is brought into memory and any sensitive attributes are accessed.

The PPC page header contains two mini-page pointers (in addition to the typical page header fields) which include the starting addresses for plaintext and ciphertext mini-pages.

Buffer Manager Support: When a PPC page is brought into a buffer slot, depending upon the nature of the access, the page may first need to be decrypted. The buffer manager, besides supporting a *write bit* to indicate whether a page has been modified, also needs to support an *encryption bit* to determine whether the ciphertext mini-page has already been decrypted. Initially, when the page is brought into a buffer slot, its write bit is off, and its encryption bit is on. Each read or update request to the buffer manager indicates whether a sensitive field needs to be accessed.

The buffer manager processes read requests in the obvious manner: if the encryption bit is on, it requests the mini-page to be decrypted and then resets the encryption bit. If the bit is off, the page is already in memory in plaintext form. Record insertion, deletion and update are also obvious: the write bit is set, while the encryption bit is only modified if any ciphertext has to be decrypted.

Whenever a page in the buffer is chosen by the page replacement policy to be sent to secondary storage, the buffer manager first checks if the page's encryption bit is off and the write bit is on. If so, the cipher mini-page is first re-encrypted before being stored.

4.3 Analysis and Comparisons of the PPC Model

We now compare NSM with the proposed PPC model. As will be seen below, PPC outperforms NSM irrespective of the encryption level of granularity in NSM. Two main advantages of PPC are: 1) considerably fewer encryption operations due to clustering of sensitive data, and 2) overhead for queries involving only non-sensitive attributes.

NSM with attribute-level encryption: The comparison is quite straightforward. NSM with attribute-level encryption requires as many encryption operations per record as there are sensitive attributes. Records are typically small enough such that a large number can fit into one page, resulting in a large number of encryption operations per page. As already stated, only one decryption is per page is needed in the PPC model.

NSM with record-level encryption: One encryption is required for each record in the page. PPC requires only one encryption per page.

NSM with page level encryption: one encryption per page is required in both models. The only difference is for queries involving both sensitive and non-sensitive attributes. NSM performs an encryption operation regardless of the types of attributes, whereas, PPC only encrypts as necessary.

Optimized NSM: We mentioned the optimized NSM model in section 1. It is similar to NSM with record-level encryption (each record requires one encryption). It only differs from NSM in that extra overhead is incurred for non-sensitive queries. Again, PPC requires only one encryption operation per page as opposed to one per record for the optimized NSM.

Note that, for each comparison, the mode of access is irrelevant, i.e., whether records within the page are accessed sequentially or randomly, as is the case with the DSS and OLTP workloads. For every implementation, other than NSM with page-level encryption, one still needs to access and perform an encryption operation on the record within the page, regardless of how the record is accessed.

From the above discussion, we establish that PPC has the same costs as the regular non-encrypted NSM when handling non-sensitive queries. On the other hand, when sensitive attributes are involved, PPC costs a single encryption operation. We thus conclude that *PPC is superior to all NSM variants* in terms of encryption-related computation overhead.

Although we have not yet performed a detailed comparison of storage overheads (due to padding), we claim that PPC requires the same (or less) amount of space than any NSM variant. In the most extreme case, encrypting at the attribute level requires each sensitive attribute to be padded. A block cipher operating on 128-bit blocks (e.g., AES) would, on the average, add 64 bits of padding to each encrypted unit. Only encrypting at page level would minimize padding overhead, since only a single one unit is encrypted. This is the case for both NSM with page-level encryption and PPC.

4.4 Database Operations in PPC

Basic database operations (insertion, deletion, update and scan) in PPC are implemented similar to their counterparts in NSM, since each record in PPC is stored as two sub-records conforming to the NSM structure. During insertion, a record is split into two sub-records and each is inserted into its corresponding mini-page (sensitive or non-sensitive). As described in Section 4.2, the buffer manager determines when the ciphertext mini-page needs to be en/de-crypted. Implementation of deletion and update operations is straight-forward.

When running a query, two scan operators are invoked, one for each mini-page. Each scan operator sequentially reads a sub-record in the corresponding mini-page. If the predicate associated with the scan operator refers to an encrypted attribute, the scan operator indicates in its request to the buffer manager that it will be accessing an encrypted attribute. Scans could be implemented either using sequential access to the file containing the table, or using an index. Indexing on encrypted attributes is discussed in section 4.6 below.

4.5 Schema Change

PPC stores the schema of each relation in the catalog file. Upon adding or deleting an attribute, PPC creates a new schema and assigns it a unique version ID. All schema versions are stored in the catalog file. The header in the beginning of each plaintext and ciphertext sub-record contains the schema version that it conforms to. The advantage of having schemas in both plaintext and ciphertext sub-records is that, when retrieving a sub-record, only one lookup is needed to determine the schema that a record conforms to.

Adding or deleting an attribute is handled similar to NSM, with two exceptions: (1) a previously non-sensitive attribute is changed to sensitive (i.e., it needs to be encrypted), and (2) a sensitive attribute is changed to non-sensitive, i.e., it needs to be stored as plaintext.

To handle the former, a new schema is first created and assigned a new version ID. Then, all records containing this attribute are updated according to the new schema. This operation can be executed in a lazy fashion (pages are read and translated asynchronously), or synchronously, in which case the entire table is locked and other transactions prevented from accessing the table until the reorganization is completed.

Changing an attribute's status from sensitive to non-sensitive can be deferred (for bulk decryption) or done in a lazy fashion, since it is generally not urgent to physically peform all decryption at once. For each accessed page, the schema comparison operation will indicate whether a change is necessary. At that time, the attribute will be decrypted and moved from the ciphertext to the plaintext mini-page.

4.6 Encrypted Index

Index data structures are crucial components of any database system, mainly to provide efficient range and selection queries. We need to assess potential impact of encryption on the performance of the index. Note that an index built upon a sensitive attribute must be encrypted, since it contains attribute values present in the actual relation.

There are basically two approaches to building an index based on sensitive attribute values. In the first, the index is based upon *ciphertext*, while, in the second, the intermediate index is based upon *plaintext* and the final index is obtained by encrypting the intermediate index. Based upon characteristics which make encryption efficient in PPC, we choose to encrypt at page level, thereby encrypting each node independently. Whenever a specific index is needed in the processing of a query, necessary parts of the data structure are brought into memory and decrypted. This approach provides full index functionality while keeping the index itself secure.

There are certain tradeoffs associated with either of the two approaches. Since encryption does not preserve order, the first approach is infeasible when index is used to process range queries. Note that exact-match selection queries are still possible if encryption is deterministic.[2] When searching for an attribute value, the value is simply encrypted under the same encryption key as used in the index

[2] Informally, if encryption is non-deterministic (randomized), the same cleartext encrypted twice yields two different ciphertexts. This is common practice for preventing ciphertext correlation and dictionary attacks.

before the search. The second approach, in contrast, can support range queries efficiently, albeit, with the additional overhead of decrypting index pages.

Given the above tradeoff, the first strategy appears preferable for hash-indices or B-tree indices over record identifiers and foreign keys where data access is expected to be over equality constraints (and not a range). The second strategy is better when creating B-trees where access may include range queries. Since the second strategy incurs additional encryption overhead, we discuss its performance in further detail.

When utilizing a B-tree index, we can assume that plaintext representation of the root node already resides in memory. With a tree of depth two, we only need to perform two I/O operations for a selection: one each for the node at level 1 and 2, and, correspondingly, two decryption operations. As described in section 3.6, we measure encryption overhead in the number of encryption operations. Since one decryption is needed for each accessed node, the total overhead is the number of accessed nodes multiplied by the start-up cost of the underlying encryption algorithm.

5 Experiments

We created a prototype implementation of the PPC model based on MySQL version 4.1.0-alpha. This version provides all the necessary DBMS components. We modified the InnoDB storage model, by altering its page and record structure to create plaintext and ciphertext mini-pages. We utilized the OpenSSL cryptographic library as the basis for our encryption-related code. For the actual measurements we used the Blowfish encryption algorithm. The experiments were conducted on a 1.8 Ghz PIV machine with 384MB of RAM running Windows XP.

5.1 PPC Details

Each page in InnoDB is, by default, 16KB. Depending on the number of encrypted attributes to be stored, we split the existing pages into two parts to accommodate the respective plaintext and ciphertext mini-pages. Partitioning of one record into plaintext and ciphertext sub-records only takes place when the record is written to its designated page. InnoDB record manager was modified to partition records and store them in their corresponding mini-pages.

If a record must be read from disk during a query execution, it is first accessed by InnoDB which converts it to MySQL record format. We modified this conversion in the record manager to determine whether the ciphertext part of the record is needed in the current query. If so, the respective ciphertext mini-page is first decrypted before the ciphertext and plaintext sub-records are combined into a regular MySQL record. The ciphertext mini-page is re-encrypted if and when it is written back to disk.

5.2 Overview of Experiments

For each experiment, we compared running times between *NSM with no encryption* (NSM), *NSM with page level encryption* (NSM-page), and *PPC* (PPC). Our goal was to verify that PPC would outperform NSM-page and, when no sensitive values are involved in a query, would perform similar to NSM. Lastly, when all attributes involved are encrypted, we expect PPC and NSM-page to perform roughly equally.

As claimed earlier, PPC handles mixed queries[3] very well. To support this, we created a schema where at least one attribute from each table – and more than one in larger tables (2 attributes in *lineitem* and 3 in *orders*) – was encrypted. Specifically, we encrypted the following attributes: *l_partkey, l_shipmode, p_name, s_acctbal, ps_supplycost, c_name, o_orderdate, o_custkey, o_totalprice, n_name, and r_name.*

We ran three experiments, all based on the TPC-H data set. First, we measured the loading time during bulk insertion of a 100-, 200-, and 500-MB database. Our second experiment consisted of running TPC-H query number 1, which is based only on the *lineitem* table, while varying the number of encrypted attributes involved in the query, in order to analyze PPC performance. Finally, we compared query response time of a sub-set of TPC-H queries, attempting to identify and highlight the properties of the PPC scheme.

5.3 Bulk Insertion

We compared bulk insertion loading time required for a 100-, 200-, and 500-MB TPC-H database for each of the three models. The schema described in section 5.2 was used to define the attributes to be encrypted in PPC. On the average, NSM-page and PPC incur a 24% and 15% overhead, respectively, in loading time as compared to plain NSM. As expected, PPC outperforms NSM-page since less data is encrypted (not all attributes are considered sensitive).

We note that a more accurate PPC implementation would perform some page reorganization if the relations contained variable length attributes, in order to make best use of space in the mini-pages. As stated in [18], the PAX model suffers a 2-10% performance penalty due to page reorganization, depending on the desired degree of space utilization in each mini-page. However, the PAX model creates as many mini-pages as there are records, while we always create only two.

5.4 Varying Number of Encrypted Attributes

In this experiment, we ran queries within a single table to analyze PPC performance while increasing the number of encrypted attributes. Query 1, which only involves table *lineitem*, was chosen for this purpose, and executed over a 200MB database. It contains 16 attributes, 7 of which are involved in the query. We then

[3] Queries involving both sensitive and non-sensitive attributes.

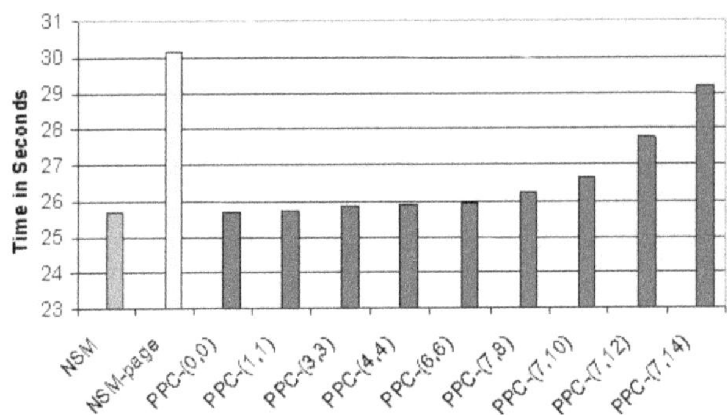

Fig. 3. Varying the number of encrypted attributes in TPC-H Query 1. PPC-(x, y) indicates that y attributes in lineitem were encrypted with x of them appearing in the query

computed the running time for NSM and NSM-page, both of which remained constant as the number of encrypted attributes varied. Eight different instances of PPC were run: the first having no encrypted attributes and the last having 14 (we did not encrypt the attributes used as primary keys). Figure 3 illustrates our results.

The results clearly show that the overhead incurred when encrypting additional attributes in PPC is rather minimal. As expected, PPC with no (or only a few) encrypted attributes exhibits performance almost identical to that of NSM. Also, as more attributes are encrypted, PPC performance begins to resemble that of NSM-page. Two last instances of PPC have relatively longer query execution times. This is due to encryption of the *lineitem* variables *l_shipinstruct and l_comment*, which are considerably larger than any other in the table.

5.5 TPC-H Queries

Recall that PPC and NSM-page each require only one encryption operation per page. However, NSM-page executes this operation whether or not there are encrypted attributes in the query. In the following experiment, we attempted to exploit the advantages of PPC, by comparing its performance with NSM-page when executing a chosen subset of TPC-H queries on a 200MB database. As in the bulk insertion experiment, we utilized a pre-defined schema (see section 5.2) to determine the attributes to encrypt when using PPC.

In figure 4, we refer to individual queries to highlight some of the interesting observations from the experiment. Queries 1 and 6 are range queries and, according to our PPC schema, have no sensitive attributes involved. The running time of NSM and PPC are, as expected, almost identical. However, since the *tables* involved contain encrypted attributes, NSM-page suffers from over-encryption and consequently has to decrypt records involved in the query, thereby adding to its running time. Due to the simplicity of these queries, the NSM-page encryption overhead is relatively small.

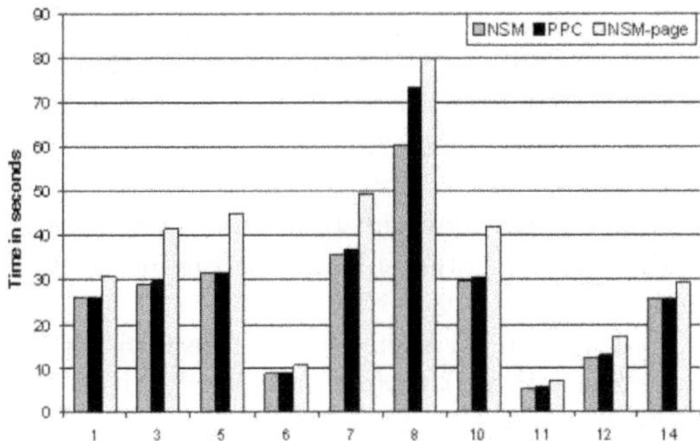

Fig. 4. Comparison of running times from selected TPC-H queries over a 200 MB database for NSM, PPC, and NSM-page.

Query 8 involved encrypted attributes from each of the three largest tables (*lineitem, partsupp, orders*), causing both PPC and NSM-page to incur relatively significant encryption-caused overhead. Again, PPC outperforms NSM-page since it has to decrypt less data. In contrast, query 10 involves encrypted attributes from four tables, only one of which is large (table *orders*). In this case, PPC performs well as compared to NSM-page, as the latter needs to decrypt *lineitem* in addition to other tables involved.

Overall, based on 10 queries shown in figure 4, PPC and NSM-page incur 6% and 33% overhead, respectively, in query response time. We feel that this experiment illustrated PPC's superior performance for queries involving both sensitive and non-sensitive attributes.

6 Conclusion

In this paper, we proposed a new DBMS storage model (PPC) that facilitates efficient incorporation of encryption. Our approach is based on grouping sensitive data in order to minimize the number of encryption operations, thus, greatly reducing encryption overhead. We compared and contrasted PPC with NSM and discussed a number of important issues regarding storage, access and query processing. Our experiments clearly illustrate advantages of the proposed PPC model.

References

1. Copeland, G. P., Khoshafian, S. F.: A Decomposition Storage Model. ACM SIGMOD International Conference on Management of Data. (1985) 268-269
2. Oracle Corporation: Database Encryption in Oracle9i. url=otn.oracle.com/deploy/security/oracle9i. (2001)
3. Department of Health and Human Services (U.S.). Gramm-Leach-Bliley (GLB) Act. FIPS PUB 81. url=www.ftc.gov/bcp/conline/pubs/buspubs/glbshort.htm. (1999)

4. Federal Trade Commission (U.S.): Health Insurance Portability and Accountability Act (HIPAA). url=www.hhs.gov/ocr/hipaa/privacy.html. (1996)
5. IBM Data Encryption for IMS and DB2 Databases, Version 1.1. url= http://www-306.ibm.com/software/data/db2imstools/html/ibmdataencryp.html. (2003)
6. He, J., Wang, M.: Cryptography and Relational Database Management Systems. Proceedings of the 5th International Database Engineering and Applications Symposium. (2001) 273-284
7. Hacigümüş, H., Iyer, B., Li, C., Mehrotra, S.: Executing SQL over Encrypted Data in the Database Service Provider Model. ACM SIGMOD Conference on Management of Data (2002)
8. Bouganim, L., Pucheral, P.: Chip-Secured Data Access: Confidential Data on Untrusted Servers. VLDB Conference, Hong Kong, China. (2002)
9. Hacigümüş, H., Iyer, B., Mehrotra, S.: Providing Database as a Service. ICDE. (2002)
10. Karlsson, J. S.: Using Encryption for Secure Data Storage in Mobile Database Systems. Friedrich-Schiller-Universitat Jena. (2002)
11. Rivest, R. L., Shamir, A., Adleman, L. M.: A Method for Obtaining Digital Signatures and Public-Key Cryptosystems. Communications of the ACM. vol. 21, (1978)
12. NIST. Advanced Encryption Standard. FIPS PUB 197. (2001)
13. TPC Transaction Processing Performance Council. url=http://www.tpc.org
14. OpenSSL Project. url=http://www.openssl.org
15. NIST. Data Encryption Standard (DES). FIPS 46-3. (1993)
16. Schneier, B.: Description of a New Variable-Length Key, 64-Bit Block Cipher (Blowfish). Fast software Encryption, Cambridge Security Workshop Proceedings. (1993) 191-204
17. Ramakrishnan, R., Gehrke, J.: Database Management Systems, 2nd Edition, WCB/McGraw-Hill. (2000)
18. Ailamaki, A., DeWitt, D. J., Hill, M. D., Skounakis, M.: Weaving Relations for Cache Performance. The VLDB Journal. (2001) 169-180

Beyond 1-Safety and 2-Safety for Replicated Databases: Group-Safety

Matthias Wiesmann and André Schiper

École Polytechnique Fédérale de Lausanne (EPFL)
CH-1015 Lausanne
{Matthias.Wiesmann,Andre.Schiper}@epfl.ch

Abstract. In this paper, we study the safety guarantees of group communication-based database replication techniques. We show that there is a model mismatch between group communication and database, and because of this, classical group communication systems cannot be used to build 2-safe database replication. We propose a new group communication primitive called *end-to-end atomic broadcast* that solves the problem, i.e., can be used to implement 2-safe database replication. We also introduce a new safety criterion, called *group-safety*, that has advantages both over 1-safety and 2-safety. Experimental results show the gain of efficiency of group-safety over lazy replication, which ensures only 1-safety.

1 Introduction

Database systems represent an important aspect of any IT infrastructure and as such require high availability. Software-based database replication is an interesting option because it promises increased availability at low cost. Traditional database replication is usually presented as a trade-off between performance and consistency [1], i.e., between eager and lazy replication. Eager replication, based on an atomic commitment protocol, is slow and deadlock prone. Lazy replication, which foregoes the atomic commitment protocol, can introduce inconsistencies, even in the absence of failures.

However, eager replication does not need to be based on atomic commitment. A different approach, which relies on group communication primitives to abstract the network functionality, has been proposed in [2,3], These techniques typically use an atomic broadcast primitive (also called total order broadcast) to deliver and order transactions in the same serial order on all replicas, and offer an answer to many problems of eager replication without the drawbacks of lazy replication: they offer good performance [4], use the network more efficiently [5] and also reduce the number of deadlocks [6].

Conceptually, group communication-based data replication systems are built by combining two modules: (1) a database module, which handles transactions and (2) a group communication module, which handles communication. When combined, these two module result in a replicated database. However, the two modules assume different failure models, which means that the failure semantics of the resulting system are unclear.

In this paper, we examine the fault tolerance guarantees offered by database replication techniques based on group communication. The model mismatch between group communication and database systems comes from the fact that they originate from two

E. Bertino et al. (Eds.): EDBT 2004, LNCS 2992, pp. 165–182, 2004.
© Springer-Verlag Berlin Heidelberg 2004

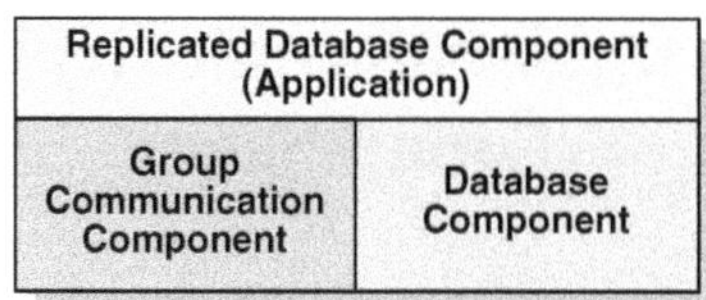

Fig. 1. Architecture

different communities. We explore this mismatch from two point of views: from the database point of view, and from the distributed system point of view. Database replication is usually specified with the *1-safety* and *2-safety* criteria. The first offers good performance, the second strong safety. However, group communication as currently specified, cannot be used to implement 2-safe database replication. The paper shows how this can be corrected. Moreover, we show that the 1-safety and 2-safety criteria can advantageously be replaced by a new safety criterion, which we call *group-safety*. Group safety ensures ensures that the databases say consistent as long as the number of server crashes are bounded. While this notion is natural for group communication, it is not for replicated databases. Simulation result show that group-safe database replication leads to improved performance over 1-safety, while at the same time offering stronger guarantees.

The rest of the paper is structured as follows. Section 2 presents the model for the database system and for group communication, and explains the use of group communication (more specifically atomic broadcast) for database replication. Section 3 shows that this solution, based on current specification of atomic broadcast, cannot be 2-safe. Section 4 proposes a new specification for atomic broadcast, in order to achieve 2-safety. Section 5 defines the new safety criterion called *group-safety*. Section 6 compares the efficiency of group-safe replication and 1-safe replication by simulation. Section 7 discusses the relationship between group-safe replication and lazy replication. Finally Sect. 8 presents related work and Sect. 9 concludes the paper.

2 Model and Definitions

We assume that the overall system is built from three components (Fig. 1): the database component, the group communication component and the replicated database component. The first two components offer the infrastructure needed to build the application – in our case a replicated database. These two infrastructure components are accessed by the application, but they have no direct interaction with each other.

The replicated database component implements the actual replicated database and is described in Sect. 2.1. The database component contains all the facilities to store the data and execute transactions locally, and is described in Sect. 2.2. The group communication component offers broadcast primitives, in particular atomic broadcast, and is described in Sect. 2.3).

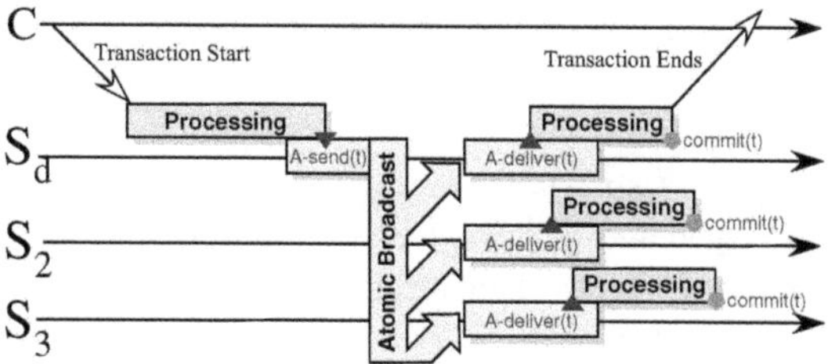

Fig. 2. Non-Voting replication

2.1 Database Replication Component

The database replication component is modelled as follows. We assume a set of servers $S_1, \ldots, S_n$, and a fully replicated database $D = \{D_1 \ldots D_n\}$, where each server S_i holds a copy D_i of the database. Since group communication does not make much sense with a replication degree of 2, we consider that $n \geq 3$. We assume update-everywhere replication [1]: clients can submit transactions to any server S_i. Clients wanting to execute transaction t send it to one server S_d that will act as the *delegate* for this transaction: S_d is responsible for executing the transaction and sending back the results to the client.[1] The correctness criterion for the replicated database is one-copy serialisability: the system appears to the outside world as one single non-replicated database.

Replication Scheme. A detailed discussion of the different database replication techniques appears in [7]. Among these techniques, we consider those that use group communication, e.g., atomic broadcast (see Sect. 2.3). As a representative, we consider the technique called *update-everywhere, non-voting, single network interaction*. Fig. 2 illustrates this technique.[2] The technique is called *non-voting* because there is no voting phase in the protocol to ensure that all servers commit or abort the transaction: this property is ensured by the atomic broadcast group communication primitive.

The processing of transaction t is done in the following way. The client C sends the transaction to the delegate server S_d. The delegate processes the transaction, and, if it contains some write operations, broadcasts the transaction to all servers using an atomic broadcast. All servers apply the writes according to delivery order of the atomic broadcast. Conflicts are detected deterministically and so, if a transaction needs to be aborted, it is aborted on all servers. Techniques that fit in this category are described in [8,9,10,4,11].

Safety Criteria for Replicated Databases. There are three safety criteria for replicated database, called *1-safe*, *2-safe* and *very safe* [12]. When a client receives a message

[1] The role of the delegate is conceptually the same than the primary server, simply any server can acts as a "primary".

[2] However, the results in this paper apply as well to the other techniques in [7] based on group communication.

indicating that his transaction committed, it means different things depending on the safety criterion.

1-safe: If the technique is *1-safe*, when the client receives the notification of t's commit, then t has been logged and will eventually commit on the delegate server of t.

2-safe: If the technique is *2-safe*, when the client receives the notification of t's commit, then t is guaranteed to have been logged on *all available* servers, and thus will eventually commit on all available servers.

Very safe: If the technique is *very safe*, when the client receives the notification of t's commit, then t is guaranteed to have been logged on *all* servers, and thus will eventually commit on all servers.

Each safety criterion shows a different tradeoff between safety and availability: the more safe a system, the less available it is. *1-safe* replication ensures that transactions can be accepted and committed even if only one server is available: synchronisation between copies is done outside of the scope of the transaction's execution. So a transaction can commit on the delegate server even if all other servers are unavailable. On the other hand, *1-safe* replication schemes can lose transactions in case of a crash. A *very safe* system ensures that a transaction is committed on all servers, but this means that a single crash renders the system unavailable. This last criterion is not very practical and most systems are therefore 1-safe or 2-safe.

The distinction between *1-safe* and *2-safe* replication is important. If the technique is *1-safe*, transactions might get lost if one server crashes and another takes over, i.e., the durability part of the ACID properties is not ensured. If the technique is *2-safe*, no transaction can get lost, even if all servers crash.

2.2 Database Component

We assume a database component on each node of the system. Each database component hosts a full copy of the database. The database component executes local transactions and enforces the ACID properties (in particular serialisability) locally.

We also assume that the local database component offers all the facilities and guarantees needed by the database replication technique (see [7]), and has a mechanism to detect and handle transactions that are submitted multiple times, e.g., *testable transactions* [13].

2.3 Group Communication Component

Each server S_i hosts one *process* p_i, which implements the group communication component. While the database model is quite well established and agreed upon, there is a large variety of group communication models [14]. Considering the context of the paper, we mention two of them. The first model is the *dynamic crash no-recovery* model, which is assumed by most group communication implementations. The other model is the *static crash-recovery* model, which has been described in the literature, but has seen little use in actual group communication infrastructure.

Dynamic crash no-recovery model. The dynamic crash no-recovery model has been introduced in the Isis system [15], and is also sometimes called the *view based model*. In this model, the group is *dynamic*: processes can join and leave after the beginning of the computation. This is handled by a list, which contains the processes that are member of the group. The list is called the *view* of the group. The history of the group is represented as a sequence of views $v_0, \ldots v_m$, a new view being installed each time a process leaves or joins the group.

In this model, processes that crash do not recover. This does not prevent crashed processes from recovering. However, a process that recovers after a crash has to take a new identity before being able the rejoin the group. When a crashed process recovers in a new incarnation, it requests a view change to join the group again. During this view change, a *state transfer* occurs: the group communication system requests that one of the current members of the view makes a checkpoint, and this checkpoint is transferred to the joining process. Most current group-communication toolkits [15,16,17,18,19,20] are based on this model or models that are similar.

Dynamic crash no-recovery group communication systems cannot tolerate the crash of *all* the members of a view. Depending on synchrony assumptions, if a view contains n processes, then at best $n - 1$ crashes can be tolerated.

Static crash recovery model. In the static crash recovery model, the group is *static*, i.e., no process can join the group after system initialisation. In this model, processes have access to stable storage, which allows them to save (part of) their state. So, crashed processes can recover, keep the same identity, and continue their computation. Most database system implement their atomic commitment protocol in this model.

While this model might seem natural, handling of recovery complicates the implementation. For this reason, in the context of group communication, this model has mostly been considered in papers [21,22]. Practical issues, like application recovery, are not well defined in this model (in [23] the recovery is log based). Because of the access to stable storage, static crash recovery group communication systems can tolerate the simultaneous crash of *all* the processes [21].

Process classes. In one system model, processes do not recover after a crash. In the other model, processes may recover after a crash, and possibly crash again, etc. Altogether this leads us to consider three classes of processes: (1) *green* processes, which never crash, (2) *yellow* processes, which might crash one or many times, but eventually stay forever up, and (3) *red* processes, which either crash forever, or are unstable (they crash and recover indefinitely). Figure 3 illustrates those three classes, along with the corresponding classes described by Aguilera *et al.* [21]. Our terminology, with the distinction between *green* and *yellow* processes, fits better the needs of this paper. In the dynamic crash no-recovery model processes are either green or red. In the static crash recovery model, processes may also be yellow.

Atomic Broadcast. We consider that the group communication component offers an atomic broadcast primitive. Informally, atomic broadcast ensures that messages are delivered in the same order by all destination processes. Formally, atomic broadcast is

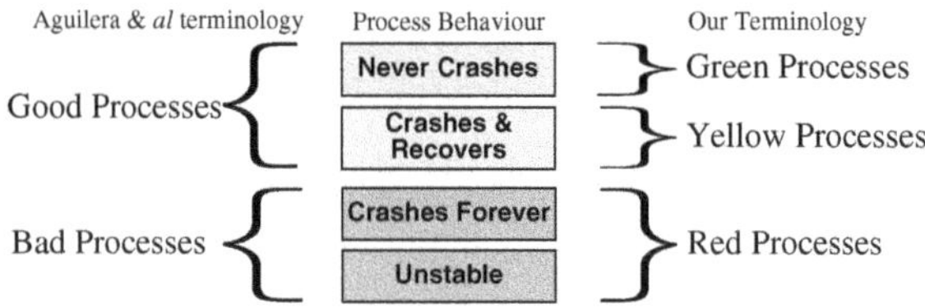

Fig. 3. Process Classes

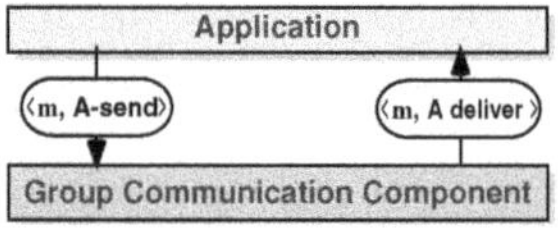

Fig. 4. Message exchange for atomic broadcast

defined by two primitives A-broadcast and A-deliver that satisfy the following properties:

Validity: If a process A-delivers m, then m was A-broadcast by some process.
Uniform Agreement: If a process A-delivers a message m, then all non-red processes eventually A-deliver m.
Uniform Integrity: For every message m, every process A-delivers m at most once.
Uniform Total Order: If two process p and q A-deliver two messages m and m', then p delivers m before m' if and only if q delivers m before m'.

In the following, we assume a system model where the atomic broadcast problem can be solved, e.g., the asynchronous system model with failure detectors [24,21], or the synchronous system model [25].

2.4 Inter-component Communications

Inter-component communication, and more specifically communication between the group communication component and the application component, is usually done using function calls. This leads to problems in case of a crash, since a message might have been delivered by the group communication component, but the application might not have processed it. To address this issue, we express the communication between the group communication layer and the application layer as *messages* (Fig. 4). When the application executes A-send(m) (A stands for Atomic Broadcast), it sends the message $\langle m, \text{A-send}\rangle$ to the group communication layer. To deliver message m to the application (i.e execute A-deliver(m)), the group communication component sends the message $\langle m, \text{A-deliver}\rangle$ to the application.

So, we model the inter-component (intra-process) communication in the same way as inter-process communication. The main difference is that all components reside in the same process, and therefore fail together. This inter-layer communication is reliable (no message loss), except in case of a crash.

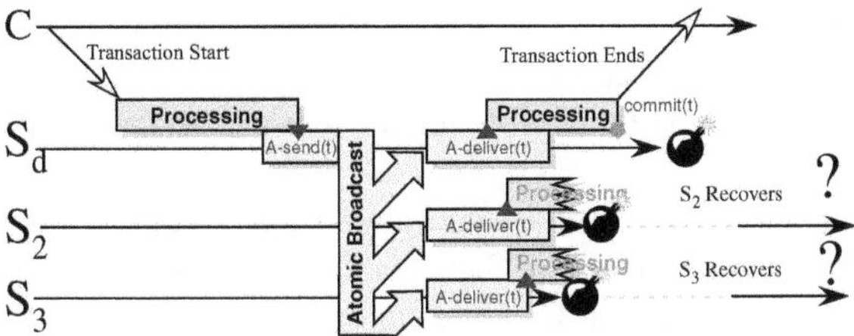

Fig. 5. Unrecoverable failure scenario

3 Group Communication-Based Database Replication Is Not 2-Safe

In this section, we show that traditional group communication systems cannot be used to implement 2-safe replication. There are two reasons for this. The first problem that arises when trying to build a 2-safe system is the number of crashes the system can tolerate. The 2-safety criterion imposes no bounds on the number of servers that may crash, but the dynamic crash no-recovery model does not tolerate the crash of all servers. This issue can be addressed by relying on the static crash recovery model.

The second problem is not linked to the model, but related to message delivery and recovery procedures. The core problem lies in the fact that the delivery of a message does not ensure the processing of that message [26]. Ignoring this fact can lead to incorrect recovery protocols [27]. Note that this second problem exists in all group communication toolkits, which rely on the state transfer mechanism for recovery regardless of the model they are implemented in.

To illustrate this problem, consider the scenario illustrated in Fig. 5. Transaction t is submitted on the delegate server S_d. When t terminates, S_d sends a message m containing t to all replicas. The message m is sent using an atomic broadcast. The delegate S_d delivers m, the local database component locally logs and commits t and confirms the commit to the client: transaction t is committed in the database component of S_d. Then S_d crashes. All other replicas (S_2 and S_3) deliver m, i.e., the group communication components of S_1, S_2 and S_3 have done their job. Finally S_2 and S_3 crash (before committing t), and later recover (before S_d).

The system cannot rebuild a consistent state that includes t's changes. Servers S_2 and S_3 recover to the state of the database D that does not include the execution of t. Message m that contained t is not kept in any group communication component (it was delivered everywhere) and t was neither committed nor logged on servers S_2 and S_3: the technique is not 2-safe.

In this replication scheme, when a client is notified of the commit of transaction t, the only guarantee is that t was committed by the delegate S_d. The use of group communication does not ensure that t *will* commit on the other servers, but merely that the message m containing t will be *delivered* on all servers in the view. If those servers crash after the time of m's delivery and before t is actually committed or logged to disk, then transaction t is lost. In the scenario of Fig. 5, if the recovery is based on the *state transfer mechanism* (Sect. 2.3), there is no available server that has a state containing t's changes. If recovery is log-based (Sect. 2.3), the group communication system cannot deliver again message m without violating the uniform integrity property (m cannot be delivered twice).

The problem lies in the lack of end-to-end guarantees of group communication systems described by Cheriton and Skeen [28] and is related to the fact that message delivery is not an atomic event. Group communication systems enforce guarantees on the delivery of messages to the application, but offer no guarantees with respect to the application level: 2-safety is an application level guarantee.

4 Group Communication with End-to-End Guarantees for 2-Safe Replication

We have shown in the previous section that it is impossible to implement a 2-safe database replication technique using a group communication toolkit that offers a traditional atomic broadcast. In order to build a 2-safe replication technique, we need to address the end-to-end issue.

4.1 Ad-hoc Solution

One way to solve the problem would be to add more messages to the protocol: for instance each server could send a message signalling that t was effectively logged and will eventually commit. The delegate S_d would confirm the commit to the client after receiving those messages. This approach has been proposed by Keidar *et al.* for implementing a group communication toolkit on top of another group communication toolkit [29]. While such an approach would work it has two drawbacks. First the technique would have a higher latency because of the additional waiting: synchronisation between replicas is expensive [5]. But most importantly, this approach ruins the modularity of the architecture. The point of using a group communication system is to have all complex network protocols implemented by the group communication component and not to clutter the application with communication issues. If additional distributed protocols are implemented in an ad-hoc fashion inside the application, they risk being less efficient (some functionality of the group communication will be duplicated inside the application, in this case, acknowledgement messages), and less reliable (distributed system protocols tend to be complex; when implemented in an ad-hoc fashion, they might be incorrect).

4.2 End-to-End Atomic Broadcast

The problem of lost transactions appears when a crash occurs between the time a message is delivered and the time it is processed by the application. When a message is delivered to the application and the application is able to process the message, we say that the delivery of the message is *successful*. However, we cannot realistically prevent servers from crashing during the time interval between delivery and successful delivery. In the event of a crash, messages that were not successfully delivered must be delivered again: we have to make sure that all messages are eventually delivered successfully.

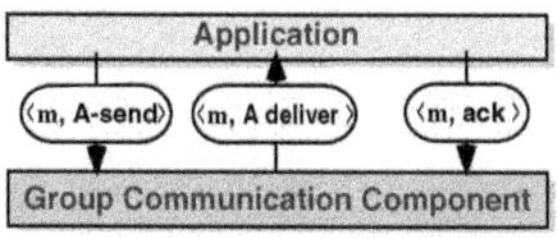

Fig. 6. Messages exchange for with successful delivery

With current group communication primitives, there is no provision for specifying successful delivery. For this reason, we introduce a new inter-component message that acknowledges the end of processing of m (i.e., successful delivery of m). We denote this message $ack(m)$. The mechanism is similar to acknowledgement messages used in inter-process communications. Figure 6 shows the exchange of messages for an atomic broadcast. First, the application sends message m, represented by the inter-component message $\langle m, \textsf{A-send}\rangle$ to the group communication system. When the group communication components is about to deliver m, it sends the inter-component message $\langle m, \textsf{A-deliver}\rangle$. Once the application has processed message m, it sends the inter-component message $\langle m, \textsf{ack}\rangle$ to signal that m is *successfully delivered.*

If a crash occurs, and the group communication component did not receive the message $\langle m, \textsf{ack}\rangle$, then $\langle m, \textsf{deliver}\rangle$ should be sent again to the application upon recovery. This requires the group communication component to log messages and to use log-based recovery (instead of checkpoint-based recovery). So after each crash, the group communication component "replays" all messages m such that $\langle m, \textsf{ack}\rangle$ was not received from the application. By replaying messages, the group communication component ensures that, if the process is eventually forever up, i.e., non-red, then all messages will eventually be successfully delivered.

We call the new primitive *end-to-end atomic broadcast.* The specification of end-to-end atomic broadcast is similar to the specification of atomic broadcast in Sect. 2.3, except for (1) a new end-to-end property, and (2) a refined uniform integrity property: a message m might be delivered multiple times, but can only be delivered *successfully once*. A message m is said to be *successful delivered* when $ack(m)$ is received. The new properties are the following:

End-to-End: If a non-red process A-delivers a message m, then it eventually *successfully* A-delivers m.

Uniform Integrity: For every message m, every process *successfully* A-delivers m at most once.

We assume a well-behaved application, that is, when the application receives message $\langle m, \textsf{A-deliver}\rangle$ from the group communication component, it sends $\langle m, \textsf{ack}\rangle$ as soon as possible.

4.3 2-Safe Database Replication Using End-to-End Atomic Broadcast

2-safe database replication can be built using end-to-end atomic broadcast. The replication technique uses the end-to-end atomic broadcast instead of the "classical" atomic

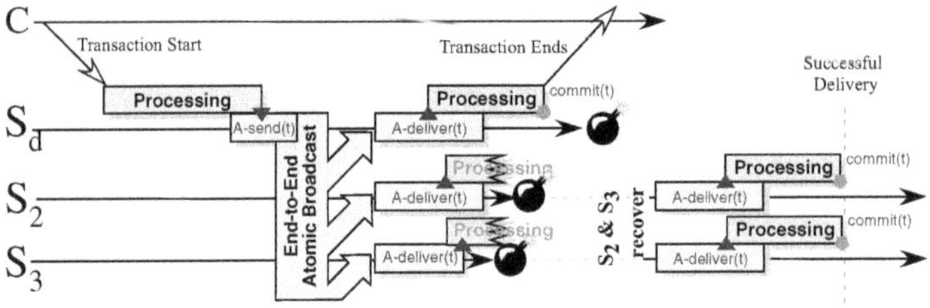

Fig. 7. Recovery with end-to-end atomic broadcast

broadcast. The only difference is that the replication technique must signal successful delivery, i.e., generate $ack(m)$. This happens when the transaction t contained in m is logged and is therefore guaranteed to commit. According to the specification of the end-to-end atomic broadcast primitive, every non-red process eventually successfully delivers m. The *testable transaction* abstraction described in Sect. 2.2 ensures that a transaction is commited at most once. So every process that is not permanently crashed or unstable eventually commits t exactly once: the technique is 2-safe.

Figure 7 shows the scenario of Fig. 5 using end-to-end atomic broadcast. After the recovery of servers S_2 and S_3, message m is delivered again. This time, S_2 and S_3 do not crash, the delivery of m is successful and t is committed on all available servers.

5 A New Safety Criterion: Group-Safety

We have shown in Sect. 3 that the techniques of Sect. 1 based on traditional group communication are not 2-safe. They are only 1-safe: when the client is notified of t's commit, t did commit on the delegate server. As shown in Sect. 4, 2-safety can be obtained by extending group communication with end-to-end guarantees. However, group communication without end-to-end guarantees, even though it does not ensure 2-safety, provides an additional guarantee that is orthogonal to 1-safety and 2-safety. We call this guarantee *group-safety*.

5.1 Group Safety

A replication technique is *group-safe* if, when a client receives confirmation of a transaction's commit, the message that contains the transaction is guaranteed to be *delivered* (but not necessarily processed) on all available servers. In contrast, 2-safety guarantees that the transaction will be *processed* (i.e., logged) on all available servers. Group-safety relies on the group of servers to ensure durability, whereas 2-safety relies on stable storage. With group-safety, if the group does not fail, i.e., enough servers remain up then durability is ensured (the number of servers depends on the system model and the algorithm used, typically a majority of the servers must stay up). Notice that group safety does not guarantee that the transaction was logged or committed on any replica. A client might be notified of the termination of some transaction t before t was actually logged on any replica.

Table 1. Summary of different safety levels

Transaction Delivered \ Transaction Logged	No Replica	1 Replica	All Replica
1 Replica	**No Safety** (0-Safe)	**1-Safe**	
All Replica	**Group-Safe**	**Group-Safe & 1-Safe** (Group-1-Safe)	**2-Safe**

The relationship between group-safety, 1-safety and 2-safety is summarised in Table 1. We use two criteria: (1) the number of servers that are guaranteed to *deliver* the (message containing the) transaction (vertical axis), and (2) the number of servers that are guaranteed to eventually *commit* the transaction (horizontal axis), that is the number of servers that have logged the transaction. We distinguish a transaction *delivered* on (*one, all*) replicas, and a transaction *logged* on (*none, one, all*) replicas. A transaction cannot be logged on a site before being delivered, so the corresponding entry in the table is grayed out. For each remaining entry in the table the corresponding safety level is indicated:

No Safety: The client is notified as soon as the transaction t is delivered on one server S_d (t did not yet commit). No safety is enforced. If S_d crashes before t's writes are flushed to stable storage, then t is lost. We call this *0-safe* replication.

1-Safe: With *1-safety*, the client is notified when transaction t is delivered and logged on one server only, the delegate server S_d. If S_d crashes, then t might get lost. Indeed, while S_d is down, the system might commit new transactions that conflict with t: t must be discarded when S_d recovers. The only alternative would be to block all new transactions while S_d is down [30].

Group-Safe: The client is notified when a transaction is guaranteed to be delivered on all available servers (but might not be logged on any servers). If the group fails because too many servers crash, then t might be lost. Group-safe replication basically allows all disk writes to be done asynchronously (outside of the scope of the transaction) thus enabling optimisations like write caching. Typically, disk writes would not be done immediately, but periodically. Writes of adjacent pages would also be scheduled together to maximise disk throughput.

Group-Safe & 1-Safe: The client is notified when transaction t is guaranteed to be delivered on all servers *and* was logged on one server, the delegate S_d and thus will eventually commit on S_d. Since the system is both group-safe and 1-safe, we call this safety level *group-1-safety*. With group-1-safety, the transaction might be lost if too many servers, **including** S_d, crash. A transaction loss occurs either if S_d never recovers, or the system accepts conflicting transactions while S_d is crashed [30]. Most proposed database replication strategies based on group communication fall in this category [31,10,32,33,34].

Table 2. Safety property and number of crashes

Tolerated Number of Crashes	Safety Property
0 crashes	0-safe, 1-safe
less than n crashes	group-safe, group-1-safe
n crashes	2-safe

Table 3. Safety of comparison between group safety and group-1-safety

	Group does not fail	Group fails S_d does not crash	Group fails S_d crashes
Group Safe	No Transaction Loss	Possible Transaction Loss	Possible Transaction Loss
Group 1-Safe	No Transaction Loss	No Transaction Loss	Possible Transaction Loss

2-Safe: The client is notified when a transaction is logged on all available servers. Even if all servers crash, the transaction will eventually commit and therefore cannot get lost.

If we consider the number of crashes that can be tolerated, we have basically three safety levels (Table 2): a) 0-safe and 1-safe replication cannot tolerate any crash, i.e., one single crash can lead to loose a transaction, b) Group-safe replication cannot tolerate the crash of all n servers, c) 2-safe replication can tolerate the crash of all n servers.

5.2 Group Safety Is Preferable to Group-1-Safety

Group-safe as well as group-1-safe replication techniques cannot tolerate the crash of all servers. So, what is the real difference between both criteria? Table 3 summarises the conditions that lead to the loss of the transaction, using two criteria: (1) failure of the group (typically failure of a majority of servers) and (2) crash of the delegate server S_d. The difference appears in the middle column (failure of the group, but not of S_d).

Group communication-based replication scheme are specially interesting in update-everywhere settings where the strong properties of atomic broadcast are used to handle concurrent transactions. If the replication is update-everywhere, then all servers $S_1 \dots S_n$ might be the delegate server for some transaction.[3] If the group fails, at least one server crashed, and this server might be the delegate server S_d for some transaction t. In this case, the middle column of Table 3 does not exist. In such settings it makes little sense to deploy a group-1-safe replication technique. It must be noted that switching between group-1-safe and group-safe can be done easily at runtime: an actual implementation might choose to switch between both modes depending on the situation.

The replication technique illustrated in Fig. 2 ensures group-1-safety. It can be transformed into group-safe-only quite easily. Figure 8 illustrates the group-safe version of the same technique. Read operations are typically done only on the delegate server S_d

[3] This is not the case with the *primary-copy* technique.

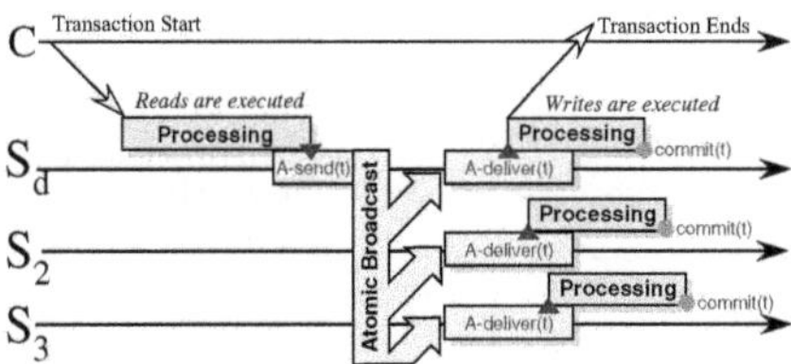

Fig. 8. Group Safe Replication

Table 4. Simulator parameters

Parameter	Value
Number of items in the database	10'000
Number of Servers	9
Number of Clients per Server	4
Disks per Server	2
CPUs per Server	2
Transaction Length	10 – 20 Operations
Probability that an operation is a write	50%
Probability that an operation is a query	50%
Buffer hit ratio	20%
Time for a read	4 - 12 *ms*
Time for a write	4 - 12 *ms*
CPU Time used for an I/O operation	0.4 *ms*
Time for a message or a broadcast on the Network	0.07 *ms*
CPU time for a network operation	0.07 *ms*

before the broadcasting, writes are executed once the transactions is delivered by the atomic broadcast. The main difference with Fig. 2 is the response to the client, which is sent back as soon as the transactions is delivered by the atomic broadcast and the decision to commit/abort the transaction is known. The observed response time by the client is shortened by the time needed to write the decision to disk. The performance gain is shown by the simulation results presented in Sect. 6.

6 Performance Evaluation

In this section we compare the performance of group-safety, group-1-safety and 1-safety (i.e., lazy replication). The evaluation is done using a replicated database simulator [5]. The group communication-based technique is the database state machine technique [10], which is an instance of the replication technique illustrated on Fig. 2 (for group-1-safety) and Fig. 8 (for group-safety). The setting of the simulator are described in Table 4. The load of the system is between 20 and 40 transactions per second; the network settings correspond to a 100 Mb/s LAN. All three techniques used the same logging setting, so they share the same throughput limits.

Figure 9 shows the results of this experiment. The X axis represents the load of the system in transactions per second, the Y axis the response time, in milliseconds.

Each replication technique is represented by one curve. The results show that group-safe replication has very good performance: it even outperforms lazy replication when

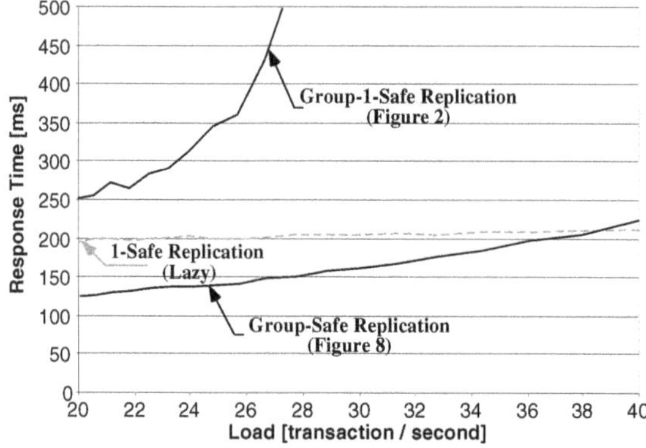

Fig. 9. Simulation results

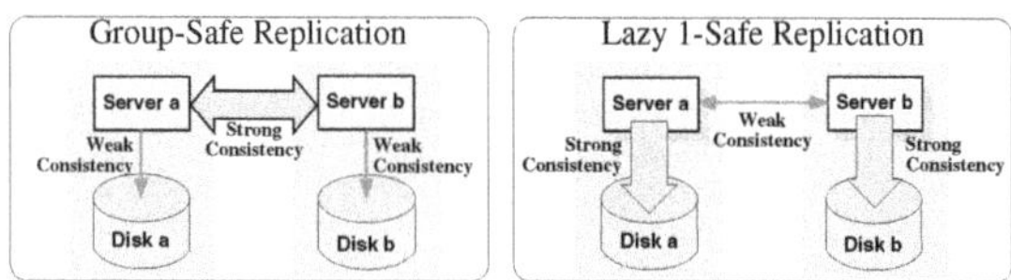

Fig. 10. group-safe replication and lazy replication

the load is below 38 transactions per second. The abort rate of the group-safe technique was constant, slightly below 7%. As the lazy technique does no conflict handling, abort rate is unknown. The very good performance of the group safe technique is due to the asynchrony of the writes (the writes to disk are done outside the scope of the transaction).

In high-load situations, group-safe replication becomes less efficient than lazy replication. The results show also that group-1-safe replication behaves significantly worse than group-safe replication: the technique scales poorly when the load increases.

To summarise, the results show that transferring the responsibility of durability from stable storage to the group is a good idea in a LAN: in our setting, writing to disk takes around 8 *ms*, while performing an atomic broadcast takes approximately 1 *ms*.

7 Group-Safe Replication *vs.* Lazy Replication

On a conceptual level, group-safe replication can be seen as a complement to lazy replication. Both approaches try to get better performance by weakening the link between some parts of the system. Figure 10 illustrates this relationship. Group-safe replication relaxes the link between server and stable storage: when a transaction t commits, the state in memory and in stable storage might be different (t's writes are not committed to disk, they are done asynchronously).

Lazy replication relaxes the link between replicas: when a transaction commits, the state in the different replicas might be different (some replicas have not seen transaction t; t's writes are sent asynchronously). The two approaches relax the synchrony that is deemed too expensive.

The main difference is the condition that leads to a violation of the ACID properties. In an update-everywhere setting, a lazy technique can violate the ACID properties even if no failure occurs. On the other hand, a group-safe replication will only violate this ACID properties if the group fails (too many servers crash). Group-safe replication has another advantage over lazy replication. With lazy replication in an update-everywhere setting, if the number of servers grow, the chances that two transaction originating from two different sites conflict grows. So the chances that the ACID properties are violated grows with the number of servers.

With group-safe replication the ACID properties might get violated if too many servers crash. If we assume that the probability of the crash of a server is independent of the number of servers, the chance of violating the ACID properties decreases when the number of servers increases. So, the chances that something *bad* happens increases with n for lazy replication, and decreases with group-safe replication.

8 Related Work

As already mentionned, traditional database replication is usually either (i) 2-safe and built around an atomic commitment protocol like 2PC, or (ii) does not rely on atomic commitment and is therefore 1-safe [12]. As the the atomic commitment protocol is implemented inside the database system, coupling between database and communication systems is not an issue. Techniques to improve atomic commitment using group communication have also been proposed [35,36,37].

The fact that 2-safety does not require atomic commitment has been hinted at in [38]. The paper explores the relationship between safety levels and the semantics of communication protocols. However, the distinction between 2-safety and the safety properties ensured by traditional group communication does not appear explicitely in [38].

While the notion of group safety is formally defined here, existing database replication protocols have in the past relied on this property, e.g., [39,27]. The trade-off between 2-safety and group-safety has never been presented before.

The COReL toolkit [29] is a group communication toolkit that is built on top of another group communication toolkit. The COReL toolkit has to cope with the absence of end-to-end guarantees of the underlying toolkit. This issue is addressed by logging incoming messages and sending explicit acknowledgement messages on the network. However, an application built on top of COReL will not get end-to-end guarantees.

The issue of end-to-end properties for application are mentioned in [40]. While the proposed solution solves the problem of partitions and partition healing, the issue of synchronisation between application and group communication toolkit is not discussed. In general, partitionable group membership systems solve some issues raised in this paper: failure of the group communication because of crashes and partitions [41]. Yet, the issue of application recovery after a crash is not handled.

The Disk Paxos[22] algorithm can also be loosely related to 2-safety, even though the paper does not address database replication issues. The paper presents an original way, using stable storage, to couple the application component with a component solving an agreement problem. However, the paper assumes a network attached storage, which is quite different from the model considered here, where each network node only has direct access to its own database.

The issue of connecting the group communication component and the database component can also be related to the *exactly once* property in three-tier applications [13]. In our case, group communication system and database system can be seen as two tiers co-located on the same machine that communicate using messages.

9 Conclusion

In this paper, we have shown that traditional group communication primitives are not suited for building 2-safe database replication techniques. This led us to introduce *end-to-end atomic broadcast* to solve the problem. We have also shown that, while traditional group communication (without end-to-end guarantees) are not suited for 2-safe replication, they offer stronger guarantees than 1-safety. To formalise this, we have introduced a new safety criterion, called *group-safety* that captures the safety guarantees of group communication-based replication techniques. While this safety criterion is natural in distributed systems, it is less in the replicated database context. Performance evaluation show that group-safe replication compares favourably to lazy replication, while providing better guarantees in terms of the ACID properties.

References

1. Gray, J.N., Helland, P., O'Neil, P., Shasha, D.: The dangers of replication and a solution. In: Proceedings of the 1996 International Conference on Management of Data, Montreal, Canada, ACM-SIGMOD (1996) 173–182
2. Schiper, A., Raynal, M.: From group communication to transactions in distributed systems. Communications of the ACM **39** (1996) 84–87
3. Agrawal, D., Alonso, G., El Abbadi, A., Stanoi, I.: Exploiting atomic broadcast in replicated databases. Technical report, Department of Computer Science, University of California, Santa Barbara, California USA (1996)
4. Kemme, B., Alonso, G.: Don't be lazy, be consistent: Postgres-R, a new way to implement database replication. In: Proceedings of the 26th International Conference on Very Large Databases (VLDB), Cairo, Egypt (2000)
5. Wiesmann, M.: Group Communications and Database Replication: Techniques, Issues and Performance. PhD thesis, École Polytechnique Fédérale de Lausanne, Switzerland (2002)
6. Holliday, J., Agrawal, D., Abbadi, A.E.: Using multicast communication to reduce deadlocks in replicated databases. In: Proceedings of the 19th Symposium on Reliable Distributed Systems SRDS'2000, Nürnberg, Germany, IEEE Computer Society, Los Alamitos, California (2000) 196–205
7. Wiesmann, M., Pedone, F., Schiper, A., Kemme, B., Alonso, G.: Database replication techniques: a three parameter classification. In: Proceedings of 19th Symposium on Reliable Distributed Systems (SRDS'2000), Nürnberg, Germany, IEEE Computer Society (2000) 206–215

8. Keidar, I.: A highly available paradigm for consistent object replication. Master's thesis, The Hebrew University of Jerusalem, Jerusalem, Israel (1994) also technical report CS94.
9. Stanoi, I., Agrawal, D., Abbadi, A.E.: Using broadcast primitives in replicated databases (abstract). In: Proceedings of the 16th Annual Symposium on Principles of Distributed Computing, Santa Barbara, California USA, ACM (1997) 283
10. Pedone, F., Guerraoui, R., Schiper, A.: The database state machine approach. Technical Report SSC/1999/008, École Polytechnique Fédérale de Lausanne, Switzerland (1999)
11. Amir, Y., Tutu, C.: From total order to database replication. Technical Report CNDS-2001-6, Departement of Computer Science John Hopkins University, Baltimore, MD 21218 USA (2001)
12. Gray, J.N., Reuter, A.: Transaction Processing: concepts and techniques. Data Management Systems. Morgan Kaufmann Publishers, Inc., San Mateo (CA), USA (1993)
13. Frølund, S., Guerraoui, R.: Implementing e-transactions with asynchronous replication. IEEE Transactions on Parallel and Distributed Systems **12** (2001)
14. Gärtner, F.C.: A gentle introduction to failure detectors and related problems. Technical Report TUD-BS-2001-01, Darmstadt University of Technology, Department of Computer Science (2001)
15. Birman, K.P., Joseph, T.A.: Exploiting virtual synchrony in distributed systems. In: Proceedings of the 11th ACM Symposium on OS Principles, Austin, TX, USA, ACM SIGOPS, ACM (1987) 123–138
16. Malloth, C.P., Felber, P., Schiper, A., Wilhelm, U.: Phoenix: A toolkit for building fault-tolerant distributed applications in large scale. In: Workshop on Parallel and Distributed Platforms in Industrial Products, San Antonio, Texas, USA, IEEE (1995) Workshop held during the 7th Symposium on Parallel and Distributed Processing, (SPDP-7).
17. van Renesse, R., Birman, K.P., Maffeis, S.: Horus: A flexible group communication system. Communications of the ACM **39** (1996) 76–83
18. Hiltunen, M.A., Schlichting, R.D.: The cactus approach to building configurable middleware services. In: Proceedings of the Workshop on Dependable System Middleware and Group Communication (DSMGC 2000), Nürnberg, Germany (2000)
19. Birman, K., Constable, R., Hayden, M., Kreitz, C., Rodeh, O., van Renesse, R., Vogels, W.: The Horus and Ensemble projects: Accomplishments and limitations. In: Proceedings of the DARPA Information Survivability Conference & Exposition (DISCEX '00), Hilton Head, South Carolina USA (2000)
20. Miranda, H., Pinto, A., Rodrigues, L.: Appia: A flexible protocol kernel supporting multiple coordinated channels. In: Proceedings of the 21st International Conference on Distributed Computing Systems (ICDCS-01), Phoenix, Arizona, USA, IEEE Computer Society (2001) 707–710
21. Aguilera, M.K., Chen, W., Toueg, S.: Failure detection and consensus in the crash recovery model. Distributed Computing **13** (2000) 99–125
22. Gafni, E., Lamport, L.: Disk paxos. Technical Report SRC 163, Compaq Systems Research Center, 130, Lytton Avenue Palo Alto, California 94301 USA (2000)
23. Rodrigues, L., Raynal, M.: Atomic broadcast in asynchronous crash-recovery distributed systems. In: Proceedings of the 20th International Conference on Distributed Systems (ICDCS'2000), Taipei, Taiwan (ROC), IEEE Computer Society, Los Alamitos USA (2000) 288–295
24. Chandra, T.D., Toueg, S.: Unreliable failure detectors for reliable distributed systems. Communications of the ACM **43** (1996) 225–267
25. Lynch, N.: Distributed Algorithms. Morgan Kaufmann, San Francisco, CS (1996)
26. Saltzer, J.H., Reed, D.P., Clark, D.D.: End-to-end arguments in system design. ACM Transactions on Computer Systems **2** (1984) 277–288

27. Holliday, J.: Replicated database recovery using multicast communications. In: Proceedings of the Symposium on Network Computing and Applications (NCA'01), Cambridge, MA, USA, IEEE (2001) 104–107
28. Cheriton, D.R., Skeen, D.: Understanding the limitations of causally and totally ordered communication. In Liskov, B., ed.: Proceedings of the 14th Symposium on Operating Systems Principles. Volume 27., Asheville, North Carolina, ACM Press, New York, NY, USA (1993) 44–57
29. Keidar, I., Dolev, D.: Totally ordered broadcast in the face of network partitions. In Avresky, D., ed.: Dependable Network Computing. Kluwer Academic Publications (2000)
30. Davidson, S.B., Garcia-Molina, H., Skeen, D.: Consistency in partitioned networks. ACM Computing Surveys **17** (1985) 341–370
31. Fu, A.W., Cheung, D.W.: A transaction replication scheme for a replicated database with node autonomy. In: Proceedings of the International Conference on Very Large Databases, Santiago, Chile (1994)
32. Kemme, B., Alonso, G.: A suite of database replication protocols based on group communication primitives. In: Proceedings of the 18th International Conference on Distributed Computing Systems (ICDCS'98), Amsterdam, The Netherlands (1998)
33. Kemme, B., Pedone, F., Alonso, G., Schiper, A.: Processing transactions over optimistic atomic broadcast protocols. In: Proceedings of the International Conference on Distributed Computing Systems, Austin, Texas (1999)
34. Holliday, J., Agrawal, D., Abbadi, A.E.: The performance of database replication with group multicast. In: Proceedings of International Symposium on Fault Tolerant Computing (FTCS29), IEEE Computer Society (1999) 158–165
35. Babao§lu, Ö., Toueg, S.: Understanding non-blocking atomic commitement. Technical Report UBLCS-93-2, Laboratory for Computer Science, University of Bologna, 5 Piazza di Porta S. Donato, 40127 Bologna (Italy) (1993)
36. Keidar, I., Dolev, D.: Increasing the resilience of distributed and replicated database systems. Journal of Computer and System Sciences (JCSS) **57** (1998) 309–224
37. Jiménez-Paris, R., Patiño-Martínez, M., Alonso, G., Arévalo, S.: A low latency non-blocking commit server. In Welch, J., ed.: Proceeedings of the 15th Internationnal Conference on Distributed Computing (DISC 2001). Volume 2180 of lecture notes on computer science., Lisbon, Portugal, Springer Verlag (2001) 93–107
38. Wiesmann, M., Pedone, F., Schiper, A., Kemme, B., Alonso, G.: Understanding replication in databases and distributed systems. In: Proceedings of 20th International Conference on Distributed Computing Systems (ICDCS'2000), Taipei, Taiwan, R.O.C., IEEE Computer Society (2000)
39. Kemme, B., Bartoli, A., Babao§lu, Ö.: Online reconfiguration in replicated databases based on group communication. In: Proceedings of the Internationnal Conference on Dependable Systems and Networks (DSN2001), Göteborg, Sweden (2001)
40. Amir, Y.: Replication using group communication over a partitioned network. PhD thesis, Hebrew University of Jerusalem, Israel (1995)
41. Ezhilchelvan, P.D., Shrivastava, S.K.: Enhancing replica management services to cope with group failures. In Krakowiak, S., Shrivastava, S.K., eds.: Advances in Distributed Systems, Advanced Distributed Computing: From Algorithms to Systems. Volume 1752 of Lecture Notes in Computer Science. Springer (1999) 79–103

A Condensation Approach to Privacy Preserving Data Mining

Charu C. Aggarwal and Philip S. Yu

IBM T. J. Watson Research Center, 19 Skyline Drive,
Hawthorne, NY 10532
{charu,psyu}@us.ibm.com

Abstract. In recent years, privacy preserving data mining has become an important problem because of the large amount of personal data which is tracked by many business applications. In many cases, users are unwilling to provide personal information unless the privacy of sensitive information is guaranteed. In this paper, we propose a new framework for privacy preserving data mining of multi-dimensional data. Previous work for privacy preserving data mining uses a perturbation approach which reconstructs data distributions in order to perform the mining. Such an approach treats each dimension independently and therefore ignores the correlations between the different dimensions. In addition, it requires the development of a new distribution based algorithm for each data mining problem, since it does not use the multi-dimensional records, but uses aggregate distributions of the data as input. This leads to a fundamental re-design of data mining algorithms. In this paper, we will develop a new and flexible approach for privacy preserving data mining which does not require new problem-specific algorithms, since it maps the original data set into a new anonymized data set. This anonymized data closely matches the characteristics of the original data including the correlations among the different dimensions. We present empirical results illustrating the effectiveness of the method.

1 Introduction

Privacy preserving data mining has become an important problem in recent years, because of the large amount of consumer data tracked by automated systems on the internet. The proliferation of electronic commerce on the world wide web has resulted in the storage of large amounts of transactional and personal information about users. In addition, advances in hardware technology have also made it feasible to track information about individuals from transactions in everyday life. For example, a simple transaction such as using the credit card results in automated storage of information about user buying behavior. In many cases, users are not willing to supply such personal data unless its privacy is guaranteed. Therefore, in order to ensure effective data collection, it is important to design methods which can mine the data with a guarantee of privacy. This has resulted to a considerable amount of focus on privacy preserving data collection and mining methods in recent years [1], [2], [3], [4], [6], [8], [9], [12], [13].

E. Bertino et al. (Eds.): EDBT 2004, LNCS 2992, pp. 183–199, 2004.
© Springer-Verlag Berlin Heidelberg 2004

A perturbation based approach to privacy preserving data mining was pioneered in [1]. This technique relies on two facts:

- Users are not equally protective of all values in the records. Thus, users may be willing to provide modified values of certain fields by the use of a (publically known) perturbing random distribution. This modified value may be generated using custom code or a browser plug in.
- Data Mining Problems do not necessarily require the individual records, but only distributions. Since the perturbing distribution is known, it can be used to reconstruct *aggregate* distributions. This aggregate information may be used for the purpose of data mining algorithms. An example of a classification algorithm which uses such aggregate information is discussed in [1].

Specifically, let us consider a set of n original data values $x_1 \ldots x_n$. These are modelled in [1] as n independent values drawn from the data distribution X. In order to create the perturbation, we generate n independent values $y_1 \ldots y_n$, each with the same distribution as the random variable Y. Thus, the perturbed values of the data are given by $x_1 + y_1, \ldots x_n + y_n$. Given these values, and the (publically known) density distribution f_Y for Y, techniques have been proposed in [1] in order to estimate the distribution f_X for X. An iterative algorithm has been proposed in the same work in order to estimate the data distribution f_X. A convergence result was proved in [2] for a refinement of this algorithm. In addition, the paper in [2] provides a framework for effective quantification of the effectiveness of a (perturbation-based) privacy preserving data mining approach.

We note that the perturbation approach results in some amount of information loss. The greater the level of perturbation, the less likely it is that we will be able to estimate the data distributions effectively. On the other hand, larger perturbations also lead to a greater amount of privacy. Thus, there is a natural trade-off between greater accuracy and loss of privacy.

Another interesting method for privacy preserving data mining is the k-anonymity model [18]. In the k-anonymity model, domain generalization hierarchies are used in order to transform and replace each record value with a corresponding generalized value. We note that the choice of the best generalization hierarchy and strategy in the k-anonymity model is highly specific to a particular application, and is in fact dependent upon the user or domain expert. In many applications and data sets, it may be difficult to obtain such precise domain specific feedback. On the other hand, the perturbation technique [1] does not require the use of such information. Thus, the perturbation model has a number of advantages over the k-anonymity model because of its independence from domain specific considerations.

The perturbation approach works under the strong requirement that the data set forming server is not allowed to learn or recover precise records. This strong restriction naturally also leads to some weaknesses. Since the former method does not reconstruct the original data values but only distributions, new algorithms need to be developed which use these reconstructed distributions in order to perform mining of the underlying data. This means that for each individual data problem such as classification, clustering, or association rule mining, a new *distribution based* data mining algorithm needs to be developed. For example, the work in [1] develops a new distribution based data mining algorithm for the classification problem, whereas the techniques in [9], and [16] develop methods for privacy preserving association rule mining. While some clever approaches have been developed for distribution based mining of data for particular problems such as association rules and classification, it is clear that using distributions instead of original records greatly restricts the range of algorithmic techniques that can be used on the data. Aside from the additional inaccuracies resulting from the perturbation itself, this restriction can itself lead to a reduction of the level of effectiveness with which different data mining techniques can be applied.

In the perturbation approach, the distribution of each data dimension is reconstructed[1] independently. This means that any distribution based data mining algorithm works under an implicit assumption of treating each dimension independently. In many cases, a lot of relevant information for data mining algorithms such as classification is hidden in the inter-attribute correlations [14]. For example, the classification technique in [1] uses a distribution-based analogue of a single-attribute split algorithm. However, other techniques such as multi-variate decision tree algorithms [14] cannot be accordingly modified to work with the perturbation approach. This is because of the independent treatment of the different attributes by the perturbation approach. This means that distribution based data mining algorithms have an inherent disadvantage of loss of implicit information available in multi-dimensional records. It is not easy to extend the technique in [1] to reconstruct multi-variate distributions, because the amount of data required to estimate multi-dimensional distributions (even without randomization) increases exponentially[2] with data dimensionality [17]. This is often not feasible in many practical problems because of the large number of dimensions in the data.

The perturbation approach also does not provide a clear understanding of the level of indistinguishability of different records. For example, for a given level of perturbation, how do we know the level to which it distinguishes the different records effectively? While the k-anonymity model provides such guarantees, it requires the use of domain generalization hierarchies, which are a constraint on their effective use over arbitrary data sets. As in the k-anonymity model, we use an approach in which a record cannot be distinguished from at least k other records in the data. The approach discussed in this paper requires the comparison of a current set of records with the current set of summary statistics. Thus, it requires a relaxation of the strong assumption of [1] that the data set

[1] Both the local and global reconstruction methods treat each dimension independently.

[2] A limited level of multi-variate randomization and reconstruction is possible in sparse categorical data sets such as the market basket problem [9]. However, this specialized form of randomization cannot be effectively applied to a generic non-sparse data sets because of the theoretical considerations discussed.

forming server is not allowed to learn or recover records. However, only aggregate statistics are *stored* or *used* during the data mining process at the server end.

A record is said to be *k-indistinguishable*, when there are at least k other records in the data from which it cannot be distinguished. The approach in this paper re-generates the anonymized records from the data using the above considerations. The approach can be applied to either static data sets, or more dynamic data sets in which data points are added incrementally. Our method has two advantages over the k-anonymity model:
(1) It does not require the use of domain generalization hierarchies as in the k-anonymity model.
(2) It can be effectively used in situations with dynamic data updates such as the data stream problem. This is not the case for the work in [18], which essentially assumes that the entire data set is available apriori.

This paper is organized as follows. In the next section, we will introduce the locality sensitive condensation approach. We will first discuss the simple case in which an entire data set is available for application of the privacy preserving approach. This approach will be extended to incrementally updated data sets in section 3. The empirical results are discussed in section 4. Finally, section 5 contains the conclusions and summary.

2 The Condensation Approach

In this section, we will discuss a condensation approach for data mining. This approach uses a methodology which condenses the data into multiple groups of pre-defined size. For each group, a certain level of statistical information about different records is maintained. This statistical information suffices to preserve statistical information about the mean and correlations across the different dimensions. Within a group, it is not possible to distinguish different records from one another. Each group has a certain minimum size k, which is referred to as the *indistinguishability level* of that privacy preserving approach. The greater the indistinguishability level, the greater the amount of privacy. At the same time, a greater amount of information is lost because of the condensation of a larger number of records into a single statistical group entity.

Each group of records is referred to as a condensed unit. Let $\mathcal{G}$ be a condensed group containing the records $\{\overline{X_1} \dots \overline{X_k}\}$. Let us also assume that each record $\overline{X_i}$ contains the d dimensions which are denoted by $(x_i^1 \dots x_i^d)$. The following information is maintained about each group of records $\mathcal{S}$:

- For each attribute j, we maintain the sum of corresponding values. The corresponding value is given by $\sum_{i=1}^{k} x_i^j$. We denote the corresponding first-order sums by $Fs_j(\mathcal{G})$. The vector of first order sums is denoted by $\overline{Fs(\mathcal{G})}$.
- For each pair of attributes i and j, we maintain the sum of the product of corresponding attribute values. This sum is equal to $\sum_{t=1}^{k} x_t^i \cdot x_t^j$. We denote the corresponding second order sums by $Sc_{ij}(\mathcal{G})$. The vector of second order sums is denoted by $\overline{Sc(\mathcal{G})}$.

– We maintain the total number of records k in that group. This number is denoted by $n(\mathcal{G})$.

We make the following simple observations:
Observation 1: *The mean value of attribute j in group $\mathcal{G}$ is given by $Fs_j(\mathcal{G})/n(\mathcal{G})$.*
Observation 2: *The covariance between attributes i and j in group $\mathcal{G}$ is given by $Sc_{ij}(\mathcal{G})/n(\mathcal{G}) - Fs_i(\mathcal{G}) \cdot Fs_j(\mathcal{G})/n(\mathcal{G})^2$.*

The method of group construction is different depending upon whether an entire database of records is available or whether the data records arrive in an incremental fashion. We will discuss two approaches for construction of class statistics:

– When the entire data set is available and individual subgroups need to be created from it.
– When the data records need to be added incrementally to the individual subgroups.

The algorithm for creation of subgroups from the entire data set is a straightforward iterative approach. In each iteration, a record $\overline{X}$ is sampled from the database $\mathcal{D}$. The closest $(k-1)$ records to this individual record $\overline{X}$ are added to this group. Let us denote this group by $\mathcal{G}$. The statistics of the k records in $\mathcal{G}$ are computed. Next, the k records in $\mathcal{G}$ are deleted from the database $\mathcal{D}$, and the process is repeated iteratively, until the database $\mathcal{D}$ is empty. We note that at the end of the process, it is possible that between 1 and $(k-1)$ records may remain. These records can be added to their nearest sub-group in the data. Thus, a small number of groups in the data may contain larger than k data points. The overall algorithm for the procedure of condensed group creation is denoted by *CreateCondensedGroups*, and is illustrated in Figure 1. We assume that the final set of group statistics are denoted by $\mathcal{H}$. This set contains the aggregate vector $(\overline{Sc(\mathcal{G})}, \overline{Fs(\mathcal{G})}, n(\mathcal{G}))$ for each condensed group $\mathcal{G}$.

2.1 Anonymized-Data Construction from Condensation Groups

We note that the condensation groups represent statistical information about the data in each group. This statistical information can be used to create *anonymized data* which has similar statistical characteristics to the original data set. This is achieved by using the following method:

– A $d * d$ co-variance matrix $C(\mathcal{G})$ is constructed for each group $\mathcal{G}$. The ijth entry of the co-variance matrix is the co-variance between the attributes i and j of the set of records in $\mathcal{G}$.
– The eigenvectors of this co-variance matrix are determined. These eigenvectors are determined by decomposing the matrix $C(\mathcal{G})$ in the following form:

$$C(\mathcal{G}) = P(\mathcal{G}) \cdot \Delta(\mathcal{G}) \cdot P(\mathcal{G})^T \tag{1}$$

```
Algorithm CreateCondensedGroups(Indistinguish. Lvl.: k,
            Database: D);
begin
  while D contains at least k points do
  begin
    Randomly sample a data point X from D;
    G = {X};
    Find the closest (k − 1) records to X and add to G;
    for each attribute j compute statistics Fs_j(G);
    for each pair of attributes i, j compute Sc_ij(G);
    Set n(G) = k;
    Add the corresponding statistics of group G to H;
    D = D − G;
  end;
  Assign each remaining point in D to the closest group
  and update the corresponding group statistics;
  end
  return(H);
end
```

Fig. 1. Creation of Condensed Groups from the Data

> The columns of $P(\mathcal{G})$ represent the eigenvectors of the covariance matrix $C(\mathcal{G})$. The diagonal entries $\lambda_1(\mathcal{G}) \ldots \lambda_d(\mathcal{G})$ of $\Delta(\mathcal{G})$ represent the corresponding eigenvalues. Since the matrix is positive semi-definite, the corresponding eigenvectors form an ortho-normal axis system. This ortho-normal axis-system represents the directions along which the second order correlations are removed. In other words, if the data were represented using this ortho-normal axis system, then the covariance matrix would be the diagonal matrix corresponding to $\Delta(\mathcal{G})$. Thus, the diagonal entries of $\Delta(\mathcal{G})$ represent the variances along the individual dimensions. We can assume without loss of generality that the eigenvalues $\lambda_1(\mathcal{G}) \ldots \lambda_d(\mathcal{G})$ are ordered in decreasing magnitude. The corresponding eigenvectors are denoted by $e_1(\mathcal{G}) \ldots e_d(\mathcal{G})$.

We note that the eigenvectors together with the eigenvalues provide us with an idea of the distribution and the co-variances of the data. In order to re-construct the anonymized data for each group, we assume that the data within each group is independently and uniformly distributed along each eigenvector with a variance equal to the corresponding eigenvalue. The statistical independence along each eigenvector is an extended approximation of the second-order statistical independence inherent in the eigenvector representation. This is a reasonable approximation when only a small spatial locality is used. Within a small spatial locality, we may assume that the data is uniformly distributed without substantial loss of accuracy. The smaller the size of the locality, the better the accuracy of this approximation. The size of the spatial locality reduces when a larger number of groups is used. Therefore, the use of a large number of groups leads to a better overall approximation in each spatial locality. On the other hand, the use of a larger number of groups also reduced the *number* of points in each group. While the use of a smaller spatial locality improves the accuracy of the approximation, the use of a smaller number of *points* affects the accuracy in the opposite direction. This is an interesting trade-off which will be explored in greater detail in the empirical section.

2.2 Locality Sensitivity of Condensation Process

We note that the error of the simplifying assumption increases when a given group does not truly represent a small spatial locality. Since the group sizes are essentially fixed, the level of the corresponding inaccuracy increases in sparse regions. This is a reasonable expectation, since outlier points are inherently more difficult to mask from the point of view of privacy preservation. It is also important to understand that the locality sensitivity of the condensation approach arises from the use of a fixed group size as opposed to the use of a fixed group radius. This is because fixing the group size fixes the privacy (indistinguishability) level over the entire data set. At the same time, the level of information loss from the simplifying assumptions depends upon the characteristics of the corresponding data locality.

3 Maintenance of Condensed Groups in a Dynamic Setting

In the previous section, we discussed a static setting in which the entire data set was available at one time. In this section, we will discuss a dynamic setting in which the records are added to the groups one at a time. In such a case, it is a more complex problem to effectively maintain the group sizes. Therefore, we make a relaxation of the requirement that each group should contain k data

Algorithm *DynamicGroupMaintenance(Database: $\mathcal{D}$,*
IncrementalStream: $\mathcal{S}$, DistinguishabilityFactor: k)
begin
$\mathcal{H}$ = *CreateCondensedGroups*(k, $\mathcal{D}$);
for each data point $\overline{X}$ received from incremental stream $\mathcal{S}$ **do**
begin
Find the nearest centroid in $\mathcal{H}$ to $\overline{X}$;
Add $\overline{X}$ to corresponding group statistics $\mathcal{M}$;
if $n(\mathcal{M}) = 2 \cdot k$ **then** $(\mathcal{M}_1, \mathcal{M}_2) = \mathit{SplitGroupStatistics}(\mathcal{M}, k)$;
Delete $\mathcal{M}$ from $\mathcal{H}$;
Add $\mathcal{M}_1$ to $\mathcal{H}$;
Add $\mathcal{M}_2$ to $\mathcal{H}$;
end
end

Fig. 2. Overall Process of Maintenance of Condensed Groups

Algorithm *SplitGroupStatistics(GroupStatistics: $\mathcal{M}$, GroupSize: k)*;
begin
Determine covariance matrix $C(\mathcal{M})$;
{ The j, kth entry of the covariance matrix is determined using the formula $C_{jk}(\mathcal{M}) = Sc_{jk}(\mathcal{M})/n(\mathcal{M}) - \overline{Fs_j(\mathcal{M})} \cdot \overline{Fs_k(\mathcal{M})}/n(\mathcal{M})^2$; }
Determine eigenvectors $\overline{e_1(\mathcal{M})} \ldots \overline{e_d(\mathcal{M})}$ with eigenvalues $\lambda_1(\mathcal{M}) \ldots \lambda_d(\mathcal{M})$;
{ Relationship is $C(\mathcal{M}) = P(\mathcal{M}) \cdot \Delta(\mathcal{M}) \cdot P(\mathcal{M})^T$
Here $\Delta(\mathcal{M})$ is a diagonal matrix; }
{ Without loss of generality we assume that $\lambda_1(\mathcal{M}) \geq \ldots \geq \lambda_d(\mathcal{M})$; }
$n(\mathcal{M}_1) = n(\mathcal{M}_2) = k$;
$\overline{Fs(\mathcal{M}_1)} = \overline{Fs(\mathcal{M})}/n(\mathcal{M} + \overline{e_1}(\mathcal{M}) \cdot \sqrt{12 \cdot \lambda_1}/4$;
$\overline{Fs(\mathcal{M}_2)} = \overline{Fs(\mathcal{M})}/n(\mathcal{M}) - \overline{e_1}(\mathcal{M}) \cdot \sqrt{12 \cdot \lambda_1}/4$;
Construct $\Delta(\mathcal{M}_1)$ and $\Delta(\mathcal{M}_2)$ by dividing diagonal entry λ_1 of $\Delta(\mathcal{M})$ by 4;
$P(\mathcal{M}_1) = P(\mathcal{M}_2) = P(\mathcal{M})$;
$C(\mathcal{M}_1) = C(\mathcal{M}_2) = P(\mathcal{M}_1) \cdot \Delta(\mathcal{M}_1) \cdot P(\mathcal{M}_1)^T$;
for each pair of attributes i, j **do**
begin
$Sc_{ij}(\mathcal{M}_1) = k \cdot C_{ij}(\mathcal{M}_1) + Fs_i(\mathcal{M}_1) \cdot Fs_j(\mathcal{M}_1)/k$;
$Sc_{ij}(\mathcal{M}_2) = k \cdot C_{ij}(\mathcal{M}_2) + Fs_i(\mathcal{M}_2) \cdot Fs_j(\mathcal{M}_2)/k$;
end;
end

Fig. 3. Splitting Group Statistics (Algorithm)

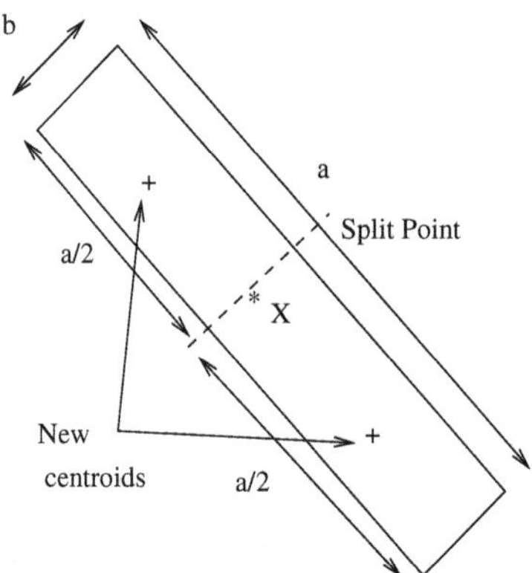

Fig. 4. Splitting Group Statistics (Illustration)

points. Rather, we impose the requirement that each group should maintain between k and $2 \cdot k$ data points.

As each new point in the data is received, it is added to the nearest group, as determined by the distance to each group centroid. As soon as the number of data points in the group equals $2 \cdot k$, the corresponding group needs to be split into two groups of k points each. We note that with each group, we only maintain the group statistics as opposed to the actual group itself. Therefore, the splitting process needs to generate two new sets of *group statistics* as opposed to the data points. Let us assume that the original set of group statistics to be split is given by $\mathcal{M}$, and the two new sets of group statistics to be generated are given by $\mathcal{M}_1$ and $\mathcal{M}_2$. The overall process of group updating is illustrated by the algorithm *DynamicGroupMaintenance* in Figure 2. As in the previous case, it is assumed that we start off with a static database $\mathcal{D}$. In addition, we have a constant stream $\mathcal{S}$ of data which consists of new data points arriving in the database. Whenever a new data point $\overline{X}$ is received, it is added to the group $\mathcal{M}$, whose centroid is closest to $\overline{X}$. As soon as the group size equals $2 \cdot k$, the corresponding group statistics needs to be split into two sets of group statistics. This is achieved by the procedure *SplitGroupStatistics* of Figure 3.

In order to split the group statistics, we make the same simplifying assumptions about (locally) uniform and independent distributions along the eigenvectors for each group. We also assume that the split is performed along the most elongated axis direction in each case. Since the eigenvalues correspond to variances along individual eigenvectors, the eigenvector corresponding to the largest eigenvalue is a candidate for a split. An example of this case is illustrated in Figure 4. The logic of choosing the most elongated direction for a split is to reduce the variance of each individual group as much as possible. This ensures that each group continues to correspond to a small data locality. This is useful in order to minimize the effects of the approximation assumptions of uniformity within a given data locality. We assume that the corresponding eigenvector is denoted by $\overline{e_1}$ and its eigenvalue by λ_1. Since the variance of the data along $\overline{e_1}$ is λ_1, then the range (a) of the corresponding uniform distribution along $\overline{e_1}$ is given[3] by $a = \sqrt{12 \cdot \lambda_1}$.

The number of records in each newly formed group is equal to k since the original group of size $2 \cdot k$ is split into two groups of equal size. We need to determine the first order and second order statistical data about each of the split groups $\mathcal{M}_1$ and $\mathcal{M}_2$. This is done by first deriving the centroid and zero (second-order) correlation directions for each group. The values of $Fs_i(\mathcal{G})$ and $Sc_{ij}(\mathcal{G})$ about each group can also be directly derived from these quantities. We will proceed to describe this derivation process in more detail.

Let us assume that the centroid of the unsplit group $\mathcal{M}$ is denoted by $\overline{Y(\mathcal{M})}$. This centroid can be computed from the first order values $\overline{Fs(\mathcal{M})}$ using the following relationship:

$$\overline{Y(\mathcal{M})} = (Fs_1(\mathcal{M}), \ldots Fs_d(\mathcal{M}))/n(\mathcal{G}) \tag{2}$$

As evident from Figure 4, the centroids of each of the split groups $\mathcal{M}_1$ and $\mathcal{M}_2$ are given by $\overline{Y(\mathcal{M})} - (a/4) \cdot \overline{e_1}$ and $\overline{Y(\mathcal{M})} + (a/4) \cdot \overline{e_1}$ respectively. Therefore, the new centroids of the groups $\mathcal{M}_1$ and $\mathcal{M}_2$ are given by $\overline{Y(\mathcal{M})} - (\sqrt{12 \cdot \lambda_1}/4) \cdot \overline{e_1}$ and $\overline{Y(\mathcal{M})} + (\sqrt{12 \cdot \lambda_1}/4) \cdot \overline{e_1}$ respectively. It now remains to compute the second order statistical values. This is slightly more tricky.

[3] This calculation was done by using the formula for the standard deviation of a uniform distribution with range a. The corresponding standard deviation is given by $\sqrt{a/12}$.

Once the co-variance matrix for each of the split groups has been computed, the second-order aggregate statistics can be derived by the use of the covariance values in conjunction with the centroids that have already been computed. Let us assume that the ijth entry of the co-variance matrix for the group $\mathcal{M}_1$ is given by $C_{ij}(\mathcal{M}_1)$. Then, from Observation 2, it is clear that the second order statistics of $\mathcal{M}_1$ may be determined as follows:

$$Sc_{ij}(\mathcal{M}_1) = k \cdot C_{ij}(\mathcal{M}_1) + Fs_i(\mathcal{M}_1) \cdot Fs_j(\mathcal{M}_1)/k \tag{3}$$

Since the first-order values have already been computed, the right hand side can be substituted, once the co-variance matrix has been determined. We also note that the eigenvectors of $\mathcal{M}_1$ and $\mathcal{M}_2$ are identical to the eigenvectors of $\mathcal{M}$, since the directions of zero correlation remain unchanged by the splitting process. Therefore, we have:

$$\begin{aligned}
e_1(\mathcal{M}_1) &= e_1(\mathcal{M}_2) = e_1(\mathcal{M}) \\
e_2(\mathcal{M}_1) &= e_2(\mathcal{M}_2) = e_2(\mathcal{M}) \\
e_3(\mathcal{M}_1) &= e_3(\mathcal{M}_2) = e_3(\mathcal{M}) \\
&\ldots \\
e_d(\mathcal{M}_1) &= e_d(\mathcal{M}_2) = e_d(\mathcal{M})
\end{aligned}$$

The eigenvalue corresponding to $\overline{e_1}(\mathcal{M})$ is equal to $\lambda_1/4$ because the splitting process along $\overline{e_1}$ reduces the corresponding variance by a factor of 4. All other eigenvectors remain unchanged. Let $P(\mathcal{M})$ represent the eigenvector matrix of $\mathcal{M}$, and $\Delta(\mathcal{M})$ represent the corresponding diagonal matrix. Then, the new diagonal matrix $\Delta(\mathcal{M}_1) = \Delta(\mathcal{M}_2)$ of $\mathcal{M}_1$ can be derived by dividing the entry $\lambda_1(\mathcal{M})$ by 4. Therefore, we have:

$$\lambda_1(\mathcal{M}_1) = \lambda_1(\mathcal{M}_2) = \lambda_1(\mathcal{M})/4$$

The other eigenvalues of $\mathcal{M}_1$ and $\mathcal{M}_2$ remain the same:

$$\begin{aligned}
\lambda_2(\mathcal{M}_1) &= \lambda_2(\mathcal{M}_2) = \lambda_2(\mathcal{M}) \\
\lambda_3(\mathcal{M}_1) &= \lambda_3(\mathcal{M}_2) = \lambda_3(\mathcal{M}) \\
&\ldots \\
\lambda_d(\mathcal{M}_1) &= \lambda_d(\mathcal{M}_2) = \lambda_d(\mathcal{M})
\end{aligned}$$

Thus, the co-variance matrixes of $\mathcal{M}_1$ and $\mathcal{M}_2$ may be determined as follows:

$$C(\mathcal{M}_1) = C(\mathcal{M}_2) = P(\mathcal{M}_1) \cdot \Delta(\mathcal{M}_1) \cdot P(\mathcal{M}_1)^T \tag{4}$$

Once the co-variance matrices have been determined, the second order aggregate information about the data is determined using Equation 3. We note that even though the covariance matrices of $\mathcal{M}_1$ and $\mathcal{M}_2$ are identical, the values of $Sc_{ij}(\mathcal{M}_1)$ and $Sc_{ij}(\mathcal{M}_2)$ will be different because of the different first order aggregates substituted in Equation 3. The overall process for splitting the group statistics is illustrated in Figure 3.

3.1 Application of Data Mining Algorithms to Condensed Data Groups

Once the condensed data groups have been generated, data mining algorithms can be applied to the anonymized data which is generated from these groups. After generation of the anonymized data, any *known* data mining algorithm can be directly applied to this new data set. Therefore, specialized data mining algorithms do not need to be developed for the condensation based approach. As an example, we applied the technique to the classification problem. We used a simple nearest neighbor classifier in order to illustrate the effectiveness of the technique. We also note that a nearest neighbor classifier cannot be effectively modified to work with the perturbation-based approach of [1]. This is because the method in [1] reconstructs aggregate distributions of each dimension independently. On the other hand, the modifications required for the case of the condensation approach were relatively straightforward. In this case, separate sets of data were generated from each of the different classes. The separate sets of data for each class were used in conjunction with a nearest neighbor classification procedure. The class label of the closest record from the set of perturbed records is used for the classification process.

4 Empirical Results

Since the aim of the privacy preserving data mining process was to create a new perturbed data set with similar data characteristics, it is useful to compare the statistical characteristics of the newly created data with the original data set. Since the proposed technique is designed to preserve the covariance structure of the data, it would be interesting to test how the covariance structure of the newly created data set matched with the original. If the newly created data set has very similar data characteristics to the original data set, then the condensed

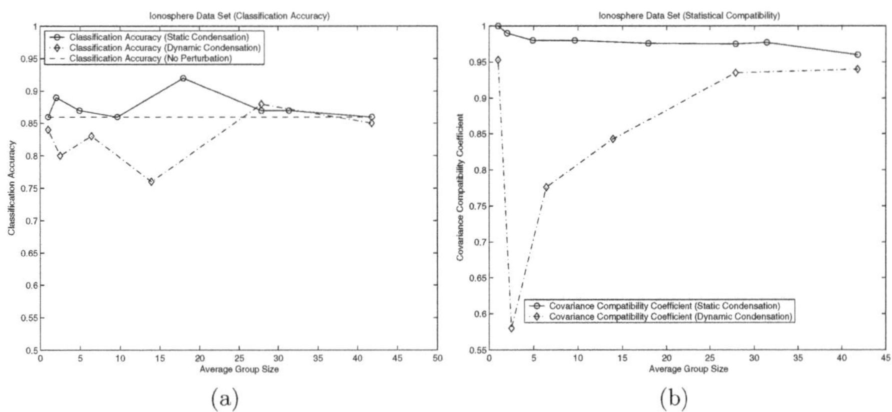

Fig. 5. (a) Classifier Accuracy and (b) Covariance Compatibility (Ionosphere)

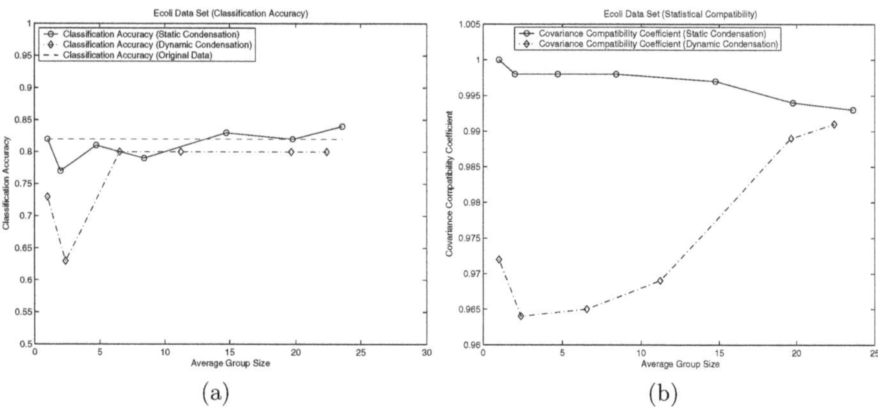

(a) (b)

Fig. 6. (a) Classifier Accuracy and (b) Covariance Compatibility (Ecoli)

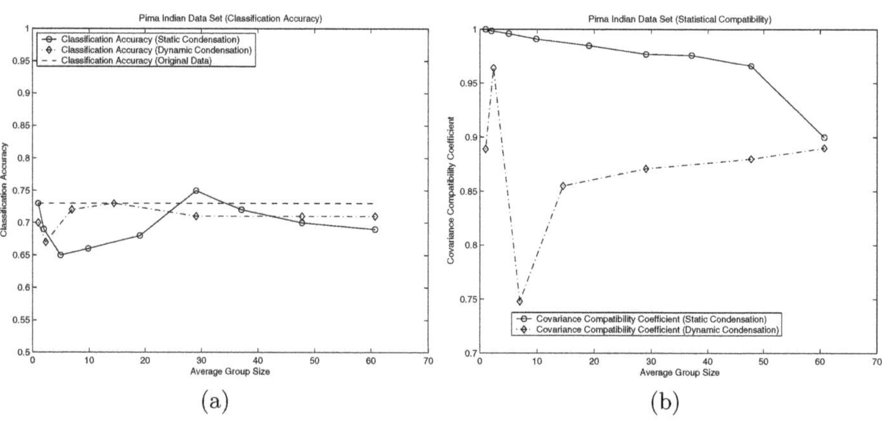

(a) (b)

Fig. 7. (a) Classifier Accuracy and (b) Covariance Compatibility (Pima Indian)

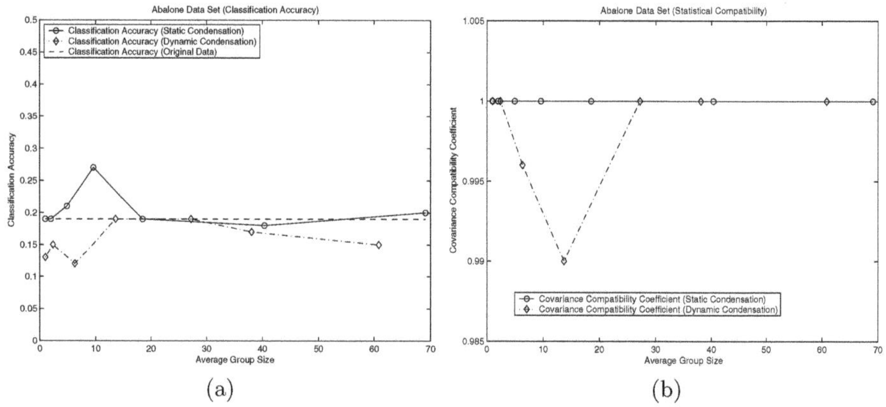

(a) (b)

Fig. 8. (a) Classifier Accuracy and (b) Covariance Compatibility (Abalone)

data set is a good substitute for privacy preserving data mining algorithms. For each dimension pair (i, j), let the corresponding entries in the covariance matrix for the original and the perturbed data be denoted by o_{ij} and p_{ij}. In order to perform this comparison, we computed the statistical coefficient of correlation between the pairwise data entry pairs (o_{ij}, p_{ij}). Let us denote this value by μ. When the two matrices are identical, the value of μ is 1. On the other hand, when there is perfect negative correlations between the entries, the value of μ is -1.

We tested the data generated from the privacy preserving condensation approach on the classification problem. Specifically, we tested the accuracy of a simple k-nearest neighbor classifier with the use of different levels of privacy. The level of privacy is controlled by varying the sizes of the groups used for the condensation process. The results show that the technique is able to achieve high levels of privacy without noticeably compromising classification accuracy. In fact, in many cases, the classification accuracy improves because of the noise reduction effects of the condensation process. These noise reduction effects result from the use of the aggregate statistics of a small local cluster of points in order to create the anonymized data. The aggregate statistics of each cluster of points often mask the effects of a particular anomaly[4] in it. This results in a more robust classification model. We note that the effect of anomalies in the data are also observed for a number of other data mining problems such as clustering [10]. While this paper studies classification as one example, it would be interesting to study other data mining problems as well.

A number of real data sets from the UCI machine learning repository[5] were used for the testing. The specific data sets used were the Ionosphere, Ecoli, Pima Indian, and the Abalone Data Sets. Except for the Abalone data set, each of these data sets correspond to a classification problem. In the abalone data set, the aim of the problem is to predict the age of abalone, which is a regression modeling problem. For this problem, the classification accuracy measure used was the percentage of the time that the age was predicted within an accuracy of less than one year by the nearest neighbor classifier.

The results on classification accuracy for the Ionosphere, Ecoli, Pima Indian, and Abalone data sets are illustrated in Figures 5(a), 6(a), 7(a) and 8(a) respectively. In each of the charts, the average group size of the condensation groups is indicated on the X-axis. On the Y-axis, we have plotted the classification accuracy of the nearest neighbor classifier, when the condensation technique was used. Three sets of results have been illustrated on each graph:

- The accuracy of the nearest neighbor classifier when static condensation was used. In this case, the static version of the algorithm was used in which the entire data set was used for condensation.
- The accuracy of the nearest neighbor classifier when dynamic condensation was used. In this case, the data points were added incrementally to the condensed groups.

[4] We note that a k-nearest neighbor model is often more robust than a 1-nearest neighbor model for the same reason.

[5] *http://www.ics.uci.edu/~mlearn*

- We note that when the group size was chosen to be one for the case of static condensation, the result was the same as that of using the classifier on the original data. Therefore, a horizontal line (parallel to the X-axis) is drawn in the graph which shows the baseline accuracy of using the original classifier. This horizontal line intersects the static condensation plot for a groups size of 1.

An interesting point to note is that when dynamic condensation is used, the result of using a group size of 1 does not correspond to the original data. This is because of the approximation assumptions implicit in splitting algorithm of the dynamic condensation process. Specifically, the splitting procedure assumed a uniform distribution of the data within a given condensed group of data points. Such an approximation tends to lose its accuracy for very small group sizes. However, it should also be remembered that the use of small group sizes is not very useful anyway from the point of view of privacy preservation. Therefore, the behavior of the dynamic condensation technique for very small group sizes is not necessarily an impediment to the effective use of the algorithm.

One of the interesting conclusions from the results of Figures 5(a), 6(a), 7(a) and 8(a) is that the static condensation technique often provided *better* accuracy than the accuracy of a classifier on the original data set. The effects were particularly pronounced in the case of the ionosphere data set. As evident from Figure 5(a), the accuracy of the classifier on the statically condensed data was higher than the baseline nearest neighbor accuracy for almost all group sizes. The reason for this was that the process of condensation affected the data in two potentially contradicting ways. One effect was to add noise to the data because of the random generation of new data points with similar statistical characteristics. This resulted in a reduction of the classification accuracy. On the other hand, the condensation process itself removed many of the anomalies from the data. This had the opposite effect of improving the classification accuracy. In many cases, this trade-off worked in favor of improving the classification accuracy as opposed to worsening it.

The use of dynamic classification also demonstrated some interesting results. While the absolute classification accuracy was not quite as high with the use of dynamic condensation, the overall accuracy continued to be almost comparable to that of the original data for modestly sized groups. The comparative behavior of the static and dynamic condensation methods is because of the additional assumptions used in the splitting process of the latter. We note that the splitting process uses a uniformly distributed assumption of the data distribution within a particular locality (group). While this is a reasonable assumption for reasonably large group sizes within even larger data sets, the assumption does not work quite as effectively when either of the following is true:

- When the group size is too small, then the splitting process does not estimate the statistical parameters of the two split groups quite as robustly.
- When the group size is too large (or a significant fraction of the overall data size), then a set of points can no longer be said to represent a locality of the data. Therefore, the use of the uniformly distributed assumption for splitting

and regeneration of the data points within a group is not as robust in this case.

These results are reflected in the behavior of the classifier on the dynamically condensed data. In many of the data sets, the classification accuracy was sensitive to the size of the group. While the classification accuracy reduced upto the use of a group size of 10, it gradually improved with increasing groups size. In most cases, the classification accuracy of the dynamic condensation process was comparable to that on the original data. In some cases such as the Pima Indian data set, the accuracy of the dynamic condensation method was even higher than that of the original data set. Furthermore, the accuracy of the classifier on the static and dynamically condensed data was somewhat similar for modest group sizes between 25 to 50. One interesting result which we noticed was for the case of the Pima Indian data set. In this case, the classifier worked more effectively with the dynamic condensation technique as compared to that of static condensation. The reason for this was that the data set seemed to contain a number of classification anomalies which were removed by the splitting process in the dynamic condensation method. Thus, in this particular case, the splitting process seemed to improve the overall classification accuracy. While it is clear that the effects of the condensation process on classification tends to be data specific, it is important to note that the accuracy of the condensed data is quite comparable to that of the original classifier.

We also compared the covariance characteristics of the data sets. The results are illustrated in Figures 5(b), 6(b), 7(b) and 8(b) respectively. It is clear that in each data set, the value of the statistical correlation μ was almost 1 for each and every data set for the static condensation method. In most cases, the value of μ was larger than 0.98 over all ranges of groups sizes and data sets. While the value of the statistical correlation reduced slightly with increasing group size, its relatively high value indicated that the covariance matrices of the original and perturbed data were virtually identical. This is a very encouraging result since it indicates that the approach is able to preserve the inter-attribute correlations in the data effectively. The results for the dynamic condensation method were also quite impressive, though not as accurate as the static condensation method. In this case, the value of μ continued to be very high (> 0.95) for two of the data sets. For the other two data sets, the value of μ reduced to the range of 0.65 to 0.75 for very small group sizes. As the average group sizes increased to about 20, this value increased to a value larger than 0.95. We note that in order for the indistinguishability level to be sufficiently effective, the group sizes also needed to be of sizes at least 15 or 20. This means that the accuracy of the classification process is not compromised in the range of group sizes which are most useful from the point of view of condensation. The behavior of the correlation statistic for dynamic condensation of small group sizes is because of the splitting process. It is a considerable approximation to split a small discrete number of discrete points using a uniform distribution assumption. As the group sizes increase, the value of μ increases because of the robustness of using a larger number of points in each group. However, increasing group sizes beyond a certain limit has the opposite effect of reducing μ (slightly). This effect is visible in both the static and dynamic condensation methods. The second effect is because of the greater levels of approximation inherent in using a uniform distribution assumption over a larger *spatial locality.* We note that when the overall data set size is large, it is more effectively possible to simultaneously achieve the seemingly contradictory goals of using the robustness of larger group sizes as well as the effectiveness of using a small locality of the data. This is because a modest group size of 30 truly represents a small data locality in a large data set of 10000 points, whereas this cannot be achieved in a data set containing only 100 points. We note that many of the data sets tested in this paper contained less than 1000 data points. These constitute difficult cases for our approach. Yet, the condensation approach continued to perform effectively both for small data sets such as the Ionosphere data set, and for larger data sets such as the Pima Indian data set. In addition, the condensed data often provided more accurate results than the original data because of removal of anomalies from the data.

5 Conclusions and Summary

In this paper, we presented a new way for privacy preserving data mining of data sets. Since the method re-generates multi-dimensional data records, existing data mining algorithms do not need to be modified to be used with the condensation technique. This is a clear advantage over techniques such as the perturbation method discussed in [1] in which a new data mining algorithm needs to be developed for each problem. Unlike other methods which perturb each dimension separately, this technique is designed to preserve the inter-attribute correlations of the data. As substantiated by the empirical tests, the condensation technique is able to preserve the inter-attribute correlations of the data quite effectively. At the same time, we illustrated the effectiveness of the system on the classification problem. In many cases, the condensed data provided a higher classification accuracy than the original data because of the removal of anomalies from the database.

References

1. Agrawal R., Srikant R.: Privacy Preserving Data Mining. Proceedings of the ACM SIGMOD Conference, (2000).
2. Agrawal D. Aggarwal C. C.: On the Design and Quantification of Privacy Preserving Data Mining Algorithms. ACM PODS Conference, (2002).
3. Benassi P. Truste: An online privacy seal program. Communications of the ACM, 42(2), (1999) 56–59.
4. Clifton C., Marks D.: Security and Privacy Implications of Data Mining. ACM SIGMOD Workshop on Research Issues in Data Mining and Knowledge Discovery, (1996) 15–19.
5. Clifton C., Kantarcioglu M., Vaidya J.: Defining Privacy for Data Mining. National Science Foundation Workshop on Next Generation Data Mining, (2002) 126–133.

6. Vaidya J., Clifton C.: Privacy Preserving Association Rule Mining in Vertically Partitioned Data. ACM KDD Conference, (2002).
7. Cover T., Thomas J.: Elements of Information Theory, John Wiley & Sons, Inc., New York, (1991).
8. Estivill-Castro V., Brankovic L.: Data Swapping: Balancing privacy against precision in mining for logic rules. Lecture Notes in Computer Science Vol. 1676, Springer Verlag (1999) 389–398.
9. Evfimievski A., Srikant R., Agrawal R., Gehrke J.: Privacy Preserving Mining Of Association Rules. ACM KDD Conference, (2002).
10. Hinneburg D. A., Keim D. A.: An Efficient Approach to Clustering in Large Multimedia Databases with Noise. ACM KDD Conference, (1998).
11. Iyengar V. S.: Transforming Data To Satisfy Privacy Constraints. ACM KDD Conference, (2002).
12. Liew C. K., Choi U. J., Liew C. J.: A data distortion by probability distribution. ACM TODS Journal, 10(3) (1985) 395-411.
13. Lau T., Etzioni O., Weld D. S.: Privacy Interfaces for Information Management. Communications of the ACM, 42(10) (1999), 89–94.
14. Murthy S.: Automatic Construction of Decision Trees from Data: A Multi-Disciplinary Survey. Data Mining and Knowledge Discovery, Vol. 2, (1998), 345–389.
15. Moore Jr. R. A.: Controlled Data-Swapping Techniques for Masking Public Use Microdata Sets. Statistical Research Division Report Series, RR 96-04, US Bureau of the Census, Washington D. C., (1996).
16. Rizvi S., Haritsa J.: Maintaining Data Privacy in Association Rule Mining. VLDB Conference, (2002.)
17. Silverman B. W.: *Density Estimation for Statistics and Data Analysis.* Chapman and Hall, (1986).
18. Samarati P., Sweeney L.: Protecting Privacy when Disclosing Information: k-Anonymity and its Enforcement Through Generalization and Suppression. Proceedings of the IEEE Symposium on Research in Security and Privacy, (1998).

Efficient Query Evaluation over Compressed XML Data

Andrei Arion[1], Angela Bonifati[2], Gianni Costa[2], Sandra D'Aguanno[1], Ioana Manolescu[1], and Andrea Pugliese[3]

[1] INRIA Futurs, Parc Club Orsay-Universite,
4 rue Jean Monod, 91893 Orsay Cedex, France
{firstname.lastname}@inria.fr
[2] Icar-CNR, Via P. Bucci 41/C,
87036 Rende (CS), Italy
{bonifati,costa}@icar.cnr.it
[3] DEIS, University of Calabria, Via P. Bucci 41/C,
87036 Rende(CS), Italy
apugliese@si.deis.unical.it

Abstract. XML suffers from the major limitation of high redundancy. Even if compression can be beneficial for XML data, however, once compressed, the data can be seldom browsed and queried in an efficient way. To address this problem, we propose *XQueC*, an [*XQue*]ry processor and [*C*]ompressor, which covers a large set of XQuery queries in the compressed domain. We shred compressed XML into suitable data structures, aiming at both reducing memory usage at query time and querying data while compressed. XQueC is the first system to take advantage of a query workload to choose the compression algorithms, and to group the compressed data granules according to their common properties. By means of experiments, we show that good trade-offs between compression ratio and query capability can be achieved in several real cases, as those covered by an XML benchmark. On average, XQueC improves over previous XML query-aware compression systems, still being reasonably closer to general-purpose query-unaware XML compressors. Finally, QETs for a wide variety of queries show that XQueC can reach speed comparable to XQuery engines on uncompressed data.

1 Introduction

XML documents have an inherent textual nature due to repeated tags and to PCDATA content. Therefore, they lend themselves naturally to compression. Once the compressed documents are produced, however, one would like to still query them under a compressed form as much as possible (reminiscent of "lazy decompression" in relational databases [1], [2]). The advantages of processing queries in the compressed domain are several: first, in a traditional query setting, access to small chunks of data may lead to less disk I/Os and reduce the query processing time; second, the memory and computation efforts in processing compressed data can be dramatically lower than those for uncompressed ones, thus even low-battery mobile devices can afford them; third, the possibility of obtaining compressed query results allows to spare network bandwidth when sending these results to a remote location, in the spirit of [3].

E. Bertino et al. (Eds.): EDBT 2004, LNCS 2992, pp. 200–218, 2004.
© Springer-Verlag Berlin Heidelberg 2004

Previous systems have been proposed recently, i.e. XGrind [4] and XPRESS [5], allowing the evaluation of simple path expressions in the compressed domain. However, these systems are based on a naive top-down query evaluation mechanism, which is not enough to execute queries efficiently. Most of all, they are not able to execute a large set of common XML queries (such as joins, inequality predicates, aggregates, nested queries etc.), without spending prohibitive times in decompressing intermediate results.

In this paper, we address the problem of compressing XML data in such a way as to allow efficient XQuery evaluation in the compressed domain. We can assert that our system, XQueC, is the first XQuery processor on compressed data. It is the first system to achieve a good trade-off among data compression factors, queryability and XQuery expressibility. To that purpose, we have carefully chosen a fragmentation and storage model for the compressed XML documents, providing selective access paths to the XML data, and thus further reducing the memory needed in order to process a query. The XQueC system has been demonstrated at VLDB 2003 [6].

The basis of our fragmentation strategy is borrowed from the XMill [7] project. XMill is a very efficient compressor for XML data, however, it was not designed to allow querying the documents under their compressed form. XMill made the important observation that data nodes (leaves of the XML tree) found on the same path in an XML document (e.g. /site/people/person/address/city in the XMark [8] documents) often exhibit similar content. Therefore, it makes sense to group all such values into a single *container* and choose the compression strategy *once per container*. Subsequently, XMill treated a container like a single "chunk of data" and compressed it as such, which disables access to any individual data node, unless the whole container is decompressed. Separately, XMill compressed and stored the structure tree of the XML document.

While in XMill a container may contain leaf nodes found under several paths, leaving to the user or the application the task of defining these containers, in XQueC the fragmentation is always dictated by the paths, i.e., we use one container per root-to-leaf path expression. When compressing the values in the container, like XMill, we take advantage of the commonalities between all container values. But most importantly, unlike XMill, *each container value is individually compressed and individually accessible*, enabling an effective query processing.

We base our work on the principle that XML compression (for saving disk space) and sophisticated query processing techniques (like complex physical operators, indexes, query optimization etc.) can be used together when properly combined. This principle has been stated and forcefully validated in the domain of relational query processing [1], [3]. Thus, it is not less important in the realm of XML.

In our work, we focus on the right compression of the *values* found in an XML document, coupled with a compact storage model for all parts of the document. Compressing the *structure* of an XML document has two facets. First, XML tags and attribute names are extremely repetitive, and practically all systems (indeed, even those not claiming to do "compression") encode such tags by means of much more compact tag numbers. Second, an existing work [9] has addressed the summarization of the tree structure itself, connecting among them parent and child nodes. While structure compression is interesting, its advantages are not very visible when considering the XML document as a whole. Indeed, for a rich corpus of XML datasets, both real and synthetic, our measures have shown that values make up 70% to 80% of the document structure. Projects like XGrind [4] and XPRESS [5] have already proposed schemes for value compression that would enable querying, but they suffer from limited query evaluation techniques (see also Section 1.2). These systems apply a fixed compression strategy regardless of the data and query set. In contrast, our system increases the compression benefits by adapting its compression strategy to the data and query workload, based on a suitable cost model.

By doing data fragmentation and compression, XQueC indirectly targets the problem of main-memory XQuery evaluation, which has recently attracted the attention of the community [9], [10]. In [10], the authors show that some current XQuery prototypes are in practice limited by their large memory consumption; due to its small footprint, XQueC scales better (see Section 5). Furthermore, some such in-memory prototypes exhibit prohibitive query execution times even for simple lookup queries. [9] focuses on the problem of fitting into memory a narrowed version of the tree of tags, which is however a small percentage of the overall document, as explained above.

XQueC addresses this problem in a two-fold way. First, in order to diminish its footprint, it applies powerful compression to the XML documents. The compression algorithms that we use allow to evaluate most predicates directly on the compressed values. Thus, decompression is often necessary only at the end of the query evaluation (see Section 4). Second, the XQueC storage model includes lightweight access support structures for the data itself, providing thus efficient primitives for query evaluation.

1.1 The XQueC System

The system we propose compresses XML data and queries them as much as possible under its compressed form, covering all real-life, complex classes of queries.

The XQueC system adheres to the following principles:

1. As in XMill, data is collected into containers, and the document structure stored separately. In XQueC, there is a container for each different $< type, pe >$, where *pe* is a distinguished root-to-leaf path expression and type is a distinguished elementary type. The set of containers is then partitioned again to allow for better sharing of compression structures, as explained in Section 2.2.
2. In contrast with previous compression-aware XML querying systems, whose storage was plainly based on files, XQueC is the first to use a complete and robust storage model for compressed XML data, including a set of access support structures. Such storage is fundamental to guarantee a fast query evaluation mechanism.
3. XQueC seamlessly extends a simple algebra for evaluating XML queries to include compression and decompression. This algebra is exploited by a cost-based optimizer, which may choose query evaluation strategies, that freely mix regular operator and compression-aware ones.
4. XQueC is the first system to exploit the *query workload* to *(i)* partition the containers into sets according to the source model[1] and to *(ii)* properly assign the most suitable

[1] The source model is the model used for the encoding, for instance the Huffman encoding tree for Huffman compression [11] and the dictionary for ALM compression [12], outlined later.

compression algorithm to each set. We have devised an appropriate cost model, which helps making the right choices.
5. XQueC is the first compressed XML querying system to use the order-preserving[2] textual compression. Among several alternatives, we have chosen to use the ALM [12] compression algorithm, which provides good compression ratios and still allows fast decompression, which is crucial for an algorithm to be used in a database setting [13]. This feature enables XQueC to evaluate, in the compressed domain, the class of queries involving inequality comparisons, which are not featured by the other compression-aware systems.

In the following sections, we will use XMark [8] documents for describing XQueC. A simplified structural outline of these documents is depicted in Figure 1 (at right). Each document describes an auction site, with people and open auctions (dashed lines represent IDREFs pointing to IDs and plain lines connect the other XML items). We describe XQueC following its architecture, depicted in Figure 1 (at left). It contains the following modules:

1. The *loader and compressor* converts XML documents in a compressed, yet queryable format. A cost analysis leverages the variety of compression algorithms and the query workload predicates to decide the partition of the containers.
2. The *compressed repository* stores the compressed documents and provides: *(i)* compressed data access methods, and *(ii)* a set of compression-specific utilities that enable, e.g., the comparison of two compressed values.
3. The *query processor* evaluates XQuery queries over compressed documents. Its complete set of physical operators (regular ones and compression-aware ones) allows for efficient evaluation over the compressed repository.

1.2 Related Work

XML data compression was first addressed by XMill [7], following the principles outlined in the previous section. After coalescing all values of a given container into a single data chunk, XMill compresses separately each container with its most suited algorithm, and then again with `gzip` to shrink it as much as possible. However, an XMill-compressed document is opaque to a query processor: thus, one must fully decompress a whole chunk of data before being able to query it.

The XGrind system [4] aims at query-enabling XML compression. XGrind does not separate data from structure: an XGrind-compressed XML document is still an XML document, whose tags have been dictionary-encoded, and whose data nodes have been compressed using the Huffman [11] algorithm and left at their place in the document. XGrind's query processor can be considered an extended SAX parser, which can handle *exact-match* and *prefix-match queries* on compressed values and *partial-match* and *range queries* on decompressed values. However, several operations are not supported by XGrind, for example, non-equality selections in the compressed domain. Therefore, XGrind cannot perform any join, aggregation, nested queries, or construct operations.

[2] Note that a compression algorithm *comp* preserves order if for any x_1, x_2, $comp(x_1) < comp(x_2)$ iff $x_1 < x_2$.

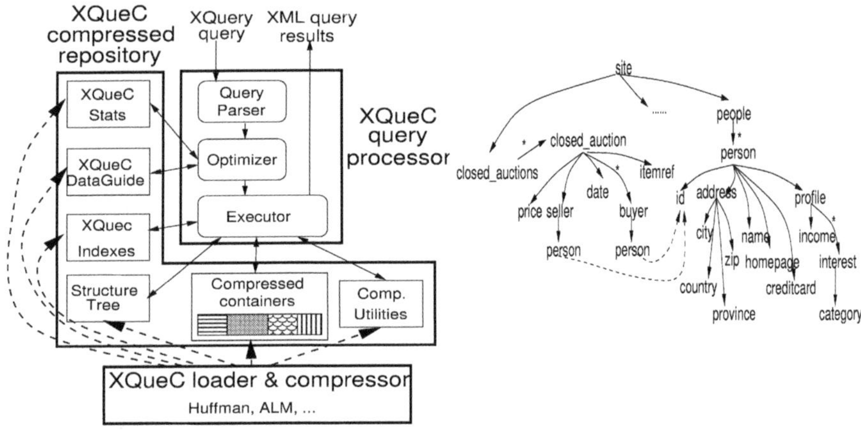

Fig. 1. Architecture of the XQueC prototype (left); simplified summary of the XMark XML documents (right).

Such operations occur in many XML query scenarios, as illustrated by XML benchmarks (e.g., all but the first two of the 20 queries in XMark [8]).

Also, XGrind uses a fixed naive top-down navigation strategy, which is clearly insufficient to provide for interesting alternative evaluation strategies, as it was done in existing works on querying compressed relational data (e.g., [1], [2]). These works considered evaluating arbitrary SQL queries on compressed data, by comparing (in the traditional framework of cost-based optimization) many query evaluation alternatives, including compression / decompression at several possible points.

A third recent work, XPRESS [5] uses a novel *reverse arithmetic encoding* method, mapping entire path expressions to intervals. Also, XPRESS uses a simple mechanism to infer the type (and therefore the compression method suited) of each elementary data item. XPRESS's compression method, like XGrind's, is homomorphic, i.e. it preserves the document structure.

To summarize, while XML compression has received significant attention [4], [5], [7], querying compressed XML is still in its infancy [4], [5]. Current XML compression and querying systems do not come anywhere near to efficiently executing complex XQuery queries. Indeed, even the evaluation of XPath queries is slowed down by the use of the fixed top-down query evaluation strategy.

Moreover, the interest towards compression even in a traditional data warehouse setting is constantly increasing in commercial systems, such as Oracle [14]. In [14], it is shown that the occupancy of raw data can be reduced while not impacting query performance. In principle, we expect that in the future a big share of this data will be expressed in XML, thus making the problem of compression very appealing.

Finally, for what concerns information retrieval systems, [15] exploits a variant of Huffman (extended to "bytes" instead of bits) in order to execute phrase matching entirely in the compressed domain. However, querying the text is obviously only a subset of the XQuery features. In particular, theta-joins are not feasible with the above variant of Huffman, whereas they can be executed by means of order-aware ALM.

1.3 Organization

The paper is organized as follows. In Section 2, we motivate the choice of our storage structures for compressed XML, and present ALM [12] and other compression algorithms, which we use for compressing the containers. Section 3 outlines the cost model used for partitioning the containers into sets, and for identifying the right compression to be applied to the values in each container set. Section 4 describes the XQueC query processor, its set of physical operators, and outlines its optimization algorithm. Section 5 shows the performance measures of our system on several data sets and XQuery queries.

2 Compressing XML Documents in a Queryable Format

In this section, we present the principles behind our approach for storing compressed XML documents, and the resulting storage model.

2.1 Compression Principles

In general, we make the observation that within XML text, strings represent a large percentage of the document, while numbers are less frequent. Thus, compression of strings, when effective, can truly reduce the occupancy of XML documents. Nevertheless, not all compression algorithms can seamlessly afford string comparisons in the compressed domain. In our system, we include both order-preserving and order-agnostic compression algorithms, and the final choice is entrusted to a suitable cost model.
Our approach for compressing XML was guided by the following principles:
Order-agnostic compression. As an order-agnostic algorithm, we chose classical Huffman [3], which is universally known as a simple algorithm which achieves the best possible redundancy among the resulting codes. The process of encoding and decoding is also faster than universal compression techniques. Finally, it has a set of fixed codewords, thus strings compressed with Huffman can be compared in the compressed domain within equality predicates. However, inequality predicates need to be decompressed. That is why in XQueC we may exploit order-preserving compression as well as not order-preserving one.
Order-preserving compression. Whereas everybody knows the potentiality of Huffman, the choice of an order-preserving algorithm is not immediate. We had initially three choices for encoding strings in an order-preserving manner: the Arithmetic [16], Hu-Tucker [17] and ALM [12] algorithms. We knew that dictionary-based encoding has demonstrated its effectiveness w.r.t. other non-dictionary approaches [18] while ALM has outperformed Hu-Tucker (as described in [19]). The former being both dictionary-based and efficient, was a good choice in our system. ALM has been used in relational databases for blank-padding (i.e. in Oracle) and for indexes compression. Due to its dictionary-based nature, ALM decompresses faster than Huffman, since it outputs bigger portions of a string at a time, when decompressing. Moreover, ALM seamlessly solved the problem of order-preserving dictionary compression, raised by encodings

[3] Here and in the remainder of the paper, by Huffman we shall mean solely the classical Huffman algorithm [11], thus disregarding its variants.

Token	Code	Interval
.....	....	
the	c	[theaa, therd]
there	d	[there, there]
the	e	[therf, thezz]
ir	b	[ir, ir]
.....	....	
se	v	[se, se]

String	Code
their	cb
there	d
these	ev

Fig. 2. An example of encoding in ALM.

such as Zilch encoding, string prefix compression and composite key compression by improving each of these. To this purpose, ALM eliminates the prefix property exhibited by those former encodings by allowing in the dictionary more than one symbol for the same prefix.

We now provide a short overview of how the ALM algorithm works. The fundamental mechanics behind the algorithm tells to consider the original set of source substrings, to split it into disjunct partitioning intervals set and to associate an interval prefix to each partitioning interval. For example, Figure 2 shows the mapping from the original source (made of the strings `there, their, these`) into some partitioning intervals and associated prefixes, which clearly do not scramble the original order among the source strings. We have implemented our own version of the algorithm, and we have obtained encouraging results w.r.t. previous compression-aware XML processors (see Section 5).

Workload-based choices of compression. Among the possible predicates writable in an XQuery query, we distinguish among the inequality, equality and wildcard. The ALM algorithm [12] allows inequality and equality predicates in the compressed domain, but not wildcards, whereas Huffman [11] supports prefix-wildcards and equality but not inequality. Thus, the choice of the algorithm can be aided by a proper query workload, whenever this turns to be available. In case, instead, the workload has not been provided, XQueC uses ALM for strings and decompresses the compared values in case of wildcard operations.

Structures for algebraic evaluation. Containers in XQueC closely resemble B+trees on values. Moreover, a light-weight structure summary allows for accessing the structure tree and the data containers in the query evaluation process. Data fragmentation allows for better exploiting all the possible evaluation plans, i.e. bottom-up, top-down, hybrid or index-based. As shown below, several queries of the XMark benchmark take advantage of the XQueC appropriate structures and of the consequent flexibility in parsing and querying these compressed structures.

2.2 Compressed Storage Structures

The XQueC loader/compressor parses and splits an XML document into the data structures depicted in Figure 1.

Node name dictionary. We use a dictionary to encode the element and attribute names present in an XML document. Thus, if there are N_t distinct names, we assign to each of

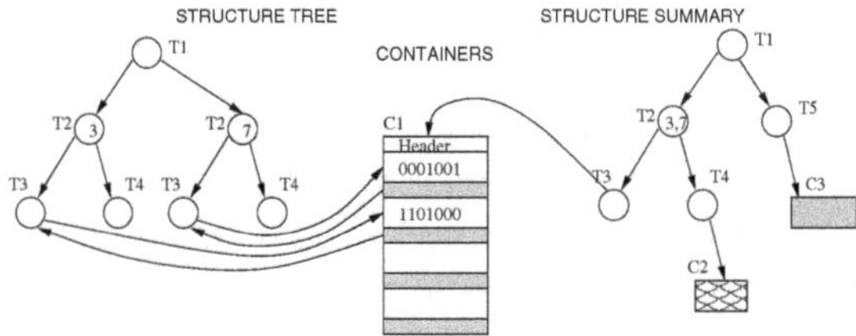

Fig. 3. Storage structures in the XQueC repository

them a bit string of length $log_2(N_t)$. For example, the XMark documents use 92 distinct names, which we encode on 7 bits.

Structure tree. We assign to each non-value XML node (element or attribute) an unique integer ID. The structure tree is stored as a sequence of *node records*, where each record contains: its own ID, the corresponding tag code; the IDs of its children; and (redundantly) the ID of its parent. For better query performance, as an access support structure, we construct and store a B+ search tree on top of the sequence of node records. Finally, each node record points to all its attribute and text children in their respective containers.

Value containers. All data values found under the same root-to-leaf path expression in the document are stored together into homogeneous containers. A container is a sequence of *container records*, each one consisting of a compressed value and a pointer to parent of this value in the structure tree. Records are not placed in the document order, but in a lexicographic order, to enable fast binary search. Note that container generation as done in XQueC is reminiscent of vertical partitioning of relational databases [20]. This kind of partitioning guarantees random access to the document content at different points, i.e. the containers access points. This choice provides interesting query evaluation strategies and leads to good query performance (see Section 5). Moreover, containers, even if kept separated, may share the same source model or, they can be compressed with different algorithms if not involved in the same queries. This is decided by a cost analysis which exploits the query workload and the similarities among containers, as described in Section 3.

Structure summary. The loader also constructs, as a redundant access support structure, a structural summary representing all possible paths in the document. For tree-structured XML documents, it will always have less nodes than the document (typically by several orders of magnitude). A structural summary of the auction documents can be derived from Figure 1, by (i) omitting the dashed edges, which brings it to a tree form, and (ii) storing in each non-leaf node in Figure 3, accessible in this tree by a path p, the list of nodes reachable in the document instance by the same path. Finally, the leaf nodes of our structure summary point to the corresponding value containers. Note that the structure summary is very small, thus it does not affect the compression rate. Indeed, in our experiments on the corpus of XML documents described in Section 5, the structure summary amounts to about 19% of the original document size.

Other indexes and statistics. When loading a document, other indexes and/or statistics can be created, either on the value containers, or on the structure tree. Our loader prototype currently gathers simple fan-out and cardinality statistics (e.g. number of person elements).

To measure the occupancy of our structures, we have used a set of documents produced by means of the *xmlgen* generator of the XMark project and ranged from 115KB to 46MB. They have been reduced by an average factor of 60% after compression (these figures include all the above access structures).

Our proposed storage structure is the simplest and most compact one that fulfills the principles listed at the beginning of Section 2; there are many ways to store XML in general [21]. If we omit our access support structures (backward edges, B+ index, and the structure summary), we shrink the database by a factor of 3 to 4, albeit at the price of deteriorated query performance.

Any storage mechanism for XML can be seamlessly adopted in XQueC, as long as it allows the presence of containers and the facilities to access container items.

2.3 Memory Issues

Data fragmentation in XQueC guarantees a wide variety of query evaluation strategies, and not solely top-down evaluation as in homomorphic compressors [4], [5]. Instead of identifying at compile-time the parts of the documents necessary for query evaluation, as given by an XQuery projection operator [10], in XQueC the path expressions are hard-coded into the containers and projection is already prepared in advance when compressing the document, without any additional effort for the loader. Consider as examples the following query Q14 of XMark:

```
FOR $i IN document("auction.xml")/site//item
WHERE CONTAINS($i/description,"gold")
RETURN $i/name/text()
```

This query would require prohibitive parsing times in XGrind and XPRESS, which basically have to load into main-memory all the document and parse it entirely in order to find the sought items. For this query, as shown in Figure 4, all the XML stream has to be parsed to find the elements `<item>`.

In XQueC, the compressor has already shredded the data and accessibility to these data from the structure summary allows to save the parsing and loading times. Thus, in XQueC the structure summary is parsed (not all the structure tree), then the involved containers are directly accessed (or alternatively their selected single items) and loaded into main-memory. More precisely, as shown in Figure 4, once the structure summary leads to the containers C_1, C_2 and C_3, only these (or part of them) need to be fetched in memory. Finally, note that in Galax, extended with the projection operator [10], the execution times for queries involving the *descendant-or-self* axis (such as XMark Q14) are significantly increased, since additional complex computation is demanded to the loader for those queries.

3 Compression Choices

XQueC exploits the query workload to choose the way containers are compressed. As already highlighted, the containers are filled up with textual data, which represents a big share of the whole documents. Thus, achieving a good trade-off between compression

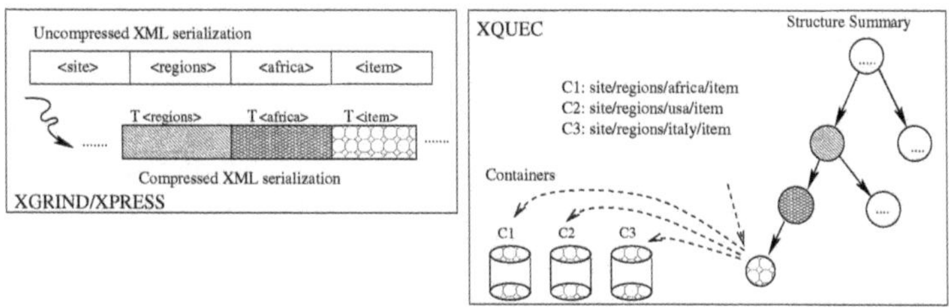

Fig. 4. Accesses to containers in case of XMark's Q14 with *descendant-or-self* axis in XPress/XGrind versus XQueC.

ratio and query execution times, must necessarily imply the capability to make a good choice for textual container compression.

First, a container may be compressed with any compression algorithm, but obviously one would like to apply a compression algorithm with nice properties. For instance, the decompression time for a given algorithm strongly influences the times of queries over data compressed with that algorithm. In addition, the compression ratio achieved by a given algorithm on a given container influences the overall compression ratio.

Second, a container can be compressed separately or can share the same source model with other containers. The latter choice would be very convenient whenever for example two containers exhibit data similarities, which will improve their common compression ratio. Moreover, the occupancy of the source model is as relevant in the choice of the algorithm as the occupancy of containers.

To understand the impact of compression choices, consider two binary-encoded containers, ct_1 and ct_2. ct_1 contains only strings composed of letters a and b, whereas ct_2 contains only strings composed of letters c and d. Suppose, as one extreme case, that two separate source models are built for the two containers; in such a case, containers are encoded with 1 bit per letter. As the other extreme case, a common source model is used for both containers, thus requiring 2 bits per letter for the encoding, and increasing the containers occupancy. This scenario may get even more complicated when we think of an arbitrary number of encodings assigned to each container. This smallish example already shows that compressing several containers with the same source model leads to losses in the compression ratio.

In the sequel, we show how our system addresses these problems, by proposing a suitable cost model, a greedy algorithm for making the right choice, and some experimental results. The cost model of XQueC is based on the set of non-numerical (textual) containers, the set of available compression algorithms $\mathcal{A}$, and the query workload $\mathcal{W}$. As it is typical of optimization problems, we will characterize the search space, define the cost function, and finally propose a simple search strategy.

3.1 Search Space: Possible Compression Configurations

Let $\mathcal{C}$ be the set of containers built from a set of documents $\mathcal{D}$. A *compression configuration* s for $\mathcal{D}$ is denoted by a tuple $< P, alg >$ where P is a partition of $\mathcal{C}$'s elements, and the function $alg : P \rightarrow \mathcal{A}$ associates a compression algorithm with each set p in the partition P. The configuration s dictates thus that all values of the containers in p will be compressed using $alg(p)$, and a single common source model. Moreover, let $\mathcal{P}$ be the set of possible partitions of $\mathcal{C}$. The cardinality of $\mathcal{P}$ is the *Bell number* $B_{|\mathcal{C}|}$, which is exponential with $|\mathcal{C}|$. For each possible partition $P_i \in \mathcal{P}$, there are $|\mathcal{A}|^{|P_i|}$ ways of assigning a compression algorithm to each set in P_i. Therefore, the size of the search space is: $\sum_{i=1}^{B_{|\mathcal{C}|}} |\mathcal{A}|^{|P_i|}$, which is exponential in $|\mathcal{A}|$.

3.2 Cost Function: Appreciating the Quality of a Compression Configuration

Intuitively, the cost function for a configuration s reflects the time needed to apply the necessary data decompressions in order to evaluate the predicates involved in the queries of $\mathcal{W}$. Reasonably, it also accounts for the compression ratios of the employed compression algorithms, and it includes the cost of storing the source model structures. The cost of a configuration s is an integer value computed as a weighted sum of storage and decompression costs.

Characterization of compression algorithms. Each algorithm $a \in \mathcal{A}$ is denoted by a tuple $< d_c, c_s(F), c_a(F),\ eq,\ ineq,\ wild >$. The *decompression cost* d_c is an estimate of the cost of decompressing a container record by using a, the *storage cost* $c_s(F)$ is a function estimating the cost of storing a container record compressed with a, and the *storage cost of the source model structures* $c_a(F)$ is a function estimating the cost of storing the source model structures for a container record. F is a symmetric *similarity matrix* whose generic element $F[i,\ j]$ is a real number ranging between 0 and 1, capturing the normalized similarity between a container ct_i and a container ct_j. F is built on the basis of data statistics, such as the number of overlapping values, the character distribution within the container entries, and possibly other type information, whenever available (e.g. the XSchema types, using results presented in [22]) [4]. Finally, the *algorithmic properties* eq, $ineq$ and $wild$ are boolean values indicating whether the algorithm supports in the compressed domain: (*i*) equality predicates without prefix-matching (eq), (*ii*) inequality predicates without prefix-matching ($ineq$) and (*iii*) equality predicates with prefix-matching ($wild$). For instance, Huffman will have $eq = true$, $ineq = false$ and $wild = true$, while ALM will have $eq = true$, $ineq = true$ and $wild = false$. We denote each parameter of algorithm a with an array notation, e.g., $a[eq]$.

Storage costs. The containers and source model storage costs are simply computed as $\sum_{p \in P} \left(alg(p)[\widehat{c}(F_p)] * \sum_{c \in p} |c| \right)$ where $\widehat{c} = c_s$ for the case of container storage and $\widehat{c} = c_a$ for source model storage[5]. Obviously, c_s and c_a need not to be evaluated on the overall F but solely on F_p, that is the projection of F over the containers of the partition p.

[4] We do not delve here into the details of F as study of similarity among data is outside the scope of this paper.

[5] We are not considering here the containers that are not involved in any query in W. Those do not incur a cost so they can be disregarded in the cost model.

Decompression cost. In order to evaluate the decompression cost associated with a given compression configuration s, we define three square matrices, E, I and D, having size $(|\mathcal{C}|+1) \times (|\mathcal{C}|+1)$. These matrices reflect the comparisons (equality, inequality and prefix-matching equality comparisons, respectively) made in $\mathcal{W}$ among container values or between container values and constants. More formally, the generic element $E_{i,j}$, with $i \neq |\mathcal{C}|+1$ and $j \neq |\mathcal{C}|+1$, is the number of equality predicates in $\mathcal{W}$ between ct_i and ct_j not involving prefix-matching, whereas with $i = |\mathcal{C}|+1$ or $j = |\mathcal{C}|+1$, it is the number of equality predicates in $\mathcal{W}$ between ct_i and a constant (if $j = |\mathcal{C}|+1$), or between ct_j and a constant (if $i = |\mathcal{C}|+1$), not involving prefix-matching. Matrices I and D have the same structure but refer to inequality and prefix-matching comparisons, respectively. Obviously, E, I and D are symmetric.

Considering the generic element of the three matrices, say $M[i, j]$, the associated decompression cost is obviously zero if ct_i and ct_j share the same source model and the algorithm they are compressed with supports the corresponding predicate in the compressed domain. A decompression cost occurs in three cases: (*i*) ct_i and ct_j are compressed using different algorithms; (*ii*) ct_i and ct_j are compressed using the same algorithm but different source models; (*iii*) ct_i and ct_j share the same source model but the algorithm does not support the needed comparison (equality in the case of E, inequality for I and prefix-matching for D) in the compressed domain. For instance, for a generic element $I[i, j]$, in the case of $i \neq j$, $i \neq |\mathcal{C}|+1$ and $j \neq |\mathcal{C}|+1$, the cost would be:

- zero, if $ct_i \in p$, $ct_j \in p$, $alg(p)[ineq] = true$;
- $|ct_i| * alg(p')[d_c] + |ct_j| * alg(p'')[d_c]$, if $ct_i \in p'$, $ct_j \in p''$, $p' \neq p''$ (cases (*i*) and (*ii*));
- $(|ct_i| + |ct_j|) * alg(p)[d_c]$, if $ct_i \in p$, $ct_j \in p$, $alg(p)[ineq] = false$ (case (*iii*)).

The decompression cost is calculated by summing up the costs associated with each element of the matrices E, I, and D. However, note that (*i*) for the cases of E and D, we consider $alg(p)[eq]$ and $alg(p)[wild]$, respectively, and that (*ii*) the term referring to the cardinality of the containers to be decompressed is adjusted in the cases of self-comparisons (i.e. $i = j$) and comparisons with constants ($i = |\mathcal{C}|+1$ or $j = |\mathcal{C}|+1$).

3.3 Devising a Suitable Search Strategy

XQueC currently uses a greedy strategy for moving into the search space. The search starts with an initial configuration $s_0 =< P_0, algo_0 >$, where P_0 is a partition of $\mathcal{C}$ having sets of exactly one container, and $algo_0$ blindly assigns to each set a generic compression algorithm (e.g. `bzip`) and a separate source model. Next, s_0 is gradually improved by a sequence of *configuration moves*.

Let $Pred$ be the set of value comparison predicates appearing in $\mathcal{W}$. A move from $s_k =< P_k, alg_k >$ to $s_{k+1} =< P_{k+1}, alg_{k+1} >$ is done by first randomly extracting a predicate $pred$ from $Pred$. Let ct_i and ct_j be the containers involved in $pred$ (for instance $pred$ makes an equality comparison, such as $ct_i = ct_j$, or an inequality one, such as $ct_i > ct_j$). Let p' and p'' the sets in P_k to which ct_i and ct_j belong, respectively. If $p' = p''$, we build a new configuration s' where $alg_{k+1}(p')$ is such that the evaluation of

$pred$ is enabled on compressed values, and alg_{k+1} has the greatest number of algorithmic properties holding $true$. Then, we evaluate the costs of s_k and s', and let s_{k+1} be the one with the minimum cost. In the case of $p' \neq p''$, we build two new configurations s' and s''. s' is obtained by dropping ct_i and ct_j from p' and p'', respectively, and adding the set $\{ct_i, ct_j\}$ to P_{k+1}. s'' is obtained by replacing p' and p'' with their union. For both s' and s'', alg_{k+1} associates to the new sets in P_{k+1} an algorithm enabling the evaluation of $pred$ in the compressed domain and having the greatest number of algorithmic properties holding $true$. Finally, we evaluate the costs of s_k, s' and s'', and let s_{k+1} be the one with the minimum cost.

Example. To give a flavor of the savings gained with partitioning the set of containers, consider an initial configuration, which has five containers on an XMark document, all of them sized about 6MB, which we initially (naively) choose to compress with ALM only; let us call this configuration NaiveConf. The workload is made of XQuery queries with inequality predicates over the path expressions leading to the above containers. The first three containers are filled with Shakespeare's sentences, the fourth is filled with person names and the fifth with dates. Using the above workload, we obtain the best partitioning, which has three partitions, one with the first three containers and a distinct partition for the fourth and fifth, let us call it *GoodConf*. The compression factor shifts from 56.14% for the *NaiveConf* to 67.14%, 71.75% and 65.15% respectively for the three partitions of *GoodConf*. While in such a case the source models sizes do not vary significantly, the decompression cost in *Good Conf* is clearly advantageous w.r.t. *NaiveConf*, leading to gain 21.42% for shakespearian text, 28.57% for person names and to loose only 6% for dates. □

Note that, for each predicate in $Pred$, the strategy explores a fixed subset of possible configuration moves, so its complexity is linear in $|Pred|$. Of course, due to this partial exploration, the search yields a locally optimal solution. Moreover, containers not involved in W are not considered by the cost model, and a reasonable choice could be to compress them using order-unaware algorithms offering good compression ratios, e.g. `bzip2` [23]. Finally, note also that the choice of a suitable compression configuration is orthogonal with respect to the choosing of an optimal XML storage model [22]; we can combine both for an automatic storage-and-compression design.

4 Evaluating XML Queries over Compressed Data

The XQueC query processor consists of a query parser, an optimizer, and a query evaluation engine. The set of physical operators used by the query evaluation engine can be divided in three classes:

- *data access operators*, retrieving information from the compressed storage structures;
- *regular data combination operators* (joins, outer joins, selections etc.);
- *compression and decompression operators*.

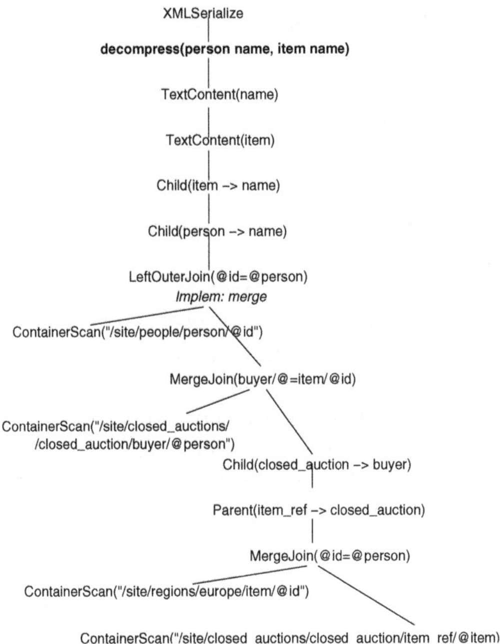

Fig. 5. Query execution plan for XMark's Q9.

Among our data access operators, there are *ContScan* and *ContAccess*, which allow, respectively, to scan all (elementID, compressed value) pairs from a container, and to access only some of them, according to an interval search criteria. *StructureSummaryAccess* provide direct access to the identifiers of all elements reachable through a given path. *Parent* and *Child* allow to fetch the parent, respectively, the children (all children, or just those with a specific tag) for a given set of elements. Finally, *TextContent* pairs element IDs with all their immediate text children, retrieved from their respective containers. *TextContent* is implemented as a hash join pairing the element IDs with the content obtained from a *ContScan*.

Due to the storage model chosen in XQueC (Section 2.2), the *StructureSummaryAccess* operator provides the identifiers of the required elements *in the correct document order*. Furthermore, the *Parent* and *Child* operator preserve the order of the elements with respect to which they are applied. Also, if the *Child* operator returns more than one child for a given node, these children are returned in correct order. The order-preserving behavior allow us to perform many path computations through comparatively inexpensive 1-pass merge joins; furthermore, many simple queries can be answered without requiring a sort to re-constitute document order.

While these operators respect document order, *ContScan* and *ContAccess* respect data order, provides fast access to elements (and values) according to a given value search criteria. Also, as soon as predicates on container values are given in the query, it is often profitable to start query evaluation by scanning (and perhaps merge-joining) a few containers.

As an example of QEP, consider query Q9 from XMark:

```
FOR $p IN document("auction.xml")/site/people/person
LET $a :=
    FOR $t IN document("auction.xml")/site/
        closed_auctions/closed_auction
    LET $n :=
        FOR $t2 IN document("auction.xml")/site/
            regions/europe/item
        WHERE $t/itemref/@item = $t2/@id
        RETURN $t2
    WHERE $p/@id = $t/buyer/@person
    RETURN <item> $n/name/text() </item>
RETURN <person name=$p/name/text()> $a </person>
```

Figure 5 shows a possible XQueC execution plan for Q9 (this is indeed the plan used in the experiments). Based on this example, we make several remarks. First, note that we only decompress the necessary pieces of information (person name and item name), only at the very end of the query execution (the decompress operators shown in bold fonts). All the way down in the QEP, we were able to compute the three-ways join between persons, buyers, and items, using directly the compressed attributes person/@id, buyer/@person, and item_ref/@item. Second, due to the order of data obtained from *ContainerScans*, we are able to make extensive use of MergeJoins, without the need for sorting. Third, this plan mixes *Parent* and *Child* operators, alternating judiciously between top-down and bottom-up strategy, in order to minimize the number of tuples manipulated at any particular moment. This feature is made possible by the usage of a full set of algebraic evaluation choices, which XQueC has, but is not available to the XGrind or XPress query processors.

Finally, note that for instance in query Q9 also an *XMLSerialize* operator is employed in order to correctly construct the new XML which the query outputs. To this purpose, we recall that XML construction plays a minor role within the XML algebraic evaluation, and, being not crucial, it can be disregarded in the whole query execution time [24]. This has been confirmed by our experiments.

5 Implementation and Experimental Evaluation

XQueC is being implemented entirely in Java, using as back-end an embedded database, Berkeley DB [25]. We have performed some interesting comparative measures, that show that XQueC is a competitor of both query-aware compressors, and of early XQuery prototypes.

In the following, we want to illustrate both XQueC good compression ratios and query execution times. To this purpose, we have done two kinds of experiments:

Compression Factors. We have performed experiments on both synthetic data (XMark documents) and on real-life data sets (in particular, we considered the ones chosen in [5] for the purpose of cross-comparison with it).

Query Execution Times. We show how our system performs on some XML benchmark queries [8] and cross-compare them with the query execution times of optimized Galax [10], an open-source XQuery prototype.

All the experiments have been executed on a *DELL Latitude C820* laptop equipped with a 2,20GHz CPU and 512MB RAM.

Table 1. Data Sets used in the experiments (XMark11 is used in QETs measures.)

Document	*Size(MB)*	*Containers*	*Distinct tags*	*Tree nodes*
Shakespeare	15.0	39	22	65621
Baseball	16.8	41	46	27181
Washington-course	12.1	12	18	99729
XMark11	11.3	432	77	76726

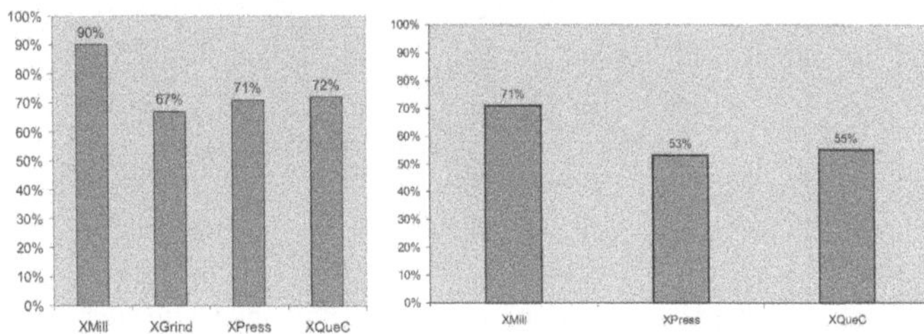

Fig. 6. Average CF for Shakespeare, WashingtonCourse and Baseball data sets (left); and for XMark synthetic data sets (right).

Compression Factors. We have compared the obtained compression factors (defined as $1-(cs/os)$), where cs and os are the sizes of the compressed and original documents, respectively) with the corresponding factors of XMill, XGrind and XPRESS. Figure 6 (left) shows the average compression factor obtained for a corpus of documents composed of *Shakespeare.xml*, *Washington-Course.xml* and *Baseball.xml*, whose main characteristics are shown in Table 1. Note that, on average, XQueC closely tracks XPRESS. It is interesting to notice that some limitations affect some of the XML compressors that we tested - for example, the documents decompressed by XPRESS have lost all their white spaces. Thus, the XQueC compression factor could be further improved if blanks were not considered.

Moreover, we have also tested the compression factors on different-sized XMark synthetic data sets (we considered documents ranging from 1MB to 25MB), generated by means of xmlgen [8]. As Figure 6 (right) shows, we have obtained again good compression factors w.r.t XPRESS and XMill.

Note also that XGrind does not appear in these experiments. Indeed, due to repetitive crashes, we were not able to upload in the XGrind system (the version available through the site *http://sourceforge.net*) any XMark document except for one sized 100KB, whose compression factor however is very low and not representative of the system (precisely equal to 17.36%).

Query Execution Times. We have tested our system against the optimized version of Galax by running XMark queries and other queries. Due to space limits, we select here a set of significant XMark queries. Indeed, XMark queries left out stress language features, on which compression will likely have no significant impact whatsoever, e.g., support for functions, deep nesting etc. The reasons why we chose Galax is that it is open-source and has an optimizer. Note that the XQueC optimizer is not finalized yet (and was indeed

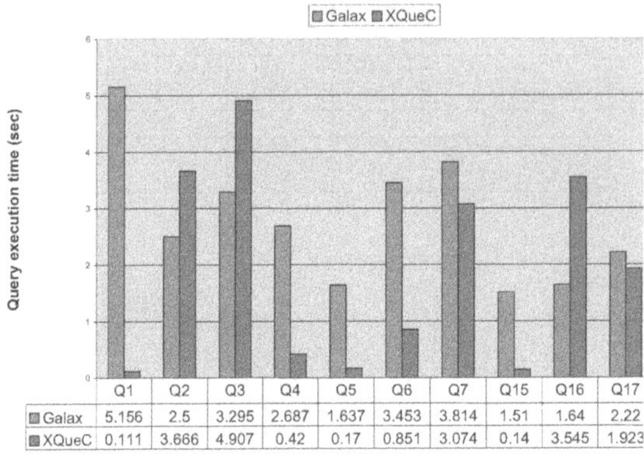

Fig. 7. Comparative execution times between us and Optimized Galax.

not used in these measures), thus our results are only due to the compression ratio, data structures, and efficient execution engine.

Figure 7 shows the executions of XQueC queries on the document XMark11, sized 11.3MB. For the sake of better readability, in Figure 7, we have omitted Q9, and Q8. These queries measured in our system 2.133 sec. and 2.142 sec. respectively, whereas in Galax Q9 could not be measured on our machine [6] and Q8 took 126.33 sec. Note also that on Q2, Q3, Q16, the QET is a little worse than the Galax one, because in the current implementation we use simple unique IDs, given that our data model imposes a large number of parent-child joins. However, even with this limitation, we are still reasonably close to Galax, and we expect much better once XQueC will migrate to 3-valued IDs, as already started in the spirit of [26], [27], [28]. Most importantly, note that the previous XQueC QETs are to be intended as the times taken to both execute the queries in the compressed and decompress the obtained results. Thus, those measures show that there is no performance penalty in XQueC w.r.t. Galax due to compression. Thus, with comparable times w.r.t. an XQuery engine over uncompressed data, XQueC exhibits the advantage of compression.

As a general remark, note that our system is implemented in Java and can be made faster by using a native code compiler, which also we plan to plug in the immediate future.

Finally, it is worth noting that comparison of XQueC with XGrind and XPress query times could not be done due to the fact that fully working versions of the latters are not publicly available. Nevertheless, that comparison would have been less meaningful, since those systems cover a limited fragment of XPath, and not full XQuery, as discussed in Section 1.2.

[6] The same query has been tested on a more powerful machine in the paper [10] and results in a rather lengthy computation.

6 Conclusions and Future Work

We have presented XQueC, a compression-aware XQuery processor. We have shown that our system exhibits a good trade-off between compression factors over different XML data sets and query evaluation times on XMark queries. XQueC works on compressed XML documents, which can be a huge advantage when query results must be shipped around a network.

In the very near future, our system will be improved in several ways: by moving to three-valued IDs for XML elements, in the spirit of [26], [27], [28] and by incorporating further storage techniques that lead to additionally reduce the occupancy of structures. The implementation of an XQuery [29] optimizer for querying XML compressed data is ongoing. Moreover, we are testing the suitability of our system w.r.t. the full-text queries [30], which are being defined for the XQuery language at W3C. Another important extension we have devised is needed for uploading in our system larger documents than currently (e.g. SwissProt, measuring about 500MB). To this purpose, we plan to access the containers during the parsing phase directly on secondary storage rather than in memory.

References

1. Westmann, T., Kossmann, D., Helmer, S., Moerkotte, G.: The Implementation and Performance of Compressed Databases. ACM SIGMOD Record **29** (2000) 55–67
2. Chen, Z., Gehrke, J., Korn, F.: Query Optimization In Compressed Database Systems. In: Proc. of ACM SIGMOD. (2000)
3. Chen, Z., Seshadri, P.: An Algebraic Compression Framework for Query Results. In: Proc. of the ICDE Conf. (2000)
4. Tolani, P., Haritsa, J.: XGRIND: A query-friendly XML compressor. In: Proc. of the ICDE Conf. (2002)
5. Min, J.K., Park, M., Chung, C.: XPRESS: A queriable compression for XML data. In: Proc. of ACM SIGMOD. (2003)
6. Arion, A., Bonifati, A., Costa, G., D'Aguanno, S., Manolescu, I., Pugliese, A.: XQueC: Pushing XML Queries to Compressed XML Data (demo). Proc. of the VLDB Conf. (2003)
7. Liefke, H., Suciu, D.: XMILL: An efficient compressor for XML data. In: Proc. of ACM SIGMOD. (2000)
8. Schmidt, A., Waas, F., Kersten, M., Carey, M., Manolescu, I., Busse, R.: XMark: A benchmark for XML data management. In: Proc. of the VLDB Conf. (2002)
9. Buneman, P., Grohe, M., Koch, C.: Path Queries on Compressed XML. In: Proc. of the VLDB Conf. (2003)
10. Marian, A., Simeon, J.: Projecting XML Documents. In: Proc. of the VLDB Conf. (2003)
11. Huffman, D.A.: A Method for Construction of Minimum-Redundancy Codes. In: Proc. of the IRE. (1952)
12. Antoshenkov, G.: Dictionary-Based Order-Preserving String Compression. VLDB Journal **6** (1997) 26–39
13. Goldstein, J., Ramakrishnan, R., Shaft, U.: Compressing Relations and Indexes. In: Proc. of the ICDE Conf. (1998) 370–379
14. Poess, M., Potapov, D.: Data Compression in Oracle. In: Proc. of the VLDB Conf. (2003)
15. Moura, E.D., Navarro, G., Ziviani, N., Baeza-Yates, R.: Fast and Flexible Word Searching on Compressed Text. ACM Transactions on Information Systems **18** (2000) 113–139

16. Witten, I.H.: Arithmetic Coding For Data Compression. Communications of ACM (1987)
17. Hu, T.C., Tucker, A.C.: Optimal Computer Search Trees And Variable-Length Alphabetical Codes. SIAM J. APPL. MATH **21** (1971) 514–532
18. Moffat, A., Zobel, J.: Coding for Compression in Full-Text Retrieval Systems. In: Proc. of the Data Compression Conference (DCC). (1992) 72–81
19. Antoshenkov, G., Lomet, D., Murray, J.: Order preserving string compression. In: Proc. of the ICDE Conf. (1996) 655–663
20. Ozsu, M.T., Valduriez, P.: Principles of Distributed Database Systems. Prentice-Hall (1999)
21. Amer-Yahia, S.: Storage Techniques and Mapping Schemas for XML. SIGMOD Record (2003)
22. Bohannon, P., Freire, J., Roy, P., Simeon, J.: From XML Schema to Relations: A Cost-based Approach to XML Storage. In: Proc. of the ICDE Conf. (2002)
23. Website: The bzip2 and libbzip2 Official Home Page (2002) http://sources.redhat.com/bzip2/.
24. Shanmugasundaram, J., Shekita, E., Barr, R., Carey, M., Lindsay, B., Pirahesh, H., Reinwald, B.: Efficiently Publishing Relational Data as XML Documents. In: Proc. of the VLDB Conf. (2000)
25. Website: Berkeley DB Data Store (2003) http://www.sleepycat.com/pro-ducts/data.shtml.
26. Paparizos, S., Al-Khalifa, S., Chapman, A., Jagadish, H.V., Lakshmanan, L.V.S., Nierman, A., Patel, J.M., Srivastava, D., Wiwatwattana, N., Wu, Y., Yu, C.: TIMBER:A Native System for Querying XML. In: Proc. of ACM SIGMOD. (2003) 672
27. T.Grust: Accelerating XPath location steps. In: Proc. of ACM SIGMOD. (2002) 109–120
28. Srivastava, D., Al-Khalifa, S., Jagadish, H.V., Koudas, N., Patel, J.M., Wu, Y.: Structural Joins: A Primitive for Efficient XML Query Pattern Matching. In: Proc. of the ICDE Conf. (2002)
29. Website: The XML Query Language (2003) http://www.w3.org/XML/Query.
30. Website: XQuery and XPath Full-text Use Cases (2003) http://www.w3.org/TR/xmlquery-full-text-use-cases.

XQzip: Querying Compressed XML Using Structural Indexing

James Cheng and Wilfred Ng

Department of Computer Science
Hong Kong University of Science and Technology
Clear Water Bay, Hong Kong
{csjames,wilfred}@cs.ust.hk

Abstract. XML makes data flexible in representation and easily portable on the Web but it also substantially inflates data size as a consequence of using tags to describe data. Although many effective XML compressors, such as XMill, have been recently proposed to solve this data inflation problem, they do not address the problem of running queries on compressed XML data. More recently, some compressors have been proposed to query compressed XML data. However, the compression ratio of these compressors is usually worse than that of XMill and that of the generic compressor gzip, while their query performance and the expressive power of the query language they support are inadequate. In this paper, we propose XQzip, an XML compressor which supports querying compressed XML data by imposing an indexing structure, which we call Structure Index Tree (SIT), on XML data. XQzip addresses both the compression and query performance problems of existing XML compressors. We evaluate XQzip's performance extensively on a wide spectrum of benchmark XML data sources. On average, XQzip is able to achieve a compression ratio 16.7% better and a querying time 12.84 times less than another known queriable XML compressor. In addition, XQzip supports a wide scope of XPath queries such as multiple, deeply nested predicates and aggregation.

1 Introduction

XML has become the de facto standard for data exchange. However, its flexibility and portability are gained at the cost of substantially inflated data, which is a consequence of using repeated tags to describe data. This hinders the use of XML in both data exchange and data archiving. In recent years, many XML compressors have been proposed to solve this data inflation problem. There are two types of compressions: *unqueriable compression* and *queriable compression*.

The unqueriable compression, such as XMill [8], makes use of the similarities between the semantically related XML data to eliminate data redundancy so that a good compression ratio is always guaranteed. However, in this approach the compressed data is not directly usable; a full chunk of data must be first decompressed in order to process the imposed queries.

E. Bertino et al. (Eds.): EDBT 2004, LNCS 2992, pp. 219–236, 2004.
© Springer-Verlag Berlin Heidelberg 2004

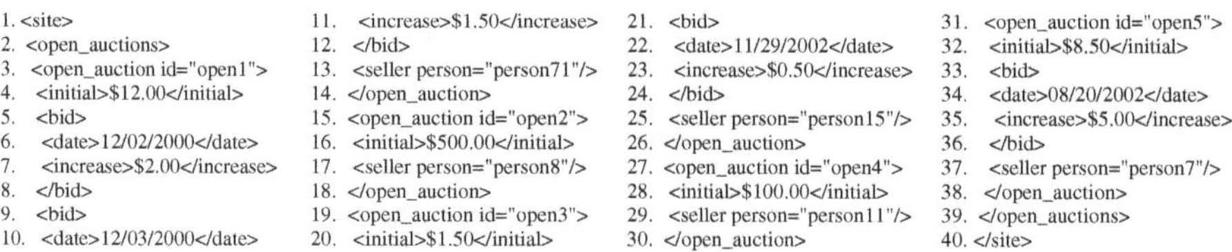

```
1. <site>
2. <open_auctions>
3. <open_auction id="open1">
4. <initial>$12.00</initial>
5. <bid>
6. <date>12/02/2000</date>
7. <increase>$2.00</increase>
8. </bid>
9. <bid>
10. <date>12/03/2000</date>
11. <increase>$1.50</increase>
12. </bid>
13. <seller person="person71"/>
14. </open_auction>
15. <open_auction id="open2">
16. <initial>$500.00</initial>
17. <seller person="person8"/>
18. </open_auction>
19. <open_auction id="open3">
20. <initial>$1.50</initial>
21. <bid>
22. <date>11/29/2002</date>
23. <increase>$0.50</increase>
24. </bid>
25. <seller person="person15"/>
26. </open_auction>
27. <open_auction id="open4">
28. <initial>$100.00</initial>
29. <seller person="person11"/>
30. </open_auction>
31. <open_auction id="open5">
32. <initial>$8.50</initial>
33. <bid>
34. <date>08/20/2002</date>
35. <increase>$5.00</increase>
36. </bid>
37. <seller person="person7"/>
38. </open_auction>
39. </open_auctions>
40. </site>
```

Fig. 1. A Sample Auction XML Extract

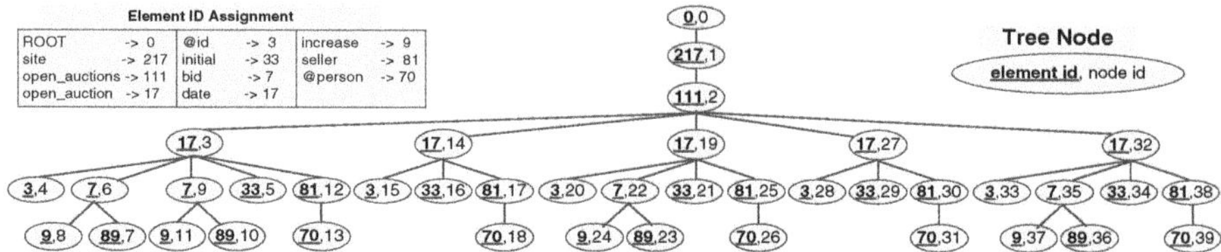

Fig. 2. Structure Tree (contents of the *exts* not shown) of the Auction XML Extract

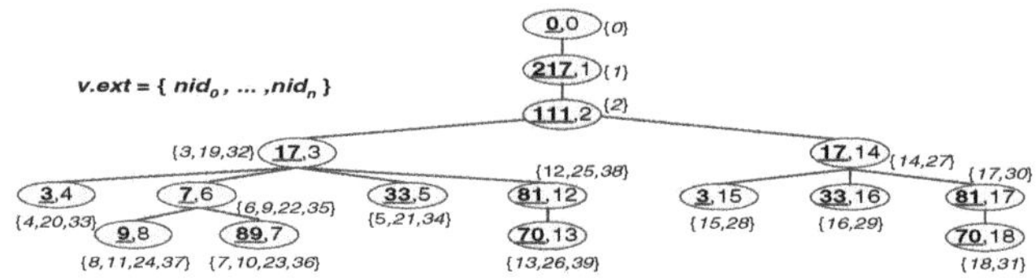

Fig. 3. SIT of the Auction Structure Tree

The queriable compression encodes each of the XML data items individually so that the compressed data item can be accessed directly without a full decompression of the entire file. However, the fine-granularity of the individually compressed data unit does not take advantage of the XML data commonalities and, hence, the compression ratio is usually much degraded with respect to the full-chunked compression strategy used in unqueriable compression.

The queriable compressors, such as XGrind [14] and XPRESS [10], adopts homomorphic transformation to preserve the structure of the XML data so that queries can be evaluated on the structure. However, the preserved structure is always too large (linear in the size of the XML document). It will be very inefficient to search this large structure space, even for simple path queries. For example, to search for bidding items with an initial price under $10 in the compressed file of the sample XML extract shown in Fig. 1, XGrind parses the entire compressed XML document and, for each encoded element/attribute parsed, it has to match its incoming path with the path of the input query. XPRESS makes an improvement as it reduces the element-by-element matching to path-by-path matching by encoding a path as a distinct interval in [0.0,1.0), so that a path can be matched using the containment relationships among the intervals. However, the path-by-path matching is still inefficient since most paths are duplicate in an XML document, especially for those *data-centric* XML documents.

Contributions. We propose XQzip, which has the following desirable features: (1) achieves a good compression ratio and a good compression/decompression time; (2) supports efficient query processing on compressed XML data; and (3) supports an expressive query language. XQzip provides feasible solutions to the problems encountered with the queriable and unqueriable compressions.

Firstly, XQzip removes the duplicate structures in an XML document to improve query performance by using an indexing structure called the *Structure Index Tree* (or *SIT*). An example of a SIT is shown in Fig. 3, which is the index of the tree in Fig. 2, the structure of the the sample XML extract in Fig. 1. Note that the duplicate structures in Fig. 2 are eliminated in the SIT. In fact, large portions of the structure of most XML documents are redundant and can be eliminated. For example, if an XML document contains 1000 repetitions of our sample XML extract (with different data contents), the corresponding tree structure will be 1000 times bigger than the tree in Fig. 2. However, its SIT will essentially have the same structure as the one in Fig. 3, implying that the search space for query evaluation is reduced 1000 times by the index.

Secondly, XQzip avoids full decompression by compressing the data into a sequence of blocks which can be decompressed individually and at the same time allow commonalities of the XML data to be exploited to achieve a good compression. XQzip also effectively reduces the decompression overhead in query evaluation by managing a buffer pool for the decompressed blocks of XML data.

Thirdly, XQzip utilizes the index to query the compressed XML data. XQzip supports a large portion of XPath [15] queries such as multiple and deeply nested predicates with mixed value-based and structure-based query conditions, and aggregations; and it extends an XPath query to select an arbitrary set of distinct elements with a single query. We also give an easy mapping scheme to make the verbose XPath queries more readable. In addition, we devise a simple algorithm to evaluate the XPath [15] queries in polynomial time in the average-case.

Finally, we evaluate the performance of XQzip on a wide variety of benchmark XML data sources and compare the results with XMill, gzip and XGrind for compression and query performance. Our results show that the compression ratio of XQzip is comparable to that of XMill and approximately 16.7% better than that of XGrind. XQzip's compression and decompression speeds are comparable to that of XMill and gzip, but several times faster than that of XGrind. In query evaluation, we record competitive figures. On average, XQzip evaluates queries 12.84 times faster than XGrind with an initially empty buffer pool, and 80 times faster than XGrind with a warm buffer pool. In addition, XQzip supports efficient processing of many complex queries not supported by XGrind. Although we are not able to compare XPRESS directly due to the unavailability of the code, we believe that both our compression and query performance are better than that of XPRESS, since XPRESS only achieves a compression ratio comparable to that of XGrind and a query time 2.83 times better than that of XGrind, according to XPRESS's experimental evaluation results [10].

Related Work. We are also aware of another XML compressor, XQueC [2], which also supports querying. XQueC compresses each data item individually and this usually results in a degradation in the compression ratio (compared to XMill). An important feature of XQueC is that it supports efficient evaluation of XQuery [16] by using a variety of structure information, such as dataguides [5], structure tree and other indexes. However, these structures, together with the pointers pointing to the individually compressed data items, would incur huge space overhead. Another queriable compression is also proposed recently in [3], which compresses the structure tree of an XML document to allow it to be placed in memory to support Core XPath [6] queries. This use of the compressed structure is similar to the use of the SIT in XQzip, i.e. [3] condenses the tree edges while the SIT indexes the tree nodes. [3] does not compress the textual XML data items and hence it cannot be served as a direct comparison.

This paper is organized as follows. We outline the XQzip architecture in Section 2. Section 3 presents the SIT and its construction algorithm. Section 4 describes a queriable, compressed data storage model. Section 5 discusses query coverage and query evaluation. We evaluate the performance of XQzip in Section 6 and give our concluding remarks and discuss our future work in Section 7.

2 The Architecture of XQzip

The architecture of XQzip consists of four main modules: the *Compressor*, the *Index Constructor*, the *Query Processor*, and the *Repository*. A simplified diagram of the architecture is shown in Fig. 4. We describe the operations related to the processes of compression and querying.

For the compression process, the input XML document is parsed by the *SAX Parser* which distributes the XML data items (element contents and attribute values) to the Compressor and the XML structure (tags and attributes) to the Index Constructor. The Compressor compresses the data into blocks which can be efficiently accessed from the *Hashtable* where the element/attribute names are stored. The Index Constructor builds the SIT for the XML structure.

For the querying process, the *Query Parser* parses an input query and then the *Query Executor* uses the index to evaluate the query. The Executor checks with the *Buffer Manager*, which applies the LRU rule to manage the *Buffer Pool* for the decompressed data blocks. If the data is already in the Buffer Pool, the Executor retrieves it directly without decompression. Otherwise, the Executor communicates with the Hashtable to retrieve the data from the compressed file.

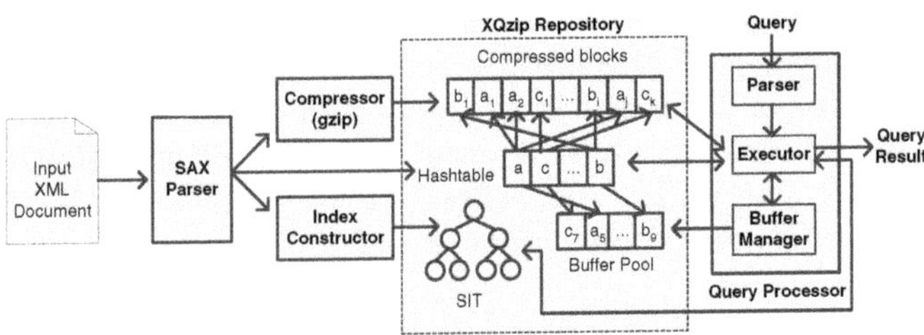

Fig. 4. Architecture of XQzip

3 XML Structure Index Trees (SITs)

In this section we introduce an effective indexing structure called a Structure Index Tree (or a SIT) for XML data. We first define a few basic terminologies used to describe the SIT and then present an algorithm to generate the SIT.

3.1 Basic Notions of XML Structures

We model the structure of an XML document as a tree, which we call the *structure tree*. The structure tree contains only a root node and element nodes. The element nodes represent both elements and attributes. We add the prefix '@' to the attribute names to distinguish them from the elements. We assign a *Hash ID* to each distinct tag/attribute name and store it in a hashtable, i.e. the *Hashtable* in Fig. 4. The XML data items are separated from the structure and are compressed into different blocks accessible via the Hashtable. Hence, no text nodes are considered in our model. We do not model namespaces, PIs and comments for simplicity, though it is a straightforward extension to include them.

Formally, the structure tree of an XML document is an unranked, ordered tree, $T = (V_T, E_T, ROOT)$, where V_T and E_T are the set of tree nodes and edges respectively, and $ROOT$ is the unique root of T. We define a tree node $v \in V_T$ by $v = (eid, nid, ext)$, where $v.eid$ is the Hash ID of the element/attribute being modelled by v; $v.nid$ is the unique node identifer assigned to v according to document order; initially $v.ext = \{v.nid\}$. We represent each node v by the pair $(v.eid, v.nid)$. The pair $(ROOT.eid, ROOT.nid)$ is uniquely assigned as $(0,0)$. In addition, if a node v has n (ordered) children $(\beta_1, \ldots, \beta_n)$, their order in T is specified as: $v.\beta_1.eid \leq v.\beta_2.eid \leq \cdots \leq v.\beta_n.eid$; and if $v.\beta_i.eid = v.\beta_{i+1}.eid$, then $v.\beta_i.nid < v.\beta_{i+1}.nid$. This node ordering accelerates node matchings in T by an approximate factor of 2, since we match two nodes by their *eids* and on average, we only need to search half of the children of a given node.

Definition 1. (Branch and Branch Ordering) *A branch of T, denoted as b, is defined by $b = v_0 \to \cdots \to v_i \to \cdots \to v_p$, where v_p is a leaf node in T and v_{i-1} is parent of v_i for $0 < i \leq p$. Let B be a set of branches of a tree or a subtree. A branch ordering $\prec$ on B is defined as: $\forall b_1, b_2 \in B$, let $b_1 = u_0 \to \cdots \to u_p$ and $b_2 = v_0 \to \cdots \to v_q$, $b_1 \prec b_2$ implies that there exists some i such that $u_i.nid = v_i.nid$ and $u_{i+1}.nid \neq v_{i+1}.nid$, and either (1) $u_{i+1}.eid < v_{i+1}.eid$, or (2) $u_{i+1}.eid = v_{i+1}.eid$ and $u_{i+1}.nid < v_{i+1}.nid$.*

For example, given b_1 = (0,0) $\to \cdots \to$ (3,4), b_2 = (0,0) $\to \cdots \to$ (9,11), b_3 = (0,0) $\to \cdots \to$ (3,20) in Fig. 2, we have $b_1 \prec b_2$, $b_2 \prec b_3$ and $b_1 \prec b_3$. We can describe a tree as the sequence of all its branches ordered by $\prec$. For example, the subtree rooted at the node (17,27) in Fig. 2 can be represented as: (17,27) $\to \cdots \to$ (3,28) $\prec$ (17,27) $\to \cdots \to$ (33,29) $\prec$ (17,27) $\to \cdots \to$ (70,31), while the tree in Fig. 3 is represented as: x(3,4) $\prec$ x(9,8) $\prec$ x(89,7) $\prec$ x(33,5) $\prec$ x(70,13) $\prec$ x(3,15) $\prec$ x(33,16) $\prec$ x(70,18), where x denotes (0,0) $\to \cdots \to$ for simplicity.

Definition 2. (Sit-Equivalence) *Two branches,* $b_1 = u_0 \rightarrow \cdots \rightarrow u_p$ *and* $b_2 = v_0 \rightarrow \cdots \rightarrow v_q$*, are SIT-equivalent if* $u_i.eid = v_i.eid$ *for* $0 \leq i \leq p$ *and* $p = q$*. Two subtrees,* $t_1 = b_{10} \prec \cdots \prec b_{1m}$ *and* $t_2 = b_{20} \prec \cdots \prec b_{2n}$*, are SIT-equivalent if* $t_1.ROOT$ *and* $t_2.ROOT$ *are siblings and,* b_{1i} *and* b_{2i} *are SIT-equivalent for* $0 \leq i \leq m$ *and* $m = n$*.*

For example, in Fig. 2, the subtrees rooted at the nodes (17,14) and (17,27) are SIT-equivalent subtrees since every pair of corresponding branches in the two subtrees are SIT-equivalent. The SIT-equivalent subtrees are duplicate structures in XML data and thus we eliminate this redundancy by using a merge operator defined as follows.

Definition 3. (Merge Operator) *A merge operator,* $Merge_T$*, is defined as:* $Merge_T$*:* $(t_1, t_2) \rightarrow t$*, where* t_1 *and* t_2 *are SIT-equivalent and* $t_1.ROOT.nid < t_2.ROOT.nid$*,* $t_1 = b_{10} \prec \cdots \prec b_{1n}$ *and* $t_2 = b_{20} \prec \cdots \prec b_{2n}$*, and* $b_{1i} = u_0 \rightarrow \cdots \rightarrow u_p$ *and* $b_{2i} = v_0 \rightarrow \cdots \rightarrow v_p$*. For* $0 \leq i \leq n$*,* $Merge_T$ *assigns* $u_j.ext = u_j.ext \cup v_j.ext$ *for* $0 \leq j \leq p$*, and then deletes* b_{2i}*.*

Thus, the merge operator merges t_1 and t_2 to produce t, where t is SIT-equivalent to both t_1 and t_2. The effect of the merge operation is that the duplicate SIT-equivalent structure is eliminated. We can remove this redundancy in the structure tree to obtain a much more concise structure representation, the *Structure Index Tree* (*SIT*), by applying $Merge_T$ iteratively on the structure tree until no two SIT-equivalent subtrees are left. For example, the tree in Fig. 3 is the SIT for the structure tree in Fig. 2. Note that all SIT-equivalent subtrees in Fig. 2 are merged into a corresponding SIT-equivalent subtree in the SIT.

A structure tree and its SIT are equivalent, since the structures of the deleted SIT-equivalent subtrees are retained in the SIT. In addition, the deleted nodes are represented by their node identifiers kept in the node *exts* while the deleted edges can be reconstructed by following the node ordering. Since the SIT is in general much smaller than its structure tree, it allows more efficient node selection than its structure tree.

3.2 SIT Construction

In this section, we present an efficient algorithm to construct the SIT for an XML document. We define four node pointers, *parent*, *previousSibling*, *nextSibling*, and *firstChild*, for each tree node. The pointers tremendously speed up node navigation for both SIT construction and query evaluation. The space incurred for these pointers is usually insignificant since a SIT is often very small.

We linear-scan (by SAX) an input XML document only once to build its SIT and meanwhile we compress the text data (detailed in Section 4). For every SAX start/end-tag event (i.e. the structure information) parsed, we invoke the procedure construct_SIT, shown in Fig. 5. The main idea is to operate on a "base" tree and a constructing tree. A constructing tree is the tree under construction for each *start-tag* parsed and it is a subtree of the "base" tree. When an *end-tag* is parsed, a constructing tree is completed. If this completed subtree

```
procedure construct_SIT (SAX-Event)
/* stack is an array keeping the start/end tag information (either START-TAG or END-TAG);
        top indicates the stack top;   c is the current node pointer;   count initially is set to 0 */
begin
1.   if (SAX-Event is a start-tag event)            /* an attribute is also a start-tag event */
2.     create a new node, u,where u.eid := hash (SAX-Event) and count := count +1, u.nid := count;
3.     if (stack [top] = START-TAG)
4.       assign u as the firstchild of c;
5.     else
6.       insert u among the siblings of c according to the SIT node ordering;
7.     top := top + 1;  stack [top] := START-TAG;
8.   else if (SAX-Event is an end-tag event)       /* an end-tag event is also passed after processing an attribute value */
9.     if (subtree (c) is SIT-equivalent to subtree (one of c's preceding siblings, u))    /* check by a parallel DFS */
10.      Merge_T( (subtree (u), subtree (c) );
11.    if (stack [top] = START-TAG)                 /* c has no child and the START-TAG was pushed for c */
12.      if (stack [top – 1] = START-TAG)           /* c is the first child of its parent */
13.        stack [top] := END-TAG;                  /* finish processing c */
14.      else                                       /* c has preceding sibling(s) (processed) */
15.        top := top – 1;                          /* use the previous END-TAG to indicate c has been processed */
16.    else    /* the END-TAG indicates c's child processed, stack [top–1] must be START-TAG indicating c not processed */
17.      if (stack [top – 2] = START-TAG)           /* c is the first child of its parent */
18.        top := top – 1; stack [top] := END-TAG;  /* remove c's child's stack and indicates c has been processed */
19.      else                                       /* c's preceding sibling(s) processed */
20.        top := top – 2;        /* use c's preceding sibling's END-TAG, i.e. stack [top–2], to indicate c has been processed */
21.  c := u;
end
```

Fig. 5. Pseudocode for the SIT Construction Procedure

is SIT-equivalent to any subtree in the "base" tree, it is merged into its SIT-equivalent subtree; otherwise, it becomes part of the "base" tree. We use a stack to indicate the parent-child or sibling-sibling relationships between the previous and the current XML element to build the tree structure. Lines 11-20 maintain the consistency of the structure information and skip redundant information. Hence, the stack size is always less than twice the height of the SIT.

The time complexity is $O(|V_T|)$ in the average-case and $O(|SIT||V_T|)$ in the worse-case, where $|V_T|$ is the number of tags and attributes in the XML document and $|SIT|$ is the number of nodes in the SIT. $O(|SIT||V_T|)$ is the worst-case complexity because we at most compare and merge $2|SIT|$ nodes for each of the $|V_T|$ nodes parsed. However, in most cases only a constant number of nodes are operated on for each new element parsed, resulting in the $O(|V_T|)$ time. The space required is $|V_T|$ for the node exts and at most $2|SIT|$ for the structure since at all time, both the "base" tree and the constructing tree can be at most as large as the final tree (i.e. the SIT).

SIT and F&B-Index. The SIT shares some similar features with the F&B-Index [1,7]. The F&B-Index uses bisimulation [7,12] to partition the data nodes while we use SIT-equivalence to index the structure tree. However, the SIT preserves the node ordering whereas bisimulation preserves no order of the nodes. This node ordering reduces the number of nodes to be matched in query evaluation and in SIT construction by an average factor of 50%. The F&B-Index can be computed in time $O(m \log n)$, where m and n are the number of edges and nodes in the original XML data graph, by first adding an inverse edge for every edge and then computing the 1-Index [9] using an algorithm proposed in [11]. However, the memory consumption is too high, since the entire structure of an XML document must be first read into the main memory.

4 A Queriable Storage Model for Compressed XML Data

In this section, we discuss a storage model for the compressed XML data. We seek to balance the full-chunked and the fine-grained storage models so that the compression algorithm is able to exploit the commonalities in the XML data to improve compression (i.e. the full-chunk approach), while allowing efficient retrieval of the compressed data for query evaluation (i.e. the fine-grain approach).

We group XML data items associated with the same tag/attribute name into a same data stream (c.f. this technique is also used in XMill [8]). Each data stream is then compressed separately into a sequence of blocks. These compressed blocks can be decompressed individually and hence full decompression is avoided in query evaluation. The problem is that if a block is small, it does not make good use of data commonalities for a better compression; on the other hand, it will be costly to decompress a block if its size is large. Therefore, it is critical to choose a suitable block size in order to attain both a good compression ratio and efficient retrieval of matching data in the compressed file.

We conduct an experiment (described in Section 6.1) and find that a block size of 1000 data records is feasible for both compression and query evaluation. Hence we use it as the default block size for XQzip. In addition, we set a limit of 2 MBytes to prevent memory exhaustion, since some data records may be long. When either 1000 data records have been parsed into a data stream or the size of a data stream reaches 2 MBytes, we compress the stream using gzip, assign an id to the compressed block and store it on disk, and then resume the process.

The start position of a block in the compressed file is stored in the Element Hashtable. (Note that gzip can decompress a block given its start position and an arbitrary data length.) We also assign an *id* to each block as the value of the maximum node identifier of the nodes whose data is compressed into that block. To retrieve the block which contains the compressed data of a node, we obtain the block position by using the containment relationship of the node's node identifier and the ids of the successive compressed blocks of the node's data stream. The position of the node's data is kept in an array and can be obtained by a binary search on the node identifier (in our case, this only takes log*1000* time since each block has at most 1000 records) and the data length is simply the difference between two successive positions.

A desirable feature of the queriable compressors XGrind [14] and XPRESS [10] is that decompression is avoided since string conditions can be encoded to match with the individually compressed data, while with our storage model (partial) decompression is always needed for the matching of string conditions. However, this is only true for exact-match and numeric range-match predicates, decompression is still inevitable in XGrind and XPRESS for any other value-based predicates such as string range-match, starts-with and substring matches.

To evaluate these predicates, our block model is much more efficient, since decompressing x blocks is far less costly than decompressing the corresponding *1000x* individually compressed data units. More importantly, as we will discuss in Section 5.2, our block model allows the efficient management of a buffer pool which significantly reduces the decompression overhead, while the compressed blocks serve naturally as input buffers to facilitate better disk reads.

5 Querying Compressed XML Using SIT

In this section, we present the queries supported by XQzip and show how they are evaluated on the compressed XML data.

5.1 Query Coverage

Our implementation of XQzip supports most of the core features of XPath 1.0 [15]. We extend XPath to select an arbitrary set of distinct elements by a single query and we also give a mapping to reduce the verbosity of the XPath syntax.

XPath Queries. A query specifies the matching nodes by the location path. A location path consists of a sequence of one or more location steps, each of which has an axis, a node test and zero or more predicates. The axis specifies the relationship between the context node and nodes selected by the location step. XQzip supports eight XPath axes: *ancestor*, *ancestor-or-self*, *attribute*, *child*, *descendant*, *descendant-or-self*, *parent* and *self*. XQzip simplifies the node test by comparing just the *eids* of the nodes. The predicates use arbitrary expressions, which can in turn be a location path containing more predicates and so on recursively, to further refine the set of nodes selected by the location step.

Apart from the comparison operators (=, ! =, >, <, >= and <=) and string operators (*contains*, i.e. substring, and *starts-with*), XQzip supports a complete set of standard aggregation operators (*count* and *sum*, *average*, *minimum* and *maximum*). XQzip also allows structure-based, value-based, and aggregation predicates to be combined by the logical operators (*not*, *or* and *and*).

XPath Group Queries. An XPath query can only specify one distinct element to be selected at a time. We modify the XPath syntax slightly to make it possible to select an arbitrary set of distinct elements by a single query, which we call an *XPath group query*. We use "(" and ")" to indicate the grouping, and "+" to represent the union of elements in a group. For example, the XPath group query "(//Orderitem[discount[. >= 20% *and* . <= 50%]]/(@id + quantity + price))" selects three elements from "Orderitem" with a "discount" of 20-50%.

Evaluating an XPath group query is much more efficient than evaluating a group of XPath queries, since all location paths inside a group share the same context node addressed by the location path just preceding the group. For example, given $(l/(l_0 + \cdots + l_n))$, we evaluate l only once for all l_i.

Abbreviated Syntax. Although the syntax of XPath is straightforward, it is rather verbose as a query language. We map the XPath axes, together with

Table 1. Abbreviated Syntax

Full Form	Abbr.	Full Form	Abbr.	Full Form	Abbr.	Full Form	Abbr.	Full Form	Abbr.
self	.	descendant	//	logical-not	!	sum()	$S	text()	$T
child	/	ancestor-or-self	.\	logical-or	|	count()	$C	wildcard	*
parent	\	descendant-or-self	/.	logical-and	&	max()	$U	contains	?=
ancestor	\\	root	..	average()	$A	min()	$L	starts-with	$=

the functions and operators, to more concise syntactic abbreviations. We show the mapping in Table 1 (Examples of mapping are given in [4], but omitted due to space limitation.). We note that the abbreviation of the axes *child*, *attribute*, *self*, *descendant-or-self* and *parent* are also given in [15], but we give different abbreviation to the last two axes as to give a complete but easy mapping for the queries covered by XQzip. In order to make parsing easier, our query parser also requires that predicates in queries be fully parenthesized.

5.2 Query Evaluation

XQzip evaluates queries in four major phases: (1) query parsing; (2) node selection; (3) data retrieval; and (4) query result output.

Query Parsing. The query parser translates an input query into a stream of events represented as integers, with positive values representing the XML elements (i.e. their Hash IDs) and negative values representing other expressions.

Node Selection. Node selection is critical in query evaluation. A survey [6] shows that contemporary XPath query engines evaluate XPath queries in exponential time. The cause of the exponential time evaluation is that for each location step, a set of nodes of size linear in the size of the document may be selected and each node in this set may in turn select a linear number of nodes for the next location step. Hence, the time complexity is $|D|^{|Q|}$, where $|D|$ is the document size and $|Q|$ the query size. Although [6] proposes a polynomial-time XPath evaluation algorithm, it is not applicable with our setting. We propose a simple algorithm which gives polynomial time complexity in the average case.

Our algorithm basically divides an axis closure into two disjoint areas. We associate each node in the SIT a *visited flag*. A subtree is *visited* if its root's visited flag is set. The union of all *visited subtrees* in an axis closure with respect to a context node forms the *visited_closure*, and the *unvisited_closure* is simply the difference between the axis closure and the visited_closure.

We give the core of our query evaluation algorithm in Fig. 6. The idea is as follows: on evaluating $s_i \ldots s_n$ where a_i is the *descendant* or *descendant-or-self* axes (and similarly if a_i is the *ancestor* or *ancestor-or-self* axes) w.r.t. a context node u, the subtree rooted at u is set to be visited when the evaluation process finishes $s_i \ldots s_n$ w.r.t. u (regardless of the evaluation result), since the result of $s_i \ldots s_n$ will always be the same for the same context node u. Moreover, an ancestor always includes its descendants and hence we set a node visited when it is included in the result set. Consequently, as the evaluation process goes on, more and more subtrees will be visited and the unvisited_closure becomes smaller and even vanishes. This implies that the nodes selected at each location step are no longer linear at later stages of the query evaluation. Hence, we have the average-case polynomial query evaluation time *in the size of the SIT*.

The worst-case time complexity is still exponential, i.e. $|SIT|^{|Q|}$, since the unvisited_closure has no effect on predicates. Nonetheless, predicate evaluation rarely checks all nodes specified by the predicate's location path but it terminates as soon as one evaluation returns true. More importantly, $|SIT|$ is often orders of magnitude smaller than $|D|$, implying that $|SIT|^{|Q|}$ is much smaller than $|D|^{|Q|}$. The space complexity is $O(|SIT| + |V_T|)$: $O(|SIT|)$ since we only hold the SIT in memory and all nodes in the result set are distinct (we do not count the space requirements for the buffer pool and for writing query result) and $O(|V_T|)$ space is needed to indicate which elements are matched for value-based predicates.

```
procedure evaluate_query ( u, i, Q )
/* u is the context node and i is initially set to 0; Q: s0 . . . si . . . sn, where si = < ai, ti, pij > */
begin
1.      for each node v in unvisited_closure ( ai (u) ) do
2.         if ( ti ( v ) is true and for all j, pij is true for v )
3.            if ( i < n )
4.               evaluate_query ( v, i + 1, Q );
5.            else    /* i = n */
6.               include v in the query result set and set v.visited_flag;
7.            if ( ai = \\ )
8.               set v.visited_flag;
9.      if ( ai = // )
10.        set u.visited_flag;
end
```

Fig. 6. Core Query Evaluation Algorithm

Data Retrieval and Decompression. We have described the retrieval of a compressed block and the retrieval of data from a decompressed block in Section 4. Although the data retrieval cost is not expensive, an element may appear in many places of a query or in a set of queries asked consecutively, resulting in a compressed block being retrieved and decompressed many times. Since we use gzip as our underlying compression tool, we cannot do much to improve the time to decompress a block. Instead, we avoid the scenario that the same block being repeatedly decompressed by introducing a buffer pool.

XQzip applies the LRU rule to manage a buffer pool for holding recently decompressed XML data. The buffer pool is modelled as a doubly-linked list with a head and tail pointer and the buffers do not have a fixed size but are allocated dynamically according to decompressed data size. When a new block is decompressed, the buffer manager appends it to the tail of the list. When a block is accessed again, the buffer manager takes it out from the list and appends it to the tail. We set a memory limit (default 16 MBytes) to the total size of the buffer pool. When the memory limit is reached, the buffer manager removes the buffers at the head of the list until memory is sufficient to allocate a new buffer.

Each buffer in the pool can be instantly accessed from the Hashtable and is assigned an *id* which is the same as the compressed block id, thus, avoiding decompressing a block again if a buffer with the same id is already in the pool.

The data access patterns of queries asked at a certain time are usually similar according to the principle of locality. Therefore, after some queries have been evaluated and the buffers have been initialized, new blocks tend to be decompressed only occasionally. Our experimental evaluation result shows that the buffer pool significantly reduces the querying time: the average querying time measured with a warm (initialized) buffer pool is 5.14 times less than that with a cold buffer pool. Moreover, restoring the original XML document from the compressed file is also much faster with a warm buffer pool.

Query Result Output. The query processor produces the query result specified by the output expression. XQzip allows the following output expressions: (1) *not specified*: all elements in the result set are returned; (2) location path/*text()*: only text contents of the result elements are returned; (3) location path/*op*: one of the five aggregation operations; and (4) [Q]: returns *true* if Q evaluates to be true, *false* otherwise.

6 Experimental Evaluation

We evaluated the performance of XQzip by an extensive set of experiments. All experiments were run on a Windows XP machine with a Pentium 4, 2.4 GHz and 256 MBytes main memory. We compared our compression performance with XMill, gzip and XGrind, and query performance with XGrind. Since XGrind is not able to compress all the datasets used in our evaluation and simply outputs query results as "found" or "not found", we modified the XGrind source code to make it work for all the datasets we used and write query results to a disk file, as XQzip does. We also made XGrind adapt to our experimental platform.

We first studied the effect of using different sized data blocks on the compression and query performance of XQzip; the aim of this experiment is to choose a feasible default block size for XQzip. We then performed, for each data source, four classes of experiments: (1) the effectiveness of the SIT; (2) compression ratios; (3) compression/decompression time; and (4) query performance. We define the compression ratio as: *Compression Ratio* = (1 − *Compressed file size*/*Original XML file size*) $*$ 100%, and we measure all the time in seconds.

We use eight data sources for our evaluation, which cover a wide range of XML data formats and structures. A description of the datasets is given in [4] due to space limit but we give their characteristics in Table 2, where E_num and A_num refer to the number of elements and attributes in the dataset respectively.

6.1 Effect of Using Different Block Size

We carried out a set of experiments to explore the effects of using different data block sizes on compression and query performance. We chose three representative

Table 2. XML Data Sources

Data Source	Size (MB)	Depth	Tags/Attrs	E_num	A_num
XMark	111	11	86	1666315	381878
OMIM	24.5	5	22	188052	0
DBLP	148	6	41	3883112	471124
SwissProt	109	5	100	2977031	2189859
Treebank	82	36	252	2437666	1
PSD	683	7	72	21305818	1052770
Shakespeare	7.3	6	23	179072	0
Lineitem	30.8	3	19	1022976	1

documents: SwissProt (which has no heavy text items), XMark (which has a lot of data and one heavy text item) and OMIM (whose data content is dominated by very heavy texts) for running the experiments.

Compression. For all datasets, compression performance is extremely poor for block sizes less than 2 KBytes and improves linearly with the increase in block size (greater than 2 KBytes), but does not improve much (within 10%) for block sizes beyond 100-150 (SwissProt: ~150, XMark: ~130, OMIM: ~100) KBytes.

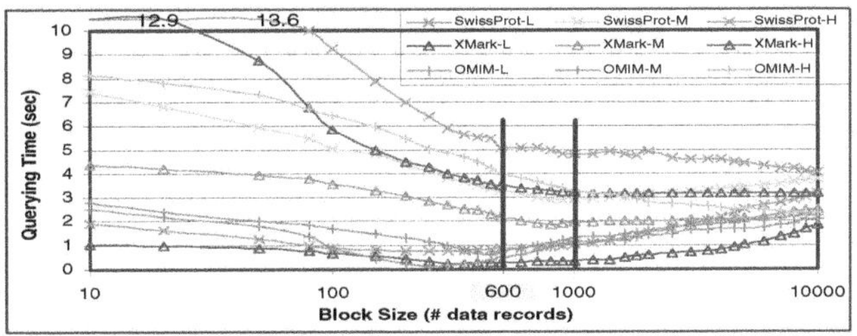

Fig. 7. Querying Time with Different Block Sizes

Query Evaluation. We use range predicates to select a set of queries (the queries are listed in [4] due to the space limit) of different selectivity for each dataset: low-selectivity (appr. 0.01%, 0.03%, 0.05%, 0.08% and 0.1%), medium-selectivity (appr. 0.3%, 0.5%, 0.7%, 1% and 3%) and high-selectivity (appr. 5%, 20%, 50%, 80% and 100%). For each dataset, we plot the average querying time of the queries of each selectivity group, represented by the prefixes L, M and H respectively in Fig. 7. We also found that the block size is actually sensitive to the number of records per block instead of number of bytes per block. We thus measure the block size in terms of number of data records per block.

For all the three data sources, query performance is poor on small block sizes (less than 100 records). High-selectivity queries have better performance on larger block sizes though performance improves only slightly for block sizes beyond 1000 records. Medium and low selectivity queries have best performance in the range of 500 to 800 records and 250 to 300 records respectively, and their querying time increases linearly for block sizes exceeding the optimal ranges. The difference in querying time of the various selectivity queries with the change in block size is mainly due to the inverse correlation between the decompression time of the different-sized blocks and the total number of blocks to be decompressed w.r.t. a particular block size, i.e. larger blocks have longer decompression time but fewer blocks need be decompressed, and vice versa. Although the optimal block size does not agree for the different data sources and different selectivity queries, we find that within the range of 600 to 1000 data records per block, the querying time of all queries is close to their optimal querying time. We also find that a block size of about 950 data records is the best average.

For most XML documents, a total size of 950 records of a distinct element is usually less than 100 KBytes, a good block size for compression. However, to facilitate query evaluation, we choose a block size of 1000 data records per block (instead of 950 for easier implementation) as the default block size for XQzip, and we demonstrate that it is a feasible choice in the subsequent subsections.

6.2 Effectiveness of the SIT

In this subsection, we show that the SIT is an effective index. In Table 3, $|T|$ represents the total number of tags and attributes in each of the eight datasets, while $|V_T|$ and $|V_I|$ show the number of nodes (presentation tags not indexed) in the structure tree and in the SIT respectively; $|V_I|/|V_T|$ is the percentage of node reduction of the index; Load Time (LT) is the time taken to load the SIT from a disk file to the main memory; and Acceleration Factor (AF) is the rate of acceleration in node selection using the SIT instead of the F&B-Index.

Table 3. Index Size

Data Source	$\|T\|$	$\|V_T\|$	$\|V_I\|$	$\|V_I\|/\|V_T\|$	LT	AF
XMark	2048193	1837608	30071	1.64%	0.67s	2.15
OMIM	188052	188052	445	0.24%	0.07s	2.16
DBLP	4354236	4350639	1877	0.04%	1.62s	2.11
SwissProt	5166890	5166890	1466332	28.38%	5.61s	1.92
Treebank	2437667	2437667	2277202	93.42%	2.26s	1.76
PSD	22358588	22358588	2425868	10.85%	9.97s	2.18
Shakespeare	179072	179072	3514	1.96%	0.07s	2.10
Lineitem	1022977	1022977	19	0.002%	0.42s	1.78

For five out of the eight datasets, the size of the SIT is only an average of 0.7% of the size of their structure tree, which essentially means that the query search space is reduced approximately 140 times. For SwissProt and PSD, although the reduction is smaller, it is still a significant one. The SIT of Treebank is almost the same size as its structure tree, since Treebank is totally irregular and very nested. We remark that there are few XML data sources in real life as irregular as Treebank. Note also that most of the SITs only need a fraction of a second to be loaded in the main memory. We find that the load time is roughly proportional to $|V_I|/|V_T|$ (i.e. irregularity) and $|V_T|$ of an XML dataset.

We built the F&B-Index (no *idrefs*, presentation tags and text nodes), using a procedure described in [7]. However, it ran out of memory for DBLP, SwissProt and PSD datasets on our experimental platform. Therefore, we performed this experiment on these three datasets on another platform with 1024 MBytes of memory (other settings being the same). On average, the construction (including parsing) of the SIT is 3.11 times faster than that of the F&B-Index. We next measured the time taken to select each distinct element in a dataset using the two indexes. The AF for each dataset was then calculated as the sum of time taken for all node selections of the dataset (e.g. 86 node selections for XMark since it has 86 distinct elements) using the F&B-Index divided by that using the SIT. On average, the AF is 2.02, which means that node selection using the SIT is faster than that using the F&B-Index by a factor of 2.02.

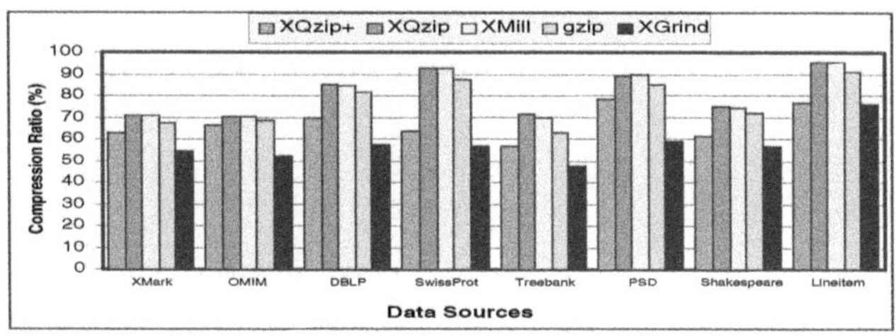

Fig. 8. Compression Ratio

6.3 Compression Ratio

Fig. 8 shows the compression ratios for the different datasets and compressors. Since XQzip also produces an index file (the SIT and data position information), we represent the sum of the size of the index file and that of the compressed file as XQzip+. On average, we record a compression ratio of 66.94% for XQzip+, 81.23% for XQzip, 80.94% for XMill, 76.97% for gzip, and 57.39% for XGrind.

When the index file is not included, XQzip achieves slightly better compression ratio than XMill, since no structure information of the XML data is kept in XQzip's compressed file. Even when the index file is included, XQzip is still able to achieve a compression ratio 16.7% higher than that of XGrind, while the compression ratio of XPRESS only levels with that of XGrind.

6.4 Compression/Decompression Time

Fig. 9a shows the compression time. Since XGrind's time is much greater than that of the others, we represent the time in logarithmic scale for better viewing. The compression time for XQzip is split into three parts: (1) parsing the input XML document; (2) applying gzip to compress data; and (3) building the SIT. The compression time for XMill is split into two parts as stated in [8]: (1)parsing and (2) applying gzip to compress the data containers. There is no split for gzip and XGrind. On average, XQzip is about 5.33 times faster than XGrind while it is about 1.58 times and 1.85 times slower than XMill and gzip respectively. But we remark that XQzip also produces the SIT, which contributs to a large portion of its total compression time, especially for the less regular data sources such as Treebank.

Fig. 9b shows the decompression time for the eight datasets. The decompression time here refers to the time taken to restore the original XML document. We include the time taken to load the SIT to XQzip's decompression time, represented as XQzip+. On average, XQzip is about 3.4 times faster than XGrind while it is about 1.43 time and 1.79 times slower than XMill and gzip respectively, when the index load time is not included. Even when the load time is included, XQzip's total time is still 3 times shorter than that of XGrind.

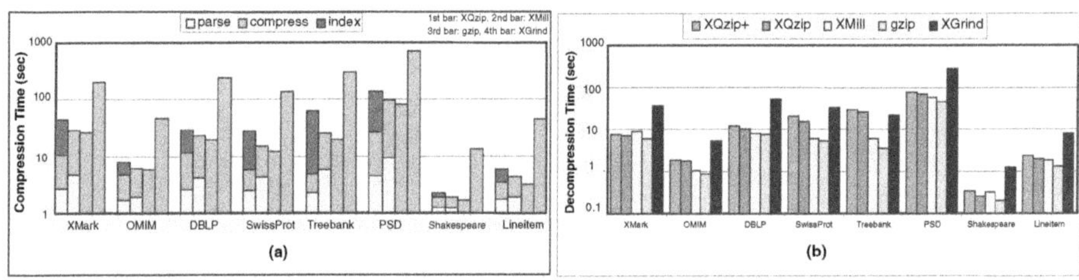

Fig. 9. (a) Compression Time (b) Decompression Time (Seconds in $\log_{10}$ scale)

6.5 Query Performance

We measured XQzip's query performance for six data sources. For each of the data sources, we give five representative queries which are listed in [4] due to the space limit. For each dataset except Treebank, Q1 is a simple path query for which no decompression is needed during node selection. Q2 is similar to Q1 but with an exact-match predicate on the result nodes. Q3 is also similar to Q1 but it uses a range predicate. The predicates are not imposed on intermediate steps of the queries since XGrind cannot evaluate such queries. Q4 and Q5 consists multiple and deeply nested predicates with mixed structure-based, value-based, and aggregation conditions. They are used to evaluate XQzip's performance on complex queries. The five queries of Treebank are used to evaluate XQzip's performance on extremely irregular and deeply nested XML data.

We recorded the query performance results in Table 4. Column (1) records the sum of the time taken to parse the input query and to select the set of result nodes. In case decompression is needed, the time taken to retrieve and decompress the data is given in Column (2). Column (3) and Column (4) give the time taken to write the textual query results (decompression may be needed) and the index of the result nodes respectively. Column (5)is the total querying time, which is the sum of Column (1) to (4) (note that each query was evaluated with an initially empty buffer pool). Column (6) records the time taken to evaluate the same queries but with the buffer pool initialized by evaluating several queries

Table 4. Query Evaluation Results

Data Sources		(1) Node Selecting Time (sec)	(2) Partial Decomp. Time (sec)	(3) Result (text) Processing Time (sec)	(4) Result (index) Processing Time (sec)	(5) Querying Time (sec) (XQzip-)	(6) Querying Time (sec) (XQzip+)	(7) Querying Time (sec) (XGrind)	(8) Query Result (text) (KBytes)	(9) Query Result (index) (KBytes)
XMark (111MB)	Q1	0.001	---	0.911	0.001	0.913	0.122	22.774	263	40
	Q2	0.001	0.920	0.012	0.001	0.934	0.295	23.067	0.8	0.09
	Q3	0.001	3.395	0.014	0.001	3.411	0.349	35.012	1.74	0.22
	Q4	0.003	---	0.551	0.030	0.584	0.118	---	14999	1256
	Q5	0.831	4.534	0.010	0.001	5.376	1.544	---	0.21	0.03
OMIM (24.5MB)	Q1	0.001	---	0.030	0.001	0.032	0.005	3.513	146	23.6
	Q2	0.001	0.021	0.011	0.001	0.034	0.014	4.690	19.1	2.7
	Q3	0.001	0.036	0.057	0.001	0.095	0.067	6.134	66.8	9.45
	Q4	0.005	---	---	---	0.005	0.005	---	---	---
	Q5	0.012	0.020	0.580	0.001	0.613	0.034	---	1666	274
DBLP (148MB)	Q1	0.001	---	0.370	0.010	0.381	0.034	19.582	7219	621
	Q2	0.001	0.330	0.013	0.001	0.345	0.029	26.108	59	6
	Q3	0.033	0.391	8.997	0.120	9.541	1.543	50.344	22940	1853
	Q4	0.001	---	0.000	0.000	0.001	0.001	---	No Match	No Match
	Q5	0.087	1.122	0.260	0.012	1.481	0.642	---	2312	205
Lineitem (30.8MB)	Q1	0.001	---	0.041	0.001	0.043	0.011	2.336	1176	175
	Q2	0.001	0.031	0.011	0.001	0.044	0.012	2.890	130	16
	Q3	0.001	0.058	0.015	0.001	0.075	0.014	3.210	393	54
	Q4	0.001	---	1.594	0.082	1.677	0.342	---	31539	4024
	Q5	0.002	0.030	---	---	0.032	0.007	---	---	---
Shakespeare (7.3MB)	Q1	0.001	---	0.035	0.001	0.037	0.014	1.311	865	89
	Q2	0.001	0.034	0.002	0.001	0.038	0.016	1.620	0.05	0.001
	Q3	0.001	0.032	0.005	0.001	0.039	0.016	2.312	48	2.3
	Q4	0.005	---	---	---	0.005	0.005	---	---	---
	Q5	0.007	0.032	---	---	0.039	0.014	---	---	---
Treebank (82MB)	Q1	0.321	---	3.304	0.120	3.745	0.674	---	21278	5659
	Q2	0.167	---	0.010	0.001	0.178	0.177	---	0.45	0.12
	Q3	0.183	---	1.012	0.064	1.259	0.453	---	785	204
	Q4	0.124	---	6.123	0.282	6.529	1.003	---	24111	6078
	Q5	0.156	---	6.004	0.274	6.434	0.985	---	24111	6078

containing some elements in the query under experiment prior to the evaluation of the query. Column (7) records the time taken by XGrind to evaluate the queries. Note that XGrind can only handle the first three queries of the first five datasets and does not give an index to the result nodes. Finally, we record the disk file size of the query results in Column (8) and (9). Note that for the queries whose output expression is an aggregation operator, the result is printed to the standard output (i.e. C++ stdout) directly and there is no disk write.

Column (1) accounts for the effectiveness of the SIT and the query evaluation algorithm, since it is the time taken for the query processor to process node selection on the SIT. Compared to Column (1), the decompression time shown in Column (2) and (3) is much longer. In fact, decompression would be much more expensive if the buffer pool is not used. Despite of this, XQzip still achieves an average total querying time 12.84 times better than XGrind, while XPRESS is only 2.83 times better than XGrind. When the same queries are evaluated with a warm buffer pool, the total querying time, as shown in Column (6), is reduced 5.14 times and is about 80.64 times shorter than XGrind's querying time.

7 Conclusions and Future Work

We have described XQzip, which supports efficient querying compressed XML data by utilizing an index (the SIT) on the XML structure. We have demonstrated by employing rich experimental evidence that XQzip (1) achieves comparable compression ratios and compression/decompression time with respect to XMill; (2) achieves extremely competitive query performance results on the compressed XML data; and (3) supports a much more expressive query language than its counterpart technologies such as XGrind and XPRESS. We notice that a lattice structure can be defined on the SIT and we are working to formulate a lattice whose elements can be applied to accelerate query evaluation.

Acknowledgements. This work is supported in part by grants HKUST 6185/02E and HKUST 6165/03E from the Research Grant Council of Hong Kong.

References

1. S. Abiteboul, P. Buneman, and D. Suciu. *Data on the web: from relations to semistructured data and XML*. San Francisco, Calif.: Morgan Kaufmann, c2000.
2. A. Arion and et. al. XQueC: Pushing Queries to Compressed XML Data. In *(Demo) Proceedings of VLDB*, 2003.
3. P. Buneman, M. Grohe, and C. Koch. Path Queries on Compressed XML. In *Proceedings of VLDB*, 2003.
4. J. Cheng and W. Ng. XQzip (long version). http://www.cs.ust.hk/~csjames/
5. R. Goldman and J. Widom. Dataguides: Enabling Query Formulation and Opeimization in Semistructured Databases. In *Proceedings of VLDB*, 1997.
6. G. Gottlob, C. Koch, and R. Pichler. Efficient Algorithms for Processsing XPath Queries. In *Proceedings of VLDB*, 2002.
7. R. Kaushik, P. Bohannon, J. F. Naughton and H. F. Korth. Covering Indexes for Branching Path Queries. In *Proceedings of SIGMOD*, 2002.
8. H. Liefke and D. Suciu. XMill: An Efficient Compressor for XML Data. In *Proceedings of SIGMOD*, 2000.
9. T. Milo and D. Suciu. Index Structures for Path Expressions. In *Proceedings of ICDT*, 1999.
10. J. K. Min, M. J. Park, C. W. Chung. XPRESS: A Queriable Compression for XML Data. In *Proceedings of SIGMOD*, 2003.
11. R. Paige and R. E. Tarjan. Three partition refinement algorithms. *SIAM Journal on Computing*, 16(6): 973-989, Decemember 1987.
12. D. Park. Concurrency and automata on infinite sequences. In *Theoretical Computer Science, 5th GI-Conf.*, LNCS 104, 176-183. Springer-Verlag, Karlsruhe, 1981.
13. A. R. Schmidt and F. Waas and M. L. Kersten and M. J. Carey and I. Manolescu and R. Busse. XMark: A Benchmark for XML Data Management. In *Proceedings of VLDB*, 2002.
14. P. M. Tolani and J. R. Haritsa. XGRIND: A Query-friendly XML Compressor. In *Proceedings of ICDE*, 2002.
15. World Wide Web Consortium. XML Path Language (XPath) Version 1.0. http://www.w3.org/TR/xpath/, W3C Recommendation 16 November 1999.
16. World Wide Web Consortium. XQuery 1.0: An XML Query Language. http://www.w3.org/TR/xquery/, W3C Working Draft 22 August 2003.

HOPI: An Efficient Connection Index for Complex XML Document Collections

Ralf Schenkel, Anja Theobald, and Gerhard Weikum

Max Planck Institut für Informatik
Saarbrücken, Germany
`http://www.mpi-sb.mpg.de/units/ag5/`
`{schenkel,anja.theobald,weikum}@mpi-sb.mpg.de`

Abstract. In this paper we present *HOPI*, a new connection index for XML documents based on the concept of the 2–hop cover of a directed graph introduced by Cohen et al. In contrast to most of the prior work on XML indexing we consider not only paths with child or parent relationships between the nodes, but also provide space– and time–efficient reachability tests along the ancestor, descendant, and link axes to support path expressions with wildcards in our XXL search engine. We improve the theoretical concept of a 2–hop cover by developing scalable methods for index creation on very large XML data collections with long paths and extensive cross–linkage. Our experiments show substantial savings in the query performance of the HOPI index over previously proposed index structures in combination with low space requirements.

1 Introduction

1.1 Motivation

XML data on the Web, in large intranets, and on portals for federations of databases usually exhibits a fair amount of heterogeneity in terms of tag names and document structure even if all data under consideration is thematically coherent. For example, when you want to query a federation of bibliographic data collections such as DBLP, Citeseer, ACM Digital Library, etc., which are not a priori integrated, you have to cope with structural and annotation (i.e., tag name) diversity. A query looking for authors that are cited in books could be phrased in XPath-style notation as `//book//citation//author` but would not find any results that look like `/monography/bibliography/reference/paper/writer`. To address this issue we have developed the XXL query language and search engine [24] in which queries can include similarity conditions for tag names (and also element and attribute contents) and the result is a ranked list of approximate matches. In XXL the above query would look like `//~book//~citation//~author` where ~ is the symbol for "semantic" similarity of tag names (evaluated in XXL based on quantitative forms of ontological relationships, see [23]).

When application developers do not have complete knowledge of the underlying schemas, they would often not even know if the required information can

E. Bertino et al. (Eds.): EDBT 2004, LNCS 2992, pp. 237–255, 2004.
© Springer-Verlag Berlin Heidelberg 2004

be found within a single document or needs to be composed from multiple, connected documents. Therefore, the paths that we consider in XXL for queries of the above kind are not restricted to a single document but can span different documents by following XLink [12] or XPointer kinds of links. For example, a path that starts as `/monography/bibliography/reference/URL` in one document and is continued as `/paper/authors/person` in another document would be included in the result list of the above query. But instead of following a URL-based link an element of the first document could also point to non-root elements of the second documents, and such cross-linkage may also arise within a single document.

To efficiently evaluate path queries with wildcards (i.e., // conditions in XPath), one needs an appropriate index structure such as Data Guides [14] and its many variants (see related work in Section 2). However, prior work has mostly focused on constructing index structures for paths without wildcards, with poor performance for answering wildcard queries, and has not paid much attention to document-internal and cross-document links. The current paper addresses this problem and presents a new path index structure that can efficiently handle path expressions over arbitrary graphs (i.e., not just trees or nearly-tree-like DAGs) and supports the efficient evaluation of queries with path wildcards.

1.2 Framework

We consider a graph $G_d = (V_d, E_d)$ for each XML document d that we know about (e.g., that the XXL crawler has seen when traversing an intranet or some set of Web sites), where 1) the vertex set V_d consists of all elements of d plus all elements of other documents that are referenced within d and 2) the edge set E_d includes all parent-child relationships between elements as well as links from elements in d to external elements.

Then, a collection of XML documents $X = \{d_1, \ldots, d_n\}$ is represented by the union $G_X = (V_X, E_X)$ of the graphs $G_1, ..., G_n$ where V_X is the union of the V_{d_i} and E_X is the union of the E_{d_i}. We represent both document–internal and cross–document links by an edge between the corresponding elements. Let $L_X = \{(v, w) \in E_X | v \in V_{d_i}, w \in V_{d_j} : i \neq j\}$ be the set of links that span different documents.

In addition to this element-granularity global graph, we maintain the document graph $DG_X = (DV_X, DE_X)$ with $DV_X = \{d_1, ..., d_n\}$ and $DE_X = \{(d_i, d_j) \mid \exists u \in d_i, v \in d_j \text{ s.t. } (u, v) \in L_X\}$. Both the vertices and the edges of the document graph are augmented with weights: the vertex weight vw_i for the vertex d_i is the number of elements that document d_i contains, and the edge weight ew_{ij} for the edge between d_i and d_j is the total number of links that exist from elements of d_i to elements of d_j.

Note that this framework disregards the ordering of an element's children and the possible ordering of multiple links that originate from the same element. The rationale for this abstraction is that we primarily address schema-less or highly heterogeneous collections of XML documents (with old-fashioned and

XML-wrapped HTML documents and href links being a special case, still interesting for Web information retrieval). In such a context, it is extremely unlikely that application programmers request accesss to the second author of the fifth reference and the like, simply because they do not have enough information about how to interpret the ordering of elements.

1.3 Contribution of the Paper

This paper presents a new index structure for path expressions with wildcards over arbitrary graphs. Given a path expression of the form `//A1//A2//...//Am`, the index can deliver all sequences of element ids $(e_1, \ldots, e_m)$ such that element e_i has tag name A_i (or, with the similarity conditions of XXL, a tag name A_i' that is "semantically" close to A_i). As the XXL query processor gradually binds element ids to query variables after evaluating subqueries, an important variation is that the index retrieves all sequences $(x, e_2, \ldots, e_m)$ or $(e_1, \ldots, y)$ that satisfy the tag-name condition and start or end with a given element with id x or y, respectively. Obviously, these kinds of reachability conditions could be evaluated by materializing the transitive closure of the element graph G_X. The concept of a 2-hop cover, introduced by Edith Cohen et al. in [9], offers a much better alternative that is an order of magnitude more space-efficient and has similarly good time efficiency for lookups, by encoding the transitive closure in a clever way. The key idea is to store for each node n a subset of the node's ancestors (nodes with a path to n) and descendants (nodes with a path from n). Then, there is a path from node x to y if and only if there is middle-man z that lies in the descendant set of x and in the ancestor set of y. Obviously, the subset of descendants and ancestors that are explicitly stored should be as small as possible, and unfortunately, the problem of choosing them is NP-hard.

Cohen et al. have studied the concept of 2-hop covers from a mostly theoretical perspective and with application to all sorts of graphs in mind. Thus they disregarded several important implementation and scalability issues and did not consider XML-specific issues either. Specifically, their construction of the 2-hop cover assumes that the full transitive closure of the underlying graph has initially been materialized and can be accessed as if it were completely in memory. Likewise, the implementation of the 2-hop cover itself assumes standard main-memory data structures that do not gracefully degrade into disk-optimized data structures when indexes for very large XML collections do not entirely fit in memory.

In this paper we introduce the HOPI index (2-HOP-cover-based Index) that builds on the excellent theoretical work of [9] but takes a systems-oriented perspective and successfully addresses the implementation and scalability issues that were disregarded by [9]. Our methods are particularly tailored to the properties of large XML data collections with long paths and extensive cross-linkage for which index build time is a critical issue. Specifically, we provide the following important improvements over the original 2–hop-cover work:

- We provide a heuristic but highly scalable method for efficiently constructing a complete path index for large XML data collections, using a divide-

and-conquer approach with limited memory. The 2-hop cover that we can compute this way is not necessarily optimal (as this would require solving an NP-hard problem) but our experimental studies show that it is usually near-optimal.
- We have implemented the index in the XXL search engine. The index itself is stored in a relational database, which provides structured storage and standard B-trees as well as concurrency control and recovery to XXL, but XXL has full control over all access to index data. We show how the necessary computations for 2-hop-cover lookups and construction can be mapped to very efficient SQL statements.
- We have carried out experiments with real XML data of substantial size, using data from DBLP [20], as well as experiments with synthetic data from the XMach benchmark [5]. The results indicate that the HOPI index is efficient, scalable to large amounts of data , and robust in terms of the quality of the underlying heuristics.

2 Related Work

We start with a short classification of structure indexes for semistructured data by the navigational axes they support. A *structure index* supports all navigational XPath axes. A *path index* supports the navigational XPath axes (`parent`, `child`, `descendants-or-self`, `ancestors-or-self`, `descendants`, `ancestors`). A *connection index* supports the XPath axes that are used as wildcards in path expressions (`ancestors-or-self`, `descendantsor-self`, `ancestors`, `descendants`).

All three index classes traditionally serve to support navigation within the internal element hierarchy of a document only, but they can be generalized to include also navigation along links both within and across documents. Our approach focuses on connection indexes to support queries with path wildcards, on arbitrary graphs that capture element hierarchies and links. axis):

Structure Indexes. Grust et al. [16,15] present a database index structure designed to support the evaluation of XPath queries. They consider an XML document as a rooted tree and encode the tree nodes using a pre– and post–order numbering scheme. Zezula et al. [26,27] propose tree signatures for efficient tree navigation and twig pattern matching. Theoretical properties and limits of pre–/post-order and similar labeling schemes are discussed in [8,17]. All these approaches are inherently limited to trees only and cannot be extended to capture arbitrary link structures.

Path Indexes. Recent work on path indexing is based on structural summaries of XML graphs. Some approaches represent all paths starting from document roots, e.g., Data Guide [14] and Index Fabric [10]. T–indexes [21] support a pre–defined subset of paths starting at the root. APEX [6] is constructed by utilizing data mining algorithms to summarize paths that appear frequently in the query workload. The Index Definition Scheme [19] is based on bisimilarity of nodes. Depending on the application, the index definition scheme can be used to define special indexes (e.g. 1–Index, A(k)–Index, D(k)–Index [22], F&B–Index) where k is the maximum length of the supported paths. Most of these approaches can handle arbitrary graphs or can be easily extended to this end.

Connection Indexes. Labeling schemes for rooted trees that support ancestor queries have recently been developed in the following papers. Alstrup and Rauhe [2] enhance the pre–/postorder scheme using special techniques from tree clustering and alphabetic codes for efficient evaluation of ancestor queries. Kaplan et al. [8,17] describe a labeling scheme for XML trees that supports efficient evaluation of ancestor queries as well as efficient insertion of new nodes. In [1, 18] they present a tree labeling scheme based on a two level partition of the tree, computed by a recursive algorithm called prune&contract algorithm.
All these approaches are, so far, limited to trees. We are not aware of any index structure that supports the efficient evaluation of ancestor and descendant queries on arbitrary graphs. The one, but somewhat naive, exception is to precompute and store the transitive closure $C_X = (V_X, E_X^+)$ of the complete XML graph $G_X = (V_X, E_X)$. C_X is a very time-efficient connection index, but is wasteful in terms of space. Therefore, its effectiveness with regard to memory usage tends to be poor (for large data that does not entirely fit into memory) which in turn may result in excessive disk I/O and poor response times.

To compute the transitive closure, time $O(|V|^3)$ is needed using the Floyd-Warshall algorithm (see Section 26.2 of [11]). This can be lowered to $O(|V|^2 + |V| \cdot |E|)$ using Johnson's algorithm (see Section 26.3 of [11]). Computing transitive closures for very large, disk-resident relations should, however, use disk-block-aware external storage algorithms. We have implemented the "semi-naive" method [3] that needs time $O(|E'_X| \cdot |V|)$.

3 Review of the 2–Hop Cover

3.1 Example and Definition

A *2–hop cover* of a graph is a compact representation of connections in the graph that has been developed by Cohen et al. [9]. Let $T = \{(u,v) | \textit{there is a path from } u \textit{ to } v \textit{ in } G\}$ the set of all connections in a directed graph $G = (V, E)$ (i.e., T is the transitive closure of the binary relation given by E). For each connection (u, v) G (i.e., $(u, v) \in T$) choose a node w on a path from u to v as a center node and add w to a set $L_{out}(u)$ of descendants of u and to a set $L_{in}(v)$ of ancestors of v. Now we can test efficiently if two nodes u and v are connected by a path by checking if $L_{out}(u) \cap L_{in}(v) = \emptyset$. There is a path from u to v iff $L_{out}(u) \cap L_{in}(v) \neq \emptyset$; and this connection from u to v is given by a first hop from u to some $w \in L_{out}(u) \cap L_{in}(v)$ and a second hop from w to v, hence the name of the method.

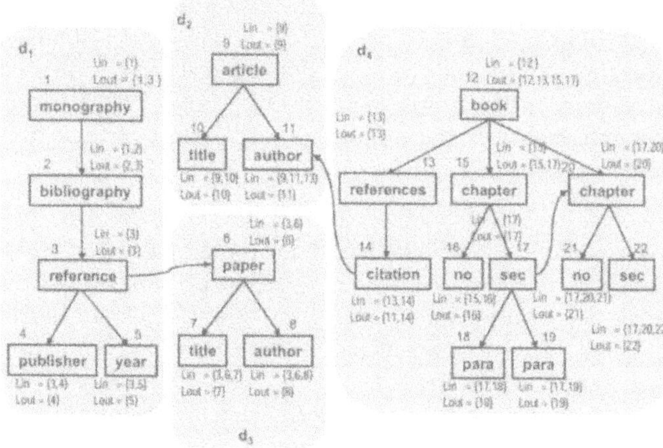

Fig. 1. Collection of XML Documents which include 2–hop labels for each node

As an example consider the XML document collection in Figure 1 with information for the 2–hop cover added. There is a path from u=(2,bibliography) to v=(6,paper), and we can easily test this because the intersection $L_{out}(u) \cap L_{in}(v) = \{3\}$ is not empty.

Now we can give a formal definition for the 2–hop cover of a directed graph. Our terminology slightly differs from that used by Cohen et al. While their concepts are more general, we adapted the definitions to better fit our XML application, leaving out many general concepts that are not needed here.

A 2–hop label of a node v of a directed graph captures a set of ancestors and a set of descendants of v. These sets are usually far from exhaustive; so they do not need to capture all ancestors and descendants of a node.

Definition 1 (2–Hop Label). *Let $G = (V, E)$ be a directed graph. Each node $v \in V$ is assigned a* 2–hop label *$L(v) = (L_{in}(v), L_{out}(v))$ where $L_{in}(v)$,$L_{out}(v) \subseteq V$ such that for each node $x \in L_{in}(v)$ there is a path $\langle x \dots v \rangle$ in G and for each node $y \in L_{out}(v)$, there is a path $\langle v \dots y \rangle$ in G.* □

The idea of building a connection index using 2–hop labels is based on the following property.

Theorem 1. *For a directed graph $G = (V, E)$ let $u, v \in V$ be two nodes with 2–hop labels $L(u)$ and $L(v)$. If there is a node $w \in V$ such that $w \in L_{out}(u) \cap L_{in}(v)$ then there is a path from u to v in G.* □

Proof. This is an obvious consequence of Definition 1. □

A *2–hop labeling* of a directed graph G assigns to each node of G a 2–hop label as described in Definition 1. A *2–hop cover* of a directed graph G is a 2–hop labeling that covers all paths (i.e., all connections) of G .

Definition 2 (2–Hop Cover). *Let $G = (V, E)$ be a directed graph. A 2–hop cover is a 2–hop labeling of graph G such that if there is a path from a node u to a node v in G then $L_{out}(u) \cap L_{in}(v) \neq \emptyset$.* □

We define the size of the 2–hop cover to be the sum of the sizes of all node labels: $\sum_{v \in V}(|L_{in}(v)| + |L_{out}(v)|)$.

3.2 Computation of a 2–Hop Cover

To represent the transitive closure of a graph, we are, of course, interested in a 2–hop cover with minimal size. However, as the minimum set cover problem can be reduced to the problem of finding a minimum 2–hop cover for a graph, we are facing an NP–hard problem [11,9]. So we need an approximation algorithm for large graphs. Cohen et al. introduce a polynomial-time algorithm that computes a 2–hop cover for a graph $G = (V, E)$ whose size is at most by a factor of $O(\log |V|)$ larger than the optimal size. We now sketch this algorithm.

Let $G = (V, E)$ be a directed graph and $G' = (V, T)$ be the transitive closure of G. For a node $w \in V$, $C_{in}(w) = \{v \in V | (v, w) \in T\}$ is the set of nodes $v \in V$ for which there is a path from v to w in G (i.e., the ancestors of w). Analogously, for a node $w \in V$, $C_{out}(w) = \{v \in V | (w, v) \in T\}$ is the set of nodes $v \in V$ for which there is a path from w to v in G (i.e., the descendants of w).

For a node $w \in V$ let $S(C_{in}(w), w, C_{out}(w)) = \{(u, v) \in T | u \in C_{in}(w) \text{ and } v \in C_{out}(w)\} = \{(u, v) \in T | (u, w) \in T \text{ and } (w, v) \in T\}$ denote the set of paths in G that contain w. The node w is called *center* of the set $S(C_{in}(w), w, C_{out}(w))$.

For a given 2-hop labeling that is not yet a 2-hop cover let $T' \subseteq T$ be the set of connections that are not yet covered. Thus, the set $S(C_{in}(w), w, C_{out}(w)) \cap T'$ contains all connections of G that contain w and are not covered. The ratio

$$r(w) = \frac{|S(C_{in}(w), w, C_{out}(w)) \cap T'|}{|C_{in}(w)| + |C_{out}(w)|}$$

describes the relation between the number of connections via w that are not yet covered and the total number of nodes that lie on such connections.

The algorithm for computing a nearly optimal 2–hop cover starts with $T' = T$ and empty 2–hop labels for each node of G. The set T' contains, at each stage, the set of connections that are not yet covered. In a greedy manner the algorithm chooses the "best" node $w \in V$ that covers as many not yet covered connections as possible using a small number of nodes. If we choose w with the highest value of $r(w)$, we arrive at a small set of nodes that covers many of the not yet covered connections but does not increase the size of the 2–hop labeling too much. After $w, C_{in}(w), C_{out}(w)$ are selected, its nodes are used to update the 2–hop labels:

$$\textit{for all } v \in C_{in}(w) : L_{out}(v) := L_{out}(v) \cup \{w\}$$

$$\textit{for all } v \in C_{out}(w) : L_{in}(v) := L_{in}(v) \cup \{w\}$$

and then $S(C_{in}(w), w, C_{out}(w))$ will be removed from T'. The algorithm terminates when the set T' is empty, i.e., when all connections in T are covered by the resulting 2–hop cover.

For a node $w \in V$ there are an exponential number of subsets $C_{in}(w), C_{out}(w) \subseteq V$ which must be considered in a single computation step. So, the above algorithm would require exponential time for computing a 2–hop cover for a given set T, and thus needs further considerations to achieve polynomial run-time.

The problem of finding the sets $C_{in}(w), C_{out}(w) \subseteq V$ for a given node $w \in V$ that maximizes the quotient r is exactly the problem of finding the *densest subgraph* of the *center graph* of w. We construct an auxiliary undirected bipartite center graph $CG_w = (V_w, E_w)$ of node w as follows. The set V_w contains two nodes v_{in} and v_{out} for each node $v \in V$ of the original graph. There is an undirected edge $(u_{out}, v_{in}) \in E_w$ if and only if $(u, v) \in T'$ is still not covered and $u \in C_{in}(w)$ and $v \in C_{out}(w)$. Finally, all isolated nodes can be removed from CG_w.

Figure 2 shows the center graph of node $w = 6$ for the graph given in Figure 1.

Definition 3 (Center Graph). *Let $G = (V, E)$ be a directed graph. For a given 2-hop labeling let $T' \subseteq T$ be the set of not yet covered connections in G, and let $w \in V$. The center graph $CG_w = (V_w, E_w)$ of w is an undirected, bipartite graph with node set V_w and edge set E_w. The set of nodes is $V_w = V_{in} \cup V_{out}$ where $V_{in} = \{u_{in} | u \in V : \exists v \in V : (u, v) \in T'$ and $u \in C_{in}(w)$ and $v \in C_{out}(w)\}$ and $V_{out} = \{v_{out} | v \in V : \exists u \in V : (u, v) \in T'$ and $u \in C_{in}(w)$ and $v \in C_{out}(w)\}$. There is a undirected edge $(u_{in}, v_{out}) \in E_w$ if and only if $(u, v) \in T'$ and $u \in C_{in}(w)$ and $v \in C_{out}(w)$.*

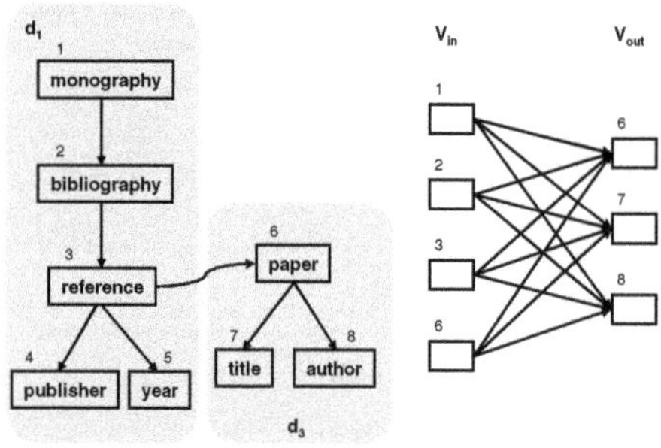

Fig. 2. Center graph of node $w = 6$ (labeled "paper")

The density of a subgraph is the average degree (i.e., number of incoming and outgoing edges) of its nodes. The densest subgraph of a given center graph CG_w can be computed by a linear-time 2–approximation algorithm which iteratively removes a node of minimum degree from the graph. This generates a sequence of subgraphs and their densities. The algorithm returns the subgraph with the highest density, i.e., the densest subgraph $CG'_w = (V'_w, E'_w)$ of the given center graph CG_w where density is the ratio of the number of edges to the number of nodes in the subgraph. We denote the density of this subgraph by d_w.

Definition 4 (Densest Subgraph). *Let $CG = (V, E)$ be an undirected graph. The densest subgraph problem is to find a subset $V' \subseteq V$ such that the average degree d of nodes of the subgraph $CG' = (V', E')$ is maximized where $d = |E'|/|V'|$. Here, E' is the set of edges of E that connect two nodes of V'.*

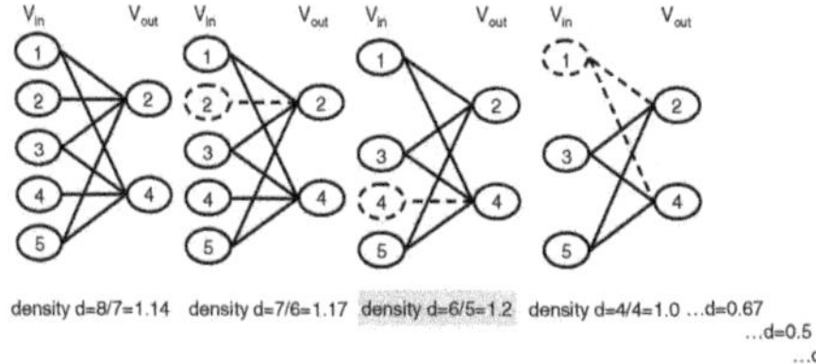

Fig. 3. Densest subgraph of a given center graph

The refined algorithm for computing a 2-hop cover chooses the "best" node w out of the remaining nodes in descending order of the density of the densest subgraph $CG'_w = (V'_{in} \cup V'_{out}, E'_w)$ of the center graph $CG_w = (V_{in} \cup V_{out}, E_w)$ of w. Thus, we efficiently obtain the sets $C_{in}(w) = V'_{in}$, $C_{out}(w) = V'_{out}$ for a given node w with maximum quotient $r(w)$.

So this consideration yields a polynomial-time algorithm for computing a 2–hop cover for the set T of connections of the given graph G.

Constructing the 2–hop cover has time complexity $O(|V|^3)$, because for computing the transitive closure of the given graph G using the Floyd–Warshall–Algorithm [11] the algorithm needs time $O(|V|^3)$ and for computing the 2–hop cover from the transitive closure the algorithm needs time $O(|V|^3)$. (The first step computes the densest subgraphs for —V— nodes, the second step computes the densest subgraphs for —V— nodes, etc., yielding $O(|V|^2)$ computations each with worst-case complexity $O(|V|)$.)

The 2-hop cover requires at most space $O(|V| \cdot \sqrt{|E|})$, yielding $O(|V|^2)$ in the worst case. However, it can be shown that for undirected trees the worst-case space complexity is $O(n \cdot \log n)$; Cohen et al. state in [9] that the complexity tends to remain that favorable for graphs that are very tree-similar (i.e., that can be transformed into trees by removing a small number of edges), which would be the case for XML documents with few links. Testing the connectivity of two nodes, using the 2-hop cover, requires time $O(L)$ on average, where L is the average size of the label sets of nodes. Experiments show that this number is very small for most nodes in our XML application (see Section 6).

4 Efficient and Scalable Construction of the HOPI Index

The algorithm by Cohen et al. for computing the 2–hop cover is very elegant from a theoretical viewpoint, but it has problems when applied to large graphs such as large-scale XML collections:

- Exhaustively computing the densest subgraph for all center graphs in each step of the algorithm is very time-consuming and thus prohibitive for large graphs.
- Operating on the precomputed transitive closure as an input parameter is very space-consuming and thus a potential problem for index creation on large graphs.

Although both problems arise only during index construction (and are no longer issues for index lookups once the index has been built), they are critical in practice for many applications require online index creation in parallel to the regular workload so that the processing power and especially the memory that is available to the index builder may be fairly limited. In this section we show how to overcome these problems and present the scalable HOPI index construction method. In Subsection 4.1 we develop results that can dramatically reduce the number of densest-subgraph computations. In Subsection 4.2 we develop a divide-and-conquer method that can drastically alleviate the space-consumption problem of initially materializing the transitive closure and also speeds up the actual 2–hop-cover computation.

4.1 Efficient Computation of Densest Subgraphs

A naive implementation of the polynomial-time algorithm of Cohen et al. would recompute the densest subgraph of all center graphs in each step of the algorithm, yielding $O(|V|^2)$ such computations in the worst case. However, as in each step only a small fragment of all connections is removed, only a few center graphs change; so it is unnecessary to recompute the densest subgraphs of unchanged center graphs. Additionally, it is easy to see that the density of the densest subgraph of a centergraph will not increase if we remove some connections.

We therefore propose to precompute the density d_w of the densest subgraph of the center graph of each node w of the graph G at the beginning of the algorithm. We insert each node w in a priority queue with d_w as priority. In each step of the algorithm, we then extract the node m with the current maximum density from the queue and check if the stored density is still valid (by recomputing d_m for this node). If they are different, i.e., the extracted value is larger than d_m, another node w may have a larger d_w; so we reinsert m with its newly computed d_w as priority into the queue and extract the current maximum. We repeat this procedure until we find a node where the stored density equals the current density. Even though this modification does not change the worst-case complexity, our experiments show that we have to recompute d_w for each node w only about 2 to 3 times on average, as opposed to $O(|V|)$ computations for each node in the original algorithm. Cohen et al. also discuss a similar approach to maintaining precomputed densest subgraphs in a heap, but their technique requires more space as they keep all centergraphs in memory.

In addition, there is even more potential for optimization. In our experiments, it turned out that precomputing the densest subgraphs took significant time for large graphs. This precomputation step can be dramatically accelerated by exploiting additional properties of center graphs that we will now derive.

We say that a center graph is *complete* if there are edges between each node $u \in V_{in}$ and each node $v \in V_{out}$. We can then show the following lemma:

Lemma 1. *Let G=(V,E) a directed graph and T' a set of connections that are not yet covered. A complete subgraph CG'_w of the center graph CG_w of a node $w \in V$ is always its densest subgraph.* □

Proof. For a complete subgraph CG'_w, $|V'_{in}| \cdot |V'_{out}| = |E'_w|$ holds. A simple computation shows that the density $d = (|V'_{in}| \cdot |V'_{out}|)/(|V'_{in}| + |V'_{out}|)$ of this graph is maximal. □

Using this lemma, we can show that the initial center graphs are always their densest subgraph. Thus we do not have to run the algorithm to find densest subgraphs but can immediately use the density of the center graphs.

Lemma 2. *Let G=(V,E) a directed graph and $T' = T$ the set of connections that are not yet covered. The center graph CG_w of a node $w \in V$ is itself its densest subgraph.* □

Proof. We show that the center graph is always complete, so that the claim follows from the previous lemma. Let T the set of all connections of a directed graph G. We assume there is a node w such that the corresponding center graph is not complete. Thus, the following three conditions hold:

1. there are two nodes $u \in V_{in}, v \in V_{out}$ such that $(u, v) \notin E_w$
2. there is at least one node $x \in V_{out}$ such that $(u, x) \in E_w$
3. there is at least one node $y \in V_{in}$ such that $(y, v) \in E_w$

As described in Definition 3 the second and third condition induce that (u, w), $(w, x) \in T$ and $(y, w), (w, v) \in T$. But if $(u, w) \in T$ and $(w, v) \in T$ then $(u, v) \in E_w$. This is a contradiction to our first condition. Therefore, the initial center graph of any node w is complete. □

Initially, the density of the densest subgraph of center graph for a node w can be computed as $d_w = |E_w|/(|V_w|)$. Although our little lemma applies only to the initial center graphs, it does provide significant savings in the precomputation: our experiments have shown that the densest subgraphs of 100,000 nodes can be computed in less than one second.

4.2 Divide-and-Conquer Computation of the 2–Hop Cover

Since materializing the transitive closure as the input of the 2–hop-cover computation can be very critical in terms of memory consumption, we propose a divide-and-conquer technique based on partitioning the original XML graph so that the transitive closure needs to be materialized only for each partition separately. Our technique works in three steps:

1. Compute a partitioning of the original XML graph. Choose the size of each partition (and thus the number of partitions) such that the 2-hop-cover computation for each partition can be carried out with memory-based data structures.
2. Compute the transitive closure and the 2-hop cover for each partition and store the 2–hop cover on disk.
3. Merge the 2-hop covers for partitions that have one or more cross-partition edges, yielding a 2–hop cover for the entire graph.

In addition to eliminating the bottleneck in transitive closure materialization, the divide-and-conquer algorithm also makes very efficient use of the available memory during the 2-hop-cover computation and scales up well, and it can even be parallelized in a straightforward manner. We now explain how steps 1 and 3 of the algorithm are implemented in our prototype system; step 2 simply applies the algorithm of Section 3 with the optimizations presented in the previous subsection.

Graph Partitioning. The general partitioning problem for directed graphs can be stated as follows: given a graph $G = (V, E)$, a node weight function $f_V : V \to \mathbf{N}$, an edge weight function $f_E : E \to \mathbf{N}$ and a maximal partition weight M, compute a set $P = \{V_1, \ldots, V_p\}$ of partitions of G such that $V = \cup_{i=1}^{p} V_i$, for each V_i $\sum_{v \in V_i} f_V(v) < M$, and the cost

$$c := \sum_{e \in E \cap \cup_{i \neq j} V_i \times V_j} f_E(e)$$

of the partitioning is minimized. We call the set $E_c := E \bigcap (\cup_{i \neq j} V_i \times V_j)$ the set of *cross-partition edges.*

This partitioning problem is known to be NP-hard, so the optimal partitioning for a large graph cannot be efficiently computed. However, the literature offers many good approximation algorithms. In our prototype system, we implemented a greedy partitioning heuristics based on [13] and [7]. This algorithm builds one partition at a time by selecting a seed node and greedily accumulating nodes by traversing the graph (ignoring edge direction) while trying to keep E_c as small as possible. This process is repeated until the partition has reached a predefined maximum size (e.g., the size of the available memory). We considered several approaches for selecting seeds, but none of them consistently won. Therefore, seeds are selected randomly from the nodes that have not yet been assigned to a partition, and the partitioning is recomputed several times, finally choosing the partitioning with minimal cost as the result.

In principle, we could invoke this partitioning algorithm on the XML element graph with all node and edge weights uniformly set to 1. However, the size of this graph may still pose efficiency problems. Moreover, we can exploit the fact that we consider XML data where most of the edges can be expected to be intra-document parent-child edges. So we actually consider only the much more compact document graph (introduced in Subsection 1.2) in the partitioning algorithm. The node weight of a document is the number of its elements, and the weight of an edge is the number of links from elements of edge-source document to elements of the edge-target document. This choice of weights is obviously heuristic, but our experiments show that it leads to fairly good performance.

Cover Merging. After the 2-hop covers for the partitions have been computed, the cover for the entire graph is built by forming the union of the partitions' covers and adding information about connections induced by cross-partition edges. A cross-partition edge $x \to y$ may establish new connections from the ancestors of x to the descendants of y if x and y have not been known to be connected before. To reflect this new connection in the 2-hop cover for the entire graph, we choose x as a center node and update the labels of other nodes as follows:

$$\text{for all } a \in \text{ancestors}(x) : L_{out}(a) := L_{out}(a) \cup \{x\}$$

$$\text{for all } d \in \text{descendants}(y) \cup \{y\} : L_{in}(d) := L_{in}(d) \cup \{x\}$$

As x may not be the optimal choice for the center node, the resulting index may be larger than necessary, but it correctly reflects all connections.

5 Implementation Details

As we aim at very large, dynamic XML collections, we implemented HOPI as a database-backed index structure, by storing the 2–hop cover in database tables and running SQL queries against these tables to evaluate XPath-like queries. Our implementation is based on Oracle 9i, but could be easily carried over to other database platforms. Note that this approach automatically provides us with all the dependability and manageability benefits of modern database systems, particularly, recovery and concurrency control. For storing the 2–hop cover, we need two tables LIN and LOUT that capture L_{in} and L_{out}:

```
CREATE TABLE LIN(                  CREATE TABLE LOUT(
            ID     NUMBER(10),                 ID     NUMBER(10),
            INID   NUMBER(10));                OUTID  NUMBER(10));
```

Here, ID stores the ID of the node and INID/OUTID store the node's label, with one entry in LIN/LOUT for each entry in the node's corresponding L_{in}/L_{out} sets. To minimize the number of entries, we do not store the node itself as INID or OUTID values. For efficient evaluation of queries, additional database indexes are built on both tables: a *forward index* on the concatentation of ID and INID for LIN and on the concatentation of ID and OUTID for LOUT, and a *backward index* on the concatentation of INID and ID for LIN and on the concatentation of OUTID and ID for LOUT. In our implementation, we store both LIN and LOUT as index-organized tables in Oracle sorted in the order of the forward index, so the additional backward indexes double the disk space needed for storing the tables.

Additionally we maintain information about nodes in G_X in the table NODES that stores for each node its unique ID, its XML tag name, and the url of its document.

Connection Test. To test if two nodes identified by their ID values ID1 and ID2 are connected, the following SQL statement would be used if we stored the complete node labels (i.e., did not omit the nodes themselves from the stored L_{in} and L_{out} labels):

```
SELECT COUNT(*) FROM LIN, LOUT WHERE LOUT.ID=ID1 AND LIN.ID=ID2
                                 AND LOUT.OUTID=LIN.INID
```

This query performs the intersection of the L_{out} set of the first node with the L_{in} set of the second node. Whenever the query returns a non-zero value, the nodes are connected. It is evident that the backward indexes are helpful for an efficient evaluation of this query. As we do not store the node itself in its label, the system executes the following two additional, very efficient, queries that capture this case:

```
SELECT COUNT(*) FROM LIN, LOUT WHERE LOUT.ID=ID1 AND LOUT.OUTID=ID2
SELECT COUNT(*) FROM LIN, LOUT WHERE LIN.ID=ID2  AND LIN.INID=ID1
```

Again it is evident that the backward and the forward index speed up query execution. For ease of presentation, we will not mention these additional queries in the remainder of this section anymore.

Compute Descendants. To compute all descendants of a given node with ID `ID1`, the following SQL query is submitted to the database:

```
SELECT LIN.ID FROM LIN, LOUT WHERE LOUT.ID=ID1
                                   AND LOUT.OUTID=LIN.INID
```

It returns the IDs of the descendants of the given node. Using the forward index on `LOUT` and the backward index on `LIN`, this query can be efficiently evaluated.

Descendants with a Given Tag Name. As the last case in this subsection, we consider how to determine the descendants of a given node with ID `ID` that have a given tag name `N`. The following SQL query solves this case:

```
SELECT LIN.ID FROM LIN, LOUT, NODES WHERE LOUT.ID=ID1
   AND LOUT.OUTID=LIN.INID AND LIN.ID=NODES.ID AND NODES.NAME=N
```

Again, the query can be answered very efficiently with an additional index on the `NAMES` column of the `NODES` table.

6 Experimental Evaluation

6.1 Setup

In this section, we compare the storage requirements and the query performance of HOPI with other, existing path index approaches, namely

- the pre- and postorder encoding scheme [15,16] for tree-structured XML data,
- a variant of APEX [6] without optimization for frequently used queries (APEX-0) that was adapted to our model for the XML graph,
- using the transitive closure as a connection index.

We implemented all strategies as indexes of our XML search engine XXL [24,25]. However, to exclude any possible influences of the XXL system on the measurements, we measured the performance independently from XXL by immediately calling the index implementations. As we want to support large-scale data that do not fit into main memory, we implemented all strategies as database applications, i.e., they read all information from database tables without explicit caching (other than the usual caching in the database engine).

All our experiments were run on a Windows-based PC with a 3GHz Pentium IV processor, and 4 GByte RAM. We used a Oracle 9.2 database server than ran on a second Windows-based PC with a 3GHz Pentium IV, 1GB of RAM, and a single IDE hard disk.

6.2 Results with Real-Life Data

Index Size. As a real-life example for XML data with links we used the XML version of the DBLP collection [20]. We generated one XML doc for each 2nd-level element in DBLP (`article`, `inproceedings`, ...) plus one document for the top-level `dblp` document and added XLinks that correspond to `cite` and `crossref` entries. The resulting document collection consists of 419,334 documents with 5,244,872 elements and 63,215 links (plus the 419,333 links from the top-level document to the other documents). To see how large HOPI gets for real-life data, we built the index for two fragments of DBLP:

- *The fragment consisting of all publications in EDBT, ICDE, SIGMOD and VLDB.* It consists of 5,561 documents with totally 141,140 nodes and 9,105 links. The transitive closure for this data has 5,651,952 connections that require about 43 Megabytes of storage (2x4 bytes for each entry, without distance information). HOPI built without partitioning the document graph resulted in a cover of size 231,596 entries requiring about 3.5 Megabytes of storage (2x4 bytes for each entry plus the same amount for the backward index entry); so HOPI is about 12 times more compact than the transitive closure. Partitioning the graph into three partitions and then merging the computed covers yielded a cover of size 251,315 entries which is still about 11 times smaller than the transitive closure. Computing this cover took about 16 minutes.
- *The complete DBLP set.* The transitive closure for the complete DBLP set has 306,637,532 entries requiring about 2.4 Gigabytes of storage. With partitioning the document graph into 53 partitions of size 100,000 elements, we arrived at an overall cover size of 27,190,122 entries that require about 415 Megabytes of storage; this is a compression factor of about 5.8. Computing this cover took about 24 hours without any parallelization. About $\frac{1}{3}$ of the time was spent on computing the partition covers; merging the covers consumed most of the time because of many SQL statements executed against the PC-based low-end database server used in our experiments (where especially the slow IDE disk became the main bottleneck).

Storage needed for the pre- and postorder labels for the tree part of the data (i.e., disregarding links which are not supported by this approach) was 2x4 bytes per node, yielding about 1 Megabyte for the small set and about 40

Megabytes for complete DBLP. For APEX-0, space was dominated by the space needed for storing the edge extents, that required in our implementation storing 4 additional bytes per node (denoting the node of the APEX graph in which this node resides) and 2x4 bytes for each edge of the XML graph (node that HOPI does not need this information), yielding an overall size of about 1.7 megabytes for the small set and about 60.5 megabytes for complete DBLP.

Query Performance. For studying query performance, we concentrated on comparing HOPI against the APEX-0 path index, one of the very best index structures that supports parent-child and ancestor-descendant axes on arbitrary graphs.

Figure 4 shows the wall-clock time to test whether two given elements are connected, averaged over many randomly chosen `inproceedings` and `author` element pairs, as a function of the distance between the elements. The figure shows that HOPI performs one or two orders of magnitude better than APEX-0 and was immune to increases in the distance.

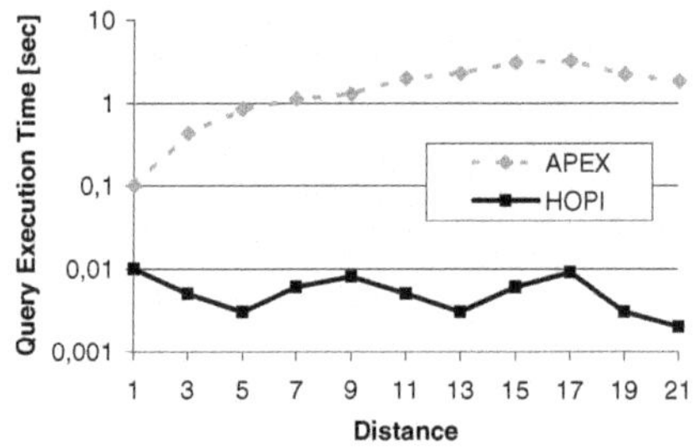

Fig. 4. Time to test connection of two nodes at varying distances

For path queries with wildcards but without any additional conditions, such as `//inproceedings//author`, HOPI outperformed APEX-0 only marginally. Note, however, that such queries are rare in practice. Rather we would expect additional filter predicates for the source and/or target elements; and with conventional index lookups for these conditions the connection index would be primarily used to test connectivity between two given elements as shown in Figure 4 above.

Figure 5 shows the wall-clock time to compute all descendants of a given node, averaged over randomly chosen nodes, as a function of the number of descendants. (We first randomly selected source nodes, computed their descendants, and later sorted the results by the number of descendants.) Again, HOPI can beat APEX-0 by one or two orders of magnitude. But, of course, we should recall that APEX has not been optimized for efficient descendant lookups, but is primarily designed for parent-child navigation.

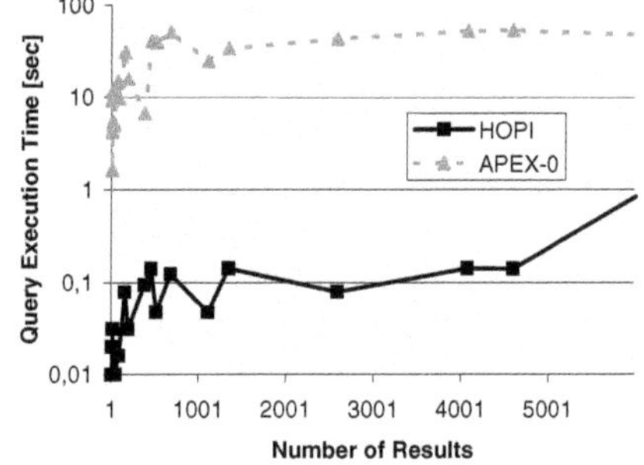

Fig. 5. Time to compute all descendants for a given node

Finally, for finding all descendants of a given node that have a given tag name, HOPI was about 4 to 5 times faster than APEX-0 on average. This was measured with randomly chosen `inproceedings` elements and finding all their `author` descendants.

6.3 Scalability Results with Synthetic Data

To systematically assess our index with respect to document size and fraction of links, we used the XMach benchmark suite [5] to generate a collection of synthetic documents. A document had about 165 elements on average. We randomly added links between documents, where both the number of incoming and outgoing links for each document was chosen from a Zipf distribution with skew parameter 1.05, choosing high numbers of outgoing links ("hubs") for documents with low ID and high numbers of incoming links ("authorities") for documents with high ID. For each link, the element from which it starts was chosen uniformly among all elements within the source document, and the link's destination was chosen as the root element of the target document, reflecting the fact that the majority of links in the Web point to the root of documents.

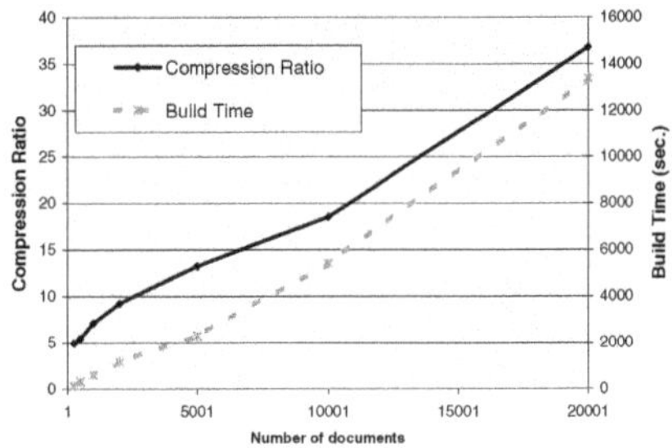

Fig. 6. Compression factor of HOPI vs. transitive closure, with varying number of documents

Figure 6 shows the compression ratio that HOPI achieves compared to the materialized transitive closure as the number of documents increases, with one outgoing and one incoming link per document on average (but with the skewed distribution discussed above). The dashed curve in the figure is the index build time for HOPI. For the collection of 20,001 documents that consisted of about 3.22 million elements, HOPI's size was about 96 megabytes as compared to about 37 megabytes for APEX-0.

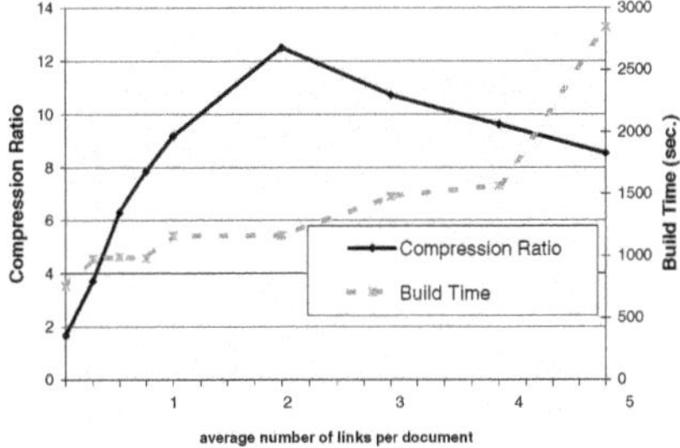

Fig. 7. Compression factor of HOPI vs. transitive closure, with varying number of links per document

Figure 7 shows the compression ratio and the index build time as the number of links per document increases, for a fixed number, 1001, of documents. At an average link density of five links per document, HOPI's size was about 60 megabytes, whereas APEX-0 required about 4 megabytes. The compression ratio ranges from about 5 to more than an order of magnitude.

These results demonstrate the dramatic space savings that HOPI can achieve as compared to the transitive closure. As for index build time, HOPI nicely scales up with increasing number of documents when the number of links is kept constant, whereas Figure 7 reflects the inevitable superlinear increase in the cost as the graph density increases.

7 Conclusion

Our goal in this work has been to develop a space- and time-efficient index structure that supports XML path queries with wildcards such as `/book//author`, regardless of whether the qualifying paths are completely within one document or span documents. We believe that HOPI has achieved this goal and significantly outperforms previously proposed XML index structures for this type of queries while being competitive for all other operations on XML indexes. Our experimental results show that HOPI is an order of magnitude more space-efficient than an index based on materializing the transitive closure of the XML graph, and still significantly smaller than the APEX index. In terms of query performance, HOPI substantially outperforms APEX for path queries with wildcards and is competitive for child and parent axis navigation.

The seminal work by Cohen et al. on the 2-hop cover concept provided excellent algorithmic foundations to build on, but we had to address a number of important implementation issues that are decisive for a practically viable system solution that scales up with very large collections of XML data. Most importantly, we developed new solutions to the issues of efficient index construction with limited memory. Our future work on this theme will include efficient algorithms for incremental updates and further improvements of index building by using more sophisticated algorithms for graph partitioning.

References

[1] S. Abiteboul et al. Compact labeling schemes for ancestor queries. In *SODA 2001*, pages 547–556, 2001.
[2] S. Alstrup and T. Rauhe. Improved labeling scheme for ancestor queries. In *SODA 2002*, pages 947–953, 2002.
[3] F. Bancilhon and R. Ramakrishnan. An amateur's introduction to recursive query processing strategies. In *SIGMOD 1986*, pages 16–52, 1986.
[4] H. Blanken, T. Grabs, H.-J. Schek, R. Schenkel, and G. Weikum (eds.). *Intelligent Search on XML Data.* LNCS 2818, Springer, Sept. 2003.
[5] T. Böhme and E. Rahm. Multi-user evaluation of XML data management systems with XMach-1. In *EEXTT 2002*, pages 148–158, 2003.
[6] C.-W. Chung, J.-K. Min, and K. Shim. APEX: An adaptive path index for XML data. In *SIGMOD 2002*, pages 121–132, 2002.
[7] P. Ciarlet, Jr and F. Lamour. On the validity of a front oriented approach to partitioning lage sparse graphs with a connectivity constraint. *Numerical Algorithms*, 12(1,2):193–214, 1996.
[8] E. Cohen et al. Labeling dynamic XML trees. In *PODS 2002*, pages 271–281, 2002.
[9] E. Cohen et al. Reachability and distance queries via 2-hop labels. In *SODA 2002*, pages 937–946, 2002.

[10] B. Cooper et al. A fast index for semistructured data. In *VLDB 2001*, pages 341–350, 2001.
[11] T. H. Cormen, C. E. Leiserson, and R. L. Rivest. *Introduction to Algorithms.* MIT Press, 1st edition, 1990.
[12] S. DeRose et al. XML linking language (XLink), version 1.0. W3C recommendation, 2001.
[13] C. Farhat. A simple and efficient automatic FEM domain decomposer. *Computers and Structures*, 28(5):579–602, 1988.
[14] R. Goldman and J. Widom. DataGuides: Enabling query formulation and optimization in semistructured databases. In *VLDB 1997*, pages 436–445, 1997.
[15] T. Grust. Accelerating XPath location steps. In *SIGMOD 2002*, pages 109–120, 2002.
[16] T. Grust and M. van Keulen. Tree awareness for relational DBMS kernels: Staircase join. In Blanken et al. [4].
[17] H. Kaplan et al. A comparison of labeling schemes for ancestor queries. In *SODA 2002*, pages 954–963, 2002.
[18] H. Kaplan and T. Milo. Short and simple labels for small distances and other functions. In *WADS 2001*, pages 246–257, 2001.
[19] R. Kaushik et al. Covering indexes for branching path queries. In *SIGMOD 2002*, pages 133–144, 2002.
[20] M. Ley. DBLP XML Records. Downloaded Sep 1st, 2003.
[21] T. Milo and D. Suciu. Index structures for path expressions. In *ICDT 1999*, pages 277–295, 1999.
[22] C. Qun et al. D(k)-index: An adaptive structural summary for graph-structured data. In *SIGMOD 2003*, pages 134–144, 2003.
[23] R. Schenkel, A. Theobald, and G. Weikum. Ontology-enabled XML search. In Blanken et al. [4].
[24] A. Theobald and G. Weikum. The index-based XXL search engine for querying XML data with relevance ranking. In *EDBT 2002*, pages 477–495, 2002.
[25] A. Theobald and G. Weikum. The XXL search engine: Ranked retrieval of XML data using indexes and ontologies. In *SIGMOD 2002*, 2002.
[26] P. Zezula, G. Amato, and F. Rabitti. Processing XML queries with tree signatures. In Blanken et al. [4].
[27] P. Zezula et al. Tree signatures for XML querying and navigation. In *1st Int. XML Database Symposium*, pages 149–163, 2003.

Efficient Distributed Skylining for Web Information Systems

Wolf-Tilo Balke[1], Ulrich Güntzer[2], and Jason Xin Zheng[1]

[1] Computer Science Department, University of California,
Berkeley, CA 94720, USA
{balke,xzheng}@eecs.berkeley.edu
[2] Insitut für Informatik, Universität Tübingen,
72076 Tübingen, Germany
guentzer@informatik.uni-tuebingen.de

Abstract. Though skyline queries already have claimed their place in retrieval over central databases, their application in Web information systems up to now was impossible due to the distributed aspect of retrieval over Web sources. But due to the amount, variety and volatile nature of information accessible over the Internet extended query capabilities are crucial. We show how to efficiently perform distributed skyline queries and thus essentially extend the expressiveness of querying today's Web information systems. Together with our innovative retrieval algorithm we also present useful heuristics to further speed up the retrieval in most practical cases paving the road towards meeting even the real-time challenges of on-line information services. We discuss performance evaluations and point to open problems in the concept and application of skylining in modern information systems. For the curse of dimensionality, an intrinsic problem in skyline queries, we propose a novel sampling scheme that allows to get an early impression of the skyline for subsequent query refinement.

1 Introduction

In times of the ubiquitous Internet the paradigm of Web information systems has substantially altered the world of modern information acquisition. Both in business and private life the support with information that is stored in a decentralized manner and assembled at query time, is a resource that users more and more rely on. Consider for instance Web information services accessible via mobile devices. First useful services like city guides, route planning, or restaurant booking have been developed [5], [2] and generally all these services will heavily rely on information distributed over several Internet sources possibly provided by independent content providers. Frameworks like NTT DoCoMo's i-mode [18] already provide a common platform and business model for a variety of independent content providers.

Recent research on web-based information systems has focused on employing middleware algorithms, where users had to specify weightings for each aspect of their query and a central compensation function was used to find the best matching objects [7], [1]. The lack of expressiveness of this 'top k' query model, however, has first been addressed by [8] and with the growing incorporation of user preferences into

E. Bertino et al. (Eds.): EDBT 2004, LNCS 2992, pp. 256–273, 2004.
© Springer-Verlag Berlin Heidelberg 2004

database systems [6], [10] and information services [22] the limitations of the entire model became more and more obvious. This led towards the integration of so-called 'skyline queries' (e.g. [4]) into database systems. Basically the 'skyline' is a non-discriminating combination of numerical preferences under the notion of Pareto optimality. Since it was only proposed for database systems working over a central (multi-dimensional) index structure, extending its expressiveness also to the broad class of Web information systems is most desirable. The contribution of this paper is to undertake this task and present an efficient algorithm with proven optimality. We will present a distributed skylining algorithm and show how to enhance its efficiency for most practical cases by suitable heuristics. We will also give an extensive performance evaluation and propose a scheme to cope with high-dimensional skylines.

As a running example throughout this paper we will focus on a typical Web information service scenario. Our algorithm will support a sample user interacting with a route planning service like e.g. Map-Quest's Road Trip Planner or Driving Directions [16]. This is a characteristic example of a Web service where the gathering of on-line information is tantamount: though a routing service is generally capable of finding possible routes, the quality of certain routes - and thus their desirability to the user - may heavily differ depending on current information like road blockings, traffic jams or the weather conditions. Thus we first have to collect a set of user-specified preferences and integrate them with our query to the routing system. But of course users won't be able to specify something like 'for my purposes the shortest route is 0.63 times more important than that there is no jam' in a sensible, i.e. *intuitive*, way. Queries rather tend to be formulated like 'I would prefer my route to be rather short and with little jams' giving no explicit weightings for a compensation function. Hence the *skyline* over the set of possible routes is needed for a high quality answer set. Since there often are many sources on the Internet offering current traffic information, usually the query also will have to be posed to a variety of sources needing an efficient algorithm for the distributed skyline computation. The example of a route planning service also stresses the focus on real time constraints, because most on-line information like traffic jams or accidents will have to be integrated on the fly and delivered immediately to be of use for navigation. Since such efficient algorithms for distributed retrieval are still problematic, today's web portals like Map-Quest allow only a minimum of additional information (e.g. avoiding toll roads) and use central databases, that provide necessary information. However, given the dynamic nature of the Web this does not really meet the challenges of Web information systems.

2 Web Information Systems Architecture and Related Work

Modern Web information systems feature an architecture like the one roughly sketched in figure 1. Using a (mobile) client device the user poses a query. Running on an application/Web server this query may be enriched with information about a user (e.g. taken from stored profiles) and will be posed to a set of Internet sources. Depending on the nature of the query different sources can be involved in different parts of the query, e.g. individual sources for traffic jams or weather information. Collecting the individual results the combining engine runs an algorithm to compute

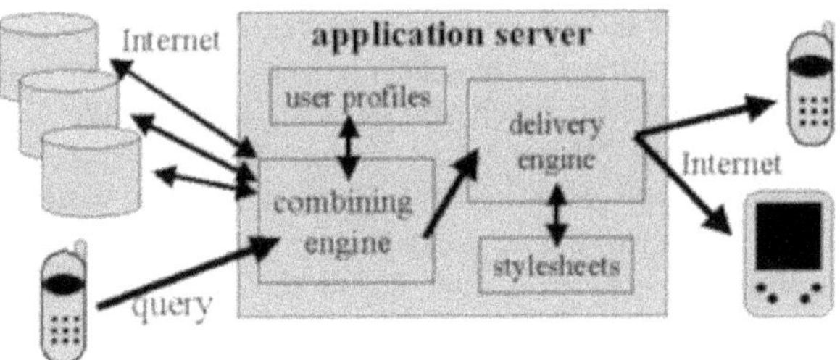

Fig. 1. Web information system architecture

the overall best matching objects. These final results have then to be aggregated according to each individual user's specifications and preferences. After a transformation to the appropriate client format (e.g. using XSLT with suitable stylesheets) the best answers will be returned to the user.

The first area to address such a distributed retrieval problem was the area of 'top k retrieval' over middleware environments, e.g. [7], [9], [19]. Especially for content-based retrieval of multimedia data these techniques have proven to be particularly helpful. Basically all algorithms distinguish between different query parts (subqueries) evaluating different characteristics, which often have to be retrieved from various subsystems or web sources. Each subsystem assesses a numerical score value (usually normalized to [0,1]) to each object in the collection. The middleware algorithms use two basic kinds of accesses that can be posed: there is the iteration over the best results from one source (or with respect to a single aspect of the query) called a '*sorted access*' and there is the so-called '*random access*' that retrieves the score value with respect to one source or aspect for a certain given object.

The physical implementation of these accesses always strongly depends on the application area and will usually differ from system to system. The gain of speeding up a single access (e.g. using a suitable index) will of course complement the total run-time improvement by reducing the overall number of accesses. Therefore minimizing the number of necessary object accesses and thus also the overall query runtimes is tantamount to build practical systems (with real-time constraints) [1]. Prototypical Web information systems of that kind are e.g. given by [3], [5] or [2]. However, all these top k retrieval systems relied on a single combining function (often called 'utility function') that is used to compensate scores between different parts of the query. Being worse in one aspect can be compensated by the object doing better in another part. However, the semantic meaning of these (user provided) combining functions is unclear and users often have to guess the 'right' weightings for their query. The area of operations research and research in the field of human preferences like [6] or [8] has already since long criticized this lack in expressiveness.

A more expressive model of non-discriminating combination has been introduced into the database community by [15]. The 'skyline' or 'Pareto set' is a set of *non-dominated* answers in the result for a query under the notion of Pareto optimality. The typical notion of Pareto optimality is that without knowing the actual database content, there can also be no precise a-priori knowledge about the most sensible optimization in each individual case (and thus something that would allow a user to choose weightings for a compensation function). The Pareto set or skyline hence contains all best matching object for all possible strictly monotonic optimization

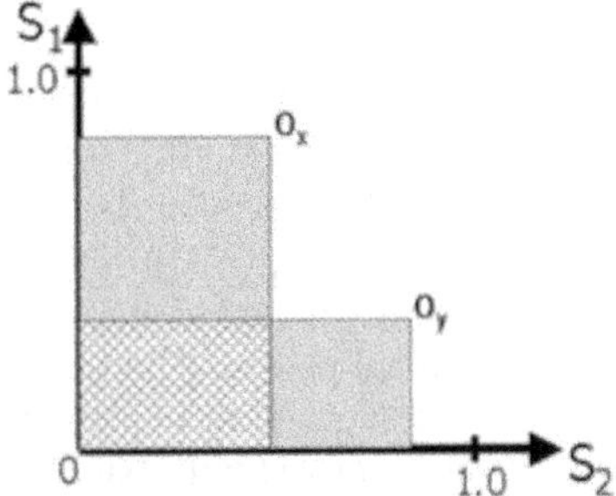

Fig. 2. Skyline objects and regions of domination

functions. An example for skyline objects with respect to two query parts and their scorings S_1 and S_2 is shown in figure 2. Each database object is seen as a point in multidimensional space characterized by its score values. For instance objects o_x =(0.9, 0.5) and o_y=(0.4, 0.9) both dominate all objects within a rectangular area (shaded). But o_x and o_y are not comparable, since o_x dominates o_y in S_1 and o_y dominates o_x in S_2. Thus both are part of the skyline.

Whereas [15] and the more recent extensive system in [12] with an algebra for integrating the concept of Pareto optimality with the top k retrieval model for preference engineering and query optimization in databases [11], are more powerful in that they do not restrict skyline queries to numerical domains, they both rely on the naïve algorithm of quadratic complexity doing pairwise comparisons of all database objects. Focusing on numerical domains [4] was able to gain logarithmic complexity along the lines of [14]. Initially skyline queries were mainly intended to be performed within a single database query engine. Thus the first algorithms and subsequent improvements all work on a central (multidimensional) index structure like R*-trees [20], certain partitioning schemes [21] or k-nearest-neighbor searches [13]. However, such central indexes cannot be applied to distributed Web information systems. Since there is still no algorithm to process distributed skyline queries, up to now the extension of expressiveness of the query model could not be integrated in Web information services. We will deal with the problem of designing an efficient distributed algorithm for computing skyline queries only relying on sorted and random accesses.

3 A Distributed Skylining Algorithm

In this section we will investigate distributed skylining and present a first basic algorithm. As we have motivated in the previous section the basic skyline consists of all non-dominated database objects. That means all database objects for which there is no object in the database that is better or equal in all dimensions, but in at least one aspect strictly better. Assuming every database object to be represented by a point in n-dimensional space with the coordinates for each dimension given by its scores for the respective aspect, we can formulate the problem as:

The Skyline Problem: Given set $O := \{o_1,...,o_N\}$ of N database objects, n score-functions $s_1,...s_n$ with $s_i : O \rightarrow [0,1]$ and n sorted lists $S_1,...,S_n$ containing all database objects and their respective score values using one of the score function for each list; all lists are sorted descending by score values starting with the highest scores. Wanted is the subset P of all non-dominated objects in O, i.e. $\{o_i \in P \mid \neg\exists\ o_j \in O : (s_1(o_i) \leq s_1(o_j) \wedge ... \wedge s_n(o_i) \leq s_n(o_j) \wedge \exists\ q \in [1,...,n] : s_q(o_i) < s_q(o_j)) \}$

We will now approach a suitable distributed algorithm to efficiently find this set. Our algorithm basically consists of three phases: The first phase (step 1) will perform sorted accesses until we have definitely seen all objects that can possibly be part of the skyline. The second phase (step 2 and 3) will extend the accesses on all objects with minimum seen scores in the lists and will prune all other database objects. The third phase (step 4) will employ focused random accesses to discard all seen objects that are dominated before returning the skyline to the user. To keep track of all accessed objects we will need a central datastructure containing all available information about all objects seen, but also group the objects with respect to the sorted lists that they have occurred in. The beauty of this design is that we only have to check for domination within the small sets for each list and can return some first results early.

Basic Distributed Skyline Algorithm

0. Initialize a datastructure $P := \emptyset$ containing records with an identifier and n real values indexed by the identifiers, initialize n lists $K_1,...,K_n := \emptyset$ containing records with an identifier and a real value, and initialize n real values $p_1,...,p_n := 1$

1. Initialize counter $i := 1$.

1.1. Get the next object o_{new} by sorted access on list S_i

1.2. If $o_{new} \in P$, update its record's i-th real value with $s_i(o_{new})$, else create such a record in P

1.3. Append o_{new} with $s_i(o_{new})$ to list K_i

1.4. Set $p_i := s_i(o_{new})$ and $i := (i \bmod n) + 1$

1.5. If all scores $s_j(o_{new})$ $(1 \leq j \leq n)$ are known, proceed with step 2 else with step 1.1.

2. For $i = 1$ to n do

2.1. While $p_i = s_i(o_{new})$ do sorted access on list S_i and handle the retrieved objects like in step 1.2 to 1.3

3. If more than one object is entirely known, compare pairwise and remove the dominated objects from P.

4. For $i = 1$ to n do

4.1. Do all necessary random accesses for the objects in K_i that are also in P, immediately discard objects that are not in P

4.2. Take the objects of K_i and compare them pairwise to the objects in K_i. If an object is dominated by another object remove it from K_i and P

5. Output P as the set of all non-dominated objects

For ease of understanding we show how the algorithm works for our running example: for mobile route planning in [2] we have shown for the case of top k retrieval how traffic information aspects can be queried from various on-line sources. Posing a query on the best route with respect to say its length (S_1) and the traffic density (S_2) our user employs functions that evaluate the different aspects, but is not sure how to compensate length and density. The following tables show two result lists with some routes R_i ordered by decreasing scores with respect to their length and current traffic density:

S_1 (length)					
R1	R3	R5	R4	R7	...
0.9	0.9	0.8	0.8	0.7	...

S_2 (traffic density)					
R2	R4	R6	R3	R8	...
0.9	0.8	0.8	0.8	0.7	...

The algorithm in step 1 will in turn perform sorted accesses on both lists until the first route R4 has been seen in both lists leading to the following potential skyline objects:

Route	R1	R2	R3	**R4**	R5	R6
Score S_1	0.9	?	0.9	**0.8**	0.8	?
Score S_2	?	0.9	?	**0.8**	?	0.8

In step 2 we will do some additional sorted accesses on all routes that possibly could also show the current minimum score in each list and find that R7 in S_1 already has a smaller score, hence we can discard it. In contrast R3 in S_2 has the current minimum score, hence we have to add it to our list, but can then discard the next object R8 in S_2, which does have a lower score. Step 3 now tests, if one of the two completely seen routes R3 and R4 is dominated: by comparing their scores we find that R4 is dominated by R3 and can thus be discarded. We can now regroup objects into sets K_i and do all necessary random accesses and the final tests for domination only within each set.

K_1		
R1	R3	R5
0.9	0.9	0.8
?	0.8	?

K_2		
R2	R6	R3
?	?	0.9
0.9	0.8	0.8

Step 4 now works on the single sets K_i. We have to make a random access on R1 with respect to S_2 and find that its score is say 0.5. Thus we get its score pair (0.9, 0.5) and have to check for domination within set K_1. Since it is obviously dominated by the score pair (0.9, 0.8) of R3, we can safely discard R1. Doing the same for object R5 we may retrieve a value of say 0.6 thus R5's pair (0.8, 0.6) is also dominated by R3 and we are finished with set K_1. Please note that we could have saved this last random access on R5, since we already know that all unknown scores in S_2 must be smaller than the current minimum of the respective list (in this case 0.8). This would already have shown R5's highest possible score pair (0.8, 0.8) to be dominated by R3. At this point we are already able to output the non-dominated objects of K_1, since lemma 2 shows that if any of the objects of set K_1 should be dominated by objects in another set K_i , they also always would be dominated by an object *in* K_1.

Dealing with K_2 we have to make random accesses for S_1 on routes R2 and R6 and find for route R2 a score value of say 0.6 leading to a score pair of (0.6, 0.9). But it cannot be dominated by R3's pair (0.9, 0.8), as its score in S_2 is higher than R3's. Finally for R6 we may find a score of say 0.2, thus it is dominated by R3 and can be discarded (also in these cases we could have saved two random accesses like shown above). We now can deliver the entire skyline to our user's query consisting of routes R3 and R2. All other routes in the database (either seen or not yet accessed) are definitely dominated by at least one of these two routes.

Independently of any weightings a user could have chosen for a compensation function thus either route R3 or R2 would have turned up as top object dominating all other routes. Delivering them both as top objects saves users from having to state unintuitive a-priori weightings and allows for an informed choice according to each individual user's preferences. But we still have to make sure, that upon termination no pruned object can belong to the skyline and no dominated object will ever be returned. We will state two lemmas and then prove the correctness of our algorithm.

Lemma 1 (Discarding unseen objects)

After an object o_x has been seen in each list and all objects down to at least score $s_i(o_x)$ $(1 \leq i \leq n)$ in each list have also been seen, the objects not yet seen cannot be part of the skyline, more precisely they are dominated by o_x.

Proof: Let o_x be the object seen in all lists. Then with p_i as the minimum score seen in each list we have due to the sorting of the lists $\forall\, i\ (1 \leq i \leq n) : s_i(o_x) \geq p_i$. Since all objects having a score of at least score p_i in list i have been collected, we can conclude that any not yet seen object o_{unseen} satisfies $\forall\, i\ (1 \leq i \leq n) : s_i(o_{unseen}) < p_i \leq s_i(o_x)$ and thus $\forall\, i\ (1 \leq i \leq n) : s_i(o_{unseen}) < s_i(o_x)$. Hence o_{unseen} is dominated by o_x and thus cannot be part of the skyline independently of o_x itself being part of the set or being dominated. ■

We can even show the somewhat stronger result that, if we have seen an object o_x in all lists and stop the sorted accesses in step 2 after seeing only a single worse object in any of the lists, we can still safely discard all unseen objects. This is because we need the strict '<' in one single list only. In the other lists '≤' would still be sufficient (since due to sorting '=' is the highest possible).

Lemma 2 (Objects can only be dominated by objects in the same set K_i)

Assume that all objects that have been seen, are divided into n sets according to the lists in which they occurred, i.e. if an object o_x occurs in list i $(1 \leq i \leq n)$ it is added to set K_i. Lets further assume that in the lists in which o_x occurred, all objects having at least the respective score value of o_x have also been seen. Then, if the object o_x in any set K_i is dominated by any other object, this object has also to be part of set K_i.

Proof: Let o_x be any dominated object already seen and assigned to at least one set K_i $(1 \leq i \leq n)$. Due to Lemma 1 o_x cannot be dominated by any unseen object, thus the dominating object o_y has already been seen and thus has also been assigned to at least one of the sets K_i $(1 \leq i \leq n)$. If o_x and o_y are in exactly the same sets there is nothing to show. Thus let us assume o_y dominates o_x and there exists at least one set K_j $(1 \leq j \leq n)$ containing object o_x, but not object o_y. Thus due to the sorting of the lists and the fact that we have seen all objects in list x having at least the respective score value $s_j(o_x)$ of object o_x, we have to conclude that $s_j(o_y) < s_j(o_x)$ in contrast to the assumption that o_y dominates o_x. ■

Theorem 1: (Correctness of the Basic Algorithm)

The basic algorithm always terminates and delivers the entire set of non-dominated objects and only the set of non-dominated objects.

Proof: Since the termination is obvious, we have to show that a) no relevant object is missed by our algorithm and that b) no object in the returned set can be dominated by any other object.

Ad a) Steps 1 and 2 of the algorithm collect all objects, until one object has been seen in all lists and all objects of the minimum score in each list have also been seen. Thus Lemma 1 applies and we can safely discard all unseen objects, since they cannot be part of the skyline. In steps 3 and 4 only dominated objects are discarded (in step 4 we also might use upper boundary estimations of some scores for discarding, but since the upper boundaries are best case estimations, it is obvious that objects discarded in step 4 would also be discarded using their actual score values). Thus the set returned in step 5 will contain all objects of the skyline.

Ad b) After steps 1 to 3 Lemma 2 applies and we can restrict the search for dominating objects to the sets K_i ($1 \leq i \leq n$). Since in any set K_i no object can be dominated by an object having a strictly smaller score with respect to the i-th list, it is sufficient to do pairwise comparisons with those objects having a larger or equal score. Thus Step 4 correctly discards all dominated objects within the sets K_i and since all objects returned in step 5 must have been part of at least one K_i, they cannot be dominated by any object. ■

Since the algorithm is supposed to work with distributed web sources thus having rather high access costs, for the optimality and complexity considerations we have to focus on the necessary object accesses instead of main memory operations. The next theorem will show that the termination condition of phase 1 is optimal, since one of the objects seen in all lists is definitely part of the skyline. Stopping earlier would thus discard possibly non-dominated objects; we therefore have to see an object in all lists.

Theorem 2 (Optimality of Sorted Accesses):
The basic algorithm uses an optimal number of sorted accesses.

Proof: Sorted accesses are only made during the first two steps. After the first step one object has been seen in all lists. In step 2 we do further sorted accesses to get all objects with at least one score equal to the respective minimum score in each list. If we can show that among these objects and the object seen in all lists there always is at least one object belonging to the skyline, we could not stop doing sorted accesses earlier and thus use an optimal number of sorted accesses.

Let o_x be the first object that has occurred in all lists and p_i ($1 \leq i \leq n$) be the minimum scores in each list. Then we get $\forall\, i\; s_i(o_x) \geq p_i$ and $s_k(o_x) = p_k$ for at least one $1 \leq k \leq n$. For every object $o \neq o_x$ seen during step 1 of our algorithm there is at least one list S_j ($1 \leq j \leq n$) in which o has not been seen and hence we have either $s_j(o) < p_j \leq s_j(o_x)$ *(A)* or $s_j(o) = p_j$ *(B)*.

If case *(A)* applies for an object o, it cannot dominate the object o_x. Thus object o_x can only be dominated by an object for which case *(B)* applies, i.e. one of those objects that have occurred during step 2 of our algorithm. Choose among those objects the maximum object o_m dominating o_x. We will then show by contradiction that o_m belongs to the skyline:

If o_m would not be part of the skyline, it would have to be dominated by another object. Due to Lemma 1 o_m cannot be dominated by any unseen object, and due to being maximal among those objects occurring in step 2, it would have to be dominated by an object o seen in step 1and not seen in step 2 of the algorithm. This means, that there is an index j, such that $s_j(o)$ is smaller than p_j (cf. case 1 above). Therefore o can dominate neither o_x nor o_m leading to the contradiction. ■

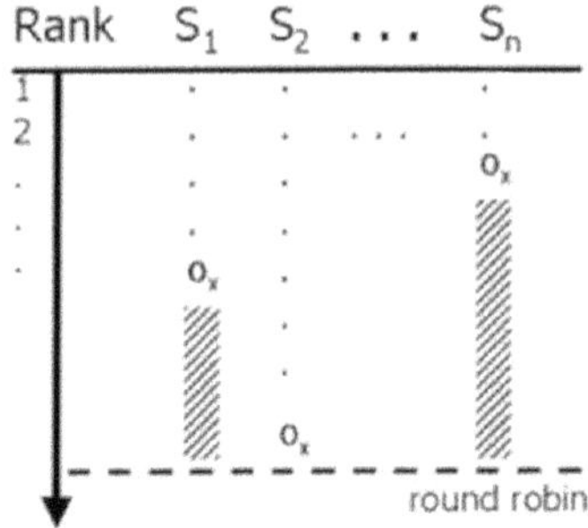

Fig. 3. Savings implemented by heuristic 1

4 Improvements by Advanced Heuristics

Having shown that we will have to see at least one object in all the lists we will now focus on heuristics to find this object that causes the first phase to terminate more quickly and will try to minimize the necessary comparisons within the sets K_i.

Consider the situation shown in figure 3. Having adopted a round robin strategy in our basic algorithm, we have to expand all the lists until an object (e.g. o_x) occurs in all lists. But our proof of correctness allows us to immediately disregard even all those objects that have only occurred in any list *after* o_x (i.e. the shaded areas). Thus using all information about discovered objects at an early stage and employing a sophisticated control flow, we can improve our algorithm by immediately focusing on objects that can be assumed to foster early termination by being the first object to occur in all lists with reasonably high probability. Having chosen such an object we will no longer do sorted accesses on lists in which this object has already occurred, but rather expand lists in which its score is still unknown. Therefore we need to know how to find an object that is most probable to terminate our algorithm. In case studies on multi-objective optimization like [3] one of the most effective functions in estimating dominating objects is a greedy strategy called 'maximin' function. Our heuristic for estimating an appropriate object has been built along the lines of this function. But whereas the 'maximin' function only focuses on the maximum value after evaluating the minimum scores for each object and thus advocates the smallest possible expansion in every list, our heuristic additionally will take advantage of the fact that because of the sorting of the lists and recent sorted accesses on it, we *exactly know* the current score value in each list and thus can better estimate the necessary expansion.

Heuristic 1: If all scores of an object are known (either by sorted or by random access) consider all scores value in lists where it has not yet been seen by sorted access. If we sum up the difference between these values and the last score value seen by sorted access on the respective list, we get an aggregated value for each object. The object with a minimum value can be considered the most promising object. It still needs the least expansion in all lists. Therefore it is probable to be the object that will first occur in all of the lists. If there are more objects with the same minimum score, the one with the minimum sum of scores will need the least expansion of all lists.

To find these objects, we will mix sorted and random accesses already in the first phase to immediately get all information about an object. Since these accesses would have been necessary in the third phase of the basic algorithm anyway, by doing them immediately we just spend a few random accesses too much for those objects that we might already have seen by sorted access in more than one list. Knowing all scores we can now estimate how far we would have to expand all the lists, if we had to see the latest object in all lists adding up the differences between values seen by random access and the current score in the respective list. Focusing only on the best object with respect to necessary list expansions, we will employ indicators that tell us which lists to expand next, avoiding those lists our object has already occurred in.

Since we gather all information about an object at its first occurrence and immediately assess its probable utility for termination, we will not expand any list more than necessary. If we can choose several lists for the next sorted access, we can either pick one randomly, or, if we expect non-uniform data distributions a complementing indicator technique e.g. using the derivatives of the score distribution function in each list along the lines of [9] may be employed to estimate the expected gain in each list. Please note that our heuristic 1 will not affect the abstract order of complexity from our previously stated optimality results, because the maximum improvement factor over the round robin strategy can only be the number of lists (n). But, given the rather expensive costs of object accesses over the Internet even small numbers of accesses saved will improve the overall run-time behavior like shown in [5] or [1]. Thus, also improvements taking only constant factors off the algorithm's complexity should be employed towards meeting real-time constraints.

Our second heuristic will focus on the necessary comparisons within the sets K_i. Obviously no object having a smaller score with respect to S_i will be able to dominate any object having a larger score. Thus we do not really need the pairwise comparisons like suggested in the basic algorithm. We only have to compare pairwise between objects within the same set Ki having equal scores and can otherwise test, if the objects with smaller scores are dominated by ones having larger score values.

Heuristic 2: Start with the objects first seen in each set K_i and compare pairwise all objects with the same score value. Then only test for domination by objects with higher scores.

To implement this we employ the fact that since the lists are ordered, also all K_i are ordered. We will use two counters q and b and divide each K_i into subsets grouping same score values. Starting with the first set we will assume the objects as enumerated and set q to the number of the first object of a subset and b to the number of the last. According to heuristic 2 we don't need any comparisons with objects on numbers larger than b, we need pairwise comparisons for all objects between q and b and we need a test for domination by all objects with numbers smaller than q.

Using our heuristics we will now present our improved algorithm for distributed skyline queries. Again we need the initialization of a central datastructure for the set of possible skyline objects and sets containing the objects for each sorted list as before. Additionally we need a variable for the object that is considered most promising to terminate our algorithm. Note that all necessary random accesses are now already performed in step 1 in order to derive a greedy estimation of the object most probable to foster early termination.

Improved Distributed Skyline Algorithm

0. Initialize a datastructure P := ∅ containing records with an identifier and n real values for scores indexed by the identifiers, initialize n lists $K_1,\dots,K_n$:= ∅ containing records with an identifier and one real value, initialize a record term_oid containing an identifier and a real value := 0 and initialize n real values $p_1,\dots,p_n$:= 1
1. Initialize counter i := 1.
1.1. Get the next object o_{new} by sorted access on list S_i, set $p_i := s_i(o_{new})$ and update the real value in term_oid according to step 1.3
1.2. If $o_{new} \notin P$
1.2.1. Create a record in P containing oid and score in S_i in the i-th entry in its record.
1.2.2. Do random accesses on all missing scores and update the record in P like above
1.3. Add up the difference between o_{new}'s score values in lists, where it has not yet been seen, and the p_i in these lists
1.4. If this sum is smaller than the value in term_oid, replace the oid and the value in term_oid with the oid and new value of o_{new}
1.5. If the sum is equal to the value in term_oid, replace like in 1.4 only, if the total sum of scores for o_{new} is larger than the sum for the object given by term_oid
1.6. Append o_{new} with $s_i(o_{new})$ to list K_i
1.7. Set i to any number of a set K_i in which the object given by term_oid has not yet occurred. If it is element of all K_i proceed with step 2 else with step 1.1.
2. Let o_{term} be the object given by term_oid. For i = 1 to n do
2.1. While $p_i = s_i(o_{term})$ do sorted access on list S_i and update p_i like in step 1.4, append it to list K_i like in step 1.3 and if the retrieved objects is not in P handle it like in step 1.2.1 and 1.2.2
3. For i = 1 to n do
3.1. q :=0, b:= 0
3.2. While there is an q+1-th entry in K_i do
3.2.1. Repeat (collect an object of K_i and set b:= b+1) until the value of the b+1-th entry in K_i is strictly smaller than the b-th entry or there is no b+1-th entry
3.2.2. If any collected object does not exist in P, discard the object and remove it from K_i and set b := b-1
3.2.3. Compare the collected objects pairwise. If any of these objects is dominated, discard it and remove it from K_i and P and set b := b-1
3.2.4. Compare all collected objects pairwise to all objects being on a position smaller or equal than q in K_i. If any collected object is dominated, discard it and remove it from K_i and P and set b := b-1
3.2.5. Set q := b
4. Output P as the set of all non-dominated objects, i.e. the skyline.

Since the correctness of the improved algorithm is straightforward along the lines of the basic algorithm and also the optimality holds, we will again return to our example to show how the algorithm works. Again we pose a query on the best route with respect to its length (S_1) and the traffic density (S_2). The following tables show our result lists with routes ordered by scores:

S_1 (length)					
R1	R3	R5	R4	R7	...
0.9	0.9	0.8	0.8	0.7	...

S_2 (traffic density)					
R2	R4	R6	R3	R8	...
0.9	0.8	0.8	0.8	0.7	...

The algorithm in step 1 will perform sorted accesses on S_1 and finds route R1. A random access will reveal R1's second score 0.5 and that its sum of unseen values is (1.0-0.5)=0.5. That means our first estimation is that we will have to expand the list S_2 down to score 0.5 in order to see R1 in all lists. Thus we have to do a sorted access on list S_2 trying to decrease the scores to find R1's second score, and we get route R2. The second score of R2 leads to a sum of differences of 0.3. Thus it is more promising than R1 and we will focus on lists where R2 has not yet occurred. Accessing S_1 we encounter object R3, whose second score 0.8 again leads to a change in our term_oid to R3 with value 0.1. After we have also accessed R4 and R6 in list S_2 who both show larger sums, we finally encounter R3 and can terminate step 1.

Route	R1	R2	R3	R4	R6
Score S_1	0.9	0.6	0.9	0.8	0.2
Score S_2	0.5	0.9	0.8	0.8	0.8
term_oid	R1	R2	R3	R3	R3
next access	S_2	S_1	S_2	S_2	S_2

In step 2 we will do some additional accesses on all routes also showing the current minimum score in each list and find that R5 in S_1 already has a smaller score, hence we can discard it, and we can also discard the next object R8 in S_2.

K_1	
R1	R3
0.9	0.9

K_2			
R2	R6	R4	R3
0.9	0.8	0.8	0.8

Step 3 now focuses on the sets K_i and finds that in K_1 R3 dominates R1 and in K_2 we first have to compare R6, R4 and R3 pairwise and find that R3 dominates all and then only have to test, if R3 is dominated by R2. However, as R2 does not dominate R3 we can return them as the skyline. Please note that besides more efficient comparisons within the K_i, even in this limited example our indicator technique already saved us expensive object accesses on routes R5 and R7, which now remain unseen.

5 Evaluation of Distributed Skylining

The presented algorithm for the first time addresses the problem of distributed skylining in Web information systems, thus in our evaluation we obviously cannot compare it to similar algorithms. Since comparisons with algorithms over central indexes (which of course will be faster not having to deal with network latencies) will also yield no sensible results, we will concentrate on the necessary number of object accesses, the total number of objects in the skyline for some practical cases and the

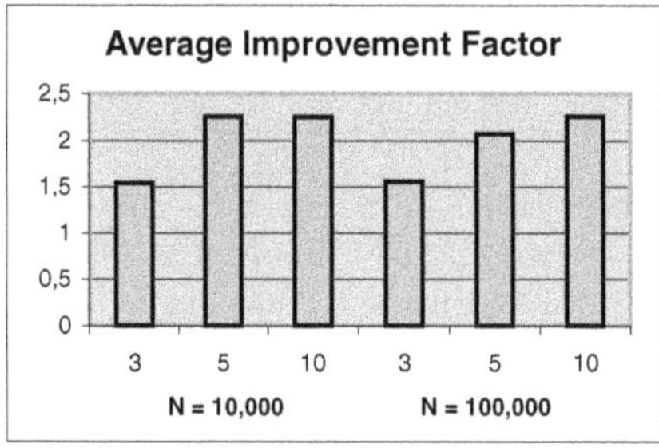

Fig. 4. Improvement due to heuristics

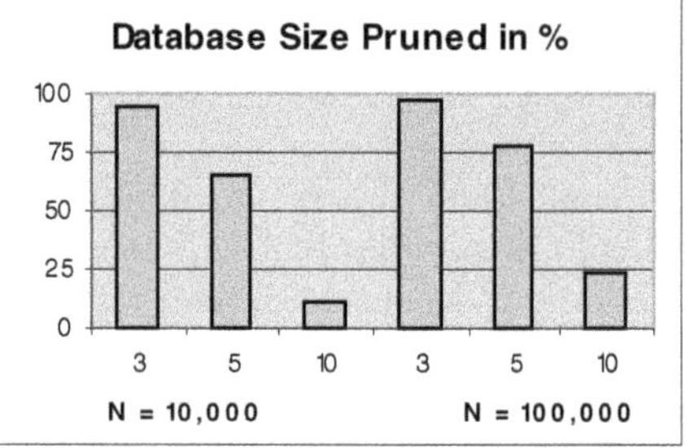

Fig. 5. Saved accesses w.r.t. database size

improvements that can be gained over the basic algorithm by using our advanced heuristics. For all experiments we used an independent data distribution of scores.

Let us first take a glance on the savings due to our heuristics and then evaluate the performance of our improved algorithm. We will focus on the improvement factors in terms of overall object accesses saved. Figure 4 shows the average improvement factors for different numbers of lists (3,5, and 10) and two different database sizes of 10000 and 100000 database objects. We can clearly see that independent of the database size the average improvement factors for our experiments range between 1.5 for small numbers of lists and around 2.5 for higher numbers. Thus, even using just these simple heuristics without any tuning we instantly halve the necessary object accesses. We can even expect higher factors by tuning the given heuristic to adapt more closely to the data distribution like shown e.g. in [9].

Now we can concentrate on the object accesses that our algorithm saves with respect to the database size. Figure 5 shows what percentage of the database can be pruned, again for different numbers of lists and different database sizes. We can see clearly that our algorithm scales well with the database size and for lower numbers of lists works well, e.g. prunes more than 95% over 3 lists. However, we can also see that the performance quickly deteriorates with a growing number of lists. To explain this behavior we have to consider the portions of skyline objects among all objects that have been accessed (cf. figure 6). We find that, though our algorithm's performance seems to deteriorate with growing numbers of lists, its precision in terms of how many objects that are not part of the skyline have to be accessed, heavily increases with growing numbers of lists. For instance in the case of 10 lists over a database of 10000 objects almost 60% of the accesses are definitely necessary to see the entire skyline, i.e. to terminate the algorithm correctly. Considering this instance

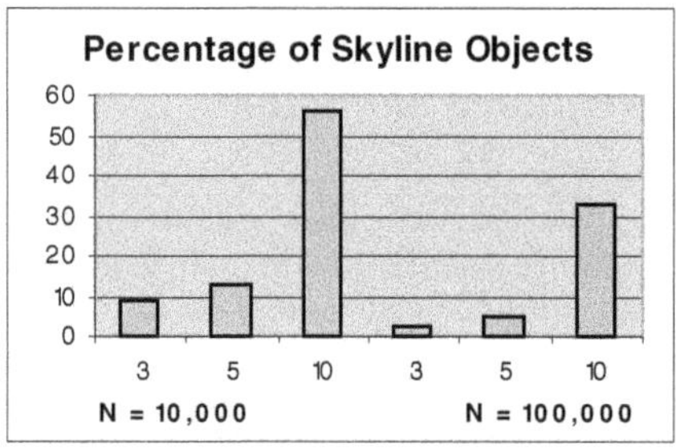

Fig. 6. Skyline objects among all objects accessed

Table 1. Size of the skyline with respect to different numbers of database objects and lists

Size of database (N)	Number of lists	Size of skyline (in % of database size)
10,000	3	0.51
	5	4.44
	10	49.25
100,000	3	0.07
	5	1.00
	10	25.11

further we can conclude that, if we access about 90% of 10000 objects and about 55% of them are necessary, the skyline has to be about 49.5% of the entire database.

To support these considerations we performed more experiments on the actual average size of the skyline for varying numbers of lists and different database sizes. In table 1 we can see that our considerations have been correct (also confirmed by experiments in [4]). Indeed the size of the skyline rapidly increases with larger numbers of lists. We are forced to conclude that, though the concept of skylining may be a very intuitive model for querying, its output behavior seems only to be feasible for rather small numbers of lists to combine. In fact skyline sizes grow exponentially with the number of dimensions. Thus, independently of the retrieval algorithms the problem itself does not scale and we still need a effective dimensionality reduction for skyline queries that are probable to retrieve huge results.

6 Sampling the Efficient Frontier for Improved Scalability

So even if an algorithm could compute high-dimensional skylines in acceptable time, it would still not be sensible to return something like 50% of database objects to the user for manual processing. If on the other hand, users first aggregate all lists in which a compensation between scores can be defined, and then use the skyline query model only for modest numbers of these aggregated lists, the skyline will consist of sensible numbers of elements and can be retrieved reasonably well. But how to know, which dimensions can be compensated and over which dimensions we still need a skyline? As pointed out in [4] specific characteristics of dimensions like correlation have an essential influence on the manageability of the resulting skyline. Correlated data usually results in smaller skylines than the independently distributed case. In contrast anti-correlated distributions amount in a vast increase of the number of skyline objects. Measures to assess such characteristics that hint at the size of the result, are for example the objects' average *consistency of performance*, i.e. if scores for each object show similar absolute values in all different dimensions. The hope is to see *in advance* e.g. if there are correlations between some dimensions, which in turn could be condensed into a single dimension. Since computing skylines of small numbers of dimensions (say 3) are still not at all problematic, our main idea is to get an impression of the original characteristics of the skyline by investigating skylines of some representative low-dimensional subsets of the original dimensions. The following theorem states that -without having to calculate the high-dimensional skyline- our sampling can nevertheless rely on actual skyline objects, which in turn improves the sampling's quality.

Theorem 3 (Skyline of Subsets of Dimensions):
For each object *o* in the skyline of a subset of the dimensions (i.e. a subset of score lists) there is always a corresponding object *o'* in the skyline of all dimensions having exactly the same scores as *o* with respect to the subset of dimensions.

Proof: Assume that we have chosen an arbitrary subset of score lists. We can then calculate the skyline *P* of this subset. Let *o* be any object of *P*. We have to show that there is a corresponding object o' in the skyline *Q* for all score lists having same scores in the chosen subset. If *o* already is also part of *Q* the statement is trivially true. Thus let us assume that *o* is not element of *Q* and therefore must be dominated by at least one object *p*. That means for all lists $s_i(p) \geq s_i(o)$ holds. If, however, considering only the chosen lists there would be any some list for which 'strictly better' holds, i.e. $s_i(p) > s_i(o)$, object *o* would already be dominated by *p* with respect to our subset. Since this would be in contradiction to our assumption of *o* being part of the skyline of the subset, for the entire subset $s_i(p) = s_i(o)$ has to hold and *p* is our object *o'*. ■

Using this result we will now propose the sampling scheme. We will sample the skyline in three steps: choosing *q* subsets of the lists, calculating their lower-dimensional skylines and merging the results as the subsequent sampling. Since skylines can already grow large for only 4 to 5 dimensions, we will always sample with three-dimensional subsets. Values of $q = 5$ for 10 score lists and $q = 15$-20 for 15 score lists in our experiments have provided sufficient sampling quality. For simplicity we just take the entire low-dimensional skyline (2.1)and merge it (2.2). As theorem 3 shows, should two objects feature the same score within a low-dimensional skyline, random accesses on all missing dimensions could be used to rule out a few dominated objects sometimes. We experimented with this (more exact) approach, but found it to perform much worse, while improving the sampling quality only slightly.

Sampling Skylines by Reduced Dimensions

1. Given *m* score lists randomly select *q* three-dimensional subsets, such that all lists occur in at least one of the subsets. Initialize the sampling set $P := \emptyset$
2. For each three-dimensional subset do
   2.1. Calculate the skyline P_i of the subset
   2.2. Union with the sampling set $P := P \cup P_i$
3. The set P is a sample of the skyline for all *m* score lists

Now we have to investigate the quality of our sampling. An obvious quality measure is the *manageability* of the sample; its number of objects should be far smaller than the actual skyline. Also the *consistency of performance* is also an interesting measure, because larger number of consistent objects will mean some amount of correlation and therefore hints at rather small skylines. Our actual measurement here takes the perpendicular distance between each skyline object and the diagonal in score space $[0,1]^n$ normalized to a value between 0 and 100% and aggregated within 10% intervals. The third measure will be a *cluster analysis* dividing each score dimension into upper and lower half, thus getting 2^m buckets. Our cluster analysis counts the elements in each bucket and groups the buckets according to the number of 'upper halves' (i.e. score values > 0.5) they contain. Again having more elements in the clusters with either higher or lower numbers of 'upper halves' indicate correlation, whereas objects in the buckets with medium numbers hint at anti-correlation.

Our experiments on how adequately the proposed sampling technique predicts the actual skyline, will focus on a 10-dimensional skyline for a database containing

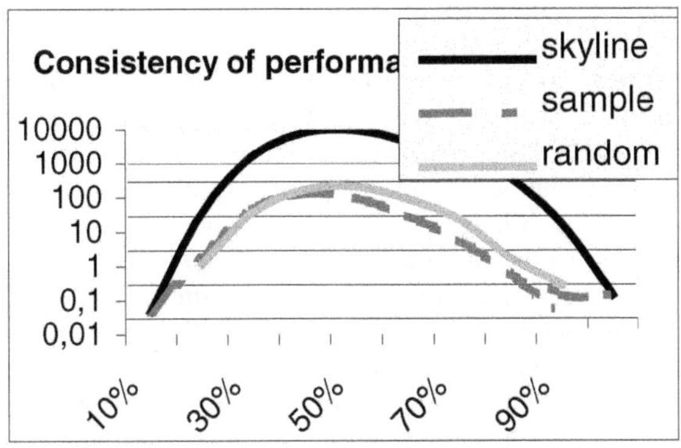

Fig. 7. Consistency of performance

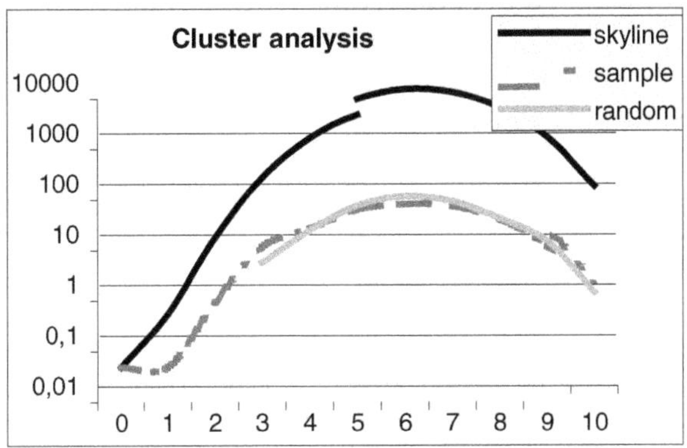

Fig. 8. Cluster analysis for the 10-dim sample

N=100,000 objects. Score values over all dimensions have been uniformly distributed and statistical averages over multiple runs and distributions have been taken. We have fixed $q := 5$ and compare our measurement against the quality of a random sample of the actual 10-dimensional skyline, i.e. the best sample possible (which, however, in contrast to our sample cannot be taken without inefficiently calculating the high-dimensional skyline). Since our sample is expected to essentially reduce the number of objects, we will use a logarithmic axis for the numbers of objects in all diagrams.

We have randomly taken 5 grips of 3 score lists and processed their respective skylines like shown in our algorithm. Measuring the manageability we have to compare the average size of the 10-dim skyline and our final sample: the actual size of the skyline is on average 25133.3 objects whereas our sample consists of only 313.4 objects, i.e. 1.25% of the original size. Figure 7 shows the consistency of performance measure for the actual skyline, our sample and a random sample of about the same size as our sample. The shapes of the graphs are quite accurate, but whereas the peaks of the actual set (dark line) and its random sample (light line) are aligned, the peak for our sampling (dashed line) is slightly shifted to the left. We thus underestimate the consistency of performance a little, because when focusing on only a subset of dimensions, some quite consistent objects may 'hide' behind optimal objects with respect to these dimensions, having only slightly smaller scores, but nevertheless a better consistency. But this effect only can lead to a slight overestimation of the skyline's size and thus is in tune with our intentions of preventing the retrieval of huge skylines. Figure 8 addresses our cluster analysis. Again we can see that our sampling graph snugly aligns with the correct random sampling and the actual skyline graph. Only for the buckets of count 3 there is a slight irritation, which is due to the fact that we have sampled using three dimensions and thus have definitely seen all optimal objects with scores >0.5 in these three dimensions. Thus we slightly overestimate their total count. Overall we see that our sampling strategy with reduced dimensions promises -without having to calculate the entire skyline- to give us an impression of the number of elements of the skyline almost as accurate as a random sample of the actual skyline would provide. Using this information for either safely executing queries or passing them back to the user for reconsideration in the case of too many estimated skyline objects seems promising to lead to a better understanding and manageability of skyline queries.

7 Summary and Outlook

We addressed the important problem of skyline queries in Web information systems. Skylining extends the expressiveness of the conventional 'exact match' or the 'top k' retrieval models by the notion of Pareto optimality. Thus it is crucial for intuitive querying in the growing number of Internet-based applications. Distributed Web Information services like [5] or [2] are premium examples benefiting from our contributions. In contrast to traditional skylining, we presented a first algorithm that allows to retrieve the skyline over distributed data sources with basic middleware access techniques and have proven that it features an optimal complexity in terms of object accesses. We also presented a number of advanced heuristics further improve performance towards real-time applications. Especially in the area of mobile information services [22] using information from various content providers that is assembled on the fly for subsequent use, our algorithm will allow for more expressive queries by enabling users to specify even complex preferences in an intuitive way. Confirming our optimality results our performance evaluation shows that our algorithm scales with growing database sizes and already performs well for reasonable numbers of lists to combine. To overcome the deterioration for higher numbers of lists (curse of dimensionality) we also proposed an efficient sampling technique enabling us to estimate the size of a skyline by assessing the degree of data correlation. This sampling can be performed efficiently without computing high-dimensional skylines and its quality is comparable to a correct random sample of the actual skyline.

Our future work will focus on the generalization of skylining and numerical top k retrieval towards the problem of multi-objective optimization in information systems, e.g. over multiple scoring functions like in [10]. Besides we will focus more closely on quality aspects of skyline queries. In this context especially a-posteriori quality assessments along the lines of our sampling technique and qualitative assessments like in [17] may help users to cope with large result sets. We will also investigate our proposed quality measures in more detail and evaluate their individual usefulness.

Acknowledgements. We are grateful to Werner Kießling, Mike Franklin and to the German Research Foundation (DFG), whose Emmy-Noether-program funded part of this research.

References

1. W.-T. Balke, U. Güntzer, W. Kießling. On Real-time Top k Querying for Mobile Services, In *Proc. of the Int. Conf. on Coop. Information Systems (CoopIS'02)*, Irvine, USA, 2002
2. W.-T. Balke, W. Kießling, C. Unbehend. A situation-aware mobile traffic information prototype. In *Hawaii Int. Conf. on System Sciences (HICSS-36)*, Big Island, Hawaii, USA, 2003
3. R. Balling. The Maximin Fitness Function: Multi-objective City and Regional Planning. In *Conf. on Evol. Multi-Criterion Optimization (EMO'03),* LNCS 2632, Faro, Portugal, 2003
4. S. Börzsönyi, D. Kossmann, K. Stocker. The Skyline Operator. In *Proc. of the Int. Conf. on Data Engineering (ICDE'01)*, Heidelberg, Germany, 2001
5. N. Bruno, L. Gravano, A. Marian. Evaluating Top-k Queries over Web-Accessible Databases. In *Proc. of the Int. Conf. on Data Engineering (ICDE'02)*, San Jose, USA, 2002.
6. J. Chomicki. Querying with intrinsic preferences. In *Proc. of the Int. Conf. on Advances in Database Technology (EDBT)*, Prague, Czech Republic, 2002
7. R. Fagin, A. Lotem, M. Naor. Optimal Aggregation Algorithms for Middleware. *ACM Symp. on Principles of Database Systems (PODS'01)*, Santa Barbara, USA, 2001
8. P. Fishburn. *Preference Structures and their Numerical Representations.* Theoretical Computer Science, 217:359-383, 1999
9. U. Güntzer, W.-T. Balke, W. Kießling. Optimizing Multi-Feature Queries for Image Databases. In *Proc. of the Int. Conf. on Very Large Databases (VLDB'00)*, Cairo, Egypt, 2000
10. R. Keeney, H. Raiffa. Decisions with Multiple Objectives: Preferences and Value Tradeoffs. Wiley & Sons, 1976
11. W. Kießling. Foundations of Preferences in Database Systems. In *Proc. of the Int. Conf. on Very Large Databases (VLDB'02)*, Hong Kong, China, 2002
12. W. Kießling, G. Köstler. Preference SQL - Design, Implementation, Experiences. In *Proc. of the Int. Conf. on Very Large Databases (VLDB'02)*, Hong Kong, China, 2002
13. D. Kossmann, F. Ramsak, S. Rost. Shooting Stars in the Sky: An Online Algorithm for Skyline Queries. In *Conf. on Very Large Data Bases (VLDB'02)*, Hong Kong, China, 2002
14. H. Kung, F. Luccio, F. Preparata. On Finding the Maxima of a Set of Vectors. *Journal of the ACM*, vol. 22(4), ACM, 1975
15. M. Lacroix, P.Lavency. Preferences: Putting more Knowledge into Queries. In *Proc. of the Int. Conf. on Very Large Databases (VLDB'87)*, Brighton, UK, 1987
16. Map-Quest Roadtrip Planner. www.map-quest.com, 2003
17. M. McGeachie, J. Doyle. Efficient Utility Functions for Ceteris Paribus Preferences. In *Conf. on AI and Innovative Applications of AI (AAAI/IAAI'02)*, Edmonton, Canada, 2002
18. NTT DoCoMo home page. http://www.nttdocomo.com/home.html, 2003
19. M. Ortega, Y. Rui, K. Chakrabarti, et al. Supporting ranked boolean similarity queries in MARS. *IEEE Trans. on Knowledge and Data Engineering (TKDE)*, Vol. 10 (6), 1998
20. D. Papadias, Y. Tao, G. Fu, et.al. *An Optimal and Progressive Algorithm for Skyline Queries.* In *Proc. of the Int. ACM SIGMOD Conf. (SIGMOD'03),* San Diego, USA, 2003
21. K.-L. Tan, P.-K. Eng, B. C. Ooi. *Efficient Progressive Skyline Computation.* In Proc. *of Conf. on Very Large Data Bases (VLDB'01)*, Rome, Italy, 2001
22. M. Wagner, W.-T. Balke, et al.. A Roadmap to Advanced Personalization of Mobile Services. In *Proc. of the. DOA/ODBASE/CoopIS (Industry Program), Irvine,* USA, 2002.

Query-Customized Rewriting and Deployment of DB-to-XML Mappings

Oded Shmueli[1], George Mihaila[2], and Sriram Padmanabhan[2]

[1] Technion Israel Institute of Technology, Haifa 32000, Israel
oshmu@cs.technion.ac.il
[2] IBM T.J. Watson Research Center,
P.O. Box 704, Yorktown Heights, NY 10598, USA
{mihaila,srp}@us.ibm.com

Abstract. Given the current trend towards application interoperability and XML-based data integration, there is an increasing need for XML interfaces to relational database management systems. In this paper we consider the problem of rewriting a DB-to-XML mapping, into several modified mappings in order to support clients that require various portions of the mapping-defined data. Mapping rewriting has the effect of reducing the amount of shipped data and, potentially, query processing time at the client. We ship sufficient data to correctly answer the client queries. Various techniques to further limit the amount of shipped data are examined. We have conducted experiments to validate the usefulness of our shipped data reduction techniques in the context of the TPC-W benchmark. The experiments confirm that in reasonable applications, data reduction is indeed significant (60-90%).

1 Introduction

Due to the increasing popularity of XML, enterprise applications need to efficiently generate and process XML data. Hence, native support for XML data is being built into commercial database engines. Still, a large part of today's data currently resides in relational databases and will probably continue to do so in the foreseeable future. This is mainly due to the extensive installed base of relational databases and the availability of the skills associated with them. However, mapping between relational data and XML is not simple. The difficulty in performing the transformation arises from the differences in the data models of relational databases (relational model) and XML objects (a hierarchical model of nested elements).

Currently, this mapping is usually performed as part of the application code. A significant portion of the effort for enabling an e-business application lies in developing the code to perform the transformation of data from relational databases into an XML format or to store the information in an XML object in a relational database, increasing the cost of e-business development. Moreover, specifying the mapping in the application code makes the maintenance of the

E. Bertino et al. (Eds.): EDBT 2004, LNCS 2992, pp. 274–291, 2004.
© Springer-Verlag Berlin Heidelberg 2004

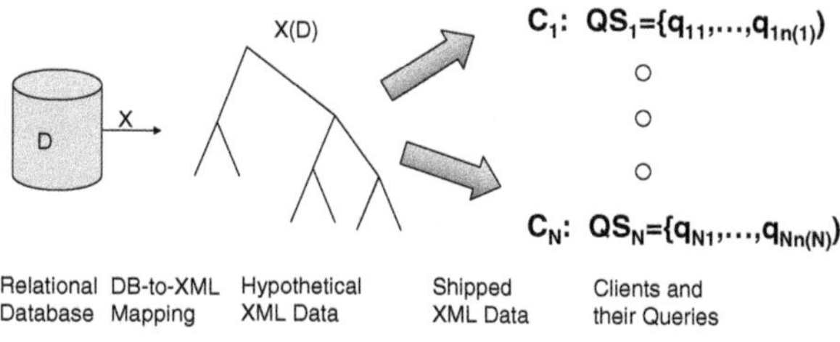

Fig. 1. Typical scenario

application difficult, since any change in the database schema, the XML schema or the business logic requires a new programming effort.

A better approach is to externalize the specification of the mapping, and replace the programming effort by the simpler effort of writing a declarative mapping that describes the relationship between the XML constructs and the corresponding RDBMS constructs. Several notations for defining mappings have been proposed: some are based on DTD or XMLSchema annotations [LCPC01,Mic], others are based on extensions to SQL or XQuery [XQ]. Indeed, all major commercial DBMS products (e.g., Oracle 8i, IBM DB2 and Microsoft SQLServer) support some form of XML data extraction from relational data. All of these notations specify mappings between the rows and columns of tables in the relational model onto the elements and attributes of the XML object. Our objective is not to define yet another mapping notation. Instead, we introduce an abstract, notation-neutral, internal representation for mappings, named *tagged tree*, which models the constructs of the existing notations.

Consider the following typical enterprise usage scenario. An e-commerce company A owns a large relational database containing order related information. A has signed contracts with a number of companies, which may be divisions of A, $C_1, C_2, \ldots, C_N$ that would like to use A's data (for example, they want to mine it to discover sales trends). The contracts specify that the data is to be delivered as XML. So, A needs to expose the content of its database as XML. The database administrator will therefore define a generic mapping, called the *DB-to-XML mapping* that converts the key-foreign key relationships between the various tables to parent-child relationships among XML elements. This is illustrated in Figure 1.

Let us now describe typical use cases for clients:

- Pre-defined queries (that perhaps can be parameterized) against periodically generated official versions of the data (e.g., price tables, addresses, shipping rates).
- Ad-hoc queries that are applied against the XML data.

In most enterprises, the first kind by far dominates the second kind. We therefore focus on the periodical generation of official data versions. We note that ad-hoc queries can also be handled by dynamically applying the techniques we explore in this paper, on a per-query basis.

An obvious option is to execute the DB-to-XML mapping and ship each client the result. Since the mappings are defined in a generic fashion in order to accommodate all possible users, they may contain a large amount of irrelevant data for any particular user. Thus such a strategy would result in huge XML documents which will not only be expensive to transmit over the network but also will be expensive to query by the interested parties. We therefore need to analyze alternative deployment strategies.

Consider a client C with set of (possibly parameterizable) queries QS. [1] Let X be the DB-to-XML mapping defined by A over its database D. Instead of shipping to C the whole XML data, namely $X(D)$, A would like to ship only data that is *relevant* for QS (and that should produce, for queries in QS, the same answers as those on $X(D)$). We show that determining the *minimum* amount of data that can be shipped is NP-hard and most probably cannot be done efficiently. Nevertheless, we devise efficient methods that for many common applications generate significantly smaller amounts of shipped data as compared with $X(D)$.

1.1 An Example

Consider the DB-to-XML mapping X defined by the tagged tree in Figure 2. Intuitively, the XML data tree specified by this mapping is generated by a depth-first traversal of the tagged tree, where each SQL query is executed and the resulting tuples are used to populate the text nodes (we defer the formal definition of data tree generation to Section 2).

Now, consider the following query set QS = { /polist/po[status = 'processing'] /orderline/item, /polist/po[status = 'processing']/customer, /polist/po[status = 'pending']/billTo, /polist/po[status = 'pending']/customer }.

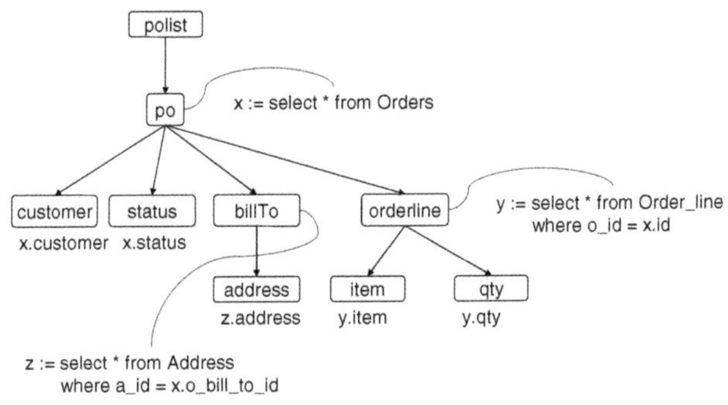

Fig. 2. Original tagged tree

[1] QS may be a generalization of the actual queries which may be too sensitive to disclose.

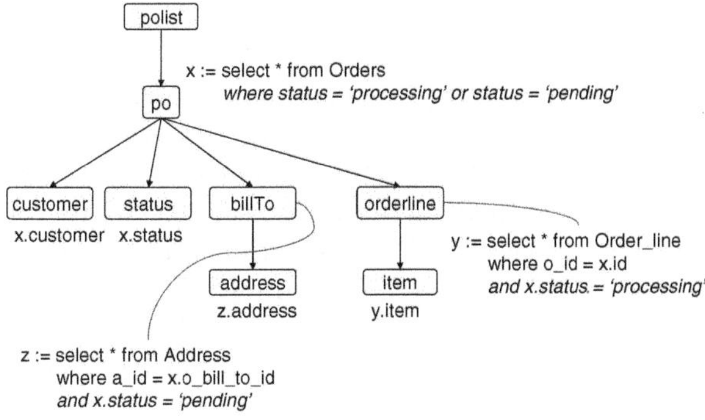

Fig. 3. Modified tagged tree

Clearly, in order to support the query set QS, we do not need to compute the full data tree defined by the mapping X, because only some parts of the resulting data tree will be used by these queries, while others are completely ignored by these queries (and therefore useless). By examining the query set, we realize that the only purchase orders (po) that need to be generated are those whose status is either "processing" or "pending". Moreover, for the "pending" purchase orders, the queries are only looking for the "customer" and "billTo" information, but do not need any "orderline" information. On the other hand, for the purchase orders whose status is "processing", the queries need the "item" branch of "orderline" and the "customer" information.

The aim of our mapping rewriting is to analyze a query set QS and a mapping definition X and produce a custom mapping definition X' that provides sufficient data for all the queries in QS and, when materialized, does not generate "useless data". For the above mapping and query set, for example, the algorithm will produce the mapping X' defined by the rewritten tagged tree depicted in Figure 3.

There are several features of this modified tagged tree that we would like to point out:

1. the query associated with the "po" node has been augmented with a disjunction of predicates on the order status that effectively cause only relevant purchase orders to be generated;
2. the query associated with the "billTo" node has been extended with a predicate that restricts the generation of this type of subtrees to pending orders;
3. the query associated with the "orderline" node has been extended with a predicate that restricts the generation of these subtrees to processing purchase orders;
4. the "qty" node has been eliminated completely, as it is not referenced in the query set.

This rewritten DB-to-XML mapping definition, X', when evaluated against a TPCW benchmark database instance, reduces the size of the generated data tree by more than 60% compared to the generated data tree for the original mapping X.

1.2 Main Contributions and Paper Structure

Our main contribution is in devising a practical method to rewrite DB-to-XML mappings so as to reflect a client's (Xpath) query workload and generate data likely to be relevant to that workload. *We never ship more data than the naive ship $X(D)$ approach.* Realistic experimentation shows a very significant amount of data generation savings. Various optimizations, both at the mapping level and at the generated data level, are outlined. We also prove that generating the minimum amount of data is intractable (NP-hard).

In Section 2 we define our DB-to-XML definition language, trees whose nodes are tagged with element names and, optionally, with a tuple variable binding formula or a column extraction formula. In Section 3 we show how an Xpath expression can be converted into an equivalent set of normalized queries that only navigate on child:: and self:: axes. Given a normalized query and a matching to the tagged tree, we show in Section 4 how to modify the original tagged tree so as to retrieve data that is relevant for *one* matching. Usually, a single query may result in many matchings with the tagged tree. We explain how rewritten tagged trees resulting from such mappings may be superimposed. A crucial issue is how to ensure that the superimposition does not result in loss of selectivity. We explore two basic kinds of Optimizations: in Section 5 we focus on modifications to the resulting tagged trees so as to further limit generated XML data. Section 6 presents our experimental results. We consider a realistic query workload and show that our method results in significant savings. Conclusions and future work are in Section 7.

1.3 Related Work

We have recently witnessed an increasing interest in the research community in the efficient processing of XML data. There are essentially two main directions: designing native semi-structured and XML databases (e.g., Natix [KM00], Lore [GMW00], Tamino [Sch01]) and using off-the-shelf relational database systems.

While we do recognize the potential performance benefits of native storage systems, in this work we focus on systems that publish existing relational data as XML. In this category, the XPERANTO system [SSB+00,CKS+00] provides an XMLQuery-based mechanism for defining virtual XML views over a relational schema and translates XML queries against the views to SQL. A similar system, SilkRoute [FMS01] introduces another view definition language, called RXL, and transforms XML-QL queries on views to a sequence of SQL queries. SilkRoute is designed to handle one query at a time. Our work extends SilkRoute's approach by taking a more general approach: rather than solving each individual query, we consider a group of queries and rewrite the mapping to efficiently support that group.

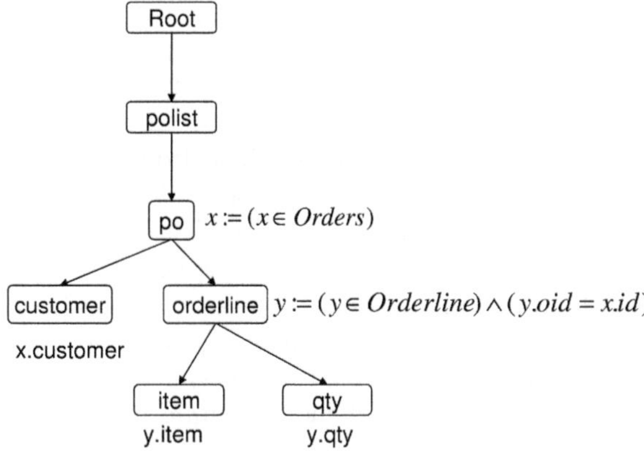

Fig. 4. A simple tagged tree

2 A Simple Relational to XML Mapping Mechanism

In this section we introduce a simple DB-to-XML mapping mechanism called *tagged trees.*

Definition 1. *Consider a relational database D. A* tagged tree *over D is a tree whose root node is labeled "Root" and each non-root node v is labeled by an XML element or attribute name and may also have an annotation, $v.annotation$, of one of the following two types:*

- *$x := Q$, where x is a tuple variable and Q is a query on D; intuitively, x is a tuple ranging over the result of query Q; we say that this node* binds *variable x; a node cannot bind the same variable as bound by one of its ancestors but Q may make references to variables bound by its ancestor nodes; we refer to Q as $v.formula$ and to x as $v.var$;*
- *$x.C$, where C is a database column name and x is a variable bound in an annotation of an ancestor node; we call this type of annotation "value annotation", because it assigns values to nodes; in this case $v.formula$ is defined as $x.C \neq NULL$.*

A tagged tree T defines a DB-to-XML mapping X_T over a relational database; the result of applying the mapping X_T to a database instance D is an XML tree $XT = X_T(D)$, called *a data tree image* of T, inductively defined as follows:

1. the root of XT is the "document root" node; we say that the root of XT is the *image* of the root of T. In general, each tagged tree node expands into a set of image nodes in XT;
2. if T is obtained from another tree T' by adding a child v to a node w of T' then:

a) if v has no annotation, then XT is obtained from $XT' = X_{T'}(D)$ by attaching a child node, with the same label as v, to each image node of w in XT'; the set of these nodes are the image of v in XT;
b) if v has a binding annotation $x := Q$ and Q does not contain ancestor variable references then XT is obtained from XT' as follows: for each node in the image of w, we attach a set of $|Q(D)|$ nodes with the same label as v; each of these nodes corresponds to a binding of the variable x to a specific tuple in $Q(D)$ (called the *current binding* of that variable);
c) if v has a binding annotation $x := Q$ and Q contains ancestor variable references, then for each node in the image of w there are current binding tuples for the variables that are referenced in Q; we replace each variable reference $y.C$ by the value of the C column in the current binding of y and proceed as in the case with no variable references;
d) if v has a value annotation $x.C$, then we attach a child node, with the same label as v, to every image of w in XT' and set the text value of each such new node to the value of the C column in the current binding tuple for x.

The data tree image can be generated by a simple depth-first traversal of the tagged tree and separate execution of each query. However, this evaluation strategy is very inefficient, especially if the queries return many results, since it involves a large number of requests to the DBMS. A better strategy is to combine all the queries into a single "sorted outer union" query and use the result to produce the XML document. Since the resulting tuples come in the same order as the final XML document no in-memory buffering is necessary and the result can be pipelined to a tagger component (as in XPERANTO [SKS+01]).

3 Xpath Expression Normalization

Xpath [XP] is a simple yet powerful language for querying XML data trees. In particular it includes "traversal steps" that traverse a number of edges at a time (for example *descendant-or-self*) and ones that utilize non-parent child edges (such as *preceding-sibling* and *following-sibling*). Even more complex are the *following* and *preceding* axes. Our goal in normalizing the Xpath expression is to bring it to a form in which the only allowed axes are *child::* and *self::*. To illustrate our ideas we first define the *simple Xpath expressions (SXE)* fragment of Xpath and later on extend it. The grammar for the main fragment we treat, SXE, is defined as follows:

```
EXP       ::= Root | Root '/' RLP
RLP       ::= Step | Step '/' RLP
Step      ::= AxisName NodeTest
                          Predicate*
Predicate ::= '[' PredExp ']'
PredExp   ::= RLP | RLP '/ self::node()' Op Value
            | 'self::node()' Op Value
```

Op ::= '=' | '<' | '≤' | '>' | '≥' | '≠'
NodeTest ::= NodeName | 'node()' | 'text()'
AxisName ::= 'ancestor::'
| 'ancestor-or-self::'
| 'child::' | 'descendant::'
| 'descendant-or-self::'
| 'parent::' | 'self::'

We can extend Op with 'eq', 'neq' etc., however as these operators imply uniqueness some of our techniques may not apply[2].

Example 1. The following are examples of SXE path expressions:

1. Root /child:: polist /child:: po [child:: orderline /child:: item /self:: node() = "Thinkpad"]. Find po elements that contain at least one orderline element whose item subelement is "Thinkpad".
2. Root /child:: polist /child:: po [child:: orderline [child:: item = "Thinkpad"][child:: qty /self::node()> 5]]. Find po elements that contain an orderline element whose item subelement is "Thinkpad" and its qty element is greater than 5.

An SXE expression e is *normalized* if child:: and self:: are the only axes appearing in e. Let T be a tagged tree and let e be an SXE expression to be evaluated on data tree images of T. We convert e into an expression set $E = \{e_1, \ldots, e_n\}$, such that each e_i is normalized, and for all images T_d of T, $e(T_d) = \bigcup_{i=1}^{n} e_i(T_d)$. Such an expression set E is said to be T-*equivalent* to e. To produce E, we simulate matching e on T_d via a traversal of T. In general, there may be a number of possible such traversals. However, since T_d is an image of T, each such traversal identifies a traversal in T (that may re-traverse some edges and nodes more than once).

At this point we have a set E of expressions. Let e be an expression in E. Consider applying e to a data tree T_d. The semantics of path expressions is captured by the concept of an *expression mapping* which is a function from normalized expression components (steps, predicates and comparisons) to data tree nodes. For a normalized expression e and a data tree T_d, an expression mapping ψ from e to T_d satisfies the following conditions:

1. (Step Mapping) Each step is mapped to a node in T_d, intuitively, this is the node to which the step leads. ψ maps Root to the root of T_d.
2. (Node Test Consistency) Let nt be a node test in a step mapped by ψ to node v in T_d, then nt is true at v.
3. (Edge Consistency) If a step is mapped into a node u of T_d and the immediately following step has axis child:: (respectively, self::) and is mapped to node v in T, then (u, v) is an edge of T_d (respectively, $u = v$).
4. (Predicate Mapping) ψ maps each Predicate to the node to which it maps the step within which the Predicate appears.

[2] In our rewriting a single axis may be substituted for by several child:: or self:: axis sequences. Since each such sequence gives rise to a separate Xpath expression, we "lose track" of the fact that only one of these expressions should be satisfied.

5. (Step-Predicate Consistency) If ψ maps a Predicate to node u in T_d and ψ maps the first step of the RLP of the PredExp of the Predicate to node v in T_d, then (u, v) is an edge in T_d.
6. (Comparison Mapping) ψ maps the 'Op Value' part of a predicate 'self::node() Op Value' to the node it maps the self:: step and the condition 'Op Value' is satisfied by this node.

Similarly to an expression mapping, a *matching map* is also a function from expression components into tree nodes, this time nodes of T rather than T_d. A matching map satisfies the same six conditions listed above[3]. As we shall see, the existence of an expression mapping function from e to T_d implies the existence of a matching map from e to T.

Let T be a tagged tree, T_d an image data tree of T and e a normalized expression. Suppose there exists an element occurrence *elem*, in T_d, computed by e on T_d as evidenced by an expression mapping ψ from e to T_d. We associate with ψ a matching map ψ_p such that if ψ maps a component c of e to a node v in T_d then ψ_p maps c to the node u in T such that v is an image of u. Because of the way images of tagged trees are defined, if ψ maps c_1 to u and c_2 to v and (u, v) is an edge in T_d, then $(\psi_p(c_1), \psi_p(c_2))$ is an edge in T. Furthermore, the node tests that hold true in T_d must be "true" in T, that is Node Names are the same and if text() holds on the T_d node then the corresponding T node "manufactures" text. We also call ψ_p a *matching* of e and T.

Observe that there may be a number of distinct matching maps from the same normalized expression e to T. Perhaps the simplest example is a tagged tree T having a root and two children tagged with 'A'. Let e be Root/child::A, we can match the step child::A with either of the two A children of the root of T. Observe that these two matching maps correspond to different ways of constructing an expression mapping from e to a data tree T_d of T.

4 Tagged Tree Rewriting

Rewriting is done as follows:

- Based on a matching map for an expression the tagged tree is modified (subsection 4.1).
- A collection of rewritten tagged trees is superimposed into a single tagged tree (subsection 4.2).

We shall present the obvious option of combining *all* rewritten trees for all expressions and their matching maps. We note that, in general, the collection of superimposed trees may be any subset of these trees, giving rise to various strategies as to how many superimposed trees to generate. Our techniques apply in this more general setting as well.

[3] Except the 'Op Value' satisfaction requirement.

4.1 Node Predicate Modification

Our goal is to modify T so as to restrict the corresponding image data to data that is relevant to the normalized expressions in $E = \{e_1, \ldots, e_n\}$. Consider $e \in E$. Let M_e be the set of matching maps from e to T. Consider $\psi_p \in M_e$. We next describe how to modify the formulas attached to the nodes of T based on ψ_p.

Algorithm 1 examines the parsed normalized expression and the tree T in the context of a matching map ψ_p. Inductively, once the algorithm is called with a node v in T and a parsed sub-expression, it returns a formula F which represents conditions that must hold at that T node for the recursive call to succeed in a data tree T_d for T (at a corresponding image node). Some of these returned formulas, the ones corresponding to Predicate* sequences on the *major* steps of e, are attached to tree nodes (in lines 20 and 25), the others are simply returned to the caller with no side effect. The information about whether the algorithm is currently processing a major step is encoded in the Boolean parameter $isMajor$. Let $v.formula$ be the original formula labeling v in T; in case of a data annotation, the formula is $v.annotation \neq NULL$ (and $True$ if no formula originally labels v in T). Initially, the algorithm is invoked as follows: AssociateF$(root, e, True)$.

At this point let us review the effect of AssociateF. Consider a matching map $m \in M_e$ for normalized expression e. Let $Step_1/\ldots/Step_a$ be the *major steps* in the *major path* of e, i.e., those steps not embedded within any $[\ldots]$. Let $v_1, \ldots, v_a$ be the respective nodes of T to which m maps $Step_1, \ldots, Step_a$. Algorithm AssociateF attaches formulas $G_1, \ldots, G_a$ that will specify the generation of image data for node v_i only if all predicates applied at $Step_i$ are guaranteed to hold. In other words, image data generation for nodes along the major path of e is filtered. Note, that this filtering holds only for *this* matching. We shall therefore need to carefully superimpose rewritings so as not to undo the filtering effect.

Example 2. Let T be the tagged tree in Figure 4 and expression e = Root /child:: polist /child:: po [child:: customer /self::node()= "ABC"]. In this case, there is only one possible matching of e to T. The call AssociateF(Root, e, True) will recursively call AssociateF on the node *polist*, then *po*, and then on the predicate at node *po*. The call on the predicate expression will return the formula $\exists z[x.customer \neq NULL \wedge x.customer =$ "ABC"$]$[4] which will be conjoined with the original binding annotation formula $x \in Orders$ at node *po*, thus effectively limiting the data tree generation to purchase orders of company "ABC".

4.2 Superimposing Rewritings

Algorithm AssociateF handles one matching $m \in M_e$ of an expression e. Let m' be another matching of e and T. Intuitively, each such matching should be

[4] z here is a dummy variable as no variable is bound at this node.

Algorithm 1 Associate Formulas to Tree Nodes

```
ASSOCIATEF(Node v, Parsed String s, Boolean isMajor)
 1  /* ψ_p is the matching map */
 2  switch (s)
 3    case EXP = Root :
 4        F ← (v is root)
 5    case EXP = Root '/' RLP :
 6        u ← ψ_p(RLP)/* Current node for RLP */
 7        F ← ASSOCIATEF(u, RLP, isMajor)
 8        F ← F ∧ ASSOCIATEF(v, Root, isMajor)
 9    case RLP = Step '/' RLP :
10        u ← ψ_p(RLP)/* Current node for RLP */
11        F ← ASSOCIATEF(u, RLP, isMajor)
12        F ← F ∧ ASSOCIATEF(v, Step, isMajor)
13    case RLP = Step :
14        F ← ASSOCIATEF(v, Step, isMajor)
15    case Step = child:: NodeTest Predicate* :
16        u ← ψ_p(Step)/* Current node */
17        F ← ASSOCIATEF(u, Predicate*, isMajor)
18        F ← v.formula ∧ ∃u.var(u.formula ∧ F)
19        if (isMajor)
20          then v.formula ← F
21    case Step = self:: NodeTest Predicate* :
22        F ← ASSOCIATEF(v, Predicate*, isMajor)
23        F ← v.formula ∧ F
24        if (isMajor)
25          then v.formula ← F
26    case Predicate* = [PredExp_1] ... [PredExp_k] :
27        F ← True/* Note: For k = 0 F is true */
28        for i ← 1  to  k do
29         F ← F ∧ ASSOCIATEF(v, PredExp_i, False)
30        end for
31    case PredExp = RLP :
32        F ← ASSOCIATEF(v, RLP, False)
33    case PredExp = RLP '/' self::node() Op Value :
34        F ← ASSOCIATEF(v, RLP, False)
35        /* Point data node, e.g., y.qty */
36        v ← ψ_p(self::node() Op Value)
37        F ← F ∧ (v.annotation Op Value)
38    case PredExp = self::node() Op Value :
39        /* Already pointing data node, e.g., y.qty */
40        F ← (v.annotation Op Value)
41   Return F
```

supported independently of the other. We now consider superimposing rewritings due to such independent matching maps. A straightforward approach is to rewrite a formula at a node v that is in the range of some matching maps, say $m_1, \ldots, m_a$, to $v.formula \wedge \bigvee_{i=1}^{a} \phi_i$ where $v.formula$ is the original formula tagging v and ϕ_i is the formula assigned to v by AssociateF based on matching m_i, $1 \leq I \leq a$.

The approach above may lead to unnecessary image data generation. Consider a tree T, with *Root*, a child u of root at which variable x is bound, and a child v of u in which variable y is bound via formula $v.formula$ depending on x. Suppose map m_1 results in a single binding $x = t$ on the current relational data. Suppose map m_2 results in no x bindings on the current relational data. Now consider generating image data at v. The formula at v is of the form $v.formula \wedge (\phi_1 \vee \phi_2)$ where ϕ_1 corresponds to m_1 and ϕ_2 to m_2. Suppose that $v.formula$ and ϕ_2 are true on some other tuple $t' \neq t$ on which ϕ_1 is false. Then, an image data is generated for v based on the resultant y binding. However, had we applied the rewritings separately, no such image data would be generated. This phenomenon in which a formula for one matching map generates image data based on a binding due to another matching map is called *tuple crosstalk.*

The solution is to add an additional final step to algorithm $AssociateF$. In this step the rewritten tree is transformed into a *qual-tagged tree* (definition follows). This transformation is simple and results in the elimination of tuple crosstalk. Essentially, it ensures that each disjunct ϕ_i in $v.formula \wedge \bigvee_{i=1}^{a} \phi_i$ will be true only for bindings that are relevant to ϕ_i. For example, in subsection 1.1 this solution was used in obtaining the final superimposed tree.

We now define the concept of a *qual-tagged* trees. Consider a variable, say x, bound by a formula Q_x. Define $qual(x)$ to be Q_x from which all atoms of the form $(x \in R_i)$ are eliminated. For example, suppose $Q_x = (x \in Orderline) \wedge (x.oid = y.oid)$. Then $qual(x) = (x.oid = y.oid)$. Consider a node v in tagged tree T with ancestor variables $x_1, \ldots, x_n$. If we replace $v.formula$ with $v.formula \wedge qual(x_1) \ldots qual(x_n)$, the meaning of the tagged tree remains unchanged. This is because, intuitively, the restrictions added are guaranteed to hold at that point. A tree in which this replacement is applied to all nodes is called a *qual-tagged tree.*

5 Tagged Tree Optimizations

5.1 Node Marking and Mapping Tree Pruning

Consider a tagged tree T and a normalized expression e. Each node in T which is in the range of some matching map m_i is marked as *visited.* Each such node that is the last one to be visited along the major path of the corresponding path expression e and all its descendants are marked as *end nodes.* Nodes that are not marked at all are *useless for* e. No image data generated for such nodes will ever be explored by e in an image data tree T_d. If for all client queries ec, for all normalized expressions e for ec, node v is useless for e, then node v may be deleted from T.

One may wonder whether we can further prune the tagged tree; consider the following example.

Example 3. Let T be a chain-like tagged tree, with a root, a root child A tagged with a formula ϕ binding a variable x, and a child B (of A) containing data extracted from, say, $x.B$. Suppose our set of queries consists of the following normalized expression $e =$ Root / child:: A [child::B /self:: node() > 10]. Observe that there is but a single matching map m from e to T. After performing AssociateF based on m, the formula at node A is modified to reflect the requirement for the existence of the B node whose data can be interpreted as an integer greater than 10. So, when image data is produced for A, only such data tuples t having $t.B > 10$ are extracted. Since the B elements are not part of the answer (just a predicate on the A elements), one is tempted to prune node B from T. This however will result in an error when applying e to T_d, the predicate [child::B > 10] will not be satisfied as there will simply be no B elements!

5.2 Formula Pushing

Consider a tagged tree T_m produced by an application of algorithm AssociateF using matching mapping m. A node in T_m is *relevant* if it is an image under m. A relevant node in T_m is *essential* if either it (i) is an end node, or (ii) has an end node descendant, or (iii) is the image of a last step in a predicate expression. (Observe that this definition implies that all relevant leaves are essential.) A relevant node that is not essential is said to be *dependent.* Intuitively, a dependent node is an internal node of the subtree defined by m and that has no end node descendant.

Let us formalize the notion of a *formula's push up step.* Let v be a dependent node in T_m tagged with formula F. Let $v_1 \ldots v_c$ be v's relevant children, associated respectively with formulas $f_1 \ldots f_c$. Let x_i be the variable bound at v_i, if any and some new "dummy" variable otherwise. Modify F to $F' = F \wedge \bigvee_{i=1}^{c} \exists x_i f_i$. The intuition is that the data generated as the image of node v is filtered by its formula as well as the requirement that this data will embed generated data for *some* child. There is no point in generating a data element e for v that does not "pass" this filtering. Such a data element e cannot possibly be useful for data tree matching by the expression mapping implied by m.

Push up steps may be performed in various parts of the tree T_m. In fact, if we proceed bottom-up, handling a dependent node only once all its dependent children nodes (if any) were handled, the result will be a tagged tree in which each generated image data, for a dependent node, can potentially be used by the expression mapping implied by m (on the resulting data tree). In other words, image data that certainly cannot lead to generation of image data that may be used by the expression mapping are not produced.

The benefit of pushing lies in the further filtering of image data node generation. The cost of extensive filtering is that (a) the resulting formulas are complex (they need eventually be expressed in SQL), and (b) some computations are repeated (that is, a condition is ensured, perhaps as part of a disjunction, and then rechecked for a filtering effect further down the tree). Therefore, there is a tradeoff; less "useless" image data is generated, but the computation is more extensive. Further work is needed to quantify this tradeoff so as to decide when is it profitable to apply push up steps.

We have explained formula push up as applied to a tagged tree that reflects a single matching. Recall that such trees, for various queries and matching mappings, may be superimposed. The superimposition result reflects the push up steps of the various matching mappings as well. An alternative approach is to first superimpose and then do push up steps. For example, view a node as essential if it is essential for any of the relevant mappings. Clearly, the resulting filtering will be less strict (analogous to the tuple "cross-talk" phenomenon").

5.3 Minimum Data Generation

For a tree T let $|T|$ denote the number of nodes in T. For tree T', $T' \subseteq T$ denotes that T' may be obtained from T by deleting some sub-trees of T.

Given a data tree T_d and a query Q, we would like to compute a minimum data tree $T'_d \subseteq T_d$ for which $Q(T'_d) = Q(T_d)$. This problem is related to the following decision problem:

BOUNDED TREE
INSTANCE: A data tree T_d, a query Q, an integer $k < |T_d|$
QUESTION: Is there a data tree $T'_d \subseteq T_d$ with k nodes such that $Q(T'_d) = Q(T_d)$?

Theorem 1. *The BOUNDED TREE problem is NP-complete.*

Proof. By reduction from SET COVER (ommited).

Corollary 1. *Finding a minimum data tree is NP-hard.*

6 Experimental Evaluation

In order to validate our approach, we applied our selective mapping materialization techniques to relational databases conforming to the TPC-W benchmark [TPC]. The TPC-W benchmark specifies a relational schema for a typical e-commerce application, containing information about orders, customers, addresses, items, authors, etc. We have designed a mapping from this database schema to an XML schema consisting of a `polist` element that contains a list of `po` elements, each of which contains information about the `customer` and one or more `orderline`-s, which in turn contain the `item` bought and its `author` (an extension of the simple tagged tree example in Section 2).

In the first experiment, we examine the effect of tagged tree pruning for XPath queries without predicates. Thus, we simulated a client workloads $QS_1 =$ {/polist/po/orderline/item, //item/subject, //item/author, //title} (we use the abbreviated XPath syntax for readability). For each XPath expression in this workload, the ASSOCIATEF algorithm found a single matching in the original tagged tree and, after eliminating all the unmarked nodes, it resulted in a tagged

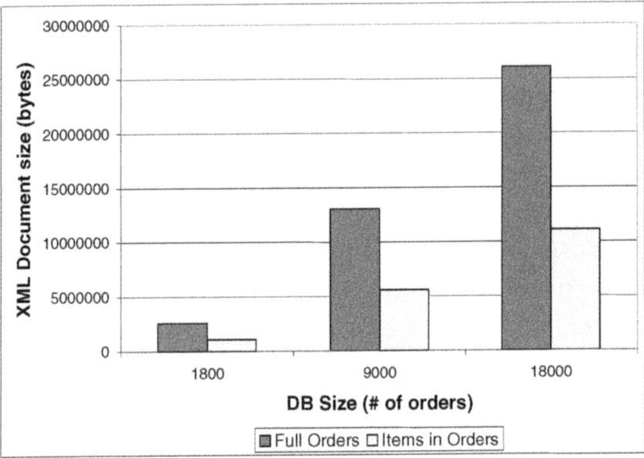

Fig. 5. Data Tree Reductions (no predicates)

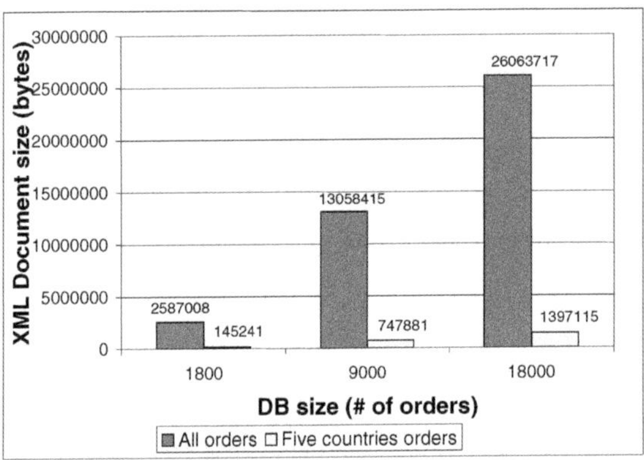

Fig. 6. Data Tree Reduction (with predicates)

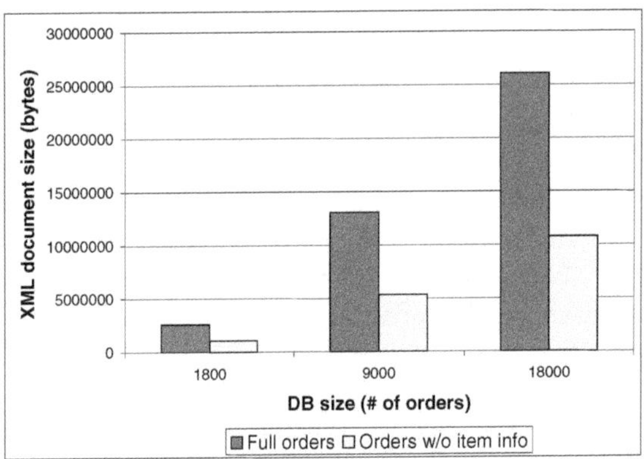

Fig. 7. Data Tree Reduction (no orderlines)

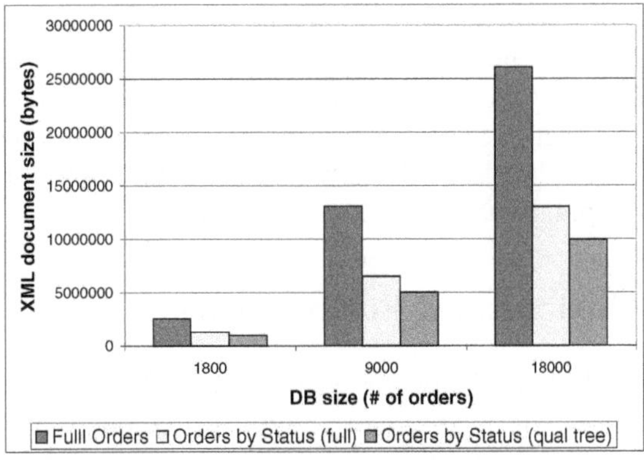

Fig. 8. Data Tree Reduction (predicates and structure)

tree that enabled a data reduction of about 58%. The sizes of the generated documents are shown in Figure 5 (for three database sizes).

In the second experiment (see Figure 6), we simulated a client that is interested only in the orders with shipping address in one of the following five countries: USA, UK, Canada, Germany and France QS_2 = { /polist/po[ship_to/country = 'USA'], /polist/po[ship_to/country = 'Canada'], /polist/po[ship_to/country = 'UK'], Root/polist/po[ship_to/country = 'Germany'], Root/polist/po[ship_to/country = 'France'] }. This time, all the order information is needed for the qualifying orders, so no nodes are eliminated from the tagged tree. Instead, the disjunction of all the country selection predicates is attached to the po node, which reduced the data tree size by about 94% (because only about 5.6% of the orders were shipped to one of these countries). In general, the magnitude of data reduction for this type of query is determined by the selectivity of the predicate.

In the third experiment (see Figure 7), we simulated a client that wants to mine order data, but does not need the actual details of the ordered items (QS_3 = { Root/polist/po/customer, /polist/po//date,/polist/po/price, /polist/po/shipping, /polist/po/ship_to, /polist/po/status}. In this case, the AssociateF algorithm eliminated the entire subtree rooted at `orderline` resulting in a data reduction of about 60%.

Finally, in the fourth experiment (see Figure 8), we simulated the combined effect of predicate-based selection and conditional prunning of different portions of the tagged tree. Thus, we considered the workload described in the Introduction (Section 1.1): QS_4 = { /polist/po[status = 'processing']/orderline/item, /polist/po[status = 'processing']/customer, /polist/po[status = 'pending']/billTo, /polist/po[status = 'pending']/customer}. This time, the data reduction amounted to about 62% when a qual-tree was generated, compared to about 50% for the non qual-tree option (the predicates applied only at the "po" node), which demonstrates the usefulness of qual-trees.

Our experiments show that, in practice, our mapping rewriting algorithms manage to reduce the generated data tree size by significant amounts for typical query workloads. Of course, there are cases when the query workload "touches" almost all the tagged tree nodes, in which case the data reduction would be minimal. Our algorithms can identify such cases and advise the data administrator that full mapping materialization is preferable.

7 Conclusions and Future Work

We considered the problem of rewriting an XML mapping, defined by the tagged tree mechanism, into one or more modified mappings. We have laid a firm foundation for rewriting based on a set of client queries, and suggested various techniques for optimization - at the tagged tree level as well as at the data tree level. We confirmed the usefulness of our approach with realistic experimentation.

The main application we consider is XML data deployment to clients requiring various portions of the mapping-defined data. Based on the queries in which a client is interested, we rewrite the mapping to generate image data that is relevant for the client. This image data can then be shipped to the client that may apply to the data an ordinary Xpath processor. The main benefit is in reducing the amount of shipped data and potentially of query processing time at the client. In all cases, we ship sufficient amount of data to correctly support the queries at the client. We also considered various techniques to further limit the amount of shipped data. We have conducted experiments to validate the usefulness of our shipped data reduction ideas. The experiments confirm that in reasonable applications, data reduction is indeed significant (60-90%)

The following topics are worthy of further investigation: developing a formula-label aware Xpath processor; quantifying a cost model for tagged trees, and rules for choosing transformations, for general query processing; and extending rewriting techniques to a full-fledged query language (for example, a useful fragment of Xquery).

References

[CKS+00] M. J. Carey, J. Kiernan, J. Shanmugasundaram, E. J. Shekita, and S. N. Subramanian. XPERANTO: Middleware for publishing object-relational data as XML documents. In *VLDB 2000*, pages 646–648. Morgan Kaufmann, 2000.

[FMS01] Mary Fernandez, Atsuyuki Morishima, and Dan Suciu. Efficient evaluation of XML middleware queries. In *SIGMOD 2001*, pages 103–114, Santa Barbara, California, USA, May 2001.

[GMW00] Roy Goldman, Jason McHugh, and Jennifer Widom. Lore: A database management system for XML. *Dr. Dobb's Journal of Software Tools*, 25(4):76–80, April 2000.

[KM00] Carl-Christian Kanne and Guido Moerkotte. Efficient storage of XML data. In *ICDE 2000*, pages 198–200, San Diego, California, USA, March 2000. IEEE.

[LCPC01] Ming-Ling Lo, Shyh-Kwei Chen, Sriram Padmanabhan, and Jen-Yao Chung. XAS: A system for accessing componentized, virtual XML documents. In *ICSE 2001*, pages 493–502, Toronto, Ontario, Canada, May 2001.

[Mic] Microsoft. SQLXML and XML mapping technologies. msdn.microsoft.com/sqlxml.

[MS02] G. Miklau and D. Suciu. Containment and equivalence for an xpath fragment. In *PODS 2002*, pages 65–76, Madison, Wisconsin, May 2002.

[Sch01] H. Schöning. Tamino - A DBMS designed for XML. In *ICDE 2001*, pages 149–154, Heidelberg, Germany, April 2001. IEEE.

[SKS+01] J. Shanmugasundaram, J. Kiernan, E. J. Shekita, C. Fan, and J. Funderburk. Querying xml views of relational data. In *VLDB 2001*, pages 261–270, Roma, Italy, September 2001.

[SSB+00] Jayavel Shanmugasundaram, Eugene J. Shekita, Rimon Barr, Michael J. Carey, Bruce G. Lindsay, Hamid Pirahesh, and Berthold Reinwald. Efficiently publishing relational data as XML documents. In *VLDB 2000*, pages 65–76. Morgan Kaufmann, 2000.

[TPC] TPC-W: a transactional web c-commerce performace benchmark. www.tpc.org/tpcw.

[XP] XPath. www.w3.org/TR/xpath.

[XQ] XQuery. www.w3c.org/XML/Query.

LexEQUAL: Supporting Multiscript Matching in Database Systems*

A. Kumaran and Jayant R. Haritsa

Department of Computer Science and Automation
Indian Institute of Science, Bangalore 560012, INDIA
{kumaran,haritsa}@csa.iisc.ernet.in

Abstract. To effectively support today's global economy, database systems need to store and manipulate text data in multiple languages simultaneously. Current database systems do support the storage and management of multilingual data, but are not capable of querying or matching text data across different scripts. As a first step towards addressing this lacuna, we propose here a new query operator called LexEQUAL, which supports multiscript matching of proper names. The operator is implemented by first transforming matches in multiscript text space into matches in the equivalent phoneme space, and then using standard approximate matching techniques to compare these phoneme strings. The algorithm incorporates tunable parameters that impact the phonetic match quality and thereby determine the match performance in the multiscript space. We evaluate the performance of the LexEQUAL operator on a real multiscript names dataset and demonstrate that it is possible to simultaneously achieve good *recall* and *precision* by appropriate parameter settings. We also show that the operator run-time can be made extremely efficient by utilizing a combination of *q-gram* and database indexing techniques. Thus, we show that the LexEQUAL operator can complement the standard lexicographic operators, representing a first step towards achieving complete multilingual functionality in database systems.

1 Introduction

The globalization of businesses and the success of mass-reach *e-Governance* solutions require database systems to store and manipulate text data in many different natural languages simultaneously. While current database systems do support the storage and management of multilingual data [13], they are not capable of *querying* or *matching* text data across languages that are in *different scripts*. For example, it is not possible to automatically match the English string *Al-Qaeda* and its equivalent strings in other scripts, say, Arabic, Greek or Chinese, even though such a feature could be immensely useful for news organizations or security agencies.

We take a first step here towards addressing this lacuna by proposing a new query operator – LexEQUAL – that matches *proper names* across different scripts, hereafter referred to as *Multiscript Matching*. Though restricted to proper names, multiscript matching nevertheless gains importance in light of the fact that *a fifth of normal text*

* A poster version of this paper appears in the Proc. of the 20th IEEE Intl. Conf. on Data Engineering, March 2004.

E. Bertino et al. (Eds.): EDBT 2004, LNCS 2992, pp. 292–309, 2004.
© Springer-Verlag Berlin Heidelberg 2004

Author	Author_FN	Title	Price	Language
Descartes	René	Les Méditations Metaphysiques	€ 49.00	French
நேரு	ஜவஹர்லால்	ஆசிய ஜோதி	INR 250	Tamil
Σαρρη	Κατερινα	Παιχνίδια στο Πιανο	€ 15.50	Greek
Nero	Bicci	The Coronation of the Virgin	$ 99.00	English
بهنسي ، د	عفيف	العمارة عبر التاريخ	SAR 75	Arabic
Nehru	Jawaharlal	Discovery of India	$ 9.95	English
寺井正博	著	秋の風 普及版	¥ 7500	Japanese
नेहरु	जवाहरलाल	भारत एक खोज	INR 175	Hindi

Fig. 1. Multilingual *Books.com*

```
select Author, Title from Books
where Author = 'Nehru'
   or Author = 'नेहरु' or Author = 'நேரு' or Author = 'Νηρυ'
```

Fig. 2. SQL:1999 Multiscript Query

corpora is generic or proper names [16]. To illustrate the need for the LexEQUAL operator, consider *Books.com*, a hypothetical e-Business that sells books in different languages, with a sample product catalog as shown in Figure 1[1].

In this environment, an SQL:1999 compliant query to retrieve all works of an author (say, `Nehru`), across multiple languages (say, in `English`, `Hindi`, `Tamil` and `Greek`) would have to be written as shown in Figure 2. This query suffers from a variety of limitations: Firstly, the user has to specify the search string `Nehru` in all the languages in which she is interested. This not only entails the user to have access to lexical resources, such as fonts and multilingual editors, in each of these languages to input the query, but also requires the user to be proficient enough in all these languages, to provide all close variations of the query name. Secondly, given that the storage and querying of proper names is significantly error-prone due to lack of dictionary support during data entry even in monolingual environments [10], the problem is expected to be much worse for multilingual environments. Thirdly, and very importantly, it would not permit a user to retrieve all the works of `Nehru`, *irrespective* of the language of publication. Finally, while selection queries involving multi-script *constants* are supported, queries involving multi-script *variables*, as for example, in join queries, cannot be expressed.

The LexEQUAL operator attempts to address the above limitations through the specification shown in Figure 3, where the user has to input the name in only one language, and then either explicitly specify only the *identities* of the target match languages, or even use * to signify a wildcard covering *all languages* (the `Threshold` parameter in the query helps the user *fine-tune* the quality of the matched output, as discussed later in the paper). When this LexEQUAL query is executed on the database of Figure 1, the result is as shown in Figure 4.

[1] Without loss of generality, the data is assumed to be in Unicode [25] with each attribute value tagged with its language, or in an equivalent format, such as *Cuniform* [13].

```
select Author, Title from Books
where Author LexEQUAL 'Nehru' Threshold 0.25
      inlanguages { English, Hindi, Tamil, Greek }
```

Fig. 3. LexEQUAL Query Syntax

Author	Title	Price
Nehru	Discovery of India	$ 9.95
நேரு	ஆசிய ஜோதி	INR 250
नेहरू	भारत एक खोज	INR 175

Fig. 4. Results of LexEQUAL Query

Our approach to implementing the LexEQUAL operator is based on transforming the match in *character space* to a match in *phoneme space*. This phonetic matching approach has its roots in the classical Soundex algorithm [11], and has been previously used successfully in monolingual environments by the information retrieval community [28]. The transformation of a text string to its equivalent *phonemic* string representation can be obtained using common linguistic resources and can be represented in the canonical IPA format [9]. Since the phoneme sets of two languages are seldom identical, the comparison of phonemic strings is *inherently fuzzy*, unlike the standard uniscript lexicographic comparisons, making it only possible to produce a likely, but not perfect, set of answers with respect to the user's intentions. For example, the record with English name `Nero` in Figure 1, could appear in the output of the query shown in Figure 3, based on threshold value setting. Also, in theory, the answer set may not include all the answers that would be output by the equivalent (if feasible) $SQL:1999$ query. However, we expect that this limitation would be virtually eliminated in practice by employing high-quality Text-to-Phoneme converters.

Our phoneme space matches are implemented using standard *approximate string matching* techniques. We have evaluated the matching performance of the LexEQUAL operator on a real multiscript dataset and our experiments demonstrate that it is possible to simultaneously achieve good *recall* and *precision* by appropriate algorithmic parameter settings. Specifically, a recall of over 95 percent and precision of over 85 percent were obtained for this dataset.

Apart from output quality, an equally important issue is the *run-time* of the LexEQUAL operator. To assess this quantitatively, we evaluated our first implementation of the LexEQUAL operator as a User-Defined Function (UDF) on a commercial database system. This straightforward implementation turned out to be extremely slow – however, we were able to largely address this inefficiency by utilizing one of Q-Gram filters [6] or Phoneme Indexing [27] techniques that inexpensively weed out a large number of *false positives*, thus optimizing calls to the more expensive UDF function. Further performance improvements could be obtained by internalizing our "outside-the-server" implementation into the database engine.

In summary, we expect the phonetic matching technique outlined in this paper to effectively and efficiently complement the standard lexicographic matching, thereby representing a first step towards the ultimate objective of achieving complete multilingual functionality in database systems.

```
select Author from Books B1, Books B2
where B1.Author LexEQUAL B2.Author Threshold 0.25
  and B1.Language <> B2.Language
```

Fig. 5. LexEQUAL Join Syntax

1.1 Organization of This Paper

The rest of the paper is organized as follows: The scope and issues of multiscript matching, and the support currently available, are discussed in Section 2. Our implementation of the LexEQUAL operator is presented in Section 3. The match quality of LexEQUAL operator is discussed with experimental results in Section 4. The run-time performance of LexEQUAL and techniques to improve its efficiency are discussed in in Section 5. Finally, we summarize our conclusions and outline future research avenues in Section 6.

2 Multiscript Query Processing

In multiscript matching, we consider the matching of text attributes across multiple languages arising from different scripts. We restrict our matching to attributes that contain *proper names* (such as attributes containing names of *individuals, corporations, cities, etc.*) which are assumed not to have any semantic value to the user, other than their vocalization. That is, we assume that when a name is queried for, the primary intention of the user is in retrieving all names that match *aurally*, in the specified target languages. Though restricted to proper names, multiscript matching gains importance in light of the fact that *a fifth of normal text corpora is generic or proper names* [16].

A sample multiscript selection query was shown earlier in Figure 3. The LexEQUAL operator may also be used for *equi-join* on multiscript attributes, as shown in the query in Figure 5, where all authors who have published in multiple languages are retrieved.

The multiscript matching we have outlined here is applicable to many user domains, especially with regard to *e-Commerce* and *e-Governance* applications, web search engines, digital libraries and multilingual data warehouses. A real-life *e-Governance* application that requires a join based on the phonetic equivalence of multiscript data is outlined in [12].

2.1 Linguistic Issues

We hasten to add that multiscript matching of proper names is, not surprisingly given the diversity of natural languages, fraught with a variety of linguistic pitfalls, accentuated by the attribute level processing in the database context. While simple lexicographic and accent variations may be handled easily as described in [14], issues such as language-dependent vocalizations and context-dependent vocalizations, discussed below, appear harder to resolve – we hope to address these issues in our future work.

Language-dependent Vocalizations. A single text string (say, Jesus) could be different phonetically in different languages ("Jesus" in English and "Hesus" in Spanish). So, it is not clear when a match is being looked for, which vocalization(s) should be used. One plausible solution is to take the vocalization that is appropriate to the language in which the base data is present. But, automatic language identification is not a straightforward issue, as many languages are not uniquely identified by their associated Unicode character-blocks. With a large corpus of data, IR and NLP techniques may perhaps be employed to make this identification.

Context-dependent Vocalizations. In some languages (especially, Indic), the vocalization of a set of characters is dependent on the surrounding context. For example, consider the Hindi name Rama. It may have different vocalizations depending on the gender of the person (pronounced as Rāmā for males and Ramā for females). While it is easy in running text to make the appropriate associations, it is harder in the database context, where information is processed at the attribute level.

2.2 State of the Art

We now briefly outline the support provided for multiscript matching in the database standards and in the currently available database engines.

While Unicode, the multilingual character encoding standard, specifies the semantics of comparison of a pair of multilingual strings at three different levels [3]: using *base characters*, *case*, or *diacritical marks*, such schemes are applicable only between strings in languages that share a common script – comparison of multilingual strings across scripts is only *binary*. Similarly, the SQL:1999 standard [8,17] allows the specification of *collation sequences* (to correctly sort and index the text data) for individual languages, but comparison across collations is *binary*.

To the best of our knowledge, none of the commercial and open-source database systems currently support multiscript matching. Further, with regard to the specialized techniques proposed for the LexEQUAL operator, their support is as follows:

Approximate Matching. Approximate matching is not supported by any of the commercial or open-source databases. However, all commercial database systems allow *User-defined Functions* (*UDF*) that may be used to add new functionality to the server. A major drawback with such addition is that UDF-based queries are not easily amenable to optimization by the query optimizer.

Phonetic Matching. Most database systems allow matching text strings using pseudo-phonetic *Soundex* algorithm originally defined in [11], primarily for Latin-based scripts.

In summary, while current databases are effective and efficient for monolingual data (that is, within a collation sequence), they do not currently support processing multilingual strings across languages in any unified manner.

2.3 Related Research

To our knowledge, the problem of matching multiscript strings has not been addressed previously in the database research literature. Our use of a phonetic matching scheme for multiscript strings is inspired by the successful use of this technique in the *mono-script* context by the information retrieval and pharmaceutical communities. Specifically, in [23] and [28], the authors present their experience in phonetic matching of uniscript text strings, and provide measures on correctness of matches with a suite of techniques. Phonemic searches have also been employed in pharmaceutical systems such as [15], where the goal is to find *look-alike sound-alike* (*LASA*) drug names.

The approximate matching techniques that we use in the phonetic space are being actively researched and a large body of relevant literature is available (see [19] for a comprehensive survey). We use the well known *dynamic programming* technique for approximate matching and the standard *Levenshtein* edit-distance metric to measure the *closeness* of two multiscript strings in the phonetic space. The dynamic programming technique is chosen for its flexibility in simulating a wide range of different edit distances by appropriate parameterization of the cost functions.

Apart from being multiscript, another novel feature of our work is that we not only consider the *match quality* of the LexEQUAL operator (in terms of recall and precision) but also quantify its *run-time efficiency* in the context of a commercial state-of-the-art database system. This is essential for establishing the viability of multilingual matching in online e-commerce and e-governance applications. To improve the efficiency of LexEQUAL, we resort to Q-Gram filters [6], which have been successfully used recently for approximate matches in monolingual databases to address the problem of names that have many variants in spelling (example, `Cathy` and `Kathy` or variants due to input errors, such as `Catyh`). We also investigate the phonetic indexes to speed up the match process – such indexes have been previously considered in [27] where the phonetic closeness of English lexicon strings is utilized to build simpler indexes for text searches. Their evaluation is done with regard to in-memory indexes, whereas our work investigates the performance for persistent on-disk indexes. Further, we extend these techniques to multilingual domains.

3 LexEQUAL: Multiscript Matching Operator

In this section, we first present the strategy that we propose for matching multilingual strings, and then detail our multiscript matching algorithm.

3.1 Multiscript Matching Strategy

Our view of ontology of text data storage in database systems is shown in Figure 6. The semantics of *what* gets stored is outlined in the top part of the figure, and *how* the information gets stored in the database systems is provided by the bottom part of the figure. The important point to note is that a *proper name*, which is being stored currently as a character string (shown by the dashed line) may be complemented with a phoneme string (shown by the dotted line), that can be derived on demand, using standard linguistic resources, such as *Text-To-Phoneme (TTP)* converters.

As mentioned earlier, we assume that when a name is queried for, the primary intention of the user is in retrieving all names that match *aurally*, irrespective of the language. Our strategy is to capture this intention by matching the equivalent *phonemic* strings of

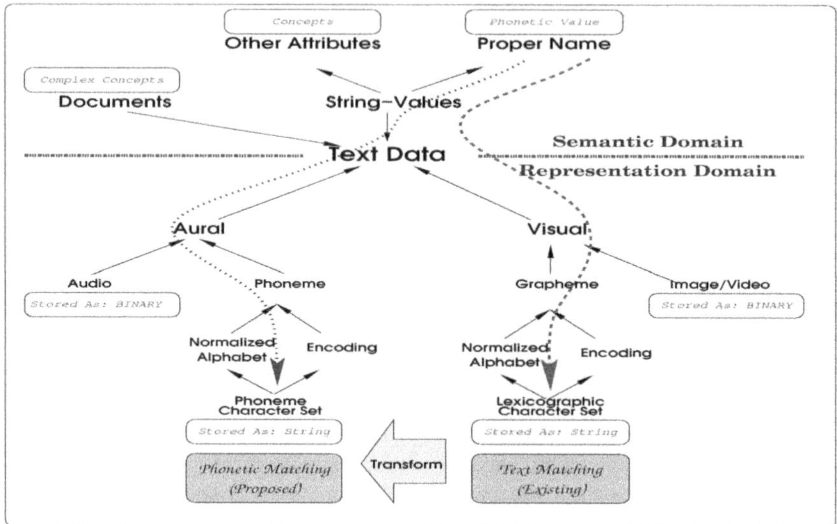

Fig. 6. Ontology for Text Data

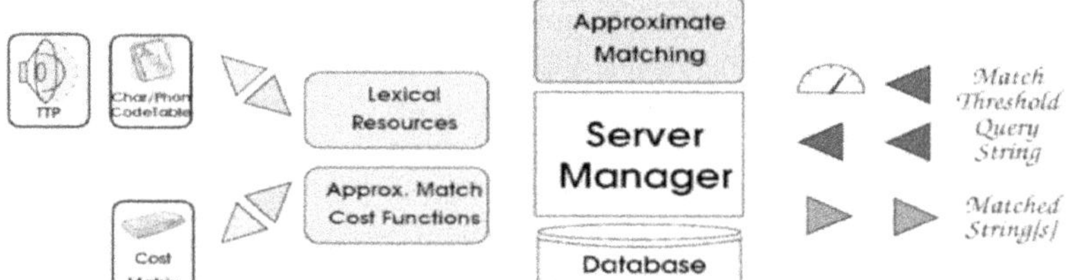

Fig. 7. Architecture

the multilingual strings. Such phoneme strings represent a normalized form of proper names across languages, thus providing a means of comparison. Further, when the text data is stored in multiple scripts, this may be the *only* means for comparing them. We propose complementing and enhancing the standard lexicographic equality operator of database systems with a matching operator that may be used for approximate matching of the equivalent phonemic strings. Approximate matching is needed due to the inherent fuzzy nature of the representation and due to the fact that phoneme sets of different languages are seldom identical.

3.2 LexEQUAL Implementation

Our implementation for querying multiscript data is shown as shaded boxes in Figure 7. Approximate matching functionality is added to the database server as a UDF. Lexical resources (e.g., script and IPA code tables) and relevant TTP converters that convert a given language string to its equivalent phonemes in IPA alphabet are integrated with the query processor. The cost matrix is an installable resource intended to tune the quality of match for a specific domain.

Ideally the LexEQUAL operator should be implemented inside the database engine for optimum performance. However, as a pilot study and due to lack of access to the internals in the commercial database systems, we have currently implemented LexEQUAL as a *user-defined function (UDF)* that can be called in SQL statements. As shown later in this paper, even such an *outside-the-server* approach can, with appropriate optimizations, be engineered to provide viable performance. A related advantage is that LexEQUAL can be easily integrated with current systems and usage semantics while the more involved transition to an inside-the-engine implementation is underway.

3.3 LexEQUAL Matching Algorithm

The LexEQUAL algorithm for comparing multiscript strings is shown in Figure 8. The operator accepts two multilingual text strings and a match threshold value as input. The strings are first transformed to their equivalent phonemic strings and the edit distance between them is then computed. If the edit distance is less than the threshold value, a positive match is flagged.

The `transform` function takes a multilingual string in a given language and returns its phonetic representation in IPA alphabet. Such transformation may be easily imple-

LexEQUAL (S_l, S_r, e)
Input: Strings S_l, S_r, *Match Threshold e*
Languages with IPA transformations, $\mathcal{S}_\mathcal{L}$ *(as global resource)*
Output: TRUE, FALSE or NORESOURCE

1. $L_l \leftarrow$ Language of S_l;$L_r \leftarrow$ Language of S_r;
2. **if** $L_l \in \mathcal{S}_\mathcal{L}$ and $L_r \in \mathcal{S}_\mathcal{L}$ **then**
3. $T_l \leftarrow$**transform**(S_l,L_l); $T_r \leftarrow$**transform**(S_r,L_r);
4. $Smaller \leftarrow (|\, T_l \,| \leq |\, T_r \,| \;?\; |T_l| : |T_r|)$;
5. **if** editdistance$(T_l, T_r) \leq (e * Smaller)$ **then**
   return TRUE **else return** FALSE;
6. **else return** NORESOURCE;

editdistance(S_L, S_R)
Input: String S_L, String S_R
Output: Edit-distance k

1. $L_l \leftarrow |\, S_L \,|$; $L_r \leftarrow |\, S_R \,|$;
2. Create *DistMatrix*$[L_l, L_r]$ and initialize to $Zero$;
3. **for** i **from** 0 **to** L_l **do** *DistMatrix*$[i, 0] \leftarrow i$;
4. **for** j **from** 0 **to** L_r **do** *DistMatrix*$[0, j] \leftarrow j$;
5. **for** i **from** 1 **to** L_l **do**
6. **for** j **from** 1 **to** L_r **do**
7. $DistMatrix[i,j] \leftarrow \textbf{Min} \left\{ \begin{array}{c} DistMatrix[i-1, j] + InsCost(S_{L_i}) \\ DistMatrix[i-1, j-1] + SubCost(S_{R_j}, S_{L_i}) \\ DistMatrix[i, j-1] + DelCost(S_{R_j}) \end{array} \right\}$
8. **return** *DistMatrix*$[L_l, L_r]$;

Fig. 8. The LexEQUAL Algorithm

mented by integrating standard TTP systems that are capable of producing phonetically equivalent strings. The `editdistance` function [7] takes two strings and returns the *edit distance* between them. A *dynamic programming* algorithm is implemented for this computation, due to, as mentioned earlier, the flexibility that it offers in experimenting with different cost functions.

Match Threshold Parameter. A user-settable parameter, *Match Threshold*, as a fraction between 0 and 1, is an additional input for the phonetic matching. This parameter specifies the user tolerance for approximate matching: 0 signifies that only perfect matches are accepted, whereas a positive threshold specifies the allowable error (that is, edit distance) as the fraction of the size of query string. The appropriate value for the threshold parameter is determined by the requirements of the application domain.

Intra-Cluster Substitution Cost Parameter. The three cost functions in Figure 8, namely *InsCost, DelCost* and *SubsCost*, provide the costs for inserting, deleting and substituting characters in matching the input strings. With different cost functions, different flavors of edit distances may be implemented easily in the above algorithm. We support a *Clustered Edit Distance* parameterization, by extending the *Soundex* [11] algorithm to the phonetic domain, under the assumptions that clusters of like phonemes exist and a substitution of a phoneme from within a cluster is more acceptable as a match than a substitution from across clusters. Hence, near-equal phonemes are clustered, based on the similarity measure as outlined in [18], and the substitution cost within a cluster is made a tunable parameter, the *Intra-Cluster Substitution Cost*. This parameter may be varied between 0 and 1, with 1 simulating the standard *Levenshtein* cost function and lower values modeling the *phonetic proximity* of the like-phonemes. In addition, we also allow user customization of clustering of phonemes.

4 Multiscript Matching Quality

In this section, we first describe an experimental setup to measure the quality (in terms of precision and recall) of the LexEQUAL approach to multiscript matching, and then the results of a representative set of experiments executed on this setup. Subsequently, in Section 5, we investigate the run-time efficiency of the LexEQUAL operator.

4.1 Data Set

With regard to the datasets to be used in our experiments, we had two choices: experiment with multilingual lexicons and verify the match quality by *manual relevance judgement*, or alternatively, experiment with tagged multilingual lexicons (that is, those in which the expected matches are marked beforehand) and verify the quality mechanically. We chose to take the second approach, but because no tagged lexicons of multiscript names were readily available[2], we created our own lexicon from existing monolingual ones, as described below.

[2] Bi-lingual dictionaries mark *semantically*, and not *phonetically*, similar words.

Lexicographic String	Language	Phonetic Representation (in IPA)
University	English	junəvɜrsɪti
நேரு	Tamil	neiru
École	French	eikøl
இந்தியா	Tamil	ɪndɪyɑ
हैड्रोजन	Hindi	haɪdrədʒən
Espanõl	Spanish	ɛspɑnjøl

Fig. 9. Phonemic Representation of Test Data

We selected proper names from three different sources so as to cover common names in English and Indic domains. The first set consists of randomly picked names from the *Bangalore Telephone Directory*, covering most frequently used Indian names. The second set consists of randomly picked names from the *San Francisco Physicians Directory*, covering most common American first and last names. The third set consisting of generic names representing Places, Objects and Chemicals, was picked from the *Oxford English Dictionary*. Together the set yielded about 800 names in English, covering three distinct name domains. Each of the names was hand converted to two Indic scripts – Tamil and Hindi. As the Indic languages are phonetic in nature, conversion is fairly straight forward, barring variations due to the mismatch of phoneme sets between English and the Indic languages. All phonetically equivalent names (but in different scripts) were manually tagged with a common *tag-number*. The tag-number is used subsequently in determining quality of a match – any match of two multilingual strings is considered to be correct if their tag-numbers are the same, and considered to be a *false-positive* otherwise. Further, the fraction of *false-dismissals* can be easily computed since the expected set of correct matches is known, based on the tag-number of a given multilingual string.

To convert English names into corresponding phonetic representations, standard linguistic resources, such as the *Oxford English Dictionary* [22] and TTP converters from [5], were used. For Hindi strings, *Dhvani* TTP converter [4] was used. For Tamil strings, due to the lack of access to any TTP converters, the strings were hand-converted, assuming phonetic nature of the Tamil language. Further those symbols specific to speech generation, such as the supra-segmentals, diacritics, tones and accents were removed. Sample phoneme strings for some multiscript strings are shown in Figure 9.

The frequency distribution of the data set with respect to string length is shown in Figure 10, for both lexicographic and (generated) phonetic representations. The set had an average lexicographic length of 7.35 and an average phonemic length of 7.16. Note that though Indic strings are typically visually much shorter as compared to English strings, their character lengths are similar owing to the fact that most Indic characters are composite glyphs and are represented by multiple Unicode characters.

We implemented a prototype of LexEQUAL on top of the *Oracle 9i (Version 9.1.0)* database system. The multilingual strings and their phonetic representations (in IPA alphabet) were both stored in Unicode format. The algorithm shown in Figure 8 was implemented, as a UDF in the PL/SQL language.

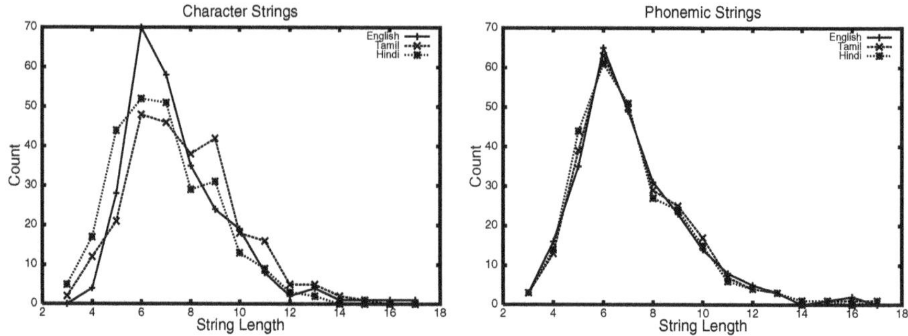

Fig. 10. Distribution of Multiscript Lexicon (for Match Quality Experiments)

4.2 Performance Metrics

We ran multiscript selection queries (as shown in Figure 3). For each query, we measured two metrics – *Recall*, defined as *the fraction of correct matches that appear in the result*, and *Precision*, defined as *the fraction of the delivered results that are correct*. The recall and the precision figures were computed using the following methodology: We matched each phonemic string in the data set with every other phonemic string, counting the number of matches (m_1) that were correctly reported (that is, the tag-numbers of multiscript strings being matched are the same), along with the total number of matches that are reported as the result (m_2). If there are n equivalent groups (with the same tag-number) with n_i of multiscript strings each (note that both n and n_i are known during the tagging process), the *precision* and *recall* metrics are calculated as follows:

$$\textit{Recall} = m_1 / \sum_{i=1}^{n} ({}^{n_i}C_2) \quad \text{and} \quad \textit{Precision} = m_1 / m_2$$

The expression in the denominator of *recall* metric is the ideal number of matches, as every pair of strings (*i.e.*, ${}^{n_i}C_2$) with the same tag-number must match. Further, for an ideal answer for a query, both the metrics should be 1. Any deviation indicates the inherent fuzziness in the querying, due to the differences in the phoneme set of the languages and the losses in the transformation to phonemic strings. Further, the two query input parameters – *user match threshold* and *intracluster substitution cost* (explained in Section 3.3) were varied, to measure their effect on the quality of the matches.

4.3 Experimental Results

We conducted our multiscript matching experiments on the lexicon described above. The plots of the *recall* and *precision* metrics against *user match threshold*, for various *intracluster substitution costs*, between 0 and 1, are provided in Figure 11.

The curves indicate that the recall metric improves with increasing user match threshold, and asymptotically reaches perfect recall, after a value of 0.5. An interesting point to note is that the recall gets better with reducing intracluster substitution costs, validating the assumption of the *Soundex* algorithm [11].

In contrast to the recall metric, and as expected, the precision metric drops with increasing threshold – while the drop is negligible for threshold less than 0.2, it is rapid

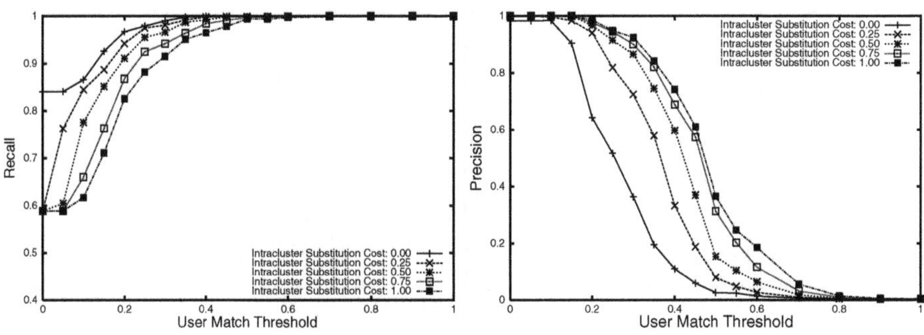

Fig. 11. Recall and Precision Graphs

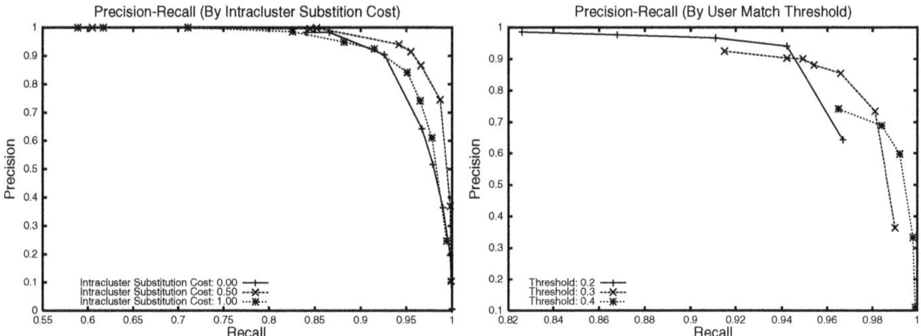

Fig. 12. Precision-Recall Graphs

in the range `0.2` to `0.5`. It is interesting to note that with an intracluster substitution cost of 0, the precision drops very rapidly at a user match threshold of `0.1` itself. That is, the *Soundex* method, which is good in recall, is very ineffective with respect to precision, as it introduces a large number of false-positives even at low thresholds.

Selection of Ideal Parameters for Phonetic Matching. Figure 12 shows the *precision-recall* curves, with respect to each of the query parameters, namely, *intracluster substitution cost* and *user match threshold*. For the sake of clarity, we show only the plots corresponding to the costs `0`, `0.5` and `1`, and plots corresponding to thresholds `0.2`, `0.3` and `0.4`. The top-right corner of the precision-recall space corresponds to a perfect match and the closest points on the precision-recall graphs to the top-right corner correspond to the query parameters that result in the best match quality. As can be seen from Figure 12, the best possible matching is achieved by a substitution cost between `0.25` and `0.5`, and for thresholds between `0.25` and `0.35`, corresponding to the knee regions of the respective curves. With such parameters, the *recall* is ≈95%, and *precision* is ≈85%. That is, ≈5% of the real matches would be *false-dismissals*, and about ≈15% of the results are *false-positives*, which must be discarded by post-processing, using non-phonetic methods.

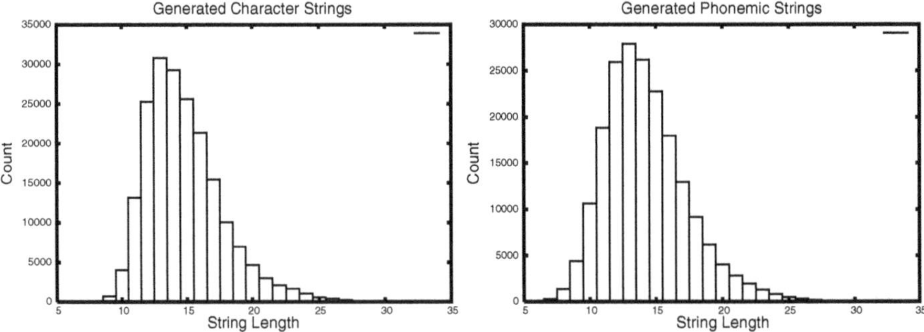

Fig. 13. Distribution of Generated Data Set (for Performance Experiments)

We also would like to emphasize that quality of approximate matching depends on phoneme sets of languages, the accuracy of the phonetic transformations, and more importantly, on the data sets themselves. Hence the matching needs to be tuned as outlined in this section, for specific application domains. In our future work, we plan to investigate techniques for automatically generating the appropriate parameter settings based on dataset characteristics.

5 Multiscript Matching Efficiency

In this section, we analyze the query processing efficiency using the LexEQUAL operator. Since the real multiscript lexicon used in the previous section was not large enough for performance experiments, we synthetically generated a large dataset from this multiscript lexicon. Specifically, we concatenated each string with all remaining strings *within a given language*. The generated set contained about 200,000 names, with an average lexicographic length of 14.71 and average phonemic length of 14.31. The Figure 13 shows the frequency distribution of the generated data set – in both character and (generated) phonetic representations with respect to string lengths.

5.1 Baseline LexEQUAL Runs

To create a baseline for performance, we first ran the selection and equi-join queries using the LexEQUAL operator (samples shown in Figures 3 and 5), on the large generated data set. Table 1 shows the performance of the native equality operator (for exact matching of character strings) and the LexEQUAL operator (for approximate matching of phonemic strings), for these queries[3]. The performance of the standard database equality operator is shown only to highlight the inefficiency of the approximate matching operator. As can be seen clearly, the UDF is orders of magnitude slower compared with native database equality operators. Further, the optimizer chose a *nested-loop* technique for the join query, irrespective of the availability of indexes or optimizer hints, indicating that no optimization was done on the UDF call in the query.

[3] The join experiment was done on a 0.2% subset of the original table, since the full table join using UDF took about 3 days.

Table 1. Relative Performance of Approximate Matching

Query	Matching Methodology	Time
Scan	*Exact (= Operator)*	0.59 *Sec*
Scan	*Approximate (*LexEQUAL *UDF)*	1418 *Sec*
Join	*Exact (= Operator)*	0.20 *Sec*
Join	*Approximate (*LexEQUAL *UDF)*	4004 *Sec*

To address the above problems and to improve the efficiency of multiscript matching with LexEQUAL operator, we implemented two alternative optimization techniques, *Q-Grams* and *Phonetic Indexes*, described below, that cheaply provide a candidate set of answers that is checked for inclusion in the result set by the accurate but expensive LexEQUAL UDF. These two techniques exhibit different quality and performance characteristics, and may be chosen depending on application requirements.

5.2 Q-Gram Filtering

We show here that *Q-Grams*[4], which are a popular technique for approximate matching of standard text strings [6], are applicable to phonetic matching as well.

The database was first augmented with a table of *positional q-grams* of the original phonemic strings. Subsequently, the three filters described below, namely *Length* filter that depends only on the length of the strings, and *Count* and *Position* filters that use special properties of q-grams, were used to filter out a majority of the non-matches using standard database operators only. Thus, the filters weed out most non-matches cheaply, leaving the accurate, but expensive LexEQUAL UDF to be invoked (to weed out *false-positives*) on a vastly reduced candidate set.

Length Filter leverages the fact that strings that are within an edit distance of *k* cannot differ in length, by more than *k*. This filter does not depend on the q-grams.

Count Filter ensures that the number of matching q-grams between two strings σ_1 and σ_2 of lengths $|\sigma_1|$ and $|\sigma_2|$, must be at least $(max(|\sigma_1|, |\sigma_2|) - 1 - (k-1) * q)$, a necessary condition for two strings to be within an *edit-distance* of k.

Position Filter ensures that a positional q-gram of one string does not get matched to a positional q-gram of the second that differs from it by more than k positions.

A sample SQL query using q-grams is shown in Figure 14, assuming that the query string is transformed into a record in table Q, and the auxiliary q-gram table of Q is created in AQ. The *Length Filter* is implemented in the fourth condition of the SQL statement, the *Position Filter* by the fifth condition, and the *Count Filter* by the `GROUP BY/HAVING` clause. As can be noted in the above SQL expression, the *UDF* function, LexEQUAL, is called at the end, *after* all three filters have been utilized.

[4] Let σ be a string of size n in a given alphabet Σ and $\sigma[i,j]$, $1 \leq i \leq j \leq n$, denote a substring starting at position i and ending at position j of σ. A *Q-gram* of σ is a substring of σ of length q. A *Positional Q-gram* of a string σ is a pair $(i, \sigma_{extended}[i, i+q-1])$ where $\sigma_{extended}$ is the augmented string of σ, which is appended with (q-1) start symbols(say, ◁) and (q-1) end symbols (say, ▷), where the start and end symbols are not in the original alphabet. For example, a string `LexEQUAL` will have the following *positional q-grams*: {(1,◁◁L), (2, ◁Le), (3, Lex), (4, exE), (5, xEQ), (6, EQU), (7, QUA), (8, UAL), (9, AL▷), (10, L▷▷)}.

```
SELECT N.ID, N.Name
FROM Names N, AuxNames AN, Query Q, AuxQuery AQ
WHERE N.ID = AN.ID
    AND Q.ID = AQ.ID
    AND AN.Qgram = AQ.Qgram
    AND |len(N.PName) – len(Q.str)| ≤ e * length(Q.str)
    AND |AN.Pos – AQ.Pos| ≤ (e * length(Q.str))
GROUP BY N.ID, N.PName
HAVING count(*) ≥ (len(N.PName) – 1 – ((e * len(Q.str) – 1) * q))
    AND LexEQUAL(N.PName, Q.str, e)
```

Fig. 14. SQL using *Q-Gram* Filters

Table 2. Q-Gram Filter Performance

Query	Matching Methodology	Time
Scan	LexEQUAL *UDF + q-gram filters*	13.5 *Sec*
Join	LexEQUAL *UDF + q-gram filters*	856 *Sec*

The performance of the selection and equi-join queries, after including the Q-gram optimization, are given in Table 2. Comparing with figures in Table 1, the use of this optimization improves the *selection* query performance by an order of magnitude and the *join* query performance by five-fold. The improvement in join performance is not as dramatic as in the case of scans, due to the additional joins that are required on the large q-gram tables. Also, note that the performance improvements are not as high as those reported in [6], perhaps due to our use of a standard commercial database system and the implementation of LexEQUAL using slow dynamic programming algorithm in an interpreted PL/SQL language environment.

5.3 Phonetic Indexing

We now outline a *phonetic indexing* technique that may be used for accessing the *near-equal* phonemic strings, using a standard database index. We exploit the following two facts to build a compact database index: First, the substitutions of *like* phonemes keeps the recall high (refer to Figure 11), and second, phonemic strings may be transformed into smaller numeric strings for indexing as a database number. However, the downside of this method is that it suffers from a drop in recall (that is, *false-dismissals* are introduced).

To implement the above strategy, we need to transform the phoneme strings to a number, such that phoneme strings that are *close* to each other map to the same number. For this, we used a modified version of the *Soundex* algorithm [11], customized to the phoneme space: We first grouped the phonemes into equivalent clusters along the lines outlined in [18], and assigned a unique number to each of the clusters. Each phoneme string was transformed to a unique numeric string, by concatenating the cluster identifiers of each phoneme in the string. The numeric string thus obtained was converted into an integer – *Grouped Phoneme String Identifier* – which is stored along with the phoneme string. A standard database B-Tree index was built on the grouped phoneme string identifier attribute, thus creating a compact index structure using only integer datatype.

For a LexEQUAL query using phonetic index, we first transform the operand multiscript string to its phonetic representation, and subsequently to its grouped phoneme string identifier. The index on the grouped phoneme string identifier of the lexicon is used to retrieve all the candidate phoneme strings, which are then tested for a match invoking the LexEQUAL UDF with the user specified match tolerance. The invocation of the LexEQUAL operator in a query maps into an internal query that uses the phonetic index, as shown in Figure 15 for a sample join query. Note that any two strings that match in the above scheme are *close phonetically*, as the differences between individual phonemes are from only within the pre-defined cluster of phonemes. Any changes across the groups will result in a non-match. Also, it should be noted that those strings that are within the classical definition of *edit-distance*, but with substitutions across groups, will not be reported, resulting in *false-dismissals*. While some of such false-dismissals may be corrected by a more robust design of phoneme clusters and cost functions, not all *false-dismissals* can be corrected in this method.

We created an index on the grouped phoneme string identifier attribute and re-ran the same selection and equi-join queries on the large synthetic multiscript dataset. The LexEQUAL operator is modified to use this index, as shown in the SQL expression in Figure 15, and the associated scan and join performance is given in Table 3.

While the performance of the queries with phonetic index is an order of magnitude better than that achieved with q-gram technique, the phonetic index introduces a small, but significant 4 - 5% *false-dismissals*, with respect to the classical edit-distance metric. A more robust grouping of like phonemes may reduce this drop in quality, but may not nullify it. Hence, the phonetic index approach may be suitable for applications which can tolerate false-dismissals, but require a very fast response times (such as, web search engines).

```
SELECT N.ID, N.Name
FROM Names N, Query Q
WHERE N.GroupedPhonStringID = Q.GroupedPhonStringID
    AND LexEQUAL(N.PName, Q.PName, e)
```

Fig. 15. SQL using Phonetic Indexes

Table 3. Phonemic Index Performance

Query	Matching Methodology	Time
Scan	LexEQUAL *UDF + phonetic index*	0.71 *Sec*
Join	LexEQUAL *UDF + phonetic index*	15.2 *Sec*

6 Conclusions and Future Research

In this paper we specified a multilingual text processing requirement – *Multiscript Matching* – that has a wide range of applications from *e-Commerce* applications to search engines to multilingual data warehouses. We provided a survey of the support provided by SQL standards and current database systems. In a nutshell, multiscript processing is not supported in any of the database systems.

We proposed a strategy to solve the multiscript matching problem, specifically for proper name attributes, by transforming matching in the *lexicographic space* to the equivalent *phonetic space*, using standard linguistic resources. Due to the inherent fuzzy nature of the phonetic space, we employ approximate matching techniques for matching the transformed phonemic strings. Currently, we have implemented the multiscript matching operator as a UDF, for our initial pilot implementation. We confirmed the feasibility of our strategy by measuring the quality metrics, namely *Recall* and *Precision*, in matching a real, tagged multilingual data set. The results from our initial experiments on a representative multiscript nouns data set, showed good recall ($\approx$95%) and precision ($\approx$85%), indicating the potential of such an approach for practical query processing. We also showed how the parameters may be tuned for optimal matching for a given dataset. Further, we showed that the poor performance associated with the UDF implementation of approximate matching may be improved significantly, by employing one of the two alternate methods: the *Q-Gram* technique, and a *Phonemic Indexing* technique. These two techniques exhibit different quality and performance characteristics, and may be chosen depending on the requirements of an application. However, both the techniques, as we have demonstrated, are capable of improving the multiscript matching performance by orders of magnitude.

Thus, we show that the LexEQUAL operator outlined in this paper is effective in multiscript matching, and can be made efficient as well. Such an operator may prove to be a valuable first step in achieving full multilingual functionality in database systems.

In our future work, we plan to investigate techniques for automatically generating the optimal matching parameters, based on a given dataset, its domain and a training set. Also, we plan to explore extending the approximate indexing techniques outlined in [1, 21] for creating a metric index for phonemes. We are working on an *inside-the-engine* implementation of LexEQUAL on an open-source database system, with the expectation of further improving the runtime efficiency.

Acknowledgements. This work was partially supported by a Swarnajayanti Fellowship from the Department of Science and Technology, Government of India.

References

1. R. Baeza-Yates and G. Navarro. Faster Approximate String Matching. *Algorithmica*, Vol 23(2):127-158, 1999.
2. E. Chavez, G. Navarro, R. Baeza-Yates and J. Marroquin. Searching in Metric Space. *ACM Computing Surveys*, Vol 33(3):273-321, 2001.
3. M. Davis. Unicode collation algorithm. *Unicode Consortium Technical Report*, 2001.

4. Dhvani - A Text-to-Speech System for Indian Languages. *http://dhvani.sourceforge.net/.*
5. The Foreign Word – The Language Site, Alicante, Spain. *http://www.ForeignWord.com.*
6. L. Gravano, P. Ipeirotis, H. Jagadish, N. Koudas, S. Muthukrishnan and D. Srivastava. Approximate String Joins in a Database (almost) for Free. *Proc. of 27th VLDB Conf.*, September 2001.
7. D. Gusfield. Algorithms on Strings, Trees and Sequences. *Cambridge University Press*, 2001.
8. International Organization for Standardization. ISO/IEC 9075-1-5:1999, Information Technology – Database Languages – SQL (parts 1 through 5). 1999.
9. The International Phonetic Association. Univ. of Glasgow, Glasgow, UK. *http://www.arts.gla.ac.uk/IPA/ipa.html.*
10. D. Jurafskey and J. Martin. Speech and Language Processing. *Pearson Education*, 2000.
11. D. Knuth. The Art of Computer Programming, Volume 3: Sorting and Searching. *Addison-Wesley*, 1993.
12. A. Kumaran and J. Haritsa. On Database Support for Multilingual Environments. *Proc. of 9th IEEE RIDE Workshop*, March 2003.
13. A. Kumaran and J. Haritsa. On the Costs of Multilingualism in Database Systems. *Proc. of 29th VLDB Conference*, September 2003.
14. A. Kumaran and J. Haritsa. Supporting Multilexical Matching in Database Systems. *DSL/SERC Technical Report TR-2004-01*, 2004.
15. B. Lambert, K. Chang and S. Lin. Descriptive analysis of the drug name lexicon. *Drug Information Journal*, Vol 35:163-172, 2001.
16. M. Liberman and K. Church. Text Analysis and Word Pronunciation in TTS Synthesis. *Advances in Speech Processing*, 1992.
17. J. Melton and A. Simon. SQL 1999: Understanding Relational Language Components. *Morgan Kaufmann*, 2001.
18. P. Mareuil, C. Corredor-Ardoy and M. Adda-Decker. Multilingual Automatic Phoneme Clustering. *Proc. of 14th Intl. Congress of Phonetic Sciences*, August 1999.
19. G. Navarro. A Guided Tour to Approximate String Matching. *ACM Computing Surveys*, Vol 33(1):31-88, 2001.
20. G. Navarro, E. Sutinen, J. Tanninen, J. Tarhio. Indexing Text with Approximate q-grams. *Proc. of 11th Combinatorial Pattern Matching Conf.*, June 2000.
21. G. Navarro, R. Baeza-Yates, E. Sutinen and J. Tarhio. Indexing Methods for Approximate String Matching. *IEEE Data Engineering Bulletin*, Vol 24(4):19-27, 2001.
22. The Oxford English Dictionary. *Oxford University Press*, 1999.
23. U. Pfeifer, T. Poersch and N. Fuhr. Searching Proper Names in Databases. *Proc. Conf. Hypertext-Information Retrieval-Multimedia*, April 1995.
24. L. Rabiner and B. Juang. *Fundamentals of Speech Processing*. Prentice Hall, 1993.
25. The Unicode Consortium. The Unicode Standard. *Addison-Wesley*, 2000.
26. The Unisyn Project. The Center for Speech Technology Research, Univ. of Edinburgh, United Kingdom. *http://www.cstr.ed.ac.uk/projects/unisyn/.*
27. J. Zobel and P. Dart. Finding Approximate Matches in Large Lexicons. *Software – Practice and Experience*, Vol 25(3):331-345, March, 1995.
28. J. Zobel and P. Dart. Phonetic String Matching: Lessons from Information Retrieval. *Proc. of 19th ACM SIGIR Conf.*, August 1996.

A Model for Ternary Projective Relations between Regions

Roland Billen[1] and Eliseo Clementini[2]

[1] Dept. of Geography and Geomatics
University of Glasgow
Glasgow G12 8QQ, Scotland, UK
rbillen@geog.gla.ac.uk

[2] Dept. of Electrical Engineering
University of L'Aquila
I-67040 Poggio di Roio (AQ), Italy
eliseo@ing.univaq.it

Abstract. Current spatial database systems offer limited querying capabilities beyond topological relations. This paper introduces a model for projective relations between regions to support other qualitative spatial queries. The relations are ternary because they are based on the collinearity invariant of three points under projective geometry. The model is built on a partition of the plane in five regions that are obtained from projective properties of two reference objects: then, by considering the empty/non empty intersections of a primary object with these five regions, the model is able to distinguish between 31 different projective relations.

1 Introduction

A formal geometric definition of spatial relations is needed to build reasoning systems on them and facilitate a standard implementation in spatial database systems. This is what happens for some models of topological relations, like the 9-intersection [6] and the calculus-based method – CBM [3]. These models provide formal definitions for the relations, establish reasoning mechanisms to find new relations from a set of given ones [5] and, as part of the OpenGIS specifications [17] and ISO/TC 211 standard, have been implemented in several commercial geographic information systems (GISs) and spatial database systems.

Topological relations take into account an important part of geometric knowledge and can be used to formulate qualitative queries about the connection properties of close spatial objects, like "retrieve the lakes that are *inside* Scotland". Other qualitative queries that involve disjoint objects cannot be formulated in topological terms, for example: "the cities that are *between* Glasgow and Edinburgh", "the lakes that are *surrounded* by the mountains", "the shops that are on the *right* of the road", the building that is *before* the crossroad". All these examples can be seen as semantic interpretations of underlying projective properties of spatial objects. As discussed in [1], geometric properties can be subdivided in three groups: topological, projective and metric. Most qualitative relations between spatial objects can be defined in terms

E. Bertino et al. (Eds.): EDBT 2004, LNCS 2992, pp. 310–328, 2004.
© Springer-Verlag Berlin Heidelberg 2004

of topological or projective properties [24], with the exception of qualitative distance and direction relations (such as *close*, *far*, *east*, *north*) that are a qualitative interpretation of metric distances and angles [2].

Invariants are geometric properties that do not change after a certain class of transformations: topological invariants are properties that are maintained after a topological transformation (a bicontinuous mapping or homeomorphism) and projective invariants are properties that are maintained after a projective transformation (projection). Likewise topological relations, which are defined by using the connectedness topological invariant, projective relations are defined by using the collinearity projective invariant, which is the property of three collinear points being still collinear after an arbitrary number of projections. A main difference in the treatment of topological relations and projective relations is that, while basic topological relations are binary, basic projective relations are ternary because they are defined on the collinearity of three objects. Still, we can identify some special cases of binary projective relations (e.g., an object is inside the convex hull of another). Other binary relations, such as *surrounded by*, can be derived as a consequence of the model of ternary relations. In the present paper, we will limit the treatment to the basic ternary relations, while unary projective operators and binary projective relations will be part of further developments of the model. To have a qualitative understanding of projective relations, it is sufficient to think to different two-dimensional views of a three-dimensional real world scene of objects: changing the point of view, metric aspects such distances and angles among the objects appear to be different, but there are properties that are common in all the views. These common properties are projective properties.

In this paper, we propose a model for representing the projective relations between any three regions of the plane. One of these regions acts as the primary object and the other two as reference objects for the relation. We will show how by using only projective concepts it is possible to partition the plane in five regions with respect to the reference objects. Then, the model, called the 5-intersection, is able to differentiate between 31 different projective relations that are obtained by computing the intersection of the primary object with the five regions that are determined by the reference objects. Though in this paper we discuss the model for regions, the 5-intersection can be applied to other spatial objects such as points and lines. Other developments not treated in this paper will be to establish a reasoning system with projective relations to infer unknown relations from a set of given relations: this will be based on the algebraic properties of projective relations.

In first approximation, this work can be compared to research on qualitative relations dealing with relative positioning or cardinal directions [8, 10, 15, 16, 19, 20] and also path relations [13]. Most approaches consider binary relations to which is associated a frame of reference [11]. But most of them, even when explicitly related to projective geometry, never avoid the use of metric properties (minimum bounding rectangles, angles, etc.) and external frames of reference (such as a grid). To this respect, the main difference in our approach is that we only deal with projective invariants, disregarding distances and angles. Most work on projective relations deals with point abstractions of spatial features and limited work has been devoted to extended objects [10, 14, 23]. In [4], the authors use spheres surrounding the objects to take into account the shape of objects in relative orientation. The projective relations that are introduced in our paper are influenced by the size and shape of the three objects involved in a relation. The acceptance areas of the relations are truly based on the projective properties of the objects. Early work on projective relations such as "between" was developed by [9]. Freksa's double-cross calculus [7] is similar to our approach in the case of points. Such a calculus, as it has been further discussed in [12, 21], is based on ternary directional relations between points. However, in Freksa's model, an intrinsic frame of reference centred in a given point partitions the plane in four quadrants that are given by the front-back and right-left dichotomies. This leads to a greater number of qualitative distinctions with different algebraic properties and composition tables.

The paper is organized as follows. We start in Section 2 with developing a model for ternary projective relations between points: this is a natural starting point because the collinearity invariant applies to three points. Such a model is a simplified version of the model for regions and is very useful to understand the plausibility of the relations. In Section 3, we introduce the 5-intersection model for ternary projective relations between regions, giving the definitions, the algebraic properties and examples of the geometric configurations. In Section 4, we draw short conclusions and discuss the future developments of this model.

2 Projective Relations between Points

Our basic set of projective relations is based on the most important geometric invariant in a projective space: the collinearity of three points. Therefore, the nature of projective relations is intrinsically ternary. It is not possible to speak about binary projective relations except in some special or derived cases, and also in this cases the third object cannot be said to be absent, but rather to be hidden. For example, an "object *A* is in front of object *B*": this is linguistically a binary relation, but it implies that object *B* has an intrinsic frame of reference [18] that determines which is its front and that takes the role of the 'third point'. Analogously, considering the proposition "point *P* is to the right of line *L*", we have a derived binary relation because the direction of the line is defined by two points.

As a first step, we are going to define the basic ternary projective relations between points. Projective relations between points have a straightforward definition because they are related to common concepts of projective geometry [22]. The results of this section will be the basis for introducing the more complex definitions of projective relations between regions in Section 3.

2.1 "Collinear" Relation

The collinearity relation can be considered the most important relation from which all the others are obtained. The embedding space we are considering is R^2.

Definition 1. A point P_1 is *collinear* to two given points P_2 and P_3, $collinear(P_1, P_2, P_3)$, if one of the following conditions holds:

(a) $P_2 = P_3$;

(b) $P_1 \in \overline{P_2 P_3}$.

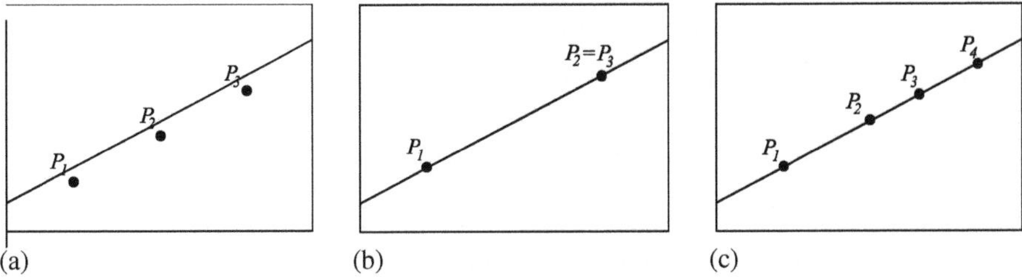

Fig. 1. The relation *collinear* between three points (a); the special case of coincidence of points P_2 and P_3 (b); illustration of the transitivity property (c)

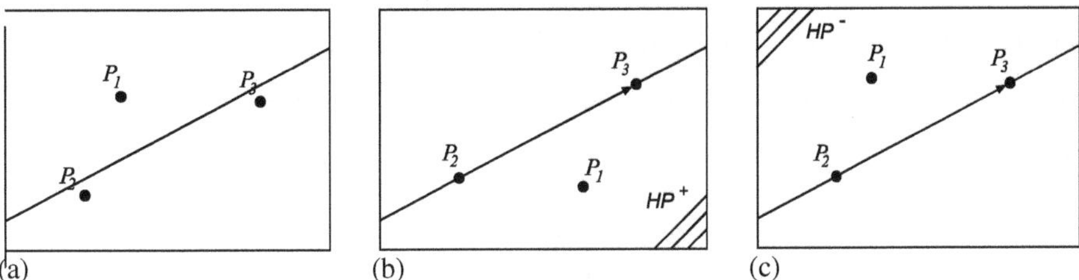

Fig. 2. The relation *aside* (a) and the relations *rightside* (b) and *leftside* (c)

Rephrasing Definition 1, the first point P_1 is collinear to two other points P_2 and P_3 if P_1 belongs to the line that passes through P_2 and P_3 (part (b)). The part (a) of the definition takes into account the trivial case where P_2 and P_3 are coincident and therefore they cannot define a line. Because there is always a line that passes through two points, we assume that the collinearity is also true in this case. The relation *collinear* is illustrated in Fig. 1(a-b).

Whenever we write the notation $collinear(P_1, P_2, P_3)$, the first of the three points corresponds to the one that holds the relation with the other two points and the other two points are defining a line. This order in the arguments of the relation is valid also for other ternary relations.

The properties of collinearity allow us to conclude that it is an equivalence relation. An equivalence relation is usually defined for binary relations by showing that they are reflexive, symmetric and transitive. An equivalence relation generates a partition in equivalence classes. With regard to the ternary collinearity relation, analogously we give below the properties that are divided in three groups (reflexivity, symmetry and transitivity). The equivalence classes that are generated are the classes of all collinear points, which are also all the lines of the space.

1. The *collinear* relation is reflexive. For all $P_1, P_2 \in R^2$:
   a. $collinear(P_1, P_1, P_1)$;
   b. $collinear(P_1, P_2, P_2)$;
   c. $collinear(P_1, P_1, P_2)$;
   d. $collinear(P_1, P_2, P_1)$.

2. The *collinear* relation is symmetric. For all $P_1, P_2, P_3 \in R^2$:
   a. $collinear(P_1, P_2, P_3) \Rightarrow collinear(P_1, P_3, P_2)$;
   b. $collinear(P_1, P_2, P_3) \Rightarrow collinear(P_2, P_1, P_3)$;
   c. $collinear(P_1, P_2, P_3) \Rightarrow collinear(P_3, P_1, P_2)$.
3. The *collinear* relation is transitive (see Fig. 1(c)). For all $P_1, P_2, P_3, P_4 \in R^2$:
   $collinear(P_1, P_2, P_3) \wedge collinear(P_2, P_3, P_4) \Rightarrow collinear(P_1, P_3, P_4)$.

2.2 "Aside" Relation

The *aside* relation is the complement of the *collinear* relation (see Fig. 2(a)).

Definition 2. A point P_1 is *aside* of two given points P_2 and P_3, $aside(P_1, P_2, P_3)$, if $P_1 \notin \overline{P_2 P_3}$ and $P_2 \neq P_3$.

The *aside* relation could simply be defined as $aside(P_1, P_2, P_3) \Leftrightarrow \neg collinear(P_1, P_2, P_3)$. The properties of the *aside* relation are restricted to the symmetry group:

1. The *aside* relation is symmetric.
   $aside(P_1, P_2, P_3) \Rightarrow aside(P_1, P_3, P_2)$
   $aside(P_1, P_2, P_3) \Rightarrow aside(P_2, P_1, P_3)$
   $aside(P_1, P_2, P_3) \Rightarrow aside(P_3, P_1, P_2)$

2.3 "Rightside" and "Leftside" Relations

By considering the two halfplanes determined by the oriented line $\overrightarrow{P_2 P_3}$, respectively the halfplane to the right of the line, which we indicate with $HP^+(\overrightarrow{P_2 P_3})$, and the halfplane to the left of the line, which we indicate with $HP^-(\overrightarrow{P_2 P_3})$, we refine the configurations described by the relation $aside(P_1, P_2, P_3)$ in two distinct parts that are described by the relations rightside and leftside (see Fig. 2(b-c)).

Definition 3. A point P_1 is *rightside* of two given points P_2 and P_3, $rightside(P_1, P_2, P_3)$, if $P_1 \in HP^+(\overrightarrow{P_2 P_3})$.

Definition 4. A point P_1 is *leftside* of two given points P_2 and P_3, $leftside(P_1, P_2, P_3)$, if $P_1 \in HP^-(\overrightarrow{P_2 P_3})$.

The order of the three arguments of the relations *rightside* and *leftside* is meaningful: the first argument is the point that is said to be on the rightside (or leftside) of the other two points; the second and third arguments are the points defining a direction that goes from the second point towards the third point.

It may be observed that three non collinear points are arranged in a triangle. Further, with relations *rightside* and *leftside*, it is possible to define an order in the triangles. In particular, if *rightside* (P_1,P_2,P_3), then the triangle $\overset{\Delta}{P_1P_2P_3}$ is a clockwise ordered triangle. If *leftside* (P_1,P_2,P_3), then the triangle $\overset{\Delta}{P_1P_2P_3}$ is a counter-clockwise ordered triangle (see Fig. 2(b-c)).

In the following, we give the properties of relations *rightside* and *leftside*. The first property enables to pass from *rightside* to *leftside* and vice versa, while the remaining properties define a cyclic order:

1. $rightside(P_1,P_2,P_3) \Leftrightarrow leftside(P_1,P_3,P_2)$;
2. $rightside(P_1,P_2,P_3) \Rightarrow rightside(P_2,P_3,P_1)$;
3. $rightside(P_1,P_2,P_3) \Rightarrow rightside(P_3,P_1,P_2)$;
4. $leftside(P_1,P_2,P_3) \Rightarrow leftside(P_2,P_3,P_1)$;
5. $leftside(P_1,P_2,P_3) \Rightarrow leftside(P_3,P_1,P_2)$.

2.4 "Between" and "Nonbetween" Relations

The collinear relation can be refined in two relations that are called *between* and *nonbetween*. This is possible by assessing whether the first point P_1 falls inside the segment $[P_2P_3]$ or outside it.

Definition 5. A point P_1 is *between* two given points P_2 and P_3, $between(P_1,P_2,P_3)$, if one of the following conditions hold:

(a) $P_1 = P_2 = P_3$;

(b) $P_1 \in [P_2P_3]$ with $P_2 \neq P_3$.

The relation *between* is illustrated in Fig. 3.

Definition 6. A point P_1 is *nonbetween* two given points P_2 and P_3, $nonbetween(P_1,P_2,P_3)$, if $collinear(P_1,P_2,P_3)$ and:

(a) $P_1 \notin [P_2P_3]$ with $P_2 \neq P_3$;

(b) $P_1 \neq P_2$ with $P_2 = P_3$.

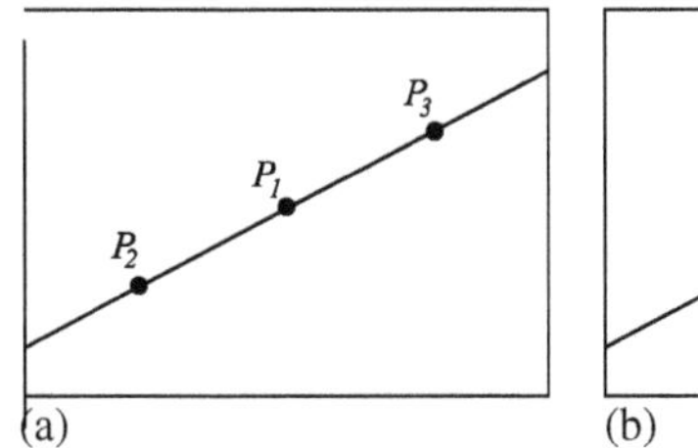

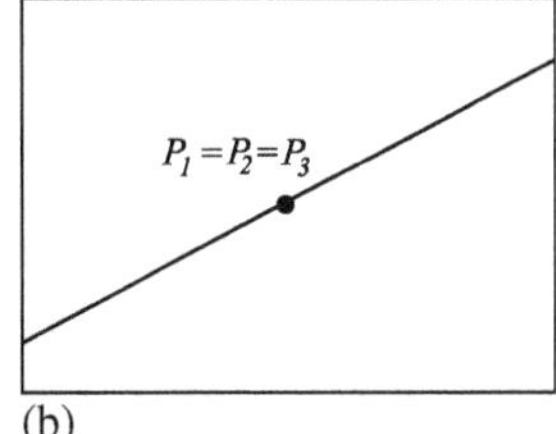

Fig. 3. The relation *between* in the general case (a) and in the special case of coincidence of points P_2 and P_3 (b)

The following properties hold. As we can see, if compared to *collinear*, the relation *between* is not an equivalence relation anymore, even if some of the properties in the reflexivity, symmetry and transitivity groups are maintained:

1. from the reflexivity group:
   a. $between(P_1, P_1, P_1)$;
   b. $nonbetween(P_1, P_2, P_2)$;
   c. $between(P_1, P_1, P_2)$;
   d. $between(P_1, P_2, P_1)$.
2. from the symmetry group:
   a. $between(P_1, P_2, P_3) \Rightarrow between(P_1, P_3, P_2)$;
   b. $between(P_1, P_2, P_3) \Rightarrow nonbetween(P_2, P_1, P_3)$;
   c. $between(P_1, P_2, P_3) \Rightarrow nonbetween(P_3, P_1, P_2)$;
   d. $nonbetween(P_1, P_2, P_3) \Rightarrow nonbetween(P_1, P_3, P_2)$.
3. transitivity:
   a. $between(P_1, P_2, P_3) \wedge between(P_2, P_3, P_4) \Rightarrow between(P_1, P_3, P_4)$;
   b. $between(P_1, P_2, P_3) \wedge between(P_2, P_3, P_4) \Rightarrow between(P_2, P_1, P_4)$.

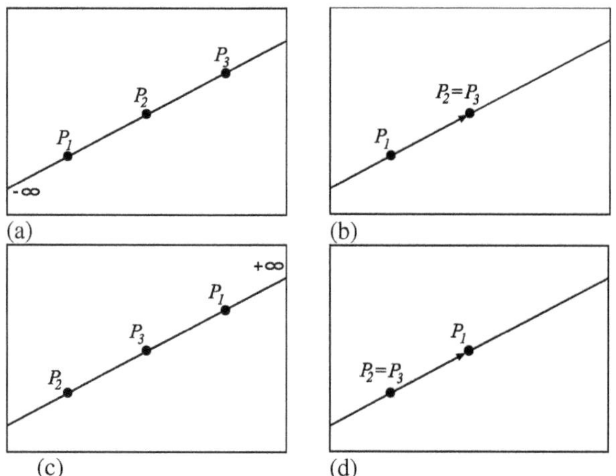

Fig. 4. The relations *before* (a-b) and *after* (c-d)

2.5 "Before" and "After" Relations

The *nonbetween* relation can be refined in the two relations *before* and *after* by considering the oriented line $\overrightarrow{P_2 P_3}$ and checking whether the point P_1 falls inside the interval $(-\infty, P_2)$ or the interval $(P_3, +\infty)$, respectively.

Definition 7. A point P_1 is *before* points P_2 and P_3, $before(P_1, P_2, P_3)$, if $collinear(P_1, P_2, P_3)$ and:

(a) $P_1 \in (-\infty, P_2)$, with $P_2 \neq P_3$;

(b) $P_1 \in \overrightarrow{P_1P_2}$, with $(P_2 = P_3) \wedge (P_1 \neq P_2)$.

Definition 8. A point P_1 is *after* points P_2 and P_3, $after(P_1, P_2, P_3)$ if $collinear(P_1, P_2, P_3)$ and:

(a) $P_1 \in (P_3, +\infty)$, with $P_2 \neq P_3$;

(b) $P_1 \in \overrightarrow{P_2P_1}$, with $(P_2 = P_3) \wedge (P_1 \neq P_2)$.

In Definitions 7 and 8, part (a) represents the plain case of distinct points P_2 and P_3, while part (b) is related to the case of coincident P_2 and P_3. For distinct points P_2 and P_3 the oriented line $\overrightarrow{P_2P_3}$ is considered. For coincident P_2 and P_3, we consider the line $\overline{P_1P_2}$ and an arbitrary orientation on this line: if the orientation $\overrightarrow{P_1P_2}$ is chosen, the relation $before(P_1, P_2, P_3)$ holds; all the way round, if the orientation $\overrightarrow{P_2P_1}$ is chosen, the relation $after(P_1, P_2, P_3)$ holds (see Fig. 4).

The properties of *before* and *after* relations are the following:

1. $before(P_1, P_2, P_3) \Rightarrow before(P_3, P_2, P_1)$;
2. $before(P_1, P_2, P_3) \Leftrightarrow after(P_1, P_3, P_2)$;
3. $before(P_1, P_2, P_3) \Leftrightarrow after(P_3, P_1, P_2)$;
4. $before(P_1, P_2, P_3) \Rightarrow between(P_2, P_1, P_3)$;
5. $after(P_1, P_2, P_3) \Rightarrow after(P_2, P_1, P_3)$;
6. $after(P_1, P_2, P_3) \Rightarrow between(P_3, P_2, P_1)$;
7. $before(P_1, P_2, P_3) \wedge before(P_2, P_3, P_4) \Rightarrow before(P_1, P_3, P_4)$;
8. $before(P_1, P_2, P_3) \wedge before(P_2, P_3, P_4) \Rightarrow before(P_1, P_2, P_4)$;
9. $after(P_1, P_2, P_3) \wedge after(P_3, P_4, P_2) \Rightarrow after(P_1, P_4, P_2)$;
10. $after(P_1, P_2, P_3) \wedge after(P_3, P_4, P_2) \Rightarrow after(P_1, P_4, P_3)$.

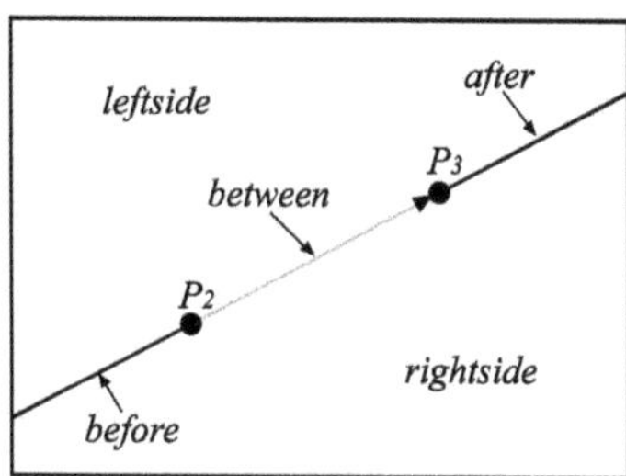

Fig. 5. The five low-level projective relations between points

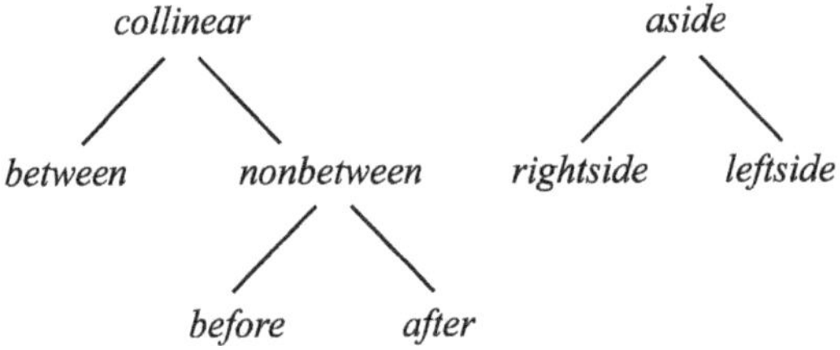

Fig. 6. The hierarchy of projective relations

To summarize, we have built a set of five projective relations between three points of the plane (*before, between, after, rightside, leftside*) – see Fig. 5. This set is a complete set in the sense that, given any three points, the projective relation between them must be one of the five, and is an independent set of relations, in the sense that, if a given relation between three points is true, then the other four relations must be false. These relations can be hierarchically structured, so to have more general levels of relations: *nonbetween* is *before* or *after*, *collinear* is *between* or *nonbetween*, *aside* is *rightside* or *leftside* (see Fig. 6).

3 Projective Relations between Regions

The results of Section 2 were useful to understand the hierarchy of ternary projective relations between three points. Such results immediately followed from the definition of collinearity in a projective space. In this section, we are going to define ternary projective relations between three objects of type region. We will show that it is possible to find plausible definitions for these relations. The definitions for points will be a special case of the definitions for regions. Not all the properties of the relations are maintained passing from points to regions.

3.1 "Collinear" Relation

For regions, we will assume the definition given in the OpenGIS Specifications [17], that is, a region is regular closed point set possibly with holes and separate components. For any relation $r(A,B,C)$, the first argument acts as the primary object, while the second and third arguments are reference objects. As a first step, let us introduce the *collinear* relation between a point and two regions.

Definition 9. A point P is *collinear* to two regions B and C, $collinear(P,B,C)$, if there exists a line l intersecting B and C that is also passing trough P:

$$\exists l, (l \cap B \neq \varnothing) \wedge (l \cap C \neq \varnothing) \mid l \cap P \neq \varnothing .$$

If the convex hulls of regions B and C are not disjoint, there is always a line passing through P and intersecting B and C. Therefore, in this case, we have a degenerate case of collinearity. To avoid it, in the definition of projective relations between three regions, we assume that the regions B and C have disjoint convex hulls. We indicate the convex hull of a region with a unary function $CH()$.

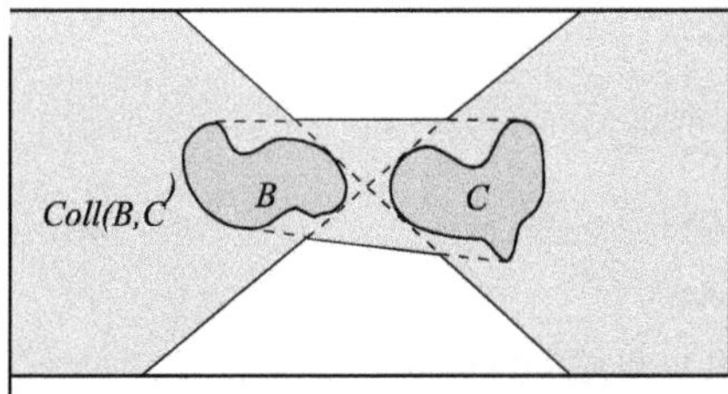

Fig. 7. The part of the plane corresponding to the collinearity region of B and C

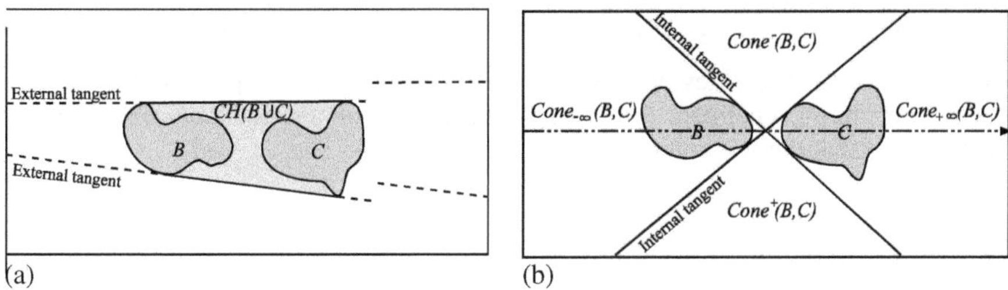

(a) (b)

Fig. 8. The construction to obtain the collinearity region: (a) the common external tangents make up the convex hull of the union of regions B and C and (b) the common internal tangents partition the plane in four cones

Definition 10. Given two regions B and C, with $CH(B) \cap CH(C) = \varnothing$, a region A is *collinear* to regions B and C, $collinear(A,B,C)$, if for every point $P \in A$, there exists a line l intersecting B and C that also intersects P, that is:

$$\forall P \in A, \exists l, (l \cap B \neq \varnothing) \wedge (l \cap C \neq \varnothing) \,|\, l \cap P \neq \varnothing .$$

For every two regions B and C, the relation *collinear* identifies a part of the plane where a region A completely contained into it is called collinear to B and C (see Fig. 7). Let us call this part of the plane the collinearity region of B and C, *Coll(B,C)*. The collinearity region of B and C can be built by considering all the lines that are intersecting both B and C. The boundary of the collinearity region is delimited by four lines that are the common external tangents and the common internal tangents. Common external tangents of B and C are defined by the fact that they also are tangent to the convex hull of the union of B and C (see Fig. 8(a)). Common internal tangents intersect inside the convex hull of the union of regions B and C and divide the plane in four cones (see Fig. 8(b)). In order to distinguish the four cones, we consider an oriented line from region B to region C and we call $Cone_{-\infty}(B,C)$ the cone that contains region B, $Cone_{+\infty}(B,C)$ the cone that contains region C, $Cone^{+}(B,C)$ the cone that is to the right of the oriented line, $Cone^{-}(B,C)$ the cone that is to the left of the oriented line. In terms of these subregions, the collinearity region is equivalent to the following:

$$Coll(B,C) = Cone_{-\infty}(B,C) \,\cup\, Cone_{+\infty}(B,C) \,\cup\, CH(B \cup C) .$$

We showed in Section 2 that the relation *collinear* among points is a ternary equivalence relation. The relation *collinear* for regions is not an equivalence relation because we lose transitivity. The only remaining properties are reflexivity and symmetry:

1. The *collinear* relation is reflexive:
   a. $collinear(A, A, A)$;
   b. $collinear(A, B, B)$;
   c. $collinear(A, A, B)$;
   d. $collinear(A, B, A)$.
2. The *collinear* relation is symmetric:
   a. $collinear(A, B, C) \Rightarrow collinear(A, C, B)$;
   b. $collinear(A, B, C) \Rightarrow collinear(B, A, C)$;
   c. $collinear(A, B, C) \Rightarrow collinear(C, A, B)$.

When discussing properties of relations, the role of primary object and the reference objects are often exchanged: therefore, to avoid degenerate cases of collinearity, we must assume that the two reference objects have disjoint convex hulls.

3.2 "Aside" Relation

If a region *A* is collinear to regions *B* and *C*, it means that it is entirely contained in the collinearity region of *B* and *C*. If the relation *aside* is true, it means that region *A* is entirely contained in the complement of the collinearity region. We will see at the end of this section how the model takes into account configurations where region *A* is partly inside and partly outside the collinearity region.

Definition 11. A region *A* is *aside* two regions *B* and *C*, $aside(A, B, C)$, if there is no line *l* intersecting *B* and *C* that also intersects *A*:

$$\forall l, (l \cap B \neq \varnothing) \wedge (l \cap C \neq \varnothing) \Rightarrow l \cap A = \varnothing .$$

The *aside* relation is symmetric:

$aside(A, B, C) \Rightarrow aside(A, C, B)$;

$aside(A, B, C) \Rightarrow aside(B, A, C)$;

$aside(A, B, C) \Rightarrow aside(C, A, B)$.

3.3 "Rightside" and "Leftside" Relation

The *rightside* and *leftside* relations are refinements of the *aside* relation, which are obtained by considering a region *A* that falls inside the two cones $Cone^{+}(B, C)$ or $Cone^{-}(B, C)$, respectively.

Definition 12. A region *A* is *rightside* of two regions *B* and *C*, $rightside(A, B, C)$, if *A* is contained inside $Cone^{+}(B, C)$ minus the convex hull of the union of regions *B* and *C*, that is, if $A \subset (Cone^{+}(B, C) - CH(B \cup C))$.

Definition 13. A region A is *leftside* of two regions B and C, $leftside(A,B,C)$, if A is contained inside $Cone^{-}(B,C)$ minus the convex hull of the union of regions B and C, that is, if $A \subset (Cone^{-}(B,C) - CH(B \cup C))$.

The following are the properties of relations *leftside* and *rightside* for regions. With respect to the corresponding properties we had for points, there is no more a strict cyclic order but a more permissive form of it:

1. $rightside(A,B,C) \Leftrightarrow leftside(A,C,B)$;
2. $rightside(A,B,C) \Rightarrow rightside(B,C,A) \vee (rightside(B,C,A) \wedge between(B,C,A))$;
3. $rightside(A,B,C) \Rightarrow rightside(C,A,B) \vee (rightside(C,A,B) \wedge between(C,A,B))$;
4. $leftside(A,B,C) \Rightarrow leftside(B,C,A) \vee (leftside(B,C,A) \wedge between(B,C,A))$;
5. $leftside(A,B,C) \Rightarrow leftside(B,C,A) \vee (leftside(B,C,A) \wedge between(B,C,A))$.

3.4 "Between" and "Nonbetween" Relations

The *between* and *nonbetween* relations are a refinement of the *collinear* relation. If region A falls inside the convex hull of the union of regions B and C, then by definition it is *between* B and C, otherwise is *nonbetween.*

Definition 14. A region A is *between* two regions B and C, $between(A,B,C)$, if $A \subseteq CH(B \cup C)$

Definition 15. A region A is *nonbetween* two regions B and C, $nonbetween(A,B,C)$, if $A \subset (Cone_{-\infty}(B,C) \cup Cone_{+\infty}(B,C)) - CH(B \cup C)$.

As we did for points, the following are the properties from the reflexive, symmetric and transitive groups that are maintained for the relation *between* among regions:

1. from the reflexivity group:
   a. $between(A,A,A)$; b. $between(A,A,B)$; c. $between(A,B,A)$.
2. from the symmetry group:
   a. $between(A,B,C) \Rightarrow between(A,C,B)$;
   b. $between(A,B,C) \Rightarrow nonbetween(B,A,C)$;
   c. $between(A,B,C) \Rightarrow nonbetween(C,A,B)$;
   d. $nonbetween(A,B,C) \Rightarrow nonbetween(A,C,B)$.
3. transitivity:
   $between(A,B,C) \wedge between(B,C,D) \Rightarrow between(A,C,D)$.

3.5 "Before" and "After" Relations

The relation nonbetween can be refined by checking whether region A falls inside $Cone_{-\infty}(B,C)$ or $Cone_{+\infty}(B,C)$, obtaining the relations *before* and *after*, respectively.

Definition 16. A region A is *before* two regions B and C, $before(A,B,C)$, if $A \subset Cone_{-\infty}(B,C) - CH(B \cup C)$.

Definition 17. A region A is *after* two regions B and C, $after(A,B,C)$, if $A \subset Cone_{+\infty}(B,C) - CH(B \cup C)$.

We can identify the following properties for the relations *before* and *after* among regions:

1. $before(A,B,C) \Rightarrow before(C,B,A) \vee (before(C,B,A) \wedge aside(C,B,A))$;
2. $before(A,B,C) \Leftrightarrow after(A,C,B)$;
3. $before(A,B,C) \Rightarrow after(C,A,B) \vee (after(C,A,B) \wedge aside(C,A,B))$;
4. $before(A,B,C) \Rightarrow between(B,A,C) \vee (between(B,A,C) \wedge aside(B,A,C))$;
5. $after(A,B,C) \Rightarrow after(B,A,C) \vee (after(B,A,C) \wedge aside(B,A,C))$;
6. $after(A,B,C) \Rightarrow before(B,C,A) \vee (before(B,C,A) \wedge aside(B,C,A))$;
7. $after(A,B,C) \Rightarrow between(C,B,A) \vee (between(C,B,A) \wedge aside(C,B,A))$;
8. $before(A,B,C) \wedge before(B,C,D) \Rightarrow$
   $before(A,C,D) \vee (before(A,C,D) \wedge aside(A,C,D)) \vee aside(A,C,D)$;
9. $before(A,B,C) \wedge before(B,C,D) \Rightarrow$
   $before(A,B,D) \vee (before(A,B,D) \wedge aside(A,B,D)) \vee aside(A,B,D)$;
10. $after(A,B,C) \wedge after(C,D,B) \Rightarrow$
    $after(A,D,B) \vee (after(A,D,B) \wedge aside(A,D,B)) \vee aside(A,D,B)$.
11. $after(A,B,C) \wedge after(C,D,B) \Rightarrow$
    $after(A,D,C) \vee (after(A,D,C) \wedge aside(A,D,C)) \vee aside(A,D,C)$.

The set of five projective relations *before*, *between*, *after*, *rightside*, and *leftside* can be used as a set of basic relations to build a model for all projective relations between three regions of the plane. For the sake of simplicity, let us give a name to the regions of the plane corresponding to the basic relations (see also Fig. 9):

$Before(B,C) = Cone_{-\infty}(B,C) - CH(B \cup C)$;

$After(B,C) = Cone_{+\infty}(B,C) - CH(B \cup C)$;

$Rightside(B,C) = Cone^{+}(B,C) - CH(B \cup C)$;

$Leftside(B,C) = Cone^{-}(B,C) - CH(B \cup C)$;

$Between(B,C) = CH(B \cup C)$.

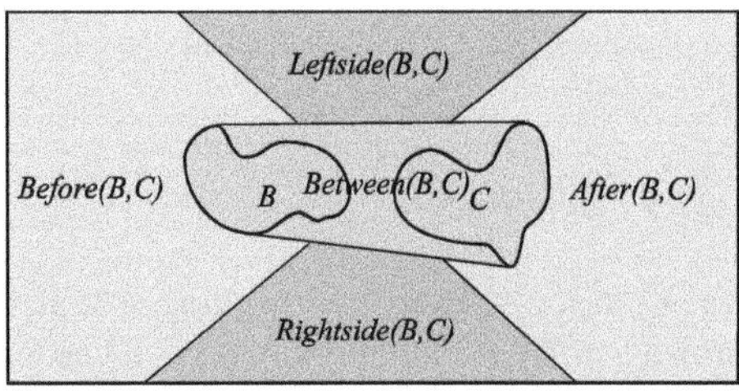

Fig. 9. The partition of the plane in five regions

The model, that we call the *5-intersection*, is synthetically expressed by a matrix of five values that are the empty/non-empty intersections of a region A with the five regions defined above:

	$A \cap$ *Leftside(B,C)*	
$A \cap$ *Before(B,C)*	$A \cap$ *Between(B,C)*	$A \cap$ *After(B,C)*
	$A \cap$ *Rightside(B,C)*	

In the matrix, a value 0 indicates an empty intersection, while a value 1 indicates a non-empty intersection. The five basic relations correspond to values of the matrix with only one non-empty value:

$$before(A,B,C)\colon \begin{pmatrix} & 0 & \\ 1 & 0 & 0 \\ & 0 & \end{pmatrix};\quad between(A,B,C)\colon \begin{pmatrix} & 0 & \\ 0 & 1 & 0 \\ & 0 & \end{pmatrix};\quad after(A,B,C)\colon \begin{pmatrix} & 0 & \\ 0 & 0 & 1 \\ & 0 & \end{pmatrix};$$

$$rightside(A,B,C)\colon \begin{pmatrix} & 0 & \\ 0 & 0 & 0 \\ & 1 & \end{pmatrix};\quad leftside(A,B,C)\colon \begin{pmatrix} & 1 & \\ 0 & 0 & 0 \\ & 0 & \end{pmatrix}.$$

In total, the 5-intersection matrix can have 2^5 different values that correspond to the same theoretical number of projective relations. Excluding the configuration with all zero values which cannot exist, we are left with 31 different projective relations between the three regions A, B and C. In Fig. 10-13, we have some examples of the 31 projective relations. Previously defined *nonbetween*, *collinear* and *aside* relations can be expressed in terms of the 5-intersection as follows:

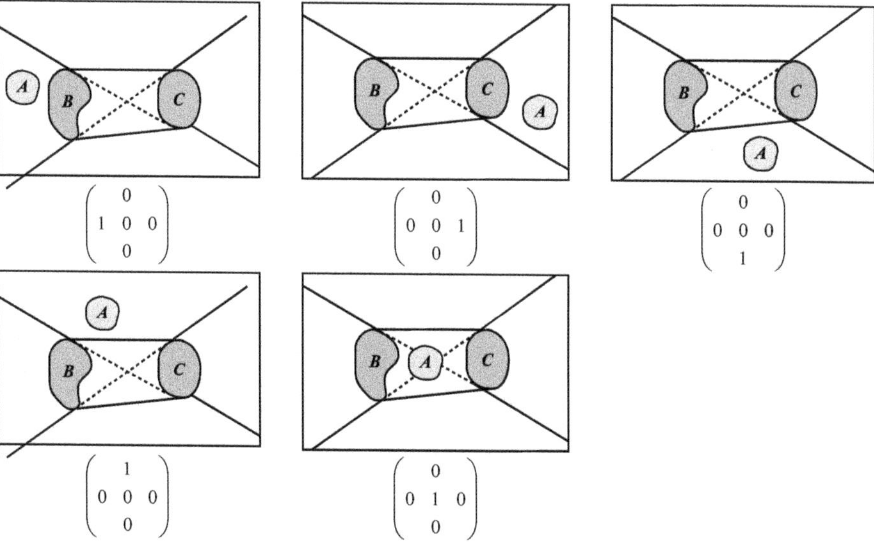

Fig. 10. The projective relations with object A intersecting only one of the regions of the plane

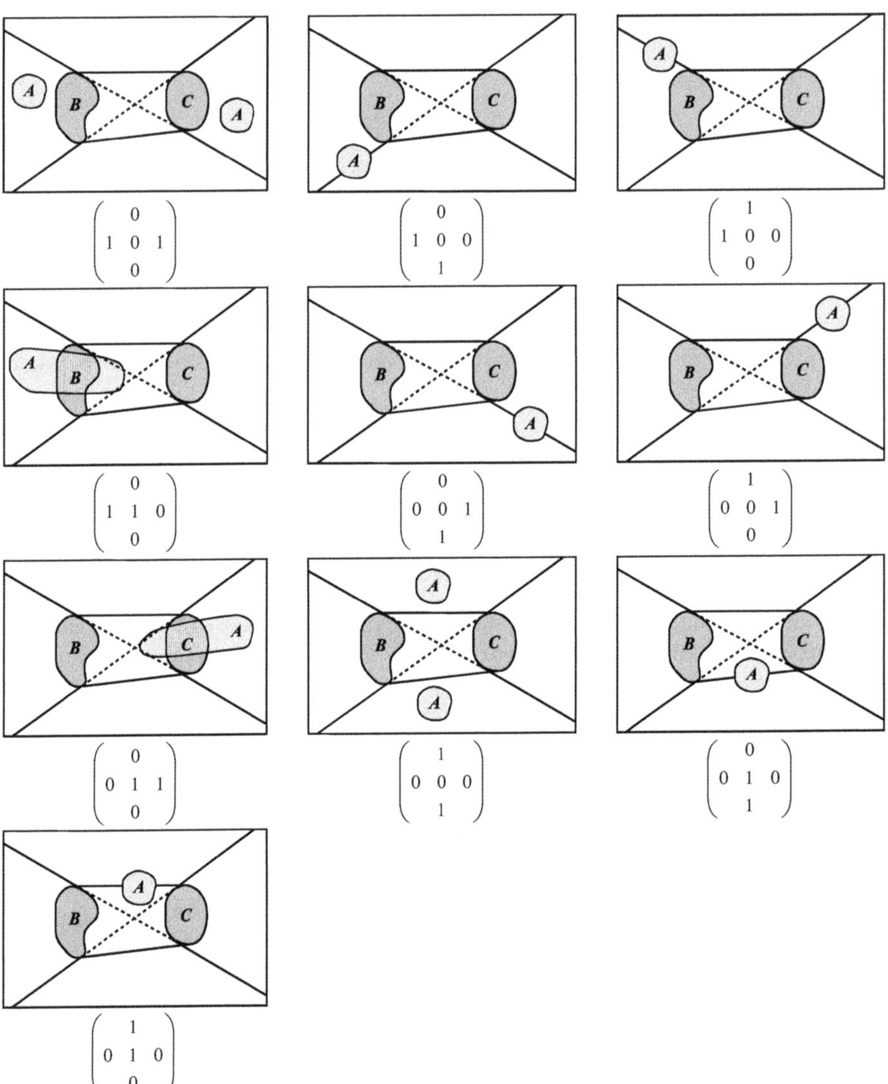

Fig. 11. The projective relations with object A intersecting two regions of the plane

$$nonbetween(A,B,C): \begin{pmatrix} & 0 & \\ 1 & 0 & 0 \\ & 0 & \end{pmatrix} \vee \begin{pmatrix} & 0 & \\ 0 & 0 & 1 \\ & 0 & \end{pmatrix} \vee \begin{pmatrix} & 0 & \\ 1 & 0 & 1 \\ & 0 & \end{pmatrix};$$

$$collinear(A,B,C): \begin{pmatrix} & 0 & \\ 1 & 0 & 0 \\ & 0 & \end{pmatrix} \vee \begin{pmatrix} & 0 & \\ 0 & 1 & 0 \\ & 0 & \end{pmatrix} \vee \begin{pmatrix} & 0 & \\ 0 & 0 & 1 \\ & 0 & \end{pmatrix} \vee \begin{pmatrix} & 0 & \\ 1 & 1 & 0 \\ & 0 & \end{pmatrix} \vee$$

$$\begin{pmatrix} & 0 & \\ 1 & 0 & 1 \\ & 0 & \end{pmatrix} \vee \begin{pmatrix} & 0 & \\ 0 & 1 & 1 \\ & 0 & \end{pmatrix} \vee \begin{pmatrix} & 0 & \\ 1 & 1 & 1 \\ & 0 & \end{pmatrix};$$

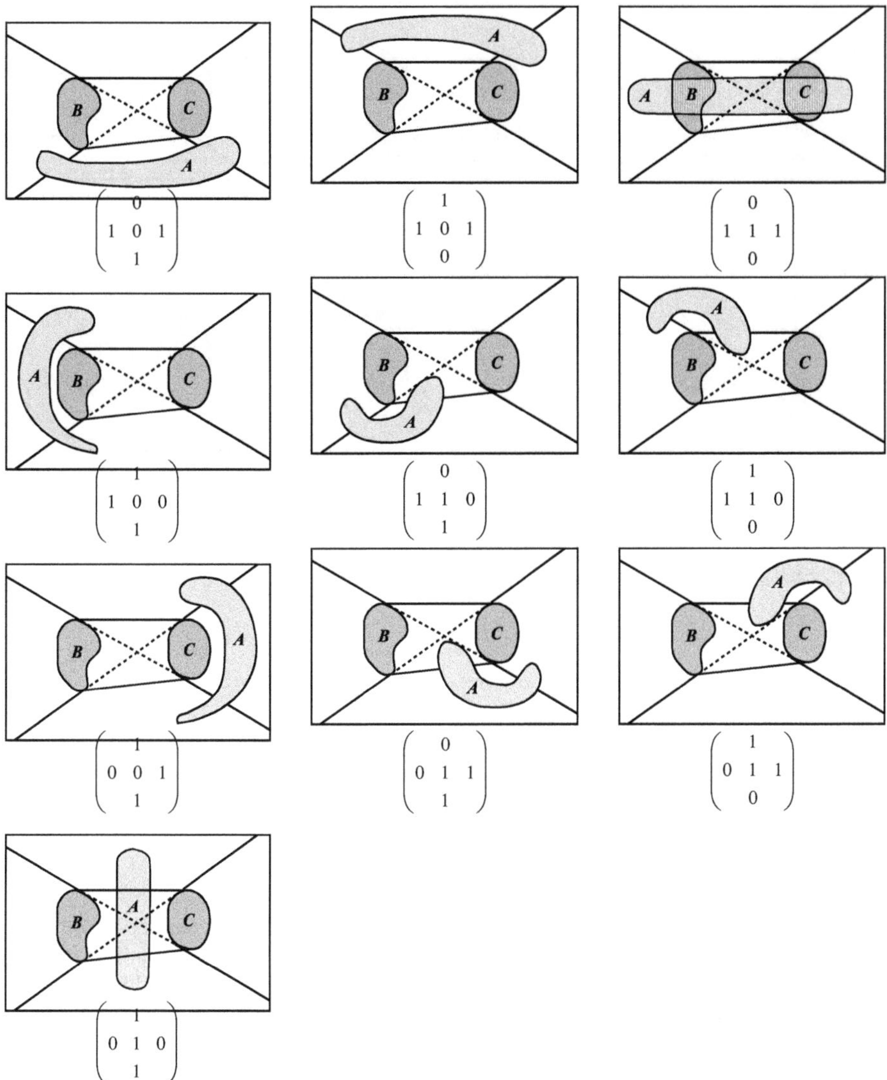

Fig. 12. The projective relations with object A intersecting three regions of the plane

$$aside(A,B,C): \begin{pmatrix} & 0 & \\ 0 & 0 & 0 \\ & 1 & \end{pmatrix} \vee \begin{pmatrix} & 1 & \\ 0 & 0 & 0 \\ & 0 & \end{pmatrix} \vee \begin{pmatrix} & 1 & \\ 0 & 0 & 0 \\ & 1 & \end{pmatrix}.$$

Besides the relations above, it is possible to assign a name to other relations by using a combination of the basic relation names, for example, the following relation would be a "before and rightside":

$$\begin{pmatrix} & 0 & \\ 1 & 0 & 0 \\ & 1 & \end{pmatrix}.$$

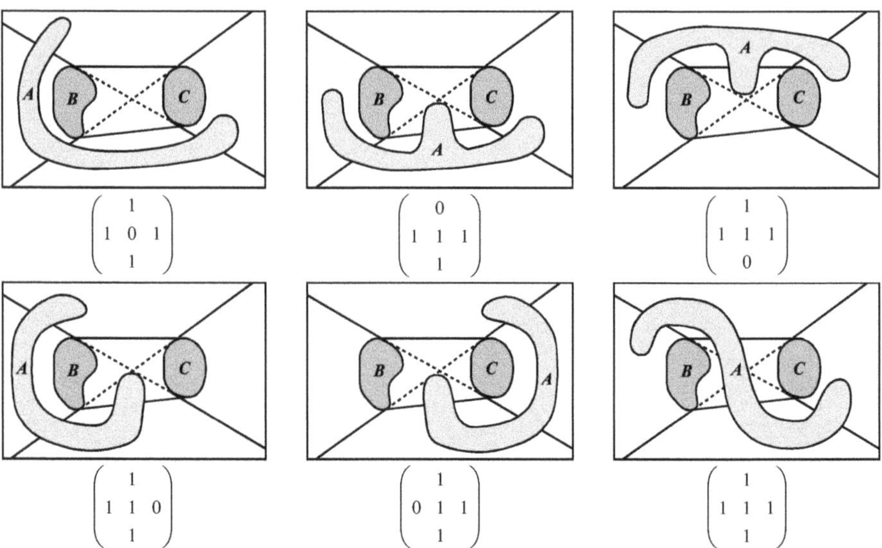

Fig. 13. The projective relations with object *A* intersecting four or five regions of the plane

4 Further Research

This paper introduces a set of jointly exhaustive and pairwise disjoint projective relations between three regions of the plane. The number of relations is 31 and is obtained by considering the collinearity of three points as the basic projective invariant. The strengths of this model are the independence from any external frame of reference and the capacity of taking the actual size and shape of objects into account for defining the relations.

The model presented in this paper is the first step of future research on projective relations. The proofs of the formal properties of relations will be given. The relations for lines and also mixed cases (region/point, region/line, line/point) will be developed as well as a 3D extension of the model. The reasoning system will be improved to have rules for symmetry and transitivity by means of composition tables: with regard to symmetric properties, given the projective relation $r(A,B,C)$, the rules will give $r(A,C,B)$, $r(B,A,C)$ and $r(C,A,B)$; with regard to transitive properties, given the relations $r(A,B,C)$ and $r(B,C,D)$, the rules will give $r(A,C,D)$.

Furthermore, the relations will be extended for scenes of more than three objects: as a combination of ternary relations, it will be possible to express relations such as "surrounded by" or "in the middle of". Another step will be the evaluation of algorithms to find out the partition of the plane in five regions for any pair of reference objects and the implementation of projective relations in a spatial database system.

Acknowledgements. This work was supported by M.I.U.R. under project "Representation and management of spatial and geographic data on the Web".

References

1. Clementini, E. and P. Di Felice, *Spatial Operators.* ACM SIGMOD Record, 2000. **29**(3): p. 31-38.
2. Clementini, E., P. Di Felice, and D. Hernández, *Qualitative representation of positional information.* Artificial Intelligence, 1997. **95**: p. 317-356.
3. Clementini, E., P. Di Felice, and P. van Oosterom, *A Small Set of Formal Topological Relationships Suitable for End-User Interaction*, in *Advances in Spatial Databases - Third International Symposium, SSD '93*, D. Abel and B.C. Ooi, Editors. 1993, Springer-Verlag: Berlin. p. 277-295.
4. Dugat, V., P. Gambarotto, and Y. Larvor. *Qualitative Theory of Shape and Orientation.* in *Proc. of the 16th Int. Joint Conference on Artificial Intelligence (IJCAI'99).* 1999. Stockolm, Sweden: Morgan Kaufmann Publishers. p. 45-53.
5. Egenhofer, M.J., *Deriving the composition of binary topological relations.* Journal of Visual Languages and Computing, 1994. **5**(1): p. 133-149.
6. Egenhofer, M.J. and J.R. Herring, *Categorizing Binary Topological Relationships Between Regions, Lines, and Points in Geographic Databases.* 1991, Department of Surveying Engineering, University of Maine, Orono, ME.
7. Freksa, C., *Using Orientation Information for Qualitative Spatial Reasoning*, in *Theories and Models of Spatio-Temporal Reasoning in Geographic Space*, A.U. Frank, I. Campari, and U. Formentini, Editors. 1992, Springer-Verlag: Berlin. p. 162-178.
8. Gapp, K.-P. *Angle, Distance, Shape, and their Relationship to Projective Relations.* in *Proceedings of the 17th Conference of the Cognitive Science Society.* 1995. Pittsburgh, PA.
9. Gapp, K.-P. *From Vision to Language: A Cognitive Approach to the Computation of Spatial Relations in 3D Space.* in *Proc. of the First European Conference on Cognitive Science in Industry.* 1994. Luxembourg. p. 339-357.
10. Goyal, R. and M.J. Egenhofer, *Cardinal directions between extended spatial objects.* IEEE Transactions on Knowledge and Data Engineering, 2003. (in press).
11. Hernández, D., *Qualitative Representation of Spatial Knowledge.* Lecture Notes in Artificial Intelligence. Vol. LNAI 804. 1994, Berlin: Springer-Verlag.
12. Isli, A. *Combining Cardinal Direction Relations and other Orientation Relations in QSR.* in *AI&M 14-2004, Eighth International Symposium on Artificial Intelligence and Mathematics.* January 4-6, 2004. Fort Lauderdale, Florida.
13. Kray, C. and A. Blocher. *Modeling the Basic Meanings of Path Relations.* in *Proc. of the 16th International Joint Conference on Artificial Intelligence (IJCAI-99).* 1999. Stockolm, Sweden: Morgan Kaufmann Publishers. p. 384-389.
14. Kulik, L., et al. *A graded approach to directions between extended objects.* in *Proc. of the 2nd Int. Conf. on Geographic Information Science.* 2002. Boulder, CO: Springer. p. 119-131.
15. Kulik, L. and A. Klippel, *Reasoning about Cardinal Directions Using Grids as Qualitative Geographic Coordinates*, in *Spatial Information Theory. Cognitive and Computational Foundations of Geographic Information Science: International Conference COSIT'99*, C. Freksa and D.M. Mark, Editors. 1999, Springer. p. 205-220.
16. Moratz, R. and K. Fischer. *Cognitively Adequate Modelling of Spatial Reference in Human-Robot Interaction.* in *Proc. of the 12th IEEE International Conference on Tools with Artificial Intelligence, ICTAI 2000.* 2000. Vancouver, BC, Canada. p. 222-228.
17. OpenGIS Consortium, *OpenGIS Simple Features Specification for SQL.* 1998.
18. Retz-Schmidt, G., *Various Views on Spatial Prepositions.* AI Magazine, 1988. **9**(2): p. 95-105.
19. Schlieder, C., *Reasoning about ordering*, in *Spatial Information Theory: A Theoretical Basis for GIS - International Conference, COSIT'95*, A.U. Frank and W. Kuhn, Editors. 1995, Springer-Verlag: Berlin. p. 341-349.

20. Schmidtke, H.R., *The house is north of the river: Relative localization of extended objects*, in *Spatial Information Theory. Foundations of Geographic Information Science: International Conference, COSIT 2001*, D.R. Montello, Editor. 2001, Springer. p. 415-430.
21. Scivos, A. and B. Nebel, *Double-Crossing: Decidability and Computational Complexity of a Qualitative Calculus for Navigation*, in *Spatial Information Theory. Foundations of Geographic Information Science: International Conference, COSIT 2001*, D.R. Montello, Editor. 2001, Springer. p. 431-446.
22. Struik, D.J., *Projective Geometry*. 1953, London: Addison-Wesley.
23. Vorwerg, C., et al. *Projective relations for 3D space: Computational model, application, and psychological evaluation*. in *Proc. of the 14th National Conference on Artificial Intelligence and 9th Innovative Applications of Artificial Intelligence Conference, AAAI 97, IAAI 97*. 1997. Providence, Rhode Island: AAAI Press / The MIT Press. p. 159-164.
24. Waller, D., et al., *Place learning in humans: The role of distance and direction information*. Spatial Cognition and Computation, 2000. **2**: p. 333-354.

Computing and Handling Cardinal Direction Information

Spiros Skiadopoulos[1], Christos Giannoukos[1], Panos Vassiliadis[2], Timos Sellis[1], and Manolis Koubarakis[3]

[1] School of Electrical and Computer Engineering
National Technical University of Athens
Zographou 157 73 Athens, Hellas
{spiros,chgian,timos}@dblab.ece.ntua.gr
[2] Dept. of Computer Science
University of Ioannina, Ioannina 451 10, Hellas
pvassil@cs.uoi.gr
[3] Dept. of Electronic and Computer Engineering
Technical University of Crete, Chania 731 00 Crete, Hellas
manolis@intelligence.tuc.gr

Abstract. Qualitative spatial reasoning forms an important part of the commonsense reasoning required for building intelligent Geographical Information Systems (GIS). Previous research has come up with models to capture cardinal direction relations for typical GIS data. In this paper, we target the problem of efficiently computing the cardinal direction relations between regions that are composed of sets of polygons and present the first two algorithms for this task. The first of the proposed algorithms is purely qualitative and computes, in linear time, the cardinal direction relations between the input regions. The second has a quantitative aspect and computes, also in linear time, the cardinal direction relations with percentages between the input regions. The algorithms have been implemented and embedded in an actual system, CARDIRECT, that allows the user to annotate regions of interest in an image or a map, compute cardinal direction relations and retrieve combinations of interesting regions on the basis of a query.

1 Introduction

Recent developments in the fields of mobile and collaborative computing, require that intelligent Geographical Information Systems (GIS) should support real-time response to complex queries. Related research in the field of spatiotemporal data management and reasoning has provided several results towards this problem. Among these research topics, qualitative spatial reasoning has received a lot of attention with several kinds of useful spatial relations being studied so far, e.g., topological relations [2,17], cardinal direction relations [6,8,11] and distance relations [3]. The uttermost aim in these lines of research is to define new categories of spatial operators as well as to build efficient algorithms for the automatic processing of queries that use such operators.

E. Bertino et al. (Eds.): EDBT 2004, LNCS 2992, pp. 329–347, 2004.
© Springer-Verlag Berlin Heidelberg 2004

The present paper concentrates on *cardinal direction relations* [6,8]. Cardinal direction relations are qualitative spatial relations characterizing the relative position of a region with respect to another (e.g., region a is *north of* region b). Our starting point is the cardinal direction framework presented in [5,6,20,21]. To express the cardinal direction relation between a region a and with respect to region b, this model approximates only region b (using its minimum bounding box – MBB) while it uses the exact shape of region a. This offers a more precise and expressive model than previous approaches that approximate both extended regions using points or MBB's [4,8,13]. Particularly, in this paper we will employ the cardinal direction model presented in [21] because it is formally defined and can be applied to a wide set of regions (like disconnected regions and regions with holes). Additionally, we also study the interesting extension of cardinal directions relations that adds a quantitative aspect using percentages [6].

The goal of this paper is to address the problem of efficiently computing the cardinal direction relations between regions that are composed of sets of polygons (stored as lists of their edges). To the best of our knowledge, this is the first effort handling the aforementioned problem for the cardinal direction relations that can be expressed in [6,21]. On the contrary, for other models of directions such algorithms do exist. For instance, Peuquet and Ci-Xiang [15] capture cardinal direction on polygons using points and MBB's approximations and present linear algorithms that compute the relative direction. Moreover, we present an implemented system, CarDirect that encapsulates the cardinal direction relations computation functionality in order to answer interesting user queries. The scenario for CarDirect usage is based on a simple scheme, where the user identifies and annotates interesting areas in an image or a map (possibly with the use of special segmentation software) and requires to retrieve regions that satisfy (spatial and thematic) criteria.

The technical contributions of this paper can be summarized as follows:

1. We present an algorithm for the efficient computation of cardinal direction relations. The proposed algorithm calculates the purely qualitative cardinal direction relations between the input regions and can be executed in linear time with respect to the number of input polygon's edges.
2. We complement the previous result with an algorithm for the linear computation of cardinal direction relations in a quantitative fashion with percentages. The computation is performed through a novel technique for the computation of areas of polygons.
3. We discuss the implementation of a tool, CarDirect that encapsulates the above algorithms. Using CarDirect the user can specify, edit and annotate regions of interest in an image or a map and compute the cardinal direction relations between these regions using the aforementioned linear algorithms. The configuration of the image (formed by the annotated regions and the calculated relations) are persistently stored using a simple XML description. Finally, the user is allowed to query the stored XML configuration of the image and retrieve combinations of interesting regions.

The rest of the paper is organized as follows. Section 2 presents the cardinal direction relations model. In Section 3, we present two algorithms for the problem of computing cardinal direction relations. Proofs of correctness and more details about the two algorithms can be found in the extended version of this paper [19]. Section 4 presents the CARDIRECT tool. Finally, Section 5 offers conclusions and lists topics of future research.

2 A Formal Model for Cardinal Direction Information

Cardinal direction relations, for various types of regions, have been defined in [5,6,20,21]. Goyal and Egenhofer [5] first presented a set of cardinal direction relations for connected regions. Skiadopoulos and Koubarakis [20] formally define the above cardinal direction relations, propose composition algorithms and prove that these algorithm are correct. Moreover, Skiadopoulos and Koubarakis [21] presented an extension that handles disconnected regions and region with holes, and study the consistency problem for a given set of cardinal direction constraints. In this paper, we will start with the cardinal direction relations for the composite regions presented in [21] and then we will present an extension with percentages in the style of [5,6].

We consider the Euclidean space $\Re^2$. *Regions* are defined as non-empty and bounded sets of points in $\Re^2$. Let a be a region. The *infimum* (greatest lower bound) [9] of the *projection* of region a on the x-axis (resp. y-axis) is denoted by $inf_x(a)$ (resp. $inf_y(a)$). The *supremum* (least upper bound) of the *projection* of region a on the x-axis (resp. y-axis) is denoted by $sup_x(a)$ (resp. $sup_y(a)$). The *minimum bounding box* of a region a, denoted by $mbb(a)$, is the rectangular region formed by the straight lines $x = inf_x(a)$, $x = sup_x(a)$, $y = inf_y(a)$ and $y = sup_y(a)$ (see Fig. 1a). Obviously, the projections on the x-axis (resp. y-axis) of a region and its minimum bounding box have the same infimums and supremums.

Throughout this paper we will consider the following types of regions [20,21]:

- Regions that are homeomorphic to the *closed unit disk* ($\{(x, y) : x^2 + y^2 \leq 1\}$). The set of these regions will be denoted by *REG*. Regions in *REG* are *closed, connected* and have *connected boundaries* (for definitions of closeness and connectness see [9]). Class *REG* excludes disconnected regions, regions with holes, points, lines and regions with emanating lines. Notice that our results are not affected if we consider regions that are homeomorphic to the *open unit disk* (as in [14]).
- Regions in *REG* cannot model the variety and complexity of geographic entities [1]. Thus, we consider class *REG**, an extension of class *REG*, that accommodates *disconnected regions* and *regions with holes*. The set of these regions will be denoted by *REG**. Set *REG** is a natural extension of *REG*. The regions that we consider are very common, for example, countries are made up of separations (islands, exclaves, external territories) and holes (enclaves) [1].

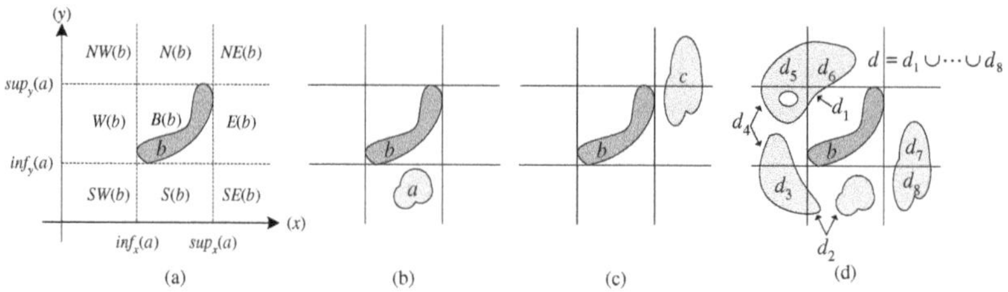

Fig. 1. Reference tiles and relations

In Fig. 1, regions a, b and c are in *REG* (also in *REG**) and region $d = d_1 \cup \dots \cup d_8$ is in *REG**. Notice that region d is disconnected and has a hole.

Let us now consider two arbitrary regions a and b in *REG**. Let region a be related to region b through a cardinal direction relation (e.g., a is north of b). Region b will be called the *reference* region (i.e., the region which the relation refers to) while region a will be called the *primary* region (i.e., the region for which the relation is introduced). The axes forming the minimum bounding box of the reference region b divide the space into 9 areas which we call *tiles* (Fig. 1a). The peripheral tiles correspond to the eight cardinal direction relations *south*, *southwest*, *west*, *northwest*, *north*, *northeast*, *east* and *southeast*. These tiles will be denoted by $S(b)$, $SW(b)$, $W(b)$, $NW(b)$, $N(b)$, $NE(b)$, $E(b)$ and $SE(b)$ respectively. The central area corresponds to the region's minimum bounding box and is denoted by $B(b)$. By definition each one of these tiles includes the parts of the axes forming it. The union of all 9 tiles is $\Re^2$.

If a primary region a is included (in the set-theoretic sense) in tile $S(b)$ of some reference region b (Fig. 1b) then we say that *a is south of b* and we write $a\ S\ b$. Similarly, we can define *southwest* (SW), *west* (W), *northwest* (NW), *north* (N), *northeast* (NE), *east* (E), *southeast* (SE) and *bounding box* (B) relations. If a primary region a lies partly in the area $NE(b)$ and partly in the area $E(b)$ of some reference region b (Fig. 1c) then we say that *a is partly northeast and partly east of b* and we write $a\ NE{:}E\ b$.

The general definition of a cardinal direction relation in our framework is as follows.

Definition 1. *A* cardinal direction relation *is an expression* $R_1{:}\cdots{:}R_k$ *where (a)* $1 \le k \le 9$, *(b)* $R_1, \dots, R_k \in \{B, S, SW, W, NW, N, NE, E, SE\}$ *and (c)* $R_i \ne R_j$ *for every* i, j *such that* $1 \le i, j \le k$ *and* $i \ne j$. *A cardinal direction relation* $R_1{:}\cdots{:}R_k$ *is called* single-tile *if* $k = 1$; *otherwise it is called* multi-tile.

Let a and b be two regions in REG. Single-tile cardinal direction relations are defined as follows:*

$$a\ B\ b \text{ iff } inf_x(b) \le inf_x(a),\ sup_x(a) \le sup_x(b),\ inf_y(b) \le inf_y(a) \text{ and } sup_y(a) \le sup_y(b).$$

$$a\ S\ b \text{ iff } sup_y(a) \le inf_y(b),\ inf_x(b) \le inf_x(a) \text{ and } sup_x(a) \le sup_x(b).$$

$a\ SW\ b$ *iff* $sup_x(a) \leq inf_x(b)$ *and* $sup_y(a) \leq inf_y(b)$.
$a\ W\ b$ *iff* $sup_x(a) \leq inf_x(b)$, $inf_y(b) \leq inf_y(a)$ *and* $sup_y(a) \leq sup_y(b)$.
$a\ NW\ b$ *iff* $sup_x(a) \leq inf_x(b)$ *and* $sup_y(b) \leq inf_y(a)$.
$a\ N\ b$ *iff* $sup_y(b) \leq inf_y(a)$, $inf_x(b) \leq inf_x(a)$ *and* $sup_x(a) \leq sup_x(b)$.
$a\ NE\ b$ *iff* $sup_x(b) \leq inf_x(a)$ *and* $sup_y(b) \leq inf_y(a)$.
$a\ E\ b$ *iff* $sup_x(b) \leq inf_x(a)$, $inf_y(b) \leq inf_y(a)$ *and* $sup_y(a) \leq sup_y(b)$.
$a\ SE\ b$ *iff* $sup_x(b) \leq inf_x(a)$ *and* $sup_y(a) \leq inf_y(b)$.

In general, each multi-tile $(2 \leq k \leq 8)$ *relation is defined as follows:*

$$a\ R_1{:}\cdots{:}R_k\ b \text{ iff there exist regions } a_1, \ldots, a_k \in REG^* \text{ such that } a_1\ R_1\ b, \ldots, a_k\ R_k\ b \text{ and } a = a_1 \cup \cdots \cup a_k.$$

In Definition 1 notice that for every i, j such that $1 \leq i, j \leq k$ and $i \neq j$, a_i and a_j have disjoint interiors but may share points in their boundaries.

Example 1. S, $NE{:}E$ and $B{:}S{:}SW{:}W{:}NW{:}N{:}E{:}SE$ are cardinal direction relations. The first relation is single-tile while the others are multi-tile. In Fig. 1, we have $a\ S\ b$, $c\ NE{:}E\ b$ and $d\ B{:}S{:}SW{:}W{:}NW{:}N{:}E{:}SE\ b$. For instance in Fig. 1d, we have $d\ B{:}S{:}SW{:}W{:}NW{:}N{:}SE{:}E\ b$ because there exist regions $d_1, \ldots, d_8$ in REG^* such that $d = d_1 \cup \cdots \cup d_8$, $d_1\ B\ b$, $d_2\ S\ b$, $d_3\ SW\ b$, $d_4\ W\ b$, $d_5\ NW\ b$, $d_6\ N\ b$, $d_7\ SE\ b$ and $d_8\ E\ b$.

In order to avoid confusion, we will write the single-tile elements of a cardinal direction relation according to the following order: B, S, SW, W, NW, N, NE, E and SE. Thus, we always write $B{:}S{:}W$ instead of $W{:}B{:}S$ or $S{:}B{:}W$. Moreover, for a relation such as $B{:}S{:}W$ we will often refer to B, S and W as its *tiles.*

The set of cardinal direction relations for regions in REG^* is denoted by $\mathcal{D}^*$. Relations in $\mathcal{D}^*$ are jointly exhaustive and pairwise disjoint, and can be used to represent *definite information* about cardinal directions, e.g., $a\ N\ b$. Using the relations of $\mathcal{D}^*$ as our basis, we can define the *powerset* $2^{\mathcal{D}^*}$ of $\mathcal{D}^*$ which contains 2^{511} relations. Elements of $2^{\mathcal{D}^*}$ are called *disjunctive cardinal direction relations* and can be used to represent not only definite but also *indefinite information* about cardinal directions, e.g., $a\ \{N, W\}\ b$ denotes that region a is north *or* west of region b.

Notice that the inverse of a cardinal direction relation R, denoted by $inv(R)$, is not always a cardinal direction relation but, in general, it is a disjunctive cardinal direction relation. For instance, if $a\ S\ b$ then it is possible that $b\ NE{:}N{:}NW\ a$ or $b\ NE{:}S\ a$ or $b\ N{:}NW\ a$ or $b\ N\ a$. Specifically, the relative position of two regions a and b is fully characterized by the pair (R_1, R_2), where R_1 and R_2 are cardinal directions such that (a) $a\ R_1\ b$, (b) $b\ R_2\ a$, (c) R_1 is a disjunct of $inv(R_2)$ and (d) R_2 is a disjunct of $inv(R_1)$. An algorithm for computing the inverse relation is discussed in [21]. Moreover, algorithms that calculate the composition of two cardinal direction relations and the consistency of a set of cardinal direction constraints are discussed in [20,21,22].

Goyal and Egenhofer [5,6] use *direction relation matrices* to represent cardinal direction relations. Given a cardinal direction relation $R = R_1{:}\cdots{:}R_k$ the

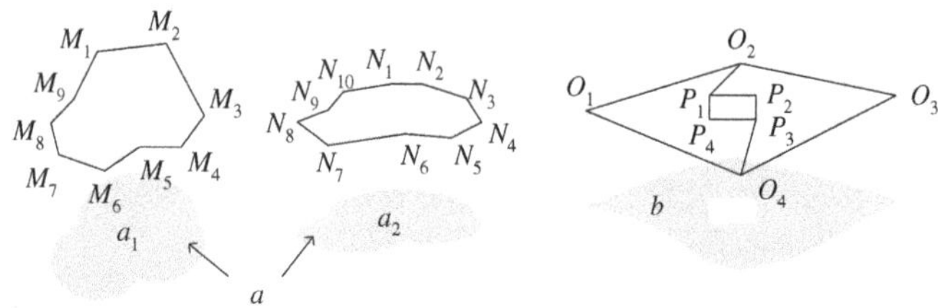

Fig. 2. Using polygons to represent regions

cardinal direction relation matrix that corresponds to R is a 3×3 matrix defined as follows:

$$R = \begin{bmatrix} P_{NW} & P_N & P_{NE} \\ P_W & P_B & P_E \\ P_{SW} & P_S & P_{SE} \end{bmatrix} \quad \text{where} \quad P_{dir} = \begin{cases} \square \text{ if } dir \notin \{R_1, \ldots, R_k\} \\ \blacksquare \text{ if } dir \in \{R_1, \ldots, R_k\} \end{cases}.$$

For instance, the direction relation matrices that correspond to relations S, $NE{:}E$ and $B{:}S{:}SW{:}W{:}NW{:}N{:}E{:}SE$ of Example 1 are as follows:

$$S = \begin{bmatrix} \square\square\square \\ \square\square\square \\ \square\blacksquare\square \end{bmatrix}, \; NE{:}E = \begin{bmatrix} \square\blacksquare\blacksquare \\ \square\square\square \\ \square\square\square \end{bmatrix} \text{ and } B{:}S{:}SW{:}W{:}NW{:}N{:}E{:}SE = \begin{bmatrix} \blacksquare\blacksquare\square \\ \blacksquare\blacksquare\blacksquare \\ \blacksquare\blacksquare\blacksquare \end{bmatrix}.$$

At a finer level of granularity, the model of [5,6] also offers the option to record how much of the a region falls into each tile. Such relations are called *cardinal direction relations with percentages* and can be represented with *cardinal direction matrices with percentages*. Let a and b be two regions in REG^*. The cardinal direction matrices with percentages can be defined as follows:

$$a \quad \frac{100\%}{area(a)} \cdot \begin{bmatrix} area(NW(b) \cap a) & area(N(b) \cap a) & area(NE(b) \cap a) \\ area(W(b) \cap a) & area(B(b) \cap a) & area(E(b) \cap a) \\ area(SW(b) \cap a) & area(S(b) \cap a) & area(SE(b) \cap a) \end{bmatrix} \quad b$$

where $area(r)$ denotes the area of region r.

Consider for example regions c and b in Fig. 1c; region a is 50% northeast and 50% east of region b. This relation is captured with the following cardinal direction matrix with percentages.

$$c \begin{bmatrix} 0\% & 0\% & 50\% \\ 0\% & 0\% & 50\% \\ 0\% & 0\% & 0\% \end{bmatrix} b$$

In this paper, we will use simple assertions (e.g., S, $B{:}S{:}SW$) to capture cardinal direction relations [20,21] and direction relations matrices to capture cardinal direction relations with percentages [5,6].

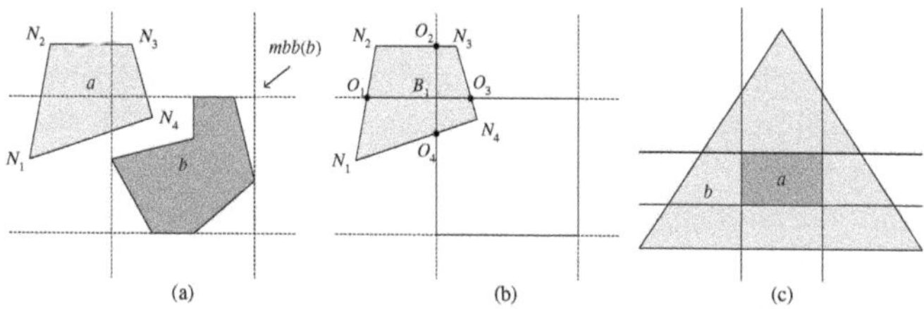

Fig. 3. Polygon clipping

3 Computing Cardinal Direction Relations

Typically, in Geographical Information Systems and Spatial Databases, the connected regions in REG are represented using single polygons, while the composite regions in REG^* are represented using sets of polygons [18,23]. In this paper, the edges of polygons are taken in a clockwise order. For instance, in Fig. 2 region $a_1 \in REG$ is represented using polygon $(M_1 M_2 \cdots M_9)$ and region $a = a_1 \cup a_2 \in REG^*$ is represented using polygons $(M_1 M_2 \cdots M_9)$ and $(N_1 N_2 \cdots N_{10})$. Notice than using sets of polygons, we can even represent regions with holes. For instance, in Fig. 2 region $b \in REG^*$ is represented using polygons $(O_2 O_3 O_4 P_3 P_2 P_1)$ and $(O_1 O_2 P_1 P_4 P_3 O_4)$.

Given the polygon representations of a primary region a and a reference region b, the *computation of cardinal direction relations problem* lies in the calculation of the cardinal direction relation R, such that $a \ R \ b$ holds. Similarly, we can define the *computation of cardinal direction relations with percentages problem.*

Let us consider a primary region a and a reference region b. According to Definition 1, in order to calculate the cardinal direction relation between region a and b, we have to divide the primary region a into segments such that each segment falls exactly into one tile of b. Furthermore, in order to calculate the cardinal direction relation with percentages we also have to measure the area of each segment. Segmenting polygons using *bounded boxes* is a well-studied topic of Computational Geometry called *polygon clipping* [7,10]. A polygon clipping algorithm can be extended to handle *unbounded boxes* (such as the tiles of reference region b) as well. Since polygon clipping algorithms are very efficient (linear in the number of polygon edges), someone would be tempted to use them for the calculation of cardinal direction relations and cardinal direction relations with percentages. Let us briefly discuss the disadvantages of such an approach.

Let us consider regions a and b presented in Fig. 3a. Region a is formed by a quadrangle (i.e., a total of 4 edges). To achieve the desired segmentation, polygon clipping algorithms introduce to a new edges [7,10]. After the clipping algorithms are performed (Fig. 3b), region a is formed by 4 quadrangles (i.e., a total of 16 edges). The worst case that we can think (illustrated in Fig. 3c) starts with 3 edges (a triangle) and ends with 35 edges (2 triangles, 6 quadrangles and 1 pentagon). These new edges are only used for the calculation of cardinal direction relations and are discarded afterwards. Thus, it would be important to minimize their number. Moreover, in order to perform the clipping the edges of the primary region a must be scanned 9 times (one time for every tile of the reference region b). In real GIS applications, we expect that the average number of edges is high. Thus, each scan of the edges of a polygon can be quite time consuming. Finally, polygon clipping algorithms sometimes require complex floating point operations which are costly.

In Sections 3.1 and 3.2, we consider the problem of calculating cardinal direction relations and cardinal direction relations with percentages respectively. We provide algorithms specifically tailored for this task, which avoid the drawbacks of polygon clipping methods. Our proposal does not segment polygons; instead it only divides some of the polygon edges. In Example 2, we show that such a division is necessary for the correct calculation. Interestingly, the resulting number of introduced edges is significantly smaller than the respective number of polygon clipping methods. Furthermore, the complexity of our algorithms is not only linear in the number of polygon edges but it can be performed with a single pass. Finally, our algorithms use simple arithmetic operations and comparisons.

3.1 Cardinal Direction Relations

We will start by considering the calculation of cardinal constraints relations problem. First, we need the following definition.

Definition 2. *Let $R_1, \ldots, R_k$ be basic cardinal direction relations. The* tile-union *of $R_1, \ldots, R_k$, denoted by tile-union$(R_1, \ldots, R_k)$, is a relation formed from the union of the tiles of $R_1, \ldots, R_k$.*

For instance, if $R_1 = S{:}SW$, $R_2 = S{:}E{:}SE$ and $R_3 = W$ then we have *tile-union*$(R_1, R_2) = S{:}SW{:}E{:}SE$ and *tile-union*$(R_1, R_2, R_3) = S{:}SW{:}W{:}E{:}SE$.

Let $S_a = \{p_1, \ldots, p_k\}$ and $S_b = \{q_1, \ldots, q_l\}$ be sets of polygons representing a primary region a and a reference region b. To calculate the cardinal direction R between the primary region a and the reference region b, we first record the tiles of region b where the points forming the edges of the polygons $p_1, \ldots, p_k$ fall in. Unfortunately, as the following example presents, this is not enough.

Example 2. Let us consider the region a (formed by the single polygon $(N_1 N_2 N_3 N_4)$) and the region b presented in Fig. 4a. Clearly points N_1, N_2, N_3 and N_4 lie in $W(b)$, $NW(b)$, $NW(b)$ and $NE(b)$ respectively, but the relation between p and b is $B{:}W{:}NW{:}N{:}NE$ and not $W{:}NW{:}NE$.

The problem of Example 2 arises because there exist edges of polygon $(N_1 N_2 N_3 N_4)$ that expand over three tiles of the reference region b. For instance, $N_3 N_4$ expands over tiles $NW(b)$, $N(b)$ and $NE(b)$. In order to handle such situations, we use the lines forming the minimum bounding box of the reference region b to divide the edges of the polygons representing the primary region a and create new edges such that (a) region a does not change and (b) every new edge lies in exactly one tile. To this end, for every edge AB of region a, we compute the set of intersection points $\mathcal{I}$ of AB with the lines forming box b. We use the intersection

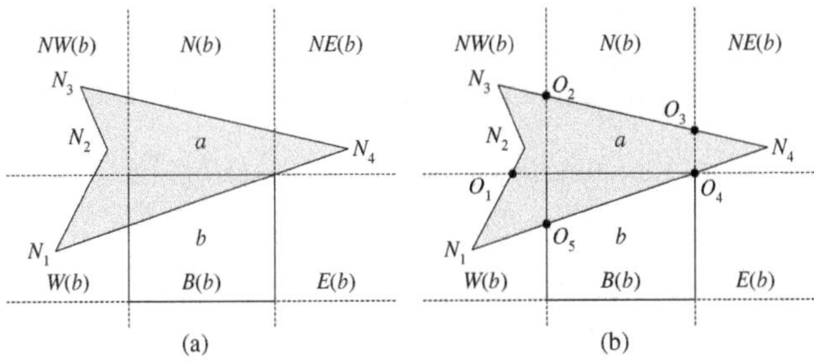

Fig. 4. Illustration of Examples 2 and 3

points of $\mathcal{I}$ to divide AB into a number of segments $\mathcal{S} = AO_1, \ldots, O_kB$. Each segment $AO_1, \ldots, O_kB$ lies in exactly one tile of b and the union of all tiles is AB. Thus, we can safely replace edge AB with $AO_1, \ldots O_kB$ without affecting region a. Finally, to compute the cardinal direction between regions a and b we only have to record the tile of b where each new segment lies. Choosing a single point from each segment is sufficient for this purpose; we choose to pick the middle of the segment as a representative point. Thus, the tile where the middle point lies gives us the tile of the segment too. The above procedure is captured in Algorithm COMPUTE-CDR (Fig. 5) and is illustrated in the following example.

Example 3. Let us continue with the regions of Example 2 (see also Fig. 4). Algorithm COMPUTE-CDR considers every edge of region a (polygon $(N_1N_2N_3N_4)$) in turn and performs the replacements presented in the following table.

Edge	Replace with (new edges)	Edge	Replace with (new edges)
N_1N_2	$N_1O_1,\ O_1N_2$	N_2N_3	N_2N_3
N_3N_4	$N_3O_2,\ O_2O_3,\ O_3N_4$	N_4N_1	$N_3O_4,\ O_4O_5,\ O_5N_4$

It easy to verify that every new edge lies in exactly one tile of b (Fig. 4b). The middle points of the new edges lie in $B(b)$, $W(b)$, $NW(b)$, $N(b)$, $NE(b)$ and $E(b)$. Therefore, Algorithm COMPUTE-CDR returns $B{:}W{:}NW{:}N{:}NE{:}E$, which precisely captures the cardinal direction relation between regions a and b.

Notice that in Example 3, Algorithm COMPUTE-CDR takes as input a quadrangle (4 edges) and returns 9 edges. This should be contrasted with the polygon clipping method that would have resulted in 19 edges (2 triangles, 2 quadrangles and 1 pentagon). Similarly, for the shapes in Fig. 3b-c, Algorithm COMPUTE-CDR introduces 8 and 11 edges respectively while polygon clipping methods introduce 16 and 34 edges respectively.

The following theorem captures the correctness of Algorithm COMPUTE-CDR and measures its complexity.

Theorem 1. *Algorithm* COMPUTE-CDR *is correct, i.e., it returns the cardinal direction relation between two regions a and b in REG^* that are represented using two sets of polygons S_a and S_b respectively. The running time of Algorithm*

Algorithm COMPUTE-CDR
Input: Two sets of polygons S_a and S_b representing regions a and b in REG^*.
Output: The cardinal direction relation R such that $a\ R\ b$ holds.
Method:
Use S_b to compute the minimum bounding box $mbb(b)$ of b.
Let R be the empty relation.
For every polygon p of S_a
  For every edge AB of polygon p
    Let $\mathcal{I}$ be the set of intersection points of AB with the lines forming box b.
    Let $\mathcal{S} = AO_1, \dots O_k B$ be the segments that points in $\mathcal{I}$ divide AB.
    Replace AB with $AO_1, \dots O_k B$ in the representation of polygon p.
    Let $T_1, \dots, T_k$ be the tiles of b in which the middle points of
    edges $AO_1, \dots O_k B$ lie.
    $R = \textit{tile-union}(\ R,\ T_1, \dots, T_k\ )$
  EndFor
  If the center of $mbb(b)$ is in p Then $R = \textit{tile-union}(\ R,\ B\ )$
EndFor
Return R

Fig. 5. Algorithm COMPUTE-CDR

COMPUTE-CDR *is* $\mathcal{O}(k_a + k_b)$ *where* k_a *(respectively* k_b*) is the total number of edges of all polygons in* S_a *(respectively* S_b*).*

Summarizing this section, we can use Algorithm COMPUTE-CDR to compute the cardinal direction relation between two sets of polygons representing two regions a and b in REG^*. The following section considers the case of cardinal direction relations with percentages.

3.2 Cardinal Direction Relations with Percentages

In order to compute cardinal direction relations with percentages, we have to calculate the area of the primary region that falls in each tile of the reference region. A naive way for this task is to segment the polygons that form the primary region so that every polygon lies in exactly one tile of the reference region. Then, for each tile of the reference region we find the polygons of the primary region that lie inside it and compute their area. In this section, we will propose an alternative method that is based on Algorithm COMPUTE-CDR. This method simply computes the area between the edges of the polygons that represent the primary region and an appropriate reference line without segmenting these polygons.

We will now present a method to compute the area between a line and an edge. Then, we will see how we can extend this method to compute the area of a polygon. We will first need the following definition.

Definition 3. *Let* AB *be an edge and* e *be a line. We say that* e does not cross AB *if and only if one of the following holds: (a)* AB *and* e *do not intersect, (b)* AB *and* e *intersect only at point* A *or* B*, or (c)* AB *completely lies on* e*.*

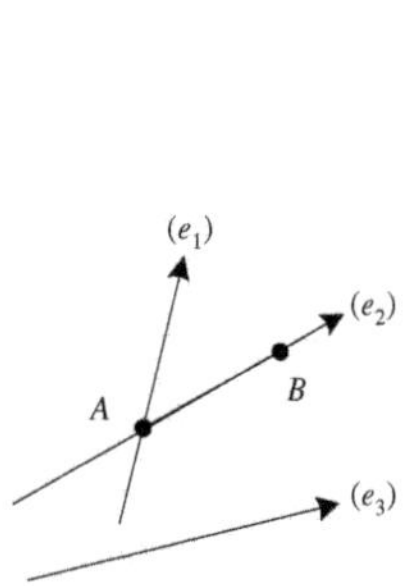

Fig. 6. Lines not crossing AB

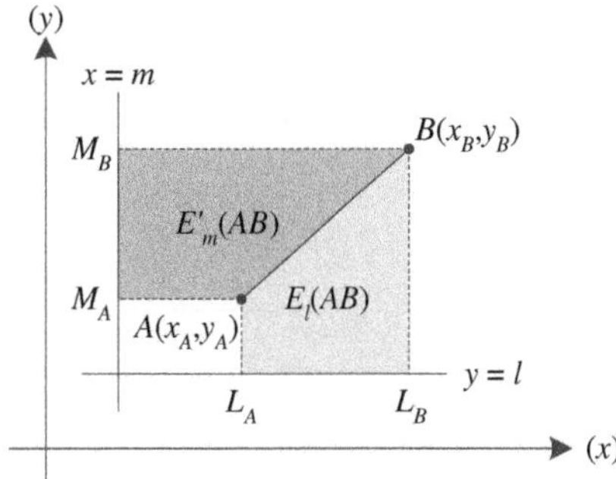

Fig. 7. Area between an edge and a line

For example, in Fig. 6 lines e_1, e_1 and e_3 do not cross edge AB. Let us now calculate the area between an edge and a line.

Definition 4. *Let $A(x_A, y_A)$ and $B(x_B, y_B)$ be two points forming edge AB, $y = l$ and $x = m$ be two lines that do not cross AB. Let also L_A and L_B (respectively M_A and M_B) be the projections of points A,B to line $y = l$ (respectively $x = m$) – see also Fig. 7. We define expression $E_l(AB)$ and $E'_m(AB)$ as follows:*

$$E_l(AB) = \frac{(x_B - x_A)(y_A + y_B - 2l)}{2} \text{ and } E'_m(AB) = \frac{(y_B - y_A)(x_A + x_B - 2l)}{2}.$$

Expressions $E_l(AB)$ and $E'_m(AB)$ can be positive or negative depending on the direction of vector $\overrightarrow{AB}$. It is easy to verify that $E_l(AB) = -E_l(BA)$ and $E'_m(AB) = -E'_m(BA)$ holds. The absolute value of $E_l(AB)$ equals to the area between edge AB and line $y = l$, i.e., the area of polygon (ABL_BL_A). In other words, the following formula holds.

$$area(\ (ABL_BL_A)\ ) = E_l(AB) = \frac{(x_B - x_A)(y_A + y_B - 2l)}{2}$$

Symmetrically, area between edge AB and line $x = m$, i.e., the area of polygon (ABM_BM_A), equals to the absolute value of $E'_m(AB)$.

$$area(\ (AM_AM_BB)\ ) = E'_m(AB) = \frac{(y_B - y_A)(x_A + x_B - 2l)}{2}$$

Expressions E_l and E'_m can be used to calculate the area of polygons. Let $p = (N_1 \cdots N_k)$ be a polygon, and $y = l$, $x = m$ be two lines that do not cross with any edge of polygon p. The area of polygon p, denoted by $area(p)$, can be calculated as follows:

$$area(p) = |\ E_l(N_1N_2) + \cdots + E_l(N_kN_1)\ | = |\ E'_m(N_1N_2) + \cdots + E'_m(N_kN_1)\ |.$$

Notice that Computational Geometry algorithms, in order to calculate the area of a polygon p use a similar method that is based on a reference point

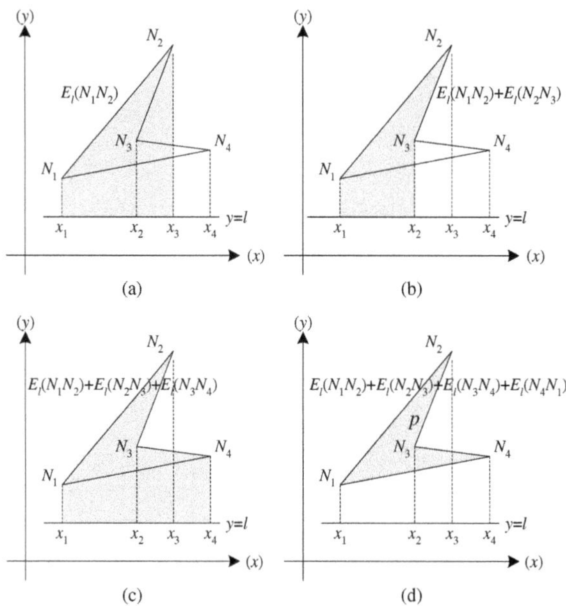

Fig. 8. Using expression E_l to calculate the area of a polygon

(instead of a line) [12,16]. This method is not appropriate for our case because it requires to segment the primary region using polygon clipping algorithms (see also the discussion at the beginning of Section 3). In the rest of this section, we will present a method that utilizes expressions E_l and E'_m and does not require polygon clipping.

Example 4. Let us consider polygon $p = (N_1N_2N_3N_4)$ and line $y = l$ presented in Fig. 8d. The area of polygon p can be calculated using formula $area(p) = \mid E_l(N_1N_2)+E_l(N_2N_3)+E_l(N_3N_4)+E_l(N_4N_1) \mid$. All the intermediate expressions $E_l(N_1N_2)$, $E_l(N_1N_2)+E_l(N_2N_3)$, $E_l(N_1N_2)+E_l(N_2N_3)+E_l(N_3N_4)$, $E_l(N_1N_2) + E_l(N_2N_3) + E_l(N_3N_4) + E_l(N_4N_1)$ are presented as the gray areas of Fig. 8a-d respectively.

We will use expressions E_l and E_m to compute the percentage of the area of the primary region that falls in each tile of the reference region. Let us consider region a presented Fig. 9. Region a is formed by polygons $(N_1N_2N_3N_4)$ and $(M_1M_2M_3)$. Similarly to Algorithm COMPUTE-CDR, to compute the cardinal direction relation with percentages of a with b we first use the $mbb(b)$ to divide the edges of region a. Let $x = m_1$, $x = m_2$, $y = l_1$ and $y = l_2$ be the lines forming $mbb(b)$. These lines divide the edges of polygons $(N_1N_2N_3N_4)$ and $(M_1M_2M_3)$ as shown in Fig. 9.

Let us now compute the area of a that lies in the NW tile of b (i.e., $area(NW(b) \cap a)$). Notice that $area(NW(b) \cap a) = area((O_1N_2O_2B_1))$. To compute the area of polygon $(O_1N_2O_2B_1)$ it is convenient to use as a reference line

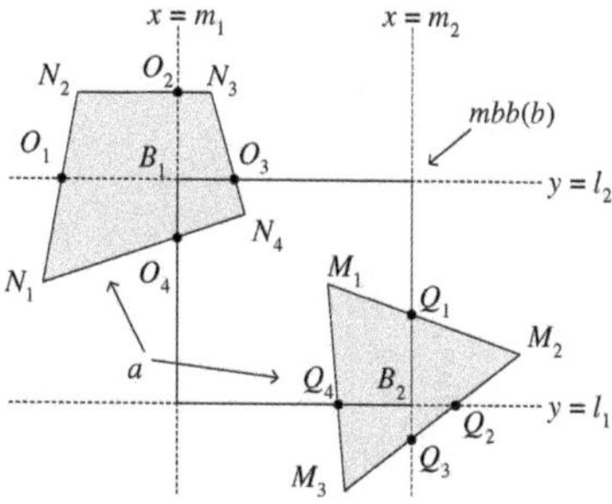

Fig. 9. Computing cardinal direction relations with percentages

$x = m_1$. Doing so, we do not have to compute edges B_1O_1 and O_2B_1 because $E'_{m_1}(B_1O_1) = 0$ and $E'_{m_1}(O_2B_1) = 0$ hold and thus the area we are looking for can be calculated with the following formula:

$$area(NW(b) \cap a) = area((O_1N_2O_2B_1)) = \mid E'_{m_1}(O_1N_2) + E'_{m_1}(N_2O_2) \mid$$

In other words, to compute the area of a that lies in $NW(b)$ $(area(NW(b) \cap a))$ we calculate the area between the west line of $mbb(b)$ $(x = m_1)$ and every edge of a that lies in $NW(b)$, i.e., the following formula holds:

$$area(NW(b) \cap a) = \mid \sum_{AB \in NW(b)} E'_{m_1}(AB) \mid.$$

Similarly, to calculate the area of a that lies in the $W(b)$ and $SW(b)$ we can use the expressions:

$$area(W(b) \cap a) = \mid \sum_{AB \in W(b)} E'_{m_1}(AB) \mid, \; area(SW(b) \cap a) = \mid \sum_{AB \in SW(b)} E'_{m_1}(AB) \mid$$

For instance, in Fig. 9 we have $area(W(b) \cap a) = |E'_{m_1}(N_1O_1) + E'_{m_1}(O_1B_1)|$ and $area(SW(b) \cap a) = 0$

To calculate the area of a that lies in $NE(b)$, $E(b)$, $SE(b)$, $S(b)$ and $N(b)$ we simply have to change the line of reference that we use. In the first three cases, we use the east line of $mbb(b)$ (i.e., $x = m_2$ in Fig. 9), in the fourth case, we use the south line of $mbb(b)$ $(y = l_1)$ and in the last case, we use the north line of $mbb(b)$ $(y = l_2)$. In all cases, we use the edges of a that fall in the tile of b that we are interested in. Thus, have:

$$\begin{array}{ll} area(T(b) \cap a) = \mid \sum_{AB \in T(b)} E'_{m_2}(AB) \mid & \text{if} \quad T \in \{NE, E, SE\} \\ area(S(b) \cap a) = \mid \sum_{AB \in S(b)} E_{l_1}(AB) \mid & \\ area(N(b) \cap a) = \mid \sum_{AB \in N(b)} E_{l_2}(AB) \mid & \end{array}.$$

For instance, in Fig. 9 we have $area(N(b) \cap a) = \mid E_{l_2}(O_2N_3) + E'_{m_1}(N_3O_3) \mid$ and $area(W(b) \cap a) = \mid E'_{m_2}(Q_1M_2) + E'_{m_2}(M_2Q_2) \mid$.

Let us now consider the area of a that lies in $B(b)$. None of the lines of $mbb(b)$ can help us compute $area(B(b) \cap a)$ without segmenting the polygons that represent region a. For instance, in Fig. 9 using line $y = l_1$ we have:

$$area(B(b) \cap a) = | \, E_{l_1}(Q_4M_1) + E_{l_1}(M_1Q_4) + E_{l_1}(O_4N_4) + E_{l_1}(N_4O_4) + E_{l_1}(O_4B_1) + E_{l_1}(B_1O_3) \, |.$$

Edge B_1O_3 is not an edge of any of the polygons representing a. To handle such situations, we employ the following method. We use the south line of $mbb(b)$ $(y = l_1)$ as the reference line and calculate the areas between $y = l_1$ and all edges that lie *both* in $N(b)$ and $B(b)$. This area will be denoted by $area((B+N)(b) \cap a)$ and is practically the area of a that lies on $N(b)$ and $B(b)$, i.e., $area((B+N)(b) \cap a) = area(N(b) \cap a) + area(B(b) \cap a)$. Since $area(N(b) \cap a)$ has been previously computed, we just have to subtract it from $area((B + N)(b) \cap a)$ in order to derive $area(B(b) \cap a)$. For instance, in Fig. 9 we have:

$$area((B+N)(b) \cap a) = | \, \textstyle\sum_{AB \in B(b) \cup N(b)} E_{l_1}(AB) \, | = | \, E_{l_1}(O_2N_3) + E_{l_1}(O_3N_4) + E_{l_1}(N_4O_4) + E_{l_1}(Q_4M_1) + E_{l_1}(M_1Q_4) \, | = area(\, (O_2N_3O_3N_4O_4) + (M_1Q_1B_2Q_4) \,)$$

and

$$area(N(b) \cap a) = | \sum_{AB \in N(b)} E_{l_2}(AB)| = area((O_2N_3O_3N_4O_4)).$$

Therefore, $area(B(b) \cap a) = area((B + N)(b) \cap a) - area(N(b) \cap a)$ holds.

The above described method is summarized in Algorithm COMPUTE-CDR% presented in Fig. 10. The following theorem captures the correctness of Algorithm COMPUTE-CDR% and measures its complexity.

Theorem 2. *Algorithm* COMPUTE-CDR% *is correct, i.e., it returns the cardinal direction relation with percentages between two regions a and b in REG^* that are represented using two sets of polygons S_a and S_b respectively. The running time of Algorithm* COMPUTE-CDR% *is $O(k_a + k_b)$ where k_a (respectively k_b) is the total number of edges of all polygons in S_a (respectively S_b).*

In the following section, we will present an actual system, CARDIRECT, that incorporates and implements Algorithms COMPUTE-CDR and COMPUTE-CDR%.

4 A Tool for the Manipulation of Cardinal Direction Information

In this section, we will present a tool that implements the aforementioned reasoning tasks for the computation of cardinal direction relationships among regions. The tool, CARDIRECT, has been implemented in C++ over the Microsoft Visual Studio toolkit. Using CARDIRECT, the user can define regions of interest over some underlying image (e.g., a map), compute their relationships (with and

Algorithm COMPUTE-CDR%
Input: Two sets of polygons S_a and S_b representing regions a and b in REG^* resp.
Output: The cardinal direction relation with percentages R, such that $a\ R\ b$ holds.
Method:
Use S_b to compute the minimum bounding box $mbb(b)$ of b.
Divide all the edges in S_a so that every new edge lies in exactly one tile of b.
Let $y = l_1$, $y = l_2$, $x = m_1$ and $x = m_2$ be the lines forming $mbb(b)$.
$a_{B+N} = a_S = a_{SW} = a_W = a_{NW} = a_N = a_{NE} = a_E = a_{SE} = 0$
<u>For</u> every edge AB of S_a
  Let t be the tile of b that AB falls in.
  <u>Case</u> t // Expressions E' and E are defined in Definition 4
    NW, W, SW: $a_t = a_t + E'_{m_1}(AB)$
    NE, E, SE: $a_t = a_t + E'_{m_1}(AB)$
    S: $a_t = a_t + E_{l_1}(AB)$
    N: $a_t = a_t + E_{l_2}(AB)$
  <u>EndCase</u>
  <u>If</u> $(t = N)$ or $(t = B)$ <u>Then</u> $a_{B+N} = a_{B+N} + E_{l_1}(AB)$
<u>EndFor</u>
$a_B = |a_{B+N}| - |a_N|$
$totalArea = |a_B| + |a_S| + |a_{SW}| + |a_W| + |a_{NW}| + |a_N| + |a_{NE}| + |a_E| + |a_{SE}|$
<u>Return</u> $\frac{100\%}{totalArea} \cdot \begin{bmatrix} |a_{NW}| & |a_N| & |a_{NE}| \\ |a_S| & |a_B| & |a_E| \\ |a_{SW}| & |a_S| & |a_{SE}| \end{bmatrix}$

Fig. 10. Algorithm COMPUTE-CDR%

without percentages) and pose queries. The tool implements an XML interface, through which the user can import and export the configuration he constructs (i.e., the underlying image and the sets of polygons that form the regions); the XML description of the configuration is also employed for querying purposes.

The XML description of the exported scenarios is quite simple: A configuration (`Image`) is defined upon an image file (e.g., a map) and comprises a set of regions and a set of relations among them. Each region comprises a set of polygons of the same color and each polygon comprises a set of edges (defined by x- and y-coordinates). The direction relations among the different regions are all stored in the XML description of the configuration. The DTD for CARDIRECT configurations is as follows.

```
<?xml version="1.0" encoding="UTF-8"?>
<!ELEMENT Image (Region+, Relation*)>
<!ATTLIST Image name CDATA #IMPLIED file CDATA #IMPLIED>
<!ELEMENT Region (Polygon*)>
<!ATTLIST Region id ID #REQUIRED name CDATA #IMPLIED color CDATA #IMPLIED>
<!ELEMENT Polygon (Edge, Edge, Edge, Edge*)>
<!ATTLIST Polygon id CDATA #REQUIRED>
<!ELEMENT Edge EMPTY>
<!ATTLIST Edge x CDATA #REQUIRED y CDATA #REQUIRED>
<!ELEMENT Relation EMPTY>
<!ATTLIST Relation type CDATA #REQUIRED
        primary IDREF #REQUIRED reference IDREF #REQUIRED>
```

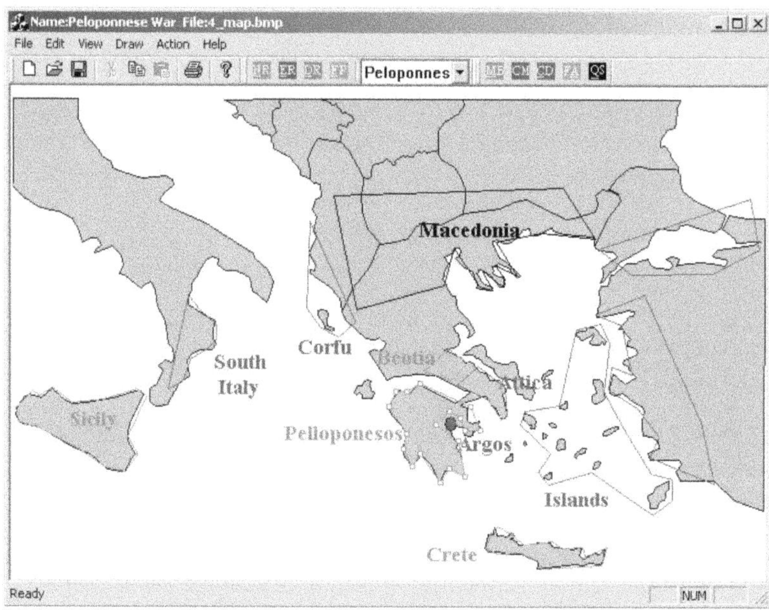

Fig. 11. Using CARDIRECT to annotate images

Observe Fig. 11. In this configuration, the user has opened a map of Ancient Greece at the time of the Peloponnesian war as the underlying image. Then, the user defined three sets of regions: the "Athenean Alliance" in blue, comprising of Attica, the Islands, the regions in the East, Corfu and South Italy; (b) the "Spartan Alliance" in red, comprising of Peloponnesos, Beotia, Crete and Sicely; and (c) the "Pro-Spartan" in black, comprising of Macedonia.

Moreover, using CARDIRECT, the user can compute the cardinal direction relations and the cardinal direction relations with percentages between the identified regions. In Fig. 12, we have calculated the relations between the regions of Fig. 11. For instance, Peloponnesos is $B{:}S{:}SW{:}W$ of Attica (left side of Fig. 12) while Attica is

$$\begin{bmatrix} 0\% & 19\% & 12\% \\ 0\% & 19\% & 50\% \\ 0\% & 0\% & 0\% \end{bmatrix}$$

of Peloponnesos (right-hand side of Fig. 12).

The query language that we employ is based on the following simple model. Let $A = \{a_1, \ldots, a_n\}$ be a set of regions in REG^* over a configuration. Let C be a finite set of thematic attributes for the regions of REG^* (e.g., the color of each region) and f a function, $f : REG^* \rightarrow dom(C)$, practically relating each of the regions with a value over the domain of C (e.g., the fact that the Spartan Alliance is colored red).

A *query condition* over variables $x_1, \ldots, x_k$ is a conjunction the following types of formulae $x_i = a$, $f(x_i) = c$, $x_i \ R \ x_j$ where $1 \leq i, j \leq n$, $a \in A$ is a

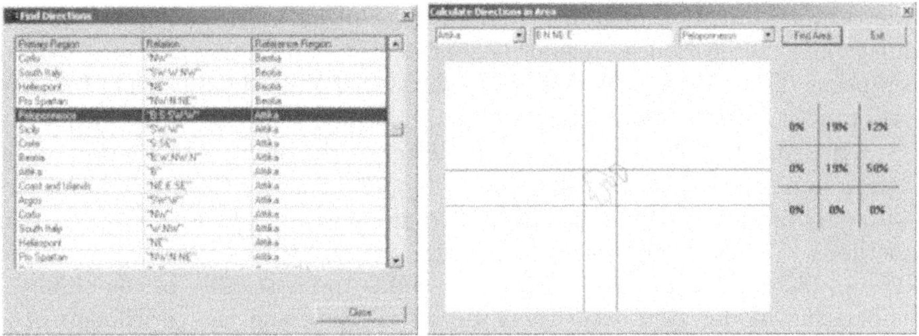

Fig. 12. Using CARDIRECT to extract cardinal direction relations

region of the configuration, $c \in dom(C)$ is a value of a thematic attribute and $R \in 2^{\mathcal{D}^*}$ is a (possibly disjunctive) cardinal direction relation. A *query* q over variables $x_1, \ldots, x_n$ is a formula of the form

$$q = \{(x_1, \ldots, x_n) \mid \phi(x_1, \ldots, x_n)\}$$

where $\phi(x_1, \ldots, x_n)$ is a query condition.

Intuitively, the query returns a set of regions in the configuration of an image that satisfy the query condition, which can take the form of: (a) a cardinal direction constraint between the query variables (e.g., x_1 $B{:}SE{:}S$ x_2); (b) a restriction in the thematic attributes of a variable (e.g., $color(x_1) = blue$) and (c) direct reference of a particular region (e.g., $x_1 = Attica$).

For instance, for the configuration of Fig. 11 we can pose the following query: "Find all regions of the Athenean Alliance which are surrounded by a region in the Spartan Alliance". This query can be expressed as follows:

$$q = \{(a, b) \mid color(a) = red,\ color(b) = blue,\ a\ S{:}SW{:}W{:}NW{:}N{:}NE{:}E{:}SE\ b\}$$

5 Conclusions and Future Work

In this paper, we have addressed the problem of efficiently computing the cardinal direction relations between regions that are composed of sets of polygons (a) by presenting two linear algorithms for this task, and (b) by explaining their incorporation into an actual system. These algorithms take as inputs two sets of polygons representing two regions respectively. The first of the proposed algorithms is purely qualitative and computes the cardinal direction relations between the input regions. The second has a quantitative aspect and computes the cardinal direction relations with percentages between the input regions. To the best of our knowledge, these are the first algorithms that address the aforementioned problem. The algorithms have been implemented and embedded in an actual system, CARDIRECT, which allows the user to specify, edit and annotate regions of interest in an image. Then, CARDIRECT automatically computes the cardinal direction relations between these regions. The configuration of the image and the introduced regions is persistently stored using a simple XML description. The user is allowed to query the stored XML description of the image and retrieve combinations of interesting regions on the basis of the query.

Although this part of our research addresses the problem of relation computation to a sufficient extent, there are still open issues for future research. First, we would like to evaluate experimentally our algorithm against polygon clipping methods. A second interesting topic is the possibility of combining topological [2] and distance relations [3]. Another issue is the possibility of combining the underlying model with extra thematic information and the enrichment of the employed query language on the basis of this combination. Finally, a long term goal would be the integration of CARDIRECT with image segmentation software, which would provide a complete environment for the management of image configurations.

References

1. E. Clementini, P. Di Fellice, and G. Califano. Composite Regions in Topological Queries. *Information Systems*, 7:759–594, 1995.
2. M.J. Egenhofer. Reasoning about Binary Topological Relationships. In *Proceedings of SSD'91*, pages 143–160, 1991.
3. A.U. Frank. Qualitative Spatial Reasoning about Distances and Directions in Geographic Space. *Journal of Visual Languages and Computing*, 3:343–371, 1992.
4. A.U. Frank. Qualitative Spatial Reasoning: Cardinal Directions as an Example. *International Journal of GIS*, 10(3):269–290, 1996.
5. R. Goyal and M.J. Egenhofer. The Direction-Relation Matrix: A Representation for Directions Relations Between Extended Spatial Objects. In *the annual assembly and the summer retreat of University Consortium for Geographic Information Systems Science*, June 1997.
6. R. Goyal and M.J. Egenhofer. Cardinal Directions Between Extended Spatial Objects. *IEEE Transactions on Data and Knowledge Engineering*, (in press), 2000. Available at `http://www.spatial.maine.edu/~max/RJ36.html`.
7. Y.-D. Liang and B.A. Barsky. A New Concept and Method for Line Clipping. *ACM Transactions on Graphics*, 3(1):868–877, 1984.
8. G. Ligozat. Reasoning about Cardinal Directions. *Journal of Visual Languages and Computing*, 9:23–44, 1998.
9. S. Lipschutz. *Set Theory and Related Topics*. McGraw Hill, 1998.
10. P.-G. Maillot. A New, Fast Method For 2D Polygon Clipping: Analysis and Software Implementation. *ACM Transactions on Graphics*, 11(3):276–290, 1992.
11. A. Mukerjee and G. Joe. A Qualitative Model for Space. In *Proceedings of AAAI'90*, pages 721–727, 1990.
12. J. O'Rourke. *Computational Geometry in C*. Cambridge University Press, 1994.
13. D. Papadias, Y. Theodoridis, T. Sellis, and M.J. Egenhofer. Topological Relations in the World of Minimum Bounding Rectangles: A Study with R-trees. In *Proceedings of ACM SIGMOD'95*, pages 92–103, 1995.
14. C.H. Papadimitriou, D. Suciu, and V. Vianu. Topological Queries in Spatial Databases. *Journal of Computer and System Sciences*, 58(1):29–53, 1999.

15. D.J. Peuquet and Z. Ci-Xiang. An Algorithm to Determine the Directional Relationship Between Arbitrarily-Shaped Polygons in the Plane. *Pattern Recognition*, 20(1):65–74, 1987.
16. F. Preparata and M. Shamos. *Computational Geometry: An Introduction.* Springer Verlag, 1985.
17. J. Renz and B. Nebel. On the Complexity of Qualitative Spatial Reasoning: A Maximal Tractable Fragment of the Region Connection Calculus. *Artificial Intelligence*, 1-2:95–149, 1999.
18. P. Rigaux, M. Scholl, and A. Voisard. *Spatial Data Bases.* Morgan Kaufman, 2001.
19. S. Skiadopoulos, C. Giannoukos, P. Vassiliadis, T. Sellis, and M. Koubarakis. Computing and Handling Cardinal Direction Information (Extended Report). Technical Report TR-2003-5, National Technical University of Athens, 2003. Available at `http://www.dblab.ece.ntua.gr/publications`.
20. S. Skiadopoulos and M. Koubarakis. Composing Cardinal Directions Relations. In *Proceedings of the 7th International Symposium on Spatial and Temporal Databases (SSTD'01)*, volume 2121 of *LNCS*, pages 299–317. Springer, July 2001.
21. S. Skiadopoulos and M. Koubarakis. Qualitative Spatial Reasoning with Cardinal Directions. In *Proceedings of the 7th International Conference on Principles and Practice of Constraint Programming (CP'02)*, volume 2470 of *LNCS*, pages 341–355. Springer, September 2002.
22. S. Skiadopoulos and M. Koubarakis. Composing Cardinal Direction Relations. *Artificial Intelligence*, 152(2):143–171, 2004.
23. M. Zeiler. *Modelling our World. The ESRI Guide to Geodatabase Design.* ESRI-Press, 1999.

A Tale of Two Schemas: Creating a Temporal XML Schema from a Snapshot Schema with τXSchema

Faiz Currim[1], Sabah Currim[1], Curtis Dyreson[2], and Richard T. Snodgrass[1]

[1]University of Arizona, Tucson, AZ, USA
{fcurrim,scurrim}@bpa.arizona.edu, rts@cs.arizona.edu
[2]Washington State University, Pullman, WA, USA
cdyreson@wsu.edu

Abstract. The W3C XML Schema recommendation defines the structure and data types for XML documents. XML Schema lacks explicit support for time-varying XML documents. Users have to resort to ad hoc, non-standard mechanisms to create schemas for time-varying XML documents. This paper presents a data model and architecture, called τXSchema, for creating a temporal schema from a non-temporal (snapshot) schema, a temporal annotation, and a physical annotation. The annotations specify which portion(s) of an XML document can vary over time, how the document can change, and where timestamps should be placed. The advantage of using annotations to denote the time-varying aspects is that logical and physical data independence for temporal schemas can be achieved while remaining fully compatible with both existing XML Schema documents and the XML Schema recommendation.

1 Introduction

XML is becoming an increasingly popular language for documents and data. XML can be approached from two quite separate orientations: a *document-centered* orientation (e.g., HTML) and a *data-centered* orientation (e.g., relational and object-oriented databases). *Schemas* are important in both orientations. A schema defines the building blocks of an XML document, such as the types of elements and attributes. An XML document can be *validated* against a schema to ensure that the document conforms to the formatting rules for an XML document (is well-formed) and to the types, elements, and attributes defined in the schema (is valid). A schema also serves as a valuable guide for querying and updating an XML document or database. For instance, to correctly construct a query, e.g., in XQuery, a user will (usually) consult the schema rather than the data. Finally, a schema can be helpful in query optimization, e.g., in constructing a path index [24].

Several schema languages have been proposed for XML [22]. From among these languages, XML Schema is the most widely used. The syntax and semantics of XML Schema 1.0 are W3C recommendations [35, 36].

Time-varying data naturally arises in both document-centered and data-centered orientations. Consider the following wide-ranging scenarios. In a university, students take various courses in different semesters. At a company, job positions and salaries change. At a warehouse, inventories evolve as deliveries are made and good are

E. Bertino et al. (Eds.): EDBT 2004, LNCS 2992, pp. 348–365, 2004.
© Springer-Verlag Berlin Heidelberg 2004

shipped. In a hospital, drug treatment regimes are adjusted. And finally at a bank, account balances are in flux. In each scenario, querying the current state is important, e.g., "how much is in my account right now", but it also often useful to know how the data has changed over time, e.g., "when has my account been below $200".

An obvious approach would have been to propose changes to XML Schema to accommodate time-varying data. Indeed, that has been the approach taken by many researchers for the relational and object-oriented models [25, 29, 32]. As we will discuss in detail, that approach inherently introduces difficulties with respect to document validation, data independence, tool support, and standardization. So in this paper we advocate a novel approach that retains the non-temporal XML schema for the document, utilizing a series of separate schema documents to achieve data independence, enable full document validation, and enable improved tool support, while not requiring any changes to the XML Schema standard (nor subsequent extensions of that standard; XML Schema 1.1 is in development).

The primary contribution of this paper is to introduce the *τXSchema* (Temporal XML Schema) data model and architecture. τXSchema is a system for constructing schemas for time-varying XML documents[1]. A time-varying document records the evolution of a document over time, i.e., all of the versions of the document. τXSchema has a three-level architecture for specifying a schema for time-varying data[2]. The first level is the schema for an individual version, called the *snapshot schema*. The snapshot schema is a conventional XML Schema document. The second level is the *temporal annotations* of the snapshot schema. The temporal annotations identify which elements can vary over time. For those elements, the temporal annotations also effect a temporal semantics to the various integrity constraints (such as uniqueness) specified in the snapshot schema. The third level is the *physical annotations*. The physical annotations describe how the time-varying aspects are represented. Each annotation can be independently changed, so the architecture has (logical and physical) *data independence* [7]. Data independence allows XML documents using one representation to be automatically converted to a different representation while preserving the semantics of the data. τXSchema has a suite of auxiliary tools to manage time-varying documents and schemas. There are tools to convert a time-varying document from one physical representation to a different representation, to extract a time slice from that document (yielding a conventional static XML document), and to create a time-varying document from a sequence of static documents, in whatever representation the user specifies.

As mentioned, τXSchema *reuses* rather than extends XML Schema. τXSchema is consistent and compatible with both XML Schema and the XML data model. In τXSchema, a temporal validator augments a conventional validator to more comprehensively check the validity constraints of a document, especially temporal constraints that cannot be checked by a conventional XML Schema validator. We describe a means of validating temporal documents that ensures the desirable property of *snapshot validation subsumption*. We show elsewhere how a temporal document can be smaller and faster to validate than the associated XML snapshots [12].

---

[1] We embrace both the document and data centric orientations of XML and will use the terms "document" and "database" interchangeably.

[2] Three-level architectures are a common architecture in both databases [33] and spatio-temporal conceptual modeling [21].

While this paper concerns temporal XML Schema, we feel that the general approach of separate temporal and physical annotations is applicable to other data models, such as UML [28]. The contribution of this paper is two-fold: (1) introducing a three-level approach for logical data models and (2) showing in detail how this approach works for XML Schema in particular, specifically concerning a theoretical definition of snapshot validation subsumption for XML, validation of time-varying XML documents, and implications for tools operating on realistic XML schemas and data, thereby exemplifying in a substantial way the approach. While we are confident that the approach could be applied to other data models, designing the annotation specifications, considering the specifics of data integrity constraint checking, and ascertaining the impact on particular tools remain challenging (and interesting) tasks.

τXSchema focuses on *instance versioning* (representing a time-varying XML instance document) and not *schema versioning* [15, 31]. The schema can describe which aspects of an instance document change over time. But we assume that the schema itself is fixed, with no element types, data types, or attributes being added to or removed from the schema over time. *Intensional XML data* (also termed dynamic XML documents [1]), that is, parts of XML documents that consist of programs that generate data [26], are gaining popularity. Incorporating intensional XML data is beyond the scope of this paper.

The next section motivates the need for a new approach. Section 0 provides a theoretical framework for τXSchema, while an overview of its architecture is in Section 0. Details of the `τValidator` may be found in Section 0. Related work is reviewed in Section 0. We end with a summary and list of future work in Section 0.

2 Motivation

This section discusses whether conventional XML Schema is appropriate and satisfactory for time-varying data. We first present an example that illustrates how a time-varying document differs from a conventional XML document. We then pinpoint some of the limitations of XML Schema. Finally we state the desiderata for schemas for time-varying documents.

2.1 Motivating Example

Assume that the history of the Winter Olympic games is described in an XML document called `winter.xml`. The document has information about the athletes that participate, the events in which they participate, and the medals that are awarded. Over time the document is edited to add information about each new Winter Olympics and to revise incorrect information. Assume that information about the athletes participating in the 2002 Winter Olympics in Salt Lake City, USA was added on 2002-01-01. On 2002-03-01 the document was further edited to record the medal winners. Finally, a small correction was made on 2002-07-01.

To depict some of the changes to the XML in the document, we focus on information about the Norwegian skier Kjetil Andre Aamodt. On 2002-01-01 it was known that Kjetil would participate in the games and the information shown in Fig. 1

was added to `winter.xml`. Kjetil won a medal; so on 2002-03-01 the fragment was revised to that shown in Fig. 2. The edit on 2002-03-01 incorrectly recorded that Kjetil won a silver medal in the Men's Combined; Kjetil won a gold medal. Fig. 3 shows the correct medal information.

```
...
<athlete>
  <athName>Kjetil Andre Aamodt</athName>
</athlete>
...
```

Fig. 1. A fragment of `winter.xml` on 2002-01-01

```
<athlete>
  <athName>Kjetil Andre Aamodt</athName> won a medal in
  <medal mtype="silver">Men's Combined</medal>
</athlete>
```

Fig. 2. Kjetil won a medal, as of 2002-03-01

```
<athlete>
  <athName>Kjetil Andre Aamodt</athName> won a medal in
  <medal mtype="gold">Men's Combined</medal>
</athlete>
```

Fig. 3. Medal data is corrected on 2002-07-01

A *time-varying document* records a *version history*, which consists of the information in each version, along with timestamps indicating the lifetime of that version. Fig. 4 shows a fragment of a time-varying document that captures the history of Kjetil. The fragment is *compact* in the sense that each edit results in only a small, localized change to the document. The history is also *bi-temporal* because both the *valid time* and *transaction time* lifetimes are captured [20]. The *valid time* refers to the time(s) when a particular fact is true in the modeled reality, while the *transaction time* is the time when the information was edited. The two concepts are orthogonal. Time-varying documents can have each kind of time. In Fig. 4 the valid- and transaction-time lifetimes of each element are represented with an optional `<rs:timestamp>` sub-element[3]. If the timestamp is missing, the element has the same lifetime as its enclosing element. For example, there are two `<athlete>` elements with different lifetimes since the content of the element changes. The last version of `<athlete>` has two `<medal>` elements because the medal information is revised. There are many different ways to represent the versions in a time-varying document; the methods differ in which elements are timestamped, how the elements are timestamped, and how changes are represented (e.g., perhaps only differences between versions are represented).

Keeping the history in a document or data collection is useful because it provides the ability to recover past versions, track changes over time, and evaluate temporal queries [17]. But it changes the nature of validating against a schema. Assume that the

[3] The introduced `<rs:timestamp>` element is in the "`rs`" namespace to distinguish it from any `<timestamp>` elements already in the document. This namespace will be discussed in more detail in Sections 0 and 0.

```
...
<athlete>
  <rs:timestamp ttStart="2002-01-01" ttStop="2002-02-28"
    vtBegin="2002-02-01" vtEnd="2002-02-28"/>
  <athName>Kjetil Andre Aamodt</athName>
  ...
</athlete>
<athlete>
  <rs:timestamp ttStart="2002-03-01" ttStop="now"
    vtBegin="2002-03-01" vtEnd="now"/>
  <athName>Kjetil Andre Aamodt</athName> won a medal in
  <medal mtype="silver">
   <rs:timestamp ttStart="2002-03-01" ttStop="2002-06-30"
     vtAt="2002-03-01"/>
    Men's Combined
  </medal>
  <medal mtype="gold">
    <rs:timestamp ttStart="2002-07-01" ttStop="now" vtAt="2002-03-01"/>
    Men's Combined
  </medal>
...
```

Fig. 4. A fragment of a time-varying document

```
<element name="athlete">
  <complexType mixed="true">
    <sequence>
      <element name="athName" type="string"/>
      <element ref="medal" minOccurs="0" maxOccurs="unbounded"/>
      <element name="birthPlace" type="string" minOccurs="1"
        maxOccurs="1"/>
      <element name="phone" type="phoneNumType" minOccurs="0"
        maxOccurs="unbounded"/>
    </sequence>
    <attribute name="age" type="nonNegativeInteger" use="required"/>
  </complexType>
</element>
```

Fig. 5. An extract from the winOlympic schema

file `winOlympic.xsd` contains the *snapshot schema* for `winter.xml`. The snapshot schema is the schema for an individual version. The snapshot schema is a valuable guide for editing and querying individual versions. A fragment of the schema is given in Fig. 5. Note that the schema describes the structure of the fragment shown in Fig. 1, Fig. 2, and Fig. 3. The problem is that although individual versions conform to the schema, the time-varying document does not. So `winOlympic.xsd` cannot be used (directly) to validate the time-varying document of Fig. 4.

The snapshot schema could be used *indirectly* for validation by individually reconstituting and validating each version. But validating every version can be expensive if the changes are frequent or the document is large (e.g., if the document is a database). While the Winter Olympics document may not change often, contrast this with, e.g., a Customer Relationship Management database for a large company. Thousands of calls and service interactions may be recorded each day. This would lead to a very large number of versions, making it expensive to instantiate and validate each individually. The number of versions is further increased because there can be both valid time and transaction time versions.

To validate a time-varying document, a new, different schema is needed. The schema for a time-varying document should take into account the elements (and attributes) and their associated timestamps, specify the kind(s) of time involved, provide hints on how the elements vary over time, and accommodate differences in version and timestamp representation. Since this schema will express how the time-varying information is *represented*, we will call it the *representational schema*. The representational schema will be related to the underlying snapshot schema (Fig. 5), and allows the time-varying document to be validated using a conventional XML Schema validator (though not fully, as discussed in the next section).

2.2 Moving beyond XML Schema

Both the snapshot and representational schemas are needed for a time-varying document. The snapshot schema is useful in queries and updates. For example, a current query applies to the version valid now, a current update modifies the data in the current version, creating a new version, and a timeslice query extracts a previous version. All of these apply to a single version of a time-varying document, a version described by the snapshot schema. The representational schema is essential for validation and representation (storage). Many versions are combined into a single temporal document, described by the representational schema.

Unfortunately the XML Schema validator is *incapable* of fully validating a time-varying document using the representational schema. First, XML Schema is not sufficiently expressive to enforce *temporal constraints*. For example, XML Schema cannot specify the following (desirable) schema constraint: the transaction-time lifetime of a `<medal>` element should always be contained in the transaction-time lifetime of its parent `<athlete>` element. Second, a conventional XML Schema document augmented with timestamps to denote time-varying data cannot, in general, be used to validate a snapshot of a time-varying document. A snapshot is an instance of a time-varying document at a single point in time. For instance, if the schema asserts that an element is mandatory (`minOccurs=1`) in the context of another element, there is no way to ensure that the element is in every snapshot since the element's timestamp may indicate that it has a shorter lifetime than its parent (resulting in times during which the element is not there, violating this integrity constraint); XML Schema provides no mechanism for reasoning about the timestamps.

Even though the representational and snapshot schemas are closely related, there are no existing techniques to automatically derive a representational schema from a snapshot schema (or vice-versa). The lack of an automatic technique means that users have to resort to ad hoc methods to construct a representational schema. Relying on ad hoc methods limits data independence. The designer of a schema for time-varying data has to make a variety of decisions, such as whether to timestamp with periods or with *temporal elements* [16], which are sets of non-overlapping periods and which elements should be time-varying. By adopting a tiered approach, where the snapshot XML Schema, temporal annotations, and physical annotations are separate documents, individual schema design decisions can be specified and changed, often without impacting the other design decisions, or indeed, the processing of tools. For example, a tool that computes a snapshot should be concerned primarily with the snapshot schema; the logical and physical aspects of time-varying information should only affect (perhaps) the efficiency of that tool, not its correctness. With physical data independence, few applications that are unconcerned with representational details would need to be changed.

Finally, improved tool support for representing and validating time-varying information is needed. Creating a time-varying XML document and representational schema for that document is potentially labor-intensive. Currently a user has to manually edit the time-varying document to insert timestamps indicating when versions of XML data are valid (for valid time) or are present in the document (for transaction time). The user also has to modify the snapshot schema to define the syntax and semantics of the timestamps. The entire process would be repeated if a new timestamp representation were desired. It would be better to have automated tools to create, maintain, and update time-varying documents when the representation of the timestamped elements changes.

2.3 Desiderata

In augmenting XML Schema to accommodate time-varying data, we had several goals in mind. At a minimum, the new approach would exhibit the following desirable features.

- Simplify the representation of time for the user.
- Support a three-level architecture to provide data independence, so that changes in the logical and physical level are isolated.
- Retain full upward compatibly with existing standards and not require any changes to these standards.
- Augment existing tools such as validating parsers for XML in such a way that those tools are also upward compatible. Ideally, any off-the-shelf validating parser (for XML Schema) can be used for (partial) validation.
- Support both valid time and transaction time.
- Accommodate a variety of physical representations for time-varying data.
- Support instance versioning.

Note that while ad hoc representational schemas may meet the last three desiderata, they certainly don't meet the first four. Other desirable features, outside the scope of this paper, include supporting schema versioning and accommodating temporal indeterminacy and granularity.

3 Theoretical Framework

This section sketches the process of constructing a schema for a time-varying document from a snapshot schema. The goal of the construction process is to create a schema that satisfies the *snapshot validation subsumption* property, which is described in detail below. In the relational data model, a schema defines the structure of each relation in a database. Each relation has a very simple structure: a relation is a list of attributes, with each attribute having a specified data type. The schema also includes integrity constraints, such as the specification of primary and foreign keys. In a similar manner, an XML Schema document defines the valid structure for an XML document. But an XML document has a far more complex structure than a relation. A document is a (deeply) nested collection of elements, with each element potentially having (text) content and attributes.

3.1 Snapshot Validation Subsumption

Let D^T be an XML document that contains *timestamped elements*. A timestamped element is an element that has an associated timestamp. (A *timestamped attribute* can be modeled as a special case of a timestamped element.) Logically, the timestamp is a collection of times (usually periods) chosen from one or more temporal dimensions (e.g., valid time, transaction time). Without loss of generality, we will restrict the discussion in this section to lifetimes that consist of a single period in one temporal dimension[4]. The timestamp records (part of) the lifetime of an element[5]. We will use the notation x^T to signify that element x has been timestamped. Let the lifetime of x^T be denoted as $lifetime(x^T)$. One constraint on the lifetime is that the lifetime of an element must be contained in the lifetime of each element that encloses it[6].

The *snapshot operation* extracts a complete *snapshot* of a time-varying document at a particular instant. Timestamps are *not* represented in the snapshot. A snapshot at time t replaces each timestamped element x^T with its non-timestamped copy x if t is in $lifetime(x^T)$ or with the empty string, otherwise. The *snapshot* operation is denoted as

$$snp(t, D^T) = D$$

where D is the snapshot at time t of the time-varying document D^T.

Let S^T be a representational schema for a time-varying document D^T. The *snapshot validation subsumption property* captures the idea that, at the very least, the representational schema must ensure that every snapshot of the document is valid with respect to the *snapshot schema*. Let $vldt(S,D)$ represent the validation *status* of document D with respect to schema S. The status is true if the document is *valid* but false otherwise. Validation also applies to time-varying documents, e.g., $vldt^T(S^T, D^T)$ is the validation status of D^T with respect to a representational schema, S^T, using a temporal validator.

Property [Snapshot Validation Subsumption]. Let S be an XML Schema document, D^T be a time-varying XML document, and S^T be a representational schema, also an

[4] The general case is that a timestamp is a collection of periods from multiple temporal dimensions (a multidimensional temporal element).

[5] Physically, there are myriad ways to represent a timestamp. It could be represented as an `<rs:timestamp>` subelement in the content of the timestamped element as is done in the fragment in Fig. 4. Or it could be a set of additional attributes in the timestamped element, or it could even be a `<rs:version>` element that wraps the timestamped element.

[6] Note that the lifetime captures only when an element appears in the context of the enclosing elements. The same element can appear in other contexts (enclosed by different elements) but clearly it has a different lifetime in those contexts.

XML Schema document. S^T is said to have *snapshot validation subsumption* with respect to S if

$$vldt^T(S^T, D^T) \Leftrightarrow \forall t[t \in lifetime(D^T) \Rightarrow vldt(S, snp(t, D^T))]$$

Intuitively, the property asserts that a *good* representational schema will validate only those time-varying documents for which every snapshot conforms to the snapshot schema. The subsumption property is depicted in the following correspondence diagram.

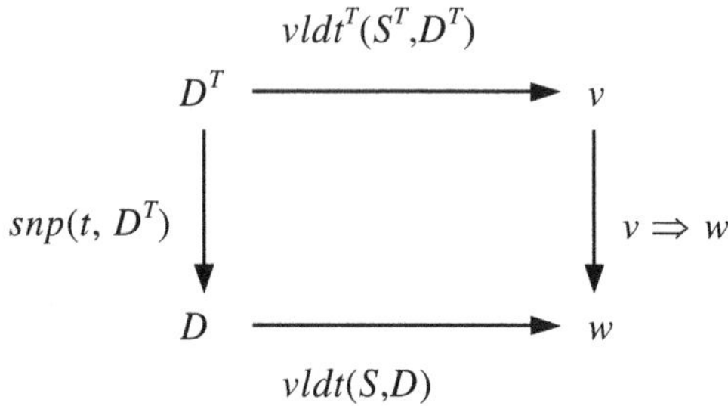

Fig. 6. Snapshot validation subsumption

Details of the process for constructing a schema for a time-varying document that conforms to the snapshot validation subsumption property from a snapshot schema are available in a technical report by the authors [12].

4 Architecture

The architecture of τXSchema is illustrated in Fig. 7. This figure is central to our approach, so we describe it in detail and illustrate it with the example. We note that although the architecture has many components, only those components shaded gray in the figure are specific to an individual time-varying document and need to be supplied by a user. New time-varying schemas can be quickly and easily developed and deployed. We also note that the representational schema, instead of being the only schema in an ad hoc approach, is merely an artifact in our approach, with the snapshot schema, temporal annotations, and physical annotations being the crucial specifications to be created by the designer.

The designer annotates the snapshot schema with *temporal annotations* (box 6). The temporal annotations together with the snapshot schema form the *logical* schema. Fig. 8 provides an extract of the temporal annotations on the winOlympic schema. The temporal annotations specify a variety of characteristics such as whether an element or attribute varies over valid time or transaction time, whether its lifetime is described as a continuous state or a single event, whether the item itself may appear at certain times (and not at others), and whether its content changes. For example, `<athlete>` is described as a state element, indicating that the `<athlete>` will be valid over a period (continuous) of time rather than a single instant. Annotations can be nested, enabling the target to be relative to that of its parent, and inheriting as

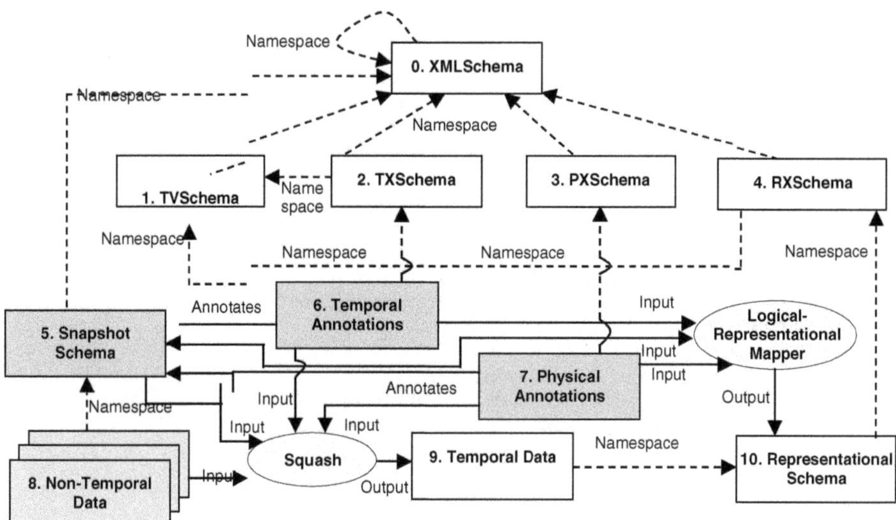

Fig. 7. Architecture of τXSchema

defaults the `kind`, `contentVarying`, and `existenceVarying` attribute values specified in the parent. The attribute `existenceVarying` indicates whether the element can be absent at some times and present at others. As an example, the presence of `existenceVarying` for an athlete's `phone` indicates that an athlete may have a phone at some points in time and not at other points in time. The attribute `contentVarying` indicates whether the element's content can change over time. An element's content is a string representation of its *immediate content*, i.e., text, sub-element names, and sub-element order.

Elements that are not described as time-varying are static and must have the same content and existence across every XML document in box 8. For example, we have assumed that the birthplace of an athlete will not change with time, so there is no annotation for `<birthPlace>` among the temporal annotations. The schema for the temporal annotations document is given by TXSchema (box 2), which in turn utilizes temporal values defined in a short XML Schema TVSchema (box 1). (Due to space limitations, we can't describe in detail these annotations, but it should be clear what aspects are specified here.)

The next design step is to create the *physical annotations* (box 7). In general, the physical annotations specify the timestamp representation options chosen by the user. An excerpt of the physical annotations for the winOlympic schema is given in Fig. 9. Physical annotations may also be nested, inheriting the specified attributes from their parent; these values can be overridden in the child element.

Physical annotations play two important roles.

1. They help to define where the physical timestamps will be placed (versioning level). The location of the timestamps is independent of which components vary over time (as specified by the temporal annotations). Two documents with the same logical information will look very different if we change the location of the physical timestamp. For example, although the elements `phone` and `athName` are time-varying, the user may choose to place the physical timestamp at the

```
<temporalAnnotations
  xmlns="http://www.cs.arizona.edu/tau/tauXSchema/TXSchema"
   xmlns:xsi="http://www.w3.org/2001/XMLSchema-instance"
   xsi:schemaLocation="http://www.cs.arizona.edu/tau/tauXSchema/TXSchema.xsd">
<snapshotSchema schemaLocation="http://www.cs.arizona.edu/
   tau/tauXSchema/examples/schemas/winOlympic.xsd"/>
...
  <validTime target="/winOlympic/…/athlete" kind="state" contentVarying="true">
     <validTime target="@age"/>
     <validTime target="athName"/>
     <validTime target="medal" kind="event"/>
     <validTime target="phone" existenceVarying="true"/>
  </validTime>
...
  <transactionTime target="/winOlympic"/>
  <transactionTime target="/winOlympic/…/athlete/@age"/>
  <transactionTime target="/winOlympic/…/athlete/athName"/>
...
</temporalAnnotations>
```

Fig. 8. Sample temporal annotations

```
<physicalAnnotations xmlns= "http://www.cs.arizona.edu/tau/tauXSchema/PXSchema"
  xmlns:xsi="http://www.w3.org/2001/XMLSchema-instance"
  xsi:schemaLocation="http://www.cs.arizona.edu/tau/tauXSchema/PXSchema.xsd">

  <temporalAnnotations schemaLocation="http://www.cs.arizona.edu/
    tau/tauXSchema/examples/schemas/winOlympicTemporal.xml"/>
...
  <stampPosition target="/winOlympic" transactionTimeStampType="step" />
  <stampPosition target="/winOlympic/.../athlete" validTimeStampType="extent">
     <stampPosition target="@age" validTimeStampType="step"
        transactionTimeStampType="step"/>
     <stampPosition target="athName" transactionTimeStampType="step"/>
     <stampPosition target="medal" validTimeStampType="none" />
     <stampPosition target="phone" transactionTimeStampType="extent"/>
  </stampPosition>
...
</physicalAnnotations>
```

Fig. 9. Sample physical annotations

athlete level. Whenever any element below athlete changes, the entire athlete element is repeated.

2. The physical annotations also define the type of timestamp (for both valid time and transaction time). A timestamp can be one of two types: step or extent. An extent timestamp specifies both the start and end instants in the timestamp's period. In contrast a step-wise constant (step) timestamp represents only the start instant. The end instant is implicitly assumed to be just prior to the start of the next version, or *now* for the current version. However, one cannot use step timestamps when there might be "gaps" in time between successive versions. Extent timestamps do not have this limitation. Changing even one timestamp from step to extent can make a big difference in the representation.

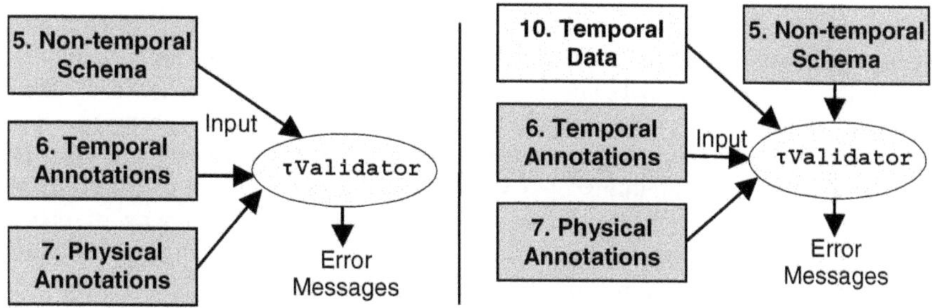

Fig. 10. τValidator: Checking the schemas and instance

The schema for the physical annotations document is PXSchema (box 3). τXSchema supplies a default set of physical annotations, which is to timestamp the root element with valid and transaction time using `step` timestamps, so the physical annotations are optional. (Again, space limitations do not allow us to describe these annotations in detail.)

We emphasize that our focus is on capturing relevant aspects of physical representations, not on the specific representations themselves, the design of which is itself challenging. Also, since the temporal and physical annotations are orthogonal and serve two separate goals, we choose to maintain them independently. A user can change where the timestamps are located, independently of specifying the temporal characteristics of that particular element. In the future, when software environments for managing changes to XML files over time are available, the user could specify temporal and physical annotations for an element together (by annotating a particular element to be temporal and also specifying that a timestamp should be located at that element), but these would remain two distinct aspects from a conceptual standpoint.

At this point, the designer is finished. She has written one conventional XML schema (box 5) and specified two sets of annotations (boxes 6 and 7). We provide boxes 1, 2, 3, and 4; XML Schema (box 0) is of course provided by W3C.

Let's now turn our attention to the tools that operate on these various specifications. The temporal annotations document (box 6) is passed through the `τValidator` (see the left half of Fig. 10) which checks to ensure that the annotations are consistent with the snapshot schema. The `Validator` utilizes the conventional validator for many of its checks. For instance, it validates the temporal annotations against the TXSchema. But it also checks that the temporal annotations are not inconsistent. Similarly, the physical annotations document is passed through the `τValidator` to ensure consistency of the physical annotations.

Once the annotations are found to be consistent, the *Logical to Representational Mapper* (software oval, Fig. 7) generates the *representational schema* (box 10) from the original snapshot schema and the temporal and physical annotations. The representational schema (mentioned in Section 0 as "`rs:`") is needed to serve as the schema for a time-varying document/data (box 9). The time-varying data can be created in four ways: 1) automatically from the non-temporal data (box 8) using τXSchema's `squash` tool (described in our technical report [12]), 2) automatically from the data stored in a database, i.e., as the result of a "temporal" query or view, 3) automatically from a third-party tool, or 4) manually.

The time-varying data is validated against the representational schema in two stages. First, a conventional XML Schema validating parser is used to parse and validate the time-varying data since the representational schema is an XML Schema document that satisfies the snapshot validation subsumption property. But as emphasized in Section 0, using a conventional XML Schema validating parser is not sufficient due to the limitations of XML Schema in checking temporal constraints. For example, a regular XML Schema validating parser has no way of checking something as basic as "the valid time boundaries of a parent element must encompass those of its child". These types of checks are implemented in the `τValidator`. So the second step is to pass the temporal data to `τValidator` as shown in the right half of Fig. 10. A temporal XML data file (box 9) is essentially a timestamped representation of a sequence of non-temporal XML data files (box 8). The namespace is set to its associated XML Schema document (i.e. representational schema). The timestamps are based on the characteristics defined in the temporal and physical annotations (boxes 6 and 7). The `τValidator`, by checking the temporal data, effectively checks the non-temporal constraints specified by the snapshot schema simultaneously on all the instances of the non-temporal data (box 8), as well as the constraints *between* snapshots, which cannot be expressed in a snapshot schema.

To reiterate, the conventional approach has the user start with a representational schema (box 10); our proposed approach is to have the user design a snapshot schema and two annotations, with the representational schema automatically generated.

5 Tools

Our three-level schema specification approach enables a suite of tools operating both on the schemas and the data they describe. The tools are open-source and beta versions are available[7]. The tools were implemented in Java using the DOM API [34]. We now turn to a central tool, the temporal validator.

The logical and physical temporal annotations (Fig. 7, boxes 6 and 7) for a non-temporal XML Schema (Fig. 7, box 5) are XML documents and hence can be validated as such. However, a validating XML parser cannot perform all of the necessary checks to ensure that the annotations are correctly specified. For example it cannot check that elements that have a `minOccurs` of 0 do not use a step-wise constant timestamp representation (i.e. a compact representation that assumes continuous existence, and where only the begin/start time of a timestamp is specified and the end/stop time of a timestamp is assumed to be the same as the begin/start point of the succeeding timestamp). This motivates the need for a special validator for the temporal and physical annotations. We implemented a tool, called `Validator`, to check the annotations. First, `τValidator` validates the temporal and physical annotations against the TXSchema and PXSchema, respectively. Then it performs additional tests to ensure that the snapshot schema and the temporal and physical annotations are all consistent.

---

[7] `http://www.cs.arizona.edu/tau/txschema/` and `http://www.cs.arizona.edu/tau/tdom/`

τValidator also validates time-varying data. A temporal data validator must ensure that every snapshot of the time-varying document conforms to the snapshot schema. It does this, in part, by using an existing XML Schema validating parser to validate the temporal document against the representational schema. Validator then performs two additional kinds of checks: representational checks and checks to compensate for differences in the semantics of temporal and non-temporal constraints. For instance it needs to check that there are no gaps in the lifetimes of versions for elements that have minOccurs=1 in the representational schema.

Additional details about other tools developed—including results of experiments performed on the tools—are available elsewhere [12].

6 Review of Related Work

While there have been a number of research efforts that have identified methods to detect and represent changes in XML documents over time [18], none have addressed the issue of validating a time-varying document.

There are various XML schemas that have been proposed in the literature and in the commercial arena. We chose to extend XML Schema in τXSchema because it is backed by the W3C and supports most major features available in other XML schemas [22]. It would be relatively straightforward to apply the concepts in this paper to develop time support for other XML schema languages; less straightforward but possible would be to apply our approach of temporal and physical annotations to other data models, such as UML [28].

Garcia-Molina and Cho [10] provide evidence that some web pages change on every access, whereas other pages change very infrequently, with a coarse average change interval of a web page of 4 months. Nguyen et al. [27] describe how to detect changes in XML documents that are accessible via the web. In the Xyleme system [37], the XML Alerter module periodically (with a periodicity specified by the user) accesses the XML document and compares it with a cached version of the document. The result is a sequence of static documents, each with an associated existence period. Dyreson [13] describes how a web server can capture some of the versions of a time-varying document, by caching the document as it is served to a client, and comparing the cached version against subsequent requests to see if anything has changed. Amagasa et al. [2] classify the methods used to access XML documents into two general categories: (i) using specialized APIs for XML documents, such as DOM, and (ii) directly editing documents, e.g., with an editor. In the former case, to access and modify temporal XML documents, DOM can be extended to automatically capture temporal information (and indeed, we have implemented such functionality in τDOM). It is also possible to capture transaction time information in the documents through change analysis, as discussed above and elsewhere [4, 11].

There has been a lot of interest in representing time-varying documents. Marian et al. [23] discuss versioning to track the history of downloaded documents. Chien, Tsotras and Zaniolo [9] have researched techniques for compactly storing multiple versions of an evolving XML document. Chawathe et al. [8] described a model for representing changes in semi-structured data and a language for querying over these changes. For example, the *diff* based approach [4, 11] focuses on an efficient way to store time-varying data and can be used to help detect transaction time changes in the document at the physical level. Buneman et al. [6] provide another means to store a single copy of an element that occurs in many snapshots. Grandi and Mandreoli [19] propose a `<valid>` tag to define a validity context that is used to timestamp part of a document. Finally, Chawathe et al. [8] and Dyreson et al. [14] discuss timestamps on edges in a semi-structured data model.

Recently there has been interest in incremental validation of XML documents [3, 5, 30]. These consider validating a snapshot that is the result of updates on the previous snapshot, which has already been validated. In a sense, this is the dual to the problem we consider, which is validating a (compressed) temporal document all at once, rather than once per snapshot (incrementally or otherwise).

None of the approaches above focus on the extensions required in XML Schema to adequately specify the nature of changes permissible in an XML document over time, and the corresponding validation of the extended schema. In fact, some of the previous approaches that attempt to identify or characterize changes in documents do not consider a schema. As our emphasis is on logical and physical data modeling, we assume that a schema is available from the start, and that the desire is for that schema to capture both the static and time-varying aspects of the document. If no schema exists, tools can derive the schema from the base documents, but that is beyond the scope of this paper. Our approach applies at the logical view of the data, while also being able to specify the physical representation. Since our approach is independent of the physical representation of the data, it is possible to incorporate the *diff*-based approach and other representational approaches [6] in our physical annotations.

7 Conclusion

In this paper we introduce the τXSchema model and notation to annotate XML Schemas to support temporal information. τXSchema provides an efficient way to annotate temporal elements and attributes. Our design conforms to W3C XML Schema definition and is built on top of XML Schema. Our approach ensures data independence by separating (i) the snapshot schema document for the instance document, (ii) information concerning which portion(s) of the instance document can vary over time, and (iii) where timestamps should be placed and precisely how the time-varying aspects should be represented. Since these three aspects are orthogonal, our approach allows each aspect to be changed independently. A small change to the physical annotations (or temporal annotations) can effect a large change in the (automatically generated) representational schema and the associated XML file.

This separation of concerns may be exploited in supporting tools; several new, quite useful tools are discussed that exploit the logical and physical data independence provided by our approach. Additionally, this independence enables existing tools (e.g., the XML Schema validator, XQuery, and DOM) to be used in the implementation of their temporal counterparts.

Future work includes extending the τXSchema model to fulfill the remaining issues in the desiderata and beyond. Indeterminacy and granularity are two significant and related issues, and should be fully supported by τXSchema. We anticipate that providing this support would require additions to the TVSchema / TXSchema / PXSchema / RXSchema (Fig. 7, boxes 1–4), but no changes to the user-designed schemas (Fig. 7, boxes 5–7). These augmentations would be upward compatibile with this version of τXSchema and be transparent to the user. Schema versioning is another important capability. For simplicity, we assume that the XML document changes, but the schema remains stable over time. However, in reality, the schema will also change with time. We are designing an extension that takes into account schema versioning.

We plan to extend our approach to also accommodate intensional XML data [26] which refer to programs that generate data. Some of these programs may be evaluated (a process termed *materialization*), with the results replacing the programs in the document. There are several interesting time-varying aspects of intensional XML data: (i) the programs themselves may change over time, (ii) even if the programs are static, the results of program evaluations may change over time, as external data the programs access changes, and (iii) even if the programs and the external data are static, different versions of the program evaluators (e.g., Java compiler) may be present, may generate different results due to incompatibilities between versions. It is challenging to manage this combination of schema and instance versioning over time.

Another broad area of work is optimization and efficiency. Currently there is no separation of elements or attributes based on the relative frequency of update. In the situation that some elements (for example) vary at a significantly different rate than other elements, it may prove more efficient to split the schema up into pieces such that elements with similar "rates of change" are together [25, 29, 32]. This would avoid redundant repetition of elements that do not change as frequently. Related to optimization is the issue of optimizing the use of time-varying text content. For instance it may be desirable to capture order among different pieces of text content within an element (e.g., different pieces may be used to describe a particular sub-element and may therefore vary with a frequency strongly correlated to the sub-element's temporal characteristics). We want to incorporate recently proposed representations (e.g., [4, 6, 9, 11]) into our physical annotations. Finally, the efficiency of the tools mentioned in Section 5 can be improved. For example, it would be interesting to investigate whether incremental validation approaches [3, 5, 30] are applicable in the temporal schema validator.

References

[1] Abiteboul, S., Bonifati, A., Cobena, G., Manolescu, I. and Milo, T., Dynamic XML Documents with Distribution and Replication. *Proceedings of the ACM SIGMOD International Conference on Management of Data*, (San Diego, CA, 2003), 527-538.

[2] Amagasa, T., Yoshikawa, M. and Uemura, S., A Data Model for Temporal XML Documents. *Proceedings of the 11th International Workshop on Database and Expert Systems Applications*, (London, England, 2000), Springer, Berlin, New York, 334-344.

[3] Barbosa, D., Mendelzon, A., Libkin, L., Mignet, L. and Arenas, M., Efficient Incremental Validation of XML Documents. *Proceedings of the 20th International Conference on Data Engineering*, (Boston, MA, 2004), IEEE Computer Society.

[4] Birsan, D., Sluiman, H. and Fernz, S.-A. XML Diff and Merge Tool, IBM alphaWorks, 1999. http://www.alphaworks.ibm.com/tech/xmldiffmerge.

[5] Bouchou, B. and Halfeld-Ferrari, M., Updates and Incremental Validation of XML Documents. *Proceedings of the 9th International Workshop on Data Base Programming Languages*, (Potsdam, Germany, 2003), Springer.

[6] Buneman, P., Khanna, S., Tajima, K. and Tan, W.C., Archiving scientific data. *Proceedings of the ACM SIGMOD International Conference on Management of Data*, (Madison, WI, 2002), ACM, 1-12.
[7] Burns, T., Fong, E.N., Jefferson, D., Knox, R., Mark, L., Reedy, C., Reich, L., Roussopoulos, N. and Truszkowski, W. Reference Model for DBMS Standardization, Database Architecture Framework Task Group of the ANSI/X3/SPARC Database System Study Group. *SIGMOD Record*, *15* (1). 19-58, 1986.
[8] Chawathe, S., Abiteboul, S. and Widom, J., Representing and Querying Changes in Semistructured Data. *Proceedings of the 14th International Conference on Data Engineering*, (Orlando, FL, USA, 1998), IEEE Computer Society, 4-13.
[9] Chien, S., Tsotras, V. and Zaniolo, C. Efficient schemes for managing multiversion XML documents. *VLDB Journal*, *11* (4). 332-353, 2002.
[10] Cho, J. and Garcia-Molina, H., The Evolution of the Web and Implications for an Incremental Crawler. *Proceedings of the 26th International Conference on Very Large Data Bases*, (Cairo, Egypt, 2000), Morgan Kaufmann, 200-209.
[11] Cobena, G., Abiteboul, S. and Marian, A., Detecting Changes in XML Documents. *Proceedings of the 18th International Conference on Data Engineering*, (San Jose, California, 2002), IEEE Computer Society, 41-52.
[12] Currim, F., Currim, S., Snodgrass, R.T. and Dyreson, C.E. τXSchema: Managing Temporal XML Schemas, Technical Report TR-77, TimeCenter, 2003.
[13] Dyreson, C., Towards a Temporal World-Wide Web: A Transaction Time Web Server. *Proceedings of the 12th Australasian Database Conference*, (Gold Coast, Australia, 2001), 169-175.
[14] Dyreson, C.E., Bohlen, M. and Jensen, C.S., Capturing and Querying Multiple Aspects of Semistructured Data. *Proceedings of the 25th International Conference on Very Large Data Bases*, (Edinburgh, Scotland, UK, 1999), Morgan Kaufmann, 290-301.
[15] Franconi, E., Grandi, F. and Mandreoli, F., Schema Evolution and Versioning: A Logical and Computational Characterisation. *Database Schema Evolution and Meta-Modeling, Proceedings of the 9th International Workshop on Foundations of Models and Languages for Data and Objects, FoMLaDO/DEMM*, (Dagstuhl, Germany, 2000), Springer, 85-99.
[16] Gadia, S. A Homogeneous Relational Model and Query Languages for Temporal Databases. *ACM Transactions on Database Systems*, *13* (4). 418-448, 1988.
[17] Gao, D. and Snodgrass, R.T., Temporal Slicing in the Evaluation of XML Queries. *Proceedings of the 29th International Conference on Very Large Databases*, (Berlin, Germany, 2003), Morgan Kaufmann, 632-643.
[18] Grandi, F. An Annotated Bibliography on Temporal and Evolution Aspects in the WorldWideWeb, Technical Report TR-77, TimeCenter, 2003.
[19] Grandi, F. and Mandreoli, F. The Valid Web: its time to Go…, Technical Report TR-46, TimeCenter, 1999.
[20] Jensen, C.S. and Dyreson, C.E. (eds.). A Consensus Glossary of Temporal Database Concepts. in Etzion, O., Jajodia, S. and Sripada, S. (eds.). *Temporal Databases: Research and Practice*, Springer-Verlag, 1998, 367-405.
[21] Khatri, V., Ram, S. and Snodgrass, R.T. Augmenting a Conceptual Model with Spatio-Temporal Annotations. *IEEE Transactions on Knowledge and Data Engineering*, forthcoming, 2004.
[22] Lee, D. and Chu, W. Comparative Analysis of Six XML Schema Languages. *SIGMOD Record*, *29* (3). 76-87, 2000.
[23] Marian, A., Abiteboul, S., Cobena, G. and Mignet:, L., Change-Centric Management of Versions in an XML Warehouse. *Proceedings of the Very Large Data Bases Conference*, (Roma, Italy, 2001), Morgan Kaufmann, 581-590.
[24] McHugh, J. and Widom, J., Query Optimization for XML. *Proceedings of the 25th International Conference on Very Large Databases*, (Edinburgh, Scotland, UK, 1999), Morgan Kaufmann, 315-326.

[25] McKenzie, E. and Snodgrass, R.T. An Evaluation of Relational Algebras Incorporating the Time Dimension in Databases. *ACM Computing Surveys*, *23* (4). 501-543, 1991.
[26] Milo, T., Abiteboul, S., Amann, B., Benjelloun, O. and Ngoc, F.D., Exchanging Intensional XML Data. *Proceedings of the ACM SIGMOD International Conference on Management of Data*, (San Diego, CA, 2003), 289-300.
[27] Nguyen, B., Abiteboul, S., Cobena, G. and Preda, M., Monitoring XML Data on the Web. *Proceedings of the ACM SIGMOD International Conference on Management of Data*, (Santa Barbara, CA, 2001), 437-448.
[28] OMG. Unified Modeling Language (UML), v1.5, 2003. http://www.omg.org/technology/documents/formal/uml.htm.
[29] Ozsoyoglu, G. and Snodgrass, R.T. Temporal and Real-Time Databases:A Survey. *IEEE Transactions on Knowledge and Data Engineering*, *7* (4). 513-532, 1995.
[30] Papakonstantinou, Y. and Vianu, V., Incremental Validation of XML Documents. *Proceedings of the 9th International Conference on Database Theory*, (Siena, Italy, 2003), Springer, 47-63.
[31] Roddick, J.F. A Survey of Schema Versioning Issues for Database Systems. *Information and Software Technology*, *37* (7). 383-393, 1995.
[32] Snodgrass, R.T. Temporal Object-Oriented Databases: A Critical Comparison. in Kim, W. ed. *Modern Database Systems: The Object Model, Interoperability and Beyond*, Addison-Wesley/ACM Press, 1995, 386-408.
[33] Steel, T.B., Jr., Chairman Interim Report: ANSI/X3/SPARC Study Group on Data Base Management Systems 75-02-08. *FDT-Bulletin of ACM SIGMOD*, *7* (2). 1-140, 1975.
[34] W3C. Document Object Model (DOM) Level 2 HTML Specification Version 1.0. Hors, A.L. ed., W3C, 2002. http://www.w3.org/TR/2002/PR-DOM-Level-2-HTML-20021108/.
[35] W3C. XML Schema Part 1: Structures. Mendelsohn, N. ed., W3C, 2001. http://www.w3.org/TR/2001/REC-xmlschema-1-20010502/.
[36] W3C. XML Schema Part 2: Datatypes. Malhotra, A. ed., W3C, 2001. http://www.w3.org/TR/2001/REC-xmlschema-2-20010502/.
[37] Xyleme, L. A dynamic warehouse for XML Data of the Web. *IEEE Data Engineering Bulletin*, *24* (2). 40-47, 2001.

Spatial Queries in the Presence of Obstacles

Jun Zhang, Dimitris Papadias, Kyriakos Mouratidis, and Manli Zhu

Department of Computer Science
Hong Kong University of Science and Technology
Clear Water Bay, Hong Kong
{zhangjun,dimitris,kyriakos,cszhuml}@cs.ust.hk

Abstract. Despite the existence of obstacles in many database applications, traditional spatial query processing utilizes the Euclidean distance metric assuming that points in space are directly reachable. In this paper, we study spatial queries in the presence of obstacles, where the obstructed distance between two points is defined as the length of the shortest path that connects them without crossing any obstacles. We propose efficient algorithms for the most important query types, namely, range search, nearest neighbors, e-distance joins and closest pairs, considering that both data objects and obstacles are indexed by R-trees. The effectiveness of the proposed solutions is verified through extensive experiments.

1 Introduction

This paper presents the first comprehensive approach for spatial query processing in the presence of obstacles. As an example of an "obstacle nearest neighbor query" consider Fig. 1 that asks for the closest point of q, where the definition of distance must now take into account the existing obstacles (shaded areas). Although point a is closer in terms of Euclidean distance, the actual nearest neighbor is point b (i.e., it is closer in terms of the *obstructed distance*). Such a query is typical in several scenarios, e.g., q is a pedestrian looking for the closest restaurant and the obstacles correspond to buildings, lakes, streets without crossings etc. The same concept applies to any spatial query, e.g., range search, spatial join and closest pair.

Despite the lack of related work in the Spatial Database literature, there is a significant amount of research in the context of Computational Geometry, where the

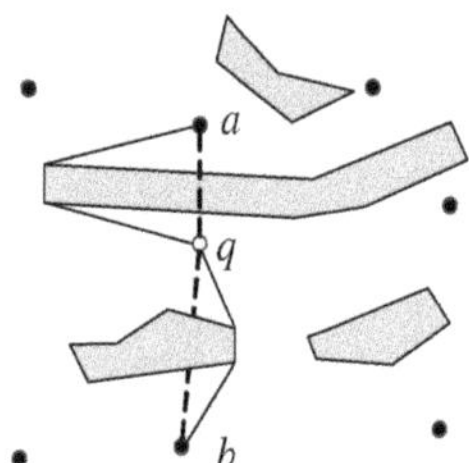

Fig. 1. An obstacle nearest neighbor query example

E. Bertino et al. (Eds.): EDBT 2004, LNCS 2992, pp. 366–384, 2004.
© Springer-Verlag Berlin Heidelberg 2004

problem is to devise main-memory, shortest path algorithms that take obstacles into account (e.g., find the shortest path from point *a* to *b* that does not cross any obstacle). Most existing approaches (reviewed in Section 2) construct a *visibility graph*, where each node corresponds to an obstacle vertex and each edge connects two vertices that are not obstructed by any obstacle. The algorithms pre-suppose the maintenance of the entire visibility graph in main memory. However, in our case this is not feasible due to the extreme space requirements for real spatial datasets. Instead we maintain local visibility graphs only for the obstacles that may influence the query result (e.g., for obstacles around point *q* in Fig. 1).

In the data clustering literature, *cod-clarans* [THH01] clusters objects into the same group with respect to the obstructed distance using the visibility graph, which is pre-computed and materialized. In addition to the space overhead, materialization is unsuitable for large spatial datasets due to potential updates in the obstacles or data (in which case a large part or the entire graph has to be re-reconstructed). Estivill-Castro and Lee [EL01] discuss several approaches for incorporating obstacles in spatial clustering. Despite some similarities with the problem at hand (e.g., visibility graphs), the techniques for clustering are clearly inapplicable to spatial query processing.

Another related topic regards query processing in spatial network databases [PZMT03], since in both cases movement is restricted (to the underlying network or by the obstacles). However, while obstacles represent areas where movement is prohibited, edges in spatial networks explicitly denote the permitted paths. This fact necessitates different query processing methods for the two cases. Furthermore, the target applications are different. The typical user of a spatial network database is a driver asking for the nearest gas station according to driving distance. On the other hand, the proposed techniques are useful in cases where movement is allowed in the whole data space except for the stored obstacles (vessels navigating in the sea, pedestrians walking in urban areas). Moreover, some applications may require the integration of both spatial network and obstacle processing techniques (e.g., a user that needs to find the best parking space near his destination, so that the sum of travel and walking distance is minimized).

For the following discussion we assume that there is one or more datasets of *entities*, which constitute the points of interest (e.g., restaurants, hotels) and a single obstacle dataset. The extension to multiple obstacle datasets or cases where the entities also represent obstacles is straightforward. Similar to most previous work on spatial databases, we assume that the entity and the obstacle datasets are indexed by R-trees [G84, SRF87, BKSS90], but the methods can be applied with any data partition index. Our goal is to provide a complete set of algorithms covering all common query types. The rest of the paper is organized as follows: Section 2 surveys the previous work focusing on directly related topics. Sections 3, 4, 5 and 6 describe the algorithms for range search, nearest neighbors, *e*-distance joins and closest pairs, respectively. Section 7 provides a thorough experimental evaluation and Section 8 concludes the paper with some future directions.

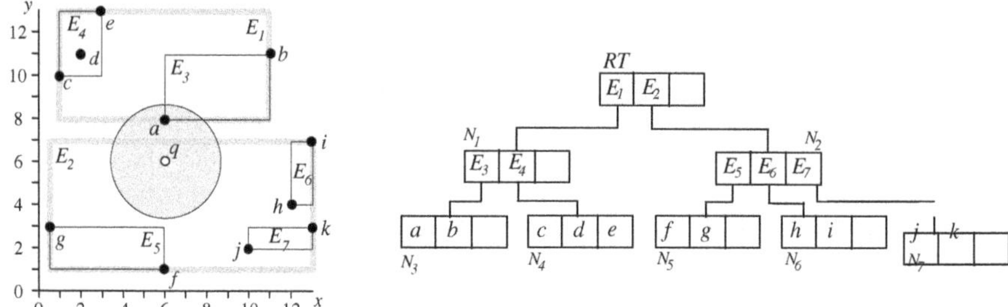

Fig. 2. An R-tree example

2 Related Work

Sections 2.1 and 2.2 discuss query processing in conventional spatial databases and spatial networks, respectively. Section 2.3 reviews obstacle path problems in main memory, and describes algorithms for maintaining visibility graphs. Section 2.4 summarizes the existing work and identifies the links with the current problem.

2.1 Query Processing in the Euclidean Space

For the following examples we use the R-tree of Fig. 2, which indexes a set of points $\{a,b,\ldots,k\}$, assuming a capacity of three entries per node. Points that are close in space (e.g., *a* and *b*) are clustered in the same leaf node (N_3), represented as a minimum bounding rectangle (MBR). Nodes are then recursively grouped together following the same principle until the top level, which consists of a single root. R-trees (like most spatial access methods) were motivated by the need to efficiently process *range queries*, where the range usually corresponds to a rectangular window or a circular area around a query point. The R-tree answers the range query *q* (shaded area) in Fig. 2 as follows. The root is first retrieved and the entries (e.g., E_1, E_2) that intersect the range are recursively searched because they may contain qualifying points. Non-intersecting entries (e.g., E_4) are skipped. Notice that for non-point data (e.g., lines, polygons), the R-tree provides just a *filter* step to prune non-qualifying objects. The output of this phase has to pass through a *refinement* step that examines the actual object representation to determine the actual result. The concept of filter and refinement steps applies to all spatial queries on non-point objects.

A *nearest neighbor* (NN) *query* retrieves the *k* ($k\geq1$) data point(s) closest to a query point *q*. The R-tree NN algorithm proposed in [HS99] keeps a *heap* with the entries of the nodes visited so far. Initially, the heap contains the entries of the root sorted according to their minimum distance (*mindist*) from *q*. The entry with the minimum *mindist* in the heap (E_2 in Fig. 2) is expanded, i.e., it is removed from the heap and its children (E_5, E_6, E_7) are added together with their *mindist*. The next entry visited is E_1 (its *mindist* is currently the minimum in the heap), followed by E_3, where the actual 1NN result (*a*) is found. The algorithm terminates, because the *mindist* of all entries in the heap is greater than the distance of *a*. The algorithm can be easily extended for the retrieval of *k* nearest neighbors (*k*NN). Furthermore, it is optimal (it visits only the nodes necessary for obtaining the nearest neighbors) and *incremental*, i.e., it reports neighbors in ascending order of their distance to the query point, and can be applied when the number k of nearest neighbors to be retrieved is not known in advance.

The *e-distance join* finds all pairs of objects (s,t) $s \in S$, $t \in T$ within (Euclidean) distance e from each other. If both datasets S and T are indexed by R-trees, the *R-tree join* algorithm [BKS93] traverses synchronously the two trees, following entry pairs if their distance is below (or equal to) e. The *intersection join*, applicable for region objects, retrieves all intersecting object pairs (s,t) from two datasets S and T. It can be considered as a special case of the e-distance join, where e=0. Several spatial join algorithms have been proposed for the case where only one of the inputs is indexed by an R-tree or no input is indexed.

A closest-pairs query outputs the k ($k \geq 1$) pairs of points (s,t) $s \in S$, $t \in T$ with the smallest (Euclidean) distance. The algorithms for processing such queries [HS98, CMTV00] combine spatial joins with nearest neighbor search. In particular, assuming that both datasets are indexed by R-trees, the trees are traversed synchronously, following the entry pairs with the minimum distance. Pruning is based on the mindist metric, but this time defined between entry MBRs. Finally, a distance semi-join returns for each point $s \in S$ its nearest neighbor $t \in T$. This type of query can be answered either (i) by performing a NN query in T for each object in S, or (ii) by outputting closest pairs incrementally, until the NN for each entity in S is retrieved.

2.2 Query Processing in Spatial Networks

Papadias et al. [PZMT03] study the above query types for spatial network databases, where the network is modeled as a graph and stored as adjacency lists. Spatial entities are independently indexed by R-trees and are mapped to the nearest edge during query processing. The *network distance* of two points is defined as the distance of the shortest path connecting them in the graph. Two frameworks are proposed for pruning the search space: *Euclidean restriction* and *network expansion*.

Euclidean restriction utilizes the Euclidean *lower-bound property* (i.e., the fact that the Euclidean distance is always smaller or equal to the network distance). Consider, for instance, a range query that asks for all objects within network distance e from point q. The Euclidean restriction method first performs a conventional range query at the entity dataset and returns the set of objects S' within (Euclidean) distance e from q. Given the Euclidean lower bound property, S' is guaranteed to avoid false misses. Then, the network distance of all points of S' is computed and false hits are eliminated. Similar techniques are applied to the other query types, combined with several optimizations to reduce the number of network distance computations.

The network expansion framework performs query processing directly on the network without applying the Euclidean lower bound property. Consider again the example network range query. The algorithm first expands the network around the query point and finds all edges within range e from q. Then, an intersection join algorithm retrieves the entities that fall on these edges. Nearest neighbors, joins and closest pairs are processed using the same general concept.

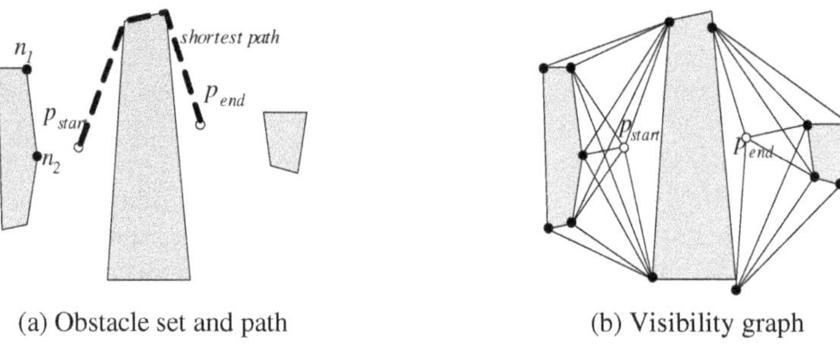

(a) Obstacle set and path (b) Visibility graph

Fig. 3. Obstacle path example

2.3 Obstacle Path Problems in Main Memory

Path problems in the presence of obstacles have been extensively studied in Computational Geometry [BKOS97]. Given a set O of non-overlapping obstacles (polygons) in 2D space, a starting point p_{start} and a destination p_{end}, the goal is to find the shortest path from p_{start} to p_{end} which does not cross the interior of any obstacle in O. Fig. 3a shows an example where O contains 3 obstacles. The corresponding *visibility graph* G is depicted in Fig. 3b. The vertices of all the obstacles in O, together with p_{start} and p_{end} constitute the nodes of G. Two nodes n_i and n_j in G are connected by an edge if and only if they are mutually visible (i.e., the line segment connecting n_i and n_j does not intersect any obstacle interior). Since obstacle edges (e.g., n_1n_2) do not cross obstacle interiors, they are also included in G.

It can be shown [LW79] that the shortest path contains only edges of the visibility graph. Therefore, the original problem can be solved by: (i) constructing G and (ii) computing the shortest path between p_{start} and p_{end} in G. For the second task any conventional shortest path algorithm [D59, KHI+86] suffices. Therefore, the focus has been on the first problem, i.e., the construction of the visibility graph. A naïve solution is to consider every possible pair of nodes in G and check if the line segment connecting them intersects the interior of any obstacle. This approach leads to $O(n^3)$ running time, where n is the number of nodes in G. In order to reduce the cost, Sharir and Schorr [SS84] perform a rotational plane-sweep for each graph node and find all the other nodes that are visible to it with total cost $O(n^2 \log n)$.

Subsequent techniques for visibility graph construction involve sophisticated data structures and algorithms, which are mostly of theoretical interest. The worst case optimal algorithm [W85, AGHI86] performs a rotational plane-sweep for all the vertices simultaneously and runs in $O(n^2)$ time. The optimal output-sensitive approaches [GM87, R95, PV96] have $O(m+n\log n)$ running time, where m is the number of edges in G. If all obstacles are convex, it is sufficient to consider the *tangent visibility graph* [PV95], which contains only the edges that are tangent to two obstacles.

2.4 Discussion

In the rest of the paper we utilize several of these findings for efficient query processing. First the Euclidean *lower-bound property* also holds in the presence of obstacles, since the Euclidean distance is always smaller or equal to the obstructed distance. Thus, the algorithms of Section 2.1 can be used to return a set of candidate entities, which includes the actual output, as well as, a set of *false hits*. This is similar to the Euclidean restriction framework for spatial networks, discussed in Section 2.2. The difference is that now we have to compute the obstructed (as opposed to network) distances of the candidate entities. Although we take advantage of visibility graphs to facilitate obstructed distance computation, in our case it is not feasible to maintain in memory the complete graph due to the extreme space requirements for real spatial datasets. Furthermore, pre-materialization is unsuitable for updates in the obstacle or entity datasets. Instead we construct visibility graphs on-line, taking into account only the obstacles and the entities relevant to the query. In this way, updates in individual datasets can be handled efficiently, new datasets can be incorporated in the system easily (as new information becomes available), and the visibility graph is kept small (so that distance computations are minimized).

3 Obstacle Range Query

Given a set of obstacles O, a set of entities P, a query point q and a range e, an obstacle range (OR) query returns all the objects of P that are within obstructed distance e from q. The OR algorithm processes such a query as follows: (i) it first retrieves the set P' of candidate entities that are within Euclidean distance e (from q) using a conventional range query on the R-tree of P; (ii) it finds the set O' of obstacles that are relevant to the query; (iii) it builds a local visibility graph G' containing the elements of P' and O'; (iv) it removes false hits from P' by evaluating the obstructed distance for each candidate object using G'. Consider the example OR query q (with e = 6) in Fig. 4a, where the shaded areas represent obstacles and points correspond to entities.

Clearly, the set P' of entities intersecting the disk C centered at q with radius e, constitutes a superset of the query result. In order to remove the false hits we need to retrieve the relevant obstacles. A crucial observation is that only the obstacles intersecting C may influence the result. By the Euclidean lower-bound property, any path that starts from q and ends at any vertex of an obstacle that lies outside C

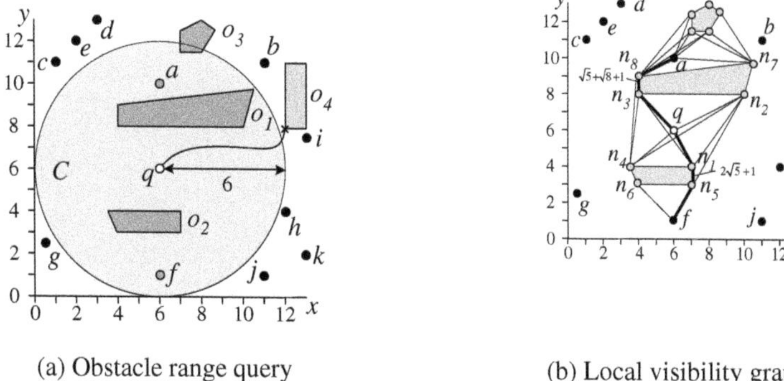

(a) Obstacle range query (b) Local visibility graph

Fig. 4. Example of obstacle range query

(e.g., curve in Fig. 4a), has length larger than the range e. Therefore, it is safe to exclude the obstacle (o_4) from the visibility graph. Thus, the set O' of relevant obstacles can be found using a range query (centered at q with radius e) on the R-tree of O. The local visibility graph G' for the example of Fig. 4a is shown in Fig. 4b. For constructing the graph, we use the algorithm of [SS84], without tangent simplification.

The final step evaluates the obstructed distance between q and each candidate. In order to minimize the computation cost, OR expands the graph around the query point q only once for all candidate points using a traversal method similar to the one employed by Dijkstra's algorithm [D59]. Specifically, OR maintains a priority queue Q, which initially contains the neighbors of q (i.e., n_1 to n_4 in Fig. 4b) sorted by their obstructed distance. Since these neighbors are directly connected to q, the obstructed distance $d_O(n_i,q)$, $1 \le i \le 4$, equals the Euclidean distance $d_E(n_i,q)$. The first node (n_1) is de-queued and inserted into a set of visited nodes V. For each unvisited neighbor n_x of n_1 (i.e., $n_x \notin V$), $d_O(n_x,q)$ is computed, using n_1 as an intermediate node i.e., $d_O(n_x,q) = d_O(n_1,q) + d_E(n_x,n_1)$. If $d_O(n_x,q) \le e$, n_x is inserted in Q. Fig. 5 illustrates the OR algorithm.

Note that it is possible for a node to appear multiple times in Q, if it is found through different paths. For instance, in Fig. 4b, n_2 may be re-inserted after visiting n_1. Duplicate elimination is performed during the de-queuing process, i.e., a node is visited only the first time that it is de-queued (with the smallest distance from q). Subsequent visits are avoided by checking the contents of V (set of already visited nodes). When the de-queued node is an entity, it is reported and removed from P'. The algorithm terminates when the queue or P' is empty.

```
Algorithm OR(RTP, RTO, q, e)
/* RTP is the entity R-tree, RTO is the obstacle R-tree, q is the
query point, e is the query range */
P' = Euclidean_range(RTP,q,e) // get qualifying entities
O' = Euclidean_range(RTO,q,e) // get relevant obstacles
G' = build_visibility_graph(q, P',O') // algorithm of [SS84]
V = Ø; R = Ø  // V is the set of visited nodes, R is the result
insert <q, 0> into Q
while Q and P' are both non-empty
    de-queue <n, dO(n,q)> from Q // n has the min dO(n,q)
    if n∉V // n is an unvisited node
        if n∈P' // n is an unreported entity
            R = R ∪ {n}; P' = P' - {n}
        for each neighbor node nx of n
            if (nx∉V)
                dO(nx,q) = dO(n,q) + dE(n,nx)
                if (dO(nx,q) ≤ e)
                    insert <nx, dO(nx,q)> into Q
        V = V ∪ n
return R
End OR
```

Fig. 5. OR algorithm

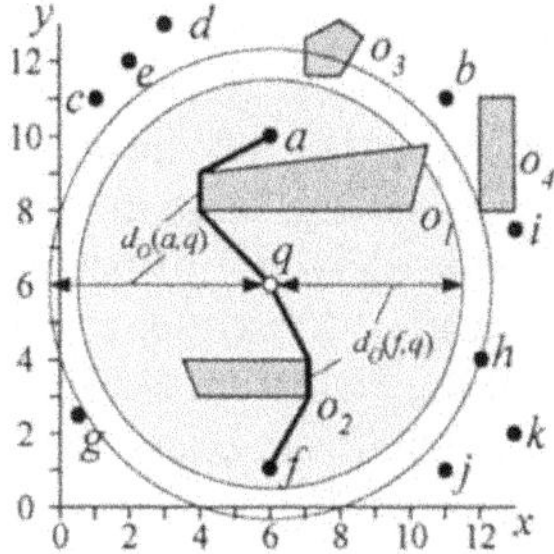

Fig. 6. Example of obstacle nearest neighbor query

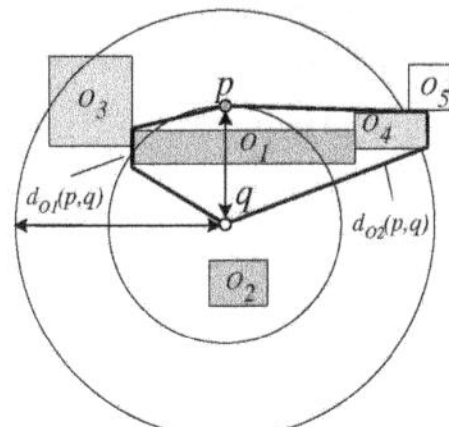

Fig. 7. Example of obstructed distance computation

4 Obstacle Nearest Neighbor Query

Given a query point q, an obstacle set O and an entity set P, an obstacle nearest neighbor (ONN) query returns the k objects of P that have the smallest obstructed distances from q. Assuming, for simplicity, the retrieval of a single neighbor (k=1) in Fig. 6, we illustrate the general idea of ONN algorithm before going into details. First the Euclidean nearest neighbor of q (object a) is retrieved from P using an incremental algorithm (e.g., [HS99] in Section 2.1) and $d_O(a,q)$ is computed. Due to the Euclidean lower-bound property, objects with potentially smaller obstructed distance than a should be within Euclidean distance $d_{Emax} = d_O(a,q)$. Then, the next Euclidean neighbor (f) within the d_{Emax} range is retrieved and its obstructed distance is computed. Since $d_O(f,q) < d_O(a,q)$, f becomes the current NN and d_{Emax} is updated to $d_O(f,q)$ (i.e., d_{Emax} continuously shrinks). The algorithm terminates when there is no Euclidean nearest neighbor within the d_{Emax} range.

It remains to clarify the obstructed distance computation. Consider, for instance, Fig. 7 where the Euclidean NN of q is point p. In order to compute $d_O(p,q)$, we first retrieve the obstacles o_1, o_2 within the range $d_E(p,q)$ and build an initial visibility graph that contains o_1, o_2, p and q. A provisional distance $d_{O1}(p,q)$ is computed using a shortest path algorithm (we apply Dijkstra's algorithm). The problem is that the graph is not sufficient for the actual distance, since there may exist obstacles (o_3, o_4) outside the range that obstruct the shortest path from q to p.

In order to find such obstacles, we perform a second Euclidean range query on the obstacle R-tree using $d_{O1}(p,q)$ (i.e., the large circle in Fig. 7). The new obstacles o_3 and o_4 are added to the visibility graph, and the obstructed distance $d_{O2}(p,q)$ is computed again. The process has to be repeated, since there may exist another obstacle (o_5) outside the range $d_{O2}(p,q)$ that intersects the new shortest path from q to p. The termination condition is that there are no new obstacles in the last range, or equivalently, the shortest path remains the same in two subsequent iterations, meaning that the last set of added obstacles does not affect $d_O(p,q)$ (note that the obstructed distance can only increase in two subsequent iterations as new obstacles are discovered). The pseudo-code of the algorithm is shown in Fig. 8. The initial visibility graph G', passed as a parameter, contains p, q and the obstacles in the Euclidean range $d_E(p,q)$.

The final remark concerns the dynamic maintenance of the visibility graph in main memory. The following basic operations are implemented, to avoid re-building the graph from scratch for each new computation:

- *Add_obstacle(o,G')* is used by the algorithm of Fig. 8 for incorporating new obstacles in the graph. It adds all the vertices of o to G' as nodes and creates new edges accordingly. It removes existing edges that cross the interior of o.
- *Add_entity(p,G')* incorporates a new point in an existing graph. If, for instance, in the example of Fig. 7 we want the two nearest neighbors, we re-use the graph that we constructed for the 1st NN to compute the distance of the second one. The operation adds p to G' and creates edges connecting it with the visible nodes in G'.
- *Delete_entity(p,G')* is used to remove entities for which the distance computations have been completed.

Add obstacle performs a rotational plane-sweep for each vertex of o and adds the corresponding edges to G'. A list of all obstacles in G' is maintained to facilitate the sweep process. Existing edges that cross the interior of o are removed by an intersection check. *Add entity* is supported by performing a rotational plane-sweep for the newly added node to reveal all its edges. The *delete entity* operation just removes p and its incident edges.

Fig. 9 illustrates the complete algorithm for retrieval of k (≥1) nearest neighbors. The k Euclidean NNs are first obtained using the entity R-tree, sorted in ascending order of their obstructed distance to q, and d_{Emax} is set to the distance of the kth point. Similar to the single NN case, the subsequent Euclidean neighbors are retrieved incrementally, while maintaining the k (obstructed) NNs and d_{Emax} (except that d_{Emax} equals the obstructed distance of the k-th neighbor), until the next Euclidean NN has larger Euclidean distance than d_{Emax}.

```
Algorithm compute_obstructed_distance(G, p, q, G', RTo)
dO(p,q)= shortest_path_dist(G',p,q)
O' = set of obstacles in G'
repeat
    Onew= Euclidean_range(RTO, q, dO(p,q))
    if O'⊂ Onew
        for each obstacle o in Onew - O'
            add_obstacle(o,G')
        dO(p,q)= shortest_path_dist(G',p,q)
        O' = Onew
    else // termination condition
        return dO(p,q)
End compute_obstructed_distance
```

Fig. 8. Obstructed distance computation

```
Algorithm ONN(RTP, RTO, q, k)
/* RTP is the entity R-tree, RTO is the obstacle R-tree, q is the
query, k is number of NN requested */
R = ∅  // R is the result
P' = Euclidean_NN(RTP, q, k); // find the k Euclidean NNs of q
O' = Euclidean_range(RTO, q, d(pk ,q))
G' = build_visibility_graph(q, P',O')
for each entity pi in P'
     dO(pi,q)= compute_obstructed_distance(G',pi,q)
     delete_entity(pi,G')
sort P' in ascending order of dO(pi,q) and insert into R
dEmax= dO(pk ,q) // pk is the farthest NN
repeat
     (p,dE(p,q))=next_Euclidean_NN(RTP, q);
     add_entity(p,G')
     dO(p,q)=compute_obstructed_distance(G',p,q)
     delete_entity(p,G')
     if (dO(p,q)<dO(pk ,q)) // p is closer than the kth NN
          R = R - {pk}
          insert p in R so that R remains sorted by dO
          dEmax = dO(pk ,q) // update the Euclidean threshold
until dE(p,q)>dEmax
return R
End ONN
```

Fig. 9. ONN algorithm

5 Obstacle *e*-Distance Join

Given an obstacle set O, two entity datasets S, T and a value e, an obstacle e-distance join (ODJ) returns all entity pairs (s,t), $s \in S$, $t \in T$ such that $d_O(s,t) \le e$. Based on the Euclidean lower-bound property, the ODJ algorithm processes an obstacle e-distance join as follows: (i) it performs an Euclidean e-distance join on the R-trees of S and T to retrieve entity pairs (s,t) with $d_E(s,t) \le e$; (ii) it evaluates $d_O(s,t)$ for each candidate pair (s,t) and removes false hits. The R-tree join algorithm [BKS93] (see Section 2.1) is applied for step (i). For step (ii) we use the obstructed distance computation algorithm of Fig. 8.

Observe that although the number of distance computations equals the cardinality of the Euclidean join, the number of applications of the algorithm can be significantly smaller. Consider, for instance, that the Euclidean join retrieves five pairs: (s_1, t_1), (s_1, t_2), (s_1, t_3), (s_2, t_1), (s_2, t_4), requiring five obstructed distance computations. However, there are only two objects $s_1, s_2 \in S$ participating in the candidate pairs, implying that all five distances can be computed by building only two visibility graphs around s_1 and s_2. Based on this observation, ODJ counts the number of distinct objects from S and T in the candidate pairs. The dataset with the smallest count is used to provide the 'seeds' for visibility graphs. Let Q be the set of points of the 'seed' dataset that appear in the Euclidean join result (i.e., in the above example $Q = \{s_1,s_2\}$). Similarly, P is the set of points of the second dataset that appear in the result (i.e., $P = \{t_1,t_2,t_3,t_4\}$). The problem can then be converted to: for each $q \in Q$ and a set $P' \subseteq P$ of candidates (paired with q in the Euclidean join), find the objects of P' that are within obstructed distance e from q. This process corresponds to the false hit elimination part of the obstacle range query and can be processed by an algorithm similar to OR (Fig. 5). To

```
Algorithm ODJ(RT_S, RT_T, RT_O, e)
/* RT_S and RT_T is the entity R-trees, RT_O is the obstacle R-tree, e is
the query range */
R = Ø
Rjoin-res = Euclidean_distance_join(RT_S, RT_T, e)
compute Q and P;
sort Q according to Hilbert order // to maximize locality
for each object q ∈ Q
    P' = set of objects ∈ P that appear with q in Rjoin-res
    O' = Euclidean_range(RT_O, q, e) // get relevant obstacles
    R' = OR(P', O', q, e) // eliminate false hits
    R  = R ∪ {<q, r>/ r ∈ R'}
return R
End ODJ
```

Fig. 10. ODJ algorithm

exploit spatial locality between subsequent accesses to the obstacle R-tree (needed to retrieve the obstacles for the visibility graph for each range), ODJ sorts and processes the seeds by their Hilbert order. The pseudo code of the algorithm is shown in Fig. 10.

6 Obstacle Closest-Pair Query

Given an obstacle set O, two entity datasets S, T and a value $k \geq 1$, an obstacle closest-pair (OCP) query retrieves the k entity pairs (s, t), $s \in S$, $t \in T$, that have the smallest $d_O(s, t)$. The OCP algorithm employs an approach similar to ONN. Assuming for example, that only the (single) closest pair is requested, OCP: (i) performs an incremental closest pair query on the entity R-trees of S and T and retrieves the Euclidean closest pair (s,t); (ii) it evaluates $d_O(s,t)$ and uses it as a bound d_{Emax} for Euclidean closest-pairs search; (iii) it obtains the next closest pair (within Euclidean distance d_{Emax}), evaluates its obstructed distance and updates the result and d_{Emax} if necessary; (iv) it repeats step (iii) until the incremental search for pairs exceeds d_{Emax}. Fig. 11 shows the OCP algorithm for retrieval of k closest-pairs.

```
Algorithm OCP(RT_S, RT_T, RT_O, k)
/* RT_S and RT_T is the entity R-trees, RT_O is the obstacle R-tree, k is
the number of pairs requested */
{(s_1, t_1), ... , (s_k, t_k)} = Euclidean_CP(RT_S, RT_T, k)
sort (s_i, t_i) in ascending order of their d_O(s_i, t_i)
d_Emax= d_O(s_k, t_k)
repeat
    (s', t') = next_Euclidean_CP(RT_S, RT_T)
    d_O(s', t') = compute_obstructed_distance(G',s',t')
    if (d_O(s', t') < d_Emax)
        delete (s_k, t_k) from {(s_1, t_1), ... , (s_k, t_k)} and insert (s',
         t') in it, so that it remains sorted by d_O
    d_Emax= d_O(s_k, t_k)
until d_E(s', t') > d_Emax
return {(s_1, t_1), ... , (s_k, t_k)}
End OCP
```

Fig. 11. OCP algorithm

```
Algorithm iOCP(RTS, RTT, RTO)
repeat
    (s, t) = next_Euclidean_CP(RTS, RTT)
    dO(s, t) = compute_obstructed_distance(s, t)
    insert < (s, t), dO(s, t)> into Q
    for each (si, tj) such that dO(si, tj)≤ dE(s, t)
        de-heap <(si, tj), dO(si, tj)> from Q
        report <(si, tj), dO(si, tj)>
until termination condition
return
End iOCP
```

Fig. 12. *i*OCP algorithm

OCP first finds the k Euclidean pairs, it evaluates their obstructed distances and treats the maximum distance as d_{Emax}. Subsequent candidate pairs are retrieved incrementally, continuously updating the result and d_{Emax} until no pairs are found within the d_{Emax} bound. Note that the algorithm (and ONN presented in Section 4) is not suitable for *incremental* processing, where the value of k is not set in advance. Such a situation may occur if a user just browses through the results of a closest pair query (in increasing order of the pair distances), without a pre-defined termination condition. Another scenario where incremental processing is useful concerns complex queries: "find the city with more than 1M residents, which is closest to a nuclear factory". The output of the top-1 CP may not qualify the population constraint, in which case the algorithm has to continue reporting results until the condition is satisfied.

In order to process incremental queries we propose a variation of the OCP algorithm, called *i*OCP (for incremental), shown in Fig. 12 (note that now there is not a k parameter). When a Euclidean CP (s, t) is obtained, its obstructed distance $d_O(s, t)$ is computed and the entry $< (s, t), d_O(s, t)>$ is inserted into a queue Q. The observation is that all the pairs (s_i, t_j) in Q such that $d_O(s_i, t_j) \leq d_E(s, t)$, can be immediately reported, since no subsequent Euclidean CP can lead to a lower obstructed distance. The same methodology can be applied for deriving an incremental version of ONN.

7 Experiments

In this section, we experimentally evaluate the CPU time and I/O cost of the proposed algorithms, using a Pentium III 733MHz PC. We employ R*-trees [BKSS90], assuming a page size of 4K (resulting in a node capacity of 204 entries) and an LRU buffer that accommodates 10% of each R-tree participating in the experiments. The obstacle dataset contains $|O| = 131,461$ rectangles, representing the MBRs of streets in Los Angeles [Web] (but as discussed in the previous sections, our methods support arbitrary polygons). To control the density of the entities, the entity datasets are synthetic, with cardinalities ranging from $0.01 \cdot |O|$ to $10 \cdot |O|$. The distribution of the entities follows the obstacle distribution; the entities are allowed to lie on the boundaries of the obstacles but not in their interior. For the performance evaluation of the range and nearest neighbor algorithms, we execute workloads of 200 queries, which also follow the obstacle distribution.

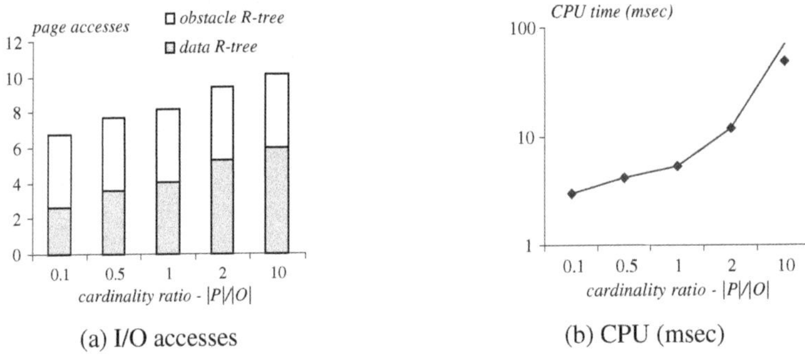

(a) I/O accesses (b) CPU (msec)

Fig. 13. Cost vs. $|P|/|O|$ (e=0.1%)

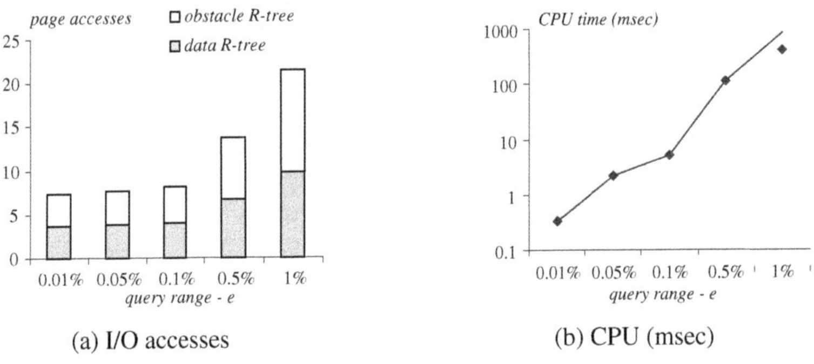

(a) I/O accesses (b) CPU (msec)

Fig. 14. Cost vs. e ($|P|$=$|O|$)

7.1 Range Queries

First, we present our experimental results on obstacle range queries. Fig. 13a and Fig. 13b show the performance of the OR algorithm in terms of I/O cost and CPU time, as functions of $|P|/|O|$ (i.e., the ratio of entity to obstacle dataset cardinalities), fixing the query range e to 0.1% of the data universe side length. The I/O cost for entity retrieval increases with $|P|/|O|$ because the nodes that lie within the (fixed) range e in the entity R-tree grows with $|P|$. However, the page accesses for obstacle retrieval remain stable, since the number of obstacles that participate in the distance computations (i.e., the ones intersecting the range) is independent of the entity dataset cardinality. The CPU time grows rapidly with $|P|/|O|$, because the visibility graph construction cost is $O(n^2 \log n)$ and the value of n increases linearly with the number of entities in the range (note the logarithmic scale for CPU cost).

Fig. 14 depicts the performance of OR as a function of e, given $|P|$=$|O|$. The I/O cost increases quadratically with e because the number of objects and nodes intersecting the Euclidean range is proportional to its area (which is quadratic with e). The CPU performance again deteriorates even faster because of the $O(n^2 \log n)$ graph construction cost.

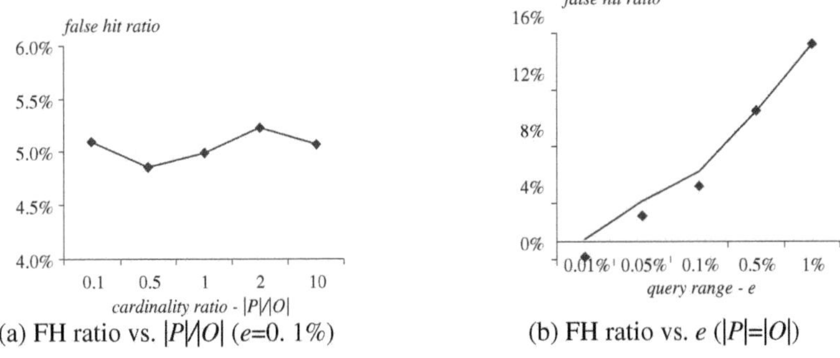

(a) FH ratio vs. $|P|/|O|$ (e=0. 1%) (b) FH ratio vs. e ($|P|$=$|O|$)

Fig. 15. False hit ratio by OR

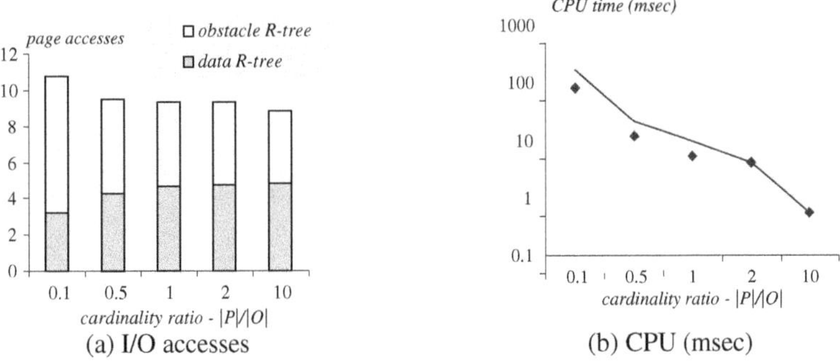

(a) I/O accesses (b) CPU (msec)

Fig. 16. Cost vs. $|P|/|O|$ (k=16)

The next experiment evaluates the number of false hits, i.e., objects within the Euclidean, but not in the obstructed range. Fig. 15a shows the false hit ratio (number of false hits / number of objects in the obstructed range) for different cardinality ratios (fixing e=0.1%), which remains almost constant (the absolute number of false hits increases linearly with $|P|$). Fig. 15b shows the false hit ratio as a function of e (for $|P|$ = $|O|$). For small e values, the ratio is low because the numbers of candidate entities and obstacles that obstruct their view is limited. As a result, the difference between Euclidean and obstructed distance is insignificant. On the other hand, the number of obstacles grows quadratically with e, increasing the number of false hits.

7.2 Nearest Neighbor Queries

This set of experiments focuses on obstacle nearest neighbor queries. Fig. 16 illustrates the costs of the ONN algorithm as function of the ratio $|P|/|O|$, fixing the number k of neighbors to 16. The page accesses of the entity R-tree do not increase fast with $|P|/|O|$ because, as the density increases, the range around the query point where the Euclidean neighbors are found decreases. As a result the obstacle search radius (and the number of obstacles that participate in the obstructed distance computations) also declines. Fig. 16b confirms this observation, showing that the CPU time drops significantly with the data density.

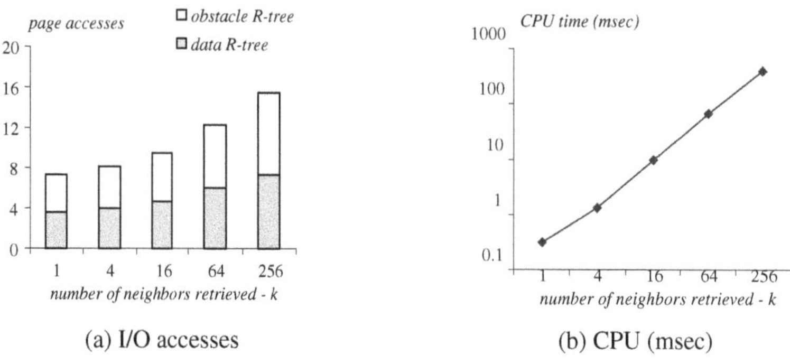

(a) I/O accesses (b) CPU (msec)

Fig. 17. Cost vs. k ($|P|=|O|$)

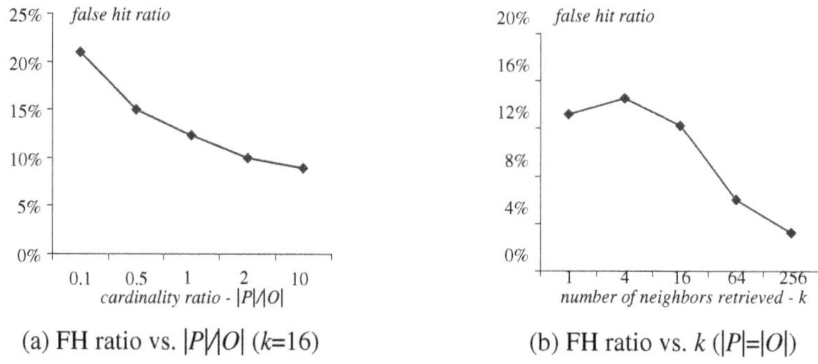

(a) FH ratio vs. $|P|/|O|$ (k=16) (b) FH ratio vs. k ($|P|=|O|$)

Fig. 18. False hit ratio by ONN

Fig. 17 shows the performance of ONN for various values of k when $|P|=|O|$. As expected, both the I/O cost and CPU time of the algorithm grow with k, because a high value of k implies a larger range to be searched (for entities and obstacles) and more distance computations. Fig. 18a shows the impact of $|P|/|O|$ on the false hit ratio ($k = 16$). A relatively small cardinality $|P|$ results in large deviation between Euclidean and obstructed distances, therefore incurring high false hit ratio, which is gradually alleviated as $|P|$ increases. In Fig. 18b we vary k and monitor the false hit ratio. Interestingly, the false hit ratio obtains its maximum value for $k \approx 4$ and starts decreasing when $k > 4$. This can be explained by the fact that, when k becomes high, the set of k Euclidean NN contains a big portion of the k actual (obstructed) NN, despite their probably different internal ordering (e.g., the 1st Euclidean NN is 3nd obstructed NN).

7.3 *e*-Distance Joins

We proceed with the performance study of the e-distance join algorithm, using $|T|=0.1|O|$ and setting the join distance e to 0.01% of the universe length. Fig. 19a plots the number of disk accesses as a function of $|S|/|O|$, ranging from 0.01 to 1. The number of page accesses for the entity R-trees grows much slower than the obstacle R-tree because the cost of the Euclidean join is not very sensitive to the data density.

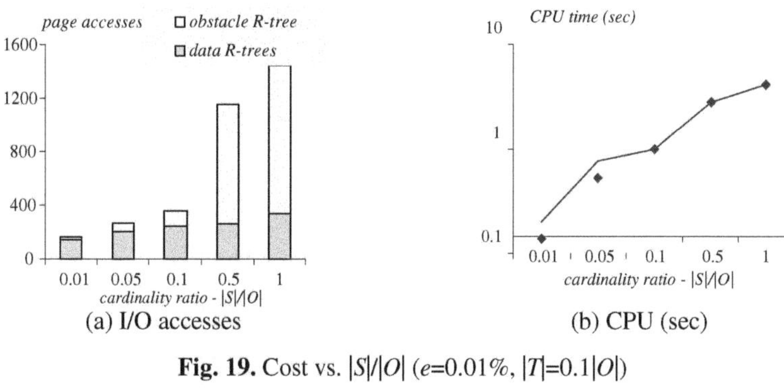

(a) I/O accesses (b) CPU (sec)

Fig. 19. Cost vs. $|S|/|O|$ (e=0.01%, $|T|$=0.1$|O|$)

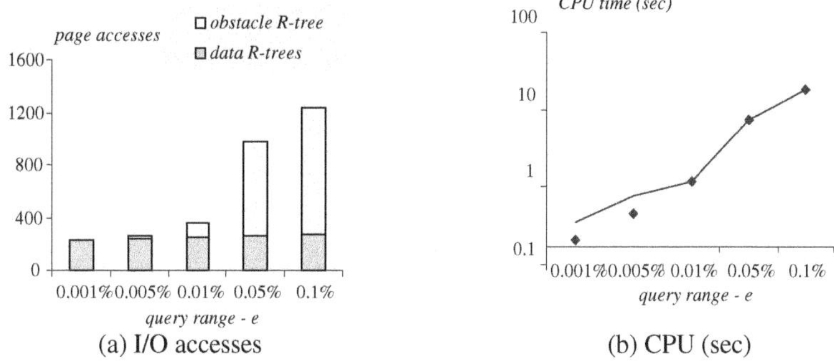

(a) I/O accesses (b) CPU (sec)

Fig. 20. Cost vs. e ($|S|$=$|T|$=0.1$|O|$)

On the other hand, the output size (of the Euclidean join) grows fast with the density, increasing the number of obstructed distance evaluations and the accesses to the obstacle R-tree (in the worst case each Euclidean pair initiates a new visibility graph). This observation is verified in Fig. 19b which shows the CPU cost as a function of $|S|/|O|$.

In Fig. 20a, we set $|S|$=$|T|$=0.1$|O|$ and measure the number of disk accesses for varying e. The page accesses for the entity R-tree do not have large variance (they range between 230 for e = 0.001% and 271 for e = 0.1%) because the node extents are large with respect to the range. However, as in the case of Fig. 20a, the output of the Euclidean joins (and the number of obstructed distance computations) grows fast with e, which is reflected in the page accesses for the obstacle R-tree and the CPU time (Fig. 20b).

7.4 Closest Pairs

Next, we evaluate the performance of closest pairs in the presence of obstacles. Fig. 21 plots the cost of the OCP algorithm as a function of $|S|/|O|$ for k=16 and $|T|$=0.1$|O|$. The I/O cost of the entity R-trees grows with the cardinality ratio (i.e., density of S), which is caused by the Euclidean closest-pair algorithm (similar observations were

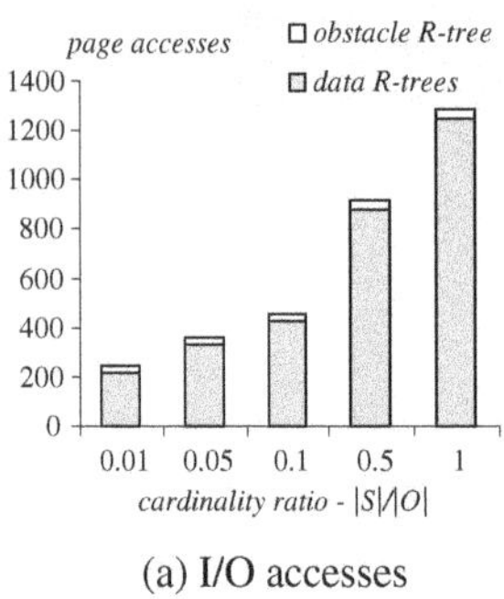

(a) I/O accesses

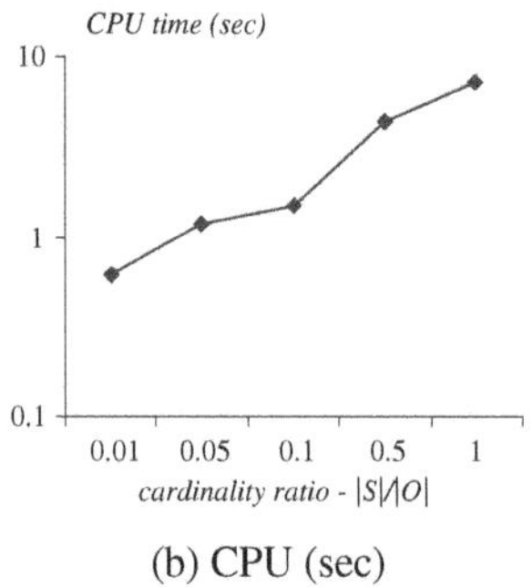

(b) CPU (sec)

Fig. 21. Cost vs. $|S|/|O|$ (k=16, $|T|$=0.1$|O|$)

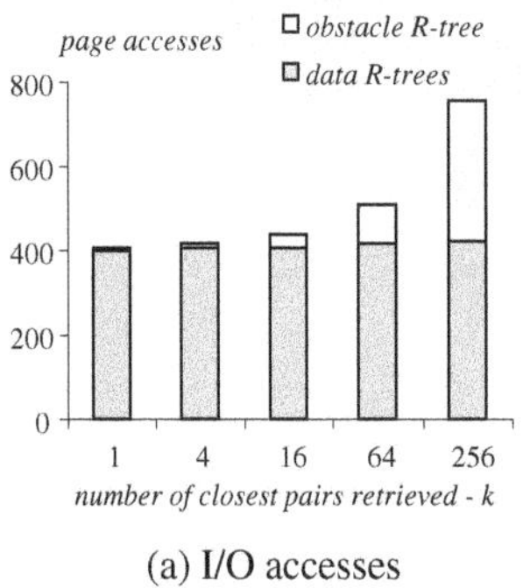

(a) I/O accesses

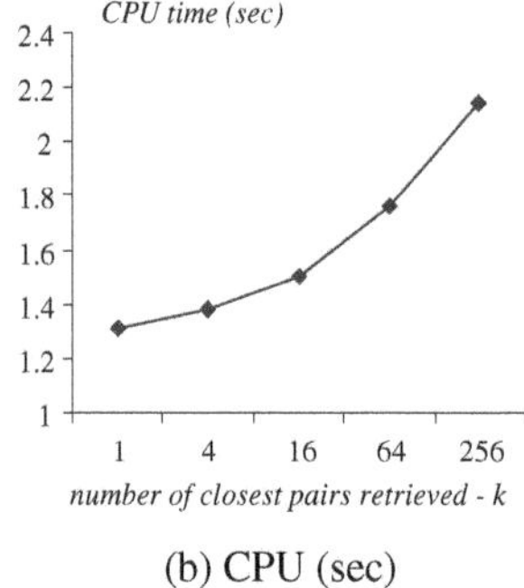

(b) CPU (sec)

Fig. 22. Cost vs. k ($|S|$=$|T|$=0.1$|O|$)

made in [CMTV00]). On the other hand, the density of S does not affect significantly the accesses to the obstacle R-tree because high density leads to closer distance between the Euclidean pairs. The CPU time of the algorithm (shown in Fig. 21b) grows fast with $|S|/|O|$, because the dominant factor is the computation required for obtaining the Euclidean closest pairs (as opposed to obstructed distances).

Fig. 22 shows the cost of the algorithm with $|S|$=$|T|$=0.1$|O|$ for different values of k. The page accesses for the entity R-trees (caused by the Euclidean CP algorithm) remain almost constant, since the major cost occurs before the first pair is output (i.e., the k closest pairs are likely to be in the heap after the first Euclidean NN is found, and are returned without extra IOs). The accesses to the obstacle R-tree and the CPU time, however, increase with k because more obstacles must be taken into account during the construction of the visibility graphs.

8 Conclusion

This paper tackles spatial query processing in the presence of obstacles. Given a set of entities P and a set of polygonal obstacles O, our aim is to answer spatial queries with respect to the obstructed distance metric, which corresponds to the length of the shortest path that connects them without passing through obstacles. This problem has numerous important applications in real life, and several main memory algorithms have been proposed in Computational Geometry. Surprisingly, there is no previous work for disk-resident datasets in the area of Spatial Databases.

Combining techniques and algorithms from both aforementioned fields, we propose an integrated framework that efficiently answers most types of spatial queries (i.e., range search, nearest neighbors, *e*-distance joins and closest pairs), subject to obstacle avoidance. Making use of local visibility graphs and effective R-tree algorithms, we present and evaluate a number of solutions. Being the first thorough study of this problem in the context of massive datasets, this paper opens a door to several interesting directions for future work. For instance, as objects move in practice, it would be interesting to study obstacle queries for moving entities and/or moving obstacles.

References

[AGHI86] Asano, T., Guibas, L., Hershberger, J., Imai, H. Visibility of Disjoint Polygons. Algorithmica 1, 49-63, 1986.

[BKOS97] de Berg, M., van Kreveld, M., Overmars, M., Schwarzkopf, O. Computational Geometry. pp. 305-315, Springer, 1997.

[BKS93] Brinkhoff, T., Kriegel, H., Seeger, B. Efficient Processing of Spatial Joins Using R-trees. SIGMOD, 1993.

[BKSS90] Becker, B., Kriegel, H., Schneider, R, Seeger, B. The R*-tree: An Efficient and Robust Access Method. SIGMOD, 1990.

[CMTV00] Corral, A., Manolopoulos, Y., Theodoridis, Y., Vassilakopoulos, M. Closest Pair Queries in Spatial Databases. SIGMOD, 2000.

[D59] Dijkstra, E. A Note on Two Problems in Connection with Graphs. Numeriche Mathematik, 1, 269-271, 1959.

[EL01] Estivill-Castro, V., Lee, I. Fast Spatial Clustering with Different Metrics in the Presence of Obstacles. ACM GIS, 2001.

[G84] Guttman, A. R-trees: A Dynamic Index Structure for Spatial Searching. SIGMOD, 1984.

[GM87] Ghosh, S., Mount, D. An Output Sensitive Algorithm for Computing Visibility Graphs. FOCS, 1987.

[HS98] Hjaltason, G., Samet, H. Incremental Distance Join Algorithms for Spatial Databases. SIGMOD, 1998.

[HS99] Hjaltason, G., Samet, H. Distance Browsing in Spatial Databases. TODS, 24(2), 265-318, 1999.

[KHI+86] Kung, R., Hanson, E., Ioannidis, Y., Sellis, T., Shapiro, L. Stonebraker, M. Heuristic Search in Data Base Systems. Expert Database Systems, 1986.

[LW79] Lozano-Pérez, T., Wesley, M. An Algorithm for Planning Collision-free Paths among Polyhedral Obstacles. CACM, 22(10), 560-570, 1979.

[PV95] Pocchiola, M., Vegter, G. Minimal Tangent Visibility Graph. Computational Geometry: Theory and Applications, 1995.

[PV96] Pocchiola, M., Vegter, G. Topologically Sweeping Visibility Complexes via Pseudo-triangulations. Discrete Computational Geometry, 1996.

[PZMT03] Papadias, D., Zhang, J., Mamoulis, N., Tao, Y. Query Processing in Spatial Network Databases. VLDB, 2003.

[R95] Rivière, S. Topologically Sweeping the Visibility Complex of Polygonal Scenes. Symposium on Computational Geometry, 1995.

[SRF87] Sellis, T., Roussopoulos, N. Faloutsos, C. The R+-tree: a Dynamic Index for Multi-Dimensional Objects. VLDB, 1987.

[SS84] Sharir, M., Schorr, A. On Shortest Paths in Polyhedral Spaces. STOC, 1984.

[THH01] Tung, A., Hou, J., Han, J. Spatial Clustering in the Presence of Obstacles. ICDE, 2001.

[W85] Welzl, E. Constructing the Visibility Graph for *n* Line Segments in $O(n^2)$ Time, Information Processing Letters 20, 167-171, 1985.

[Web] http://www.maproom.psu.edu/dcw.

NNH: Improving Performance of Nearest-Neighbor Searches Using Histograms

Liang Jin[1*], Nick Koudas[2], and Chen Li[1*]

[1] Information and Computer Science, University of California, Irvine, CA 92697, USA
{liangj,chenli}@ics.uci.edu
[2] AT&T Labs Research, 180 Park Avenue, Florham Park, NJ 07932, USA
koudas@research.att.com

Abstract. Efficient search for nearest neighbors (NN) is a fundamental problem arising in a large variety of applications of vast practical interest. In this paper we propose a novel technique, called NNH ("Nearest Neighbor Histograms"), which uses specific histogram structures to improve the performance of NN search algorithms. A primary feature of our proposal is that such histogram structures can co-exist in conjunction with a plethora of NN search algorithms without the need to substantially modify them. The main idea behind our proposal is to choose a small number of pivot objects in the space, and pre-calculate the distances to their nearest neighbors. We provide a complete specification of such histogram structures and show how to use the information they provide towards more effective searching. In particular, we show how to construct them, how to decide the number of pivots, how to choose pivot objects, how to incrementally maintain them under dynamic updates, and how to utilize them in conjunction with a variety of NN search algorithms to improve the performance of NN searches. Our intensive experiments show that nearest neighbor histograms can be efficiently constructed and maintained, and when used in conjunction with a variety of algorithms for NN search, they can improve the performance dramatically.

1 Introduction

Nearest-neighbor (NN) searches arise in a large variety of applications such as image and video databases [1], CAD, information retrieval (IR) [2], data compression [3], and string matching/searching [4]. The basic version of the k-NN problem is to find the k nearest neighbors of a query object in a database, according to a distance measurement. In these applications, objects are often characterized by features and represented as points in a multi-dimensional space. For instance, we often represent an image as a multi-dimensional vector using features such as histograms of colors and textures. A typical query in an image database is to find images most similar to a given query image utilizing such features. As another example, in information retrieval, one often wishes to locate

* These two authors were supported by NSF CAREER award No. IIS-0238586 and a UCI CORCLR grant.

E. Bertino et al. (Eds.): EDBT 2004, LNCS 2992, pp. 385–402, 2004.
© Springer-Verlag Berlin Heidelberg 2004

documents that are most similar to a given query document, considering a set of features extracted from the documents [2].

Variations of the basic k-NN problem include high-dimensional joins between point sets. For instance, an *all-pair k-nearest neighbor join* between two point sets seeks to identify the k closest pairs among all pairs from two sets [5,6]. An *all-pair k-nearest neighbor semi-join* between two point sets reports, for each object in one data set, its k nearest neighbors in the second set [5].

Many algorithms have been proposed to support nearest-neighbor queries. Most of them use a high-dimensional indexing structure, such as an R-tree [7] or one of its variations. For instance, in the case of an R-tree, these algorithms use a branch-and-bound approach to traverse the tree top down, and use distance bounds between objects to prune branches (minimum-bounding rectangles, MBR's) that do not need to be considered [8,9]. A priority queue of interior nodes is maintained based on their distances to the query object. In the various forms of high-dimensional joins between point sets, a queue is maintained to keep track of pairs of objects or nodes in the two data sets.

One of the main challenges in these algorithms is to perform effective pruning of the search space, and subsequently achieve good search performance. The performance of such an algorithm heavily depends on the number of disk accesses (often determined by the number of branches visited in the traversal) and its runtime memory requirements, which indicates memory (for priority-queue storage) and processor requirements for maintaining and manipulating the queue. Performance can deteriorate if too many branches are visited and/or too many entries are maintained in the priority queue, especially in a high-dimensional space due to the well-known "curse of dimensionality" problem [1].

In this paper we develop a novel technique to improve the performance of these algorithms by keeping histogram structures (called "NNH"). Such structures record the nearest-neighbor distances for a preselected collection of objects ("pivots"). These distances can be utilized to estimate the distance at which the k-nearest neighbors for each query object can be identified. They can subsequently be used to improve the performance of a variety of nearest-neighbor search and related algorithms via more effective pruning. The histogram structures proposed can co-exist in conjunction with a plethora of NN algorithms without the need to substantially modify these algorithms.

There are several challenges associated with the construction and use of such structures. (1) The construction time should be small, their storage requirements should be minimal, and the estimates derived from them should be precise. (2) They should be easy to use towards improving the performance of a variety of nearest-neighbor algorithms. (3) Such structures should support efficient incremental maintenance under dynamic updates. In this paper we provide a complete specification of such histogram structures, showing how to efficiently and accurately construct them, how to choose pivots effectively, how to incrementally maintain them under dynamic updates, and how to utilize them in conjunction with a variety of NN algorithms to improve the performance of searches.

The rest of the paper is organized as follows. Section 2 outlines the formal definition of a nearest-neighbor histogram (NNH) structure. In Section 3 we show how to use such histograms to improve the performance for a variety of NN algorithms. Section 4 discusses how to choose pivots in such a structure. In Section 5 we discuss how to incrementally maintain an NN histogram structure in the presence of dynamic updates. In Section 6 we report our extensive experimental results, evaluating the construction time, maintenance algorithms, and the efficiency of our proposed histograms when used in conjunction with a variety of algorithms for NN search to improve their performance. Due to space limitation, we provide more results in [10].

Related Work: Summary structures in the form of histograms have been utilized extensively in databases in a variety of important problems, such as selectivity estimation [11,12] and approximate query answering [13,14]. In these problems, the main objective is to approximate the distribution of frequency values using specific functions and a limited amount of space.

Many algorithms exist for efficiently identifying the nearest neighbors of low and high-dimensional data points for main memory data collections in the field of computational geometry [15]. In databases, many different families of high-dimensional indexing structures are available [16], and various techniques are known for performing NN searches tailored to the specifics of each family of indexing structures. Such techniques include NN searches for the *entity grouping* family of indexing structures (e.g., R-trees [7]) and NN searches for the *space partitioning* family (e.g., Quad-trees [17]). In addition to the importance of NN queries as stand-alone query types, a variety of other query types make use of NN searches. *Spatial or multidimensional* joins [18] are a representative example of such query types. Different algorithms have been proposed for spatial NN semi-joins and all-pair NN joins [5]. NN search algorithms can benefit from the histogram structures proposed in this paper enabling them to perform more effective pruning. For example, utilizing a good estimate to the distance of the k-th nearest neighbor of a query point, one can form essentially a range query to identify nearest neighbors, using the query object and the estimated distance and treating the search algorithm as a "black box" without modifying its code.

Various studies [19,20,21,22] use notions of pivots or anchors or foci for efficient indexing and query processing. We will compare our approach with these methods in Section 6.4.

2 NNH: Nearest-Neighbor Histograms

Consider a data set $D = \{p_1, \dots, p_n\}$ with n objects in a Euclidean space $\Re^d$ under some l_p form. Formally, there is a distance function $\Delta : \Re^d \times \Re^d \rightarrow \Re$, such that given two objects p_i and p_j, their distance is defined as

$$\Delta(p_i, p_j) = \Big(\sum_{1 \le l \le d} |x_l^i - x_l^j|^p \Big)^{1/p} \qquad (1)$$

$(x_1^i, \dots, x_d^i)$ and $(x_1^j, \dots, x_d^j)$ are coordinates of objects p_i and p_j, respectively.

Definition 1. *(NN Search) Given a query object, a j-Nearest Neighbor (NN) search returns the j points in the database that are closest to the query object.*

Given an object p in the space, its *NN distance vector* of size t is a vector $v(p) = \langle r_1, \ldots, r_t \rangle$, in which each r_i is the distance of p's i-th nearest neighbor in the database D. A *nearest-neighbor histogram* (NNH) of the data set, denoted H, is a collection of objects (called "pivots") with their NN vectors. In principle, these pivot points may or may not correspond to points in the database. In the rest of the paper, we assume that the pivots are *not* part of the data set for the purpose of easy dynamic maintenance, as discussed in Section 5. Initially all the vectors have the same length, denoted T, which is a design parameter and forms an upper bound on the number of neighbors NN queries specify as their desired result. We choose to fix the value of T in order to control the storage requirement for the NNH structure [23]. For any pivot p, let $H(p, j)$ denote the j-NN distance of p recorded in H. Let

$$H(p) = \langle H(p, 1), \ldots, H(p, T) \rangle \tag{2}$$

denote the NN vector for a pivot p in the histogram H.

Pivot IDs	Coordinates	NN Vectors					
1	$(0.3, 1.2, \ldots, 2.5)$	1.34	1.50	1.57	1.67	1.97	2.23
2	$(3.6, 2.8, \ldots, 0.7)$	0.95	1.62	1.84	1.98	2.04	2.31
$\vdots$	$\vdots$			$\vdots$			
50	$(1.7, 0.2, \ldots, 3.0)$	1.36	1.49	1.87	2.02	2.15	2.34

$T = 6$

Fig. 1. An NN histogram structure H.

Figure 1 shows such a structure. It has $m = 50$ pivots, each of which has an NN vector of size $T = 6$. For instance, $H(p_1, 3) = 1.57$, $H(p_2, 6) = 2.31$, and $H(p_{50}, 5) = 2.15$. In Section 4 we discuss how to choose pivots to construct a histogram. Once we have chosen pivots, for each p of them, we run a T-NN search to find all its T nearest neighbors. Then, for each $j \in \{1, \ldots, T\}$, we calculate the distance from the j-th nearest neighbor to the object p, and use these T distances to construct an NN vector for p.

3 Improving Query Performance

In this section we discuss how to utilize the information captured by nearest neighbor histograms to improve query performance. A number of important queries could benefit from such histograms, including k-nearest neighbor search (k-NN) and various forms of high-dimensional joins between point sets, such as *all-pair k-nearest neighbor joins* (i.e., finding k closest pairs among all the pairs between two data sets), and k-nearest neighbor semi-joins (i.e., finding k NN's in the second data set for each object in the first set). The improvements to such algorithms are twofold: (a) the processor time can be reduced substantially due to advanced pruning. This reduction is important since for data sets of high dimensionality, distance computations are expensive and processor time becomes a significant fraction of overall query-processing time [24]; and (b) the memory requirement can be reduced significantly due to the much smaller queue size. Most NN algorithms assume a high-dimensional indexing structure on the data set. To simplify our presentation, we choose to highlight how to utilize our histogram structures to improve the performance of common queries involving R-trees [7]. Similar concepts carry out easily to other structures (e.g. SS-tree [25], SR-tree [26], etc.) and algorithms as well.

3.1 Utilizing Histograms in k-NN Queries

A typical k-NN search involving R-trees follows a branch-and-bound strategy traversing the index top down. It maintains a priority queue of active minimum bounding rectangles (MBR's) [8,9]. At each step, it maintains a bound to the k-NN distance, δ, from the query point q. This bound is initialized to infinity when the search starts. Using the geometry of an MBR mbr and the coordinates of query object q, an upper-bound distance of q to the nearest point in the mbr, namely $MINMAXDIST(q, mbr)$, can be derived [27]. In a similar fashion, a lower bound, namely $MINDIST(q, mbr)$, is derived. Using these estimates, we can prune MBR's from the queue as follows: (1) For an MBR mbr, if its $MINDIST(q, mbr)$ is greater than $MINMAXDIST(q, mbr')$ of another MBR mbr', then mbr can be pruned. (2) If $MINDIST(q, mbr)$ for an MBR mbr is greater than δ, then this mbr can be pruned.

In the presence of NN histograms, we can utilize the distances to estimate an upper bound of the k-NN of the query object q. Recall that the NN histogram includes the NN distances for selected pivots only, and it does not convey immediate information about the NN distances of objects not encoded in the histogram structure. We can estimate the distance of q to its k-NN, denoted δ_q, using the triangle inequality between q and any pivot p_i in the histogram:

$$\delta_q \leq \Delta(q, p_i) + H(p_i, k), 1 \leq i \leq m.^1 \tag{3}$$

Thus, we can obtain an upper bound estimate δ_q^{est} of δ_q as

$$\delta_q^{est} = \min_{1 \leq i \leq m} \left(\Delta(q, p_i) + H(p_i, k) \right) \tag{4}$$

The complexity of this estimation step is $O(m)$. Since the histogram structure is small enough to fit in the memory, and the number of pivots is small, the above estimation can be conducted efficiently. After computing the initial estimate δ_q^{est},

[1] Note that we use $H(p_i, k)$ instead of $H(p_i, k-1)$ because in this paper we assume that the pivots are *not* part of the database.

we can use this distance to help the search process prune MBR's. That is, the search progresses by evaluating $MINMAXDIST$ and $MINDIST$ between q and an R-tree MBR mbr as before. Besides the standard pruning steps discussed above, the algorithm also checks if

$$MINDIST(q, mbr) > \delta_q^{est} \tag{5}$$

is true. If so, then this mbr can be pruned. Thus we do not need to insert it into the queue, reducing the memory requirement (queue size) and the later operations of this MBR in the queue.

Notice that the algorithm in [8,9] is shown to be IO optimal [28]. Utilizing our NNH structure may not reduce the number of IOs during the R-tree traversal. However, our structure can help reduce the size of the priority queue, and the number of queue operations. This reduction can help reduce the running time of the algorithm, as shown in our experiments in Section 6. In addition, if the queue becomes too large to fit into memory, this reduction could even help us reduce the IO cost since part of the queue needs to be paged on disk.

3.2 Utilizing Histograms in k-NN Joins

A related methodology could also be applied in the case of all-pairs k-NN join queries using R-trees. The bulk of algorithms for this purpose progress by inserting pairs of MBR's between index nodes from corresponding trees in a priority queue and recursively (top-down) refining the search. In this case, using k-NN histograms, one could perform, in addition to the type of pruning highlighted above, even more powerful pruning.

More specifically, let us see how to utilize such a histogram to do pruning in a k-NN semi-join search [5]. This problem tries to find for each object o_1 in a data set D_1, all o_1's k-nearest neighbors in a data set D_2. (This pruning technique can be easily generalized to other join algorithms.) If the two data sets are the same, the join becomes a self semi-join, i.e., finding k-NN's for all objects in the data set. Assume the two data sets are indexed in two R-trees, R_1 and R_2, respectively. A preliminary algorithm described in [5] keeps a priority queue of MBR pairs between index nodes from the two trees. In addition, for each object o_1 in D_1, we can keep track of objects o_2 in D_2 whose pair $\langle o_1, o_2 \rangle$ has been reported. If $k = 1$, we can just keep track of D_1 objects whose nearest neighbor has been reported. For $k > 1$, we can output its nearest neighbors while traversing the trees, thus we only need to keep a counter for this object o_1. We stop searching for neighbors of this object when this counter reaches k.

Suppose we have constructed a histogram H_2 for data set D_2. We can utilize H_2 to prune portions of the search space in bulk by pruning pairs of MBR's from the priority queue as follows. For each object o_1 in D_1, besides the information kept in the original search algorithm, we also keep an estimated radius δ_{o_1} of the k-NN in D_2 for this object. We can get an initial estimate for δ_{o_1} as before (Section 3.1). Similarly, we will not insert a pair (o_1, mbr_2) into the queue if $MINDIST(o_1, mbr_2) \geq \delta_{o_1}$. In this way we can prune more object-MBR pairs.

Now we show that this histogram is even capable to prune MBR-MBR pairs. For each MBR mbr_1 in tree R_1, consider a pivot p_i in the NN histogram H_2 of dataset D_2. For each possible object o_1 in mbr_1, using the triangle inequality between o_1 and p_i, we know that the k-NN distance to o_1:

$$\delta_{o_1} \leq \Delta(o_1, p_i) + H_2(p_i, k) \leq MAXDIST(mbr_1, p_i) + H_2(p_i, k). \tag{6}$$

$MAXDIST(mbr_1, p_i)$ is an upper bound of the distance between any object in mbr_1 and object p_i. Therefore,

$$\delta^{est}_{mbr_1} = \min_{p_i \in H_2} (MAXDIST(mbr_1, p_i) + H_2(p_i, k)) \tag{7}$$

is an upper bound for the k-NN distance for any object o_1 in mbr_1. It can be used to prune any (mbr_1, mbr_2) from the queue, if $\delta^{est}_{mbr_1} \leq MINDIST(mbr_1, mbr_2)$ is true, where $MINDIST(mbr_1, mbr_2)$ is the lower bound of the distance between any pair of objects from mbr_1 and mbr_2 respectively. In order to use this technique to do pruning, in addition to keeping an estimate for the distance of the k-NN for each object in data set D_1, we also keep an estimate of distance δ_{mbr_1} for each MBR mbr_1 in R_1. This number tends to be smaller than the number of objects in D_1. These MBR-distance estimates can be used to prune many MBR-MBR pairs, reducing the queue size and the number of disk IO's.

Pruning in all-pair k-nearest neighbor joins: The pruning techniques described above can be adapted to perform more effective pruning when finding the k-nearest pairs among all pairs of objects from two data sets [5,6]. Notice that so far we have assumed that only D_2 has a histogram H_2. If the first data set D_1 also has a histogram H_1, similar pruning steps using H_1 can be done to do more effective pruning, since the two sets are symmetric in this join problem.

4 Constructing NNH Using Good Pivots

Pivot points are vital to NNH for obtaining distance estimates in answering NN queries. We now turn to the problems associated with the choice of pivot points, and the number of pivots. Assume we decide to choose m pivot points. The storage requirement for NNH becomes $O(mT)$, since for each pivot point p we will associate a vector of p's distances to its T-NN's. Let the m pivot points be $p_1, \dots, p_m$. Given a query point q, we can obtain an estimate to the distance of q's k-NN, δ^{est}_q, by returning

$$\min_{1 \leq i \leq m} \big(\Delta(q, p_i) + H(p_i, k)\big) \tag{8}$$

This estimate is an upper bound of the real distance of q to its k-NN point and is obtained utilizing the triangle inequality, among q, a pivot point p_i, and p_i's k-NN point. Assuming that the true distance of q to its k-NN is $\Delta_k(q)$. This estimation incurs an error of

$$\min_{1 \leq i \leq m} \big(\Delta(q, p_i) + H(p_i, k)\big) - \Delta_k(q). \tag{9}$$

The expected error for the estimation of any k-NN query q ($1 \leq k \leq T$) becomes:

$$\frac{1}{T}\sum_{k=1}^{T}\Big(\min_{1\leq i\leq m}\left(\Delta(q,p_i)+H(p_i,k)\right)-\Delta_k(q)\Big) \tag{10}$$

The larger the number of pivot points m, the larger the space requirements of the corresponding NNH structure. However, the larger m, the higher the chances of obtaining a more accurate estimate δ_q^{est}. It is evident that by increasing the number of pivot points, we increase the storage overhead of NNH, but potentially improve its estimation accuracy.

4.1 Choosing Pivots

Given the number of pivot points m devoted to the NNH, we want to choose the best m pivots to minimize the expected distance estimation error for any query q. Query points are not known in advance, and any query point q on the data set D could be equally likely. Moreover, the parameter k in a k-NN distance estimate is also not known in advance, but provided at run time. At best we are aware of an upper bound for it. For this reason, we decide to minimize the term

$$\Delta(q,p_i)+H(p_i,k), 1\leq i\leq m \tag{11}$$

providing the estimate to the k-NN query, by choosing as pivot points the set S of m points that minimize the quantity:

$$\sum_{q\in D, p_i\in S}\Delta(q,p_i) \tag{12}$$

That is, we minimize distances to pivot points assuming queries are points of D. This goal is the well-known objective of the clustering problem and consequently we obtain the m cluster centroids of D, as pivots. It is, in expectation, the best choice of m pivots, provided that query points q belong to D, assuming no knowledge of the number of NN points k-NN queries specify. This choice has the added utility of enabling a plethora of known clustering algorithms (e.g., [29, 30]) to be applied in our problem of selecting the pivots.

4.2 Choosing the Number of Pivots

We now present our methodology for deciding the number of pivots m to use when constructing an NNH structure. We start by describing a way to quantify the benefits of an NNH with a given number of pivots. Consider an NN search for a query object q. We use both the standard algorithm [8] and the improved one described in Section 3.1. The *queue-size-reduction ratio* of the NNH with m pivots for this search is:

$$\text{reduction ratio} = 1 - \frac{\text{max queue size of improved algorithm}}{\text{max queue size of standard algorithm}} \tag{13}$$

This ratio indicates how much memory the NNH can save by reducing the queue size. Notice that we could also use the kNN semi-join operation to define the corresponding queue-size-reduction ratio. Our experiments showed no major difference between the results of these two definitions, so we adopt the former operation for defining queue-size-reduction.

Given a number m, we use the approach in Section 4.1 to find m good pivots. We randomly select a certain number (say, 10) of objects in the data set to perform NN searches, and calculate the average of their queue-size-reduction ratios. The average value, denoted B_m, is a good measurement of the benefits of the NNH with m pivots. In particular, using standard tail inequality theory [31] one can show that such an estimate converges (is an unbiased estimate) to the true benefit for random queries as the size of the sample grows. We omit the details due to lack of space.

Our algorithm for deciding the m value for a data set is shown in Figure 2. Its main idea is as follows: we first initialize m to a small number (e.g., 5) and measure the average queue-size-reduction ratio B_m. Then we increment the number of pivots (using the parameter SP) and judge how much benefit (in terms of the reduction ratio) the increased number of pivots can achieve. When there is no big difference (using the parameter ε) between consecutive rounds, the algorithm terminates and reports the current number of pivots.

One potential problem of this iterative algorithm is that it could "get stuck" at a local optimal number of pivots (since the local gain on the reduction ratio becomes small), although it is still possible to achieve a better reduction ratio using a larger pivot number. We can modify the algorithm slightly to solve this

Algorithm
Input: • D: data set.
• SP: step for incrementing the number of pivots.
• ε: Condition to stop searching.
Output: a good number of pivots.
Variables: • B_{new}: reduction ratio in current iteration.
• B_{old}: reduction ratio in last iteration.
• m: number of pivots.
Method:
$B_{new} \leftarrow 0.0$; $m \leftarrow 0$;
DO {
  $B_{old} \leftarrow B_{new}$;
  $m \leftarrow m + SP$;
  Choose m pivots to construct an NNH;
  Perform kNN queries for sampled objects using the NNH;
  $B_{new} \leftarrow$ average reduction ratio of the searches;
}
WHILE (B_{new} - $B_{old} > \varepsilon$);
RETURN m;

Fig. 2. Algorithm for deciding pivot number

problem. Before the algorithm terminates, it "looks forward" to check a larger pivot number, and see if we can gain a better reduction ratio. Techniques for doing so are standard in hill-climbing type of algorithms [32] and they can be readily incorporated if required.

5 Incremental Maintenance

In this section we discuss how to maintain an NN histogram in the presence of dynamic updates (insertions/deletions) in the underlying database. Under dynamic updates, a number of important issues arise. When a new object is inserted, it could affect the structure of the nearest neighbors of many pivots, possibly prompting changes to their NN vectors. Similarly, when an object is deleted, it could also change the NN structure of pivots. We associate a separate value E_i for each pivot p_i, which identifies the number of positions (starting from the beginning) in the vector $H(p_i)$ that can be utilized to provide distance estimates. All the distances after the E_i-th position cannot be used for NN distance-estimation purposes, since as a result of some update operations they are not valid anymore. Initially, $E_i = T$ for all the pivots.

Insertion: Upon insertion of an object o_{new} into the data set, we perform the following task. For each pivot p_i whose E_i nearest neighbors may include o_{new}, we need to update their NN vectors. We scan all the pivots in the histogram, and for each pivot p_i, we compute the distance between p_i and the new object, i.e., $\Delta(p_i, o_{new})$. Consider the distance vector of p_i in the NN histogram: $H(p_i) = \langle r_1, \ldots, r_{E_i} \rangle$. We locate the position of $\Delta(p_i, o_{new})$ in this vector. Assume

$$r_{j-1} \leq \Delta(p_i, o_{new}) < r_j$$

where $j \leq E_i$. There are two cases. (1) Such a position cannot be found. Then this new object cannot be among the E_i nearest neighbors of p_i and we do not need to update this NN vector. (2) Such a position is found. o_{new} cannot be among the (j-1)-NN objects of p_i. Therefore, we can insert this distance $\Delta(p_i, o_{new})$ to the j-th slot in the NN vector, and shift the $(E_i - j)$ distances after the slot to the right. Correspondingly, we increment the number of valid distances for this vector E_i by 1. If E_i becomes larger than T, we set $E_i = T$.

Deletion: When deleting an object o_{del}, we need to update the vectors for the pivots whose nearest neighbors may have included o_{del}. For each pivot p_i, similarly to the insertion case, we consider the distance vector of p_i in H. We locate the position of $\Delta(p_i, o_{del})$ in this vector and update the vector similarly to the insertion case, except now we need to shrink the vector if necessary. Notice that in this paper we assume that the pivots are *not* part of the database, deleting a data point from the database will not affect the formation of pivots. It only could change the values in the NN vectors.

The worst case complexity of each procedure above for insertions and deletions is $O(m * T * log(T))$, where m is the number of pivots in the histogram, and T is the maximal length of each distance vector. The reason is that we can do a binary search to find the inserting position of $\Delta(p_i, o_{new})$ or $\Delta(p_i, o_{del})$ in the NN vector of p_i, which takes $O(log(T))$ time. If the position is found, we need $O(T)$ time to shift the rest of the vector (if we use a simple array implementation of the vector in memory). This operation is executed for all the m pivots in the histogram. Since the number of pivots is small and the histogram can fit in memory, the maintenance cost is low (see Section 6.3). After many insertions and deletions, if the valid length of an NN vector becomes too small, we can recompute a new NN distance for this pivot by doing a T-NN search. In addition, we can periodically run the algorithms in Section 4 to choose a new collection of pivots and construct the corresponding NN histogram.

6 Experiments

In this section we present the results of an experimental evaluation assessing the utility of the proposed NNH techniques when used in conjunction with algorithms involving NN searches. We used two datasets in the evaluation. (1) A Corel image database (Corel). It consists of $60,000$ color histogram features. Each feature is a 32-dimensional float vector. (2) A time-series data set from the AT&T Labs. It consists of 5 million numerical values generated for a fixed time span. We constructed datasets with different dimensionalities by using different time-window sizes. Both datasets exhibit similar trend in the results. We mainly focus on reporting the results of the Corel image database. We will use the time-series data to show the effects of dimensionality in our NNH approach and evaluate different approaches to choosing pivots.

All experiments were performed on a SUN Ultra 4 workstation with four 300MHz CPU's and 3GB memory, under the SUN OS 4.7 operating system. The software was compiled using GNU C++, using its maximum optimization ("-O4"). For the priority queue required in the algorithm described in [8,9], we used a heap implementation from the Standard Template Library [33].

6.1 Improving k-NN Search

We present experiments showing the effectiveness of NNH for NN searches using R-trees on the Corel database. In general, any indexing technique that follows a branch-and-bound strategy to answer NN queries can be used. As an example, we implemented the k-NN algorithm described in [8,9], using an R-tree with a page size of $8,192$ bytes. We refer to this algorithm as the "standard version" of the NN search. We assume that a query object may not belong to the data set. We performed pruning as described in Section 3.1. We refer to it as the "improved version" of the NN algorithm.

Reducing Memory Requirements and Running Time: Several important factors affect the performance of a k-NN search including memory usage, running time, and number of IO's. Memory usage impacts running time significantly, since the larger the priority queue gets, the more distance comparisons the algorithm has to perform. At large dimensionality, distance comparisons are a significant fraction of the algorithm's running time.

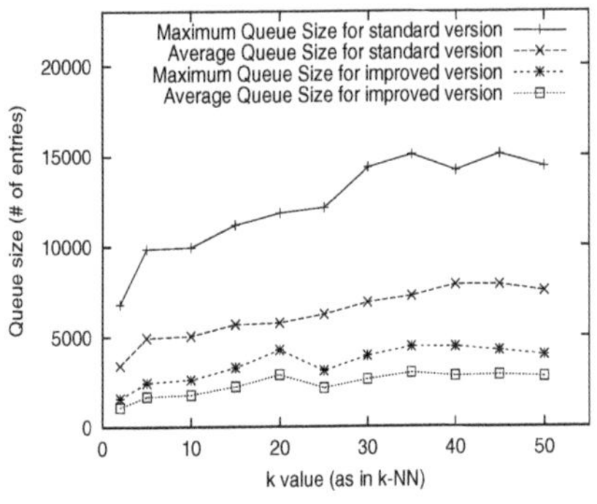

Fig. 3. Queue size of k-NN search.

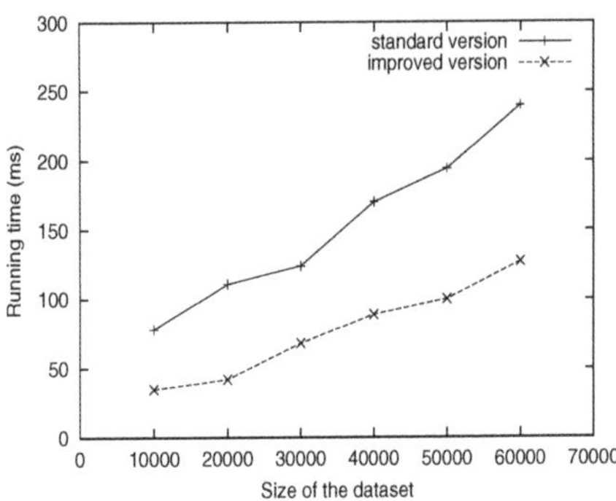

Fig. 4. Running Time for 10-NN queries.

We use the size of the priority queue to measure memory usage, since additional memory requirements are relatively small. Figure 3 shows the maximal queue size and the average queue size for the standard and improved versions of the NN algorithm. We first ran a k-means algorithm to generate 100 pivots, and constructed the NN histogram with $T = 50$. Then we performed 10-NN queries for 100 randomly generated query objects, and calculated the average number for both the maximal queue size and the average queue size. We observe that we can reduce both the queue sizes dramatically by utilizing the NNH to prune the search. For instance, when searching for the 10-NN's for a query object, the average queue size of the standard version was $5,036$, while it was only $1,768$ for the improved version, which was only about 35% of that of the standard version.

Figure 4 shows the running times for different dataset sizes for both versions, when we ran 10-NN queries. The improved version can always speed up the query as the size increases. This improvement increases as the size of the dataset increases. The reason is that, increasing the size of the dataset increases the size of the priority queue maintained in the algorithm. As a result, the standard version has to spend additional processor time computing distances between points and MBR's of the index. In contrast the effective pruning achieved by the improved version reduces this overhead.

Choosing the Number of Pivots: As discussed in Section 4, by choosing the pivots using cluster centroids, the larger the number of pivots, the better the distance estimates, and as a result the better performance improvement. Figure 5 shows the performance improvement for different numbers of pivots when we ran 10-NN queries for the $60,000$-object Corel data set. The first data point in the figure represents the standard version: its maximum queue size is $13,772$, its average queue size is $6,944$. It is shown that as the number of pivots increases, both the maximal queue size and the average queue size decrease. For instance, by keeping only 100 pivots, we can reduce the memory requirement by more than 66%. This improvement increases as we have more pivots. The extra gain for this data set is not significant, exhibiting a diminishing-returns phenomenon. As a result, it is evident that for this data set, an NNH of very small size can offer very large performance advantages. Our algorithm in Section 4.2 reported

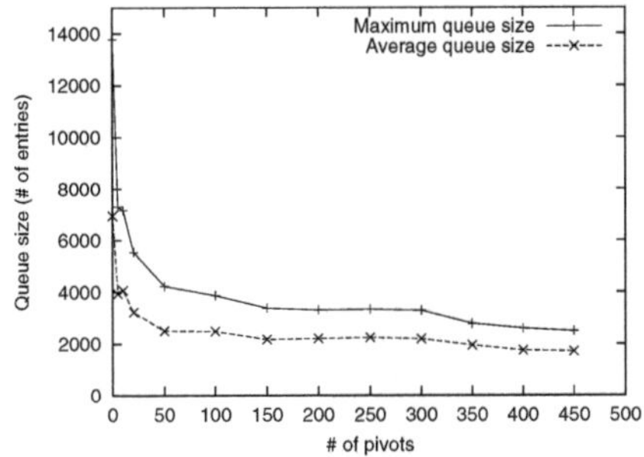

Fig. 5. Performance for different # of pivots

100 as the "optimal" number of pivots with $\epsilon = 0.1\%$ and $SP = 5$. This result is consistent with the intuition obtained by the observation of Figure 5. We also deployed the suitable queue-size-reduction ratio definition for k-NN semi-join, and obtained similar results.

6.2 Improving k-NN Joins

We implemented the k-NN semi-join algorithm in [5]. We performed a semi-join using two different subsets D_1 and D_2 (with the same size) of objects in the Corel data set, to find k-nearest neighbors for each object in D_1, allowing k to vary from 1 to 50. We constructed an NNH H_2 for D_2, with 100 pivots and $T = 50$. We implemented the approach in Section 3.2 to prune the priority queue. During the traversal, we tried to perform a depth-first search on the R-tree of the first data set, so that pruning for the objects in the trees enabled by the histograms can be used as early as possible.

Reducing Memory Requirements and Running Time: We collected the maximal and average queue sizes for both the standard version and the improved one. Figure 6(a) presents the results. It is shown that additional pruning using the NNH histograms makes the semi-join algorithm much more efficient. For instance, when we performed a 10-NN semi-join search, the maximal and average queue size of the standard version were 10.2M (million) and 6.3M respectively, while it was only 2.1M and 1.2M for the improved version.

We also measured the running time for both versions. The results are shown in Figure 6(b). Clearly by using the improved version, we can reduce the running time dramatically. For instance, when performing a 10-NN semi-join, utilizing the NNH structure we can reduce the time from 1,132 seconds to 219 seconds. Figure 7(a) and (b) show the running times and queue sizes for different $|D_1| = |D_2|$ data sizes. The figures show that as the data size increases, the semi-join with pruning achieves significant performance advantages.

To evaluate the effect of different dimensionalities, we used the time-series dataset. We constructed each record with different window sizes from the dataset to achieve different dimensionalities. We extracted two data sets D_1 and D_2,

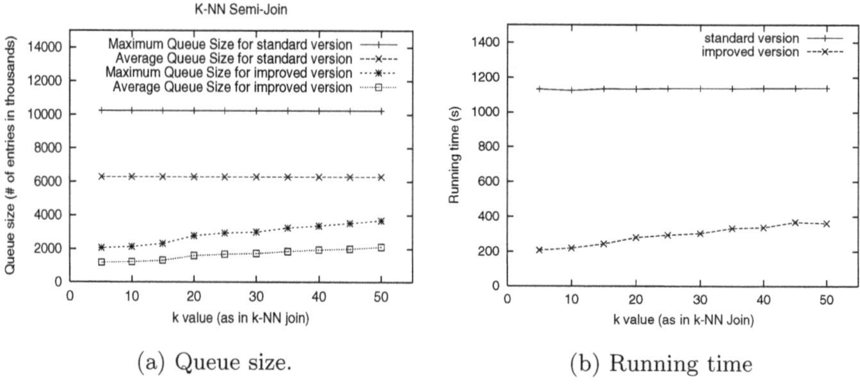

(a) Queue size. (b) Running time

Fig. 6. Semi-join performance improvement for different k values.

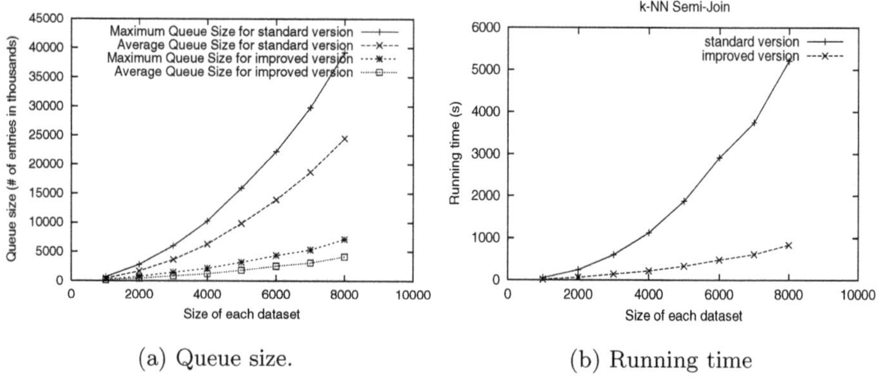

(a) Queue size. (b) Running time

Fig. 7. Semi-join performance for different data sizes.

and each contained 2000 records. Figure 8(a) shows that the NNH structure can consistently help to reduce the maximal and average queue sizes. As shown in Figure 8(a), it appears that there is no strong correlation between the dimensionality and the effect of the NNH structure. The reason is that for the range of dimensions shown in the figure, the number of clusters in the underlying datasets remains stable. Figure 8(b) shows the same trend for the running time for different dimensionalities. The running time of the improved version takes around 33% of the time of the standard version. The effectiveness of our NNH structure remains stable for different dimensionalities. We also evaluated the effect of different numbers of pivots in the k-NN semi-join, and observed similar results as the single k-NN case.

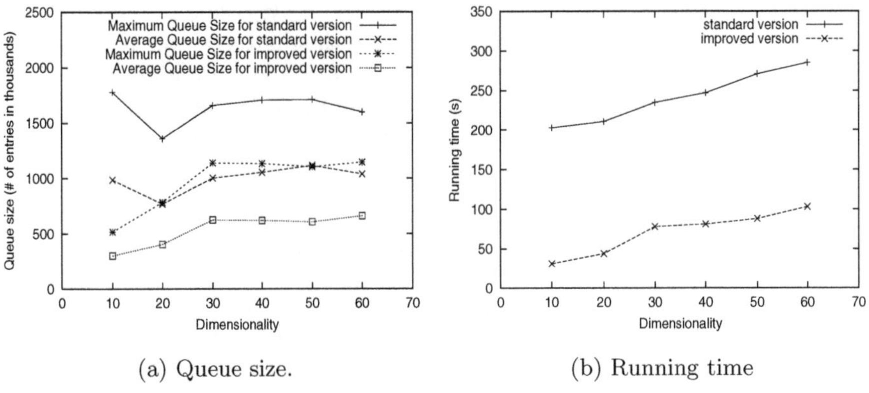

(a) Queue size. (b) Running time

Fig. 8. Semi-join performance for different dimensionalities.

6.3 Costs and Benefits of NN Histograms

While it is desirable to have a large number of pivots in an NNH, we should also consider the costs associated with such a structure. In particular, we should pay attention to (1) the storage space; (2) the initial construction cost (off-line); and (3) the incremental-maintenance cost in the case of database updates (online).

We measured these different costs, as well as the performance improvement for different numbers of pivots. We performed 10-NN queries and semi-joins on our 60,000-object Corel dataset with different numbers of pivots, and measured the costs. For each pivot, we maintain its 50 NN radii, thus, $T = 50$. Table 1 shows the time to construct the NNH, the required storage space for NNH, and the time for a single dynamic maintenance operation (insertion or deletion). Notice that entries for the maintenance time per each update are all zero, corresponding to times below the precision of our timing procedures. The two queue-size rows represent the ratio of the improved maximal queue sizes versus that of the standard version. For instance, when we had 100 pivots in the NNH, the maximal-queue-size-reduction ratio was 72% for a single 10-NN query. We do not include the numbers for the average-queue size since they follow the same trend as the maximal queue sizes.

Table 1. Costs and benefits of an NNH structure.

Number of pivots	10	50	100	150	200	250	300	350	400
Construction Time (sec)	2.1	10.2	19.8	28.2	34.1	40.8	48.6	53.4	60.2
Storage space (kB)	2	10	20	30	40	50	60	70	80
Time for dynamic maintenance (ms $\approx$)	0	0	0	0	0	0	0	0	0
Queue reduction ratio(k-NN) (%)	60	70	72	76	76	76	77	80	82
Queue reduction ratio (semi-join) (%)	70	72	74	77	77	78	79	79	80

From the table we can see that the size of the NNH is small, compared to the size of the data set, 28.5MB. The construction time is very short (e.g., less than 20 seconds for an NNH with 100 pivots). The incremental-maintenance time is almost negligible. The performance improvement is substantial: for instance, by keeping 100 pivots we can reduce the maximal queue size by 72% in a 10-NN search, and 74% in a semi join.

6.4 Comparison with Other Methods of Choosing Pivots

The final set of experiments we present compares our clustering approach of choosing pivots to existing methods of selecting pivots to improve similarity search in metric spaces [19,20,21,34]. The studies in [20,21] claim that it is desirable to select pivots that are far away from each other and from the rest of the elements in the database. These studies converge on the claim that the number of pivots should be related to the "intrinsic dimensionality" of a dataset [35]. Although such an approach makes sense in the context of the problem these works address, it is not suitable for the problem at hand. The reason is that, an NNH relies on the local information kept by each pivot to estimate the distances of the nearest neighbors to a query object, so that effective pruning can be performed. Thus, the way we choose the number of pivots depends on how clustered the objects are, so does the way we choose the pivots. In particular, the number of pivots depends on how many clusters data objects form. In addition, it is desirable to choose a pivot that is very close to many objects, so that it can capture the local distance information about these objects. Thus, the selected pivots might not be too far from each other, depending upon the distribution of the objects. Clearly outliers are not good pivots for NNH, since they cannot capture the local information of the neighboring objects.

We chose the approach presented in [21] as a representative of these methods, denoted as "OMNI." We compared this approach and our clustering approach of choosing pivots in NNH in terms of their effect of reducing the queue size and running time in an NN search. Our experiments showed that our clustering approach of choosing pivots is more effective in reducing the queue size and the running time than the OMNI approach. See [10] for more details.

Summary: our intensive experiments have established that the improved pruning enabled via the use of an NNH structure can substantially improve the performance of algorithms involving k-NN searches, while the costs associated with such a structure are very low. These improvements increase as the size of the data sets increases, leading to more effective and scalable algorithms. It is evident that standard algorithms for k-NN search and join problems are significantly challenged when the size of the data sets increases. Their run-time memory requirements increase significantly and performance degrades rapidly. The improved pruning techniques via the use of NNH can alleviate these problems, reducing the run-time memory requirements (and subsequently processor requirements) significantly.

7 Conclusions

In this paper we proposed a novel technique that uses nearest-neighbor histogram structures to improve the performance of NN search algorithms. Such histogram structures can co-exist in conjunction with a plethora of NN search algorithms without the need to substantially modify them. The main idea is to preprocess the data set, and selectively obtain a set of pivot points. Using these points, the NNH is populated and then used to estimate the NN distances for each object, and make use of this information towards more effective searching. We provided a complete specification of such histogram structures, showing how to efficiently and accurately construct them, how to incrementally maintain them under dynamic updates, and how to utilize them in conjunction with a variety of NN search algorithms to improve the performance of NN searches. Our intensive experiments showed that such a structure can be efficiently constructed and maintained, and when used in conjunction with a variety of NN-search algorithms, could offer substantial performance advantages.

References

1. Faloutsos, C., Ranganathan, M., Manolopoulos, I.: Fast Subsequence Matching in Time Series Databases. Proceedings of ACM SIGMOD (1994) 419–429
2. Salton, G., McGill, M.J.: Introduction to modern information retrieval. McGraw-Hill (1983)
3. Gersho, A., Gray, R.: Vector Quantization and Data Compression. Kluwer (1991)
4. Ferragina, P., Grossi, R.: The String B-Tree: A New Data Structure for String Search in External Memory and Its Applications. Journal of ACM 46,2, pages 237–280, Mar. 1999 (1999)
5. Hjaltason, G.R., Samet, H.: Incremental distance join algorithms for spatial databases. In: SIGMOD. (1998)
6. Shin, H., Moon, B., Lee, S.: Adaptive multi-stage distance join processing. In: SIGMOD. (2000)
7. Guttman, A.: R-trees: A dynamic index structure for spatial searching. In: Proceedings of ACM SIGMOD. (1984) 47–57
8. Hjaltason, G.R., Samet, H.: Ranking in spatial databases. In: Symposium on Large Spatial Databases. (1995) 83–95
9. Hjaltason, G.R., Samet, H.: Distance browsing in spatial databases. ACM Transactions on Database Systems **24** (1999) 265–318
10. Jin, L., Koudas, N., Li, C.: NNH: Improving performance of nearest-neighbor searches using histograms (full version). Technical report, UC Irvine (2002)
11. Jagadish, H.V., Koudas, N., Muthukrishnan, S., Poosala, V., Sevcik, K.C., Suel, T.: Optimal Histograms with Quality Guarantees. VLDB (1998) 275–286
12. Mattias, Y., Vitter, J.S., Wang, M.: Dynamic Maintenance of Wavelet-Based Histograms. Proceedings of VLDB, Cairo, Egypt (2000) 101–111
13. Acharya, S., Gibbons, P., Poosala, V., Ramaswamy, S.: The Aqua Approximate Query Answering System. Proceedings of ACM SIGMOD (1999) 574–578
14. Vitter, J., Wang, M.: Approximate computation of multidimensional aggregates on sparse data using wavelets. Proceedings of SIGMOD (1999) 193–204

15. Preparata, F.P., Shamos, M.I.: Computational Geometry. Springer-Verlag, New York-Heidelberg-Berlin (1985)
16. Gaede, V., Gunther, O.: Multidimensional Access Methods. ACM Computing Surveys (1998)
17. Samet, H.: The Design and Analysis of Spatial Data Structures. Addison Wesley (1990)
18. Brinkhoff, T., Kriegel, H.P., Seeger, B.: Efficient Processing of Spatial Joins using R-trees. Proceedings of ACM SIGMOD (1993) 237–246
19. Brin, S.: Near neighbor search in large metric spaces. In: The VLDB Journal. (1995) 574–584
20. Bustos, B., Navarro, G., Ch'avez, E.: Pivot selection techniques for proximity searching in metric spaces. In: Proc. of the XXI Conference of the Chilean Computer Science Society (SCCC'01). (2001)
21. Filho, R.F.S., Traina, A.J.M., Jr., C.T., Faloutsos, C.: Similarity search without tears: The OMNI family of all-purpose access methods. In: ICDE. (2001) 623–630
22. Vleugels, J., Veltkamp, R.C.: Efficient image retrieval through vantage objects. In: Visual Information and Information Systems. (1999) 575–584
23. Tsaparas, P., Palpanas, T., Kotidis, Y., Koudas, N., Srivastava, D.: Ranked Join Indicies. ICDE (2003)
24. Weber, R., Schek, H., Blott, S.: A Quantitative Analysis and Performance Study for Similarity Search Methods in High Dimensional Spaces. VLDB (1998)
25. White, D.A., Jain, R.: Similarity indexing with the ss-tree. In: ICDE. (1996) 516–523
26. Katayama, N., Satoh, S.: The SR-tree: an index structure for high-dimensional nearest neighbor queries. In: Proceedings of ACM SIGMOD. (1997) 369–380
27. Roussopoulos, N., Kelley, S., Vincent, F.: Nearest neighbor queries. In: SIGMOD. (1995) 71–79
28. Berchtold, S., Böhm, C., Keim, D.A., Kriegel, H.P.: A cost model for nearest neighbor search in high-dimensional data space. In: PODS. (1997) 78–86
29. Guha, S., Rastogi, R., Shim, K.: CURE: An Efficient Clustering Algorithm for Large Databases. Proceedings of ACM SIGMOD (1998) 73–84
30. Ng, R.T., Han, J.: Efficient and effective clustering methods for spatial data mining. In: VLDB, Los Altos, USA, Morgan Kaufmann Publishers (1994) 144–155
31. Motwani, R., Raghavan, P.: Randomized Algorithms. Prentice Hall (1997)
32. Bishop, C.: Neural Networks for Pattern Recognizion. Oxford University Press (1996)
33. Standard Template Library: http://www.sgi.com/tech/stl/ (2003)
34. Yianilos: Data structures and algorithms for nearest neighbor search in general metric spaces. In: SODA: ACM-SIAM. (1993)
35. Chavez, E., Navarro, G., Baeza-Yates, R.A., Marroquin, J.L.: Searching in metric spaces. ACM Computing Surveys **33** (2001) 273–321

Clustering Multidimensional Extended Objects to Speed Up Execution of Spatial Queries

Cristian-Augustin Saita and François Llirbat

INRIA-Rocquencourt
Domaine de Voluceau, B.P. 105
78153 Le Chesnay Cedex, France
firstname.lastname@inria.fr

Abstract. We present a cost-based adaptive clustering method to improve average performance of spatial queries (intersection, containment, enclosure queries) over large collections of multidimensional extended objects (hyper-intervals or hyper-rectangles). Our object clustering strategy is based on a cost model which takes into account the spatial object distribution, the query distribution, and a set of database and system parameters affecting the query performance: object size, access time, transfer and verification costs. We also employ a new grouping criterion to group objects in clusters, more efficient than traditional approaches based on minimum bounding in all dimensions. Our cost model is flexible and can accommodate different storage scenarios: in-memory or disk-based. Experimental evaluations show that our approach is efficient in a number of situations involving large spatial databases with many dimensions.

1 Introduction

In this paper we present a cost-based adaptive clustering solution to faster answer *intersection, containment, or enclosure-based spatial queries* over large collections of *multidimensional extended objects.* While a multidimensional point defines single values in all dimensions, a *multidimensional extended object* defines range intervals in its dimensions. A multidimensional extended object is also called *hyper-interval* or *hyper-rectangle.* Although a point can be also represented as an extended object (with zero-length extensions over dimensions), we are interested in collections of objects with real (not null) extensions.

Motivation. Our work is motivated by the development of new dissemination-based applications (SDI or Selective Dissemination of Information) [1][8][12]. Such applications involve timely delivery of information to large sets of subscribers and include stock exchange, auctions, small ads, and service delivery. Let us consider a publish-subscribe notification system dealing with small ads. An example of subscription is "Notify me of all new apartments within 30 miles from Newark, with a rent price between 400$ and 700$, having between 3 and 5 rooms, and 2 baths". In this example, most subscription attributes specify range intervals instead of single values. Range subscriptions are more suitable for notification systems. Indeed, subscribers often wish to consult the set of alternative

E. Bertino et al. (Eds.): EDBT 2004, LNCS 2992, pp. 403–421, 2004.
© Springer-Verlag Berlin Heidelberg 2004

offers that are close to their wishes. Range intervals allow them to express more flexible matching criteria. High rates of new offers (events), emitted by publishers, need to be verified against the subscription database. The role of the system is to quickly retrieve and notify all the subscribers matching the incoming events. The events can define either single values or range intervals for their attributes. An example of range event is "Apartments for rent in Newark: 3 to 5 rooms, 1 or 2 baths, 600-900". In such context, subscriptions and events can be represented as *multidimensional extended objects.* The matching subscriptions are retrieved based on *intersection, containment, or enclosure queries* (spatial range or window queries). In some applications the reactivity of the notification system is crucial (stock exchange, auctions). As the number of subscriptions can be large (millions) and the number of possible attributes significant (tens of dimensions), an indexing method is required to ensure a good response time. Such method should cope with large collections of multidimensional extended objects, with many dimensions, and with high rates of events (actually spatial queries).

Problem Statement. Most multidimensional indexing methods supporting spatial queries over collections of multidimensional extended objects descend from the R-tree approach[11]. R-tree employs minimum bounding boxes (MBBs) to hierarchically organize the spatial objects in a height-balanced tree. Construction constraints like preserving tree height balance or ensuring minimal page utilization, corroborated with the multidimensional aspect, lead to significant overlap between MBBs at node level. During searches, this overlap determines the exploration of multiple tree branches generating serious performance degradation (notably for range queries). Because the probability of overlap increases with the number of dimensions [2][4], many techniques have been proposed to alleviate the "dimensional curse". Despite this effort, experiments show that, for more than 5-10 dimensions, a simple database Sequential Scan outperforms complex R-tree implementations like X-tree[4], or Hilbert R-tree[9]. This was reported for range queries over collections of hyper-space points [3]. When dealing with spatially-extended data, the objects themselves may overlap each others, further increasing the general overlap and quickly leading to poor performance. For these reasons, R-tree-based methods can not be used in practice on collections of multidimensional extended objects with more than a few dimensions.

Contributions. We propose a new approach to cluster multidimensional extended objects, to faster answer spatial range queries (intersection, containment, enclosure), and to satisfy the requirements outlined in our motivation section: large collections of objects, many dimensions, high rates of spatial queries, and frequent updates. Our main contributions are:

1. An adaptive cost-based clustering strategy: Our cost-based clustering strategy takes into account the spatial data distribution and the spatial query distribution. It is also parameterized by a set of database and system parameters affecting the query performance: object size, disk access time, disk transfer rate, and object verification cost. The cost model is flexible and can easily adapt different storage scenarios: in-memory or disk-based. Using the cost-based clustering we always guarantee better average performance than Sequential Scan.

2. An original criterion for clustering objects: Our adaptive clustering strategy is enabled by a new approach to cluster objects, which consists in clustering together objects with "similar" intervals on a restrained number of dimensions. The grouping intervals/dimensions are selected based on local statistics concerning cluster-level data distribution and cluster access probability, aiming to minimize the cluster exploration cost. Our object clustering proves to be more efficient than classical methods employing minimum bounding in all dimensions.

Paper Organization. The rest of the paper is organized as follows: Section 2 reviews the related work. Section 3 presents our adaptive cost-based clustering solution and provides algorithms for cluster reorganization, object insertion, and spatial query execution. Section 4 presents our grouping criterion. Section 5 provides details on the cost model supporting the clustering strategy. Section 6 considers implementation-related aspects like model parameters and storage utilization. Section 7 experimentally evaluates the efficiency of our technique, comparing it to alternative solutions. Finally, conclusions are presented in Section 8.

2 Related Work

During last two decades numerous indexing techniques have been proposed to improve the search performance over collections of multidimensional objects. Recent surveys review and compare many of existing multidimensional access methods [10][6][17]. From these surveys, two families of solutions can be distinguished. First family descends from the K-D-tree method and is based on recursive space partitioning in disjoint regions using one or several, alternating or not, split dimensions: quad-tree, grid file, K-D-B-tree, hB-tree, but also Pyramid-tree and VA-file [1]. These indexing methods work only for multidimensional points. Second family is based on the R-tree technique introduced in [11] as a multidimensional generalization of B-tree. R-tree-based methods evolved in two directions. One aimed to improve performance of nearest neighbor queries over collection of multidimensional points: SS-tree, SR-tree, A-tree [2]. Since we deal with extended objects, these extensions do not apply in our case. The other direction consisted in general improvements of the original R-tree approach, still supporting spatial queries over multidimensional extended objects: R^+-tree[14], R^*-tree[2]. Although efficient in low-dimensional spaces (under 5-10 dimensions), these techniques fail to beat Sequential Scan in high dimensions due to the large number of nodes/pages that need to be accessed and read in a random manner. Random disk page read is much more expensive than sequential disk page read. In general, to outperform Sequential Scan, no more than 10% of tree nodes should be (randomly) accessed, which is not possible for spatial range queries over extended objects with many dimensions. To transform the random access into sequential scan, the concept of *supernode* was introduced in X-tree[4]. Multiple pages are assigned to directory nodes for which the split would generate too much overlap. The size of a supernode is determined based

[1] See surveys [10][6] for further references.

[2] See surveys [6][17] for further references.

on a cost model taking into account the actual data distribution, but not considering the query distribution. A cost-based approach is also employed in [7] to dynamically compute page sizes based on data distribution. In [15] the authors propose a general framework for converting traditional indexing structures to adaptive versions exploiting both data and query distributions. Statistics are maintained in a global histogram dividing the data space into bins/cells of equal extent/volume. Although efficient for B-trees, this technique is impractical for high-dimensional R-trees: First, because the number of histogram bins grows exponentially with the number of dimensions. Second, the deployed histogram is suitable for hyper-space points (which necessarily fit the bins), but is inappropriate for hyper-rectangles that could expand over numerous bins. Except for the node size constraint, which is relaxed, both X-tree and Adaptive R-tree preserve all defining properties of the R-tree structure: height balance, minimum space bounding, balanced split, and storage utilization. In contrast, we propose an indexing solution which drops these constraints in favor of a cost-based object clustering. In high-dimensional spaces, VA-File method[16] is a good alternative to tree-based indexing approaches. It uses approximated (compressed) data representation and takes advantage of Sequential Scan to faster perform searches over collections of multidimensional points. However, this technique can manage only point data. An interesting study regarding the optimal clustering of a static collection of spatial objects is presented in [13]. The static clustering problem is solved as a classical optimization problem, but data and query distributions need to be known in advance.

3 Cost-Based Database Clustering

Our database clustering takes into consideration both data and query distributions, and allows clusters to have variable sizes. Statistical information is associated to each cluster and employed in the cost model, together with other database and system parameters affecting the query performance: object size, disk access cost, disk transfer rate, and object check rate. The cost model supports the creation of new clusters and the detection and removal of older inefficient clusters.

3.1 Cluster Description

A *cluster* represents a group of objects accessed and checked together during spatial selections. The grouping characteristics are represented by the *cluster signature*. The cluster signature is used to verify (a) if an object can become a member of the cluster: only objects matching the cluster signature can become cluster members; (b) if the cluster needs to be explored during a spatial selection: only clusters whose signatures are matched by the spatial query are explored. To evaluate the average query cost, we also associate each cluster signature with two performance indicators:

1. The number of queries matching the cluster signature over a period of time: This statistics represents a good indicator for the *cluster access probability*. Indeed, the access probability can be estimated as the ratio between the number of queries exploring the cluster and the total number of queries addressed to the system over a period of time.

2. The number of objects matching the cluster signature: When combined with specific database and system parameters (object size, object access, transfer and verification costs), this statistics allows to estimate the *cluster exploration cost*. Indeed, cluster exploration implies individual checking of each of its member objects.

3.2 Clustering Strategy

The clustering process is recursive in spirit and is accomplished by relocating objects from existing clusters in new (sub)clusters when such operation is expected to be profitable. Initially, the collection of spatial objects is stored in a single cluster, *root cluster*, whose general signature accepts any spatial object. The access probability of the root cluster is always 1 because all the spatial queries are exploring it. At root cluster creation we invoke the *clustering function* to establish the signatures of the potential subclusters of the root cluster. The potential subclusters of an existing cluster are further referred as *candidate (sub)clusters*. Performance indicators are maintained for the root cluster and all its candidate subclusters. Decision of cluster reorganization is made periodically after a number of queries are executed and after performance indicators are updated accordingly. Clustering decision is based on the *materialization benefit function* which applies to each candidate subcluster and evaluates the potential profit of its materialization. Candidate subclusters with the best expected profits are selected and materialized. A subcluster materialization consists in two actions: First, a new cluster with the signature of the corresponding candidate subcluster is created: all objects matching its signature are moved from the parent cluster. Second, the clustering function is applied on the signature of the new cluster to determine its corresponding candidate subclusters. Performance indicators are attached to each of the new candidate subclusters in order to gather statistics for future re-clustering. Periodically, clustering decision is re-considered for all materialized clusters. As a result, we obtain a tree of clusters, where each cluster is associated with a signature and a set of candidate subclusters with the corresponding performance indicators. Sometimes, the separate management of an existing cluster can become inefficient. When such situation occurs, the given cluster is removed from the database and its objects transferred back to the parent cluster (direct ancestor in the clustering hierarchy). This action is called *merging operation* and permits the clustering to adapt changes in object and query distributions. A merging operation is decided using the *merging benefit function* which evaluates its impact on the average spatial query performance. To facilitate merging operations, each database cluster maintains a reference to the direct parent, and a list of references to the child clusters. The root cluster has no parent and can not be removed from the spatial database.

3.3 Functions Supporting the Clustering Strategy

Clustering Function. Based on the signature σ_c of the database cluster c, the *clustering function* γ produces the set of signatures $\{\sigma_s\}$ associated to the candidate subclusters $\{s\}$ of c. Formally, $\gamma(\sigma_c) \to \{\sigma_s\}$; $\sigma_s \in \gamma(\sigma_c)$ is generated such that any spatial object qualifying for the subcluster s also qualifies for the cluster c. It is possible for a spatial object from the cluster c to satisfy the signatures of several subclusters of c. The clustering function ensures a backward object compatibility in the clustering hierarchy. This property enables merging operations between child and parent clusters.

Materialization Benefit Function. Each database cluster is associated with a set of candidate subclusters potentially qualifying for materialization. The role of the *materialization benefit function* β is to estimate for a candidate subcluster the impact on the query performance of its possible materialization. For this purpose, β takes into consideration the performance indicators of the candidate subcluster, the performance indicators of the original cluster, and the set of database and system parameters affecting the query response time. Formally, if $\sigma_s \in \gamma(\sigma_c)$ (s is a candidate subcluster of the cluster c) then

$$\beta(s,c) \to \begin{cases} > 0 \text{ if materialization of } s \text{ is profitable;} \\ \leq 0 \text{ otherwise.} \end{cases}$$

Merging Benefit Function. The role of the *merging benefit function* μ is to evaluate the convenience of the merging operation. For this purpose, μ takes into consideration the performance indicators of the considered cluster, of the parent cluster, and the set of system parameters affecting the query response time. Formally, if $\sigma_c \in \gamma(\sigma_a)$ (a is the parent cluster of the cluster c) then

$$\mu(c,a) \to \begin{cases} > 0 \text{ if merging } c \text{ to } a \text{ is profitable;} \\ \leq 0 \text{ otherwise.} \end{cases}$$

Table 1. Notations

$\mathcal{C}$	set of materialized clusters	$parent(\mathtt{c})$	parent cluster of cluster c
$\sigma(\mathtt{c})$	signature of cluster c	$children(\mathtt{c})$	set of child clusters of cluster c
$n(\mathtt{c})$	nb. of objects in cluster c	$candidates(\mathtt{c})$	set of candidate subclusters of c
$q(\mathtt{c})$	nb. of exploring queries of c	$objects(\mathtt{c})$	set of objects from cluster c
$p(\mathtt{c})$	access probability of c	$\beta(), \mu()$	benefit functions

3.4 Cluster Reorganization

Regarding an existent cluster, two actions might improve the average query cost: the cluster could be split by materializing some of its candidate subclusters, or the cluster could be merged with its parent cluster. Figures 1, 2, and 3 depict the procedures invoked during the cluster reorganization process. Table 1 summarizes the notations used throughout the presented algorithms.

The main cluster reorganization schema is sketched in Fig. 1. First, the merging benefit function μ is invoked to estimate the profit of the merging operation.

```
ReorganizeCluster ( cluster c )
  1.  if μ(c, parent(c)) > 0 then MergeCluster(c);
  2.  else TryClusterSplit(c);
End.
```

Fig. 1. Cluster Reorganization Algorithm

```
MergeCluster ( cluster c )
  1.  let a ← parent(c);
  2.  Move all objects from c to a;
  3.  let n(a) ← n(a) + n(c);
  4.  for each s in candidates(a) do
  5.     let M(s, c) ← {o ∈ objects(c) | o matches σ(s)};
  6.     let n(s) ← n(s) + card(M(s, c));
  7.  for each s in children(c) do
  8.     let parent(s) ← a;
  9.  Remove c from database;
End.
```

Fig. 2. Cluster Merge Algorithm

If a positive profit is expected the merging procedure is executed. Otherwise, a cluster split is attempted. When none of the two actions is beneficial for the query performance, the database cluster remains unchanged.

The merging procedure is detailed in Fig. 2. The objects from the input cluster are transferred to the parent cluster (step 2). This requires actualization of the performance indicators associated to the clusters involved: the number of objects in the parent cluster, as well as the number of objects for each candidate subcluster of the parent cluster (steps 4-6). To preserve the clustering hierarchy, the parent cluster becomes the parent of the children of the input cluster (steps 7-8). Finally, the input cluster is removed from database (step 9).

The cluster split procedure is depicted in Fig. 3. The candidate subclusters promising the best materialization profits are selected in step 1: $\mathcal{B}$ is the set of the best candidate subclusters exhibiting positive profits. If $\mathcal{B}$ is not empty (step 2), one of its members becomes subject to materialization (step 3): a new database cluster is created (step 4), the objects qualifying for the selected candidate are identified (step 5) and moved from the input cluster to the new cluster (step 6), the configuration of the new cluster is set in step 7 (signature, number of objects, parent cluster), the number of remaining objects in the input cluster is updated (step 10), as well as the number of objects in the candidate subclusters of the input cluster (steps 11-13). Steps 11-13 are necessary because objects from the input cluster might qualify for several candidate subclusters. This is possible because the candidate subclusters are virtual clusters. However, once removed from the input cluster, an object can no more qualify for the candidate subclusters. The split procedure continues with the selection of the next best candidate subclusters. The materialization process repeats from step 1 until no profitable candidate is found. The selection is performed in a greedy manner

```
TryClusterSplit ( cluster c )
  1.  let B ← {b ∈ candidates(c) | β(b,c) > 0 ∧
                 β(b,c) ≥ β(d,c), ∀d ≠ b ∈ candidates(c)};
  2.  if (B ≠ ∅) then
  3.     let b ∈ B;
  4.     Create new database cluster d;
  5.     let M(b,c) = {o ∈ objects(c) | o matches σ(b)};
  6.     Move M(b,c) objects from c to d;
  7.     let σ(d) ← σ(b); let n(d) ← n(b); let parent(d) ← c;
  8.     let n(c) ← n(c) − n(d);
  9.     for each s in candidates(c) do
 10.        let M(s,d) ← {o ∈ objects(d) | o matches σ(s)};
 11.        let n(s) ← n(s) − card(M(s,d));
 12.     go to 1.
End.
```

Fig. 3. Cluster Split Algorithm

and the most profitable candidates are materialized first. To take into consideration the changes from the input cluster and from the candidate subclusters, induced by subsequent materializations, the set of best candidates $\mathcal{B}$ needs to be re-computed each time (step 1). At the end, the input cluster will host the objects not qualifying for any of the new materialized subclusters.

3.5 Object Insertion

When inserting a new object in the spatial database, beside the root cluster whose general signature accepts any object, other database clusters might also accommodate the corresponding object. These candidate clusters are identified based on their signatures. Among them, we choose to place the object in the one with the lowest access probability. Fig. 4 depicts our simple insertion strategy (steps 1-3). Object insertion needs to update statistics n of the selected cluster, and of the candidate subclusters of the selected cluster (steps 4-6).

```
ObjectInsertion ( object o )
  1.  let B ← {b ∈ C | o matches σ(b) ∧ p(b) ≤ p(c), ∀c ≠ b ∈ C};
  2.  let b ∈ B;
  3.  Insert object o in selected cluster b;
  4.  let n(b) ← n(b) + 1;
  5.  let S ← {s ∈ candidates(b) | o matches σ(s)};
  6.  for each s in S do
  7.     let n(s) ← n(s) + 1;
End.
```

Fig. 4. Object Insertion Algorithm

```
SpatialQuery ( query object ρ ) : object set
  1.  R ← ∅; // query answer set
  2.  let X ← {c ∈ C | ρ matches σ(c)};
  3.  for each cluster c ∈ X do
  4.      for each object o in objects(c) do
  5.          if (ρ matches o) then
  6.              let R ← R ∪ {o};
  7.      q(c) ← q(c) + 1;
  8.      let S ← {s ∈ candidates(c) | ρ matches σ(s)};
  9.      for each s in S do
 10.          q(s) ← q(s) + 1;
 11.  return R;
End.
```

Fig. 5. Spatial Query Execution Algorithm

3.6 Spatial Query Execution

A *spatial query* (or *spatial selection*) specifies the *query object* and the *spatial relation* (*intersection, containment, or enclosure*) requested between the query object and the database objects from the answer set. Answering a spatial query implies the exploration of the materialized clusters whose signatures satisfy the spatial relation with respect to the query object. The objects from the explored clusters are individually checked against the spatial selection criterion. The spatial query execution algorithm is straightforward and is depicted in Fig. 5. The number of exploring queries is incremented for each explored cluster, as well as for the corresponding candidate subclusters virtually explored (steps 7-10).

4 Clustering Criterion

This section presents our approach to group objects, more flexible than traditional methods which are based on minimum bounding in all dimensions. Basically, it consists in clustering together objects with "similar" intervals on a restrained number of dimensions. We first define the cluster signatures used to implement our clustering criterion. Then we present an instantiation of the clustering function which applies on such cluster signatures.

4.1 Cluster Signatures

Let N_d be the data space dimensionality. We consider each dimension taking values in the domain $[0, 1]$. A spatial object specifies an interval for each dimension: $o = \{d_1[a_1, b_1], d_2[a_2, b_2], \ldots, d_{N_d}[a_{N_d}, b_{N_d}]\}$ where $[a_i, b_i]$ represents the interval defined by the spatial object o in dimension d_i $(0 \leq a_i \leq b_i \leq 1, \forall i \in \{1, 2, \ldots, N_d\})$.

A *cluster* represents a group of spatial objects. To form a cluster we put together objects defining *similar intervals* for the same dimensions. By *similar intervals* we understand intervals located in the same domain regions (for instance in the first quart of the domain). The grouping intervals/dimensions are represented in the cluster signature. The cluster signature is defined as

$$\sigma = \{d_1\ [a_1^{min}, a_1^{max}] : [b_1^{min}, b_1^{max}],\quad d_2\ [a_2^{min}, a_2^{max}] : [b_2^{min}, b_2^{max}],\quad \ldots,\quad d_{N_d}\ [a_{N_d}^{min}, a_{N_d}^{max}] : [b_{N_d}^{min}, b_{N_d}^{max}]\ \}$$

where σ regroups spatial objects whose intervals in dimensions d_i start between a_i^{min} and a_i^{max}, and end between b_i^{min} and b_i^{max}, $\forall i \in \{1, 2, \ldots, N_d\}$. The *intervals of variation* $[a^{min}, a^{max}]$ and $[b^{min}, b^{max}]$ are used to precisely define the notion of interval similarity: All the intervals starting in $[a^{min}, a^{max}]$ and ending in $[b^{min}, b^{max}]$ are considered similar with respect to $a^{min}, a^{max}, b^{min}$ and b^{max}.

Example 1. The signature of the *root cluster* must accept any spatial object. For this reason, the intervals of variation corresponding to the signature of the root cluster are represented by complete domains in all dimensions:

$$\sigma_r = \{d_1[0, 1] : [0, 1], \ldots, d_{N_d}[0, 1] : [0, 1]\}.$$

Example 2. Considering the objects $O_1, O_2, O_3, \ldots, O_8$ from the 2-dimensional space depicted in Fig. 6, we can form 3 sample clusters as follows:

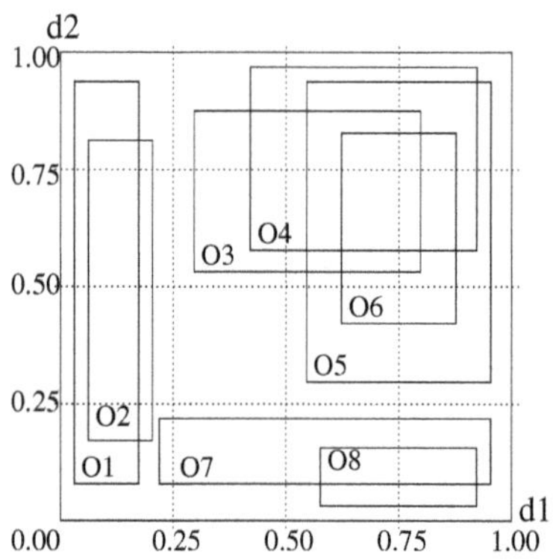

O_1 and O_2 in a cluster represented by σ_1:

$$\sigma_1 = \{d_1[0.00, 0.25) : [0.00, 0.25),\ d_2[0.00, 1.00] : [0.00, 1.00]\};$$

O_3 and O_4 in a cluster represented by σ_2:

$$\sigma_2 = \{d_1[0.25, 0.50) : [0.75, 1.00],\ d_2[0.50, 0.75) : [0.75, 1.00]\};$$

O_5 and O_6 and O_8 in a cluster repres. by σ_3:

$$\sigma_3 = \{d_1[0.50, 0.75) : [0.75, 1.00],\ d_2[0.00, 1.00] : [0.00, 1.00]\}.$$

Fig. 6. Example 2

4.2 Clustering Function

The role of the clustering function is to compute the signatures of the candidate subclusters of a given cluster. Many possible signatures can be used to group objects. A good clustering function should solve the following trade-off: On one hand, the number of candidate subclusters should be sufficiently large to ensure good opportunities of clustering. On the other hand, if this number is too large, it will increase the cost of maintaining statistics (recall that performance indicators are maintained for each candidate subcluster). Our clustering function works as follows: Given a cluster signature we iteratively consider each dimension. For each dimension we divide both intervals of variation in a fixed number of subintervals. We call *division factor* and note f the number of subintervals. We then replace the pair of intervals of variation by each possible combination of subintervals. We have f^2 combinations of subintervals for each dimension and thus f^2 subsignatures[3]. Since we apply this transformation on each dimension we obtain $N_d \cdot f^2$ subsignatures. As a result, the number of candidate subclusters keeps linear with the number of dimensions.

Example 3. We consider σ_1 from the preceding example and apply the clustering function on dimension d_1 using a division factor $f = 4$. The signatures of the corresponding candidate subclusters are:

$\sigma_1^1 = \{d_1[0.0000, 0.0625) : [0.0000, 0.0625), d_2[0, 1] : [0, 1]\};$
$\sigma_1^2 = \{d_1[0.0000, 0.0625) : [0.0625, 0.1250), d_2[0, 1] : [0, 1]\};$
$\sigma_1^3 = \{d_1[0.0000, 0.0625) : [0.1250, 0.1875), d_2[0, 1] : [0, 1]\};$
$\sigma_1^4 = \{d_1[0.0000, 0.0625) : [0.1875, 0.2500], d_2[0, 1] : [0, 1]\};$
$\sigma_1^5 = \{d_1[0.0625, 0.1250) : [0.0625, 0.1250), d_2[0, 1] : [0, 1]\};$
$\sigma_1^6 = \{d_1[0.0625, 0.1250) : [0.1250, 0.1875), d_2[0, 1] : [0, 1]\};$
$\sigma_1^7 = \{d_1[0.0625, 0.1250) : [0.1875, 0.2500], d_2[0, 1] : [0, 1]\};$
$\sigma_1^8 = \{d_1[0.1250, 0.1875) : [0.1250, 0.1875), d_2[0, 1] : [0, 1]\};$
$\sigma_1^9 = \{d_1[0.1250, 0.1875) : [0.1875, 0.2500], d_2[0, 1] : [0, 1]\};$
$\sigma_1^{10} = \{d_1[0.1875, 0.2500] : [0.1875, 0.2500], d_2[0, 1] : [0, 1]\}.$

There are 16 possible subintervals combinations, but only 10 are valid because of the symmetry. Similarly, applying the clustering function on d_2 we use the subintervals $[0.00, 0.25)$, $[0.25, 0.50)$, $[0.50, 0.75)$ and $[0.75, 1.00]$ and obtain 10 more candidate subclusters.

5 Cost Model and Benefit Functions

Our database clustering is based on a cost model evaluating the average query performance in terms of execution time. The expected query execution time associated to a database cluster c can be generally expressed as:

$$T_c = A + p_c \cdot (B + n_c \cdot C) \quad (1)$$

where p_c represents the access probability associated to the cluster c, n_c the number of objects hosted by c, and A, B and C three parameters depending on the database and system characteristics. The access probability and the number of objects are performance indicators we maintain for each database cluster. Regarding parameters A, B and C, we consider the following scenarios:

i. Memory Storage Scenario. The spatial database fits the main memory, the objects from the same clusters are sequentially stored in memory in order to maximize the data locality and benefit from the memory cache line and read ahead capabilities of the nowadays processors. In this case:

[3] When the intervals of variation of the selected dimension are identical, only $N_f = \frac{f \cdot (f+1)}{2}$ subintervals combinations are distinct because of the symmetry.

A represents the time spent to check the cluster signature in order to decide or not the cluster exploration (signature verification time);

B includes the time required to prepare the cluster exploration (call of the corresponding function, initialization of the object scan) and the time spent to update the query statistics for the current cluster and for the candidate subclusters of the current cluster;

C represents the time required to check one object against the selection criterion (object verification time).

ii. Disk Storage Scenario. The signatures of the database clusters, as well as the associated statistics and parameters, are managed in memory, while the cluster members are stored on external support. The objects from the same clusters are sequentially stored on disk in order to minimize the disk head repositioning and benefit from the the better performance of the sequential data transfer between disk and memory. In this case:

$A' = A$ the same as in the first scenario;

$B' = B$ plus the time required to position the disk head at the beginning of the cluster in order to prepare the object read (disk access time), because the cluster is stored on external support.

$C' = C$ plus the time required to transfer one object from disk to memory (object read time).

Materialization Benefit Function. The materialization benefit function β takes a database cluster c and one of its candidate subclusters s, and evaluates the impact on the query performance, of the potential materialization of s. To obtain the expression of β, we consider the corresponding query execution times before and after the materialization of the candidate subcluster: $T_{bef} = T_c$ and $T_{aft} = T_{c'} + T_s$. T_{bef} represents the execution time associated to the original database cluster c, and T_{aft} represents the joint execution time associated to the clusters c' and s resulted after the materialization of the candidate s of c. The materialization benefit function is defined as

$$\beta(s,c) = T_{bef} - T_{aft} = T_c - (T_{c'} + T_s) \tag{2}$$

and represents the profit in terms of execution time, expected from the materialization of the candidate s of c. Using (1) to expand $T_c = A + p_c \cdot (B + n_c \cdot C)$, $T_{c'} = A + p_{c'} \cdot (B + n_{c'} \cdot C)$, and $T_s = A + p_s \cdot (B + n_s \cdot C)$, and assuming i. $p_{c'} = p_c$ and ii. $n_{c'} = n_c - n_s$, (2) becomes:

$$\beta(s,c) = ((p_c - p_s) \cdot n_s \cdot C) - (p_s \cdot B) - A \tag{3}$$

The interest of the materialization grows when the candidate subcluster has a lower access probability, and when enough objects from the original cluster qualify for the considered candidate subcluster.

Merging Benefit Function. The merging benefit function μ takes a cluster c and its parent cluster a, and evaluates the impact on the query performance of the possible merging of the two clusters. To obtain the expression of μ, we consider the corresponding query execution times before and after the merging operation: $T_{bef} = T_c + T_a$ and $T_{aft} = T_{a'}$. T_{bef} represents the joint execution time associated to the original database cluster c and to the parent cluster a, and T_{aft} represents the execution time associated to the cluster a' resulted from merging c to a. The materialization benefit function is defined as

$$\mu(c, a) = T_{bef} - T_{aft} = (T_c + T_a) - T_{a'} \tag{4}$$

and represents the profit in terms of execution time, expected from the merging operation between clusters c and a. Using (1) to expand $T_c = A + p_c \cdot (B + n_c \cdot C)$, $T_a = A + p_a \cdot (B + n_a \cdot C)$, and $T_{a'} = A + p_{a'} \cdot (B + n_{a'} \cdot C)$, and assuming i. $p_{a'} = p_a$ and ii. $n_{a'} = n_a + n_c$, (4) becomes:

$$\mu(c, a) = A + (p_c \cdot B) - ((p_a - p_c) \cdot n_c \cdot C) \tag{5}$$

The interest in a merging operation grows when the access probability of the child cluster approaches the one of the parent cluster (for instance due to changes in query patterns), or when the number of objects in the child cluster decreases too much (due to object removals).

6 Implementation Considerations

Cost Model Parameters. Parameters A, B, and C are part of the cost model supporting the clustering strategy and depend on the system performance with respect to the adopted storage scenario. They can be either experimentally measured and hard-coded in the cost model, or dynamically evaluated for each database cluster and integrated as model variables to locally support the clustering decision. Cost values for I/O and CPU operations corresponding to our system are presented as reference in Table 2.

Table 2. I/O and CPU Operations Costs

I/O	Cost	CPU	Cost
Disk Access Time	15ms	Cluster Signature Check	$5 \cdot 10^{-7}$ms
Disk Transfer Rate	20MBytes/sec	Object Verification Rate	300Mbytes/sec
Transfer Time per Byte	$4.77 \cdot 10^{-5}$ms	Verification Time per Byte	$3.18 \cdot 10^{-6}$ms

Clustering Function. For the clustering function we used a domain division factor $f = 4$. According to Section 4, the number of candidate subclusters associated to a database cluster is between $10 * N_d$ and $16 * N_d$ where N_d represents the space dimensionality. For instance, considering a 16-dimensional space, we have between 160 and 256 candidate subclusters for each database cluster. Because the candidate subclusters are virtual, only their performance indicators have to be managed.

Storage Utilization. As part of our clustering strategy, each cluster is sequentially stored in memory or on external support. This placement constraint can trigger expensive cluster moving operations during object insertions. To avoid frequent cluster moves, we reserve a number of places at the end of each cluster created or relocated. For the number of reserved places, we consider between 20% and 30% of the cluster size, thus taking into account the data distribution. Indeed, larger clusters will have more free places than smaller clusters. In all cases, a storage utilization factor of at least 70% is ensured.

Fail Recovery. In the disk-based storage case, maintaining the search structure across system crashes can be an important consideration. For recovery reasons, we can store the cluster signatures together with the member objects and use an one-block disk directory to simply indicate the position of each cluster on disk. Performance indicators associated to clusters might be also saved, on a regular basis, but this is optional since new statistics can be eventually gathered.

7 Performance Evaluation

To evaluate our adaptive cost-based clustering solution, we performed extensive experiments executing intersection-based and point-enclosing queries over large collections of spatial objects (hyper-rectangles with many dimensions and following uniform and skewed spatial distributions). We compare our technique to Sequential Scan and to R*-tree evaluating the query execution time, the number of cluster/node accesses, and the size of verified data.

7.1 Experimental Setup

Competitive Techniques. R*-tree is the most successful R-tree variant still supporting multidimensional extended objects. It has been widely accepted in literature and often used as reference for performance comparison. Sequential Scan is a simple technique: it scans the database and checks all the objects against the selection criterion. Although quantitatively expensive, Sequential Scan benefits of good data locality, and of sustained data transfer rate between disk and memory. Sequential Scan is considered a reference in high-dimensional spaces because it often outperforms complex indexing solutions [3][5].

Experimental Platform. All experiments are executed on a Pentium III workstation with i686 CPU at 650MHz, 768MBytes RAM, several GBytes of secondary storage, and operating under Red Hat Linux 8.0. The system has a SCSI disk with the following characteristics: disk access time = 15ms, sustained transfer rate = 20MBps. To test the disk-based storage scenario, we limited the main memory capacity to 64MBytes and used experimental databases of multidimensional extended objects whose sizes were at least twice larger than the available memory. This way we forced data transfer between disk and memory.

Data Representation. A spatial object consists of an object identifier and of N_d pairs of real values representing the intervals in the N_d dimensions. The interval limits and the object identifier are each represented on 4 bytes. The R*-tree implementation follows [2]. In our tests we used a node page size of 16KBytes. Considering a storage utilization of 70%, a tree node accommodates 35 objects with 40 dimensions, and 86 objects with 16 dimensions. Using smaller page sizes would trigger the creation of too many tree nodes resulting in high overheads due to numerous node accesses, both in memory and on disk.

Execution Parameters and Performance Indicators. The following parameters are varied in our tests: number of database objects (up to 2,000,000), number of dimensions (from 16 to 40), and query selectivity (between 0.00005% and 50%). In each experiment, a large number of spatial queries is addressed to the indexing structure and average values are raised for the following performance indicators: query execution time (combining all costs), number of accessed clusters/nodes (relevant for the cost due to disk access operations), size of verified data (relevant for data transfer and check costs).

Experimental Process. For Sequential Scan, the database objects are loaded and stored in a single cluster. Queries are launched, and performance indicators are raised. For R*-tree, the objects are first inserted in the indexing structure, then query performance is evaluated. For Adaptive Clustering, the database objects are inserted in the root cluster, then a number of queries are launched to trigger the object organization in clusters. A database reorganization is triggered every 100 spatial queries. If the query distribution does not change, the clustering process reaches a stable state (in less than 10 reorganization steps). We then evaluate the average query response time. The reported time also includes the time spent to update query statistics associated to accessed clusters.

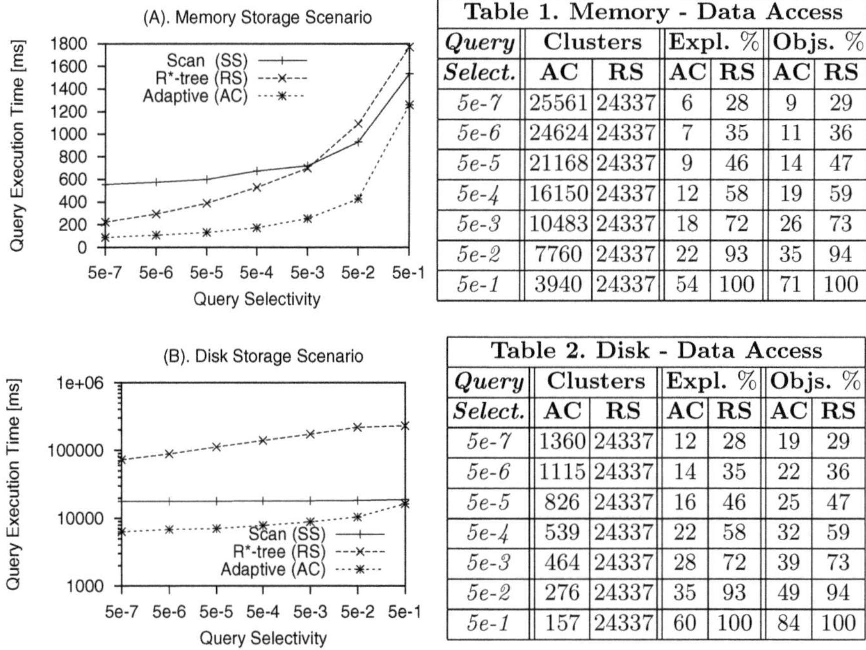

Table 1. Memory - Data Access

Query	Clusters		Expl. %		Objs. %	
Select.	**AC**	**RS**	**AC**	**RS**	**AC**	**RS**
5e-7	25561	24337	6	28	9	29
5e-6	24624	24337	7	35	11	36
5e-5	21168	24337	9	46	14	47
5e-4	16150	24337	12	58	19	59
5e-3	10483	24337	18	72	26	73
5e-2	7760	24337	22	93	35	94
5e-1	3940	24337	54	100	71	100

Table 2. Disk - Data Access

Query	Clusters		Expl. %		Objs. %	
Select.	**AC**	**RS**	**AC**	**RS**	**AC**	**RS**
5e-7	1360	24337	12	28	19	29
5e-6	1115	24337	14	35	22	36
5e-5	826	24337	16	46	25	47
5e-4	539	24337	22	58	32	59
5e-3	464	24337	28	72	39	73
5e-2	276	24337	35	93	49	94
5e-1	157	24337	60	100	84	100

Fig. 7. Query Performance when Varying Query Selectivity (Uniform Workload)

7.2 Experiments

Uniform Workload and Varying Query Selectivity (2,000,000 objects). In the first experiment we examine the impact of the query selectivity on the query performance. We consider 2,000,000 database objects uniformly-distributed in a 16-dimensional data space (251MBytes of data) and evaluate the query response time for intersection queries with selectivities varying from 0.00005% to 50%. Each database object defines intervals whose sizes and positions are randomly distributed in each dimension. The intervals of the query objects are also uniformly generated in each dimension, but minimal/maximal interval sizes are enforced in order to control the query selectivity. Performance results are presented in Fig. 7 for both storage scenarios: in-memory and disk-based. Charts A and B illustrate average query execution times for the three considered methods: Sequential Scan (SS), Adaptive Clustering (AC), and R*-tree (RS). Tables 1 and 2 compare AC and RS in terms of total number of clusters/nodes, average ratio of explored clusters/nodes, and average ratio of verified objects. Unlike RS for which the number of nodes is constant, AC adapts the object clustering to the actual data and query distribution. When the queries are very selective many clusters are formed because few of them are expected to be explored. In contrast, when the queries are not selective fewer clusters are created. Indeed, their frequent exploration would otherwise trigger significant cost overhead. The cost model supporting the adaptive clustering always ensures better performance for AC compared to SS[4]. RS is much more expensive than SS on disk, but also in memory for queries with selectivities over 0.5%. The bad performance of RS confirms our expectations: RS can not deal with high dimensionality (16 in this case) because the MBBs overlap within nodes determines the exploration of many tree nodes[5]. AC systematically outperforms RS, exploring fewer clusters and verifying fewer objects both in memory and on disk. Our object grouping is clearly more efficient. In memory, for instance, we verify three times fewer objects than RS in most cases. Even for queries with selectivities as low as 50%, when RS practically checks the entire database, only 71% of objects are verified by AC. The difference in number of verified objects is not so substantial on disk, but the cost overhead due to expensive random I/O accesses is remarkably inferior[6]. This happens because the number of AC clusters is much smaller than the number of RS nodes. Compared to the memory storage scenario, the small number of clusters formed on disk is due to the cost model that takes into consideration the negative impact of expensive random I/O accesses. This demonstrates the flexibility of our adaptive cost-based clustering strategy. Thanks to it AC succeeds to outperform SS on disk in all cases.

---

[4] The cost of SS in memory increases significantly (up to 3x) for lower query selectivities. This happens because an object is rejected as soon as one of its dimensions does not satisfy the intersection condition. When the query selectivity is low, more attributes have to be verified on average.

[5] See ratio of explored nodes in Tables 1 and 2.

[6] Note the logarithmic time scale from Chart 7-B.

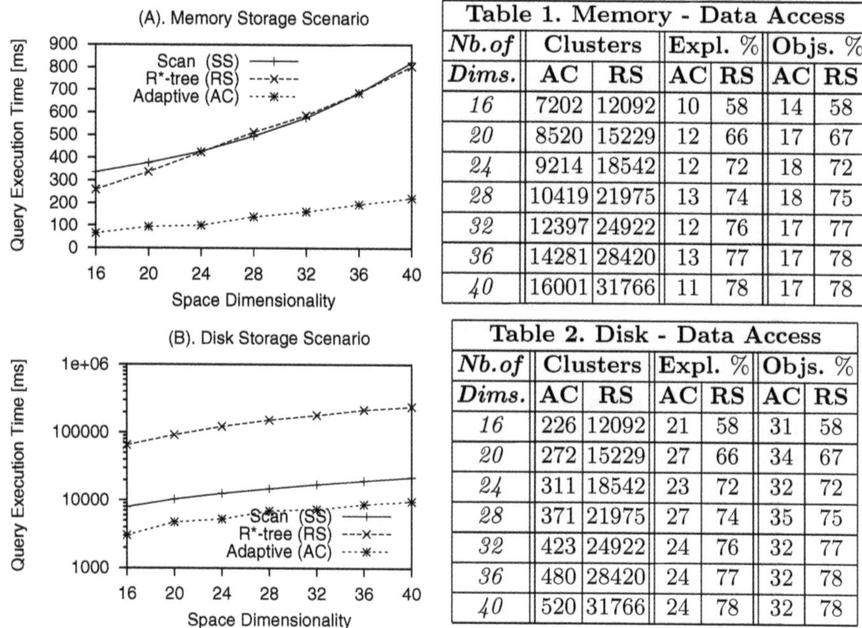

Table 1. Memory - Data Access

Nb.of	Clusters		Expl. %		Objs. %	
Dims.	AC	RS	AC	RS	AC	RS
16	7202	12092	10	58	14	58
20	8520	15229	12	66	17	67
24	9214	18542	12	72	18	72
28	10419	21975	13	74	18	75
32	12397	24922	12	76	17	77
36	14281	28420	13	77	17	78
40	16001	31766	11	78	17	78

Table 2. Disk - Data Access

Nb.of	Clusters		Expl. %		Objs. %	
Dims.	AC	RS	AC	RS	AC	RS
16	226	12092	21	58	31	58
20	272	15229	27	66	34	67
24	311	18542	23	72	32	72
28	371	21975	27	74	35	75
32	423	24922	24	76	32	77
36	480	28420	24	77	32	78
40	520	31766	24	78	32	78

Fig. 8. Query Performance when Varying Space Dimensionality (Skewed Data)

Skewed Workload and Varying Space Dimensionality (1,000,000 objects). With this experiment we intend to demonstrate both the good behavior with increasing dimensionality and the good performance under skewed data. Skewed data is closer to reality where different dimensions exhibit different characteristics. For this test, we adopted the following skewed scenario: we generate uniformly-distributed query objects with no interval constraints, but consider 1,000,000 database objects with different size constraints over dimensions. We vary the number of dimensions between 16 and 40. For each database object, we randomly choose a quart of dimensions that are two times more selective than the rest of dimensions. We still control the global query selectivity because the query objects are uniformly distributed. For this experiment we ensure an average query selectivity of 0.05%. Performance results are illustrated in Fig. 8. We first notice that the query time increases with the dimensionality. This is normal because the size of the dataset increases too from 126MBytes (16d) to 309MBytes (40d). Compared to SS, AC again exhibits good performance, scaling well with the number of dimensions, both in memory and on disk. AC resists to increasing dimensionality better than RS. RS fails to outperform SS due to the large number of accessed nodes (> 72%). AC takes better advantage of the skewed data distribution, and groups objects in clusters whose signatures are based on the most selective similar intervals and dimensions of the objects regrouped. In contrast, RS does not benefit from the skewed data distribution, probably due to the minimum bounding constraint, which increases the general overlap. In memory, for instance, RS verifies four times more objects than AC.

Point-Enclosing Queries. Because queries like "find the database objects containing a given point" can also occur in practice (for instance, in a publish-subscribe application where subscriptions define interval ranges as attributes, and events can be points in these ranges), we also evaluated point-enclosing queries considering different workloads and storage scenarios. We do not show here experimental details, but we report very good performance: up to 16 times faster than SS in memory, and up to 4 times on disk, mostly due to the good selectivity. Compared to spatial range queries (i.e. intersections with spatial extended objects), point-enclosing queries are best cases for our indexing method thanks to their good selectivity.

Conclusion on Experiments. While R*-tree fails to outperform Sequential Scan in many cases, our cost-based clustering follows the data and the query distribution and always exhibits better performance in both storage scenarios: in-memory and disk-based. Experimental results show that our method is scalable with the number of objects and has good behavior with increasing dimensionality (16 to 40 in our tests), especially when dealing with skewed data or skewed queries. For intersection queries, performance is up to 7 times better in memory, and up to 4 times better on disk. Better gains are obtained when the query selectivity is high. For point-enclosing queries on skewed data, gain can reach a factor of 16 in memory.

8 Conclusions

The emergence of new applications (such as SDI applications) brings out new challenging performance requirements for multidimensional indexing schemes. An advanced subscription system should support spatial range queries over large collections of multidimensional extended objects with many dimensions (millions of subscriptions and tens to hundreds of attributes). Moreover, such system should cope with workloads that are skewed and varying in time. Existing structures are not well suited for these new requirements. In this paper we presented a simple clustering solution suitable for such application contexts. Our clustering method uses an original grouping criterion, more efficient than traditional approaches. The cost-based clustering allows us to scale with large number of dimensions and to take advantage of skewed data distribution. Our method exhibits better performance than competitive solutions like Sequential Scan or R*-tree both in memory and on disk.

References

1. M. Altimel and M. J. Franklin. Efficient filtering of XML documents for selective dissemination of information. In *Proc. 26th VLDB Conf., Cairo, Egypt*, 2000.
2. N. Beckmann, H.-P. Kriegel, R. Schneider, and B. Seeger. The R*-tree: An efficient and robust access method for points and rectangles. In *Proc. ACM SIGMOD Conf., Atlantic City, NJ*, 1990.

3. S. Berchtold, C. Böhm, and H.-P. Kriegel. The Pyramid-technique: Towards breaking the curse of dimensionality. In *Proc. ACM SIGMOD Conf., Seattle, Washington*, 1998.
4. S. Berchtold, D. A. Keim, and H.-P. Kriegel. The X-tree: An index structure for high-dimensional data. In *Proc. 22nd VLDB Conf., Bombay, India*, 1996.
5. K. Beyer, J. Goldstein, R. Ramakrishnan, and U. Shaft. When is "nearest neighbor" meaningful? *Lecture Notes in Computer Science*, 1540:217–235, 1999.
6. C. Böhm, S. Berchtold, and D. A. Keim. Searching in high-dimensional spaces: Index structures for improving the performance of multimedia databases. *ACM Computing Surveys*, 33(3):322–373, 2001.
7. C. Böhm and H.-P. Kriegel. Dynamically optimizing high-dimensional index structures. In *Proc. 7th EDBT Conf., Konstanz, Germany*, 2000.
8. F. Fabret, H. Jacobsen, F. Llirbat, J. Pereira, K. Ross, and D. Shasha. Filtering algorithm and implementation for very fast publish/subscribe systems. In *Proc. ACM SIGMOD Conf., Santa Barbara, California, USA*, 2001.
9. C. Faloutsos and P. Bhagwat. Declustering using fractals. *PDIS Journal of Parallel and Distributed Information Systems*, pages 18–25, 1993.
10. V. Gaede and O. Günther. Multidimensional access methods. *ACM Computing Surveys*, 30(2):170–231, 1998.
11. A. Guttman. R-trees: A dynamic index structure for spatial searching. In *Proc. ACM SIGMOD Conf., 47-57*, 1984.
12. H. Liu and H. A. Jacobsen. Modelling uncertainties in publish/subscribe systems. In *Proc. 20th ICDE Conf., Boston, USA*, 2004.
13. B.-U. Pagel, H.-W. Six, and M. Winter. Window query-optimal clustering of spatial objects. In *Proc. ACM PODS Conf., San Jose*, 1995.
14. T. Sellis, N. Roussopoulos, and C. Faloustos. The R+-tree: A dynamic index for multi-dimensional objects. In *Proc. VLDB Conf., Brighton, England*, 1987.
15. Y. Tao and D. Papadias. Adaptive index structures. In *Proc. 28th VLDB Conf., Hong Kong, China*, 2002.
16. R. Weber, H.-J. Schek, and S. Blott. A quantitative analysis and performance study for similarity-search methods in high-dimensional spaces. In *Proc. 24th VLDB Conf., New York, USA*, 1998.
17. C. Yu. *High-dimensional indexing. Transformational approaches to high-dimensional range and similarity searches.* LNCS 2341, Springer-Verlag, 2002.

Processing Unions of Conjunctive Queries with Negation under Limited Access Patterns

Alan Nash[1] and Bertram Ludäscher[2]

[1] Department of Mathematics, anash@math.ucsd.edu
[2] San Diego Supercomputer Center, ludaesch@sdsc.edu
University of California, San Diego

Abstract. We study the problem of answering queries over sources with limited access patterns. The problem is to decide whether a given query Q is *feasible*, i.e., equivalent to an *executable* query Q' that observes the limited access patterns given by the sources. We characterize the complexity of deciding feasibility for the classes $\mathrm{CQ}^\neg$ (conjunctive queries with negation) and $\mathrm{UCQ}^\neg$ (unions of $\mathrm{CQ}^\neg$ queries): Testing feasibility is just as hard as testing containment and therefore $\mathbf{\Pi}_2^{\mathrm{P}}$-complete. We also provide a uniform treatment for CQ, UCQ, $\mathrm{CQ}^\neg$, and $\mathrm{UCQ}^\neg$ by devising a single algorithm which is optimal for each of these classes. In addition, we show how one can often avoid the worst-case complexity by certain approximations: At compile-time, even if a query Q is not feasible, we can find efficiently the minimal executable query containing Q. For query answering at runtime, we devise an algorithm which may report complete answers even in the case of infeasible plans and which can indicate to the user the degree of completeness for certain incomplete answers.

1 Introduction

We study the problem of answering queries over sources with limited query capabilities. The problem arises naturally in the context of database integration and query optimization in the presence of limited source capabilities (e.g., see [PGH98,FLMS99]). In particular, for any database mediator system that supports not only conventional SQL databases, but also sources with *access pattern restrictions* [LC01,Li03], it is important to come up with query plans which observe those restrictions. Most notably, the latter occurs for sources which are modeled as *web services* [WSD03]. For the purposes of query planning, a web service operation can be seen as a remote procedure call, corresponding to a limited query capability which requires certain arguments of the query to be bound (the input arguments), while others may be free (the output arguments).

Web Services as Relations with Access Patterns. A *web service operation* can be seen as a function *op*: $x_1, \ldots, x_n \to y_1, \ldots, y_m$ having an *input message* (*request*) with n arguments (*parts*), and an *output message* (*response*) with m parts [WSD03, Part 2, Sec. 2.2]. For example, op_B: *author* $\to$ $\{(isbn, title)\}$ may implement a book search service, returning for a given author A a list of books

E. Bertino et al. (Eds.): EDBT 2004, LNCS 2992, pp. 422–440, 2004.
© Springer-Verlag Berlin Heidelberg 2004

authored by A. We model such operations as *relations with access pattern*, here: $B^{oio}(isbn, author, title)$, where the access pattern 'oio' indicates that a value for the second attribute must be given as input, while the other attribute values can be retrieved as output. In this way, a family of web service operations over k attributes can be concisely described as a relation $R(a_1, \ldots, a_k)$ with an associated set of access patterns. Thus, queries become declarative specifications for web service composition.

An important problem of query planning over sources with access pattern restrictions is to determine whether a query Q is *feasible*, i.e., equivalent to an *executable query plan* Q' that observes the access patterns.

Example 1 The following conjunctive query[1] with negation

$$Q(i, a, t) \longleftarrow B(i, a, t), C(i, a), \neg L(i)$$

asks for books available through a store B which are contained in a catalog C, but not in the local library L. Let the only access patterns be B^{ioo}, B^{oio}, C^{oo}, and L^{o}. If we try to execute Q from left to right, neither pattern for B works since we either lack an ISBN i or an author a. However, Q is *feasible* since we can execute it by first calling $C(i, a)$ which binds both i and a. After that, calling $B^{ioo}(i, a, t)$ or $B^{oio}(i, a, t)$ will work, resulting in an executable plan. In contrast, calling $\neg L(i)$ first and then B does not work: a negated call can only filter out answers, but cannot produce any new variable bindings.

This example shows that for some queries which are not executable, simple reordering can yield an executable plan. However there are queries which cannot be reordered yet are feasible.[2] This raises the question of how to determine whether a query is feasible and how to obtain "good approximations" in case the query is *not* feasible. Clearly, these questions depend on the class of queries under consideration. For example, feasibility is undecidable for Datalog queries [LC01] and for first-order queries [NL04]. On the other hand, feasibility is decidable for subclasses such as conjunctive queries (CQ) and unions of conjunctive queries (UCQ) [LC01].

Contributions. We show that deciding feasibility for conjunctive queries with negation ($\text{CQ}^{\neg}$) and unions of conjunctive queries with negation ($\text{UCQ}^{\neg}$) is $\mathbf{\Pi}_2^{\mathrm{P}}$-complete, and present a corresponding algorithm, FEASIBLE. Feasibility of CQ and UCQ was studied in [Li03]. We show that our uniform algorithm performs optimally on all these four query classes.

We also present a number of practical improvements and approximations for developers of database mediator systems: PLAN* is an efficient polynomial-time algorithm for computing two plans Q^u and Q^o, which at runtime produce *underestimates* and *overestimates* of the answers to Q, respectively. Whenever PLAN* outputs two identical Q^u and Q^o, we know at compile-time that Q is

[1] We write variables in lowercase.

[2] Li and Chang call this notion *stable* [LC01,Li03].

feasible without actually incurring the cost of the $\mathbf{\Pi}_2^{\mathrm{P}}$-complete feasibility test. In addition, we present an efficient runtime algorithm ANSWER* which, given a database instance D, computes underestimates ANSWER(Q^u, D) and overestimates ANSWER(Q^o, D) of the exact answer. If Q is not feasible, ANSWER* may still compute a complete answer and signal the completeness of the answer to the user at runtime. In case the answer is incomplete (or not known to be complete), ANSWER* can often give a lower bound on the relative completeness of the answer.

Outline. The paper is organized as follows: Section 2 contains the preliminaries. In Section 3 we introduce our basic notions such as executable, orderable, and feasible. In Section 4 we present our main algorithms for computing execution plans, determining the feasibility of a query, and runtime processing of answers. In Section 5 we present the main theoretical results, in particular a characterization of the complexity of deciding feasibility of UCQ$^\neg$ queries. Also we show how related algorithms can be obtained as special cases of our uniform approach. We summarize and conclude in Section 6.

2 Preliminaries

A *term* is a variable or constant. We use lowercase letters to denote terms. By $\bar{x}$ we denote a finite sequence of terms $x_1, \ldots, x_k$. A *literal* $\hat{R}(\bar{x})$ is an atom $R(\bar{x})$ or its negation $\neg R(\bar{x})$.

A *conjunctive query* Q is a formula of the form $\exists \bar{y}\ R_1(\bar{x}_1) \wedge \ldots \wedge R_n(\bar{x}_n)$. It can be written as a Datalog rule $Q(\bar{z}) \longleftarrow R_1(\bar{x}_1), \ldots, R_n(\bar{x}_n)$. Here, the existentially-quantified variables $\bar{y}$ are among the $\bar{x}_i$ and the distinguished (answer) variables $\bar{z}$ in the head of Q are the remaining *free variables* of Q, denoted free(Q). Let vars(Q) denote all variables of Q; then we have free$(Q) =$ vars$(Q) \setminus \{\bar{y}\} = \{\bar{z}\}$. Conjunctive queries (CQ) are also known as SPJ (select-project-join) queries.

A *union of conjunctive queries* (UCQ) is a query Q of the form $Q_1 \vee \ldots \vee Q_k$ where each $Q_i \in$ CQ. If free$(Q) = \{\bar{z}\}$, then Q in rule form consists of k rules, one for each Q_i, all with the same head $Q(\bar{z})$.

A *conjunctive query with negation* (CQ$^\neg$) is defined like a conjunctive query, but with literals $\hat{R}_i(\bar{x}_i)$ instead of atoms $R_i(\bar{x}_i)$. Hence a CQ$^\neg$ query is an existentially quantified conjunction of positive or negated atoms.

A *union of conjunctive queries with negation* (UCQ$^\neg$) is a query $Q_1 \vee \ldots \vee Q_k$ where each $Q_i \in$ CQ$^\neg$; the rule form consists of k CQ$^\neg$-rules having the same head $Q(\bar{z})$.

For $Q \in$ CQ$^\neg$, we denote by Q^+ the conjunction of the positive literals in Q in the same order as they appear in Q and by Q^- the conjunction of the negative literals in Q in the same order as they appear in Q.

A CQ or CQ$^\neg$ query is *safe* if every variable of the query appears in a positive literal in the body. A UCQ or UCQ$^\neg$ query is safe if each of its CQ or CQ$^\neg$ parts is safe and if all of them have the same free variables. In this paper we only consider safe queries.

3 Limited Access Patterns and Feasibility

Here we present the basic definitions for source queries with limited access patterns. In particular, we define the notions executable, orderable, and feasible. While the former two notions are syntactic in the sense that they can be decided by a simple inspection of a query, the latter notion is semantic, since feasibility is defined up to logic equivalence. An executable query can be seen as a *query plan*, prescribing how to execute the query. An orderable query can be seen as an "almost executable" plan (it just needs to be reordered to yield a plan). A feasible query, however, does not directly provide an execution plan. The problem we are interested in is how to determine whether such an executable plan exists and how to find it. These are two different, but related, problems.

Definition 1 (Access Pattern) An *access pattern* for a k-ary relation R is an expression of the form R^α where α is word of length k over the alphabet $\{\mathrm{i}, \mathrm{o}\}$.

We call the jth position of P an *input slot* if $\alpha(j) = \mathrm{i}$ and an *output slot* if $\alpha(j) = \mathrm{o}$.[3] At runtime, we *must* provide values for input slots, while for output slots such values are not required, i.e., "*bound is easier*" [Ull88].[4] In general, with access pattern R^α we may retrieve the set of tuples $\{\bar{y} \mid R(\bar{x}, \bar{y})\}$ as long as we supply the values of $\bar{x}$ corresponding to all input slots in R.

Example 2 (Access Patterns) Given the access patterns B^{ioo} and B^{oio} for the book relation in Example 1 we can obtain, e.g., the set $\{\langle a, t\rangle \mid B(i, a, t)\}$ of authors and titles given an ISBN i and the set $\{t \mid \exists i\, B(i, a, t)\}$ of titles given an author a, but we cannot obtain the set $\{\langle a, t\rangle \mid \exists i\, B(i, a, t)\}$ of authors and titles, given no input.

Definition 2 (Adornment) Given a set $\mathcal{P}$ of access patterns, a $\mathcal{P}$*-adornment* on $Q \in \mathrm{UCQ}^\neg$ is an assignment of access patterns from $\mathcal{P}$ to relations in Q.

Definition 3 (Executable) $Q \in \mathrm{CQ}^\neg$ is $\mathcal{P}$*-executable* if $\mathcal{P}$-adornments can be added to Q so that every variable of Q appears first in an output slot of a non-negated literal. $Q \in \mathrm{UCQ}^\neg$ with $Q := Q_1 \vee \ldots \vee Q_k$ is $\mathcal{P}$*-executable* if every Q_i is $\mathcal{P}$-executable.

We consider the query which returns no tuples, which we write `false`, to be (vacuously) executable. In contrast, we consider the query with an empty body, which we write `true`, to be non-executable. We may have both kinds of queries in ans(Q) defined below. From the definitions, it follows that executable queries are safe. The converse is false.

An executable query provides a query *plan*: execute each rule separately (possibly in parallel) from left to right.

[3] Other authors use 'b' and 'f' for bound and free, but we prefer to reserve these notions for variables under or not under the scope of a quantifier, respectively.

[4] If a source does *not* accept a value, e.g., for y in $R^{\mathrm{io}}(x, y)$, one can ignore the y binding and call $R(x, y')$ with y' unbound, and afterwards execute the join for $y' = y$.

Definition 4 (Orderable) $Q \in \text{UCQ}^\neg$ with $Q := Q_1 \vee \ldots \vee Q_k$ is $\mathcal{P}$-*orderable* if for every $Q_i \in \text{CQ}^\neg$ there is a permutation Q'_i of the literals in Q_i so that $Q' := Q'_1 \vee \ldots \vee Q'_k$ is $\mathcal{P}$-executable.

Clearly, if Q is executable, then Q is orderable, but not conversely.

Definition 5 (Feasible) $Q \in \text{UCQ}^\neg$ is $\mathcal{P}$-*feasible* if it is equivalent to a $\mathcal{P}$-executable $Q' \in \text{UCQ}^\neg$.

Clearly, if Q is orderable, then Q is feasible, but not conversely.

Example 3 (Feasible, Not Orderable) Given access patterns B^{ioo}, B^{oio}, L^{o},

$$Q(a) \longleftarrow B(i,a,t), L(i), B(i',a',t)$$
$$Q(a) \longleftarrow B(i,a,t), L(i), \neg B(i',a',t)$$

is not orderable since i' and a' cannot be bound, but feasible because this query is equivalent to the executable query $Q'(a) \longleftarrow L(i), B(i,a,t)$.

Usually, we have in mind a fixed set $\mathcal{P}$ of access patterns and then we simply say executable, orderable, and feasible instead of $\mathcal{P}$-executable, $\mathcal{P}$-orderable, and $\mathcal{P}$-feasible. The following two definitions and the algorithm in Figure 1 are small modifications of those presented in [LC01].

Definition 6 (Answerable Literal) Given $Q \in \text{CQ}^\neg$, we say that a literal $\hat{R}(\bar{x})$ (not necessarily in Q) is Q-*answerable* if there is an executable $Q^R \in \text{CQ}^\neg$ consisting of $\hat{R}(\bar{x})$ and literals in Q.

Definition 7 (Answerable Part ans(Q)) If $Q \in \text{CQ}^\neg$ is unsatisfiable then $\text{ans}(Q) = \texttt{false}$. If Q is satisfiable, $\text{ans}(Q)$ is the query given by the Q-answerable literals in Q, in the order given by the algorithm ANSWERABLE (see Figure 1). If $Q \in \text{UCQ}^\neg$ with $Q = Q_1 \vee \ldots \vee Q_k$ then $\text{ans}(Q) = \text{ans}(Q_1) \vee \ldots \vee \text{ans}(Q_k)$.

Notice that the answerable part $\text{ans}(Q)$ of Q is executable whenever it is safe.

Proposition 1 *$Q \in \text{CQ}^\neg$ is orderable iff every literal in Q is Q-answerable.*

Proposition 2 *There is a quadratic-time algorithm for computing* $\text{ans}(Q)$.

The algorithm is given in Figure 1.

Corollary 3 *There is a quadratic-time algorithm for checking whether $Q \in \text{UCQ}^\neg$ is orderable.*

In Section 5.1 we define and discuss containment of queries and in Section 5.2 we prove the following proposition. Query P is said to be *contained* in query Q (in symbols, $P \sqsubseteq Q$) if for every instance D, $\text{ANSWER}(P,D) \subseteq \text{ANSWER}(Q,D)$.

Proposition 4 *If $Q \in \text{UCQ}^\neg$, then $Q \sqsubseteq$* $\text{ans}(Q)$.

Corollary 5 *If $Q \in \text{UCQ}^\neg$,* $\text{ans}(Q)$ *is safe, and* $\text{ans}(Q) \sqsubseteq Q$*, then Q is feasible.*

PROOF If $\text{ans}(Q) \sqsubseteq Q$ then $\text{ans}(Q) \equiv Q$ and therefore, since $\text{ans}(Q)$ is safe and thus executable, Q is feasible.

We show in Section 5 that the converse also holds; this is one of our main results.

```
Input:  – CQ¬ query Q = L1 ∧ ... ∧ Lk over a schema with access patterns P
Output: – ans(Q), the answerable part A of Q

procedure ANSWERABLE(Q, P)
  if UNSATISFIABLE(Q) then return false
  A := ∅;   B := ∅   /* initialize answerable literals and bound variables */
  repeat
    done := true
    for i := 1 to k do
      if Li ∉ A and ( vars(Li) ⊆ B or (positive(Li) and invars(Li) ⊆ B) ) then
        A := A ∧ Li ;   B := B ∪ vars(Li);   done := false
  until done
  return A
```

Fig. 1. Algorithm ANSWERABLE for $\mathrm{CQ}^{\neg}$ queries

4 Computing Plans and Answering Queries

Given a $\mathrm{UCQ}^{\neg}$ query $Q = Q_1 \vee \cdots \vee Q_n$ over a relational schema with access pattern restrictions $\mathcal{P}$, our goal is to find executable plans for Q which satisfy $\mathcal{P}$. As we shall see such plans may not always exist and deciding whether Q is feasible, i.e., equivalent to some executable Q' is a hard problem ($\mathbf{\Pi}_2^{\mathrm{P}}$-complete). On the other hand, we will be able to obtain efficient approximations, both at compile-time and at runtime. By *compile-time* we mean the time during which the query is being processed, before any specific database instance D is considered or available. By *runtime* we mean the time during which the query is executed against a specific database instance D. For example, feasibility is a compile-time notion, while completeness (of an answer) is a runtime notion.

4.1 Compile-Time Processing

Let us first consider the case of an individual $\mathrm{CQ}^{\neg}$ query $Q = L_1 \wedge \ldots \wedge L_k$ where each L_i is a literal. Figure 1 depicts a simple and efficient algorithm ANSWERABLE to compute $\mathrm{ans}(Q)$, the answerable part of Q: First we handle the special case that Q is unsatisfiable. In this case we return `false`. Otherwise, at every stage, we will have a set of input variables (i.e., variables with bindings) B and an executable sub-plan A. Initially, A and B are empty. Now we iterate, each time looking for at least one more answerable literal L_i that can be handled with the bindings B we have so far ($\mathrm{invars}(L_i)$ gives the variables in L_i which are in input slots). If we find such answerable literal L_i, we add it to A and we update our variable bindings B. When no such L_i is found, we exit the outer loop. Obviously, ANSWERABLE is polynomial (quadratic) time in the size of Q.

We are now ready to consider the general case of computing execution plans for a $\mathrm{UCQ}^{\neg}$ query Q (Figure 2). For each $\mathrm{CQ}^{\neg}$ query Q_i of Q, we compute its answerable part $A_i := \mathrm{ans}(Q_i)$ and its unanswerable part $U_i := Q_i \setminus A_i$. As the underestimate of Q_i^u, we consider A_i if U_i is empty; else we dismiss Q_i

```
Input:  – UCQ¬ query Q(x̄) = Q_1 ∨ ··· ∨ Q_n over a schema with access patterns P
Output: – execution plans Q^u (underestimates), Q^o (overestimates)

procedure PLAN*(Q)
  for i := 1 to n do
      A_i := ANSWERABLE(Q_i, P);  U_i := Q_i \ A_1
      if U_i = ∅ then Q_i^u := A_i else Q_i^u := false
      v̄ := x̄ \ vars(A_i)
      Q_i^o := A_i ∧ ( v̄ = null )
  Q^u := Q_1^u ∨ ··· ∨ Q_n^u;  Q^o := Q_1^o ∨ ··· ∨ Q_n^o
  output Q^u, Q^o
```

Fig. 2. Algorithm PLAN* for UCQ¬ queries

altogether for the underestimate. Either way, we ensure that $Q_i^u \sqsubseteq Q_i$. For the overestimate Q_i^o we give U_i the "benefit of doubt" and consider that it could be true. However, we need to consider the case that not all variables $\bar{x}$ in the head of the query occur in the answerable part A_i: some may appear only in U_i, so we cannot return a value for them. Hence we set the variables in $\bar{x}$ which are not in A_i to `null`. This way we ensure that $Q_i \sqsubseteq Q_i^o$, except when Q_i^o has null values. We have to interpret tuples with nulls carefully (see Section 4.2). Clearly, if all U_i are empty, then $Q^u = Q^o$ and all Q_i can be executed in the order given by ANSWERABLE, so Q is orderable and thus feasible. Also note that PLAN* is efficient, requiring at most quadratic time.

Example 4 (Underestimate, Overestimate Plans) Consider the following query $Q = Q_1 \vee Q_2$ with the access patterns $\mathcal{P} = \{S^{\text{o}}, R^{\text{oo}}, B^{\text{ii}}, T^{\text{oo}}\}$.

$$Q_1(x,y) \longleftarrow \neg S(z), R(x,z), B(x,y)$$
$$Q_2(x,y) \longleftarrow T(x,y)$$

Although we can use $S(z)$ to produce bindings for z, this is not the case for its negation $\neg S(z)$. But by moving $R(x,z)$ to the front of the first disjunct, we can first bind z and then test against the filter $\neg S(z)$. However, we cannot satisfy the access pattern for B. Hence, we will end up with the following plans for $Q^u = Q_1^u \vee Q_2^u$ and $Q^o = Q_1^o \vee Q_2^o$.

$$Q_1^u(x,y) \longleftarrow \texttt{false}$$
$$Q_2^u(x,y) \longleftarrow T(x,y)$$
$$Q_1^o(x,y) \longleftarrow R(x,z), \neg S(z), y = \texttt{null}$$
$$Q_2^o(x,y) \longleftarrow T(x,y)$$

Note that the unanswerable part $U_1 = \{B(x,y)\}$ results in an underestimate Q_1^u equivalent to `false`, so Q_1^u can be dropped from Q^u (the unanswerable $B(x,y)$ is also responsible for the infeasibility of this plan). In the overestimate, $R(x,z)$ is moved in front of $\neg S(z)$, and $B(x,y)$ is replaced by a special condition equating the unknown value of y with `null`.

Input: – UCQ$^{\neg}$ query $Q(\bar{x}) = Q_1 \vee \cdots \vee Q_n$ over a schema with access patterns
Output: – true if Q is feasible, false otherwise

```
procedure FEASIBLE(Q)
  (Q^u, Q^o) := PLAN*(Q)
  if Q^u = Q^o then return true
  if Q^o contains null then return false else return Q^o ⊑ Q
```

Fig. 3. Algorithm FEASIBLE for UCQ$^{\neg}$ queries

Feasibility Test. While PLAN* is an efficient way to compute plans for a query Q, if it returns $Q^u \neq Q^o$ then we do not know whether Q is feasible. One way, discussed below, is to not perform any static analysis in addition to PLAN* and just "wait and see" what results Q^u and Q^o produce at runtime. This approach is particularly useful for ad-hoc, one-time queries.

On the other hand, when designing integrated views of a mediator system over distributed sources and web services, it is desirable to establish at view definition time that certain queries or views are feasible and have an equivalent executable plan for all database instances. For such "view design" and "view debugging" scenarios, a full static analysis using algorithm FEASIBLE in Figure 3 is desirable. First, FEASIBLE calls PLAN* to compute the two plans Q^u and Q^o. If Q^u and Q^o coincide, then Q is feasible. Similarly, if the overestimate contains some CQ$^{\neg}$ sub-query in which a `null` value occurs, we know that Q cannot be feasible (since then ans(Q) is unsafe). Otherwise, Q may still be feasible, i.e., if ans(Q) (= overestimate Q^o in this case) is contained in Q. The complexity of FEASIBLE is dominated by the $\mathbf{\Pi}_2^{\mathrm{P}}$-complete containment check $Q^o \sqsubseteq Q$.

4.2 Runtime Processing

The worst-case complexity of FEASIBLE seems to indicate that in practice and for large queries there is no hope to obtain plans having complete answers. Fortunately, the situation is not that bad after all. First, as indicated above, we may use the outcome of the efficient PLAN* algorithm to at least in some cases decide feasibility at compile-time (see first part of FEASIBLE up to the containment test). Perhaps even more important, from a practical point of view, is the ability to decide completeness of answers dynamically, i.e., at runtime.

Consider algorithm ANSWER* in Figure 4. We first let PLAN* compute the two plans Q^u and Q^o and evaluate them on the given database instance D to obtain the underestimate and overestimate ans_u and ans_o, respectively. If the difference Δ between them is empty, then we know the answer is complete even though the query may not be feasible. Intuitively, the reason is that an unanswerable part which causes the infeasibility may in fact be irrelevant for a specific query.

Input: – UCQ$^\neg$ query $Q(\bar{x}) = Q_1 \vee \cdots \vee Q_n$ over schema $\mathbf{R}$ with access patterns
– D a database instance over $\mathbf{R}$
Output: – underestimate ans_u
– difference Δ to overestimate ans_o
– completeness information

```
procedure ANSWER*(Q)
  (Q^u, Q^o) := PLAN*(Q)
  ans_u := ANSWER(Q^u, D);   ans_o := ANSWER(Q^o, D);   Δ := ans_o \ ans_u
  output ans_u
  if Δ = ∅ then output "answer is complete"
  else
      output "answer is not known to be complete"
      output "these tuples may be part of the answer:" Δ
      if Δ has no null values then
        output "answer is at least" |ans_u|/|ans_o| "complete"
   /* optional: minimize Δ using domain enumeration for U_i */
```

Fig. 4. Algorithm ANSWER*(UCQ$^\neg$) for runtime handling of plans

Example 5 (Not Feasible, Runtime Complete) Consider the plans created for the query in Example 4 (here we dropped the unsatisfiable Q_1^u):

$$\begin{aligned} Q_2^u(x,y) &\longleftarrow T(x,y) \\ Q_1^o(x,y) &\longleftarrow R(x,z), \neg S(z), y = \texttt{null} \\ Q_2^o(x,y) &\longleftarrow T(x,y) \end{aligned}$$

Given that B^{ii} is the only access pattern for B, the query Q_1 in Example 4 is not feasible since we cannot create y bindings for $B(x,y)$. However, for a given database instance D, it may happen that the answerable part $R(x,z), \neg S(z)$ does not produce any results. In that case, the unanswerable part $B(x,z)$ is irrelevant and the answer obtained is still complete.

Sometimes it is not accidental that certain disjuncts evaluate to false, but rather it follows from some underlying semantic constraints, in which case the omitted unanswerable parts do not compromise the completeness of the answer.

Example 6 (Dependencies) In the previous example, if $R.z$ is a foreign key referencing $S.z$, then always $\{z \mid R(x,z)\} \subseteq \{z \mid S(z)\}$. Therefore, the first disjunct $Q_1^o(x,y)$ can be discarded at compile-time by a semantic optimizer. However, even in the absence of such checks, our runtime processing can still recognize this situation and report a complete answer for this infeasible query.

In the BIRN mediator [GLM03], when unfolding queries against global-as-view defined integrated views into UCQ$^\neg$ plans, we have indeed experienced query plans with a number of unsatisfiable (with respect to some underlying, implicit integrity constraints) CQ$^\neg$ bodies. In such cases, when plans are redundant or partially unsatisfiable, our runtime handling of answers allows to report complete answers even in cases when the feasibility check fails or when the semantic optimization cannot eliminate the unanswerable part. In Figure 4, we know that ans_u is complete if Δ is empty, i.e., the overestimate plan Q^o has not contributed new answers. Otherwise we cannot know whether the answer is complete. However, if Δ does not contain `null` values, we can quantify the completeness of the underestimate relative to the overestimate.

We have to be careful when interpreting tuples with nulls in the overestimate.

Example 7 (Nulls) Let us now assume that $R(x,z), \neg S(z)$ from above holds for some variable binding. Such a binding, say $\beta = \{x/\mathtt{a}, z/\mathtt{b}\}$, gives rise to an overestimate tuple $Q_1^o(\mathtt{a}, \mathtt{null})$.

How should we interpret a tuple like $(\mathtt{a}, \mathtt{null}) \in \Delta$? The given variable binding $\beta = \{x/\mathtt{a}, z/\mathtt{b}\}$ gives rise to the following partially instantiated query:

$$Q_1^o(\mathtt{a}, y) \longleftarrow R(\mathtt{a}, \mathtt{b}), \neg S(\mathtt{b}), B(\mathtt{a}, y).$$

Given the access pattern B^{ii} we cannot know the contents of $\{y \mid B(\mathtt{a}, y)\}$. So our special `null` value in the answer means that there may be one or more y values such that $(\mathtt{a}, y)$ is in the answer to Q. On the other hand, there may be no such y in B which has `a` as its first component. So when $(\mathtt{a}, \mathtt{null})$ is in the answer, we can only infer that $R(\mathtt{a}, \mathtt{b})$ and $\neg S(\mathtt{b})$ are true for some value `b`; but we do not know whether indeed there is a matching $B(\mathtt{a}, y)$ tuple. The incomplete information on B due to the `null` value also explains why in this case we cannot give a numerical value for the completeness information in ANSWER*.

From Theorem 16 below it follows that the overestimates ans_o computed via Q^o cannot be improved, i.e., the construction is optimal. This is not the case for the underestimates as presented here.

Improving the Underestimate. The ANSWER* algorithm computes under- and overestimates ans_u, ans_o for UCQ$^\neg$ queries at runtime. If a query is feasible, then we will always have $ans_u = ans_o$, which is detected by ANSWER*. However, in the case of infeasible queries, there are still additional improvements that can be made. Consider the algorithm PLAN* in Figure 2: it divides a CQ$^\neg$ query Q_i into two parts, the answerable part A_i and the unanswerable part U_i. For each variable x_j which requires input bindings in U_i not provided by U_i, we can create a *domain enumeration view* $\mathsf{dom}(x_j)$ over the relations of the given schema and provide the bindings obtained in this way as partial domain enumerations to U_i.

Example 8 (Domain Enumeration) For our running example from above, instead of Q_1^u being `false`, we obtain an improved underestimate as follows:

$$Q_1^u(x,y) \longleftarrow R(x,z), \neg S(z), \mathsf{dom}(y), B(x,y)$$

where $\mathsf{dom}(y)$ could be defined, e.g., as the union of the projections of various columns from other relations for which we have access patterns with output slots: $\mathsf{dom}(x) \longleftarrow R(x,y) \vee R(z,x) \vee \ldots$

This domain enumeration approach has been used in various forms [DL97]. Note that in our setting of ANSWER* we can create a very dynamic handling of answers: if ANSWER* determines that $\Delta \neq \emptyset$, the user may want to decide at that point whether he or she is satisfied with the answer or whether the possibly costly domain enumeration views should be used. Similarly, the relative answer completeness provided by ANSWER* can be used to guide the user and/or the system when introducing domain enumeration views.

5 Feasibility of Unions of Conjunctive Queries with Negation

We now establish the complexity of deciding feasibility for safe $\mathrm{UCQ}^\neg$ queries.

5.1 Query Containment

We need to consider query containment for $\mathrm{UCQ}^\neg$ queries. In general, query P is said to be *contained* in query Q (in symbols, $P \sqsubseteq Q$) if for all instances D, ANSWER$(P, D) \subseteq$ ANSWER(Q, D). We write $\mathrm{CONT}(\mathcal{L})$ for the following decision problem: For a class of queries $\mathcal{L}$, given $P, Q \in \mathcal{L}$ determine whether $P \sqsubseteq Q$.

For $P, Q \in \mathrm{CQ}$, a function σ: $\mathrm{vars}(Q) \to \mathrm{vars}(P)$ is a *containment mapping* if P and Q have the same free (distinguished) variables, σ is the identity on the free variables of Q, and, for every literal $R(\bar{y})$ in Q, there is a literal $R(\sigma\bar{y})$ in P.

Some early results in database theory are:

Proposition 6 *[CM77]* $\mathrm{CONT}(\mathrm{CQ})$ *and* $\mathrm{CONT}(\mathrm{UCQ})$ *are* **NP**-*complete.*

Proposition 7 *[SY80,LS93]* $\mathrm{CONT}(\mathrm{CQ}^\neg)$ *and* $\mathrm{CONT}(\mathrm{UCQ}^\neg)$ *are* $\mathbf{\Pi}_2^{\mathrm{P}}$-*complete.*

For many important special cases, testing containment can be done efficiently. In particular, the algorithm given in [WL03] for containment of safe $\mathrm{CQ}^\neg$ and $\mathrm{UCQ}^\neg$ uses an algorithm for $\mathrm{CONT}(\mathrm{CQ})$ as a subroutine. Chekuri and Rajaraman [CR97] show that containment of acyclic CQs can be solved in polynomial time (they also consider wider classes of CQs) and Saraiya [Sar91] shows that containment of CQs, in the case where no relation appears more than twice in the body, can be solved in linear time. By the nature of the algorithm in [WL03], these gains in efficiency will be passed on directly to the test for containment of CQs and UCQs (so the check will be in **NP**) and will also improve the test for containment of $\mathrm{CQ}^\neg$ and $\mathrm{UCQ}^\neg$.

5.2 Feasibility

Definition 8 (Feasibility Problem) $\mathrm{FEASIBLE}(\mathcal{L})$ is the following decision problem: given $Q \in \mathcal{L}$ decide whether Q is feasible for the given access patterns.

Before proving our main results, Theorems 16 and 18, we need to establish a number of auxiliary results. Recall that we assume queries to be safe; in particular Theorems 12 and 13 hold only for safe queries.

Proposition 8 *$Q \in \mathrm{CQ}^\neg$ is unsatisfiable iff there exists a relation R and terms $\bar{x}$ so that both $R(\bar{x})$ and $\neg R(\bar{x})$ appear in Q.*

PROOF Clearly if there are such R and $\bar{x}$ then Q is unsatisfiable. If not, then consider the frozen query $[Q^+]$ ($[Q^+]$ is a Herbrand model of Q^+). Clearly $[Q^+] \models Q$ so Q is satisfiable.

Therefore, we can check whether $Q \in \mathrm{CQ}^\neg$ is satisfiable in quadratic time: for every $R(\bar{x})$ in Q^+, look for $\neg R(\bar{x})$ in Q^-.

Proposition 9 *If $\hat{R}(\bar{x})$ is Q-answerable, then it is Q^+-answerable.*

Proposition 10 *If $Q \in \mathrm{CQ}^\neg$, $\hat{S}(\bar{x})$ is Q-answerable, and for every literal $R(\bar{x})$ in Q^+, $\neg R(\bar{x})$ is P-answerable, then $\hat{S}(\bar{x})$ is P-answerable.*

PROOF If $\hat{S}(\bar{x})$ is Q-answerable, it is Q^+-answerable by Proposition 9. By definition, there must be executable Q' consisting of $\hat{S}(\bar{x})$ and literals from Q^+. Since every literal $R(\bar{x})$ in Q^+ is P-answerable, there must be executable P^R consisting of $R(\bar{x})$ and literals from P. Then the conjunction of all P^Rs is executable and consists of $\hat{S}(\bar{x})$ and literals from P. That is, $\hat{S}(\bar{x})$ is P-answerable.

Proposition 11 *If $P, Q \in \mathrm{CQ}$, σ: $\mathrm{vars}(Q) \to \mathrm{vars}(P)$ is a containment mapping (so $P \sqsubseteq Q$), and $\hat{R}(\sigma\bar{x})$ is Q-answerable, then $\hat{R}(\bar{x})$ is P-answerable.*

PROOF If the hypotheses hold, there must be executable Q' consisting of $\hat{R}(\sigma\bar{x})$ and literals from Q. Then $P' = \sigma Q'$ consists of $\hat{R}(\bar{x})$ and literals from P. Since we can use the same adornments for P' as the ones we have for Q', P' is executable and therefore, $\hat{R}(\bar{x})$ is P-answerable.

Given $P, R \in \mathrm{CQ}^\neg$ where $P = (\exists\bar{x})\, P'$ and $Q = (\exists\bar{y})\, Q'$ and where P' and Q' are quantifier free (i.e., consist only of joins), we write P, Q to denote the query $(\exists\bar{x}, \bar{y})\, (P' \wedge Q')$. Recently, [WL03] gave the following theorems.

Theorem 12 *[WL03, Theorem 2] If $P, Q \in \mathrm{CQ}^\neg$ then $P \sqsubseteq Q$ iff P is unsatisfiable or there is a containment mapping σ: $\mathrm{vars}(Q) \to \mathrm{vars}(P)$ witnessing $P^+ \sqsubseteq Q^+$ such that, for every negative literal $\neg R(\bar{y})$ in Q, $R(\sigma\bar{y})$ is not in P and $P, R(\sigma\bar{y}) \sqsubseteq Q$.*

Theorem 13 *[WL03, Theorem 5] If $P \in \mathrm{CQ}^\neg$ and $Q \in \mathrm{UCQ}^\neg$ with $Q = Q_1 \vee \ldots \vee Q_k$ then $P \sqsubseteq Q$ iff P is unsatisfiable or if there is i $(1 \leqslant i \leqslant k)$ and a containment mapping σ: $\mathrm{vars}(Q_i) \to \mathrm{vars}(P)$ witnessing $P^+ \sqsubseteq Q^+$ such that, for every negative literal $\neg R(\bar{y})$ in Q_i, $R(\sigma\bar{y})$ is not in P and $P, R(\sigma\bar{y}) \sqsubseteq Q$.*

Therefore, if $P \in \mathrm{CQ}^\neg$ and $Q \in \mathrm{UCQ}^\neg$ with $Q = Q_1 \vee \ldots \vee Q_k$, we have that $P \sqsubseteq Q$ iff there is a tree with root $P^+ \sqsubseteq Q_r^+$ for some r and where each node is of the form $P^+, N_1(\bar{x}_1), \ldots, N_m(\bar{x}_m) \sqsubseteq Q_s^+$ and represents a true containment except when $P, N_1(\bar{x}_1), \ldots, N_m(\bar{x}_m)$ is unsatisfiable, in which case also the node has no children. Otherwise, for some containment mapping

$$\sigma_s\colon \mathrm{vars}(Q_s^+) \to \mathrm{vars}(P^+, N_1(\bar{x}_1), \ldots, N_m(\bar{x}_m))$$

witnessing the containment, there is one child for every negative literal in Q_s. Each child is of the form $P^+, N_1(\bar{x}_1), \ldots, N_m(\bar{x}_m), N_{m+1}(\bar{x}_{m+1}) \sqsubseteq Q_t^+$ where $\bar{x}_{m+1} = \sigma_s(\bar{y})$ and $\neg N_{m+1}(\bar{y})$ appears in Q_s.

We will need the following two facts about this tree, in the special case where $Q \sqsubseteq E$ with E executable, in the proof of Theorem 16.

Lemma 14 *If $\hat{R}(\bar{x})$ is $Q^+, N_1(\bar{x}_1), \ldots, N_m(\bar{x}_m)$-answerable, it is Q^+-answerable.*

Proof By induction. It is obvious for $m = 0$. Assume that the lemma holds for m and that $\hat{R}(\bar{x})$ is $Q^+, N_1(\bar{x}_1), \ldots, N_{m+1}(\bar{x}_{m+1})$-answerable.

We have $Q^+, N_1(\bar{x}_1), \ldots, N_m(\bar{x}_m) \sqsubseteq E_s^+$ for some s witnessed by a containment mapping σ and $\bar{x}_{m+1} = \sigma(\bar{y})$ for some literal $\neg N_{m+1}(\bar{y})$ appearing in E_s. Since E_s is executable, by Propositions 1 and 9, $\neg N_{m+1}(\bar{y})$ is E_s^+-answerable. Therefore by Proposition 11, $\neg N_{m+1}(\bar{x})$ is $Q^+, N_1(\bar{x}_1), \ldots, N_m(\bar{x}_m)$-answerable and by the induction hypothesis, Q^+-answerable. Therefore, by Proposition 10 and the induction hypothesis, $\hat{R}(\bar{x})$ is Q^+-answerable.

Lemma 15 *If the conjunction $Q, N_1(\bar{x}_1), \ldots, N_m(\bar{x}_m)$ is unsatisfiable, then the conjunction* $\mathrm{ans}(Q), N_1(\bar{x}_1), \ldots, N_m(\bar{x}_m)$ *is also unsatisfiable.*

Proof If Q is satisfiable, but $Q, N_1(\bar{x}_1), \ldots, N_m(\bar{x}_m)$ is unsatisfiable, then by Proposition 8 we must have some $\neg N_i(\bar{x}_i)$ in Q. $N_i(\bar{x}_i)$ must have been added from some $N_i(\bar{y})$ in E_s and some containment map

$$\sigma_s\colon \mathrm{vars}(E_s^+) \to \mathrm{vars}(Q^+, N_1(\bar{x}_1), \ldots, N_{i-1}(\bar{x}_{i-1}))$$

satisfying $\sigma_s \bar{y} = \bar{x}$. Since E_s is executable, by Propositions 1 and 9, $\neg N_i(\bar{y})$ is E_s^+-answerable. Therefore by Proposition 11, $\neg N_i(\bar{x}_i)$ is $Q^+, N_1(\bar{x}_1), \ldots, N_m(\bar{x}_m)$-answerable and by Lemma 14, Q^+-answerable. Therefore, we must have $\neg N_i(\bar{x}_i)$ in $\mathrm{ans}(Q)$, so $\mathrm{ans}(Q), N_1(\bar{x}_1), \ldots, N_m(\bar{x}_m)$ is also unsatisfiable.

We include here the proof of Proposition 4 and then prove our main results, Theorems 16 and 18.

Proof (**Proposition 4**) For $Q \in \mathrm{CQ}$ this is clear since $\mathrm{ans}(Q)$ contains only literals from Q and therefore the identity map is a containment mapping from $\mathrm{ans}(Q)$ to Q. If $Q \in \mathrm{CQ}^\neg$ and Q is unsatisfiable, the result is obvious. Otherwise the identity is a containment mapping from $(\mathrm{ans}(Q))^+$ to Q^+. If a negative literal $\neg R(\bar{y})$ appears in $\mathrm{ans}(Q)$, then since $\neg R(\bar{y})$ also appears in Q, we have that $Q, R(\bar{y})$ is unsatisfiable, and therefore $Q \sqsubseteq \mathrm{ans}(Q)$ by Theorem 12.

Theorem 16 *If $Q \in \text{UCQ}^\neg$, E is executable, and $Q \sqsubseteq E$, then $Q \sqsubseteq \text{ans}(Q) \sqsubseteq E$. That is, $\text{ans}(Q)$ is a minimal feasible query containing Q.*

PROOF We have $Q \sqsubseteq \text{ans}(Q)$ from Proposition 4. Set $A_i = \text{ans}(Q_i)$. We know that for all i, $Q_i \sqsubseteq E$. We will show that $Q_i \sqsubseteq E$ implies $A_i \sqsubseteq E$, from which it follows that $\text{ans}(Q) \sqsubseteq E$.

If Q_i is unsatisfiable, then A_i is also unsatisfiable, so $A_i \sqsubseteq E$ holds trivially, Therefore assume, to get a contradiction, that Q_i is satisfiable, $Q_i \sqsubseteq E$, and $A_i \not\sqsubseteq E$. Since Q_i is satisfiable and $Q_i \sqsubseteq E$, by [WL03, Theorem 4.3] we must have a tree with root $Q_i^+ \sqsubseteq E_r^+$ for some r and where each node is of the form $Q_i^+, N_1(\bar{x}_1), \ldots, N_m(\bar{x}_m) \sqsubseteq E_s^+$ and represents a true containment except when $Q_i, N_1(\bar{x}_1), \ldots, N_m(\bar{x}_m)$ is unsatisfiable, in which case also the node has no children. Otherwise, for some containment mapping

$$\sigma_s\colon \text{vars}(E_s^+) \to \text{vars}(Q_i^+, N_1(\bar{x}_1), \ldots, N_m(\bar{x}_m))$$

witnessing the containment there is one child for every negative literal in E_s. Each child is of the form $Q_i^+, N_1(\bar{x}_1), \ldots, N_m(\bar{x}_m), N_{m+1}(\bar{x}_{m+1}) \sqsubseteq E_t^+$ where $\bar{x}_{m+1} = \sigma_s(\bar{y})$ and $\neg N_{m+1}(\bar{y})$ appears in E_s.

Since $A_i \not\sqsubseteq E$, if in this tree we replace every Q_i^+ by A_i^+, by Lemma 15 we must have some non-terminal node where the containment doesn't hold. Accordingly, assume that $Q_i^+, N_1(\bar{x}_1), \ldots, N_m(\bar{x}_m) \sqsubseteq E_s^+$ and $A_i^+, N_1(\bar{x}_1), \ldots, N_m(\bar{x}_m) \not\sqsubseteq E_s^+$. For this to hold, there must be a containment mapping

$$\sigma_s\colon \text{vars}(E_s^+) \to \text{vars}(Q_i^+, N_1(\bar{x}_1), \ldots, N_m(\bar{x}_m))$$

which maps into some literal $R(\bar{x})$ which appears in Q_i^+ but not in A_i^+. That is, there must be some $\bar{y}$ so that $R(\bar{y})$ appears in E_s and $\sigma(\bar{y}) = \bar{x}$. By Propositions 1 and 9, since E_s is executable, $R(\bar{y})$ is E_s^+-answerable. By Proposition 11, $R(\bar{x})$ is $Q_i^+, N_1(\bar{x}_1), \ldots, N_m(\bar{x}_m)$-answerable and so, by Lemma 14, Q_i^+-answerable. Therefore, $R(\bar{x})$ is in A_i^+, which is a contradiction.

Corollary 17 *Q is feasible iff* $\text{ans}(Q) \sqsubseteq Q$.

Theorem 18 $\text{FEASIBLE}(\text{UCQ}^\neg) \equiv_m^{\text{P}} \text{CONT}(\text{UCQ}^\neg)$.

That is, determining whether a $\text{UCQ}^\neg$ query is feasible is polynomial-time many-one equivalent to determining whether a $\text{UCQ}^\neg$ query is contained in another $\text{UCQ}^\neg$ query.

PROOF One direction follows from Corollary 17 and Proposition 2. For the other direction, consider two queries $P, Q \in \text{UCQ}^\neg$ where $P = P_1 \vee \ldots \vee P_k$. The query

$$P' := P_1, B(y) \vee \ldots \vee P_k, B(y)$$

where y is a variable not appearing in P or Q and B is a relation not appearing in P or Q with access pattern B^{i}. We give relations R appearing in P or Q output access patterns (i.e., $R^{\text{ooo}\cdots}$). As a result, P and Q are both executable, but $P' \sqsubset P$ and P' is not feasible. We set $Q' := P' \vee Q$. Clearly, $\text{ans}(Q') \equiv P \vee Q$. If $P \sqsubseteq Q$, then $\text{ans}(Q') \equiv P \vee Q \equiv Q \sqsubseteq Q'$ so by Corollary 17, Q' is feasible. If $P \not\sqsubseteq Q$, then since $P' \sqsubset P$ and $P' \not\sqsubseteq Q$ we have $\text{ans}(Q') \equiv P \vee Q \not\sqsubseteq P' \vee Q \equiv Q'$ so again by Corollary 17, Q' is not feasible.

Since CONT($\text{UCQ}^{\neg}$) is $\mathbf{\Pi}_2^{\text{P}}$-complete, we have

Corollary 19 FEASIBLE($\text{UCQ}^{\neg}$) *is* $\mathbf{\Pi}_2^{\text{P}}$*-complete.*

$\text{UCQ}^{\neg}$ includes the classes CQ, UCQ, and $\text{CQ}^{\neg}$. We have the following strict inclusions $\text{CQ} \subsetneq \text{UCQ}, \text{CQ}^{\neg} \subsetneq \text{UCQ}^{\neg}$. Algorithm FEASIBLE essentially consists of two steps: (i) compute $\text{ans}(Q)$, and (ii) test $\text{ans}(Q) \sqsubseteq Q$. Below we show that FEASIBLE provides optimal processing for all the above subclasses of $\text{UCQ}^{\neg}$. Also, we compare FEASIBLE to the algorithms given in [LC01].

5.3 Conjunctive Queries

Li and Chang [LC01] show that FEASIBLE(CQ) is **NP**-complete and provide two algorithms for testing feasibility of $Q \in \text{CQ}$:

- Find a minimal $M \in \text{CQ}$ so $M \equiv Q$, then check that $\text{ans}(M) = M$ (they call this algorithm CQstable).
- Compute $\text{ans}(Q)$, then check that $\text{ans}(Q) \sqsubseteq Q$ (they call this algorithm CQstable*).

The advantage of the latter approach is that $\text{ans}(Q)$ may be equal to Q, eliminating the need for the equivalence check. For conjunctive queries, algorithm FEASIBLE is exactly the same as CQstable*.

Example 9 (CQ Processing) Consider access patterns F^{o} and B^{i} and the conjunctive query

$$Q(x) \longleftarrow F(x), B(x), B(y), F(z)$$

which is not orderable. Algorithm CQstable first finds the minimal $M \equiv Q$

$$M(x) \longleftarrow F(x), B(x)$$

then checks M for orderability (M is in fact executable). Algorithms CQstable* and FEASIBLE first find $A := \text{ans}(Q)$

$$A(x) \longleftarrow F(x), B(x), F(z)$$

then check that $A \sqsubseteq Q$ holds (which is the case).

5.4 Conjunctive Queries with Union

Li and Chang [LC01] show that FEASIBLE(UCQ) is **NP**-complete and provide two algorithms for testing feasibility of $Q \in \text{UCQ}$ with $Q = Q_1 \vee \ldots \vee Q_k$:

- Find a minimal (with respect to union) $M \in \text{UCQ}$ so $M \equiv Q$ with $M = M_1 \vee \ldots \vee M_\ell$, then check that every M_i is feasible using either CQstable or CQstable* (they call this algorithm UCQstable)
- Take the union P of all the feasible Q_is, then check that $Q \sqsubseteq P$ (they call this algorithm UCQstable*). Clearly, $P \sqsubseteq Q$ holds by construction.

For UCQs, algorithm FEASIBLE is different from both of these and thus provides an alternate algorithm. The advantage of CQstable* and FEASIBLE over CQstable is that P or ans(Q) may be equal to Q, eliminating the need for the equivalence check.

Example 10 (UCQ Processing) Consider access patterns F^{o}, G^{o}, H^{o}, and B^{i} and the query

$$\begin{aligned} Q(x) &\longleftarrow F(x), G(x) \\ Q(x) &\longleftarrow F(x), H(x), B(y) \\ Q(x) &\longleftarrow F(x) \end{aligned}$$

Algorithm UCQstable first finds the minimal (with respect to union) $M \equiv Q$

$$M(x) \longleftarrow F(x)$$

then checks that M is feasible (it is). Algorithm UCQstable* first finds P, the union of the feasible rules in Q

$$\begin{aligned} P(x) &\longleftarrow F(x), G(x) \\ P(x) &\longleftarrow F(x) \end{aligned}$$

then checks that $Q \sqsubseteq P$ holds (it does). Algorithm FEASIBLE finds $A := \text{ans}(Q)$ the union of the answerable part of each rule in Q

$$\begin{aligned} A(x) &\longleftarrow F(x), G(x) \\ A(x) &\longleftarrow F(x), H(x) \\ A(x) &\longleftarrow F(x) \end{aligned}$$

then checks that $A \sqsubseteq Q$ holds (it does).

5.5 Conjunctive Queries with Negation

Proposition 20 $\text{CONT}(\text{CQ}^{\neg}) \leqslant_m^{\text{P}} \text{FEASIBLE}(\text{CQ}^{\neg})$

PROOF Assume $P, Q \in \text{CQ}^{\neg}$ are given by

$$\begin{aligned} P(\bar{x}) &:= (\exists \bar{x}_0)(\hat{R}_1(\bar{x}_1) \wedge \ldots \wedge \hat{R}_k(\bar{x}_k)) \\ Q(\bar{x}) &:= (\exists \bar{y}_0)(\hat{S}_1(\bar{y}_1) \wedge \ldots \wedge \hat{S}_\ell(\bar{y}_\ell)) \end{aligned}$$

where the R_is and S_is are not necessarily distinct and the x_is and y_is are also not necessarily distinct. Then define

$$L(\bar{x}) := (\exists \bar{x}_0, \bar{y}_0, u, v)(T(u) \wedge \hat{R}_1'(u, \bar{x}_1) \wedge \ldots \wedge \hat{R}_k'(u, \bar{x}_k) \wedge \hat{S}_1'(v, \bar{y}_1) \wedge \ldots \wedge \hat{S}_\ell'(v, \bar{y}_\ell))$$

with access patterns T^{o}, $R_i'^{\mathrm{ioo}\ldots}$, $S_i'^{\mathrm{ioo}\ldots}$. Then clearly

$$\mathrm{ans}(L) = (\exists \bar{x}_0, u)(T(u) \wedge \hat{R}_1'(u, \bar{x}_1) \wedge \ldots \wedge \hat{R}_k'(u, \bar{x}_k))$$

and therefore $P \sqsubseteq Q$ iff $P \sqsubseteq P \wedge Q$ iff $\mathrm{ans}(L) \sqsubseteq L$ iff L is feasible. The second iff follows from the fact that every containment mapping η: $P \wedge Q \to P$ corresponds to a unique containment mapping η': $L \to \mathrm{ans}(L)$ and vice versa.

Since CONT(CQ$^\neg$) is $\mathbf{\Pi}_2^{\mathrm{P}}$-complete, we have

Corollary 21 FEASIBLE(CQ$^\neg$) *is* $\mathbf{\Pi}_2^{\mathrm{P}}$*-complete.*

6 Discussion and Conclusions

We have studied the problem of producing and processing executable query plans for sources with limited access patterns. In particular, we have extended the results by Li et al. [LC01,Li03] to conjunctive queries with negation (CQ$^\neg$) and unions of conjunctive queries with negation (UCQ$^\neg$). Our main theorem (Theorem 18) shows that checking feasibility for CQ$^\neg$ and UCQ$^\neg$ is equivalent to checking containment for CQ$^\neg$ and UCQ$^\neg$, respectively, and thus is $\mathbf{\Pi}_2^{\mathrm{P}}$-complete. Moreover, we have shown that our treatment for UCQ$^\neg$ nicely unifies previous results and techniques for CQ and UCQ respectively and also works optimally for CQ$^\neg$. In particular, we have presented a new uniform algorithm which is optimal for all four classes. We have also shown how we can often avoid the theoretical worst-case complexity, both by approximations at compile-time and by a novel runtime processing strategy. The basic idea is to avoid performing the computationally hard containment checks and instead (i) use two efficiently computable approximate plans Q^u and Q^o, which produce tight underestimates and overestimates of the actual query answer for Q (algorithm PLAN*), and defer the containment check in the algorithm FEASIBLE if possible, and (ii) use a runtime algorithm ANSWER*, which may report complete answers even in the case of infeasible plans, and which can sometimes quantify the degree of completeness. [Li03, Sec.7] employs a similar technique to the case of CQ. However, since union and negation are not handled, our notion of bounding the result from above and below is not applicable there (essentially, the underestimate is always empty when not considering union).

Although technical in nature, our work is driven by a number of practical engineering problems. In the Bioinformatics Research Network project [BIR03], we are developing a database mediator system for federating heterogeneous brain data [GLM03,LGM03]. The current prototype takes a query against a global-as-view definition and unfolds it into a UCQ$^\neg$ plan. We have used ANSWERABLE and a simplified version (without containment check) of PLAN* and ANSWER* in the system. Similarly, in the SEEK and SciDAC projects [SEE03,SDM03] we are building distributed scientific workflow systems which can be seen as procedural variants of the declarative query plans which a mediator is processing.

We are interested in extending our techniques to larger classes of queries and to consider the addition of integrity constraints. Even though many questions become undecidable when moving to full first-order or Datalog queries, we are interested in finding analogous compile-time and runtime approximations as presented in this paper.

Acknowledgements. Work supported by NSF-ACI 9619020 (NPACI), NIH 8P41 RR08605-08S1 (BIRN-CC), NSF-ITR 0225673 (GEON), NSF-ITR 0225676 (SEEK), and DOE DE-FC02-01ER25486 (SciDAC).

References

[BIR03] Biomedical Informatics Research Network Coordinating Center (BIRN-CC), University of California, San Diego. http://nbirn.net/, 2003.

[CM77] A. K. Chandra and P. M. Merlin. Optimal Implementation of Conjunctive Queries in Relational Data Bases. In *ACM Symposium on Theory of Computing (STOC)*, pp. 77–90, 1977.

[CR97] C. Chekuri and A. Rajaraman. Conjunctive query containment revisited. In *Intl. Conf. on Database Theory (ICDT)*, Delphi, Greece, 1997.

[DL97] O. M. Duschka and A. Y. Levy. Recursive plans for information gathering. In *Proc. IJCAI*, Nagoya, Japan, 1997.

[FLMS99] D. Florescu, A. Y. Levy, I. Manolescu, and D. Suciu. Query Optimization in the Presence of Limited Access Patterns. In *SIGMOD*, pp. 311–322, 1999.

[GLM03] A. Gupta, B. Ludäscher, and M. Martone. BIRN-M: A Semantic Mediator for Solving Real-World Neuroscience Problems. In *ACM Intl. Conference on Management of Data (SIGMOD)*, 2003. System demonstration.

[LC01] C. Li and E. Y. Chang. On Answering Queries in the Presence of Limited Access Patterns. In *Intl. Conference on Database Theory (ICDT)*, 2001.

[LGM03] B. Ludäscher, A. Gupta, and M. E. Martone. Bioinformatics: Managing Scientific Data. In T. Critchlow and Z. Lacroix, editors, *A Model-Based Mediator System for Scientific Data Management.* Morgan Kaufmann, 2003.

[Li03] C. Li. Computing Complete Answers to Queries in the Presence of Limited Access Patterns. *Journal of VLDB*, 12:211–227, 2003.

[LS93] A. Y. Levy and Y. Sagiv. Queries Independent of Updates. In *Proc. VLDB*, pp. 171–181, 1993.

[NL04] A. Nash and B. Ludäscher. Processing First-Order Queries under Limited Access Patterns. submitted for publication, 2004.

[PGH98] Y. Papakonstantinou, A. Gupta, and L. M. Haas. Capabilities-Based Query Rewriting in Mediator Systems. *Distributed and Parallel Databases*, 6(1):73–110, 1998.

[Sar91] Y. Saraiya. *Subtree elimination algorithms in deductive databases.* PhD thesis, Computer Science Dept., Stanford University, 1991.

[SDM03] Scientific Data Management Center (SDM). http://sdm.lbl.gov/sdmcenter/ and http://www.er.doe.gov/scidac/, 2003.

[SEE03] Science Environment for Ecological Knowledge (SEEK). http://seek.ecoinformatics.org/, 2003.

[SY80] Y. Sagiv and M. Yannakakis. Equivalences Among Relational Expressions with the Union and Difference Operators. *Journal of the ACM*, 27(4):633–655, 1980.

[Ull88] J. Ullman. The Complexity of Ordering Subgoals. In *ACM Symposium on Principles of Database Systems (PODS)*, 1988.

[WL03] F. Wei and G. Lausen. Containment of Conjunctive Queries with Safe Negation. In *Intl. Conference on Database Theory (ICDT)*, 2003.

[WSD03] Web Services Description Language (WSDL) Version 1.2. http://www.w3.org/TR/wsdl12, June 2003.

Projection Pushing Revisited*

Benjamin J. McMahan[1], Guoqiang Pan[1], Patrick Porter[2], and Moshe Y. Vardi[1]

[1] Department of Computer Science, Rice University,
Houston, TX 77005-1892, U.S.A.
{mcmahanb,gqpan}@rice.edu, vardi@cs.rice.edu
[2] Scalable Software
Patrick.Porter@scalablesoftware.com

Abstract. The join operation, which combines tuples from multiple relations, is the most fundamental and, typically, the most expensive operation in database queries. The standard approach to join-query optimization is cost based, which requires developing a cost model, assigning an estimated cost to each query-processing plan, and searching in the space of all plans for a plan of minimal cost. Two other approaches can be found in the database-theory literature. The first approach, initially proposed by Chandra and Merlin, focused on minimizing the number of joins rather then on selecting an optimal join order. Unfortunately, this approach requires a homomorphism test, which itself is NP-complete, and has not been pursued in practical query processing. The second, more recent, approach focuses on structural properties of the query in order to find a project-join order that will minimize the size of intermediate results during query evaluation. For example, it is known that for Boolean project-join queries a project-join order can be found such that the arity of intermediate results is the treewidth of the join graph plus one.

In this paper we pursue the structural-optimization approach, motivated by its success in the context of constraint satisfaction. We chose a setup in which the cost-based approach is rather ineffective; we generate project-join queries with a large number of relations over databases with small relations. We show that a standard SQL planner (we use PostgreSQL) spends an exponential amount of time on generating plans for such queries, with rather dismal results in terms of performance. We then show how structural techniques, including projection pushing and join reordering, can yield exponential improvements in query execution time. Finally, we combine early projection and join reordering in an implementation of the bucket-elimination method from constraint satisfaction to obtain another exponential improvement.

1 Introduction

The join operation is the most fundamental and, typically, the most expensive operation in database queries. Indeed, most database queries can be expressed as select-project-join queries, combining joins with selections and projections. Choosing an optimal *plan*, i.e., the particular order in which to perform the select, project, and join operations

* Work supported in part by NSF grants CCR-9988322, CCR-0124077, CCR-0311326, IIS-9908435, IIS-9978135, and EIA-0086264.

E. Bertino et al. (Eds.): EDBT 2004, LNCS 2992, pp. 441–458, 2004.
© Springer-Verlag Berlin Heidelberg 2004

in the query, can have a drastic impact on query processing time and is therefore a key focus in query-processing research [32,19]. The standard approach is that of *cost-based optimization* [22]. This approach requires the development of a cost model, based on database statistics such as relation size, block size, and selectivity, which enables assigning an estimated cost to each plan. The problem then reduces to searching the space of all plans for a plan of minimal cost. The search can be either exhaustive, for search spaces of limited size (cf. [4]), or incomplete, such as simulated annealing or other approaches (cf. [25]). In constructing candidate plans, one takes into account the fact that the join operation is associative and commutative, and that selections and projections commute with joins under certain conditions (cf. [34]). In particular, selections and projections can be "pushed" downwards, reducing the number of tuples and columns in intermediate relations [32]. Cost-based optimizations are effective when the search space is of manageable size and we have reasonable cost estimates, but it does not scale up well with query size (as our experiments indeed show).

Two other approaches can be found in the database-theory literature, but had little impact on query-optimization practice. The first approach, initially proposed by Chandra and Merlin in [8] and then explored further by Aho, Ullman, and Sagiv in [3,2], focuses on minimizing the number of joins rather than on selecting a plan. Unfortunately, this approach generally requires a *homomorphism* test, which itself is NP-hard [20], and has not been pursued in practical query processing.

The second approach focuses on structural properties of the query in order to find a project-join order that will minimize the size of intermediate results during query evaluation. This idea, which appears first in [34], was first analytically studied for acyclic joins [35], where it was shown how to choose a project-join order in a way that establishes a linear bound on the size of intermediate results. More recently, this approach was extended to general project-join queries. As in [35], the focus is on choosing the project-join order in such a manner so as to polynomially bound the size of intermediate results [10,21,26,11]. Specific attention was given in [26,11] to *Boolean* project-join queries, in which all attributes are projected out (equivalently, such a query simply tests the nonemptiness of a join query). For example, [11] characterizes the minimal arity of intermediate relations when the project-join order is chosen in an optimal way and projections are applied as early as possible. This minimal arity is determined by the *join graph*, which consists of all attributes as nodes and all relation schemes in the join as cliques. It is shown in [11] that the minimal arity is the *treewidth* of the join graph plus one. The treewidth of a graph is a measure of how close this graph is to being a tree [16] (see formal definition in Section 5). The arity of intermediate relations is a good proxy for their size, since a constant-arity bound translates to a polynomial-size bound. This result reveals a theoretical limit on the effectiveness of projection pushing and join reordering in terms of the treewidth of the join graph. (Note that the focus in [28] is on projection pushing in recursive queries; the non-recursive case is not investigated.)

While acyclicity can be tested efficiently [31], finding the treewidth of a graph is NP-hard [5]. Thus, the results in [11] do not directly lead to a feasible way of finding an optimal project-join order, and so far the theory of projection pushing, as developed in [10,21,26,11], has not contributed to query optimization in practice. At the same time, the projection-pushing strategy has been applied to solve constraint-satisfaction problems in Artificial Intelligence with good experimental results [29,30]. The input to a constraint-satisfaction problem consists of a set of variables, a set of possible values for the variables, and a set of constraints between the variables; the question is to determine whether there is an assignment of values to the variables that satisfies the given constraints. The study of constraint satisfaction occupies a prominent place in Artificial Intelligence, because many problems that arise in different areas can be modeled as constraint-satisfaction problems in a natural way; these areas include Boolean satisfiability, temporal reasoning, belief maintenance, machine vision, and scheduling [14]. A general method for projection pushing in the context of constraint satisfaction is the *bucket-elimination* method [15,14]. Since evaluating Boolean project-join queries is essentially the same as solving constraint-satisfaction problems [26], we attempt in this paper to apply the bucket-elimination approach to approximate the optimal project-join order (i.e., the order that bounds the arity of the intermediate results by the treewidth plus one).

In order to focus solely on projection pushing in project-join expressions, we choose an experimental setup in which the cost-based approach is rather ineffective. To start, we generate project-join queries with a large number (up to and over 100) of relations. Such expressions are common in mediator-based systems [36]. They challenge cost-based planners, because of the exceedingly large size of the search space, leading to unacceptably long query compile time. Furthermore, to factor out the influence of cost information we consider small databases, which fit in main memory and where cost information is essentially irrelevant. (Such databases arise naturally in query containment and join minimization, where the query itself is viewed as a database [8]. For a survey of recent applications of query containment see [23].) We show experimentally that a standard SQL planner (we use PostgreSQL) spends an exponential amount of time on generating plans for such queries, with rather dismal results in terms of performance and without taking advantage of projection pushing (and neither do the SQL planners of DB2 and Oracle, despite the widely held belief that projection pushing is a standard query-optimization technique).

Our experimental test suite consists of a variety of project-join queries. We take advantage of the correspondence between constraint satisfaction and project-join queries [26] to generate queries and databases corresponding to instances of 3-COLOR problems [20]. Our main focus in this paper is to study the scalability of various projection-pushing methods. Thus, our interest is in comparing the performance of different optimization techniques when the size of the queries is increased. We considered both random queries as well as a variety of queries with specific structures, such as "augmented paths", "ladders", "augmented ladders", and "augmented circular ladders" [27]. To study the effectiveness of the bucket-elimination approach, we start with a straightforward plan that joins the relations in the order in which they are listed, without applying projection pushing. We then proceed to apply projection pushing and join reordering in a greedy fashion. We demonstrate experimentally that this yields exponential improvement in query execution time over the straightforward approach. Finally, we combine projection pushing and join reordering in an implementation of the bucket-elimination method. We first prove that this method is optimal for general project-join queries with respect to intermediate-result arity, provided the "right" order of "buckets" is used (this was previously known only for Boolean project-join queries [15,17,26,11]). Since finding such an order is NP-hard [5], we use the "maximum cardinality" order of [31], which is often used to approximate the optimal order [7,29,30]. We demonstrate experimentally that this approach yields an exponential improvement over the greedy approach for the complete range of input queries in our study. This shows that applying bucket elimination is highly effective even when applied heuristically and it significantly dominates greedy heuristics, without incurring the excessive cost of searching large plan spaces.

The outline of the paper is as follows. Section 2 describes the experimental setup. We then describe a naive and straightforward approach in Section 3, a greedy heuristic approach in Section 4, and the bucket-elimination approach in Section 5. We report on our scalability experiments in Section 6, and conclude with a discussion in Section 7.

2 Experimental Setup

Our goal is to study join-query optimization in a setting in which the traditional cost-based approach is ineffective, since we are interested in using the structure of the query to drive the optimization. Thus, we focus on project-join queries with a large number of relations over a very small database, which not only easily fits in main memory, but also where index or selectivity information is rather useless. First, to neutralize the effect of query-result size we consider Boolean queries in which all attributes are projected out, so the final result consists essentially of one bit (empty result vs. nonempty result). Then we also consider queries where a fraction of attributes are not projected out, to simulate more closely typical database usage. We work with project-join queries, also known as *conjunctive queries* (conjunctive queries are usually defined as positive, existential conjunctive first-order formulas [1]). Formally, an n-ary project-join query is a query definable by the project-join fragment of relational algebra; that is, by an expression of the form $\pi_{x_1,\ldots,x_n}(R_1 \bowtie \ldots \bowtie R_m)$, where the R_js are relations and $x_1,\ldots,x_n$ are the free variables (we use the terms "variables" and "attributes" interchangably). Initially, we focus on Boolean project-join queries, in which there are no free variables. We emulate Boolean queries by including only a single variable in the projection (i.e., $n = 1$). Later we consider non-Boolean queries where there are a fixed fraction of free variables by listing them in the projection.

In our experiments, we generate queries with the desired characteristics by translating graph instances of 3-COLOR into project-join queries, cf. [8]. This translation yields queries over a single binary relation with six tuples. It is important to note, however, that our algorithms do not rely on the special structure of the queries that we get from 3-COLOR instances (i.e., bounded arity of relations and bounded domain size)–they are applicable to project-join queries in general. An instance of 3-COLOR is a graph $G = (V, E)$ and a set of colors $C = \{1, 2, 3\}$, where $|V| = n$ and $|E| = m$. For each edge $(u, v) \in E$, there are six possible colorings of (u, v) to satisfy the requirement of no monochromatic edges. We define the relation *edge* as containing all six tuples corresponding to all pairs of distinct colors. The query Q_G is then expressed as the project-join expression $\pi_{v_1} \bowtie_{(v_i,v_j)\in E} edge(v_i, v_j)$. This query returns a nonempty result over the *edge* relation iff G is 3-colorable [8].

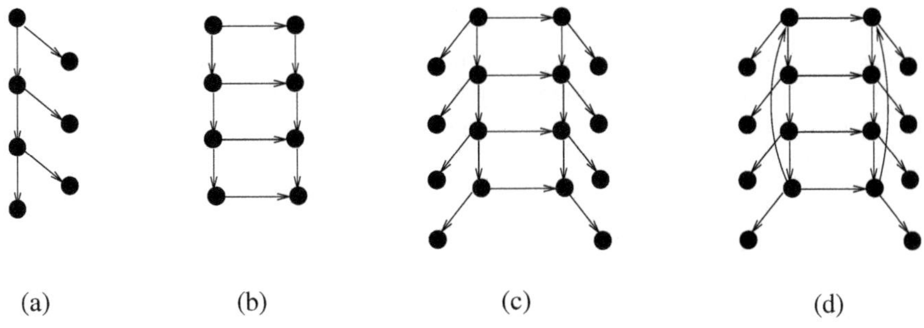

Fig. 1. Augmented path, ladder, augmented ladder, and augmented circular ladder

We note that our queries have the following features (see our concluding remarks):

- Projecting out a column from our relation yields a relation with all possible tuples. Thus, in our setting, *semijoins*, as in the Wong-Youssefi algorithm [34], are useless. This enables us to focus solely on ordering joins and projections.
- Since we only have one relation of fixed arity, differences between the various notions of width, such as treewidth, query width, and hypertree widths are minimized [10, 21], enabling us to focus in this paper on treewidth.

To generate a range of queries with varying structural properties, we start by generating random graph instances. For a fixed number n of vertices and a fixed number m of edges, instances are generated uniformly. An edge is generated by choosing uniformly at random two distinct vertices. Edges are generated (without repetition) until the right number of edges is arrived at. We measure the performance of our algorithms by scaling up the size of the queries (note that the database here is fixed). We focus on two types of scalability. First, we keep the *order* (i.e. the number of vertices) fixed, while scaling up the *density*, which is the ratio m/n of edges to vertices. Second, we keep the density fixed while scaling up the order. Clearly, a low density suggests that the instance is underconstrained, and therefore is likely to be 3-colorable, while a high density suggests that the instance is overconstrained and is unlikely to be 3-colorable. Thus, density scaling yields a spectrum of problems, going from underconstrained to overconstrained. We studied orders between 10 and 35 and densities between 0.5 and 8.0.

We also consider non-random graph instances for 3-COLOR. These queries, suggested in [27], have specific structures. An *augmented path* (Figure 1a) is a path of length n, where for each vertex on the path a dangling edge extends out of the vertex. A *ladder* (Figure 1b) is a ladder with n rungs. An *augmented ladder* (Figure 1c) is a ladder where every vertex has an additional dangling edge, and an *augmented circular ladder* (Figure 1d) is an augmented ladder where the top and bottom vertices are connected together with an edge. For these instances only the order is scaled; we used orders from 5 to 50.

All experiments were performed on the Rice Tersascale Cluster[1], which is a Linux cluster of Itanium II processors with 4GB of memory each, using PostgreSQL[2] 7.2.1.

[1] `http://www.citi.rice.edu/rtc/`

[2] `http://www.postgresql.org/`

For each run we measured the time it took to generate the query, the time the PostgreSQL Planner took to optimize the query, and the execution time needed to actually run the query. For lack of space we report only median running times. Using command-line parameters we selected hash joins to be the default, as hash joins proved most efficient in our setting.

3 Naive and Straightforward Approaches

Given a conjunctive query $\varphi = \pi_{v_1} \bowtie_{(v_i,v_j) \in E} edge(v_i, v_j)$, we first use a *naive* translation of φ into SQL:

SELECT DISTINCT $e_1.u_1$
FROM *edge* e_1 (u_1, w_1), ..., *edge* e_m (u_m, w_m)
WHERE $\bigwedge_{j=1}^{m} (e_j.u_j = e_{p(u_j)}.u_j$ AND $e_j.w_j = e_{p(w_j)}.w_j)$

As SQL does not explicitly allow us to express Boolean queries, we instead put a single vertex in the SELECT section. The FROM section simply enumerates all the atoms in the query, referring to them as $e_1, \ldots, e_m$ and renames the columns to match the vertices of the query. The WHERE section enforces equality of different occurrences of the same vertex. More precisely, we enforce equality of each occurrence to the first occurrence of the same vertex; $p(v_i)$ points to the first occurrence of the vertex v_i.

We ran these queries for instances of order 5 and integral densities from 1 to 8 (the database engine could not handle larger orders with the naive approach). The PostgreSQL Planner found the naive queries exceedingly difficult to compile; compile time was four orders of magnitude longer than execution time. Furthermore, compile time scaled exponentially with the density as shown in Figure 2. We used the PostgreSQL Planner's genetic algorithm option to search for a query plan, as an exhaustive search for our queries was infeasible. This algorithm proved to be quite slow as well as ineffective for our queries. The plans generated by the Planner showed that it does not utilize at all projection pushing; it simply chooses some join order.

In an attempt to get around the Planner's ineffectiveness, we implemented a *straightforward* approach. We explicitly list the joins in the FROM section of the query, instead of using equalities in the WHERE section as in the naive approach.

SELECT DISTINCT $e_1.u_1$
FROM *edge* e_1 (u_1, w_1) JOIN ... JOIN *edge* e_m (u_m, w_m)
ON $(e_1.u_1 = e_{p(u_1)}.u_1$ AND $e_1.w_1 = e_{p(w_1)})$ ON ... ON $(e_m.u_m = e_{p(u_m)}.u_m$ AND $e_m.w_m = e_{p(w_m)})$

Parentheses forces the evaluation to proceed from e_1 to e_2 and onwards (i.e., $(\ldots(e_1 \bowtie e_2)\ldots \bowtie e_m)$). We omit parentheses here for sake of readability.

The order in which the relations are listed then becomes the order that the database engine evaluates the query. This effectively limits what the Planner can do and therefore drastically decreases compile time. As is shown in Figure 2, compile time still scales exponentially with density, but more gracefully than the compile time for the naive approach.

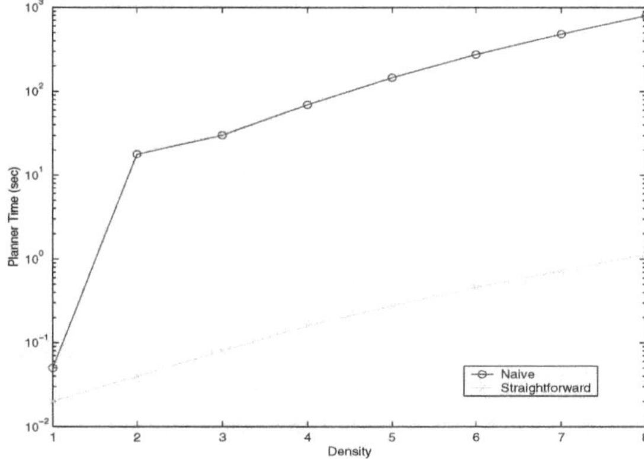

Fig. 2. Naive and straightforward approaches: density scaling of compile time, 3-SAT, 5 variables, logscale

We note that the straightforward approach also does not take advantage of projection pushing. We found query execution time for the naive and straightforward approaches to be essentially identical; the join order chosen by the genetic algorithm is apparently no better than the straightforward order.

In the rest of the paper we show how we can take advantage of projection pushing and join reordering to improve query execution time dramatically. As a side benefit, since we use subqueries to enforce a particular join and projection order, compile time becomes rather negligible, which is why we do not report it.

4 Projection Pushing and Join Reordering

The conjunctive queries we are considering have the form $\pi_{v_1}(e_1 \bowtie e_2 \bowtie \ldots \bowtie e_m)$. If v_j does not appear in the relations $e_{k+1}, \ldots, e_m$, then we can rewrite the formula into an equivalent one:

$$\pi_{v_1}(\pi_{livevars}(e_1 \bowtie \ldots \bowtie e_k) \bowtie \ldots \bowtie e_m)$$

where $livevars$ are all the variables in the scope minus v_j. This means we can write a query to join the relations $e_1, \ldots, e_k$, project out v_j, and join the result with relations $e_{k+1}, \ldots, e_m$. We then say that the projection of v_j has been pushed in and v_j has been *projected early*. The hope is that early projection would reduce the size of intermediate results by reducing their arity, making further joins less expensive, and thus reducing the execution time of the query. Note that the reduction in size of intermediate results has to offset the overhead of creating a copy of the projected relations. We implemented early projection in SQL using subqueries. The subformula found in the scope of each nested existential quantifier is itself a conjunctive query, therefore each nested existential quantifier becomes a subquery. Suppose that k and j above are minimal. Then the SQL query can be rewritten as:

SELECT DISTINCT $e_m.u_m$
FROM *edge* e_m (u_m, w_m) JOIN ... JOIN *edge* e_{k+1} (u_{k+1}, w_{k+1}) JOIN (subquery$_k$)
AS t_k
ON $(e_{k+1}.u_{k+1} = e_{p(u_{k+1})}.u_{p(u_{k+1})}$ AND $e_{k+1}.w_{k+1} = e_{p(w_{k+1})}.w_{p(w_{k+1})})$ ON ...
ON $(e_m.u_m = e_{p(u_m)}.u_{p(u_m)}$ AND $e_m.w_m = e_{p(w_m)}.w_{p(w_m)})$

where subquery$_k$ is obtained by translating the subformula $\pi_{livevars}(e_1 \bowtie \ldots \bowtie e_k)$ into SQL according to the straightforward approach (with $p(v_l)$ updated to point toward t_k, when appropriate, for occurrences of v_l in $e_{k+1}, \ldots, e_m$). The only difference between the subquery and the full query is the SELECT section. In the subquery the SELECT section contains all *live* variables within its scope, i.e. all variables except for v_j. Finally, we proceed recursively to apply early projection to the join of $e_{k+1}, \ldots, e_m$.

The early projection method processes the relations of the query in a linear fashion. Since the goal of early projection is to project variables as soon as possible, reordering the relations may enable us to project early more aggressively. For example, if a variable v_j appears only in the first and the last relation, early projection will not quantify v_j out. But had the relations been processed in a different order, v_j could have been projected out very early. In general, instead of processing the relations in the order $e_1, \ldots, e_m$, we can apply a permutation ρ and process the relations in the order $e_{\rho(1)}, \ldots, e_{\rho(m)}$. The permutation ρ should be chosen so as to minimize the number of live variables in the intermediate relations. This observation was first made in the context of symbolic model checking, cf. [24]. Finding an optimal permutation for the order of the relations is a hard problem in and of itself. So we have implemented a greedy approach, searching at each step for an atom that would result in the maximum number of variables to be projected early. The algorithm incrementally computes an atom order. At each step, the algorithm searches for an atom with the maximum number of variables that occur only once in the remaining atoms. If there is a tie, the algorithm chooses the atom that shares the least variables with the remaining atoms. Further ties are broken randomly. Once the permutation ρ is computed, we construct the same SQL query as before, but this time with the order suggested by ρ. We then call this method *reordering*.

5 Bucket Elimination

The optimizations applied in Section 4 correspond to a particular rewriting of the original conjunctive query according to the algebraic laws of the relational algebra [32]. By using projection pushing and join reordering, we have attempted to reduce the arity of intermediate relations. It is natural to ask what the limit of this technique is, that is, if we consider all possible join orders and apply projection pushing aggressively, what is the minimal upper bound on the arity of intermediate relations?

Consider a project-join query $Q = \pi_{x_1,\ldots,x_n}(R_1 \bowtie \ldots \bowtie R_m)$ over the set $\mathcal{R} = \{R_j | 1 \leq j \leq m\}$ of relations, where A is the set of attributes in $\mathcal{R}$, and the target schema $S_Q = \{x_1, \ldots, x_n\}$ is a subset of A. A *join-expression tree* of Q can be defined as a tuple $J_Q = (T = (V_Q, E_Q, v_0), L_w, L_p)$ where T is a tree, with nodes V_Q and edges E_Q, rooted at v_0, and both $L_w : V_Q \to 2^A$ and $L_p : V_Q \to 2^A$ label the nodes of T with sets of attributes. For each node $v \in V_Q$, $L_w(v)$ is called v's *working label* and $L_p(v)$ is called v's *projected label*. For every leaf node $u \in V_Q$ there is some $R_j \in \mathcal{R}$ such that

$L_w(u) = R_j$. For every nonleaf node $v \in V_Q$, we define $L_w(v) = \bigcup_{\{x|(v,x)\in E_Q\}} L_p(x)$ as the union of the projected labels of its children. The projected label $L_p(u)$ of a node u is the subset of $L_w(u)$ that consists of all $a \in L_w(u)$ that appear outside the subtree of T rooted at u. All other attributes are said to be *unnecessary* for u. Intuitively, the join-expression tree describes an evaluation order for the join, where the joins are evaluated bottom up and projection is applied as early as possible for that particular evaluation order. The *width* of the join-expression tree J_Q is defined as $\max_{v\in V_Q} |L_w(v)|$, the maximum size of the working label. The *join width* of Q is the width over all possible join-expression trees of Q.

To understand the power of join reordering and projection pushing, we wish to characterize the join width of project-join queries. We now describe such a characterization in terms of the *join graph* of Q. In the join graph $G_Q = (V, E)$, the node set V is the set A of attributes, and the edge set E consists of all pairs (x, y) of attributes that co-occur in some relation $R_j \in \mathcal{R}$. Thus, each relation $R_j \in \mathcal{R}$ yields a clique over its attributes in G_Q. In addition, we add an edge (x, y) for every pair of attributes in the schema S_Q. The important parameter of the join graph is its *treewidth* [16].

Let $G = (V, E)$ be a graph. A *tree decomposition* of G is a pair (T, X), where $T = (I, F)$ is a tree with node set I and edge set F, and $X = \{X_i : i \in I\}$ is a family of subsets of V, one for each node of T, such that (1) $\bigcup_{i\in I} X_i = V$, (2) for every edge $(v, w) \in E$, there is an $i \in I$ with $v \in X_i$ and $w \in X_i$, and (3) for all $i, j, k \in I$, if j is on the path from i to k in T, then $X_i \cap X_k \subseteq X_j$. The *width* of a tree decomposition is $\max_{i\in I} |X_i| - 1$. The *treewidth* of a graph G, denoted by $tw(G)$, is the minimum width over all possible tree decompositions of G. For each fixed $k > 0$, there is a linear-time algorithm that tests whether a given graph G has treewidth k. The algorithms actually constructs a tree decomposition of G of width k [16].

We can now characterize the join width of project-join queries:

Theorem 1. *The join width of a project-join query Q is $tw(G_Q) + 1$.*

Proof Sketch: We first show that the join width of Q provides a bound for $tw(G_Q) + 1$. Given a join-expression tree J_Q of Q with width k, we construct a tree decomposition of G_Q of width $k - 1$. Intuitively, we just drop all the projected labels and use the working label as the tree decomposition labeling function.

Lemma 1. *Given a project-join query Q and join-expression tree J_Q of width k, there is a tree decomposition $T_{J_Q} = ((I, F), X)$ of the join graph G_Q such that the width of T_{J_Q} is $k - 1$.*

In the other direction, we can go from tree decompositions to join-expression trees. First the join graph G_Q is constructed and a tree decomposition of width k for this graph is constructed. Once we have a tree decomposition, we simplify it to have only the nodes needed for the join-expression tree without increasing the width of the tree decomposition. In other words, the leaves of the simplified tree decomposition each correspond to a relation in $\mathcal{R} \cup \mathcal{S}_Q$, and the nodes between these leaves still maintain all the tree-decomposition properties.

Lemma 2. *Given a project-join query Q, its join graph G_Q, and a tree decomposition $(T = (I, F), X)$ of G_Q of width k, there is a simplified tree decomposition $(T' =$*

$(I', F'), X')$ of G_Q of width k such that every leaf node of T' has a label containing an R_j for some $R_j \in \mathcal{R}$.

Lemma 3. *Given a project-join query Q, a join graph G_Q, and a simplified tree decomposition of G_Q of treewidth k, there is a join-expression tree of Q with join width $k+1$.* ∎

Theorem 1 offers a graph-theoretic characterization of the power of projection pushing and join reordering. The theorem extends results in [11] regarding rewriting of Boolean conjunctive queries, expressed in the syntax of first-order logic. That work explores rewrite rules whose purpose is to rewrite the original query Q into a first-order formula using a smaller number of variables. Suppose we succeeded to rewrite Q into a formula of L^k, which is the fragment of first-order logic with k variables, containing all atomic formulas in these k variables and closed only under conjunction and existential quantification over these variables. We then know that it is possible to evaluate Q so that all intermediate relations are of width at most k, yielding a polynomial upper bound on query execution time [33]. Given a Boolean conjunctive query Q, we'd like to characterize the minimal k such that Q can be rewritten into L^k, since this would describe the limit of variable-minimization optimization. It is shown in [11] that if k is a positive integer and Q a Boolean conjunctive query, then the join graph of Q has treewidth $k-1$ iff there is an L^k-sentence ψ that is a rewriting of Q. Theorem 1 not only uses the more intuitive concepts of join width (rather than expressibility in L^k), but also extend the characterization to non-Boolean queries.

Unfortunately, we cannot easily turn Theorem 1 into an optimization method. While determining if a given graph G has treewidth k can be done in linear time, this depends on k being fixed. Finding the treewidth is known to be NP-hard [5]. An alternative strategy to minimizing the width of intermediate results is given by the *bucket-elimination* approach for constraint-satisfaction problems [13], which are equivalent to Boolean project-join queries [26]. We now rephrase this approach and extend it to general project-join queries. Assume that we are given an order $x_1, \ldots, x_n$ of the attributes of a query Q. We start by creating n "buckets", one for each variable x_i. For an atom $r_i(x_{i_1}, \ldots, x_{i_k})$ of the query, we place the relation r_i with attributes $x_{i_1}, \ldots, x_{i_k}$ in bucket $\max\{i_1, \ldots, i_k\}$. We now iterate on i from n to 1, eliminating one bucket at a time. In iteration i, we find in bucket i several relations, where x_i is an attribute in all these relations. We compute their join, and project out x_i if it is not in the target schema. Let the result be r_i'. If r_i' is empty, then the result of the query is empty. Otherwise, let j be the largest index smaller than i, such that x_j is an attribute of r_i'; we move r_i' to bucket j. Once all the attributes that are not in the target schema have been projected out, we join the remaining relations to get the answer to the query. For Boolean queries (for which bucket elimination was originally formulated), the answer to the original query is 'yes' if none of the joins returns an empty result.

The maximal arity of the relations computed during the bucket-elimination process is called the *induced width* of the process relative to the given variable order. Note that the sequence of operations in the bucket-elimination process is independent of the actual relations and depends only on the relation's schemas (i.e., the attributes) and the order of the variables [17]. By permuting the variables we can perhaps minimize the induced width. The *induced width of the query* is the induced width of bucket elimination with respect to the best possible variable order.

Theorem 2. *The induced width of a project-join query is its treewidth.*

This theorem extends the characterization in [15,17] for Boolean project-join queries.

Theorem 2 tells us that we can optimize the width of intermediate results by scheduling the joins and projections according to the bucket-elimination process, using a subquery for each bucket, if we are provided with the optimal variable order. Unfortunately, since determining the treewidth is NP-hard [5], it follows from Theorem 2 that finding optimal variable order is also NP-hard. Nevertheless, we can still use the bucket-elimination approach, albeit with a heuristically chosen variable order. We follow here the heuristic suggested in [7,29,30], and use the *maximum-cardinality search order* (MCS order) of [31]. We first construct the join graph G_Q of the query. We now number the variables from 1 to n, where the variables in the target schema are chosen as initial variables and then the i-th variable is selected to maximize the number of edges to variables already selected (breaking ties randomly).

6 Experimental Results

6.1 Implementation Issues

Given a k-COLOR graph instance, we convert the formula into an SQL query. For the non-Boolean case, before we convert the formula we pick 20% of the vertices randomly to be free. The query is then sent to the PostgreSQL backend, which returns a nonempty answer iff the graph is k-colorable. Most of the implementation issues arise in the construction of the optimized query from the graphs formulas. We describe these issues here. The *naive* implementation of this conversion starts by creating an array E of edges, where for each edge $E[i]$ we store its vertices. We also construct an array min_occur such that for every vertex v_j, we have that $min\_occur[j] = \min\{k | j \in E[k]\}$ is the minimal edge containing an occurrence of j. For the SQL query, we SELECT the first vertex that occurs in an edge, and list in the FROM section all the edges and their vertices using the $edge$ relation. Finally, for the WHERE section we traverse the edges and for each edge E_i and each vertex $v_j \in E[i]$ we add the condition $E_i.v_j = E_l.v_j$, where $l = min\_occur[j]$. For the non-Boolean case, the only change is to list the free vertices in the SELECT clause. The *straightforward* implementation uses the same data structures as the naive implementation. The SELECT statement remains the same, but the FROM statement now first lists the edges in reverse order, separated by the keyword JOIN. Then, traversing E as before, we list the equalities $E_i.v_j = E_l.v_j$ as ON conditions for the JOINs (parentheses are used to ensure the joins are performed in the same order as in the naive implementation).

For the *early-projection* method, we create another array max_occur such that for every vertex v_j, we have $max\_occur[j] = \max\{k | j \in E[k]\}$ is the last edge containing v_j. Converting the formula to an SQL query starts the same way as in the straightforward implementation, listing all the edges in the FROM section in reverse order. Before listing an edge $E[i]$ we check whether $i \in max\_occur[j]$ for some vertex v_j (we sort the vertices according to max_occur to facilitate this check). In such a case, we generate a subquery recursively. In the subquery, the SELECT statement lists all *live* vertices at this point minus the vertex v_j, effectively projecting out v_j. We define the set of live vertices as all the vertices $k \in E[l]$ such that $min\_occur[j] \leq l \leq max\_occur[j]$. This subquery is then given a temporary name and is joined with the edges that have already been listed in the FROM section. In the non-Boolean case we initially set, for a free vertex v_j, the $max\_occur[j] = |E| + 1$. This effectively keeps these vertices *live*, so they are kept throughout the subqueries and they are then listed in the outer most SELECT clause. The *reordering* method is a variation of the early-projection method. We first construct a permutation π of the edges, using the greedy approach described in Section 4. We then follow the early-projection method, processing the edges according to the permutation π.

Finally, for the *bucket-elimination* method, we first find the MCS order of the vertices (see Section 5). Given that order, for each vertex v_j we create a bucket that stores the edges and subqueries for v_j. The live vertices of the bucket are the vertices that appear in the edges and in the SELECT sections of the subqueries. Initially, the bucket for v_j contains all edges E_i such that v_j is the maximal vertex in E_i. We now create the SQL query by processing the buckets in descending order. A bucket for v_j is processed by creating a subquery in which we SELECT all the live variables in the bucket (minus v_j if v_j is not free), then listing all the edges and subqueries of the bucket in the FROM section of the subquery and JOINing them using ON conditions as in the straightforward approach. The subquery is then given a temporary name and moved to bucket $v_{j'}$, where $v_{j'}$ is the maximal vertex in the SELECT section of the subquery. The final query is obtained by processing the last bucket, SELECTing only one vertex in the Boolean case or SELECTing the free vertices in the non-Boolean case.

6.2 Density and Order Scaling

In order to test the scalability of our optimization techniques, we varied two parameters of the project-join queries we constructed. In these experiments we measured query execution time (recall that query compilation time is significant only for the straightforward approach). In the first experiment, we fixed the order of the 3-COLOR queries to 20 and compared how the optimizations performed as the density of the formula increased. This tested how, as the structure of the queries changes, the methods used scaled with the structural change. Figure 3 shows the median running times (logscale) of each optimization method as we increase the density of the generated 3-COLOR instances. The left side shows the Boolean query, and the right side considers the non-Boolean case with 20% of the vertices in the target schema. The shape of the curve for the greedy methods are roughly the same. At first, running time increases as density increases, since the number of joins increases with the density. Eventually, the size of the intermediate result becomes quite small (or even empty), so additional joins have little effect on overall running time.

Note that at low densities each optimization method improves upon the previous methods. The sparsity of the instances at low densities allow more aggressive application of the early projection optimization. For denser instances, these optimizations lose their effectiveness, since there are fewer opportunites for early projection. Nevertheless, bucket elimination was able to find opportunities for early projection even for dense instances. As the plot shows, bucket elimination completely dominates the greedy

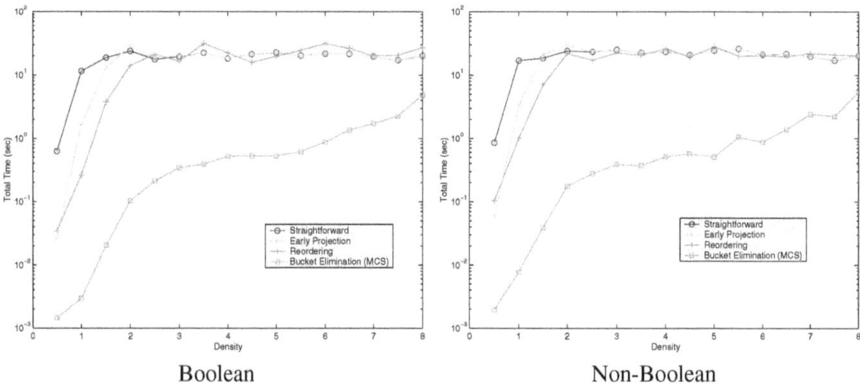

Fig. 3. 3-COLOR Density Scaling, Order = 20 – Logscale

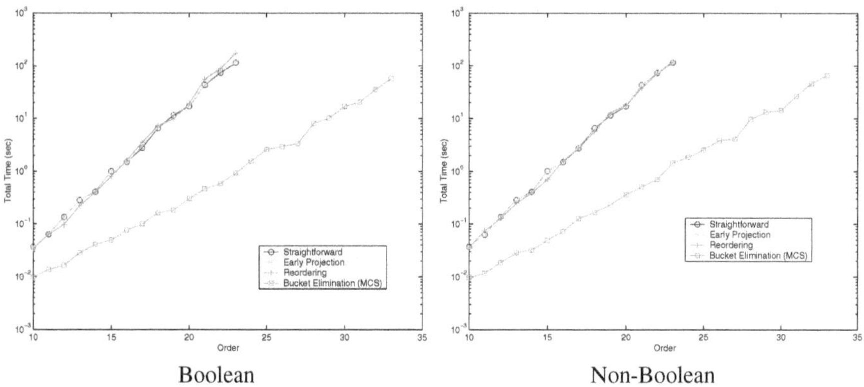

Fig. 4. 3-COLOR Order Scaling, Density = 3.0 – Logscale

methods in running time for both the underconstrained and overconstrained regions. The non-Boolean instances demonstrate a similar behaviour.

For the next experiment, we fixed the density, and looked to see how the optimizations scaled as order is increased. For 3-COLOR we looked at two densities, 3.0 and 6.0; the lower density is associated with (most likely) 3-colorable queries while the high density is associated with (most likely) non-3-colorable queries. Figure 4 shows the running times (logscale) for several optimization methods for density 3.0 as order is scaled from 10 to 35. Notice that all the methods are exponential (linear slope in logscale), but bucket elimination maintains a lower slope. This means that the exponent of the method is strictly smaller and we have an exponential improvement. Figure 5 shows the experiment for density 6.0 as order is scaled from 15 to 30. We see that the greedy heuristics do not improve upon the straightforward approach for both the underconstrained and the overconstrained densities, while bucket elimination still finds opportunities for early projection and shows exponential improvement over the other optimizations.

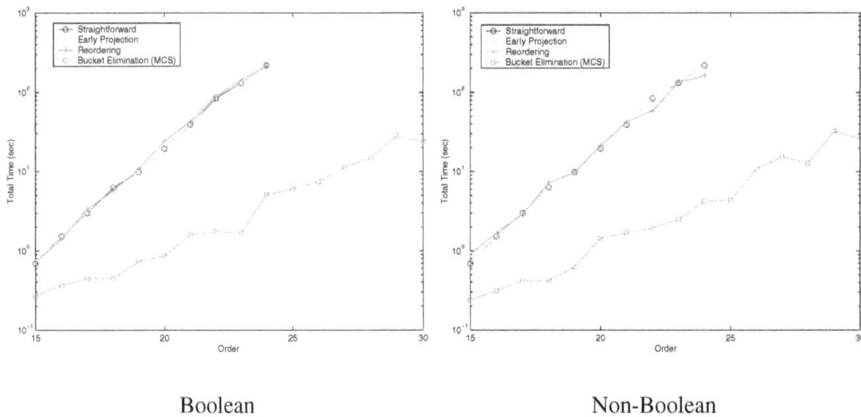

Boolean Non-Boolean

Fig. 5. 3-COLOR Order Scaling, Density = 6.0 – Logscale

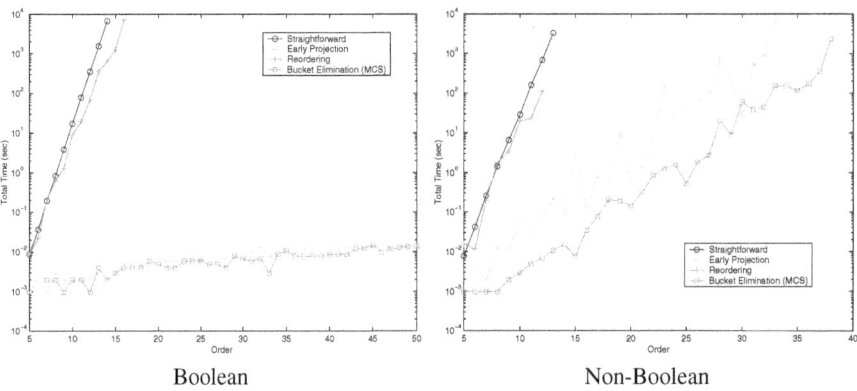

Boolean Non-Boolean

Fig. 6. 3-COLOR Augmented Path Queries – Logscale

Our next focus was to run order-scaling experiments for the structured queries. Figure 6 shows the running time (logscale) for the optimization methods as the augmented path instances scaled. The early projection and bucket elimination methods dominate. Unlike the random graph problems, early projection is competitive for these instances because the problem has a natural order that works well. But bucket elimination is still able to run slightly better. Here we start to see a considerable difference between the Boolean and non-Boolean case. The optimizations do not scale as well when we move to the non-Boolean queries. This is due to the fact that there are 20% less vertices to exploit in the optimization, and each optimization method suffers accordingly. It should be noted that early projection and bucket elimination still dominate over the straightforward approach. Figure 7 shows the running time (logscale) for the methods when applied to the ladder graph instances. These results are very similar to the augmented path results, but notice that now reordering is even slower than the straightforward approach. At this point, not only is the heuristic unable to find a better order, but it actually finds a worse

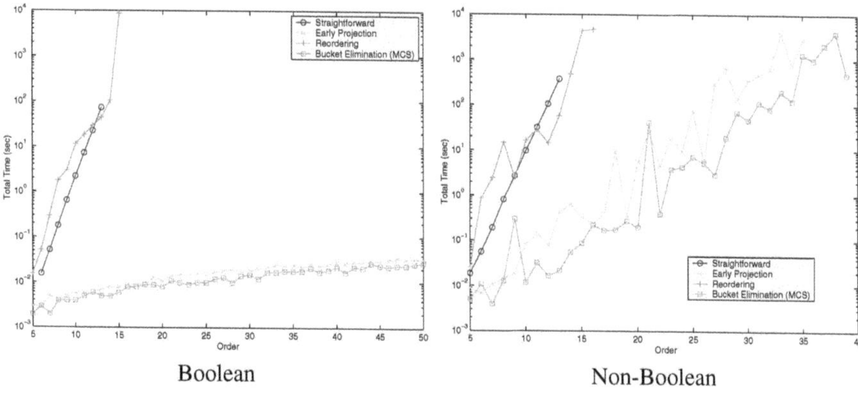

Fig. 7. 3-COLOR Ladder Queries – Logscale

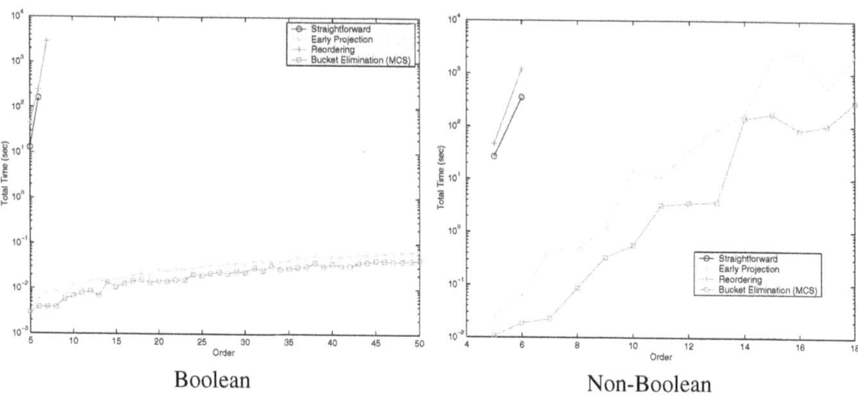

Fig. 8. 3-COLOR Augmented Ladder Queries – Logscale

one. As we move to the augmented ladder instances in Figure 8 and the augmented circular ladder instances in Figure 9, the differences between the optimization methods become even more stark, with the straightforward and reordering methods timing out at around order 7. Also the difference between the Boolean and non-Boolean case becomes more drastic with the non-Boolean case struggling to reach order 20 with the faster optimization methods. But throughout both the random and structured graph instances, bucket elimination manages to dominate the field with an exponential improvement at every turn.

7 Concluding Remarks

We demonstrated in this paper some progress in moving structural query optimization from theory, as developed in [10,21,26,11], to practice, by using techniques from constraint satisfaction. In particular, we demonstrated experimentally that projection pushing can yield an exponential improvement in performance, and that bucket elimination yields

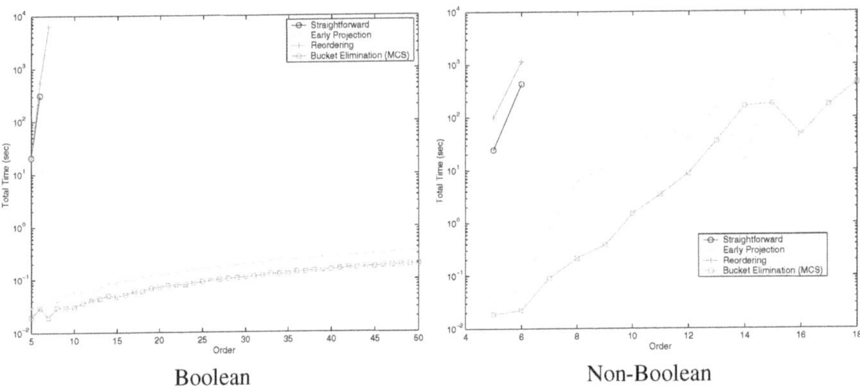

Fig. 9. 3-COLOR Augmented Circular Ladder Queries – Logscale

an exponential improvement not only over naive and straightforward approaches, but also over various greedy approaches. In this paper, we focused on queries constructed from 3-COLOR; we have also tested our algorithms on queries constructed from 3-SAT and 2-SAT and have obtained results that are consistent with those reported here. This shows that NP-hardness results at the heart of structural query optimization theory need not be considered an insurmountable barrier to the applicability of these techniques. Our work is, of course, merely the first step in moving structural query optimization from theory to practice. First, further experiments are needed to demonstrate the benefit of our approach for a wider variety of queries. For example, we need to consider relations of varying arity and sizes. In particular, one need is to study queries that could arise in mediator-based systems [36] as well as to study scalability with respect to relation size. Second, further ideas should be explored, from the theory of structural query optimization, e.g., semijoins [34] and hypertree width [21], from constraint satisfaction, e.g., mini-buckets [12], from symbolic model checking, e.g, partitioning techniques [9], and from algorithmic graph theory, e.g., treewidth approximation [6]. Third, heuristic approaches to join *minimization* (as in [8]) should also be explored. Since join minimization requires evaluating a conjunctive query over a *canonical query database* [8], the techniques in this paper should be applicable to the minimization problem, cf. [27]. Fourth, structural query optimization needs to be combined with cost-based optimization, which is the prevalent approach to query optimization. In particular, we need to consider queries with *weighted* attributes, reflecting the fact that different attributes may have different widths in bytes. In particular, a variety of practical settings needs to be explored, such as nested queries, "exists" subqueries, and the like. Finally, there is the question of how our optimization technique can be integrating into the framework of rule-based optimization [18].

Acknowledgement. We are grateful to Phokion Kolaitis for useful discussions and comments.

References

1. S. Abiteboul, R. Hull, and V. Vianu. *Foundations of databases.* Addison-Wesley, 1995.
2. A. Aho, Y. Sagiv, and J.D. Ullman. Efficient optimization of a class of relational expressions. *ACM Trans. on Database Systems*, 4:435–454, 1979.
3. A. Aho, Y. Sagiv, and J.D. Ullman. Equivalence of relational expressions. *SIAM Journal on Computing*, 8:218–246, 1979.
4. P. Apers, A. Hevner, and S. Yao. Optimization algorithms for distributed queries. *IEEE Trans. Software Engineering*, 9(1):57–68, 1983.
5. Arnborg, Corneil, and Proskurowski. Complexity of finding embeddings in a k-tree. *SIAM Journal of Algebraic and Discrete Methods*, 8(2):277–284, 1987.
6. H.L. Bodlaender. A tourist guide through treewidth. *Acta Cybernetica*, 11:1–21, 1993.
7. F. Bouquet. *Gestion de la dynamicité et énumération d'implicants premiers: une approche fondée sur les Diagrammes de Décision Binaire.* PhD thesis, Université de Provence, France, 1999.
8. A.K. Chandra and P.M. Merlin. Optimal implementation of conjunctive queries in relational databases. In *Proc. 9th ACM Symp. on Theory of Computing*, pages 77–90, 1977.
9. P. Chauhan, E.M. Clarke, S. Jha, J.H. Kukula, H. Veith, and Dong Wang. Using combinatorial optimization methods for quantification scheduling. In *Proc. 11th Conf. on Correct Hardware Design and Verification Methods*, pages 293–309, 2001.
10. C. Chekuri and A. Ramajaran. Conjunctive query containment revisited. Technical report, Stanford University, November 1998.
11. V. Dalmau, P.G. Kolaitis, and M.Y. Vardi. Constraint satisfaction, bounded treewidth, and finite-variable logics. In *Proc. Principles and Practice of Constraint Programming (CP'2002)*, pages 311–326, 2002.
12. R. Dechter. Mini-buckets: A general scheme for generating approximations in automated reasoning. In *International Joint Conference on Artificial Intelligence*, pages 1297–1303, 1997.
13. R. Dechter. Bucket elimination: a unifying framework for reasoning. *Artificial Intelligence*, 113(1–2):41–85, 1999.
14. R. Dechter. *Constraint Processing.* Morgan Kaufmann, 2003.
15. R. Dechter and J. Pearl. Network-based heuristics for constraint-satisfaction problems. *Artificial Intelligence*, 34:1–38, 1987.
16. R.G. Downey and M.R. Fellows. *Parametrized Complexity.* Springer-Verlag, 1999.
17. E.C Freuder. Complexity of k-tree structured constraint satisfaction problems. In *Proc. AAAI-90*, pages 4–9, 1990.
18. J.C. Freytag. A rule-based view of query optimization. In *Proceedings of the 1987 ACM SIGMOD international conference on Management of data*, pages 173–180, 1987.
19. H. Garcia-Molina, J.D. Ullman, and J. Widom. *Database System Implementation.* Prentice Hall, 2000.
20. M. R. Garey and D. S. Johnson. *Computers and Intractability, A Guide to the Theory of NP-Completeness.* W. H. Freeman, New York, NY, 1979.
21. G. Gottlob, N. Leone, and F. Scarcello. Hypertree decompositions and tractable queries. In *Proc. 18th ACM Symp. on Principles of Database Systems*, pages 21–32, 1999.
22. P.P. Griffiths, M.M. Astrahan, D.D. Chamberlin, R.A. Lorie, and T.G. Price. Access path selection in a relational database management system. In *ACM SIGMOD International Conference on Management of Data*, pages 23–34, 1979.
23. A. Halevy. Answering queries using views: A survey. *VLDB Journal*, pages 270–294, 2001.
24. R. Hojati, S. C. Krishnan, and R. K. Brayton. Early quantification and partitioned transition relations. In *Proc. 1996 Int'l Conf. on Computer Design*, pages 12–19, 1996.

25. Y. Ioannidis and E. Wong. Query optimization by simulated annealing. In *ACM SIGMOD International Conference on Management of Data*, pages 9–22, 1987.
26. Ph.G. Kolaitis and M.Y. Vardi. Conjunctive-query containment and constraint satisfaction. *Journal of Computer and System Sciences*, pages 302–332, 2000. Earlier version in: Proc. 17th ACM Symp. on Principles of Database Systems (PODS '98).
27. I.K. Kunen and D. Suciu. A scalable algorithm for query minimization. Technical report, University of Washington, 2002.
28. R. Ramakrishnan, C. Beeri, and R. Krishnamurthi. Optimizing existential datalog queries. In *Proceedings of the ACM Symposium on Principles of Database Systems*, pages 89–102, 1988.
29. I. Rish and R. Dechter. Resolution versus search: Two strategies for SAT. *Journal of Automated Reasoning*, 24(1/2):225–275, 2000.
30. A. San Miguel Aguirre and M.Y. Vardi. Random 3-SAT and BDDs – the plot thickens further. In *Proc. Principles and Practice of Constraint Programming (CP'2001)*, pages 121–136, 2001.
31. R. E. Tarjan and M. Yannakakis. Simple linear-time algorithms to tests chordality of graphs, tests acyclicity of hypergraphs, and selectively reduce acyclic hypergraphs. *SIAM J. on Computing*, 13(3):566–579, 1984.
32. J. D. Ullman. *Database and Knowledge-Base Systems, Volumes I and II.* Computer Science Press, 1989.
33. M.Y. Vardi. On the complexity of bounded-variable queries. In *Proc. 14th ACM Symp. on Principles of Database Systems*, pages 266–276, 1995.
34. E. Wong and K. Youssefi. Decomposition - a strategy for query processing. *ACM Trans. on Database Systems*, 1(3):223–241, 1976.
35. M. Yannakakis. Algorithms for acyclic database schemes. In *Proc. 7 Int'l Conf. on Very Large Data Bases*, pages 82–94, 1981.
36. R. Yerneni, C. Li, J.D. Ullman, and H. Garcia-Molina. Optimizing large join queries in mediation systems. *Lecture Notes in Computer Science*, 1540:348–364, 1999.

On Containment of Conjunctive Queries with Arithmetic Comparisons

Foto Afrati[1], Chen Li[2*], and Prasenjit Mitra[3]

[1] National Technical University of Athens, 157 73 Athens, Greece
afrati@cs.ece.ntua.gr
[2] Information and Computer Science, University of California, Irvine, CA 92697, U.S.A
chenli@ics.uci.edu
[3] School of Information Sciences and Techonology
The Pennsylvania State University, University Park, PA 16802, U.S.A
pmitra@ist.psu.edu

Abstract. We study the following problem: how to test if Q_2 is contained in Q_1, where Q_1 and Q_2 are conjunctive queries with arithmetic comparisons? This problem is fundamental in a large variety of database applications. Existing algorithms first normalize the queries, then test a logical implication using multiple containment mappings from Q_1 to Q_2. We are interested in cases where the containment can be tested more efficiently. This work aims to (a) reduce the problem complexity from Π_2^P-completeness to NP-completeness in these cases; (b) utilize the advantages of the homomorphism property (i.e., the containment test is based on a single containment mapping) in applications such as those of answering queries using views; and (c) observing that many real queries have the homomorphism property. The following are our results. (1) We show several cases where the normalization step is not needed, thus reducing the size of the queries and the number of containment mappings. (2) We develop an algorithm for checking various syntactic conditions on queries, under which the homomorphism property holds. (3) We further reduce the conditions of these classes using practical domain knowledge that is easily obtainable. (4) We conducted experiments on real queries, and show that most of the queries pass this test.

1 Introduction

The problem of testing query containment is as follows: how to test whether a query Q_2 is *contained* in a query Q_1, i.e., for any database D, is the set of answers to Q_2 a subset of the answers to Q_1? This problem arises in a large variety of database applications, such as query evaluation and optimization [1], data warehousing [2], and data integration using views [3]. For instance, an important problem in data integration is to decide how to answer a query using source views. Many existing algorithms are based on query containment [4].

* Supported by NSF CAREER award No. IIS-0238586.

E. Bertino et al. (Eds.): EDBT 2004, LNCS 2992, pp. 459–476, 2004.
© Springer-Verlag Berlin Heidelberg 2004

A class of queries of great significance is conjunctive queries (select-project-join queries and Cartesian products). These queries are widely used in many database applications. Often, users need to pose queries with arithmetic comparisons (e.g., year > 2000, price ≤ 5000). Thus testing for containment of conjunctive queries with arithmetic comparisons becomes very important. Several algorithms have been proposed for testing containment in this case (e.g., [5,6]). These algorithms first normalize the queries by replacing constants and shared variables, each with new unique variables and add arithmetic comparisons to equate those new variables to the original constants or shared variables. Then, they test the containment by checking a logical implication using *multiple* containment mappings. (See Section 2 for detail.)

We study how to test containment of conjunctive queries with arithmetic comparisons. In particular, we focus on the following two problems: (1) In what cases is the normalization step not needed? (2) In what cases does the *homomorphism property* hold, i.e., the containment test is based on a single containment mapping [6]?

We study these problems for three reasons. The first is the efficiency of this test procedure. Whereas the problem of containment of pure conjunctive queries is known to be NP-complete [7], the problem of containment of conjunctive queries with arithmetic comparisons is Π_2^P-complete [6,8]. In the former case, the containment test is in NP, because it is based on the existence of a *single* containment mapping, i.e., the homomorphism property holds. In the latter case, the test needs multiple containment mappings, which significantly increases the problem complexity. We find large classes of queries where the homomorphism property holds; thus we can reduce the problem complexity to NP. Although the saving on the normalization step does not put the problem in a different complexity class (i.e., it is still in NP), it can still reduce the sizes of the queries and the number of containment mappings in the containment test.

The second reason is that the homomorphism property can simplify many problems such as that of answering queries using views [9], in which we want to construct a plan using views to compute the answer to a query. It is shown in [10] that if both the query and the views are conjunctive queries with arithmetic comparisons, and the homomorphism property does not hold, then a plan can be recursive. Hence, if we know the homomorphism property holds by analyzing the query and the views, we can develop efficient algorithms for constructing a plan using the views.

The third motivation is that, in studying realistic queries (e.g., in TPC benchmarks), we found it hard to construct examples that need multiple mappings in the containment test. We observed that most real query pairs only need a single containment mapping to test the containment. To easily detect such cases, we want to derive syntactic conditions on queries, under which the homomorphism property holds. These syntactic conditions should be easily checked in polynomial time. In this paper, we develop such conditions.

The following are our contributions of this work. (Table 1 is a summary of results.)

Table 1. Results on containment test. The classes in NP have the homomorphism property. (See Table 2 for symbol definitions.)

Contained Query	Containing Query	Complexity	References
CQ	CQ	NP	[7]
CQ with closed LSI	CQ with closed LSI	NP	[5,6]
CQ with open LSI	CQ with open LSI	NP	[5,6]
CQ with AC	CQ with closed LSI	NP	Section 4
CQ with AC Constraints	CQ with LSI (i)-lsi, (ii)-lsi, (iii)-lsi	NP	Section 4 Theorem 4
CQ with SI Constraints	CQ with LSI, RSI (i)-lsi,rsi, (ii)-lsi,rsi, (iii)-lsi,rsi, (iv)	NP	Section 4 Theorem 5
CQ with SI Constraints	CQ with LSI, RSI, PI as above and (v),(vi),(vii)	NP	Section 4 Theorem 6
CQ with AC	CQ with AC	Π_2^P	[8]

1. We show cases where the normalization step is not needed (Section 3).
2. When the containing query Q_1 has only arithmetic comparisons between a variable and a constant (called "semi-interval," or "SI" for short), we present cases where the homomorphism property holds (Section 4). If the homomorphism property does not hold, then some "heavy" constraints must be satisfied. Such a constraint could be: An ordinary subgoal of Q_1, an ordinary subgoal of Q_2, an open-left-semi-interval subgoal of Q_2, and a closed-left-semi-interval subgoal of Q_2 all use the same constant. (See Table 1 for the definitions of these terms.) Notice that these conditions are just syntactic constraints, and can be checked in time polynomial in the size of the queries.
3. We further relax the conditions of the homomorphism property using practical domain knowledge that is easily obtainable (Section 5).
4. We conducted experiments on real queries, and show many of them satisfy the conditions under which the homomorphism property holds (Section 6).

Due to space limitation, we leave theorem proofs and more experimental results in the complete version [11].

1.1 Related Work

For conjunctive queries, restricted classes of queries are known for which the containment problem is polynomial. For instance, if every database predicate occurs in the contained query at most twice, then the problem can be solved in linear time [12], whereas it remains NP-complete if every database predicate occurs at least three times in the body of the contained query. If the containing query is acyclic, i.e., the predicate hypergraph has a certain property, then the containment problem is polynomial [13].

Klug [6] has shown that containment for conjunctive queries with comparison predicates is in Π_2^P, and it is proven to be Π_2^P-hard in [8]. The reduction only used $\neq$. This result is extended in [14] to use only $\neq$ and at most three occurrences of the same predicate name in the contained query. The same reduction shows that it remains Π_2^P-complete even in the case where the containing query is acyclic, thus the results in [13] do not extend to conjunctive queries with $\neq$. The complexity is reduced to co-NP in [14] if every database predicate occurs at most twice in the body of the contained query and only $\neq$ is allowed.

The most relevant to our setting is the work in [5,6]. It is shown that if only left or right semi-interval comparisons are used, the containment problem is in NP. It is stated as an open problem to search for other classes of conjunctive queries with arithmetic comparisons for which containment is in NP. Furthermore, query containment has been studied also for recursive queries. For instance, containment of a conjunctive query in a datalog query is shown to be EXPTIME-complete [15,16]. Containment among recursive and nonrecursive datalog queries is also studied in [17,18].

In [10] we studied the problem of how to answer a query using views if both the query and views are conjunctive queries with arithmetic comparisons. Besides showing the necessity of using recursive plans if the homomorphism property does not hold, we also developed an algorithm in the case where the property holds. Thus the results in [10] are an application of the contributions of this paper. Clearly testing query containment efficiently is a critical problem in many data applications as well.

2 Preliminaries

In this section, we review the definitions of query containment, containment mappings, and related results in the literature. We also define the homomorphism property.

Definition 1. *(Query containment) A query Q_2 is contained in a query Q_1, denoted $Q_2 \sqsubseteq Q_1$, if for any database D, the set of answers to Q_2 is a subset of the answers to Q_1. The two queries are equivalent, denoted $Q_1 \equiv Q_2$, if $Q_1 \sqsubseteq Q_2$ and $Q_2 \sqsubseteq Q_1$.*

We consider conjunctive queries that are in the following form: $h(\bar{X})$:- $g_1(\bar{X}_1), \ldots, g_k(\bar{X}_k)$. In each subgoal $g_i(\bar{X}_i)$, predicate g_i is a *base relation*, and every predicate argument $\bar{X}_i$ is either a variable or a constant. Chandra and Merlin [7] showed that for two conjunctive queries Q_1 and Q_2, $Q_2 \sqsubseteq Q_1$ if and only if there is a *containment mapping* from Q_1 to Q_2, such that the mapping maps a constant to the same constant, and maps a variable to either a variable or a constant. Under this mapping, the head of Q_1 becomes the head of Q_2, and each subgoal of Q_1 becomes *some* subgoal in Q_2.

Let Q be a conjunctive query with arithmetic comparisons (CQAC). We consider the following arithmetic comparisons: $<$, $\leq$, $>$, $\geq$, and $\neq$. We assume that database instances are over densely totally ordered domains. In addition, without loss of generality, throughout the paper we make the following assumptions about the comparisons. (1) The comparisons are not contradictory, i.e., there exists an instantiation of the variables such that all the comparisons are true. (2) All the comparisons are safe, i.e., each variable in the comparisons appears

Table 2. Symbols used in the paper. X denotes a variable and c is a constant. The RSI cases are symmetrical to those of LSI.

Symbol	Meaning
CQ	Conjunctive Query
AC	Arithmetic Comparison ($X\ \theta\ Y$)
CQAC	Conjunctive Query with ACs
core(Q)	Set of ordinary subgoals of query Q
AC(Q)	Set of arithmetic-comparison subgoals of query Q
SI	Semi-interval: $X\ \theta\ c$, $\theta \in \{<, \leq, >, \geq\}$
LSI	Left-semi-interval: $X\ \theta\ c$, $\theta \in \{<, \leq\}$
closed-LSI	$X \leq c$
open-LSI	$X < c$
PI	Point Inequalities ($X \neq c$)
SI-PI	Some subgoals are SI, and some are PI

in some ordinary subgoal. (3) The comparisons do not imply equalities. If they imply an equality $X = Y$, we rewrite the query by substituting X for Y.

We denote *core*(Q) as the set of ordinary (uninterpreted) subgoals of Q that do not have comparisons, and denote $AC(Q)$ as the set of subgoals that are arithmetic comparisons in Q. We use the term *closure* of a set of arithmetic comparisons S, to represent the set of all possible arithmetic comparisons that can be logically derived from S. For example, for the set of arithmetic comparisons $S = \{X \leq Y, Y = c\}$, we have $Closure(S) = \{X \leq Y, Y = c, X \leq c\}$. In addition, for convenience, we will denote Q_0 as the corresponding conjunctive query whose head is the head of Q, and whose body is *core*(Q). See Table 2 for a complete list of definitions and notations on special cases of arithmetic comparisons such as semi-interval, point inequalities, and others.

2.1 Testing Containment

Let Q_1 and Q_2 be two conjunctive queries with arithmetic comparisons (CQACs). Throughout the paper, we study how to test whether $Q_2 \sqsubseteq Q_1$. To do the testing, according to the results in [5,6], we first *normalize* both queries Q_1 and Q_2 to Q'_1 and Q'_2 respectively as follows.

- For all occurrences of a shared variable X in the normal subgoals except the first occurrence, replace the occurrence of X by a new distinct variable X_i, and add $X = X_i$ to the AC's of the query; and
- For each constant c in the query, replace the constant by a new distinct variable Z, and add $Z = c$ to the AC's of the query.

The testing is illustrated in Figure 1. For simplicity, we denote $\beta_1 = AC(Q_1)$, $\beta_2 = AC(Q_2)$, $\beta'_1 = AC(Q'_1)$, and $\beta'_2 = AC(Q'_2)$. Let $\mu_1, \ldots, \mu_k$ be all the containment mappings from $Q'_{1,0}$ to $Q'_{2,0}$. Let $\gamma_1, \ldots, \gamma_l$ be all the containment mappings from $Q_{1,0}$ to $Q_{2,0}$. There are a few important observations: (1) The

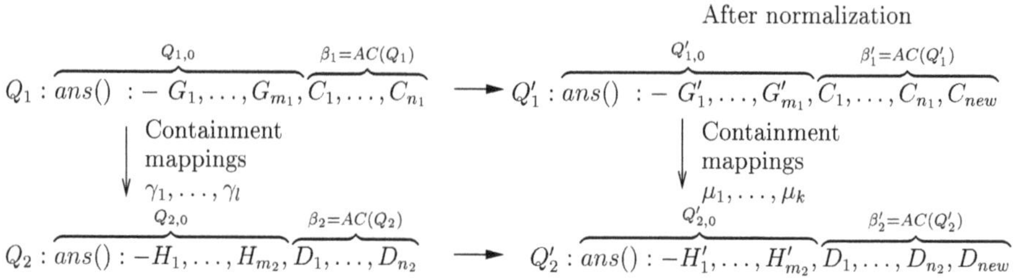

$$Q_1 : ans() :- \overbrace{G_1, \ldots, G_{m_1}}^{Q_{1,0}}, \overbrace{C_1, \ldots, C_{n_1}}^{\beta_1 = AC(Q_1)} \longrightarrow Q'_1 : ans() :- \overbrace{G'_1, \ldots, G'_{m_1}}^{Q'_{1,0}}, \overbrace{C_1, \ldots, C_{n_1}, C_{new}}^{\beta'_1 = AC(Q'_1)}$$

After normalization

Containment mappings $\gamma_1, \ldots, \gamma_l$ | Containment mappings $\mu_1, \ldots, \mu_k$

$$Q_2 : ans() : -\overbrace{H_1, \ldots, H_{m_2}}^{Q_{2,0}}, \overbrace{D_1, \ldots, D_{n_2}}^{\beta_2 = AC(Q_2)} \longrightarrow Q'_2 : ans() : -\overbrace{H'_1, \ldots, H'_{m_2}}^{Q'_{2,0}}, \overbrace{D_1, \ldots, D_{n_2}, D_{new}}^{\beta'_2 = AC(Q'_2)}$$

Fig. 1. Containment testing ([5,6]).

number of ordinary subgoals in Q_1 (resp. Q_2) does not change after the normalization. Each subgoal G_i (resp. H_i) has changed to a new subgoal G'_i (resp. H'_i). (2) While the comparisons $C_1, \ldots, C_{n_1}$ (resp. $D_1, \ldots, D_{n_2}$) are kept after the normalization, we may have introduced new comparions C_{new} (resp. D_{new}) after the normalization. Note C_{new} and D_{new} contain only equalities. (3) There can be more containment mappings for the normalized queries than the original queries, i.e., $k \geq l$. The reason is that a containment mapping cannot map a constant to a variable, nor map different instances of the same variable to different variables. However, after normalizing the queries, their ordinary subgoals only have distinct variables, making any variable in Q'_1 mappable to any variable in Q'_2 (for the same position of the same predicate).

Theorem 1. *$Q_2 \sqsubseteq Q_1$ if and only if the following logical implication ϕ is true:*

$$\phi : \beta'_2 \Rightarrow \mu_1(\beta'_1) \vee \ldots \vee \mu_k(\beta'_1)$$

That is, the comparisons in the normalized query Q'_2 logically implies (denoted "$\Rightarrow$") the disjunction of the images of the comparisons of the normalized query Q'_1 under these mappings [5,6].

Example 1. These two queries show that the normalization step in Theorem 1 is critical [19].

$Q_1 : h(W)$:- $q(W), p(X, Y, Z, Z', U, U), X < Y, Z > Z'$.
$Q_2 : h(W)$:- $q(W), p(X, Y, 2, 1, U, U), p(1, 2, X, Y, U, U), p(1, 2, 2, 1, X, Y)$.

There are two containment mappings from $Q_{1,0}$ to $Q_{2,0}$.

$\mu_1 : W \to W, X \to X, Y \to Y, Z \to 2, Z' \to 1, U \to U.$
$\mu_2 : W \to W, X \to 1, Y \to 2, Z \to X, Z' \to Y, U \to U.$

Notice we do not have a containment mapping from the p subgoal in Q_1 to the last p subgoal in Q_2, since we cannot map the two instances of variable U to both X and Y.

We can show $Q_2 \sqsubseteq Q_1$, but the following implication

$$TRUE \Rightarrow \mu_1(X < Y, Z > Z') \vee \mu_2(X < Y, Z > Z')$$

is not true, since it is possible $X = Y$. However, when $X = Y$, we would have a new "containment mapping" from Q_1 to Q_2:

$$\mu_3 : W \to W, X \to 1, Y \to 2, Z \to 2, Z' \to 1, U \to X = Y$$

After normalizing the two queries, we will have three (instead of two) containment mappings from the normalized query of Q_1 to that of Q_2.

Example 2. These two queries show that the $\vee$ operation in the implication in Theorem 1 is critical.

$$Q_1 : ans() \text{ :- } p(X,4), X < 4.$$
$$Q_2 : ans() \text{ :- } p(A,4), p(3,A), A \leq 4.$$

Their normalized queries are:

$$Q'_1 : ans() \text{ :- } p(X,Y), X < 4, Y = 4.$$
$$Q'_2 : ans() \text{ :- } p(A,B), p(C,D), A \leq 4, B = 4, C = 3, A = D.$$

There are two containment mappings from $Q'_{1,0}$ to $Q'_{2,0}$: $\mu_1 : X \to A, Y \to B$, and $\mu_2 : X \to C, Y \to D$. We can show that:

$$A \leq 4, B = 4, C = 3, A = D \Rightarrow \mu_1(X < 4, Y = 4) \vee \mu_2(X < 4, Y = 4)$$

Thus, $Q_2 \sqsubseteq Q_1$. Note both mappings are needed to prove the implication.

There are several challenges in using Theorem 1 to test whether $Q_2 \sqsubseteq Q_1$. (1) The queries look less intuitive after the normalization. The computational cost of testing the implication ϕ increases since we need to add more comparisons. (2) The implication needs the disjunction of the images of multiple containment mappings. In many cases it is desirable to have a single containment mapping to satisfy the implication. (3) There can be more containment mappings between the normalized queries than those between the original queries. In the rest of the paper we study how to deal with these challenges. In Section 3 we study in what cases we do not need to normalize the queries. That is, even if Q_1 and Q_2 are not normalized, we still have $Q_2 \sqsubseteq Q_1$ if and only if $\beta_2 \Rightarrow \gamma_1(\beta_1) \vee \ldots \vee \gamma_l(\beta_1)$.

2.2 Homomorphism Property

Definition 2. *(Homomorphism property) Let $\mathcal{Q}_1$, $\mathcal{Q}_2$ be two classes of queries. We say that containment testing* on the pair $(\mathcal{Q}_1, \mathcal{Q}_2)$ has the homomorphism property *if for any pair of queries (Q_1, Q_2) with $Q_1 \in \mathcal{Q}_1$ and $Q_2 \in \mathcal{Q}_2$, the following holds: $Q_2 \sqsubseteq Q_1$ iff there is a homomorphism μ from $core(Q_1)$ to $core(Q_2)$ such that $AC(Q_2) \Rightarrow \mu(AC(Q_1))$. If $\mathcal{Q}_1 = \mathcal{Q}_2 = \mathcal{Q}$, then we say containment testing has the homomorphism property for class $\mathcal{Q}$.*

Although the property is defined for two classes of queries, in the rest of the paper we refer to the homomorphism property holding for two queries when the two classes contain only one query each. The containment test of Theorem

1 for general CQACs considers normalized queries. However, in Theorem 3, we show that in the cases where a single mapping suffices to show containment between normalized queries, it also suffices to show containment between these queries when they are not in normalized form and vice versa. Hence, whenever the homomorphism property holds, we need not distinguish between normalized queries and non-normalized ones.

In cases where the homomorphism property holds, we have the following non-deterministically polynomial algorithm that checks if $Q_2 \sqsubseteq Q_1$. Guess a mapping μ from $core(Q_1)$ to $core(Q_2)$ and check whether μ is a containment mapping with respect to the AC subgoals too (the latter meaning that an AC subgoal g maps on an AC subgoal g' so that $g' \Rightarrow g$ holds). Note that the number of mappings is exponential on the size of the queries.

Klug [6] has shown that for the class of conjunctive queries with only open-LSI (open-RSI respectively) comparisons, the homomorphism property holds. In this paper, we find more cases where the homomorphism property holds. Actually, we consider pairs of classes of queries such as (LSI-CQ, CQAC) and we look for constraints which, if satisfied, the homomorphism property holds.

Definition 3. *(Homomorphism property under constraints) Let $\mathcal{Q}_1$, $\mathcal{Q}_2$ be two classes of queries and $\mathcal{C}$ be a set of constraints. We say that containment testing* on the pair $(\mathcal{Q}_1, \mathcal{Q}_2)$ w.r.t. the constraints in $\mathcal{C}$ has the homomorphism property *if for any pair of queries (Q_1, Q_2) with $Q_1 \in \mathcal{Q}_1$ and $Q_2 \in \mathcal{Q}_2$ and for which the constraints in $\mathcal{C}$ are satisfied, the following holds: $Q_2 \sqsubseteq Q_1$ iff there is a homomorphism μ from $core(Q_1)$ to $core(Q_2)$ such that $AC(Q_2) \Rightarrow \mu(AC(Q_1))$.*

The constraints we use are given as *syntactic conditions* that relate subgoals, in both queries. The satisfaction of the constraints can be checked in polynomial time in the size of the queries. When the homomorphism property holds, then the query containment problem is in NP.

3 Containment of Non-normalized Queries

To test the containment of two queries Q_1 and Q_2, using the result in Theorem 1, we need to normalize them first. Introducing more comparisons to the queries in the normalization can make the implication test computationally more expensive. Thus, we want to have a containment result that does not require the queries to be normalized. In this section, we present two cases, in which even if Q_1 and Q_2 are not normalized, we still have $Q_2 \sqsubseteq Q_1$ if and only if $\beta_2 \Rightarrow \gamma_1(\beta_1) \vee \ldots \vee \gamma_l(\beta_1)$.

Case 1: The following theorem says that Theorem 1 is still true even for non-normalized queries Q_1, if two conditions are satisfied by the queries: (1) β_1 contains only $\leq$ and $\geq$, and (2) β_1 (correspondingly β_2) do not imply equalities. In this case we can restrict the space of mappings because of the monotonicity property: For a query Q whose AC's only include $\leq, \geq$, if a tuple t of a database D is an answer to Q, then on any database D' obtained from D, by identifying some elements, the corresponding tuple t' is in the answer to $Q(D')$. Due to space limitations, we give the proofs of all theorems in [11].

Theorem 2. *Consider two CQAC queries Q_1 and Q_2 shown in Figure 1 that may not be normalized. Suppose β_1 contains only $\leq$ and $\geq$, and β_1 (correspondingly β_2) do not imply "=" restrictions. Then $Q_2 \sqsubseteq Q_1$ if and only if:*

$$\beta_2 \Rightarrow \gamma_1(\beta_1) \vee \ldots \vee \gamma_l(\beta_1)$$

where $\gamma_1, \ldots, \gamma_l$ are all the containment mappings from $Q_{1,0}$ to $Q_{2,0}$.

Case 2: The following theorem shows that we do not need to normalize the queries if they have the homomorphism property.

Lemma 1. *Assume the comparisons in Q_1 and Q_2 do not imply equalities. If there is a containment mapping μ from $Q'_{1,0}$ to $Q'_{2,0}$, such that $\beta'_2 \Rightarrow \mu(\beta'_1)$, then there must be a containment mapping γ from $Q_{1,0}$ to $Q_{2,0}$, such that $\beta_2 \Rightarrow \gamma(\beta_1)$.*

Using the lemma above, we can prove:

Theorem 3. *Suppose the comparisons in Q_1 and Q_2 do not imply equalities. The homomorphism property holds between Q_1 and Q_2 iff it holds between Q'_1 and Q'_2.*

4 Conditions for Homomorphism Property

Now we look for constraints in the form of syntactic conditions on queries Q_1 and Q_2, under which the homomorphism property holds. The conditions are sufficiently tight in that, if at least one of them is violated, then there exist queries Q_1 and Q_2 for which the homomorphism property does not hold. The conditions are syntactic and can be checked in polynomial time. We consider the case where the containing query (denoted by Q_1 all through the section) is a conjunctive query with only arithmetic comparisons between a variable and a constant; i.e., all its comparisons are *semi-interval* (SI), which are in the forms of $X > c$, $X < c$, $X \geq c$, $X \leq c$, or $X \neq c$. We call $X \neq c$ a *point inequality* (PI).

This section is structured as follows. Section 4.1 discusses technicalities on the containment implication, and in particular in what cases we do not need a disjunction. In Section 4.2 we consider the case where the containing query has only left-semi-interval (LSI) subgoals. We give a main result in Theorem 4. In Section 4.3, we extend Theorem 4 by considering the general case, where the containing query may use any semi-interval subgoals and point inequality subgoals. In Section 4.4, we discuss the case for more general inequalities than SI. Section 4.5 gives an algorithm for checking whether these conditions are met. In [11], we include many examples to show that the conditions in the main theorems are tight.

4.1 Containment Implication

In this subsection, we will focus on the implication

$$\phi : \beta_2' \Rightarrow \mu_1(\beta_1') \vee \ldots \vee \mu_k(\beta_1')$$

in Theorem 1. We shall give some terminology and some basic technical observations. The left-hand side (lhs) is a conjunction of arithmetic comparisons (in Example 2, the lhs is: $A \leq 4 \wedge B = 4 \wedge C = 3 \wedge A = D$). The right-hand side (rhs) is a disjunction and each disjunct is a conjunction of arithmetic comparisons. For instance, in Example 2, the rhs is: $(A < 4 \wedge B = 4) \vee (C < 4 \wedge D = 4)$, which has two disjuncts, and each is the conjunction of two comparisons. Given an integer i, we shall call **containment implication** any implication of this form: i) the lhs is a conjunction of arithmetic comparisons, and ii) the rhs is a disjunction and each disjunct is a conjunction of i arithmetic comparisons.

Observe that the rhs can be equivalently written as a conjunction of disjunctions (using the distributive law). Hence this implication is equivalent to a conjunction of implications, each implication keeping the same lhs as the original one, and the rhs is one of the conjuncts in the implication that results after applying the distributive law. We call each of these implications a **partial containment implication.**[1] In Example 2, we write equivalently the rhs as: $(A < 4 \vee C < 4) \wedge (A < 4 \vee D = 4) \wedge (B = 4 \vee C < 4) \wedge (B = 4 \vee D = 4)$. Thus, the containment implication in Example 2 can be equivalently written as

$$\begin{array}{l}(A \leq 4, B = 4, C = 3, A = D \Rightarrow A < 4 \vee C < 4)\ \wedge \\ (A \leq 4, B = 4, C = 3, A = D \Rightarrow A < 4 \vee D = 4)\ \wedge \\ (A \leq 4, B = 4, C = 3, A = D \Rightarrow B = 4 \vee C < 4)\ \wedge \\ (A \leq 4, B = 4, C = 3, A = D \Rightarrow B = 4 \vee D = 4).\end{array}$$

Here we get four partial containment implications.

A partial containment implication $\alpha \Rightarrow (\alpha_1 \vee \alpha_2 \vee \ldots \vee \alpha_k)$ is called a *direct implication* if there exists an i, such that if this implication is true, then $\alpha \Rightarrow \alpha_i$ is also true. Otherwise, it is called a *coupling implication.* For instance,

$$(A \leq 4, B = 4, C = 3, A = D \Rightarrow B = 4 \vee D = 4)$$

is a direct implication, since it is logically equivalent to $(A \leq 4, B = 4, C = 3, A = D \Rightarrow B = 4)$. On the contrary, $(A \leq 4, B = 4, C = 3, A = D \Rightarrow A < 4 \vee D = 4)$ is a coupling implication. The following lemma is used as a basis for many of our results.

Lemma 2. *Consider a containment implication $\alpha \Rightarrow (\alpha_1 \vee \alpha_2 \vee \ldots \vee \alpha_k)$ that is true, where each of the α and α_i's is a conjunction of arithmetic comparisons. If all its partial containment implications are direct implications, then there exists a single disjunct α_i in the rhs of the containment implication such that $\alpha \Rightarrow \alpha_i$.*

[1] Notice that containment implications and their partial containment implications are not necessarily related to mappings and query containment, only the names are borrowed.

We give conditions to guarantee direct implications in containment test.

Corollary 1. *Consider the normalized queries Q'_1 and Q'_2 in Theorem 1. Suppose all partial containment implications are direct. Then there is a mapping μ_i from $Q'_{1,0}$ to $Q'_{2,0}$ such that $\beta'_2 \Rightarrow \mu_i(\beta'_1)$.*

4.2 Left Semi-interval Comparisons (LSI) for Q_1

We first consider the case where Q_1 is a conjunctive query with left semi-interval arithmetic comparison subgoals only (i.e., one of the form $X < c$ or $X \leq c$ or both may appear in the same query). The following theorem is a main result describing the conditions for the homomorphism property to hold in this case.

Theorem 4. *Let Q_1 be a conjunctive query with left semi-interval arithmetic comparisons and Q_2 a conjunctive query with any arithmetic comparisons. If they satisfy all the following conditions, then the homomorphism property holds:*

- Condition (i)-lsi*: There do not exist subgoals as follows which all share the same constant: An open-LSI subgoal in $AC(Q_1)$, a closed-LSI subgoal in closure of $AC(Q_2)$, and a subgoal in $core(Q_1)$.*
- Condition (ii)-lsi*: Either $core(Q_1)$ has no shared variables or there do not exist subgoals as follows which all share the same constant: An open-LSI subgoal in $AC(Q_1)$, a closed-LSI subgoal in the closure of $AC(Q_2)$ and, a subgoal in $core(Q_2)$.*
- Condition (iii)-lsi*: Either $core(Q_1)$ has no shared variables or there do not exist subgoals as follows which all share the same constant: An open-LSI subgoal in $AC(Q_1)$ and two closed-LSI subgoals in the closure of $AC(Q_2)$.*

It is straightforward to construct corollaries of Theorem 4 with simpler conditions. The following is an example.

Corollary 2. *Let Q_1 be a conjunctive query with left semi-interval arithmetic comparisons and Q_2 a conjunctive query with any arithmetic comparisons. If the arithmetic comparisons in Q_1 do not share a constant with the closure of the arithmetic comparisons in Q_2, then the homomorphism property holds.*

The results in Theorem 4 can be symmetrically stated for RSI queries as containing queries. The symmetrical conditions of Theorem 4 for the RSI case will be referred to as conditions (i)-rsi, (ii)-rsi, and (iii)-rsi, respectively.

4.3 Semi-interval (SI) and Point-Inequalities (PI) Queries for Q_1

Now we extend the result of Theorem 4 to treat both LSI and RSI subgoals occurring in the same containing query. We further extend it to include point inequalities (of the form $X \neq c$). The result is the following.

SI Queries for Q_1: We consider the case where Q_1 has both LSI and RSI inequalities called "SI inequalities," i.e., any of the $<$, $>$, $\leq$, and $\geq$. In this case we need one more condition, namely Condition (iv), in order to avoid coupling implications. Thus Theorem 4 is extended to the following theorem, which is the second main result of this section.

Theorem 5. *Let Q_1 be a conjunctive query with left semi-interval and right semi-interval arithmetic comparisons and Q_2 a conjunctive query with SI arithmetic comparisons. If they satisfy all the following conditions, then the homomorphism property holds:*

- *Conditions (i)-lsi, (ii)-lsi, (iii)-lsi, (i)-rsi, (ii)-rsi, and (iii)-rsi.*
- *Condition (iv)-si: Any constant in an RSI subgoal of Q_1 is strictly greater than any constant in an LSI subgoal of Q_1.*

We refer to the last conditin as (iv)-si.

PI Queries for Q_1: If the containing query Q_1 has point inequalities, three more forms of coupling implications can occur. Thus Theorem 5 is further extended to Theorem 6, which is the third main result of this section.

Theorem 6. *Let Q_1 be a conjunctive query with left semi-interval and right semi-interval and point inequality arithmetic comparisons and Q_2 a conjunctive query with SI arithmetic comparisons. If Q_1 and Q_2 satisfy all the following conditions, then the homomorphism property holds:*

- *Conditions (i)-lsi, (ii)-lsi, (iii)-lsi, (i)-rsi, (ii)-rsi, (iii)-rsi and (iv)-si.*
- *Condition (v)-pi: Either Q_1 has no repeated variables, or it does not have point inequalities.*
- *Condition (vi)-pi: Point-Inequality(Q_1) does not have a constant that occurs in core(Q_1), or Closed-LSI(Q_1), or Closed-RSI(Q_1).*

4.4 Beyond Semi-interval Queries for Q_1

Our results have already captured subtle cases where the homomorphism property holds. There is not much hope beyond those cases, unless we restrict the number of subgoals of the contained query, which is known in the literature (e.g., [14]). Couplings due to the implication:

$$TRUE \Rightarrow ((X \leq Y) \vee (Y \leq X))$$

indicate that if the containing query has closed comparisons, then the homomorphism does not hold. The following is such an example:

$$Q_1 : ans() \text{ :- } p(X,Y), X \leq Y.$$
$$Q_2 : ans() \text{ :- } p(X,Y), p(Y,X).$$

Clearly Q_2 is contained in Q_1, but the homomorphism property does not hold.

4.5 A Testing Algorithm

We summarize the results in this section in an algorithm shown in Figure 2. Given two CQAC queries Q_1 and Q_2, the algorithm tests if the homomorphism property holds in checking $Q_2 \sqsubseteq Q_1$. Queries may not satisfy these conditions but still the

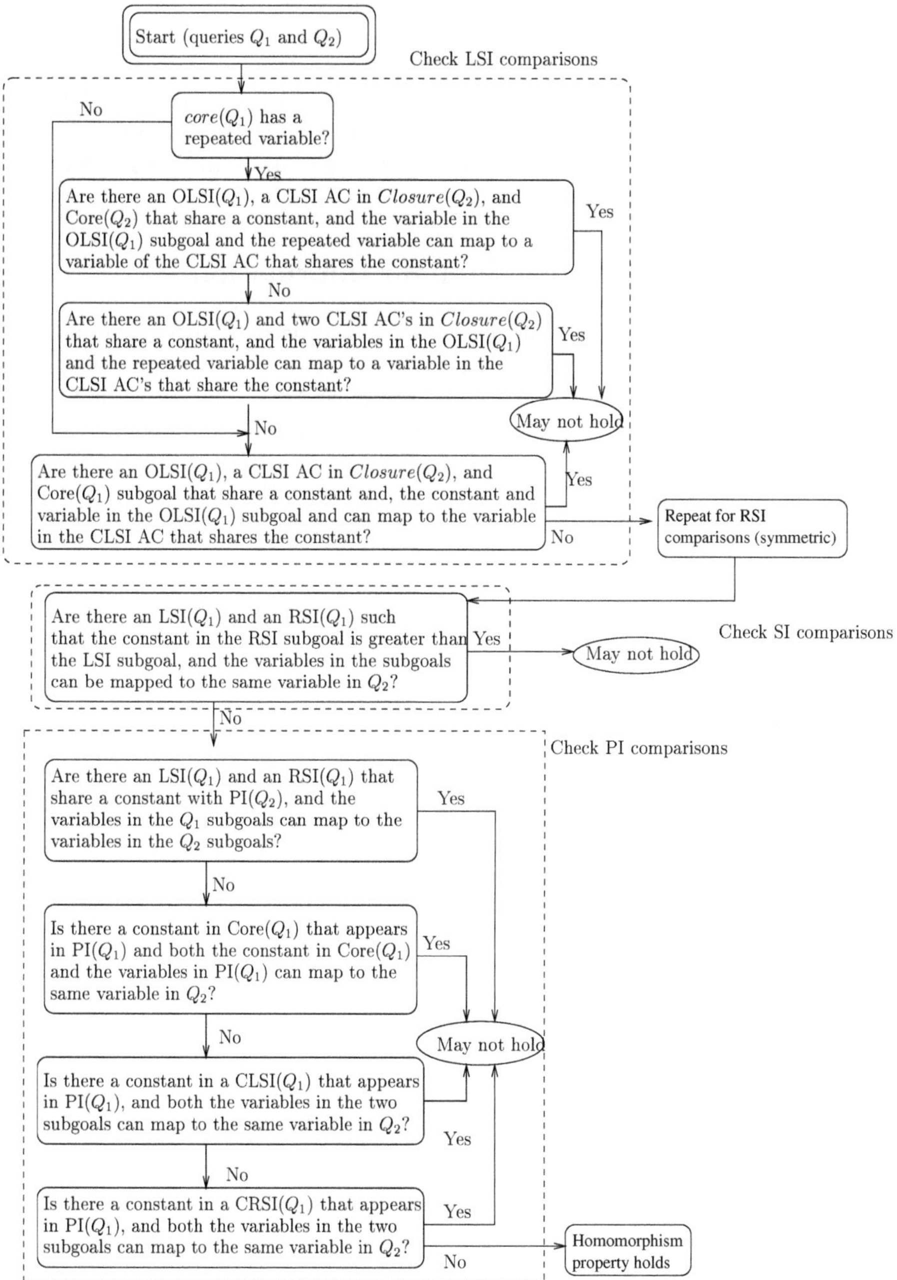

Fig. 2. An algorithm for checking homomorphism property in testing $Q_2 \sqsubseteq Q_1$.

homomorphism property may hold. For instance, it could happen if they do not have self-joins, or if domain information yields that certain mappings are not possible (see Section 5). Hence, in the diagram, we can also put this additional check: Whenever one of the conditions is not met, we also check whether there are mappings that would enable a coupling implication. We did not include the formal results for this last test for brevity, as they are a direct consequence of the discussion in the present section.

5 Improvements Using Domain Information

So far we have discussed in what cases we do not need to normalize queries in the containment test, and in what cases we can reduce the containment test to checking the existence of a single homomorphism. If a query does not satisfy these conditions, the above results become inapplicable. For instance, often a query may have both $<$ and $\geq$ comparisons, not satisfying the conditions in Theorem 2. In this section, we study how to relax these conditions by using domain knowledge of the relations and queries.

The intuition of our approach is the following. We partition relation attributes into different domains, such as "car models," "years," and "prices." We can safely assume that for realistic queries, their conditions respect these domains. In particular, for a comparison $X\ \theta\ A$, where X is a variable, A is a variable or a constant, the domain of A should be the same as that of X. For example, it may be meaningless to have conditions such as "carYear = \$6,000." Therefore, in the implication of testing query containment, it is possible to partition the implication into different domains. The domain information about the attributes is collected only once before queries are posed. For instance, given the following implication ϕ: $year > 2000 \wedge price \leq \$5,000 \Rightarrow year > 1998 \wedge price \leq \$6,000$. We do not need to consider implication between constants or variables in different domains, such as between "1998" and "\$6,000," and between "year" and "price." As a consequence, this implication can be projected to the following implications in two domains:

Year domain ϕ_y: $year > 2000 \Rightarrow year > 1998$.
Price domain ϕ_p: $price \leq \$5,000 \Rightarrow price \leq \$6,000$.

We can show that ϕ is true iff both ϕ_y and ϕ_p are true. In this section, we first formalize this domain idea, and then show how to partition an implication into implications of different domains.

5.1 Domains of Relation Attributes and Query Arguments

Assume each attribute A_i in a relation $R(A_1, \ldots, A_k)$ has a domain $Dom(R.A_i)$. Consider two tables: `house(seller, street, city, price)` and `crimerate(city, rate)`. Relation `house` has housing information, and relation `crimerate` has information about crime rates of cities. The following table shows the domains of different attributes in these relations. Notice that attributes `house.city` and `crimerate.city` share the same domain: $D_3 = \{\text{city names}\}$.

Attribute	Domain
`house.seller`	$D_1 = \{\text{person names}\}$
`house.street`	$D_2 = \{\text{street names}\}$
`house.city`	$D_3 = \{\text{city names}\}$
`house.price`	$D_4 = \{\text{float numbers in dollars}\}$
`crimerate.city`	$D_3 = \{\text{city names}\}$
`crimerate.rate`	$D_5 = \{\text{crime-rate float numbers}\}$

We equate domains of variables and constants using the following rules:

- For each argument X_i (either a variable or a constant) in a subgoal $R(X_1, \dots, X_k)$ in query Q, the domain of X_i, $Dom(X_i)$, is the corresponding domain of the j-th attribute in relation R.
- For each comparison $X \ \theta \ c$ between variable X and constant c, we set $Dom(c) = Dom(X)$. Constants from different domains are always treated as different constants. For instance, in two conditions $carYear = 2000$ and $carPrice = \$2000$, constants "2000" and "\$2000" are different constants.

We perform this process on all subgoals and comparisons in the query. In this calculation we make the following realistic assumptions: (1) If X is a shared variable in two subgoals, then the corresponding attributes of the two arguments of X have the same domain. (2) If we have a comparison $X \ \theta \ Y$, where X and Y are variables, then $Dom(X)$ and $Dom(Y)$ are always the same.

Consider the following queries on the relations above.

P_1: $ans(t_1, c_1)$:- $house(s_1, t_1, c_1, p_1), crimerate(c_1, r_1), p_1 \leq \$300,000, r_1 \geq 3.0\%$.
P_2: $ans(t_2, c_2)$:- $house(s_2, t_2, c_2, p_2), crimerate(c_2, r_2), p_2 \leq \$250,000, r_2 \geq 3.5\%$.

The computed domains of the variables and constants are shown in the table below. It is easy to see that the domain information as defined in this section can be obtained in polynomial time.

P_1: Variable/constant	P_1: Domain	P_2: Variable/constant	P_2: Domain
s_1	D_1	s_2	D_1
t_1	D_2	t_2	D_2
c_1	D_3	c_2	D_3
p_1	D_4	p_2	D_4
r_1	D_5	r_2	D_5
\$300,000	D_4	\$250,000	D_4
3.0%	D_5	3.5%	D_5

5.2 Partitioning Implication into Domains

According to Theorem 1, to test the containment $Q_1 \sqsubseteq Q_2$ for two given queries Q_1 and Q_2, we need to test the containment implication in the theorem. We want to partition this implication to implications in different domains, since testing the implication in each domain is easier. Now we show that this partitioning idea is feasible. We say a comparison $X \ \theta \ A$ is in domain D if X and A are in domain D. The following are two important observations.

- If a mapping μ_i maps an argument X in query Q_1 to an argument Y in query Q_2, based on the calculation of argument domains, clearly X and Y are from the same domain.
- In query normalization, each new introduced variable has the same domain as the replaced argument (variable or constant).

Definition 4. *Consider the following implication ϕ in Theorem 1:*

$$\beta_2' \Rightarrow \mu_1(\beta_1') \vee \ldots \vee \mu_k(\beta_1').$$

For a domain D of the arguments in ϕ, the projection of ϕ in D*, denoted ϕ_D, is the following implication:*

$$\beta_{2,D}' \Rightarrow \mu_1(\beta_{1,D}') \vee \ldots \vee \mu_k(\beta_{1,D}').$$

$\beta_{2,D}'$ includes all comparisons of β_2' in domain D. Similarly, $\beta_{1,D}'$ includes all comparisons of β_1' in domain D.

Suppose we want to test $P_2 \sqsubseteq P_1$ for the two queries above. There is only one containment mapping from P_1 to P_2, and we need to test the implication:

$$\pi : p_2 \leq \$250,000, r_2 \geq 3.5\% \Rightarrow p_2 \leq \$300,000, r_2 \geq 3.0\%.$$

The projection of π on domain D_4 (float numbers in dollars) π_{D_4} is $p_2 \leq \$250,000 \Rightarrow p_2 \leq \$300,000$. Similarly, π_{D_5} is $r_2 \geq 3.5\% \Rightarrow r_2 \geq 3.0\%$.

Theorem 7. *Let $D_1, \ldots, D_k$ be the domains of the arguments in the implication ϕ. Then ϕ is true iff all the projected implications $\phi_{D_i}, \ldots, \phi_{D_k}$ are true.*

In the example above, by Theorem 7, π is true iff π_{D_4} and π_{D_5} are true. Since the latter two are true, π is true. Thus $P_2 \sqsubseteq P_1$. In general, we can test the implication in Theorem 1 by testing the implications in different domains, which are much cheaper than the whole implication. [11] gives formal results that relax the conditions in the theorems of the previous section to apply only on elements of the same domain.

6 Experiments

In this section we report on experiments to determine whether the homomorphism property holds for real queries. We checked queries in many introductory database courses available on the Web, some data-mining queries provided by Microsoft Research, and the TPC-H benchmark queries [20]. We have observed that, for certain applications (e.g., the data-mining queries), usually queries do not have self-joins; thus the homomorphism property holds. In addition, among the queries that use only semi-interval (SI) and point inequality (PI) comparisons, the majority have the homomorphism property.

For a more detailed discussion, we focus on our evaluation results on the TPC-H benchmark queries [20], which represent typical queries in a wide range of decision-support applications. To the best of our knowledge, our results are the first evidence that containment is easy for those queries. The following is a summary of our experiments on the TPC-H benchmark queries.

1. All, except two (Q_4 and Q_{21}) of the 22 queries use semi-interval comparisons (SI's) and point inequalities (PI's) only.
2. When the homomorphism property may not hold, it is always because of the following situation: a variable X (usually of "date" type) is bounded in an interval between two constants. In such a case, the property is guaranteed to hold if the contained query does not contain self-joins of the subgoal that uses a variable that X can map to.
3. As a consequence, if the contained query is also one of the 22 queries, since they do not have self-joins of relations that share a variable with SI predicates, the homomorphism property holds.

The detailed experimental results are in [11]. Here we use the following query adapted from TPC-H query Q_3 as an example. (For simplicity we call this query Q_3.) We show how to apply the results in the earlier sections to test the following: in testing if Q_3 is containing another CQAC query, does the homomorphism property hold in the test?

```
SELECT l_orderkey, l_extendedprice, l_discount, o_orderdate, o_shippriority
FROM   customer, orders, lineitem
WHERE  c_mktsegment = '[SEGMENT]'
       AND c_custkey = o_custkey AND l_orderkey = o_orderkey
       AND o_orderdate < date '[DATE]' AND l_shipdate > date '[DATE]';
```

Consider the case where we check for the containment of any conjunctive query with semi-interval arithmetic comparisons in the above query Q_3. We shall apply Theorem 5. Notice that the above query has shared variables (expressed by the equality $c\_custkey = o\_custkey$ in the `WHERE` clause), as well as it contains both LSI and RSI arithmetic comparisons. However the variables $o\_orderdate$ (used in a comparison) and $c\_custkey$ (a shared variable) are obviously of different domains. Hence conditions (ii)-lsi, (ii)-rsi, (iii)-lsi, (iii)-rsi are satisfied. Also using domain information, we see that (i)-lsi and (i)-rsi are satisfied.

In general, the condition (iv) in Theorem 5 may not be satisfied, but the scenario in which it is not satisfied either uses a query with a self-join on relation `lineitem` or a self-join on relation `orders`. Such a query (a) is not included in the benchmark, and (b) would ask for information that is not natural or is of a very specific and narrow interest (e.g., would ask of pairs of orders sharing a property). Consequently, to test containment of any natural SI query in Q_3, we need only one containment mapping. Notice that without using the domain information, we could not derive this conclusion.

7 Conclusion

In this paper we considered the problem of testing containment between two conjunctive queries with arithmetic comparisons. We showed in what cases the normalization step in the algorithm [5,6] is not needed. We found various syntactic conditions on queries, under which we can reduce considerably the number of mappings needed to test containment to a single mapping (homomorphism property). These syntactic conditions can be easily checked in polynomial time. Our experiments using real queries showed that many of these queries pass this test, so they do have the homomorphism property, making it possible to use more efficient algorithms for the test.

Acknowledgments. We thank Microsoft Research for providing us their data-mining queries to do our experiments.

References

1. Chaudhuri, S., Krishnamurthy, R., Potamianos, S., Shim, K.: Optimizing queries with materialized views. In: ICDE. (1995) 190–200
2. Theodoratos, D., Sellis, T.: Data warehouse configuration. In: Proc. of VLDB. (1997)
3. Ullman, J.D.: Information integration using logical views. In: ICDT. (1997) 19–40
4. Halevy, A.: Answering queries using views: A survey. In: Very Large Database Journal. (2001)
5. Gupta, A., Sagiv, Y., Ullman, J.D., Widom, J.: Constraint checking with partial information. In: PODS. (1994) 45–55
6. Klug, A.: On conjunctive queries containing inequalities. Journal of the ACM **35** (1988) 146–160
7. Chandra, A.K., Merlin, P.M.: Optimal implementation of conjunctive queries in relational data bases. STOC (1977) 77–90
8. van der Meyden, R.: The complexity of querying indefinite data about linearly ordered domains. In: PODS. (1992)
9. Levy, A., Mendelzon, A.O., Sagiv, Y., Srivastava, D.: Answering queries using views. In: PODS. (1995) 95–104
10. Afrati, F., Li, C., Mitra, P.: Answering queries using views with arithmetic comparisons. In: PODS. (2002)
11. Afrati, F., Li, C., Mitra, P.: On containment of conjunctive queries with arithmetic comparisons (extended version). Technical report, UC Irvine (2003)
12. Saraiya, Y.: Subtree elimination algorithms in deductive databases. Ph.D. Thesis, Computer Science Dept., Stanford Univ. (1991)
13. Qian, X.: Query folding. In: ICDE. (1996) 48–55
14. Kolaitis, P.G., Martin, D.L., Thakur, M.N.: On the complexity of the containment problem for conjunctive queries with built-in predicates. In: PODS. (1998) 197–204
15. Chandra, A., Lewis, H., Makowsky, J.: Embedded implication dependencies and their inference problem. In: STOC. (1981) 342–354
16. Cosmadakis, S.S., Kanellakis, P.: Parallel evaluation of recursive queries. In: PODS. (1986) 280–293
17. Chaudhuri, S., Vardi, M.Y.: On the equivalence of recursive and nonrecursive datalog programs. In: PODS. (1992) 55–66
18. Shmueli, O.: Equivalence of datalog queries is undecidable. Journal of Logic Programming **15** (1993) 231–241
19. Wang, J., Maher, M., Toper, R.: Rewriting general conjunctive queries using views. In: 13th Australasian Database Conf. (ADC), Melbourne, Australia, ACS (2002)
20. TPC-H: `http://www.tpc.org/tpch/` (2003)

XPath with Conditional Axis Relations

Maarten Marx*

Language and Inference Technology, ILLC, Universiteit van Amsterdam, The Netherlands
marx@science.uva.nl

Abstract. This paper is about the W3C standard node-addressing language for XML documents, called XPath. XPath is still under development. Version 2.0 appeared in 2001 while the theoretical foundations of Version 1.0 (dating from 1998) are still being widely studied. The paper aims at bringing XPath to a "stable fixed point" in its development: a version which is expressively complete, still manageable computationally, with a user-friendly syntax and a natural semantics. We focus on an important axis relation which is not expressible in XPath 1.0 and is very useful in practice: *the conditional axis*. With it we can express paths specified by for instance "do a `child` step, while `test` is true at the resulting node". We study the effect of adding conditional axis relations to XPath on its expressive power and the complexity of the query evaluation and query equivalence problems. We define an XPath dialect $\mathcal{X}$CPath which is expressively complete, has a linear time query evaluation algorithm and for which query equivalence given a DTD can be decided in exponential time.

1 Introduction

XPath 1.0 [38] is a variable free language used for selecting nodes from XML documents. XPath plays a crucial role in other XML technologies such as XSLT [42], XQuery [41] and XML schema constraints, e.g., [40]. The latest version of XPath (version 2.0) [39] is much more expressive and is close to being a full fledged tree query language. Version 2.0 contains variables which are used in if–then–else, for and quantified expressions. The available axes are the same in both versions. The purpose of this paper is to show that useful and more expressive variants of XPath 1.0 can be created without introducing variables. We think that the lack of variables in XPath 1.0 is one of the key features for its success, so we should not lightly give it up.

This paper uses the abstraction to the logical core of XPath 1.0 developed in [17, 16]. This means that we are discussing the expressive power of the language on XML document tree models. The central expression in XPath is axis :: *node_label*[filter] (called a *location path*) which when evaluated at node n yields an answer set consisting of nodes n' such that

- the axis relation goes from n to n',
- the node tag of n' is *node_label*, and
- the expression filter evaluates to true at n'.

* Research supported by NWO grant 612.000.106. Thanks to Patrick Blackburn, Linh Nguyen and Petrucio Viana.

E. Bertino et al. (Eds.): EDBT 2004, LNCS 2992, pp. 477–494, 2004.
© Springer-Verlag Berlin Heidelberg 2004

We study the consequences of varying the set of available axis relations on the expressive power and the computational complexity of the resulting XPath dialect. All axis relations of XPath 1.0, like child, descendant etc., are assumed as given. We single out an important axis relation which is not expressible in XPath 1.0 and is very useful in practice: *the conditional axis*. With it we can express paths specified by for instance "do a `child` step, while `test` is true at the resulting node". Such conditional axes are widely used in programming languages and temporal logic specification and verification languages. In temporal logic they are expressed by the Since and Until operators. The acceptance of temporal logic as a key verification language is based on two interrelated results. First, as shown by Kamp [21] and later generalized and given an accessible proof by Gabbay, Pnueli, Shelah and Stavi [14], temporal logic over linear structures can express every first order definable property. This means that the language is in a sense complete and finished. This is an important point in the development of a language. It means that no further expressivity (up to first order of course) needs to be added. The second important result concerned the complexity of the model checking and validity problem. Both are complete for polynomial space, while model checking can be done in time $O(2^{|Q|} \cdot |D|)$, with $|Q|$ and $|D|$, the size of the query and data, respectively [8].

The paper aims at bringing navigational XPath to a similar " fixed point" in its development: a version which is expressively complete, still manageable computationally, with a user-friendly syntax and a natural semantics. The key message of the paper is that all of this is obtainable by adding the conditional axes to the XPath syntax. Our main contributions are the following:

- A motivation of conditional paths with natural examples (Section 2).
- The definition of several very expressive variable free XPath dialects, in particular the language $\mathcal{X}$CPath (Section 3).
- A comparison of the expressive power of the different dialects (Section 4).
- An investigation of the computational complexity of the discussed dialects. The main results are that the extra expressivity comes at no (theoretical) extra cost: query evaluation is in linear time in the size of the query and the data (Section 5), and query equivalence given a DTD is decidable in exponential time (Section 6).

For succinctness and readability all proofs are put in the Appendix.

We end this introduction with a few words on related literature. The observation that languages for XML like XPath, DTD's and XSchema can be viewed as propositional temporal, modal or description logics has been made by several authors. For instance, Miklau and Suciu [25] and Gottlob et al [15] embed XPath into CTL. The group round Calvanese, de Giacomo and Lenzerini published a number of papers relating DTD's and XPath to description logic, thereby obtaining powerful complexity results cf, e.g., [7]. Demri, de Rijke and Alechina reduce certain XML constraint inference problems to propositional dynamic logic [2]. The containment problem for XPath given a set of constraints (a DTD for instance) has been studied in [36,9,25,26]. The complexity of XPath query evaluation was determined in [15,16]. We are convinced that this list is incomplete, if only for the sole reason that the connection between the formalisms and the structures in which they are interpreted is so obvious. Our work differs from most in that we consider node labeled trees, whereas (following [1]) most authors model semistructured data as edge labeled trees. This is more than just a different semantic viewpoint. It allows us to use the same syntax as standard XPath and to give simpler and more perspicuous embeddings into known formalisms. Taking this viewpoint it turns out that many results on XPath follow easily from known results: linear time query evaluation follows directly from linear time model checking for propositional dynamic logic (PDL); the exponential time query equivalence algorithm can also be deduced (with quite a bit more work) from results on PDL, and finally Gabbay's separation technique for temporal logic is directly applicable to node labeled sibling ordered trees.

2 Conditional Paths

This section motivates the addition of conditional paths to the XPath language.

Example 1. Consider an XML document containing medical data as in Figure 1. Each node describes a person with an attribute assigning a name and an attribute stating whether or not the person has or had leukemia. The child-of relation in the tree models the real child-of relation between persons. Thus the root of the tree is person a which has leukemia. Person a has a child a1 without the disease and a grandchild a12 which has it.

```
<P name=a leukemia=yes>
   <P name=a1 leukemia=no>
       <P name=a11 leukemia=no/>
       <P name=a12 leukemia=yes/>
       <P name=a13 leukemia=no/>
   </P>
   <P name=a2 leukemia=yes>
       <P name=a21 leukemia=yes/>
       <P name=a22 leukemia=no/>
   </P>
</P>
```

Fig. 1. XML document containing medical data.

Consider the following information need: *given a person x, find descendants y of x without leukemia such that all descendants of x between x and y had/have leukemia.* The answer set of this query in the example document when evaluated at the root is the set of nodes with name attribute a1 and a22. When evaluated at node a1, the answer set is {a11,a13}, when evaluated at a2 the answer set is {a22}, and at all other nodes, the answer set is empty. The information need can be expressed in first order logic using a suitable signature. Let child and descendant be binary and P and has_leukemia be unary predicates. The information need is expressed by a first order formula in two free variables:

$$\texttt{descendant}(x,y) \wedge \neg\texttt{has\_leukemia}(y) \wedge$$
$$\forall z((\texttt{descendant}(x,z) \wedge \texttt{descendant}(z,y)) \rightarrow \texttt{has\_leukemia}(z)).$$

This information need can be expressed in XPath 1.0 for arbitrarily deep documents by the infinite disjunction (for readability, we abbreviate *leukemia* to *l*)

```
child::P[@l='no'] |
child::P[@l='yes']/child::P[@l='no'] |
child::P[@l='yes']/child::P[@l='yes']/child::P[@l='no'] ...
```

Theorem 3 below states that it is not possible to express this information need in Core XPath. What seems to be needed is the notion of a *conditional path*. Let $_{[\texttt{test}]}\texttt{child}$ denote all pairs (n, n') such that n' is a child of n and the test succeeds at n. Then the information need can be expressed by

$$\texttt{child} :: \texttt{P}/({}_{[@\texttt{l}='\texttt{yes}']}\texttt{child})^* :: \texttt{P}[@\texttt{l} =' \texttt{no}'].$$

The axis $({}_{[@\texttt{l}='\texttt{yes}']}\texttt{child})^*$ describes the reflexive transitive closure of $_{[@\texttt{l}='\texttt{yes}']}\texttt{child}$, whence either the path self or a child–path $n_0, n_1, \ldots, n_k$, for $k \geq 1$ such that at all nodes $n_0, \ldots n_{k-1}$ the leukemia attribute equals yes.

The next example discusses an information need which is not expressible using conditional paths. Admittedly the example is rather contrived. In fact it is very difficult to find natural information needs on the data in Figure 1 which are not expressible using transitive closure over conditional paths. Theorem 4 below states that every first order expressible set of nodes can be described as an XPath expression with transitive closure over conditional paths. Thus the difficulty in finding not expressible natural queries arises because such queries are genuinely second order. We come back to this point in Section 4 when we discuss the expressive power of XPath dialects.

Example 2. Consider the query "find all descendants which are an even number of steps away from the node of evaluation", expressible as $(\texttt{child}; \texttt{child})^* :: *$. Note that the axis relation contains a transitive closure over a sequence of atomic paths. The proof of Theorem 3 shows that this information need is not expressible using just transitive closure over conditional paths. The information need really expresses a second order property.

3 A Brief Introduction to XPath

[16] proposes a fragment of XPath 1.0 which can be seen as its logical core, but lacks many of the functionality that account for little expressive power. In effect it supports all XPath's axis relations, except the attribute relation[1], it allows sequencing and taking unions of path expressions and full booleans in the filter expressions. It is called Core XPath. A similar logical abstraction is made in [4]. As the focus of this paper is expressive power, we also restrict XPath to its logical core. We will define four XPath languages which only differ in the axis relations allowed in their expressions. As in XPath 1.0, we distinguish a number of axis relations. Instead of the rather verbose notation of XPath 1.0, we use a self-explanatory graphical notation, together with regular expression operators $^+$ and *. For the definition of the XPath languages, we follow the presentation of XPath in [16]. The expressions obey the standard W3C unabbreviated XPath 1.0 syntax, except

[1] This is without loss of generality as instead of modeling attributes as distinct axes, as in the standard XML model, we may assign multiple labels to each node, representing whether a certain attribute-value pair is true at that node.

for the different notation of the axis relations. The semantics is as in [4] and [15], which is in line with the standard XPath semantics from [34].

Our simplest language $\mathcal{X}$Core is slightly more expressive than Core XPath (cf. Remark 1). We view $\mathcal{X}$Core as the baseline in expressive power for XPath languages. $\mathcal{X}$CPath, for *conditional* XPath, simply extends $\mathcal{X}$Core with conditional paths. The key difference between $\mathcal{X}$Core and the three other languages is the use of filter expressions inside the axis relations, in particular as conditional paths. Regular expressions[2] with tests are well studied and often applied in languages for specifying paths (see the literature on Propositional Dynamic Logic (PDL) and Kleene algebras with tests [18,23]).

Definition 1 The syntax of the XPath languages $\mathcal{X}$Core, $\mathcal{X}$CPath, $\mathcal{X}_{reg}^{\mathsf{CPath}}$, $\mathcal{X}_{reg}$ is defined by the grammar

locpath ::= axis '::'ntst | axis '::' ntst '['fexpr']' | '/' locpath | locpath '/' locpath |
locpath '|' locpath
fexpr ::= locpath | not fexpr | fexpr and fexpr | fexpr or fexpr
prim_axis ::= self | $\Downarrow$ | $\Uparrow$ | $\Rightarrow$ | $\Leftarrow$

$\mathcal{X}$Core	axis ::= prim_axis | axis*
$\mathcal{X}$CPath	axis ::= prim_axis | $_{\text{fexpr}}$prim_axis | prim_axis$_{\text{fexpr}}$ | axis*
$\mathcal{X}_{reg}^{\mathsf{CPath}}$	axis ::= prim_axis | $_{\text{fexpr}}$prim_axis | prim_axis$_{\text{fexpr}}$ | axis; axis | axis $\cup$ axis | axis*
$\mathcal{X}_{reg}$	axis ::= prim_axis |?fexpr | axis; axis | axis $\cup$ axis | axis*.

where "locpath" (pronounced as *location path*) is the start production, "axis" denotes axis relations and "ntst" denotes tags labeling document nodes or the star '*' that matches all tags (these are called node tests). The "fexpr" will be called *filter expressions* after their use as filters in location paths. With an XPath expression we always mean a "locpath".

The semantics of XPath expressions is given with respect to an XML document modeled as a finite *node labeled sibling ordered tree*[3] (tree for short). Each node in the tree is labeled with a name tag from some alphabet. Sibling ordered trees come with two binary relations, the child relation, denoted by $R_{\Downarrow}$, and the immediate_right_sibling relation, denoted by $R_{\Rightarrow}$. Together with their inverses $R_{\Uparrow}$ and $R_{\Leftarrow}$ they are used to interpret the axis relations.

Each location path denotes a binary relation (a set of paths). The meaning of the filter expressions is given by the predicate $\mathcal{E}(n, \mathsf{fexpr})$ which assigns a boolean value. Thus a filter expression fexpr is most naturally viewed as denoting sets of nodes: all n such that $\mathcal{E}(n, \mathsf{fexpr})$ is true. For examples, we refer to Section 2 and to [16]. Given a tree $\mathfrak{M}$ and an expression f, the denotation or meaning of f in $\mathfrak{M}$ is written as $[\![f]\!]_{\mathfrak{M}}$. Table 1 contains the definition of $[\![\cdot]\!]_{\mathfrak{M}}$.

---

[2] Regular expressions are strings generated by the grammar $r ::= \epsilon \mid a \mid r^+ \mid r^* \mid r;r \mid r \cup r$ with a a primitive symbol and ϵ the empty string. The operations have their usual meaning.

[3] A sibling ordered tree is a structure isomorphic to $(N, R_{\Downarrow}, R_{\Rightarrow})$ where N is a set of finite sequences of natural numbers closed under taking initial segments, and for any sequence s, if $s \cdot k \in N$, then either $k = 0$ or $s \cdot k - 1 \in N$. For $n, n' \in N$, $nR_{\Downarrow}n'$ holds iff $n' = n \cdot k$ for k a natural number; $nR_{\Rightarrow}n'$ holds iff $n = s \cdot k$ and $n' = s \cdot k + 1$.

Table 1. The semantics of $\mathcal{X}$Core and $\mathcal{X}$CPath.

$$
\begin{array}{lcl}
[\![\mathcal{X} :: t]\!]_{\mathfrak{M}} & = & \{(n,n') \mid n[\![\mathcal{X}]\!]_{\mathfrak{M}} n' \text{ and } t(n')\} \\
[\![\mathcal{X} :: t[e]]\!]_{\mathfrak{M}} & = & \{(n,n') \mid n[\![\mathcal{X}]\!]_{\mathfrak{M}} n' \text{ and } t(n') \text{ and } \mathcal{E}_{\mathfrak{M}}(n',e)\} \\
[\![/\text{locpath}]\!]_{\mathfrak{M}} & = & \{(n,n') \mid (root,n') \in [\![\text{locpath}]\!]_{\mathfrak{M}}\} \\
[\![\text{locpath}/\text{locpath}]\!]_{\mathfrak{M}} & = & [\![\text{locpath}]\!]_{\mathfrak{M}} \circ [\![\text{locpath}]\!]_{\mathfrak{M}} \\
[\![\text{locpath} \mid \text{locpath}]\!]_{\mathfrak{M}} & = & [\![\text{locpath}]\!]_{\mathfrak{M}} \cup [\![\text{locpath}]\!]_{\mathfrak{M}}
\end{array}
$$

$$
\begin{array}{lcl}
\mathcal{E}_{\mathfrak{M}}(n, \text{locpath}) = true & \Longleftrightarrow & \exists n' : (n,n') \in [\![\text{locpath}]\!]_{\mathfrak{M}} \\
\mathcal{E}_{\mathfrak{M}}(n, \text{fexpr}_1 \texttt{ and } \text{fexpr}_2) = true & \Longleftrightarrow & \mathcal{E}_{\mathfrak{M}}(n, \text{fexpr}_1) = true \text{ and } \mathcal{E}_{\mathfrak{M}}(n, \text{fexpr}_2) = true \\
\mathcal{E}_{\mathfrak{M}}(n, \text{fexpr}_1 \texttt{ or } \text{fexpr}_2) = true & \Longleftrightarrow & \mathcal{E}_{\mathfrak{M}}(n, \text{fexpr}_1) = true \text{ or } \mathcal{E}_{\mathfrak{M}}(n, \text{fexpr}_2) = true \\
\mathcal{E}_{\mathfrak{M}}(n, \texttt{not } \text{fexpr}) = true & \Longleftrightarrow & \mathcal{E}_{\mathfrak{M}}(n, \text{fexpr}) = false.
\end{array}
$$

$$
\begin{array}{ll}
[\![\Downarrow]\!]_{\mathfrak{M}} := R_{\Downarrow} & [\![\mathsf{self}]\!]_{\mathfrak{M}} := \{(x,y) \mid x = y\} \\
[\![\Rightarrow]\!]_{\mathfrak{M}} := R_{\Rightarrow} & [\![p/q]\!]_{\mathfrak{M}} := [\![p]\!]_{\mathfrak{M}} \circ [\![q]\!]_{\mathfrak{M}} \\
[\![\Uparrow]\!]_{\mathfrak{M}} := R_{\Downarrow}^{-1} & [\![p \mid q]\!]_{\mathfrak{M}} := [\![p]\!]_{\mathfrak{M}} \cup [\![q]\!]_{\mathfrak{M}} \\
[\![\Leftarrow]\!]_{\mathfrak{M}} := R_{\Rightarrow}^{-1} & [\![p^*]\!]_{\mathfrak{M}} := [\![\mathsf{self}]\!]_{\mathfrak{M}} \cup [\![p]\!]_{\mathfrak{M}} \cup [\![p]\!]_{\mathfrak{M}} \circ [\![p]\!]_{\mathfrak{M}} \cup \ldots \\
[\![p_{\mathsf{fexpr}}]\!]_{\mathfrak{M}} := [\![p]\!]_{\mathfrak{M}} \circ [\![?\text{fexpr}]\!]_{\mathfrak{M}} & [\![?e]\!]_{\mathfrak{M}} := \{(x,y) \mid x = y \text{ and } \mathcal{E}_{\mathfrak{M}}(x,e) = true\}. \\
[\![{}_{\mathsf{fexpr}}p]\!]_{\mathfrak{M}} := [\![?\text{fexpr}]\!]_{\mathfrak{M}} \circ [\![p]\!]_{\mathfrak{M}} &
\end{array}
$$

Remark 1. XPath 1.0 (and hence Core XPath) has a strange asymmetry between the vertical (parent and child) and the horizontal (sibling) axis relations. For the vertical direction, both transitive and reflexive–transitive closure of the basic steps are primitives. For the horizontal direction, only the transitive closure of the immediate_left_ and immediate_right_sibling axis are primitives (with the rather ambiguous names *following* and *preceding_sibling*). $\mathcal{X}$Core removes this asymmetry and has all four one step navigational axes as primitives. XPath 1.0 also has two primitive axis related to the document order and transitive closures of one step navigational axes. These are just syntactic sugar, as witnessed by the following definitions:

$$
\begin{array}{lcl}
\texttt{descendant} :: t[\phi] & \equiv & \Downarrow :: */\Downarrow^* :: t[\phi] \\
\texttt{following} :: t[\phi] & \equiv & \Uparrow^* :: */\Rightarrow :: */\Rightarrow* :: */\Downarrow^* :: t[\phi] \\
\texttt{preceding} :: t[\phi] & \equiv & \Uparrow^* :: */\Leftarrow :: */\Leftarrow^* :: */\Downarrow^* :: t[\phi].
\end{array}
$$

So we can conclude that $\mathcal{X}$Core is at least as expressive as Core XPath, and has a more elegant set of primitives.

The reader might wonder why the set of XPath axes was not closed under taking converses. The next theorem states that this is not needed.

Theorem 2. *The set of axes of all four XPath languages are closed under taking converses.*

4 Expressive Power

This section describes the relations between the four defined XPath dialects and two XPath dialects from the literature. We also embed the XPath dialects into first order and monadic second order logic of trees and give a precise characterization of the conditional path dialect $\mathcal{X}$CPath in terms of first order logic.

Core XPath [17] was introduced in the previous section. [4] considers the Core XPath fragment $\mathcal{X}^{\uparrow}_{r,[]}$ obtained by deleting the sibling relations and the booleans on the filter expressions.

Theorem 3. *1. $\mathcal{X}^{\uparrow}_{r,[]}$ is strictly contained in Core XPath, and Core XPath is strictly contained in $\mathcal{X}$Core.*
2. $\mathcal{X}$Core is strictly contained in $\mathcal{X}$CPath.
3. $\mathcal{X}$CPath is strictly contained in $\mathcal{X}_{reg}$.
4. $\mathcal{X}_{reg}$ and $\mathcal{X}_{reg}^{\mathsf{CPath}}$ are equally expressive.

We now view the XPath dialects as query languages over trees, and compare them to first and second order logic interpreted on trees. Before we can start, we must make clear what kind of queries XPath expresses.

In the literature on XPath it is often tacitly assumed that each expression is always evaluated at the root. Then the meaning of an expression is naturally viewed as a *set of nodes*. Stated differently, it is a query with one variable in the select clause. This tacit assumption can be made explicit by the notion of an *absolute* XPath expression `/locpath`. The answer set of `/locpath` evaluated on a tree $\mathfrak{M}$ (notation: $answer_{\mathfrak{M}}(/\mathtt{locpath})$) is the set $\{n \in \mathfrak{M} \mid (root, n) \in [\![\mathtt{locpath}]\!]_{\mathfrak{M}}\}$. The relation between filter expressions and arbitrary XPath expressions evaluated at the root becomes clear by the following equivalence. For each filter expression `fexpr`, $\mathcal{E}_{\mathfrak{M}}(n, \mathtt{fexpr})$ is true if and only if $n \in answer_{\mathfrak{M}}(/\Downarrow^* :: *[\mathtt{fexpr}])$. On the other hand, looking at Table 1 it is immediate that in general an expression denotes a *binary relation*.

Let $\mathcal{L}^{tree}_{FO}$ and $\mathcal{L}^{tree}_{MSO}$ be the first order and monadic second order languages in the signature with two binary relation symbols *Descendant* and *Sibling* and countably many unary predicates $P, Q, \ldots$ Both languages are interpreted on node labeled sibling ordered trees in the obvious manner: *Descendant* is interpreted as the descendant relation $R^+_{\Downarrow}$, *Sibling* as the strict total order $R^+_{\Rightarrow}$ on the siblings, and the unary predicates P as the sets of nodes labeled with P. For the second order formulas, we always assume that all second order variables are quantified. So a formula in two free variables means a formula in two free variables ranging over nodes.

It is not hard to see that every $\mathcal{X}_{reg}$ expression is equivalent[4] to an $\mathcal{L}^{tree}_{MSO}$ formula in two free variables, and that every filter expression is equivalent to a formula in one free variable. $\mathcal{X}_{reg}$ can express truly second order properties as shown in Example 2. A little bit harder is

Proposition 1. *Every $\mathcal{X}$CPath (filter) expression is equivalent to an $\mathcal{L}^{tree}_{FO}$ formula in two (one) free variable(s).*

The converse of this proposition would state that $\mathcal{X}$CPath is powerful enough to express every first order expressible query. For one variable queries on Dedekind complete linear structures, the converse is known as Kamp's Theorem [21]. Kamp's result is generalized to other linear structures and given a simple proof in the seminal paper [14]. [24] showed that the result can further be generalized to sibling ordered trees:

Theorem 4 ([24]). *Every $\mathcal{L}^{tree}_{FO}$ query in one free variable is expressible as an absolute $\mathcal{X}$CPath expression.*

---

[4] In fact, there is a straightforward logspace translation, see the proof of Theorem 7.(i).

Digression: Is first order expressivity enough? [5] argues for the non-counting property of natural languages. A counting property expresses that a path consists of a number of nodes that is a multiple of a given number k. Since first order definable properties of trees are non-counting [32], by Theorem 4, $\mathcal{X}$CPath has the non-counting property. Example 2 shows that with regular expressions one can express counting properties. DTD's also allow one to express these: e.g., $A \longrightarrow (B, B, B)^+$ expresses that A nodes have a number of B children divisible by 3.

It seems to us that for the node addressing language first order expressivity is sufficient. This granted, Theorem 4 means that one need not look for other (i.e., more expressive) XPath fragments than $\mathcal{X}$CPath. Whether this also holds for constraints is debatable. Fact is that many natural counting constraints can be equivalently expressed with first order constraints. Take for example, the DTD rule $couple \longrightarrow (man, woman)^*$, which describes the couple element as a sequence of man, woman pairs. Clearly this expresses a counting property, but the same constraint can be expressed by the following $\mathcal{X}$CPath (i.e., first order) inclusions on sets of nodes. Both left and right hand side of the inclusions are filter expressions. (In these rules we just write man instead of the cumbersome self :: man, and similarly for the other node labels.)

$$\begin{aligned} couple &\subseteq \mathsf{not} \Downarrow :: *[\mathsf{not}\ man\ \mathsf{and}\ \mathsf{not}\ woman] \\ man\ \mathsf{and} \Uparrow :: couple &\subseteq \mathsf{not} \Rightarrow :: *[\mathsf{not}\ woman] \\ woman\ \mathsf{and} \Uparrow :: couple &\subseteq \Leftarrow :: man\ \mathsf{and}\ \mathsf{not} \Rightarrow :: *[\mathsf{not}\ man]. \end{aligned}$$

In the next two sections on the complexity of query evaluation and containment we will continue discussing more powerful languages than $\mathcal{X}$CPath, partly because there is no difference in complexity, and partly because DTD's are expressible in them.

5 Query Evaluation

The last two sections are about the computational complexity of two key problems related to XPath: query evaluation and query containment. We briefly discuss the complexity classes used in this paper. For more thorough surveys of the related theory see [20, 27]. By PTIME and EXPTIME we denote the well-known complexity classes of problems solvable in deterministic polynomial and deterministic exponential time, respectively, on Turing machines.

$\mathcal{X}_{reg}$ queries can be evaluated in linear time in the size of the data and the query. This is the same bound as for Core XPath. This bound is optimal because the combined complexity of Core XPath is already PTIME hard [16]. It is not hard to see that the linear time algorithm for Core XPath in [15] can be extended to work for full $\mathcal{X}_{reg}$. But the result also follows from known results about Propositional Dynamic Logic model checking [3] by the translation given in Theorem 10. For a model $\mathfrak{M}$, a node n and an XPath expression q, $answer^n_{\mathfrak{M}}(q) = \{t \mid (n,t) \in [\![q]\!]_{\mathfrak{M}}\}$.

Theorem 5. *For $\mathcal{X}_{reg}$ expressions q, $answer^n_{\mathfrak{M}}(q)$ can be computed in time $O(|\mathfrak{M}| \cdot |q|)$.*

6 Query Containment under Constraints

We discuss equivalence and containment of XPath expressions in the presence of constraints on the document trees. Constraints can take the form of a Document Type Definition (DTD) [37], an XSchema [40] specification, and in general can be any statement. For XPath expressions containing the child and descendant axes and union of paths, this problem —given a DTD— is already EXPTIME-complete [26]. The containment problem has been studied in [36,9,25,26]. For example, consider the XPath expressions in abbreviated syntax[5] $q_1 := a[b]/c$ and $q_2 := a/c$. Then obviously q_1 implies q_2. But the converse does not hold, as there are trees with a nodes having just a single c child. Of course there are many situations in which the "counterexamples" to the converse containment disappear, and in which q_1 and q_2 are equivalent. For instance when

(a) every a node has a b child. This is the case when the DTD contains for instance the rule $a \rightarrow (b, d|e^*)$, or in general on trees satisfying $\mathsf{self} :: a \equiv \mathsf{self} :: a[\Downarrow :: b]$.
(b) if every c node has a b sibling. This holds in all trees in which $\mathsf{self} :: b \equiv \mathsf{self} :: b[\Rightarrow^+ :: c \text{ or } \Leftarrow^+ :: c]$.
(c) if no a has a c child. This holds in all trees satisfying $\mathsf{self} :: a[\Downarrow :: c] \equiv \emptyset$.

We consider the following decision problem: for t_i, t_i', XPath expressions, does it follow that $t_0 \equiv t_0'$ given that $t_1 \equiv t_1'$ and ... and $t_n \equiv t_n'$ (notation: $t_1 \equiv t_1', \ldots, t_n \equiv t_n' \models t_0 \equiv t_0'$). The example above gives four instances of this problem:

1. $\models a[b]/c \equiv a/c$,
2. $\mathsf{self} :: a \equiv \mathsf{self} :: a[\Downarrow :: b] \models a[b]/c \equiv a/c$,
3. $\mathsf{self} :: b \equiv \mathsf{self} :: b[\Rightarrow^+ :: c \text{ or } \Leftarrow^+ :: c] \models a[b]/c \equiv a/c$,
4. $\mathsf{self} :: a[\Downarrow :: c] \equiv \emptyset \models a[b]/c \equiv a/c$.

This first instance does not hold, all others do. A number of instructive observations can be drawn from these examples. First, the constraints are all expressed as equivalences between XPath expressions denoting *sets of nodes*, while the conclusion relates two sets of *pairs of nodes*. This seems general: constraints on trees are naturally expressed on nodes, not on edges[6]. A DTD is a prime example. From the constraints on sets of nodes we deduce equivalences about sets of pairs of nodes. In example (a) this is immediate by substitution of equivalents. In example (b), some simple algebraic manipulation is needed, for instance using the validity $x[y]/y \equiv x/y$.

That constraints on trees are naturally given in terms of nodes is fortunate because we can reason about sets of nodes instead of sets of edges. The last becomes (on arbitrary graphs) quickly undecidable. The desire for computationally well behaved languages for reasoning on graphs resulted in the development of several languages which can specify sets of nodes of trees or graphs like Propositional Dynamic Logic [19], Computation Tree Logic [11] and the propositional μ-calculus [22]. Such languages are –like XPath–

[5] In our syntax they are $q1 := \mathsf{self} :: a[\Downarrow :: b]/\Downarrow :: c$ and $q2 := \mathsf{self} :: a/\Downarrow :: c$.

[6] This does not mean that we cannot express general properties of trees. For instance, $\mathsf{self} :: *[\text{not} \Uparrow :: *] \equiv \mathsf{self} :: *[\text{not} \Downarrow :: */\Downarrow :: */\Downarrow :: *]$ expresses that the tree has depth at most two, and $\mathsf{self} :: *[\text{not} \Uparrow :: *] \equiv \mathsf{self} :: *[\text{not} \Downarrow^* :: *[\text{not} \Downarrow :: */\Rightarrow :: */\Rightarrow :: *]]$ that the tree is at most binary branching.

typically two-sorted, having a sort for the relations between nodes and a sort for sets of nodes. Concerns about computational complexity together with realistic modeling needs determine which operations are allowed on which sort. For instance, boolean intersection is useful on the set sort (and available in XPath 1.0) but not in the relational sort. Similarly, complementation on the set sort is still manageable computationally but leads to high complexity when allowed on the relation sort.

All these propositional languages contain a construct $\langle\pi\rangle\phi$ with π from the edge sort and ϕ from the set sort. $\langle\pi\rangle\phi$ denotes the set of nodes from which there *exists* a π path to a ϕ node. Full boolean operators can be applied to these constructs. Note that XPath contains exactly the same construct: the location path $\pi :: *[\phi]$ evaluated as a filter expression.

Thus we consider the constraint inference problem restricted to XPath expressions denoting sets of nodes, earlier called *filter expressions*, after their use as filters of node sets in XPath. This restriction is natural, computationally still feasible and places us in an established research tradition.

We distinguish three notions of equivalence. The first two are the same as in [4]. The third is new. Two $\mathcal{X}_{reg}$ expressions p and p' are *equivalent* if for every tree model $\mathfrak{M}$, $[\![p]\!]_{\mathfrak{M}} = [\![p']\!]_{\mathfrak{M}}$. They are *root equivalent* if the answer sets of p and p' are the same, when evaluated at the root[7]. The difference between these two notions is easily seen by the following example. The expressions $\mathsf{self} :: *[A \text{ and not } A]$ and $\mathsf{self} :: *[\Uparrow]$ are equivalent when evaluated at the root (both denote the empty set) but nowhere else. If p, p' are both filter expressions and $\mathsf{self} :: *[p] \equiv \mathsf{self} :: *[p']$, we call them *filter equivalent*. Equivalence of p and p' is denoted by $p \equiv p'$, letting context decide which notion of equivalence is meant. Root and filter equivalence are closely related notions:

Theorem 6. *Root equivalence can effectively be reduced to filter equivalence and vice verse.*

The statement $t_1 \equiv t'_1, \ldots, t_n \equiv t'_n \models t_0 \equiv t'_0$ expresses that $t_0 \equiv t'_0$ is logically implied by the set of constraints $t_1 \equiv t'_1, \ldots, t_n \equiv t'_n$. This is this case if for each model $\mathfrak{M}$ in which $[\![t_i]\!]_{\mathfrak{M}} = [\![t'_i]\!]_{\mathfrak{M}}$ holds for all i between 1 and n, also $[\![t_0]\!]_{\mathfrak{M}} = [\![t'_0]\!]_{\mathfrak{M}}$ holds. The following results follow easily from the literature.

Theorem 7. *(i) Let $t_0^{(')}, \ldots, t_n^{(')}$ be $\mathcal{X}_{reg}$ expressions.*
The problem whether $t_1 \equiv t'_1, \ldots, t_n \equiv t'_n \models t_0 \equiv t'_0$ is decidable.
(ii) Let $t_0^{(')}, \ldots, t_n^{(')}$ be $\mathcal{X}$Core filter expressions in which `child` is the only axis. The problem whether $t_1 \equiv t'_1, \ldots, t_n \equiv t'_n \models t_0 \equiv t'_0$ is EXPTIME *hard.*

Decidability for the problem in (i) is obtained by an interpretation into $S\omega S$, whence the complexity is non-elementary [30]. On the other hand, (ii) shows that a single exponential complexity is virtually unavoidable: it already obtains for filter expressions with the most popular axis. Above we argued that a restriction to filter expressions is a good idea when looking for "low" complexity, and this still yields a very useful fragment. And indeed we have

Theorem 8. *Let $t_0^{(')}, \ldots, t_n^{(')}$ be $\mathcal{X}_{reg}$ root or filter expressions. The problem whether $t_1 \equiv t'_1, \ldots, t_n \equiv t'_n \models t_0 \equiv t'_0$ is in* EXPTIME.

[7] Thus, if for every tree model $\mathfrak{M}$, $[\![/p]\!]_{\mathfrak{M}} = [\![/p']\!]_{\mathfrak{M}}$.

6.1 Expressing DTDs in $\mathcal{X}_{reg}^{\mathsf{CPath}}$

In this section we show how a DTD can effectively be transformed into a set of constraints on $\mathcal{X}_{reg}^{\mathsf{CPath}}$ filter expressions. The DTD and this set are equivalent in the sense that a tree model conforms to the DTD if and only if each $\mathcal{X}_{reg}^{\mathsf{CPath}}$ filter expression is true at every node. A regular expression is a formula r generated by the following grammar: $r \ ::= e \mid (r;r) \mid (r \cup r) \mid r^*$ with e an element name. A DTD rule is a statement of the form $e \longrightarrow r$ with e an element name and r a regular expression. A DTD consists of a set of such rules and a rule stating the label of the root. An example of a DTD rule is $family \longrightarrow wife; husband; kid^*$. A document conforms to this rule if each *family* node has a *wife*, a *husband* and zero or more *kid* nodes as children, in that order. But that is equivalent to saying that for this document, the following equivalence holds:

$$\mathsf{self} :: family \equiv \mathsf{self} :: *[\Downarrow :: wife[\mathsf{first\ and} \Rightarrow :: husband[(\Rightarrow_{[kid]})^* :: *[\mathsf{last}]]]],$$

where first and last abbreviate not $\Leftarrow$ :: $*$ and not $\Rightarrow$ :: $*$, denoting the first and the last child, respectively. This example yields the idea for an effective reduction. Note that instead of $\Rightarrow$ :: $husband[\mathsf{fexpr}]$ we could have used a conditional path: $\Rightarrow_{[husband]}$ :: $*[\mathsf{fexpr}]$. For ease of translation, we assume without loss of generality that each DTD rule is of the form $e \longrightarrow e'; r$, for e' an element name. Replace each element name a in r by $\Rightarrow_{[\mathsf{self}\ ::\ a]}$ and call the result r^t. Now a DTD rule $e \rightarrow e'; r$ is transformed into the equivalent $\mathcal{X}_{reg}^{\mathsf{CPath}}$ filter expression constraint[8]:

$$\mathsf{self} :: e \subseteq \mathsf{self} :: e[\Downarrow :: e'[\mathsf{first\ and}\ r^t :: *[\mathsf{last}]]]. \tag{1}$$

That this transformation is correct is most easily seen by thinking of the finite state automaton (FSA) corresponding to $e'; r$. The word to be recognized is the sequence of children of an e node in order. The expression in the right hand side of (1) processes this sequence just like an FSA would. We assumed that every node has at least one child, the first being labeled by e'. The transition from the initial state corresponds to making the step to the first child (done by $\Downarrow :: e'[\mathsf{first}]$). The output state of the FSA is encoded by last, indicating the last child. Now r^t describes the transition in the FSA from the first node after the input state to the output state. The expression $\Rightarrow_{[\mathsf{self}\ ::\ a]}$ encodes an a–labeled transition in the FSA. If a DTD specifies that the root is labeled by e, this corresponds to the constraint $root \subseteq self :: e$. (Here and elsewhere *root* is an abbreviation for self :: $*[\mathsf{not} \Uparrow :: *]$). So we have shown the following

Theorem 9. *Let Σ be a DTD and Σ^t the set of expressions obtained by the above transformation. Then for each tree T in which each node has a single label it holds that T conforms to the DTD Σ iff $T \models \Sigma^t$.*

This yields together with Theorem 8,

Corollary 1. *Both root equivalence and filter equivalence of $\mathcal{X}_{reg}$ expressions given a DTD can be decided in* EXPTIME.

[8] The symbol $\subseteq$ denotes set inclusion. Inclusion of node sets is definable as follows: $f_1 \subseteq f_2$ iff self :: $* \equiv$ self :: $*[\mathsf{not}\ f_1\ \mathsf{or}\ f_2]$.

7 Conclusions

We can conclude that $\mathcal{X}$CPath can be seen as a stable fixed point in the development of XPath languages. $\mathcal{X}$CPath is expressively complete for first order properties on node labeled sibling ordered trees. The extra expressive power comes at no (theoretical) extra cost: query evaluation is in linear and query equivalence given a DTD in exponential time. These results even hold for the much stronger language $\mathcal{X}_{reg}$.

Having a stable fixed point means that new research directions come easily. We mention a few. An important question is whether $\mathcal{X}$CPath is also complete with respect to first order definable paths (i.e., first order formulas in two free variables.) Another expressivity question concerns XPath with regular expressions and tests, our language $\mathcal{X}_{reg}$. Is there a natural extension of first order logic for which $\mathcal{X}_{reg}$ is complete? An empirical question related to first and second order expressivity —see the discussion at the end of Section 4— is whether second order expressivity is really needed, both for XPath and for constraint languages like DTD and XSchema. Finally we would like to have a normal form theorem for $\mathcal{X}_{reg}$ and $\mathcal{X}_{reg}^{\mathsf{CPath}}$. In particular it would be useful to have an effective algorithm transforming $\mathcal{X}_{reg}^{\mathsf{CPath}}$ expressions into directed step expressions (cf. the proof of Theorem 8.)

References

1. S. Abiteboul, P. Buneman, and D. Suciu. *Data on the web.* Morgan Kaufman, 2000.
2. N. Alechina, S. Demri, and M. de Rijke. A modal perspective on path constraints. *Journal of Logic and Computation*, 13:1–18, 2003.
3. N. Alechina and N. Immerman. Reachability logic: An efficient fragment of transitive closure logic. *Logic Journal of the IGPL*, 8(3):325–337, 2000.
4. M. Benedikt, W. Fan, and G. Kuper. Structural properties of XPath fragments. In Proc. ICDT'03, 2003.
5. R. Berwick and A. Weinberg. *The Grammatical Basis of Natural Languages.* MIT Press, Cambridge, MA, 1984.
6. P. Blackburn, B. Gaiffe, and M. Marx. Variable free reasoning on finite trees. In *Proceedings of Mathematics of Language (MOL–8), Bloomington*, 2003.
7. D. Calvanese, G. De Giacomo, and M. Lenzerini. Representing and reasoning on XML documents: A description logic approach. *J. of Logic and Computation*, 9(3):295–318, 1999.
8. E.M. Clarke and B.-H. Schlingloff. Model checking. Elsevier Science Publishers, to appear.
9. A. Deutsch and V. Tannen. Containment of regular path expressions under integrity constraints. In *Knowledge Representation Meets Databases*, 2001.
10. J. Doner. Tree acceptors and some of their applications. *J. Comput. Syst. Sci.*, 4:405–451, 1970.
11. E.M. Clarke and E.A. Emerson. Design and Synthesis of Synchronization Skeletons using Branching Time Temporal Logic. In D. Kozen, editor, *Proceedings of the Workshop on Logics of Programs*, volume 131 of *LNCS*, pages 52–71, Springer, 1981.
12. M. Fisher and R. Ladner. Propositional dynamic logic of regular programs. *J. Comput. Syst. Sci.*, 18(2):194–211, 1979.
13. D.M. Gabbay, I. Hodkinson, and M. Reynolds. *Temporal Logic.* Oxford Science Publications, 1994. Volume 1: Mathematical Foundations and Computational Aspects.
14. D.M. Gabbay, A. Pnueli, S. Shelah, and J. Stavi. On the temporal analysis of fairness. In *Proc. 7th ACM Symposium on Principles of Programming Languages*, pages 163–173, 1980.

15. G. Gottlob, C. Koch, and R. Pichler. Efficient algorithms for processing XPath queries. In *Proc. of the 28th International Conference on Very Large Data Bases (VLDB 2002)*, 2002.
16. G. Gottlob, C. Koch, and R. Pichler. The complexity of XPath query evaluation. In *PODS 2003*, pages 179–190, 2003.
17. G. Gottlob and C. Koch. Monadic queries over tree-structured data. In *Proc. LICS*, Copenhagen, 2002.
18. D. Harel. Dynamic logic. In D.M. Gabbay and F. Guenther, editors, *Handbook of Philosophical Logic*, volume 2, pages 497–604. Reidel, Dordrecht, 1984.
19. D. Harel, D. Kozen, and J. Tiuryn. *Dynamic Logic*. MIT Press, 2000.
20. D. Johnson. A catalog of complexity classes. In J. van Leeuwen, editor, *Handbook of Theoretical Computer Science*, volume B, pages 67–161. Elsevier, 1990.
21. J.A.W. Kamp. *Tense Logic and the Theory of Linear Order*. PhD thesis, University of California, Los Angeles, 1968.
22. D. Kozen. Results on the propositional mu-calculus. *Th. Comp. Science*, 27, 1983.
23. D. Kozen. Kleene algebra with tests. *ACM Transactions on Programming Languages and Systems*, 19(3):427–443, May 1997.
24. M. Marx. $\mathcal{X}$CPath, the expressively complete XPath fragment. Manuscript, July 2003.
25. G. Miklau and D. Suciu. Containment and equivalence for an XPath fragment. In *Proc. PODS'02*, pages 65–76, 2002.
26. F. Neven and T. Schwentick. XPath containment in the presence of disjunction, DTDs, and variables. In *ICDT 2003*, 2003.
27. Ch. Papadimitriou. *Computational Complexity*. Addison–Wesley, 1994.
28. V. Pratt. Models of program logics. In *Proceedings FoCS*, pages 115–122, 1979.
29. M. Rabin. Decidability of second order theories and automata on infinite trees. *Transactions of the American Mathematical Society*, 141:1–35, 1969.
30. K. Reinhardt. The complexity of translating logic to finite automata. In E. Grädel et al., editor, *Automata, Logics, and Infinite Games*, volume 2500 of *LNCS*, pages 231–238. 2002.
31. J. Rogers. *A descriptive approach to language theoretic complexity*. CSLI Press, 1998.
32. W. Thomas. Logical aspects in the study of tree languages. In B. Courcelle, editor, *Ninth Colloquium on Trees in Algebra and Programming*, pages 31–50. CUP, 1984.
33. M.Y. Vardi and P. Wolper. Automata-theoretic techniques for modal logics of programs. *Journal of Computer and System Sciences*, 32:183–221, 1986.
34. P. Wadler. Two semantics for XPath. Technical report, Bell Labs, 2000.
35. M. Weyer. Decidability of S1S and S2S. In E. Grädel et al., editor, *Automata, Logics, and Infinite Games*, volume 2500 of *LNCS*, pages 207–230. Springer, 2002.
36. P. Wood. On the equivalence of XML patterns. In *Proc. 1st Int. Conf. on Computational Logic*, volume 1861 of *LNCS*, pages 1152–1166, 2000.
37. W3C. Extensible markup language (XML) 1.0 `http://www.w3.org/TR/REC-xml`.
38. W3C. XML path language (XPath 1.0). `http://www.w3.org/TR/xpath.html`.
39. W3C. XML path language (XPpath 2.0) `http://www.w3.org/TR/xpath20/`.
40. W3C. XML schema part 1: Structures. `http://www.w3.org/TR/xmlschema-1`.
41. W3C. Xquery 1.0: A query language for XML. `http://www.w3.org/TR//xquery/`.
42. W3C. XSL transformations language XSLT 2.0. `http://www.w3.org/TR/xslt20/`.

A Appendix

A.1 XPath and Propositional Dynamic Logic

The next theorem states that PDL and the $\mathcal{X}_{reg}$ filter expressions are equally expressive and effectively reducible to each other.

For our translation it is easier to use a variant of standard PDL in which the state formulas are boolean formulas over formulas $\langle\pi\rangle$, for π a program. Now $\langle\pi\rangle$ has the same meaning as $\langle\pi\rangle\top$ in standard PDL. Clearly this variant is equally expressive as PDL by the equivalences $\langle\pi\rangle \equiv \langle\pi\rangle\top$ and $\langle\pi\rangle\phi \equiv \langle\pi; ?\phi\rangle$.

Theorem 10. *There are logspace translations t from $\mathcal{X}_{reg}$ filter expressions to PDL formulas and t' in the converse direction such that for all models $\mathfrak{M}$, for all nodes n in $\mathfrak{M}$,*

$$\mathcal{E}_{\mathfrak{M}}(n, e) = true \iff \mathfrak{M}, n \models (e)^t \tag{2}$$

$$\mathcal{E}_{\mathfrak{M}}(n, (e^{t'}) = true \iff \mathfrak{M}, n \models e. \tag{3}$$

PROOF OF THEOREM 10. Let $(\cdot)^t$ from $\mathcal{X}_{reg}$ filter expressions to PDL formulas be defined as follows:

$$\begin{aligned}
&(\text{axis} :: \text{ntst}[\text{fexpr}])^t &&= \langle \text{axis}; ?(\text{ntst} \wedge \text{fexpr}^t)\rangle \\
&(/\text{locpath})^t &&= \langle \Uparrow^*; ?root\rangle(\text{locpath})^t \\
&(\text{locpath1}/\text{locpath2})^t &&= (\text{locpath1})^t(\text{locpath2})^t \\
&(\text{locpath1} \mid \text{locpath2})^t &&= (\text{locpath1})^t \vee (\text{locpath2})^t \\
&(\cdot)^t \text{ commutes with the booleans}
\end{aligned}$$

Then (2) holds. For the other direction, let $(\cdot)^{t'}$ commute with the booleans and let $\langle\pi\rangle^{t'} = \mathsf{self} :: *[\pi^\circ :: *]$, where π° is π with each occurrence of $?\phi$ replaced by $?\mathsf{self} :: *[\phi^{t'}]$. Then (3) holds.

A.2 Proofs

PROOF OF THEOREM 2. Every axis containing converses can be rewritten into one without converses by pushing them in with the following equivalences:

$$\begin{array}{lll}
\Downarrow^{-1} \equiv \Uparrow, & (p^{-1})^{-1} \equiv p, & (p/q)^{-1} \equiv q^{-1}/p^{-1}, \\
\Uparrow^{-1} \equiv \Downarrow, & (?p)^{-1} \equiv ?p, & (p \mid q)^{-1} \equiv p^{-1} \mid q^{-1}, \\
\Leftarrow^{-1} \equiv \Rightarrow, & (p^*)^{-1} \equiv (p^{-1})^*, & \\
\Rightarrow^{-1} \equiv \Leftarrow, & & \\
\mathsf{self}^{-1} \equiv \mathsf{self}. & &
\end{array}$$

PROOF OF THEOREM 3. $\mathcal{X}^{\uparrow}_{r,[]}$ is a fragment of Core XPath, but does not have negation on predicates. That explains the first strict inclusion. The definition of $\mathcal{X}\mathsf{Core}$ given here was explicitly designed to make the connection with Core XPath immediate. $\mathcal{X}\mathsf{Core}$ does not have the Core XPath axes `following` and `preceding` as primitives, but they are definable as explained in Remark 1. All other Core XPath axes are clearly in $\mathcal{X}\mathsf{Core}$. The inclusion is strict because Core XPath does not contain the immediate right and left sibling axis.

$\mathcal{X}\mathsf{Core} \subsetneq \mathcal{X}\mathsf{CPath}$ holds already on linear structures. This follows from a fundamental result in temporal logic stating that on such structures the temporal operator *until* is not expressible by the operators *next-time*, *sometime-in-the-future* and their inverses [13]. The last two correspond to the XPath axis `child` and `descendant`, respectively. *Until(A,B)* is expressible with conditional paths as $(\Downarrow_{\mathsf{self} :: B})^* :: *[/]\Downarrow :: A$.

$\mathcal{X}\mathsf{CPath} \subsetneq \mathcal{X}_{reg}$ also holds on linear structures already. $\mathcal{X}\mathsf{CPath}$ is a fragment of the first order logic of ordered trees by Proposition 1. But Example 2 expresses a relation which is not first order expressible on trees [32].

$\mathcal{X}^{\mathsf{CPath}}_{reg} \subseteq \mathcal{X}_{reg}$, because the conditional axis can be expressed by ? and ;. For the other direction, let p be an $\mathcal{X}_{reg}$ axis. Apply to all subterms of p the following rewrite rules until no more is applicable[9]. From the axioms of Kleene algebras with tests [23] it follows that all rules state an equivalence.

$$\begin{array}{ll} (a \cup b); c \longrightarrow (a; c) \cup (b; c) & (?F)^* \longrightarrow \mathsf{self} \\ c; (a \cup b) \longrightarrow (c; a) \cup (c; b) & (a \cup ?F)^* \longrightarrow a^* \\ (a^*)^* \longrightarrow a^* & a^*; ?F \longrightarrow ?F \cup a^*; a; ?F \\ ?F_1 \cup ?F_2 \longrightarrow ?(F_1 \vee F_2) & ?F; a^* \longrightarrow ?F \cup ?F; a; a^*. \\ ?F_1; ?F_2 \longrightarrow ?(F_1 \wedge F_2) & \end{array}$$

Then all tests occurring under the scope of a $*$ or in a sequence will be conditional to an atomic axes. Now consider a location step `axes::ntst[fexpr]`. If `axes` is a $*$ expression or a sequence, the location step is in $\mathcal{X}_{reg}^{\mathsf{CPath}}$. If it is a union or a test, delete tests by the equivalences

```
?F::nst[fexpr]        ≡ self::nst[fexpr and F]
(?F∪ A)::nst[fexpr] ≡ A::nst[fexpr] | self::nst[fexpr and F].
```

PROOF OF PROPOSITION 1. The only interesting cases are transitive closures of conditional paths, like $\Downarrow^*_{\mathrm{fexpr}} :: t[E]$. This expression translates to the $\mathcal{L}_{FO}^{tree}$ formula (letting $(\cdot)^\circ$ denote the translation) ; $(x = y \vee \forall z(Descendant(x,z) \wedge Descendant(z,y) \rightarrow \mathrm{fexpr}^\circ(z))) \wedge \mathrm{fexpr}^\circ(y) \wedge t(y) \wedge E^\circ(y)$.

PROOF OF THEOREM 5. Computing the set of states in a model $\mathfrak{M}$ at which a PDL formula p is true can be done in time $O(|\mathfrak{M}| \cdot |p|)$ [3]. Thus for $\mathcal{X}_{reg}$ filter expressions, the result follows from Theorem 10. Now let q be an arbitrary expression, and we want to compute $answer^n_{\mathfrak{M}}(q)$. Expand $\mathfrak{M}$ with a new label l_n such that $[\![l_n]\!]_{\mathfrak{M}} = \{(n,n)\}$. Use the technique in the proof of Theorem 6 to obtain a filter expression q' such that $t \in answer^n_{\mathfrak{M}}(q)$ iff $\mathcal{E}_{\mathfrak{M}}(t,q') = true$ (here use the new label l_n instead of $root$.)

PROOF OF THEOREM 6. We use the fact that $\mathcal{X}_{reg}$ axis are closed under converse (Theorem 2) and that every $\mathcal{X}_{reg}$ location path is equivalent to a simple location path of the form axis $::$ t[fexpr]. The last holds as $\mathrm{axis}_1 :: t_1[\mathrm{fexpr}_1] | \mathrm{axis}_2 :: t_2[\mathrm{fexpr}_2]$ is equivalent to $(\mathrm{axis}_1; ?(\mathsf{self} :: t_1[\mathrm{fexpr}_1]) \cup \mathrm{axis}_2; ?(\mathsf{self} :: t_2[\mathrm{fexpr}_2])) :: *$, etc. We claim that for each model $\mathfrak{M}$, $\mathfrak{M} \models /\mathrm{axis}_1 :: t_1[\mathrm{fexpr}_1] \equiv /\mathrm{axis}_2 :: t_2[\mathrm{fexpr}_2]$ if and only if $\mathfrak{M} \models \mathsf{self} :: t_1[\mathrm{fexpr}_1 \text{ and } \mathrm{axis}_1{}^{-1} :: *[root]] \equiv \mathsf{self} :: t_2[\mathrm{fexpr}_2 \text{ and } \mathrm{axis}_2{}^{-1} :: *[root]]$. This is easily proved by writing out the definitions using the equivalence $(p;q)^{-1} \equiv q^{-1}; p^{-1}$. Filter equivalence can be reduced to root equivalence because $p \equiv p'$ iff $\mathsf{self} :: *[root] \equiv \mathsf{self} :: *[root \text{ and not } \Downarrow^* :: *[p \text{ and not } p']]$.

PROOF OF THEOREM 7. (i) Decidability follows from an interpretation in the monadic second order logic over variably branching trees $L^2_{K,P}$ of [31]. The consequence problem for $L^2_{K,P}$ is shown to be decidable by an interpretation into $S\omega S$. Finiteness of a tree can be expressed in $L^2_{K,P}$. The translation of $\mathcal{X}_{reg}$ expressions into $L^2_{K,P}$ is straightforward given the meaning definition. We only have to use second order quantification to define the transitive closure of a relation. This can be done by the usual definition: for R any binary relation, xR^*y holds iff

$$x = y \vee \forall X(X(x) \wedge \forall z, z'(X(z) \wedge zRz' \rightarrow X(z')) \rightarrow X(y)).$$

(ii) Theorem 10 gives an effective reduction from PDL tree formulas to $\mathcal{X}_{reg}$ filter expressions. The consequence problem for ordinary PDL interpreted on graphs is EXPTIME hard [12]. An inspection

[9] An exponential blowup cannot be avoided. Consider a composition of n expressions $(a_i \cup ?F_i)$, for the a_i atomic axis. Then the only way of rewriting this into an $\mathcal{X}_{reg}^{\mathsf{CPath}}$ axes is to fully distribute the unions over the compositions, leaving a union consisting of 2^n elements.

of the proof shows that the path $\Downarrow$ can be used as the only program and that checking consequence on finite trees is sufficient.

PROOF OF THEOREM 8. We first give a proof for $\mathcal{X}_{reg}$ by a reduction to deterministic PDL with converse. Then we give a direct algorithm which might be easier to implement. This algorithm unfortunately works only for $\mathcal{X}_{reg}^{\mathsf{CPath}}$ expressions in which there are no occurrences of an arrow and its inverse under the Kleene star.

Proof by reduction. By Theorem 10, and standard PDL reasoning we need only decide satisfiability of PDL formulas in the signature with the four arrow programs interpreted on finite trees. Call the language compass-PDL. Consider the language PDL_2, the PDL language with only the two programs $\{\downarrow_1, \downarrow_2\}$ and their inverses $\{\uparrow_1, \uparrow_2\}$. PDL_2 is interpreted on finite at most *binary-branching* trees, with $\downarrow_1$ and $\downarrow_2$ interpreted by the first and second daughter relation, respectively. We will effectively reduce compass-PDL satisfiability to PDL_2 satisfiability. PDL_2 is a fragment of deterministic PDL with converse. [33] shows that the satisfiability problem for this latter language is decidable in EXPTIME over the class of all models. This is done by constructing for each formula ϕ a tree automaton A_ϕ which accepts exactly all tree models in which ϕ is satisfied. Thus deciding satisfiability of ϕ reduces to checking emptiness of A_ϕ. The last check can be done in time polynomial in the size of A_ϕ. As the size of A_ϕ is exponential in the length of ϕ, this yields the exponential time decision procedure.

But we want satisfiability on *finite* trees. This is easy to cope with in an automata-theoretic framework: construct an automaton $A_{\mathit{fin\_tree}}$, which accepts only finite binary trees, and check emptiness of $A_\phi \cap A_{\mathit{fin\_tree}}$. The size of $A_{\mathit{fin\_tree}}$ does not depend on ϕ, so this problem is still in EXPTIME.

The reduction from compass-PDL to PDL_2 formulas is very simple: replace the compass-PDL programs $\Downarrow, \Uparrow, \Rightarrow, \Leftarrow$ by the PDL_2 programs $\Downarrow_1; \Downarrow_2^*, \Uparrow_2^*; \Uparrow_1, \Downarrow_2, \Uparrow_2$, respectively. It is straightforward to prove that this reduction preserves satisfiability, following the reduction from $S\omega S$ to $S2S$ as explained in [35]: a compass-PDL model $(T, R_\Rightarrow, R_\Downarrow, V)$ is turned into an PDL_2 model (T, R_1, R_2, V) by defining $R_1 = \{(x, y) \mid xR_\Downarrow y$ and y is the first daughter of $x\}$ and $R_2 = R_\Rightarrow$. A PDL_2 model (T, R_1, R_2, V) is turned into a compass-PDL model $(T, R_\Rightarrow, R_\Downarrow, V)$ by defining $R_\Rightarrow = R_2$ and $R_\Downarrow = R_1 \circ R_2^*$.

Direct proof. Consider $t_1 \equiv t_1', \ldots, t_n \equiv t_n' \Rightarrow t_0 \equiv t_0'$ as in the Theorem. By Theorem 6 we may assume that all terms are filter expressions. For this proof, assume also that the expressions are in $\mathcal{X}_{reg}^{\mathsf{CPath}}$ and that in each subexpression π^* of an axis, π may not contain an arrow and its inverse. We call such expressions *directed.* First we bring these expressions into a normal form. Define the set of *step paths* by the grammar $s \ =:: \ a \mid {}_{[\mathtt{test}]}a \mid a_{[\mathtt{test}]} \mid s \cup \ldots \cup s \mid p_1; \ldots; p_n; s; p_{n+1}; \ldots; p_{n+k}$, where a is one of the four arrows and the p_i can be any path. The next lemma gives the reason for considering directed step paths. Its simple proof is omitted.

Lemma 1. *Let $\mathcal{X}$ be a step path not containing an arrow axis and its inverse. Then in any model $\mathfrak{M}$, $n\mathcal{X}n'$ holds only if $n \neq n'$ and the relation $\mathcal{X}$ is conversely well-founded.*

Lemma 2. *Every $\mathcal{X}_{reg}^{\mathsf{CPath}}$ expression is effectively reducible to an $\mathcal{X}_{reg}^{\mathsf{CPath}}$ expression in which for every occurrence of π^*, π is a step path.*

Proof. Define a function G from $\mathcal{X}_{reg}^{\mathsf{CPath}}$ expressions to sets of $\mathcal{X}_{reg}^{\mathsf{CPath}}$ expressions which yields the set of step paths which "generate" the expression: for an $\mathcal{X}_{reg}^{\mathsf{CPath}}$ expression p, $G(p) = \{p\}$, if p is a step path. Otherwise set $G(p \cup q) = G(p) \cup G(q)$, $G(p; q) = G(p) \cup G(q)$ and $G(p^*) = G(p)$. Now define the translation $(\cdot)^t$ from $\mathcal{X}_{reg}^{\mathsf{CPath}}$ expressions to $\mathcal{X}_{reg}^{\mathsf{CPath}}$ expressions in which for every occurrence of π^*, π is a step path: $p^t = p$, if p is a step path. Otherwise set $(p \cup q)^t = p^t \cup q^t$, $(p; q)^t = p^t; q^t$ and $(p^*)^t = (s_1 \cup \ldots \cup s_k)^*$ for $G(p) = \{s_1, \ldots, s_k\}$. A rather straightforward induction shows that $p^t \equiv p$ and that $|p^t|$ is linear in $|p|$.

The rest of the proof is a reduction to the consequence problem for a simple language interpreted on binary trees. The language is equivalent to filter expressions with only two axis, first and second child. We could give the proof in terms of the $\mathcal{X}_{reg}^{\mathsf{CPath}}$ language, but the syntax is very cumbersome to work with. For that reason we use the effective reduction to PDL formulas from Theorem 10 and do the rest of the proof in the PDL syntax.

The proof consists of two linear reductions and a decision algorithm. The first reduction removes the transitive closure operation by adding new propositional symbols. Similar techniques are employed in [29,10] for obtaining normalized monadic second order formulas. The second reduction is based on Rabin's reduction of $S\omega S$ to $S2S$.

Let $\mathcal{L}_2$ be the modal language[10] with only two atomic paths $\{\downarrow_1, \downarrow_2\}$ and the modal constant $root$. $\mathcal{L}_2$ is interpreted on finite *binary* trees, with $\downarrow_1$ and $\downarrow_2$ interpreted by the first and second daughter relation, respectively, and $root$ holds exactly at the root. The semantics is the same as that of PDL.

The *consequence problem* for PDL and for $\mathcal{L}_2$ is the following: for $\phi_0, \ldots, \phi_n$ determine whether $\phi_1, \ldots, \phi_n \models \phi_0$ is true. The last is true if for each model $\mathfrak{M}$ with node set T in which $[\![\phi_1]\!]_{\mathfrak{M}} = \ldots [\![\phi_n]\!]_{\mathfrak{M}} = T$ it also holds that $[\![\phi_0]\!]_{\mathfrak{M}} = T$.

Lemma 3. *The $\mathcal{L}_2$ consequence problem is decidable in* EXPTIME.

Proof. A direct proof of this lemma using a bottom up version of Pratt's [28] EXPTIME Hintikka Set elimination technique was given in [6]. As $\mathcal{L}_2$ is a sublanguage of PDL_2, the lemma also follows from the argument given above in the *proof by reduction.*

A PDL formula in which the programs are $\mathcal{X}_{reg}^{\mathsf{CPath}}$ axis with the restriction that for every occurrence of π^*, π is a step path not containing an arrow and its inverse is called a *directed step PDL formula.* The next Lemma together with Lemmas 2 and 3 and Theorem 10 yield the EXPTIME result for directed $\mathcal{X}_{reg}^{\mathsf{CPath}}$ expressions.

Lemma 4. *There is an effective reduction from the consequence problem for directed step PDL formulas to the consequence problem for $\mathcal{L}_2$ formulas.*

Proof. Let χ be a directed step PDL formula. Let $Cl(\chi)$ be the Fisher–Ladner closure [12] of χ. We associate a formula $\nabla(\chi)$ with χ as follows. We create for each $\phi \in Cl(\chi)$, a new propositional variable q_ϕ and for each $\langle p_1; p_2\rangle\phi \in Cl(\chi)$ we also create $q_{\langle p_1\rangle q_{\langle p_2\rangle\phi}}$. Now $\nabla(\chi)$ "axiomatizes" these new variables as follows:

$$
\begin{array}{ll}
q_p \leftrightarrow p & q_{\langle\pi_1;\pi_2\rangle\phi} \leftrightarrow q_{\langle\pi_1\rangle q_{\langle\pi_2\rangle\phi}} \\
q_{\neg\phi} \leftrightarrow \neg q_\phi & q_{\langle\pi_1\cup\pi_2\rangle\phi} \leftrightarrow q_{\langle\pi_1\rangle\phi} \vee q_{\langle\pi_2\rangle\phi} \\
q_{\phi\wedge\psi} \leftrightarrow q_\phi \wedge q_\psi & q_{\langle\pi^*\rangle\phi} \leftrightarrow q_\phi \vee q_{\langle\pi\rangle q_{\langle\pi^*\rangle\phi}} \\
q_{\phi\vee\psi} \leftrightarrow q_\phi \vee q_\psi & \\
q_{\langle\alpha\rangle\phi} \leftrightarrow \langle\alpha\rangle q_\phi & \\
q_{\langle \mathtt{test}\,\alpha\rangle\phi} \leftrightarrow q_{\mathtt{test}} \wedge \langle\alpha\rangle q_\phi & \\
q_{\langle\alpha\,\mathtt{test}\rangle\phi} \leftrightarrow \langle\alpha\rangle(q_{\mathtt{test}} \wedge q_\phi) &
\end{array}
$$

for $\alpha \in \{\Downarrow, \Uparrow, \Leftarrow, \Rightarrow\}$, and `test` a directed step PDL formula.

We claim that for every model $\mathfrak{M}$ which validates $\nabla(\chi)$, for every node n and for every new variable q_ϕ, $[\![q_\phi]\!]_{\mathfrak{M}} = [\![\phi]\!]_{\mathfrak{M}}$. In the proof we use the usual logical notation $n \models \phi$ instead of the more cumbersome $n \in [\![\phi]\!]_{\mathfrak{M}}$.

The proof is by induction on the structure of the formula and the path and for the left to right direction of the $\langle\pi^*\rangle$ case by induction on the depth of direction of π. The case for proposition

[10] That is, the syntax is defined as that of PDL, with $\pi ::= \downarrow_1 | \downarrow_2$ and $\phi ::= l \mid \top \mid root \mid \neg\phi \mid \phi \wedge \phi \mid \phi \vee \phi \mid \langle\pi\rangle\phi$.

letters and the Boolean cases are immediate by the axioms in $\nabla(\chi)$. For the diamonds, we also need an induction on the structure of the paths, so let $n \models q_{\langle\pi\rangle\phi}$ for $\pi \in \{\Downarrow, \Uparrow, \Leftarrow, \Rightarrow\}$. Iff, by the axiom, $n \models \langle\pi\rangle q_\phi$. Iff $m \models q_\phi$ for some m such that $nR_\pi m$. Iff, by induction hypothesis, $m \models \phi$ for some m such that $nR_\pi m$. Iff $n \models \langle\pi\rangle\phi$. The cases for the conditional arrows are shown similarly. The cases for composition and union and the right to left direction of the Kleene star case follow immediately from the axioms. For the left to right direction of the Kleene star we also do an induction on the depth of the direction of π. This is possible by Lemma 1. As an example let the direction be $\Downarrow$. Let n be a leaf and let $n \models q_{\langle\pi^*\rangle\phi}$. By the axiom in $\nabla(\chi)$, $n \models q_\phi$ or $n \models q_{\langle\pi\rangle q_{\langle\pi^*\rangle\phi}}$. The latter implies, by induction on the complexity of paths, that $n \models \langle\pi\rangle q_{\langle\pi^*\rangle\phi}$. But that is not possible by Lemma 1 as n is a leaf. Thus $n \models q_\phi$, and by IH, $n \models \phi$, whence $n \models \langle\pi^*\rangle\phi$. Now let n be a node with $k+1$ descendants, and let the claim hold for nodes with k descendants. Let $n \models q_{\langle\pi^*\rangle\phi}$. Then by the axiom $n \models q_\phi$ or $n \models q_{\langle\pi\rangle q_{\langle\pi^*\rangle\phi}}$. In the first case, $n \models \langle\pi^*\rangle\phi$ by IH. In the second case, by the induction on the structure of paths, $n \models \langle\pi\rangle q_{\langle\pi^*\rangle\phi}$. As π is a directed step path, there exists a child m of n and $m \models q_{\langle\pi^*\rangle\phi}$. Whence, by the induction on the depth of the direction $\mathfrak{M}, m \models \langle\pi^*\rangle\phi$. But then also $\mathfrak{M}, n \models \langle\pi^*\rangle\phi$.

Hence for $\phi_0, \phi_1, \ldots, \phi_n$ directed step PDL formulas, we have

$$\phi_1, \ldots, \phi_n \models \phi_0 \iff q_{\phi_1}, \ldots, q_{\phi_n}, \nabla(\{\phi_0, \phi_1, \ldots, \phi_n\}) \models q_{\phi_0}.$$

As the language is closed under conjunction, we need only consider problems of the form $\phi_1 \models \phi_0$, and we do that from now on.

Note that the only modalities occurring in $\nabla(\chi)$ are $\langle\pi\rangle$ for π one of the four arrows. We can further reduce the number of arrows to only $\Downarrow, \Rightarrow$ when we add two modal constants *root* and *first* for the root and first elements, respectively. Let χ be a formula in this fragment. As before create a new variable q_ϕ for each (single negation of a) subformula ϕ of χ. Create $\nabla(\chi)$ as follows: $q_p \leftrightarrow p$, $q_{\neg\phi} \leftrightarrow \neg q_\phi$, $q_{\phi\wedge\psi} \leftrightarrow q_\phi \wedge q_\psi$ and $q_{\langle\pi\rangle\phi} \leftrightarrow \langle\pi\rangle q_\phi$, for $\pi \in \{\Downarrow, \Rightarrow\}$, and for each subformula $\langle\Uparrow\rangle\phi$ and $\langle\Leftarrow\rangle\phi$, add to $\nabla\chi$ the axioms

$$\begin{array}{lll} q_\phi \rightarrow [\Downarrow]q_{\langle\Uparrow\rangle\phi}, & \langle\Downarrow\rangle q_{\langle\Uparrow\rangle\phi} \rightarrow q_\phi, & q_{\langle\Uparrow\rangle\phi} \rightarrow \neg root, \\ q_\phi \rightarrow [\Rightarrow]q_{\langle\Leftarrow\rangle\phi}, & \langle\Rightarrow\rangle q_{\langle\Leftarrow\rangle\phi} \rightarrow q_\phi, & q_{\langle\Leftarrow\rangle\phi} \rightarrow \neg first. \end{array}$$

We claim that for every model $\mathfrak{M}$ which validates $\nabla(\chi)$, for every node n and for every subformula $\phi \in Cl(\chi)$, $\mathfrak{M}, n \models q_\phi$ iff $\mathfrak{M}, n \models \phi$. An easy induction shows this. Consider the case of $\langle\Uparrow\rangle\phi$. If $n \models \langle\Uparrow\rangle\phi$, then the parent of n models ϕ, whence by inductive hypothesis, it models q_ϕ, so by the axiom $q_\phi \rightarrow [\Downarrow]q_{\langle\Uparrow\rangle\phi}$, $n \Vdash q_{\langle\Uparrow\rangle\phi}$. Conversely, if $n \models q_{\langle\Uparrow\rangle\phi}$, then by axiom $q_{\langle\Uparrow\rangle\phi} \rightarrow \neg root$, n is not the root. So the parent of n exists and it models $\langle\Downarrow\rangle q_{\langle\Uparrow\rangle\phi}$. Then it models q_ϕ by axiom $\langle\Downarrow\rangle q_{\langle\Uparrow\rangle\phi} \rightarrow q_\phi$, and by inductive hypothesis it models ϕ. Thus $n \models \langle\Uparrow\rangle\phi$. Hence, $\gamma \models \chi \iff \nabla(\gamma \wedge \chi), q_\gamma \models q_\chi$.
Note that the formulas on the right hand side only contain the modalities $\langle\Downarrow\rangle$ and $\langle\Rightarrow\rangle$. Now we come to the second reduction: to the consequence problem of binary branching trees. Let χ be a formula, translate it to a PDL_2 formula as in the *proof by reduction*. Note that this is a directed step PDL formula. Finally use the first reduction again to reduce the consequence problem to the consequence problem of the language with just the modalities $\langle\Downarrow_1\rangle$ and $\langle\Downarrow_2\rangle$, interpreted on binary trees.

Clinching all these reductions together, we obtain the reduction stated in Lemma 4.

Declustering Two-Dimensional Datasets over MEMS-Based Storage*

Hailing Yu, Divyakant Agrawal, and Amr El Abbadi

Department of Computer Science
University of California at Santa Barbara
Santa Barbara, 93106, USA
{hailing,agrawal,amr}@cs.ucsb.edu

Abstract. Due to the large difference between seek time and transfer time in current disk technology, it is advantageous to perform large I/O using a single sequential access rather than multiple small random I/O accesses. However, prior optimal cost and data placement approaches for processing range queries over two-dimensional datasets do not consider this property. In particular, these techniques do not consider the issue of sequential data placement when multiple I/O blocks need to be retrieved from a single device. In this paper, we reevaluate the optimal cost of range queries by declustering two-dimensional datasets over multiple devices, and prove that, in general, it is impossible to achieve the new optimal cost. This is because disks cannot facilitate two-dimensional sequential access which is required by the new optimal cost. Fortunately, MEMS-based storage is being developed to reduce I/O cost. We first show that the two-dimensional sequential access requirement can not be satisfied by simply modeling MEMS-based storage as conventional disks. Then we propose a new placement scheme that exploits the physical properties of MEMS-based storage to solve this problem. Our theoretical analysis and experimental results show that the new scheme achieves almost optimal results.

1 Introduction

Multi-dimensional datasets have received a lot of attention due to their wide applications, such as relational databases, images, GIS, and spatial databases. Range queries are an important class of queries for multi-dimensional data applications. In recent years, the size of datasets has been rapidly growing, hence, fast retrieval of relevant data is the key to improve query performance. A common method of browsing geographic applications is to display a low resolution map of some area on a screen. A user may specify a rectangular bounding box over the map, and request the retrieval of the higher resolution map of the specified region. In general, the amount of data associated with different regions may be quite large, and may involve a large number of I/O transfers. Furthermore, due to advances in processor and semi-conductor technologies, the gap in access cost between main memory and disk is constantly increasing. Thus, I/O cost will dominate the cost of range query. To alleviate this problem, two-dimensional datasets are often uniformly

* This research is supported by the NSF under grants CCR-9875732, IIS-0220152, and EIA 00-80134.

E. Bertino et al. (Eds.): EDBT 2004, LNCS 2992, pp. 495–512, 2004.
© Springer-Verlag Berlin Heidelberg 2004

divided into tiles. The tiles are then declustered over multiple disks to improve query performance through parallel I/O. In [10], it is shown that strictly optimal solutions for range queries exist in only a small number of cases. Given a query that retrieves A tiles, the optimal cost is $\lceil A/M \rceil$, where M is the number of I/O devices. A data assignment scheme is said to be *strictly optimal* if it satisfies the optimal cost. Because it is impossible to find the optimal solution for the general case, several assignment schemes have been proposed [5,11,3,4,6] to achieve near optimal solutions. However, all prior research, including the optimal cost formulation itself, is based on the assumption that the retrieval of each tile takes constant time and is retrieved independently (random I/O involving both seek and transfer time). This condition does not hold when considering current disk technology. Recent trends in hard disk development favor reading large chunks of consecutive disk blocks (sequential access). Thus, the solutions for allocating two-dimensional data across multiple disk devices should also account for this factor. In this paper, we reevaluate the optimal cost for current disk devices, and show that it is still impossible to achieve the new optimal cost for the general case.

Even though the performance gap between main memory and disks is mitigated by a variety of techniques, it is still bounded by the access time of hard disks. The mechanical positioning system in disks limits the access time improvements to only about 7% per year. Therefore, this performance gap can only be overcome by inventing new storage technology. Due to advances in nano-technology, Micro-ElectroMechanical Systems (MEMS) based storage systems are appearing on the horizon as an alternative to disks [12,1,2]. MEMS are devices that have microscopic moving parts made by using techniques similar to those used in semiconductor manufacturing. As a result, MEMS devices can be produced and manufactured at a very low cost. Preliminary studies [13] have shown that stand-alone MEMS based storage devices reduce I/O stall time by 4 to 74 times over disks and improve the overall application run times by 1.9X to 4.4X.

MEMS-based storage devices have very different characteristics from disk devices. When compared to disk devices, head movement in MEMS-based storage devices can be achieved in both X and Y dimensions, and multiple probe tips (over thousands) can be activated concurrently to access data. In [8], Griffin et al. consider the problem of integrating MEMS-based storage into computers by modeling them as conventional disks. In [9], we proposed a new data placement scheme for relational data on MEMS based storage by taking its characteristics into account. The performance analysis showed that it is beneficial to use MEMS storage in a novel way. Range queries over two-dimensional data (map or images) are another data-intensive application, thus, in this paper, we explore data placement schemes for two-dimensional data over MEMS-based storage to facilitate efficient processing of range queries. In our new scheme, we tile two-dimensional datasets according to the physical properties of I/O devices. In all previous work, the dataset is divided into tiles along each dimension uniformly. Through the performance study, we show that tiling the dataset based on the properties of devices can significantly improve the performance without any adverse impact on users, since users only care about query performance, and do not need to know how or where data is stored. The significant improvement in performance further demonstrates the great potential that novel storage devices, like MEMS, have for database applications.

The rest of the paper is organized as follows. Section 2 revisits the optimal cost of a range query on a two-dimensional dataset. In Section 3, we first give a brief introduction of MEMS-based storage; then we adapt existing data placement schemes proposed for disks to MEMS-based storage. A novel scheme is proposed in Section 4. Section 5 presents the experimental results. We conclude the paper in Section 6.

2 Background

In this section, we first address the problem of existing optimal cost evaluation for range queries over two-dimensional data, then we derive the optimal cost for current disks.

2.1 Access Time versus Transfer Time

A disk is organized as a sequence of identically-sized disk pages. In general, the I/O performance of queries is expressed in terms of the number of pages accessed, assuming that the access cost is the same for each page. Access time is composed of three elements: *seek time, rotational delay, and transfer time*. We refer to the sum of the seek time and rotational delay as *access time*. Based on this assumption, the optimal cost of a query is derived as

$$\lceil A/M \rceil \times (t_{access} + t_{transfer}). \quad (1)$$

Where A is the number of tiles intersecting the query, M is the number of disk devices, t_{access} is the average access time of one page, $t_{transfer}$ is the average transfer time of one page (all the terms have the same meaning throughout the paper). We will refer to equation (1) as the *prior optimal cost*. Because each tile is retrieved by an independent random I/O, in order to improve the access cost of a query, existing data placement schemes decluster the dataset into tiles and assign neighboring tiles to different devices, thus allowing concurrent access of multiple pages.

In recent years, disk external transfer rates have improved significantly from 4MB/s to over 500MB/s; and the internal transfer rate is up to 160MB/s. However, access time has only improved by a factor of 2. For a disk with 8KB page size, 160MB/s internal

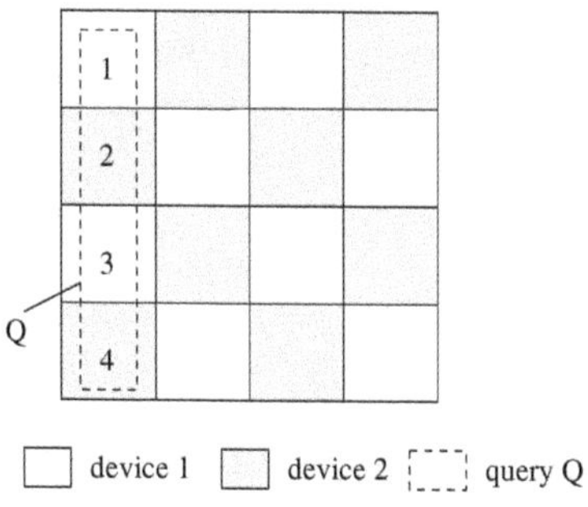

Fig. 1. An image picture is placed on two disk devices

transfer rate, and 5ms access time, the ratio of access time over transfer time is about 100. Thus, current disk technology is heavily skewed towards sequential access instead of random access due to the high cost of access time. This principle can benefit range queries over two-dimensional data, if we could place the related tiles of a query that are allocated on a single disk device sequentially. For example, Figure 1 shows an image with sixteen disk pages (or tiles). Assume that this image is placed on two disk devices. According to [10], tiles will be placed as shown in Figure 1. If tiles 1 and 3 are placed sequentially on disk device 1 and tiles 2 and 4 are placed on device 2, the access cost of query Q (given by the dashed rectangle in Figure 1) is $1 \times t_{access} + 2 \times t_{transfer}$, instead of $2 \times (t_{access} + t_{transfer})$. Based on this observation, we reevaluate the optimal cost of range queries for hard disks.

2.2 Optimal Cost Estimation

Due to the fact that current hard disks are more efficient when accessing data sequentially, the advantage of sequential access must be considered to facilitate fast retrieval of the related tiles in a range query. Ideally, if all tiles related to a query, which are allocated to the same device, are placed sequentially, then only one access time is incurred for the query. Thus the optimal retrieval cost is given by the following formula (referred to as *new optimal cost*).

$$t_{access} + \lceil A/M \rceil \times t_{transfer} + (\lceil A/N_t \rceil - 1) \times t_{trackswitch}. \tag{2}$$

where N_t is the average number of blocks in a track, $t_{trackswitch}$ is the time of switching from one track to a neighboring track. The first term in the formula is the cost of one access time, because all the related tiles on one device are placed consecutively, and all initial accesses to different disks are performed concurrently. The second term is the maximal transfer time of all devices, which is derived by considering the parallelism among multiple disk devices. The third term represents the track switching time if the number of involved tiles $\lceil A/M \rceil$ is too large to be stored on one track. However, it is impossible to achieve the optimal cost for all queries, as shown by the following argument.

In general, the two-dimensional data is divided into $N_1 \times N_2$ tiles. The number of disk devices is M. Consider a query Q_1 with A tiles. Without loss of generality, assume A is much smaller than N_t (thus there is no track switching time), and A is equal to M as shown in Figure 2 (a). Based on the new optimal cost formula (2), each tile in this query is allocated to a different device. Thus, the access cost of this query is

$$t_{access} + \lceil A/M \rceil \times t_{transfer} = t_{access} + t_{transfer}.$$

This cost is optimal. Figure 2 (b) shows query Q_2 which extends query Q_1 in the X dimension. The number of tiles in query Q_2 is $A + E_1$, and $E_1 = M$. In order to achieve the optimal cost, each device is allocated two tiles, and these two tiles need to be placed sequentially. Alternatively, we extend query Q_1 in the Y dimension to generate a new query Q_3, as shown in Figure 2 (c). Query Q_3 accesses $A + E_2$ tiles, where E_2 also equals M. Therefore, each device needs to place two tiles (one from A and one from E_2)

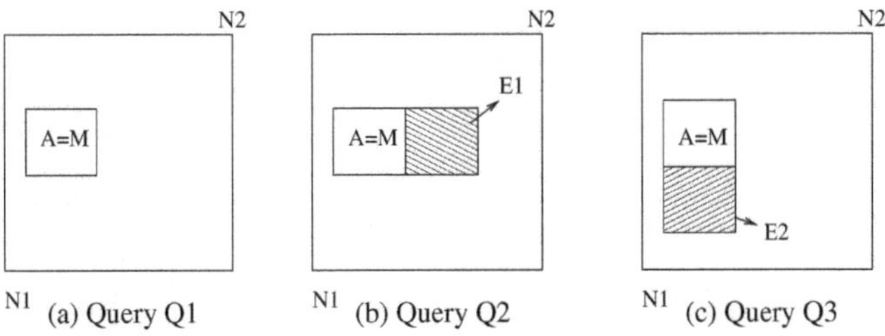

Fig. 2. Queries in a $N_1 \times N_2$ data set

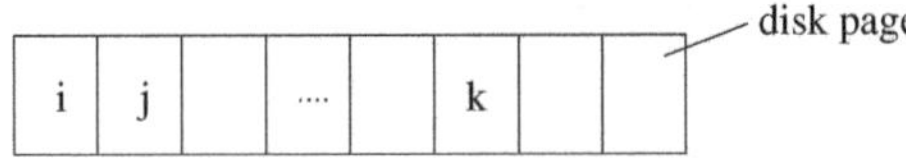

Fig. 3. Tile allocation to sequential disk pages

sequentially to achieve the optimal cost. However, it is impossible to achieve the optimal cost for both query Q_2 and Q_3. Assume tiles i, j, k are on device d, tile i intersects Q_1, tiles i, j intersect Q_2, and tiles i, k intersect Q_3. In order to achieve sequential access for query Q_2, tiles i and j need to be placed next to each other. Thus, tile k can not be placed next to i, as shown in Figure 3. Alternatively, if k is placed next to i, then j can not be placed next to i. Thus, in general, it is impossible to achieve the optimal cost for all queries of a data set, given the physical characteristics of disks.

3 Adapting Disk Allocation Scheme to MEMS Storage

MEMS storage devices are novel experimental systems that can be used as storage. Their two-dimensional structure and inherent parallel retrieval capability hold the promise of solving the problems disks face during the retrieval of two-dimensional datasets. In this section, we first briefly introduce MEMS-based storage, then show how to adapt existing disk allocation schemes to MEMS-based storage.

3.1 MEMS-Based Storage

MEMS are extremely small mechanical structures on the order of $10\mu m$ to $1000\mu m$, which are formed by the integration of mechanical elements, actuators, electronics, and sensors. These micro-structures are fabricated on the surface of silicon wafers by using photolithographic processes similar to those employed in manufacturing standard semiconductor devices. MEMS-based storage systems use MEMS for the positioning of read/write heads. Therefore, MEMS-based storage systems can be manufactured at a very low cost. Several research centers are developing real MEMS-based storage devices, such as IBM Millipede [12], Hewlett-Packard Laboratories ARS [2], and Carnegie Mellon University CHIPS [1].

Due to the difficulty of manufacturing efficient and reliable rotating parts in silicon, MEMS-based storage devices do not make use of rotating platters. All of the designs

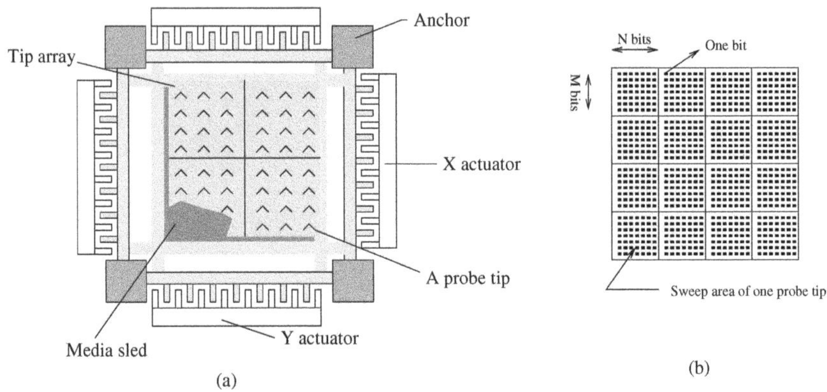

Fig. 4. The architecture of CMU CHIPS

use a large-scale MEMS array, thousands of read/write heads (called *probe tips*), and a recording media surface. The probe tips are mounted on micro-cantilevers embedded in a semiconductor wafer and arranged in a rectangular fashion. The recording media is mounted on another rectangular silicon wafer (called the *media sled*) that uses different techniques [12,1] for recording data. The IBM Millipede uses special polymers for storing and retrieving information [12]. The CMU CHIPS project adopts the same techniques as data recording on magnetic surfaces [1]. To access data under this model, the media sled is moved from its current position to a specific position defined by (x, y) coordinates. After the "seek" is performed, the media sled moves in the Y direction while the probe tips access the data. The data can be accessed sequentially in the Y dimension. The design is shown in Figure 4 (a).

The media sled is organized into rectangular regions at the lower level. Each of these rectangular regions contains $M \times N$ bits and is accessible by one tip, as shown in Figure 4 (b). Bits within a region are grouped into vertical 90-bit columns called *tip sectors*. Each tip sector contains 8 data bytes, which is the smallest accessible unit of data in MEMS-based storage [8]. In this paper, we will use the CMU CHIPS model to motivate two-dimensional data allocation techniques for MEMS-based storage. The parameters are given in Table 1. Because of heat-dissipation constraints, in this model, not all tips can be activated simultaneously even though it is feasible theoretically. In the CMU CHIPS model, the maximal number of tips that can be activated concurrently is limited to 1280 (which provides the intra-device parallelism). Each rectangular region stores 2000×2000 bits.

Table 1. Parameters of MEMS-based storage devices from CMU CHIPS

Parameter	Value
Number of regions	6400 (80×80)
Number of tips	6400
Max number of active tips	1280
Tip sector size	8 bytes
Servo overhead	10 bits per tip sector
Bits per tip region ($M \times N$)	2000×2000
Per-tip data rate	0.7Mbit/s
X axis settle time	0.125ms
Average turnaround time	0.06ms

3.2 Adapting Disk Placement Approaches

Even though MEMS-based storage has very different characteristics from disk devices, in order to simplify the process of integrating it into computing systems, some prior approaches have been proposed to map MEMS-based storage into disk-like devices. Using disk terminology, a *cylinder* is defined as the set of all bits with identical x offset within a region; i.e., a cylinder consists of all bits accessible by all tips when the sled moves only in the Y direction. Due to power and heat considerations, only a subset can be activated simultaneously. Thus cylinders are divided into tracks. A *track* consists of all bits within a cylinder that can be accessed by a group of concurrently active tips. Each track is composed of multiple tip sectors, which contain less data than sectors of disks. Sectors can be grouped into logical blocks. In [8], each logical block is 512 bytes and is striped across 64 tips. Therefore, by using the MEMS-based storage devices in Table 1, there are up to 20 logical blocks that can be accessed concurrently (1280 concurrent $\text{tips}/64$ tips $= 20$). Data is accessed based on its logical block number on the MEMS-based storage.

After this mapping, a MEMS-based storage device can be treated as a regular disk. Thus, all prior approaches for two-dimensional data allocation proposed for disk devices can be adapted to MEMS-based storage, such as Generalized Fibonacci (GFIB) scheme [11], Golden Ratio Sequences (GRS) [4], Almost optimal access [3], and other approaches based on replication [6]. All of these approaches are based on the prior optimal cost (1) and do not factor the sequential access property of current disks. Hence, when adapting them to MEMS-based storage devices, this problem still remains unsolved. For example, a two-dimensional dataset with 4×4 tiles is shown in Figure 5 (a). Two MEMS-based storage devices are used to store the data ($M = 2$). The MEMS devices in this example have four probe tips each, and only two of them can be activated concurrently. Based on the prior optimal cost (1), the tiles should be distributed evenly and alternately to the two devices, as shown in Figure 5 (a). The number d_i in a tile means that the tile is allocated to MEMS device d, and i stands for the relative position

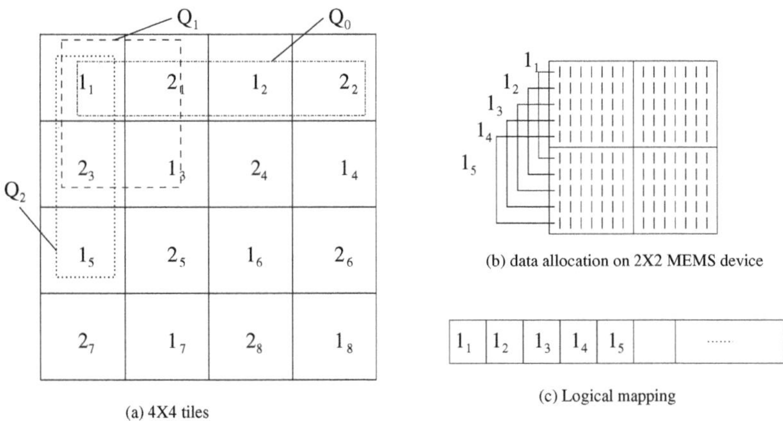

Fig. 5. An example of placing tiles on MEMS-based storage

of that tile on the device. In this example, we assume two tip sectors to contain the data of one tile (The size of one tile is determined by the maximum size of one data retrieval. In this example, it is $2 \times 8 = 16$). As a result, an allocation is shown in Figure 5 (b) based on the above mapping, tiles 1_1 to 1_5 are placed sequentially. Their logical positions are given in Figure 5 (c). This allocation is optimal according to the prior optimal cost (1). In fact, for query Q_0 in Figure 5 (a), this allocation is also optimal according to the new optimal cost (2). However, for Queries Q_1 and Q_2 shown in Figure 5 (a), both of them can not achieve the new optimal solution. Q_1 needs to retrieve tiles 1_1 and 1_3. Based on the relative layout given in Figure 5 (c), they are not placed sequentially. A similar analysis holds for query Q_2. In fact, using this mapping, MEMS-based storage devices lose some of their characteristics. The intra-device parallelism is not considered at all in this mapping. In [9], we showed that by taking these properties into account, MEMS-based storage can achieve extra performance gains in relational data placement. In the next section, we propose a new scheme for placing two-dimensional data on MEMS-based storage. This scheme exploits the physical properties of MEMS-based storage to achieve sequential-like performance for queries such as Q_1 and Q_2.

4 Parallel MEMS Storage Allocation

In this section, we propose a new data placement scheme based on the physical characteristics of MEMS storage.

4.1 Motivation and Challenges

In Section 2, we argued that it is impossible to achieve the new optimal cost for disk devices. In order to achieve the optimal cost, tiles have to be placed in both X and Y dimensions sequentially, which cannot be realized by one-dimensional storage devices (disk-like devices). Thus, in our new scheme, we need to place the dataset in such a way that tiles can be sequentially accessed in both dimensions (we refer to this as the *two-dimensional sequential access requirement*). Even though MEMS-based storage is arranged in a two-dimensional manner, data can only be accessed in the Y dimension sequentially (which gives sequential access in the Y dimension). According to the design of MEMS-based storage, any movement in the X dimension will result in a new seek. Therefore, we have to solve the two-dimensional sequential access requirement by using other properties of MEMS-based storage.

Due to power and heat constraints, only a subset of the probe tips can be activated concurrently. Even though tip sectors with the same coordinates cannot all be accessed simultaneously, they can be accessed "almost" sequentially. For example, we show a new data layout for the example in Figure 5. Instead of placing tiles 1_1 and 1_2 along the Y dimension sequentially, we place them over a group of tip sectors with the same coordinates as shown in Figure 6(b). In order to answer query Q_0, which is shown in Figure 6 (a), we first activate the tip sectors for tile 1_1 (only two out of four tips can be activated concurrently), then turn the media sled around and activate the tip sectors for tile 1_2 without moving in the X dimension. Hence, query Q_0 is processed sequentially (no extra seek cost). This layout corresponds to the logical layout given in Figure 6 (c).

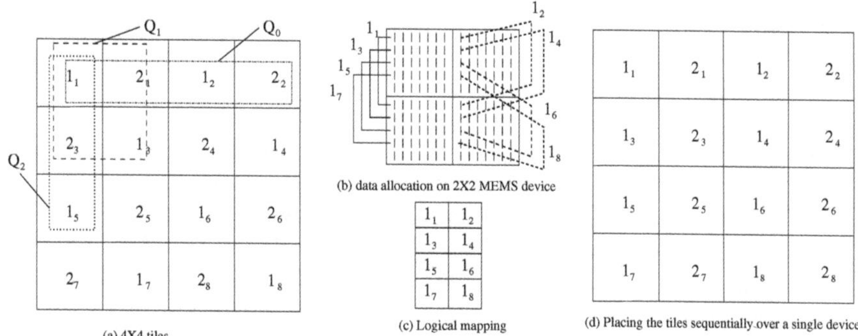

Fig. 6. An example that takes the intra-device parallelism into account

Thus, query Q_1 can also achieve an optimal answer ($t_{access} + 2 * t_{transfer}$). However, the access cost of query Q_2 is $2 * t_{access} + 2 * t_{transfer}$ (the track switching time is zero), which is still not optimal (tiles 1_1 and 1_5 are not sequentially allocated, hence it results in an extra access penalty).

In order to solve this problem and take advantage of sequential access, we could allocate the tiles sequentially along the Y dimension over a single device. The 4×4 dataset shown in Figure 5 can be allocated in a way shown in Figure 6 (d). This allocation can achieve optimal performance for both Q_0 and Q_1. Furthermore, since the tiles $1_1, 1_3, 1_5$ are placed sequentially, the access cost of query Q_2 will be reduced to $t_{access} + 3 * t_{transfer}$. Even though the new cost is reduced compared to the layout in Figure 6 (a), the data intersecting with query Q_2 are not distributed over the M given devices uniformly (the optimal cost should be $t_{access} + 2 * t_{transfer}$). Based on this discussion, we observe that sequential access and parallelism over multiple devices are conflicting goals. To address this contradiction, in our placement scheme, we first tile the dataset based on the physical properties (rather than tiling the dataset without considering the properties of devices), then we allocate the data in each tile on the M devices evenly to guarantee that each device participates almost equally in transfer time. Note that from a user's point of view, the underlying tiling is not of interest and has no effect on the user's interaction with the dataset; efficiency and fast retrieval is the user's concern.

4.2 Tiling the Data

In general, two-dimensional data are divided into tiles along each dimension uniformly, and the size of each tile corresponds to one disk page. In our scheme, we divide the data into tiles based on the physical properties of the underlying storage devices, in particular, the number of given devices, M, and their parameters. In Table 1, 1280 of 6400 probe tips can be activated concurrently. Because the smallest accessible unit is a tip sector with 8 bytes, 1280×8 bytes can be accessed concurrently. There are M devices, thus the total size of data which can be accessed simultaneously is $M \times 1280 \times 8$ bytes. This determines the size of a tile. In other words, a tile corresponds to the maximum number of bytes that can be accessed concurrently. After determining the size of a tile, the next step is to decide on the number of tiles along each dimension. In our scheme, in order to take advantage of potential concurrent access of tip sectors with the same coordinates, all the tip sectors allocated to tiles on a single row should have the same coordinates. Hence a single row will contain $6400 \times 8 \times M$ bytes. Since a tile has $1280 \times 8 \times M$ bytes, there are 5 tiles per row. Now consider a query that only intersects the 5 tiles of a single row. If the total number of tip sectors on each device in the query does not exceed 1280, they could all be retrieved by one transfer. Hence given a dataset of dimensions $W \times L = S$ bytes, we divide W into 5 columns. Each tile will have dimensions $\frac{W}{5} \times \frac{M \times 1280 \times 8}{W/5}$. After determining the number of tiles in the X dimension, the number of tiles along the Y dimension can be computed by the following formula:

$$\lceil S/\text{the data size in each row} \rceil = \lceil S/(M \times 6400 \times 8) \rceil .$$

4.3 Slicing a Tile

We now introduce how to distribute the data in each tile over M MEMS-based storage devices. In order to avoid the problem of sacrificing transfer time to achieve sequential access, we distribute the data in each tile over all M devices uniformly. However, the placement has to guarantee that the transfer time of a query on each device is the same. For example, consider a single row of a dataset with 5 tiles, and two MEMS storage devices. For the sake of argument, let us assume the top 1280 eight-byte units of each tile are allocated to device 1 and the bottom 1280 eight-byte units are allocated to device 2, as shown in Figure 7 (a). For a query Q_1 given by the dotted rectangle in Figure 10, it is impossible to achieve optimal transfer time. Even though the data of $D_{11}, D_{12}, D_{13}, D_{14}, D_{15}$ are placed on tip sectors with the same coordinates which have the potential to be accessed concurrently, if the number of tip sectors accessed by Q_1 is larger than the maximal number of concurrent tips, lets say two times larger, then answering Q_1 will take two transfer time. However, in this case, only device 1 is used. If device 2 could retrieve half of the requested data, only one transfer time is necessary (which is the optimal cost). Thus the data in each tile should be distributed over the M devices evenly at the level of tip sectors.

In each tile, the data is organized into 8-byte units which correspond to the size of each tip sector. The data allocation at this level needs to distribute the 8-byte units over the M devices evenly. Consider the dataset shown in Figure 7(a) as an example. In each

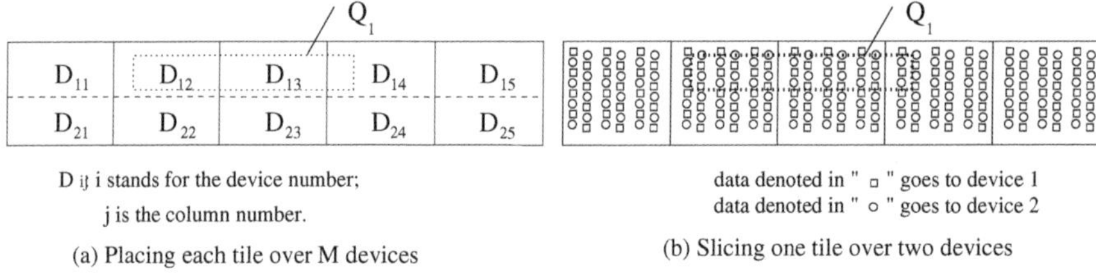

(a) Placing each tile over M devices

(b) Slicing one tile over two devices

Fig. 7. An example of placing and slicing one tile

tile, the data are organized into 8-byte units, which are highlighted by little squares and circles in Figure 7(b). We uniformly allocate all 8-byte unites to device 1 (shown as squares), and to device 2 (shown as circles), As a result, a query such as Q_1 can be processed optimally. Slicing each tile over multiple devices is similar to declustering a two-dimensional dataset over multiple disk devices, if we treat a tile as a new two-dimensional dataset and each 8-byte unit as a new tile of the dataset. Thus, all the data placement schemes proposed for two-dimensional dataset could be easily adopted. For example, in [3], the authors use a coloring scheme. It is proved that any range query over this dataset is guaranteed to access no more than $\lceil N_u/M \rceil + \gamma$ 8-byte units where $\gamma = O(logM)$ and N_u is the total number of 8-byte units in a tile. We adopt this scheme for allocating the data in one tile on multiple MEMS devices.

4.4 Algorithms

In this section, we describe the procedures for placing the data on MEMS storage devices, and given a query, how to retrieve the relevant data.

Based on the parameters given in Table 1, the number of tip sectors of a single device which are allocated to one tile is the maximal number of concurrent tips (1280). There are 6400 tips in total, as a result, all the tip sectors with the same coordinates can form 5 $(6400/1280)$ tiles of maximal concurrent tip sectors. All the tip sectors in these five tiles have the potential to be accessed simultaneously. Furthermore, any $M \times 1280 \times 8$ bytes in a row have the potential to be accessed concurrently. The generic data allocation procedure is given in Algorithm 1. We use an example to explain this algorithm. In Figure 8(a), given three MEMS storage devices ($M = 3$), a dataset is divided into a $5 \times n$ tile grid. In each tile, the circles, squares, and triangles stand for 8-byte units, that will be allocated to different devices, as shown in Figure 8(b). The 8-byte units on row 1

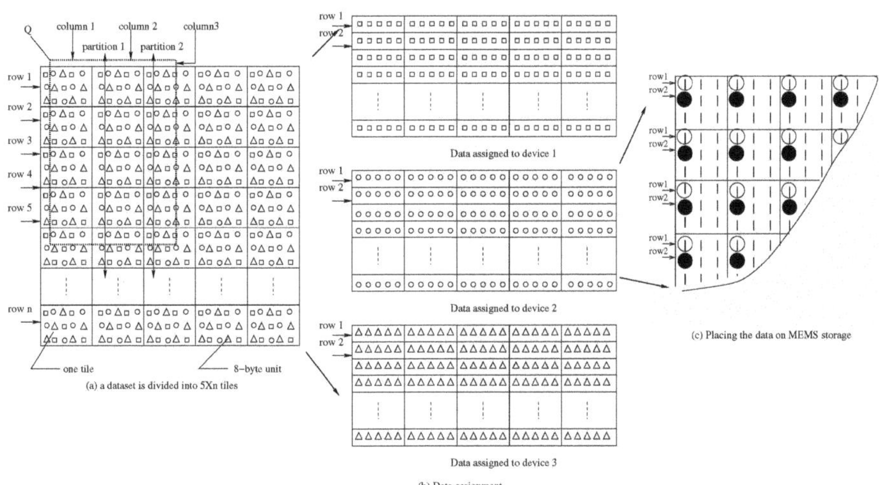

Fig. 8. Placing the tiles of a dataset over M MEMS devices

are mapped to row 1 on each device in Figure 8(b). Figure 8(c) shows how to allocate the data assigned to each device on the physical storage device, which is similar to the one used in [9]. Assume we start placing the data at the coordinates (x, y), then the data of row 1 is placed on the tip sectors with coordinates (x, y), which are highlighted by white circles in Figure 8(c). Based on the data provided in Table 1, in order to decrease seek time, we first consider the allocation of the tip sectors which have the same x coordinate as row 1, and y coordinate differs by one from row 1. As a result, row 2 is placed on the tip sectors with coordinates $(x, y + 1)$, which are highlighted by black circles in Figure 8(c). This process continues until the y coordinate reaches the boundary, when the tip sectors are allocated in the next column (coordinate x differs by one from the last row).

In general, the dataset is placed at two levels: the lower level places each tile over the M devices, while the upper level places the rows within a single device. Based on this layout, we now describe how to answer a query (data retrieval). Given a query Q, assume Q intersects rows $i, i + 1, ..., i + k$ in continuous order. The data retrieval procedure is given in Algorithm 2. In this algorithm, there are two cases to consider:

- Case 1: For any single device[1], the number of tip sectors in any row, which intersects the query, is not larger than the maximal number of concurrent tips.
  The media sled is first moved to the coordinates (x_i, y_i) of row i, then the tips which are in charge of the intersected tip sectors are activated, and the corresponding data with these coordinates are retrieved. Then the media sled moves to the coordinates of the next row, $i + 1$, to access the data. Based on Algorithm 1, we know that any two neighboring rows differ either in their x coordinate by one, or y coordinate by one, which means, data is either sequentially retrieved in the Y dimension or at most involves one track switching time (move from one column to its neighboring column). On the other hand, there is no unnecessary data (which is not included in the range of Q) retrieved.
- Case 2: For some devices, the number of tip sectors in any row involved in Q is larger than the maximal number of concurrent tips.
  In this case, the relevant data in each row can not be retrieved simultaneously. For any single device, the intersected tip sectors of each of row i, i+1,...,i+k are organized into concurrent groups[2] (the number of tip sectors in the final group may be less than the maximal number of concurrent tips). For example, Figure 8(a) gives a query Q delineated by a dotted rectangle. Partitions 1 and 2 regroup the query range into three new columns, as shown in Figure 8(a). These three new columns with the original rows, divide the query range into new tiles (the new tiles in column 3 contain less data than the other two new tiles). Based on the tile allocation scheme, the 8-byte units in the new tiles are distributed over the M devices evenly. Thus, we can adopt the same retrieval procedure as in Case 1 to access the data in each new column. After accessing one of the new columns, instead of moving the media sled back to the coordinates of row 1 every time (thus introducing a new seek), the media sled is just turned around changing its moving direction, then the tips in another

[1] The data in each tile can only be distributed over the M devices almost evenly.

[2] The tip sectors in each row have the same coordinates, thus they have the potential to be accessed simultaneously.

Algorithm 1 Data Placement

The maximum number of concurrent tips: $N_{concurrent}$; The total number of tips: N_{total};
The number of tiles in a row: $N_{row} = \lceil N_{total}/N_{concurrent} \rceil$;
The size of each tip sector: $S_{tipsector}$; The size of each row of tiles: $S_{row} = N_{total} \times M \times S_{tipsector}$;
The size of the dataset: $S_{dataset}$; The number of tiles in a column: $N_{column} = S_{dataset}/S_{row}$;
Organizing the data in each tile into $S_{tipsector}$-byte units;
Using any disk allocation scheme to distribute the data in each tile over M devices
for each device **do**
  Move the media sled to the initial position with coordinates (x, y); $moveDirection = down$; $i = 0$;
  while $i \leq N_{row}$ **do**
    Allocate tip sectors with coordinates (x, y) to data tiles at row i;
    if $moveDirection = down$ **then**
      $y = y + 1$;
      if y is out of range of movement of the media sled **then**
        $y = y - 1, x = x + 1$; Move the media sled to the position (x, y), and turn it around; $moveDirection = up$
      end if
    else
      $y = y - 1$;
      if y is out of range of movement of the media sled **then**
        $y = y + 1, x = x + 1$; Move the media sled to the position (x, y), and turn it around; $moveDirection = down$
      end if
    end if
    $i = i + 1$;
  end while
end for

Algorithm 2 Data Retrieval

A query Q intersects the dataset by rows $i, i + 1, ..., i + k$ in continuous order;
for each device **do**
  The number of involved tips in a row: $N_{involved}$;
  Move the media sled to the coordinates of tip sectors for row i: (x_{start}, y_{start});
  $x = x_{start}, y = y_{start}$; $moveDirection = down$; $retrievedrows = 0$;
  if $N_{involved} \leq N_{concurrent}$ **then**
    while $retrievedrows \leq k$ **do**
      Activate all involved tips, and retrieve the data;
      if $moveDirection = down$ **then**
        $y = y + 1$;
        if y is out of range of movement of the media sled **then**
          $y = y - 1, x = x + 1$; Move the media sled to the position (x, y), and turn it around; $moveDirection = up$
        end if
      else
        $y = y - 1$;
        if y is out of range of movement of the media sled **then**
          $y = y + 1, x = x + 1$; Move the media sled to the position (x, y), and turn it around; $moveDirection = down$
        end if
      end if
      $retrievedrow += 1$;
    end while
  else
    The number of concurrent groups: $N_{group} = \lceil N_{involved}/N_{concurrent} \rceil$;
    For each of these groups, turn around the media sled;
    if $moveDirection = down$ **then**
      $moveDirection = up$;
    else
      $moveDirection = down$;
    end if
    Use the same procedure as the one when $N_{involved} \leq N_{concurrent}$;
  end if
end for

concurrent tip group are activated to access the data (tip sectors can be accessed in both directions of the Y dimension).

As mentioned earlier, disks can not satisfy the two-dimensional sequential access property of the new optimal cost. Even though MEMS-based storage looks like a two-dimensional device, it can only facilitate sequential access along the Y dimension. Our proposed data placement scheme creates sequential access along the X dimension by using the property of concurrent tips. During query processing, our proposed method uses the maximum concurrent tips to maximize data retrieval.

5 Experimental Results

In this section, we first compare the new optimal cost (2) with the prior optimal one (1) through experiments on disks, and show that the prior data placement schemes can not achieve the new optimal cost in general. Then we evaluate our new data placement scheme for MEMS-based storage devices.

5.1 Evaluating the Optimal Cost on Disks

In this section, we experimentally explore the relationship between the prior and new optimal costs (Equation (1) and (2)). We also investigate ways in which I/O scheduling may try to take advantage of sequential I/O on disks to improve the performance of algorithms designed based on the prior optimal cost. We do not evaluate any specific existing data placement schemes, because all of them are based on the prior optimal cost, they can not outperform the prior optimal cost. We therefore assume the data placement schemes can achieve the prior optimal cost. However, these schemes based on the prior optimal cost do not discuss how data is placed on the individual disks. We therefore consider two cases, one when data is placed randomly on each disk and the other where data is allocated sequentially on the disks. Finally, we also investigate the performance when the disk access mechanism retrieves large chunks of data even though the chunks may contain unnecessary data in the middle. This is based on the fact that seek time is much more expensive than transfer time. Thus, the transfer time is sacrificed to improve seek time [14]. We refer to this approach as *bulk loading*. Hence we consider three cases.

- Random access: Tiles assigned to the same disk are placed randomly. In this case, the access of different tiles is an independent random access.
- Sequential access: Tiles allocated to a single device are placed row by row. Thus, the two-dimensional tiles are mapped onto one-dimensional I/O devices (refer to Figure 5 as an example). The tiles intersecting with queries are not retrieved sequentially if they are not placed consecutively. In this case, no unnecessary tiles are accessed (or transfered).
- Bulk loading: The data layout is the same as the one in sequential access. However, we use bulk loading, thus some unnecessary tiles may be retrieved.

The comparison is based on the average cost of all possible queries [11]. We first average the cost of all queries with the same size, i.e., the same number of tiles, then we

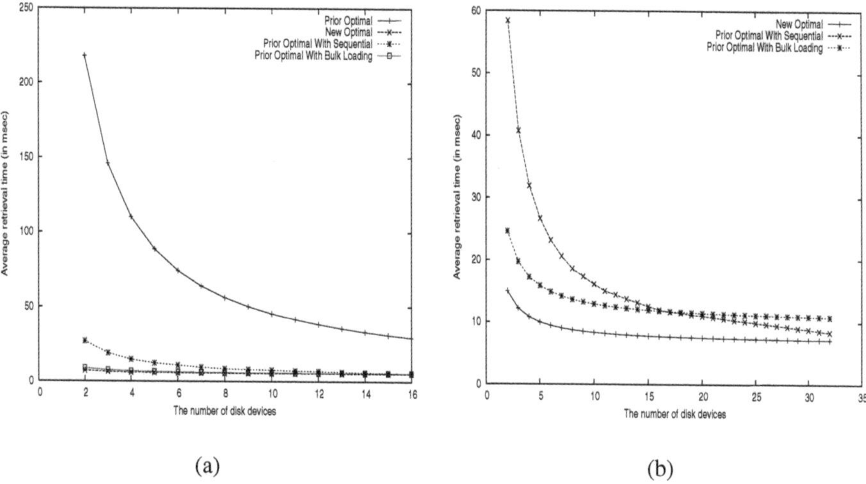

(a) (b)

Fig. 9. Performance evaluation of datasets with $N_1 = N_2 = 16$ tiles and $N_1 = N_2 = 32$ tiles

take the average of all possible queries with different sizes. In our experiments, for the sake of simplicity, we place the first tile at the beginning of a track. The disk parameters are: The transfer time is $0.05ms$, the access time is $5ms$, and the track switching time is $2.5ms$.

The first experiment is conducted on a dataset with 16×16 tiles, which can be contained on one track, thus, there is no track switching time. The result is shown in Figure 9 (a). The prior optimal cost is much larger than the other three curves, thus we do not consider it in our later experiments. Figure 9 (b) shows the results of a dataset with 32×32 tiles. The tendency of the three curves is similar to Figure 9 (a). However, the difference between the new optimal cost and the other two is larger than in Figure 9 (a), which is due to the track switching time. The prior optimal cost (1) does not consider the relative positions of involved tiles. In other words, sequential access and bulk loading involves more track switching time than the optimal cost. As the number of devices is increased, sequential access outperforms bulk loading, because sequential access has less track switching time than bulk loading.

5.2 Evaluating the New Placement Scheme on MEMS

In this section, we evaluate our new placement scheme for MEMS-based storage devices. We use the coloring scheme proposed in [3] to distribute the data in each tile. We compare our new scheme with the new optimal cost. We also evaluate the prior optimal layout for MEMS-based storage with sequential access and bulk loading. In these cases, we use the CHIPS disk-based modeling of MEMS storage described in Section 3.2. The seek time and transfer time we use for the MEMS-based storage devices are $1.46ms$ and $0.129ms$ respectively [7]. The turn-around time is $0.06ms$ which is much smaller than seek time and transfer time. The number of tip sectors in the Y dimension of a region

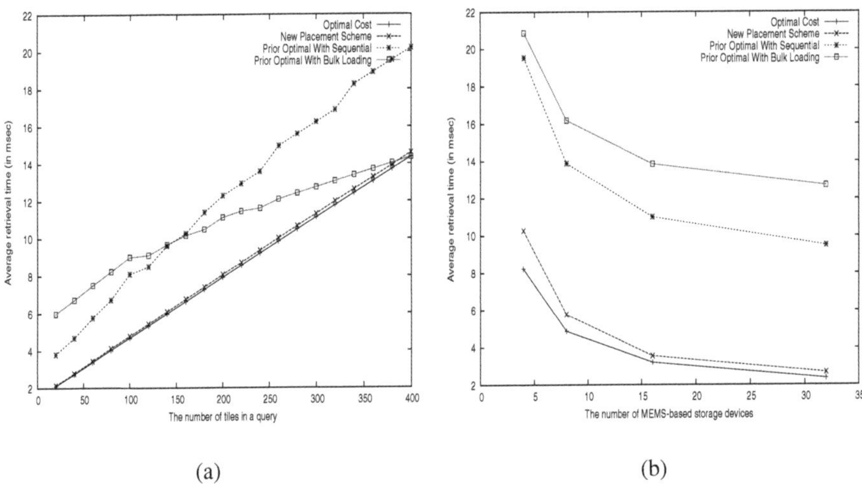

(a) (b)

Fig. 10. Performance evaluation of datasets with $N_1 = N_2 = 20$ tiles and $N_1 = N_2 = 80$ tiles

is 22 [9]. Because we use a different standard to tile the two-dimensional dataset, in our comparison we transfer the ranges of queries in the original data tiles to our new layout. Thus, we compare the same set of range queries for different schemes.

Figure 10(a) shows the performance when the number of tiles in a query is varied over 20×20 dataset and 4 MEMS storage devices. The average retrieval cost is obtained by taking the average access cost of all possible ranges with the same number of tiles. Our new placement scheme always outperforms the sequential access, and outperforms bulk loading in most queries. The little difference between our new scheme and the optimal cost is due to the turn-around time. Because the dataset is composed of 20×20 tiles, each tile contains $8K$ bytes. According to our tiling scheme, the dataset is reorganized into 5×20 tiles, each of the tiles in the new scheme contains $M \times 1280 \times 8 = 4 \times 1280 \times 8$ bytes. For the sake of simplicity, we place the rows at the beginning of regions, i.e., row 1 has coordinates $(0, 0)$. In each region, there are 22 tip sectors in the Y dimension, thus, there is no track switching time involved. In the new scheme, the media sled needs to move forwards and backwards to retrieve the tiles in different columns. When the number of tiles in a query is very large (almost the entire dataset), bulk loading slightly outperforms the new scheme. When a large number of tiles are involved in a query, then the number of unnecessary tiles retrieved in bulk loading is very small. In contrast, the new scheme incurs the extra cost of turn-around time. When the number of tiles is small, sequential access has better performance than bulk loading, because bulk loading retrieves too many unrelated tiles, as shown in Figure 10(a).

In order to further evaluate the average performance of these four methods, we compared their average retrieval cost for all sizes of queries by varying the number of MEMS-based storage devices and using a dataset with 80×80 tiles. From Figure 10(b), we observe that sequential access outperforms bulk loading which was not the case in Figure 10. This is because the ratio of access time to transfer time of MEMS-based storage is smaller than that of disk, cost of retrieving of unnecessary tiles under bulk loading results in greater penalty. Our new scheme performs better than both sequential access and bulk loading, as shown in Figure 10(b). The difference between our scheme and the optimal cost is due to the turn-around time and the column-switching time. In our scheme, the column-switching time is larger than for the optimal cost, since the column-switching time in the optimal cost is not affected by the relative positions of the accessed tiles.

6 Conclusion

The cost of range queries over two-dimensional datasets is dominated by disk I/O. Declustering and parallel I/O techniques are used to improve query performance. Since the optimal cost can not be realized in general, several approaches have been proposed to achieve near optimal cost. However, the physical properties of current disks are not considered. In this paper, we reevaluate the optimal query cost for current disks, which favor sequential accesses over random accesses. We also demonstrate that it is impossible to achieve the new optimal cost on disks in general, since the new optimal cost of range queries requires two-dimensional sequential access. This is not feasible in the context of disks, since disks are single-dimensional devices. In this paper, we propose to use MEMS-based storage to overcome this inherent problem in disks. We develop a new data placement scheme for MEMS-based storage that takes advantage of its physical properties, where the two-dimensional sequential access requirement is satisfied. The new scheme allows for the reorganization of query ranges into new tiles which contain more relevant data, thus maximizing the number of concurrent active tips to access the relevant data. In the new scheme, we also relax the traditional tiling approach (which has never been specified explicitly) by tiling datasets based on the physical properties of MEMS-based storage. Our theoretical analysis and experimental results show that our new scheme can achieve almost optimal performance.

Acknowledgment. We would like to thank Dr. Anurag Acharya for supporting this work.

References

1. CMU CHIP project. 2003. http://www.lcs.ece.cmu.edu/research/MEMS.
2. Hewlett-packard laboratories atomic resolution storage, 2003. http://www.hpl.hp.com/research/storage.html.
3. M.J. Atallah and S. Prabhakar. (almost) optimal parallel block access for range queries. *Nineteenth ACM Symposium on Principles of Database Systems, PODS*, pages 205–215, May 2000.
4. R. Bhatia, Sinha R.K., and C.M. Chen. Declustring using golden ratio sequences. *In Proc. of International Conference on Data Engineering*, pages 271–280, February 2000.
5. C. Faloutsos and P. Bhagwat. Declustring using fractals. *In Proc. of the 2nd Int. Conf. on Parallel and Distributed Information Systems*, pages 18–25, January 1993.

6. K. Frikken, M. J. Atallah, Sunil Prabhakar, and R. Safavi-Naini. Optimal parallel i/o for range queries through replication. *In Proceedings of the 13th International Conference on Database and Expert Systems Applications*, pages 669–678, September 2002.
7. J. Griffin, S. Schlosser, G. Ganger, and D. Nagle. Modeling and performance of MEMS-Based storage devices. *Proceedings of ACM SIGMETRICS*, pages 56–65, June 2000.
8. J. Griffin, S. Schlosser, G. Ganger, and D. Nagle. Operating systems management of MEMS-based storage devices. *Symposium on Operating Systems Design and Implementation(OSDI)*, pages 227–242, October 2000.
9. H.Yu, D.Agrawal, and A.El Abbadi. Tabular placement of relational data on MEMS-based storage devices. *In proceedings of the 29th Conference on Very Large Databases(VLDB)*, pages 680–693, September 2003.
10. K.A.S.Abdel-Ghaffar and A. El Abbadi. Optimal allocation of two-dimensional data. *In International Conference on Database Theory*, pages 408–418, January 1997.
11. S. Prabhakar, K.A.S.Abdel-Ghaffar, D. Agrawal, and A. El Abbadi. Cyclic allocation of two-dimensional data. *In International Conference on Data Engineering*, pages 94–101, February 1998.
12. P.Vettider, M.Despont, U.Durig, W.Haberle, M.I. Lutwyche, H.E.Rothuizen, R.Stuz, R.Widmer, and G.K.Binnig. The "millipede"-more than one thousand tips for future afm storage. *IBM Journal of Research and Development*, pages 44(3):323–340, May 2000.
13. Steven W. Schlosser, John Linwood Griffin, David F. Nagle, and Gregory R. Ganger. Designing computer systems with MEMS-based storage. *Architectural Support for Programming Languages and Operating Systems*, pages 1–12, November 2000.
14. B. Seeger. An analysis of schedules for performing multi-page requests. *Information Systems*, 21(5):387–407, 1996.

Self-tuning UDF Cost Modeling Using the Memory-Limited Quadtree

Zhen He, Byung S. Lee, and Robert R. Snapp

Department of Computer Science
University of Vermont
Burlington, VT 05405
{zhenhe,bslee,snapp}@emba.uvm.edu

Abstract. Query optimizers in object-relational database management systems require users to provide the execution cost models of user-defined functions(UDFs). Despite this need, however, there has been little work done to provide such a model. Furthermore, none of the existing work is self-tuning and, therefore, cannot adapt to changing UDF execution patterns. This paper addresses this problem by introducing a self-tuning cost modeling approach based on the quadtree. The quadtree has the inherent desirable properties to (1) perform fast retrievals, (2) allow for fast incremental updates (without storing individual data points), and (3) store information at different resolutions. We take advantage of these properties of the quadtree and add the following in order to make the quadtree useful for UDF cost modeling: the abilities to (1) adapt to changing UDF execution patterns and (2) use limited memory. To this end, we have developed a novel technique we call the *memory-limited quadtree(MLQ)*. In MLQ, each instance of UDF execution is mapped to a query point in a multi-dimensional space. Then, a prediction is made at the query point, and the actual value at the point is inserted as a new data point. The quadtree is then used to store summary information of the data points at different resolutions based on the distribution of the data points. This information is used to make predictions, guide the insertion of new data points, and guide the compression of the quadtree when the memory limit is reached. We have conducted extensive performance evaluations comparing MLQ with the existing (static) approach.

1 Introduction

A new generation of object-relational database applications, including multimedia and web-based applications, often make extensive use of user-defined functions(UDFs) within the database. Incorporating those UDFs into ORDBMSs entails query optimizers should consider the UDF execution costs when generating query execution plans. In particular, when UDFs are used in the 'where' clause of SQL select statements, the traditional heuristic of evaluating predicates as early as possible is no longer valid [1]. Moreover, when faced with multiple UDFs in the 'where' clause, the order in which the UDF predicates are evaluated can make a significant difference to the execution time of the query.

E. Bertino et al. (Eds.): EDBT 2004, LNCS 2992, pp. 513–531, 2004.
© Springer-Verlag Berlin Heidelberg 2004

Consider the following examples taken from [2,3].

```
select Extract(roads, m.SatelliteImg) from Map m
where Contained(m.satelliteImg, Circle(point, radius))
  and SnowCoverage(m.satelliteImg) <  20%;

select d.name, d.location from Document d
where Contains(d.text, string)
  and SimilarityDistance(d.image, shape) < 10;

select p.name, p.street_address, p.zip from Person p, Sales s
where HighCreditRating(p.ss_no) and p.age in [30,40]
  and Zone(p.zip) = ''bay area'' and p.name = s.buyer_name
group by p.name, p.street_address, p.zip
having sum(s.amount) > 1000;
```

In the above examples, the decision as to which UDF (e.g., `Contains()`, `SimilarityDistance()`) to execute first or whether a join should be performed before UDF execution depends on the cost of the UDFs and the selectivity of the UDF predicates. This paper is concerned with the former.

Although cost modeling of UDFs is important to the performance of query optimization, only two existing papers address this issue [3,4]. The other existing works are centered on the generation of optimal query execution plans for query optimizers catering for UDFs [1,2,5]. They assume UDF execution cost models are provided by the UDF developer. This assumption is naive since functions can often have complex relationships between input arguments and execution costs. In this regard, this paper aims to develop *automated* means of predicting the execution costs of UDFs in an ORDBMS.

No existing approach[4,3] for automatically modeling the costs of UDFs is *self-tuning*. One existing approach is the static histogram(SH)-based cost modeling approach[3]. The other approach uses curve-fitting based on neural networks[4]. Both approaches require users to train the model a-priori with previously collected data. Approaches that do not self-tune degrade in prediction accuracy as the pattern of UDF execution varies greatly from the pattern used to train the model. In contrast, we use a self-tuning query feedback-driven approach similar to that used in [6,7] for selectivity estimation of range queries and in [8] for relational database query optimization.

Figure 1 shows how self-tuning cost modeling works. When a query arrives, the query optimizer generates a query execution plan using the UDF cost estimator as one of its components. The cost estimator makes its prediction using the cost model. The query is then executed by the execution engine according to the query plan. When the query is executed, the actual cost of executing the UDF is used to update the cost model. This allows our approach to adapt to changing UDF execution patterns.

In this paper, we describe a *quadtree*-based approach to the cost modeling of UDFs. The quadtree is widely used in digital image processing and computer graphics for modeling spatial segmentation of images and surfaces[9,10,11], in the

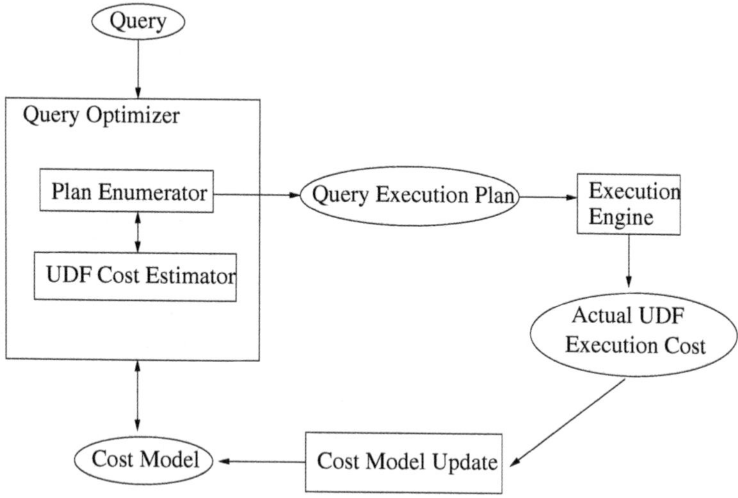

Fig. 1. Query feedback-driven UDF cost modeling.

spatial database environment for the indexing and retrieval of spatial objects [12, 13], in the on-line analytic processing context to answer aggregate queries (e.g., SUM, COUNT, MIN, MAX, AVG)[14], and so on.

The quadtree has the following inherent desirable properties. It (1) performs retrievals fast, (2) allows for fast incremental updates (without the need to store individual data points), and (3) stores information at different resolutions. The first and second properties are of particular importance to UDF cost modeling since the final goal of the cost modeling is to improve the query execution speed. Naturally, the overhead introduced by the cost estimator needs to be very low.

We take advantage of these properties of the quadtree and add the following in order to make the quadtree more useful for UDF cost modeling: the abilities to (1) adapt to changing UDF execution patterns and (2) use a limited amount of memory. The first property is important since UDF execution patterns may change over time. The second property is important since the cost estimator is likely to be allocated only a small portion of the memory allocated to the query optimizer for metadata. Moreover, the query optimizer needs to keep two cost estimators for each UDF in order to model both CPU and disk IO costs. In this regard, we call our approach the *memory-limited quadtree(MLQ)*.

In MLQ, each instance of UDF execution is mapped to a data point in a multi-dimensional space. The summary information of data points is stored in the nodes of a quadtree. The summary information consists of sum, count, and sum of squares for data points in the indexed data region. We store the summary information at every level of the quadtree, with coarser-grained information (over a larger region) at a higher level. This information is then used to make predictions and to guide the compression of the quadtree when the memory limit it reached.

Since MLQ is based on the quadtree which partitions the *entire* multi-dimensional space, it can start making predictions immediately after the first data point is inserted (with no a-priori training data). The prediction accuracy improves as more data points are inserted. Alternatively, MLQ can be trained with some a-priori training data before making the first prediction. This improves its initial prediction accuracy.

The key contributions of this paper are in (1) proposing a self-tuning UDF cost modeling approach that adapts to changing UDF execution patterns, (2) proposing a dynamic quadtree-based summary structure that works with limited memory, (3) conducting an extensive performance evaluation of MLQ against the existing static SH algorithm. To our knowledge, SH is the only existing UDF cost modeling algorithm feasibly usable in an ORDBMS.

The remainder of this paper is organized as follows. In Section 2 we outline related work. In Section 3 we formally define the problem. We then describe our MLQ approach to solving the problem in Section 4. In Section 5 we detail the experiments conducted to evaluate the performance of MLQ. Last, in Section 6 we conclude the paper.

2 Related Work

In this section we discuss existing work in two related areas: UDF cost modeling and self-tuning approaches to query optimization.

2.1 UDF Cost Modeling

As already mentioned, the SH approach in [3] is designed for UDF cost modeling in ORDBMSs. It is not self-tuning in the sense that it is trained a-priori with existing data and do not adapt to new query distributions. In SH, users define a set of variables used to train the cost model. The UDF is then executed using these variable values to build a multi-dimensional histogram. The histogram is then used to predict the cost of future UDF executions.

Specifically, two different histogram construction methods are used in [3], equi-width and equi-height. In the equi-width histogram method, each dimension is divided into N intervals of equal length. Then, N^d buckets are created, where d is the number of dimensions. The equi-height histogram method divides each dimension into intervals so that the same number of data points are kept in each interval. In order to improve storage efficiency, they propose reducing the number of intervals assigned to variables that have low influence on the cost. However, they do not specify how to find the amount of influence a variable has. It is left as future work.

In [4] Boulos proposes a curve-fitting approach based on neural networks. Their approach is not self-tuning either and, therefore, does not adapt to changing query distributions. Moreover, neural networks techniques are complex to implement and very slow to train[15], therefore inappropriate for query optimization in ORDBMSs[3]. This is the reason we do not compare MLQ with this neural networks approach.

2.2 Self-Tuning Approaches to Query Optimization

Histogram-based techniques have been used extensively in selectivity estimation of range queries in the query optimizers of relational databases [6,7,16]. STGrid[6] and STHoles[7] are two recent techniques that use a query feed-back-driven, self-tuning, multi-dimensional histogram-based approach. The idea behind both STGrid and STHoles is to spend more modeling resources in areas where there is more workload activity. This is similar to our aim of adapting to changing query distributions. However, there is a fundamental difference. Their feedback information is the actual *number of tuples* selected for a range query whereas our feedback information is the actual *cost values* of individual UDF executions. This difference presents a number of problems when trying to apply their approach to solve our problem. For example, STHoles creates a "hole" in a histogram bucket for the region defined by a range query. This notion of a region does not make sense for a point query used in UDF cost modeling.

DB2's LEarning Optimizer(LEO) offers a comprehensive way of repairing incorrect statistics and cardinality estimates of a query execution plan by using feedback information from recent query executions. It is general and can be applied to any operation – including the UDFs – in a query execution plan. It works by logging the following information of past query executions: execution plan, estimated statistics, and actual observed statistics. Then, in the background, it compares the difference between the estimated statistics and the actual statistics and stores the difference in an adjustment table. Then, it looks up the adjustment table during query execution and apply necessary adjustments. MLQ is more storage efficient than LEO since it uses a quadtree to store summary information of UDF executions and applies the feedback information directly on the statistics stored in the quadtree.

3 Problem Formulation

In this section we formally define UDF cost modeling and define our problem.

UDF Cost Modeling

Let $f(a_1, a_2, ..., a_n)$ be a UDF that can be executed within an ORDBMS with a set of input arguments $a_1, a_2, ..., a_n$. We assume the input arguments are ordinal and their ranges are given, while leaving it to future work to incorporate nominal arguments and ordinal arguments with unknown ranges. Let $T(a_1, a_2, ..., a_n)$ be a transformation function that maps some or all of $a_1, a_2, ..., a_n$ to a set of 'cost variables' $c_1, c_2, ..., c_k$, where $k \leq n$. The transformation T is *optional.* T allows the users to use their knowledge of the relationship between input arguments and the execution costs ec_{IO} (e.g., the number of disk pages fetched) and ec_{CPU} (e.g., CPU time) to produce cost variables that can be used in the model more efficiently than the input arguments themselves. An example of such a transformation is for a UDF that has the input arguments `start_time` and `end_time` which are mapped to the cost variable `elapsed_time` as `elapsed_time` = `end_time` − `start_time`.

Let us define *model variables* $m_1, m_2, .., m_k$ as either input arguments $a_1, a_2, ..., a_n$ or cost variables $c_1, c_2, ..., c_k$ depending on whether the transformation T exists or not. Then, we define *cost modeling* as the process for finding the relationship between the model variables $m_1, m_2, ..., m_k$ and ec_{IO}, ec_{CPU} for a given UDF $f(a_1, a_2, ..., a_n)$. In this regard, a cost model provides a mapping from a k-dimensional data space defined by the k model variables to a 2-dimensional space defined by ec_{IO} and ec_{CPU}. Each point in the data space has the model variables as its coordinates.

Problem Definition

Our goal is to provide a self-tuning technique for UDF cost modeling with a strict memory limit and the following performance considerations: prediction accuracy, average prediction cost(APC), and average model update costs(AUC). The AUC includes insertion costs and compression costs.

APC is defined as:

$$APC = \frac{\sum_{i=0}^{N_P-1} P(i)}{N_P} \quad (1)$$

where $P(i)$ is the time it takes to make the ith prediction using the model and N_P is the total number of predictions made.

AUC is defined as:

$$AUC = \frac{\sum_{i=0}^{N_I-1} I(i) + \sum_{i=0}^{N_C-1} C(i)}{N_P} \quad (2)$$

where $I(i)$ is the time it takes to insert the ith data point into the model and N_I is the total number of insertions, and $C(i)$ is the time it takes for the ith compression and N_C is the total number of compressions.

4 The Memory-Limited Quadtree

Section 4.1 describes the data structure of the memory-limited quadtree, Section 4.2 describes the properties that an optimal quadtree has in our problem setting, and Sections 4.3 and 4.4 elaborate on MLQ cost prediction and model update, respectively.

4.1 Data Structure

MLQ uses the conventional quadtree as its data structure to store summary information of past UDF executions. The quadtree fully partitions the multidimensional space by recursively partitioning it into 2^d equal sized blocks (or, partitions), where d is the number of dimensions. In the quadtree structure, a child node is allocated for each non-empty block and its parent has a pointer to

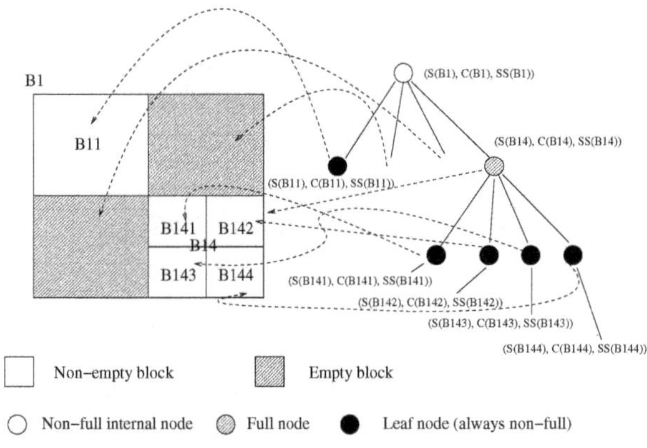

Fig. 2. The quadtree data structure.

it. Empty blocks are represented by null pointers. Figure 2 illustrates different node types of the quadtree using a two dimensional example. We call a node that has exactly 2^d children a *full node*, and a node with fewer than 2^d children a *non-full node*. Note that a leaf node is a non-full node.

Each node —internal or leaf— of the quadtree stores the summary information of the data points stored in a block represented by the node. The summary information for a block b consists of the sum $S(b)$, the count $C(b)$, the sum of squares $SS(b)$ of the values of the data points that map into the block. There is little overhead in updating these summary values incrementally as new data points are added. At prediction time, MLQ uses these summary values to compute the average value as follows.

$$AVG(b) = \frac{S(b)}{C(b)} \tag{3}$$

During data point insertion and model compression, the summary information stored in quadtree nodes are used to compute the sum of squared errors ($SSE(b)$) as follows.

$$\begin{aligned} SSE(b) &= \sum_{i=0}^{C(b)} (V_i - AVG(b))^2 \\ &= SS(b) - C(b)(AVG(b))^2 \end{aligned} \tag{4}$$

where V_i is the value of the ith data point that maps into the block b.

4.2 Optimal Quadtree

Given the problem definition in Section 3, we now define the optimality criterion of the quadtree used in MLQ. Let M_{max} denote the maximum memory available for use by the quadtree and DS denote a set of data points for training. Then, using M_{max} and DS, we now define $QT(M_{max}, DS)$ as the set of all possible quadtrees that can model DS using no more than M_{max}.

Let us define $SSENC$ as the sum of squared errors of the data points in block b excluding those in its children. That is,

$$SSENC(b) = \sum_{i=1}^{C(b_{nc})} (V_i - AVG(b))^2 \quad (5)$$

where b_{nc} is the set of data points in b that do not map into any of its children and V_i is the value of the ith data point in b_{nc}.

$SSENC(b)$ is a measure of the expected error for making a prediction using a non-full block b. This is a well-accepted error metric used for the compression of a data array[17]. It is used in [17] to define the optimal quadtree for the purpose of building the optimal *static* two-dimensional quadtree. We can use it for our purpose of building the optimal *dynamic* multi-dimensional quadtree, where the number of dimensions can be more than two.

Then, we define the optimal quadtree as one that minimizes the *total SSENC* ($TSSENC$) defined as follows.

$$TSSENC(qt) = \sum_{b \in NFB(qt)} (SSENC(b)) \quad (6)$$

where qt is the quadtree such that $qt \in QT(M_{max}, DS)$ and $NFB(qt)$ is defined as the set of the blocks of non-full nodes of qt. We use $TSSENC(qt)$ to guide the compression of the quadtree qt so that the resultant quadtree has the smallest increase in the expected prediction error. Further details of this will appear in Section 4.4.

4.3 Cost Prediction

The quadtree data structure allows cost prediction to be fast, simple, and straightforward. Figure 3 shows MLQ's prediction algorithm. The parameter β allows MLQ to be tuned based on the expected level of noise in the cost data. (We define noise as the magnitude by which the cost fluctuates at the same data point coordinate.) This is particularly useful for UDF cost modeling since disk IO costs (which is affected by many factors related to the database buffer cache) fluctuate more sharply at the same coordinates than CPU costs do. A larger value of β allows for averaging over more data points when a higher level of noise is expected.

4.4 Model Update

Model update in MLQ consists of data point insertion and compression. In this subsection we first describe how the quadtree is updated when a new data point is inserted and, then, describe the compression algorithm.

Predict_Cost (QT: quadtree, QP: query point, β: minimum number of points)

1. Find the lowest level node of QT such that QP maps into the block b of the node and the count in the node $\geq \beta$.
2. Return sum/count ($= S(b)/C(b)$) from the node found.

Fig. 3. Cost prediction algorithm of MLQ.

Data point insertion: When a new data point is inserted into the quadtree, MLQ updates the summary information in each of the existing blocks that the new data point maps into. It then decides whether the quadtree should be partitioned further in order to store the summary information for the new data point at a higher resolution. An approach that partitions more eagerly will lead to higher prediction accuracy but more frequent compressions since the memory limit will be reached earlier. Thus, there exists a trade-off between the prediction accuracy and the compression overhead.

In MLQ, we let the user choose what is more important by proposing two alternative insertion strategies: eager and lazy. In the eager strategy, the quadtree is partitioned to a maximum depth (λ) during the insertion of every new data point. In contrast, the lazy strategy delays partitioning by partitioning a block only when its SSE reaches a threshold (th_{SSE}). This has the effect of delaying the time of reaching the memory limit and, consequently, reducing the frequency of compression.

The th_{SSE}, used in the lazy insertion strategy, is defined as follows.

$$th_{SSE} = \alpha \, SSE(r) \tag{7}$$

where r is the root block and the parameter α is a *scaling factor* that helps users to set the th_{SSE}. The SSE in the root node indicates the degree of cost variations in the *entire* data space. In this regard, th_{SSE} can be determined relative to $SSE(r)$. If α is smaller, new data points are stored in a block at a higher depth and, as a result, prediction accuracy is higher. At the same time, however, the quadtree size is larger and, consequently, the memory limit is reached earlier, thus causing more frequent compressions. Thus, the α parameter is another mechanism for adjusting the trade-off between the prediction accuracy and the compression overhead.

Figure 4 shows the insertion algorithm. The same algorithm is used for both eager and lazy stategies. The only difference is that in the eager approach the th_{SSE} is set to zero whereas, in the lazy approach, it is set using Equation 7 (after the first compression). The algorithm traverses the quadtree top down while updating the summary information stored in every node it passes. If the child node that the data point maps into does not exist, a new child node is created (line 6-7). The traversal ends when the maximum depth λ is reached or the currently processed node is a leaf node with the SSE greater than the th_{SSE}.

Figure 5 illustrates how the quadtree is changed as two new data points P_1 and P_2 are inserted. In this example, we are using lazy insertion with the

Insert_point (DP: data point, QT: quadtree, th_{SSE}: SSE threshold, λ: maximum depth)

1. cn = the current node being processed, its initialized to be the root node of QT.
2. update sum, count, and sum of squares stored in cn.
3. while (($SSE(cn) \geq th_{SSE}$) and (λ has not been reached)) or
4. (cn is not a leaf node) {
5.. if DP does not map into any existing child of cn {
6. create the child in cn that DP maps into.
7. initialize sum, count, and sum of squares of the created child to zero.
8. }
9. cn = child of cn that DP maps into.
10. update sum, count, and sum of squares of cn.
11. }

Fig. 4. Insertion algorithm of MLQ.

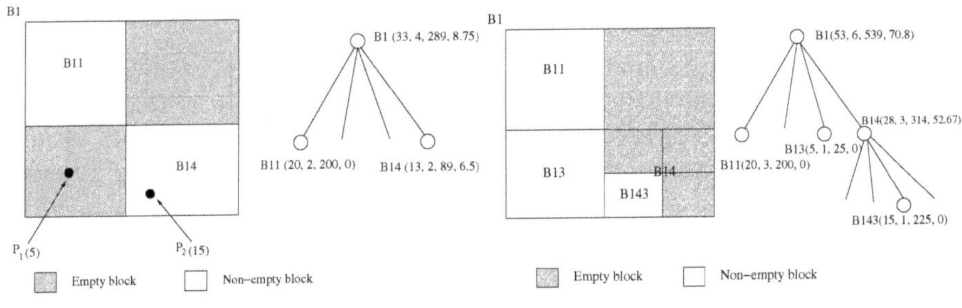

(a) Before inserting new data points. (b) After inserting new data points.

P(v), **B**(s,c,ss,sse): v = value, s = sum, c = count, ss = sum of squares, sse = sum of squared errors

Fig. 5. An example of data point lazy insertion in MLQ.

th_{SSE} of 8 and λ of 5. When P_1 is inserted, a new node is created for the block B13. Then, B13's summary information in the node is initialized to 5 for sum, 1 for the count, 25 for the sum of squares, and 0 for SSE. B13 is not further partitioned since its SSE is less than the th_{SSE}. Next, when P_2 is inserted, B14 is partitioned since its updated SSE of 67 becomes greater than the th_{SSE}.

Model compression: As mentioned in the Introduction, compression is triggered when the memory limit is reached. Let us first give an intuitive description of MLQ's compression algorithm. It aims to minimize the expected loss in prediction accuracy after compression. This is done by incrementally removing quadtree nodes in a bottom up fashion. The nodes that are more likely to be removed have the following properties: a low probability of future access and an average cost similar to its parent. Removing these nodes is least likely to degrade the future prediction accuracy.

Formally, the goal of compression is to free up memory by deleting a set of nodes such that the increase in $TSSENC$ (see definition in Equation 6) is minimized and a certain factor (γ) of the memory allocated for cost modeling is freed. γ allows the user to control the trade-off between compression frequency and prediction accuracy.

In order to achieve the goal, all leaf nodes are placed into a priority queue based on the *sum of squared error gain (SSEG)* of each node. The $SSEG$ of block b is defined as follows.

$$SSEG(b) = SSENC(p_{ac}) - (SSENC(b) + SSENC(p_{bc})) \quad (8)$$

where p_{bc} refers to the state of the parent block of b before the removal of b and p_{ac} refers to that after the removal of b. $SSEG(b)$ is a measure of the increase in the $TSSENC$ of the quadtree after block b is removed. Here, leaf nodes are removed before internal nodes to make the algorithm incremental since removing an internal node automatically removes all its children nodes as well.

Equation 8 can be simplified to the following equation. (Due to space constraints, we omit the details of the derivation and ask the readers to refer to [18].)

$$SSEG(b) = C(b)(AVG(p) - AVG(b))^2 \quad (9)$$

where p is the parent block of b. Equation 9 has three desirable properties. First, it favors the removal of leaf nodes that have fewer data points (i.e. smaller $C(b)$). This is desirable since a leaf node with fewer data points has a lower probability of being accessed in the future under the assumption that frequently queried regions are more likely to be queried again. Second, it favors the removal of leaf nodes that show a smaller difference between the average cost for the node and that for its parent. This is desirable since there is little value in keeping a leaf node that returns a predicted value similar to that from its parent. Third, computation of $SSEG(b)$ is efficient as it can be done using the sum and count values already stored in the quadtree nodes.

Figure 6 shows the compression algorithm. First, all leaf nodes are placed into the priority query PQ based on the SSEG value (line 1). Then, the algorithm iterates through PQ while removing the nodes from the top, that is, from the node with the smallest SSEG first (line 2 - 10). If the removal of a leaf node results in its parent's becoming a leaf node, then the parent node is inserted into PQ (line 5 - 7). The algorithm stops removing nodes when either PQ becomes empty or at least γ fraction of memory has been freed.

Figure 7 illustrates how MLQ performs compression. Figure 7(a) shows the state of the quadtree before the compression. Either B141 or B144 can be removed first since they both have the lowest SSEG value of 1. The tie is arbitrarily broken, resulting in, for example, the removal of B141 first and B144 next. We can see that removing both B141 and B144 results in an increase of only 2 in the $TSSENC$. If we removed B11 instead of B141 and B144, we would increase the $TSSENC$ by 2 after removing only one node.

```
Compress_tree (QT: quadtree, γ: minimum amount memory to be freed,
               total_mem: the total amount of memory allocated)
1. Traverse QT and place every leaf node into a priority queue PQ with the
   node with the smallest SSEG at its top.
2. while (PQ is not empty) and (memory_freed / total_mem < γ) {
3.     remove the top element from PQ and put it in current_leaf
4.     parent_node = the parent of current_leaf.
5.     if (parent_node is not the root node) and (parent_node is now a leaf node) {
6.         insert parent_node into PQ based on its SSEG.
7.     }
8.     deallocate memory used by current_leaf
9.     memory_freed = memory_freed + size of current_leaf
10. }
```

Fig. 6. Compression algorithm of MLQ.

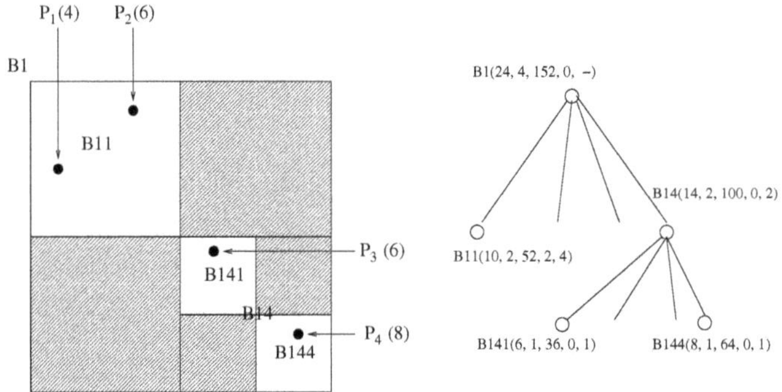

(a) Before compression.

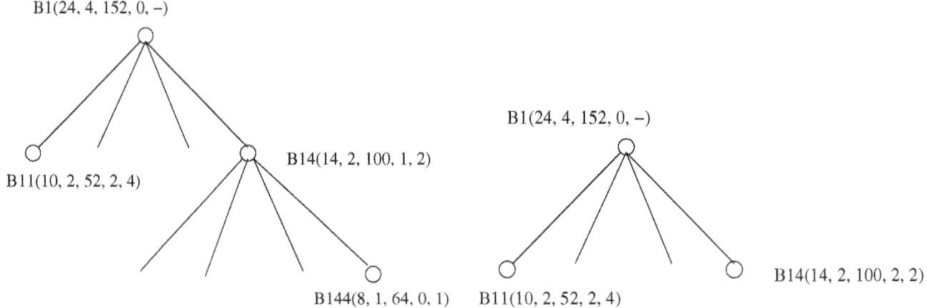

(b) After removing block B141. (c) After removing block B144.

P(e), **B**(s,c,ss,ssenc,sseg): e = execution cost, s = sum, c = count, ss = sum of square, ssenc = sum of squared error of data points not associated with any of its children, sseg = sum of squared error gain.

Fig. 7. An example of MLQ compression.

5 Experimental Evaluation

In this section we describe the experimental setup used to evaluate MLQ against existing algorithms and present the results of experiments.

5.1 Experimental Setup

Modeling methods and model training methods: We compare the performance of two MLQ variants against two variants of SH: (1) **MLQ-E**, our method using eager insertions, (2) **MLQ-L**, our method using lazy insertions, (3) **SH-H**[3] using equi-height histograms, and (4) **SH-W**[3] using equi-width histograms.

In these methods, models are trained differently depending on whether the method is self-tuning or not. The two MLQ methods, which are self-tuning, start with no data point and train the model incrementally (i.e., one data point at a time) while the model is being used to make predictions. In contrast, the two SH methods, which are not self-tuning, train the model a-priori with a set of queries that has the same distribution as the set of queries used for testing.

We limit the amount of memory allocated in each method to 1.8 Kbytes. This is similar to the amount of memory allocated in existing work[7,16,19] for selectivity estimation of range queries. All experiments allocate the same amount of memory in all methods. We have extensively tuned MLQ to achieve its best performance and used the resulting parameters values. In the case of the SH methods, there are no tuning parameters except the number of buckets used, which is determined by the memory size. The following is a specification of the MLQ parameters used in this paper: $\beta = 1$ for CPU cost experiments and 10 for disk IO cost experiments, $\alpha = 0.05$, $\gamma = 0.1\%$, and $\lambda = 6$. We show the effect of varying the MLQ parameters in [18] due to space constraints.

Synthetic UDFs/datasets: We generate synthetic UDFs/datasets in two steps. In the first step, we randomly generate a number (N) of *peaks* (i.e. extreme points within confined regions) in the multi-dimensional space. The coordinates of the peaks have the uniform distribution, and the heights (i.e. execution costs) of the peak have the Zipf distribution[20]. In the second step, we assign a randomly selected *decay function* to each peak. Here, a decay function specifies how the execution cost decreases as a function of the Euclidean distance from the peak. The decay functions we use are uniform, linear, Gaussian, log of base 2, and quadratic. They are defined so that the maximum point is at the peak and the height decreases to zero at a certain distance (D) from the peak. This suite of decay functions reflect the various computational complexities common to UDFs.

This setup allows us to vary the complexity of the data distribution by varying N and D. As N and D increase, we see more overlaps among the resulting decay regions (i.e., regions covered by the decay functions).

The following is a specification of the parameters we have used: the number of dimensions d set to 4, the range of values in each dimension set to 0 - 1000, the maximum cost of 10000 at the highest peak, the Zipf parameter (z) value of 1 for the Zipf distribution, a standard deviation of 0.2 for the Gaussian decay function, and the distance D equal to 10% of the Euclidean distance between two extreme corners of the multi-dimensional space.

Real UDFs/datasets: Two different kinds of real UDFs are used: three keyword-based text search functions (simple, threshold, proximity) and three spatial search functions (K-nearest neighbors, window, range). All six UDFs are implemented in Oracle PL/SQL using built-in Oracle Data Cartridge functions. The dataset used for the keyword-based text search functions is 36422 XML documents of news articles acquired from the Reuters. The dataset used for the spatial search functions is the maps of urban areas in all counties of Pennsylvania State [21]. We ask the readers to see [18] for a more detailed description.

Query distributions: Query points are generated using three different random distributions of their coordinates: (1) uniform, (2) Gaussian-random, and (3) Gaussian-sequential. In the uniform distribution, we generate query points uniformly in the entire multi-dimensional space. In the case of Gaussian-random, we first generate c Gaussian centroids using the uniform distribution. Then, we randomly choose one of the c centroids and generate one query point using the Gaussian distribution whose peak is at the chosen centroid. This is repeated n times to generate n query points. In the Gaussian-sequential case, we generate a centroid using the uniform distribution and generate n/c query points using the Gaussian distribution whose peak is at the centroid. This is repeated c times to generate n query points.

We use the Gaussian distribution to simulate skewed query distribution in contrast to the uniform query distribution. For this purpose, we set c to 3 and the standard deviation to 0.05. In addition, we set n to 5000 for the synthetic datasets and 2500 for the real datasets.

Error Metric: We use the *normalized absolute error*(NAE) to compare the prediction accuracy of different methods. Here, the NAE of a set of query points Q is defined as:

$$NAE(Q) = \frac{\sum_{\mathbf{q} \in Q} |PC(\mathbf{q}) - AC(\mathbf{q})|}{\sum_{\mathbf{q} \in Q} AC(\mathbf{q})} \tag{10}$$

where $PC(\mathbf{q})$ denotes the predicted cost and $AC(\mathbf{q})$ denotes the actual cost at a query point $\mathbf{q}$. This is similar to the normalized absolute error used in [7].

Note that we do not use the relative error because it is not robust to situations where the execution costs are low. We do not use the (unnormalized) absolute error either because it varies greatly across different UDFs/datasets while, in our experiments, we do compare errors across different UDFs/datasets.

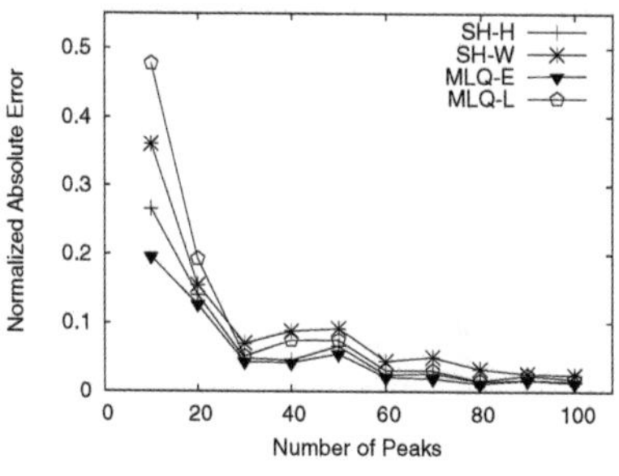

(a) Uniform query distribution

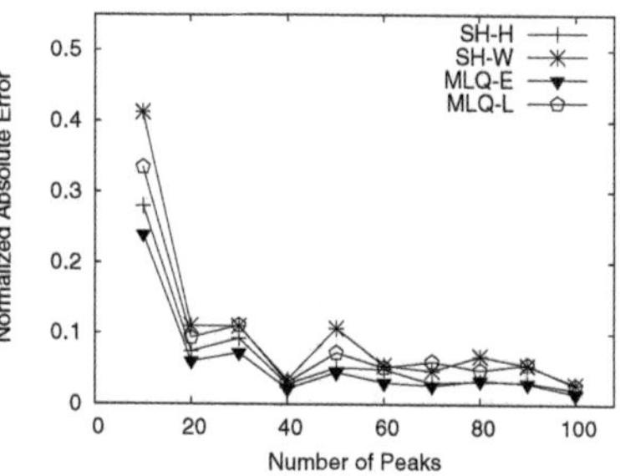

(b) Gaussian-sequential query distribution

Fig. 8. Prediction accuracy for a varying number of peaks (for synthetic data).

Computing platform: In the experiments involving real datasets, we use Oracle 9i on SunOS 5.8, installed on Sun Ultra Enterprise 450 with four 300 MHz CPUs, 16 KB level 1 I-cache, 16 KB level 1 D-cache, and 2 MB of level 2 cache per processor, 1024 MB RAM, and 85 GB of hard disk. Oracle is configured to use a 16 MB data buffer cache with direct IO. In the experiments involving synthetic datasets, we use Red Hat Linux 8 installed on a single 2.00 GHz Intel Celeron laptop with 256 KB level 2 cache, 512 MB RAM, and 40 GB hard disk.

5.2 Experimental Results

We have conducted four different sets of experiments (1) to compare the prediction accuracy of the algorithms for various query distributions and UDFs/datasets, (2) to compare the prediction, insertion, and compression costs of the algorithms, (3) to compare the effect of noise on the prediction accuracy of the algorithms, and (4) to compare the prediction accuracy of the MLQ algorithms as the number of query points processed increases.

Experiment 1 (prediction accuracy): Figure 9 shows the results of predicting the CPU costs of the real UDFs. The results for the disk IO costs will appear in Experiment 3.The results in Figure 9 show MLQ algorithms give lower error (or within 0.02 absolute error) when compared with SH-H in 10 out of 12 test cases. This demonstrates MLQ's ability to retain high prediction accuracy while dynamically 'learning' and predicting UDF execution costs.

Figure 8 shows the results obtained using the synthetic UDFs/datasets. The results show MLQ-E performs the same as or better than SH in all cases. However, the margin between MLQ-E and SH algorithms is smaller than that for the real UDFs/datasets. This is because the costs in the synthetic UDFs/datasets fluctuate less steeply than those in the real UDFs/datasets. Naturally, this causes the difference in the prediction errors of all the different methods to be smaller.

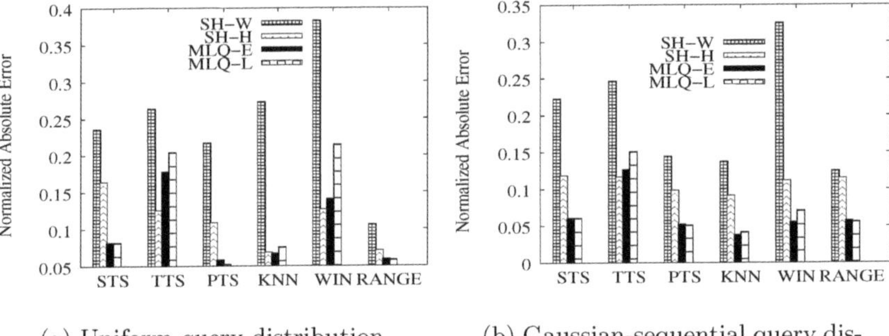

(a) Uniform query distribution

(b) Gaussian-sequential query distribution

Fig. 9. Prediction accuracy for various real UDFs/datasets.

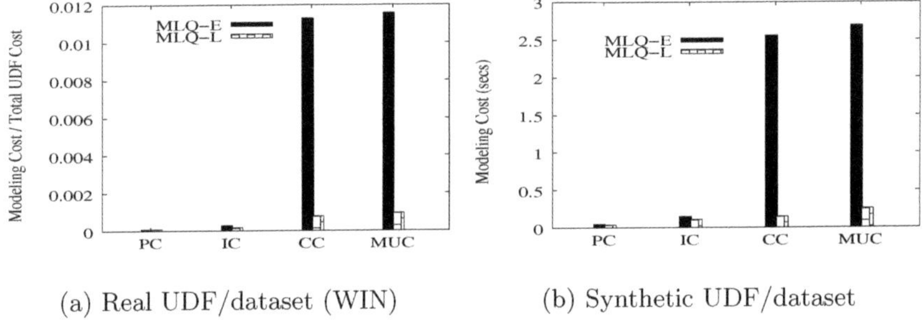

(a) Real UDF/dataset (WIN)

(b) Synthetic UDF/dataset

Fig. 10. Modeling costs (using uniform query distribution).

Experiment 2 (modeling costs): In this experiment we compare the modeling costs (prediction, insertion, and compression cost) of the cost modeling algorithms. This experiment is not applicable to SH due to its static nature and, therefore, we compare only among the MLQ algorithms. Figure 10(a) shows the results from the real UDFs/datasets. It shows the breakdown of the modeling costs into the prediction cost(PC), insertion cost(IC), compression cost(CC), and model update cost(MUC). MUC is the sum of IC and CC. All costs are normalized against the total UDF execution cost. Due to space constraints, we show only the results for WIN. The other UDFs show similar trends. The prediction costs of both MLQ-E and MLQ-L are only around 0.02% of the total UDF execution cost. In terms of the model update costs, even MLQ-E, which is slower than MLQ-L, imposes only between 0.04% and 1.2% overhead. MLQ-L outperforms MLQ-E for model update since MLQ-L delays the time the memory limit is reached and, as a result, performs compression less frequently.

Figure 10(b) shows the results from the synthetic UDFs/datasets. The results show similar trends as the real UDFs/datasets, namely MLQ-L outperforms MLQ-E for model update.

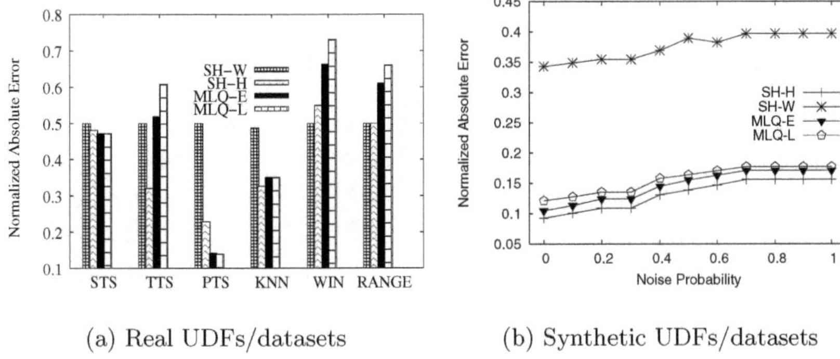

(a) Real UDFs/datasets (b) Synthetic UDFs/datasets

Fig. 11. Prediction accuracy for varying noise effect (using uniform query distribution).

Experiment 3 (noise effect on prediction accuracy): As mentioned in Section 4.3, the database buffer caching has a noise-like effect on the disk IO cost. In this experiment, we compare the accuracy of the algorithms at predicting the disk IO cost while introducing noise.

Figure 11(a) shows the results for the real UDFs/datasets. The results show MLQ-E outperforms MLQ-L. This is because MLQ-E does not delay partitioning and, thus, stores data at a higher resolution eariler than MLQ-L, thereby allowing prediction to be made using the summary information of *closer* data points. MLQ-E performs within around 0.1 normalized absolute error from SH-H in five out of the six cases. This is a good result, considering that SH-H is expected to perform better because it can absorb more noise by averaging over more data points and is trained a-prior with a complete set of UDF execution costs.

For the synthetic UDFs/datasets, we simulate the noise by varying *noise probability*, that is, the probability that a query point returns a random value instead of the true value. Due to space constraints, we omit the details of how noise is simulated and refer the readers to [18]. Figure 11(b) shows the results for the synthetic UDFs/datasets. The results show SH-H outperforms the MLQ algorithms by about 0.7 normalized absolute error irrespective of the amount of noise simulated.

Experiment 4 (prediction accuracy for an increasing number of query points processed): In this experiment we observe how fast the prediction error decreases as the number of query points processed increases in the MLQ algorithms. This experiment is not applicable to SH because it is not dynamic.

Figure 12 shows the results obtained using the same set of UDFs/datasets and query distribution as in Experiment 2. In all the results, MLQ-L reaches its minimum prediction error much earlier than MLQ-E. This is because of MLQ-L's strategy of delaying the node partitioning limits the resolution of the summary information in the quadtree and, as a result, causes the highest possible accuracy to be reached faster.

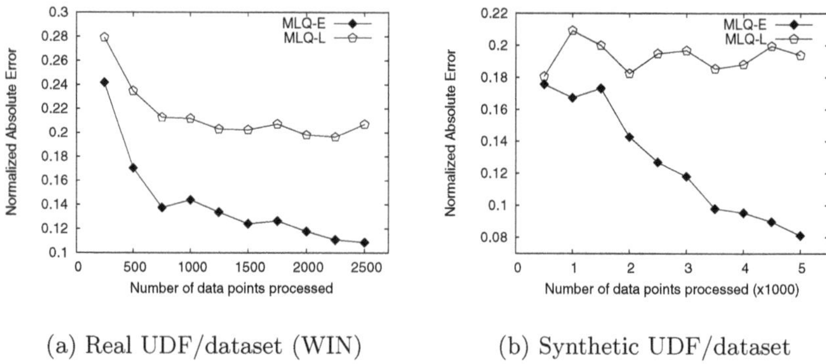

(a) Real UDF/dataset (WIN)

(b) Synthetic UDF/dataset

Fig. 12. Prediction error with an increasing number of data points processed (uniform query distribution).

6 Conclusions

In this paper we have presented a memory-limited quadtree-based approach (called MLQ) to self-tuning cost modeling with a focus on the prediction accuracy and the costs for prediction and model updates. MLQ stores and manages summary information in the blocks (or partitions) of a dynamic multi-resolution quadtree while limiting its memory usage to a predefined amount. Predictions are made using the summary information stored in the quadtree, and the actual costs are inserted as the values of new data points. MLQ offers two alternative insertion strategies: eager and lazy. Each strategy has its own merits. The eager strategy is more accurate in most cases but incurs higher compression cost (up to 50 times). When the memory limit is reached, the tree is compressed in such a way as to minimize the increase in the total expected error in subsequent predictions.

We have performed extensive experimental evaluations using both real and synthetic UDFs/datasets. The results show that the MLQ method gives higher or similar prediction accuracy compared with the SH method despite that the SH method is not self-tuning and, thus, trains the model using a complete set of training data collected a-priori. The results also show that the overhead for being self-tuning is negligible compared with the execution cost of the real UDFs.

Acknowledgments. We thank Li Chen, Songtao Jiang, and David Van Horn for setting up the real UDFs/datasets used in the experiments, and the Reuters Limited for providing Reuters Corpus, Volume 1, English Language, for use in the experiments. This research has been supported by the US Department of Energy through Grant No. DE-FG02-ER45962.

References

1. Hellerstein, J., Stonebraker, M.: Predicate migration: Optimizing queries with expensive predicates. In: Proc. of ACM-SIGMOD. (1993) 267–276
2. Chaudhuri, S., Shim, K.: Optimization of queries with user-defined predicates. In: Proc. of ACM SIGMOD. (1996) 87–98
3. Jihad, B., Kinji, O.: Cost estimation of user-defined methods in object-relational database systems. SIGMOD Record (1999) 22–28
4. Boulos, J., Viemont, Y., Ono, K.: A neural network approach for query cost evaluation. Trans. on Information Processing Society of Japan (1997) 2566–2575
5. Hellerstein, J.: Practical predicate placement. In: Proc. of ACM SIGMOD. (1994) 325–335
6. Aboulnaga, A., Chaudhuri, S.: Self-tuning histograms: building histograms without looking at data. In: Proc. of ACM SIGMOD. (1999) 181–192
7. Bruno, N., Chaudhuri, S., Gravano, L.: STHoles: A mulidimensional workload-aware histogram. In: Proc. of ACM SIGMOD. (2001) 211–222
8. Stillger, M., Lohman, G., Markl, V., Kandil, M.: LEO - DB2's LEarning optimizer. In: Proc. of VLDB. (2001) 19–28
9. Hunter, G.M., Steiglitz, K.: Operations on images using quadtrees. IEEE Trans. on Pattern Analysis and Machine Intelligence **1** (1979) 145–153
10. Strobach, P.: Quadtree-structured linear prediction models for image sequence processing. IEEE Trans. on Pattern Analysis and Machine Intelligence **11** (742-748)
11. Lee, J.W.: Joint optimization of block size and quantization for quadtree-based motion estimation. IEEE Trans. on Pattern Analysis **7** (1998) 909–911
12. Aref, W.G., Samet, H.: Efficient window block retrieval in quadtree-based spatial databases. GeoInformatica **1** (1997) 59–91
13. Wang, F.: Relational-linear quadtree approach for two-dimensional spatial representation and manipulation. IEEE Trans. on Knowledge and Data Eng. **3** (1991) 118–122
14. Lazaridis, I., Mehrotra, S.: Progressive approximate aggregate queries with a multiresolution tree structure. In: Proc. of ACM SIGMOD. (2001) 401–413
15. Han, J., Kamber, M.: 7. In: Data Mining: Concepts and Techniques. Morgan Kaufmann (2001) 303, 314–315
16. Poosala, V., Ioannidis, Y.: Selectivity estimation without the attribute value independence assumption. In: Proc. of VLDB. (1997) 486–495
17. Buccafurri, F., Furfaro, F., Sacca, D., Sirangelo, C.: A quad-tree based multiresolution approach for two-dimensional summary data. In: Proc. of SSDBM, Cambridge, Massachusetts, USA (2003)
18. He, Z., Lee, B.S., Snapp, R.R.: Self-tuning UDF cost modeling using the memory limited quadtree. Technical Report CS-03-18, Department of Computer Science, University of Vermont (2003)
19. Deshpande, A., Garofalakis, M., Rastogi, R.: Independence is good: Dependency-based histogram synopses for high-dimensional data. In: Proc. of ACM SIGMOD. (2001) 199–210
20. Zipf, G.K.: Human behavior and the principle of least effort. Addison-Wesley (1949)
21. PSADA: Urban areas of pennsylvania state. URL:http://www.pasda.psu.edu/access/urban.shtml (Last viewed:6-18-2003)

Distributed Query Optimization by Query Trading

Fragkiskos Pentaris and Yannis Ioannidis

Department of Informatics and Telecommunications, University of Athens,
Ilisia, Athens 15784, Hellas(Greece),
{frank,yannis}@di.uoa.gr

Abstract. Large-scale distributed environments, where each node is completely autonomous and offers services to its peers through external communication, pose significant challenges to query processing and optimization. Autonomy is the main source of the problem, as it results in lack of knowledge about any particular node with respect to the information it can produce and its characteristics. Inter-node competition is another source of the problem, as it results in potentially inconsistent behavior of the nodes at different times. In this paper, inspired by e-commerce technology, we recognize queries (and query answers) as commodities and model query optimization as a trading negotiation process. Query parts (and their answers) are traded between nodes until deals are struck with some nodes for all of them. We identify the key parameters of this framework and suggest several potential alternatives for each one. Finally, we conclude with some experiments that demonstrate the scalability and performance characteristics of our approach compared to those of traditional query optimization.

1 Introduction

The database research community has always been very interested in large (intranet- and internet-scale) federations of autonomous databases as these seem to satisfy the scalability requirements of existing and future data management applications. These systems, find the answer of a query by splitting it into parts (sub-queries), retrieving the answers of these parts from remote "black-box" database nodes, and merging the results together to calculate the answer of the initial query [1]. Traditional query optimization techniques are inappropriate [2,3,4] for such systems as node autonomy and diversity result in lack of knowledge about any particular node with respect to the information it can produce and its characteristics, e.g., query capabilities, cost of production, or quality of produced results. Furthermore, if inter-node competition exists (e.g., commercial environments), it results in potentially inconsistent node behavior at different times.

In this paper, we consider a new scalable approach to distributed query optimization in large federations of autonomous DBMSs. Inspired from microeconomics, we adapt e-commerce trading negotiation methods to the problem. The result is a query-answers trading mechanism, where instead of trading goods, nodes trade answers of (parts of) queries in order to find the best possible query execution plan.

Motivating example: Consider the case of a telecommunications company with thousands of regional offices. Each of them has a local DBMS, holding customer-care (CC) data of millions of customers. The schema includes the relations

E. Bertino et al. (Eds.): EDBT 2004, LNCS 2992, pp. 532–550, 2004.
© Springer-Verlag Berlin Heidelberg 2004

`customer(custid, custname, office)`, holding customer information such as the regional office responsible for them, and `invoiceline(invid, linenum, custid, charge)`, holding the details (charged amounts) of customers' past invoices. For performance and robustness reasons, each relation may be horizontally partitioned and/or replicated across the regional offices. Consider now a manager at the Athens office asking for the total amount of issued bills in the offices in the islands of Corfu and Myconos:

```
SELECT SUM(charge) FROM invoiceline i, customer c
WHERE i.custid=c.custid AND office in ('Corfu','Myconos');
```

The Athens node will ask the rest of the company's nodes whether or not they can evaluate (some part of) the query. Assume that the Myconos and Corfu nodes reply positively about the part of the query dealing with their own customers with a cost of 30 and 40 seconds, respectively. These offers could be based on the nodes actually processing the query, or having the offered result pre-computed already, or even receiving it from yet another node; whatever the case, it is no concern of Athens. It only has to compare these offers against any other it may have, and whatever has the least cost wins.

In this example, Athens effectively *purchases* the two answers from the Corfu and Myconos nodes at a cost of 30 and 40 seconds, respectively. That is, queries and query-answers are commodities and query optimization is a common trading negotiation process. The buyer is Athens and the potential sellers are Corfu and Myconos. The cost of each query-answer is the time to deliver it. In the general case, the cost may involve many other properties of the query-answers, e.g., freshness and accuracy, or may even be monetary. Moreover, the participating nodes may not be in a cooperative relationship (parts of a company's distributed database) but in a competitive one (nodes in the internet offering data products). In that case, the goal of each node would be to maximize its private benefits (according to the chosen cost model) instead of the joint benefit of all nodes.

In this paper, we present a complete query and query-answers trading negotiation framework and propose it as a query optimization mechanism that is appropriate for a large-scale distributed environment of (cooperative or competitive) *autonomous* information providers. It is inspired by traditional e-commerce trading negotiation solutions, whose properties have been studied extensively within B2B and B2C systems [5,6,7,8, 9], but also for distributing tasks over several agents in order to achieve a common goal (e.g., Contract Net [10]). Its major differences from these traditional frameworks stem primarily from two facts:

- A query is a complex structure that can be cut into smaller pieces that can be traded separately. Traditionally, only atomic commodities are traded, e.g., a car; hence, buyers do not know *a priori* what commodities (query answers) they should buy.
- The *value* of a query answer is in general multidimensional, e.g., system resources, data freshness, data accuracy, response time, etc. Traditionally, only individual monetary values are associated with commodities.

In this paper, we focus on the first difference primarily and provide details about the proposed framework with respect to the overall system architecture, negotiation protocols, and negotiation contents. We also present the results of an extended number of simulation experiments that identify the key parameters affecting query optimization in very large autonomous federations of DBMSs and demonstrate the potential efficiency and performance of our method.

To the best of our knowledge, there is no other work that addresses the problem of distributed query optimization in a large environment of purely autonomous systems. Nevertheless, our experiments include a comparison of our technique with some of the currently most efficient techniques for distributed query optimization [2,4].

The rest of the paper is organized as follows. In section 2 we examine the way a general trading negotiation frameworks is constructed. In section 3 we present our query optimization technique. In section 4 we experimentally measure the performance of our technique and compare it to that of other relevant algorithms. In section 5 we discuss the results of our experiments and conclude.

2 Trading Negotiations Framework

A trading negotiation framework provides the means for buyers to request items offered by seller entities. These items can be anything, from plain pencils to advanced gene-related data. The involved parties (buyer and sellers) assign private valuations to each traded item, which in the case of traditional commerce, is usually their cost measured using a currency unit. Entities may have different valuations for the same item (e.g. different costs) or even use different indices as valuations, (e.g. the weight of the item, or a number measuring how important the item is for the buyer).

Trading negotiation procedures follow rules defined in a negotiation protocol [9] which can be bidding (e.g., [10]), bargaining or an auction. In each step of the procedure, the protocol designates a number of possible actions (e.g., make a better offer, accept offer, reject offer, etc.). Entities choose their actions based on (a) the strategy they follow, which is the set of rules that designate the exact action an entity will choose, depending on the knowledge it has about the rest of the entities, and (b) the expected surplus(utility) from this action, which is defined as the difference between the values agreed in the negotiation procedure and these held privately. Traditionally, strategies are classified as either *cooperative* or *competitive* (*non-cooperative*). In the first case, the involved entities aim to maximize the joint surplus of all parties, whereas in the second case, they simply try to individually maximize only their personal utility.

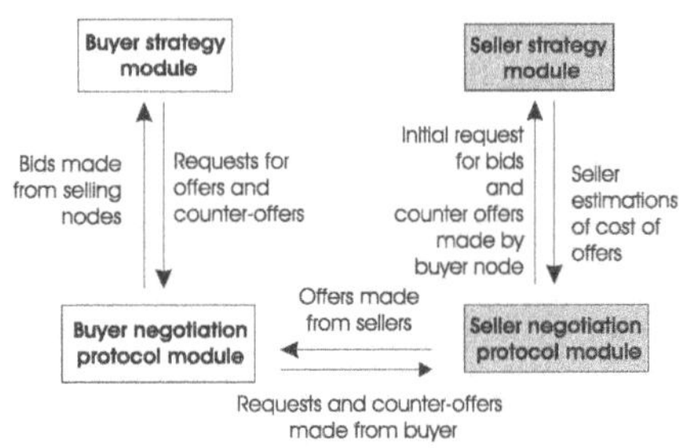

Fig. 1. Modules used in a general trading negotiations framework.

Figure 1 shows the modules required for implementing a distributed electronic trading negotiation framework among a number of network nodes. Each node uses two separate modules, a *negotiation protocol* and a *strategy* module (white and gray modules designate buyer and seller modules respectively). The first one handles inter-nodes message exchanges and monitors the current status of the negotiation, while the second one selects the contents of each offer/counter-offer.

3 Distributed Query Optimization Framework

Using the e-commerce negotiations paradigm, we have constructed an efficient algorithm for optimizing queries in large disparate and autonomous environments. Although our framework is more general, in this paper, we limit ourselves on select-project-join queries. This section presents the details of our technique, focusing on the parts of the trading framework that we have modified. The reader can find additional information on parts that are not affected by our algorithm, such as general competitive strategies and equilibriums, message congestion protocols, and details on negotiation protocol implementations in [5,6,11,12,13,7,8,9] and on standard e-commerce and strategic negotiations textbooks (e.g., [14,15,16]). Furthermore, there are possibilities for additional enhancements of the algorithm that will be covered in future work. These enhancements include the use of *contracting* to model partial/adaptive query optimization techniques, the design of a scalable *subcontracting* algorithm, the selection of advanced *cost functions*, and the examination of various *competitive and cooperative* strategies.

3.1 Overview

The idea of our algorithm is to consider queries and query-answers as commodities and the query optimization procedure as a trading of query answers between nodes holding information that is relevant to the contents of these queries. Buying nodes are those that are unable to answer some query, either because they lack the necessary resources (e.g. data, I/O, CPU), or simply because outsourcing the query is better than having it executed locally. Selling nodes are the ones offering to provide data relevant to some parts of these queries. Each node may play any of those two roles(buyer and seller) depending on the query been optimized and the data that each node locally holds.

Before going on with the presentation of the optimization algorithm, we should note that no query or part of it is physically executed during the whole optimization procedure. The buyer nodes simply ask from seller nodes for assistance in evaluating some *queries* and seller nodes make offers which contain their *estimated* properties of the answer of these queries (*query-answers*). These properties can be the total time required to execute and transmit the results of the query back to the buyer, the time required to find the first row of the answer, the average rate of retrieved rows per second, the total rows of the answer, the freshness of the data, the completeness of the data, and possibly a charged amount for this answer. The query-answer properties are calculated by the sellers' query optimizer and strategy module, therefore, they can be extremely precise, taking into account the available *network resources* and the *current workload* of sellers.

The buyer ranks the offers received using an administrator-defined weighting aggregation function and chooses those that minimize the total cost/value of the query. In the rest of this section, the valuation of the offered query-answers will be the total execution time (cost) of the query, thus, we will use the terms cost and valuation interchangeably. However, nothing forbids the use of a different cost unit, such as the total network resources used (number of transmitted bytes) or even monetary units.

3.2 The Query-Trading Algorithm

The execution plans produced by the query-trading (QT) algorithm, consist of the query-answers offered by remote seller nodes together with the processing operations required to construct the results of the optimized queries from these offers. The algorithm finds the combination of offers and local processing operations that minimizes the valuation (cost) of the final answer. For this reason, it runs iteratively, progressively selecting the best execution plan. In each iteration, the buyer node asks (Request for Bids -RFBs) for some queries and the sellers reply with offers that contain the estimations of the properties of these queries (query-answers). Since sellers may not have all the data referenced in a query, they are allowed to give offers for only the part of the data they actually have. At the end of each iteration, the buyer uses the received offers to find the best possible execution plan, and then, the algorithm starts again with a possibly new set of queries that might be used to construct an even better execution plan.

The optimization algorithm is actually a kind of bargaining between the buyer and the seller nodes. The buyer asks for certain queries and the sellers counter-offer to evaluate some (modified parts) of these queries at different values. The difference between our approach and the general trading framework, is that in each iteration of this bargaining the negotiated queries are different, as the buyer **and** the sellers progressively identify additional queries that may help in the optimization procedure. This difference, in turn, makes necessary to change selling nodes in each step of the bargaining, as these additional queries may be better offered by other nodes. This is in contrast to the traditional trading framework, where the participants in a bargaining remain constant.

Figure 2 presents the details of the distributed optimization algorithm. The input of the algorithm is a query q with an initially estimated cost of C_i. If no estimation using the available local information is possible, then C_i is a predefined constant (zero or something else depending on the type of cost used). The output is the estimated best execution plan P_* and its respective cost C_* (step B8). The algorithm, at the buyer-side, runs iteratively (steps B1 to B7). Each iteration starts with a set Q of pairs of queries and their estimated costs, which the buyer node would like to purchase from remote nodes. In the first step (B1), the buyer strategically estimates the values it should ask for the queries in set Q and then asks for bids (RFB) from remote nodes (step B2). The seller nodes after receiving this RFB make their offers, which contain query-answers concerning parts of the queries in set Q (step S2.1 - S2.2) or other relevant queries that they think it could be of some use to the buyer (step S2.3). The winning offers are then selected using a small nested trading negotiation (steps B3 and S3). The buyer uses the contents of the winning offers to find a set of candidate execution plans P_m and their respective estimated costs C_m (step B4), and an enhanced set Q of queries-costs pairs (q_e, c_e) (steps B5 and B6) which they could possibly be used in the next iteration of the algorithm for further improving the plans produced at step B4. Finally, in step B7, the best execution plan P_* out of the candidate plans P_m is selected. If this is not better than that of the previous iteration (i.e., no improvement) or if step B6 did not find any new query, then the algorithm is terminated.

As previously mentioned, our algorithm looks like a general bargaining with the difference that in each step the sellers and the queries bargained are different. In steps B2, B3 and S3 of each iteration of the algorithm, a complete (nested) trading negotiation

Buyer-side algorithm	Sellers-side algorithm
B0. Initialization, set $Q = \{\{q, C_i\}\}$	
B1. Make estimations of the values of the queries in set Q, using a trading strategy.	
B2. Request offers for the queries in set Q	
	S1. For each query q in set Q do the following:
	S2.1. Find sub-queries q_k of q that can be answered locally.
	S2.2. Estimate the cost c_k of each of these sub-queries q_k.
	S2.3. Find other (sub-)queries that may be of some help to the buyer node.
B3. Select the best offers $\{q_i, c_i\}$ using **one of the three** methods (bidding, auction, bargaining) of the query trading framework	S3. Using the query trading framework, make offers and try to sell some of the subqueries of step S2.2 and S2.3.
B4. Using the best offers, find possible execution plans P_m and their estimated cost C_m	
B5. Find possible sub-queries q_e and their estimated cost c_e that, if available, could be used in step B4.	
B6. Update set Q with sub-queries $\{q_e, c_e\}$.	
B7. Let P_* be the best of the execution plans P_m. If P_* is better than that of the previous iteration of the algorithm, or if step B6 modified the set Q, then go to step B1.	
B8. Inform the selling-nodes, which offered queries used in the best execution plan P_*, to execute these queries.	

Fig. 2. The distributed optimization algorithm.

is conducted to select the best seller nodes and offers. The protocol used can be any of the ones discussed in section 2.

3.3 Algorithm Details

Figure 3 shows the modules required for an implementation of our optimization algorithm (grayed boxes concern modules running at the seller nodes) and the processing workflow between them. As Figure 3 shows, the buyer node initially assumes that the value of query q is C_i, and asks its *buyer strategy* module to make a (strategic) estimation of its value using a traditional e-commerce trading reasoning. This estimation is given to the *buyer negotiation protocol* module that asks for bids (RFB) from the selling nodes. The seller, using its *seller negotiation protocol* module, receives this RFB and forwards it to the *partial query constructor and cost estimator* module, which builds pairs of a possible part of query q together with an estimate of its respective value. The pairs are forwarded to the *seller predicates analyser* to examine them and find additional queries (e.g., materialized views) that might be useful to the buyer. The output of this module (set of (sub-)queries and their costs) is given to the *seller strategy module* to decide (using again an e-commerce trading reasoning) which of these pairs is worth attempting to sell to the buyer node, and in what value. The *negotiation protocols* modules of both the seller and the buyer then run though the network a predefined trading protocol (e.g. bidding) to find the winning offers (q_i, c_i). These offers are used by the buyer as input to the *buyer query plan generator*, which produces a number of candidate execution plans P_m and their respective buyer-estimated costs C_m. These plans are forwarded to the *buyer*

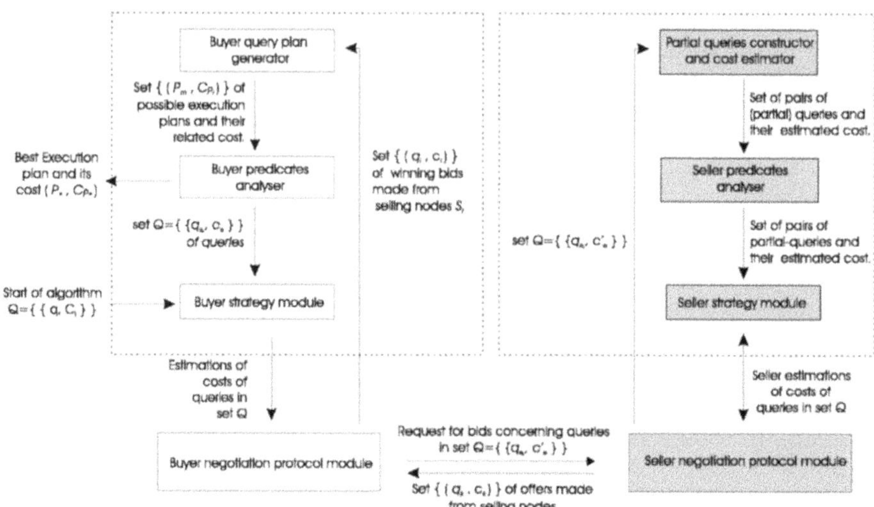

Fig. 3. Modules used by the optimization algorithm.

predicates analyser to find a new set Q of queries q_e and then, the workflow is restarted unless the set Q was not modified by the *buyer predicates analyser* and the *buyer query plan generator* failed to find a better candidate plan than that of the previous workflow iteration. The algorithm fails to find a distributed execution plan and immediately aborts, if in the first iteration, the *buyer query plan generator* cannot find a candidate execution plan from the offers received.

It is worth comparing Figure 1, which shows the typical trading framework, to Figure 3, which describes our query trading framework. These figures show that the buyer strategy module of the general framework is enhanced in the query trading framework with a query plan generator and a buyer predicates analyser. Similarly, the seller strategy module is enhanced with a partial query constructor and a seller predicates analyser. These additional modules are required, since in each bargaining step the buyer and seller nodes make (counter-)offers concerning a different set of queries, than that of the previous step.

To complete the analysis of the distributed optimization algorithm, we examine in detail each of the modules of Figure 3 below.

3.4 Partial Query Constructor and Cost Estimator

The role of the partial query constructor and cost estimator of the selling nodes is to construct a set of queries q_k offered to the buyer node. It examines the set Q of queries asked by the buyer and identifies the parts of these queries that the seller node can contribute to. Sellers may not have all necessary base relations, or relations' partitions, to process all elements of Q. Therefore, they initially examine each query q of Q and rewrite it (if possible), using the following algorithm, which removes all non-local relations and restricts the base-relation extents to those partitions available locally:

Query rewriting algorithm

1. While there is a relation R in query q that is not available locally, do
1.1. Remove R from q.
1.2. Update the SELECT-part of q adding the attributes of the rest relations of q that are used in joins with R.
1.3. Update the WHERE-part of q removing any operators referencing relation R.
1. End While
2. For each remaining relation R in query q, do
2.1 Update the WHERE-part of q adding the restriction operators of the partitions of R that are stored locally.
2. End For

As an example of how the previous algorithm works, consider the example of the telecommunications company and consider again the example of the query asked by that manager at Athens. Assume that the Myconos node has the whole invoiceline table but only the partition of the customer table with the restriction `office='Myconos'`. Then, after running the query rewriting algorithm at the Myconos node and simplifying the expression in the WHERE part, the resulting query will be the following:

```
SELECT SUM(charge) FROM invoiceline i, customer c
WHERE i.custid=c.custid AND office='Myconos';
```

The restriction `office='Myconos'` was added to the above query, since the Myconos node has only this partition of the customer table.

After running the query rewrite algorithm, the sellers use their local query optimizer to find the best possible local plan for each (rewritten) query. This is needed to estimate the properties and cost of the query-offers they will make. Conventional local optimizers work progressively pruning sub-optimal access paths, first considering two-way joins, then three-way joins, and so on, until all joins have been considered [17]. Since, these partial results may be useful to the buyer, we include the optimal two-way, three-way, etc. partial results in the offer sent to the buyer. The modified dynamic programming (DP) algorithm [18] that runs for each (rewritten) query q is the following (The queries in set D are the result of the algorithm):

Modified DP algorithm

1. Find all possible access paths of the relations of q.
2. Compare their cost and keep the least expensive.
3. Add the resulting plans into set D.
3. For i=2 to number of joins in q, do
3.1. Consider joining the relevant access paths found in previous iterations using all possible join methods.
3.2. Compare the cost of the resulting plans and keep the least expensive.
3.3. Add the resulting plans into set D.
3. End For

If we run the modified DP algorithm on the output of the previous example, we will get the following queries:

```
1. SELECT custid FROM customer
   WHERE office='Myconos';
2. SELECT custid,charge FROM invoiceline;
3. SELECT SUM(charge) FROM invoiceline i, customer c
   WHERE i.custid=c.custid AND office='Myconos';
```

The first two SQL queries are produced at steps 1-3 of the dynamic programming algorithm and the last query is produced in its first iteration (i=2) at step 3.3.

3.5 Seller Predicates Analyser

The seller predicates analyser works complementarily to the partial query constructor finding queries that might be of some interest to the buyer node. The latter is based on a traditional DP optimizer and therefore does not necessarily find all queries that might be of some help to the buyer. If there is a materialized view that might be used to quickly find a superset/subset of a query asked by the buyer, then it is worth offering (in small value) the contents of this materialized view to the buyer. For instance, continuing the example of the previous section, if Myconos node had the materialized view:

```
CREATE VIEW invoice AS
    SELECT custid, SUM(charge) FROM invoiceline
    GROUP by custid;
```

then it would worth offering it to the buyer, as the grouping asked by the manager at Athens is more coarse than that of this materialized view. There are a lot of non-distributed algorithms concerning answering queries using materialized views with or without the presence of grouping, aggregation and multi-dimensional functions, like for instance [19]. All these algorithms can be used in the seller predicates analyser to further enhance the efficiency of the QT algorithm and enable it to consider using remote materialized views. The potential of improving the distributed execution plan by using materialized views is substantial, especially in large databases, data warehouses and OLAP applications.

The seller predicates analyser has another role, useful when the seller does not hold the whole data requested. In this case, the seller, apart from offering only the data it already has, it may try to find the rest of these data using a subcontracting procedure, i.e., purchase the missing data from a third seller node. In this paper, due to lack of space, we do not consider this possibility.

3.6 Buyer Query Plan Generator

The query plan generator combines the queries q_i that won the bidding procedure to build possible execution plans P_m for the original query q. The problem of finding these plans is identical to the answering queries using materialized views [20] problem. In general, this problem is NP-Complete, since it involves searching though a possibly exponential number of rewritings.

The most simple algorithm that can be used is the dynamic programming algorithm. Other more advanced algorithms that may be used in the buyer plan generator include those proposed for the Manifold System (bucket algorithm [21]), the InfoMaster System (inverse-rules algorithm [22]) and recently the MiniCon [20] algorithm. These algorithms are more scalable than the DP algorithm and thus, they should be used if the complexity of the optimized queries, or the number of horizontal partitions per relation are large.

In the experiments presented at section 4, apart from the DP algorithm, we have also considered the use of the Iterative Dynamic Programming IDP-M(2,5) algorithm proposed in [2]. This algorithm is similar to DP. Its only difference is that after evaluating all 2-way join sub-plans, it keeps the best five of them throwing away all other 2-way join sub-plans, and then it continues processing like the DP algorithm.

3.7 Buyer Predicates Analyser

The buyer predicates analyser enriches the set Q (see Figure 3) with additional queries, which are computed by examining each candidate execution plan P_m (see previous subsection). If the queries used in these plans provide redundant information, it updates the set Q adding the restrictions of these queries which eliminate the redundancy. Other queries that may be added to the set Q are simple modifications of the existing ones with the addition/removal of sorting predicates, or the removal of some attributes that are not used in the final plan.

To make more concrete to the reader the functionality of the buyer predicate analyser, consider again the telecommunications company example, and assume that someone asks the following query:

```
SELECT custid FROM customer
WHERE office in ('Corfu', 'Myconos', 'Santorini');
```

Assume that one of the candidate plans produced from the buyer plan generator contains the union (distrinct) of the following queries:

```
1a. SELECT custid FROM customer
    WHERE office in ('Corfu', 'Myconos');
2a. SELECT custid FROM customer c
    WHERE office in ('Santorini', 'Myconos');
```

The buyer predicates analyser will see that this union has redundancy and will produce the following two queries:

```
1b. SELECT custid FROM customer WHERE office='Corfu';
2b. SELECT custid FROM customer WHERE office='Santorini';
```

In the next iteration of the algorithm, the buyer will also ask for bids concerning the above two SQL statements, which will be used in the next invocation of the buyer plan generator, to build the same union-based plan with either query (1a) or (2a) replaced with the cheaper queries (1b) or (2b) respectively.

3.8 Negotiation Protocols

All of the known negotiation protocols, such as bidding, bargaining and auctions can be used in the query trading environment. Bidding should be selected if someone wishes to keep the implementation as simple as possible. However, if the expected number of selling nodes is large, bidding will lead to flooding the buying nodes with too many bids. In this case, a better approach is to use an agent based auction mechanism, since it reduces the number of bids. On the other hand, an auction may produce sub-optimal results if the bidders are few or if some malicious nodes form a *ring* agreeing not to compete against each other. The latter is possible, if our query trading framework is used for commercial purposes. This problem affects all general e-commerce frameworks and is solved in many different ways (e.g., [23]).

Bargaining, instead of bidding, is worth using only when the number of expected offers is small and minor modifications in the offers are required (e.g., a change of a single query-answer property), since this will avoid the cost of another workflow iteration. If major modifications in the structure of the offered queries are required, the workflow (by definition) will have to run at least one more iteration and since each iteration is actually a generalized bargaining step, using a nested bargaining within a bargaining will only increase the number of exchanged messages.

4 Experimental Study

In order to assert the quality of our algorithm (QT), we simulated a large network of interconnected RDBMSs and run a number of experiments to measure the performance of our algorithm. To the best of our knowledge, there is no other work that addresses the problem of distributed query optimization in large networks of purely autonomous nodes. Hence, there is no approach to compare our algorithm against on an equal basis with respect to its operating environment.

As a matter of comparison, however, and in order to identify the potential "cost" for handling true autonomy, we have also implemented the SystemR algorithm, an instance of the optimization algorithm used by the Mariposa distributed DBMS [4] and a variant of the Iterative Dynamic Programming (IDP) algorithm [2]. These are considered three of the most effective algorithms for distributed query optimization and serve as a solid basis of our evaluation.

4.1 Experiments Setup

Simulation parameters. We used C++ to build a simulator of a large Wide Area Network (WAN). The parameters of this environment, together with their possible values, are displayed in Table 1. The network had 5,000 nodes that exchanged messages with a simulated latency of 10-240ms and a speed of 0.5-4Mbits. Each node was equipped with a single CPU at 1200Mhz (on average) that hosted an RDBMs capable of evaluating joins using the nested-loops and the merge-scan algorithms. 80% of the simulated RDBMSs could also use the hash-join method. The local I/O speed of each node was not constant and varied between 5 and 20 Mbytes/s.

Table 1. Simulation parameters.

Parameter type	Parameter	Value
Network	Total size of Network (WAN)	5,000 nodes
	Minimum duration of each network message	1 ms
	WAN network packet latency	10 - 240ms (120 ms average)
	WAN interconnection speed	0.5 - 4Mbits/s
RDBMs	Join capabilities	Nested-loops, merge-scan and Hash-join
	Operators pipelining support	Yes
	CPU resources	One 700-1500 MHz CPU
	Sorting/Hashing buffer size	10,000 tuples
	I/O Speed per node	5-20Mbytes
Dataset	Size of relations	1-400,000 tuples
	Number of attributes per relation	20 attributes
	Number of partitions per relation	1-8
	Number of mirrors per partition	1-3
	Indices per partition per node	3 single-attribute indices
Workload	Joins per query	0 - 7
	Partitions per relation	1 - 8

The data-set used in the experiment was synthetically constructed. We constructed the metadata of a large schema consisting of 10,000 relations. There was no need to actually build the data since our experiments measured the performance of query optimization, not that of query execution. Each relation had 200,000 tuples on average and was horizontally range-partitioned in 1-8 disjoint partitions that were stored in possibly different nodes in such a way that each partition had 0-3 mirrors. The nodes were allowed to create 3 local indices per locally stored partition.

In order for the nodes to be aware of all currently active RFBs, we used a directory service using a publish-subscribe mechanism, since these are widely used in existing agent-based e-commerce platforms [13] and have good scalability characteristics. This type of architecture is typical for small e-commerce negotiation frameworks [24].

Query optimization algorithms. In each experiment, we studied the execution plans produced by the following four algorithms: SystemR, IDP(2,5), Mariposa, and Query Trading. More specifically:

SystemR. The SystemR algorithm [17] was examined as it produces optimal execution plans. However, it is not a viable solution in the large autonomous and distributed environments that we consider for two reasons. The first one is that it cannot cope with the complexity of the optimization search space. The second one is that it requires cost estimations from remote nodes. Not only this makes the notes not autonomous, but for a query with n joins, it will take n rounds of message exchanges to find the required information. In each round, the remote nodes will have to find the cost of every feasible k-way join (k=1..N), which quickly leads to a network bottleneck for even very small numbers of n.

We implemented SystemR so that we have a solid base for comparing the quality of the plans produced by the rest algorithms. Our implementation assumed that nodes running the algorithm had exact knowledge of the state of the whole network. This made possible running the algorithm without the bottleneck of network throughput, which would normally dominate its execution time.

IDP-M(2,5). Recently, a heuristic extension of the SystemR algorithm, the IDP-M(k,m), was proposed for use in distributed environments [2]. Therefore, we choose to include an instance of this algorithm in our study. Given an n-way join query, it works like this [2]: First, it enumerates all feasible k-way joins, i.e., all feasible joins that contain less than or equal to k base tables and finds their costs, just like SystemR does. Then, it chooses the best m subplans out of all the subplans for these k-way joins and purges all others. Finally, it continues the optimization procedure by examining the rest $n - k$ joins in a similar to SystemR way. The IDP algorithm is not suitable for autonomous environment as it shares the problems of SystemR mentioned above. For instance, for an n-way star join query ($k \ll n$), where each relation has p horizontal partitions ($p \geq 2$) each with M mirrors ($M \geq 2$), at least $O(M2^p mn^k)$ plans [2] would have to be transmitted through the network.
Our implementation assume that nodes running the algorithm have exact knowledge of the state of the whole network and thus avoids the bottleneck of network throughput, which similar to SystemR, would normally dominate its execution time [2].

Mariposa. The Mariposa query optimization algorithm [25,26] is a two-step algorithm that considers conventional optimization factors (such as join orders) separately from distributed system factors (such as data layout and execution location). First, it uses information that it keeps locally about various aspects of the data to construct a locally optimal plan by running a local optimizer over the query, disregarding the physical distribution of the base relations and fixing such items as join order and the application of join and restriction operators. It then uses network yellow-pages information to parallelize the query operators, and a bidding protocol to select the execution sites, all in a single interaction with the remote nodes. The degree of parallelism is statistically determined by the system administrator before query execution and is independent of the available distributed resources.
The Mariposa System was initially designed to cover a large range of different requirements. In this paper, we implemented the Mariposa algorithm as described in [27] with the difference that in the second phase of the algorithm, the optimization goal was set to minimize the total execution time of the query, which is the task of interest in our experiments. We included Mariposa in our study as it is one of the fastest-running known algorithm for distributed query optimization. Nevertheless, it is not suitable for true autonomous environments as it requires information from nodes that harm their autonomy, such as their cost functions, their join capabilities, and information on the data and indices they have.

Query trading. We instantiated the Query Trading Algorithm using the following properties:
- For the Negotiation protocol, we choose the bidding protocol as the expected number of offered bids for each RFB was not large enough for an auction protocol to be beneficiary. We ranked each offer based only on the time required to return the complete query answer. In this way, our optimization algorithm produced plans that had the minimum execution time, reflecting the traditional optimization task.
- We used a plain cooperative strategy. Thus nodes replied to RFBs with offers matching exactly their available resources. The seller strategy module had a small buffer that held the last 1,000 accepted bids. These bids were collected from past

biddings that the node had participated in. Using the contents of this buffer, nodes estimated the most probable value of the offer that will win a bidding and never made offers with value more than 20% of this estimation. This strategy helped to reduce the number of exchanged messages.
- In the Buyer query plan generator we used a traditional answering queries using views dynamic programming algorithm. However, to decrease its complexity we also tested the plan generator with the IDP-M(2,5) algorithm.

Simulated scenarios. We initially run some experiments to assert the scalability of our algorithm in terms of network size. As was expected, the performance of our algorithm was not dependent on the total number of network nodes but on (a) the number of nodes which replied to RFBs and (b) the complexity of the queries. Thus we ended up running three sets of experiments: In the first set, the workload consisted of star-join queries with a varying number of 0-7 joins. The relations referenced in the joins had no mirrors and only one partition. This workload was used to test the behavior of the optimization algorithms as the complexity of queries increased. In the second set of experiments, we considered 3-way-join star-queries that referenced relations without mirrors but with a varying number of 1-8 horizontal partitions. This test measured the behavior of the algorithms as relations' data were split and stored (data spreading) in different nodes. Finally, in the last set of experiments we considered 3-way-join star-queries that referenced relations with three partitions and a varying number of mirrors (1-3). This experiment measured the behavior of the algorithms in the presence of redundancy.

We run each experiment five times and measured the average execution time of the algorithms and the average plan cost of the queries, i.e., the time in seconds required to execute the produced queries as this was estimated by the algorithms. We should note that the execution times of SystemR and IDP are not directly comparable to those of other algorithms, as they do not include the cost of network message exchanges. The numbers presented for them are essentially for a non-autonomous environment with a centralized node for query optimization.

4.2 The Results

Number of joins. Figures 4(a) and 4(b) present the results of the first set of tests. The first figure presents the average execution cost of the plans produced by the SystemR, IDP(2,5), Mariposa and the two instances of the QT algorithm. It is surprising to see that even for such simple distributed data-sets (no mirrors, no partitions) all algorithms (except SystemR) fail to find the optimal plan (the deviation is in average 5% for IDP, 8% for QT and 20% for Mariposa)). As expected, IDP(2,5) algorithm deviates from the optimal plan when the number of joins is more than two. The Mariposa algorithm makes the largest error producing plans that require on average 20% more time than those produced by SystemR. This is because in its first phase of the optimization procedure, Mariposa is not aware of network costs and delays and thus, fails to find the best joins order for the base tables. The rest of the algorithms usually selected the proper joins order, taking into account that the delay caused by slow data sources may be masked if the joins related with these sources are executed last in the subplans pipeline. The

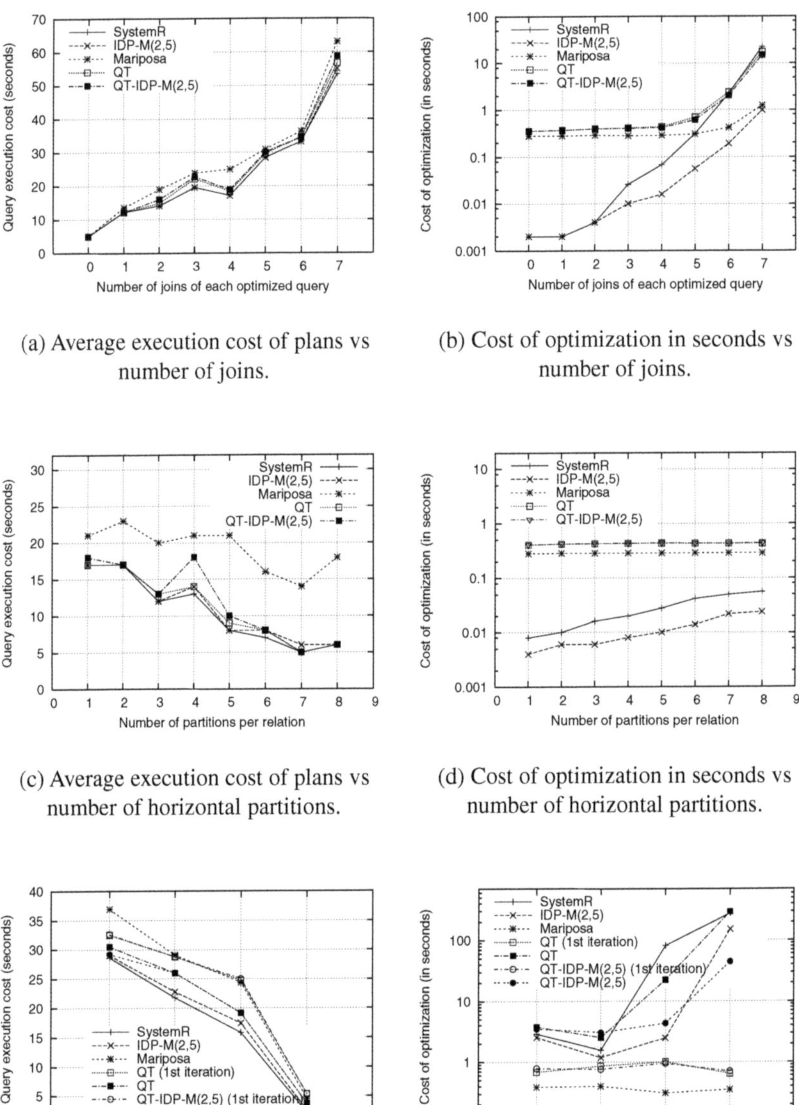

(a) Average execution cost of plans vs number of joins.

(b) Cost of optimization in seconds vs number of joins.

(c) Average execution cost of plans vs number of horizontal partitions.

(d) Cost of optimization in seconds vs number of horizontal partitions.

(e) Average execution cost of plans vs number of mirrors per partition.

(f) Cost of optimization in seconds vs number of mirrors per partition.

Fig. 4. Performance of various distributed query optimization algorithms.

QT-IDP-M algorithm produces plans that are only marginally inferior to those of plain QT.

The execution time (Figure 4(b)) of all algorithms depends exponentially on the number of joins. The QT, QT-IDP and Mariposa algorithms have a start-up cost of a single round of message exchanges (approx. 400ms and 280ms respectively) caused by the bidding procedure. The QT and QT-IDP algorithms never had to run more than one round of bids.

Data partitioning. Figures 4(c) and 4(d) summarize the results of the second set of experiments, which evaluate the algorithm as the partitioning and spreading of information varied. The first figure shows that the QT algorithm is little affected by the level of data spreading and partitioning. This was expected since the bidding procedure completely masks data spreading. The performance of the Mariposa algorithm is substantially affected by the level of data partitioning, producing plans that are up to three times slower than those of SystemR. This is because as the number of partitions increase, the chances that some remote partitions may have some useful remote indices (which are disregarded by Mariposa as each node has different indices) are increased. Moreover, Mariposa does not properly splits the join operators among the different horizontal partitions and nodes, as operators splitting is statically determined by the database administrator and not by the Mariposa algorithm itself.

The execution times of all algorithms depend on the number of relations partitions, as they all try to find the optimal join and unions orders to minimize the execution cost. Figure 4(d) shows the execution time of the QT, QT-IDP-M and Mariposa algorithm constant due to the logarithmic scale and the fact that the cost of the single bid round was much larger than that of the rest costs. Similarly to the previous set of experiments, the QT and QT-IDP-M algorithms run on average a single round of bids.

Data mirroring. Figures 4(e) and 4(f) summarize the results of the last set of experiments, where the level of data mirroring is varied. Data mirroring substantially increases the complexity of all algorithms as they have to horizontally split table-scan, join and union operators and select the nodes which allow for the best parallelization of these operators. The QT algorithm is additionally affected by data mirroring, as it has to run multiple rounds of bid procedures. On average, three rounds per query were run. For comparison reasons we captured the execution time and plan produced both at the end of the first iteration and at the end of the final one.

Figures 4(e) and 4(f) shows that although the first iteration of the QT algorithm completed in less than a second, the plans produced were on average the worse ones. Mariposa completed the optimization in the shortest possible time (less that 0.5s) and produced plans that were usually better than those produced in the first iteration of QT and QT-IDP, but worst than those produced in their last iteration. Finally, the best plans were produced by SystemR and IDP-M(2,5).

As far as the optimization cost is concerned, the SystemR, QT, and IDP-M(2,5) algorithms were the slowest ones. The QT-IDP-M algorithm was substantially faster than QT and yet, produced plans that were close to those produced by the latter. Finally,

Mariposa was the fastest of all algorithms but produced plans that were on average up to 60% slower than those of SystemR.

5 Discussion

In large database federations, the optimization procedure must be distributed, i.e., all (remote) nodes must contribute to the optimization process. This ensures that the search space is efficiently divided to many nodes. The QT algorithm cleverly distributes the optimization process in many remote nodes by asking candidate sellers to calculate the cost of any possible sub-queries that might be useful for the construction of the global plan. Network flooding is avoided using standard e-commerce techniques. For instance, in our experiments, the strategy module disallowed bids that had (estimated) few chances of being won. The degree of parallelism of the produced distributed execution plans is not statically specified, like for instance in Mariposa, but is automatically found by the DP algorithm run at the buyer query plan generator. Nevertheless, the results of the experiments indicated that the bidding procedure may severely limit the number of possible combinations.

The SystemR and IDP-M centralized algorithms attempt to find the best execution plan for a query by examining several different solutions. However, the results of the experiments (even when not counting network costs) show that the search space is too large. Thus, SystemR and IDP-M are inappropriate for optimizing (at run-time) queries in large networks of autonomous nodes when relations are mirrored and partitioned. For these environments, the Mariposa algorithm should be used for queries with small execution times, and the QT and QT-IDP algorithms should be selected when the optimized queries are expected to have long execution times.

The Mariposa algorithm first builds the execution plan, disregarding the physical distribution of base relations and then selects the nodes where the plan will be executed using a greedy approach. Working this way, Mariposa and more generally any other two-step algorithm that treats network interconnection delays and data location as second-class citizens produce plans that exhibit unnecessarily high communication costs [3] and are arbitrarily far from the desired optimum [25]. Furthermore, they violate the autonomy of remote nodes as they require all nodes to follow a common cost model and ask remote nodes to expose information on their internal state. Finally they cannot take advantage of any materialized views or advanced access methods that may exist in remote nodes.

The QT algorithm is the only one of the four algorithms examined that truly respects the autonomy and privacy of remote nodes and. It treats them as true black boxes and runs without any information (or assumption) on them, apart from that implied by their bids.

6 Conclusions and Future Work

We discussed the parameters affecting a framework for trading queries and their answers, showed how we can use such a framework to build a WAN distributed query optimizer, and thoroughly examined its performance characteristics.

References

1. Navas, J.C., Wynblatt, M.: The Network is the Database: Data Management for Highly Distributed Systems. In: Proceedings of ACM SIGMOD'01 Conference. (2001)
2. Deshpande, A., Hellerstein, J.M.: Decoupled query optimization for federated database systems. In: Proc. of 18th. ICDE, San Jose, CA. (2002) 716–727
3. Kossmann, D.: The state of the art in distributed query processing. ACM Computing Surveys (2000)
4. Stonebraker, M., Aoki, P.M., Litwin, W., Pfeller, A., Sah, A., Sidell, J., Staelin, C., Yu, A.: Mariposa: A wide-area distributed database system. VLDB Journal **5** (1996) 48–63
5. Bichler, M., Kaukal, M., Segev, A.: Multi-attribute auctions for electronic procurement. In: Proc. of the 1st IBM IAC Workshop on Internet Based Negotiation Technologies, Yorktown Heights, NY, March 18-19. (1999)
6. Collins, J., Tsvetovat, M., Sundareswara, R., van Tonder, J., Gini, M.L., Mobasher, B.: Evaluating risk: Flexibility and feasibility in multi-agent contracting. In: Proc. of the 3rd Annual Conf. on Autonomous Agents , Seattle, WA, USA. (1999)
7. Parunak, H.V.D.: Manufacturing experience with the contract net. Distributed Artificial Intelligence, Michael N. Huhns (editor), Research Notes in Artificial Intelligence, chapter 10, pages 285-310. Pitman (1987)
8. Sandholm, T.: Algorithm for optimal winner determination in combinatorial auctions. Artificial Intelligence **135** (2002) 1–54
9. Su, S.Y., Huang, C., Hammer, J., Huang, Y., Li, H., Wang, L., Liu, Y., Pluempitiwiriyawej, C., Lee, M., Lam, H.: An internet-based negotiation server for e-commerce. VLDB Journal **10** (2001) 72–90
10. Smith, R.G.: The contract net protocol: High-level communication and control in a distributed problem solver. IEEE Transactions on Computers **29** (1980) 1104–1113
11. Pentaris, F., Ioannidis, Y.: Distributed query optimization by query trading. Unpublished manuscript available at `http://www.di.uoa.gr/~frank/cqp-full.pdf` (2003)
12. Conitzer, V., Sandholm, T.: Complexity results about nash equilibria. Technical report CMU-CS-02-135, `http://www-2.cs.cmu.edu/~sandholm/Nash_complexity.pdf` (2002)
13. Ogston, E., Vassiliadis, S.: A Peer-to-Peer Agent Auction. In: Proc. of AAMAS'02, Bologna, Italy. (2002)
14. Kagel, J.H.: Auctions: A Survey of Experimental Research. The Handbook of Experimental Economics, edited by John E. Kagel and Alvin E. Roth, Princeton: Princeton University Press (1995)
15. Kraus, S.: Strategic Negotiation in Multiagent Environments (Intelligent Robotics and Autonomous Agents). The MIT Press (2001)
16. Rosenchein, J.S., Zlotkin, G.: Rules of Encounter : designing conventions for automated negotiation among computers. The MIT Press series in artificial intelligence (1994)
17. Selinger, P.G., Astrahan, M.M., Chamberlin, D.D., Lorie, R.A., Price, T.G.: Access path selection in a relational database management system. In: Proc. of 1979 ACM SIGMOD, ACM (1979) 22–34
18. Halevy, A.Y.: Answering queries using views: A survey. VLDB Journal **10** (2001) 270–294
19. Zaharioudakis, M., Cochrane, R., Lapis, G., Pirahesh, H., Urata, M.: Answering complex sql queries using automatic summary tables. In: Proceedings of ACM SIGMOD'00 Conference, pages 105-116. (2000)
20. Pottinger, R., Levy, A.: A scalable alogirthm for answering queries using views. In: Proc. of the 26th VLDB Conference, Cairo, Egypt. (2000)
21. Levy, A.Y., Rajaraman, A., Ordille, J.J.: Querying heterogeneous information sources using source descriptions. In: Proc. of 22th Int. Conf. on VLDB. (1996) 251–262

22. Qian, X.: Query folding. In: Proc. of ICDE, New Orleans, LA. (1996) 48–55
23. Vickrey, W.: Counterspeculation, auctions, and competitive sealed tenders. Journal of Finance **16** (1961) 8–37
24. Buyya, R., Abramson, D., Giddy, J., Stockinger, H.: Economic models for resource management and scheduling in grid computing. In: Proc. of Commercial Applications for High-Performance Computing Conference, SPIE International Symposium on The Convergence of Information Technologies and Communications (ITCom 2001), August 20-24, 2001, Denver, Colorado. (2001)
25. Papadimitriou, C.H., Yannakakis, M.: Multiobjective query optimization. In: Proc. of the 20th ACM SIGACT-SIGMOD-SIGART Symposium on PODS, May 21-23, 2001, Santa Barbara, CA, USA, ACM, ACM (2001)
26. Stonebraker, M., Aoki, P.M., Devine, R., Litwin, W., Olson, M.A.: Mariposa: A new architecture for distributed data. In: ICDE. (1994) 54–65
27. Mariposa: Mariposa distributed database management systems, User's Manual. Available at `http://s2k-ftp.cs.berkeley.edu:8000/mariposa/src/alpha-1/mariposa-manual.pdf` (2002)

Sketch-Based Multi-query Processing over Data Streams

Alin Dobra[1], Minos Garofalakis[2], Johannes Gehrke[3], and Rajeev Rastogi[2]

[1] University of Florida, Gainesville FL, USA
adobra@cise.ufl.edu
[2] Bell Laboratories, Lucent Technologies, Murray Hill NJ, USA
{minos,rastogi}@bell-labs.com
[3] Cornell University, Ithaca NY, USA
johannes@cs.cornell.edu

Abstract. Recent years have witnessed an increasing interest in designing algorithms for querying and analyzing streaming data (i.e., data that is seen only once in a fixed order) with only limited memory. Providing (perhaps approximate) answers to queries over such continuous data streams is a crucial requirement for many application environments; examples include large telecom and IP network installations where performance data from different parts of the network needs to be continuously collected and analyzed.

Randomized techniques, based on computing small "sketch" synopses for each stream, have recently been shown to be a very effective tool for approximating the result of a single SQL query over streaming data tuples. In this paper, we investigate the problems arising when data-stream sketches are used to process *multiple* such queries concurrently. We demonstrate that, in the presence of multiple query expressions, intelligently *sharing sketches* among concurrent query evaluations can result in substantial improvements in the utilization of the available sketching space and the quality of the resulting approximation error guarantees. We provide necessary and sufficient conditions for multi-query sketch sharing that guarantee the correctness of the result-estimation process. We also prove that optimal sketch sharing typically gives rise to $\mathcal{NP}$-hard questions, and we propose novel heuristic algorithms for finding good sketch-sharing configurations in practice. Results from our experimental study with realistic workloads verify the effectiveness of our approach, clearly demonstrating the benefits of our sketch-sharing methodology.

1 Introduction

Traditional Database Management Systems (DBMS) software is built on the concept of *persistent* data sets, that are stored reliably in stable storage and queried several times throughout their lifetime. For several emerging application domains, however, data arrives and needs to be processed continuously, without the benefit of several passes over a static, persistent data image. Such *continuous data streams* arise naturally, for example, in the network installations of large telecom and Internet service providers where detailed usage information (Call-Detail-Records, SNMP/RMON packet-flow data, etc.) from different parts of the underlying network needs to be continuously collected and analyzed

E. Bertino et al. (Eds.): EDBT 2004, LNCS 2992, pp. 551–568, 2004.
© Springer-Verlag Berlin Heidelberg 2004

for interesting trends. Other applications that generate rapid-rate and massive volumes of stream data include retail-chain transaction processing, ATM and credit card operations, financial tickers, Web-server activity logging, and so on. In most such applications, the data stream is actually accumulated and archived in the DBMS of a (perhaps, off-site) data warehouse, often making access to the archived data prohibitively expensive. Further, the ability to make decisions and infer interesting patterns *on-line* (i.e., as the data stream arrives) is crucial for several mission-critical tasks that can have significant dollar value for a large corporation (e.g., telecom fraud detection). As a result, there has been increasing interest in designing data-processing algorithms that work over continuous data streams, i.e., algorithms that provide results to user queries while looking at the relevant data items *only once and in a fixed order* (determined by the stream-arrival pattern).

Given the large diversity of users and/or applications that a generic query-processing environment typically needs to support, it is evident that any realistic stream-query processor must be capable of effectively handling *multiple* standing queries over a collection of input data streams. Given a collection of queries to be processed over incoming streams, two key effectiveness parameters are (1) the amount of *memory* made available to the on-line algorithm, and (2) the *per-item processing time* required by the query processor. Memory, in particular, constitutes an important constraint on the design of stream processing algorithms since, in a typical streaming environment, only limited memory resources are made available to each of the standing queries.

Prior Work. The recent surge of interest in data-stream computation has led to several (theoretical and practical) studies proposing novel one-pass algorithms with limited memory requirements for different problems; examples include: quantile and order-statistics computation [1]; distinct-element counting [2,3]; frequent itemset counting [4]; estimating frequency moments, join sizes, and difference norms [5,6,7]; and computing one- or multi-dimensional histograms or Haar wavelet decompositions [8,9]. All these papers rely on an approximate query-processing model, typically based on an appropriate underlying synopsis data structure. The synopses of choice for a number of the above-cited papers are based on the key idea of *pseudo-random sketches* which, essentially, can be thought of as simple, randomized linear projections of the underlying data vector(s) [10]. In fact, in our recent work [11], we have demonstrated the utility of sketch synopses in computing provably-accurate approximate answers for a *single* SQL query comprising (possibly) multiple join operators.

None of these earlier research efforts has addressed the more general problem of effectively providing accurate approximate answers to *multiple* SQL queries over a collection of input streams. Of course, the problem of *multi-query optimization* (that is, optimizing multiple queries for concurrent execution in a conventional DBMS) has been around for some time, and several techniques for extending conventional query optimizers to deal with multiple queries have been proposed [12]. The cornerstone of all these techniques is the discovery of common query sub-expressions whose evaluation can be shared among the query-execution plans produced.

Our Contributions. In this paper, we tackle the problem of efficiently processing multiple (possibly, multi-join) concurrent aggregate SQL queries over a collection of input data streams. Similar to earlier work on data streaming [5,11], our approach is based on computing small, pseudo-random sketch synopses of the data. We demonstrate that, in the presence of multiple query expressions, intelligently *sharing sketches* among concurrent (approximate) query evaluations can result in substantial improvements in the utilization of the available sketching space and the quality of the resulting approximation error guarantees. We provide necessary and sufficient conditions for multi-query sketch sharing that guarantee the correctness of the resulting sketch-based estimators. We also attack the difficult optimization problem of determining sketch-sharing configurations that are optimal (e.g., under a certain error metric for a given amount of space). We prove that optimal sketch sharing typically gives rise to $\mathcal{NP}$-hard questions, and we propose novel heuristic algorithms for finding effective sketch-sharing configurations in practice. More concretely, the key contributions of our work can be summarized as follows.

• **Multi-Query Sketch Sharing: Concepts and Conditions.** We formally introduce the concept of *sketch sharing* for efficient, approximate multi-query stream processing. Briefly, the basic idea is to share sketch computation and sketching space across several queries in the workload that can effectively use the same sketches over (a subset of) their input streams. Of course, since sketches and sketch-based estimators are probabilistic in nature, we also need to ensure that this sharing does not degrade the correctness and accuracy of our estimates by causing desirable estimator properties (e.g., unbiasedness) to be lost. Thus, we present necessary and sufficient conditions (based on the resulting multi-join graph) that fully characterize such "correct" sketch-sharing configurations for a given query workload.

• **Novel Sketch-Sharing Optimization Problems and Algorithms.** Given that multiple correct sketch-sharing configurations can exist for a given stream-query workload, our processor should be able to identify configurations that are optimal or near-optimal; for example, under a certain (aggregate) error metric for the workload and for a given amount of sketching space. We formulate these sketch-sharing optimization problems for different metrics of interest, and propose novel algorithmic solutions for the two key sub-problems involved, namely: (1) *Space Allocation:* Determine the best amount of space to be given to each sketch for a fixed sketch-sharing configuration; and, (2) *Join Coalescing:* Determine an optimal sketch-sharing plan by deciding which joins in the workload will share sketches. We prove that these optimization problems (under different error metrics) are typically $\mathcal{NP}$-hard; thus, we design heuristic approximation algorithms (sometimes with guaranteed bounds on the quality of the approximation) for finding good sketch-sharing configurations in practice.

• **Implementation Results Validating our Sketch-Sharing Techniques.** We present the results from an empirical study of our sketch-sharing schemes with several synthetic data sets and realistic, multi-query workloads. Our results clearly demonstrate the benefits of effective sketch-sharing, showing that very significant improvements in answer quality are possible compared to a naive, no-sharing approach. Specifically, our experiments indicate that sketch sharing can boost accuracy of query answers by factors ranging from 2 to 4 for a wide range of multi-query workloads.

Due to space constraints, the proofs of our analytical results and several details have been omitted; the complete discussion can be found in the full version of this paper [13].

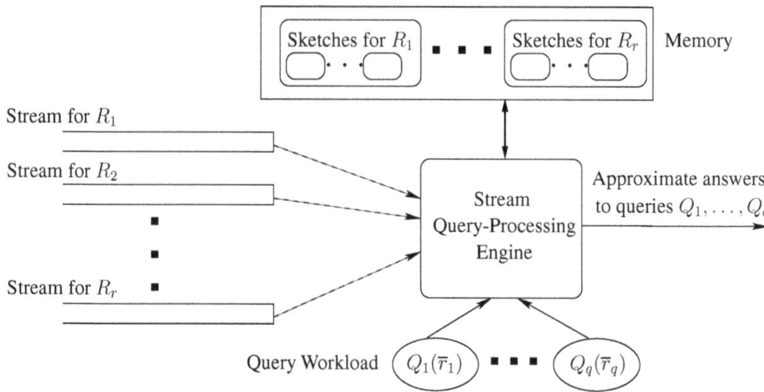

Fig. 1. Stream Multi-Query Processing Architecture.

2 Streams and Random Sketches

2.1 Stream Data-Processing Model

We now briefly describe the key elements of our generic architecture for multi-query processing over continuous data streams (depicted in Fig, 1); similar architectures (for the single-query setting) have been described elsewhere (e.g., [11,8]). Consider a workload $\mathcal{Q} = \{Q_1, \ldots, Q_q\}$ comprising a collection of (possibly) complex SQL queries $Q_1, \ldots, Q_q$ over a set of relations $R_1, \ldots, R_r$ (of course, each query typically references a subset of the relations/attributes in the input). Also, let $|R_i|$ denote the total number of tuples in R_i. In contrast to conventional DBMS query processors, our stream query-processing engine is allowed to see the data tuples in $R_1, \ldots, R_r$ *only once* and in fixed order as they are streaming in from their respective source(s). Backtracking over the data stream and explicit access to past data tuples are impossible. Further, the order of tuple arrival for each relation R_i is arbitrary and duplicate tuples can occur anywhere over the duration of the R_i stream. (Our techniques can also readily handle tuple *deletions* in the streams.)

Our stream query-processing engine is also allowed a certain amount of memory, typically significantly smaller than the total size of the data. This memory is used to maintain a set of concise *synopses* for each data stream R_i. The key constraints imposed on such synopses are that: (1) they are much smaller than the total number of tuples in R_i (e.g., their size is logarithmic or polylogarithmic in $|R_i|$); and, (2) they can be computed quickly, in a single pass over the data tuples in R_i in the (arbitrary) order of their arrival. At any point in time, our query-processing algorithms can combine the maintained collection of synopses to produce approximate answers to all queries in $\mathcal{Q}$.

2.2 Approximating Single-Query Answers with Pseudo-Random Sketches

The Basic Technique: Binary-Join Size Tracking [5,6]. Consider a simple stream-processing scenario where the goal is to estimate the size of a binary join of two streams

R_1 and R_2 on attributes $R_1.A_1$ and $R_2.A_2$, respectively. That is, we seek to approximate the result of query $Q = \texttt{COUNT}(R_1 \bowtie_{R_1.A_1=R_2.A_2} R_2)$ as the tuples of R_1 and R_2 are streaming in. Let $\texttt{dom}(A)$ denote the domain of an attribute A [1] and $f_R(i)$ be the frequency of attribute value i in $R.A$. (Note that, by the definition of the equi-join operator, the two join attributes have identical value domains, i.e., $\texttt{dom}(A_1) = \texttt{dom}(A_2)$.) Thus, we want to produce an estimate for the expression $Q = \sum_{i \in \texttt{dom}(A_1)} f_{R_1}(i) f_{R_2}(i)$. Clearly, estimating this join size exactly requires at least $\Omega(|\texttt{dom}(A_1)|)$ space, making an exact solution impractical for a data-stream setting. In their seminal work, Alon et al. [5,6] propose a randomized technique that can offer strong probabilistic guarantees on the quality of the resulting join-size estimate while using space that can be significantly smaller than $|\texttt{dom}(A_1)|$.

Briefly, the basic idea of their scheme is to define a random variable X_Q that can be easily computed over the streaming values of $R_1.A_1$ and $R_2.A_2$, such that (1) X_Q is an *unbiased* (i.e., correct on expectation) estimator for the target join size, so that $E[X_Q] = Q$; and, (2) X_Q's variance ($\text{Var}(X_Q)$) can be appropriately upper-bounded to allow for probabilistic guarantees on the quality of the Q estimate. This random variable X_Q is constructed on-line from the two data streams as follows:

- Select a family of *four-wise independent binary random variables* $\{\xi_i : i = 1, \ldots, |\texttt{dom}(A_1)|\}$, where each $\xi_i \in \{-1, +1\}$ and $P[\xi_i = +1] = P[\xi_i = -1] = 1/2$ (i.e., $E[\xi_i] = 0$). Informally, the four-wise independence condition means that for any 4-tuple of ξ_i variables and for any 4-tuple of $\{-1, +1\}$ values, the probability that the values of the variables coincide with those in the $\{-1, +1\}$ 4-tuple is exactly $1/16$ (the product of the equality probabilities for each individual ξ_i). The crucial point here is that, by employing known tools (e.g., orthogonal arrays) for the explicit construction of small sample spaces supporting four-wise independence, such families can be efficiently constructed on-line using only $O(\log |\texttt{dom}(A_1)|)$ space [6].
- Define $X_Q = X_1 \cdot X_2$, where $X_k = \sum_{i \in \texttt{dom}(A_1)} f_{R_k}(i)\xi_i$, for $k = 1, 2$. Quantities X_1 and X_2 are called the *atomic sketches* of relations R_1 and R_2, respectively. Note that each X_k is simply a randomized linear projection (inner product) of the frequency vector of $R_k.A_k$ with the vector of ξ_i's that can be efficiently generated from the streaming values of A_k as follows: Start with $X_k = 0$ and simply add ξ_i to X_k whenever the ith value of A_k is observed in the stream.

The quality of the estimation guarantees can be improved using a standard *boosting technique* that maintains several independent identically-distributed (iid) instantiations of the above process, and uses averaging and median-selection operators over the X_Q estimates to boost accuracy and probabilistic confidence [6]. (Independent instances can be constructed by simply selecting independent random seeds for generating the families of four-wise independent ξ_i's for each instance.) As above, we use the term *atomic sketch* to describe each randomized linear projection computed over a data stream. Letting SJ_k ($k = 1, 2$) denote the self-join size of $R_k.A_k$ (i.e., $\text{SJ}_k = \sum_{i \in \texttt{dom}(A_k)} f_{R_k}(i)^2$),

[1] Without loss of generality, we assume that each attribute domain $\texttt{dom}(A)$ is indexed by the set of integers $\{1, \cdots, |\texttt{dom}(A)|\}$, where $|\texttt{dom}(A)|$ denotes the size of the domain.

the following theorem [5] shows how sketching can be applied for estimating binary-join sizes in limited space. (By standard Chernoff bounds [14], using median-selection over $O(\log(1/\delta))$ of the averages computed in Theorem 1 allows the confidence in the estimate to be boosted to $1-\delta$, for any pre-specified $\delta < 1$.)

Theorem 1 ([5]). Let the atomic sketches X_1 and X_2 be as defined above. Then $E[X_Q] = E[X_1X_2] = Q$ and $\text{Var}(X_Q) \leq 2 \cdot \text{SJ}_1 \cdot \text{SJ}_2$. Thus, averaging the X_Q estimates over $O(\frac{\text{SJ}_1\text{SJ}_2}{Q^2\epsilon^2})$ iid instantiations of the basic scheme, guarantees an estimate that lies within a relative error of ϵ from Q with constant probability. □

This theoretical result suggests that the sketching technique is an effective estimation tool only for joins with reasonably high cardinality (with respect to the product of the individual self-join sizes); thus, it may perform poorly for very selective, low-cardinality joins. Note, however, that the strong lower bounds shown by Alon et al. [5] indicate that *any* approximate query processing technique is doomed to perform poorly (i.e., use large amounts of memory) for such low-cardinality joins. Thus, it appears that the only effective way to deal with such very selective joins is through exact computation.

Single Multi-Join Query Answering [11]. In our recent work [11], we have extended sketch-based techniques to approximate the result of a single *multi-join* aggregate SQL query over a collection of streams.[2] More specifically, our work in [11] focuses on approximating a multi-join stream query Q of the form: "`SELECT COUNT FROM` $R_1, R_2, \ldots, R_r$ `WHERE` $\mathcal{E}$", where $\mathcal{E}$ represents the conjunction of of n equi-join constraints of the form $R_i.A_j = R_k.A_l$ ($R_i.A_j$ denotes the jth attribute of relation R_i). The extension to other aggregate functions, e.g., `SUM`, is fairly straightforward [11]; furthermore, note that dealing with single-relation selections is similarly straightforward (simply filter out the tuples that fail the selection predicate from the relational stream).

Our development in [11] also assumes that each attribute $R_i.A_j$ appears in $\mathcal{E}$ at most once; this requirement can be easily achieved by simply renaming repeating attributes in the query. In what follows, we describe the key ideas and results from [11] based on the join-graph model of the input query Q, since this will allow for a smoother transition to the multi-query case (Section 3).

Given stream query Q, we define the *join graph* of Q (denoted by $\mathcal{J}(Q)$), as follows. There is a distinct vertex v in $\mathcal{J}(Q)$ for each stream R_i referenced in Q (we use $R(v)$ to denote the relation associated with vertex v). For each equality constraint $R_i.A_j = R_k.A_l$ in $\mathcal{E}$, we add a distinct undirected edge $e = <v, w>$ to $\mathcal{J}(Q)$, where $R(v) = R_i$ and $R(w) = R_k$; we also label this edge with the triple $< R_i.A_j, R_k.A_l, Q >$ that specifies the attributes in the corresponding equality constraint and the enclosing query Q (the query label is used in the multi-query setting). Given an edge $e = <v, w>$ with label $< R_i.A_j, R_k.A_l, Q >$, the three components of e's label triple can be obtained as $A_v(e)$, $A_w(e)$ and $Q(e)$. (Clearly, by the definition of equi-joins, $\texttt{dom}(A_v(e)) = \texttt{dom}(A_w(e))$.) Note that there may be multiple edges between a pair of vertices in the join graph, but each edge has its own distinct label triple. Finally, for a vertex v in $\mathcal{J}(Q)$, we denote

[2] [11] also describes a *sketch-partitioning* technique for improving the quality of basic sketching estimates; this technique is essentially orthogonal to the multi-query problems considered in this paper, so we do not discuss it further.

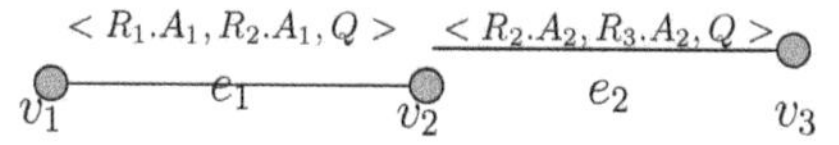

$< R_1.A_1, R_2.A_1, Q >$ $< R_2.A_2, R_3.A_2, Q >$

v_1 e_1 v_2 e_2 v_3

Fig. 2. Example Query Join Graph.

the attributes of $R(v)$ that appear in the input query (or, queries) as $\mathcal{A}(v)$; thus, $\mathcal{A}(v) = \{A_v(e) : \text{edge } e \text{ is incident on } v\}$.

The result of Q is the number of tuples in the cross-product of $R_1, \ldots, R_r$ that satisfy the equality constraints in $\mathcal{E}$ over the join attributes. Similar to the basic sketching method [5,6], our algorithm [11] constructs an unbiased, bounded-variance probabilistic estimate X_Q for Q using atomic sketches built on the vertices of the join graph $\mathcal{J}(Q)$. More specifically, for each edge $e =< v, w >$ in $\mathcal{J}(Q)$, our algorithm defines a family of four-wise independent random variables $\xi^e = \{\xi_i^e : i = 1, \ldots, |\mathtt{dom}(A_v(e))|\}$, where each $\xi_i^e \in \{-1, +1\}$. The key here is that the equi-join attribute pair $A_v(e)$, $A_w(e)$ associated with edge e shares the same ξ family; on the other hand, distinct edges of $\mathcal{J}(Q)$ use *independently-generated* ξ families (using mutually independent random seeds). The atomic sketch X_v for each vertex v in $\mathcal{J}(Q)$ is built as follows. Let $e_1, \ldots, e_k$ be the edges incident on v and, for $i_1 \in \mathtt{dom}(A_v(e_1)), \ldots, i_k \in \mathtt{dom}(A_v(e_k))$, let $f_v(i_1, \ldots, i_k)$ denote the number of tuples in $R(v)$ that match values $i_1, \ldots, i_k$ in their join attributes. More formally, $f_v(i_1, \ldots, i_k)$ is the number of tuples $t \in R(v)$ such that $t[A_v(e_j)] = i_j$, for $1 \leq j \leq k$ ($t[Aj]$ denotes the value of attribute A in tuple t). Then, the atomic sketch at v is $X_v = \sum_{i_1 \in \mathtt{dom}(A_v(e_1))} \cdots \sum_{i_k \in \mathtt{dom}(A_v(e_k))} f_v(i_1, \ldots, i_k) \prod_{j=1}^{k} \xi_{i_j}^{e_j}$. Finally, the estimate for Q is defined as $X_Q = \prod_v X_v$ (that is, the product of the atomic sketches for all vertices in $\mathcal{J}(Q)$). Note that each atomic sketch X_v is again a randomized linear projection that can be efficiently computed as tuples of $R(v)$ are streaming in; more specifically, X_v is initialized to 0 and, for each tuple t in the $R(v)$ stream, the quantity $\prod_{j=1}^{k} \xi_{t[A_v(e_j)]}^{e_j} \in \{-1, +1\}$ is added to X_v.

Example 1. Consider query $Q =$ SELECT COUNT FROM R_1, R_2, R_3 WHERE $R_1.A_1 = R_2.A_1$ AND $R_2.A_2 = R_3.A_2$. The join graph $\mathcal{J}(Q)$ is depicted in Figure 2, with vertices v_1, v_2, and v_3 corresponding to streams R_1, R_2, and R_3, respectively. Similarly, edges e_1 and e_2 correspond to the equi-join constraints $R_1.A_1 = R_2.A_1$ and $R_2.A_2 = R_3.A_2$, respectively. (Just to illustrate our notation, $R(v_1) = R_1$, $A_{v_2}(e_1) = R_2.A_1$ and $\mathcal{A}(v_2) = \{R_2.A_1, R_2.A_2\}$.) The sketch construction defines two families of four-wise independent random families (one for each edge): $\{\xi_i^{e_1}\}$ and $\{\xi_j^{e_2}\}$. The three atomic sketches X_{v_1}, X_{v_2}, and X_{v_3} (one for each vertex) are defined as: $X_{v_1} = \sum_{i \in \mathtt{dom}(R_1.A_1)} f_{v_1}(i)\xi_i^{e_1}$, $X_{v_2} = \sum_{i \in \mathtt{dom}(R_2.A_1)} \sum_{j \in \mathtt{dom}(R_2.A_2)} f_{v_2}(i,j)\xi_i^{e_1}\xi_j^{e_2}$, and $X_{v_3} = \sum_{j \in \mathtt{dom}(R_3.A_2)} f_{v_3}(j)\xi_j^{e_3}$. The value of random variable $X_Q = X_{v_1}X_{v_2}X_{v_3}$ gives the sketching estimate for the result of Q. □

Our analysis in [11] shows that the random variable X_Q constructed above is an unbiased estimator for Q, and demonstrates the following theorem which generalizes the earlier result of Alon et al. [5] to multi-join queries. ($\mathrm{SJ}_v = \sum_{i_1 \in \mathtt{dom}(A_v(e_1))} \cdots \sum_{i_k \in \mathtt{dom}(A_v(e_k))} f_v(i_1, \ldots, i_k)^2$ is the self-join size of $R(v)$.)

Theorem 2 ([11]). Let Q be a COUNT query with n equi-join predicates such that $\mathcal{J}(\mathcal{Q})$ contains no cycles of length > 2. Then, $E[X_Q] = Q$ and using sketching space of $O(\frac{\text{Var}[X_Q]\cdot\log(1/\delta)}{Q^2\cdot\epsilon^2})$, it is possible to approximate Q to within a relative error of ϵ with probability at least $1-\delta$, where $\text{Var}[X_Q] \le 2^{2n}\prod_v \text{SJ}_v$. □

3 Sketch Sharing: Basic Concepts and Problem Formulation

In this section, we turn our attention to sketch-based processing of *multiple* aggregate SQL queries over streams. We introduce the basic idea of sketch sharing and demonstrate how it can improve the effectiveness of the available sketching space and the quality of the resulting approximate answers. We also characterize the class of correct sketch-sharing configurations and formulate the optimization problem of identifying an effective sketch-sharing plan for a given query workload.

3.1 Sketch Sharing

Consider the problem of using sketch synopses for the effective processing of a query workload $\mathcal{Q} = \{Q_1, \dots, Q_q\}$ comprising multiple (multi-join) COUNT aggregate queries. As in [11], we focus on COUNT since the extension to other aggregate functions is relatively straightforward; we also assume an attribute-renaming step that ensures that each stream attribute is referenced only once in each of the Q_i's (of course, the same attribute can be used multiple times across the queries in $\mathcal{Q}$). Finally, as in [11], we do not consider single-relation selections, since they can be trivially incorporated in the model by using the selection predicates to define filters for each stream. The sketching of each relation is performed using only the tuples that pass the filter; this is equivalent to introducing virtual relations/streams that are the result of the filtering process and formulating the queries with respect to these relations. This could potentially increase the number of relations and reduce the number of opportunities to share sketches (as described in this section), but would also create opportunities similar to the ones investigated by traditional MQO (e.g., constructing sketches for common filter sub-expressions). In this paper, we focus on the novel problem of sharing sketches and we do not investigate further how such techniques can be used for the case where selection predicates are allowed. As will become apparent in this section, sketch sharing is very different from common sub-expression sharing; traditional MQO techniques do not apply for this problem.

An obvious solution to our multi-query processing problem is to build disjoint join graphs $\mathcal{J}(Q_i)$ for each query $Q_i \in \mathcal{Q}$, and construct independent atomic sketches for the vertices of each $\mathcal{J}(Q_i)$. The atomic sketches for each vertex of $\mathcal{J}(Q_i)$ can then be combined to compute an approximate answer for Q_i as described in [11] (Section 2.2). A key drawback of such a naive solution is that it ignores the fact that a relation R_i may appear in multiple queries in $\mathcal{Q}$. Thus, it should be possible to reduce the overall space requirements by *sharing* atomic-sketch computations among the vertices for stream R_i in the join graphs for the queries in our workload. We illustrate this in the following example.

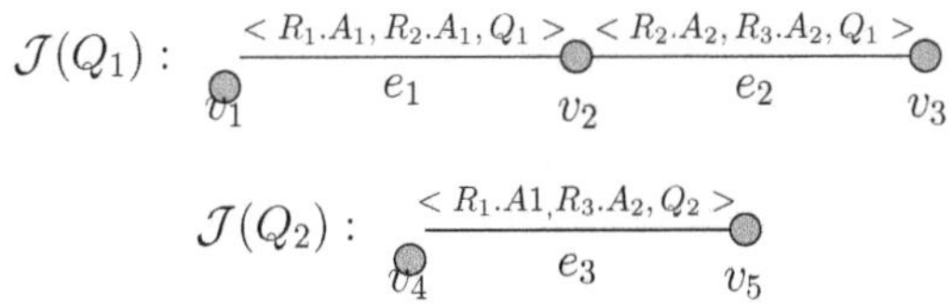

$\mathcal{J}(Q_1)$: $< R_1.A_1, R_2.A_1, Q_1 >$ $< R_2.A_2, R_3.A_2, Q_1 >$
v_1 e_1 v_2 e_2 v_3

$\mathcal{J}(Q_2)$: $< R_1.A1, R_3.A_2, Q_2 >$
v_4 e_3 v_5

Fig. 3. Example Workload with Sketch-Sharing Potential.

Example 2. Consider queries $Q_1 = \texttt{SELECT COUNT FROM } R_1, R_2, R_3 \texttt{ WHERE }$ $R_1.A_1 = R_2.A_1$ AND $R_2.A_2 = R_3.A_2$ and $Q_2 = \texttt{SELECT COUNT FROM } R_1, R_3 \texttt{ WHERE }$ $R_1.A_1 = R_3.A_2$. The naive processing algorithm described above would maintain two disjoint join graphs (Fig. 3) and, to compute a single pair (X_{Q_1}, X_{Q_2}) of sketch-based estimates, it would use three families of random variables (ξ^{e_1}, ξ^{e_2}, and ξ^{e_3}), and a total of five atomic sketches (X_{v_k}, $k = 1, \dots, 5$).

Instead, suppose that we decide to re-use the atomic sketch X_{v_1} for v_1 also for v_4, both of which essentially correspond to the same attribute of the same stream ($R_1.A_1$). Since for each $i \in \texttt{dom}(R_1.A_1)$, $f_{v_4}(i) = f_{v_1}(i)$, we get $X_{v_4} = X_{v_1} = \sum_{i \in \texttt{dom}(R_1.A_1)} f_{v_4}(i)\xi_i^{e_1}$. Of course, in order to correctly compute a probabilistic estimate of Q_2, we also need to use the same family ξ^{e_1} in the computation of X_{v_5}; that is, $X_{v_5} = \sum_{i \in \texttt{dom}(R_1.A_1)} f_{v_5}(i)\xi_i^{e_1}$. It is easy to see that both final estimates $X_{Q_1} = X_{v_1}X_{v_2}X_{v_3}$ and $X_{Q_1} = X_{v_1}X_{v_5}$ satisfy all the premises of the sketch-based estimation results in [11]. Thus, by simply sharing the atomic sketches for v_1 and v_4, we have reduced the total number of random families used in our multi-query processing algorithm to two (ξ^{e_1} and ξ^{e_2}) and the total number of atomic sketches maintained to four. □

Let $\mathcal{J}(\mathcal{Q})$ denote the collection of all join graphs in workload $\mathcal{Q}$, i.e., all $\mathcal{J}(Q_i)$ for $Q_i \in \mathcal{Q}$. Sharing sketches between the vertices of $\mathcal{J}(\mathcal{Q})$ can be seen as a transformation of $\mathcal{J}(\mathcal{Q})$ that essentially *coalesces* vertices belonging to different join graphs in $\mathcal{J}(\mathcal{Q})$. (We also use $\mathcal{J}(\mathcal{Q})$ to denote the transformed multi-query join graph.) Of course, as shown in Example 2, vertices $v \in \mathcal{J}(Q_i)$ and $w \in \mathcal{J}(Q_j)$ can be coalesced in this manner *only if* $R(v) = R(w)$ (i.e., they correspond to the same data stream) and $\mathcal{A}(v) = \mathcal{A}(w)$ (i.e., both Q_i and Q_j use exactly the same attributes of that stream). Such vertex coalescing implies that a vertex v in $\mathcal{J}(\mathcal{Q})$ can have edges from multiple different queries incident on it; we denote the set of all these queries as $Q(v)$, i.e., $Q(v) = \{Q(e) : \text{edge } e \text{ is incident on } v\}$. Figure 4(a) pictorially depicts the coalescing of vertices v_1 and v_4 as discussed in Example 2. Note that, by our coalescing rule, for each vertex v, all queries in $Q(v)$ are guaranteed to use exactly the same set of attributes of $R(v)$, namely $\mathcal{A}(v)$; furthermore, by our attribute-renaming step, each query in $Q(v)$ uses each attribute in $\mathcal{A}(v)$ exactly once. This makes it possible to share an atomic sketch built for the coalesced vertices v across all queries in $Q(v)$ but, as we will see shortly, cannot guarantee the correctness of the resulting sketch-based estimates.

Estimation with Sketch Sharing. Consider a multi-query join graph $\mathcal{J}(\mathcal{Q})$, possibly containing coalesced vertices (as described above). Our goal here is to build *atomic sketches corresponding to individual vertices* of $\mathcal{J}(\mathcal{Q})$ that can then be used for obtaining sketch-based estimates for *all* the queries in our workload $\mathcal{Q}$. Specifically, consider a query $Q \in \mathcal{Q}$, and let $V(Q)$ denote the (sub)set of vertices in $\mathcal{J}(\mathcal{Q})$ attached to a join-predicate edge corresponding to Q; that is, $V(Q) = \{v : \text{edge } e \text{ is incident on } v \text{ and } Q(e) = Q\}$. Our goal is to construct an unbiased probabilistic estimate X_Q for Q using the atomic sketches built for vertices in $V(Q)$.

The atomic sketch for a vertex v of $\mathcal{J}(\mathcal{Q})$ is constructed as follows. As before, each edge $e \in \mathcal{J}(\mathcal{Q})$ is associated with a family ξ^e of four-wise independent $\{-1, +1\}$ random variables. The difference here, however, is that edges attached to node v for the *same attribute* of $R(v)$ share the *same* ξ family since the *same* sketch of $R(v)$ corresponding to vertex v is used to estimate *all* queries in $Q(v)$; this, of course, implies that the number of *distinct* ξ families for all edges incident on v is exactly $|\mathcal{A}(v)|$ (each family corresponding to a distinct attribute of $R(v)$). Furthermore, all distinct ξ families in $\mathcal{J}(\mathcal{Q})$ are generated independently (using mutually independent seeds). For example, in Figure 4(a), since $A_{v_1}(e_1) = A_{v_1}(e_3) = R_1.A_1$, edges e_1 and e_3 share the same ξ family (i.e., $\xi^{e_3} = \xi^{e_1}$); on the other hand, ξ^{e_1} and ξ^{e_2} are distinct and independent. Assuming $\mathcal{A} = \{A_1, \ldots, A_k\}$ and letting $\xi^1, \ldots, \xi^k$ denote the k corresponding distinct ξ families attached to v, the atomic sketch X_v for node v is simply defined as $X_v = \sum_{(i_1,\ldots,i_k)\in A_1\times\cdots\times A_k} f_v(i_1, \ldots, i_k) \prod_{j=1}^{k} \xi^j_{i_j}$ (again, a randomized linear projection). The final sketch-based estimate for query Q is the product of the atomic sketches over all vertices in $V(Q)$, i.e., $X_Q = \prod_{v\in V(Q)} X_v$.

Correctness of Sketch-Sharing Configurations. The X_Q estimate construction described above can be viewed as simply "extracting" the join (sub)graph $\mathcal{J}(Q)$ for query Q from the multi-query graph $\mathcal{J}(\mathcal{Q})$, and constructing a sketch-based estimate for Q as described in Section 2.2. This is because, if we were to only retain in $\mathcal{J}(\mathcal{Q})$ vertices and edges associated with Q, then the resulting subgraph is identical to $\mathcal{J}(Q)$. Furthermore, our vertex coalescing (which completely determines the sketches to be shared) guarantees that Q references exactly the attributes $\mathcal{A}(v)$ of $R(v)$ for each $v \in V(Q)$, so the atomic sketch X_v can be utilized.

There is, however, an important complication that our vertex-coalescing rule still needs to address, to ensure that the atomic sketches for vertices of $\mathcal{J}(\mathcal{Q})$ provide unbiased query estimates with variance bounded as described in Theorem 2. Given an estimate X_Q for query Q (constructed as above), unbiasedness and the bounds on $\text{Var}[X_Q]$ given in Theorem 2 depend crucially on the assumption that the ξ families used for the edges in $\mathcal{J}(Q)$ are distinct and independent. This means that simply coalescing vertices in $\mathcal{J}(\mathcal{Q})$ that use the same set of stream attributes is insufficient. The problem here is that the constraint that all edges for the same attribute incident on a vertex v share the same ξ family may (by transitivity) force edges for the same query Q to share identical ξ families. The following example illustrates this situation.

Example 3. Consider the multi-query join graph $\mathcal{J}(\mathcal{Q})$ in Figure 4(b) for queries Q_1 and Q_2 in Example 3. ($\mathcal{J}(\mathcal{Q})$ is obtained as a result of coalescing vertex pairs v_1, v_4 and v_3, v_5 in Fig, 3.) Since $A_{v_1}(e_1) = A_{v_1}(e_3) = R_1.A_1$ and $A_{v_3}(e_2) = A_{v_3}(e_3) = R_3.A_2$, we get the constraints $\xi^{e_3} = \xi^{e_1}$ and $\xi^{e_3} = \xi^{e_2}$. By transitivity, we have $\xi^{e_1} = \xi^{e_2} = \xi^{e_3}$, i.e., all three edges of the multi-query graph share the same ξ family. This, in turn, implies that the same ξ family is used on both edges of query Q_1; that is, instead of being independent, the pseudo-random families used on the two edges of Q_1 are perfectly correlated! It is not hard to see that, in this situation, the expectation and variance derivations for X_{Q_1}

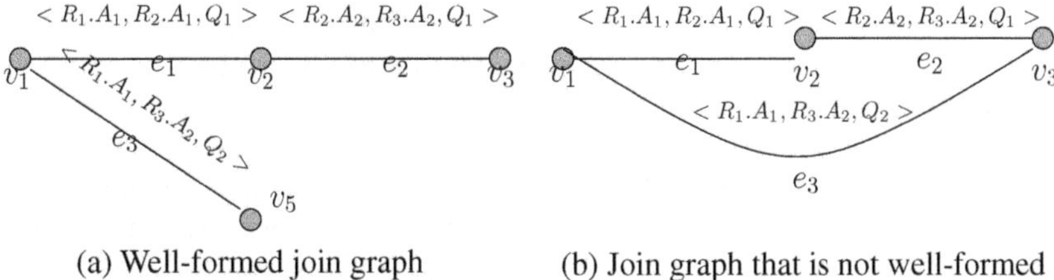

(a) Well-formed join graph (b) Join graph that is not well-formed

Fig. 4. Multi-Query Join Graphs $\mathcal{J}(\mathcal{Q})$ for Example 2.

will fail to produce the results of Theorem 2, since many of the zero cross-product terms in the analysis of [5,11] will fail to vanish. □

As is clear from the above example, the key problem is that constraints requiring ξ families for certain edges incident on each vertex of $\mathcal{J}(\mathcal{Q})$ to be identical, can transitively ripple through the graph, forcing much larger sets of edges to share the same ξ family. We formalize this fact using the following notion of (transitive) ξ*-equivalence* among edges of a multi-query graph $\mathcal{J}(\mathcal{Q})$.

Definition 1. *Two edges e_1 and e_2 in $\mathcal{J}(\mathcal{Q})$ are said to be ξ-equivalent if either (1) e_1 and e_2 are incident on a common vertex v, and $A_v(e_1) = A_v(e_2)$; or (2) there exists an edge e_3 such that e_1 and e_3 are ξ-equivalent, and e_2 and e_3 are ξ-equivalent.*

Intuitively, the classes of the ξ-equivalence relation represent exactly the sets of edges in the multi-query join graph $\mathcal{J}(\mathcal{Q})$ that need to share the same ξ family; that is, for any pair of ξ-equivalent edges e_1 and e_2, it is the case that $\xi^{e_1} = \xi^{e_2}$. Since, for estimate correctness, we require that all the edges associated with a query have distinct and independent ξ families, our sketch-sharing algorithms only consider multi-query join graphs that are *well-formed*, as defined below.

Definition 2. *A multi-query join graph $\mathcal{J}(\mathcal{Q})$ is well-formed iff, for every pair of ξ-equivalent edges e_1 and e_2 in $\mathcal{J}(\mathcal{Q})$, the queries containing e_1 and e_2 are distinct, i.e., $Q(e_1) \neq Q(e_2)$.*

It is not hard to prove that the well-formedness condition described above is actually necessary and sufficient for individual sketch-based query estimates that are unbiased and obey the variance bounds of Theorem 2. Thus, our shared-sketch estimation process over well-formed multi-query graphs can readily apply the single-query results of [5, 11] for each individual query in our workload.

3.2 Problem Formulation

Given a large workload $\mathcal{Q}$ of complex queries, there can obviously be a large number of well-formed join graphs for $\mathcal{Q}$, and all of them can potentially be used to provide approximate sketch-based answers to queries in $\mathcal{Q}$. At the same time, since the key resource constraint in a data-streaming environment is imposed by the amount of memory available to the query processor, our objective is to compute approximate answers to queries in $\mathcal{Q}$ that are as accurate as possible given a fixed amount of memory M for the sketch synopses. Thus, in the remainder of this paper, we focus on the problem of computing (1) a well-formed join graph $\mathcal{J}(\mathcal{Q})$ for $\mathcal{Q}$, and (2) an allotment of the M units of space to the vertices of $\mathcal{J}(\mathcal{Q})$ (for maintaining iid copies of atomic sketches), such that an appropriate aggregate error metric (e.g., average or maximum error) for all queries in $\mathcal{Q}$ is minimized.

More formally, let m_v denote the sketching space allocated to vertex v (i.e., number of iid copies of X_v). Also, let M_Q denote the number of iid copies built for the query estimate X_Q. Since $X_Q = \prod_{v \in V(Q)} X_v$, it is easy to see that M_Q is actually constrained by the *minimum* number of iid atomic sketches constructed for each of the nodes in $V(Q)$; that is, $M_Q = \min_{v \in V(Q)}\{m_v\}$. By Theorem 2, this implies that the (square) error for query Q is equal to W_Q/M_Q, where $W_Q = \frac{8\text{Var}[X_Q]}{E[X_Q]^2}$ is a constant for each query Q (assuming a fixed confidence parameter δ). Our sketch-sharing optimization problem can then be formally stated as follows.

Problem Statement. Given a query workload $\mathcal{Q} = \{Q_1, \ldots, Q_q\}$ and an amount of sketching memory M, compute a multi-query graph $\mathcal{J}(\mathcal{Q})$ and a space allotment $\{m_v :$ for each node v in $\mathcal{J}(\mathcal{Q})\}$ such that one of the following two error metrics is minimized:

- Average query error in $\mathcal{Q} = \sum_{Q \in \mathcal{Q}} \frac{W_Q}{M_Q}$.
- Maximum query error in $\mathcal{Q} = \max_{Q \in \mathcal{Q}}\{\frac{W_Q}{M_Q}\}$.

subject to the constraints: (1) $\mathcal{J}(\mathcal{Q})$ is well-formed; (2) $\sum_v m_v \leq M$ (i.e., the space constraint is satisfied); and, (3) For all vertices v in $\mathcal{J}(\mathcal{Q})$, for all queries $Q \in \mathcal{Q}(v)$, $M_Q \leq m_v$. □

The above problem statement assumes that the "weight" W_Q for each query $Q \in \mathcal{Q}$ is known. Clearly, if coarse statistics in the form of histograms for the stream relations are available (e.g., based on historical information or coarse a-priori knowledge of data distributions), then estimates for $E[X_Q]$ and $\text{Var}[X_Q]$ (and, consequently, W_Q) can be obtained by estimating join and self-join sizes using these histograms [11]. In the event that no prior information is available, we can simply set each $W_Q = 1$; unfortunately, even for this simple case, our optimization problem is intractable (see Section 4).

In the following section, we first consider the sub-problem of optimally allocating sketching space (such that query errors are minimized) to the vertices of a *given*, well-formed join graph $\mathcal{J}(\mathcal{Q})$. Subsequently, in Section 5, we consider the general optimization problem where we also seek to determine the best well-formed multi-query graph for the given workload $\mathcal{Q}$. Since most of these questions turn out to be $\mathcal{NP}$-hard, we propose novel heuristic algorithms for determining good solutions in practice. Our algorithm for the overall problem (Section 5) is actually an iterative procedure that uses the space-allocation algorithms of Section 4 as subroutines in the search for a good sketch-sharing plan.

4 Space Allocation Problem

In this section, we consider the problem of allocating space optimally given a well-formed join graph $J = \mathcal{J}(\mathcal{Q})$ such that the average or maximum error is minimized.

4.1 Minimizing the Average Error

The problem of allocating space to sketches in a way that minimizes the average error turns out to be $\mathcal{NP}$-hard even when $W_Q = 1$. Given the intractability of the problem, we look for an approximation based on its continuous relaxation, i.e., we allow the M_Q's and m_v's to be continuous. The continuous version of the problem is a convex optimization problem, which can be solved exactly in polynomial time using, for example, interior point methods [15]. We can then show that a near-optimal integer solution is obtained by rounding down (to integers) the optimal continuous values of the M_Q's and m_v's.

Since standard methods for solving convex optimization problems tend to be slow in practice, we developed a novel specialized solution for the problem at hand. Our solution, which we believe has applications to a much wider class of problems than the optimal space allocation problem outlined in this paper, is based on a novel usage of the Kuhn-Tucker optimality conditions (KT-conditions). We rewrite the problem using the KT conditions, and then we solve the problem through repeated application of a specific Max-Flow formulation of the constraints. Due to space limitations, we omit a detailed description of the algorithm and the analysis of its correctness; details can be found in the full version of this paper [13]. Our results are summarized in the following theorem:

Theorem 3. There is an algorithm that computes the optimal solution to the average-error continuous convex optimization problem in at most $O(\min\{|\mathcal{Q}|, |J|\} \cdot (|\mathcal{Q}| + |J|)^3)$ steps. Furthermore, rounding this optimal continuous solution results in an integer solution that is guaranteed to be within a factor of $(1 + \frac{2|J|}{M})$ of the optimal integer solution. □

4.2 Minimizing the Maximum Error

It can be easily shown (see [13] for details) that the problem of minimizing the maximum error can be solved in time $O(|J| \log |J|)$ by the following greedy algorithm: (1) take each m_v proportional to $\max_{Q \in Q(v)} W_Q$), (2) round down each m_v component to the nearest integer, and (3) take the remaining space $s \leq |J|$ and allocate one extra unit of space to each of the nodes with the s smallest values for quantity $m_v / \max_{Q \in Q(v)} W_Q$.

5 Computing a Well-Formed Join Graph

The optimization problem we are trying to solve is: find a well-formed graph $\mathcal{J}(\mathcal{Q})$ and the optimal space allocation to the vertices of $\mathcal{J}(\mathcal{Q})$ such that the average or maximum error is minimized. If we take $W_Q = 1$ for all queries and minimize the maximum error, this optimization problem reduces to the problem of finding a well-formed join graph

$\mathcal{J}(\mathcal{Q})$ with the minimum number of vertices; this problem is $\mathcal{NP}$-hard (see [13] for the proof) which makes the initial optimization problem $\mathcal{NP}$-hard as well.

In order to provide an acceptable solution in practice we designed a greedy heuristic, that we call CoalesceJoinGraphs, for computing a well-formed join graph with small error. The Algorithm CoalesceJoinGraphs iteratively merges pair of vertices in J that causes the largest decrease in error, until the error cannot be reduced any further by coalescing vertices. It uses the algorithm to compute the average (Section 4.1) or maximum error (Section 4.2) for a join graph as a subroutine, which we denote by ComputeSpace, at every step. Also, in order to ensure that graph J always stays well-formed, J is initially set to be equal to the set of all the individual join graphs for queries in $\mathcal{Q}$. In each subsequent iteration, only vertices for identical relations that have the same attribute sets and preserve the well-formedness of J are coalesced. Well-formedness testing essentially involves partitioning the edges of J' into equivalence classes, each class consisting of ξ-equivalent edges, and then verifying that no equivalence class contains multiple edges from the same join query; it can be carried out very efficiently, in time proportional to the number of edges in J'. The Algorithm CoalesceJoinGraphs needs to make at most $O(N^3)$ calls to ComputeSpace, where N is the total number of vertices in all the join graphs $\mathcal{J}(Q)$ for the queries, and this determines its time complexity.

6 Experimental Study

In this section, we present the results of an experimental study of our sketch-sharing algorithms for processing multiple COUNT queries in a streaming environment. Our experiments consider a wide range of COUNT queries on a common schema and set of equi-join constraints and with synthetically generated data sets. The reason we use synthetic data sets is that these enable us to measure the effectiveness of our sketch sharing techniques for a variety of different data distributions and parameter settings. The main findings of our study can be summarized as follows.

• **Effectiveness of Sketch Sharing.** Our experiments with various realistic workloads indicate that, in practice, sharing sketches among queries can significantly reduce the number of sketches needed to compute estimates. This, in turn, results in better utilization of the available memory, and much higher accuracy for returned query answers. For instance, for our first query set (its description is provided latter in this section), the number of vertices in the final coalesced join graph returned by our sketch-sharing algorithms decreases from 34 (with no sharing) to 16. Further, even with $W_Q = 1$ (for all queries Q), compared to naive solutions which involve no sketch sharing, our sketch-sharing solutions deliver improvements in accuracy ranging from a factor of 2 to 4 for a wide range of multi-query workloads.

• **Benefits of Intelligent Space Allocation.** The errors in the approximate query answers computed by our sketch-sharing algorithms are smaller if approximate weight information $W_Q = \frac{8\mathrm{Var}[X]}{E[X]^2}$ for queries is available. Even with weight estimates based on coarse statistics on the underlying data distribution (e.g., histograms), accuracy improvements of up to a factor of 2 can be obtained compared with using uniform weights for all queries.

Thus, our experimental results validate the thesis of this paper that sketch sharing can significantly improve the accuracy of aggregate queries over data streams, and that a careful allocation of available space to sketches is important in practice.

6.1 Experimental Testbed and Methodology

Algorithms for Answering Multiple Aggregate Queries. We compare the error performance of the following two sketching methods for evaluating query answers.

• *No sketch sharing.* This is the naive sketching technique from Section 2.2 in which we maintain separate sketches for each individual query join graph $\mathcal{J}(Q)$. Thus, there is no sharing of sketching space between the queries in the workload, and independent atomic sketches are constructed for each relation, query pair such that the relation appears in the query.

• *Sketch sharing.* In this case, atomic sketches for relations are reused as much as possible across queries in the workload for the purpose of computing approximate answers. Algorithms described in Sections 4 and 5 are used to compute the well-formed join graph for the query set and sketching space allocation to vertices of the join graph (and queries) such that either the average-error or maximum-error metric is optimized. There are two solutions that we explore in our study, based on whether prior (approximate) information on join and self-join sizes is available to our algorithms to make more informed decisions on memory allocation for sketches.

- No prior information. The weights for all join queries in the workload are set to 1, and this is the input to our sketch-sharing algorithms.
- Prior information is available. The ratio $\frac{8\mathrm{Var}(X)}{E[X]^2)}$ is estimated for each workload query, and is used as the query weight when determining the memory to be allocated to each query. We use coarse one-dimensional histograms for each relational attribute to estimate join and self-join sizes required for weight computation. Each histogram is given 200 buckets, and the frequency distribution for multi-attribute relations is approximated from the individual attribute histograms by applying the attribute value independence assumption.

Query Workload. The query workloads used to evaluate the effectiveness of sketch sharing consist of collections of JOIN-COUNT queries roughly based on the schema and queries in TPC-H benchmark; this allows us to simulate a somewhat realistic scenario in which sketches can be shared. The schema consists of six relations with one to three join attributes. Three workloads have been defined on this schema. Workload 1, inspired by the TPC-H workload, consists of twelve queries. Workload 2 extends the first workload with seventeen random queries. Workload 3 contains seven queries from the workload 1 that contain one or two join constraints together with a query from workload 3 that contains three join constraints. The full details, which we omit due to lack of space, can be found in [13].

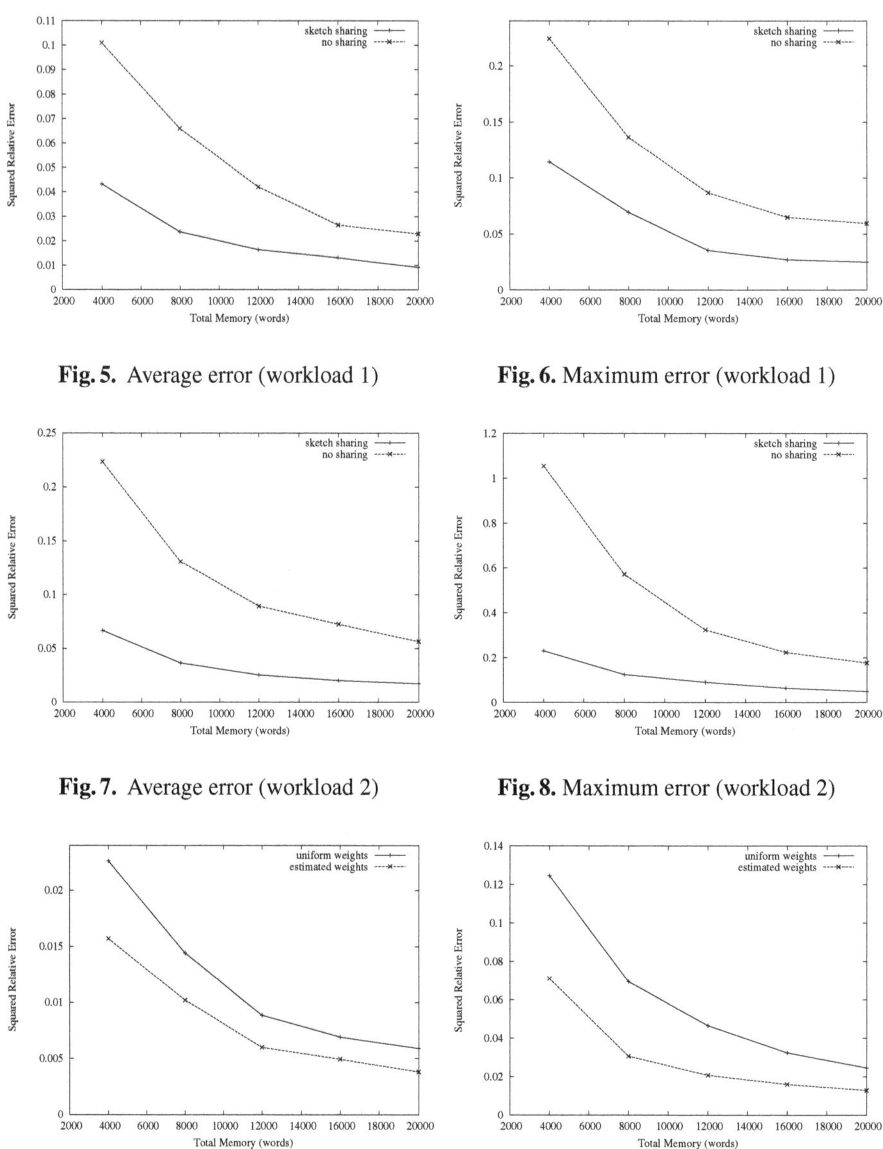

Fig. 5. Average error (workload 1)

Fig. 6. Maximum error (workload 1)

Fig. 7. Average error (workload 2)

Fig. 8. Maximum error (workload 2)

Fig. 9. Average error (workload 3)

Fig. 10. Maximum error (workload 3)

Data Set. We used the synthetic data generator from [16] to generate all the relations in our experiments. The data generator works by populating uniformly distributed rectangular regions in the multi-dimensional attribute space of each relation. Tuples are distributed across regions and within regions using a Zipfian distribution with values z_{inter} and z_{intra}, respectively. We set the parameters of the data generator to the following default values: size of each domain=1024, number of regions=10, volume of each region=1000–2000, skew across regions (z_{inter})=1.0, skew within each region (z_{intra}) =0.0–0.5 and number of tuples in each relation = 10,000,000.

Answer-Quality Metrics. In our experiments we use the square of the absolute relative error ($\frac{(actual-approx)^2}{actual^2}$) in the aggregate value as a measure of the accuracy of the approximate answer for a single query. For a given query workload, we consider both the average-error and maximum-error metrics, which correspond to averaging over all the query errors and taking the maximum from among the query errors, respectively. We repeat each experiment 100 times, and use the average value for the errors across the iterations as the final error in our plots.

6.2 Experimental Results

Results: Sketch Sharing. Figures 5 through 8 depict the average and maximum errors for query workloads 1 and 2 as the sketching space is increased from 2K to 20K words. From the graphs, it is clear that with sketch sharing, the accuracy of query estimates improves. For instance, with workload 1, errors are generally a factor of two smaller with sketch sharing. The improvements due to sketch sharing are even greater for workload 2 where due to the larger number of queries, the degree of sharing is higher. The improvements can be attributed to our sketch-sharing algorithms which drive down the number of join graph vertices from 34 (with no sharing) to 16 for workload 1, and from 82 to 25 for workload 2. Consequently, more sketching space can be allocated to each vertex, and hence the accuracy is better with sketch sharing compared to no sharing. Further, observe that in most cases, errors are less than 10% for sketch sharing, and as would be expected, the accuracy of estimates gets better as more space is made available to store sketches.

Results: Intelligent Space Allocation. We plot in Figures 9 and 10, the average and maximum error graphs for two versions of our sketch-sharing algorithms, one that is supplied uniform query weights, and another with estimated weights computed using coarse histogram statistics. We considered query workload 3 for this experiment since workloads 2 and 3 have queries with large weights that access all the underlying relations. These queries tend to dominate in the space allocation procedures, causing the final result to be very similar to the uniform query weights case, which is not happening for query workload 3. Thus, with intelligent space allocation, even with coarse statistics on the data distribution, we are able to get accuracy improvements of up to a factor of 2 by using query weight information.

7 Concluding Remarks

In this paper, we investigated the problem of processing *multiple* aggregate SQL queries over data streams concurrently. We proved correctness conditions for multi-query sketch sharing, and we developed solutions to the optimization problem of determining sketch-sharing configurations that are optimal under average and maximum error metrics for a given amount of space. We proved that the problem of optimally allocating space to sketches such that query estimation errors are minimized is $\mathcal{NP}$-hard. As a result, for a given multi-query workload, we developed a mix of near-optimal solutions (for space allocation) and heuristics to compute the final set of sketches that result in small errors. We conducted an experimental study with realistic query workloads; our findings indicate that (1) Compared to a naive solution that does not share sketches among queries, our sketch-sharing solutions deliver improvements in accuracy ranging from a factor of 2 to 4, and (2) The use of prior information about queries (e.g., obtained from coarse histograms), increases the effectiveness of our memory allocation algorithms, and can cause errors to decrease by factors of up to 2.

Acknowledgements. This work was partially funded by NSF CAREER Award 0133481, NSF ITR Grant 0205452, by NSF Grant IIS-0084762, and by the KD-D Initiative. Any opinions, findings, or recommendations expressed in this paper are those of the authors and do not necessarily reflect the views of the sponsors.

References

1. Gilbert, A.C., Kotidis, Y., Muthukrishnan, S., Strauss, M.J.: "How to Summarize the Universe: Dynamic Maintenance of Quantiles". In: VLDB 2002, Hong Kong, China (2002)
2. Bar-Yossef, Z., Jayram, T., Kumar, R., Sivakumar, D., Trevisan, L.: "Counting distinct elements in a data stream". In: RANDOM'02, Cambridge, Massachusetts (2002)
3. Gibbons, P.B., Tirthapura, S.: "Estimating Simple Functions on the Union of Data Streams". In: SPAA 2001, Crete Island, Greece (2001)
4. Manku, G.S., Motwani, R.: "Approximate Frequency Counts over Data Streams". In: VLDB 2002, Hong Kong, China (2002)
5. Alon, N., Gibbons, P.B., Matias, Y., Szegedy, M.: "Tracking Join and Self-Join Sizes in Limited Storage". In: PODS 2001, Philadelphia, Pennsylvania (1999)
6. Alon, N., Matias, Y., Szegedy, M.: "The Space Complexity of Approximating the Frequency Moments". In: STOC 1996, Philadelphia, Pennsylvania (1996) 20–29
7. Indyk, P.: "Stable Distributions, Pseudorandom Generators, Embeddings and Data Stream Computation". In: FOCS 2000, Redondo Beach, California (2000) 189–197
8. Gilbert, A.C., Kotidis, Y., Muthukrishnan, S., Strauss, M.J.: "Surfing Wavelets on Streams: One-pass Summaries for Approximate Aggregate Queries". In: VLDB 2000, Roma, Italy (2000)
9. Thaper, N., Guha, S., Indyk, P., Koudas, N.: "Dynamic Multidimensional Histograms". In: SIGMOD 2002, Madison, Wisconsin (2002)
10. Garofalakis, M., Gehrke, J., Rastogi, R.: "Querying and Mining Data Streams: You Only Get One Look". Tutorial at VLDB 2002, Hong Kong, China (2002)
11. Dobra, A., Garofalakis, M., Gehrke, J., Rastogi, R.: "Processing Complex Aggregate Queries over Data Streams". In: SIGMOD 2002, Madison, Wisconsin (2002) 61–72
12. Sellis, T.K.: "Multiple-Query Optimization". ACM Transactions on Database Systems **13** (1988) 23–52
13. Dobra, A., Garofalakis, M., Gehrke, J., Rastogi, R.: Sketch-based multi-query processing over data streams. (Manuscript available at: `www.cise.ufl.edu/~adobra/papers/sketch-mqo.pdf`)
14. Motwani, R., Raghavan, P.: "Randomized Algorithms". Cambridge University Press (1995)
15. Stefanov, S.M.: Separable Programming. Volume 53 of Applied Optimization. Kluwer Academic Publishers (2001)
16. Vitter, J.S., Wang, M.: "Approximate Computation of Multidimensional Aggregates of Sparse Data Using Wavelets". In: SIGMOD 1999, Philadelphia, Pennsylvania (1999)

Processing Data-Stream Join Aggregates Using Skimmed Sketches

Sumit Ganguly, Minos Garofalakis, and Rajeev Rastogi

Bell Laboratories, Lucent Technologies, Murray Hill NJ, USA.
{sganguly,minos,rastogi}@research.bell-labs.com

Abstract. There is a growing interest in on-line algorithms for analyzing and querying data streams, that examine each stream element only once and have at their disposal, only a limited amount of memory. Providing (perhaps approximate) answers to aggregate queries over such streams is a crucial requirement for many application environments; examples include large IP network installations where performance data from different parts of the network needs to be continuously collected and analyzed. In this paper, we present the *skimmed-sketch* algorithm for estimating the join size of two streams. (Our techniques also readily extend to other join-aggregate queries.) To the best of our knowledge, our skimmed-sketch technique is the first comprehensive join-size estimation algorithm to provide tight error guarantees while: (1) achieving the lower bound on the space required by any join-size estimation method in a streaming environment, (2) handling streams containing general update operations (inserts and deletes), (3) incurring a low logarithmic processing time per stream element, and (4) not assuming any a-priori knowledge of the frequency distribution for domain values. Our skimmed-sketch technique achieves all of the above by first skimming the dense frequencies from random hash-sketch summaries of the two streams. It then computes the subjoin size involving only dense frequencies directly, and uses the skimmed sketches only to approximate subjoin sizes for the non-dense frequencies. Results from our experimental study with real-life as well as synthetic data streams indicate that our skimmed-sketch algorithm provides significantly more accurate estimates for join sizes compared to earlier sketch-based techniques.

1 Introduction

In a number of application domains, data arrives continuously in the form of a stream, and needs to be processed in an on-line fashion. For example, in the network installations of large Telecom and Internet service providers, detailed usage information (e.g., Call Detail Records or CDRs, IP traffic statistics due to SNMP/RMON polling, etc.) from different parts of the network needs to be continuously collected and analyzed for interesting trends. Other applications that generate rapid, continuous and large volumes of stream data include transactions in retail chains, ATM and credit card operations in banks, weather measurements, sensor networks, etc. Further, for many mission-critical tasks such as fraud/anomaly detection in Telecom networks, it is important to be able to answer queries in real-time and infer interesting patterns on-line. As a result, recent years have witnessed an increasing interest in designing *single-pass* algorithms for querying and mining data streams that examine each element in the stream *only once*.

E. Bertino et al. (Eds.): EDBT 2004, LNCS 2992, pp. 569–586, 2004.
© Springer-Verlag Berlin Heidelberg 2004

The large volumes of stream data, real-time response requirements of streaming applications, and modern computer architectures impose two additional constraints on algorithms for querying streams: (1) the time for processing each stream element must be small, and (2) the amount of memory available to the query processor is limited. Thus, the challenge is to develop algorithms that can summarize data streams in a concise, but reasonably accurate, *synopsis* that can be stored in the allotted (small) amount of memory and can be used to provide *approximate answers* to user queries with some guarantees on the approximation error.

Previous Work. Recently, single-pass algorithms for processing streams in the presence of limited memory have been proposed for several different problems; examples include quantile and order-statistics computation [1,2], estimating frequency moments and join sizes [3,4,5], distinct values [6,7], frequent stream elements [8,9,10], computing one-dimensional Haar wavelet decompositions [11], and maintaining samples and simple statistics over sliding windows [12].

A particularly challenging problem is that of answering aggregate SQL queries over data streams. Techniques based on random stream sampling [13] are known to give very poor result estimates for queries involving one or more joins [14,4,15]. Alon et al. [4, 3] propose algorithms that employ small *pseudo-random sketch summaries* to estimate the size of self-joins and binary joins over data streams. Their algorithms rely on a single-pass method for computing a randomized *sketch* of a stream, which is basically a random linear projection of the underlying frequency vector. A key benefit of using such linear projections is that dealing with *delete* operations in the stream becomes straightforward [4]; this is not the case, e.g., with sampling, where a sequence of deletions can easily deplete the maintained sample summary. Alon et al. [4] also derive a *lower bound* on the (worst-case) space requirement of *any* streaming algorithm for join-size estimation. Their result shows that, to accurately estimate a join size of J over streams with n tuples, any approximation scheme requires at least $\Omega(n^2/J)$ space. Unfortunately, the worst-case space usage of their proposed sketch-based estimator is much worse: it can be as high as $O(n^4/J^2)$, i.e., the square of the lower bound shown in [4]; furthermore, the required processing time per stream element is proportional to their synopsis size (i.e., also $O(n^4/J^2)$), which may render their estimators unusable for high-volume, rapid-rate data streams.

In order to reduce the storage requirements of the basic sketching algorithm of [4], Dobra et al. [5] suggest an approach based on partitioning domain values and estimating the overall join size as the sum of the join sizes for each partition. However, in order to compute good partitions, their algorithms require a-priori knowledge of the data distribution in the form of coarse frequency statistics (e.g., histograms). This may not always be available in a data-stream setting, and is a serious limitation of the approach.

Our Contributions. In this paper, we present the *skimmed-sketch* algorithm for estimating the join size of two streams. Our skimmed-sketch technique is the first comprehensive join-size estimation algorithm to provide tight error guarantees while satisfying all of the following: (1) Our algorithm requires $O(n^2/J)$ bits of memory[1] (in the worst case) for estimating joins of size J, which matches the lower bound of [4] and, thus, the best

[1] In reality, there are additional logarithmic terms; however, we ignore them since they will generally be very small.

possible (worst-case) space bound achievable by *any* join-size estimation method in a streaming environment; (2) Being based on sketches, our algorithm can handle streams containing general update operations; (3) Our algorithm incurs very low processing time per stream element to maintain in-memory sketches – update times are only logarithmic in the domain size and number of stream elements; and, (4) Our algorithm does not assume any a-priori knowledge of the underlying data distribution. None of the earlier proposed schemes for join size estimation: sampling, basic sketching [4], or sketching with domain partitioning [5], satisfy all four of the above-mentioned properties. In fact, our skimmed-sketch algorithm achieves the same accuracy guarantees as the basic sketching algorithm of [4], using only square root of the space and guaranteed logarithmic processing times per stream element. Note that, even though our discussion here focuses on join size estimation (i.e., binary-join `COUNT` queries), our skimmed-sketch method can readily be extended to handle complex, multi-join queries containing general aggregate operators (e.g., `SUM`), in a manner similar to that described in [5]. More concretely, our key contributions can be summarized as follows.

- SKIMMED-SKETCH ALGORITHM FOR JOIN SIZE ESTIMATION. Our skimmed-sketch algorithm is similar in spirit to the *bifocal sampling* technique of [16], but tailored to a data-stream setting. Instead of samples, our skimmed-sketch method employs randomized hash sketch summaries of streams F and G to approximate the size of $F \bowtie G$ in two steps. It first skims from the sketches for F and G, all the *dense* frequency values greater than or equal to a threshold T. Thus, each *skimmed sketch*, after the dense frequency values have been extracted, only reflects *sparse* frequency values less than T. In the second step, our algorithm estimates the overall join size as the sum of the subjoin sizes for the four combinations involving dense and sparse frequencies from the two streams. As our analysis shows, by skimming the dense frequencies away from the sketches, our algorithm drastically reduces the amount of memory needed for accurate join size estimation.

- RANDOMIZED HASH SKETCHES TO REDUCE PROCESSING TIMES. Like the basic sketching method of [4], our skimmed-sketch algorithm relies on randomized sketches; however, unlike basic sketching, our join estimation algorithm arranges the random sketches in a hash structure (similar to the COUNTSKETCH data structure of [8]). As a result, processing a stream element requires only a single sketch per hash table to be updated (i.e., the sketch for the hash bucket that the element maps to), rather than updating all the sketches in the synopsis (as in basic sketching [4]). Thus, the per-element overhead incurred by our skimmed-sketch technique is much lower, and is only logarithmic in the domain and stream sizes. To the best of our knowledge, ours is the first join-size estimation algorithm for a streaming environment to employ randomized hash sketches, and incur guaranteed logarithmic processing time per stream element.

- EXPERIMENTAL RESULTS VALIDATING OUR SKIMMED-SKETCH TECHNIQUE. We present the results of an experimental study with real-life and synthetic data sets that verify the effectiveness of our skimmed-sketch approach to join size estimation. Our results indicate that, besides giving much stronger asymptotic guarantees, our skimmed-sketch technique also provides significantly more accurate estimates for join sizes compared to other known sketch-based methods, the improvement in accuracy ranging from a factor of five (for moderate data skews) to several orders of magnitude (when the skew in the frequency distribution is higher). Furthermore, even with a few kilobytes of memory, the relative error in the final answer returned by our method is generally less than 10%.

The idea of separating dense and sparse frequencies when joining two relations was first introduced by Ganguly et al. [16]. Their equi-join size estimation technique, termed *bifocal sampling*, computes samples from both relations, and uses the samples to individually estimate sizes for the four subjoins involving dense and sparse sets of frequencies from the two relations. Unfortunately, bifocal sampling is unsuitable for a one-pass, streaming environment; more specifically, for subjoins involving the sparse frequencies of a relation, bifocal sampling assumes the existence of *indices* to access (possibly multiple times) relation tuples to determine sparse frequency counts. (A more detailed etailed comparison of our skimmed-sketch method with bifocal sampling can be found in the full version of this paper [17].)

2 Streams and Random Sketches

2.1 The Stream Data-Processing Model

We begin by describing the key elements of our generic architecture for processing join queries over two continuous data streams F and G (depicted in Figure 1); similar architectures for stream processing have been described elsewhere (e.g., [5]). Each data stream is an *unordered* sequence of elements with values from the domain $\mathcal{D} = \{1, \ldots, m\}$. For simplicity of exposition, we implicitly associate with each element, the semantics of an insert operation; again, being based on random linear projections, our sketch summaries can readily handle deletes, as in [4,5].

The class of stream queries we consider in this paper is of the general form Q =AGG($F \bowtie G$), where AGG is an arbitrary aggregate operator (e.g., COUNT, SUM or AVERAGE). Suppose that f_u and g_u denote the frequencies of domain value u in streams F and G, respectively. Then, the result of the join size query COUNT($F \bowtie G$) is $\sum_{u \in \mathcal{D}} f_u \cdot g_u$. Alternately, if f and g are the frequency vectors for streams F and G, then COUNT($F \bowtie G$) = $f \cdot g$, the inner product of vectors f and g. Similarly, if each element $e \in G$ has an associated *measure* value M_e (in addition to its value u from domain $\mathcal{D}$), and h_u is the sum of the measure values of all the elements in G with value $u \in \mathcal{D}$, then SUM$_M$($F \bowtie G$) = $\sum_u f_u \cdot h_u$. Thus, SUM$_M$($F \bowtie G$) is essentially a special case of a COUNT query over streams F and H, where H is derived from G by repeating each element e, M_e number of times. Consequently, we focus exclusively on answering COUNT queries in the remainder of this paper. Without loss of generality, we use n to represent the size of each of the data streams F and G; that is, $|F| = |G| = n$. Thus, $\sum_u f_u = \sum_u g_u = n$.

In contrast to conventional DBMS query processors, our stream query-processing engine is allowed to see the elements in F and G *only once* and in fixed order as they are streaming in from their respective source(s). Backtracking over the data stream and explicit access to past elements are impossible. Further, the order of element arrival in each stream is arbitrary and elements with duplicate values can occur anywhere over the duration of the stream.

Our stream query-processing engine is also allowed a certain amount of memory, typically significantly smaller than the total size of the data stream(s). This memory is

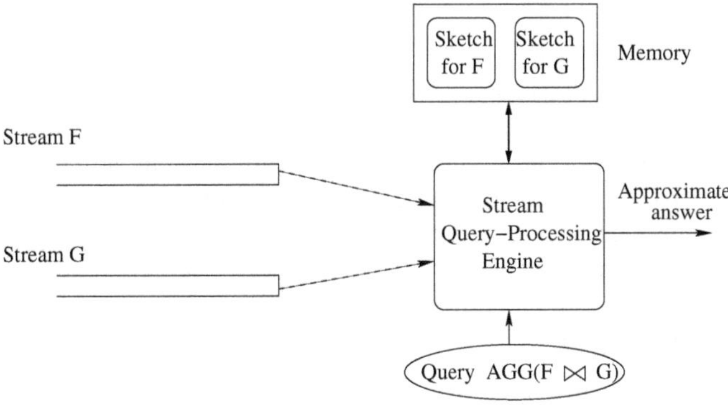

Fig. 1. Stream Query-Processing Architecture.

used to maintain a concise and accurate *synopsis* of each of the data streams F and G, denoted by $\mathcal{S}(F)$ and $\mathcal{S}(G)$, respectively. The key constraints imposed on each such synopsis, say $\mathcal{S}(F)$, are that: (1) it is much smaller than the total number of tuples in F (e.g., its size is logarithmic or polylogarithmic in $|F|$), and (2) it can be computed in a single pass over the data tuples in F in the (arbitrary) order of their arrival. At any point in time, our query-processing algorithms can combine the maintained synopses $\mathcal{S}(F)$ and $\mathcal{S}(G)$ to produce an approximate answer to the input query $Q = \texttt{COUNT}(F \bowtie G)$. Once again, we would like to point out that our techniques can easily be extended to multi-join queries, as in [5]. Also, selection predicates can easily be incorporated into our stream processing model – we simply drop from the streams, elements that do not satisfy the predicates (prior to updating the synopses).

2.2 Pseudo-Random Sketch Summaries

The Basic Technique: Self-Join Size Tracking. Consider a simple stream-processing scenario where the goal is to estimate the size of the self-join of stream F as elements of F are streaming in; thus, we seek to approximate the result of query $Q = \texttt{COUNT}(F \bowtie F)$. More specifically, since the number of elements in F with domain value u is f_u, we want to produce an estimate for the expression $f^2 = \sum_{u \in \mathcal{D}} f_u^2$ (i.e., the *second moment* of f). In their seminal paper, Alon, Matias, and Szegedy [3] prove that *any deterministic algorithm* that produces a tight approximation to f^2 requires at least $\Omega(m)$ bits of storage, rendering such solutions impractical for a data-stream setting. Instead, they propose a *randomized technique* that offers strong probabilistic guarantees on the quality of the resulting f^2 approximation while using only $O(\log(m))$ space. Briefly, the basic idea of their scheme is to define a random variable Z that can be easily computed over the streaming values of F, such that (1) Z is an *unbiased* (i.e., correct on expectation) estimator for f^2, so that $E[Z] = f^2$; and, (2) Z has sufficiently small variance $Var(Z)$ to provide strong probabilistic guarantees for the quality of the estimate. This random variable Z is constructed on-line from the streaming values of F as follows:

- Select a family of *four-wise independent binary random variables* $\{\xi_u : u = 1, \ldots, m\}$, where each $\xi_u \in \{-1, +1\}$ and $P[\xi_u = +1] = P[\xi_u = -1] = 1/2$ (i.e., $E[\xi_u] = 0$). Informally, the four-wise independence condition means that for any 4-tuple of ξ_u variables and for any 4-tuple of $\{-1, +1\}$ values, the probability that the values of the variables coincide with those in the $\{-1, +1\}$ 4-tuple is exactly $1/16$ (the product of the equality probabilities for each individual ξ_u). The crucial point here is that, by employing known tools (e.g., orthogonal arrays) for the explicit construction of small sample spaces supporting four-wise independent random variables, such families can be efficiently constructed on-line using only $O(\log(m))$ space [3].
- Define $Z = X^2$, where $X = \sum_{u \in \mathcal{D}} f_u \xi_u$. Note that X is simply a randomized linear projection (inner product) of the frequency vector of F with the vector of ξ_u's that can be efficiently generated from the streaming values of F as follows: Start with $X = 0$ and simply add ξ_u to X whenever an element with value u is observed in stream F. (If the stream element specifies a deletion of value u from F, then simply subtract ξ_u from X).

We refer to the above randomized linear projection X of F's frequency vector as an *atomic sketch* for stream F. To further improve the quality of the estimation guarantees, Alon, Matias, and Szegedy propose a standard *boosting technique* that maintains several independent identically-distributed (iid) instantiations of the random variables Z and uses averaging and median-selection operators to boost accuracy and probabilistic confidence. (Independent instances can be constructed by simply selecting independent random seeds for generating the families of four-wise independent ξ_u's for each instance.) Specifically, the synopsis $\mathcal{S}(F)$ comprises of a two-dimensional array of $s_1 \cdot s_2$ atomic sketches, where s_1 is a parameter that determines the *accuracy* of the result and s_2 determines the *confidence* in the estimate. Each atomic sketch in the synopsis array, $X[i, j]$, $1 \leq i \leq s_2$, $1 \leq j \leq s_1$, uses the same on-line construction as the variable X (described earlier), but with an independent family of four-wise independent variables $\{\xi_u^{ij} : u = 1, \ldots, m\}$. Thus, atomic sketch $X[i, j] = \sum_u f_u \xi_u^{ij}$. The final boosted estimate Y of f^2 is the median of s_2 random variables $Y_1, \ldots, Y_{s_2}$, each Y_i being the average of the squares of the s_1 iid atomic sketches $X[i, j]$, $j = 1, \ldots, s_1$. (We denote the above-described procedure as EstSJSize(X, s_1, s_2).)

The following theorem [3] demonstrates that the above sketch-based method offers strong probabilistic guarantees for the second-moment estimate while utilizing only $O(s_1 \cdot s_2 \cdot (\log(m) + \log(n)))$ space – here $O(\log(m))$ space is required to generate the ξ_u^{ij} variables for each atomic sketch, and $\log(n)$ bits are needed to store the atomic sketch value.

Theorem 1 **([3]).** The estimate Y computed by EstSJSize satisfies: $P[|Y - f^2| \leq (4/\sqrt{s_1}) f^2] \geq 1 - 2^{-s_2/2}$. This implies that EstSJSize estimates f^2 with a relative error of at most ϵ with probability at least $1 - \delta$ (i.e., $P[|Y - f^2| \leq \epsilon \cdot f^2] \geq 1 - \delta$) while using only $O\left(\frac{\log(1/\delta)}{\epsilon^2}(\log(m) + \log(n))\right)$ bits of memory. □

In the remainder of the paper, we will use the term *sketch* to refer to the overall synopsis array X containing $s_1 \cdot s_2$ atomic sketches for a stream.

Binary-Join Size Estimation. In a more recent paper, Alon et al. [4] show how their sketch-based approach applies to handling the size-estimation problem for binary joins over a pair of distinct streams. More specifically, consider approximating the result of the query $Q = \texttt{COUNT}(F \bowtie G)$ over two streams F and G. As described previously, let X_F and X_G be the sketches for streams F and G, each containing $s_1 \cdot s_2$ atomic sketches. Thus, each atomic sketch $X_F[i,j] = \sum_{u \in \mathcal{D}} f_u \xi_u^{ij}$ and $X_G[i,j] = \sum_{u \in \mathcal{D}} g_u \xi_u^{ij}$. Here, $\{\xi_u^{ij} : u = 1, \ldots, m\}$ is a family of four-wise independent $\{-1, +1\}$ random variables with $E[\xi_u^{ij}] = 0$, and f_u and g_u represent the frequencies of domain value u in streams F and G, respectively. An important point to note here is that the atomic sketch pair $X_F[i,j]$, $X_G[i,j]$ share the same family of random variables $\{\xi_u^{ij}\}$. The binary-join size of F and G, i.e., the inner product $f \cdot g = \sum_{u \in \mathcal{D}} f_u \cdot g_u$, can be estimated using sketches X_F and X_G as described in the EstJoinSize procedure (see Figure 2). (Note that EstSJSize(X, s_1, s_2) is simply EstJoinSize(X, X, s_1, s_2).)

Procedure EstJoinSize(X_F, X_G, s_1, s_2)
Input: Sketches X_F and X_G for streams F and G (respectively).
Output: Estimate of binary-join size of F and G.
begin
1. **for** $i = 1$ to s_2 **do** $Y_i := (\sum_{j=1}^{s_1} X_F[i,j] \cdot X_G[i,j])/s_1$;
2. **return** median $\{Y_1, Y_2, \ldots, Y_{s_2}\}$;

end

Fig. 2. Join-Size Estimation using Basic Sketching.

The following theorem (a variant of the result in [4]) shows how sketching can be applied for accurately estimating binary-join sizes in limited space.

Theorem 2 ([4]). The estimate Y computed by EstJoinSize satisfies: $P[|Y - (f \cdot g)| \leq 4\sqrt{\frac{f^2 \cdot g^2}{s_1}}] \leq 1 - 2^{-s_2/2}$. This implies that EstJoinSize estimates $f \cdot g$ with a relative error of at most ϵ with probability at least $1 - \delta$ (i.e., $P[|Y - (f \cdot g)| \leq \epsilon \cdot (f \cdot g)] \geq 1 - \delta$) while using only $O\left(\frac{\log(1/\delta) \cdot f^2 \cdot g^2}{\epsilon^2 \cdot (f \cdot g)^2}(\log(m) + \log(n))\right)$ bits of memory. □

Alon et al. [4] also prove that no binary-join size estimation algorithm can provide good guarantees on the accuracy of the final answer unless it stores $\Omega(n^2/(f \cdot g))$ bits. Unfortunately, their *basic sketching* procedure EstJoinSize, in the worst case, requires $O(\frac{n^4}{\epsilon^2 \cdot (f \cdot g)^2})$ space, which is the square of their lower bound. This is because, as indicated in Theorem 2, for a given s_1, the maximum cumulative error of the estimate Y returned by EstJoinSize can be as high as $O(\sqrt{\frac{f^2 \cdot g^2}{s_1}})$. Stated alternately, for a desired level of accuracy ϵ, the parameter s_1 for each sketch is $s_1 = O(\frac{f^2 \cdot g^2}{\epsilon^2 \cdot (f \cdot g)^2})$. Since, in the worst case, $f^2 = g^2 = n^2$, the required space s_1 becomes $O(\frac{n^4}{\epsilon^2 \cdot (f \cdot g)^2})$, which is the square of the lower bound, and can be quite large. Another drawback of the basic sketching procedure EstJoinSize is that processing each stream element involves updating every one of the $s_1 \cdot s_2$ atomic sketches. This is clearly undesirable given that basic sketching needs to store $O(n^4/(f \cdot g)^2)$ atomic sketches and, furthermore, *any* sketch-based join-size estimation algorithm requires at least $\Omega(n^2/(f \cdot g))$ atomic sketches. Ideally, we would like for our join size estimation technique to incur an overhead per element that is only logarithmic in m and n. So far, no known join size estimation method for streams meets the storage lower bound of $\Omega(n^2/(f \cdot g))$ while incurring at most logarithmic processing time per stream element, except for simple random sampling which, unfortunately, (1) cannot handle delete operations, and (2) typically performs *much* worse than sketches in practice [4].

3 Intuition Underlying Our Skimmed-Sketch Algorithm

In this section, we present the key intuition behind our skimmed-sketch technique which achieves the space lower bound of $\Omega(n^2/(f \cdot g))$, while providing guarantees on the quality of the $f \cdot g$ estimate. For illustrative purposes, we describe the key, high-level ideas underlying our technique using the earlier sketches X_F and X_G and the basic-sketching procedure EstJoinSize described in Section 2. As mentioned earlier, however, maintaining these sketches incurs space and time overheads proportional to $n^4/(f \cdot g)^2$, which can be excessive for data-stream settings. Consequently, in the next section, we introduce random hash sketches, which, unlike the sketches X_F and X_G, arrange atomic sketches in a hash structure; we then present our skimmed-sketch algorithm that employs these hash sketches to achieve the space lower bound of $\Omega(n^2/(f \cdot g))$ while requiring only logarithmic time for processing each stream element.

Our skimmed-sketch algorithm is similar in spirit to the *bifocal sampling* technique of [16], but tailored to a data-stream setting. Based on the discussion in the previous section, it follows that in order to improve the storage performance of the basic sketching estimator, we need to devise a way to make the self-join sizes f^2 and g^2 small. Our *skimmed-sketch* join algorithm achieves this by *skimming* from sketches X_F and X_G all frequencies greater than or equal to a certain threshold T, and then using the *skimmed* sketches (containing only frequencies less than T) to estimate $f \cdot g$. Specifically, suppose that a domain value u in F (G) is *dense* if its frequency f_u (resp., g_u) exceeds or is equal to some threshold T. Our skimmed-sketch algorithm estimates $f \cdot g$ in the following two steps.

1. Extract dense value frequencies in F and G into the frequency vectors $\hat{f}$ and $\hat{g}$, respectively. After these frequencies are *skimmed* away from the corresponding sketch, the skimmed sketches X'_F and X'_G correspond to the *residual* frequency vectors $f' = f - \hat{f}$ and $g' = g - \hat{g}$, respectively. Thus, each skimmed atomic sketch $X'_F[i,j] = \sum_u f'_u \xi_u^{ij}$ and $X'_G[i,j] = \sum_u g'_u \xi_u^{ij}$. Also note that, for every domain value u, the residual frequencies f'_u and g'_u in the corresponding skimmed sketches X'_F and X'_G, are less than T.
2. Individually estimate the subjoins $\hat{f} \cdot \hat{g}$, $\hat{f} \cdot g'$, $f' \cdot \hat{g}$, and $f' \cdot g'$. Return the sum of the four estimates as the estimate for $f \cdot g$. For each of the individual estimates,

a) Compute $\hat{f} \cdot \hat{g}$ accurately (that is, with zero error) using the extracted dense frequency vectors $\hat{f}$ and $\hat{g}$.
b) Compute the remaining three estimates by invoking procedure EstJoinSize with the skimmed sketches X'_F, X'_G, and newly constructed sketches $\hat{X}_F$ and $\hat{X}_G$ for frequency vectors $\hat{f}$ and $\hat{g}$, respectively. For instance, in order to estimate $f' \cdot \hat{g}$, invoke EstJoinSize with sketches X'_F and $\hat{X}_G$.

The maximum additive error of the final $f \cdot g$ estimate is the sum of the errors for the three estimates computed in Step 2(b) above (since $\hat{f} \cdot \hat{g}$ is computed exactly with zero error), and due to Theorem 2, is $O(\frac{\sqrt{\hat{f}^2 \cdot g'^2} + \sqrt{f'^2 \cdot \hat{g}^2} + \sqrt{f'^2 \cdot g'^2}}{\sqrt{s_1}})$. Clearly, if F and G contain many dense values that are much larger than T, then $f'^2 \ll f^2$ and $g'^2 \ll g^2$. Thus, in this case, the error for our skimmed-sketch join algorithm can be much smaller than the maximum additive error of $O(\sqrt{\frac{f^2 \cdot g^2}{s_1}})$ for the basic sketching technique (described in the previous section).

In the following section, we describe a variant of the CountSketch algorithm of [8] that, with high probability, can extract from a stream all frequencies greater than $T = O(n/s_1)$. As a result, in the worst case, f'^2 and g'^2 can be at most $n \cdot T = O(n^2/s_1)$ (which happens when there are n/T values with frequency T). Thus, in the worst case, the maximum additive error in the estimate computed by skimming dense frequencies is $O(\sqrt{\frac{n^2 \cdot (n^2/s_1)}{s_1}}) = O(n^2/s_1)$. It follows that for a desired level of accuracy ϵ, the space s_1 required in the worst case, becomes $O(n^2/(\epsilon \cdot (f \cdot g)))$, which is the square root of the space required by the basic sketching technique, and matches the lower bound achievable by any join size estimation algorithm [4].

Example 1. Consider a streaming scenario where $\mathcal{D} = \{1, 2, 3, 4\}$, and frequency vectors for streams F and G are given by: $f = [50, 50, 10, 5]$ and $g = [50, 5, 10, 50]$. The join size is $f \cdot g = 3100$, and self-join sizes are $f^2 = g^2 \approx 5000$. Thus, with the basic sketching algorithm, given space s_1, the maximum additive error is $4\sqrt{(5000)^2/s_1} = 20000/\sqrt{s_1}$. Or alternately, for a given relative error ϵ, the space s_1 required is $(20000/(\epsilon \cdot 3100))^2 \approx 42/\epsilon^2$.

Now suppose we could extract from sketches X_F and X_G all frequencies greater than or equal to a threshold $T = 10$. Let the extracted frequency vectors for the dense domain values be $\hat{f} = [40, 40, 0, 0]$ and $\hat{g} = [40, 0, 0, 40]$. In the skimmed sketches (after the dense values are extracted), the residual frequency vectors $f' = [10, 10, 10, 5]$ and $g' = [10, 5, 10, 10]$. Note that $\hat{f}^2 = \hat{g}^2 = 3200$, $f'^2 = g'^2 \approx 300$. Thus, the maximum additive errors in the estimates for $\hat{f} \cdot \hat{g}$, $f' \cdot \hat{g}$, $\hat{f} \cdot g'$ and $f' \cdot g'$ are 0, $4\sqrt{(3200 \cdot 300)/s_1} \approx 4000/\sqrt{s_1}$, $4\sqrt{(300 \cdot 3200)/s_1} \approx 4000/\sqrt{s_1}$ and $4\sqrt{(300 \cdot 300)/s_1} = 1200/\sqrt{s_1}$, respectively. Thus, the total maximum additive error due to our skimmed sketch technique is $\approx 9200/\sqrt{s_1}$. Or alternately, for a given relative error ϵ, the space s_1 required is $(9200/(\epsilon \cdot 3100))^2 = 9/\epsilon^2$, which is smaller than the memory needed for the basic sketching algorithm by more than a factor of 4. □

4 Join Size Estimation Using Skimmed Sketches

We are now ready to present our skimmed-sketch algorithm for tackling the join size estimation problem in a streaming environment. To the best of our knowledge, ours is the first known technique to achieve the space lower bound[2] of $\Omega(n^2/(f \cdot g))$ while requiring only logarithmic time for processing each stream element. The key to achieving the low element handling times is the hash sketch data structure, which we describe in Section 4.1. While hash sketches have been used before to solve a variety of data-stream computation problems (e.g., top-k frequency estimation [8]), we are not aware of any previous work that uses them to estimate join sizes. In Section 4.2, we first show how hash sketches can be used to extract dense frequency values from a stream, and then in Section 4.3, we present the details of our skimmed-sketch join algorithm with an analysis of its space requirements and error guarantees.

4.1 Hash Sketch Data Structure

The hash sketch data structure was first introduced in [8] for estimating the top-k frequency values in a stream F. It consists of an array H of s_2 hash tables, each with s_1 buckets. Each hash bucket contains a single counter for the elements that hash into the bucket. Thus, H can be viewed as a two-dimensional array of counters, with $H[p,q]$ representing the counter in bucket q of hash table p. Associated with each hash table p, is a pair-wise independent hash function h_p that maps incoming stream elements uniformly over the range of buckets $\{1,\ldots,s_1\}$; that is, $h_p : \{1,\ldots,m\} \rightarrow \{1,\ldots,s_1\}$. For each hash table p, we also maintain a family of four-wise independent variables $\{\xi_u^p : u = 1,\ldots,m\}$.

Initially, all counters $H[p,q]$ of the hash sketch H are 0. Now, for each element in stream F, with value say u, we perform the following action for each hash table p: $H[p,q] = H[p,q] + \xi_u^p$, where $q = h_p(u)$. (If the element specifies to delete value u from F, then we simply subtract ξ_u from $H[p,q]$). Thus, since there are s_2 hash tables, the time to process each stream element is $O(s_2)$ – essentially, this is the time to update a single counter (for the bucket that the element value maps to) in each hash table. Later in Section 4.3, we show that it is possible to obtain strong probabilistic error guarantees for the join size estimate as long as $s_2 = O(\log m)$. Thus, maintaining the hash sketch data structure for a stream requires only logarithmic time per stream element.

Note that each counter $H[p,q]$ is essentially an *atomic sketch* constructed over the stream elements that map to bucket q of hash table p.

4.2 Estimating Dense Frequencies

In [8], the authors propose the COUNTSKETCH algorithm for estimating the top-k frequencies in a stream F. In this section, we show how the COUNTSKETCH algorithm can be adapted to extract, with high probability, all dense frequencies greater than or equal to a threshold T. The COUNTSKETCH algorithm maintains a hash sketch structure H over the streaming values in F. The key idea here is that by randomly distributing domain

[2] Ignoring logarithmic terms since these are generally small.

Procedure SKIMDENSE(H)
Input: Hash sketch H for stream F.
Output: Skimmed sketch and frequency estimates $\hat{f}$ for dense values.
begin
1. **for** every domain value $u \in \mathcal{D}$ **do** $\hat{f}_u := 0$;
2. $E := \phi$; $T' := \Theta(n/s_1)$;
3. **for** every domain value $u \in \mathcal{D}$ **do** {
4. **for** each hash table p **do** { $q := h_p(u)$; $\hat{f}_u^p := H[p,q] \cdot \xi_u^p$; }
5. $\text{EST}(u) := \text{median}\{\hat{f}_u^1, \ldots, \hat{f}_u^{s_2}\}$;
6. **if** ($\text{EST}(u) \geq 2T'$) **then** { $\hat{f}_u := \text{EST}(u)$; $E := E \cup \{u\}$; }
7. }
8. **for** every domain value u such that $\hat{f}_u > 0$ **do**
9. **for** each hash table p **do** { $q := h_p(u)$; $H[p,q] := H[p,q] - (\hat{f}_u \cdot \xi_u^p)$; }
10. **return** $(H, \hat{f}, E)$;
end

Fig. 3. Variant of COUNTSKETCH Algorithm [8] for Skimming Dense Frequencies.

values across the s_1 buckets, the hash functions h_p help to separate the dense domain values. As a result, the self-join sizes (of the stream projections) within each bucket are much smaller, and the dense domain values u spread across the buckets of a hash table p can be estimated fairly accurately (and with constant probability) by computing the product $H[p,q] \cdot \xi_u^p$, where $q = h_p(u)$. The probability can then be boosted to $1-\delta$ by selecting the median of the $s_2 = O(\log(m/\delta))$ different frequency estimates for u, one per table. Procedure SKIMDENSE, depicted in Figure 3, extracts into vector $\hat{f}$, all dense frequencies $f_u \geq T = 3T'$, where $T' = \Theta(n/s_1)$. In order to show this, we first present the following adaptation of a result from [8].

Theorem 3 ([8]). Let $s_2 = O(\log(m/\delta))$, and $T' = \Theta(n/s_1)$. Then, for every domain value u, procedure SKIMDENSE computes an estimate $\text{EST}(u)$ of f_u (in Step 5) with an additive error of at most T' with probability at least $1-\delta$ (i.e., $P[|\text{EST}(u) - f_u| \leq T'] \geq 1-\delta$) while using only $O(s_1 \cdot s_2 \cdot (\log(m) + \log(n)))$ bits of memory. □

Based on the above property of estimates $\text{EST}(u)$, it is easy to show that, in Step 6, procedure SKIMDENSE extracts (with high probability) into $\hat{f}$ all frequencies $f_u \geq T$, where $T = 3T'$. Furthermore, the residual element frequencies can be upper-bounded as shown in the following theorem (the proof can be found in [17]).

Theorem 4. Let $s_2 = O(\log(m/\delta))$, $T' = \Theta(n/s_1)$ and $T = 3T'$. Then, with probability at least $1-\delta$, procedure SKIMDENSE returns a frequency vector $\hat{f}$ such that for every domain value u, (1) $|\hat{f}_u - f_u| \leq T$ and (2) $|\hat{f}_u - f_u| \leq f_u$. □

Note that Point (1) in Theorem 4 ensures that the residual frequency $|\hat{f}_u - f_u|$ does not exceed T for all domain values, while Point (2) ensures that the residual frequency $|\hat{f}_u - f_u|$ is no larger than the original frequency f_u. Also, observe that, in Steps 8–9, procedure SKIMDENSE skims the dense frequencies from the s_2 hash tables, and returns (in addition to the dense frequency vector $\hat{f}$) the final skimmed hash sketch containing only the residual frequencies.

The runtime complexity of procedure SKIMDENSE is $O(m)$ since it examines every domain value u. This is clearly a serious problem when domain sizes are large (e.g., 64-bit IP addresses). Fortunately, it is possible to reduce the execution time of procedure SKIMDENSE to $O(s_1 \log m)$ using the concept of *dyadic intervals* as suggested in [9]. Consider a hierarchical organization of domain values $\mathcal{D} = \{1, \ldots, m\}$ into $\log(m)$ levels[3]. At level l, $0 \leq l < \log(m)$, the domain $\mathcal{D}$ is split into a sequence of $\frac{m}{2^l}$ dyadic intervals of size 2^l, and all domain values in the uth dyadic interval $[(u-1)\cdot 2^l + 1, u \cdot 2^l]$ are mapped to a single value u at level l. Thus, for level $l = 0$, each domain value u is mapped to u itself. For $l = 1$, the sequence of intervals is $[1, 2], [3, 4], \ldots, [\frac{m}{2}\cdot 2-1, \frac{m}{2}\cdot 2]$, which are mapped to values $1, 2, \ldots, \frac{m}{2}$ at level 1. For $l = 2$, the sequence of intervals is $[1, 4]$, $[5, 8], \ldots, [\frac{m}{4} \cdot 4 - 3, \frac{m}{4} \cdot 4]$, which are mapped to values $1, 2, \ldots, \frac{m}{4}$ at level 2, and so on. Let $\mathcal{D}^l = \{1, \ldots, \frac{m}{2^l}\}$ denote the set of values at level l, and for every $u \in \mathcal{D}^l$, let f_u^l be the frequency of value u at level l. Thus, $f_u^0 = f_u$, and in general, $f_u^l = \sum_{v=(u-1)\cdot 2^l+1}^{u\cdot 2^l} f_v$. For example, $f_2^2 = \sum_{v=5}^{8} f_v$.

The key observation we make is the following: for a level l, if f_u^l is less than threshold value T, then for every domain value v in the interval $[(u-1)\cdot 2^l + 1, u \cdot 2^l]$, f_v must be less than T. Thus, our optimized SKIMDENSE procedure simply needs to maintain hash sketches at $\log(m)$ levels, where the sketch at level l is constructed using values from $\mathcal{D}^l$. Then, beginning with level $\log(m) - 1$, the procedure estimates the dense frequency values at each level, and uses this to prune the set of values estimated at each successive lower level, until level 0 is reached. Specifically, if for a value u at level $l > 0$, the estimate $\hat{f}_u^l$ is $< 2T'$, then we know that $f_u^l < T = 3T'$ (due to Theorem 3), and thus, we can prune the entire interval of values $[(u-1)\cdot 2^l + 1, u \cdot 2^l]$ since these cannot be dense. Only if $\hat{f}_u^l \geq 2T'$, do we recursively check values $2u - 1$ and $2u$ at level $l - 1$ that correspond to the two sub-intervals $[(2u-2)\cdot 2^{l-1} + 1, (2u-1)\cdot 2^{l-1}]$ and $[(2u-1)\cdot 2^{l-1} + 1, 2u \cdot 2^{l-1}]$ contained within the interval for value u at level l. Thus, since at each level, there can be at most $O(n/T')$ values with frequency T' or higher, we obtain that the worst-case time complexity of our optimized SKIMDENSE algorithm is $O(s_1 \log m)$.

4.3 Join Size Estimation Using Skimmed Sketches

We now describe our skimmed-sketch algorithm for computing $f \cdot g = \sum_u f_u \cdot g_u$. Let H_F and H_G be the hash sketches for streams F and G, respectively. (Sketches H_F and H_G use identical hash functions h_p). The key idea of our algorithm is to first skim all the dense frequencies from sketches H_F and H_G using SKIMDENSE, and then use the skimmed sketches (containing no dense frequencies) to estimate $f \cdot g$. Skimming enables our algorithm to estimate the join size more accurately than the basic sketching algorithm of [4] that uses sketches X_F and X_G directly (without skimming). As already discussed in Section 3, the reason for this is that skimming causes every residual frequency in the skimmed sketches to drop below T (see Theorem 4), and thus the self-join sizes of

[3] For simplicity of exposition, we assume that m is a power of 2.

Procedure EstSkimJoinSize(H_F, H_G)
Input: H_F and H_G are the hash sketches for streams F and G.
Output: Estimate of join size.
begin
1. $(H'_F, \hat{f}, E_F)$:= SkimDense(H_F); $(H'_G, \hat{g}, E_G)$:= SkimDense(H_G);
2. $\hat{J}_{d,d}$:= $\hat{f} \cdot \hat{g}$; $\hat{J}_{ds}$:= EstSubJoinSize($\hat{f}, H'_G$); $\hat{J}_{sd}$:= EstSubJoinSize($\hat{g}, H'_F$);
3. **for** $p = 1$ to s_2 **do** {
4. $\quad\hat{J}^p_{ss}$:= 0;
5. $\quad$**for** $q = 1$ to s_1 **do** $\hat{J}^p_{ss}$:= $\hat{J}^p_{ss}$ + $H'_F[p,q] \cdot H'_G[p,q]$;
6. }
7. $\hat{J}_{ss}$:= median $\{\hat{J}^1_{ss}, \ldots, \hat{J}^{s_2}_{ss}\}$;
8. $\hat{J}$:= $\hat{J}_{dd} + \hat{J}_{ds} + \hat{J}_{sd} + \hat{J}_{ss}$;
9. **return** $\hat{J}$;
end

Procedure EstSubJoinSize($\hat{v}, H'$)
Input: Frequency vector $\hat{v}$ of dense frequencies and hash sketch H'.
Output: Estimate of subjoin size.
begin
1. **for** $p = 1$ to s_2 **do** {
2. $\quad\hat{J}^p$:= 0;
3. $\quad$**for** each domain value u s.t. $\hat{v}_u > 0$ **do** { q := $h_p(u)$; $\hat{J}^p$:= $\hat{J}^p + H'[p,q] \cdot (\hat{v}_u \cdot \xi^p_u)$; }
4. }
5. **return** median$\{\hat{J}^1, \ldots, \hat{J}^{s_2}\}$;
end

Fig. 4. Skimmed-sketch Algorithm to Estimate Join Size.

the residual frequency vectors in the skimmed sketches become significantly smaller. Consequently, the join size estimate computed using skimmed sketches can potentially be more accurate (because of the dependence of the maximum additive error on self-join sizes), and the space requirements of our skimmed-sketch algorithm can be shown to match the lower bound of $\Omega(n^2/(f \cdot g))$ for the join-size estimation problem.

Skimmed-Sketch Algorithm. Our skimmed-sketch algorithm for estimating the join size of streams F and G from their hash sketches H_F and H_G is described in Figure 4. Procedure EstSkimJoinSize begins by extracting into vectors $\hat{f}$ and $\hat{g}$, all frequencies in f and g (respectively) that exceed the threshold $T = \Theta(n/s_1)$. For each domain value u, let $f'_u = f_u - \hat{f}_u$ and $g'_u = g_u - \hat{g}_u$ be the residual frequencies for u in the skimmed sketches H'_F and H'_G (returned by SkimDense). We will refer to f'_u as the sparse component, and to $\hat{f}_u$ as the dense component of the frequency for value u.

The first observation we make is that the join size $J = f \cdot g$ can be expressed entirely in terms of the sparse and dense frequency components. Thus, if $J_{dd} = \hat{f} \cdot \hat{g}$, $J_{ds} = \hat{f} \cdot g'$, $J_{sd} = f' \cdot \hat{g}$, and $J_{ss} = f' \cdot g'$, then $J = J_{dd} + J_{ds} + J_{sd} + J_{ss}$. Consequently, our skimmed-sketch algorithm estimates the join size $\hat{J}$ by summing the individual estimates $\hat{J}_{dd}$, $\hat{J}_{ds}$, $\hat{J}_{sd}$ and $\hat{J}_{ss}$ for the four terms J_{dd}, J_{ds}, J_{sd} and J_{ss}, respectively.

The second observation is that the subjoin size J_{dd} between the dense frequency components can be computed accurately (that is, with zero error) since $\hat{f}$ and $\hat{g}$ are known exactly. Thus, sketches are only needed to compute subjoin sizes for the cases when one of the components is sparse. Let us consider the problem of estimating the subjoin size $J_{ds} = \hat{f} \cdot g'$. For each domain value u that is non-zero in $\hat{f}$, an estimate for the quantity $\hat{f}_u \cdot g'_u$ can be generated from each hash table p by multiplying $(\hat{f}_u \cdot \xi_u^p)$ with $H'_G[p,q]$, where $q = h_p(u)$. Thus, by summing these individual estimates for hash table p, we can obtain an estimate $\hat{J}_{ds}^p$ for J_{ds} from hash table p. Finally, we can boost the confidence of the final estimate $\hat{J}_{ds}$ by selecting it to be the median of the set of estimates $\{\hat{J}_{ds}^1, \ldots, \hat{J}_{ds}^{s_2}\}$. Estimating the subjoin size $J_{sd} = f' \cdot \hat{g}$ is completely symmetric; see the pseudo-code for procedure ESTSUBJOINSIZE in Figure 4. To estimate the subjoin size $J_{ss} = f' \cdot g'$ (Steps 3–7 of procedure ESTSKIMJOINSIZE), we again generate estimates $\hat{J}_{ss}^p$ for each hash table p, and then select the median of the estimates to boost confidence. Since the pth hash tables in the two hash sketches H_F and H_G employ the same hash function h_p, the domain values that map to a bucket q in each of the two hash tables are identical. Thus, estimate $\hat{J}_{ss}^p$ for each hash table p can be generated by simply summing $H'_F[p,q] \cdot H'_G[p,q]$ for all the buckets q of hash table p.

Analysis. We now give a sketch of the analysis for the accuracy of the join size estimate $\hat{J}$ returned by procedure ESTSKIMJOINSIZE. First, observe that on expectation, $\hat{J} = J$. This is because $\hat{J}_{dd} = J_{dd}$, and for all other i, j, $E[\hat{J}_{ij}] = J_{ij}$ (shown in [4]). Thus, $E[\hat{J}] = J_{dd} + J_{ds} + J_{sd} + J_{ss} = J$. In the following, we show that, with high probability, the additive error in each of the estimates $\hat{J}_{ij}$ (and thus, also the final estimate $\hat{J}$) is at most $\Theta((n^2/s_1)(\log n)^{1/2})$. Intuitively, the reason for this is that these errors depend on hash bucket self-join sizes, and since every residual frequency f'_u in H'_F and H'_G is at most $T = \Theta(n/s_1)$, each bucket self-join size is proportional to $\Theta(n^2/s_1^2)$ with high probability. Due to space constraints, the detailed proofs have been omitted – they can be found in the full version of this paper [17].

Lemma 1. Let $s_2 = O(\log(m/\delta))$. Then, the estimate $\hat{J}_{sd}$ computed by ESTSKIMJOINSIZE satisfies: $P[|\hat{J}_{sd} - J_{sd}| \leq \Theta((n^2/s_1)(\log n)^{1/4})] \geq 1 - \Theta(\delta)$. □

Lemma 2. Let $s_2 = O(\log(m/\delta))$. Then, the estimate $\hat{J}_{ss}$ computed by ESTSKIMJOINSIZE satisfies: $P[|\hat{J}_{ss} - J_{ss}| \leq \Theta((n^2/s_1^{1.5})(\log n)^{1/2})] \geq 1 - \Theta(\delta)$. □

Note that a result similar to that in Lemma 1 above can also be shown for $\hat{J}_{ds}$ [17]. Using the above lemmas, we are now ready to prove the analytical bounds on worst-case additive error and space requirements for our skimmed-sketch algorithm.

Theorem 5. Let $s_2 = O(\log(m/\delta))$. Then the estimate $\hat{J}$ computed by ESTSKIMJOINSIZE satisfies: $P[|\hat{J} - (f \cdot g)| \leq \Theta((n^2/s_1)(\log n)^{1/2})] \geq 1 - \delta$. This implies that ESTSKIMJOINSIZE estimates $f \cdot g$ with a relative error of at most ϵ with probability at least $1 - \delta$ (i.e., $P[|\hat{J} - (f \cdot g)| \leq \epsilon \cdot (f \cdot g)] \geq 1 - \delta$) while using only $O\left(\frac{n^2 \cdot \log(m/\delta) \cdot (\log n)^{1/2}}{\epsilon \cdot (f \cdot g)} (\log(m) + \log(n))\right)$ bits of memory (in the worst case). □

Proof. Due to Lemmas 1 and 2, it follows that with probability at least $1 - \delta$, the total additive error in the estimates $\hat{J}_{ds}$, $\hat{J}_{sd}$ and $\hat{J}_{ss}$ is at most $\Theta((n^2/s_1)(\log n)^{1/2})$. Thus, since $\hat{J} = \hat{J}_{dd} + \hat{J}_{ds} + \hat{J}_{sd} + \hat{J}_{ss}$, and the error in estimate $\hat{J}_{dd}$ is 0, the statement of the theorem follows. □

Thus, ignoring the logarithmic terms since these will generally be small, we obtain that in the worst case, our skimmed-sketch join algorithm requires approximately $O(\frac{n^2}{\epsilon \cdot (f \cdot g)})$ amount of space, which is equal to the lower bound achievable by any join size estimation algorithm [4]. Also, since maintenance of the hash sketch data structure involves updating s_2 hash bucket counters per stream element, the processing time per element of our skimmed-sketch algorithm is $O(\log(m/\delta))$.

5 Experimental Study

In this section, we present the results of our experimental study in which we compare the accuracy of the join size estimates returned by our skimmed-sketch method with the basic sketching technique of [4]. Our experiments with both synthetic and real-life data sets indicate that our skimmed-sketch algorithm is an effective tool for approximating the size of the join of two streams. Even with a few kilobytes of memory, the relative error in the final answer is generally less than 10%. Our experiments also show that our skimmed-sketch method provides significantly more accurate estimates for join sizes compared to the the basic sketching method, the improvement in accuracy ranging from a factor of five (for moderate skew in the data) to several orders of magnitude (when the skew in the frequency distribution is higher).

5.1 Experimental Testbed and Methodology

Algorithms for Query Answering. We consider two join size estimation algorithms in our performance study: the basic sketching algorithm of [4] and a variant of our skimmed-sketch technique. We do not consider histograms or random-sample data summaries since these have been shown to perform worse than sketches for queries with one or more joins [4,5]. We allocate the same amount of memory to both sketching methods in each experiment.

Data Sets. We used a single real-life data set, and several synthetically generated data sets with different characteristics in our experiments.

• *Census data set (www.bls.census.gov).* This data set was taken from the Current Population Survey (CPS) data, which is a monthly survey of about 50,000 households conducted by the Bureau of the Census for the Bureau of Labor Statistics. Each month's data contains around 135,000 tuples with 361 attributes, of which we used two numeric attributes to join, in our study: weekly wage and weekly wage overtime, each with domain size 288416. In our study, we use data from the month of September 2002 containing 159,434 records[4].

• *Synthetic data sets.* The experiments involving synthetic data sets evaluate the size of the join between a Zipfian distribution and a right-shifted Zipfian distribution with the

[4] We excluded records with missing values.

same Zipf parameter z. A right-shifted Zipfian distribution with Zipf parameter z and shift parameter s is basically the original distribution shifted right by the shift parameter s. Thus, the frequency of domain values between 1 and s in the shifted Zipfian distribution is identical to the frequencies in the original Zipfian distribution for domain values between $m - s + 1$ to m, where m, the domain size, is chosen to be 2^{18} (or 256 K). We generate 4 million elements for each stream.

In our experiments, we use the shift parameter s to control the join size; a shift value of 0 causes the join to become equivalent to a self-join, while as the shift parameter is increased, the join size progressively decreases. Thus, parameter s provides us with a knob to "stress-test" the accuracy of the two algorithms in a controlled manner. We expect the accuracy of both algorithms to fall as the shift parameter is increased (since relative error is inversely proportion to join size), which is a fact that is corroborated by our experiments. The interesting question then becomes: how quickly does the error performance of each algorithm degenerate?

Due to space constraints, we omit the presentation of our experimental results with the real-life Census data; they can be found in the full paper [17]. In a nutshell, our numbers with real-life data sets are qualitatively similar to our synthetic-data results, demonstrating that our skimmed-sketch technique offers roughly half the relative error of basic sketching, even though the magnitude of the errors (for both methods) is typically significantly smaller [17].

Answer-Quality Metrics. In our experiments, we compute the error of the join size estimate $\hat{J}$ as $\frac{|J-\hat{J}|}{\min\{J,\hat{J}\}}$, where J is the actual join size. The reason we use this alternate error metric instead of the standard relative error $(|J - \hat{J}|)/J$, is that the relative error measure is biased in favor of underestimates, and penalizes overestimates more severely. For example, the relative error for a join size estimation algorithm that always returns 0 (the smallest possible underestimate of the join size), can never exceed 1. On the other hand, the relative error of overestimates can be arbitrarily large. The error metric we use remedies this problem, since by being symmetric, it penalizes underestimates and overestimates about equally. Also, in some cases when the amount of memory is low, the join size estimates $\hat{J}$ returned by the sketching algorithms are very small, and at times even negative. When this happens, we simply consider the error to be a large constant, say 10 (which is equivalent to using a sanity bound of $J/10$ for very small join size results).

We repeat each experiment between 5 and 10 times, and use the average value for the errors across the iterations as the final error in our plots. In each experiment, for a given amount of space s, we consider s_1 values between 50 and 250 (in increments of 50), and s_2 from 11 to 59 (in increments of 12) such that $s_1 \cdot s_2 = s$, and take the average of the results for s_1, s_2 pairs.

5.2 Experimental Results

Figures 5(a) and 5(b) depict the error for the two algorithms as the amount of available memory is increased. The Zipf parameters for the Zipfian distributions joined in Figures 5(a) and 5(b) are 1.0 and 1.5, respectively. The results for three settings of the shift parameter are plotted in the graph of Figure 5(a), namely, 100, 200, and 300. On the

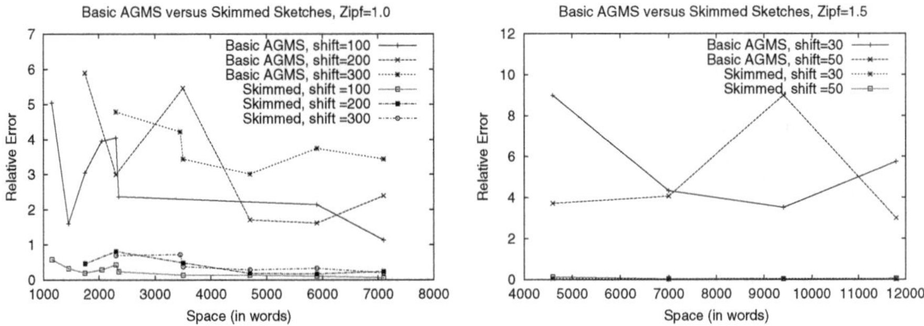

Fig. 5. Results for Synthetic Data Sets: (a) $z = 1.0$, (b) $z = 1.5$.

other hand, smaller shifts of 30 and 50 are considered for the higher Zipf value of 1.5 in 5(b). This is because the data is more skewed when $z = 1.5$, and thus, larger shift parameter values cause the join size to become too small.

It is interesting to observe that the error of our skimmed-sketch algorithm is almost an order of magnitude lower than the basic sketching technique for $z = 1.0$, and several orders of magnitude better when $z = 1.5$. This is because as the data becomes more skewed, the self-join sizes become large and this hurts the accuracy of the basic sketching method. Our skimmed-sketch algorithm, on the other hand, avoids this problem by eliminating from the sketches, the high frequency values. As a result, the self-join sizes of the skimmed sketches never get too big, and thus the errors for our algorithm are small (e.g., less than 10% for $z = 1$, and almost zero when $z = 1.5$). Also, note that the error typically increases with the shift parameter value since the join size is smaller for larger shifts. Finally, observe that there is much more variance in the error for the basic sketching method compared to our skimmed-sketch technique – we attribute this to the high self-join sizes with basic sketching (recall that variance is proportional to the product of the self-join sizes).

6 Conclusions

In this paper, we have presented the *skimmed-sketch* algorithm for estimating the join size of two streams. (Our techniques also naturally extend to complex, multi-join aggregates.) Our skimmed-sketch technique is the first comprehensive join-size estimation algorithm to provide tight error guarantees while (1) achieving the lower bound on the space required by any join-size estimation method, (2) handling general streaming updates, (3) incurring a guaranteed small (i.e., logarithmic) processing overhead per stream element, and (4) not assuming any a-priori knowledge of the data distribution. Our experimental study with real-life as well as synthetic data streams has verified the superiority of our skimmed-sketch algorithm compared to other known sketch-based methods for join-size estimation.

References

1. Greenwald, M., Khanna, S.: "Space-efficient online computation of quantile summaries". In: Proceedings of the 2001 ACM SIGMOD International Conference on Management of Data, Santa Barbara, California (2001)
2. Gilbert, A., Kotidis, Y., Muthukrishnan, S., Strauss, M.: "How to Summarize the Universe: Dynamic Maintenance of Quantiles". In: Proceedings of the 28th International Conference on Very Large Data Bases, Hong Kong (2002)
3. Alon, N., Matias, Y., Szegedy, M.: "The Space Complexity of Approximating the Frequency Moments". In: Proceedings of the 28th Annual ACM Symposium on the Theory of Computing, Philadelphia, Pennsylvania (1996) 20–29
4. Alon, N., Gibbons, P.B., Matias, Y., Szegedy, M.: "Tracking Join and Self-Join Sizes in Limited Storage". In: Proceedings of the Eighteenth ACM SIGACT-SIGMOD-SIGART Symposium on Principles of Database Systems, Philadeplphia, Pennsylvania (1999)
5. Dobra, A., Garofalakis, M., Gehrke, J., Rastogi, R.: "Processing Complex Aggregate Queries over Data Streams". In: Proceedings of the 2002 ACM SIGMOD International Conference on Management of Data, Madison, Wisconsin (2002)
6. Gibbons, P.: "Distinct Sampling for Highly-accurate Answers to Distinct Values Queries and Event Reports". In: Proceedings of the 27th International Conference on Very Large Data Bases, Roma, Italy (2001)
7. Cormode, G., Datar, M., Indyk, P., Muthukrishnan, S.: "Comparing Data Streams Using Hamming Norms". In: Proceedings of the 28th International Conference on Very Large Data Bases, Hong Kong (2002)
8. Charikar, M., Chen, K., Farach-Colton, M.: "Finding frequent items in data streams". In: Proceedings of the 29th International Colloquium on Automata Languages and Programming. (2002)
9. Cormode, G., Muthukrishnan, S.: "What's Hot and What's Not: Tracking Most Frequent Items Dynamically". In: Proceedings of the Twentysecond ACM SIGACT-SIGMOD-SIGART Symposium on Principles of Database Systems, San Diego, California (2003)
10. Manku, G., Motwani, R.: "Approximate Frequency Counts over Data Streams". In: Proceedings of the 28th International Conference on Very Large Data Bases, Hong Kong (2002)
11. Gilbert, A.C., Kotidis, Y., Muthukrishnan, S., Strauss, M.J.: "Surfing Wavelets on Streams: One-pass Summaries for Approximate Aggregate Queries". In: Proceedings of the 27th International Conference on Very Large Data Bases, Roma, Italy (2001)
12. Datar, M., Gionis, A., Indyk, P., Motwani, R.: "Maintaining Stream Statistics over Sliding Windows". In: Proceedings of the 13th Annual ACM-SIAM Symposium on Discrete Algorithms, San Francisco, California (2002)
13. Vitter, J.: Random sampling with a reservoir. ACM Transactions on Mathematical Software **11** (1985) 37–57
14. Acharya, S., Gibbons, P.B., Poosala, V., Ramaswamy, S.: "Join Synopses for Approximate Query Answering". In: Proceedings of the 1999 ACM SIGMOD International Conference on Management of Data, Philadelphia, Pennsylvania (1999) 275–286
15. Chakrabarti, K., Garofalakis, M., Rastogi, R., Shim, K.: "Approximate Query Processing Using Wavelets". In: Proceedings of the 26th International Conference on Very Large Data Bases, Cairo, Egypt (2000) 111–122
16. Ganguly, S., Gibbons, P., Matias, Y., Silberschatz, A.: "Bifocal Sampling for Skew-Resistant Join Size Estimation". In: Proceedings of the 1996 ACM SIGMOD International Conference on Management of Data, Montreal, Quebec (1996)
17. Ganguly, S., Garofalakis, M., Rastogi, R.: "Processing Data-Stream Join Aggregates Using Skimmed Sketches". Bell Labs Tech. Memorandum (2004)

Joining Punctuated Streams

Luping Ding, Nishant Mehta, Elke A. Rundensteiner, and George T. Heineman

Department of Computer Science, Worcester Polytechnic Institute
100 Institute Road, Worcester, MA 01609
{lisading,nishantm,rundenst,heineman}@cs.wpi.edu

Abstract. We focus on stream join optimization by exploiting the constraints that are dynamically embedded into data streams to signal the end of transmitting certain attribute values. These constraints are called *punctuations*. Our stream join operator, PJoin, is able to remove no-longer-useful data from the state in a timely manner based on punctuations, thus reducing memory overhead and improving the efficiency of probing. We equip PJoin with several alternate strategies for purging the state and for propagating punctuations to benefit down-stream operators. We also present an extensive experimental study to explore the performance gains achieved by purging state as well as the trade-off between different purge strategies. Our experimental results of comparing the performance of PJoin with XJoin, a stream join operator without a constraint-exploiting mechanism, show that PJoin significantly outperforms XJoin with regard to both memory overhead and throughput.

1 Introduction

1.1 Stream Join Operators and Constraints

As stream-processing applications, including sensor network monitoring [14], online transaction management [18], and online spreadsheets [9], to name a few, have gained in popularity, continuous query processing is emerging as an important research area [1] [5] [6] [15] [16]. The join operator, being one of the most expensive and commonly used operators in continuous queries, has received increasing attention [9] [13] [19]. Join processing in the stream context faces numerous new challenges beyond those encountered in the traditional context. One important new problem is the *potentially unbounded runtime join state*. Since the join needs to maintain in its join state the data that has already arrived in order to compare it against the data to be arriving in the future. As data continuously streams in, the basic stream join solutions, such as symmetric hash join [22], will indefinitely accumulate input data in the join state, thus easily causing memory overflow.

XJoin [19] [20] extends the symmetric hash join to avoid memory overflow. It moves part of the join state to the secondary storage (disk) upon running out of memory. However, as more data streams in, a large portion of the join state will be paged to disk. This will result in a huge amount of I/O operations. Then the performance of XJoin may degrade in such circumstances.

E. Bertino et al. (Eds.): EDBT 2004, LNCS 2992, pp. 587–604, 2004.
© Springer-Verlag Berlin Heidelberg 2004

In many cases, it is not practical to compare every tuple in a potentially infinite stream with all tuples in another also possibly infinite stream [2]. In response, the recent work on window joins [4] [8] [13] extends the traditional join semantics to only join tuples within the current time windows. This way the memory usage of the join state can be bounded by timely removing tuples that drop out of the window. However, choosing an appropriate window size is non-trivial. The join state may be rather bulky for large windows.

[3] proposes a k-constraint-exploiting join algorithm that utilizes *statically specified constraints*, including clustered and ordered arrival of join values, to purge the data that have finished joining with the matching cluster from the opposite stream, thereby shrinking the state.

However, the static constraints only characterize restrictive cases of real-world data. In view of this limitation, a new class of constraints called *punctuations* [18] has been proposed to dynamically provide meta knowledge about data streams. Punctuations are embedded into data streams (hence called *punctuated streams*) to signal the end of transmitting certain attribute values. This should enable stateful operators like *join* to discard partial join state during the execution and blocking operators like *group-by* to emit partial results.

In some cases punctuations can be provided actively by the applications that generate the data streams. For example, in an *online auction management system* [18], the *sellers portal* merges items for sale submitted by sellers into a stream called *Open*. The *buyers portal* merges the bids posted by bidders into another stream called *Bid*. Since each item is open for bid only within a specific time period, when the open auction period for an item expires, the auction system can insert a punctuation into the *Bid* stream to signal the end of the bids for that specific item.

The query system itself can also derive punctuations based on the semantics of the application or certain static constraints, including the join between key and foreign key, clustered or ordered arrival of certain attribute values, etc. For example, since each tuple in the *Open* stream has a unique *item_id* value, the query system can then insert a punctuation after each tuple in this stream signaling no more tuple containing this specific *item_id* value will occur in the future. Therefore punctuations cover a wider realm of constraints that may help continuous query optimization. [18] also defines the rules for algebra operators, including join, to purge runtime state and to propagate punctuations down-stream. However, no concrete punctuation-exploiting join algorithms have been proposed to date. This is the topic we thus focus on in this paper.

1.2 Our Approach: PJoin

In this paper, we present the first punctuation-exploiting stream join solution, called PJoin. PJoin is a binary hash-based equi-join operator. It is able to exploit punctuations to achieve the optimization goals of reducing memory overhead and of increasing the data output rate. Unlike prior stream join operators stated above, PJoin can also propagate appropriate punctuations to benefit down-stream operators. Our contributions of PJoin include:

1. We propose alternate strategies for purging the join state, including eager and lazy purge, and we explore the trade-off between different purge strategies regarding the memory overhead and the data output rate experimentally.
2. We propose various strategies for propagating punctuations, including eager and lazy index building as well as propagation in push and pull mode. We also explore the trade-off between different strategies with regard to the punctuation output rate.
3. We design an event-driven framework for accommodating all PJoin components, including memory and disk join, state purge, punctuation propagation, etc., to enable the flexible configuration of different join solutions.
4. We conduct an experimental study to validate our preformance analysis by comparing the performance of PJoin with XJoin [19], a stream join operator without a constraint-exploiting mechanism, as well as the performance of using different state purge strategies in terms of various data and punctuation arrival rates. The experimental results show that PJoin outperforms XJoin with regard to both memory overhead and data output rate.

In Section 2, we give background knowledge and a running example of punctuated streams. In Section 3 we describe the execution logic design of PJoin, including alternate strategies for state purge and punctuation propagation. An extensive experimental study is shown in Section 4. In Section 5 we explain related work. We discuss future extensions of PJoin in Section 6 and conclude our work in Section 7.

2 Punctuated Streams

2.1 Motivating Example

We now explain how punctuations can help with continuous query optimization using the *online auction* example [18] described in Section 1.1. Fragments of *Open* and *Bid* streams with punctuations are shown in Figure 1 (a). The query in Figure 1 (b) joins all items for sale with their bids on *item_id* and then sum up bid-increase values for each item that has at least one bid. In the corresponding query plan shown in Figure 1 (c), an *equi-join* operator joins the *Open* stream with the *Bid* stream on *item_id*. Our PJoin operator can be used to perform this equi-join. Thereafter, the *group-by* operator groups the output stream of the join (denoted as Out_1) by *item_id*. Whenever a punctuation from *Bid* is obtained which signals the auction for a particular item is closed, the tuple in the state for the *Open* stream that contains the same *item_id* value can then be purged. Furthermore, a punctuation regarding this *item_id* value can be propagated to the Out_1 stream for the *group-by* to produce the result for this specific item.

2.2 Punctuations

Punctuation semantics. A punctuation can be viewed as a predicate on stream elements that must evaluate to *false* for every element *following* the

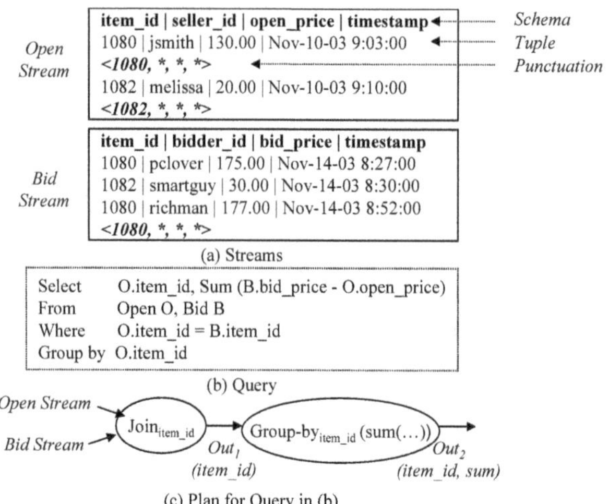

(a) Streams

(b) Query

(c) Plan for Query in (b)

Fig. 1. Data Streams and Example Query.

punctuation, while the stream elements that appear *before* the punctuation can evaluate either to *true* or to *false*. Hence a punctuation can be used to detect and purge the data in the join state that *won't* join with any future data.

In PJoin, we use the same punctuation semantics as defined in [18], i.e., a punctuation is an ordered set of *patterns*, with each pattern corresponding to an attribute of a tuple. There are five kinds of patterns: wildcard, constant, range, enumeration list and empty pattern. The "and" of any two punctuations is also a punctuation. In this paper, we only focus on exploiting punctuations over the join attribute. We assume that for any two punctuations p_i and p_j such that p_i arrives before p_j, if the patterns for the join attribute specified by p_i and p_j are Ptn_i and Ptn_j respectively, then either $Ptn_i \wedge Ptn_j = \emptyset$ or $Ptn_i \wedge Ptn_j = Ptn_i$. We denote all tuples that arrived before time T from stream A and B as tuple sets $TS_A(T)$ and $TS_B(T)$ respectively. All punctuations that arrived before time T from stream A and B are denoted as punctuation sets $PS_A(T)$ and $PS_B(T)$ respectively. According to [18], if a tuple t has a join value that matches the pattern declared by the punctuation p, then t is said to match p, denoted as $match(t, p)$. If there exists a punctuation p_A in $PS_A(T)$ such that the tuple t matches p_A, then t is defined to also match the set $PS_A(T)$, denoted as $setMatch(t, PS_A(T))$.

Purge rules for join. Given punctuation sets $PS_A(T)$ and $PS_B(T)$, the purge rules for tuple sets $TS_A(T)$ and $TS_B(T)$ are defined as follows:

$$\begin{aligned} &\forall t_A \in TS_A(T),\ purge(t_A)\ \ if\ \ setMatch(t_A, PS_B(T)) \\ &\forall t_B \in TS_B(T),\ purge(t_B)\ \ if\ \ setMatch(t_B, PS_A(T)) \end{aligned} \tag{1}$$

Propagation rules for join. To propagate a punctuation, we must guarantee that no more tuples that match this punctuation will be generated later. The propagation rules are derived based on the following theorem.

Theorem 1. *Given $TS_A(T)$ and $PS_A(T)$, for any punctuation p_A in $PS_A(T)$, if at time T, no tuple t_A exists in $TS_A(T)$ such that match(t_A,p_A), then no tuple t_R such that match(t_R, p_A) will be generated as a join result at or after time T.*

Proof by contradiction. Assume that at least one tuple t_R such that match(t_R, p_A) will be generated as a join result at or after time T. Then there must exist at least one tuple t in $TS_A(T_k)$ ($T_k \geq T$) such that match(t, p_A). Based on the definition of punctuation, there will not be any tuple t_A to be arriving from stream A after time T such that match(t_A, p_A). Then t must have been existing in $TS_A(T)$. This contradicts the premise that no tuple t_A exists in $TS_A(T)$ such that match(t_A, p_A). Therefore, the assumption is wrong and no tuple t_R such that match(t_R, p_A) will be generated as a join result at or after time T. Thus p_A can be propagated safely at or after time T. □

The propagation rules for $PS_A(T)$ and $PS_B(T)$ are then defined as follows:

$$\begin{aligned} &\forall p_A \in PS_A(T),\ propagate(p_A)\ \ if\ \ \forall t_A \in TS_A(T), \neg match(t_A, p_A) \\ &\forall p_B \in PS_B(T),\ propagate(p_B)\ \ if\ \ \forall t_B \in TS_B(T), \neg match(t_B, p_B) \end{aligned} \tag{2}$$

3 PJoin Execution Logic

3.1 Components and Join State

Components. Join algorithms typically involve multiple subtasks, including: (1) probe in-memory join state using a new tuple and produce result for any match being found (*memory join*), (2) move part of the in-memory join state to disk when running out of memory (*state relocation*), (3) retrieve data from disk into memory for join processing (*disk join*), (4) purge no-longer-useful data from the join state (*state purge*) and (5) propagate punctuations to the output stream (*punctuation propagation*).

The frequencies of executing each of these subtasks may be rather different. For example, *memory join* runs on a per-tuple basis, while *state relocation* executes only when memory overflows and *state purge* is activated upon receiving one or multiple punctuations. To achieve a fine-tuned, adaptive join execution, we design separate components to accomplish each of the above subtasks. Furthermore, for each component we explore a variety of alternate strategies that can be plugged in to achieve optimization in different circumstances, as further elaborated upon in Section 3.2 through Section 3.5. To increase the throughput, several components may run concurrently in a multi-threaded mode. Section 3.6 introduces our event-based framework design for PJoin.

Join state. Extending from the symmetric hash join [22], PJoin maintains a separate state for each input stream. All the above components operate on this shared data storage. For each state, a *hash table* holds all tuples that have arrived but have not yet been purged. Similar to XJoin [19], each hash bucket has an in-memory portion and an on-disk portion. When memory usage of the join state reaches a *memory threshold*, some data in the memory-resident portion will be moved to the on-disk portion. A *purge buffer* contains the tuples which should be purged based on the present punctuations, but cannot yet be purged safely because they may possibly join with tuples stored on disk. The purge buffer will be cleaned up by the disk join component. The punctuations that have arrived but have not yet been propagated are stored in a *punctuation set*.

3.2 Memory Join and Disk Join

Due to the memory overflow resolution explained in Section 3.3 below, for each new input tuple, the matching tuples in the opposite state could possibly reside in two different places: memory and disk. Therefore, the join operation can happen in two components. The *memory join* component will use the new tuple to probe the memory-resident portion of the matching hash bucket of the opposite state and produce the result, while the *disk join* component will fetch the disk-resident portion of some or all the hash buckets and finish the left-over joins due to the state relocation (Section 3.3). Since the disk join involves I/O operations which are much more expensive than in-memory operations, the policies for scheduling these two components are different. The memory join is executed on a per-tuple basis. Only when the memory join cannot proceed due to the slow delivery of the data or when punctuation propagation needs to finish up all the left-over joins, will the disk join be scheduled to run. Similar to XJoin [19], we associate an *activation threshold* with the disk join to model how aggressively it is to be scheduled for execution.

3.3 State Relocation

PJoin employs the same memory overflow resolution as XJoin, i.e., moving part of the state from memory to secondary storage (disk) when the memory becomes full (reaches the *memory threshold*). The corresponding component in PJoin is called *state relocation*. Readers are referred to [19] for further details about the state relocation.

3.4 State Purge

The state purge component removes data that will no longer contribute to any future join result from the join state by applying the purge rules described in Section 2. We propose two state purge strategies, *eager (immediate) purge* and *lazy (batch) purge*. *Eager purge* starts to purge the state whenever a punctuation is obtained. This can guarantee the minimum memory overhead caused by the join state. Also by shrinking the state in an aggressive manner, the state probing can be done more efficiently. However, since the state purge causes the extra overhead for scanning the join state, when punctuations arrive very frequently so that the cost of state scan exceeds the saving of probing, eager purge may instead slow down the data output rate. In response, we propose a *lazy purge* which will start purging when the number of new punctuations since the last purge reaches a *purge threshold*, which is the number of punctuations to be arriving between two state purges. We can view eager purge as a special case of lazy purge, whose purge threshold is 1. Accordingly, finding an appropriate purge threshold becomes an important task. In Section 4 we experimentally assess the effect on PJoin performance posed by different purge thresholds.

3.5 Punctuation Propagation

Besides utilizing punctuations to shrink the runtime state, in some cases the operator can also propagate punctuations to benefit other operators down-stream in the query plan, for example, the *group-by* operator in Figure 1 (c). According to the propagation rules described in Section 2, a join operator will propagate punctuations in a *lagged* fashion, that is, before a punctuation can be released to the output stream, the join must wait until all result tuples that match this punctuation have been safely output. Hence we consider to initiate propagation periodically. However, each time we invoke the propagation, each punctuation in the *punctuation sets* needs to be evaluated against all tuples currently in the same state. Therefore, the punctuations which were not able to be propagated in the previous propagation run may be evaluated against those tuples that have already been compared with last time, thus incurring duplicate expression evaluations. To avoid this problem and to propagate punctuations correctly, we design an incrementally maintained *punctuation index* which arranges the data in the join state by punctuations.

Punctuation index. To construct a punctuation index (Figure 2 (c)), each punctuation in the punctuation set is associated with a unique ID (*pid*) and a *count* recording the number of matching tuples that reside in the same state (Figure 2 (a)). We also augment the structure of each tuple to add the *pid* which denotes the punctuation that matches the tuple (Figure 2 (b)). If a tuple matches multiple punctuations, the *pid* of the tuple is always set as the *pid* of the first arrived punctuation found to be matched. If the tuple is not valid for any existing punctuations, the *pid* of this tuple is null. Upon arrival of a new punctuation p, only tuples with *pid* field being *null* need to be evaluated against p. Therefore the punctuation index is constructed incrementally so to avoid the duplicate expression evaluations. Whenever a tuple is purged from the state, the punctuation whose *pid* corresponds the *pid* contained by the purged tuple will deduct its *count* field. When the *count* of a punctuation reaches 0 which means no tuple matching this punctuation exists in the state, according to Theorem 1 in Section 2, this punctuation becomes propagable. The punctuations being propagated are immediately removed from the punctuation set.

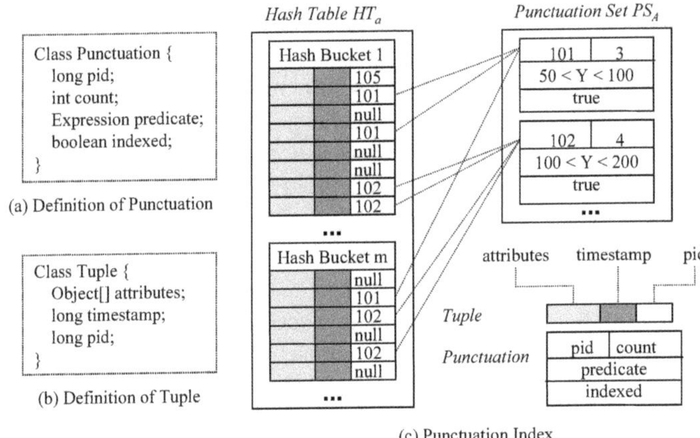

Fig. 2. Data Structures for Punctuation Propagation.

Algorithms for index building and propagation. We can see that punctuation propagation involves two important steps: *punctuation index building* which associates each tuple in the join state with a punctuation and *propagation* which outputs the punctuations with the *count* field being zero. Clearly, propagation relies on the index building process. Figure 3 shows the algorithm for constructing a punctuation index for tuples from stream B (Lines 1-14) and the algorithm for propagating punctuations from stream B to the output stream (Lines 16-21).

```
1.  Procedure Index-Build-B () {
2.     ArrayList pIndexSet = new ArrayList();
3.     /* Select all punctuations from B punctuation set PS_B not being used for indexing tuples. */
4.     foreach p_i in PS_B
5.         if (! (p_i.indexed))
6.             pIndexSet.add(p_i);
7.     /* Index all tuples in the B hash table HT_b that have not yet been indexed. */
8.     foreach bucket_k in HT_b
9.         foreach t_j in bucket_k
10.            if (t_j.pid == null)
11.                foreach p_i in pIndexSet
12.                    if (match(t_j, p_i)) {
13.                        t_j.pid = p_i.pid; /* Assign pid to the matching tuple. */
14.                        continue; } }
15.
16. Procedure Propagate-B () {
17.    /* Output and remove all punctuations whose count field is 0 in B punctuation set PS_B. */
18.    foreach p_i in PS_B
19.        if (p_i.count == 0) {
20.            output(p_i); /* Release p_i to output stream. */
21.            remove(PS_B, p_i); /* Remove p_i from B punctuation set PS_B */ } }
```

Fig. 3. Algorithms of Punctuation Index Building and Propagation.

Eager and lazy index building. Although our incrementally constructed punctuation index avoids duplicate expression evaluations, it still needs to scan the entire join state to search for the tuples whose *pids* are null each time it is executed. We thus propose to batch the index building for multiple punctuations in order to share the cost of scanning the state. Accordingly, instead of

triggering the index building upon the arrival of each punctuation, which we call *eager index building*, we run it only when the punctuation propagation is invoked, called *lazy index building*. However, eager index building is still preferred in some cases. For example, it can help guarantee the steady instead of bursty output of punctuations whenever possible. In the eager approach, since the index is incrementally built right upon receiving each punctuation and the index is indirectly maintained by the state purge, some punctuations may be detected to be propagable much earlier than the next invocation of propagation.
Propagation mode. PJoin is able to trigger punctuation propagation in either *push* or *pull* mode. In the *push* mode, PJoin actively propagates punctuations when either a fixed time interval since the last propagation has gone by, or a fixed number of punctuations have been received since the last propagation. We call them *time propagation threshold* and *count propagation threshold* respectively. On the other hand, PJoin is also able to propagate punctuations upon the request of the down-stream operators, which would be the beneficiaries of the propagation. This is called the *pull* mode.

3.6 Event-Driven Framework of PJoin

To implement the PJoin execution logic described above, with components being tunable, a join framework which incorporates the following features is desired.

1. The framework should keep track of a variety of runtime parameters that serve as the triggering conditions for executing each component, such as the size of the join state, the number of punctuations that arrived since the last state purge, etc. When a certain parameter reaches the corresponding threshold, such as the purge threshold, the appropriate components should be scheduled to run.
2. The framework should be able to model the different coupling alternatives among components and easily switch from one option to another. For example, the lazy index building is coupled with the punctuation propagation, while the eager index building is independent of the punctuation propagation strategy selected by a given join execution configuration.

To accomplish the above features, we have designed an *event-driven* framework for PJoin as shown in Figure 4. The memory join runs as the main thread. It continuously retrieves data from the input streams and generates results. A *monitor* is responsible for keeping track of the status of various runtime parameters about the input streams and the join state being changed during the execution of the memory join. Once a certain threshold is reached, for example the size of the join state reaches the memory threshold or both input streams are temporarily stuck due to network delay and the disk join activation threshold is reached, the monitor will invoke the corresponding event. Then the listeners of the event, which may be either disk join, state purge, state relocation, index build or punctuation propagation component, will start running as a second thread. If an event has multiple listeners, these listeners will be executed in an order specified in the event-listener registry described below.

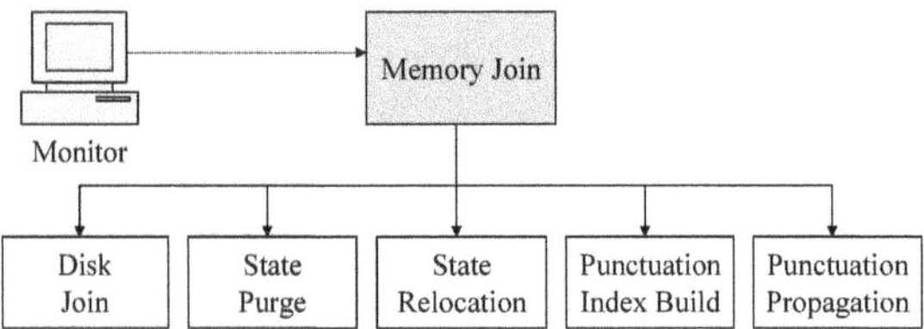

Fig. 4. Event-Driven Framework of PJoin.

Table 1. Example Event-Listener Registry.

Events	*Conditions*	*Listeners (Activated In Order)*
StreamEmptyEvent	Activation threshold is reached.	Disk Join
PurgeThresholdReachEvent	none	State Purge
StateFullEvent	C1*	State Purge
StateFullEvent	C2*	State Relocation
PropagateCountReachEvent	none	Index Build, Propagation
C1*: There exists punctuations which haven't been used to purge the state.		
C2*: No punctuations exist that haven't been used to purge the state.		

The following events have been defined to model the status changes of monitored *runtime parameters* that may cause a component to be activated.

1. *StreamEmptyEvent* signals both input streams run out of tuples.
2. *PurgeThresholdReachEvent* signals the *purge threshold* is reached.
3. *StateFullEvent* signals the size of the in-memory join state reaches the *memory threshold*.
4. *NewPunctReadyEvent* signals a new punctuation arrives.
5. *PropagateRequestEvent* signals a propagation request is received from downstream operators.
6. *PropagateTimeExpireEvent* signals the *time propagation threshold* is reached.
7. *PropagateCountReachEvent* signals the *count propagation threshold* is reached.

PJoin maintains an *event-listener registry*. Each entry in the registry lists the event to be generated, the additional conditions to be checked and the listeners (components) which will be executed to handle the event. The registry while initiated at the static query optimization phase can be updated at runtime. All parameters for invoking the events, including the *purge*, *memory* and *propagation threshold*, are specified inside the monitor and can also be changed at runtime.

Table 1 gives an example of this registry. This configuration of PJoin is used by several experiments shown in Section 4. In this configuration, we apply the *lazy purge* strategy, that is, to purge state whenever the purge threshold is reached. Also the *lazy index building* and the *push* mode propagation are applied, that is, when the count propagation threshold is reached, we first construct the punctuation index for all newly-arrived punctuations since the last index building and then start propagation.

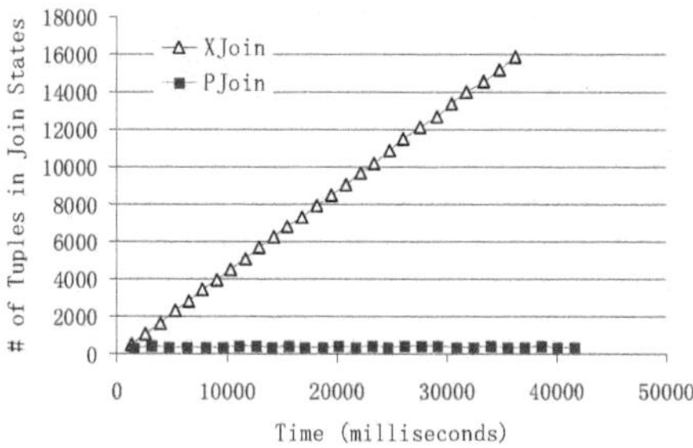

Fig. 5. PJoin vs. XJoin, Memory Overhead, Punctuation Inter-arrival: 40 tuples/punctuation.

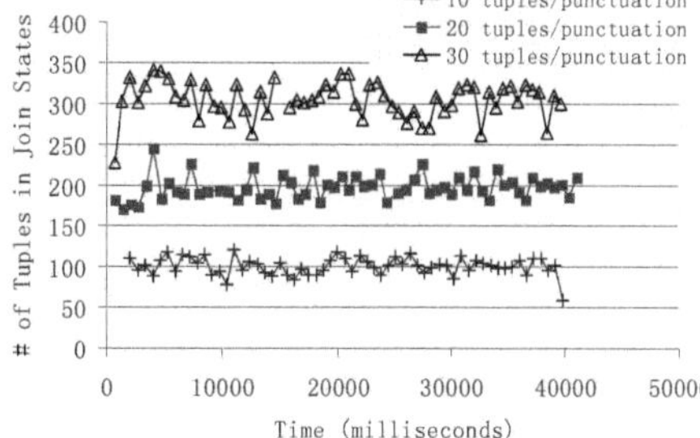

Fig. 6. PJoin Memory Overhead, Punctuation Inter-arrival: 10, 20, 30 tuples/punctuation.

4 Experimental Study

We have implemented the PJoin operator in Java as a query operator in the Raindrop XQuery subscription system [17] based on the event-based framework presented in Section 3.6. Below we describe the experimental study we have conducted to explore the effectiveness of our punctuation-exploiting stream join optimization. The test machine has a 2.4GHz Intel(R) Pentium-IV processor and a 512MB RAM, running Windows XP and Java 1.4.1.01 SDK. We have created a benchmark system to generate synthetic data streams by controlling the arrival patterns and rates of the data and punctuations. In all experiments shown in this section, the tuples from both input streams have a Poisson inter-arrival time with a mean of 2 milliseconds. All experiments run a many-to-many join over two input streams, which, we believe, exhibits the most general cases of our solution. In the charts, we denote the PJoin with purge threshold n as PJoin-n. Accordingly, PJoin using eager purge is denoted as PJoin-1.

4.1 PJoin versus XJoin

First we compare the performance of PJoin with XJoin [19], a stream join operator without a constraint-exploiting mechanism. We are interested in exploring two questions: (1) how much memory overhead can be saved and (2) to what degree can the tuple output rate be improved. In order to be able to compare these two join solutions, we have also implemented XJoin in our system and applied the same optimizations as we did for PJoin.

To answer the first question, we compare PJoin using the eager purge with XJoin regarding the total number of tuples in the join state during the length of the execution. The input punctuations have a Poisson inter-arrival with a mean of 40 tuples/punctuation. From Figure 5 we can see that the memory requirement for the PJoin state is almost insignificant compared to that of XJoin.

As the punctuation inter-arrival increases, the size of the PJoin state will increase accordingly. When the punctuation inter-arrival reaches infinity so that

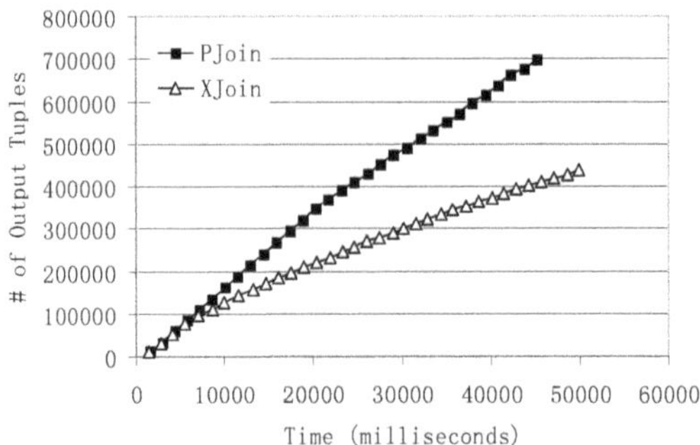

Fig. 7. PJoin vs. XJoin, Tuple Output Rates, Punctuation Inter-arrival: 30 tuples/punctuation.

no punctuations exist in the input stream, the memory requirement of PJoin becomes the same as that of XJoin.

In Figure 6, we vary the punctuation inter-arrival to be 10, 20 and 30 tuples/punctuation respectively for three different runs of PJoin accordingly. We can see that as the punctuation inter-arrival increases, the average size of the PJoin state becomes larger correspondingly.

To answer the second question, Figure 7 compares the tuple output rate of PJoin to that of XJoin. We can see that as time advances, PJoin maintains an almost steady output rate whereas the output rate of XJoin drops. This decrease in XJoin output rate occurs because the XJoin state increases over time thereby leading to an increasing cost for probing state. From this experiment we conclude that PJoin performs better or at least equivalent to XJoin regarding both the output rate and the memory resources consumption.

4.2 State Purge Strategies for PJoin

Now we explore how the performance of PJoin is affected by different state purge strategies. In this experiment, the input punctuations have a Poisson inter-arrival with a mean of 10 tuples/punctuation. We vary the *purge threshold* to start purging state after receiving every 10, 100, 400, 800 punctuations respectively and measure its effect on the output rate and memory overhead of the join.

Figure 8 shows the state requirements for the eager purge (PJoin-1) and the lazy purge with purge threshold 10 (PJoin-10). The chart confirms that the eager purge is the best strategy for minimizing the join state, whereas the lazy purge requires more memory to operate.

Figure 9 compares the PJoin output rate using different purge strategies. We plot the number of output tuples against time summarized over four experiment runs, each run with a different purge threshold (1,100,400 and 800 respectively). We can see that up to some limit, the higher the *purge threshold*, the higher the output rate. This is because there is a cost associated with purge, and thus purging very frequently such as the eager strategy leads to a loss in performance. But this gain in output rate is at the cost of the increase in memory overhead.

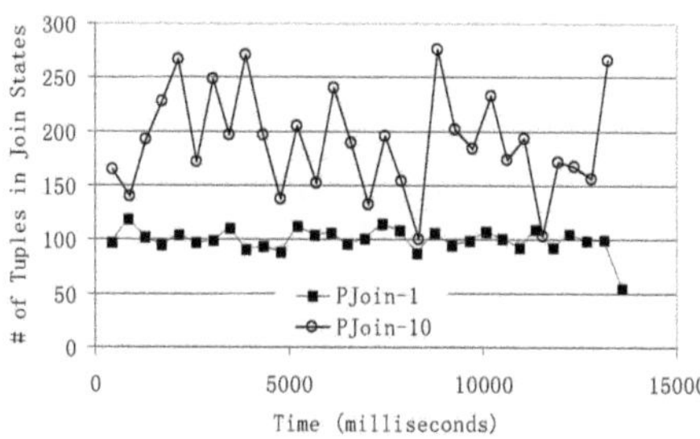

Fig. 8. Eager vs. Lazy Purge, Memory Overhead, Punctuation Inter-arrival: 10 tuples/punctuation.

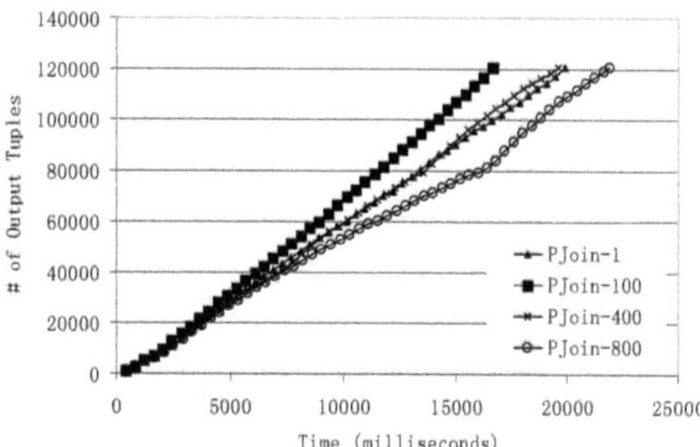

Fig. 9. Eager vs. Lazy Purge, Tuple Output rates, Punctuation Inter-arrival: 10 tuples/punctuation.

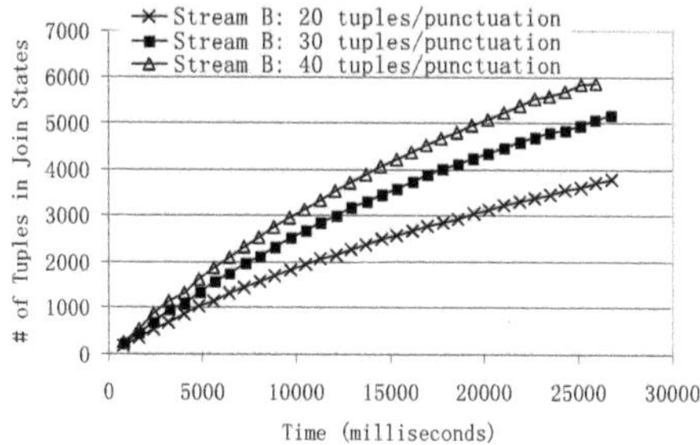

Fig. 10. Memory Overhead, Asymmetric Punctuation Inter-arrival Rates, A Punctuation Inter-arrival: 10 tuples/punctuation, B Punctuation Inter-arrival: 20, 30, 40 tuples/punctuation.

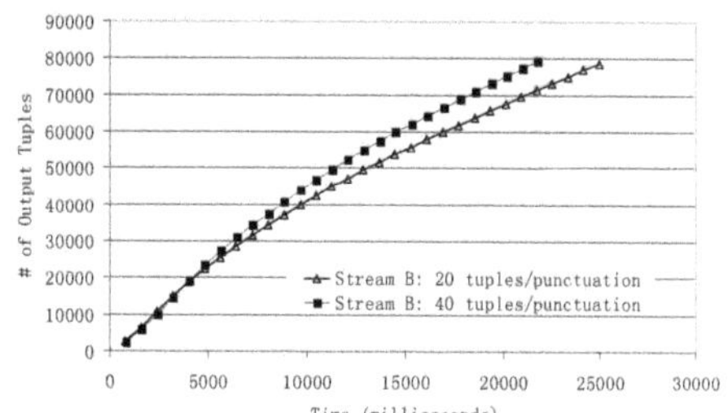

Fig. 11. Tuple Output Rates, Asymmetric Punctuation Inter-arrival Rates, A Punctuation Inter-arrival: 10 tuples/punctuation, B Punctuation Inter-arrival: 20, 40 tuples/punctuation.

When the increased cost of probing the state exceeds the cost of purge, we start to lose on performance, such as the case of PJoin-400 and PJoin-800. This is the same problem as encountered by XJoin, that is, every new tuple enlarges the state, which in turn increases the cost of probing the state.

4.3 Asymmetric Punctuation Inter-arrival Rate

Now we explore the performance of PJoin in terms of input streams with asymmetric punctuation inter-arrivals. We keep the punctuation inter-arrival of stream A constant at 10 tuples/punctuation and vary that of stream B. Figure 10 shows the state requirement of PJoin using eager purge. We can see that the larger the difference in the punctuation inter-arrival of the two input streams, the larger will be the memory requirement. Less frequent punctuations from stream B cause the A state to be purged less frequently. Hence the A state becomes larger.

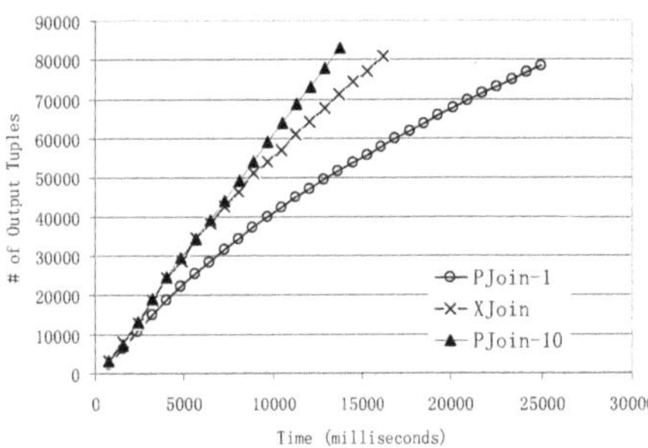

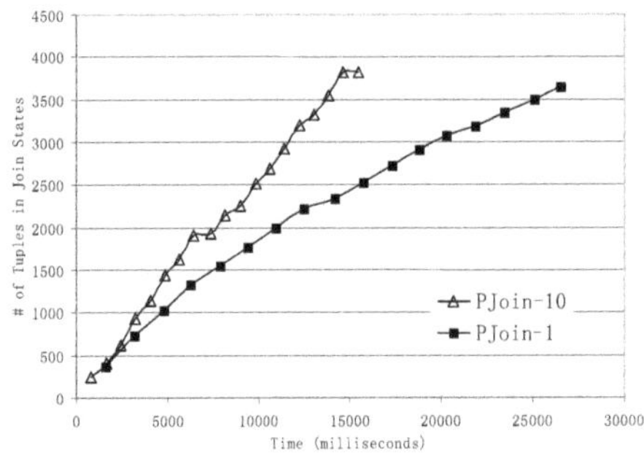

Fig. 12. Eager vs. Lazy Purge, Output Rates, Asymmetric Punctuation Inter-arrival Rates, A Punctuation Inter-arrival: 10 tuples/punctuation, B Punctuation Inter-arrival: 20 tuples/punctuation.

Fig. 13. Eager vs. Lazy Purge, Memory Overhead, Asymmetric Punctuation Inter-arrival Rates, A Punctuation Inter-arrival: 10 tuples/punctuation, B Punctuation Inter-arrival: 20 tuples/punctuation.

Another interesting phenomenon not shown here is that the B state is very small or insignificant compared to the A state. This happens because punctuations from stream A arrive at a faster rate. Thus most of the time when a B tuple is received, there already exists an A punctuation that can drop this B tuple on the fly [7]. Therefore most B tuples never become a part of the state.

Figure 11 gives an idea about the tuple output rate of PJoin for the above cases. The slower the punctuation arrival rate, the greater is the tuple output rate. This is because the slow punctuation arrival rate means a smaller number of purges and hence the less overhead caused by purge.

Figure 12 shows the comparison of PJoin against XJoin in terms of asymmetric punctuation inter-arrivals. The punctuation inter-arrival of stream A is 10 tuples/punctuation and that of stream B is 20 tuples/punctuation. We can see that the output rate of PJoin with the eager purge (PJoin-1) lags behind that of XJoin. This is mainly because of the cost of purge associated with PJoin. One way to overcome this problem is to use the lazy purge together with an appropriate setting of the *purge threshold*. This will make the output rate of PJoin better or at least equivalent to that of XJoin. Figure 13 shows the state requirements for this case. We conclude that if the goal is to minimize the memory overhead of the join state, we can use the eager purge strategy. Otherwise the lazy purge with an appropriate purge threshold value can give us a significant advantage in tuple output rate, at the expense of insignificant increase in memory overhead.

4.4 Punctuation Propagation

Lastly, we test the punctuation propagation ability of PJoin. In this experiment, both input streams have a punctuation inter-arrival with a mean of 40 tuples/punctuation. We show the ideal case in which punctuations from both input streams arrive in the same order and of same granularity, i.e., each punctuation contains a constant pattern. PJoin is configured to start propagation after a pair of equivalent punctuations has been received from both input streams.

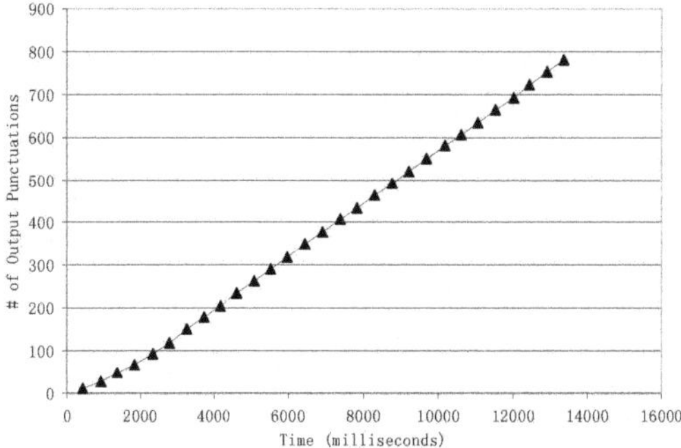

Fig. 14. Punctuation Propagation, Punctuation Inter-arrival: 40 tuples/punctuation

Figure 14 shows the number of punctuations being output over time. We can see that PJoin can guarantee a steady punctuation propagation rate in the ideal case. This property can be very useful for the down-stream operators such as *group-by* that themselves rely on the availability of input punctuations.

5 Related Work

As the data being queried has expanded from finite and statically available datasets to distributed continuous data streams ([1] [5] [6] [15]), new problems have arisen. Specific to the join processing, two important problems need to be tackled: potentially unbounded growing join state and dynamic runtime features of data streams such as widely-varying data arrival rates. In response, the *constraint-based join optimization* [16] and *intra-operator adaptivity* [11] [12] are proposed in the literature to address these two issues respectively.

The main goal of constraint-based join optimization is to in a timely manner detect and purge the no-longer-useful data from the state. *Window joins* exploit *time-based constraints* called sliding windows to remove the expired data from the state whenever a time window passes. [1] defines formal semantics for a binary join that incorporates a window specification. Kang et al. [13] provide a unit-time-basis cost model for analyzing the performance of a binary window join. They also propose strategies for maximizing the join efficiency in various scenarios. [8] studies algorithms for handling sliding window multi-join processing. [10] researches the shared execution of multiple window join operators. They provide alternate strategies that favor different window sizes. The *k-constraint-exploiting algorithm* [3] exploits clustered data arrival, a *value-based constraint* to help detect stale data. However, both window and k-constraints are statically specified, which only reflect the restrictive cases of the real-world data.

Punctuations [18] are a new class of constraints embedded into the stream dynamically at runtime. The static constraints such as one-to-many join cardinality and clustered arrival of join values can also be represented by punctuations. Beyond the general concepts of punctuations, [18] also lists all rules for algebra operators, namely, pass, keep (equal to purge) and propagation. In our PJoin design, we apply these functional rules to achieve join optimization, including the exploration of alternate modes for applying these rules.

Adaptive join operators can adjust their behavior in response to the changing conditions of data and computing resources as well as the runtime statistics. *Ripple joins* [9] are a family of physical pipelining join operators which are designed for producing partial results quickly. Ripple joins adjust their behavior during processing in accordance with the statistical properties of the data. They also consider the user preferences about the accuracy of the partial result and the time between updates of the running aggregate to adaptively set the rate of retrieving tuples from each input stream. *XJoin* [19] [20] is able to adapt to insufficient memory by moving part of the in-memory join state to the secondary storage. It also hides the intermittent delays in data arrival from slow remote resources by reactively scheduling background processing.

We apply the ideas of constraint-driven join optimization and intra-operator adaptivity in our work. PJoin is able to exploit constraints presented as punctuations to achieve the optimization goals of reducing memory overhead and increasing data output rates. PJoin also adopts almost all features of XJoin. We differ in that no previous work incorporates both constraint-exploiting mechanism and adaptivity into join execution logic itself. Unlike the k-constraint-exploiting algorithm, PJoin does not always start to purge state upon receiving a punctuation. Instead, it allows tuning options in order to do it in an optimized way, such as the lazy purge strategy. The user can adjust the behavior of PJoin by specifying a set of parameters statically or at runtime. PJoin can also propagate appropriate punctuations to benefit the down-stream operators, which neither window joins nor k-constraint-exploiting algorithms do.

6 Discussion: Extending PJoin Beyond Punctuations

The current implementation of PJoin is a binary equi-join without exploiting window specifications because we want to first focus on exploring the impact of punctuations on the join performance. As we have experimentally shown, simply by making use of appropriate punctuations, the join state may already be kept bounded this way. However, the design of PJoin being based on a flexible event-driven framework is easily-extendible to support alternate join components, tuning options, sliding windows and to handle n-ary join.

Extension for supporting sliding window. To support sliding window, additional tuple dropping operation needs to be introduced to purge expired tuples as the window moves. This operation can be performed in combination with the state probing in the memory join and the disk join components. In addition, the tuples in each hash bucket can be arranged by their timestamps so that the early-arrived tuples are always accessed first. This way the tuple invalidation by window can perform more effectively. Whenever the first time-valid tuple according to the current window is encountered, the tuple invalidation for this

hash bucket can stop. Furthermore, the interaction between punctuations and windows may enable further optimization such as early punctuation propagation.
Extension for handling n-ary join. It is also straightforward to extend the current binary join implementation of PJoin to handle n-ary joins [21]. The modifications to be made for the state purge component are as follows: instead of purging the state of stream B by punctuations from stream A, in an n-ary join, for punctuations from the ith stream, the state purge component needs to purge the states of all other (n-1) streams. The punctuation index building and propagation algorithms for each input stream could remain the same. The memory join component needs to be modified as well. If the join value of a new tuple from one stream is detected to match the punctuations from all other (n-1) streams, this tuple can be on-the-fly dropped after the memory join. Otherwise we need to insert this tuple into its state. There exist prolific optimization tasks in terms of forming partial join results, designing a correlated purge threshold, designing a correlated propagation threshold, to name a few.

7 Conclusion

In this paper, we presented the design of a punctuation-exploiting stream join operator called PJoin. We sketched six components to accomplish the PJoin execution logic. For state purge and propagation, we designed alternate strategies to achieve different optimization goals. We implemented PJoin using an event-driven framework to enable the flexible configuration of join execution for coping with the dynamic runtime environment. Our experimental study compared PJoin with XJoin, explores the impact of different state purge strategies and evaluates the punctuation propagation ability of PJoin. The experimental results illustrated the benefits achieved by our punctuation-exploiting join optimization.

Acknowledgment. The authors wish to thank Leonidas Fegaras for many useful comments on our work, which lead to improvements of this paper.

References

1. D. Abadi, D. Carney, U. Cetintemel, M. Cherniack, C. Convey, S. Lee, M. Stonebraker, N. Tatbul, and S. Zdonik. Aurora: A new model and architecture for data stream management. *VLDB Journal*, 12(2):120–139, August 2003.
2. A. Arasu, B. Babcock, S. Babu, J. McAlister, and J. Widom. Characterizing memory requirements for queries over continuous data streams. In *PODS*, pages 221–232, June 2002.
3. S. Babu and J. Widom. Exploiting k-constraints to reduce memory overhead in continuous queries over data streams. Technical report, Stanford Univ., Nov 2002.
4. D. Carney, U. Cetintemel, M. Cherniack, C. Convey, S. Lee, G. Seidman, M. Stonebraker, N. Tatbul, and S. Zdonik. Monitoring streams - a new class of data management applications. In *VLDB*, pages 215–226, August 2002.

5. S. Chandrasekaran, O. Cooper, A. Deshpande, M. Franklin, J. Hellerstein, W. Hong, S. Krishnamurthy, S. Madden, V. Raman, F. Reiss, and M. Shah. TelegraphCQ: Continuous dataflow processing for an uncertain world. In *CIDR*, pages 269–280, Jan 2003.
6. J. Chen, D. DeWitt, F. Tian, and Y. Wang. NiagaraCQ: A scalable continuous query system for internet databases. In *ACM SIGMOD*, pages 379–390, June 2002.
7. L. Ding, E. A. Rundensteiner, and G. T. Heineman. MJoin: A metadata-aware stream join operator. In *DEBS*, June 2003.
8. L. Golab and M. T. Ozsu. Processing sliding window multi-joins in continuous queries over data streams. In *VLDB*, pages 500–511, Sep 2003.
9. P. Haas and J. Hellerstein. Ripple joins for online aggregation. In *ACM SIGMOD*, pages 287–298, June 1999.
10. M. A. Hammad, M. J. Franklin, W. G. Aref, and A. K. Elmagarmid. Scheduling for shared window joins over data streams. In *VLDB*, pages 297–308, Sep 2003.
11. J. M. Hellerstein, M. J. Franklin, S. Chandrasekaran, A. Deshpande, K. Hildrum, S. Madden, V. Raman, and M. Shah. Adaptive query processing: Technology in evolution. *IEEE Data Engineering Bulletin*, 23(2):7–18, Jun 2000.
12. Z. G. Ives, D. Florescu, M. Friedman, A. Levy, and D. S. Weld. An adaptive query execution system for data integration. In *ACM SIGMOD*, pages 299–310, 1999.
13. J. Kang, J. F. Naughton, and S. D. Viglas. Evaluating window joins over unbounded streams. In *ICDE*, pages 341–352, March 2003.
14. S. Madden and M. Franklin. Fjording the stream: An architecture for queries over streaming sensor data. In *ICDE*, pages 555–566, Feb 2002.
15. S. Madden, M. Shah, J. M. Hellerstein, and V. Raman. Continuously adaptive continuous queries over streams. In *ACM SIGMOD*, pages 49–60, June 2002.
16. R. Motwani, J. Widom, A. Arasu, B. Babcock, S. Babu, M. Datar, G. Manku, C. Olston, J. Rosenstein, and R. Varma. Query processing, resource management, and approximation in a data stream management system. In *CIDR*, pages 245–256, Jan 2003.
17. H. Su, J. Jian, and E. A. Rundensteiner. Raindrop: A uniform and layered algebraic framework for XQueries on XML streams. In *CIKM*, pages 279–286, Sep 2003.
18. P. A. Tucker, D. Maier, T. Sheard, and L. Fegaras. Exploiting punctuation semantics in continuous data streams. *IEEE Transactions on Knowledge and Data Engineering*, 15(3):555–568, May/June 2003.
19. T. Urhan and M. Franklin. XJoin: A reactively scheduled pipelined join operator. *IEEE Data Engineering Bulletin*, 23(2):27–33, 2000.
20. T. Urhan and M. J. Franklin. Dynamic pipeline scheduling for improving interactive query performance. In *VLDB*, pages 501–510, Sep 2001.
21. S. Viglas, J. Naughton, and J. Burger. Maximizing the output rate of multi-way join queries over streaming information. In *VLDB*, pages 285–296, Sep 2003.
22. A. N. Wilschut and P. M. G. Apers. Dataflow query execution in a parallel main-memory environment. *Distributed and Parallel Databases*, 1(1):103–128, 1993.

Using Convolution to Mine Obscure Periodic Patterns in One Pass*

Mohamed G. Elfeky, Walid G. Aref, and Ahmed K. Elmagarmid

Department of Computer Sciences, Purdue University
{mgelfeky,aref,ake}@cs.purdue.edu

Abstract. The mining of periodic patterns in time series databases is an interesting data mining problem that can be envisioned as a tool for forecasting and predicting the future behavior of time series data. Existing periodic patterns mining algorithms either assume that the periodic rate (or simply the period) is user-specified, or try to detect potential values for the period in a separate phase. The former assumption is a considerable disadvantage, especially in time series databases where the period is not known a priori. The latter approach results in a multi-pass algorithm, which on the other hand is to be avoided in online environments (e.g., data streams). In this paper, we develop an algorithm that mines periodic patterns in time series databases with unknown or obscure periods such that discovering the period is part of the mining process. Based on convolution, our algorithm requires only one pass over a time series of length n, with $O(n \log n)$ time complexity.

1 Introduction

A time series database is one that abounds with data evolving over time. Life embraces several examples of time series databases such as meteorological data containing several measurements, e.g., temperature and humidity, stock prices depicted in financial market, and power consumption data reported in energy corporations. Data mining is the process of discovering patterns and trends by sifting through large amounts of data using technology that employs statistical and mathematical techniques.

Research in time series data mining has concentrated on discovering different types of patterns: sequential patterns [3,18,10,5], temporal patterns [7], periodic association rules [17], partial periodic patterns [12,11,4], surprising patterns [14] to name a few. These periodicity mining techniques require the user to specify a period that determines the rate at which the time series is periodic. They assume that users either know the value of the period beforehand or are willing to try various period values until satisfactory periodic patterns emerge. Since the mining process must be executed repeatedly to obtain good results, this trial-and-error scheme is clearly not efficient. Even in the case of time series data

* This work has been supported in part by the National Science Foundation under grants IIS-0093116, EIA-9972883, IIS-0209120, and by grants from NCR and Wal-Mart.

E. Bertino et al. (Eds.): EDBT 2004, LNCS 2992, pp. 605–620, 2004.
© Springer-Verlag Berlin Heidelberg 2004

with a priori known periods, there may be obscure periods, and consequently interesting periodic patterns that will not be discovered. The solution to these problems is to devise techniques for discovering potential periods in time series data. Research in this direction has focused either on devising general techniques for discovering potential periods [13,6], or on devising special techniques for specific periodicity mining problems [20,16]. Both approaches turn out to require multiple passes over the time series in order to output the periodic patterns themselves. However, real-time systems, which draw the attention of database researchers recently (e.g., as in data streams), cannot abide the time nor the storage needed for multiple passes over the data.

In this paper, we address the problem of mining periodic patterns in time series databases of unknown or obscure periods, hereafter referred to as *obscure periodic patterns*. We define the periodicity of the time series in terms of its symbols, and subsequently define the obscure periodic patterns where the period is a variable rather than an input parameter (Sect. 2). We develop a convolution-based algorithm for mining the obscure periodic patterns in one pass (Sect. 3). To the best of our knowledge, our proposed algorithm is the first algorithm in the literature (Sect. 1.1) that mines the periodic patterns with unknown period in one pass. In Sect. 4, the performance of our proposed algorithm is extensively studied verifying its correctness, examining its resilience to noise, and justifying its practicality. We summarize our findings in Sect. 5.

1.1 Related Work

Discovering the period of time series data has drawn the attention of the data mining research community very recently. Indyk et al. [13] have addressed this problem under the name *periodic trends*, and have developed an $O(n \log^2 n)$ time algorithm, where n is the length of the time series. Their notion of a periodic trend is the relaxed period of the entire time series, and their output is a set of candidate period values. In order to output the periodic patterns of the time series, a periodic patterns mining algorithm should be incorporated using each candidate period value, resulting in a multi-pass periodicity mining process.

Specific to partial periodic patterns, Ma and Hellerstein [16] have developed a linear distance-based algorithm for discovering the potential periods regarding the symbols of the time series. However, their algorithm misses some valid periods since it only considers the adjacent inter-arrivals. For example, consider a symbol that occurs in a time series in positions 0, 4, 5, 7, and 10. Although the underlying period should be 5, the algorithm only considers the periods 4, 1, 2, and 3. Should it be extended to include all possible inter-arrivals, the complexity of the algorithm of [16] will increase to $O(n^2)$. In [20], a similar algorithm has been proposed with some pruning techniques. Yet, both algorithms of [20,16] require at least two passes over the time series in order to output the periodic patterns.

Berberidis et al. [6] have solved the problem of the distance-based algorithms by developing a multi-pass algorithm for discovering the potential periods regarding the symbols of the time series, one symbol at a time. Their algorithm suffers from the need for incorporating a periodic patterns mining algorithm to output the periodic patterns of the time series.

2 Problem Definition

2.1 Notation

Assume that a sequence of n timestamped feature values is collected in a time series database. For a given feature t, let t_i be the value of the feature at timestamp i. The time series of feature t is represented as $T = t_0, t_1, \ldots, t_{n-1}$. For example, the feature in a time series database for power consumption might be the hourly power consumption rate of a certain customer, while the feature in a time series database for stock prices might be the final daily stock price of a specific company. If we discretize [14] the time series feature values into nominal discrete levels and denote each level (e.g., high, medium, low, etc.) by a symbol (e.g., a, b, c, etc.), then the set of collected feature values can be denoted $\Sigma = \{a, b, c, \cdots\}$, where T is a string of length n over Σ.

A time series database may also be a sequence of n timestamped events drawn from a finite set of nominal event types, e.g., the event log in a computer network monitoring the various events that can occur. Each event type can be denoted by a symbol (e.g., a, b, c, etc.), and hence we can use the same notation above.

2.2 Symbol Periodicity

In a time series T, a symbol s is said to be periodic with a period p if s exists "almost" every p timestamps. For example, in the time series $T = abcabbabcb$, the symbol b is periodic with period 4 since b exists every four timestamps (in positions 1, 5 and 9). Moreover, the symbol a is periodic with period 3 since a exists almost every three timestamps (in positions 0, 3, and 6 but not 9). We define symbol periodicity as follows.

Let $\pi_{p,l}(T)$ denote the projection of a time series T according to a period p starting from position l; that is

$$\pi_{p,l}(T) = t_l, t_{l+p}, t_{l+2p}, \ldots, t_{l+(m-1)p},$$

where $l < p$, $m = \lceil (n-l)/p \rceil$, and n is the length of T. For example, if $T = abcabbabcb$, then $\pi_{4,1}(T) = bbb$, and $\pi_{3,0}(T) = aaab$. Intuitively, the ratio of the number of occurrences of a symbol s in a certain projection $\pi_{p,l}(T)$ to the length of this projection indicates how often this symbol occurs every p timestamps. However, this ratio is not quite accurate since it captures all the occurrences even the outliers. In the example above, the symbol b will be considered periodic with period 3 with a frequency of 1/4, which is not quite true. As another example, if for a certain T, $\pi_{p,l}(T) = abcbac$, this means that the symbol changes every p timestamp and so no symbol should be periodic with a period p. We remedy this problem by considering only the consecutive occurrences. A consecutive occurrence of a symbol s in a certain projection $\pi_{p,l}(T)$ indicates that the symbol s reappeared in T after p timestamps from the previous appearance, which means that p is a potential period for s. Let $\mathcal{F}_2(s, T)$ denote the number of times the symbol s occurs in two consecutive positions in the time series T. For example, if $T = abbaaabaa$, then $\mathcal{F}_2(a, T) = 3$ and $\mathcal{F}_2(b, T) = 1$.

Definition 1. *If a time series T of length n contains a symbol s such that $\exists l, p$ where $l < p$, and $\frac{\mathcal{F}_2(s,\pi_{p,l}(T))}{\lceil (n-l)/p \rceil - 1} \geq \psi$ where $0 < \psi \leq 1$; then s is said to be periodic in T with period p at position l with respect to a periodicity threshold equal to ψ.*

For example, in the time series $T = abcabbabcb$, $\frac{\mathcal{F}_2(a,\pi_{3,0}(T))}{\lceil 10/3 \rceil - 1} = 2/3$, thus the symbol a is periodic with period 3 at position 0 with respect to a periodicity threshold $\psi \leq 2/3$. Similarly, the symbol b is periodic with period 3 at position 1 with respect to a periodicity threshold $\psi \leq 1$.

2.3 Obscure Periodic Patterns

The main advantage of the definition of symbol periodicity is that not only does it determine the candidate periodic symbols, but it also determines their corresponding periods and locates their corresponding positions. Thus, there are no presumptions of the period value, and so obscure periodic patterns can be defined as follows.

Definition 2. *If a time series T of length n contains a symbol s that is periodic with period p at position l with respect to an arbitrary periodicity threshold, then a periodic single-symbol pattern of length p is formed by putting the symbol s in position l and putting the "don't care" symbol § in all other positions. The support of such periodic single-symbol pattern is estimated by $\frac{\mathcal{F}_2(s,\pi_{p,l}(T))}{\lceil (n-l)/p \rceil - 1}$.*

For example, in the time series $T = abcabbabcb$, the pattern a§§ is a periodic single-symbol pattern of length 3 with a support value of 2/3, and so is the single-symbol pattern §b§ with a support value of 1. However, we cannot deduce that the pattern ab§ is also periodic since we cannot estimate its support[1]. The only thing we know for sure is that its support value will not exceed 2/3.

Definition 3. *In a time series T of length n, let $S_{p,l}$ be the set of all the symbols that are periodic with period p at position l with respect to an arbitrary periodicity threshold. Let S^p be the Cartesian product of all $S_{p,l}$ in an ascending order of l, that is $S^p = (S_{p,0} \cup \{\S\}) \times (S_{p,1} \cup \{\S\}) \times \ldots \times (S_{p,p-1} \cup \{\S\})$. Every ordered pair $(s_0, s_1, \ldots, s_{p-1})$ that belongs to S^p corresponds to a candidate periodic pattern of the form $s_0 s_1 \ldots s_{p-1}$ where $s_i \in S_{p,i} \cup \{\S\}$.*

For example, in the time series $T = abcabbabcb$, we have $S_{3,0} = \{a\}$, $S_{3,1} = \{b\}$, and $S_{3,2} = \{\}$, then the candidate periodic patterns are a§§, §b§, and ab§, ignoring the "*don't care*" pattern §§§.

[1] This is similar to the Apriori property of the association rules [2], that is if A and B are two frequent itemsets, then AB is a candidate frequent itemset that may turn out to be infrequent.

3 Mining Obscure Periodic Patterns

Assume first that the period p is known for a specific time series T. Then, the problem is reduced to mining the periodic patterns of length p. In other words, the problem is to detect the symbols that are periodic with period p. A way to solve this simpler problem is to shift the time series p positions, denoted as $T^{(p)}$, and compare this shifted version $T^{(p)}$ to the original version T. For example, if $T = abcabbabcb$, then shifting T three positions results in $T^{(3)} = \S\S\S abcabba$. Comparing T to $T^{(3)}$ results in four symbol matches that. If the symbols are mapped in a particular way, we can deduce that those four matches are actually two for the symbol a both at position 0, and two for the symbol b both at position 1.

Therefore, our proposed algorithm for mining obscure periodic patterns relies on two main ideas. The first is to obtain a mapping scheme for the symbols, which reveals, upon comparison, the symbols that match and their corresponding positions. Turning back to the original problem where the period is unknown, the second idea is to use the concept of convolution in order to shift and compare the time series for all possible values of the period. Hence, all the symbol periodicities can be detected in one pass. The remaining part of this section describes those ideas in detail starting by defining the concept of convolution (Sect. 3.1) as it derives our mapping scheme (Sect. 3.2).

3.1 Convolution

A convolution [8] is defined as follows. Let $x = [x_0, x_1, \ldots, x_{n-1}]$ and $y = [y_0, y_1, \ldots, y_{n-1}]$ be two finite length sequences of numbers[2], each of length n. The convolution of x and y is defined as another finite length sequence $x \otimes y$ of length n such that $(x \otimes y)_i = \sum_{j=0}^{i} x_j y_{i-j}$ for $i = 0, 1, \ldots, n-1$. Let $x' = [x'_0, x'_1, \ldots, x'_{n-1}]$ denote the reverse of the vector x, i.e., $x'_i = x_{n-1-i}$. Taking the convolution of x' and y, and obtaining its reverse leads to the following:

$$(x' \otimes y)'_i = (x' \otimes y)_{n-1-i} = \sum_{j=0}^{n-1-i} x'_j y_{n-1-i-j} = \sum_{j=0}^{n-1-i} x_{n-1-j} y_{n-1-i-j},$$

i.e.,

$$\begin{aligned}
(x' \otimes y)'_0 &= x_0 y_0 + x_1 y_1 + \cdots + x_{n-1} y_{n-1}, \\
(x' \otimes y)'_1 &= x_1 y_0 + x_2 y_1 + \cdots + x_{n-1} y_{n-2}, \\
&\vdots \\
(x' \otimes y)'_{n-1} &= x_{n-1} y_0.
\end{aligned}$$

[2] The general definition of convolution does not assume equal length sequences. We adapted the general definition to conform to our problem, in which convolutions only take place between equal length sequences.

In other words, the component of the resulting sequence at position i corresponds to positioning one of the input sequences in front of position i of the other input sequence.

Based on the mapping scheme described in the next section, our proposed algorithm converts the time series into two identical finite sequences of numbers, reverses one of them, performs the convolution between them, and then reverses the output. The component values of the resulting sequence will be analyzed exhaustively to get the periodic symbols and their corresponding periods and positions (Sect. 3.2).

It is well known that convolution can be calculated by fast Fourier transform (FFT) [15] as follows:

$$x \otimes y = \mathrm{FFT}^{-1}\Big(\mathrm{FFT}(x) \cdot \mathrm{FFT}(y)\Big).$$

Therefore, this allows us to achieve two key benefits. First, the time complexity is reduced to $O(n \log n)$ rather than the $O(n^2)$ time complexity of the brute force approach of shifting and comparing the time series for all possible values. Second, an external FFT algorithm [19] can be used for large sizes of databases mined while on disk.

3.2 Mapping Scheme

Let $T = t_0, t_1, \ldots, t_{n-1}$ be a time series of length n, where t_i's are symbols from a finite alphabet Σ of size σ. Let Φ be a mapping for the symbols of T such that $\Phi(T) = \Phi(t_0), \Phi(t_1), \ldots, \Phi(t_{n-1})$. Let $C^T = (\Phi(T)' \otimes \Phi(T))'$, and c_i^T be the ith component of C^T. The challenge to our one pass algorithm is to obtain a mapping Φ of the symbols, which satisfies two conditions: (i) when the symbols match, this should contribute a non-zero value in the product $\Phi(t_j) \cdot \Phi(t_{i-j})$, otherwise it should contribute 0, and (ii) the value of each component of C^T, $c_i^T = \sum_{j=0}^{i} \Phi(t_j) \cdot \Phi(t_{i-j})$, should identify the symbols that cause the occurrence of this value and their corresponding positions.

We map the symbols to the binary representation of increasing powers of two [1]. For example, if the time series contains only the 3 symbols a, b, and c, then a possible mapping could be $a : 001$, $b : 010$, and $c : 100$, corresponding to power values of 0, 1, and 2, respectively. Hence, a time series of length n is converted to a binary vector of length σn. For example, let $T = acccabb$, then T is converted to the binary vector $\bar{T} = 001100100100001010010$. Adopting regular convolution, defined previously, results in a sequence $C^{\bar{T}}$ of length σn. Considering only the n positions $0, \sigma, 2\sigma, \ldots, (n-1)\sigma$, which are the exact start positions of the symbols, gives back the sequence C^T. The latter derivation of C^T can be written as $C^T = \pi_{\sigma,0}(C^{\bar{T}})$ using the projection notation defined in Sect. 2.2.

The first condition is satisfied since the only way to obtain a value of 1 contributing to a component of C^T is that this 1 comes from the same symbol. For example, for $T = acccabb$, although $c_1^{\bar{T}} = 1$, this is not considered one of C^T components. However, $c_3^{\bar{T}} = 3$ and so $c_1^T = 3$, which corresponds to

$\bar{T}$:	0 0 1 1 0 0 1 0 0 1 0 0 0 0 1 0 1 0 0 1 0
$\bar{T}^{(3)}$:	0 0 1 1 0 0 1 0 0 1 0 0 0 0 1 0 1 0
$c_3^{\bar{T}} = c_1^T =$	2^{14} + 2^{11} + 2^1
$\bar{T}$:	0 0 1 1 0 0 1 0 0 1 0 0 0 0 1 0 1 0 0 1 0
$\bar{T}^{(12)}$:	0 0 1 1 0 0 1 0 0
$c_{12}^{\bar{T}} = c_4^T =$	2^6

Fig. 1. A clarifying example for the mapping scheme

three matches when T is compared to $T^{(1)}$. Those matches are seen from the manual inspection of T to be two c's and one b. Nevertheless, it is not possible to determine those symbols only by examining the value of c_1^T, i.e., the second condition is not yet satisfied. Therefore, we modify the convolution definition to be $(x \otimes y)_i = \sum_{j=0}^{i} 2^j x_j y_{i-j}$. The reason for adding the coefficient 2^j is to get a different contribution for each match, rather than an unvarying contribution of 1. For example, when the new definition of convolution is used for the previous example, $c_1^T = 2^1 + 2^{11} + 2^{14} = 18434$. Figure 1 illustrates this calculation. The powers of 2 for this value are 1, 11, and 14. Examining those powers modulo 3, which is the size of the alphabet in this particular example, results in 1, 2 and 2, respectively, which correspond to the symbols b, c, and c, respectively.

Figure 1 gives another example for c_4^T containing only one power of 2, which is 6, that corresponds to the symbol a since $6 \bmod 3 = 0$ and a was originally mapped to the binary representation of 2^0. This means that comparing T to $T^{(4)}$ results in only one match of the symbol a. Moreover, the power value of 6 reveals that the symbol a is at position 0 in $T^{(4)}$. Note that in the binary vector, the most significant bit is the leftmost one, whereas the most significant position of the time series T is the rightmost one. Therefore, not only can the power values reveal the number of matches of each symbol at each period, they also reveal their corresponding starting positions. This latter observation complies with the definition of symbol periodicity.

Formally, let $s_0, s_1, \ldots, s_{\sigma-1}$ be the symbols of the alphabet of a time series T of length n. Assume that each symbol s_k is mapped to the σ-bit binary representation of 2^k to form $\bar{T}$. The sequence $C^{\bar{T}}$ is computed such that $c_i^{\bar{T}} = \sum_{j=0}^{i} 2^j \bar{t}_j \cdot \bar{t}_{i-j}$ for $i = 0, 1, \ldots, \sigma n - 1$. Thus, $C^T = \pi_{\sigma,0}(C^{\bar{T}})$. Assume that c_p^T is a non-zero component of C^T. Let W_p denote the set of powers of 2 contained in c_p^T, i.e.,

$$W_p = \{w_{p,1}, w_{p,2}, \ldots\}$$

where $c_p^T = \sum_h 2^{w_{p,h}}$, and let

$$W_{p,k} = \{w_{p,h} : w_{p,h} \in W_p \wedge w_{p,h} \bmod \sigma = k\}.$$

As shown in the previous example, the cardinality of each $W_{p,k}$ represents the number of matches of the symbol s_k when T is compared to $T^{(p)}$. Moreover, let

$$W_{p,k,l} = \{w_{p,h} : w_{p,h} \in W_{p,k} \wedge (n - p - 1 - \lfloor w_{p,h}/\sigma \rfloor) \bmod p = l\}.$$

Revisiting the definition of symbol periodicity, we observe that the cardinality of each $W_{p,k,l}$ is equal to the desired value of $\mathcal{F}_2(s_k, \pi_{p,l}(T))$. Working out the example of Sect. 2.2 where $T = abcabbabcb$, $n = 10$, and $\sigma = 3$, let $s_0, s_1, s_2 = a, b, c$, respectively. Then, for $p = 3$, $W_3 = \{18, 16, 9, 7\}$, $W_{3,0} = \{18, 9\}$, $W_{3,0,0} = \{18, 9\} \Rightarrow \mathcal{F}_2(a, \pi_{3,0}(T)) = 2$ which conforms to the results obtained previously. As another example, if $T = cabccbacd$ where $n = 9$, $\sigma = 4$, and $s_0, s_1, s_2, s_3 = a, b, c, d$, respectively, then for $p = 4$, $W_4 = \{18, 6\}$, $W_{4,2} = \{18, 6\}$, $W_{4,2,0} = \{18\} \Rightarrow \mathcal{F}_2(c, \pi_{4,0}(T)) = 1$, and $W_{4,2,3} = \{6\} \Rightarrow \mathcal{F}_2(c, \pi_{4,3}(T)) = 1$ which are correct since $\pi_{4,0}(T) = ccd$ and $\pi_{4,3}(T) = cc$.

One final detail about our algorithm is the use of the values $w_{p,h}$ to estimate the support of the candidate periodic patterns formed according to Definition 3. Let $s_{j_0} s_{j_1} \dots s_{j_{p-1}}$ be a candidate periodic pattern that is not a single-symbol pattern nor the "*don't care*" pattern, i.e., at least 2 s_{j_i}'s are not §. The set $W_{p,j_i,i}$ contains the values responsible for the symbol $s_{j_i} \neq$ §. Let W^p be a subset of the Cartesian product of the sets $W_{p,j_i,i}$ for all i where $s_{j_i} \neq$ § such that all the values in an ordered pair should have the same value of $\lfloor \frac{n-p-1-\lfloor w_{p,h}/\sigma \rfloor}{p} \rfloor$. The support estimate of that candidate periodic pattern is $\frac{|W^p|}{\lfloor n/p \rfloor}$. For example, if $T = abcabbabcb$, $W_{3,0,0} = \{18, 9\}$ corresponds to the symbol a, and $W_{3,1,1} = \{16, 7\}$ corresponds to the symbol b, then for the candidate periodic pattern ab§, $W^p = \{(18, 16), (9, 7)\}$, and the support of this pattern is 2/3.

Therefore, our algorithm scans the time series once to convert it into a binary vector according to the proposed mapping, performs the modified convolution on the binary vector, and analyzes the resulting values to determine the symbol periodicities and consequently the periodic single-symbol patterns. Then, the set of candidate periodic patterns is formed and the support of each pattern is estimated.

The complexity of our algorithm is the complexity of the convolution step, which is $O(n \log n)$ when performed using FFT. Note that adding the coefficient 2^j to the convolution definition still preserves that

$$x \otimes y = \text{FFT}^{-1}\Big(\text{FFT}(x) \cdot \text{FFT}(y)\Big).$$

The complete algorithm is sketched in Fig. 2.

4 Experimental Study

This section contains the results of an extensive experimental study that examines the proposed obscure periodic patterns mining algorithm for different aspects. The most important aspect is the correctness of the symbol periodicity detection phase, which is studied solely in Sect. 4.1. Then, the time performance of the proposed obscure periodic patterns mining algorithm is studied in Sect. 4.2. As data inerrancy is inevitable, Sect. 4.3 scrutinizes the resilience of the proposed algorithm to various kinds of noise that can occur in time series data. The practicality and usefulness of the results are explored using real data experiments shown in Sect. 4.4. Moreover, the periodic trends algorithm of [13]

Input : a time series $T = t_0, t_1, \ldots, t_{n-1}$, and the periodicity threshold ψ.

Output : candidate periodic patterns for T (a pattern and its support value).

Algorithm :

1. Select an arbitrary ordering for the symbols $s_0, s_1, \ldots, s_{\sigma-1}$.
2. From T, obtain a binary vector $\bar{T}$ by replacing every symbol s_k by the σ-bit binary representation of 2^k.
3. Compute the sequence $C^{\bar{T}}$ where $c_i^{\bar{T}} = \sum_{j=0}^{i} 2^j \bar{t}_j \cdot \bar{t}_{i-j}$, and consequently $C^T = \pi_{\sigma,0}(C^{\bar{T}})$.
4. For $p = 1, 2, \ldots, n/2$,
   a) compute the set $W_p = \{w_{p,1}, w_{p,2}, \ldots\}$ where $c_p^T = \sum_h 2^{w_{p,h}}$,
   b) for $k = 0, 1, \ldots, \sigma-1$, and $l = 0, 1, \ldots, p-1$, compute the sets $W_{p,k}$ and $W_{p,k,l}$ as defined, and consequently the values of $\mathcal{F}_2(s_k, \pi_{p,l}(T))$,
   c) if $\frac{\mathcal{F}_2(s_k, \pi_{p,l}(T))}{\lceil (n-l)/p \rceil - 1} \geq \psi$, then p is a candidate period for the symbol s_k at position l.
   d) form and output the periodic single-symbol patterns according to Definition 2.
   e) form the set of candidate periodic patterns according to Definition 3, calculate the support of each as defined, and output those whose support values are not less than the periodicity threshold.

Fig. 2. The obscure periodic patterns mining algorithm

is chosen to be compared versus our proposed algorithm throughout the experiments. As discussed earlier in Sect. 1.1, the periodic trends algorithm of [13] is the fastest among the ones in the literature that detects all the valid candidate periods.

In our experiments, we exploit synthetic data as well as real data. We generate controlled synthetic time series data by tuning some parameters, namely, data distribution, period, alphabet size, type, and amount of noise. Both uniform and normal data distributions are considered. Types of noise include replacement, insertion, deletion, or any combination of them. Inerrant data is generated by repeating a pattern, of length equal to the period, that is randomly generated from the specified data distribution. The pattern is repeated till it spans the specified time series length. Noise is introduced randomly and uniformly over the whole time series. Replacement noise is introduced by altering the symbol at a randomly selected position in the time series by another. Insertion or deletion noise is introduced by inserting a new symbol or deleting the current symbol at a randomly selected position in the time series.

Two databases serve the purpose of real data experiments. The first one is a relatively small database that contains the daily power consumption rates of some customers over a period of one year. It is made available through the CIMEG[3] project. The database size is approximately 5 Megabytes. The second database is a Wal-Mart database of 70 Gigabytes, which resides on an NCR Teradata Server running the NCR Teradata Database System. It contains sanitized data of timed sales transactions for some Wal-Mart stores over a period of 15 months. The timed sales transactions data has a size of 130 Megabytes. In both databases, the numeric data values are discretized[4] into five levels, i.e., the alphabet size equals to 5. The levels are *very low*, *low*, *medium*, *high*, and *very high*. For the power consumption data, discretizing is based on discussions with domain experts (*very low* corresponds to less than 6000 Watts/Day, and each level has a 2000 Watts range). For the timed sales transactions data, discretizing is based on manual inspection of the values (*very low* corresponds to zero transactions per hour, *low* corresponds to less than 200 transactions per hour, and each level has a 200 transactions range).

4.1 Verification of Correctness

Synthetic data, both inerrant and noisy, are used in this experiment in order to inspect the correctness of the proposed algorithm. The correctness measure will be the ability of the algorithm to detect the symbol periodicities that are artificially embedded into the synthetic data. Figure 3 gives the results of this experiment. We use the symbols "U" and "N" to denote the uniform and the normal distributions, respectively; and the symbol "P" to denote the period. Recall that inerrant synthetic data is generated in such a way that it is perfectly periodic, i.e., the symbol periodicities are embedded at periods $P, 2P, \ldots$. The confidence is the minimum periodicity threshold value required to detect a specific period. If the data is perfectly periodic, the confidence of all the periodicities should be 1. Time series lengths of 1M symbols are used with alphabet size of 10. The values collected are averaged over 100 runs. Figure 3(a) shows that the algorithm is able to detect all the embedded periodicities in the inerrant time series data with the highest possible confidence. Although Fig. 3(b) shows an expected decrease in the confidence values due to the presence of noise, the values are still high enough (above 70%) to consider the algorithm as correct. Figure 3(b) shows also an unbiased behavior of the algorithm with respect to the period unlike the algorithm of [13] as shown in Fig. 4.

Figure 4 gives the results of the same experiment for the periodic trends algorithm of [13]. However, in order to inspect the correctness of that algorithm, we will briefly discuss its output. The algorithm computes an absolute value for each possible period, and then it outputs the periods that correspond to the minimum absolute values as the most candidate periods. In other words,

[3] CIMEG: Consortium for the Intelligent Management of the Electric Power Grid. http://helios.ecn.purdue.edu/~cimeg.

[4] The problem of discretizing time series into a finite alphabet is orthogonal to our problem and is beyond the scope of this paper (see [9] for an exhaustive overview of discretizing techniques).

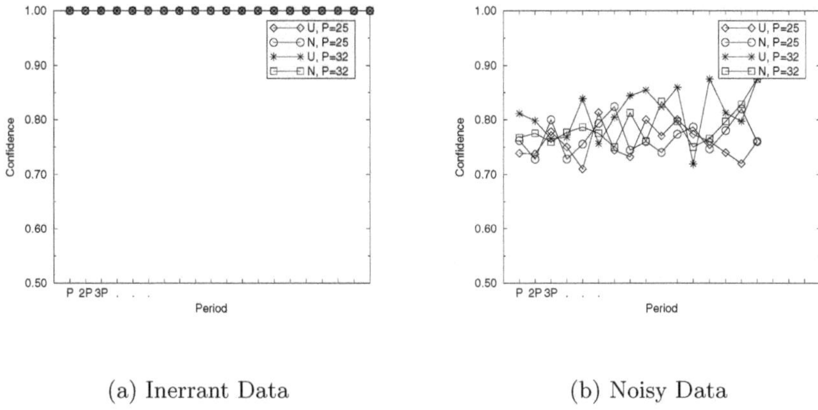

(a) Inerrant Data (b) Noisy Data

Fig. 3. Correctness of the obscure periodic patterns mining algorithm

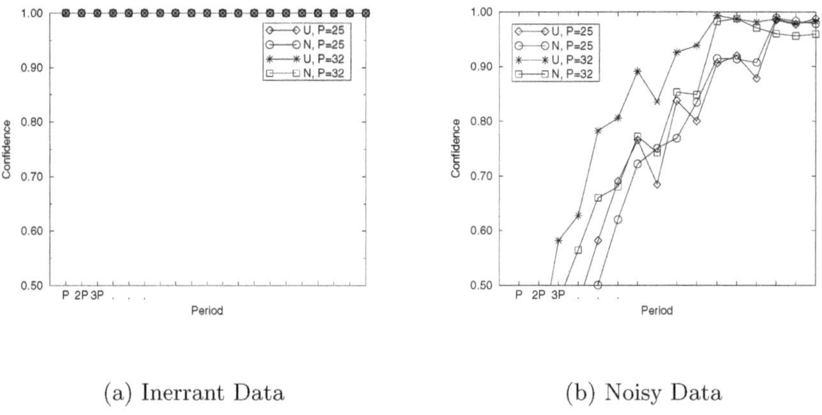

(a) Inerrant Data (b) Noisy Data

Fig. 4. Correctness of the periodic trends algorithm

if the absolute values are sorted in ascending order, the corresponding periods will be ordered from the most to the least candidate. Therefore, it is the rank of the period in this candidacy order that favors a period over another rather than its corresponding absolute value. Normalizing the ranks to be real-valued ranging from 0 to 1 is trivial. The normalized rank can be considered as the confidence value of each period (the most candidate period that has rank 1 will have normalized rank value of 1, and less candidate periods that have lower ranks will have lower normalized rank values). This means that if the data is perfectly periodic, the embedded periodicities should have the highest ranks

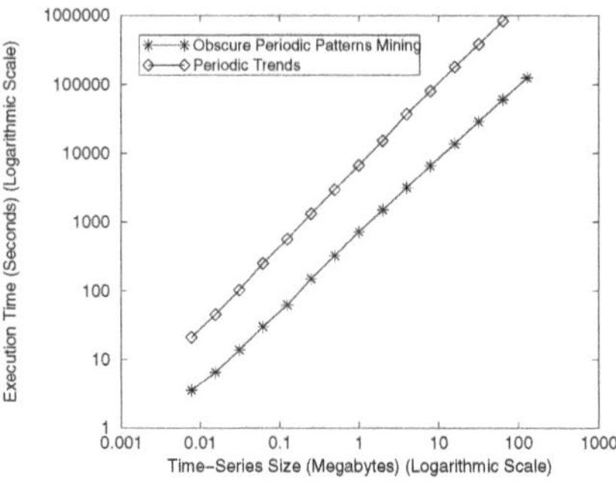

Fig. 5. Time behavior of the obscure periodic patterns mining algorithm

and so confidence values close to 1. Figure 4(b) shows a biased behavior of the periodic trends algorithm with respect to the period, as it favors the higher period values. However, we believe that the smaller periods are more accurate than the larger ones since they are more informative. For example, if the power consumption of a specific customer has a weekly pattern, it is more informative to report the period of 7 days than to report the periods of 14, 21, or other multiples of 7.

4.2 Time Performance

As mentioned earlier, our proposed algorithm is the only one that mines periodic patterns with unknown period in one pass. Having said that, there is no direct time performance comparison between our proposed algorithm and the ones in the literature. However, we compare the time behavior of the periodic trends algorithm of [13] to that of the periodicity detection phase of our proposed algorithm.

Figure 5 exhibits the time behavior of both algorithms with respect to the time series length. Wal-Mart timed sales transactions data is used in different portion lengths of powers of 2 up to 128 Megabytes. Figure 5 shows that the execution time of our proposed algorithm is linearly proportional to the time series length. More importantly, the figure shows that our proposed algorithm outperforms the periodic trends algorithm of [13]. This experimental result agrees with the theoretical results as the periodic trends algorithm [13] performs in $O(n \log^2 n)$ time whereas our proposed algorithm performs in $O(n \log n)$ time.

4.3 Resilience to Noise

As mentioned before, there are three types of noise: replacement, insertion and deletion noise. This set of experiments studies the behavior of the proposed obscure periodic patterns mining algorithm towards these types of noise as well

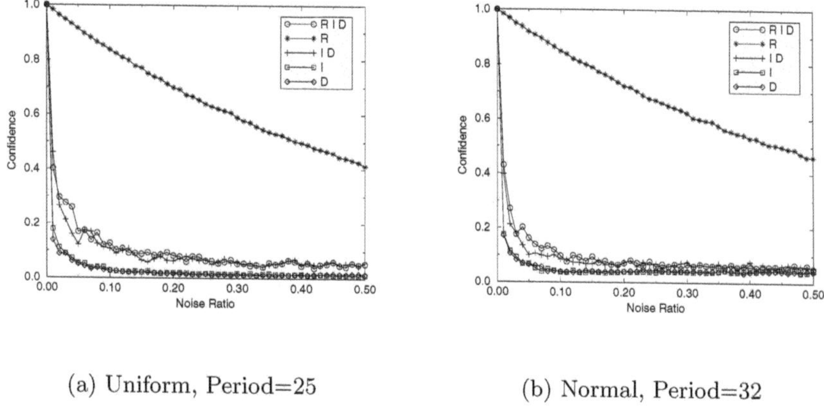

(a) Uniform, Period=25 (b) Normal, Period=32

Fig. 6. Resilience to noise of the obscure periodic patterns mining algorithm

as different combinations of them. Results are given in Fig. 6 in which we use the symbols "R", "I", and "D" to denote the three types of noise, respectively. Two or more types of noise can be combined, e.g., "R I D" means that the noise ratio is distributed equally among replacement, insertion, and deletion, while "I D" means that the noise ratio is distributed equally among insertion and deletion only. Time series lengths of 1M symbols are used with alphabet size of 10. The values collected are averaged over 100 runs. Since the behaviors were similar regardless of the period or the data distribution, an arbitrarily combination of period and data distribution is chosen. Figure 6 shows that the algorithm is very resilient to replacement noise. At 40% periodicity threshold, the algorithm can tolerate 50% replacement noise in the data. When the other types of noise get involved separately or with replacement noise, the algorithm performs poorly. However, the algorithm can still be considered roughly resilient to those other types of noise since periodicity thresholds in the range 5% to 10% are not uncommon.

4.4 Real Data Experiments

Tables 1, 2 and 3 display the output of the obscure periodic patterns mining algorithm for the Wal-Mart and CIMEG data for different values of the periodicity threshold. We examine first the symbol periodicities in Table 1 and then the periodic patterns in Tables 2 and 3. Clearly, the algorithm outputs fewer periodic patterns for higher threshold values, and the periodic patterns detected with respect to a certain value of the periodicity threshold are enclosed within those detected with respect to a lower value. To verify its correctness, the algorithm should at least output the periodic patterns of periods that are expected in the time series. Wal-Mart data has an expected period value of 24 that cor-

Table 1. Period values

Periodicity Threshold (%)	Wal-Mart Data		CIMEG Data	
	# Periods	Some Periods	# Periods	Some Periods
50	3164	263, 409	103	20, 34
55	2777	337, 385	95	128
60	2728	481	95	7, 46
65	2612	503	87	14, 54
70	2460	505	80	32
75	2447	577	79	28, 52
80	2328	647	74	38
85	2289	791	72	116
90	2285	721	72	21
95	2281	24, 168	71	35, 73

Table 2. Periodic single-symbol patterns

Periodicity Threshold (%)	Wal-Mart Data Period=24		CIMEG Data Period=7	
	# Patterns	Patterns	# Patterns	Patterns
50	13	(*b*,5), (*d*,17)	2	(*a*,3)
55	11	(*b*,8)	1	(*b*,2)
60	10	(*b*,6), (*c*,9)	1	
65	8	(*a*,21)	0	
70	7	(*a*,3)	0	
75	6	(*b*,7)	0	
80	6		0	
85	5	(*a*,0), (*a*,1),	0	
90	5	(*a*,2), (*a*,22)	0	
95	5	(*a*,23)	0	

Table 3. Periodic patterns for Wal-Mart data

Periodic Pattern	Support (%)
aaaa§§§§§§§§§§§§§§§§§*aaa*	49.78166
aaaa§§§*b*§§§§§§§§§§§§§*aaa*	42.57642
aaaa§§§*b*§§§§§§§§§*d*§§§*aaa*	38.56768
§§§§§*bbbbc*§§§§§§§§§§§§*aa*	35.80786

responds to the daily pattern of number of transactions per hour. CIMEG data has an expected period value of 7 that corresponds to the weekly pattern of power consumption rates per day.

Table 1 shows that for Wal-Mart data, a period of 24 hours is detected when the periodicity threshold is 70% or less. In addition, the algorithm detects many more periods, some of which are quite interesting. A period of 168 hours (24×7) can be explained as the weekly pattern of number of transactions per hour. A period of 3961 hours shows a periodicity of exactly 5.5 months plus one hour, which can be explained as the daylight savings hour. One may argue against the clarity of this explanation, yet this proves that there may be obscure periods, unknown a priori, that the algorithm can detect. Similarly, for CIMEG data, the period of 7 days is detected when the threshold is 60% or less. Other clear periods are those that are multiples of 7. However, a period of 123 days is difficult to explain.

Exploring the period of 24 hours for Wal-Mart and that of 7 days for CIMEG data produces the results given in Table 2. Note that periodic single-symbol pattern is reported as a pair, consisting of a symbol and a starting position for a certain period. For example, $(b,7)$ for Wal-Mart data with respect to a periodicity threshold of 80% or less represents the periodic single-symbol pattern $\S\S\S\S\S\S\S b\S\S\S\S\S\S\S\S\S\S\S\S\S\S\S\S$. Knowing that the symbol b represents the *low* level for Wal-Mart data (less than 200 transactions per hour), this periodic pattern can be interpreted as *less than 200 transactions per hour occur in the 7th hour of the day (between 7:00am and 8:00am) for* 80% *of the days.* As another example, $(a,3)$ for CIMEG data with respect to a periodicity threshold of 50% or less represents the periodic single-symbol pattern $\S\S\S a\S\S\S$. Knowing that the symbol a represents the *very low* level for CIMEG data (less than 6000 Watts/Day), this periodic pattern can be interpreted as *less than 6000 Watts/Day occur in the 4th day of the week for* 50% *of the days.* Finally, Table 3 gives the final output of periodic patterns of Wal-Mart data for the period of 24 hours for periodicity threshold of 35%. Each pattern can be interpreted in a similar way to the above.

5 Conclusions

In this paper, we have developed a one pass algorithm for mining periodic patterns in time series of unknown or obscure periods, where discovering the periods is part of the mining algorithm. Based on an adapted definition of convolution, the algorithm is computationally efficient as it scan the data only once and takes $O(n \log n)$ time, for a time series of length n. We have defined the periodic pattern in a novel way that the period is a variable rather than an input parameter. An empirical study of the algorithm using real-world and synthetic data proves the practicality of the problem, validates the correctness of the algorithm, and the usefulness of its output patterns.

References

1. K. Abrahamson. Generalized String Matching. *SIAM Journal on Computing*, Vol. 16, No. 6, pages 1039-1051, 1987.
2. R. Agrawal and R. Srikant. Fast Algorithms for Mining Association Rules. In *Proc. of the 20th Int. Conf. on Very Large Databases*, Santiago, Chile, September 1994.
3. R. Agrawal and R. Srikant. Mining Sequential Patterns. In *Proc. of the 11th Int. Conf. on Data Engineering*, Taipei, Taiwan, March 1995.
4. W. Aref, M. Elfeky, and A. Elmagarmid. Incremental, Online, and Merge Mining of Partial Periodic Patterns in Time-Series Databases. To appear in *IEEE Transactions on Knowledge and Data Engineering.*

5. J. Ayres, J. Gehrke, T. Yiu, and J. Flannick. Sequential Pattern Mining using A Bitmap Representation. In *Proc. of the 8th Int. Conf. on Knowledge Discovery and Data Mining*, Edmonton, Alberta, Canada, July 2002.
6. C. Berberidis, W. Aref, M. Atallah, I. Vlahavas, and A. Elmagarmid. Multiple and Partial Periodicity Mining in Time Series Databases. In *Proc. of the 15th Euro. Conf. on Artificial Intelligence*, Lyon, France, July 2002.
7. C. Bettini, X. Wang, S. Jajodia, and J. Lin. Discovering Frequent Event Patterns with Multiple Granularities in Time Sequences. *IEEE Transactions on Knowledge and Data Engineering*, Vol. 10, No. 2, pages 222-237, 1998.
8. T. Cormen, C. Leiserson, and R. Rivest. *Introduction to Algorithms.* The MIT Press, Cambridge, MA, 1990.
9. C. Daw, C. Finney, and E. Tracy. A Review of Symbolic Analysis of Experimental Data. *Review of Scientific Instruments*, Vol. 74, No. 2, pages 915-930, 2003.
10. M. Garofalakis, R. Rastogi, and K. Shim. SPIRIT: Sequential Pattern Mining with Regular Expression Constraints. In *Proc. of the 25th Int. Conf. on Very Large Databases*, Edinburgh, Scotland, UK, September 1999.
11. J. Han, G. Dong, and Y. Yin. Efficient Mining of Partial Periodic Patterns in Time Series Databases. In *Proc. of the 15th Int. Conf. on Data Engineering*, Sydney, Australia, March 1999.
12. J. Han, W. Gong, and Y. Yin. Mining Segment-Wise Periodic Patterns in Time Related Databases. In *Proc. of the 4th Int. Conf. on Knowledge Discovery and Data Mining*, New York City, New York, August 1998.
13. P. Indyk, N. Koudas, and S. Muthukrishnan. Identifying Representative Trends in Massive Time Series Data Sets Using Sketches. In *Proc. of the 26th Int. Conf. on Very Large Data Bases*, Cairo, Egypt, September 2000.
14. E. Keogh, S. Lonardi, and B. Chiu. Finding Surprising Patterns in a Time Series Database in Linear Time and Space. In *Proc. of the 8th Int. Conf. on Knowledge Discovery and Data Mining*, Edmonton, Alberta, Canada, July 2002.
15. D. Knuth. *The Art of Computer Programming, Vol. 2.* Addison-Wesley, Reading, MA, 1981.
16. S. Ma and J. Hellerstein. Mining Partially Periodic Event Patterns with Unknown Periods. In *Proc. of the 17th Int. Conf. on Data Engineering*, Heidelberg, Germany, April 2001.
17. B. Ozden, S. Ramaswamy, and A. Silberschatz. Cyclic Association Rules. In *Proc. of the 14th Int. Conf. on Data Engineering*, Orlando, Florida, February 1998.
18. R. Srikant and R. Agrawal. Mining Sequential Patterns: Generalizations and Performance Improvements. In *Proc. of the 5th Int. Conf. on Extending Database Technology*, Avignon, France, March 1996.
19. J. Vitter. External Memory Algorithms and Data Structures: Dealing with Massive Data. *ACM Computing Surveys*, Vol. 33, No. 2, pages 209-271, June 2001.
20. J. Yang, W. Wang, and P. Yu Mining Asynchronous Periodic Patterns in Time Series Data. In *Proc. of the 6th Int. Conf. on Knowledge Discovery and Data Mining*, Boston, Massachusetts, August 2000.

CUBE File: A File Structure for Hierarchically Clustered OLAP Cubes

Nikos Karayannidis, Timos Sellis, and Yannis Kouvaras

Institute of Communication and Computer Systems and
School of Electrical and Computer Engineering,
National Technical University of Athens,
Zographou 15773, Athens, Hellas
{nikos,timos,jkouvar}@dblab.ece.ntua.gr

Abstract. Hierarchical clustering has been proved an effective means for physically organizing large fact tables since it reduces significantly the I/O cost during ad hoc OLAP query evaluation. In this paper, we propose a novel multidimensional file structure for organizing the most detailed data of a cube, the CUBE File. The CUBE File achieves hierarchical clustering of the data, enabling fast access via hierarchical restrictions. Moreover, it imposes a low storage cost and adapts perfectly to the extensive sparseness of the data space achieving a high compression rate. Our results show that the CUBE File outperforms the most effective method proposed up to now for hierarchically clustering the cube, resulting in 7-9 times less I/Os on average for all workloads tested. Thus, it achieves a higher degree of hierarchical clustering. Moreover, the CUBE File imposes a 2-3 times lower storage cost.

1 Introduction

On Line Analytical Processing (OLAP) has caused a significant shift in the traditional database query paradigm. Queries have become more complex and entail the processing of large amounts of data. Considering the size of the data stored in contemporary data warehouses, as well as the processing-intensive nature of OLAP queries, there is a strong need for an effective physical organization of the data. In this paper, we are dealing with the physical organization of OLAP cubes. In particular, we are interested in primary organizations for the most detailed data of a cube, since *ad hoc* OLAP queries are usually evaluated by directly accessing the most detailed data of the cube. Therefore an appropriate primary organization must guarantee the efficient retrieval of these data. Moreover it must correspond to the peculiarities of the cube data space.

Hierarchical clustering, organizes data on disk with respect to the dimension hierarchies. The primary goal of hierarchical clustering is to reduce the I/O cost for queries containing restrictions and/or grouping operations on hierarchy attributes. The problem of evaluating the appropriateness of a primary organization for the cube can be formulated based on the following criteria, which must be fulfilled. A primary organization for the most detailed data of the cube must:

E. Bertino et al. (Eds.): EDBT 2004, LNCS 2992, pp. 621–638, 2004.
© Springer-Verlag Berlin Heidelberg 2004

- Be natively multidimensional
- Support dimension hierarchies, i.e., to enable access to the data via hierarchical restrictions.
- Impose appropriate data clustering for minimizing the I/O cost of queries.
- Adapt well to the extensive sparseness of the cube data space.
- Impose low storage overhead.
- Achieve high space utilization.

The most recent proposals [8, 16] in the literature for cube data structures deal with the computation and storage of the *data cube operator* [4]. These methods omit a significant aspect in OLAP, which is that usually dimensions are not flat but are organized in hierarchies of different aggregation levels (e.g., *store, city, area, country* is such a hierarchy for a *Location* dimension). The most popular approach for organizing the most detailed data of a cube is the so-called *star schema*. In this case the cube data are stored in a relational table, called the *fact table*. Furthermore, various indexing schemes have been developed [2, 10, 12, 15], in order to speed up the evaluation of the join of the central (and usually very large) fact table with the surrounding dimension tables (also known as a *star join*). However, even when elaborate indexes are used, due to the arbitrary ordering of the fact table tuples, there might be as many I/Os as are the tuples resulting from the fact table.

To reduce this I/O cost, hierarchical clustering of the fact table tuples appears to be a very promising solution. In [7], we have proposed a processing framework for *star queries* over hierarchical clustering primary organizations that showed significant speedups (up to 24 times faster on average) compared to conventional execution plans based on bitmap indexes. Moreover, with appropriate optimizations [13, 19] this speedup can be multiplied further. The primary organization that we used in the above for clustering hierarchically the fact table was the UB-tree [1] in combination with a clustering technique called *multidimensional hierarchical clustering* (MHC) [9].

In this paper, we propose a novel primary organization for the most detailed data of the cube, called the *CUBE File*. Our focus is the evaluation of queries from the base data. The pre-computation of data cube aggregates is an orthogonal problem that we do not address in this paper. Note also that a description of the full processing entailed for the evaluation of OLAP queries over the CUBE File or other hierarchical clustering-enabling organizations is outside the scope of this paper. The interested reader can find all the details in [7]. In this paper, our focus is on the efficient retrieval of the cube data through restrictions on the hierarchies. The relational counterpart of this is the evaluation of a star-join.

This paper is organized as follows. Section 2 addresses hierarchical chunking and the chunk-tree representation of the cube. Section 3 addresses the allocation of chunks into buckets. Section 4 discusses our experimental evaluation. Section 5 concludes.

2 The Hierarchically Chunked Cube

Clearly, what we are aiming for is to define a multidimensional file organization that natively supports hierarchies. We need a data structure that can efficiently lead us to the corresponding data subset based on hierarchical restrictions. A key observation at this point is that all restrictions on the hierarchies intuitively define a subcube or a cube-slice. Therefore, we exploit the intuitive representation of a cube as a multidimensional array and apply a *chunking* scheme in order to create subcubes, i.e., *chunks*. Our method of chunking is based on the dimension hierarchies' structure and thus we call it *hierarchical chunking*.

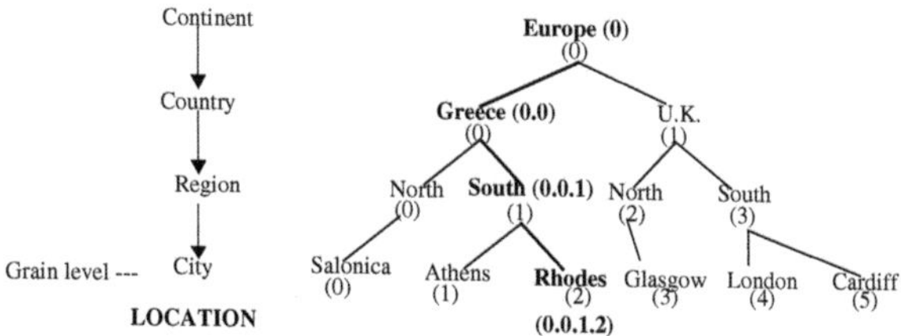

Fig. 1. Example of hierarchical surrogate keys assigned to an example hierarchy

2.1 Hierarchical Chunking

In order to apply hierarchical chunking, we first assign a surrogate key to each dimension hierarchy value. This key uniquely identifies each value within the hierarchy. More specifically, we order the values in each hierarchy level so that sibling values occupy consecutive positions and perform a mapping to the domain of positive integers. The resulting values are depicted in Fig. 1 for an example of a dimension hierarchy. The simple integers appearing under each value in each level are called *order-codes*. In order to identify a value in the hierarchy, we form the path of order-codes from the root-value to the value in question. This path is called a *hierarchical surrogate key*, or simply *h-surrogate*. For example the h-surrogate for the value "*Rhodes*" is *0.0.1.2*. H-surrogates convey hierarchical information for each cube data point, which can be greatly exploited for the efficient processing of star-queries [7, 13, 19].

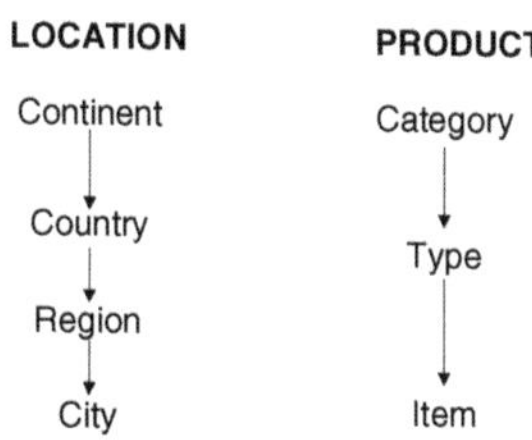

Fig. 2. Dimensions of our example cube

The basic incentive behind hierarchical chunking is to partition the data space by forming a *hierarchy of chunks* that is based on the dimensions' hierarchies. We model the cube as a large multidimensional array, which *consists only of the most detailed data*. Initially, we partition the cube in a very few chunks corresponding to the most aggregated levels of the dimensions' hierarchies. Then we recursively partition each chunk as we drill-down to the hierarchies of all dimensions in parallel. We define a measure in order to distinguish each recursion step, *chunking depth D*. Due to lack of space we will not describe in detail the process of hierarchical chunking. Rather we will illustrate it with an example. A more detailed description of the method can be found in [5, 6]. The dimensions of our example cube are depicted in Figure 2.

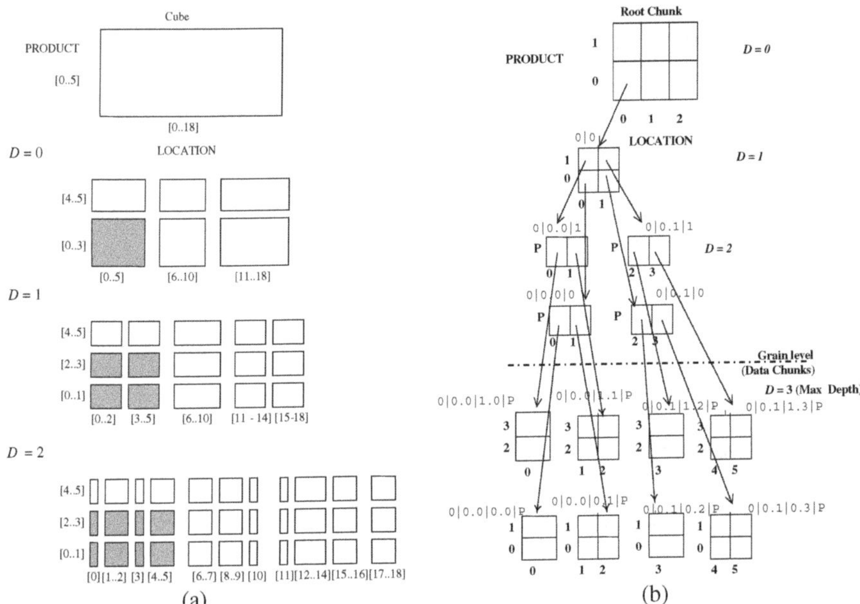

Fig. 3. (a) The cube from our running example hierarchically chunked. (b) The whole subtree up to the data chunks under chunk 0 | 0

The result of hierarchical chunking on our example cube is depicted in Fig. 3(a). Chunking begins at chunking depth $D = 0$ and proceeds in a top-down fashion. To define a chunk, we define discrete ranges of grain-level members (i.e., values) on each dimension, denoted in the figure as *[a..b]*, where *a* and *b* are grain-level order-codes. Each such range is defined as the set of members with the same parent (member) in the corresponding parent level (called *pivot* level). The total number of chunks created at each depth D equals the product of the cardinalities of the pivot levels.

The procedure ends when the next levels to include as pivot levels are the grain levels. Then we do not need to perform any further chunking, because the chunks that would be produced from such a chunking would be the cells of the cube themselves. In this case, we have reached the *maximum chunking depth* D_{MAX}. In our example, chunking stops at $D = 2$ and the maximum depth is $D = 3$. Notice the shaded chunks in Fig. 3(a) depicting chunks belonging in the same chunk hierarchy.

In order to apply our method, we need to have hierarchies of equal length. For this reason, we insert *pseudo-levels P* into the shorter hierarchies until they reach the length of the longest one. This "padding" is done at the level that is just above the grain (most detailed) level. In our example, the *PRODUCT* dimension has only three levels and needs one pseudo-level in order to reach the length of the *LOCATION* dimension. The rationale for inserting the pseudo levels above the grain level lies in that we wish to apply chunking the soonest possible and for all possible dimensions. Since, the chunking proceeds in a top-to-bottom fashion, this “eager chunking” has the advantage of reducing very early the chunk size and also provides faster access to the underlying data, because it increases the fan-out of the intermediate nodes. If at a particular depth one (or more) pivot-level is a pseudo-level, then this level *does not* take part in the chunking (in our example this occurs at $D = 2$ for the *PRODUCT* dimension.). Therefore, since pseudo levels restrict chunking in the dimensions that are applied, we must insert them to the lowest possible level. Consequently, since there is no chunking below the grain level (a data cell cannot be further partitioned), the pseudo level insertion occurs just above the grain level.

We use the intermediate depth chunks as *directory chunks* that will guide us to the D_{MAX} depth chunks containing the data and thus called *data chunks*. This leads to a *chunk-tree* representation of the hierarchically chunked cube and is depicted in Fig. 3(b) for our example cube. In Fig. 3(b), we have expanded the chunk-subtree corresponding to the family of chunks that has been shaded in Fig. 3(a). Pseudo-levels are marked with "P" and the corresponding directory chunks have reduced dimensionality (i.e., one dimensional in this case). If we interleave the h-surrogates of the pivot level members that define a chunk, then we get a code that we call *chunk-id*. This is a unique identifier for a chunk within a CUBE File. Moreover, this identifier depicts the whole path in the chunk hierarchy of a chunk. In Fig. 3(b), we note the corresponding chunk-id above each chunk. The root chunk does not have a chunk-id because it represents the whole cube and chunk-ids essentially denote subcubes. The part of a chunk-id that is contained between consecutive dots and corresponds to a specific depth D is called *D-domain*.

2.2 Advantages of the Chunk-Tree Representation

Direct access to cube data through hierarchical restrictions: One of the main advantages of the chunk-tree representation of a cube is that it explicitly supports hierarchies. This means that any cube data subset defined through restrictions on the dimension hierarchies can be accessed directly. This is achieved by simply accessing the qualifying cells at each depth and following the intermediate chunk pointers to the appropriate data. Note that the vast majority of OLAP queries contain an equality restriction on a number of hierarchical attributes and more commonly on hierarchical attributes that form a complete path in the hierarchy. This is reasonable since the core of analysis is conducted along the hierarchies. We call this kind of restrictions *hierarchical prefix path* (HPP) restrictions.

Adaptation to cube's native sparseness: The cube data space is extremely sparse [15]. In other words, the ratio of the number of real data points to the product of the dimension grain–level cardinalities is a very small number. Values for this ratio in the range of 10^{-12} to 10^{-5} are more than typical (especially for cubes with more than 3 dimensions). It is therefore, imperative that a primary organization for the cube adapts well to this sparseness, allocating space conservatively. Ideally, the allocated space must be comparable to the size of the existing data points. The chunk-tree representation adapts perfectly to the cube data space. The reason is that the empty regions of a cube are not arbitrarily formed. On the contrary, specific combinations of dimension hierarchy values form them. For instance, in our running example, if no music products are sold in Greece, then a large empty region is formed. Consequently, the empty regions in the cube data space translate naturally to one or more empty chunk-subtrees in the chunk-tree representation. Therefore, empty subtrees can be discarded altogether and the space allocation corresponds to the real data points and only.

Storage efficiency: A chunk is physically represented by a multidimensional array. This enables an offset-based access, rather than a search-based one, which speedups the cell access mechanism considerably. Moreover, it gives us the opportunity to exploit chunk-ids in a very effective way. A chunk-id essentially consists of interleaved coordinate values. Therefore, we can use a chunk-id in order to calculate the appropriate offset of a cell in a chunk but we do not have to store the chunk-id along with each cell. Indeed, a search-based mechanism (like the one used by conventional B-tree indexes, or the UB-tree [1]) requires that the dimension values (or the corresponding h-surrogates), which form the search-key, must be also stored within each cell (i.e., tuple) of the cube. In the CUBE File only the measure values of the cube are stored in each cell. Hence notable space savings are achieved. In addition, further compression of chunks can be easily achieved, without affecting the offset-based accessing (see [6] for the details).

2.3 Handling Multiple Hierarchies per Dimension and Updating

It is typical for a dimension to consist of more than one aggregation paths, i.e., hierarchies. Usually, all the possible hierarchies of a dimension have always a common grain level. The CUBE File is based on a *single* hierarchy from each dimension. We call this hierarchy the *primary hierarchy (or the primary path)* of the dimension. Data will be physically clustered according to the dimensions' primary paths. Since queries based on primary paths (either by imposing restrictions on them, or by requiring some grouping based on their levels) are very likely to be favored in terms of response time, it is crucial for the designer to decide on the paths that will play the role of the primary paths based on the query workload. Thus access to the cube data via non-primary hierarchy attribute restrictions can be supported simply by providing a mapping to the corresponding h-surrogates. However, such a query will not benefit from the underlying clustering of the data.

Unfortunately, the only way to include more than one path (per dimension) in physical clustering is to maintain redundant copies of the cube [17]. This is equivalent with trying to store the tuples of a relational table sorted by different attributes, while maintaining a single physical copy of the table. There is always one ordering per stored copy and only secondary indexes can give the "impression" of multiple orderings. Handling different hierarchies of the same dimension as two different dimensions is a work around to this problem. However, it might lead to an excessive increase of dimensionality which can deteriorate any clustering scheme altogether [20].

Finally, a discussion on the CUBE File updating issues is out of the scope of this paper. The interested reader can find a thorough description of all CUBE File maintenance operations in [5]. Here we only wish to pinpoint that the CUBE File supports bulk updating in an incremental mode, which is essentially the main requirement of all OLAP/DW applications. For example, the advent of the new data at the end of the day, or the insertion of new dimension values, or even the reclassification of dimension values will trigger only local reorganizations of the stored cube and not overall restructuring that would impose a significant time penalty.

3 Laying Chunks on the Disk

Any physical organization of data must determine how these are distributed in disk pages. A CUBE File physically organizes its data by allocating chunks into a set of buckets. A *bucket* constitutes the I/O transfer unit. The primary goal of this chunk-to-bucket allocation is to achieve the hierarchical clustering of data. We summarize the goals of such an allocation in the following:

1. Low I/O cost in the evaluation of queries containing restrictions on the dimension hierarchies.
2. Minimum storage cost.
3. High space utilization.

An allocation scheme that respects the first goal must ensure that the access of the subtrees hanging under a specific chunk must be done with a minimal number of bucket reads. Intuitively, if we could store whole subtrees in each bucket (instead of single chunks), then this would result to a better hierarchical clustering since all the restrictions on the specific subtree, as well as on any of its children subtrees, would be evaluated with a single bucket I/O. For example, the subtree hanging from the root-chunk in Fig. 3(b), at the leaf level contains all the sales figures corresponding to the continent "Europe" (order code *0*) and to the product category "Books" (order code *0*). By storing this tree into a single bucket, we can answer all queries containing hierarchical restrictions on the combination "Books" and "Europe" and on any children-members of these two, with just a single disk I/O. Therefore, each subtree in this chunk-tree corresponds to a "hierarchical family" of values. Moreover, the smaller is the chunking depth of this subtree the more value combinations it embodies. Intuitively, we can say that *the hierarchical clustering achieved can be assessed by the degree of storing small-depth whole chunk subtrees into each storage unit.*

Turning to the other two elements, the low storage cost is basically guaranteed by the chunk-tree adaptation to the data space sparseness and by the exclusion of h-surrogates from each cell, as described in the previous section. High space utilization is achieved by trying to fill each bucket to capacity.

3.1 An Allocation Algorithm

We propose a greedy algorithm for performing the chunk-to-bucket allocation in the CUBE File. Given a hierarchically chunked cube *C*, represented by a chunk-tree *CT* with a maximum chunking depth of D_{MAX}, the algorithm tries to find an allocation of the chunks of *CT* into a set of fixed-size buckets that corresponds to the criteria posed in the beginning of this section. We assume as input to this algorithm the storage cost of *CT* and any of its subtrees *t* (in the form of a function *cost(t)*) and the bucket size S_B. The output of this algorithm is a set of *K* buckets, $S = \{B_1, B_2 \ldots B_K\}$, so that each bucket contains at least one subtree of *CT* and a root-bucket B_R that contains all the rest part of *CT* (part with no whole subtrees). Note that the root-bucket can have a size greater than S_B. The algorithm assumes that this size is always sufficient for the storage of the corresponding chunks.

In each step the algorithm tries "greedily" to make an allocation decision that will maximize the hierarchical clustering of the current bucket. For example, in lines 1 to

5 of Fig. 4, the algorithm tries to store the whole input tree in a single bucket thus aiming at a maximum degree of hierarchical clustering for the corresponding bucket. If this fails, then it allocates the root R to the root-bucket and tries to allocate the subtrees at the next depth, i.e., the children of *R* (lines: 7-19). This is achieved by including all direct children subtrees with size less than (or equal to) the size of a bucket (S_B) into a list of candidate trees for inclusion into bucket-regions (*buckRegion*) (lines: 11-13). A *bucket-region* is a group of chunk-trees of the same depth having a common parent node, which are stored in the same bucket. The routine *formBucketRegions* is called upon this list and tries to include the corresponding trees in a minimum set of buckets, by forming bucket-regions (lines: 14-16). A detailed analysis of the issues involved in the formation of bucket regions can be found in [5].

```
        GreedyPutChunksIntoBuckets(R,SB)
        //Input: Root R of a chunk-tree CT, bucket size S
        //BOutput: Updated R, list of allocated buckets Buck
        // List, root bucket BR, directory entry dirEnt
        // pointing at R
        {List buckRegion // Bucket-region Candidates list
0:      IF (cost(CT) < SB){
1:         Allocate new bucket Bn
2:         Store CT in Bn
3:         dirEnt = addressOf(R)
4:         RETURN }
5:      //R will be stored in the root-bucket BR
6:      IF (R is a directory chunk) {
7:         FOR EACH child subtree CTC of R {
8:            IF (CTC is empty){
9:               Mark with empty tag corresponding R's entry}
10:           IF (cost(CTC) ≤ SB){
11:     // Insert CTC into list for bucket-region candidates
12:              buckRegion.push(CTC)}}
13:        IF(buckRegion != empty){
14:           // Formulate the bucket-regions
15:           formBucketRegions(buckRegion, BuckList, R)}
16:        WHILE (there is a child CTC : cost(CTC) > SB){
17:              GreedyPutChunkIntoBuckets(root(CTC),SB)
18:              Update corresponding R entry for CTC}
19:        Store R in the root-bucket BR
20:        dirEnt = addressOf(R)}
21:     ELSE { //R is a data chunk and cost(R) > B
22:        Artificially chunk R, create 2-level chunk-tree CTA
23:        GreedyPutChunkIntoBuckets(root(CTA),SB)
24:     //storage of R will be taken cared of by previous call
25:        dirEnt = addressOf(root(CTA))}
26:     RETURN }
27:
```

Fig. 4. A greedy algorithm for the chunk-to-bucket allocation in a CUBE File

Finally, for the children subtrees of root *R* with total size greater than the size of a bucket, we recursively try to solve the corresponding chunk-to-bucket allocation subproblem for each one of them (lines: 17-19). Very important is also the fact that no bucket space is allocated for empty subtrees (lines: 9-10); only a special entry is inserted in the parent node to denote an empty subtree. Therefore, the allocation performed by the greedy algorithm adapts perfectly to the data distribution, coping effectively with the native sparseness of the cube. The recursive calls might lead us eventually all the way down to a data chunk (at depth D_{MAX}). Indeed, if the *GreedyPutChunksIntoBuckets* is called upon a root *R*, which is a data chunk, then this means that we have come upon a data chunk with size greater than the bucket size. This is called a *large data chunk*. In order to resolve the storage of such a chunk we extend the chunking further (beyond the existing hierarchy levels) with a technique called *artificial chunking* [5]. Artificial chunking applies a normal grid on a large data chunk, in order to transform it into a 2-level chunk tree. Then, we solve the allocation subproblem for this tree (lines: 22-26). The termination of the algorithm is guaranteed by the fact that each recursive call deals with a subproblem of a smaller in size chunk-tree than the parent problem. Thus, the size of the input chunk-tree is continuously reduced.

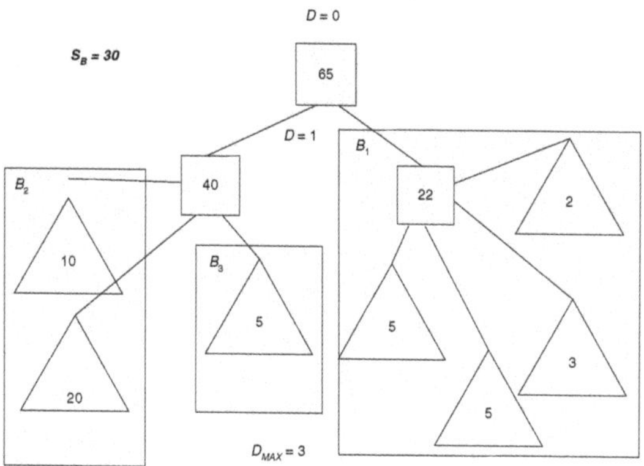

Fig. 5. The chunk-to-bucket allocation for the chunk-tree of our running example for $S_B = 30$

In Fig. 5, we depict an instance of the chunk-tree in our running example showing the non-empty subtrees. The numbers inside each node represent the storage cost for the corresponding subtree, e.g., the whole chunk-tree has a cost of 65 units. For a bucket size $S_B = 30$ units the greedy algorithm yields an allocation, which comprises three buckets B_1, B_2 and B_3, depicted as rectangles in the figure. B_1 is the first bucket to be created. Compared to the other two buckets it has achieved a better hierarchical clustering degree since it stores a subtree of smaller depth. B_2 is filled next with a bucket region consisting of two sibling subtrees. Finally, the algorithm fills B_3 with a single subtree. The nodes not included in a rectangle are allocated to the root-bucket B_R. The nodes of the root-bucket form a separate chunk-tree. This is called the *root-directory* and its storage is the topic of the next subsection.

3.2 Storage of the Root Directory

The *root directory* is an unbalanced chunk-tree, whose root is the root-chunk and consists of all the directory chunks that are allocated to the root-bucket by the greedy allocation algorithm. The basic idea for the storage of the root directory is based on the simple heuristic that if we impose hierarchical clustering to the root directory, as if it was a chunk-tree on its own, the evaluation of queries with hierarchical restrictions would benefit, because all queries need at some point to access a node of the root directory. Therefore, treating the directory entries in the root directory pointing to already allocated subtrees as pointers to empty trees, (in the sense that their storage cost is not taken into account for the storage of the root directory), we apply the greedy allocation algorithm directly on the root directory. In addition, since the root directory always contains the root chunk of the whole chunk tree as well as certain higher level (i.e., smaller depth) directory chunks, we can assume that these nodes are permanently resident in main memory during a querying session on a cube. This is of course a common practice for all index structures in databases. What is more, it is the norm for all multidimensional data structures originating from the grid file [11].

Moreover, in [5] we prove that the size of the root directory becomes very fast negligible (reduces exponentially with the number of dimensions) compared to the size of the cube at the most detailed level as dimensionality increases. Nevertheless, if the available main memory cannot hold the whole root directory, then we can traverse the latter in a breadth-first way and allocate each visited node to the root-bucket, until it is filled, assuming that the size of the root-bucket equals that of the available memory. Therefore the root-bucket stores the part of the root-directory that is cached in main memory. Then, for each unallocated subtree of the root directory we run the greedy allocation algorithm again. This continues until every part of the root-directory is allocated to a bucket. In Fig. 6, we depict the resulting allocation for the chunk-tree of the running example assuming a smaller bucket size (in order to make the root directory taller) and a cache area that cannot accommodate the whole root-directory.

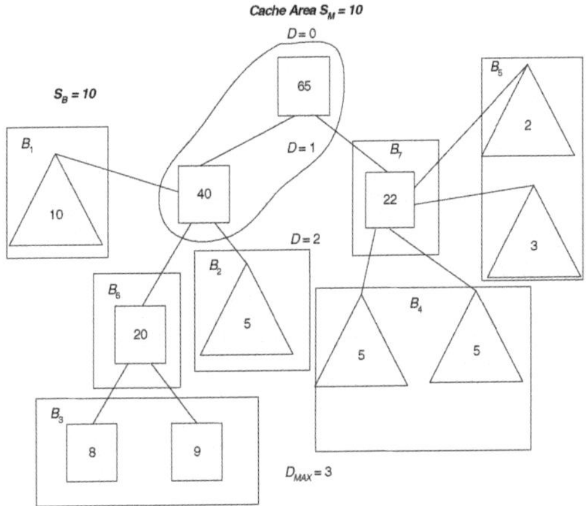

Fig. 6. Resulting allocation of the running example cube for a bucket size S_B = 10 and a cache area equal to a single bucket

4 Experimental Evaluation

In order to evaluate the CUBE File, we have run a large set of experiments that cover both the structural and the query evaluation aspects of the data structure. In addition we wanted to compare the CUBE File with the UB-tree/MHC, which to our knowledge is the only multidimensional structure that achieves hierarchical clustering with the use of h-surrogates.

4.1 Setup and Methodology

For the experimental evaluation of the CUBE File we used SISYPHUS [6]. SISYPHUS is a specialized OLAP storage manager, which incorporates the CUBE File as its primary organization for cubes. Due to lack of a CUBE File based execution engine, we simulated the evaluation of queries over the chunk-to-bucket allocation log produced by SISYPHUS. For the UB-tree experiments we used a commercial system [18] that provides the UB-tree as a primary organization for fact tables [14], enhanced with the multidimensional hierarchical clustering technique MHC [9]. We conducted experiments on an AMD Athlon processor running at 800MHz and using 768MB of main memory. For data storage we used a 60GB IDE disk. The operating system used was Linux (kernel 2.4.x). In particular, we conducted structure experiments on various data sets and query experiments on various workloads. The goal of the structure experiments was to evaluate the storage cost and the compression ability of the CUBE File, as well as the adaptation of the structure in sparse data spaces. Furthermore, we wanted to assess the relative size of the root-bucket with respect to the whole CUBE File size. Finally, we wanted to compare the storage overhead of the CUBE File with that of the UB-tree/MHC.

The first series of experiments, denoted by the acronym DIM, comprises the construction of a CUBE File, over data sets with increasing dimensionality, while maintaining a constant number of cube data points. Naturally, this increases substantially the cube sparseness. The cube sparseness is measured as the ratio of the actual cube data points to the product of the cardinalities of the dimension grain levels. The second series of structure experiments, denoted by the acronym SCALE, attempts to evaluate the scalability of the structure in the number of input data points (tuples). To this end, we build the CUBE File for data sets with increasing data point cardinality, while maintaining a constant number of dimensions.

Table 1. Dimension hierarchy configuration for the experimental data sets

Dimension	D_1	D_2	D_3	D_4	D_5	D_6	D_7	D_8	D_9
#Levels	4	5	7	3	9	2	10	8	6
Grain Level Cardinality	2000	3125	6912	500	8748	36	7776	6561	4096

The query experiments', denoted by the acronym QUERY, primary goal was to assess the hierarchical clustering achieved by the CUBE File organization and compare it with UB-tree/MHC. The most indicative measure for this assessment is the number of I/Os performed during the evaluation of queries containing hierarchical restrictions. We have decided to focus on *hierarchical prefix path (HPP)* queries, because these demonstrate better the hierarchical clustering effect and constitute the most common type of OLAP query. HPP queries consist of restrictions on the dimensions that form paths in the hierarchy levels. These paths include always the topmost (most aggregated) level. The workload comprises single (or multiple) multidimensional range queries, where the range(s) result directly from the restrictions on the hierarchy levels. Moreover, by changing the chunking depth where these restrictions are imposed, we vary the number of retrieved data points (cube selectivity).

Table 2. Data set configuration for the three series of experiments

	DIM	SCALE	QUERY
#Dimensions	Varying	5	5
#Tuples	100,000	Varying	1,142,527
#Facts	1	1	1
Maximum chunking depth	Depends on longest hierarchy	8	8
Bucket size (bytes)	8,192	8,192	8,192
UB-tree page size (bytes)	8,192	8,192	8,192
Bucket filling rate	80%	80%	80%
UB-tree leaf filling rate	80%	80%	80%

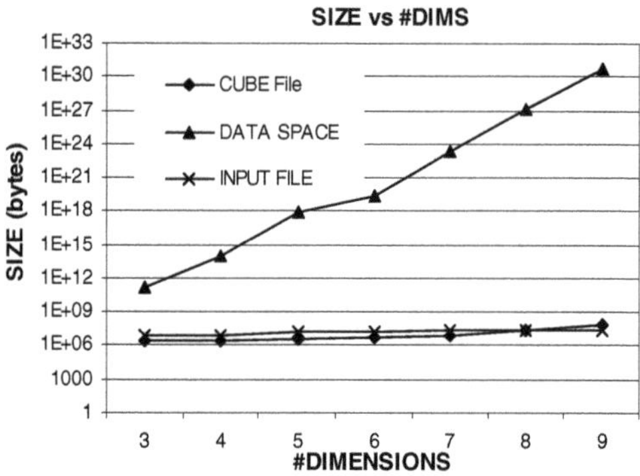

Fig. 7. Impact of cube dimensionality increase to the CUBE File size

We used synthetic data sets that were produced with an OLAP data generator that we have developed. Our aim was to create data sets with a realistic number of dimensions and hierarchy levels. In Table 1, we present the hierarchy configuration for each dimension used in the experimental data sets. The shortest hierarchy consists of 2 levels, while the longest consists of 10 levels. We tried each data set to consist of a good mixture of hierarchy lengths. Table 2 shows the data set configuration for each series of experiments. In order to evaluate the adaptation to sparse data spaces, we created cubes that were very sparse. Therefore the number of input tuples was kept from a small to a moderate level. To simulate the cube data distribution, for each cube we created ten hyper-rectangular regions as data point containers. These regions are defined randomly at the most detailed level of the cube and not by combination of hierarchy values (although this would be more realistic), in order not to favor the CUBE File particularly, due to the hierarchical chunking. We then filled each region with data points uniformly spread and tried to maintain the same number of data points in each region.

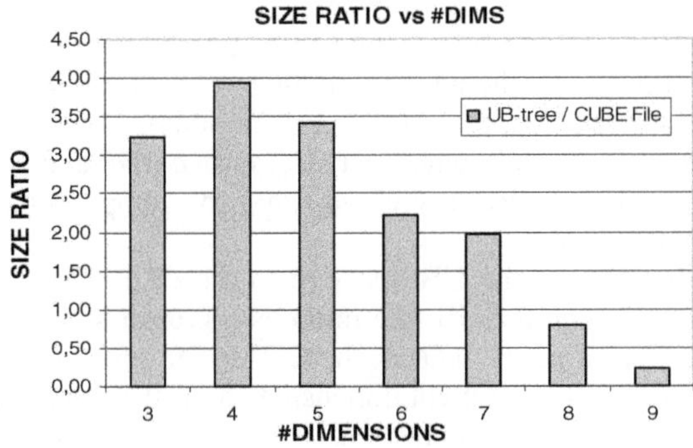

Fig. 8. Size ratio between the UB-tree and the CUBE File for increasing dimensionality

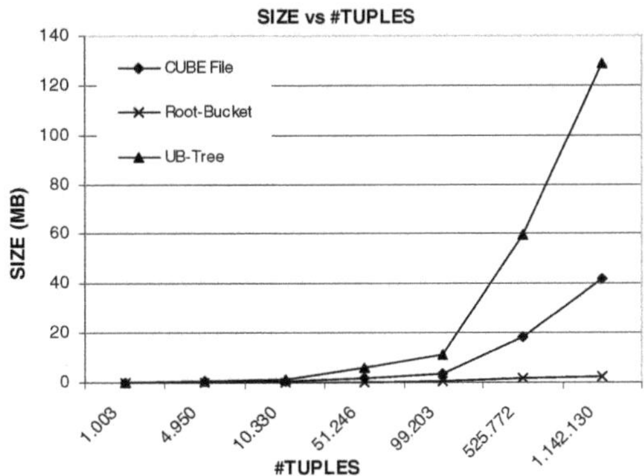

Fig. 9. Size scalability in the number of input tuples (i.e., stored data points)

4.2 Structure Experiments

Fig. 7 shows the size of the CUBE File as the dimensionality of the cube increases. The vertical axe is in logarithmic scale. We see the cube data space size (i.e., the product of the dimension grain-level cardinalities) "exploding" exponentially as the number of dimensions increases. The CUBE File size remains many orders of magnitude smaller than the data space. Moreover, the CUBE File size is also smaller than the ASCII file, containing the input tuples to be loaded into SISYPHUS. This clearly shows that the CUBE File:

1. Adapts to the large sparseness of the cube allocating space comparable to the *actual number* of data points
2. Achieves a compression of the input data since it does not store the data point coordinates (i.e., the h-surrogate keys of the dimension values) in each cell but only the measure values.

Furthermore, we wish to pinpoint that the current CUBE File implementation ([6]) does not impose any compression to the intermediate nodes (i.e., the directory chunks). Only the data chunks are compressed by means of a bitmap representing the cell offsets, which however is stored uncompressed also. This was a deliberate choice in order to evaluate the compression achieved merely by the "pruning ability" of our chunk-to-bucket allocation scheme, according to which no space is allocated for empty chunk-trees (i.e., empty data space regions). Therefore, regarding the compression achieved the following could improve the compression ratio even further: (a) compression of directory chunks and (b) compression of offset-bitmaps (e.g., with run-length encoding).

Fig. 8 shows the ratio of the UB-tree size to the CUBE File size for increasing dimensionality. We see that the UB-tree imposes a greater storage overhead than the CUBE File for almost all cases. Indeed, the CUBE file remains 2-3 times smaller in size than the UB-tree/MHC. For eight dimensions both structures have approximately the same size but for nine dimensions the CUBE File size is four times larger. This is primarily due to the increase of the size of the intermediate nodes in the CUBE File, since for 9 dimensions and 100,000 data points the data space has become extremely sparse (sparseness $\approx 10^{-27}$). As we noted above, our implementation does not apply any compression to the directory chunks. Therefore, it is reasonable that for such extremely sparse data spaces the overhead from these chunks becomes significant, since a single data point might trigger the allocation of all the cells in the parent nodes. An implementation that would incorporate the compression of directory chunks as well would eliminate this effect substantially.

Fig. 9 depicts the size of the CUBE File as the number of cube data points (i.e., input tuples) scales up, while the cube dimensionality remains constant (five dimensions with a good mixture of hierarchy lengths – see Table 1). In the same graph we show the corresponding size of the UB-tree/MHC and the size of the root-bucket. The CUBE File maintains a lower storage cost for all tuple cardinalities. Moreover, the UB-tree size increases in a faster rate making the difference of the two larger as the number of tuples increases. The root-bucket size is substantially lower than the CUBE File and demonstrates an almost constant behaviour. Note that in our implementation we store the whole root-directory in the root-bucket and thus the whole root-directory is kept in main memory during query evaluation. Thus the graph also shows that the root-directory size becomes very fast negligible compared to the CUBE File size as the number of data points increase. Indeed, for cubes containing more than 1 million tuples the root-directory size is below 5% of the CUBE File size, although the directory chunks are stored uncompressed in our current implementation. Hence it is feasible to keep the whole root-directory in main memory.

4.3 Query Experiments

For the query experiments we ran a total of 5,234 HPP queries both on the CUBE File and the UB-tree/MHC. These queries were classified in three classes: (a) 1,593 prefix queries, (b) 1,806 prefix range queries and (c) 1,835 prefix multi-range queries. A *prefix query* is one in which we access the data points by a specific chunk-id prefix. For example the following prefix query is represented by the shown chunk expression, which denotes the restriction on each hierarchy of a 3-dimensional cube of 4 chunking depth levels ($D_{MAX} = 3$).

$$\mathbf{4|7|4.37|58|}*.*|*|*.*|*|* \quad . \tag{1}$$

This expression represents a chunk-id access pattern, denoting the cells that we need to access in each chunk. '*' means "any", i.e., no restriction is imposed on this dimension level. The greatest depth containing at least one restriction is called the *maximum depth of restrictions* (D_{MAX-R}). In this example it corresponds to the *D-domain 37|58|** and thus D_{MAX-R} equals 1. The greater the maximum depth of restrictions the less are the returned data points (smaller cube selectivity) and vice-versa. A *prefix range query* is a prefix query that includes at least one range selection on a hierarchy level, thus resulting in a larger selection hyper-rectangle at the grain level of the cube. For example:

4|7|4.**[37-49]**|58|*.*|*|*.*|*|* . (2)

Finally, a *prefix multi-range query* is a prefix range query that includes at least one multiple range restriction on a hierarchy level of the form *{[a-b],[c-d]...}*. This results in multiple *disjoint* selection hyper-rectangles at the grain level. For example:

4|[7-15]|[4-8].**{[37-49],[54-60],[70-72]}**|58|*.*|*|*.*|*|* . (3)

As mentioned earlier, our goal was to evaluate the hierarchical clustering achieved by means of the performed I/Os for the evaluation of these queries. To this end, we ran two series of experiments: the *hot-cache* experiments and the *cold-cache* ones. In the hot-cache experiments we assumed that the root-bucket (containing the whole root-directory) is cached in main memory and counted only the remaining bucket I/Os. For the UB-tree in the hot-cache case, we counted only the page I/Os at the leaf level omitting the intermediate node accesses altogether. In contrast, for the cold-cache experiments for *each query* on the CUBE File we counted also the size of the whole root-bucket, while for the UB-tree we counted both intermediate and leaf-level page accesses. The root-bucket size equals to 295 buckets according to the following, which shows the sizes for the two structures for the data set used:

UB-tree total num of pages:	15,752
CUBE File total num of buckets:	4,575
Root bucket number of buckets:	295

Fig. 11, shows the I/O ratio between the UB-tree and the CUBE File for all three classes of queries for the hot-cache case. This ratio is calculated from the total number of I/Os for all queries of the same maximum depth of restrictions for each data structure. As D_{MAX-R} increases, essentially the cube selectivity decreases (i.e., less data points are returned in the result set). We see that the UB-tree performs more I/Os for all depths and for all query classes. For small-depth restrictions where the selection rectangles are very large the CUBE File performs 3 times less I/Os than the UB-tree. Moreover, for more restrictive queries the CUBE file is multiple times better achieving up to 37 times less I/Os. An explanation for this is that the smaller the selection hyper-rectangle the greater becomes the percentage of UB-tree leaf-pages containing very few (or even none) of the qualifying data points in the total number of accessed pages. Thus more I/Os are required on the whole, in order to evaluate the restriction, and for large-depth restrictions the UB-tree performs even worse, because essentially it fails to cluster the data with respect to the more detailed hierarchy levels. This behaviour was also observed in [7], where for queries with small cube selectivities the UB-tree performance was worse and the hierarchical clustering effect reduced. We believe this is due to the way data are clustered into z-regions (i.e., disk pages) along the z-curve [1]. In contrast, the hierarchical chunking applied in the CUBE File, creates groups of data (i.e., chunks) that belong in the same "hierarchical family" even for the most detailed levels. This, in combination with the chunk-to-bucket allocation that guarantees that hierarchical families will be clustered together, results in better hierarchical clustering of the cube even for the most detailed levels of the hierarchies.

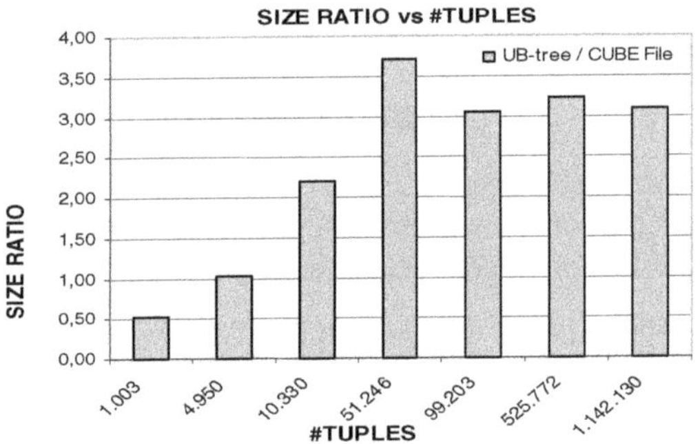

Fig. 10. Size ratio between the UB-tree and the CUBE File for increasing tuple cardinality

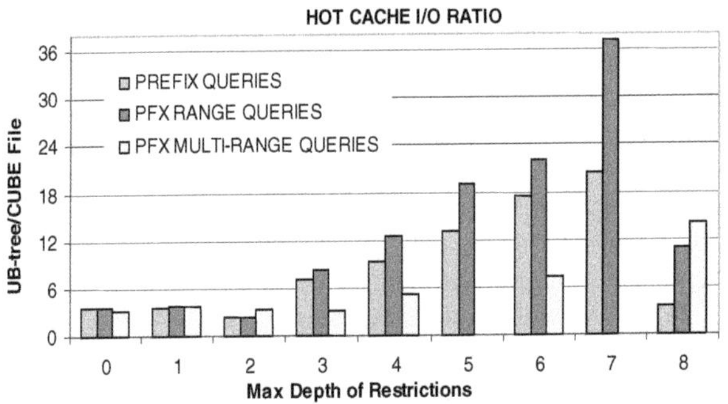

Fig. 11. I/O ratios for the hot-cache experiments

Note that in two subsets of queries the returned result set was empty (prefix multi-range queries for $D_{MAX-R} = 5$ and $D_{MAX-R} = 7$). The UB-tree had to descend down to the leaf level and access the corresponding pages, performing I/Os essentially for nothing. In contrast, the CUBE File performed no I/Os, since directly from a root directory node it could identify an empty subtree and thus terminate the search immediately. Since the denominator was zero, we depict the corresponding ratios for these two cases in Fig. 11 with a zero value.

Fig. 12, shows the I/O ratios for the cold-cache experiments. In this figure we can observe the impact of having to read the whole root directory in memory for each query on the CUBE File. For queries of small-depth restrictions (large result set) the difference in the performed I/Os for the two structures remains essentially the same with the hot-cache case. However, for larger-depth restrictions (smaller result set) the overhead imposed by the root-directory reduces the difference between the two, as it was expected. Nevertheless, the CUBE File is still multiple times better in all cases, clearly demonstrating a better hierarchical clustering. Furthermore, note that even if no cache area is available, in reality there will never be a case where the whole root directory is accessed for answering a single query. Naturally, only the relative buckets of the root-directory are accessed for each query.

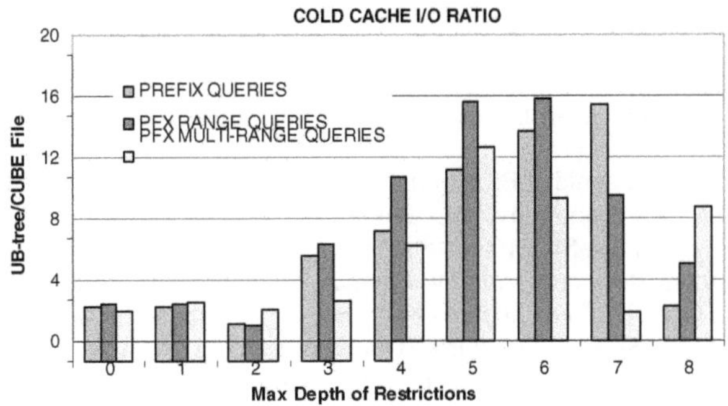

Fig. 12. I/O ratios for the cold-cache experiments

5 Summary and Conclusions

In this paper we presented the CUBE File, a novel file structure for organizing the most detailed data of an OLAP cube. This structure is primarily aimed at speeding up ad hoc OLAP queries containing restrictions on the hierarchies, which comprise the most typical OLAP workload.

The key features of the CUBE File are that it is a natively multidimensional data structure. It explicitly supports dimension hierarchies, enabling fast access to cube data via a directory of chunks formed exactly from the hierarchies. It clusters data with respect to the dimension hierarchies resulting in reduced I/O cost for query evaluation. It imposes a low storage overhead basically for two reasons: (a) it adapts perfectly to the extensive sparseness of the cube, not allocating space for empty regions, and (b) it does not need to store the dimension values along with the measures of the cube, due to its location-based access mechanism of cells. These two result in a significant compression of the data space. Moreover this compression can increase even further, if compression of intermediate nodes is employed. Finally, it achieves a high space utilization filling the buckets to capacity. We have verified the aforementioned performance aspects of the CUBE File by running an extensive set of experiments and we have also shown that the CUBE File outperforms UB-Tree/MHC, the most effective method proposed up to now for hierarchically clustering the cube, in terms of storage cost and number of disk I/Os. Furthermore, the CUBE File fits perfectly to the processing framework for ad hoc OLAP queries over hierarchically clustered fact tables (i.e., cubes) proposed in our previous work [7]. In addition, it supports directly the effective *hierarchical pre-grouping transformation* [13, 19], since it uses hierarchically encoded surrogate keys. Finally, it can be used as a physical base for implementing a chunk-based caching scheme [3].

Acknowledgements. We wish to thank Transaction Software GmbH for providing us Transbase Hypercube to run the UB-tree/MHC experiments. This work has been partially funded by the European Union's Information Society Technologies Programme (IST) under project EDITH (IST-1999-20722).

References

1. R. Bayer: The universal B-Tree for multi-dimensional Indexing: General Concepts. WWCA 1997.
2. C. Y. Chan, Y. E. Ioannidis: Bitmap Index Design and Evaluation. SIGMOD 1998.
3. P. Deshpande, K. Ramasamy, A. Shukla, J. F. Naughton: Caching Multidimensional Queries Using Chunks. SIGMOD 1998.
4. Jim Gray, Adam Bosworth, Andrew Layman, Hamid Pirahesh: Data Cube: A Relational Aggregation Operator Generalizing Group-By, Cross-Tab, and SubTotal. ICDE 1996.
5. N. Karayannidis: Storage Structures, Query Processing and Implementation of On-Line Analytical Processing Systems, Ph.D. Thesis, National Technical University of Athens, 2003. Available at: http://www.dblab.ece.ntua.gr/~ni kos/thesis/PhD_thesis_en.pdf.
6. N. Karayannidis, T. Sellis: SISYPHUS: The Implementation of a Chunk-Based Storage Manager for OLAP Data Cubes. Data and Knowledge Engineering, 45(2): 155-188, May 2003.
7. N. Karayannidis et al: Processing Star-Queries on Hierarchically-Clustered Fact-Tables. VLDB 2002.
8. L. V. S. Lakshmanan, J. Pei, J. Han: Quotient Cube: How to Summarize the Semantics of a Data Cube. VLDB 2002.
9. V. Markl, F. Ramsak, R. Bayern: Improving OLAP Performance by Multidimensional Hierarchical Clustering. IDEAS 1999.
10. P. E. O'Neil, G. Graefe: Multi-Table Joins Through Bitmapped Join Indices. SIGMOD Record 24(3): 8-11 (1995).
11. J. Nievergelt, H. Hinterberger, K. C. Sevcik: The Grid File: An Adaptable, Symmetric Multikey File Structure. TODS 9(1): 38-71 (1984).
12. P. E. O'Neil, D. Quass: Improved Query Performance with Variant Indexes. SIGMOD 1997.
13. R. Pieringer et al: Combining Hierarchy Encoding and Pre-Grouping: Intelligent Grouping in Star Join Processing. ICDE 2003.
14. F. Ramsak et al: Integrating the UB-Tree into a Database System Kernel. VLDB 2000.
15. S. Sarawagi: Indexing OLAP Data. Data Engineering Bulletin 20(1): 36-43 (1997).
16. Y. Sismanis, A. Deligiannakis, N. Roussopoulos, Y. Kotidis: Dwarf: shrinking the PetaCube. SIGMOD 2002.
17. S. Sarawagi, M. Stonebraker: Efficient Organization of Large Multidimensional Arrays. ICDE 1994
18. The Transbase Hypercube® relational database system (http://www.transaction.de).
19. Aris Tsois, Timos Sellis: The Generalized Pre-Grouping Transformation: Aggregate-Query Optimization in the Presence of Dependencies. VLDB 2003.
20. Roger Weber, Hans-Jörg Schek, Stephen Blott: A Quantitative Analysis and Performance Study for Similarity-Search Methods in High-Dimensional Spaces. VLDB 1998: 194-205.

Efficient Schema-Based Revalidation of XML

Mukund Raghavachari[1] and Oded Shmueli[2]

[1] IBM T.J. Watson Research Center, Yorktown Heights, NY 10598, USA,
raghavac@us.ibm.com,
[2] Technion – Israel Institute of Technology, Haifa, Israel,
oshmu@cs.technion.ac.il

Abstract. As XML schemas evolve over time or as applications are integrated, it is sometimes necessary to validate an XML document known to conform to one schema with respect to another schema. More generally, XML documents known to conform to a schema may be modified, and then, require validation with respect to another schema. Recently, solutions have been proposed for incremental validation of XML documents. These solutions assume that the initial schema to which a document conforms and the final schema with which it must be validated after modifications are the same. Moreover, they assume that the input document may be preprocessed, which in certain situations, may be computationally and memory intensive. In this paper, we describe how knowledge of conformance to an XML Schema (or DTD) may be used to determine conformance to another XML Schema (or DTD) efficiently. We examine both the situation where an XML document is modified before it is to be revalidated and the situation where it is unmodified.

1 Introduction

The ability to validate XML documents with respect to an XML Schema [21] or DTD is central to XML's emergence as a key technology for application integration. As XML data flow between applications, the conformance of the data to either a DTD or an XML schema provides applications with a guarantee that a common vocabulary is used and that structural and integrity constraints are met. In manipulating XML data, it is sometimes necessary to validate data with respect to more than one schema. For example, as a schema evolves over time, XML data known to conform to older versions of the schema may need to be verified with respect to the new schema. An intra-company schema used by a business might differ slightly from a standard, external schema and XML data valid with respect to one may need to be checked for conformance to the other.

The validation of an XML document that conforms to one schema with respect to another schema is analogous to the cast operator in programming languages. It is useful, at times, to access data of one type as if it were associated with a different type. For example, XQuery [20] supports a validate operator which converts a value of one type into an instance of another type. The type safety of this conversion cannot always be guaranteed statically. At runtime,

E. Bertino et al. (Eds.): EDBT 2004, LNCS 2992, pp. 639–657, 2004.
© Springer-Verlag Berlin Heidelberg 2004

XML fragments known to correspond to one type must be verified with respect to another. As another example, in XJ [9], a language that integrates XML into Java, XML variables of a type may be updated and then cast to another type. A compiler for such a language does not have access to the documents that are to be revalidated. Techniques for revalidation that rely on preprocessing the document [3,17] are not appropriate.

The question we ask is how can one use knowledge of conformance of a document to one schema to determine whether the document is valid according to another schema? We refer to this problem as the *schema cast validation* problem. An obvious solution is to revalidate the document with respect to the new schema, but in doing so, one is disregarding useful information. The knowledge of a document's conformance to a schema can help determine its conformance to another schema more efficiently than full validation. The more general situation, which we refer to as *schema cast with modifications validation*, is where a document conforming to a schema is modified slightly, and then, verified with respect to a new schema. When the new schema is the same as the one to which the document conformed originally, schema cast with modifications validation addresses the same problem as the incremental validation problem for XML [3,17]. Our solution to this problem has different characteristics, as will be described.

The scenario we consider is that a *source* schema A and a *target* schema B are provided and may be preprocessed statically. At runtime, documents valid according to schema A are verified with respect to schema B. In the modification case, inserts, updates, and deletes are performed to a document before it is verified with respect to B. Our approach takes advantage of similarities (and differences) between the schemas A and B to avoid validating portions of a document if possible. Consider the two XML Schema element declarations for purchaseOrder shown in Figure 1. The only difference between the two is that whereas the billTo element is optional in the schema of Figure 1a, it is required in the schema of Figure 1b. Not all XML documents valid with respect to the first schema are valid with respect to the second — only those with a billTo element would be valid. Given a document valid according to the schema of Figure 1a, an ideal validator would only check the presence of a billTo element and ignore the validation of the other components (they are guaranteed to be valid).

This paper focuses on the validation of XML documents with respect to the structural constraints of XML schemas. We present algorithms for schema cast validation with and without modifications that avoid traversing subtrees of an XML document where possible. We also provide an optimal algorithm for revalidating strings known to conform to a deterministic finite state automaton according to another deterministic finite state automaton; this algorithm is used to revalidate content model of elements. The fact that the content models of XML Schema types are deterministic [6] can be used to show that our algorithm for XML Schema cast validation is optimal as well. We describe our algorithms in terms of an abstraction of XML Schemas, *abstract XML schemas*, which model the structural constraints of XML schema. In our experiments, our algorithms achieve 30-95% performance improvement over Xerces 2.4.

```
<xsd:element name="purchaseOrder"
    type="POType1"/>
<xsd:complexType name="POType1">
  <xsd:sequence>
    <xsd:element name="shipTo" type="USAddress"/>
    <xsd:element name="billTo" type="USAddress"
      minOccurs="0"/>
    <xsd:element name="items" type="Items"/>
  </xsd:sequence>
</xsd:complexType>
```

(a)

```
<xsd:element name="purchaseOrder"
    type="POType2"/>
<xsd:complexType name="POType2">
  <xsd:sequence>
    <xsd:element name="shipTo"
        type="USAddress"/>
    <xsd:element name="billTo"
        type="USAddress"/>
    <xsd:element name="items"
        type="Items"/>
  </xsd:sequence>
</xsd:complexType>
```

(b)

Fig. 1. Schema fragments defining a purchaseOrder element in (a) Source Schema (b) Target Schema.

The contributions of this paper are the following:

1. An abstraction of XML Schema, *abstract XML Schema*, which captures the structural constraints of XML schema more precisely than specialized DTDs [16] and regular type expressions [11].
2. Efficient algorithms for schema cast validation (with and without updates) of XML documents with respect to XML Schemas. We describe optimizations for the case where the schemas are DTDs. Unlike previous algorithms, our algorithms do not preprocess the documents that are to be revalidated.
3. Efficient algorithms for revalidation of strings with and without modifications according to deterministic finite state automata. These algorithms are essential for efficient revalidation of the content models of elements.
4. Experiments validating the utility of our solutions.

Structure of the Paper: We examine related work in Section 2. In Section 3, we introduce abstract XML Schemas and provide an algorithm for XML schema revalidation. The algorithm relies on an efficient solution to the problem of string revalidation according to finite state automata, which is provided in Section 4. We discuss the optimality of our algorithms in Section 5. We report on experiments in Section 6, and conclude in Section 7.

2 Related Work

Papakonstantinou and Vianu [17] treat incremental validation of XML documents (typed according to specialized DTDs). Their algorithm keeps data structures that encode validation computations with document tree nodes and utilizes these structures to revalidate a document. Barbosa *et al.* [3] present an algorithm that also encodes validation computations within tree nodes. They take advantage of the 1-unambiguity of content models of DTDs and XML Schemas [6], and structural properties of a restricted set of DTDs, to revalidate documents. Our algorithm is designed for the case where schemas can be preprocessed, but the documents to be revalidated are not available *a priori* to be preprocessed.

Examples include message brokers, programming language and query compilers, etc. In these situations, techniques that preprocess the document and store state information at each node could incur unacceptable memory and computing overhead, especially if the number of updates is small with respect to the document, or the size of the document is large. Moreover, our algorithm handles the case where the document must be revalidated with respect to a different schema. Kane *et al.* [12] use a technique based on query modification for handling the incremental update problem. Bouchou and Halfeld-Ferrari [5] present an algorithm that validates each update using a technique based on tree automata. Again, both algorithms consider only the case where the schema to which the document must conform after modification is the same as the original schema.

The subsumption of XML schema types used in our algorithm for schema cast validation is similar to Kuper and Siméon's notion of type subsumption [13]. Their type system is more general than our abstract XML schema. They assume that a subsumption mapping is provided between types such that if one schema is subsumed by another, and if a value conforming to the subsumed schema is annotated with types, then by applying the subsumption mapping to these type annotations, one obtains an annotation for the subsuming schema. Our solution is more general in that we do not require either schema to be subsumed by the other, but do handle the case where this occurs. Furthermore, we do not require type annotations on nodes. Finally, we consider the notion of disjoint types in addition to subsumption in the revalidation of documents.

One approach to handling XML and XML Schema has been to express them in terms of formal models such as tree automata. For example, Lee *et al.* describe how XML Schema may be represented in terms of deterministic tree grammars with one lookahead [15]. The formalism for XML Schema and the algorithms in these paper are a more direct solution to the problem, which obviates some of the practical problems of the tree automata approach, such as having to encode unranked XML trees as ranked trees.

Programming languages with XML types [1,4,10,11] define notions of types and subtyping that are enforced statically. XDuce [10] uses tree automata as the base model for representing XML values. One difference between our work and XDuce is that we are interested in dynamic typing (revalidation) where static analysis is used to *reduce* the amount of needed work. Moreover, unlike XDuce's regular expression types and specialized DTDs [17], our model for XML values captures exactly the structural constraints of XML Schema (and is not equivalent to regular tree automata). As a result, our subtyping algorithm is polynomial rather than exponential in complexity.

3 XML Schema and DTD Conformance

In this section, we present the algorithm for revalidation of documents according to XML Schemas. We first define our abstractions for XML documents, *ordered labeled trees*, and for XML Schema, *abstract XML Schema*. Abstract XML Schema captures precisely the structural constraints of XML Schema.

Ordered Labeled Trees. We abstract XML documents as *ordered labeled trees*, where an ordered labeled tree over a finite alphabet Σ is a pair $T = (t, \lambda)$ where $t = (N, E)$ is an ordered tree consisting of a finite set of nodes, N, and a set of edges E, and $\lambda : N \rightarrow \Sigma \cup \{\chi\}$ is a function that associates a label with each node n of N. The label, χ, which can only be associated with leaves of the tree t, represents XML Schema simple values. We use $root(T)$ to denote the root of tree t. We shall abuse notation slightly to allow $\lambda(T)$ to denote the label of the root node of the ordered labeled tree T. We use $r(t_1, t_2, \ldots, t_k)$ to denote an ordered tree with root r and subtrees $t_1 \ldots t_k$, where $r()$ denotes an ordered tree with a root r that has no children. We use $\mathfrak{T}_\Sigma$ to represent the set of all ordered labeled trees.

Abstract XML Schema. XML Schemas, unlike DTDs, permit the decoupling of an element tag from its type; an element may have different types depending on context. XML Schemas are not as powerful as regular tree automata. The XML Schema specification places restrictions on the decoupling of element tags and types. Specifically, in validating a document according to an XML Schema, each element of the document can be assigned a single type, based on the element's label and the type of the element's parent (without considering the content of the element). Furthermore, this type assignment is guaranteed to be unique.

We define an abstraction of XML Schema, an *abstract XML Schema*, as a 4-tuple, $(\Sigma, \mathcal{T}, \rho, \mathcal{R})$, where

- Σ is the alphabet of element labels (tags).
- $\mathcal{T}$ is the set of types defined in the schema.
- ρ is a set of type declarations, one for each $\tau \in \mathcal{T}$, where τ is either a *simple* type of the form τ : *simple*, or a *complex type* of the form $\tau : (regexp_\tau, types_\tau)$, where:
  - $regexp_\tau$ is a regular expression over Σ. $L(regexp_\tau)$ denotes the language associated with $regexp_\tau$.
  - Let $\Sigma_\tau \subseteq \Sigma$ be the set of element labels used in $regexp_\tau$. Then, $types_\tau : \Sigma_\tau \rightarrow \mathcal{T}$ is a function that assigns a type to each element label used in the type declaration of τ. The function, $types_\tau$, abstracts the notion of XML Schema that each child of an element can be assigned a type based on its label without considering the child's content. It also models the XML Schema constraint that if two children of an element have the same label, they must be assigned the same type.
- $\mathcal{R} : \Sigma \rightarrow \mathcal{T}$ is a partial function which states which element labels can occur as the root element of a valid tree according to the schema, and the type this root element is assigned.

Consider the XML Schema fragment of Figure 1a. The function $\mathcal{R}$ maps global element declarations to their appropriate types, that is, $\mathcal{R}$(purchaseOrder) = POType1. Table 1 shows the type declaration for POType1 in our formalism.

Abstract XML Schemas do not explicitly represent atomic types, such as xsd:integer. For simplicity of exposition, we have assumed that all XML Schema atomic and simple types are represented by a single simple type. Handling atomic

Table 1. Abstract XML Schema type for XML Schema type POType1 of Figure 1a.

Type	Σ_τ	$regexp_\tau$	$types_\tau$
POType1	shipTo billTo items	(shipTo billTo? items)	shipTo → USAddress billTo → USAddress items → Items

and simple types, restrictions on these types and relationships between the values denoted by these types is a straightforward extension. We do not address the identity constraints (such as key and keyref constraints) of XML Schema in this paper. This is an area of future work. Other features of XML Schema such as substitution groups, subtyping, and namespaces can be integrated into our model. A discussion of these issues is beyond the scope of the paper.

We define the validity of an ordered, labeled tree with respect to an abstract XML Schema as follows:

Definition 1. *The set of ordered labeled trees that are valid with respect to a type is defined in terms of the least solution to a set of equations, one for each $\tau \in \rho$, of the form (n, n_1, n_2 are nodes):*

$$valid(\tau) = \begin{cases} \{(t,\lambda) \in \mathfrak{T}_\Sigma | t = n_1(n_2()), \lambda(n_1) \in \Sigma, \lambda(n_2) = \chi\} & \text{if } \tau \text{ is simple} \\ \\ \{(t,\lambda) \in \mathfrak{T}_\Sigma | t = n(), \lambda(n) \in \Sigma, \epsilon \in L(regexp_\tau)\} \cup & \text{otherwise} \\ \{(t,\lambda) \in \mathfrak{T}_\Sigma | t = n(t_1, t_2, \ldots, t_k) & \\ \quad \lambda(n), \lambda(t_1), \ldots, \lambda(t_k) \in \Sigma, k > 0 & \\ \quad \lambda(t_1) \cdot \lambda(t_2) \cdot \ldots \cdot \lambda(t_k) \in L(regexp_\tau) & \\ \quad t_i \in valid(types_\tau(\lambda(t_i))), 1 \leq i \leq k\} & \end{cases}$$

An ordered labeled tree, T, is valid with respect to a schema $S = (\Sigma, \mathcal{T}, \rho, \mathcal{R})$ if $\mathcal{R}(\lambda(T))$ is defined and $T \in valid(\mathcal{R}(\lambda(T)))$. If τ is a complex type, and $L(regexp_\tau)$ contains the empty string ϵ, $valid(\tau)$ contains all trees of height 0, where the root node has a label from Σ, that is, τ may have an *empty content model.*

We are interested only in *productive* types, that is types, τ, where $valid(\tau) \neq \emptyset$. We assume that for a schema $S = (\Sigma, \mathcal{T}, \rho, \mathcal{R})$, all $\tau \in \mathcal{T}$ are productive. Whether a type is productive can be verified easily as follows:

1. Mark all simple types as productive since by the definition of *valid*, they contain trees of height 1 with labels from Σ.
2. For complex types, τ, compute the set $ProdLabels_\tau \subseteq \Sigma$ defined as $\{\sigma \in \Sigma \mid types_\tau(\sigma)$ is productive$\}$.
3. Mark τ as productive if $ProdLabels_\tau^* \cap L(regexp_\tau) \neq \emptyset$. In other words, a type τ is productive if $\epsilon \in L(regexp_\tau)$ or there is a string in $L(regexp_\tau)$ that uses only labels from $ProdLabels_\tau$.
4. Repeat Steps 2 and 3 until no more types can be marked as productive.

This procedure identifies all productive types defined in a schema. There is a straightforward algorithm for converting a schema with types that are non-productive into one that contains only productive types. The basic idea is to modify $regexp_\tau$ for each productive τ so that the language of the new regular expression is $L(regexp_\tau) \cap ProdLabels_\tau^*$.

Pseudocode for validating an ordered, labeled tree with respect to an abstract XML Schema is provided below. *constructstring* is a utility method (not shown) that creates a string from the labels of the root nodes of a sequence of trees (it returns ϵ if the sequence is empty). Note that if a node has no children, the body of the **foreach** loop will not be executed.

boolean $validate(\tau : \text{type}, e : \text{node})$
  if (τ is a simple type)
    if $(children(e) = \{n()\}, \lambda(n) = \chi)$ **return** true
    else return false
  if $(\neg constructstring(children(e)) \in L(regexp_\tau))$
      return false
  foreach child e' of e
    if $(\neg validate(types_\tau(\lambda(e')), e'))$
      return false
  return true

boolean $doValidate(S : \text{schema}, T : \text{tree})$
  return $validate(\mathcal{R}(\lambda(T)), root(T))$

A *DTD* can be viewed as an abstract XML Schema, $D = (\Sigma, \mathcal{T}, \rho, \mathcal{R})$, where each $\sigma \in \Sigma$ is assigned a unique type irrespective of the context in which it is used. In other words, for all $\sigma \in \Sigma$, there exists $\tau' \in \mathcal{T}$ such that for all $\tau : (regexp_\tau, types_\tau) \in \rho$, $types_\tau(\sigma)$ is either not defined or $types_\tau(\sigma) = \tau'$. If $\mathcal{R}(\sigma)$ is defined, then $\mathcal{R}(\sigma) = \tau'$ as well.

3.1 Algorithm Overview

Given two abstract XML Schemas, $S = (\Sigma, \mathcal{T}, \rho, \mathcal{R})$ and $S' = (\Sigma, \mathcal{T}', \rho', \mathcal{R}')$, and an ordered labeled tree, T, that is valid according to S, our algorithm validates T with respect to S and S' in parallel. Suppose that during the validation of T with respect to S' we wish to validate a subtree of T, T', with respect to a type τ'. Let τ be the type assigned to T' during the validation of T with respect to S. If one can assert that every ordered labeled tree that is valid according to τ is also valid according to τ', then one can immediately deduce the validity of T' according to τ'. Conversely, if no ordered labeled tree that is valid according to τ is also valid according to τ', then one can stop the validation immediately since T' will not be valid according to τ'.

We use *subsumed type* and *disjoint type* relationships to avoid traversals of subtrees of T where possible:

Definition 2. *A type τ is subsumed by a type τ', denoted $\tau \preceq \tau'$ if $valid(\tau) \subseteq valid(\tau')$. Note that τ and τ' can belong to different schemas.*

Definition 3. *Two types τ and τ' are disjoint, denoted $\tau \oslash \tau'$, if $valid(\tau) \cap valid(\tau') = \emptyset$. Again, note that τ and τ' can belong to different schemas.*

In the following sections, we present algorithms for determining whether an abstract XML Schema type is subsumed by another or is disjoint from another. We present an algorithm for efficient schema cast validation of an ordered labeled tree, with and without updates. Finally, in the case where the abstract XML Schemas represent DTDs, we describe optimizations that are possible if additional indexing information is available on ordered labeled trees.

3.2 Schema Cast Validation

Our algorithm relies on relations, R_{sub} and R_{dis}, that capture precisely all subsumed type and disjoint type information with respect to the types defined in $\mathcal{T}$ and $\mathcal{T}'$. We first describe how these relations are computed, and then, present our algorithm for schema cast validation.

Computing the R_{sub} Relation

Definition 4. *Given two schemas,* $S = (\Sigma, \mathcal{T}, \rho, \mathcal{R})$ *and* $S' = (\Sigma, \mathcal{T}', \rho', \mathcal{R}')$, *let* $R_{sub} \subseteq \mathcal{T} \times \mathcal{T}'$ *be the* largest *relation such that for all* $(\tau, \tau') \in R_{sub}$ *one of the following two conditions hold:*

i. τ, τ' *are both simple types.*
ii. τ, τ' *are both complex types,* $L(regexp_{\tau}) \subseteq L(regexp_{\tau'})$, *and* $\forall \sigma \in \Sigma$, *where* $types_{\tau}(\sigma)$ *is defined,* $(types_{\tau}(\sigma), types_{\tau'}(\sigma)) \in R_{sub}$.

As mentioned before, for exposition reasons, we have chosen to merge all simple types into one common *simple type.* It is straightforward to extend the definition above so that the various XML Schema atomic and simple types, and their derivations are used to bootstrap the definition of the subsumption relationship. Also, observe that R_{sub} is a finite relation since there are finitely many types.

The following theorem states that the R_{sub} relation captures precisely the notion of subsumption defined earlier:

Theorem 1. $(\tau, \tau') \in R_{sub}$ *if and only if* $\tau \preceq \tau'$. □

We now present an algorithm for computing the R_{sub} relation. The algorithm starts with a subset of $\mathcal{T} \times \mathcal{T}'$ and refines it successively until R_{sub} is obtained.

1. Let $R_{sub} \subseteq \mathcal{T} \times \mathcal{T}'$, such that $(\tau, \tau') \in R_{sub}$ implies that both τ and τ' are simple types, or both of them are complex types.
2. For $(\tau, \tau') \in R_{sub}$, if $L(regexp_{\tau}) \not\subseteq L(regexp_{\tau'})$, remove (τ, τ') from R_{sub}.
3. For each (τ, τ') if there exists $\sigma \in \Sigma, types_{\tau}(\sigma) = \omega$ and $types_{\tau'}(\sigma) = \nu$ and $(\omega, \nu) \notin R_{sub}$, remove (τ, τ') from R_{sub}.
4. Repeat Step 3 until no more tuples can be removed from the relation R_{sub}.

Computing the R_{dis} relation. Rather than computing R_{dis} directly, we compute its complement. Formally:

Definition 5. *Given two schemas, $S = (\Sigma, \mathcal{T}, \rho, \mathcal{R})$ and $S' = (\Sigma, \mathcal{T}', \rho', \mathcal{R}')$, let $R_{nondis} \subseteq \mathcal{T} \times \mathcal{T}'$ be defined as the smallest relation (least fixpoint) such that $(\tau, \tau') \in R_{nondis}$ if:*

i. τ and τ' are both simple types.
ii. τ and τ' are both complex types, $P = \{\sigma \in \Sigma \mid (types_\tau(\sigma), types_{\tau'}(\sigma)) \in R_{nondis}\}$, $L(regexp_\tau) \cap L(regexp_{\tau'}) \cap P^* \neq \emptyset$.

To compute the R_{nondis} relation, the algorithm begins with an empty relation and adds tuples until R_{nondis} is obtained.

1. Let $R_{nondis} = \emptyset$.
2. Add all (τ, τ') to R_{nondis} such that $\tau : simple \in \rho, \tau' : simple \in \rho'$.
3. For each $(\tau, \tau') \in \mathcal{T} \times \mathcal{T}'$, let $P = \{\sigma \in \Sigma \mid (types_\tau(\sigma), types_{\tau'}(\sigma)) \in R_{nondis}\}$. If $L(regexp_\tau) \cap L(regexp_{\tau'}) \cap P^* \neq \emptyset$ add (τ, τ') to R_{nondis}.
4. Repeat Step 3 until no more tuples can be added to R_{nondis}.

Theorem 2. *$\tau \oslash \tau'$ if and only if $(\tau, \tau') \notin R_{nondis}$.* □

Algorithm for Schema Cast Validation. Given the relations R_{sub} and R_{dis}, if at any time, a subtree of the document that is valid with respect to τ from S is being validated with respect to τ' from S', and $\tau \preceq \tau'$, then the subtree need not be examined (since by definition, the subtree belongs to $valid(\tau')$). On the other hand, if $\tau \oslash \tau'$, the document can be determined to be invalid with respect to S' immediately. Pseudocode for incremental validation of the document is provided below. Again, *constructstring* is a utility method (not shown) that creates a string from the labels of the root nodes of a sequence of trees (returning ϵ if the sequence is empty). We can efficiently verify the content model of e with respect to $regexp_{\tau'}$ by using techniques for finite automata schema cast validation, as will be described in the Section 4.

boolean $validate(\tau : \text{type}, \tau' : \text{type}, e : \text{node})$
  if $\tau \preceq \tau'$ **return** true
  if $\tau \oslash \tau'$ **return** false
  if (τ is a simple type)
    if ($children(e) = \{n()\}, \lambda(n) = \chi$) **return** true
    else return false
  if ($\neg constructstring(children(e)) \in L(regexp_{\tau'})$)
      return false
  foreach child e' of e, in order,
    if ($\neg validate(types_\tau(\lambda(e')), types_{\tau'}(\lambda(e')), e')$)
      return false
  return true

boolean $doValidate(S : \text{schema}, S' : \text{schema}, T : \text{tree})$
  return $validate(\mathcal{R}(\lambda(T)), \mathcal{R}'(\lambda(T)), root(T))$

3.3 Schema Cast Validation with Modifications

Given an ordered, labeled tree, T, that is valid with respect to an abstract XML Schema S, and a sequence of insertions and deletions of nodes, and modifications of element tags, we discuss how the tree may be validated efficiently with respect to a new abstract XML Schema S'. The updates permitted are the following:

1. Modify the label of a specified node with a new label.
2. Insert a new leaf node before, or after, or as the first child of a node.
3. Delete a specified leaf node.

Given a sequence of updates, we perform the updates on T, and at each step, we encode the modifications on T to obtain T' by extending Σ with special element tags of the form Δ^a_b, where $a, b \in \Sigma \cup \{\epsilon, \chi\}$. A node in T' with label Δ^a_b represents the modification of the element tag a in T with the element tag b in T'. Similarly, a node in T' with label Δ^ϵ_b represents a newly inserted node with tag b, and a label Δ^a_ϵ denotes a node deleted from T. Nodes that have not been modified have their labels unchanged. By discarding all nodes with label Δ^a_ϵ and converting the labels of all other nodes labeled Δ^*_b into b, one obtains the tree that is the result of performing the modifications on T.

We assume the availability of a function *modified* on the nodes of T', that returns for each node whether any part of the subtree rooted at that node has been modified. The function *modified* can be implemented efficiently as follows. We assume we have the Dewey decimal number of the node (generated dynamically as we process). Whenever a node is updated we keep it in a trie [7] according to its Dewey decimal number. To determine whether a descendant of a node v was modified, the trie is searched according to the Dewey decimal number of v. Note that we can navigate the trie in parallel to navigating the XML tree.

The algorithm for efficient validation of schema casts with modifications validates $T' = (t', \lambda')$ with respect to S and S' in parallel. While processing a subtree of T', t'', with respect to types τ from S and τ' from S', one of the following cases apply:

1. If *modified*(t'') is *false*, we can run the algorithm described in the previous subsection on this subtree. Since the subtree t'' is unchanged and we know that $t'' \in valid(\tau)$ when checked with respect to S, we can treat the validation of t'' as an instance of the schema cast validation problem (without modifications) described in Section 3.2.
2. Otherwise, if $\lambda'(t'') = \Delta^a_\epsilon$, we do not need to validate the subtree with respect to any τ' since that subtree has been deleted.
3. Otherwise, if $\lambda'(t'') = \Delta^\epsilon_b$, since the label denotes that t'' is a newly inserted subtree, we have no knowledge of its validity with respect to any other schema. Therefore, we must validate the whole subtree explicitly.
4. Otherwise, if $\lambda'(t'') = \Delta^a_b, a, b \in \Sigma \cup \{\chi\}$, or $\lambda'(t'') = \sigma, \sigma \in \Sigma \cup \{\chi\}$, since elements may have been added or deleted from the original content model of the node, we must ensure that the content of t'' is valid with respect to τ'. If τ' is a simple type, the content model must satisfy (1) of

Definition 1. Otherwise, if $t'' = n(t_1, \ldots, t_k)$, one must check that $t_1, \ldots, t_k$ fit into the content model of τ' as specified by $regexp_{\tau'}$. In verifying the content model, we check whether $Proj_{new}(t_1) \ldots Proj_{new}(t_k) \in L(regexp_{\tau'})$, where $Proj_{new}(t_i)$ is defined as:

$$\sigma \text{ , if } \lambda'(t_i) = \sigma, \sigma \in \Sigma \cup \{\chi\} \quad (1)$$

$$b \text{ , if } \lambda'(t_i) = \Delta_b^a, a, b \in \Sigma \cup \{\epsilon, \chi\} \quad (2)$$

$Proj_{old}$ is defined analogously. If the content model check succeeds, and τ is also a complex type, then we continue recursively validating $t_i, 1 \leq i \leq k$ with respect to $types_\tau(Proj_{old}(t_i))$ from S and $types_{\tau'}(Proj_{new}(t_i))$ from S' (note that if $Proj_{new}(t_i)$ is ϵ, we do not have to validate that t_i since it has been deleted in T'). If τ is not a complex type, we must validate each t_i explicitly.

3.4 DTDs

Since the type of an element in an XML Schema may depend on the context in which it appears, in general, it is necessary to process the document in a top-down manner to determine the type with which one must validate an element (and its subtree). For DTDs, however, an element label determines uniquely the element's type. As a result, there are optimizations that apply to the DTD case that cannot be applied to the general XML Schema case. If one can access all instances of an element label in an ordered labeled tree directly, one need only visit those elements e where the types of e in S and S' are neither subsumed nor disjoint from each other and verify their immediate content model.

4 Finite Automata Conformance

In this section, we examine the schema cast validation problem (with and without modifications) for strings verified with respect to finite automata. The algorithms described in this section support efficient content model checking for DTDs and XML Schemas (for example, in the statement of the method *validate* of Section 3.2: **if** $(\neg constructstring(children(e)) \in L(regexp_{\tau'}))$). Since XML Schema content models correspond directly to deterministic finite state automata, we only address that case. Similar techniques can be applied to non-deterministic finite state automata, though the optimality results do not hold. For reasons of space, we omit details regarding non-deterministic finite state automata.

4.1 Definitions

A deterministic finite automaton is a 5-tuple $(Q, \Sigma, \delta, q^0, F)$, where Q is a finite set of states, Σ is a finite alphabet of symbols, $q^0 \in Q$ is the start state, $F \subseteq Q$ is a set of final, or accepting, states, and δ is the transition relation. δ is a map from $Q \times \Sigma$ to Q. Without loss of generality, we assume that for all $q \in Q, \sigma \in$

$\Sigma, \delta(q, \sigma)$ is defined. We use $\delta(q, \sigma) \rightarrow q'$, where $q, q' \in Q, \sigma \in \Sigma$ to denote that δ maps (q, σ) to q'. For string s and state q, $\delta(q, s) \rightarrow q'$ denotes the state q' reached by operating on s one symbol at a time. A string s is *accepted* by a finite state automaton if $\delta(q^0, s) \rightarrow q', q' \in F$; s is *rejected* by the automaton if s is not accepted by it.

The language accepted (or recognized) by a finite automaton a, denoted $L(a)$, is the set of strings accepted by a. We also define $L_a(q), q \in Q$, as $\{s \mid \delta(q, s) \rightarrow q', q' \in F\}$. Note that for a finite state automaton a, if a string $s = s_0 \cdot s_1 \cdot \ldots \cdot s_n$ is in $L(a)$, and $\delta(q^0, s_0 \cdot s_1 \cdot \ldots \cdot s_i) = q', 1 \leq i < n$, then $s_{i+1} \cdot \ldots \cdot s_n$ is in $L_a(q')$. We shall drop the subscript a from L_a when the automaton is clear from the context.

A state $q \in Q$ is a *dead state* if either:

1. $\forall s \in \Sigma^*$, if $\delta(q^0, s) \rightarrow q'$ then $q \neq q'$, or
2. $\forall s \in \Sigma^*$, if $\delta(q, s) \rightarrow q'$ then $q' \notin F$.

In other words, either the state is not reachable from the start state or no final state is reachable from it. We can identify all dead states in a finite state automaton in time linear in the size of the automaton via a simple graph search.

Intersection Automata. Given two automata, $a = (Q_a, \Sigma_a, \delta_a, q_a^0, F_a)$ and $b = (Q_b, \Sigma_b, \delta_b, q_b^0, F_b)$, one can derive an intersection automaton c, such that c accepts exactly the language $L(a) \cap L(b)$. The intersection automaton evaluates a string on both a and b in parallel and accepts only if both would. Formally, $c = (Q_c, \Sigma, \delta_c, q_c^0, F_c)$, where $q_c^0 = (q_a^0, q_b^0), Q_c = Q_a \times Q_b, F_c = F_a \times F_b$, and $\delta_c((q_1, q_2), \sigma) \rightarrow q'$, where $q' = (\delta_a(q_1, \sigma), \delta_b(q_2, \sigma))$. Note that if a and b are deterministic, c is deterministic as well.

Immediate Decision Automata. We introduce *immediate decision automata* as modified finite state automata that accept or reject strings as early as possible. Immediate decision automata can accept or reject a string when certain conditions are met, without scanning the entire string. Formally, an immediate decision automaton d_{immed} is a 7-tuple, $(Q, \Sigma, \delta, q^0, F, IA, IR)$, where IA, IR are disjoint sets and $IA, IR \subseteq Q$ (each member of IA and IR is a state). As with ordinary finite state automata, a string s is accepted by the automaton if $\delta(q^0, s) \rightarrow q', q' \in F$. Furthermore, d_{immed} also accepts s after evaluating a strict prefix x of s (that is $x \neq s$) if $\delta(q^0, x) \rightarrow q', q' \in IA$. d_{immed} rejects s after evaluating a strict prefix x of s if $\delta(q^0, x) \rightarrow q', q' \in IR$. We can derive an immediate decision automaton from a finite state automaton so that both automata accept the same language.

Definition 6. *Let $d = (Q_d, \Sigma, \delta_d, q_d^0, F_d)$ be a finite state automaton. The derived immediate decision automaton is $d_{immed} = (Q_d, \Sigma, \delta_d, q_d^0, F_d, IA_d, IR_d)$, where:*

- $IA_d = \{q' \mid q' \in Q_d \wedge L_d(q') = \Sigma^*\}$, *and*
- $IR_d = \{q' \mid q' \in Q_d \wedge L_d(q') = \emptyset\}$.

It can be easily shown that d_{immed} and d accept the same language.

For deterministic automata, we can determine all states that belong to IA_d and IR_d efficiently in time linear in the number of states of the automaton. The members of IR_d can be derived easily from the dead states of d.

4.2 Schema Cast Validation

The problem that we address is the following: Given two deterministic finite-state automata, $a = (Q_a, \Sigma_a, \delta_a, q_a^0, F_a)$, and $b = (Q_b, \Sigma_b, \delta_b, q_b^0, F_b)$, and a string $s \in L(a)$, does $s \in L(b)$? One could, of course, scan s using b to determine acceptance by b. When many strings that belong to $L(a)$ are to be validated with respect to $L(b)$, it can be more efficient to prepreprocess a and b so that the knowledge of s's acceptance by a can be used to determine its membership in $L(b)$. Without loss of generality, we assume that $\Sigma_a = \Sigma_b = \Sigma$.

Our method for the efficient validation of a string $s = s_1 \cdot s_2 \cdot \ldots \cdot s_n$ in $L(a)$ with respect to b relies on evaluating s on a and b in parallel. Assume that after parsing a prefix $s_1 \cdot \ldots \cdot s_i$ of s, we are in a state $q_1 \in Q_a$ in a, and a state $q_2 \in Q_b$ in b. Then, we can:

1. Accept s immediately if $L(q_1) \subseteq L(q_2)$, because $s_{i+1} \cdot \ldots \cdot s_n$ is guaranteed to be in $L(q_1)$ (since a accepts s), which implies that $s_{i+1} \cdot \ldots \cdot s_n$ will be in $L(q_2)$. By definition of $L(q)$, b will accept s.
2. Reject s immediately if $L(q_1) \cap L(q_2) = \emptyset$. Then, $s_{i+1} \cdot \ldots \cdot s_n$ is guaranteed not to be in $L(b)$, and therefore, b will not accept s.

We construct an immediate decision automaton, c_{immed} from the intersection automaton c of a and b, with IR_c and IA_c based on the two conditions above:

Definition 7. *Let $c = (Q_c, \Sigma, \delta_c, q_c^0, F_c)$ be the intersection automaton derived from two finite state automata a and b. The derived immediate decision automaton is $c_{immed} = (Q_c, \Sigma, \delta_c, q_c^0, F_c, IA_c, IR_c)$, where:*

- $IA_c = \{ (q_a, q_b) \mid ((q_a, q_b) \in Q_c) \wedge L(q_a) \subseteq L(q_b)\}$.
- $IR_c = \{ (q_a, q_b) \mid ((q_a, q_b) \in Q_c) \wedge (q_a, q_b) \text{ is a dead state } \}$.

Theorem 3. *For all $s \in L(a)$, c_{immed} accepts s if and only if $s \in L(b)$.* □

The determination of the members of IA_c can be done efficiently for deterministic finite state automata. The following proposition is useful to this end.

Proposition 1. *For any state, $(q_a, q_b) \in Q_c, L(q_a) \subseteq L(q_b)$ if and only if $\forall s \in \Sigma^*$, there exist states q_1 and q_2 such that $\delta_c((q_a, q_b), s) \rightarrow (q_1, q_2)$ and if $q_1 \in F_a$ then $q_2 \in F_b$.* □

We now present an alternative, equivalent definition of IA_c.

Definition 8. *For all $q' = (q_a, q_b)$, $q' \in IA_c$ if $\forall s \in \Sigma^*$, there exist states (q_1, q_2), such that $\delta_c((q_a, q_b), s) \rightarrow (q_1, q_2)$ and if $q_1 \in F_a$ then $q_2 \in F_b$.*

In other words, a state $(q_a, q_b) \in IA_c$ if for all states (q'_a, q'_b) reachable from (q_a, q_b), if q'_a is a final state of a, then q'_b is a final state of b. It can be shown that the two definitions, 7 and 8, of IA_c are equivalent.

Theorem 4. *For deterministic immediate decision automata, Definition 7 and Definition 8 of IA_c are equivalent, that is, they produce the same set IA_c.* □

Given two automata a and b, we can preprocess a and b to efficiently construct the immediate automaton c_{immed}, as defined by Definition 7, by finding all dead states in the intersection automaton of a and b to determine IR_c. The set of states, IA_c, as defined by Definition 8, can also be determined, in linear time, using an algorithm similar to that for the identification of dead states. At runtime, an efficient algorithm for schema cast validation without modifications is to process each string $s \in L(a)$ for membership in $L(b)$ using c_{immed}.

4.3 Schema Casts with Modifications

Consider the following variation of the schema cast problem. Given two automata, a and b, a string $s \in L(a)$, $s = s_1 \cdot s_1 \cdot \ldots \cdot s_n$, is modified through insertions, deletions, and the renaming of symbols to obtain a string $s' = s'_1 \cdot s'_1 \cdot \ldots \cdot s'_m$. The question is does $s' \in L(b)$? We also consider the special case of this problem where $b = a$. This is the single schema update problem, that is, verifying whether a string is still in the language of an automaton after a sequence of updates.

As the updates are performed, it is straightforward to keep track of the leftmost location at which, and beyond, no updates have been performed, that is, the *least* $i, 1 \leq i \leq m$ such that $s'_i \cdot \ldots \cdot s'_m = s_{n-m+i} \cdot \ldots \cdot s_n$. The knowledge that $s \in L(a)$ is generally of no utility in evaluating $s'_0 \cdot \ldots \cdot s'_{i-1}$ since the string might have changed drastically. The validation of the substring, $s'_i \cdot \ldots \cdot s'_m$, however, reduces to the schema cast problem without modifications.

Specifically, to determine the validity of s' according to b, we first process b to generate an immediate decision automaton, b_{immed}. We also process a and b to generate an immediate decision automata, c_{immed} as described in the previous section. Now, given a string s' where the leftmost unmodified position is i, we:

1. Evaluate $s'_1 \cdot \ldots s'_{i-1}$ using b_{immed}. That is, determine $q_b = \delta_b(q^0_a, s'_1 \cdot \ldots \cdot s'_{i-1})$. While scanning, b_{immed} may immediately accept or reject, at which time, we stop scanning and return the appropriate answer.
2. Evaluate $s_1 \cdot \ldots \cdot s_{n-m+i-1}$ using a. That is, determine $q_a = \delta_a(q^0_a, s_1 \cdot \ldots \cdot s_{n-m+i-1})$.
3. If b_{immed} scans $i-1$ symbols of s' and does not immediately accept or reject, we proceed scanning $s'_i \cdot \ldots \cdot s'_m$ using c_{immed} starting in state $q' = (q_a, q_b)$.
4. If c_{immed} accepts, either immediately or by scanning all of s', then $s' \in L(b)$, otherwise the string is rejected, possibly by entering an immediate reject state.

Proposition 2. *Given automata a and b, an immediate decision automaton constructed from the intersection automaton of a and b, and strings $s = s_1 \cdot \ldots \cdot$*

$s_n \in L(a)$ and $s' = s'_1 \cdot \ldots \cdot s'_m$ such that $s'_i \cdot \ldots \cdot s'_m = s_{n-m+i} \cdot \ldots \cdot s_n$. If $\delta_a(q_a^0, s_1 \cdot \ldots \cdot s_{n-m+i-1}) = q_a$ and $\delta_b(q_b^0, s'_1 \cdot \ldots \cdot s'_{i-1}) = q_b$, then $s' \in L(b)$ if and only if c_{immed}, starting in the state (q_a, q_b) recognizes $s'_i \cdot \ldots \cdot s'_m$.

The algorithm presented above functions well when most of the updates are in the beginning of the string, since all portions of the string up to the start of the unmodified portion must be processed by b_{immed}. In situations where appends are the most likely update operation, the algorithm as stated will not have any performance benefit. One can, however, apply a similar algorithm to the reverse automata[1] of a and b by noting the fact that a string belongs to $L(b)$ if and only if the reversed string belongs to the language that is recognized by the reverse automaton of b. Depending on where the modifications are located in the provided input string, one can choose to process it in the forward direction or in the reverse direction using an immediate decision automaton derived from the reverse automata for a and b. In case there is no advantage in scanning forward or backward, the string should simply be scanned with b_{immed}.

5 Optimality

An immediate decision automaton c_{immed} derived from deterministic finite state automata a and b as described previously, and with IA_c and IR_c as defined in Definition 7 is optimal in the sense that there can be no other deterministic immediate decision automaton d_{immed} that can determine whether a string s belongs to $L(b)$ earlier than c_{immed}.

Proposition 3. *Let d_{immed} be an arbitrary immediate decision automaton that recognizes exactly the set $L(a) \cap L(b)$. For every string $s = s_1 \cdot s_2 \cdot \ldots \cdot s_n$ in Σ^*, if d_{immed} accepts or rejects s after scanning i symbols of $s, 1 \leq i \leq n$, then c_{immed} will scan at the most i symbols to make the same determination.* □

Since we can efficiently construct IA_c as defined in Definition 7, our algorithm is optimal. For the case with modifications, our mechanism is optimal in that there exists no immediate decision automaton that can accept, or reject, s' while scanning fewer symbols than our mechanism.

For XML Schema, as with finite state automata, our solution is optimal in that there can be no other algorithm, which preprocesses only the XML Schemas, that validates a tree faster than the algorithm we have provided. Note that this optimality result assumes that the document is not preprocessed.

Proposition 4. *Let $T = (t, \lambda)$ be an ordered, labeled tree valid with respect to an abstract XML Schema S. If the schema cast validation algorithm accepts or rejects T after processing node n, then no other deterministic algorithm that:*

- *Accepts precisely $valid(S) \cap valid(S')$.*
- *Traverses T in a depth-first fashion.*
- *Uses an immediate decision automaton to validate content models.*

can accept or reject T before visiting node n. □

[1] The reverse automata of a deterministic automata may be non-deterministic.

6 Experiments

We demonstrate the performance benefits of our schema cast validation algorithm by comparing our algorithm's performance to that of Xerces [2]. We have modified Xerces 2.4 to perform schema cast validation as described in Section 3.2. The modified Xerces validator receives a DOM [19] representation of an XML document that conforms to a schema S_1. At each stage of the validation process, while validating a subtree of the DOM tree with respect to a schema S_2, the validator consults hash tables to determine if it may skip validation of that subtree. There is a hash table that stores pairs of types that are in the subsumed relationship, and another that stores the disjoint types. The unmodified Xerces validates the entire document. Due to the complexity of modifying the Xerces code base and to perform a fair comparison with Xerces, we do not use the algorithms mentioned in Section 4 to optimize the checking of whether the labels of the children of a node fit the node's content model. In both the modified Xerces and the original Xerces implementation, the content model of a node is checked by executing a finite state automaton on the labels of the node's children.

We provide results for two experiments. In the first experiment, a document known to be valid with respect to the schema of Figure 1a is validated with respect to the schema of Figure 1b. The complete schema of Figure 1b is provided in Figure 2. In the second experiment, we modify the quantity element declaration (in items) in the schema of Figure 2 to set xsd:maxExclusive to "200" (instead of "100"). Given a document conforming to this modified schema, we check whether it belongs to the schema of Figure 2. In the first experiment, with our algorithm, the time complexity of validation does not depend on the size of the input document — the document is valid if it contains a billTo element. In the second experiment, the quantity element in every item element must be checked to ensure that it is less than "100". Therefore, our algorithm scales linearly with the number of item elements in the document. All experiments were executed on a 3.0Ghz IBM Intellistation running Linux 2.4, with 512MB of memory.

We provide results for input documents that conform to the schema of Figure 2. We vary the number of item elements from 2 to 1000. Table 2 lists the file size of each document. Figure 3a plots the time taken to validate the document versus the number of item elements in the document for both the modified and the unmodified Xerces validators for the first experiment. As expected, our implementation has constant processing time, irrespective of the size of the document, whereas Xerces has a linear cost curve. Figure 3b shows the results of the second experiment. The schema cast validation algorithm is about 30% faster than the unmodified Xerces algorithm. Table 3 lists the number of nodes visited by both algorithms. By only traversing the quantity child of item and not the other children of item, our algorithm visits about 20% fewer nodes than the unmodified Xerces validator. For larger files, especially when the data are out-of-core, the performance benefits of our algorithms would be even more significant.

```
<xsd:schema xmlns:xsd="...">
<xsd:element name="purchaseOrder" type="POType2"/>
<xsd:element name="comment" type="xsd:string"/>

<xsd:complexType name="POType2">
  <xsd:sequence>
    <xsd:element name="shipTo" type="USAddress"/>
    <xsd:element name="billTo" type="USAddress"/>
    <xsd:element name="items" type="Items"/>
  </xsd:sequence>
</xsd:complexType>

<xsd:complexType name="USAddress">
  <xsd:sequence>
    <xsd:element name="name" type="xsd:string"/>
    <xsd:element name="street" type="xsd:string"/>
    <xsd:element name="city" type="xsd:string"/>
    <xsd:element name="state" type="xsd:string"/>
    <xsd:element name="zip" type="xsd:decimal"/>
    <xsd:element name="country" type="xsd:string"/>
  </xsd:sequence>
</xsd:complexType>
<xsd:complexType name="Items">
  <xsd:sequence>
    <xsd:element name="item" type="Item"
      minOccurs="0" maxOccurs="unbounded">
    </xsd:element>
  </xsd:sequence>
</xsd:complexType>
<xsd:complexType name="Item">
  <xsd:sequence>
    <xsd:element name="productName"
      type="xsd:string"/>
    <xsd:element name="quantity">
      <xsd:simpleType>
      <xsd:restriction base="xsd:positiveInteger">
      <xsd:maxExclusive value="100"/>
      </xsd:restriction>
      </xsd:simpleType>
    </xsd:element>
    <xsd:element name="USPrice"
      type="xsd:decimal"/>
    <xsd:element name="shipDate"
      type="xsd:date" minOccurs="0"/>
  </xsd:sequence>
</xsd:complexType>
</xsd:schema>
```

Fig. 2. Target XML Schema.

Table 2. File sizes for input documents.

# Item Nodes	Size (Bytes)
2	990
50	11,358
100	22,158
200	43,758
500	108,558
1000	216,558

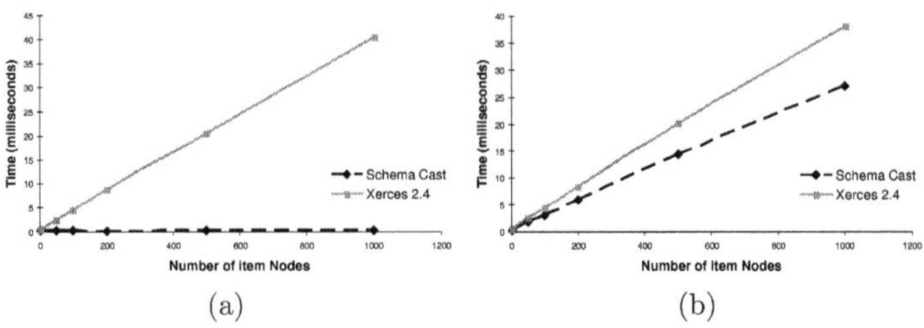

Fig. 3. (a) Validation times from first experiment. (b) Validation times from second experiment.

Table 3. Number of nodes traversed during validation in Experiment 2.

# Item Nodes	Schema Cast	Xerces 2.4
2	35	74
50	611	794
100	1,211	1,544
200	2,411	3,044
500	6,011	7,544
1000	12,011	15,044

7 Conclusions

We have presented efficient solutions to the problem of enforcing the validity of a document with respect to a schema given the knowledge that it conforms to another schema. We examine both the case where the document is not modified before revalidation, and the case where insertions, updates and deletions are applied to the document before revalidation. We have provided an algorithm for the case where validation is defined in terms of XML Schemas (with DTDs as a special case). The algorithm relies on a subalgorithm to revalidate content models efficiently, which addresses the problem of revalidation with respect to deterministic finite state automata. The solution to this schema cast problem is useful in many contexts ranging from the compilation of programming languages with XML types, to handling XML messages and Web Services interactions. The practicality and the efficiency of our algorithms has been demonstrated through experiments. Unlike schemes that preprocess documents (that handle a subset of our schema cast validation problem), the memory requirement of our algorithm does not vary with the size of the document, but depends solely on the sizes of the schemas. We are currently extending our algorithms to handle key constraints, and exploring how a system may automatically correct a document valid according to one schema so that it conforms to a new schema.

Acknowledgments. We thank the anonymous referees for their careful reading and precise comments. We also thank John Field, Ganesan Ramalingam, and Vivek Sarkar for comments on earlier drafts.

References

1. S. Alagic and D. Briggs. Semantics of objectified XML. In *Proceedings of DBPL*, September 2003.
2. Apache Software Foundation. *Xerces2 Java Parser*. `http://xml.apache.org/`.
3. D. Barbosa, A. Mendelzon, L. Libkin, L. Mignet, and M. Arenas. Efficent incremental validation of XML documents. In *Proceedings of ICDE*, 2004. To Appear.
4. V. Benzaken, G. Castagna, and A. Frisch. Cduce: an XML-centric general-purpose language. In *Proceedings of ICFP*, pages 51–63, 2003.
5. B. Bouchou and M. Halfeld-Ferrari. Updates and incremental validation of XML documents. In *Proceedings of DBPL*, September 2003.

6. A. Bruggemann-Klein and D. Wood. One-unambiguous regular languages. *Information and Computation*, 142(2):182–206, May 1998.
7. T. H. Cormen, C. E. Leiserson, and R. L. Rivest. *Introduction to Algorithms*. The MIT Press, 1989.
8. *Galax: An implementation of XQuery*. `http://db.bell-labs.com/galax`.
9. M. Harren, M. Raghavachari, O. Shmueli, M. Burke, V. Sarkar, and R. Bordawekar. XJ: Integration of XML processing into Java. Technical Report RC23007, IBM T.J. Watson Research Center, 2003. Submitted for Publication.
10. H. Hosoya and B. C. Pierce. XDuce: A statically typed XML processing language. *ACM Transactions on Internet Technology*, 2002.
11. H. Hosoya, J. Vouillon, and B. C. Pierce. Regular expression types for XML. In *Proceedings of ICFP*, 2000.
12. B. Kane, H. Su, and E. A. Rundensteiner. Consistently updating XML documents using incremental constraint check queries. In *Proceedings of the Workshop on Web Information and Data Management (WIDM'02)*, pages 1–8, November 2002.
13. G. Kuper and J. Siméon. Subsumption for XML types. In *Proceedings of ICDT*, January 2001.
14. T. Milo, D. Suciu, and V. Vianu. Typechecking for XML transformers. In *Proceedings of PODS*, pages 11–22. ACM, 2000.
15. M. Murata, D. Lee, and M. Mani. Taxonomy of XML schema languages using formal language theory. In *Extreme Markup Languages*, Montreal, Canada, 2001.
16. Y. Papakonstantinou and V. Vianu. DTD inference for views of XML data. In *Proceedings of PODS*, pages 35–46. ACM, 2000.
17. Y. Papakonstantinou and V. Vianu. Incremental validation of XML documents. In *Proceedings of ICDT*, pages 47–63, January 2003.
18. J. Siméon and P. Wadler. The essence of XML. In *Proceedings of POPL*, pages 1–13. ACM Press, January 2003.
19. World Wide Web Consortium. *Document Object Model Level 2 Core*, November 2000.
20. World Wide Web Consortium. *XQuery 1.0: An XML Query Language*, November 2000.
21. World Wide Web Consortium. *XML Schema, Parts 0,1, and 2*, May 2001.

Hierarchical In-Network Data Aggregation with Quality Guarantees

Antonios Deligiannakis[1]*, Yannis Kotidis[2], and Nick Roussopoulos[1]

[1] University of Maryland, College Park MD 20742, USA,
{adeli,nick}@cs.umd.edu
[2] AT&T Labs-Research, Florham Park NJ 07932, USA,
kotidis@research.att.com

Abstract. Earlier work has demonstrated the effectiveness of in-network data aggregation in order to minimize the amount of messages exchanged during continuous queries in large sensor networks. The key idea is to build an aggregation tree, in which parent nodes aggregate the values received from their children. Nevertheless, for large sensor networks with severe energy constraints the reduction obtained through the aggregation tree might not be sufficient. In this paper we extend prior work on in-network data aggregation to support approximate evaluation of queries to further reduce the number of exchanged messages among the nodes and extend the longevity of the network. A key ingredient to our framework is the notion of the residual mode of operation that is used to eliminate messages from sibling nodes when their cumulative change is small. We introduce a new algorithm, based on potential gains, which adaptively redistributes the error thresholds to those nodes that benefit the most and tries to minimize the total number of transmitted messages in the network. Our experiments demonstrate that our techniques significantly outperform previous approaches and reduce the network traffic by exploiting the super-imposed tree hierarchy.

1 Introduction

Technological advances in recent years have made feasible the deployment of hundreds or thousands of sensor nodes in an ad-hoc fashion, that are able to coordinate and perform a variety of monitoring applications ranging from measurements of meteorological data (like temperature, pressure, humidity), noise levels, chemicals etc. to complex military vehicle surveillance and tracking applications. Independently of the desired functionality of the sensors, all the above applications share several similar characteristics. First of all, processing is often driven by designated nodes that monitor the behavior of either the entire, or parts of the network. This monitoring is typically performed by issuing queries, which are propagated through the network, over the data collected by the sensor nodes. The output of the queries is then collected by the monitoring node(s) for further processing. While typical database queries are executed once, queries in monitoring applications are long-running and executed over a specified period, or until explicitly being terminated. These types of queries are known as *continuous queries* [3,14].

* Work partially done while author was visiting AT&T Labs-Research. Author also supported by the DoD-Army Research Office under Awards DAAD19-01-2-0011 and DAAD19-01-1-0494.

E. Bertino et al. (Eds.): EDBT 2004, LNCS 2992, pp. 658–675, 2004.
© Springer-Verlag Berlin Heidelberg 2004

Another common characteristic of sensor node applications revolves around the severe energy and bandwidth constraints that are met in such networks. In many applications sensor nodes are powered by batteries, and replacing them is not only very expensive but often impossible (for example, sensors in a disaster area). In such cases, energy-aware protocols involving the operation of the nodes need to be designed to ensure the longevity of the network. This is the focus of the work in [9,10], where energy-based query optimization is performed. The bandwidth constraints arise from the wireless nature of the communication among the nodes, the short-ranges of their radio transmitters and the high density of network nodes in some areas.

Recent work [8,9,15] has focused on reducing the amount of transmitted data by performing in-network data aggregation. The main idea is to build an aggregation tree, which the results will follow. Non-leaf nodes of that tree aggregate the values of their children before transmitting the aggregate result to their parents. At each epoch, ideally, a parent node coalesces all partial aggregates from its child nodes and transmits upwards a single partial aggregate for the whole subtree.

All the above techniques try to limit the number of transmitted data while always providing accurate answers to posed queries. However, there are many instances where the application is willing to tolerate a specified error, in order to reduce the bandwidth consumption and increase the lifetime of the network. In [11], Olston et al. study the problem of error-tolerant applications, where the users register continuous queries along with strict precision constraints at a central *stream processor*. The stream processor then dynamically distributes the error budget to the remote data sources by installing filters on them that necessitate the transmission of a data value from each source only when the source's observed value deviates from its previously transmitted value by more that a threshold specified by the filter.

The algorithms in [11] cannot be directly applied to monitoring applications over sensor networks. While the nodes in sensor networks form an aggregation tree where messages are aggregated and, therefore, the number of transmitted messages depends on the tree topology, [11] assumes a flat setup of the remote data sources, where the cost of transmitting a message from each source is independent to what happens in the other data sources. Moreover, as we will show in this paper, the algorithms in [11] may exhibit several undesirable characteristics for sensor networks, such as:

- The existence of a few volatile data sources will make the algorithms of [11] distribute most of the available budget to these nodes, without any significant benefit, and at the expense of all the other sensor nodes.
- The error distribution assumes a worst-case behavior of the sensor nodes. If any node exceeds its specified threshold, then its data needs to be propagated to the monitoring node. However, there might be many cases when changes from different data sources effectively cancel-out each other. When this happens frequently, our algorithms should exploit this fact and, therefore, prevent unnecessary messages from being propagated all the way to the root node of the aggregation tree.

In this paper we develop new techniques for data dissemination in sensor networks when the monitoring application is willing to tolerate a specified error threshold. Our techniques operate by considering the potential benefit of increasing the error threshold at a sensor node, which is equivalent to the amount of messages that we expect to save

by allocating more resources to the node. The result of using this gain-based approach is a robust algorithm that is able to identify volatile data sources and eliminate them from consideration. Moreover, we introduce the *residual mode of operation*, during which a parent node may eliminate messages from its children nodes in the aggregation tree, when the cumulative change from these sensor nodes is small. Finally, unlike the algorithms in [11], our algorithms operate with only local knowledge, where each node simply considers statistics from its children nodes in the aggregation tree. This allows for more flexibility in designing adaptive algorithms, and is a more realistic assumption for sensors nodes with very limited capabilities [9].
Our contributions are summarized as follows:

1. We present a detailed analysis of the current protocols for data dissemination in sensor networks in the case of error-tolerant applications along with their shortcomings.
2. We introduce the notion of the *residual* mode of operation. When the cumulative change in the observed quantities of multiple sensor nodes is small, this operation mode helps filter out messages close to the sensors, and prevents these messages from being propagated all the way to the root of the aggregation tree. We also extend previous algorithms to make use of the residual mode and explore their performance.
3. We introduce the notion of the *potential gain* of a node or an entire subtree and employ it as an indicator of the benefit of increasing the error thresholds in some nodes of the subtree. We then present an adaptive algorithm that dynamically determines how to rearrange the error thresholds in the aggregation tree using simple, local statistics on the potential gains of the nodes. Similarly to [11], the sensor nodes in our techniques periodically shrink their error thresholds to create an error "budget" that can be re-distributed amongst them. This re-distribution of the error is necessary to account for changes in the behavior of each sensor node. Unlike [11], where nodes are treated independently, our algorithm takes into account the tree hierarchy and the resulting interactions among the nodes.
4. We present an extensive experimental analysis of our algorithms in comparison to previous techniques. Our experiments demonstrate that, for the same maximum error threshold of the application, our techniques have a profound effect on reducing the number of messages exchanged in the network and outperform previous approaches, up to a factor of 7 in some cases.

The rest of the paper is organized as follows. Section 2 presents related work. In Sect. 3 we describe the algorithms presented in [11] and provide a high level description of our framework. In Sect. 4 we discuss the shortcomings of previous techniques when applied to sensor networks. Section 5 presents our extensions and algorithms for dynamically adjusting the error thresholds of the sensor nodes. Section 6 contains our experiments, while Sect. 7 contains concluding remarks.

2 Related Work

The development of powerful and inexpensive sensors in recent years has spurred a flurry of research in the area of sensor networks, with particular emphasis in the topics of network self-configuration [2], data discovery [6,7] and in-network query processing [8,

9,15]. For monitoring queries that aggregate the observed values from a group of sensor nodes, [8] suggested the construction of a greedy aggregation tree that seeks to maximize the number of aggregated messages and minimize the amount of the transmitted data. To accomplice this, nodes may delay sending replies to a posed query in anticipation of replies from other queried nodes. A similar approach is followed in the TAG [9], TinyDB [10] and Cougar [15] systems. In [5], a framework for compensating for packet loss and node failures during query evaluation is proposed. The work in [9] also addressed issues such as query dissemination, sensor synchronization to reduce the amount of time a sensor is active and therefore increase its expected lifetime, and also techniques for optimizations based on characteristics of the used aggregate function. Similar issues are addressed in [10], but the emphasis is on reducing the power consumption by determining appropriate sampling rates for each data source. The above work complements our in many cases, but our optimizations methods are driven by the error bounds of the application at hand.

The work in [11] addressed applications that tolerate a specified error threshold and presented a novel, dynamic algorithm for minimizing the number of transmitted messages. While our work shares a similar motivation with the work in [11], our methods apply over a hierarchical topology, such as the ones that are typically met in continuous queries over sensor networks. Similarly, earlier work in distributed constraint checking [1,13] cannot be directly applied in our setting, because of the different communication model and the limited resources at the sensors. The work of [12] provides quality guarantees during in-network aggregation, like our framework, but this is achieved through a uniform allocation strategy and does not make use of the residual mode of operation that we introduce in this paper. The evaluation of probabilistic queries over imprecise data was studied in [4]. Extending this work to hierarchical topologies, such as the ones studied in our paper, is an open research topic.

3 Basics

We first describe Olston's framework and algorithms [11] for error-tolerant monitoring applications in flat, non-hierarchical, topologies, and then provide a high-level description of our framework. The notation that we will use in the description of our algorithms is presented in Table 1. A short description of the characteristics of sensor nodes, and sensor networks in general can be found in the full version of this paper.

3.1 Olston's Framework for Error Tolerant Applications

Consider a node *Root*, which initiates a continuous query over the values observed by a set of data sources. This continuous query aggregates values observed by the data sources, and produces a single aggregate result. For each defined query, a maximum error threshold, or equivalently a precision constraint E_Global that the application is willing to tolerate is specified. The algorithm will install filters at each queried data source, that will help limit the number of transmitted messages from the data source. The selection process for the filters enforces that at any moment t after the installation of the query to the data sources, the aggregate value reported at node *Root* will lie within

the specified error threshold from the true aggregate value (ignoring network delays, or lost messages).

Initially, a filter F_i is installed in every data source S_i, such that the initial error guarantees are not violated. Each filter F_i is an interval of real values $[L_i, H_i]$ of width $W_i = H_i - L_i$, such that any source S_i whose current observed value $Current_i$ lies outside its filter F_i will need to transmit its current value to the *Root* node and then re-center its filter around this transmitted value, by setting $L_i = Current_i - W_i/2$ and $H_i = Current_i + W_i/2$. However, if $Current_i$ lies within the interval specified by the filter F_i, then this value does not need to be transmitted.

In order for the algorithm to be able to adapt to changes in the characteristics of the data sources, the widths W_i of the filters are periodically adjusted. Every *Upd* time units, *Upd* being the *adjustment period*, each filter shrinks its width by a *shrink percentage* ($shrinkFactor$). At this point, the *Root* node obtains an *error budget* equal to $(1 - shrinkFactor) \times E\_Global$, which it can then distribute to the data sources. The decision of which data sources will increase their window W_i is based on the calculation of a *Burden Score* metric B_i for each data source, which is defined as: $B_i = \frac{C_i}{P_i \times W_i}$. In this formula, C_i is the cost of sending a value from the data source S_i to the *Root* and P_i is the *estimated streamed update period*, defined as the estimated amount of time between consecutive transmissions for S_i over the last period *Upd*. For a single query over the data sources, it is shown in [11] that the goal would be to try and have all the burden scores be equal. Thus, the *Root* node selects the data sources with the largest deviation from the target burden score (these are the ones with the largest burden scores in the case of a single query) and sends them messages to increase the width of their windows by a given amount. The process is repeated every *Upd* time units.

A key drawback of the approach, when applied over sensor networks, is the requirement from each node that makes a transmission because its measured value was outside its error filter to also transmit its burden score. In hierarchical topologies, where messages from multiple nodes are aggregated on their path to the *Root* node, this may result in a significant amount of side-information that needs to be communicated along with the aggregate value (one burden score for each node that made a transmission), which defeats the purpose of the algorithm, namely the reduction in the amount of information being transmitted in the network.

3.2 A Framework for Hierarchical Data Aggregation

The model that we consider in this paper is a mixture of the Olston [11] and TAG [9] models. Similarly to [11], we consider error-tolerant applications where precision constraints are specified and filters are installed at the data sources. Unlike [11], we consider a hierarchical view of the data sources, based on the paths that the aggregate values follow towards the *Root* node.

We assume that the aggregation tree (ex: Fig. 1) for computing and propagating the aggregate has already been established. Techniques for discovering and modifying the aggregation tree are illustrated in [9]. There are two types of nodes in the tree. *Active* nodes, marked grey in the figure, are nodes that collect measurements. *Passive* nodes (for example, node 2 in the figure) are intermediate nodes in the tree that do not record any data for the query but rather aggregate partial results from their descendant nodes. By

Table 1. Symbols Used in our Algorithms

Symbol	Description
N_i	Sensor node i
W_i	The width of the filter of sensor N_i
$E_i = W_i/2$	Maximum permitted error in node N_i
E_Sub_i	Maximum permitted error in entire subtree of node N_i
E_Global	Maximum permitted error of the application
Upd	Update period of adjusting error filters
$shrinkFactor$	Shrinking Factor of filter widths
T	Number of nodes in the aggregation tree
$Root$	The node initiating the continuous query
$Gain$	The estimated gain of allocating additional error to the node
$CumGain$	The estimated gain of allocating additional error to the the node's entire subtree
$CumGain\_Sub[i]$	The estimated gain of allocating additional error to the the node's i-th subtree

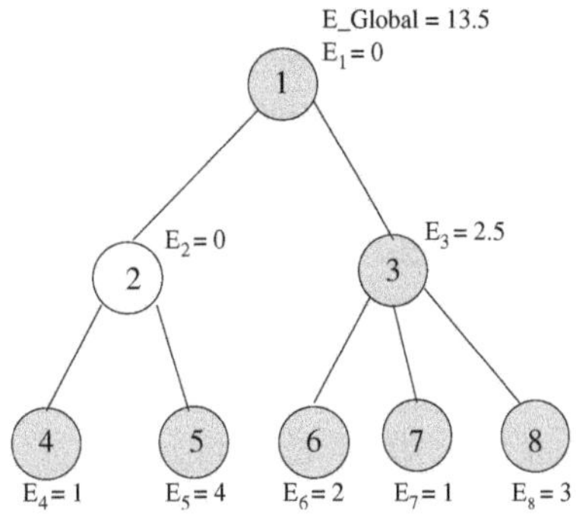

Fig. 1. Sample Aggregation Tree

default all leaf nodes are active, while intermediate nodes may be either active or passive. Our algorithms will install a filter to any node N_i in the aggregation tree, independently on whether the node is an active or passive one. This is a distinct difference from the framework of [11], where filters are assigned only to active nodes.

Similarly to the work in [11], our work covers queries containing any of the five standard aggregate functions: SUM, AVG, COUNT, MIN and MAX. The COUNT function can always be computed exactly, while the AVG function can be computed by the SUM and COUNT aggregates. The use of MIN and MAX is symmetric. The work in [11] demonstrated how these queries can be treated as a collection of AVG queries. The same observations apply in our case as well. In this paper, the focus of our discussion will thus be on queries involving the SUM aggregate function.

Figure 1 shows the maximum error of each filter for a query calculating the SUM aggregate over the active nodes of the tree. Notice that the sum of the errors specified is equal to the maximum error that the application is willing to accept (E_Global). Moreover, there is no point in placing an error filter in the $Root$ node, since this is where the result of the query is being collected.

We now describe the propagation of values in the aggregation tree, using a radio synchronization process similar to the one in [9]. During an epoch duration and within the time intervals specified in [9] the sensor nodes in our framework operate as follows:

- An active leaf node i obtains a new measurement and forwards it to its parent if the new measurement lies outside the interval $[L_i, H_i]$ specified by its filter.
- A passive (non-leaf) node awaits for messages from its children. If one or more messages are received, they are combined and forwarded to its own parent only if the new partial aggregate value of the node's subtree does not lie within the interval specified by the node's filter. Otherwise, the node remains idle.
- An active non-leaf node obtains a new measurement and waits for messages from its children nodes as specified in [9]. The node then recomputes the partial aggregate on its subtree (which is the aggregation of its own measurement with the values received by its child-nodes) and forwards it to its parent only if the new partial aggregate lies outside the interval specified by the node's filter.

Along this process, the value sent from a node to its parent is either (i) the node's measurement if the node is a leaf or (ii) the partial aggregate of all measurements in the node's subtree (including itself) if the node is an intermediate node. In both cases, a node remains idle during an epoch if the newly calculated partial aggregate value lies within the interval $[L_i, H_i]$ specified by the node's filter. This is a distinct difference from [11], where the error filters are applied to the values of the data sources, and not on the partial aggregates calculated by each node.

Details on the operation of the sensor nodes will be provided in the following sections. In our discussion hereafter, whenever we refer to Olston's algorithm we will assume the combination of its model with the model of TAG, which aggregates messages within the aggregation tree. Compared to [11], we introduce two new ideas:

1. A new algorithm for adjusting the widths of filters in the nodes: Our algorithm bases its decisions on estimates of the expected gain of allocating additional error to different subtrees. In this way, our algorithm is more robust to the existence of volatile nodes, nodes where the value of the measured quantity changes significantly in each epoch. Moreover, the estimation of gains is performed based only on local statistics for each node (*that take into account the tree topology*), in contrast to Olston's framework where sources are independent and a significant amount of information needs to be propagated to the *Root* node. These statistics are a single value for each node, which can be piggy-backed at the transmitted messages. The details of this process are presented in Sect. 5.
2. A hierarchical-based mode of operation: The filters in non-leaf nodes are used in a mode that may potentially filter messages transmitted from their children nodes, and not just from the node itself. We denote this type of operation as *residual-based* operation, and also denote the error assigned to each node in this case as a *residual* error. We show that under the *residual-based* mode nodes may transmit significantly fewer messages than in a *non-residual* operation because of the coalescing of updates that cancel out and are not propagated all the way to the *Root* node.

4 Problems of Existing Techniques

We now discuss in detail the shortcomings of the algorithms of [11] when applied in the area of sensor networks, and motivate the solutions that we present in the following section.

Hierarchical Structure of Nodes. As we have mentioned above, the sensor nodes that either measure or forward data relevant to a posed continuous query form an aggregation tree, which messages follow on their path to the node that initiated the query. Due to the hierarchical structure of this tree, transmitted values by some node in the tree may be aggregated at some higher level (closer to the *Root* node) with values transmitted by other sensor nodes. This has two main consequences: (1) While each data transmission by a node N_i may in the worst case require transmitting as many messages as the distance of N_i from the *Root* node, the actual cost in most cases will be much smaller; and (2) The actual cost of the above transmission is hard to estimate, since this requires knowledge of which sensors transmitted values, and their exact topology. However, this is an unrealistic scenario in sensor networks, since the additional information required would have to be transmitted along with the aggregate values. The cost of transmitting this additional information would outweight all the benefits of our (or Olston's) framework.

The calculation of the *Burden Score* in [11] (see Sect. 3.1) requires knowledge of the cost of each transmission, since this is one of the three variables used in the formula. Therefore, the techniques introduced in [11] can be applied in our case only by using a heuristic function for the cost of the message. However, it is doubtful that any heuristic would be an accurate one. Consider, for example, the following two cases: (1) All the nodes in the tree need to transmit their observed value. Then, if the tree contains T nodes, under the TAG [9] model exactly $T - 1$ messages will be transmitted (the $Root$ node does not need to transmit a message), making the average cost of each transmission to be equal to 1; and (2) If just one node needs to transmit its observed value, then this value may be propagated all the way to the $Root$. This always happens under the framework of [11], but not in our framework. In this case, the cost of the message will be equal to the distance (in number of hops or tree edges) of the node from the $Root$, since this is the number of messages that will ultimately be transmitted.

In our algorithms we will thus seek to use a metric that will not be dependent on the cost of each transmission, since this is not only an estimate that is impractical to calculate, but also because it varies substantially over time, due to the adaptive nature of our algorithms, and the (possibly) changing characteristics of the data observed by the sensor nodes.

Robustness to Volatile Nodes. One of the principle ideas behind the adaptive algorithms presented in [11] is that an increase in the width of a filter installed in a node will result in a decrease at the number of transmitted messages by that node. While this is an intuitive idea, there are many cases, even when the underlying distribution of the observed quantity does not change, where an increase in the width of the filter does not have any impact in the number of transmitted messages. To illustrate this, consider a node whose values follow a random step pattern, meaning that the observed value at each epoch differs by the observed value in the previous epoch by either $+\Delta$ or $-\Delta$. In this case, any filter with a window whose width is less than $2 \times \Delta$ will not be able to reduce the number of transmitted messages. A similar behavior may be observed in cases where the measured quantity exhibits a large variance. In such cases, even a filter with considerable width may not be able to reduce but a few, if any, transmissions.

The main reason why this occurs in Olston's algorithm is because the Burden Score metric being used does not give any indication about the expected benefit that we will achieve by increasing the width of the installed filter at a node. In this way, a significant amount of the maximum error budget that the application is willing to tolerate may be spent on a few nodes whose measurements exhibit the aforementioned volatile behavior, without any real benefit.

In the algorithms that are presented in the next section we propose a method for distributing the available error using a gain-based policy, which will distribute the error budget to subtrees and nodes based on the expected gain of each decision. Our algorithms identify very volatile nodes which incur very small potential gains and isolate them. Even though the result of this approach is a constant transmission by these nodes, the cost of these transmissions is amortized due to the aggregation of messages that we described above. Our experiments validate that such an approach may result in a significant decrease in the number of transmitted messages, due to the more efficient utilization of the error budget in other non-volatile sensor nodes.

Negative Correlations in Neighboring Areas. According to the algorithms in [11], each time the value of a measured quantity at a node N_i lies outside the interval specified by the filter installed at N_i, then the new value is transmitted and propagated to the $Root$ node. However, there might be cases when changes from nodes belonging to different subtrees of the aggregation tree either cancel out each other, or result in a very small change in the value of the calculated aggregate. This may happen either because of a random behavior of the data, or because of some properties of the measured quantity. Consider for example the aggregation tree of Fig. 1, and assume that each node observes the number of items moving within the area that it monitors. If some objects move from the area of node 4 to the area of node 5, then the changes that will be propagated to node 2 will cancel out each other. Even in cases when the overall change of the aggregate value is non-zero, but relatively small, and such a behavior occurs frequently, we would like our algorithms to be able to detect this and filter these messages without having them being propagated to the $Root$ node.

The algorithm that we will present in the next section introduces the notion of a *residual* mode of operation to deal with such cases. The width of the filters installed in non-leaf nodes is increased in cases when it is detected that such an action may result in filtering out a significant number of messages from descendant nodes.

5 Our Algorithms

In this section we first describe in detail our framework and demonstrate the operation of the nodes. We then present the details of our algorithms for dynamically modifying the widths of the filters installed in the sensor nodes.

5.1 Operation of Nodes

We now describe the operation of each sensor node using the notation of Table 1. Detailed pseudocode for this operation can be found in the full version of this paper. A filter is initially installed in each node of the aggregation tree, except from the Root node. The initial width of each filter is important only for the initial stages of the network's operation, as our dynamic algorithm will later adjust the sizes of the filters appropriately. For example, another alternative would have been to install filters with non-zero width in the initialization phase only to active nodes of the network. In our algorithms we initialize the widths of the error filters similarly to the *uniform allocation* method. For example, in the case when the aggregate function is the function SUM, then each of the $T-1$ nodes in the aggregation tree besides the Root node is assigned the same fraction $E\_Global/(T-1)$ of the error E_Global that the application is willing to tolerate.

In each epoch, the node obtains a measurement (V_Curr) related to the observed quantity only if it is an active node, and then waits for messages from its children nodes containing updates to their measured aggregate values. We here note that each node computes a partial aggregate based on the values reported by its children nodes in the tree. This is a recursive procedure which ultimately results in the evaluation of the aggregate query at the *Root* node. After waiting for messages from its children nodes, the current node computes the new value of the partial aggregate based on the most current partial aggregate values $LastReceived[i]$ it has received from its children.

The new aggregate is calculated using a $Combine$ function, which depends on the aggregate function specified by the query. In Table 2 we provide its implementation for the most common aggregate functions. In the case of the AVG aggregate function, we calculate the sum of the values observed at the active nodes, and then the *Root* node will divide this value with the number of active nodes participating in the query.

After calculating the current partial aggregate, the node must decide whether it needs to transmit a measurement to its parent node or not. This depends on the operation mode being used. In a *non-residual* mode, the node would have to transmit a message either when the value of the measured quantity at the node itself lies outside its filter, or when at least one of the subtrees has transmitted a message and the new changes do not exactly cancel out each other. This happens because in the *non-residual* mode (e.g. the original algorithm of [11]) the error filters are applied to the values measured by each node, and not to the partial aggregates of the subtree. On the contrary, in a *residual* mode of operation, which is the mode used in our algorithms, the node transmits a message only when the value of the new partial aggregate lies outside the node's filter. In both modes of operation the algorithm that distributes the available error enforces that for any node N_i, its calculated partial aggregate will never deviate by more than E_Sub_i from the actual partial aggregate of its subtree (ignoring propagation delays and lost messages). At each epoch the node also updates some statistics which will be later used to adjust the widths of the filters. The *cumulative gain* of the node, which is a single value, is the only statistic propagated to the parent node at each transmission. This adjustment phase is performed every Upd epochs. The first step is for all nodes to shrink the widths of their filters by a shrinking factor $shrinkFactor$ ($0 \leq shrinkFactor < 1$). After this process, the *Root* node has an error budget of size $E\_Global \times (1 - shrinkFactor)$, where E_Global is the maximum error of the application, that it can redistribute recursively to the nodes of the network. Details of the adjustment process will be given later in this section.

5.2 Calculating the Gain of Each Node

Our algorithm updates the width of the filter installed in each node by considering the potential gain of increasing the error threshold at a sensor node, which is defined as the amount of messages that we expect to save by allocating more resources to the node. The result of using this gain-based approach is a robust algorithm that respects the hierarchy imposed by the aggregation tree and, at the same time, is able to identify volatile data sources and eliminate them from consideration. This computation of potential gains, as we will show, requires only local knowledge, where each node simply considers statistics from its children nodes in the aggregation tree. In Fig. 2 we show the expected behavior of a sensor node N_i, varying the width of the its filter W_i. The y-axis plots the number of messages sent from this node to its parent in the aggregation tree in a period of Upd epochs. Assuming that the measurement on the node is not constant, a zero width filter ($W_i = E_i = 0$) results in one message for each of the Upd epochs. By increasing the

Table 2. Definition of the `Combine` function

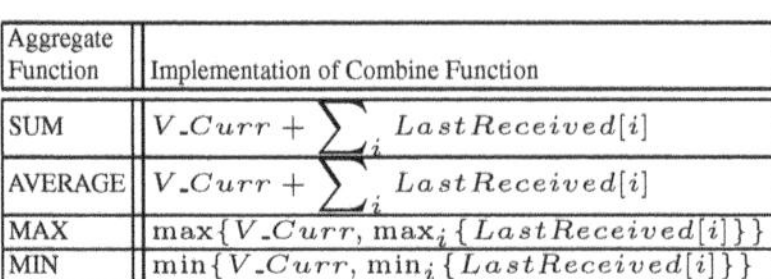

Aggregate Function	Implementation of Combine Function
SUM	$V\_Curr + \sum_i LastReceived[i]$
AVERAGE	$V\_Curr + \sum_i LastReceived[i]$
MAX	$\max\{V\_Curr, \max_i\{LastReceived[i]\}\}$
MIN	$\min\{V\_Curr, \min_i\{LastReceived[i]\}\}$

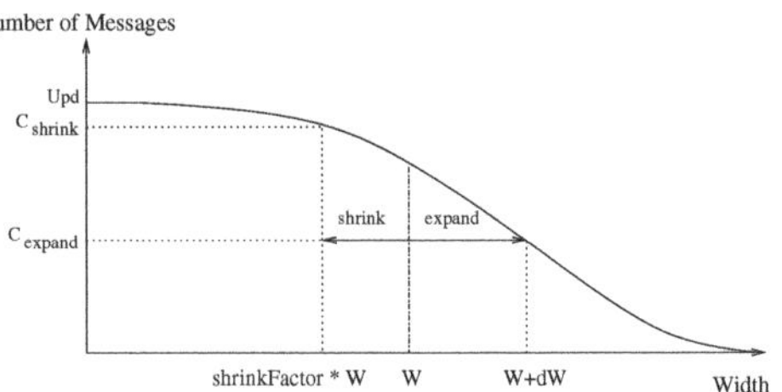

Fig. 2. Potential Gain of a Node

width of the filter, the number of messages is reduced, up to the point that no messages are required. Of course, in practice, this may never happen as the width of the filter required may exceed the global error constraint E_Global. Some additional factors that can make a node deviate from the typical behavior of Fig. 2 also exist. As an example, the measurement of the node may not change for some period of time exceeding Upd. In such a case, the curve becomes a straight line at y=0 and no messages are being sent (unless there are changes on the subtree rooted at the node). In such cases of very stable nodes, we would like to be able to detect this behavior and redistribute the error to other, more volatile nodes. At the other extreme, node N_i may be so volatile that even a filter of considerable width will not be able suppress any messages. In such a case the curve becomes a straight line at y=Upd. Notice that the same may happen because of a highly volatile node N_j that is a descendant of N_i in the aggregation tree.

In principle, we can not fully predict the behavior of a node N_i unless we take into account its interaction will all the other nodes in its subtree. Of course, a complete knowledge of this interaction is infeasible, due to the potentially large amounts of information that are required, as described in Sect. 4. We will thus achieve this by computing the potential gains of adjusting the width of the node's filter W_i, using simple, *local* statistics that we collect during the query evaluation.

Let W_i be the width of the filter installed at node N_i at the last update phase. The node also knows the $shrinkFactor$ that is announced when the query is initiated. Unless the adaptive procedure decides to increase the error of the node, its filter's width is scheduled to be reduced to $shrinkFactor \times W_i$ in the next update phase, which takes place every Upd epochs. The node can estimate the effects of this change as follows. At the same time that the node uses its filter W_i to decide whether or not to send a message to its parent, it also keeps track of its decision assuming a filter of a smaller width of $shrinkFactor \times W_i$. This requires a single counter C_{shrink} that will keep track of the number of messages that the node would have sent if its filter was reduced. C_{shrink} gives as an estimate of the negative effect of reducing the filter of N_i. Since we would also like the node to have a chance to increase its filter, the node also computes the number of messages C_{expand} in case its filter was increased by a factor dW to be defined later.[1]

[1] Even though this computation, based on two anchor points, may seem simplistic, there is little more that can truly be accomplished with only local knowledge, since the node cannot possibly know exactly which partial aggregates it would have received from its children in the case of either a smaller or a larger filter, because these partial aggregates would themselves depend on the corresponding width changes in the filters of the children nodes.

Our process is demonstrated in Fig. 2. Let $\delta G \geq 0$ be the reduction in the number of messages by changing the width from $shrinkFactor \times W_i$ (which is the default in the next update phase) to $W_i + dW$. The *potential gain* for the node is defined as:

$$Gain_i = \delta G = C_{shrink} - C_{expand} \ .$$

It is significant to note that our definition of the *potential gain* of a node is independent on whether the node is active or not, since the algorithm for deciding whether to transmit a message or not is only based on the value of the partial aggregate calculated for the node's entire subtree. Moreover, the value of dW is not uniquely defined in our algorithms. In our implementation we use the following heuristic for the computation of gains:

- For leaf nodes, we use $dW = \frac{E\_Global}{N_{active}}$, N_{active} being the number of active nodes in the aggregation tree.
- For non-leaf nodes, in the residual mode, we need a larger value of dW, since the expansion of the node's filter should be large enough to allow the node to coalesce negative correlations in the changes of the aggregates on its children nodes. As a heuristic, we have been using $dW = num\_children_i \times \frac{E\_Global}{N_{active}}$, where $num\_children_i$ is the number of children of node N_i.

These values of dW have been shown to work well in practice on a large variety of tested configurations. We need to emphasize here that these values are used to give the algorithm an estimate on the behavior of the sensor and that the actual change in the widths W_i of the filters will also be based on the amount of "error budget" available and the behavior of all the other nodes in the tree.

Computation of Cumulative Gains. The computation of the potential gains, as explained above, may provide us with an idea of the effect that modifying the size of the filter in a node may have, but is by itself inadequate as a metric for the distribution of the available error to the nodes of its subtree. This happens because this metric does not take into account the corresponding gains of descendant nodes in the aggregation tree. Even if a node may have zero potential gain (this may happen, for example, if either the node itself or some of its descendants are very volatile), this does not mean that we cannot reduce the number of transmitted messages in some areas of the subtree rooted at that node.

Because of the top-down redistribution of the errors that our algorithm applies, if no budget is allocated to N_i by its parent node then all nodes in the subtree of N_i will not get a chance to increase their error thresholds and this will eventually lead to every node in that subtree to send a new message on each epoch, which is clearly an undesirable situation. Thus, we need a way to compute the *cumulative gain* on the subtree of N_i and base the redistribution process on that value. In our framework we define the cumulative gain on a node N_i as:

$$CumGain_i = \begin{cases} Gain_i & N_i \text{ is a leaf node} \\ Gain_i + \sum_{N_j \in children(N_i)} CumGain\_Sub[j] & \text{otherwise} \end{cases} \ .$$

This definition of the cumulative gain has the following desirable properties: (1) It is based on the computed gains ($Gain_i$) that is purely a local statistic on a node N_i; and (2)

The recursive formula can be computed in a bottom-up manner by having nodes piggy-back the value of their cumulative gain in each message that they transmit to their parent along with their partial aggregate value. This is a single number that is being aggregated in a bottom-up manner, and thus poses a minimal overhead.[2] Moreover, transmitting the cumulative gain is necessary only if its value has changed (and in most cases only if this change is significant) since the last transmission of the node.

5.3 Adjusting the Filters

The algorithm for adjusting the widths of the filters is based on the cumulative gains calculated at each node. Every Upd epochs, we mentioned before that all the filters shrink by a factor of $shrinkFactor$. This results in an error budget of $E\_Global \times (1 - shrinkFactor)$ which the $Root$ node can distribute to the nodes of the tree. Each node N_i has statistics on the potential gain of allocating error to the node itself ($Gain_i$), and the corresponding cumulative gain of allocating error to each of its subtrees. Using these statistics, the allocation of the errors is performed as follows, assuming that the node can distribute a total error of $E\_Additional$ to itself and its descendants:

1. For each subtree j of node N_i, allocate error E_Sub_j proportional to its cumulative gain: $E\_Additional_j = \frac{E\_Additional \times CumGain\_Sub[j]}{Gain_i + \sum_{N_j \in children(N_i)} CumGain\_Sub[j]}$. This distribution is performed only when this quantity is at least equal to E_Global/N_{active}.
2. The remaining error budget is distributed to the node itself.

The fraction of the error budget allocated to the node itself and to each of the subtrees is analogous to the expected benefit of each choice. The only additional detail is that in case when the error allocated to a subtree of node N_i is less than the E_Global/N_{active} value, then we do not allocate any error in that subtree, and allocate this error to node N_i itself. This is done to avoid sending messages for adjusting the filters when the error budget is too small.

6 Experiments

We have developed a simulator for sensor networks that allows us to vary several parameters like the number of nodes, the topology of the aggregation tree, the data distribution etc. The synchronization of the sensor nodes is performed, for all algorithms, as described in TAG [9]. In our experiments we compare the following algorithms:

1. BBA (Burden-Based Adjustment): This is an implementation of the algorithm presented in [11] for the adaptive precision setting of cached approximate values.
2. Uni: This is a static setting where the error is evenly distributed among all active sensor nodes, and therefore does not incur any communication overhead for adjusting the error thresholds of the nodes.

[2] In contrast, the algorithm of [11], requires each node to propagate the burden scores of all of its descendant nodes in the aggregation tree whose observed values was outside their error filters.

3. PGA (Potential Gains Adjustment): This is our precision control algorithm, based on the potential gains (see Sect. 5), for adjusting the filters of the sensor nodes.

For the PGA and BBA algorithms we made a few preliminary runs to choose their internal parameters (*adjustment period*, *shrink percentage*). Notice that the *adjustment period* determines how frequently the precision control algorithm is invoked, while the *shrink percentage* determines how much of the overall error budget is being redistributed. Based on the observed behavior of the algorithms, we have selected the combination of values of Table 3(a) as the most representative ones for revealing the "preferences" of each algorithm. The first configuration (Conf1) consistently produced good results, in a variety of tree topologies and datasets, for the PGA algorithm, while the second configuration (Conf2) was typically the best choice for the BBA algorithm. In the BBA algorithm we also determined experimentally that distributing the available error to 10% of the nodes with the highest burden scores was the best choice for the algorithm.

The initial allocation of error thresholds was done using the uniform policy. We then used the first 10% of epochs as a warm-up period for the algorithms to adjust their thresholds and report the results (number of transmitted messages) for the later 90%. We used synthetic data, similar in spirit to the data used in [11]. For each simulated active node, we generated values following a random walk pattern, each with a randomly assigned step size in the range $(0 \ldots 2]$. We further added in the mix a set of "unstable nodes" whose step size is much larger: $(0 \ldots 200]$. These volatile nodes allow us to investigate how the different algorithms adapt to noisy sensors. Ideally, when the step-size of a node is comparable to the global error threshold, we would like the precision control algorithm to restrain from giving any of the available budget to that node at the expense of all the other sensor nodes in the tree. We denote with $P_{unstable}$ the probability of an active node being unstable.

$P_{unstable}$ describes the volatility of a node in terms of the magnitude of its data values. Volatility can also be expressed in the orthogonal temporal dimension. For instance some nodes may not update their values frequently, while others might be changing quite often (even by small amounts, depending on their step size). To capture this scenario, we further divide the sensor nodes in two additional classes: *workaholics* and *regulars*. Regular sensors make a random step with a fixed probability of 1% during an epoch. Workaholics, on the other hand, make a random step on every epoch. We denote with $P_{workaholic}$ the probability of an active node being workaholic.

We used three different network topologies denoted as T_{leaves}, T_{all} and T_{random}. In T_{leaves} the aggregation tree was a balanced tree with 5 levels and a fan-out of 4 (341 nodes overall). For this configuration all active nodes were at the leaves of the tree. In T_{all}, for the same tree topology, all nodes (including the *Root*) were active. Finally in T_{random} we used 500 sensor nodes, forming a random tree each time. The maximum fan-out of a node was in that case 8 and the maximum depth of the tree 6. Intermediate nodes in T_{random} were active with probability 20% (all leaf nodes are active by default).

In all experiments presented here, we executed the simulator 10 times and present here the averages. In all runs we used the SUM aggregate function (the performance of AVG was similar).

Benefits of Residual Operation and Sensitivity Analysis. The three precision control algorithms considered (Uni, PGA, BBA) along with the mode of operation (residual: Res, non-residual: $NoRes$) provide us with six different choices (Uni+Res, Uni+ $NoRes$ ...). We note that BBA+$NoRes$ is the original algorithm of [11] running over TAG, while BBA+Res is our extension of that algorithm using the residual mode of operation. The combination PGA+Res denotes our algorithm. In this first experiment we investigate whether the precision control algorithms benefit from the use of the residual mode of operation. We also seek their preferences in terms of the values of parameters *adjustment period* and *shrink percentage*.

We used a synthetic dataset with $P_{unstable}$=0 and $P_{workaholic}$=0.2. We then let the sensors operate for 40,000 epochs using a fixed error constraint E_Global=500. The average value of the SUM aggregate was 25,600, meaning that this E_Global value corresponds to a relative error of about 2%. In Table 3(b) we show the total number of messages in the sensor network for each choice of algorithm and tree topology and each selection of parameters. We also show the number of messages for an exact computation of the SUM aggregate using one more method, entitled as (E_Global=0)+Res, which places a zero width filter in every node and uses our residual mode of operation for propagating changes. Effectively, a node sends a message to its parent only when the partial aggregate on its subtree changes. This is nothing more than a slightly enhanced version of TAG. The following observations are made:

- Using a modest E_Global value of 500 (2% relative error), we are able to reduce the number of messages by 7.6-9.9 times (in PGA+Res) compared to (E_Global=0)+ Res. Thus, error-tolerate applications can significantly reduce the number of transmissions, resulting in great savings on both bandwidth and energy consumption.
- Algorithm PGA seems to require fewer invocations (larger *adjustment period*) but with a larger percentage of the error to be redistributed (a smaller *shrink percentage* results in a wider reorganization of the error thresholds). In the table we see that the number of messages for the selection of values of Conf1 is always smaller. Intuitively, larger adjustment periods, allow for more reliable statistics on the computation of potential gains. On the contrary, BBA seems to behave better when filters are adjusted more often by small increments. We also note that BBA results in a lot more messages than PGA, no matter which configuration is used.
- The PGA algorithm, when using the residual operation (PGA+Res), results in substantially fewer messages that all the other alternatives. Even when using the non-residual mode of operation, PGA outperforms, significantly, the competitive algorithms.
- BBA seems to benefit only occasionally from the use of the residual operation. The adjustment of thresholds based on the burden of a node can not distinguish on the true cause of a transmission (change on local measurement or change in the subtree) and does not seem to provide a good method of adjusting the filters with respect to the tree hierarchy.

In the rest of the section we investigate in more details the performance of the algorithms based on the network topology and the data distribution. For PGA we used the residual mode of operation. For BBA we tested both the residual and non-residual modes and present here the best results. (as seen on Table 3(b), the differences were very small) We configured PGA using the values of Conf1 and BBA using the values of Conf2 that provided the best results per case.

Sensitivity on Temporal Volatility of Sensor Measurements. We here investigate the performance of the algorithms when varying $P_{workaholic}$ and for $P_{unstable}$=0. We first fixed $P_{workaholic}$ to be 20%, as in the previous experiment. In Fig. 3 we plot the total number of messages in the network (y-axis) for 40,000 epochs when varying the error constraint E_Global from 100 to 2,000 (8% in terms of relative error). Depending on E_Global, PGA results in up to 4.8 times fewer messages than BBA and up 6.4 times fewer than Uni. These differences arise from the ability of PGA to place, judiciously, filters on passive intermediate sensor nodes and exploit negative correlations on their subtree based on the computed potential gains. Algorithm BBA may also place filters on the intermediate nodes (when the residual mode is used) but the selection of the widths of the filters based on the burden scores of the nodes was typically not especially successful in our experiments.

Figures 4 and 5 repeat the experiment for the T_{all} and T_{random} configurations. For the same global error threshold, PGA results in up to 4 times and 6 times fewer messages than BBA and Uni respectively. In Fig. 6 we vary $P_{workaholic}$ between 0 and 1 for T_{all} (best network topology for BBA). Again PGA outperforms the other algorithms. An important observation is that when the value of $P_{workaholic}$ is either 0 or 1, all the methods behave similarly. In this case all the nodes in the network have the same characteristics, so it is not surprising that Uni performs so well. The PGA and BBA algorithms managed to filter just a few more messages than Uni for these cases, but due to their overhead for updating the error thresholds of the nodes, the overall number of transmitted messages was about the same for all techniques.

Sensitivity in Magnitude of Sensor Measurements. In Figs. 7, 8 we vary the percentage of unstable nodes (nodes that make very large steps) from 0 to 100% and plot the total number of messages for T_{all} and T_{random} ($P_{workaholic}$=0, E_Global=500). For $P_{unstable}$=1 the error threshold (500) is too small to have an effect on the number of messages and all algorithms have practically the same behavior. For smaller values of $P_{unstable}$, algorithm PGA results in a reduction in the total number of messages by a factor of up to 3.8 and 5.5 compared to BBA and Uni respectively.

7 Conclusions

In this paper we proposed a framework for in-network data aggregation that supports the evaluation of aggregate queries in error-tolerant applications over sensor networks. Unlike previous approaches, our algorithms exploit the tree hierarchy that messages follow in such applications to significantly reduce the number of transmitted messages and, therefore, increase the lifetime of the network. Our algorithms are based on two key ideas that we presented in this paper. Firstly, the residual mode of operation for nodes in the aggregation tree allows nodes to apply their error filters to the partial aggregates of their subtrees and, therefore, potentially suppress messages from being transmitted towards the root node of the tree. A second key idea is the use of simple

Table 3. (a) Used Configurations; (b) First number is total number of messages (in thousands) in the network when using parameters of Conf1, second for Conf2. Uni does not use these parameters. Best numbers for each algorithm in bold

Parameters	Configuration Conf1	Conf2
Upd	50	20
shrinkFactor	0.6	0.95
Invocations	Fewer	Frequent
Error Amount Redistributed	Significant	Smaller

(a)

	T_{leaves}	T_{all}	T_{random}
PGA+Res	**423** / 978	**479** / 903	**677** / 1,207
PGA+$NoRes$	463 / 924	558 / 894	830 / 1,454
BBA+Res	2,744 / 1,654	2,471 / **1,426**	3,775 / 2,657
BBA+$NoRes$	3,203 / **1,394**	2,967 / 1,481	4,229 / **2,474**
Uni+Res	**2,568**	**2,451**	**3,906**
Uni+$NoRes$	**2,568**	2,642	4,044
(E_Global=0)+Res	**4,176**	**4,176**	**5,142**

(b)

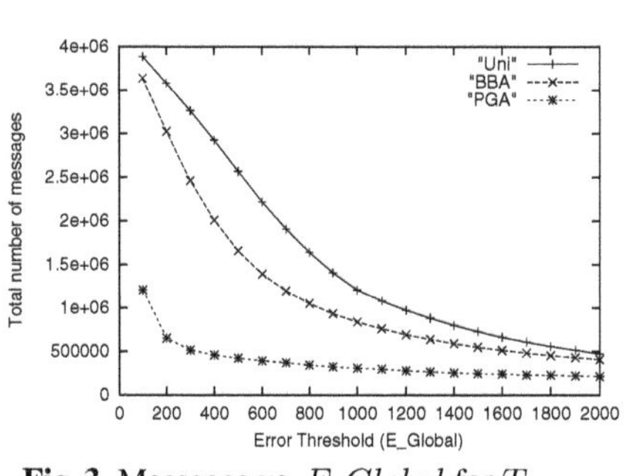

Fig. 3. Messages vs. E_Global for T_{leaves}

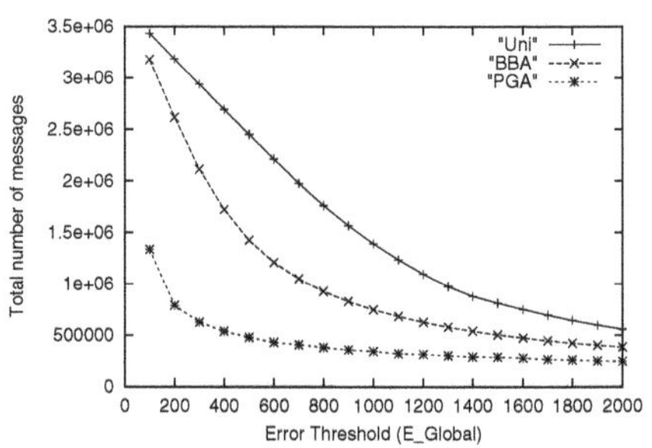

Fig. 4. Messages vs. E_Global for T_{all}

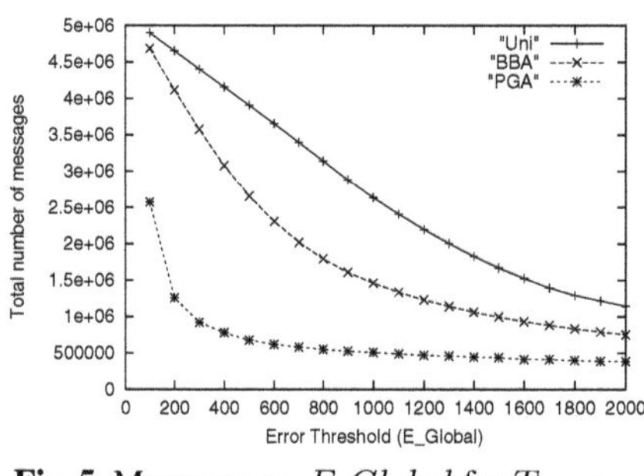

Fig. 5. Messages vs. E_Global for T_{random}

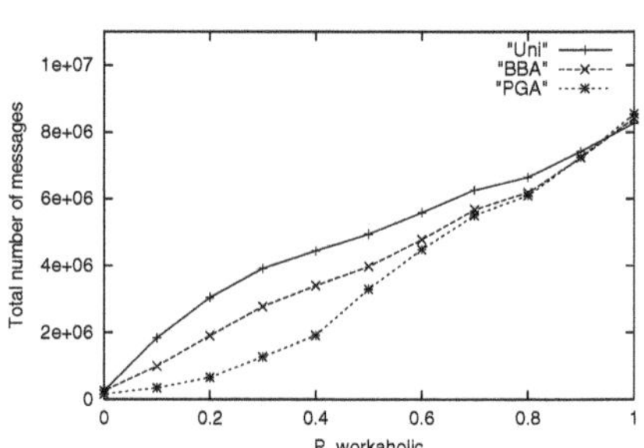

Fig. 6. Messages vs. $P_{workaholic}$ for T_{all}

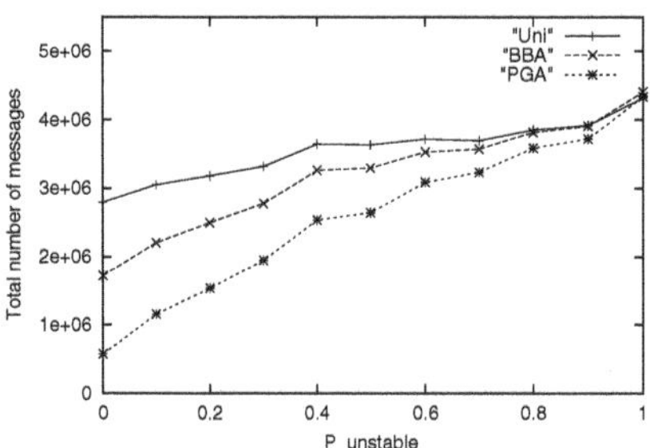

Fig. 7. Messages vs. $P_{unstable}$ for T_{all}

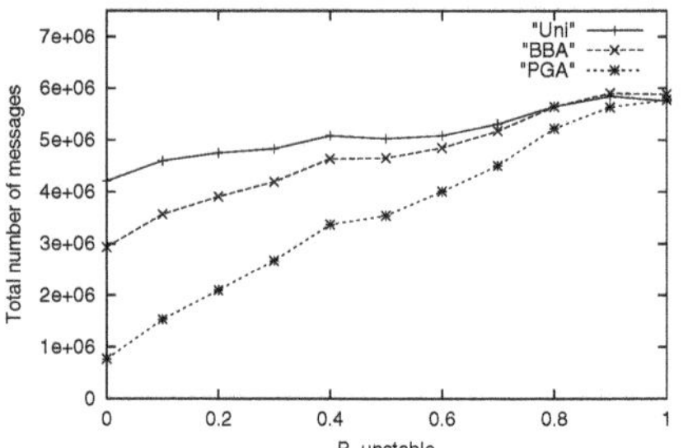

Fig. 8. Messages vs. $P_{unstable}$ for T_{random}

and local statistics to estimate the potential gain of allocating additional error to nodes in a subtree. This is a significant improvement over previous approaches that require a large amount of information to be continuously transmitted to the root node of the tree, therefore defeating their purpose, namely the reduction in the amount of transmitted information in the network. Through an extensive set of experiments, we have shown in this paper that while the distribution of the error based on the computed gains is the major factor for the effectiveness of our techniques compared to other approaches, the fusion of the two ideas provides even larger improvements.

References

1. D. Barbará and H. Garcia-Molina. The Demarcation Protocol: A Technique for Maintaining Linear Arithmetic Constraints in Distributed Database Systems. In *EDBT*, 1992.
2. A. Cerpa and D. Estrin. ASCENT: Adaptive Self-Configuring sEnsor Network Topologies. In *INFOCOM*, 2002.
3. J. Chen, D.J. Dewitt, F. Tian, and Y. Wang. NiagaraCQ: A Scalable Continuous Query System for Internet Databases. In *ACM SIGMOD*, 2000.
4. R. Cheng, D. V. Kalashnikov, and S. Prabhakar. Evaluating Probabilistic Queries over Imprecise Data. In *ACM SIGMOD Conference*, pages 551–562, 2003.
5. J. Considine, F. Li, G. Kollios, and J. Byers. Approximate Aggregation Techniques for Sensor Databases. In *ICDE*, 2004.
6. D. Estrin, R. Govindan, J. Heidermann, and S. Kumar. Next Century Challenges: Scalable Coordination in Sensor Networks. In *MobiCOM*, 1999.
7. J. Heidermann, F. Silva, C. Intanagonwiwat, R. Govindanand D. Estrin, and D. Ganesan. Building Efficient Wireless Sensor Networks with Low-Level Naming. In *SOSP*, 2001.
8. C. Intanagonwiwat, D. Estrin, R. Govindan, and J. Heidermann. Impact of Network Density on Data Aggregation in Wireless Sensor Networks. In *ICDCS*, 2002.
9. S. Madden, M. J. Franklin, J. M. Hellerstein, and W. Hong. Tag: A Tiny Aggregation Service for ad hoc Sensor Networks. In *OSDI Conf.*, 2002.
10. S. Madden, M. J. Franklin, J. M. Hellerstein, and W. Hong. The Design of an Acquisitional Query processor for Sensor Networks. In *ACM SIGMOD Conf*, June 2003.
11. C. Olston, J. Jiang, and J. Widom. Adaptive Filters for Continuous Queries over Distributed Data Streams. In *ACM SIGMOD Conference*, pages 563–574, 2003.
12. M. A. Sharaf, J. Beaver, A. Labrinidis, and P. K. Chrysanthis. TiNA: A Scheme for Temporal Coherency-Aware in-Network Aggregation. In *MobiDE*, 2003.
13. N. Soparkar and A. Silberschatz. Data-value Partitioning and Virtual Messages. In *Proceedings of PODS*, pages 357–367, Nashville, Tennessee, April 1990.
14. D.B. Terry, D. Goldberg, D. Nichols, and B.M. Oki. Continuous Queries over Append-Only Databases. In *ACM SIGMOD*, 1992.
15. Y. Yao and J. Gehrke. The Cougar Approach to In-Network Query Processing in Sensor Networks. *SIGMOD Record*, 31(3):9–18, 2002.

Efficient Similarity Search for Hierarchical Data in Large Databases

Karin Kailing[1], Hans-Peter Kriegel[1], Stefan Schönauer[1], and Thomas Seidl[2]

[1] University of Munich
Institute for Computer Science
{kailing,kriegel,schoenauer}@informatik.uni-muenchen.de
[2] RWTH Aachen University
Department of Computer Science IX
seidl@informatik.rwth-aachen.de

Abstract. Structured and semi-structured object representations are getting more and more important for modern database applications. Examples for such data are hierarchical structures including chemical compounds, XML data or image data. As a key feature, database systems have to support the search for similar objects where it is important to take into account both the structure and the content features of the objects. A successful approach is to use the edit distance for tree structured data. As the computation of this measure is NP-complete, constrained edit distances have been successfully applied to trees. While yielding good results, they are still computationally complex and, therefore, of limited benefit for searching in large databases. In this paper, we propose a filter and refinement architecture to overcome this problem. We present a set of new filter methods for structural and for content-based information in tree-structured data as well as ways to flexibly combine different filter criteria. The efficiency of our methods, resulting from the good selectivity of the filters is demonstrated in extensive experiments with real-world applications.

1 Introduction

Recently, databases are used more and more to store complex objects from scientific, engineering or multimedia applications. In addition to a variety of content-based attributes, complex objects typically carry some kind of internal structure which often forms a hierarchy. Examples of such data include chemical compounds, CAD drawings, XML documents, web sites or color images. The efficient search for similar objects in such databases, for example to classify new objects or to cluster database objects, is a key feature in those application domains. Beside the internal structure of the objects, the content information stored in the tree structure determines the similarity of different objects, too. Whereas the concept of feature vectors has proven to be very successful for unstructured content data, we particularly address the internal structure of similar objects. For this purpose we discuss several similarity measures for trees as proposed in the literature [1,2,3]. These measures are well suited for hierarchical objects and have been applied to web site analysis [4], structural similarity of XML documents [5], shape recognition [6] and chemical substructure search [4], for instance. A general problem

E. Bertino et al. (Eds.): EDBT 2004, LNCS 2992, pp. 676–693, 2004.
© Springer-Verlag Berlin Heidelberg 2004

of all those measures is their computational complexity, which makes them unsuitable for large databases. The core idea of our approach is to apply a filter criterion to the database objects in order to obtain a small set of candidate answers to a query. The final result is then retrieved from this candidate set through the use of the original complex similarity measure. This filter-refinement architecture reduces the number of expensive similarity distance calculations and speeds up the search process. To extend this concept to the new problem of searching similar tree structures, efficient and effective filters for structural properties are required. In this paper, we propose several new filter methods for tree structures and also demonstrate how to combine them with filters for content information in order to obtain a high filter selectivity.

In the next section, we discuss several measures for structural similarity. In section 3, the concept of a filter-refinement architecture is presented, while section 4 deals with our filter methods. Finally, we present an experimental evaluation of our filters, before we conclude the paper.

2 Structural Similarity

Quantifying the similarity of two trees requires a structural similarity measure. There exist several similarity measures for general graphs in the literature [7,8,9]. All of them either suffer from a high computational complexity or are limited to special graph types. Papadopoulos and Manolopoulos presented a measure based on certain edit operations for general graphs [10]. They use the degree sequence of a graph as feature vector and the Manhattan distance between the feature vectors as similarity measure. While their measure can be calculated efficiently, it is not applicable to attributed graphs. Consequently, special distance measures for labeled trees which exploit the structure and content of trees become necessary. Jiang, Wang and Zhang [1] suggested a measure based on a structural alignment of trees. They also prove that the structural alignment problem for trees is NP-hard if the degree of the trees is not bounded. Selkow [2] presented a tree-to-tree editing algorithm for ordered labeled trees. It is a first step towards the most common approach to measure tree similarity, which is the edit distance. The edit distance, well known from string matching [11,12], is the minimal number of edit operations necessary to transform one tree into the other. There are many variants of the edit distance known, depending on which edit operations are allowed. The basic form allows two edit operations, i.e. the insertion and the deletion of a tree node. The insertion of a node n in a tree below a node p means that p becomes the parent of n and a subset of p's children become n's children. The deletion of a node is the inverse operation to the insertion of the node. In the case of attributed nodes, as they appear in most real world applications, the change of a node label is introduced as a third basic operation. Using those operations, we can define the edit distance between two trees as follows.

Definition 1 (edit sequence, cost of an edit sequence). *An edit operation e is the insertion, deletion or relabeling of a node in a tree t. Each edit operation e is assigned a non-negative cost $c(e)$. The cost of a sequence of edit operations $S = \langle e_1, \ldots, e_m \rangle$, $c(S)$, is defined as the sum of the cost of each edit operation in S, i.e. $c(S) = c(e_1) + \ldots + c(e_m)$.*

Definition 2 (edit distance). *The edit distance between two trees* t_1 *and* t_2, $ED(t_1, t_2)$, *is the minimum cost of all edit sequences that transform* t_1 *into* t_2*:*
$ED(t_1, t_2) = min\{c(S)|S\, a\, sequence\, of\, edit\, operations\, transforming\, t_1\, into\, t_2\}$

A great advantage of using the edit distance as a similarity measure is that along with the distance value, a mapping between the nodes in the two trees is provided in terms of the edit sequence. The mapping can be visualized and can serve as an explanation of the similarity distance to the user. This is especially important in the context of similarity search, as different users often have a different notion of similarity in mind. Here, an explanation component can help the user to adapt weights for the distance measure in order to reflect the individual notion of similarity. Zhang, Statman and Shasha, however, showed that computing the edit distance between unordered labeled trees is NP-complete [13]. Obviously, such a complex similarity measure is unsuitable for large databases. To overcome this problem, Zhang proposed a constrained edit distance between trees, the degree-2 edit distance. The main idea behind this distance measure is that only insertions or deletions of nodes with a maximum number of two neighbors are allowed.

Definition 3 (degree-2 edit distance). *The edit distance between two trees* t_1 *and* t_2, $ED_2(t_1, t_2)$, *is the minimum cost of all degree-2 edit sequences that transform* t_1 *into* t_2 *or vice versa. A degree-2 edit sequence consists only of insertions or deletions of nodes* n *with* $degree(n) \leq 2$*, or of relabelings:*
$ED_2(t_1, t_2) = min\{c(S)|S\ is\ a\ degree\text{-}2\ edit\ sequence\ transforming\ t_1\ into\ t_2\}$

One should note that the degree-2 edit distance is well defined in the sense that two trees can always be transformed into each other by using only degree-2 edit operations. In [14] an algorithm is presented to compute the degree-2 edit distance in $O(|t_1||t_2|D)$ time, where D is the maximum of the degrees of t_1 and t_2 and $|t_i|$ denotes the number of nodes in t_i. Whereas this measure has a polynomial time complexity, it is still too complex for the use in large databases. To overcome this problem, we extend the paradigm of filter-refinement architectures to the context of structural similarity search.

3 Multistep Query Processing

The main goal of a filter-refinement architecture, as depicted in figure 1, is to reduce the number of complex and time consuming distance calculations in the query process. To achieve this goal, query processing is performed in two or more steps. The first step is a filter step which returns a number of candidate objects from the database. For those candidate objects the exact similarity distance is then determined in the refinement step and the objects fulfilling the query predicate are reported. To reduce the overall search time, the filter step has to fulfill certain constraints. First, it is essential, that the filter predicate is considerably easier to determine than the exact similarity measure. Second, a substantial part of the database objects must be filtered out. Obviously, it depends on the complexity of the similarity measure what filter selectivity is sufficient. Only if both conditions are satisfied, the performance gain through filtering is greater than the cost for the extra processing step.

Additionally, the completeness of the filter step is an important property. Completeness in this context means that all database objects satisfying the query condition are

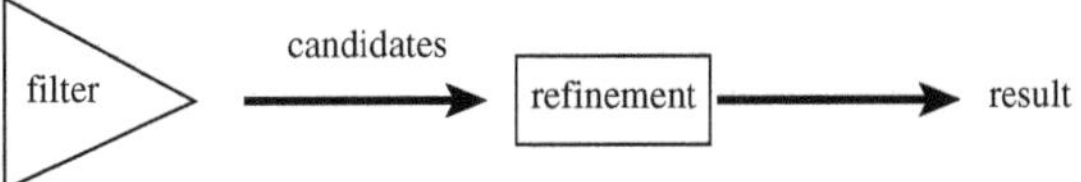

Fig. 1. The filter-refinement architecture.

included in the candidate set. Available similarity search algorithms guarantee completeness if the distance function in the filter step fulfills the following lower-bounding property. For any two objects p and q, a lower-bounding distance function d_{lb} in the filter step has to return a value that is not greater than the exact distance d_e of p and q, i.e. $d_{lb}(p,q) \leq d_e(p,q)$. With a lower-bounding distance function it is possible to safely filter out all database objects which have a filter distance greater than the current query range because the similarity distance of those objects cannot be less than the query range.

Using a multi-step query architecture requires efficient algorithms which actually make use of the filter step. Agrawal, Faloutsos and Swami proposed such an algorithm for range search [15]. In [16] a multi-step algorithm for k-nearest-neighbor search is presented, which is optimal in the sense that the minimal number of exact distance calculations are performed during query processing.

4 Structural and Content-Based Filters for Unordered Trees

In this section, we introduce several filtering techniques that support efficient similarity search for tree-structured data. Whereas single-valued features including the height of a tree, the number of nodes, or the degree of a tree, are of limited use, as we learned from preliminary experiments, we propose the use of feature histograms The advantage of this extension is that there is more information provided to the filter step for the purpose of generating candidates and, thus, the discriminative power is increased. Additionally, a variety of multidimensional index structures and efficient search algorithms are available for vector data including histograms. The particular feature histograms which we propose in the following are based on the height, the degree or the label of individual nodes.

4.1 Filtering Based on the Height of Nodes

A promising way to filter unordered trees based on their structure is to take the height of nodes into account. A very simple technique is to use the height of a tree as a single feature. The difference of the height of two trees is an obvious lower bound for the edit distance between those trees, but this filter clearly is very coarse, as two trees with completely different structure but the same height cannot be distinguished.

A more fine-grained and more sensitive filter can be obtained by creating a histogram of node heights in a tree and using the difference between those histograms as a filter distance. A first approach is to determine the distance of each node in the tree to the root node and then to store the distribution of those values in a histogram. Unfortunately, the distance between two such histograms is not guaranteed to be a lower bound for the edit

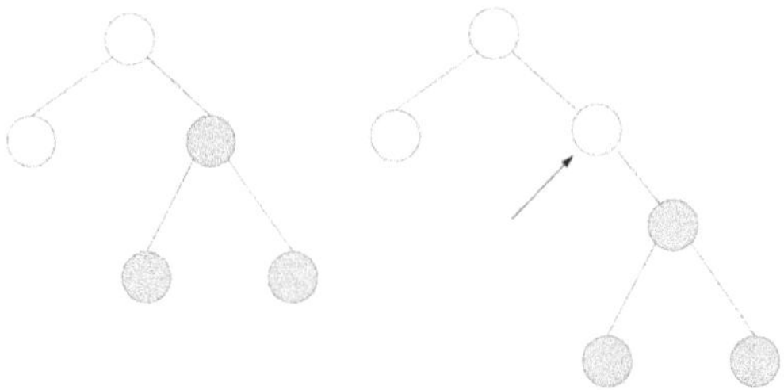

Fig. 2. A single insertion can change the distance to the root for several nodes.

distance or the degree-2 edit distance between the original trees. As can be seen in figure 2, the insertion of a single node may change the height of all nodes in its subtree. Thus, the number of affected histogram bins is only bounded by the height of the tree.

Therefore, we propose a different approach to consider the height of a node. Instead of the distance of a node from the root, its leaf distance is used to approximate the structure of a tree.

Definition 4 (leaf distance). *The leaf distance $d_l(n)$ of a node n is the maximum length of a path from n to any leaf node in the subtree rooted at n.*

Based on this definition, we introduce the leaf distance histogram of a tree as illustrated in figure 3.

Definition 5 (leaf distance histogram). *The leaf distance histogram $h_l(t)$ of a tree t is a vector of length $k = 1 + height(t)$ where the value of any bin $i \in 0, \ldots, k$ is the number of nodes that share the leaf distance i, i.e. $h_l(t)[i] = |n \in t, d_l(n) = i|$.*

For the proof of the following theorem the definition of a maximum leaf path is useful:

Definition 6 (maximum leaf path). *A maximum leaf path (MLP) of a node n in a tree t is a path of maximum length from n to a leaf node in the subtree rooted by n.*

An important observation is that adjacent nodes on an MLP are mapped to adjacent bins in the leaf distance histogram as illustrated in figure 4.

Theorem 1. *For any two trees t_1 and t_2, the L_1-distance of the leaf distance histograms is a lower bound of the edit distance of t_1 and t_2:*

$$L_1(h_l(t_1), h_l(t_2)) \leq ED(t_1, t_2)$$

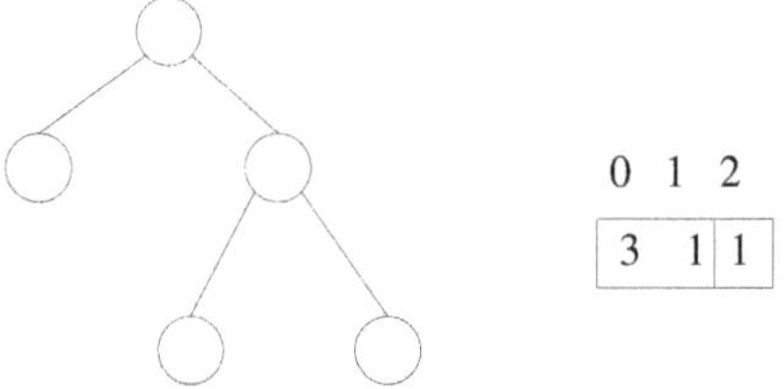

Fig. 3. Leaf distance of nodes and leaf distance histogram.

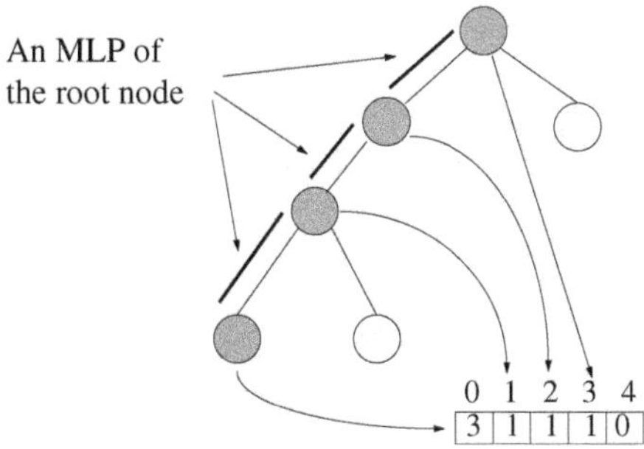

Fig. 4. A maximum leaf path.

Proof. Given two arbitrary trees t_0 and t_m, let us consider an edit sequence $S = \langle S_1, \ldots, S_m \rangle$ that transforms t_0 to t_m. We proceed by induction over the length $m = |S|$. If $m = 0$, i.e. $S = \langle\rangle$ and $t_0 = t_m$, the values of $L_1(h_l(t_0), h_l(t_m))$ and of $c(S)$ both are equal to zero. For $m > 0$, let us assume that the lower-bounding property already holds for the trees t_0 and t_{m-1}, i.e. $L_1(h_l(t_0), h_l(t_{m-1})) \leq c(\langle S1, \ldots, S_{m-1} \rangle)$. When extending the sequence $\langle S_1, \ldots, S_{m-1} \rangle$ by S_m to S, the right hand side of the inequality is increased by $c(S_m) = 1$.

The situation on the left hand side is as follows. The edit step S_m may be a relabeling, an insertion or a deletion. Obviously, the effect on the leaf distance histogram $h_l(t_{m-1})$ is void in case of a relabeling, i.e. $h_l(t_m) = h_l(t_{m-1})$, and the inequality $L_1(h_l(t_0), h_l(t_m)) = L_1(h_l(t_0), h_l(t_{m-1})) \leq c(S)$ holds.

The key observation for an insert or a delete operation is that only a single bin is affected in the histogram in any case. When a node ν is inserted, for all nodes below the insertion point, clearly, the leaf distance does not change. Only the leaf distance of any predecessor of the inserted node may or may not be increased by the insertion. Therefore, if ν does not belong to an MLP of any of its predecessors, only the bin affected by the inserted node is increased by one. This means that in the leaf distance histogram exactly one bin is increased by one. On the other hand, if an MLP of any of the predecessors of ν containing ν exists, then we only have to consider the longest of those MLPs. Due to the insertion, this MLP grows in size by one. As all nodes along the MLP are mapped into consecutive histogram bins, exactly one more bin than before is influenced by the nodes on the MLP. This means that exactly one bin in the leaf distance histogram changes due to the insertion. As insertion and deletion are symmetric operations, the same considerations hold for the deletion of a node.

The preceding considerations hold for all edit sequences transforming a tree t_1 into a tree t_2 and particularly include the minimum cost edit sequence. Therefore, the lower-bounding relationship immediately holds for the edit distance $ED(t_1, t_2)$ of two trees t_1 and t_2, too.

It should be noticed that the above considerations do not only hold for the edit distance but also for the degree-2 edit distance. Therefore, the following theorem allows us also to use leaf-distance histograms for the degree-2 edit distance.

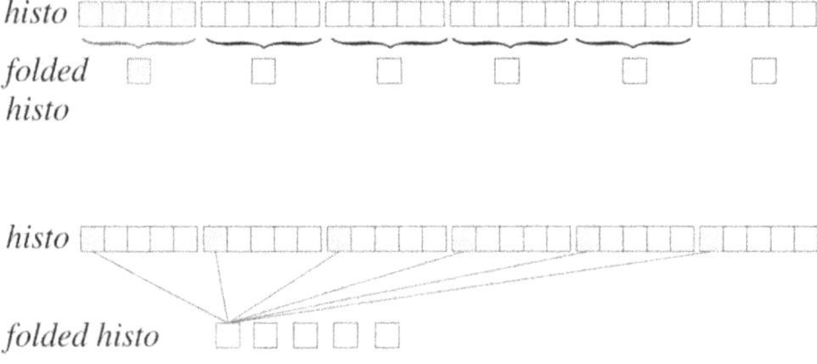

Fig. 5. Folding techniques for histograms: The technique of Papadopoulos and Manolopoulos (top) and the modulo folding technique (bottom).

Theorem 2. *For any two trees t_1 and t_2, the L_1-distance of the leaf distance histograms is a lower bound of the degree-2 edit distance of t_1 and t_2:*

$$L_1(h_l(t_1), h_l(t_2)) \leq ED_2(t_1, t_2)$$

Proof. Analogously to the proof of theorem 1.

Theorem 1 and 2 also allow us to use leaf distance histograms as a filter for the weighted edit and weighted degree-2 edit distance. This statement is justified by the following considerations. As shown above, the L_1-distance of two leaf distance histograms gives a lower bound for the insert and delete operations that are necessary to transform the two corresponding trees into each other. This fact also holds for weighted relabeling operations, as weights do not have any influence on the necessary structural modifications. But even when insert/delete operations are weighted, our filter can be used as long as their exists a smallest possible weight w_{min} for an insert or delete operation. In this case, the term $(L_1(h_l(t_1), h_l(t_2)) \cdot w_{min})$ is a lower bound for the weighted edit and degree-2 edit distance between the trees t_1 and t_2. Since we assume metric properties as well as the symmetry of insertions and deletions for the distance, the triangle inequality guarantees the existence of such a minimum weight. Otherwise, any relabeling of a node would be performed cheaper by a deletion and a corresponding insertion operation. Moreover, structural differences of objects would be reflected only weakly if structural changes are not weighted properly.

Histogram folding. Another property of leaf distance histograms is that their size is unbounded as long as the height of the trees in the database is also unbounded. This problem arises for several feature vector types, including the degree histograms presented in section 4.2. Papadopoulos and Manolopoulos [10] address this problem by folding the histograms into vectors with fixed dimension. This is done in a piecewise grouping process. For example, when a 5-dimensional feature vector is desired, the first one fifth of the histogram bins is summed up and the result is used as the first component of the feature vector. This is done analogously for the rest of the histogram bins. The above approach could also be used for leaf distance histograms, but it has the disadvantage that the maximal height of all trees in the database has to be known in advance. For dynamic data sets, this precondition cannot be fulfilled. Therefore, we propose a different technique that yields fixed-size n-dimensional histograms by adding up the values of certain entries in the leaf distance histogram. Instead of summing up adjacent bins in the histogram, we add up those with the same index modulo n, as depicted in figure 5. This way, histograms of distinct length can be compared, and there is no bound for the length of the original histograms.

Definition 7 (folded histogram). *A folded histogram $h_{fn}(h)$ of a histogram h for a given parameter n is a vector of size n where the value of any bin $i \in 0, \ldots, n-1$ is the sum of all bins k in h with $k \bmod n = i$, i.e.*

$$h_{fn}(h)[i] = \sum_{k=0 \ldots (|h|-1) \wedge k \bmod n = i} h[k]$$

The following theorem justifies to use folded histograms in a multi-step query processing architecture.

Theorem 3. *For any two histograms h_1 and h_2 and any parameter $n \geq 1$, the L_1-distance of the folded histograms of h_1 and h_2 is a lower bound for the L_1-distance of h_1 and h_2:*

$$L_1(h_{fn}(h_1), h_{fn}(h_2)) \leq L_1(h_1, h_2)$$

Proof. Let $len = n \cdot \lceil \frac{max(h_1,h_2)}{n} \rceil$ be the length of h_1 and h_2. If necessary, h_1 and h_2 are extended with bins containing 0 until $|h_1| = len$ and $|h_2| = len$. Then the following holds:

$$\begin{aligned}
& L_1(h_{fn}(h_1), h_{fn}(h_2)) \\
&= \sum_{i=0}^{n-1} \left| \sum_{\substack{k=0\ldots((|h_1|-1) \\ \wedge k\ MOD\ n=i}} h_1[k] - \sum_{\substack{k=0\ldots((|h_2|-1) \\ \wedge k\ MOD\ n=i}} h_2[k] \right| \\
&= \sum_{i=0}^{n-1} \left| \sum_{j=0}^{(len\ DIV\ n)-1} h_1[i+j \cdot n] - \sum_{j=0}^{(len\ DIV\ n)-1} h_2[i+j \cdot n] \right| \\
&\leq \sum_{i=0}^{n-1} \sum_{j=0}^{(len\ DIV\ n)-1} |h_1[i+j \cdot n] - h_2[i+j \cdot n]| \\
&= \sum_{j=0}^{len} |h_1[k] - h_2[k]| \\
&= L_1(h_1, h_2)
\end{aligned}$$

4.2 Filtering Based on Degree of Nodes

The degrees of the nodes are another structural property of trees which can be used as a filter for the edit distances. Again, a simple filter can be obtained by using the maximal degree of all nodes in a tree t, denoted by $degree_{max}(t)$, as a single feature. The difference between the maximal degrees of two trees is an obvious lower bound for the edit distance as well as for the degree-2 edit distance. As before, this single-valued filter is very coarse and using a degree histogram clearly increases the selectivity.

Definition 8 (degree histogram). *The degree histogram $h_d(t)$ of a tree t is a vector of length $k = 1 + degree_{max}(t)$ where the value of any bin $i \in 0, \ldots, k$ is the number of nodes that share the degree i, i.e. $h_d(t)[i] = |n \in t, degree(n) = i|$.*

Theorem 4. *For any two trees t_1 and t_2, the L_1-distance of the degree histograms divided by three is a lower bound of the edit distance of t_1 and t_2:*

$$\frac{L_1(h_d(t_1), h_d(t_2))}{3} \leq ED(t_1, t_2)$$

Proof. Given two arbitrary trees t_0 and t_m, let us consider an edit sequence $S = \langle S1, \ldots, S_m \rangle$ that transforms t_0 into t_m. We proceed by induction over the length of the sequence $m = |S|$. If $m = 0$, i.e. $S = \langle\rangle$ and $t_0 = t_m$, the values of $\frac{L_1(h_d(t_0), h_d(t_m))}{3}$ and of $c(S)$ both are equal to zero. For $m > 0$, let us assume that the lower-bounding property already holds for t_0 and t_{m-1}, i.e. $\frac{L_1(h_d(t_0), h_d(t_{m-1}))}{3} \leq c(\langle S1, \ldots, S_{m-1} \rangle)$. When extending the sequence $\langle S_1, \ldots, S_{m-1} \rangle$ by S_m to S, the right hand side of the inequality is increased by $c(S_m) = 1$. The situation on the left hand side is as follows. The edit step S_m may be a relabeling, an insert or a delete operation. Obviously, for a relabeling, the degree histogram $h_d(t_{m-1})$ does not change, i.e. $h_d(t_m) = h_d(t_{m-1})$ and the inequality $\frac{L_1(h_d(t_0), h_d(t_m))}{3} = \frac{L_1(h_d(t_0), h_d(t_{m-1}))}{3} \leq c(S)$ holds.

The insertion of a single node affects the histogram and the L_1-distance of the histograms in the following way:

1. The inserted node n causes an increase in the bin of n's degree. That may change the L_1-distance by at most one.
2. The degree of n's parent node p may change. In the worst case this affects two bins. The bin of p's former degree is decreased by one while the bin of its new degree is increased by one. Therefore, the L_1-distance may additionally be changed by at most two.
3. No other nodes are affected.

From the above three points it follows that the L_1-distance of the two histograms $h_d(t_{m-1})$ and $h_d(t_m)$ changes by at most three. Therefore, the following holds:

$$\frac{L_1(h_d(t_0), h_d(t_m))}{3} \leq \frac{L_1(h_d(t_0), h_d(t_{m-1})) + 3}{3}$$

$$\frac{L_1(h_d(t_0), h_d(t_m))}{3} \leq \frac{L_1(h_d(t_0), h_d(t_{m-1})}{3} + 1$$

$$\frac{L_1(h_d(t_0), h_d(t_m))}{3} \leq c(\langle S1, \ldots, S_{m-1} \rangle) + 1$$

$$\frac{L_1(h_d(t_0), h_d(t_m))}{3} \leq c(\langle S1, \ldots, S_{m-1}, S_m \rangle)$$

$$\frac{L_1(h_d(t_1), h_d(t_2))}{3} \leq ED(t_1, t_2)$$

As the above considerations also hold for the degree-2 edit distance, theorem 4 holds analogously for this similarity measure.

4.3 Filtering Based on Node Labels

Apart from the structure of the trees, the content features, expressed through node labels, have an impact on the similarity of attributed trees. The node labels can be used to define a filter function. To be useful in our filter-refinement architecture, this filter method has to deliver a lower bound for the edit cost when transforming two trees into each other. The difference between the distribution of the values within a tree and the distribution of the values in another tree can be used to develop a lower-bounding filter. To ensure efficient evaluation of the filter, the distribution of those values has to be approximated for the filter step.

One way to approximate the distribution of values is to use histograms. In this case, an n-dimensional histogram is derived by dividing the range of the node label into n bins. Then, each bin is assigned the number of nodes in the tree whose value is in the range of the bin. To estimate the edit distance or the degree-2 edit distance between two trees, half of the L_1-distance of their corresponding label histograms is appropriate. A single insert or delete operation changes exactly one bin of such a label histogram, a single relabeling operation can influence at most two histogram bins. If a node is assigned to a new bin after relabeling, the entry in the old bin is decreased by one and the entry in the new bin is increased by one (cf. figure 6). Otherwise, a relabeling does not change the histogram. This method also works for weighted variants of the edit distance and the degree-2 edit distance as long as there is a minimal weight for a relabeling operation. In this case, the calculated filter value has to be multiplied by this minimal weight in order to gain a lower-bounding filter.

This histogram approach applies to discrete label distributions very well. However, for continuous label spaces, the use of a continuous weight function which may become arbitrarily small, can be reasonable. In this case, a discrete histogram approach can not be used. An example for such a weight function is the Euclidean distance in the color space, assuming trees where the node labels are colors. Here, the cost for changing a color value is proportional to the Euclidean distance between the original and the target color. As this distance can be infinitely small, it is impossible to estimate the relabeling cost based on a label histogram as in the above cases.

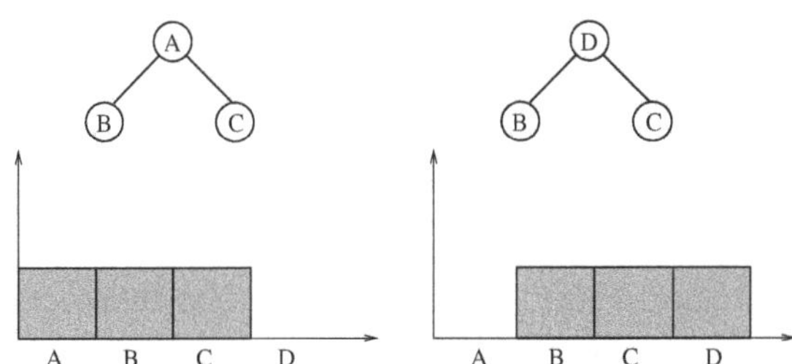

Fig. 6. A single relabeling operation may result in a label histogram distance of two.

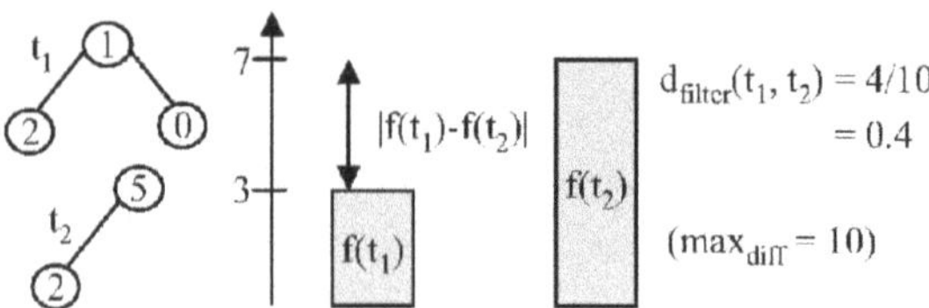

Fig. 7. Filtering for continuous weight functions.

More formally, when using the term 'continuous weight function' we mean that the cost for changing a node label from value x_1 to value x_2 is proportional to $|x_1 - x_2|$. Let max_{diff} be the maximal possible difference between two attribute values. Then $|x_1 - x_2|$ has to be normalized to $[0, 1]$ by dividing it through max_{diff}, assuming that the maximal cost for a single insertion, deletion or relabeling is one. To develop a filter method for attributes with such a weight function, we exploit the following property of the edit distance measure. The cost-minimal edit sequence between two trees removes the difference between the distributions of attribute values of those two trees. It does not matter whether this is achieved through relabelings, insertions or deletions.

For our filter function we define the following feature value $f(t)$ for a tree t:

$$f(t) = \sum_{i=1}^{|t|} |x_i|$$

Here x_i is the attribute value of the i-th node in t and $|t|$ is the size of tree t. The absolute difference between two such feature values is an obvious lower bound for the difference between the distribution of attribute values of the corresponding trees. Consequently, we use

$$d_{filter}(t_1, t_2) = \frac{|f(t_1) - f(t_2)|}{max_{diff}}$$

as a filter function for continuous label spaces, see figure 7 for an illustration. Once more, the above considerations also hold for the degree-2 edit distance.

To simplify the presentation we assumed that a node label consists of just one single attribute. But usually a node will carry several different attributes. If possible, the attribute with the highest selectivity can be chosen for filtering. In practice, there is often no such single attribute. In this case, filters for different attributes can be combined with the technique described in the following section.

4.4 Combining Filter Methods

All of the above filters use a single feature of an attributed tree to approximate the edit distance or degree-2 edit distance. As the filters are not equally selective in each situation, we propose a method to combine several of the presented filters.

A very flexible way of combining different filters is to follow the inverted list approach, i.e. to apply the different filters independently from each other and then intersect the resulting candidate sets. With this approach, separate index structures for the different filters have to be maintained and for each query, a time-consuming intersection step is necessary. To avoid those disadvantages, we concatenate the different filter histograms and filter values for each object and use a combined distance function as a similarity function.

Definition 9 (Combined distance function). *Let $C = d_i$ be a set of distance functions for trees. Then, the combined distance function d_c is defined to be the maximum of the component functions:*

$$d_C(t_1, t_2) = max\{d_i(t_1, t_2)\}$$

Theorem 5. *For every set of lower-bounding distance functions $C = \{d_{low}(t_1, t_2)\}$, i.e. for all trees t_1 and t_2 $d_i(t_1, t_2) \leq ED(t_1, t_2)$, the combined distance function d_C is a lower bound of the edit distance function d_{ED}:*

$$d_C(t_1, t_2) \leq ED(t_1, t_2)$$

Proof. For all trees t_1 and t_2, the following equivalences hold:

$$\begin{aligned} d_C(t_1, t_2) \leq ED(t_1, t_2) \Leftrightarrow \\ max\{d_i(t_1, t_2)\} \leq ED(t_1, t_2) \Leftrightarrow \\ \forall d_i : d_i(t_1, t_2) \leq ED(t_1, t_2) \end{aligned}$$

The final inequality represents the precondition.

Justified by theorem 5, we apply each separate filter function to its corresponding component of the combined histogram. The combined distance function is derived from the results of this step.

5 Experimental Evaluation

For our tests, we implemented a filter and refinement architecture according to the optimal multi-step k-nearest-neighbor search approach as proposed in [16]. Naturally, the positive effects which we show in the following experiments for k-nn-queries also hold for range queries and for all data mining algorithms based on range queries or k-nn-queries (e.g. clustering, k-nn-classification). As similarity measure for trees, we implemented the degree-2 edit distance algorithm as presented in [14]. The filter histograms were organized in an X-tree [17]. All algorithms were implemented in Java 1.4 and the experiments were run on a workstation with a Xeon 1,7 GHz processor and 2 GB main memory under Linux.

To show the efficiency of our approach, we chose two different applications, an image database and a database of websites which are described in the following.

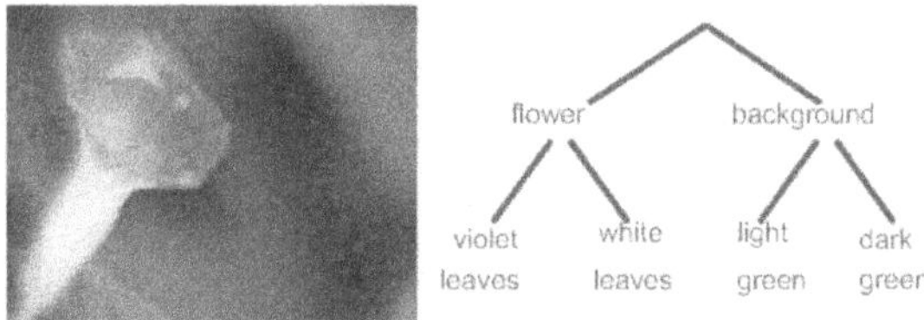

Fig. 8. Structural and content-based information of a picture represented as a tree.

5.1 Image Databases

As one example of tree structured objects we chose images, because for images, both, content-based as well as structural information are important. Figure 8 gives an idea of the two aspects which are present in a picture.

The images we used for our experiments were taken from three real-world databases: a set of 705 black and white pictographs, a set of 8,536 commercially available color images and a set of 43,000 color TV-Images. We extracted trees from those images in a two-step process. First, the images were divided into segments of similar color by a segmentation algorithm. In the second step, a tree was created from those segments by iteratively applying a region-growing algorithm which merges neighboring segments if their colors are similar. This is done until all segments are merged into a single node. As a result, we obtain a set of labeled unordered trees where each node label describes the color, size and horizontal as well as vertical extension of the associated segment. Table 1 shows some statistical information about the trees we generated.

Table 1. Statistics of the data set.

	number of images	number of nodes			height			maximal degree		
		max	min	Ø	max	min	Ø	max	min	Ø
commercial color images	8,536	331	1	30	24	0	3	206	0	18
color TV-images	43,000	109	1	24	13	0	3	71	0	11
black and white pictographs	705	113	3	13	2	1	1	112	2	12

For the first experiments, we used label histograms as described in section 4.3. To derive a discrete label distribution, we reduced the number of different attribute values to 16 different color values for each color channel and 4 different values each for size and extensions. We used a relabeling function with a minimal weight of 0.5. Later on we also show some experiments where we did not reduce the different attribute values and used a continuous weight function for relabeling.

Comparison of our filter types. For our first experiment we used 10,000 TV-images. We created 10-dimensional height and degree histograms and combined them as described in section 4.4. We also built a 24-dimensional combined label histogram which considered the color, size and extensions of all node labels (6 attributes with histograms of size 4).

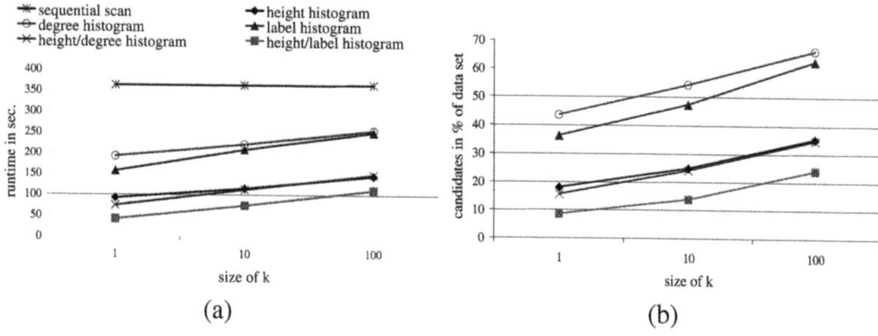

(a) (b)

Fig. 9. Runtime and number of candidates for k-nn-queries on 10,000 color TV-images.

Finally, the combination of this combined label histogram and a 4-dimensional height histogram was taken as another filter criterion. Let us note, that the creation of the filter X-trees took between 25 sec. for the height histogram and 62 sec. for the combined height-label histogram.

We ran 70 k-nearest-neighbor queries (k = 1, 10, 100) for each of our filters. Figure 9 shows the selectivity of our filters, measured in the average number of candidates with respect to the size of the data set. The figures show that filtering based solely on structural (height or degree histogram) or content-based features (label histogram) is not as effective as their combination. Figure 9 also shows that for this data the degree filter is less selective than the height filter. The method which combines the filtering based on the height of the nodes and on content features is most effective. Figure 5.1 additionally depicts the average runtime of our filters compared to the sequential scan. As one can see, we reduced the runtime by a factor of up to 5. Furthermore, the comparison of the two diagrams in figure 9 shows that the runtime is dominated by the number of candidates, whereas the additional overhead due to the filtering is negligible.

Influence of histogram size. In a next step we tested to what extent the size of the histogram influences the size of the candidate set and the corresponding runtime. The results for nearest neighbor queries on 10,000 color TV-images are shown in figure 10. With increasing dimension, the number of candidates as well as the runtime decrease. The comparison of the two diagrams in figure 10 shows that the runtime is again dominated

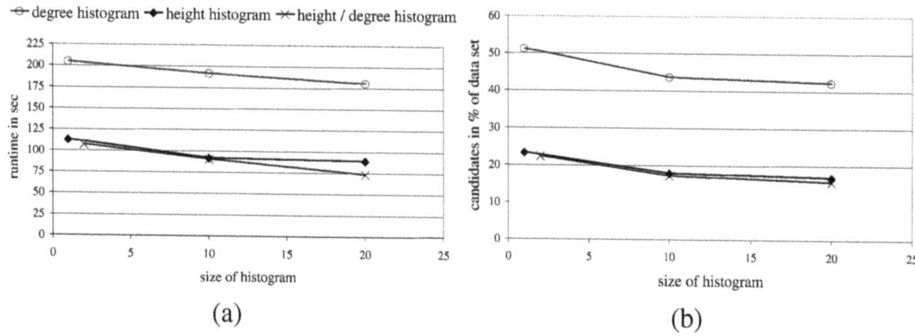

(a) (b)

Fig. 10. Influence of dimensionality of histograms.

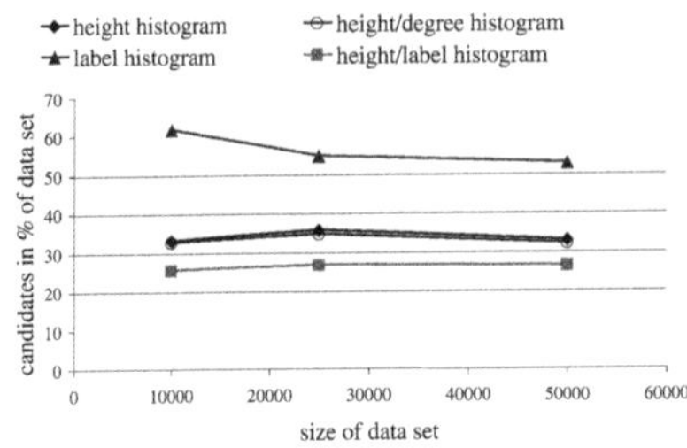

Fig. 11. Scalability versus size of data set.

by the number of candidates, while the additional overhead due to higher dimensional histograms is negligible.

Scalability of filters versus size of data set. For this experiment we united all three image data sets and chose three subsets of size 10,000, 25,000 and 50,000. On these subsets we performed several representative 5-nn queries. Figure 11 shows that the selectivity of our structural filters does not depend on the size of the data set.

Comparison of different filters for a continuous weight function. As mentioned above, we also tested our filters when using a continuous weight function for relabeling. For this experiment, we used the same 10,000 color images as in 5.1. Figure 12 shows the results averaged over 200 k-nn queries. In this case, both the height histogram and the label filter are very selective. Unfortunately, the combination of both does not further enhance the runtime. While there is a slight decrease in the number of candidates, this is used up by the additional overhead of evaluating two different filter criteria.

Comparison with a metric tree. In [18] other efficient access methods for similarity search in metric spaces are presented. In order to support dynamic datasets, we use the X-tree that can be updated at any time. Therefore, we chose to compare our filter methods to the M-tree which analogously is a dynamic index structure for metric spaces.

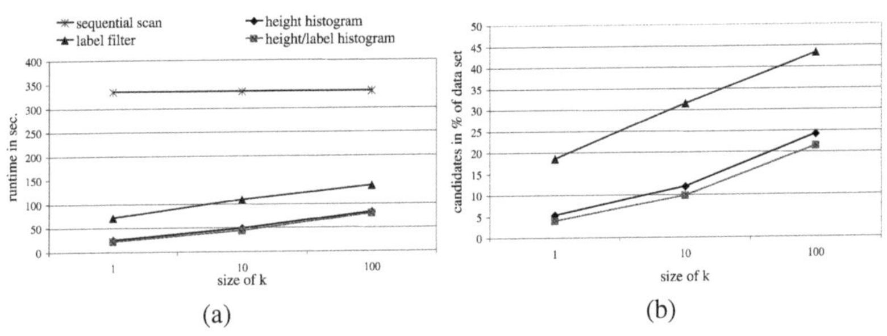

Fig. 12. Runtime and number of candidates when using a continuous weight function.

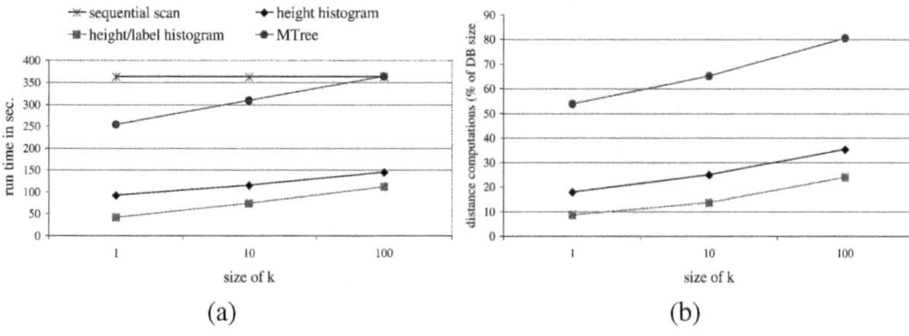

Fig. 13. Runtime and number of distance computations of filter methods compared to the M-Tree.

We implemented the M-tree as described in [19] by using the best split policy mentioned there.

The creation of an M-tree for 1,000 tree objects already took more than one day, due to the split policy that has quadratic time-complexity. The time for the creation of the filter vectors, on the other hand, was in the range of a few seconds. As can be seen in figure 13, the M-tree outperformed the sequential scan for small result sizes. However, all of our filtering techniques significantly outperform the sequential scan and the M-tree index for all result set sizes. This observation is mainly due to the fact that the filtering techniques reduce the number of necessary distance calculations far more than the M-tree index. This behavior results in speed-up factors between 2.5 and 6.2 compared to the M-tree index and even higher factors compared to a simple sequential scan. This way, our multi-step query processing architecture is a significant improvement over the standard indexing approach.

5.2 Web Site Graphs

As demonstrated in [20], the degree-2 edit distance is well suitable for approximate website matching. In website management it can be used for searching similar websites. In [21] web site mining is described as a new way to spot competitors, customers and suppliers in the world wide web.

By choosing the main page as the root, one can represent a website as a rooted, labeled, unordered tree. Each node in the tree represents a webpage of the site and is labeled with the URL of that page. All referenced pages are children of that node and the borders of the website where chosen carefully. See figure 14 for an illustration.

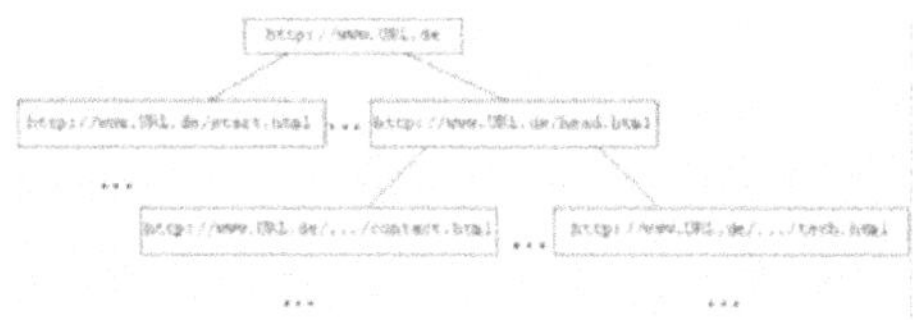

Fig. 14. Part of a website tree.

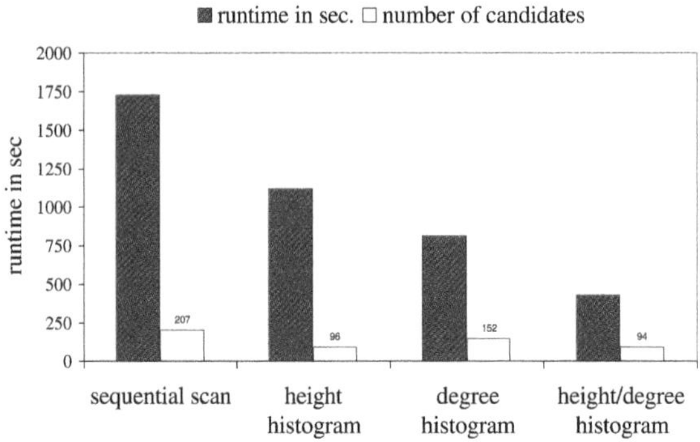

Fig. 15. Average runtime and number of candidates for 5-nn queries.

For our experiment, we used a compressed form of the 207 web sites described in [21], resulting in trees that have 67 nodes on the average. We ran 5-nn-queries on this data. The results are shown in figure 15. We notice that even if the degree filter produces a lot more candidates than the height filter, it results in a better run time. This is due to the fact that it filters out those trees, where the computation of the degree-2 edit distance is especially time-consuming. Using the combination of both histograms, the runtime is reduced by a factor of 4.

6 Conclusions

In this paper, we presented a new approach for efficient similarity search in large databases of tree structures. Based on the degree-2 edit distance as similarity measure, we developed a multi-step query architecture for similarity search in tree structures. For structural as well as for content-based features of unordered attributed trees, we suggested several filter methods. These filter methods significantly reduce the number of complex edit distance calculations necessary for a similarity search. The main idea behind our filter methods is to approximate the distribution of structural and content-based features within a tree by means of feature histograms. Furthermore, we proposed a new technique for folding histograms and a new way to combine different filter methods in order to improve the filter selectivity. We performed extensive experiments on two sets of real data from the domains of image similarity and website mining. Our experiments showed that filtering significantly accelerates the complex task of similarity search for tree-structured objects. Moreover, it turned out that no single feature of a tree is sufficient for effective filtering, but only the combination of structural and content-based filters yields good results.

In our future work, we will explore how different weights for edit operations influence the selectivity of our filter methods. Additionally, we intend to investigate other structural features of trees for their appropriateness in the filter step. In a recent publication [5], an edit distance for XML-documents has been proposed. An interesting question is, how our architecture and filters can be applied to the problem of similarity search in large databases of XML-documents.

References

1. Jiang, T., Wang, L., Zhang, K.: Alignment of trees - an alternative to tree edit. Proc. Int. Conf. on Combinatorial Pattern Matching (CPM), LNCS **807** (1994) 75–86
2. Selkow, S.: The tree-to-tree editing problem. Information Processing Letters **6** (1977) 576–584
3. Zhang, K.: A constrained editing distance between unordered labeled trees. Algorithmica **15** (1996) 205–222
4. Wang, J.T.L., Zhang, K., Chang, G., Shasha, D.: Finding approximate pattersn in undirected acyclic graphs. Pattern Recognition **35** (2002) 473–483
5. Nierman, A., Jagadish, H.V.: Evaluating structural similarity in XML documents. In: Proc. 5th Int. Workshop on the Web and Databases (WebDB 2002), Madison, Wisconsin, USA. (2002) 61–66
6. Sebastian, T.B., Klein, P.N., Kimia, B.B.: Recognition of shapes by editing shock graphs. In: Proc. 8th Int. Conf. on Computer Vision (ICCV'01), Vancouver, BC, Canada. Volume 1. (2001) 755–762
7. Bunke, H., Shearer, K.: A graph distance metric based on the maximal common subgraph. Pattern Recognition Letters **19** (1998) 255–259
8. Chartrand, G., Kubicki, G., Schultz, M.: Graph similarity and distance in graphs. Aequationes Mathematicae **55** (1998) 129–145
9. Kubicka, E., Kubicki, G., Vakalis, I.: Using graph distance in object recognition. In: Proc. ACM Computer Science Conference. (1990) 43–48
10. Papadopoulos, A., Manolopoulos, Y.: Structure-based similarity search with graph histograms. In: Proc. DEXA/IWOSS Int. Workshop on Similarity Search. (1999) 174–178
11. Levenshtein, V.: Binary codes capable of correcting deletions, insertions and reversals. Soviet Physics-Doklady **10** (1966) 707–710
12. Wagner, R.A., Fisher, M.J.: The string-to-string correction problem. Journal of the ACM **21** (1974) 168–173
13. Zhang, K., Statman, R., Shasha, D.: On the editing distance between unordered labeled trees. Information Processing Letters **42** (1992) 133–139
14. Zhang, K., Wang, J., Shasha, D.: On the editing distance between undirected acyclic graphs. International Journal of Foundations of Computer Science **7** (1996) 43–57
15. Agrawal, R., Faloutsos, C., Swami, A.N.: Efficient similarity search in sequence databases. In: Proc. 4th Int. Conf. of Foundations of Data Organization and Algorithms (FODO). (1993) 69–84
16. Seidl, T., Kriegel, H.P.: Optimal multi-step k-nearest neighbor search. In Haas, L.M., Tiwary, A., eds.: Proc. ACM SIGMOD Int. Conf. on Managment of Data, ACM Press (1998) 154–165
17. Berchtold, S., Keim, D., Kriegel, H.P.: The X-tree: An index structure for high-dimensional data. In: 22nd Conference on Very Large Databases, Bombay, India (1996) 28–39
18. Chavez, E., Navarro, G., Baeza-Yates, R., Marroquin, J.: Searching in metric spaces. ACM Computing Surveys **33** (2001) 273–321
19. Ciaccia, P., Patella, M., Zezula, P.: M-tree: An efficient access method for similarity search in metric spaces. In: VLDB'97, Proc. 23rd Int. Conf. on Very Large Databases, August 25-29, 1997, Athens, Greece. (1997) 426–435
20. Wang, J., Zhang, K., Jeong, K., Shasha, D.: A system for approximate tree matching. IEEE Transactions on Knowledge and Data Engineering **6** (1994) 559–571
21. Ester, M., Kriegel, H.P., Schubert, M.: Web site mining: A new way to spot competitors, customers and suppliers in the world wide web. In: Proc. 8th Int. Conf on Knowledge Discovery in Databases (SIGKDD'02), Edmonton, Alberta, Canada. (2002) 249–258

QuaSAQ: An Approach to Enabling End-to-End QoS for Multimedia Databases

Yi-Cheng Tu, Sunil Prabhakar, Ahmed K. Elmagarmid, and Radu Sion

Purdue University, West Lafayette IN 47907, USA

Abstract. The paper discusses the design and prototype implementation of a QoS-aware multimedia database system. Recent research in multimedia databases has devoted little attention to the aspect of the integration of QoS support at the user level. Our proposed architecture to enable end-to-end QoS control, the QoS-Aware Query Processor (QuaSAQ), satisfies user specified quality requirements. The users need not be aware of detailed low-level QoS parameters, but rather specifies high-level, qualitative attributes. In addition to an overview of key research issues in the design of QoS-aware databases, this paper presents our proposed solutions, and system implementation details. An important issue relates to the enumeration and evaluation of alternative plans for servicing QoS-enhanced queries. This step follows the conventional query execution which results in the identification of objects of interest to the user. We propose a novel *cost model* for media delivery that explicitly takes the resource utilization of the plan and the current system contention level into account. Experiments run on the QuaSAQ prototype show significantly improved QoS and system throughput.

1 Introduction

As compared to traditional applications, multimedia applications have special requirements with respect to search and playback with satisfactory quality. The problem of searching multimedia data has received significant attention from researchers with the resulting development of content-based retrieval for multimedia databases. The problem of efficient delivery and playback of such data (especially video data), on the other hand, has not received the same level of attention. From the point of view of multimedia DBMS design, one has to be concerned about not only the *correctness* but also the *quality* of the query results. The set of quality parameters that describes the temporal/spatial constraints of media-related applications is called *Quality of Service* (QoS) [1]. Guaranteeing QoS for the user requires an end-to-end solution – all the way from the retrieval of data at the source to the playback of the data at the user.

In spite of the fact that research in multimedia databases has covered many key issues such as data models, system architectures, query languages, algorithms for effective data organization and retrieval [2], little effort has been devoted to the aspect of the integration of QoS support. In the context of general multimedia system, research on QoS has concentrated on system and network support

E. Bertino et al. (Eds.): EDBT 2004, LNCS 2992, pp. 694–711, 2004.
© Springer-Verlag Berlin Heidelberg 2004

with little concern for QoS control on the higher (user, application) levels. High-level QoS support is essential in any multimedia systems because the satisfaction of human users is the primary concern in defining QoS [3]. Simply deploying a multimedia DBMS on top of a QoS-provisioning system will not provide end-to-end QoS. Moreover, such a solution is unable to exploit the application level flexibility such as the user's acceptable range of quality. For example, for a physician diagnosing a patient, the jitter-free playback of very high frame rate and resolution video of the patient's test data is critical; whereas a nurse accessing the same data for organization purposes may not require the same high quality. Such information is only available at the user or application levels.

We envision users such as medical professionals accessing these databases via a simple user interface. In addition to specifying the multimedia items of interest (directly or via content-based similarity to other items), the user specifies a set of desired quality parameter bounds. The quality bounds could be specified explicitly or automatically generated based upon the user's profile. The user should not need to be aware of detailed system QoS parameters but rather specifies high-level qualitative attributes (e.g. "high resolution", or "CD quality audio"). Thus a QoS-enabled database will search for multimedia objects that satisfy the content component of the query and at the same time can be delivered to the user with the desired level of quality.

In this paper we discuss the design and prototype implementation of our QoS-aware multimedia DBMS. We describe the major challenges to enabling end-to-end QoS, and present our proposed solutions to these problems. To the best of our knowledge, this is the first prototype system that achieves end-to-end QoS for multimedia databases. We present experimental results from our prototype that establish the feasibility and advantages of such a system. Our implementation builds upon the VDBMS prototype multimedia database system developed by our group at Purdue University [4]. Among other enhancements, QuaSAQ extends VDBMS to build a distributed QoS-aware multimedia DBMS with multiple copies of storage/streaming manager.

To address the structure of a QoS-provisioning networked multimedia system, four levels of QoS have been proposed: user QoS, application QoS, system QoS, and network QoS [1,5]. We consider a series of QoS parameters in our research as shown in Table 1. QoS guarantees for individual requests and the overall system performance are in most cases two conflicting goals since the entire QoS problem is caused by scarcity of resources. Most current research on QoS fail to address the optimization of system performance. In this paper, we highlight the key elements of our proposed approach to supporting end-to-end QoS and achieving high performance in a multimedia database environment. The approach is motivated by query processing and optimization techniques in conventional distributed databases.

The key idea of our approach is to augment the query evaluation and optimization modules of a distributed database management system (D-DBMS) to directly take QoS into account. To incorporate QoS control into the database, user-level QoS parameters are translated into application QoS and become an

Table 1. Examples of QoS parameters in video databases.

QoS Level	QoS Parameter
Application	*Frame Width, Frame Height, Color Resolution, Time Guarantee, Signal-to-noise ratio (SNR), Security*
System	*CPU cycles, Memory buffer, Disk space and bandwidth*
Network	*Delay, Jitter, Reliability, Packet loss, Network Topology, Bandwidth*

augmented component of the query. For each raw media object, a number of copies with different application QoS parameters are generated offline by transcoding and these copies are replicated on the distributed servers. Based on the information of data replication and runtime QoS adaptation options (e.g. frame dropping), the query processor generates various plans for each query and evaluates them according to a predefined *cost model*. The query evaluation/optimization module also takes care of resource reservation to satisfy low-level QoS. For this part, we propose the design of a unified API and implementation module that enables negotiation and control of the underlying system and network QoS APIs, thereby providing a single entry-point to a multitude of QoS layers (system and network). The major contributions of this paper are: 1) We propose a query processing architecture for multimedia databases for handling queries enhanced with QoS parameters; 2) We propose a cost model that evaluates QoS-aware queries by their resource utilization with consideration of current system status; 3) We implement the proposed query processor within a multimedia DBMS and evaluate our design via experiments run on this prototype.

The paper is organized as follows: Section 2 deals with the main issues encountered in the process of designing and implementing the system. Section 3 presents the actual architecture of the Quality of Service Aware Query Processor (QuaSAQ). We also discuss details pertaining to the design of individual components in the architecture. The prototype implementation of QuaSAQ is detailed in Section 4. Section 5 presents the evaluation of the proposed QuaSAQ architecture. In Section 6, we compare our work with relevant research efforts. Section 7 concludes the paper.

2 Issues

Building a distributed multimedia DBMS requires a careful design of many complex modules as well as effective interactions between these components. This becomes further complicated if the system is to support non-trivial aspects such as QoS. In order to extend the D-DBMS approach to address end-to-end QoS, several important requirements have to be met. These include:

1. Smart QoS-aware data replication algorithms have to be developed. Individual multimedia objects need to be replicated on various nodes of the

database. Each replica may satisfy different application QoS in order to closely meet the requirements of user inputs. The total number and choice of QoS of pre-stored media replicas should reflect the access pattern of media content. Therefore, dynamic online replication and migration has to be performed to make the system converge to the current status of user requests. Another concern in replication is the storage space.

2. Mapping of QoS parameters between different layers has to be achieved. First of all, user-level qualitative QoS inputs (e.g. DVD-quality video) need to be translated into application QoS (e.g. spatial resolution) since the underlying query processor only understands the latter. One critical point here is that the mapping from user QoS to application QoS highly depends on the user's personal preference. Resource consumption of query plans is essential for cost estimation and query optimization in QoS-aware multimedia databases. This requires mapping application QoS in our QoS-enhanced queries to QoS parameters on the system and network level.
3. A model for the *search space* of possible execution plans. The search space is of a very different structure from that of a traditional D-DBMS. In the latter, the primary data model for search space comprises a *query tree*. The query optimizer then explores the space using strategies such as *dynamic programming* and *randomized search* to find the "best" plan according to a *cost model* [6]. In our system, various components such as encryption, encoding, and filtering must be individually considered in addition to the choice of database server and physical media object. Depending on the system status, any of the above components can be the dominant factor in terms of cost.
4. A cost estimation model is needed to evaluate the generated QoS-aware plans. Unlike the static cost estimates in traditional D-DBMS, it is critical that the costs under current system status (e.g. based upon current load on a link) be factored into the choice of an acceptable plan. Furthermore, the cost model in our query processor should also consider optimization criteria other than the *total time*[1], which is normally the only metric used in D-DBMS. A very important optimization goal in multimedia applications is system throughput. Resource consumption of each query has to be estimated and controlled for the system to achieve maximum throughput and yet QoS constraints of individual requests are not violated.
5. Once an acceptable quality plan has been chosen, the playback of the media objects in accordance with the required quality has to be achieved. Generally, QoS control in multimedia systems are achieved in two ways: *resource reservation* and *adaptation* [1]. Both strategies require deployment of a QoS-aware resource management module, which is featured with *admission control* and *reservation* mechanisms. There may also be need for *renegotiation (adaptation)* of the QoS constraints due to user actions during playback.

Our research addresses all above challenges. In the next section, we present a framework for QoS provisioning in a distributed multimedia database environment with the focus on our solutions to items 3 and 4 listed above. For items

[1] Sometimes *response time* is also used, as in distributed INGRES.

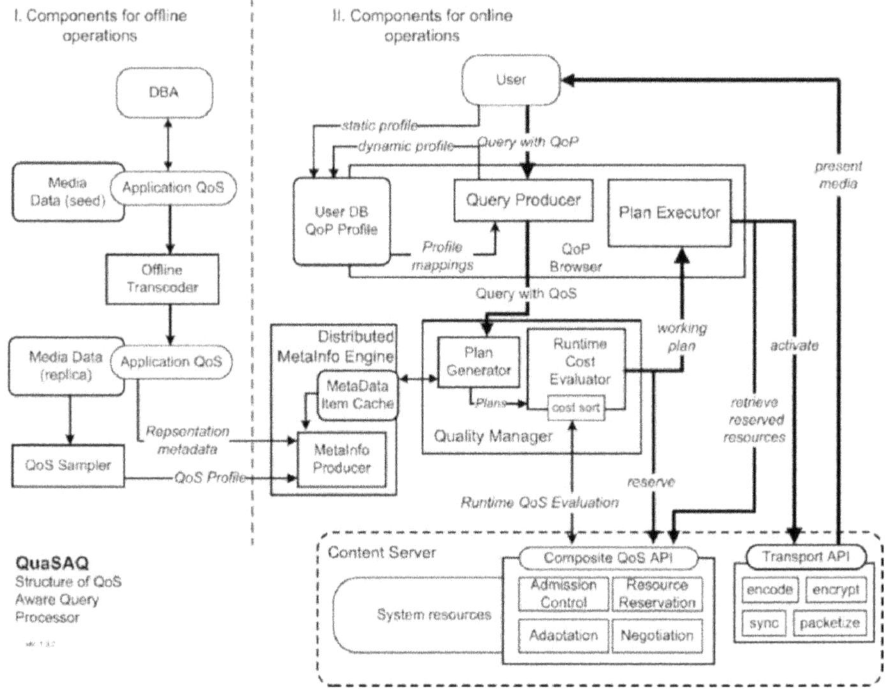

Fig. 1. QuaSAQ architecture

2 and 5, we concentrate on the implementation and evaluation of known approaches within the context of multimedia databases. Item1 will be covered in a follow-up paper.

3 Quality-of-Service Aware Query Processor (QuaSAQ)

Figure 1 describes in detail the proposed architecture of our QoS-aware distributed multimedia DBMS, which we call Quality-of-Service Aware Query Processor (QuaSAQ). In this section, we present detailed descriptions of the various components of QuaSAQ.

3.1 Offline Components

The offline components of QuaSAQ provide a basis for the database administrators to accomplish QoS-related database maintenance. Two major activities, *offline replication* and *QoS sampling*, are performed for each media object inserted into the database. As a result of those, relevant information such as the quality, location and resource consumption pattern of each replica of the newly-inserted object is fed into the *Distributed Metadata Engine* as metadata. Please refer to [7] for more details of replication and QoS mapping in QuaSAQ.

3.2 QoP Browser

The QoP Browser is the user interface to the underlying storage, processing and retrieval system. It enables certain QoP parameter control, generation of QoS-aware queries, and execution of the resulting presentation plans. The main entities of the QoP Browser include: The *User Profile* contains high-level QoP parameter mappings to lower level QoS parameter settings as well as various user related statistics acquired over time, enabling better renegotiation decisions in case of resource failure. The *Query Producer* takes as input some user actions (requests with QoP inputs) and the current settings from the user profile and generates a query. As compared to those of traditional DBMS, the queries generated in QuaSAQ are enhanced with QoS requirements. We call them *QoS-aware queries.* The *Plan Executor* is in charge of actually running the chosen plan. It basically performs actual presentation, synchronization as well as runtime maintenance of underlying QoS parameters.

Quality of Presentation. From a user's perspective, QoS translates into the more qualitative notion of *Quality of Presentation* (QoP). The user is not expected to understand low level quality parameters such as frame rates or packet loss rate. Instead, the user specifies high-level qualitative parameters to the best of his/her understanding of QoS. Some key QoP parameters that are often considered in multimedia systems include: spatial resolution, temporal resolution or period, color depth, reliability, and audio quality. Before being integrated into a database query, the QoP inputs are translated into application QoS based on the information stored in the *User Profile.* For example, a user input of "VCD-like spatial resolution" can be interpreted as a resolution range of $320 \times 240 - 352 \times 288$ pixels. The application QoS parameters are quantitative and we achieve some flexibility by allowing one QoP mapped to a range of QoS values. QoS requirements are allowed to be modified during media playback and a renegotiation is expected. Another scenario for renegotiation is when the user-specified QoP is rejected by the admission control module due to low resource availability. Under such circumstances, a number of admittable alternative plans will be presented as a "second chance" for the query to be serviced.

One important weakness of these qualitative formulations of QoP is their lack of flexibility (i.e. failure to capture differences between users). For example, when renegotiation has to be performed, one user may prefer reduction in the temporal resolution while another user may prefer a reduction in the spatial resolution. We remedy this by introducing a *per-user weighting* of the quality parameters as part of the User Profile.

3.3 Distributed Metadata Engine

In a multimedia DBMS, operations such as content-based searching depend heavily, if not exclusively, on the metadata of the media objects [2]. As mentioned in Section 2, video objects are stored in several locations, each copy with different representation characteristics. This requires more items in the metadata collection. Specifically, we require at least the following types of metadata for a QoS-aware DBMS:

- *Content Metadata:* describe the content of objects to enable multimedia query, search, and retrieval. In our system, a number of visual and semantic descriptors such as shot detection, frame extraction, segmentation, and camera motion are extracted.
- *Quality Metadata:* describe the quality characteristics (in the form of application level QoS) of physical media objects. For our QoS-aware DBMS, the following parameters are kept as metadata for each video object: resolution, color depth, frame rate, and file format.
- *Distribution Metadata:* describe the physical locations (i.e. paths, servers, proxies, etc.) of the media objects. It records the OIDs of objects and the mapping between media content and media file.
- *QoS profile:* describe the resource consumption in the delivery of individual media objects. The data in QoS profiles is obtained via static QoS mapping performed by the *QoS sampler.* The QoS profiles are the basis for cost estimation of QoS-aware query execution plans.

We distribute the metadata in various locations enabling ease of use and migration. Caching is used to accelerate non-local metadata accesses.

3.4 Quality Manager

The Quality Manager is the focal point of the entire system. It is heavily integrated with the *Composite QoS APIs* in order to enable reservation and negotiation. It has the following main components:

Plan Generator. The *Plan Generator* is in charge of generating plans that enable the execution of the query from the Query Producer. The Content Metadata is used to identify logical objects that satisfy the content component of the query (e.g. videos with images of George Bush or Sunsets). A given logical object may be replicated at multiple sites and further with different formats. For example, a given video may be stored in different resolutions and color depth at two different sites. The plan generator determines which of the alternatives can be used to satisfy the request and also the necessary steps needed to present it to the user.

The final execution of QoS-aware query plans can be viewed as a series of *server activities* that may include retrieval, decoding, transcoding between different formats and/or qualities, and encryption. Therefore, the search space of alternative QoS-aware plans consists of all possible combinations of media repositories, target objects, and server activities mentioned above. We can model the search space as a universe of disjoint sets. Each set represents a target media object or a server activity whose possible choices serve as elements in the set. Suppose we have n such sets $A_1, A_2, \ldots, A_n$, then an execution plan is an ordered set $a_1, a_2, \ldots, a_m$ satisfying the following conditions:

(1) $m \leq n$;
(2) $\forall a_i \ (1 \leq i \leq m), \ \exists \ A_j \ni a_i \ (1 \leq i \leq n)$;
(3) For any $i \neq j$ with $a_i \in A_k$ and $a_j \in A_l$, we have $k \neq l$.

The semantics of the above conditions are: (1) The total number of components in a plan cannot exceed the number of possible server activities; (2) All components in a plan come from some disjoint set; and (3) No two components in a plan come from the same set. The size of the search space is huge even with the above restrictions. Suppose each set of server activity has d elements, the number of possible plans is $O(n!d^n)$. Fortunately, there are also some other system-specific rules that further reduce the number of alternative plans. One salient rule is related to the order of server activities. For example, the first server activity should always be the retrieval of a media object from a certain site, all other activities such as transcoding, encryption have to follow the the media retrieval in a plan. If the order of all server activity sets are fixed, the size of search space decreases to $O(d^n)$.

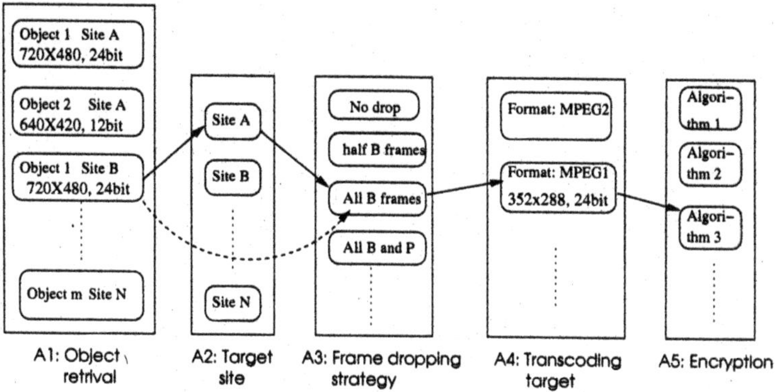

Fig. 2. Illustrative plan generation in QuaSAQ

Runtime QoS Evaluation and Plan Drop. The Plan Generator described above does not check generated plans for any QoS constraints. We can perform those verifications by applying a set of static and dynamic rules. First of all, decisions can be made instantly based on QoS inputs in the query. For example, we cannot retrieve a video with resolution lower than that required by the user. Similarly, it makes no sense to transcode from low resolution to high resolution. Therefore, QoS constraints help further reduce the size of search space by decreasing the appropriate set size d. In practice, d can be regarded as a constant. Some of the plans can be immediately dropped by the *Plan Generator* if their costs are intolerably high. This requires QuaSAQ to be aware of some obvious performance pitfalls. For example, encryption should always follow the frame dropping since it is a waste of CPU cycles to encrypt the data in frames that will be dropped. Once a suitable plan has been discovered, the Plan Generator computes its resource requirements (in the form of a *resource vector*) and feeds it to the next component down the processing pipe-line.

Illustrative examples of plans. The path in solid lines shown in Figure 2 represents a query plan with the following details: 1. retrieve physical copy number 1 of the requested media from the disk of server B; 2. transfer the media to server A; 3. transcode to MPEG1 format with certain target QoS; 4. drop all the B frames during delivery; 5. encrypt the media data using algorithm 1. The dotted line corresponds to a simpler plan: retrieve the same object and transcode with the same target QoS, no frame dropping or encryption is needed. An even simpler plan would be a single node in set $A1$, meaning the object is sent without further processing.

Runtime Cost Evaluator. The *Runtime Cost Evaluator* is the main component that computes (at runtime) estimated costs for generated plans. It sorts the plans in ascending cost order and passes them to the Plan Executor in the QoP Browser. The first plan in this order that satisfies the QoS requirements is used to service the query. In a traditional D-DBMS, the cost of a query is generally expressed as the sum of time spent on CPU, I/O and data transferring. In QuaSAQ, the total time for executing any query plans is exactly the same since the streaming time for a media object is fixed. As a result, processing time is no longer a valid metric for cost estimation of the QoS-aware query plans.

We propose a cost model that focuses on the resource consumption of alternative query execution plans. Multimedia delivery is generally resource intensive, especially on the network bandwidth. Thus, to improve system throughput is an important design goal of media systems. Intuitively, the execution plan we may choose should be one that consumes as few resources as possible and yet meets all the QoS requirements. Our cost model is designed to capture the 'amount' of resources used in each plan. Furthermore, the cost model id also valid for other global optimization goals such as minimal waste of resources, maximized user satisfaction, and fairness. Our ultimate goal is to build a configurable query optimizer whose optimization goal can be configured according to user (DBA) inputs. We then evaluate plans by their *cost efficiency* that can be denoted as:

$$E = \frac{G}{C(\boldsymbol{r})}$$

where C is the cost function, $\boldsymbol{r}$ the resource vector of the plan being evaluated, and G the *gain* of servicing the query following the plan of interest. An optimal plan is the one with the highest cost efficiency. The generation of the G value of a plan depends on the optimization goal used. For instance, a *utility function* can be used when our goal is to maximize the satisfiability of user perception of media streams [8]. A detailed discussion of the configurable cost model mentioned above is beyond the scope of this paper. Instead, we present a simple cost model that aims to maximize system throughput.

Lowest Resource Bucket (LRB) model. Suppose there are n types of resources to be considered in QuaSAQ, we denote the total amount of resource i

as R_i. In our algorithm, we build a virtual *resource bucket* for each individual resource. All R_i values are standardized into the height of the buckets. Therefore, the height of all buckets is 1 (or 100%). The buckets are filled when the relevant resources are being used and drained when the resources are released. Therefore, the height of the filled part of any bucket i is the percentage of resource i that is being used. For example, the filled part of bucket $R2$ in Figure 3d has height 42, which means 42% of R_2 is currently in use. The cost evaluation is done as follows: for any plan p, we first transform the items in p's resource vector into standardized heights related to the corresponding bucket (denoted as $r_1, r_2, \ldots, r_n$); we then fill the buckets accordingly using the transformed resource vector and record the largest height among all the buckets. The query that leads to the smallest such maximum bucket height wins. In Figure 3, the cost of three plans (a, b, c) are marked by dotted lines. Putting them all together, we found the filled height of plan 2 is the lowest and plans 2 is chosen for execution. Formally, the *cost function* of the LRB model can be expressed as

$$f(r_1, r_2, \ldots, r_n) = \max_{i=1}^{n} \left\{ \frac{U_i + r_i}{R_i} \right\} \tag{1}$$

where U_i is the current usage of resource i. The input is the resource vector of the plan being evaluated.

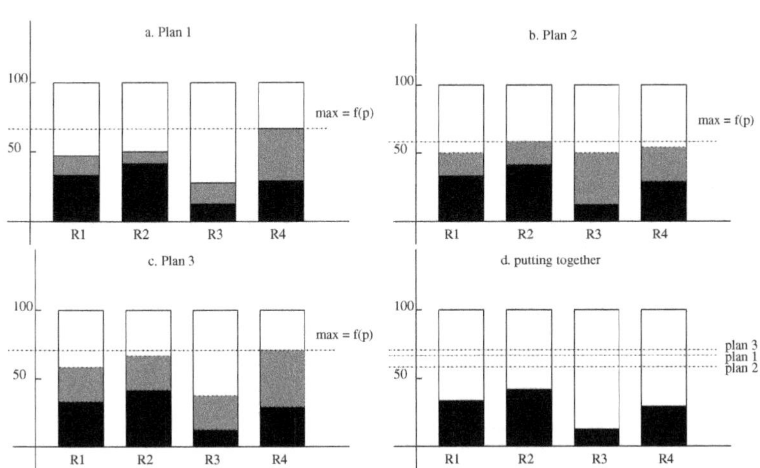

Fig. 3. Cost evaluation by the Lowest Resource Bucket model

The reasoning of the above algorithm is easy to understand: the goal is to make the filling rate of all the *buckets* distribute evenly. Since no queries can be served if we have an overflowing bucket, we should prevent any single bucket from growing faster than the others. This algorithm is not guaranteed to be optimal, it works fairly well, as shown by our experiments (Section 5.2).

3.5 QoS APIs

The *Composite QoS API* hides implementation and access details of underlying APIs (i.e. system and network) and offers control to upper layers (e.g. *Plan Generator*) at the same time. The major functionality provided by the *Composite QoS API* is QoS-related resource management, which is generally accomplished in the following aspects: 1.*Admission control*, which determines whether a query/plan can be accepted under current system status; 2.*Resource reservation*, an important strategy toward QoS control by guaranteeing resources needed during the lifetime of media delivery jobs; 3.*Renegotiation* that are mainly performed under two scenarios mentioned in Section 3.2.

Transport API. It is basically composed of the underlying packetization and synchronization mechanisms of continuous media, similar to those found in general media servers. The Transport API has to honor the full reservation of resources. This is done through interactions with the Composite QoS API. The interface to some of the other *server activities* such as encryption, transcoding, and filtering are also integrated into the Transport API.

4 QuaSAQ Implementation

We implement a prototype of QuaSAQ on top of the Video Database Management System (VDBMS) developed at Purdue University [4]. The QuaSAQ development is done using C++ under the Solaris 2.6 environment. Figure 4 shows the architecture of VDBMS enhanced with the QuaSAQ prototype.

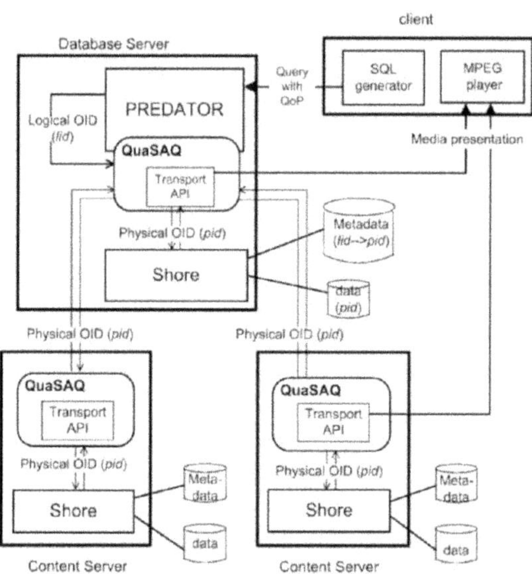

Fig. 4. System architecture for QoS-aware multimedia DBMS prototype

QuaSAQ and VDBMS. Developed from the object-relational database engine PREDATOR[9] with Shore[10] as the underlying storage manager (SM), VDBMS is a multimedia DBMS that supports full-featured video operations (e.g. content-based searching, streaming) and complex queries. Most of the VDBMS development was done by adding features to PREDATOR. We extended the current release of VDBMS, which runs only on a single node, to a distributed version by realizing communication and data transferring functionalities among different sites. As shown in Figure 4, QuaSAQ augments VDBMS and sits between Shore and PREDATOR in the query processing path. In our QuaSAQ-enhanced database, queries on videos are processed in two steps: 1. searching and identification of video objects done by the original VDBMS; 2. QoS-constrained delivery of the video by QuaSAQ [3]. In VDBMS, the query processor returns an object ID (OID), by which Shore retrieves the video from disk. With QuaSAQ, these OIDs refer to the video content (represented by logical OID) rather than the entity in storage (physical OID) since multiple copies of the same video exist. In QuaSAQ, the mapping between logical OIDs and physical OIDs are stored as part of the metadata (Section 3.3). Upon receiving the logical OID of the video of interest from PREDATOR, the Quality Manager of QuaSAQ annotates a series of plans for QoS-guaranteed delivery and chooses one to execute. It communicates with either QuaSAQ modules in remote sites or local Shore component (depending on the plan it chooses) to initiate the video transmission. Note the sender of the video data is not necessarily the site at which the query was received and processed.

QuaSAQ Components. Most of the QuaSAQ components are developed by modifying and augmenting relevant modules in VDBMS (e.g. client program, SQL parser, query optimizer). Replicas for all videos in the database are generated using a commercial video transcoding/encoding software VideoMach[2]. The choice of quality parameters is determined in a way that the bitrate of the resulting video replicas fit the bandwidth of typical network connections such as T1, DSL, and modems [7]. To obtain an online video transcoder, we modified the source code of the popular Linux video processing tool named *transcode*[3] and integrated it into the *Transport API* of our QuaSAQ prototype. The major part of the *Transport API* is developed on the basis of a open-source media streaming program[4]. It decodes the layering information of MPEG stream files and leverages the synchronization functionality of the Real Time Protocol (RTP). We also implement various frame dropping strategies for MPEG1 videos as part of the Transport API. We build the Composite QoS APIs using a QoS-aware middleware named GARA [11] as substrate. GARA contains separate managers for individual resources (e.g. CPU, network bandwidth and storage bandwidth). The CPU manager in GARA is based on the application-level CPU scheduler DSRT [12] developed in the context of the QualMan project [13]. QoS-aware network protocols are generally the solution to network resource management,

[2] Release 2.6.3, http://www.gromada.com
[3] Release 0.6.4, http://www.theorie.physik.uni-goettingen.de/~ostreich/transcode/
[4] http://www.live.com

which requires participation of both end-systems and routers. In GARA, the *DiffSrv* mechanism provided by the Internet Protocol (IP) is used.

5 Experimental Results

We evaluated the performance of QuaSAQ in comparison with the original VDBMS system. The experiments are focused on the QoS in video delivery as well as system throughput. An important metric in measuring QoS of networked video streaming tasks is the *inter-frame delay*, which is defined as the interval between the *processing time* of two consecutive frames in a video stream [12, 14]. Ideally, the inter-frame delay should be the reciprocal of the frame rate of the video. For the system throughput, we simply use the number of concurrent streaming sessions and the reject rate of queries.

Experimental setup. The experiments are performed on a small distributed system containing three servers and a number of client machines. The servers are all Intel machines (one Pentium 4 2.4GHz CPU and 1GB memory) running Solaris 2.6. The servers are located at three different 100Mbps Ethernets in the domain of purdue.edu. Each server has a total streaming bandwidth of 3200KBps. The clients are deployed on machines that are generally 2-3 hops away from the servers. Due to lack of router support of the *DiffSrv* mechanism, only *admission control* is performed in network management. A reasonable assumption here is that the bottlenecking link is always the outband link of the severs and those links are dedicated for our experiments. Instead of user inputs from a GUI-based client program [4], the queries for the experiments are from a traffic generator. Our experimental video database contains 15 videos in MPEG-1 format with playback time ranging from 30 seconds to 18 minutes. For each video, three to four copies with different quality are generated and fully replicated on three servers so that each server has all copies.

5.1 Improvement of QoS by QuaSAQ

Figure 5 shows the inter-frame delay of a representative streaming session for a video with frame rate of 23.97 fps. The data is collected on the server side, e.g. the *processing time* is when the video frame is first handled. Only end-point system resources should be considered in analyzing server-side results. The left two graphs of Figure 5 represent the result of the original VDBMS while the right two graphs show those with QuaSAQ. We compare the performance of both systems by their response to various contention levels. On the first row, streaming is done without competition from other programs (low contention) while the number of concurrent video streams are high (high contention) for experiments on the second row.

Under low contention, both systems (Fig 5a and 5b) demonstrated timely processing of almost all the frames, as shown by their relatively low variance of inter-frame delay (Table 2). Note that some variance are inevitable in dealing with Variable Bitrate (VBR) media streams such as MPEG video because the

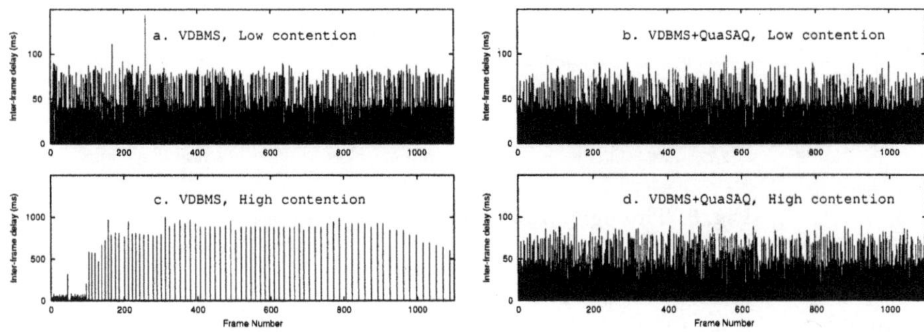

Fig. 5. Inter-frame delays on the server side under different system contentions

Table 2. Statistics of Inter-frame and Inter-GOP delays shown in Figure 5. Unit for all data is millisecond, S.D. = Standard Deviation.

Experiment	*Inter-frame*		*Inter-GOP*	
	Mean	*S. D.*	*Mean*	*S. D.*
VDBMS, Low Contention	42.07	34.12	622.82	64.51
VDBMS, High Contention	48.84	164.99	722.83	246.85
QuaSAQ, Low Contention	42.16	30.89	624.84	10.13
QuaSAQ, High Contention	42.25	30.29	626.18	8.68

frames are of different sizes and coding schemes (e.g. I, B, P frames in a Group of Pictures (GOP) in MPEG). Such intrinsic variance can be smoothed out if we collect data on the GOP level (Table 2).

VDBMS is unable to maintain QoS under high contention. Its variance of inter-frame delays (Fig 5c) are huge as compared to those of QuaSAQ (Fig 5d). Note the scale of the vertical axis in Figure 5c is one magnitude higher than those of three other diagrams. The reason for such high variance is poor guarantee of CPU cycles for the streaming jobs. The job waits for its turn of CPU utilization at most of the time. Upon getting control over CPU, it will try to process all the frames that are overdue within the quantum assigned by the OS (10ms in Solaris). Besides high variance, the average inter-frame delay is also large for VDBMS under high contention (Table 2). Note the theoretical inter-frame delay for the sample video is $1/23.97 = 41.72ms$. On the contrary, QuaSAQ achieves similar performance when system contention level changes. With the help of QoS APIs, the CPU needs in QuaSAQ are highly guaranteed, resulting in timely processing of video frames on the end-point machines. Data collected on the client side show similar results [7].

5.2 System Throughput

We compare the throughput of QuaSAQ and the original VDBMS (Fig 6). The same set of queries are fed into the tested systems. Queries are generated such that the access rate to each individual video is the same and each QoS parameter

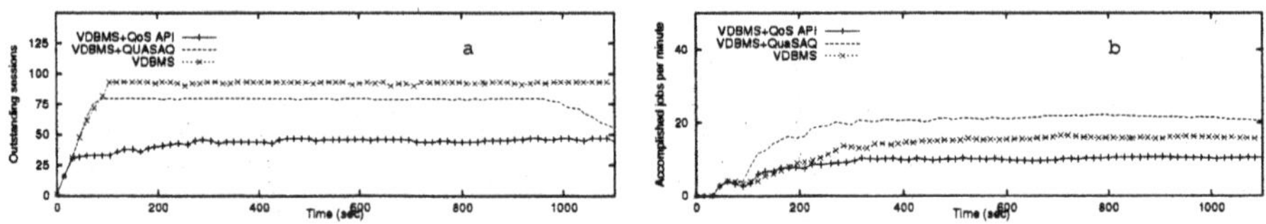

Fig. 6. Throughput of different video database systems

(QuaSAQ only) is uniformly distributed in its valid range. The inter-arrival time for queries is exponentially distributed with an average of 1 second. The original VDBMS obviously keeps the largest number of concurrent streaming sessions (Fig 6a). However, the seemingly high throughput of VDBMS is just a result of lack of QoS control: all video jobs were admitted and it took much longer time to finish each job (Table 2). To avoid an unfair comparison between VDBMS and QuaSAQ, a VDBMS enhanced with QoS APIs is introduced. The streaming sessions in this system are of the same (high) quality as those in QuaSAQ (data not shown). According to Figure 6a, throughput for all three systems stabilize after a short initial stage. QuaSAQ beats the "VDBMS + QoS API" system by about 75% on the stable stage in system throughput. This clearly shows the advantages of QoS-specific replication and Quality Manager that are unique in QuaSAQ. The superiority of QuaSAQ is also demonstrated in Figure 6b where we interpret throughput as the number of succeeded sessions per unit time.

We also evaluate our resource-based cost model (Fig 7). We compare the throughput of two QuaSAQ systems using different cost models: one with LRB and one with a simple randomized algorithm. The latter randomly selects one execution plan from the search space. The randomized approach is a frequently-used query optimization strategy with fair performance. Without performance being significantly better than that of the randomized approach, a newly-proposed cost model can hardly be regarded successful. The queries are generated in the same way as those in the previous experiment (Fig 6). It is easy to see that the resource-based cost model achieves much better throughput (Fig 7a). The number of sessions supported is 27% to 89% higher than that of the system with the randomized method. The high system throughput caused by the proposed cost model is also consistent with its low reject rate shown in Figure 7b.

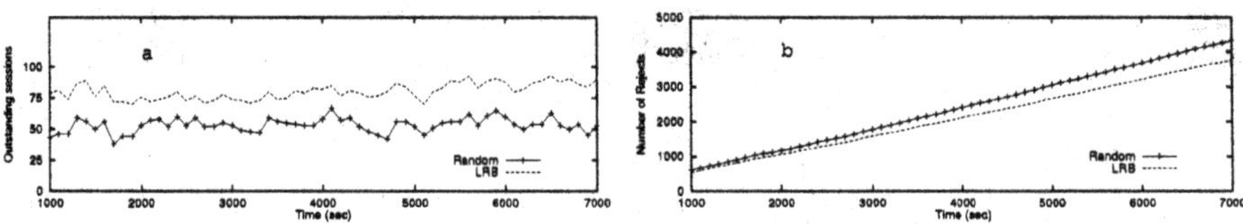

Fig. 7. Throughput of QuaSAQ systems with different cost models

Overhead of QuaSAQ. QuaSAQ is a light-weight extension to VDBMS. The throughput data in Section 5.2 already show that the overhead for running QuaSAQ does not affect performance. The major cost of QuaSAQ comes from the CPU cycles used for maintenance of the underlying QoS resource management modules. The DSRT scheduler reports an overhead of $0.4-0.8ms$ for every $10ms$ [12]. This number is only $0.16ms$ in the machines we used for experiments (1.6% overhead). The CPU use for processing each query (a few milliseconds) in QuaSAQ is negligible.

6 Related Work

Numerous research projects have been dedicated to the theory and realization of QoS control on the lower (system, network) levels [13,11,14]. The software releases of QualMan [13] and GARA [11] projects are the foundations upon which we build our low level QoS APIs. On the contrary, research on user-level QoS has attracted less attention and left us many open issues.

The following pieces of work are directly related to our QoS-aware multimedia DBMS. In [15], a QoS management framework for distributed multimedia applications is proposed with the focus of dynamic negotiation and translation of user-level QoS by QoS profiling. The same group also presents a generic framework for processing queries with QoS constraints in the context of conventional DBMS [16]. They argue for the need to evaluate queries based on a *QoS-based cost model* that takes system performance into account. However, the paper lacks technical details on how to develop and evaluate these cost models. A conceptual model for QoS management in multimedia database systems is introduced in [8]. In this paper, QoS is viewed as the distance between an actual presentation and the ideal presentation (with perfect quality) of the same media content. The metric space where the distances are defined consists of n dimensions, each of which represents a QoS parameter. *Utility functions* are used to map QoS into a satisfaction value, either on a single dimension or all QoS as a whole. The paper also proposes a language for QoS specification. Although the architecture of a prototype utilizing their QoS model is illustrated, further details on implementation and evaluation of the system are not discussed. Our work on QoS differs from [8] in two aspects: we focus on the change of query processing mechanisms in multimedia DBMS while they are more inclined to QoS semantics on a general multimedia system; we invest much effort in experimental issues while they introduce only a theoretical framework. The design and realization of QuaSAQ is motivated by a previous work [3]. The main contribution of [3] is to specify QoS in video database queries by a query language based on constraint logic programming. They propose the *content* and *view* specifications of queries. The former addresses correctness while the latter captures the quality of the query results. Similar to [8], the paper concentrates on building a logical framework rather than the design and implementation of a real system.

Other related efforts include: The idea of *Dynamic Query Optimization* [17] is analogous to QoS renegotiation in QuaSAQ; [18] studies cost estimation of queries under dynamic system contentions; and [19] discusses QoS control for general queries in real-time databases.

7 Conclusions and Future Work

We have presented an overview of our approach to enabling end-to-end QoS for distributed multimedia databases. We discussed various issues pertaining to design and implementation of a QoS-aware query processor (QuaSAQ) with the focus of novel query evaluation and optimization strategies. As a part of the query processing scheme of QuaSAQ, we presented a novel cost model that evaluates query plans by their resource consumption. QuaSAQ was implemented and evaluated on the context of the VDBMS project. Experimental data demonstrated the advantages of QuaSAQ in two aspects: highly improved QoS guarantee and system throughput.

We are currently in the process of implementing a more complete version of QuaSAQ as part of our ongoing projects. This includes efforts to add more resource managers in the Composite QoS API, security mechanisms, and more refined plan generator and cost models. The QuaSAQ idea also needs to be validated on distributed systems with scales larger than the one we deployed the prototype on. On the theoretical part, we believe the refinement and analysis of the resource-based cost model is a topic worthy of further research.

References

1. L. Wolf, C. Gridwodz, and R. Steinmetz. Multimedia Communication. *Proceedings of the IEEE*, 85(12):1915–1933, December 1997.
2. H. Jiang and A. K. Elmagarmid. Spatial and Temporal Content-Based Access to Hyper Video Databases. *The VLDB Journal*, 7(4):226–238, 1998.
3. Elisa Bertino, Ahmed Elmagarmid, and Mohand-Saïd Hacid. A Database Approach to Quality of Service Specification in Video Databases. *SIGMOD Record*, 32(1):35–40, 2003.
4. W. Aref, A. C. Catlin, A. Elmagarmid, J. Fan, J. Guo, M. Hammad, I. F. Ilyas, M.S. Marzouk, S. Prabhakar, A. Rezgui, E. Terzi, Y. Tu, A. Vakali, and X.Q. Zhu. A Distributed Database Server for Continuous Media. In *Proceedings of the 18th ICDE Conference*, pages 490–491, February 2002.
5. Klara Nahrstedt and Ralf Steinmetz. Resource Management in Networked Multimedia Systems. *IEEE Computer*, 28(5):52–63, 1995.
6. M. T. Özsu and P. Valduriez. *Principles of Distributed Database Systems*, chapter 9, pages 228–273. Prentice Hall, 1999.
7. Y. Tu, S. Prabhakar, and A. Elmagarmid. A Database-centric Approach to Enabling End-to-end QoS in Multimedia Repositories. Technical Report CSD TR 03-031, Purdue University, 2003.
8. J. Walpole, C. Krasic, L. Liu, D. Maier, C. Pu, D. McNamee, and D. Steere. Quality of Service Semantics for Multimedia Database Systems. In *Proceedings of Data Semantics 8: Semantic Issues in Multimedia Systems IFIP TC-2 Working Conference*, volume 138, 1998.

9. P. Seshadri. Enhanced Abstract Data Types in Object-Relational Databases. *The VLDB Journal*, 7(3):130–140, 1998.
10. M. Carey, D. DeWitt, M. Franklin, N. Hall, M. McAuliffe, J. Naughton, D. Schuh, M. Solomon, C. Tan, O. Tsatalos, S. White, and M. Zwilling. Shoring Up Persistent Applications. In *Proceedings of ACM SIGMOD*, pages 383–394, 1994.
11. I. Foster, A. Roy, and V. Sander. A Quality of Service Architecture that Combines Resources Reservation and Application Adaptation. In *Proceedings of IWQOS*, pages 181–188, June 2000.
12. H-H. Chu and K. Nahrstedt. A Soft Real Time Scheduling Server in UNIX Operating System. In *Proceedings of IDMS*, pages 153–162, 1997.
13. K. Nahrstedt, H. Chu, and S. Narayan. QoS-Aware Resource Management for Distributed Multimedia Applications. *Journal on High-Speed Networking, Special Issue on Multimedia Networking*, 8(3–4):227–255, 1998.
14. D. Yau and S. Lam. Operating System Techniques for Distributed Multimedia. *International Journal of Intelligent Systems*, 13(12):1175–1200, December 1998.
15. A. HAfiD and G. Bochmann. An Approach to Quality of Service Management in Distributed Multimedia Application: Design and Implementation. *Multimedia Tools and Applications*, 9(2):167–191, 1999.
16. H. Ye, B. Kerhervé, and G. v. Bochmann. Quality of Service Aware Distributed Query Processing. In *Proceedings of DEXA Workshop on Query Processing in Multimedia Information Systems(QPMIDS)*, September 1999.
17. N. Kabra and D. DeWitt. Efficient Mid-Query Re-Optimization of Sub-Optimal Query Execution Plans. In *Proceedings of ACM SIGMOD*, pages 106–117, 1998.
18. Q. Zhu, S. Motheramgari, and Y Sun. Cost Estimation for Queries Experiencing Multiple Contention States in Dynamic Multidatabase Environments. *Knowledge and Information Systems*, 5(1):26–49, 2003.
19. J. Stankovic, S. Son, and J. Liebeherr. BeeHive: Global Multimedia Database Support for Dependable, Real-Time Applications. In A. Bestavros and V. Fay-Wolfe, editors, *Real-Time Database and Information Systems: Research Advances*, chapter 22, pages 409–422. Kluwer Academic Publishers, 1997.

On Indexing Sliding Windows over Online Data Streams*

Lukasz Golab[1], Shaveen Garg[2], and M. Tamer Özsu[1]

[1] School of Computer Science, University of Waterloo, Canada.
{lgolab,tozsu}@uwaterloo.ca
[2] Department of Computer Science and Engineering, IIT Bombay, India.
shaveen@cse.iitb.ac.in

Abstract. We consider indexing sliding windows in main memory over on-line data streams. Our proposed data structures and query semantics are based on a division of the sliding window into sub-windows. By classifying windowed operators according to their method of execution, we motivate the need for two types of windowed indices: those which provide a list of attribute values and their counts for answering set-valued queries, and those which provide direct access to tuples for answering attribute-valued queries. We propose and evaluate indices for both of these cases and show that our techniques are more efficient than executing windowed queries without an index.

1 Introduction

Data management applications such as Internet traffic measurement, sensor networks, and transaction log analysis, are expected to process long-running queries (known in the literature as *continuous queries*) in real time over high-volume data streams. In order to emphasize recent data and to avoid storing potentially infinite streams in memory, the range of continuous queries may be restricted to a sliding window of the N most recent items (count-based windows) or those items whose timestamps are at most as old as the current time minus T (time-based windows). For example, an Internet traffic monitoring system may calculate the average Round Trip Time (RTT) over a sliding window to determine an appropriate value for the TCP timeout. A sliding window RTT average is appropriate because it emphasizes recent measurements and acts to smooth out the effects of any sudden changes in network conditions.

Windowed queries are re-evaluated periodically, yet the input streams arrive continuously, possibly at a high rate. This environment, in which insertions and deletions caused by high-speed data streams heavily outweigh query invocations, contrasts traditional DBMSs where queries are more frequent than updates. In light of this workload change, we pose the following questions in this paper. Given the usefulness of indices in traditional databases, is it beneficial to index sliding

* This research is partially supported by the Natural Sciences and Engineering Research Council of Canada (NSERC).

E. Bertino et al. (Eds.): EDBT 2004, LNCS 2992, pp. 712–729, 2004.
© Springer-Verlag Berlin Heidelberg 2004

windows over on-line data streams or will the cost of maintaining indices over volatile data negate their advantages? Further, how can we exploit the update patterns of sliding windows to design more efficient indices?

1.1 System Model and Assumptions

We define a data stream as a sequence of relational tuples with a fixed schema. Each tuple has a timestamp that may either be implicit (generated by the system at arrival time) or explicit (inserted by the source at creation time), and is used to determine the tuple's position in the stream. We divide the sliding window into n sub-windows, called *Basic Windows* [16]. To ensure constant sliding window size, each basic window stores the same number of tuples (count-based windows) or spans an equal time interval (time-based windows). Each sub-window may store individual tuples, aggregated summaries, or both. When the newest basic window fills up, it is appended to the sliding window, the oldest basic window is evicted, and queries are re-evaluated. This allows for inexpensive window maintenance as we need not scan the entire window to check for expired tuples, but induces a "jumping window" rather than a gradually sliding window. Finally, we assume that sliding windows are stored in main memory.

1.2 Related Work

Broadly related to our research is the work on data stream management; see [8] for a survey. Windowed algorithms are particularly relevant as simple queries may become non-trivial when constrained to a sliding window. For example, computing the maximum value in an infinite stream requires $O(1)$ time and memory, but doing so in a sliding window with N tuples requires $\Omega(N)$ space and time. The main issue is that as new items arrive, old items must be simultaneously evicted from the window and their contribution discarded from the answer. The basic window technique [16] may be used to decrease memory usage and query processing time by storing summary information rather than individual tuples in each basic window. For instance, storing the maximum value for each basic window may be used to incrementally compute the windowed maximum.

In the basic window approach, results are refreshed after the newest basic window fills up. *Exponential Histograms* (EH) have been proposed in [4] to bound the error caused by over-counting those elements in the oldest basic window which should have expired. The EH algorithm, initially proposed for counting the number of ones in a binary stream, has recently been extended to maintain a histogram in [13], and to time-based windows in [2].

Recent work on windowed joins includes binary join algorithms for count-based windows [11] and heuristics for load shedding to maximize the result size of windowed joins [3]. In previous work, we addressed the issue of joining more than two streams in the context of time-based and count-based windows [9].

Our work is also related to main memory query processing, e.g. [5,12], especially the domain storage model and ring indexing [1]. However, these works test a traditional workload of mostly searches and occasional updates. Research in bulk insertion and deletion in relational indices is also of interest, e.g. [6,15], though not directly applicable because the previous works assume a disk-resident database. Moreover, *Wave Indices* have been proposed in [14] for indexing sliding windows stored on disk. We will make further comparisons between our work and wave indices later on in this paper.

1.3 Contributions

To the best of our knowledge, this paper is the first to propose storage structures and indexing techniques specifically for main-memory based sliding windows. Our specific contributions are as follows.

- Using the basic window model as a window maintenance technique and as a basis for continuous query semantics, we propose main-memory based storage methods for sliding windows.
- We classify relational operators according to their evaluation techniques over sliding windows, and show that two types of indices are potentially useful for speeding up windowed queries: set-valued and attribute-valued indices.
- We propose and evaluate the performance of indexing techniques for answering set-valued windowed queries as well as novel techniques for maintaining a windowed ring index that supports attribute-valued queries.

1.4 Roadmap

In the remainder of the paper, Sect. 2 outlines physical storage methods for sliding windows, Sect. 3 classifies relational operators in the windowed scenario and motivates the need for indices, Sect. 4 proposes indices for set-valued queries, Sect. 5 discusses ring indices for attribute-valued queries, Sect. 6 presents experimental results regarding index performance, and Sect. 7 concludes the paper with suggestions for future work.

2 Physical Storage Methods for Sliding Windows

2.1 General Storage Structure for Sliding Windows

As a general window storage structure, we propose a circular array of pointers to basic windows; implementing individual basic windows is an orthogonal problem, as long as the contents of basic windows can be accessed via pointers. When the newest basic window fills up, its pointer is inserted in the circular array by overwriting the pointer to the oldest basic window. To guarantee constant window size, a new basic window is stored in a separate buffer as it fills up so that queries do not access new tuples until the oldest basic window has been replaced. Furthermore, since the window slides forward in units of one basic window, we remove timestamps from individual tuples and only store one timestamp per basic window, say the timestamp of its oldest tuple. With this approach, some accuracy is lost (e.g. when performing a windowed join, tuples which should have expired may be joined; however, this error is bounded by the basic window size), but space usage is decreased. Our data structure is illustrated in Fig. 1.

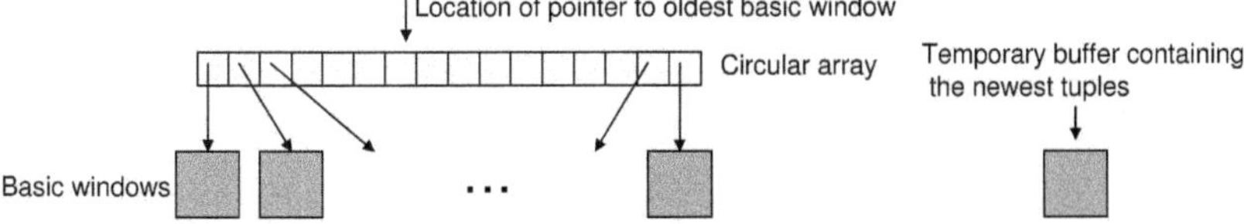

Fig. 1. Sliding window implemented as a circular array of pointers to basic windows

2.2 Storage Structures for Individual Basic Windows

The simplest storage method for individual basic windows is a linked list of tuples, abbreviated as LIST[1]. Again, implementing tuple storage is orthogonal to the basic window data structure. Moreover, the tuples inside a basic window could be linked in chronological order (newest tuple at the tail) or in reverse chronological order (newest tuple at the head). In fact, if basic windows contain tuples with the same attribute value, we can aggregate out one or more attributes, leading to three additional storage methods. In AGGR, each basic window consists of a sorted linked list of frequency counts for every distinct value appearing in this basic window. If tuples have more than one attribute, a separate AGGR structure is needed for each attribute. Alternatively, we may retain a LIST structure to store attributes which we do not want to aggregate out and use AGGR structures for the remaining attributes. Since inserting tuples in an AGGR structure may be expensive, it is more efficient to use a hash table rather than a sorted linked list. That is, (every attribute that we want to aggregate out in) each basic window could be a hash table, with each bucket storing a sorted linked list of counts for those attribute values which hash to this bucket. We call this technique HASH. Finally, further space reduction may be achieved by using AGGR structures, but only storing counts for groups of values (e.g. value ranges) rather than distinct values. We call this structure GROUP. Figure 2 illustrates the four basic window implementations, assuming that each tuple has one attribute and that tuples with the following values have arrived in the basic window: 12,14,16,17,15,4,19,17,16,23,12,19,1,12,5,23.

2.3 Window Maintenance and Query Processing

Let d be the number of distinct values and b be the number of tuples in a basic window, let g be the number of groups in GROUP, and let h be the number of buckets in HASH. Assume that b and d do not vary across basic windows. The worst-case, per-tuple cost of inserting items in the window is $O(1)$ for LIST, $O(d)$ for AGGR, $O(\frac{d}{h})$ for HASH, and $O(g)$ for GROUP. The space requirements are $O(b)$ for LIST, $O(d)$ for AGGR, $O(d{+}h)$ for HASH, and $O(g)$ for GROUP. Hence, AGGR and HASH save space over LIST, but are more expensive to maintain, while GROUP is efficient in both space and time at the expense of lost accuracy.

[1] Time-based windows usually do not store the same number of tuples in each basic window, so we cannot use another circular array.

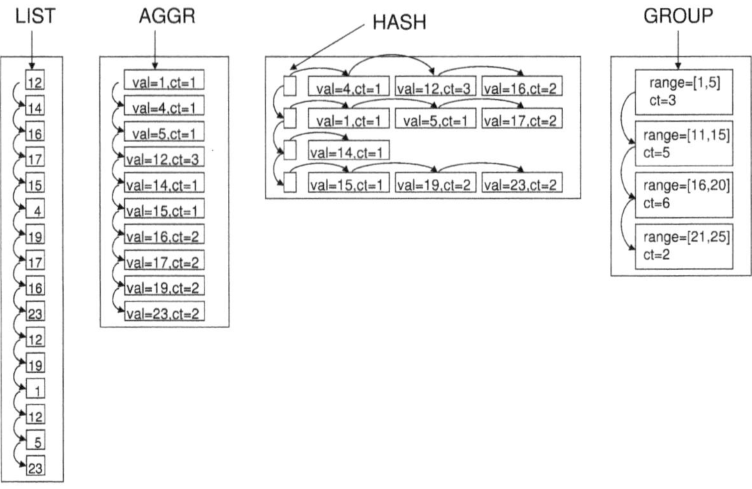

Fig. 2. Our four basic window data structures, assuming that attribute values are stored inside tuples (rather than in an index to which the tuples point, as in the *domain storage* model [1])

In general, window maintenance with the basic window approach is faster than advancing the window upon arrival of each new tuple. However, there is a delay between the arrival of a new tuple and its inclusion in the query result. If t_b is the time span of a basic window, the contribution of a new tuple to the answer will be reflected in the result with a delay of at least t_b and at most $2t_b$—the query must be re-evaluated before the next basic window fills up in order to keep up with the stream. If, however, we are falling behind, we may continue to advance the window after the newest basic window fills up, but we re-execute queries every k basic windows. We may also evaluate easy or important queries often and others more rarely, and adjust the query re-evaluation frequency dynamically in response to changing system conditions.

3 Classification of Sliding Window Operators

We now present a classification of windowed relational operators, revealing that many interesting operators require access to the entire window during query re-execution. We will show that two types of window indices may be useful: those which cover set-valued queries such as intersection, and those which cover attribute-valued queries such as joins.

3.1 Input and Output Modes

We define two input types and two output types—windowed and non-windowed—which give rise to four operator evaluation modes:

1. In the non-windowed input and non-windowed output mode, each tuple is processed on-the-fly, e.g. selection.
2. In the windowed input and non-windowed output mode, we store a window of tuples for each input stream and return new results as new items arrive, e.g. sliding window join.
3. In the non-windowed input and windowed output mode, we consume tuples as they arrive and materialize the output as a sliding window, e.g. we could store a sliding window of the result of a selection predicate.
4. In the windowed input and windowed output mode, we define windows over the input streams and materialize the output as a sliding window. For example, we can maintain a sliding window of the results of a windowed join.

Only Mode 1 does not require the use of a window; our storage techniques are directly applicable in all other cases. Furthermore, Modes 2 and 4 may require one of two index types on the input windows, as will be explained next.

3.2 Incremental Evaluation

An orthogonal classification considers whether an operator may be incrementally updated without accessing the entire window. Mode 1 and 3 operators are incremental as they do not require a window on the input. In Modes 2 and 4, we distinguish three groups: incremental operators, operators that become incremental if a histogram of the window is available, and non-incremental operators. The first group includes aggregates computable by dividing the data into partitions (e.g. basic windows) and storing a partial aggregate for each partition. For example, we may compute the windowed sum by storing a cumulative sum and partial sums for each basic window; upon re-evaluation, we subtract the sum of the items in the oldest basic window and add the sum of the items in the newest basic window. The second group contains some non-distributive aggregates (e.g. median) and set expressions. For instance, we can incrementally compute a windowed intersection by storing a histogram of attribute value frequencies: we subtract frequency counts of items in the oldest basic window, add frequency counts of items in the newest basic window, and re-compute the intersection by scanning the histogram and returning values with non-zero counts in each window. The third group includes operators such as join and some non-distributive aggregates such as variance, where the entire window must be probed to update the answer. Thus, many windowed operators require one of two types of indices: a histogram-like summary index that stores attribute values and their multiplicities, or a full index that enables fast retrieval of tuples in the window.

4 Indexing for Set-Valued Queries

We begin our discussion of sliding window indices with five techniques for set-valued queries on one attribute. This corresponds to Mode 2 and 4 operators that are not incremental without an index, but become incremental when a histogram is available. Our indices consist of a set of attribute values and their frequency counts, and all but one make use of the domain storage model. In this model, attribute values are stored in an external data structure to which tuples point.

4.1 Domain Storage Index as a List (L-INDEX)

The L-INDEX is a linked list of attribute values and their frequencies, sorted by value. It is compatible with LIST, AGGR, and HASH as the underlying basic window implementations. When using LIST and the domain storage model, each tuple has a pointer to the entry in the L-INDEX that corresponds to the tuple's attribute value—this configuration is shown in Fig. 3 (a). When using AGGR or HASH, each distinct value in every basic window has a pointer to the corresponding entry in the index. There are no pointers directed from the index back to the tuples; we will deal with attribute-valued indices, which need pointers from the index to the tuples, in the next section.

Insertion in the L-INDEX proceeds as follows. For each tuple arrival (LIST) or each new distinct value (AGGR and HASH), we scan the index and insert a pointer from the tuple (or AGGR node) to the appropriate index node. This can be done as tuples arrive, or after the newest basic window fills up; the total cost of each is equal, but the former spreads out the computation. However, we may not increment counts in the index until the newest basic window is ready to be attached, so we must perform a final scan of the basic window when it has filled up, following pointers to the index and incrementing counts as appropriate. To delete from the L-INDEX, we scan the oldest basic window as it is being removed, follow pointers to the index, and decrement the counts. There remains the issue of deleting an attribute value from the index when its count drops to zero. We will discuss this problem separately in Sect. 4.4.

4.2 Domain Storage Index as a Search Tree (T-INDEX) or Hash Table (H-INDEX)

Insertion in the L-INDEX is expensive because the entire index may need to be traversed before a value is found. This can be improved by implementing the index as a search tree, whose nodes store values and their counts. An example using an AVL tree [10] is shown in Fig. 3 (b); we will assume that a self-balancing tree is used whenever referring to the T-INDEX in the rest of the paper. A hash table index is another alternative, with buckets containing linked lists of values and frequency counts, sorted by value. An example is shown in Fig. 3 (c).

4.3 Grouped Index (G-INDEX)

The G-INDEX is an L-INDEX that stores frequency counts for groups of values rather than for each distinct value. It is compatible with LIST and GROUP, and may be used with or without the domain storage model. Using domain storage, each tuple (LIST) or group of values (GROUP) contains a pointer to the

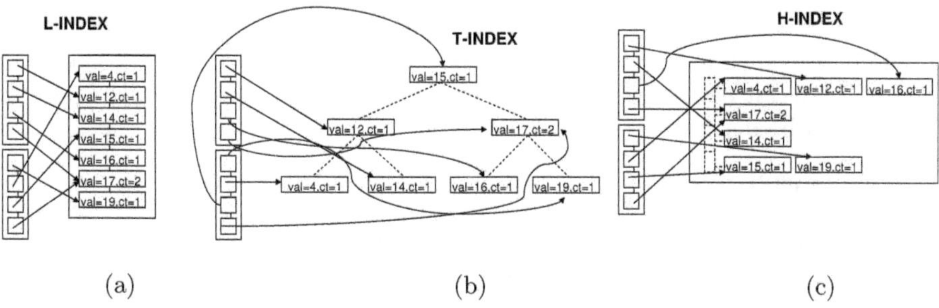

Fig. 3. Illustration of the (a) L-INDEX, (b) T-INDEX, and (c) H-INDEX, assuming that the sliding window consists of two basic windows with four tuples each. The following attribute values are present in the basic windows: 12,14,16,17 and 19,4,15,17

G-INDEX node that stores the label for the group; only one copy of the label is stored. However, with a small number of groups, we may choose not to use the domain storage model and instead store group labels in each basic window. At a price of higher space usage, we benefit from simpler maintenance as follows. When the newest basic window fills up, we merge the counts in its GROUP structure with the counts in the oldest basic window's GROUP structure, in effect creating a sorted delta-file that contains changes which need to be applied to the index. We then merge this delta-file with the G-INDEX, adding or subtracting counts as appropriate. In the remainder of the paper, we will assume that domain storage is not used when referring to the G-INDEX.

4.4 Purging Unused Attribute Values

Each of our indices stores frequency counts for attribute values or groups thereof. A new node must be inserted in the index if a new value appears, but it may not be wise to immediately delete nodes whose counts reach zero. This is especially important if we use a self-balancing tree as the indexing structure, because delayed deletions should decrease the number of required re-balancing operations. The simplest solution is to clean up the index every n tuples, in which case every nth tuple to be inserted invokes an index scan and removal of zero counts, or to do so periodically. Another alternative is to maintain a data structure that points to nodes which have zero counts, thereby avoiding an index scan.

4.5 Analytical Comparison

We will use the following variables: d is the number of distinct values in a basic window, g is the number of groups in GROUP and the G-INDEX, h is the number of hash buckets in HASH and the H-INDEX, b is the number of tuples in a basic window, N is the number of tuples in the window, and D is the number of distinct values in the window. We assume that d and b are equal across basic windows and that N and D are equal across all instances of the sliding window. The G-INDEX is expected to require the least space, especially if the number of groups is small, followed by the L-INDEX. The T-INDEX requires additional parent-child pointers while the H-INDEX requires a hash directory. The per-tuple time complexity can be divided into four steps (except the GROUP implementation, which will be discussed separately):

1. Maintaining the underlying sliding window, as derived in Sect. 2.3.
2. Creating pointers from new tuples to the index, which depends on two things: how many times we scan the index and how expensive each scan is. The former costs 1 for LIST, and $\frac{d}{b}$ for AGGR and HASH (in AGGR and HASH, we only make one access into the index for each distinct value in the basic window). The latter costs D for the L-INDEX, $\log D$ for the T-INDEX, and $\frac{D}{h}$ for the H-INDEX.
3. Scanning the newest basic window when it has filled up, following pointers to the index, and incrementing the counts in the index. This is 1 for LIST, and $\frac{d}{b}$ for AGGR and HASH.
4. Scanning the oldest basic window when it is ready to be expired, following pointers to the index, and decrementing the counts. This costs the same as in Step 3, ignoring the cost of periodic purging of zero-count values.

The cost of the G-INDEX over GROUP consists of inserting into the GROUP structure (g per tuple), and merging the delta-file with the index, which is g per basic window, or $\frac{g}{b}$ per tuple (this is the merging approach where the domain storage model is not used). Table 1 summarizes the per-tuple time complexity of maintaining each type of index with each type of basic window implementation, except the G-INDEX. The G-INDEX is expected to be the fastest, while the T-INDEX and the H-INDEX should outperform the L-INDEX if basic windows contain multiple tuples with the same attribute values.

Table 1. Per-tuple cost of maintaining each type of index using each type of basic window implementation

	L-INDEX	T-INDEX	H-INDEX
LIST	$O(D)$	$O(\log D)$	$O(\frac{D}{h})$
AGGR	$O(d + \frac{d}{b}D)$	$O(d + \frac{d}{b}\log D)$	$O(d + \frac{d}{b}\frac{D}{h})$
HASH	$O(\frac{d}{h} + \frac{d}{b}D)$	$O(\frac{d}{h} + \frac{d}{b}\log D)$	$O(\frac{d}{h} + \frac{d}{b}\frac{D}{h})$

We now compare our results with disk-based wave indices [14], which split a windowed index into sub-indices, grouped by time. This way, batch insertions and deletions of tuples are cheaper, because only one or two sub-indices need to be accessed and possibly re-clustered. We are not concerned with disk accesses and clustering in memory. Nevertheless, the idea of splitting a windowed index (e.g. one index stores the older half of the window, the other stores the newer half) may be used in our work. The net result is a decrease in update time, but an increase in memory usage as an index node corresponding to a particular attribute value may now appear in each of the sub-indices.

5 Indexing for Attribute-Valued Queries

In this section, we consider indexing for attribute-valued queries, which access individual tuples, i.e. Mode 2 and 4 operators that are not incremental. Because we need to access individual tuples that possibly have more than one attribute, LIST is the only basic window implementation available as we do not want to aggregate out any attributes. In what follows, we will present several methods of maintaining an attribute-valued index, each of which may be added on to any of the index structures proposed in the previous section.

5.1 Windowed Ring Index

To extend our set-valued indices to cover attribute-valued queries, we add pointers from the index to some of the tuples. We use a ring index [1], which links all tuples with the same attribute value; additionally, the first tuple is pointed to by a node in the index that stores the attribute value, while the last tuple points back to the index, creating a ring for each attribute value. One such ring, built on top of the L-INDEX, is illustrated in Fig. 4 (a). The sliding window is on the left, with the oldest basic window at the top and the newest (not yet full) basic window at the bottom. Each basic window is a LIST of four tuples. Shaded boxes indicate tuples that have the same attribute value of five and are connected by ring pointers. We may add new tuples to the index as they arrive, but we must ensure that queries do not access tuples in the newest basic window until it is full. This can be done by storing end-of-ring pointers, as seen in Fig. 4, identifying the newest tuple in the ring that is currently active in the window.

Let N be the number of tuples and D be the number of distinct values in the sliding window, let b be the number of basic windows, and let d be the average number of distinct values per basic window. When a new tuple arrives, the index is scanned for a cost of D (assuming the L-INDEX) and a pointer is created from the new tuple to the index. The youngest tuple in the ring is linked to the new tuple, for a cost $\frac{N}{D}$ as we may have to traverse the entire ring in the worst case. When the newest basic window fills up, we scan the oldest basic window and remove expired tuples from the rings. However, as shown in Fig. 4 (b), deleting the oldest tuple (pointed to by the arrow) entails removing its pointer in the ring (denoted by the dotted arrow) and following the ring all the way back to the index in order to advance the pointer to the start of the ring (now pointing to the next oldest tuple). Thus, deletion costs $\frac{N}{D}$ per tuple. Finally, we scan the index and update end-of-ring pointers for a cost of D. Figure 4 (c) shows the completed update with the oldest basic window removed and the end-of-ring pointer advanced. The total maintenance cost per tuple is $D + 2\frac{N}{D} + \frac{D}{b}$.

5.2 Faster Insertion with Auxiliary Index (AUX)

Insertion can be cheaper with the auxiliary index technique (AUX), which maintains a temporary local ring index for the newest basic window, as shown in Fig. 5 (a). When a tuple arrives with an attribute value that we have not seen before

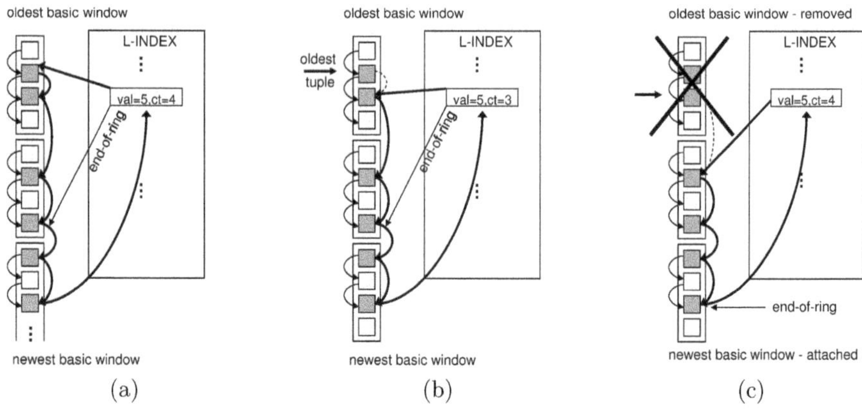

(a) (b) (c)

Fig. 4. Maintenance of a windowed ring index

in this basic window, we create a node in the auxiliary index for a cost of d. We then link the new node with the appropriate node in the main index for a cost of D. As before, we also connect the previously newest tuple in the ring with the newly arrived tuple for a cost of $\frac{N}{D}$. If another tuple arrives with the same distinct value, we only look up its value in the auxiliary index and append it to the ring. When the newest basic window fills up, advancing the end-of-ring pointers and linking new tuples to the main index is cheap as all the pointers are already in place. This can be seen in Fig. 5 (b), where dotted lines indicate pointers that can be deleted. The temporary index can be re-used for the next new basic window. The additional storage cost of the auxiliary index is $3d$ because three pointers are needed for every index node, as seen in Fig. 5. The per-tuple maintenance cost is $d+\frac{d}{b}(1+D+\frac{N}{D})$ for insertion plus $\frac{N}{D}$ for deletion.

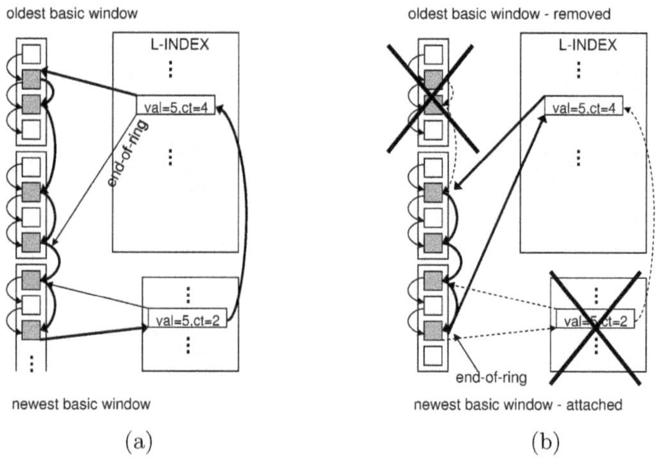

(a) (b)

Fig. 5. Maintenance of an AUX ring index

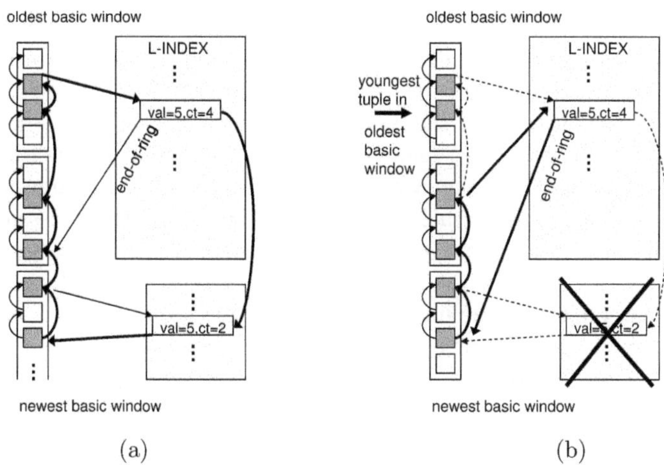

Fig. 6. Maintenance of a BW ring index

5.3 Faster Deletion with Backward-Linked Ring Index (BW)

The AUX method traverses the entire ring whenever deleting a tuple, which could be avoided by storing separate ring indices for each basic window. However, this is expensive. Moreover, we cannot traverse the ring and delete all expired tuples at once because we do not store timestamps within tuples, so we would not know when to stop deleting. We can, however, perform bulk deletions with the following change to the AUX method: we link tuples in reverse-chronological order in the LISTs and in the rings. This method, to which we refer as the backward-linked ring index (BW), is illustrated in Fig. 6 (a). When the newest basic window fills up, we start the deletion process with the youngest tuple in the oldest basic window, as labeled in Fig. 6 (b). This is possible because tuples are now linked in reverse chronological order. We then follow the ring (which is also in reverse order) until the end of the basic window and remove the ring pointers. This is repeated for each tuple in the basic window, but some of the tuples will have already been disconnected from their rings. Lastly, we create new pointers from the oldest active tuple in each ring to the index. However, to find these tuples, it is necessary to follow the rings all the way back to the index. Nevertheless, we have decreased the number of times the ring must be followed from one per tuple to one per distinct value, without any increase in space usage over the AUX method! The per-tuple maintenance cost of the BW method is $d + \frac{d}{b}(1 + D + \frac{N}{D})$ for insertion (same as AUX), but only $\frac{d}{b}\frac{N}{D}$ for deletion.

5.4 Backward-Linked Ring Index with Dirty Bits (DB)

If we do not traverse the entire ring for each distinct value being deleted, we could reduce deletion costs to $O(1)$ per tuple. The following is a solution that requires additional D bits and D tuples of storage, and slightly increases the query processing time. We use the BW technique, but for each ring, we do not delete the youngest tuple in the oldest basic window. Rather than traversing each ring to find the oldest active tuple, we create a pointer from the youngest tuple in the oldest basic window to the index, as seen in Fig. 6 (b). Since we normally delete the entire oldest basic window, we now require additional storage for up to D expired tuples (one from each ring). Note that we cannot assume that the oldest tuple in each ring is stale and ignore it during query processing—this is true only for those attribute values which appeared in the oldest basic window. Otherwise, all the tuples in the ring are in fact current. Our full solution, then, is to store "dirty bits" in the index for each distinct value, and set these bits to zero if the last tuple in the ring is current, and to one otherwise. Initially, all the bits are zero. During the deletion process, all the distinct values which appeared in the oldest basic window have their bits set to one. We call this algorithm the backward-linked ring index with dirty bits (DB).

6 Experiments

In this section, we experimentally validate our analytical results regarding the maintenance costs of various indices and basic window implementations. Further, we examine whether it is more efficient to maintain windowed indices or to re-execute continuous queries from scratch by accessing the entire window. Due to space constraints, we present selected results here and refer the reader to an extended version of this paper for more details [7].

6.1 Experimental Setting and Implementation Decisions

We have implemented our proposed indices and basic window storage structures using Sun Microsystems JDK 1.4.1, running on a Windows PC with a 2 GHz Pentium IV processor and one gigabyte of RAM. To test the T-INDEX, we adapted an existing AVL tree implementation from `www.seanet.com/users/arsen`. Data streams are synthetically generated and consist of tuples with two integer attributes and uniform arrival rates. Thus, although we are testing time-based windows, our sliding windows always contain the same number of tuples. Each experiment is repeated by generating attribute values from a uniform distribution, and then from a power law distribution with the power law coefficient equal to unity. We set the sliding window size to 100000 tuples, and in each experiment, we first generate 100000 tuples to fill the window in order to eliminate transient effects occurring when the windows are initially non-full. We then generate an additional 100000 tuples and measure the time taken to process the latter. We repeat each experiment ten times and report the average processing time.

With respect to periodic purging of unused attribute values from indices, we experimented with values between two and five times per sliding window roll-over without noticing a significant difference. We set this value to five times per window roll-over (i.e. once every 20000 tuples). In terms of the number of hash buckets in HASH and the H-INDEX, we observed the expected result that increasing the number of buckets improves performance. To simplify the experiments, we set the number of buckets in HASH to five (a HASH structure is needed for every basic window, so the number of buckets cannot be too large), and the number of buckets in the H-INDEX to one hundred. All hash functions are modular divisions of the attribute value by the number of buckets. The remaining variables in our experiments are the number of basic windows (50, 100, and 500) and the number of distinct values in the streams (1000 and 10000).

6.2 Experiments with Set-Valued Queries

Index Maintenance. Relative index maintenance costs are graphed in Fig. 7 (a) when using LIST and AGGR as basic window implementations; using HASH is cheaper than using AGGR, but follows the same pattern. As expected, the L-INDEX is the slowest and least scalable. The T-INDEX and the H-INDEX perform similarly, though the T-INDEX wins more decisively when attribute values are generated from a power law distribution, in which case our simple hash function breaks down (not shown). AGGR fails if there are too few basic windows because it takes a long time to insert tuples into the AGGR lists, especially if the number of distinct values is large. Moreover, AGGR and HASH only show noticeable improvement when there are multiple tuples with the same attribute values in the same basic window. This happens when the number of distinct values and the number of basic windows are fairly small, especially when values are generated from a power law distribution.

The performance advantage of using the G-INDEX, gained by introducing error as the basic windows are summarized in less detail, is shown in Fig. 7 (b). We compare the cost of four techniques: G-INDEX with GROUP for 10 groups, G-INDEX with GROUP for 50 groups, no index with LIST, and T-INDEX with LIST, the last being our most efficient set-valued index that stores counts for each distinct value. For 1000 distinct values, even the G-INDEX with 10 groups is cheaper to maintain than a LIST without any indices or the T-INDEX. For 10000 distinct values, the G-INDEX with 50 groups is faster than the T-INDEX and faster than maintaining a sliding window using LIST without any indices.

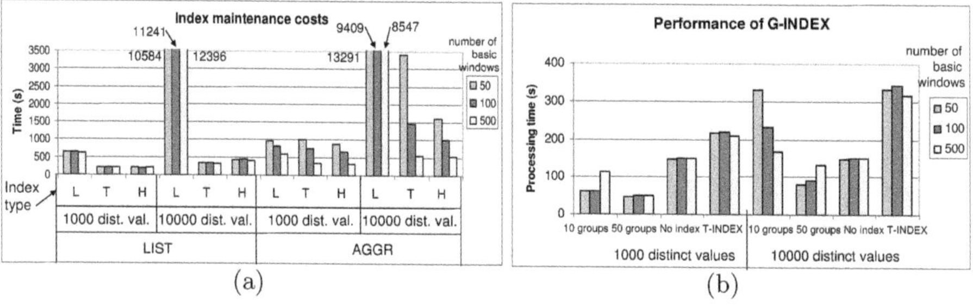

Fig. 7. Index maintenance costs. Chart (a) compares the L-INDEX (L), the T-INDEX (T), and the H-INDEX (H). Chart (b) shows the efficiency of the G-INDEX

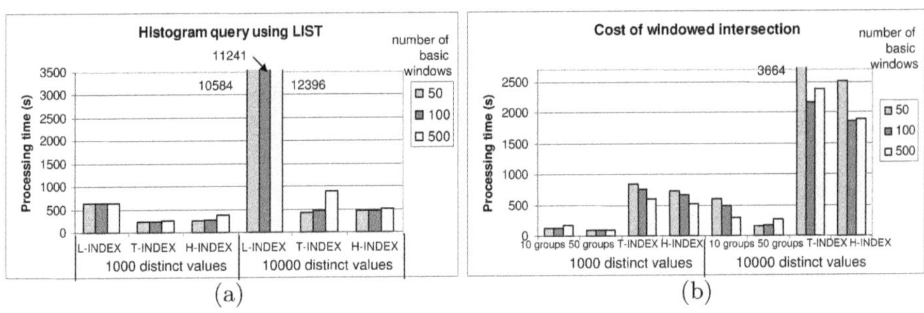

Fig. 8. Query processing costs of (a) the windowed histogram, and (b) the windowed intersection

Cost of Windowed Histogram. We now use our indices for answering continuous set-valued queries. First, we test a windowed histogram query that returns a (pointer to the first element in a) sorted list of attribute values and their multiplicities. This is a set-valued query that is not incrementally computable without a summary index. We evaluate three basic window implementations: LIST, AGGR, and HASH, as well as three indices: L-INDEX (where the index contains the answer to the query), T-INDEX (where an in-order traversal of the tree must be performed to generate updated results), and H-INDEX (where a merge-sort of the sorted buckets is needed whenever we want new results). We also execute the query without indices in two ways: using LIST as the basic window implementation and sorting the window, and using AGGR and merge-sorting the basic windows. We found that the former performs several orders of magnitude worse than any indexing technique, while the latter is faster but only outperforms an indexing technique in one specific case—merge-sorting basic windows implemented as AGGRs was roughly 30 percent faster than using the L-INDEX over AGGR for fifty basic windows and 10000 distinct values, but much slower than maintaining a T-INDEX or an H-INDEX with the same parameters. This is because the L-INDEX is expensive to maintain with a large number of distinct values, so it is cheaper to implement basic windows as AGGRs without an index and merge-sort them when re-evaluating the query. Results are shown in Fig. 8 (a) when using LIST as the basic window implementation; see [7] for results with other implementations. The T-INDEX is the overall winner, followed closely by the H-INDEX. The L-INDEX is the slowest because it is expensive to maintain, despite the fact that it requires no post-processing to answer the query. This is particularly noticeable when the number of distinct values is large—processing times of the L-INDEX extend beyond the range of the graph. In terms of basic window implementations, LIST is the fastest if there are many basic windows and many distinct values (in which case there are few repetitions in any one basic window), while HASH wins if repetitions are expected (see [7]).

Cost of Windowed Intersection. Our second set-valued query is an intersection of two windows, both of which, for simplicity, have the same size, number of basic windows, and distinct value counts. We use one index with each node storing two counts, one for each window; a value is in the result set of the intersection if both of its counts are non-zero. Since it takes approximately equal time to sequentially scan the L-INDEX, the T-INDEX, or the H-INDEX, the relative performance of each technique is exactly as shown in Fig. 7 in the index maintenance section—we are simply adding a constant cost to each technique by scanning the index and returning intersecting values. What we want to show in this experiment is that G-INDEX over GROUP may be used to return an approximate intersection (i.e. return a list of value ranges that occur in both windows) at a dramatic reduction in query processing cost. In Fig. 8 (b), we compare the G-INDEX with 10 and 50 groups against the fastest implementation of the T-INDEX and the H-INDEX. G-INDEX over GROUP is the cheapest for two reasons. Firstly, it is cheaper to insert a tuple in a GROUP structure because its list of groups and counts is shorter than an AGGR structure with a list of counts for each distinct value. Also, it is cheaper to look up a range of values in the G-INDEX than a particular distinct value in the L-INDEX.

6.3 Experiments with Attribute-Valued Queries

To summarize our analytical observations from Sect. 5, the traditional ring index is expected to perform poorly, AUX should be faster at the expense of additional memory usage, while BW should be faster still. DB should beat BW in terms of index maintenance, but query processing with DB may be slower. In what follows, we only consider an underlying L-INDEX, but our techniques may be implemented on top of any other index; the speed-up factor is the same in each case. We only compare the maintenance costs of AUX, BW, and DB as our experiments with the traditional ring index showed its maintenance costs to be at least one order of magnitude worse than our improved techniques.

Since AUX, BW, and DB incur equal tuple insertion costs, we first single out tuple deletion costs in Fig. 9 (a). As expected, deletion in DB is the fastest, followed by BW and FW. Furthermore, the relative differences among the techniques are more noticeable if there are fewer distinct values in the window and consequently, more tuples with the same attribute values in each basic window. In this case, we can delete multiple tuples from the same ring at once when the oldest basic window expires. In terms of the number of basic windows, FW is expected to be oblivious to this parameter and so we attribute the differences in FW maintenance times to experimental randomness. BW should perform better as we decrease the number of basic windows, which it does. Finally, DB incurs constant deletion costs, so the only thing that matters is how many deletions (one per distinct value) are preformed. In general, duplicates are more likely with fewer basic windows, which is why DB is fastest with 50 basic windows. Similar results were obtained when generating attribute values from a power law distribution, except that duplicates of popular items were more likely, resulting in a greater performance advantage of BW and DB over FW (not shown).

Next, we consider tuple insertion and overall query processing costs. We run a query that sorts the window on the first attribute and outputs the second

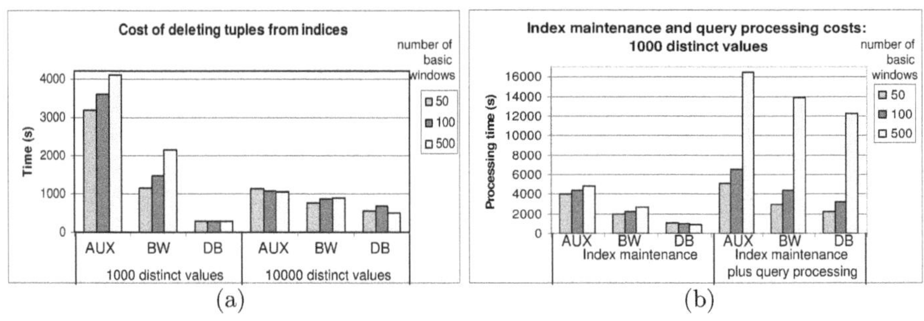

(a) (b)

Fig. 9. Performance of AUX, BW, and DB in terms of (a) deleting tuples from the index, and (b) processing an attribute-valued query

attribute in sorted order of the first. This query benefits from our attribute-valued indices because it requires access to individual tuples. In Fig. 9 (b), we graph index maintenance costs and cumulative processing costs for the case of 1000 distinct values; see [7] for results with 10000 distinct values. Since insertion costs are equal for AUX, BW, and DB, total index maintenance costs (first three sets of bars) grow by a constant. In terms of the total query processing cost (last three sets of bars), DB is faster than BW by a small margin. This shows that complications arising from the need to check dirty bits during query processing are outweighed by the lower maintenance costs of DB. Nevertheless, one must remember that BW is more space-efficient than DB. Note the dramatic increase in query processing times when the number of basic windows is large and the query is re-executed frequently.

6.4 Lessons Learned

We showed that it is more efficient to maintain our proposed set-valued windowed indices than it is to re-evaluate continuous queries from scratch. In terms of basic window implementations, LIST works well due to its simplicity, while the advantages of AGGR and HASH only appear if basic windows contain many tuples with the same attribute values. Of the various indexing techniques, the T-INDEX works well in all situations, though the H-INDEX also performs well. The L-INDEX is slow. Moreover, G-INDEX over GROUP is very efficient at evaluating approximate answers to set-valued queries.

Our improved attribute-valued indexing techniques are considerably faster than the simple ring index, with DB being the overall winner, as long as at least some repetition of attribute values exists within the window. The two main factors influencing index maintenance costs are the multiplicity of each distinct value in the sliding window (which controls the sizes of the rings, and thereby affects FW and to a lesser extent BW), and the number of distinct values, both in the entire window (which affects index scan times) and in any one basic window (which affects insertion costs). By far, the most significant factor in attribute-valued query processing cost is the basic window size.

7 Conclusions and Open Problems

This paper began with questions regarding the feasibility of maintaining sliding window indices. The experimental results presented herein verify that the answer is affirmative, as long as the indices are efficiently updatable. We addressed the problem of efficient index maintenance by making use of the basic window model, which has been the main source of motivation behind our sliding window query semantics, our data structures for sliding window implementations, and our windowed indices. In future work, we plan to develop techniques for indexing materialized views of sliding window results and sharing them among similar queries. We are also interested in approximate indices and query semantics for situations where the system cannot keep up with the stream arrival rates and is unable to process every tuple.

References

1. C. Bobineau, L. Bouganim, P. Pucheral, P. Valduriez. PicoDMBS: Scaling down database techniques for the smartcard. *VLDB'00*, pp. 11–20.
2. E. Cohen, M. Strauss. Maintaining time-decaying stream aggregates. *PODS'03*, pp. 223–233.
3. A. Das, J. Gehrke, M. Riedewald. Approximate join processing over data streams. *SIGMOD'03*, pp. 40–51.
4. M. Datar, A. Gionis, P. Indyk, R. Motwani. Maintaining stream statistics over sliding windows. *SODA'02*, pp. 635–644.
5. D. J. DeWitt et al. Implementation techniques for main memory database systems. *SIGMOD'84*, pp. 1–8.
6. A. Gärtner, A. Kemper, D. Kossmann, B. Zeller. Efficient bulk deletes in relational databases. *ICDE'01*, pp. 183–192.
7. L. Golab, S. Garg, M. T. Özsu. On indexing sliding windows over on-line data streams. University of Waterloo Technical Report CS-2003-29. Available at `db.uwaterloo.ca/~ddbms/publications/stream/cs2003-29.pdf`.
8. L. Golab, M. T. Özsu. Issues in data stream management. *SIGMOD Record*, 32(2):5–14, 2003.
9. L. Golab, M. T. Özsu. Processing sliding window multi-joins in continuous queries over data streams. *VLDB'03*, pp. 500–511.
10. E. Horowitz, S. Sahni. Fundamentals of Data Structures. Computer Science Press, Potomac, Maryland, 1987
11. J. Kang, J. Naughton, S. Viglas. Evaluating window joins over unbounded streams. *ICDE'03*.
12. T. J. Lehman, M. J. Carey. Query processing in main memory database management systems. *SIGMOD'86*, pp. 239–250.
13. L. Qiao, D. Agrawal, A. El Abbadi. Supporting sliding window queries for continuous data streams. *SSDBM'03*.
14. N. Shivakumar, H. García-Molina. Wave-indices: indexing evolving databases. *SIGMOD'97*, pp. 381–392.
15. J. Srivastava, C. V. Ramamoorthy. Efficient algorithms for maintenance of large database. *ICDE'88*, pp. 402–408.
16. Y. Zhu and D. Shasha. StatStream: Statistical monitoring of thousands of data streams in real time. *VLDB'02*, pp. 358–369.

A Framework for Access Methods for Versioned Data

Betty Salzberg*[1], Linan Jiang[2], David Lomet[3], Manuel Barrena[4]**, Jing Shan[1], and Evangelos Kanoulas[1]

[1] College of Computer & Information Science, Northeastern University, Boston, MA 02115
[2] Oracle Corporation, Oracle Parkway, Redwood Shores, CA 94404
[3] Microsoft Research, One Microsoft Way, Redmond, WA 98052
[4] Universidad de Extremadura, Cáceres, Spain

Abstract. This paper presents a framework for understanding and constructing access methods for versioned data. Records are associated with version ranges in a version tree. A minimal representation for the end set of a version range is given. We show how, within a page, a compact representation of a record can be made using start version of the version range only. Current-version splits, version-and-key splits and consolidations are explained. These operations preserve an invariant which allows visiting only one page at each level of the access method when doing exact-match search (no backtracking). Splits and consolidations also enable efficient stabbing queries by clustering data alive at a given version into a small number of data pages. Last, we survey the methods in the literature to show in what ways they conform or do not conform to our framework. These methods include temporal access methods, branched versioning access methods and spatio-temporal access methods. Our contribution is not to create a new access method but to bring to light fundamental properties of version-splitting access methods and to provide a blueprint for future versioned access methods. In addition, we have not made the unrealistic assumption that transactions creating a new version make only one update, and have shown how to treat multiple updates.

1 Introduction

Many applications such as medical records databases and banking require historical archives to be retained. Some applications such as software libraries additionally require the ability to reconstruct different historical versions, created along different versioning branches. For this reason, a number of access methods for versioned data, for example [11,4,1,10,7,13,8], have been proposed.

In this paper, we present a framework for constructing and understanding versioned access methods. The foundation of this framework is the study of *version splitting* of units of data storage (usually disk pages).

* This work was partially supported by NSF grant IRI-9610001 and IIS-0073063 and by a grant for hardware and software from Microsoft Corp.
** This work was partially supported by DGES grant PR95-426.

E. Bertino et al. (Eds.): EDBT 2004, LNCS 2992, pp. 730–747, 2004.
© Springer-Verlag Berlin Heidelberg 2004

Version splitting takes place when a storage unit becomes full. However, unlike in B-tree page splitting, some data items are *copied* to a new storage unit. Thus the data items are in both the old storage unit and the new storage unit. The motivation for copying some of the data when a storage unit is too full to accept a new insertion is to make the **stabbing query** (sometimes called "version-slice query", "time-slice query" or "snapshot query") ("Find all data alive at this version") efficient. Version splitting (and version-and-key splitting and page consolidation, both of which include version-splitting) cluster data in storage units so that when a storage unit P is accessed, a large fraction of the data items in P will satisfy the stabbing query.Many access methods for versioned data [11,4,1,10,7,13,8,12,6,9] use version-splitting techniques.

Our contribution is to explain version-splitting access methods as a general framework which can be applied in a number of circumstances. We also consider a more general situation where one transaction that creates a version can have more than one operation.(Many existing papers assume that a new version is created after each update. This is an unrealistic assumption.) It is hoped that the clearer understanding of the principles behind this technique will simplify implementation in future versioned access methods. In particular, it should become obvious that several methods which have been described in very different ways in the literature share fundamental properties.

Outline of Paper

The paper is organized as follows. In the next section, we will describe what we mean by versioned data and how it can be represented. Version splitting, version-and-key splitting and page consolidation is presented in section 3. In section 4, we describe operations on upper levels of the access method. In section 5, we will show how the related work fits into our framework. Section 6 concludes the paper with a summary. **Boldface** is used when making definitions of terms and *italics* is used for emphasis.

2 Versions, Versioned Data, and Version Ranges

In this section, we discuss versions, versioned data and version ranges. To illustrate our concepts, we begin with a database with three data objects or *records*, which are updated over time. We will start our first example with only two versions, followed by the second one with three versions. After presenting these examples, we will give some formal definitions.

2.1 Two-Version Example

First we suppose we have only two versions of the database. The first version is labeled v_1 and the second version is labeled v_2. In this example we have three distinct record keys. Each record is represented by a triple: a version label, a

version v_1
(v_1, k_1, d_1)
(v_1, k_2, d_2)
(v_1, k_3, d_3)

Fig. 1. Database starting with one version.

version v_1	version v_2
(v_1, k_1, d_1)	(v_2, k_1, d_1')
(v_1, k_2, d_2)	(v_2, k_2, d_2)
(v_1, k_3, d_3)	(v_2, k_3, d_3)

Fig. 2. Database with two versions.

(v_1, k_1, d_1) (v_2, k_1, d_1')
$(\{v_1, v_2\}, k_2, d_2)$
$(\{v_1, v_2\}, k_3, d_3)$

Fig. 3. Records are associated with a set of versions.

key, and the data. So with two versions, we get six records. **Keys** are version-invariant fields which do not change when a record is updated. For example, if records represent employees, the key might be the social security number of the employee. When the employee's salary is changed in a new version of the database, a new record is created with the new version label and the new data, but with the old social security number as key.

Figure 1 gives the records in version v_1. The k_i's are the version-invariant keys, which do not change from version to version. The d_i's are the data fields. These can change. Now let us suppose that in the second version of the database, v_2, only the first record changes. The other two records are not updated. We indicate this by using d_1' instead of d_1 to show that the data in the record with key k_1 has changed. We now list the records of both v_1 and v_2 in Figure 2 so they can be compared.

Note that there is redundancy here. The records with keys k_2 and k_3 have the same data in v_1 and v_2. The data has not changed.

What if instead of merely three records in the database there were a million records in the database and only one of them was updated in version v_2? This motivates the idea that the records should have a representation which indicates the set of versions for which they are unchanged. Then there are far fewer records. We could, for example, list the records in Figure 3.

Indicating the set of versions for which a record is unchanged is in fact what we shall do. However, in the case that there are a large number of versions for which a record does not change, we would like a shorter way to express this than listing all the versions where there is no change. For example, suppose the record with key k_2 is not modified for versions v_1 to v_{347} and then at version v_{348} an update to the record is made. We want some way to express this without writing down 347 version labels. One solution is to list the start and the end version labels, only. But there is another complication. There can be more than one end version since in some application areas, versions can branch [10,7,8].

2.2 Three-Version Example with Branching

Now we suppose we have three versions in the database. When we create version v_3, it can be created from version v_2 or from version v_1. In the example in Figure 4, we have v_3 created from v_1 by updating the record with key k_2. The record with key k_1 is unchanged in v_3. We illustrate the version derivation history for

version v_1	version v_2	version v_3
(v_1, k_1, d_1)	(v_2, k_1, d'_1)	(v_3, k_1, d_1)
(v_1, k_2, d_2)	(v_2, k_2, d_2)	(v_3, k_2, d'_2)
(v_1, k_3, d_3)	(v_2, k_3, d_3)	(v_3, k_3, d_3)

Fig. 4. Database with three versions.

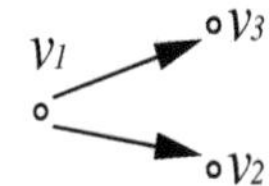

Fig. 5. Version tree for the three-version example.

$(\{v_1, v_3\}, k_1, d_1)$ (v_2, k_1, d'_1)
$(\{v_1, v_2\}, k_2, d_2)$ (v_3, k_2, d'_2)
$(\{v_1, v_2, v_3\}, k_3, d_3)$

Fig. 6. Records are listed with a set of versions.

this example in Figure 5. Now we show the representation of the records in this example using a single version label with each record.

We list with each record the set of versions for which they are unchanged in Figure 6.

We see that we cannot express a unique end version for a set of versions when there is branching. There is a possible end version on each branch. So instead of a list of versions we might keep the start version and the end version *on each branch.*

However, we also want to be able to express "open-endedness". For example, suppose the record with key k_3 is never updated in a branch. Do we want to keep updating the database with a new version label as an "end version" for k_3 every time there is a new version of the database in that branch? And what if there are a million records which do not change in the new version? We would have to find them all and change the end version set for each record. We shall give a representation for end sets with the property that only when a new version updates a record need we indicate this in the set of end versions for the original record.

To explain these concepts more precisely, we now introduce some formal definitions.

2.3 Versions

We start with an initial version of the database, with additional versions being created over time. **Versions V** is a set of versions. Initially $V = \{v_1\}$, where v_1 is called the **initial version**. New versions are obtained by updating or inserting records in an old version of V or deleting records from an old version in V. (Records are never physically deleted. Instead, a kind of tombstone or null record is inserted in the database.)

The set of versions can be represented by a tree, called the **version tree**. The nodes in the version tree are the versions and they are indicated by version labels such as v_1 and v_2. There is an edge from v_j to v_k if v_k is created by modifying (inserting, deleting or updating the data) some records of v_j. At the time a new version is created, the new version becomes a leaf on the version tree. There are many different ways to represent versions and version trees, e.g.[2]. We do not discuss these versioning algorithms here because our focus is an access method for versioned data, not how to represent versions. The version tree of our three-version example is illustrated in Figure 5.

Temporal databases are a special case of versioned databases where the versions are totally ordered (by timestamp). In this case, the version tree is a simple linked list.

We denote the partial order (resp. total order for a temporal database) on the nodes (versions) of the version tree with the "less than" symbol. We say that for $v \in V$, $\mathbf{anc(v)} = \{a|a < v\}$ is the set of **ancestors** of v. The set $\mathbf{desc(v)} = \{d|v < d\}$ is the set of **descendents** of v. A version v_k is **more recent** than v_j if $v_j < v_k$ (i.e. $v_k \in desc(v_j)$).This is standard terminology. For our three-version tree in Figure 5, $\text{desc}(v_1) = \{v_2, v_3\}$, $\text{anc}(v_3) = \text{anc}(v_2) = \{v_1\}$ and v_2 and v_3 are more recent than v_1.

2.4 Version Ranges

As we have seen in the two-version and three-version example above, records correspond to sets of versions, over which they do not change. Such a set of versions (and the edges between them) forms a connected subset of the version tree. We call a connected subset of the version tree a **version range**. (In the special case of a temporal database a version range is a time interval.) We wish to represent records in the database with a triple which is a version range, a key and the record data. We show here how to represent version ranges for records in a correct and efficient way.

A connected subset of a tree is itself a tree which has a root. This root is the **start version** of a version range. Part of our representation for a version range is the start version. We have seen that listing all the versions in a version range is inefficient in space use. Thus, we wish to represent the version range using the start version and *end versions on each branch.*

The major concern in representing end versions along a branch is that we do not want to have to update the end versions for every new version for which the record does not change. We give an example to illustrate our concern.

Let us look at Figure 7(a). Here we see a version tree with four nodes. Suppose the version v_4 is derived from v_3 and the record R with key k_3 in our (three-record) database example is updated in v_4. So we might say that v_3 is an end version for the version range of R. However, the Figure 7(b) shows that a new version (version v_5) can be derived from version v_3. If v_5 does not modify R, v_3 is no longer an end version for R. This example motivates our choice of "end versions" for a version range to be the versions where the record has been modified. The end versions will be "stop signs" along a branch, saying "you can't go beyond here." End versions of a version range will not belong to the version range.

For our example with R in Figure 7(b), we say the version range has start version $= v_1$ and end version $= v_4$. The set of versions inside the version range where R is not modified is $S = \{v_1, v_2, v_3, v_5\}$. Later, any number of descendents of versions in S could be created. If these new descendents do not modify R, one need not change the end set for the version range of R, even though the

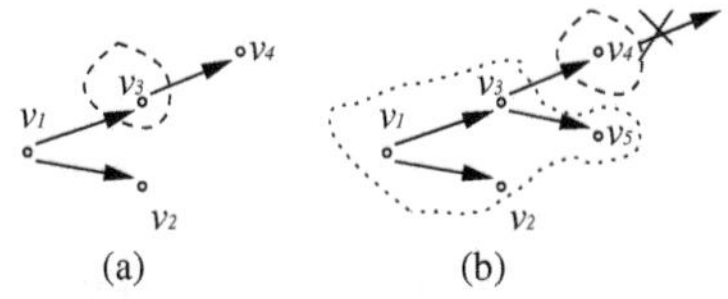

Fig. 7. Version range of R can not go further along the branch of v_4.

$((v_1, \{v_2\}), k_1, d_1)$ $((v_2, \{\}), k_1, d_1')$
$((v_1, \{v_3\}), k_2, d_2)$ $((v_3, \{\}), k_2, d_2')$
$((v_1, \{\}), k_3, d_3)$

Fig. 8. The three-version example with version range[1].

version range of R has been expanded. No descendent of v_4, however, can join the version range of R. Now we give a formal definition for end versions of a version range.

Let vr be a version range (hence a connected subset of the version tree). Let $start(vr)$ be the start version for vr. Remember that "<" is a partial order, so saying $\neg(a <= b)$ does not imply that $a > b$. Given these preliminaries we state our definition as a minimality constraint on a set of versions.

The **set of end versions for** vr (denoted $end(vr)$) is the minimal set of versions ev with the property that $v \in vr$ if and only if $start(vr) <= v$ and $\forall ev \in end(vr), \neg(ev <= v)$. That is, the set of end versions is the smallest set of versions such that elements of vr other than start(vr) are descendents of start(vr) which are not end versions nor descendents of end versions.

Saying that the set of end versions with this property is minimal implies two interesting properties of end versions:

1. End versions must be descendents of the start version. Otherwise they could be on some other branch, neither a descendent nor an ancestor of the start version and hence redundant.
2. End versions cannot be ancestors or descendents of one another. Otherwise, the more recent one would be redundant.

Using the definitions in this section, we represent records with a three-tuple: (version range vr, key, data). The version range is in turn a pair $(start(vr), end(vr))$. The three-version example is thus represented in Figure 8.

3 Pagination

In this section, we show how to store records in storage units (usually disk pages) which partition the version-key space and produce good access properties. Let us call the storage units "pages". We will only look at data pages in this section. In the next section we will look at the index pages which direct search to data pages.

[1] In figures we use { } to represent the null set, whereas in the text we use $\emptyset$

3.1 Data Pages

Data pages correspond to one version range and one key range. A **key range** for a page P is of form $[LowKey(P), HighKey(P))$. (Key ranges are half-open.) (We consider only one-dimensional key spaces in this discussion.) Keys of records stored in a data page P always lie within the key range of P. Version ranges of a record stored in P always have a non-empty intersection with the version range of P.

A **key-version range** (kr, vr) is a combination of key range kr and version range vr. We denote **KR(P)** as the key range of page P, **VR(P)** as the version range of page P and **KVR(P)** as the key-version range of page P. Using this notation, a data page D with $KVR(D) = (kr, vr)$ stores all records (vr', k, d) such that $k \in kr$ and $vr \cap vr' \neq \emptyset$.

Two key-version ranges (kr_1, vr_1) and (kr_2, vr_2) **intersect** when $kr_1 \cap kr_2 \neq \emptyset$ and $vr_1 \cap vr_2 \neq \emptyset$. The set of data pages partitions the key-version space. This implies no two distinct data pages have intersecting key-version ranges and every point in key-version space is in exactly one data page.

3.2 Compact Record Representation in Pages

It is possible to omit the end versions of a version range when storing a record in a data page and still have correct search. When we do this we say that we have a **compact-record representation**. This not only saves space, it makes updates very easy. The record being updated does not need to be found or modified; one only inserts the new record with the new data and the new start version and the same key.

In the three-version example, if we use the usual representation of version ranges as a pair (start version, set of end versions) we have Figure 9(a).

In this example, the end version set for the first record, $R1$, with key k_1 is $\{v_2\}$, indicating that $R1$ was updated in version v_2 to create a new record. The start version of a new record (updating a previous record) is the same as an end version of the previous record with the same key. We use this redundancy to eliminate listing end versions of version ranges for records in data pages. Let vr be a version range and let (vr, k, d) be a record in a page P. We say $(start(vr), k, d)$ is a **compact record**. The representation of the three-version example using compact records is shown in Figure 9 (b). As we can see, the two different representations of version ranges can be constructed from one other. So in the rest of the paper, without lose of generality, we will adopt the compact record representation.

Search for a given key k and version v which has been directed to page P must look at all the records in P with key k and find the one whose start version sv is the most recent one such that $sv \leq v$.

If only the start versions, and not the end versions are stored, one must explicitly mark deletion events to indicate that along some branch, a record is no longer there. For this reason we define null records.

A **null record** is a triple $(vr, k, null)$ where for each $v \in vr$, the versioned record corresponding to key k has been deleted. A null record is really a marker indicating that there is no data associated with version range vr and key k. If $(vr', k, null)$ is a null record we say $(start(vr'), k, null)$ is a **null compact record.**

From now on, (v, k, d) means a compact record, and in the special case when $d = null$, $(v, k, null)$ is a null compact record. Here, v is the start version for the version range of the record.

3.3 Operation Properties for Efficiency

In the next few subsections, we discuss page splitting and page consolidation. The goal in these operations is to produce efficient stabbing queries without too much replication. We will show the operations do yield efficient queries. The replication factor has been measured experimentally in many papers (in particular, [11]) not to be "too bad"; at most an average of three times the size of the database with no replication and no empty space, a good trade-off for the query efficiency.

To be deemed "efficient for stabbing queries" the access method should have the property that whenever a data page is accessed in a stabbing query for version v, a substantial percentage of the records in the page are alive for v. (A record is **alive for** v if its version range contains v.) After describing current-version splitting, key splitting, version-and-key splitting and page consolidation, we shall show under what conditions efficiency guarantees for the stabbing query can be made.

3.4 Splitting by Current Version

A **current version** is a leaf of the version tree. When new updates, deletes or inserts are made by a version v which is a current version, they should be inserted into the data page P whose key range contains the key of the update and whose version range contains the parent of the new (current) version v in the version tree. However, if P is full, a new page P' must be allocated. The page P' will contain the new record. The records of P which were updated by v will be moved to page P' and some of the records in P will be copied to page P'.

The new version v will become an end version for VR(P). The version range for P' will be $(v,\emptyset)$. This is called **current-version splitting.** In this section, we always split by a current version, i.e., a leaf of the version tree. (In some papers we discuss in the related work section [11,8] splitting by non-current versions is suggested.)

Records Copied or Moved to the New Page. The records which are copied to the new page P' are those whose version range intersects both the version range of P' and the version range of the old page P. The records which are

$((v_1, \{v_2\}), k_1, d_1)$
$((v_1, \{v_3\}), k_2, d_2)$
$((v_1, \{\}), k_3, d_3)$
$((v_2, \{\}), k_1, d_1')$
$((v_3, \{\}), k_2, d_2')$

(a)

(v_1, k_1, d_1)
(v_1, k_2, d_2)
(v_1, k_3, d_3)
(v_2, k_1, d_1')
(v_3, k_2, d_2')

(b)

Fig. 9. Three version example with its compact record representation.

(v_1, k_1, d_1)
(v_1, k_2, d_2)
(v_1, k_3, d_3)
(v_2, k_1, d_1')

(a)

(v_1, k_1, d_1)	(v_1, k_1, d_1)
(v_1, k_2, d_2)	(v_3, k_2, d_2')
(v_1, k_3, d_3)	(v_1, k_3, d_3)
(v_2, k_1, d_1')	

(b)

Fig. 10. When (v_3, k_2, d_2') is inserted, page D is split by current version v_3.

moved are records in P whose start version is v, and which are not null records. Null records only mark the end of a version range for another record, so there is no need to copy them to the new page if they do not have that function there.

More precisely, Let D be a data page identified by a key version range (kr, vr). We define **contents**$(D) = \{(v, k, d) | (v, k, d)$ is a compact record in $D\}$. We now define the subset of contents(D) which will be moved or copied to a new page during a current-version split.

Let v_n be the new version which makes an update causing D to be current-version split. The set of compact records *moved* from D to the new page is:

$$\{(v', k, d) | (v', k, d) \in contents(D) \wedge ((v' = v_n) \wedge (d \neq null))\}$$

This is the set of records created by v_n. This happens when the new version updated several records in D and the first few fit in the page, but at some point the page D became full and further updates by v_n required a split. No null records are moved.

Let T be a logical (not physical) temporary page holding records created by v_n with key in KR(D). The set of compact records of page D to be copied to the new page is defined to be:

$$\{(v', k, d) | ((v', k, d) \in contents(D)) \wedge (v' < v_n \wedge d \neq null) \wedge$$

$$(\forall (v'', k, d') \in contents(D \cup T) \text{ such that } (v'' \leq v_n \wedge v'' \neq v'), v'' < v')\}$$

When we copy records from D to the new page, we do not want to copy any with the same key as any record in T. The above definition for copied records has this property. In the case, where a key k is *not* a key of a record in T, the record in D with key k having start version as the most recent ancestor of v_n is copied. Null records are not copied.

Let us give an illustration using the two version example and the three-version example. Suppose we have in page D our two-version records, create by v_1 and v_2 and represented as compact records as in Figure 10 (a).

Suppose D can only hold 4 records. Now we update the record with key k_2 in v_3 as before. We then have the records in the new page, D' as shown in Figure 10 (b).

We have copied the two records which are not changed by v_3 and we have inserted the new updated record. The record created by version v_2 is not included in the new page because its start version is not an ancestor of v_3. All three records in D' are alive for v_3. The upper levels of the index will be directing search for v_1 and for v_2 to D and for v_3 to D'.

When we copy a compact record to a new page, we do not change its start version even if the start version is not in the version range of the new page. In the example in Figure 10(b), we retained the start version v_1 in the two moved records even though v_1 is not in $VR(D') = (v_3, \emptyset)$. There are several reasons for this:

1. If a version range (or time interval) query (rather than a stabbing query) is made, we will be able to recognize identical records obtained from different data pages. (This is a query to find all the records alive in a version range.)
2. Copying is easier. No changes are made to the copied records.
3. Search within a page is unchanged and still correct.
4. Finding the set of historical records with the same key may have less disk accesses. For example, given the most recent version number sv, to find all historical records of key k_1, we can search the index pages for key k_1 and version $v < sv$ to find the previous versions. Otherwise, search will be less efficient if a record of this version is copied over many pages.

3.5 Key Splits and Version-and-Key Splits

We will also be splitting data pages by key. For this we define subsets of contents of pages which fall within a given key range. Splitting pages by key is done exactly like in B-trees: a split key sk is chosen in KR(P). Then all records with key less than sk remain in P and all records with key greater or equal to sk are *moved* to the new page.

If the number of records copied or moved to a new data page during a current-version split is above a certain threshold value T_k, a version-and-key split is made. Here a current-version split is followed by a key split. Note that $T_c < \lfloor T_k/2 \rfloor$ where T_c is the threshold for consolidation and T_k is the threshold for version-and-key split.

A key split instead of version-and-key split will be used if the full page has version range $(v, \emptyset)$, where v is the current version. This can happen when a transaction makes multiple updates. Figure 11 is an example. Assume v_2 is the current version. VR(P_2) = $(v_2, \emptyset)$. Assume maximum page capacity is 4. When a record (v_2, k_7, d_7) is inserted into P_2, a version-and-key split will be triggered, as shown in figure 11(b). Actually the version split is not necessary since the version range of P_2 is only one version. In this situation, a pure key split, as shown in figure 11(c), should be used instead. After the split, P_3 will be posted to the same parent as P_2. It is the only parent of P_3. The pure-key-split problems mentioned later in this section and in section 4.1 will not happen in this situation because the version range here contains only the current version. Note that this is the only situation where a key split is not combined with a version split. We call this a **restricted key split**. It is restricted to the case when the (old) full page version range contains only one version.

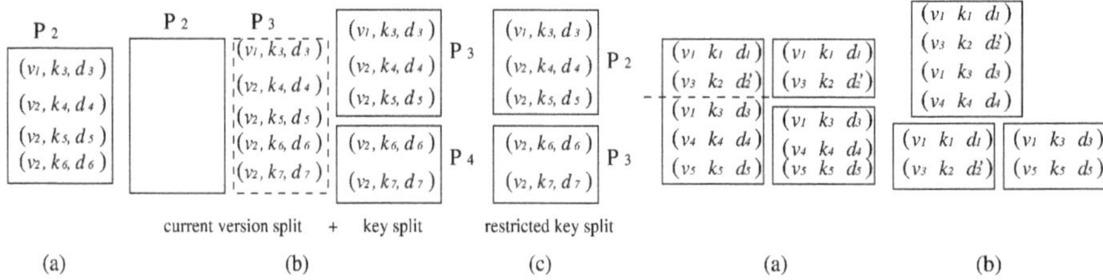

Fig. 11. When (v_2, k_7, d_7) is inserted, a restricted key split instead of a version and key split is used.

Fig. 12. After (v_4, k_4, d_4) and (v_5, k_5, d_5) are inserted, D' need to be split. (a) Pure key split with split key $= k_3$. (b) Version-and-key split: first split at version v_5 and then key split at k_3.

Our framework does not include pure key splits other than restricted key splits as in figure 11, only version-and-key splits and version splits. Here is an example to explain why we never do non-restricted key splits.

Look at D' in Figure 10(b). There are three records in D', all alive for v_3. Now suppose we insert into D' the record (v_4, k_4, d_4) using the version tree from Figure 7(b). At this point there are three records alive in D' for v_3 and four for v_4.

Now we wish to insert (v_5, k_5, d_5) in D' but D' is full. We shall use the version tree in Figure 7(b) for v_5 also, so we have v_4 and v_5 in $desc(v_3)$. Suppose we do a pure key split by split key $sk = k_3$, assuming $k_1 < k_2 < k_3 < k_4 < k_5$.

As shown in Figure 12(a), in the old page D' we have two records alive for v_3, v_4 and v_5. In D'', the new page with the higher key values, (v_1, k_3, d_3) is the only record alive for v_3, and (v_1, k_3, d_3) and (v_4, k_4, d_4) are alive for v_4 and (v_1, k_3, d_3) and (v_5, k_5, d_5) for v_5. The point is that in D'' we now have *only one record* alive for v_3. *Pure key splits cannot give good guarantees for numbers of records alive for a given version after the split unless the version range of the original page contains just one version (the restricted key split case).*

If we had split by v_5 first, and then done a key split by k_3, as we do in Figure 12(b), we would get two pages whose version ranges are both $(v_5, \emptyset)$ and both would have two records alive for v_5. The original D' would have 4 records, three alive for v_3 and four for v_4 as before.

3.6 Consolidation

In B-trees, pages are consolidated when their *contents* falls below a certain level. In versioned access methods, pages never lose contents from record deletions, which are logical, not physical. However, the number of records in the page satisfying the "stabbing" query ("Find all data alive for this version") may fall below an acceptable threshold T_c.

Let **pageSlice**(D, v) be the set of records in D whose version range contains v. This is the set of records **alive** in D at version v. After a record is deleted from

D, one checks to see if $|pageSlice(D, v)| < T_c$ where v is the version of the delete operation and T_c is the threshold. If so, we say D is **sparse** and we attempt to perform a page consolidation on D.

Consolidation is allowed when there is a suitable **sibling** with which to consolidate: another page with the same parent index page and with an adjacent key range. In this case, a current-version split is made first, both on the sparse page and on its sibling. The two new pages are then combined. If the combined page has too many records, a key split is made.

There are very few scenarios where a suitable sibling would not be available. This would happen when the whole database for a given version v fits in one data page and then only current-version splits are made (no version-and-key splits). This could happen near the creation time of the database until a sufficient number of insertions are made, or it could happen in a highly degenerate case when so many deletions were made that either one data page would hold all the records alive for some version v or there are too many null records to fit in one data page. (It is not possible that one data page becomes sparse when deleting at v and has no sibling while another data page (with a different parent) has records alive at v because upper levels would have consolidated before that happened.)

In the case when a transaction makes a large number of deletes, a special problem occurs. Let us look at an example in figure 13. Assume a transaction that creates the current version v_2 deletes all four records in page P_1 and inserts one record with key k_3. Assume the maximum page capacity is 5. After record $(v_2, k_1, null)$ is inserted in P_1 and an attempt is made to insert (v_2, k_3, d_3) in P_1, P_1 is version split as shown in figure 13(b). Now P_1 has v_2 as the end version of its version range. VR(P_2) is $(v_2, \emptyset)$. Some of the records in P_2 in figure 13(b) are "temporary records", which will be replaced by records of the current version with the same key. For example, (v_1, k_2, d_2) will be replaced by $(v_2, k_2, null)$ and (v_1, k_4, d_4) will be replaced by $(v_2, k_4, null)$. Note that this replacement only happens when the page's version range is $(v_{current}, \emptyset)$. After replacing these records, P_2 becomes sparse as shown in figure 13(c). Say that there is a sibling P_5, described in figure 13(d), with which P_2 can be consolidated. We do a version split on v_2 for P_5 and a version split on v_2 for P_2 (meaning here, we only copy live records) and obtain a new consolidated page P_3 with version range $(v_2, \emptyset)$. We now have two pages P_2 and P_3 with the same version range and overlapping key ranges. For this case, consolidating a sparse page whose version range is only one version, we call P_2, as in figure 13(d), a **ghost page**. A ghost page has a **ghost mark** in its parent indicating that it is NOT to be used in any search not **strictly including** its one version. (A range strictly includes a version v if v is in the range and is not the start version of the range.) This rules out using ghost pages in exact match search. The purpose of maintaining ghost pages is merely to facilitate version range searches in determining end versions of records. We anticipate few ghost pages in most applications since massive deletions are rare. Following our policy for moving records created by split versions, P_2 now contains only null records as in figure 13(d).

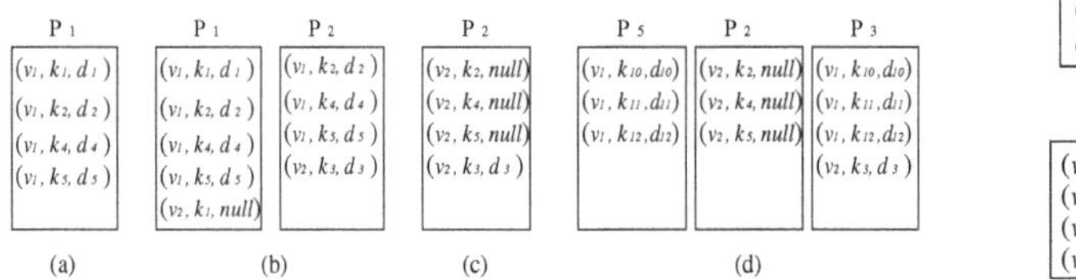

Fig. 13. After deletions and consolidation with P_5, all records in P_2 will be null records. P_2 is called ghost page.

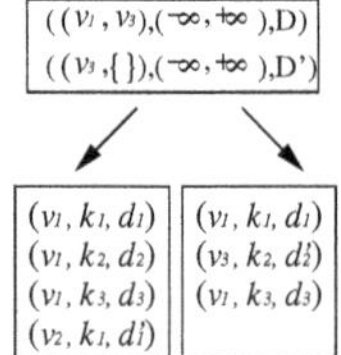

Fig. 14. Index page and data pages for the three-version example.

3.7 Stabbing Query Efficiency

The following assertions illustrate why copying some records as we do in version splitting, version-and-key splitting and consolidation helps stabbing queries to be efficient. In what follows, we assume that we start with one page D with the initial version v_1 having n alive records. The first assertion arises from the observation that if only inserts and updates are made, no version can have less than the number of records alive for v_1, the initial version. If, in addition, only version-splits are made, all the records alive for the split version are copied or moved into the new page.

Assertion 1 *If only version splits are made and there are only inserts and updates (no deletes), then for any data page D and any version $v \in VR(D)$, there will be at least n records in D satisfying the stabbing query for v.*

If we also do version-and-key splits, and assume T_k is the threshold for version-and-key splits, we get our second assertion. This is due to the observation that version-and-key splits only occur when the number of records alive for the splitting version to be copied or moved is greater than T_k, so the number in each of the two new pages is at least $T_k/2$.

Assertion 2 *If we do only updates and insertion and have only current-version or version-and-key or restricted-key splits, the stabbing query for $v \in VR(D)$ will obtain at least $min(n, T_k/2)$ records in P.*

Now allow deletes and let T_k be the threshold for version-and-key split and let T_c be the threshold for consolidation. We get a third assertion.

Assertion 3 *If it is always possible to find a sibling for node consolidation when $|pageSlice(v)| < T_c$ then we can guarantee the stabbing query for $v \in VR(D)$ will obtain at least $min(T_c, n)$ records in D, allowing version splits, version-and-key splits, restricted-key splits and node consolidation. (Note that ghost page will be not used for consolidation or stabbing query.)*

This shows that the stabbing query for v will be efficient since search in upper levels of the access method, as we show in the next section, will only retrieve data pages D with $v \in VR(D)$. In each of these accessed data pages, we have shown that at least $min(T_c, n)$ records satisfying the query will be found (provided that consolidation siblings are always available when needed).

4 Upper Levels

In this section we consider index pages, which direct search, as well as data pages. Let P, C be two (index or data) pages. We say page C is a **child page** of page P if the disk address of page C and some description of the key-version range of C is stored in page P. We will use **children(P)** to denote the set of child pages of page P. If $C \in children(P)$, we say page P is a **parent page** of page C. We will use **parents(C)** to denote the set of parent pages of page C.

The set of index pages and data pages form a Directed Acyclic Graph, or DAG. If C is a child page of P, there is an edge from P to C. Data pages do not have any outgoing edges. They are all leaves of the DAG. Two pages which are the same distance from the set of data pages are said to be at the same **level**. All the pages at levels above the data pages are index pages.

Index pages also correspond to key-version ranges. The set of index pages at a given level partitions the key-version space. An index page P with $KVR(P) = (kr, vr)$ channels searches for the version, key pair (v, k) with $v \in vr$ and $k \in kr$.

The contents of an index page are references to its children and we will use a list of the children of an index page I as **contents(I)**. In Figure 14, we show the index page and two data pages for the three-version example when the data page has split at v_3. An entry in an index page referencing a child C is of the form (start($VR(C)$), end($VR(C)$), $KR(C)$, disk page address(C)). (In the related work section, we will discuss some alternative forms for child entries in index pages.)

Access methods that fit our framework satisfy the following:

Invariant 1 *If page C is one level below page P and $KVR(P)$ intersects $KVR(C)$, then page $C \in children(P)$.*

At each level, since Invariant 1 is true, it is possible to decide exactly which page to access on the next level. For exact match search (search on one version and one key) there is only one page to visit at each level.

4.1 Index Page Splits and Consolidations

Index page splits and consolidations are similar to those of data pages. A current version split *copies* entries whose version ranges intersect the version range of both the old page P and the new page N. Any child entry whose version range lies only in $VR(P)$ stays in P. Any child entry whose version range lies only in $VR(N)$ is *moved* to N.

Since, in index page version splits, children entries can be copied from P to N, this creates multiple parents for these children. This is why the access method is a DAG and not a tree.

Now for index pages, we need to take into account that children pages have a key *range*, unlike data records, which have only a single key value. In this case there is an additional reason why it is desirable to do no pure key split without a version split first.

It is unlikely that for a given index page I, there is a key value k such that for every child C of I, either $k >= HighKey(KR(C))$ or else $k <= LowKey(KR(C))$. Thus, if we do a pure key split, we will probably have to copy child entries whose key range intersects the key range of both the new and old index page. Consider for example a database which starts with one data page D and then does a version-and-key split with split key sk, creating new data pages D' and D''. If we use sk as a split key for the parent index page I, some records in D will have keys greater than sk and others will have keys larger than sk. Thus, D will be a child both of I and of the new index page I'.

If, on the other hand, we do a current-version split first, we can choose a split key which is a boundary between two of the children and all the other children also have key ranges strictly above or strictly below the split key. In this case, we need not have copies of the same children entries in both two pages resulting from the key split.

When version splits occur on root nodes, previous work has considered two strategies. One is to increase the height by creating a new root with the old root as its child [7,8,11]. The other strategy is to maintain multiple roots and create a forest with shared subtrees [1,4,10]. In this case, when a version split occurs at a root, the new page becomes an additional root. A directory is kept with the addresses and version ranges of each root. Different trees have different heights and cover disjoint version ranges. Single root methods have the property that pages on each level partition the version-key sparce. Multiple root methods have the property that pages of each level within a given tree (under one root) partition the version range of the tree and the key range.

Consolidation of an index page I is indicated when consolidation of some of children(I) at some current version v has resulted in too few children of I alive for v. That is,

$$|\{P|(P \in children(I)) \text{ and } (v \in VR(P))\}| < T_{ci},$$

where T_{ci} is a threshold for index page consolidation. We say that the **fan-out** of I at v is **sparse**. In this case, as with data page consolidation, we find a sibling and do a current-version split on both the sparse page and its sibling and combine the result into one or two new index pages.

Before children are unable to consolidate because there is no suitable sibling for a given version v, the parent must have sparse fan-out at v. Thus the parent will consolidate with another index page on the same level, gaining suitable siblings for its child. This is why not finding suitable siblings for consolidation is unusual and only occurs in the degenerate cases we discussed before.

The index page splitting and consolidation definitions above guarantee the following: if any index page P satisfies Invariant 1, then any resulting page R from splitting or consolidating page P satisfies Invariant 1 too.

4.2 Posting

In order to have correct search, when a split or a consolidation takes place, information about the new page(s) N and the new boundaries of the old page

P must be posted to the parents of P. If this information were posted to all the parents of P, it is clear that Invariant 1 would still hold. But in fact, if we do current-version splitting and no pure key splits (no key splits that are not version-and-key splits nor restricted-key splits) less is needed. Posting need take place to only one parent.

Let v be a current version. If N is a new page created from any split or consolidation, $\mathrm{VR}(N) = (v, \phi)$. (This is *not* true if we allow pure key splits or splitting at other than current versions.) Further, since there are no pure key splits on index pages, for all index pages I, if $P \in \mathrm{children}(I)$, $\mathrm{KR}(P) \subseteq \mathrm{KR}(I)$. So there is one index page I among the parents of P such that $\mathrm{KVR}(N) \subseteq \mathrm{KVR}(I)$. This is the only parent where posting takes place.

5 Related Work

In this section, we outline how the methods proposed in the literature fit or do not fit our framework. Note that most of these methods are called "trees" although they are DAGs. (When restricted to one version, each of these DAGs is a tree.) None of these methods consider the problems of versions with multiple updates as we have done.

In [4], a write-once optical disk is used and the storage units are sets of optical disk pages. Since an update of optical disk data at the time the paper was written required indelibly burning about 1Kbyte of data and 300 bytes of checksum, it was not possible to go back and insert endpoints to version ranges of records. So the compact representation of records is used. This is a linear version tree, or temporal access method. It is presented as a way to store a B-tree and update it even though old versions had to be kept (because they could not be erased). There is no page consolidation. The multiple root strategy is used. This is called the Write-Once B-tree, or WOBT.

Another paper, [1] does have page consolidation and it does not have compact record representation in data pages. This is also a temporal access method with multiple roots. It is called MVBT, or Multi-version B-tree.

The paper [13] is based on the observation that page consolidation is done on *sparse* pages which however are not necessarily *full* pages. There is empty space in these pages. This paper places two or more logical pages (with a key range and time interval) in one physical page. There are then multiple references to a physical child page in a parent page. This increases space utilization. This is a temporal method.

The Fully Persistent B-tree [10] has page consolidation. It does not use the compact record representation. It has extra "version blocks" in the index levels which make the height of the "tree" larger than need be. It uses multiple roots.

(Versioned access methods are called **fully persistent** [3] if any version can be updated creating a new version. This causes branching in the version tree. A **partially persistent** access method only allows update on a current version, creating a linear version tree. Temporal access methods are partially persistent.)

The BT-tree, or Branched and Temporal tree [7] is also a fully persistent (branched) access method. It does page consolidation and it uses the compact data record representation. In index pages, instead of using the child entries we have described, a small binary tree called a **split history** or **sh** tree is used. This directs search depending on the key values and version values in the internal sh-tree nodes. The leaves of the sh-tree are child page addresses. The BT-tree has a single root.

All of the above methods do only current-version splits and version-and-key splits and no pure key splits. The next two methods allow splitting at versions other than the current version. As in current-version splitting, records whose version range is in the version range of both pages are copied and records whose version range is only in the new page are moved to the new page. The difference is that the set of moved records is larger than just those created by the splitting version.

The TSB-tree [11] is a temporal method and uses compact representation of records. It has no page consolidation. It has a single root. To save space and make retrieval quicker, pure key splits and non-current version splitting are allowed. In order to make posting to only one parent possible, it is required to split index pages I at a version v with the property that for all *current* children C of I, $v \leq start(VR(C))$. (**Current pages in a temporal access method** have $end(vr) = \emptyset$.) This results in current pages (the only ones that are split in a temporal access method) having only one parent.

The other paper to consider non-current version splits is the BTR-tree [8]. This is done to reduce the number of copies of records made when there is a great deal of branching. To achieve single-parent posting, only certain versions can be used for splitting. The set of possible splitting versions is derived from information gathered during the search. The BTR-tree uses compact data record representation and it supports page consolidation. It uses an sh-tree in index pages. It has a single root.

Recently, there have been some methods proposed for spatial and moving objects data (spatial-temporal data) which use current-version splitting. For example, [12] [6] both do version-splitting on an R-tree. Since the R-tree has spatial overlapping, neither satisfies Invariant 1 (with the key range understood to be a spatial key range). Thus exact match search (for a key and version) requires backtracking. On the other hand [9] is based on [5] (the hB-Pi tree), which is a spatial method without overlapping, so Invariant 1 is satisfied. The paper [9] uses the compact data record representation.

6 Summary

In this paper, we have presented a framework for versioned access methods. Records are associated with version ranges, which are connected subsets of the version tree. A definition for end sets for version ranges using minimality was given. Compact record representation, using only the start version of the version range, was introduced with its benefits in algorithmic simplicity and space usage.

We have shown, for the first time, how to handle versions which contain multiple updates. Previous work made the unrealistic assumption that each update was in a different version, created by a different transaction.

Current-version splits, version-and-key splits and consolidations were discussed and their effects on stabbing query efficiency were presented. For upper levels of the index, an invariant was introduced which allows visiting only one page at each level of the access method when doing exact-match search (no backtracking). Splits and consolidations of index pages preserve this invariant.

References

1. B. Becker, S. Gschwind, T. Ohler, B. Seeger, and P. Widmayer. On optimal multiversion access structures. In *Proc. Int. Symp. on Spatial Databases*, pages 123–141, Singapore, 1993.
2. Paul F. Dietz and Daniel D. Sleator. Two algorithms for maintaining order in a list. In *Proceedings of the nineteenth annual ACM conference on Theory of computing*, 1987.
3. James R. Driscoll, Neil Sarnak, and Daniel D. Sleator. Making data structure persistent. *Journal of Computer and System Sciences*, 38, February 1989.
4. M. C. Easton. Key-sequence data sets on indelible storage. *IBM J. Res. Development*, pages 230–241, 1986.
5. Georgios Evangelidis, David B. Lomet, and Betty Salzberg. The hB-Pi-Tree: A multi-attribute index supporting concurrency, recovery and node consolidation. *The VLDB Jounal*, pages 1–25, January 1997.
6. Marios Hadjieleftheriou, George Kollios, Vassilis J. Tsotras, and Dimitrios Gunopulos. Efficient indexing of spatiotemporal objects. In *EDBT 2002, LNCS 2287*, pages 251–268, 2002.
7. Linan Jiang, Betty Salzberg, David Lomet, and Manuel Barrena. The BT-Tree: A branched and temporal access method. In *International Conference on Very Large Data Bases*, pages 451–460, 2000.
8. Linian Jiang, Betty Salzberg, David Lomet, and Manuel Barrena. The BTR-Tree: Path-defined version-range splitting in a branched and temporal structure. In *Proceedings of the Eighth International Symposium on Spatial and Temporal Databases, SSTD 2003, Santorini Island, Greece, LNCS 2750.*
9. Evangelos Kanoulas and Georgios Evangelidis. Indexing of spatiotemporal data with the hB-Pi Tree. In *HDMS'02 1st Hellenic Data Management Symposium*, Athens, Hellas, July 2002.
10. Sitaram Lanka and Eric Mays. Fully persistent B^+-trees. In *Proceedings of ACM/SIGMOD Annual Conference on Management of Data*, pages 426–435, 1991.
11. D. Lomet and B. Salzberg. The performance of a multiversion access method. In *Proceedings of ACM/SIGMOD Annual Conference on Management of Data*, pages 354–363, 1990.
12. Yufei Tao and Dimitris Papadias. The MV3R-Tree: A spatio-temporal access method for timestamp and interval queries. In *VLDB 2001, Proceedings of 27th International Conference on Very Large Data Bases*, pages 431–440, Sep. 2001.
13. Peter J. Varman and Rakesh M. Verma. An efficient multiversion access structure. In *IEEE Transaction on Knowledge and Data Engineering*, pages 391–409, May/June 1997.

Management of Highly Dynamic Multidimensional Data in a Cluster of Workstations

Vassil Kriakov[1], Alex Delis[2], and George Kollios[3]

[1] Polytechnic University, Brooklyn NY 11201
vassil@milos.poly.edu
[2] The Univ. of Athens, Athens GR15771, Greece
ad@di.uoa.gr
[3] Boston University, Boston, MA 02215
gkollios@cs.bu.edu

Abstract. Due to the proliferation and widespread use of mobile devices and satellite based sensors there has been increased interest in storing and managing spatio-temporal and sensory data. It has been recognized that centralized and monolithic index structures are not scalable enough to address the highly dynamic nature (high update rates) and the unpredictable access patterns in such datasets. In this paper, we propose an adaptive networked index method designed to address the above challenges. Our method not only facilitates fast query and update response times via dynamic data partitioning but is also able to self-tune highly loaded sites. Our contributions consist of techniques that offer dynamic load balancing of computing sites, non-disruptive on-the-fly addition/removal of storing sites, distributed collaborative decision making for the self-administering of the manager, and statistics-based data reorganization. These features are incorporated into a distributed software layer prototype used to evaluate the design choices made. Our experimentation compares the performance of a baseline configuration with our multi-site system, examines the attained speed-up as a function of the sites participating, investigates the effect of data reorganization on query/update response times, asserts the effectiveness of our proposed dynamic load balancing method, and examines the behavior of the system under diverse types of multi-dimensional data.

Keywords: Data Management in Cluster of Workstations, Networked Storage Manager, Self-tuning Storage Nodes, and Multi-dimensional Data.

1 Introduction

Modern applications have to manage continuously growing and morphing volumes of data [2,19,9,26,7]. The high update rates and unpredictable access patterns in such applications make it challenging to provide short and consistent

E. Bertino et al. (Eds.): EDBT 2004, LNCS 2992, pp. 748–764, 2004.
© Springer-Verlag Berlin Heidelberg 2004

database response times. For example, the Terra spacecraft (EOSDIS project [7]) produces around 200 GB/day and Landsat 7 another 150 GB/day of geophysical data [30]. As pointed out in [29], *science is becoming very data intensive* for many fields. A wide range of integrated medical instrumentation and patient-care systems also produce massive spatio-temporal data [5,24,23]. The management of data networks and content delivery networks calls for efficient data visualization of network datasets [1] to help track changes and maintain good levels of resource provisioning for applications. Finally, critical areas that involve continuously changing and voluminous spatio-temporal data include intelligent transportation and traffic systems, fleet and movement-aware information systems, and management of digital battlefields. The inherent multi-dimensional nature of this data calls for the use of indexing methods that are capable of providing efficient data access [21,25,22]. It is worth pointing out that in the aforementioned areas data access as well as update patterns vary over time due to a number of reasons including ever-changing user interests, weather conditions, formation of new traffic congestion points, production of updated medical records, sensor failures, and network topology changes.

In order to facilitate the continuous, yet incremental growth of data without resorting to specialized hardware, we develop a networked storage manager based on a Cluster of Workstations (COW) connected via a high speed LAN. Portions of data are assigned to and indexed at these workstations (sites). We use R*-trees to index multidimensional data [9,4] because their leaf-level nodes are not correlated (in contrast, there is an absolute order of the leaves of a B^+-tree). This feature is leveraged by our system to extract a subset of the data indexed by one of the sites in the COW, insert it in the R*-tree of another site, and preserve the overall integrity of the dataset [18]. This load balancing through data migration involves a number of challenging trade-off questions: should data be moved at all, which data should be migrated, how much data is it necessary to ship and finally, between which sites is data to be migrated. We resolve these questions by adopting soft lower/upper limits on load variations, maintaining access statistics for nodes in the R*-trees, and continually controlling the load of the COW sites.

Our proposal builds on prior research [18,20,27,28]. However, a number of salient features substantially differentiate our work and include: support for high update rates; decentralized collaborative decision making to improve scalability; hot spots identification for efficient load balancing; graceful upscaling without any down-time; and lastly, evaluation of the usefulness of a Top-k-Level variable indexing scheme in the COW environment. We develop a full-fledged prototype in C++/BSD-sockets and carry out an extensive experimental study to demonstrate the benefits of our proposed techniques. Our main performance indicator is the average response time (ART) of requests (queries or updates) [8]. The main results of our evaluation are: a) achieved speedups of up to 50 times as compared to identical non-self-tuning systems (eg. [28]); b) sizable (10-50%) concurrent updates of the data set impose only minimal degradation of the average query response times; c) robust scalability characteristics are exhibited with minimal human intervention; d) the proposed Top-k-Level indexing scheme establishes that query redirection is best achieved through broadcasting.

The remainder of this paper is structured as follows: Section 2 discusses related work. Section 3 describes the architecture of our system and outlines the proposed load-sharing and data migration techniques. Our experimental analyses are discussed in Section 4 while conclusions and future research directions can be found in Section 5.

2 Related Work

In [6,16] distributed extendible and linear hashing are examined. A combined distributed index-hashing approach for one-dimensional data is proposed in [10]. Indexing suitable for shared-memory multiprocessor systems appears in [17], while [3] discusses issues pertinent to the reliability of distributed structures. In [11] the B-link tree is introduced which provides multiple levels of parallelism for accessing one-dimensional data. The levels of parallelism are achieved by a shared-nothing distributed approach, locking mechanisms working off individual sites, and partial replication of data. A load-conscious approach is also proposed in [14]. Load balancing techniques for parallel disks that allow for judicious file allocation and dynamic redistributions when page access patterns change are discussed in [27].

In [13] a "semi-distributed" version of R-Trees is proposed and formulae regarding optimality of data sizes and response times are derived. In [12] parallelism is exploited by distributing an R-Tree across several disks managed by a single processor and in [28] this concept is extended to a shared-nothing R-tree architecture. For one dimensional dataset, a globally height-balanced adaptive parallel B^+-tree (AB^+-tree) is introduced in [15]. An improved version based on R-trees is proposed in [18], where the strength of the approach is evaluated via a simulation study. Finally, on-line reorganization of a centralized B^+-tree is investigated in [31].

Our proposal and development work introduce a number of innovations including: a) a dynamic load balancing component facilitates data reorganization among the distributed computing sites due to random and heavily mixed workloads; b) we use on-the-fly fine-tuning of data distributions to tailor for high-rate access patterns and frequently occurring sizable updates; c) data selection during migration occurs in a way that minimizes the amount of data shipped, while maximizing the improvement on performance. The scalable LAN-based architecture reaps the benefits of a centralized global view at a master site, without impeding scalability. System upscaling can occur on demand, without any downtime, by simply adding more COW client sites which are gracefully populated.

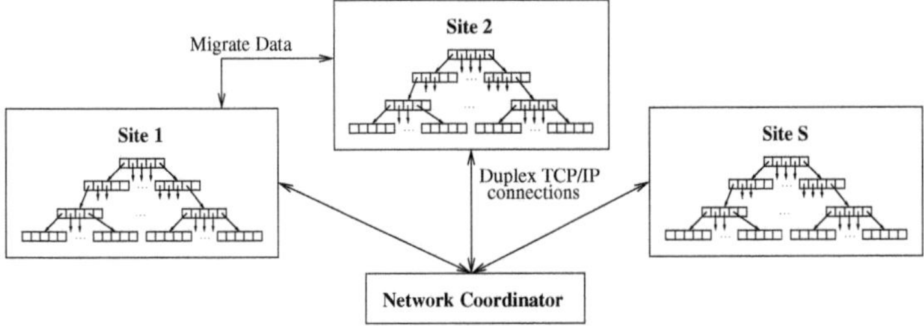

Fig. 1. Logical Architecture

3 System Architecture, Models, and Heuristics

The ultimate design goal of our COW-based manager is for it to exhibit superior performance under very intensive workloads, where skewed access patterns shift load conditions, and sustainable update rates increase resource demands.

3.1 Distributed Storage Manager Architecture

Our model consists of a cluster of workstations (COW) which communicate over a high-speed network and host the underlying data set. The COW storage manager functionality is divided between the the clients and a network coordinator (or simply coordinator) as depicted in Figure 1. The responsibilities of the network coordinator are reduced to a minimum to eliminate any bottleneck effects. The coordinator keeps a global load table which is used when making load balancing decisions. Any of the sites can also act as a coordinator.

Each site's basic tool for autonomous data management is an R*-tree which indexes the local data set fragment assigned to it. Furthermore, each client receives and executes requests which are submitted locally (through APIs), forwarded from other clients, or forwarded from the coordinator. The supported request operations are the containment or intersection queries and data insertions and deletions (updates).

In the following sections we look more closely at the reasons for some of our design choices and describe the client-client and client-coordinator interactions.

3.2 Evaluation of Top-k-Level Indexing

Past research efforts propose that a server holds a "distribution catalog" which contains partial information about the data located at the client sites. In [28, 13] the coordinator holds copies of all non-leaf-level nodes of the index structure of each client, with the postulation that this portion of the index comprises a negligible part of the total index space. This approach suffers under heavy and frequent updates as these trees have to be modified continually. In an ad-hoc manner, [18] suggests that only the root level nodes of each client site should be held at the coordinator. Empirically, we establish that the wide overlap in root nodes renders this method inefficient.

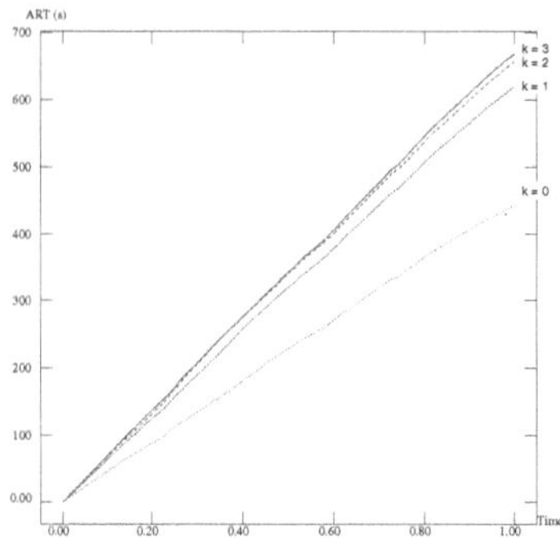

Fig. 2. Evaluating the costs of maintaining a central distribution catalog: response time is seriously affected under high update rates.

A more general approach is to keep the Top-k-Levels for each tree in the coordinator. We conduct a series of experiments to evaluate this approach for values of k ranging from 0 (no catalog) to $TreeHeight - 1$ (full catalog). Figure 2 shows the results for an experiment involving ten million elements distributed among six sites where one million insertions are intermixed with a sustained high workload of 200,000 queries each retrieving 0.1-1% of the dataset. Results for other experiments are similar but are omitted for brevity. The y-axis represents the average response time (ART), which is our primary performance measure. Our experimental results show that, under conditions involving heavy update loads, the best performance is achieved when Top-k-Level Indexing is not used and requests are broadcast to all client sites (i.e. $k = 0$). Based on this finding and under the assumption of heavy update workloads, we adopt the approach where the coordinator holds no information on data placement at client sites. Another significant benefit of this scheme is that any site may be an entry point of data requests which reduces the centralized role of the coordinator and, consequently, improves on scalability.

3.3 Self-Tuning Principles

Dynamic load balancing is required in a COW environment subject to changing access patterns as it helps achieve the following goals:

1. Detection of hot spots due to skewed access patterns and redistribution of loads without service disruption and performance degradation.
2. The overhead of self-tuning is more than compensated for by the resultant performance gains after completion of balancing.
3. No administrative work is involved during the redistribution process.

To our knowledge, this is the first work to address this issue in the described shared-nothing environment. In [27], the matter is discussed in a shared-memory parallel-disk system where device statistics are readily available. The data migration algorithms in [18] do not identify how queries are handled during the redistribution process and do not deal extensively with the issue of skewed access patterns on a per-site basis.

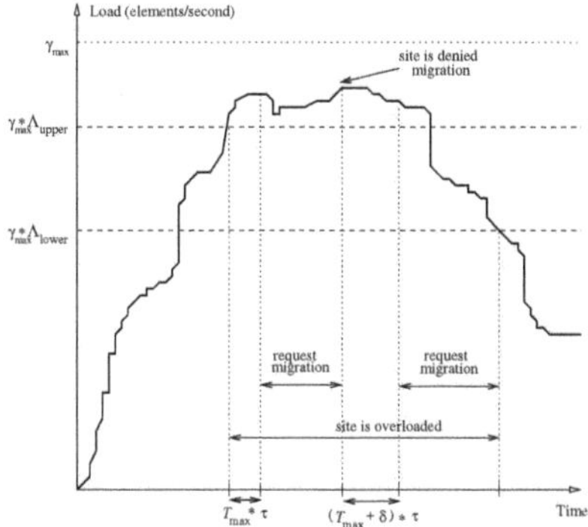

Fig. 3. Sample load variations for a given client site.

Parameter	Symbol	Values
load capacity	γ	3k - 30k
max load	γ_{max}	3k - 30k
load pct	λ	γ/γ_{max}
sampling period	τ	1 second
max samples	T_{max}	3 - 5
load increment	δ	1 - 3
upper threshold	Λ_{upper}	50-85%
lower threshold	Λ_{lower}	40-75%
load deviation	Δ	5-25%
sites	N	1 - 20
dataset size	D	0.1M - 10M

Fig. 4. System parameters and values for individual sites.

In our network storage manager, dynamic load balancing is facilitated through on-line data reorganization. To avoid disruptions to user requests, we employ a concurrency control mechanism between the client sites involved in the data migration. The overhead of self-tuning is minimized through quick but careful selection of data for migration such that the balance achieved is near-optimal, while the amount of data migrated is minimal. In addition, we employ a distributed collaborative decision making process during the load balancing phase which reduces processing at the network coordinator and minimizes the number of load-balancing considerations. These points are discussed in detail in the following sections.

3.4 Component Interaction

We define "client site load" as the number of data elements retrieved per second by a client site. This measurement is derived in connection with the CPU usage, disk I/O, and memory paging operations and implicitly reflects a workstation's resource utilization. In our experiments this value ranged from 3,000 to 30,000 elements per second (see table in Figure 4).

Each client i continuously measures its current load γ^i for each epoch elapsed (a sampling period of 1 second as indicated in the table in Figure 4). Clients have a fixed maximum sustainable load capacity γ^i_{max}, which can be determined a-priori by running a test benchmark[1] and is used to compute the current load percentage $\lambda^i = \gamma^i/\gamma^i_{max}$. Clients use the two system-wide parameters Λ_{upper} and Λ_{lower} to determine whether they are overloaded. Site i is considered overloaded as long as the condition

$$(\gamma^i > \gamma^i_{max} * \Lambda_{upper})$$

[1] To establish the value of γ^i_{max} for a site i, we retrieve all data stored at that site. Assuming that sufficient amount of data is present, the site operates at its maximum sustainable load γ^i_{max} as reported by the *Load Monitor*.

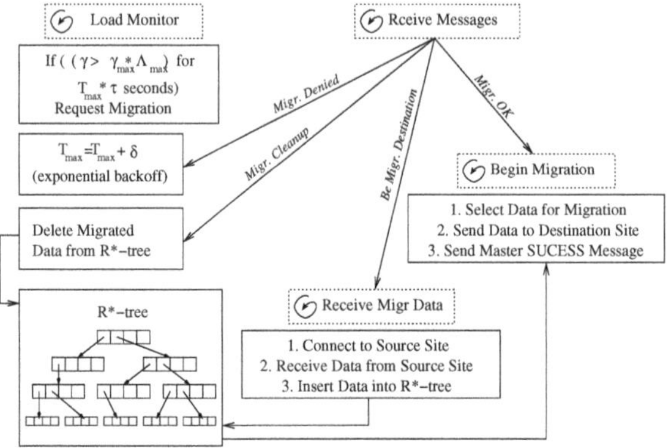

Fig. 5. Overloaded client sites request permission to perform migration. If the request is denied, T_{max} is incremented and no migration occurs. If the request is granted, data is shipped to the recipient site

holds true for an epoch. Using this epoch prevents load balancing from occurring during spurious high loads. Prior to a client site's first migration request, the epoch must last at least $T_{max} * \tau$ seconds, where τ is the load measurement time interval in seconds, and T_{max} is the number of load measurements. If a site requests migration but the coordinator decides that the system is balanced and denies the request, the site increases its value of T_{max} by δ. T_{max} is reset to its original value when a migration request is granted. When a client considers itself to be overloaded it sends a *Request Migration* message to the network coordinator as indicated in Figure 5. This triggers the self-tuning mechanism and the coordinator evaluates the system's state of balance as shown in Figure 6. It is important to note that there is no continuous processing or polling at the coordinator. This certainly aids in the scalability of our architecture.

Effectively, the set of measurements and parameters in the table in Figure 4 provides soft thresholds for determining a site's load state. This reduces the number of migration requests during system-wide overloads when self-tuning is not possible. In essence, the dynamic tuning of T_{max} allows client sites to "learn" about the overall state of the system and attempt to adjust accordingly. A sample load situation for a client site is given in Figure 3, where it can be seen that the client requests migration only after its load has crossed $\gamma^i_{max} * \Lambda_{upper}$ for $T_{max} * \tau$ seconds, and discontinues its migration requests after its load line crosses $\gamma^i_{max} * \Lambda_{lower}$.

The coordinator records each site's load in the Global Load Table (GLT) shown in Figure 6 and uses this information to decide whether the COW manager is balanced. The network coordinator computes the difference between the loads of the most (λ_{max}) and least (λ_{min}) loaded sites in $O(N)$ time where N is the number of active client sites. When the condition:

$$(\lambda_{max} - \lambda_{min}) < \Delta$$

qualifies, the system is balanced. The parameter Δ constitutes the system's tolerance for imbalance in terms of percentage and can be configured according

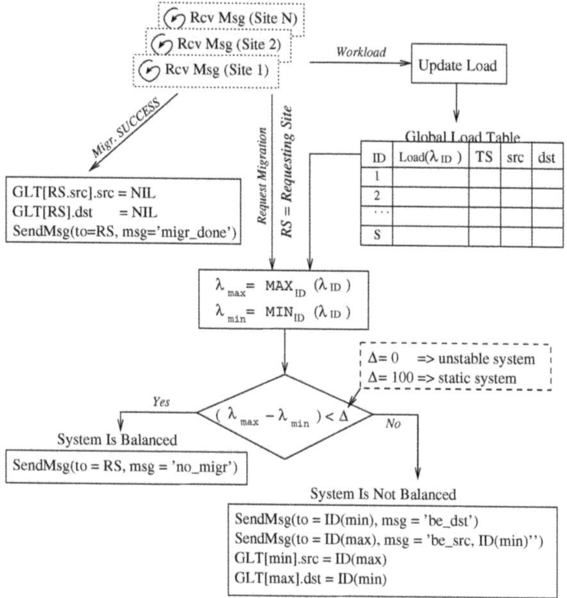

Fig. 6. The coordinator qualifies data migration based on the current load of each site, and selects for destination sites with the least load.

to the specific application needs. Finding an optimal value for Δ is beyond the scope of this paper, but we provide an empirical approach and experiment with values (5% - 25%) that are deemed representative for the parameter.

When the system is balanced, the requesting site is denied migration. Otherwise, the least loaded client is selected to be the destination site and the requesting site is redirected to continue negotiations with that client. The details of these negotiations are discussed in the next section. Since concurrent requests for migration may be issued by multiple client sites, the coordinator marks current destination/source pairs in the GLT, indicated by the 'dst' and 'src' columns in Figure 6. Such pairs of clients are not considered for destination candidates until the migration process between them completes.

3.5 Data Migration

The data migration scheme must be very efficient: data must be selected quickly and it must be shipped to the recipient site fast. To achieve these goals, each site collects access and update statistics for each node in its R*-tree tree. This information helps select minimal amount of data for migration, while maximizing the effect on load redistribution. This reduces the overhead of data transfers among the client sites and increases the system's self-tuning responsiveness.

In the context of skewed access patterns following Zipfian or Gaussian distribution we maintain that it is of significant importance *what* data is claimed

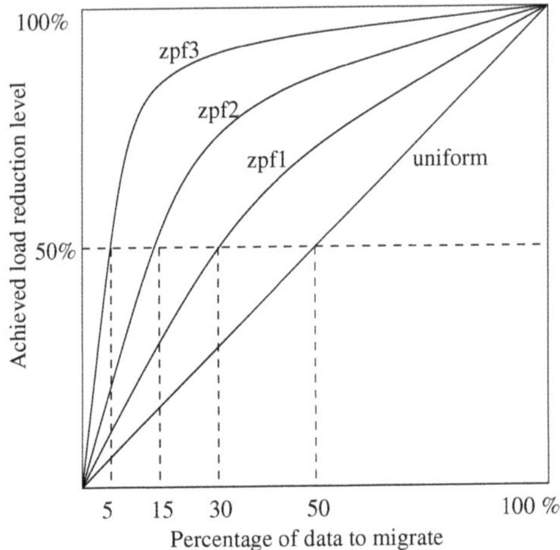

Fig. 7. With skewed access patterns, the amount of data that must be migrated to achieve a desired load reduction sharply decreases as compared to uniform access distributions. Therefore it is important to identified skewed access patterns when dealing with data redistribution.

for migration. If data accesses are uniformly distributed in space, to achieve a desired load reduction, say 50%, a client has to migrate an equivalent proportion (50%) of data. When access patterns are skewed, the degree of skew determines the amount of data to be migrated. Figure 7 depicts the relationship between load reduction rates and data migration size for various types of access skew. It can be seen that for a desired load reduction, very few elements must be redistributed under higher skews as compared to a uniform access distribution. Thus, by exploiting access pattern information, migration overheads can be reduced substantially.

Prior to selecting migration data, the overloaded client determines a target load reduction λ_{target}. This is the equilibrium point between the local load and the destination site's load: $\lambda_{target} = (\lambda_{src} - \lambda'_{dst})/2$. λ_{target} represents the load percentage that the overloaded site would like to reduce its load by while λ'_{dst} is λ_{dst} normalized to the source's maximum load capacity γ^{src}_{max}. This normalization is necessary when the COW is composed of heterogeneous sites with different capacities γ_{max}.

To select data for migration, a client first examines its root in the R*-tree and using its access statistics determines the total R*-tree load over all subtrees st:

$$TotalLoad = \sum_{st \, \epsilon \, root} (\alpha * st.read\_count + \beta * st.write\_count)/\Delta t$$

where α and β are weight coefficients for adjusting the significance of reads relative to writes since writes are usually more costly. The $TotalLoad$ represents the frequency of reads and writes applied to the tree.

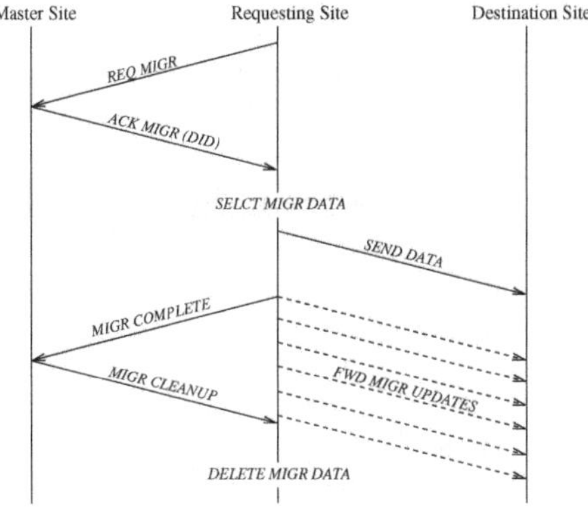

Fig. 8. Concurrency Control

Consequently, the most loaded subtree at the root is discovered. If this subtree's load is not sufficient to reach the target load reduction (i.e. if *MaxLoadedSubtreeLoad / TotalLoad* $< \lambda_{target}\%$), the subtree is selected for migration to the destination site and the selection process terminates. Otherwise, that subtree is examined: its most loaded subtree is found and the evaluation process is repeated recursively. Note that the *TotalLoad* is determined only at the root level. If the leaf-level is reached and no subtree has been selected for migration, the most loaded node in that leaf is selected for migration. To select data for migration, a site navigates its R*-tree tree, following the most loaded branches. Therefore, the data selection process runs in time proportional to the height of the tree, which is logarithmic with the number of elements indexed.

3.6 Concurrency Control and Upscaling of the COW Manager

Once a subtree is selected for migration, a concurrency mechanism allows for data migration and query execution to proceed simultaneously. This concurrent execution is important not only from a synchronization standpoint but also because of the overheads involved during data reorganization. Thus, we allow request processing and data migration to occur simultaneously. To facilitate this, the subtree chosen for migration is marked prior to any data migration. Queries are allowed to enter the marked subtree at no cost. When updates enter a marked subtree, they are propagated to the destination site which received the migrated data as Figure 8 shows.

Once migration commences, two copies of the data exist: one at the destination site and one at the source site. The forwarding of updates guarantees that the two sets are synchronized. When migration is completed, the requesting site sends a "Migration Complete" message to the coordinator. The coordinator immediately enqueues a "Migration Cleanup" message on the outgoing queue for the requesting site. When the requesting site receives this message, it safely deletes the migrated data and stops forwarding messages to the destination site.

At this stage, the data migration process is complete and there is only one copy of the migrated data at the destination site.

Due to this concurrency control mechanism, our COW manager provides a flexible environment for automatic system upscaling with the growth of the data set. New sites can be introduced into the distributed system by attaching them to the same network cluster. Gradually, part of the data set is relocated to the new site, alleviating the workload on the other sites. Down-scaling of the system is accomplished in a similar manner.

4 Experimental Results

4.1 Experimental Setup

Our prototype system is entirely developed in C++. The computing sites consist of a cluster of SPARC-stations connected through a dedicated high-speed (100Mbps) LAN.

The experiments were performed using both synthetically generated and real-life data. The synthetic data was either uniformly distributed (hyper-squares with sides of length 0.0005) or exponentially distributed (using Gaussian distribution with $\sigma = 1.0$ and $\mu = 0$) in unit space. Furthermore, the experiments were performed with data of three dimensionalities: 2D, 4D, and 8D. The number of synthetic data elements (rectangles and hyper-cubes) used in the experiments ranged from one-hundred thousand to ten million. The queries were also synthetically generated (hyper-) rectangles, distributed uniformly or exponentially in the unit square. Three types of queries were used with sides of length 0.005 (small), 0.015 (medium), and 0.05 (large). The main factors affecting the experiment's workload are the query area and the query inter-arrival rate. The real-life data[2] consisted of 208,688 points in two-dimensional space representing functional densities of a computational-fluid-dynamics experiment on the wing of an airplane (Boeing 737).

Our main performance metric is the turnaround time for a given query (measured in seconds). We refer to this as the average response time (ART). The experimental objective was to evaluate the performance of the COW-based self-tuning manager under skewed access patterns and compare it to a system which does not employ dynamic load balancing. By "skewed access patterns" we refer to accesses which create hot spots in the distributed COW-manager. For persistently high workloads, speed-ups of a factor of 50 were achieved. Under short peak workloads, the performance improvements were a factor of 5.

Moreover, we evaluated experimentally the benefits of the combination of the dynamic load balancing algorithm with our selective data migration technique. Although the technique incurs extra overhead on the R*-tree processing, it resulted in migration of up to 3 times fewer data elements as compared to when no access information was tracked.

[2] This and additional multi-dimensional data can be found at Scott Leutenegger's web page: http://www.cs.du.edu/~leut/MultiDimData.html.

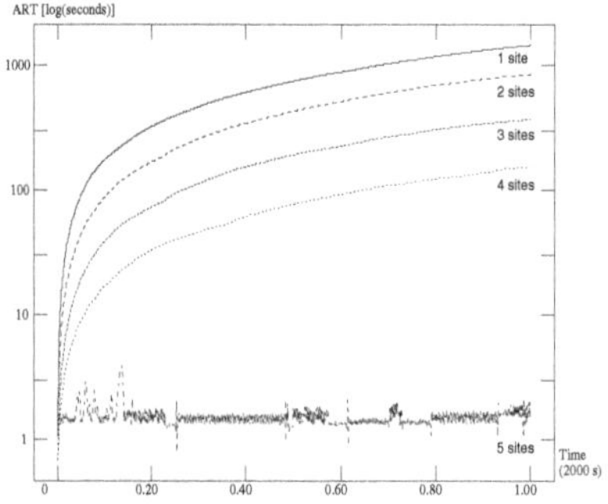

Fig. 9. Response times of a static system with 1 million 2-D elements for varying number of sites (log scale).

4.2 Results

Multi-Site Gains: Figure 9 depicts the performance gains achieved by increasing the parallelism of the COW-based manager by introducing new sites. For the cases when one to four sites were used, the system's query processing time was slower than the query arrival time. When a fifth site was introduced, the system was able to deliver optimal performance for the specific dataset, and the response times were only affected by the processing of each query at the five sites (since queries did not wait on the queue for previously submitted queries to complete). On a multi-site system there is an additional improvement for insertions and updates due to the smaller amount of data managed at each site (approximately n/N records, as opposed to n records on a single site system). This reduces some of the processing costs for data management.

Self Tuning Improvements: Figure 10 shows the response times for a two site system indexing 100,000 two-dimensional rectangles. During the experiment 10% of the stored data was modified. For the given workload, which was skewed to retrieve 70% of the requested data from one of the two sites and the remaining data from the other site, the system could not cope with the requests when self-tuning was turned off. Because the data retrieval time was greater than the query inter-arrival rate, the response time of the system increased progressively. However, with dynamic load balancing, during the first one-third of the experiment, the system automatically migrated data from the overloaded site to the underloaded site, resulting in significant improvements (up to a factor of 25).

The loads of the two sites for the duration of the experiment with migration are shown in Figure 11. The skewed query workloads cause the loads on the two sites to differ by about 50%. This is a typical unbalanced system. When the overloaded site requests migration permission from the coordinator, it is granted the request and the site begins migrating data to the underloaded site. This is seen in the gradual increase of the load of the underloaded site as it begins to index more and more data. When the two loads converge (at the 50% mark) data migration ceases and the system is optimally balanced. This corresponds to the steady low response time in Figure 10.

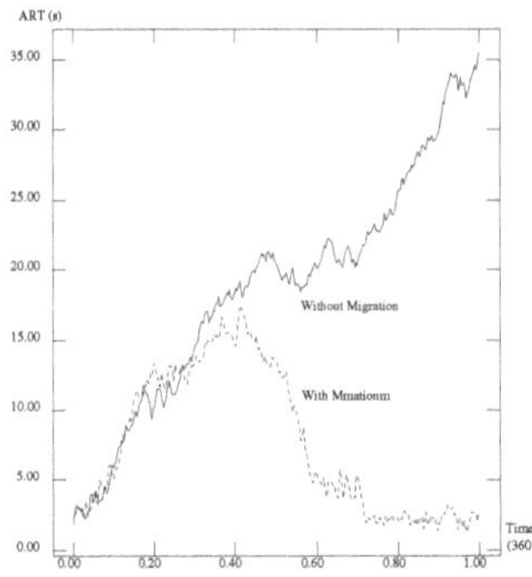

Fig. 10. 100k 2-D Expo. records, 10k updates on 2 sites (Speed-up: 5.12)

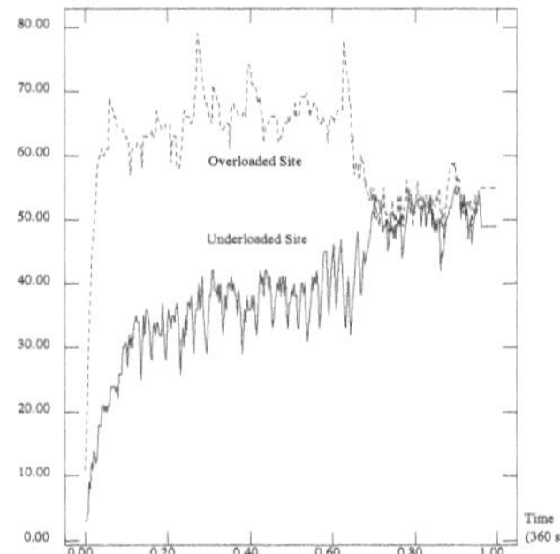

Fig. 11. Data migration effect on site load: gradual load balancing

Similar results were achieved with the real-life data set although the results are not shown due to space limitations. Surprisingly, the performance improvements were higher when operating on the real-life data: the speed-up was a factor of 9.23 on average.

With uniformly distributed data set (Figure 12) data migration again resulted in overall better performance. However, the gain ratio was much lower. This was due to two factors. Firstly, in general the response times for the uniformly distributed data set were much shorter than in the previous two cases (5.5 seconds vs. 35 seconds with exponential and 110 seconds with real-life data). Second, the overhead of data migration in the first half of the experiment was higher than the compensation achieved by moving the data to the overloaded site. However, the eventual balancing out of the load between the two sites resulted in a steady low response time (approximately 2 seconds).

The results of dynamic load balancing were comparable when data of higher dimensionalities was indexed as can be seen in Figures 13 and 14. With self-tuning, the system was slower at balancing out the load among the two sites than in the case of two-dimensional data. The spikes of the graph in the self-tuning case are result of the occurring data migration–the periods when the site is busy selecting data for migration, shipping it to the destination site, and removing it locally. These are periods when incoming requests are not processed, hence the short spikes.

When more sites are available (Figures 18, and 15), it takes more time to balance the system load because the dataset size is larger. For example, Figure 15 shows the response times of a system with ten client sites, two of which are overloaded (processing 70% of the workload) and eight underloaded (processing the remaining 30% of the workload). In such environment, it took almost 20 minutes for the system to achieve a balanced state. As larger amounts of data are stored on more sites, the "migration spikes" become more prominent, resulting in larger delays. However, it is important to note that when the system does reach a balanced state, the query response times decrease significantly, whereas

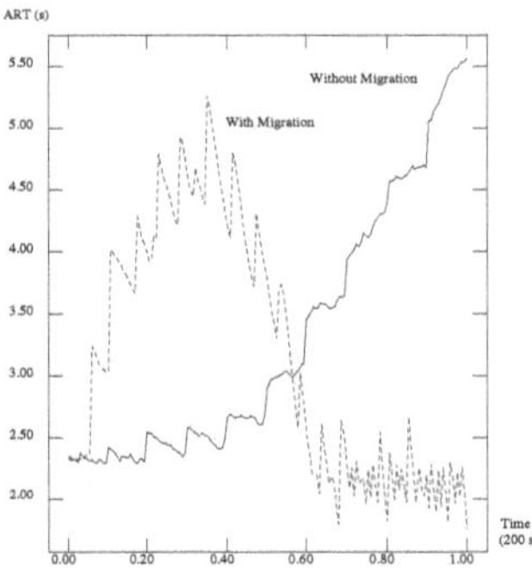

Fig. 12. 100k 2-D Uni. records, 10k updates, 2 sites (Speed-up: avg. 1.23, max. 3.14)

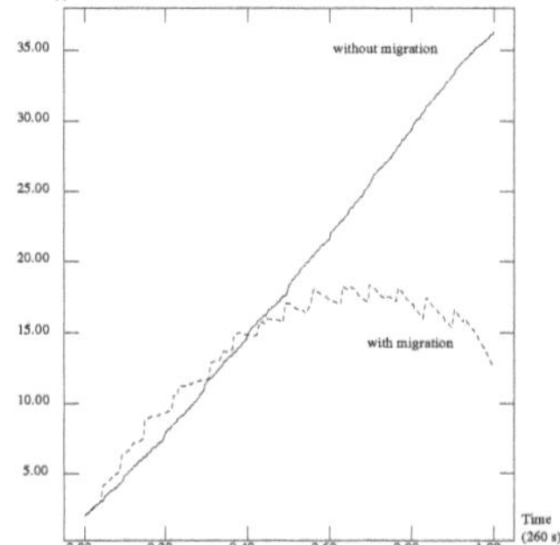

Fig. 13. 100k 4-D Uni. records, 10k updates, 2 sites (Speed-up: avg. 1.29, max. 2.88)

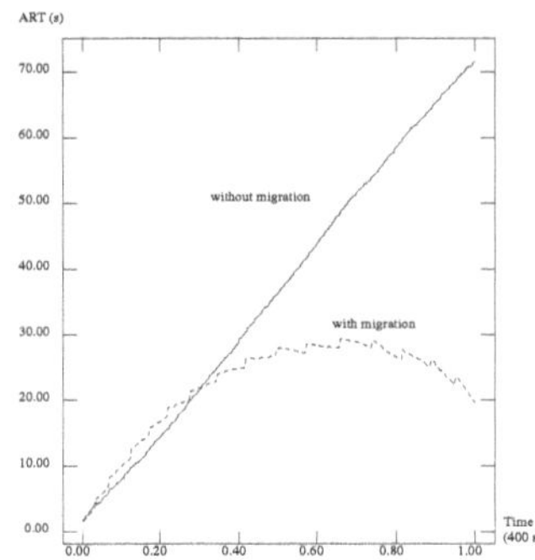

Fig. 14. 100k 8-D Uni. records, 10k updates, 2 sites (Speed-up: avg. 1.85, max. 3.99)

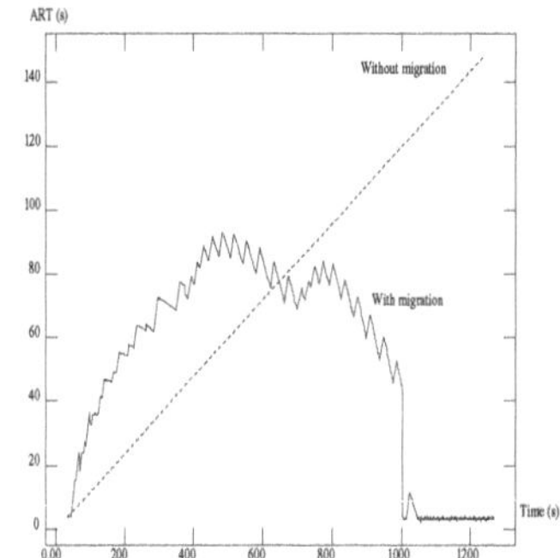

Fig. 15. 3M records, 0.5M updates, 10 sites, speed-up: 8.86

in the case of no data migration, there is no prospect for such a decrease unless the query workload decreases.

In the case of system upscaling Figure 16 depicts the load percentage of one of the sites of a working system where at time 50 seconds, a new site was introduced in the system. At that point, load balancing was initiated and through a series of data migrations, the load on the specific site was more than halved as its data was relocated to the newly introduced site.

Previously discussed experiments were performed under constant workload conditions. To evaluate the COW-based manager's performance under more realistic conditions we created a workload consisting of relatively infrequent requests (see Table 17 for details on the workload), with two instances of high workloads in the duration of the experiment. Under normal workloads, the self-tuning system under-performed due to the occurring data migrations. However, the load balancing paid off handsomely during peak loads (see Figure 19), where the self-tuning system performed up to 8 times better.

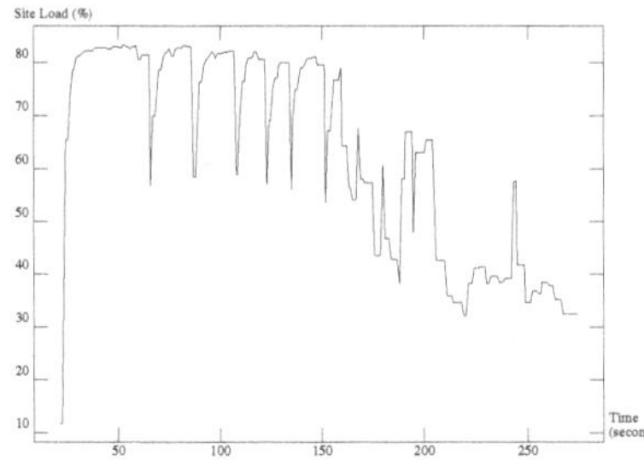

Fig. 16. System upscaling: a new site introduced at t = 50 seconds.

area (mu^2)	No. queries	delay (μs)	avg. gain
0.025	100000	2000	0.83
0.225	36000	3000	5.16
0.025	60000	2000	0.97
0.225	36000	3000	5.38
0.025	60000	2000	0.88

Fig. 17. Query workload distribution for peak workloads.

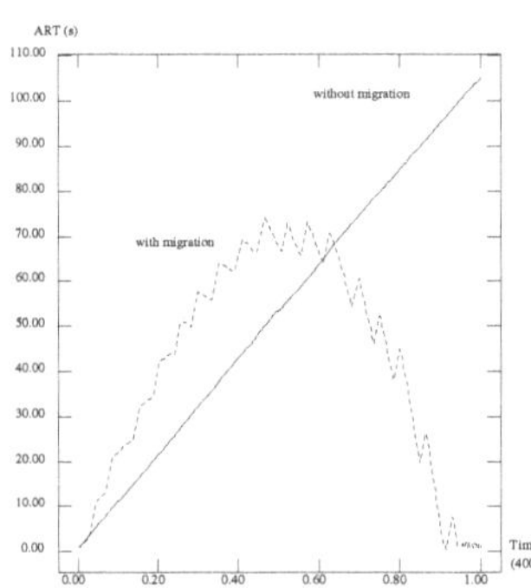

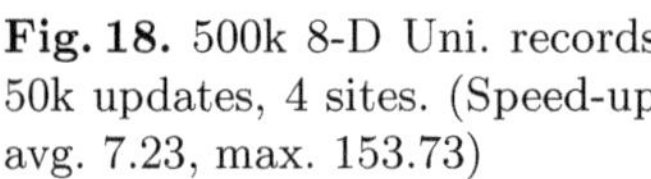
Fig. 18. 500k 8-D Uni. records, 50k updates, 4 sites. (Speed-up: avg. 7.23, max. 153.73)

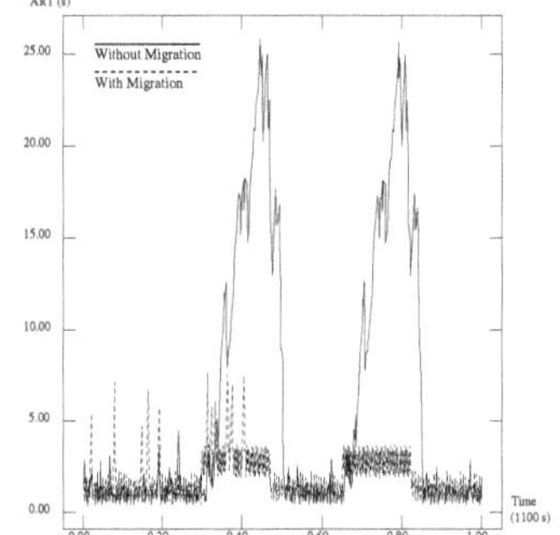

Fig. 19. Effect of migration during normal vs. peak workloads.

5 Conclusions and Future Work

We have presented a self-tuning storage management system for multi-dimensional data distributed on a cluster of commodity workstations. Compared to prior approaches, our network-based system exhibits significant performance improvements due to a number of techniques: 1) dynamic data reorganization for load balancing identifies hot spots in the COW to efficiently manage data migrations; 2) distributed collaboration in the self-tuning decision process avoids the bottleneck of the central site; 3) a variable-level distribution catalog reveals the system's scalability issues when managing high volumes of frequently updated data. The above provide for robustness and consistent performance in a variety of settings, especially in conditions of unpredictably changing access patterns and high frequency updates to the underlying data. Our prototype helped us to evaluate empirically the key features of our proposal and the trade-offs of our system design. Future work includes extension of the prototype to incorporate bulk-loading mechanisms for data migration, replication schemes, and a server-less architecture.

References

1. J. Abello and J. Korn. MGV: A System for Visualizing Massive Multidigraphs. *IEEE Trans. on Visualization and Computer Graphics*, 8(1), Jan-March 2002.
2. T. Barclay, D. Slutz, and J. Gray. TerraServer: A Spatial Data Warehouse. In *Proc. of ACM SIGMOD*, pages 307–318, 2000.
3. F. Bastani, S. Iyengar, and I. Yen. Concurrent Maintenance of Data Structures in a Distributed Environment. *The Computer Journal*, 31(12):165–174, 1988.
4. N. Beckmann, H. Kriegel, R. Schneider, and B. Seeger. The R*-Tree: An Efficient and Robust Access Method for Points and Rectangles. In *Proc. of ACM SIGMOD 1990*, pages 322–331. ACM Press, 1990.
5. V. Calhoun, T. Adali, and G. Pearlson. (Non)stationarity of Temporal Dynamics in fMRI. In *21st Annual Conference of Engineering in Medicine and Biology*, volume 2, Atlanta, GA, October 1999.
6. C. Ellis. Distributed Data Structures: A Case Study. *IEEE Transactions on Computers*, 34(12):1178–1185, 1985.
7. The Earth Observing System Data and Information System. http://spsosun.gsfc.nasa.gov/eosinfo/EOSDIS_Site/ index.html.
8. J. Gray and A. Reuter. *Transaction Processing: Concepts and Techniques.* Morgan–Kaufman, San Mateo, CA, 1992.
9. A. Guttman. R-Trees: A Dynamic Index Structure for Spatial Searching. In *SIGMOD'84, Proceedings of Annual Meeting, Boston, Massachusetts, June 18-21, 1984*, pages 47–57. ACM Press, 1984.
10. T. Honishi, T. Satoh, and U. Inoue. An Index Structure for Parallel Database Processing. In *IEEE Second International Workshop on Research Issues on Data Engineering*, pages 224–225, 1992.
11. T. Johnson, P. Krishna, and A. Colbrook. Distributed Indices for Accessing Distributed Data. In *IEEE Symposium on Mass Storage Systems (MSS '93)*, pages 199–208, Los Alamitos, Ca., USA, April 1993. IEEE Computer Society Press.
12. I. Kamel and C. Faloutsos. Parallel R-trees. In *Proceedings of the 1992 ACM SIGMOD International Conference on Management of Data, San Diego, California, June 2-5, 1992*, pages 195–204. ACM Press, 1992.
13. N. Koudas, C. Faloutsos, and I. Kamel. Declustering Spatial Databases on a Multi-Computer Architecture. In *Advances in Database Technology - EDBT'96, 5th International Conference on Extending Database Technology, Avignon, France, March 25-29, 1996, Proceedings.*
14. B. Kroll and P. Widmayer. Distributing a Search Structure Among a Growing Number of Processors. In *Proceedings of the 1994 ACM SIGMOD Conference*, pages 265–276, 1994.
15. M. Lee, M. Kitsuregawa, B. Ooi, K. Tan, and A. Mondal. Towards Self-Tuning Data Placement in Parallel Database Systems. In *Proc. of ACM SIGMOD 2000*, pages 225–236, 2000.
16. W. Litwin, M.A. Neimat, and D. Schneider. Linear Hashing for Distributed Files. In *Proceedinsg of the 1993 SIGMOD Conference*, Washington D.C., May 1993.
17. G. Matsliach and O. Shmueli. An Efficient Method for Distributing Search Structures. In *First International Conference on Parallel and Distributed Information Systems*, pages 159–166, 1991.
18. A. Mondal, M. Kitsuregawa, B. C. Ooi, and K. L. Tan. R-tree-based Data Migration and Self-tuning Strategies in Shared-nothing Spatial Databases. In *Proceedings of ACM Geographic Information Systems*, pages 28–33. ACM Press, 2001.

19. Ousterhout, J. K. G. T. Hamachi, R. N. Mayo, W. S. Scott, and G. S. Taylor. Magic: A VLSI Layout System. In *21st Design Automation Conference*, pages 152–159, June 1984.
20. E. Panagos and A. Biliris. Synchronization and Recovery in a Client-Server Storage System. *The VLDB Journal*, 6(3):209–223, 1997.
21. J. Patel, J.-B. Yu, N. Kabra, and K. Tufte. Building a Scaleable Geo-Spatial DBMS: Technology, Implementation, and Evaluation. In *Proc. of the ACM SIGMOD*, pages 336–347, 1997.
22. K. Porkaew, I. Lazaridis, and S. Mehrotra. Querying Mobile Objects in Spatio-Temporal Databases. In *Proc. of 7th SSTD*, July 2001.
23. M. Prado, L. Roa, J. Reina-Tosina, A. Palma, and J.A. Milan. Virtual Center for Renal Support: Technological Approach to Patient Physiological Image. *IEEE Transactions on Biomedical Engineering*, 49(12):1420 –1430, December 2002.
24. J. Reina-Tosina, L.M. Roa, J. Caceres, and T. Gomez-Cia. New Approaches Toward the Fully Digital Integrated Management of a Burn Unit. *IEEE Transactions on Biomedical Engineering*, 49(12):1470– 1476, December 2002.
25. S. Saltenis, C. Jensen, S. Leutenegger, and Mario A. Lopez. Indexing the Positions of Continuously Moving Objects. In *Proc. of the ACM SIGMOD*, pages 331–342, May 2000.
26. B. Salzberg and V.J. Tsotras. Comparison of Access Methods for Time-Evolving Data. *ACM Computing Surveys*, 31(2):158–221, 1999.
27. P. Scheuermann, G. Weikum, and P. Zabback. Data Partitioning and Load Balancing in Parallel Disk Systems. *VLDB Journal*, 7(1), 1998.
28. B. Schnitzer and S. Leutenegger. Master-Client R-Trees: A New Parallel R-Tree Architecture. In *Statistical and Scientific Database Management*, pages 68–77, 1999.
29. A. Szalay, J. Gray, and J. van den Berg. Petabyte Scale Data Mining: Dream or Reality. In *Proc. of SIPE Astronmy Telescopes and Instruments*, August 2002.
30. T.L. Zeiler. LANDSAT Program Report 2002. Technical report, U.S. Geological Survey - U.S. Department of Interior, Sioux Falls, SD, 2002. EROS Data Center.
31. C. Zou and B. Salzberg. Safely and Efficiently Updating References During On-line Reorganization. In *Proc. of VLDB*, pages 512–522, 1998.

Spatiotemporal Compression Techniques for Moving Point Objects

Nirvana Meratnia[1] and Rolf A. de By[2]

[1] Department of Computer Science
University of Twente
P.O. Box 217, 7500 AE, Enschede
The Netherlands
meratnia@cs.utwente.nl

[2] Intl. Inst. for Geo-information Science & Earth Observation (ITC)
P.O. Box 6, 7500 AA, Enschede
The Netherlands
deby@itc.nl

Abstract. Moving object data handling has received a fair share of attention over recent years in the spatial database community. This is understandable as positioning technology is rapidly making its way into the consumer market, not only through the already ubiquitous cell phone but soon also through small, on-board positioning devices in many means of transport and in other types of portable equipment. It is thus to be expected that all these devices will start to generate an unprecedented data stream of time-stamped positions. Sooner or later, such enormous volumes of data will lead to storage, transmission, computation, and display challenges. Hence, the need for compression techniques.
Although previously some work has been done in compression for time series data, this work mainly deals with one-dimensional time series. On the other hand, they are good for short time series and in absence of noise, two characteristics not met by moving objects.
We target applications in which present and past positions of objects are important, so focus on the compression of moving object trajectories. The paper applies some older techniques of line generalization, and compares their performance against algorithms that we specifically designed for compressing moving object trajectories.

1 Database Support for Moving Objects Is Wanting

This is a crowded world with mobile inhabitants. Their mobility gives rise to traffic, which, due to various behavioural characteristics of its agents, is a phenomenon that displays patterns. It is our aim to provide tools to study, analyse and understand these patterns. We target traffic in the widest sense: commuters in urban areas (obviously), a truck fleet at the continental scale, pedestrians in shopping malls, airports or railway stations, shopping carts in a supermarket, pieces of luggage in airport logistics, even migratory animals, under the assumption that one day we will have the techniques to routinely equip many of them

E. Bertino et al. (Eds.): EDBT 2004, LNCS 2992, pp. 765–782, 2004.
© Springer-Verlag Berlin Heidelberg 2004

with positioning devices. Fundamental in our approach is that we are not only interested in present position, but also in positional history.

In recent years, positioning technology, location-based services and ubiquitous applications have become a focus of attention in different disciplines. Perhaps, most importantly, positioning technology is becoming increasingly more available — cheaper, smaller, less power consumption — and more accurate. This development does not depend on GPS technology alone: in-house tracking technology applies various techniques for up-to-date positional awareness, and adaptable antenna arrays can do accurate positioning on cell phones [1].

Databases have not very well accommodated such data in the past, as their design paradigm was always one of 'snapshot representation'. Their present support for *spatial* time series is at best rudimentary. Consequently, database support for *moving object* representation and computing has become an active research domain. See, for instance [2,3,4,5,6].

As indicated above, there is a multitude of moving object applications. We use the phrase as a container term for various organic and inorganic entities that demonstrate mobility that itself is of interest to the application. Our principal example is urban traffic, specifically commuter traffic, and rush hour analysis. The mobile object concept, however, doesn't stop there.

Monitoring and analysing moving objects necessitates the availability of complete geographical traces to determine locations that objects have had, have or will have. Due to the intrinsic limitations of data acquisition and storage devices such inherently continuous phenomena are acquired and stored (thus, represented) in a discrete way. Right from the start, we are dealing with approximations of object trajectories. Intuitively, the more data about the whereabouts of a moving object is available, the more accurate its true trajectory can be determined. Availability of data is by no means a problem as the coming years will witness an explosion of such positional data for all sorts of moving objects. Moreover, there seem to be few technological barriers to high position sampling rates. However, such enormous volumes of data lead to storage, transmission, computation, and display challenges. Hence, there is a definite need for *compression techniques* of moving object trajectories.

Perhaps an example could help to better illustrate the essence of an effective compression technique. Let us assume that a moving object data stream is a sequence of $\langle t, x, y \rangle$, in which x, y represent coordinates of the moving object at time t, respectively. If such data is collected every 10 seconds, a simple calculation shows that 100 Mb of storage capacity is required to store the data for just over 400 objects for a single day, barring any data compression. We obviously want to be monitoring many more moving objects, and for much longer time periods.

In this paper, various compression techniques for streams of time-stamped positions are described and compared. We compare them against two new spatio-temporal compression techniques, which are described in Sect. 3.3. The superiority of the proposed methods for our application is demonstrated in Sect. 4.3. We have previously reported on this work in [7].

2 Spatial Compression Techniques

Object movement is continuous in nature. Acquisition, storage and processing technology, however, force us to use discrete representations. In its simplest form, an object trajectory is a positional time series, i.e., a (finite) sequence of time-stamped positions. To determine the object's position at time instants not explicitly available in the time series, approximation techniques are used. Piecewise linear approximation is one of the most widely used methods, due to its algorithmic simplicity and low computational complexity.

Intuitively, a piecewise linear approximation of a positional time series assumes that successive data points are connected by straight segments. There exist non-linear approximation techniques, e.g., using Bézier curves or splines [8], but we do not consider these here. In many of the applications we have in mind, object movement appears to be restricted to an underlying transportation infrastructure that itself has linear characteristics. This work, however, makes no assumption as to such positional restrictions.

Our objectives for data compression are:

- to obtain a lasting reduction in data size;
- to obtain a data series that still allows various computations at acceptable (low) complexity;
- to obtain a data series with known, small margins of error, which are preferably parametrically adjustable.

As a consequence our interest is with lossy compression techniques. The reasons for the last objective are that (i) we know our raw data to already contain error, (ii) depending on the application, we could permit additional error, as long as we understand the behaviour of error under settings of the algorithmic parameters.

Compression algorithms can be classified on another basis as well. They are either *batch* or *online* algorithms, based on whether they require the availability of the full data series. Batch algorithms do; online algorithms do not, and are typically used to compress data streams in real-time. Batch algorithms consistently produce higher quality results [9] when compared to online algorithms.

Appearing under different names, most compression algorithms relevant here can be grouped into one of the following four categories [10]:

Top-Down: The data series is recursively partitioned until some halting condition is met.

Bottom-up: Starting from the finest possible representation, successive data points are merged until some halting condition is met. The algorithm may not visit all data points in sequence.

Sliding Window: Starting from one end of the data series, a window of fixed size is moved over the data points, and compression takes place only on the data points inside the window.

Opening Window: Starting from one end of the data series, a data segment, i.e., a subseries of the data series, is grown until some halting condition is met. Then, a compression takes place on the data points inside the window. This will decrease the window size, after which the process is continued. The 'window' size is the number of data points under consideration at any one point during the execution of the algorithm.

We have coined the term 'opening window' to do justice to the dynamic nature of the size of the window in such algorithms. They are, however, elsewhere sometimes considered 'sliding window' algorithms.

Various halting conditions may be applied. Possible conditions are:

- The number of data points, thus the number of segments, exceeds a user-defined value.
- The maximum error for a segment exceeds a user-defined threshold.
- The sum of the errors of all segments exceeds a user-defined threshold.

An obvious class of candidate algorithms for our problem are the line generalization algorithms. Some of these algorithms are very simple in nature and do not take into account any relationship between neighbouring data points. They may eliminate all data points except some specific ones, e.g., leaving in every i^{th} data point [11]. Another sort of compression algorithm utilizes the characteristics of the neighbouring data points in deciding whether to eliminate one of them. Particulary, these algorithms may use the Euclidean distance between two neighbour points. If it is less than a predefined threshold, one is eliminated. All these algorithms are sequential in nature, that is they gradually process a line from the beginning to the end.

Although these two groups of algorithms are computationally efficient, they are not so popular or widely used. Their primary disadvantage is the frequent elimination or misrepresentation of important points such as sharp angles. A secondary limitation is that straight lines are still over-represented [12], unless small differences in angle are used as another discarding condition. An algorithm to overcome the first limitation was reported by Jenks [13], and involved evaluating the perpendicular distance from a line connecting two consecutive data points to an intermediate data point against a user threshold. To tackle the second disadvantage, [14] utilized the angular change between each three consecutive data points.

The most important compression algorithms that seem to hold conceptual promise are reviewed in Sects. 2.1 and 2.2.

2.1 Top-Down Compression Algorithms

The top-down algorithms work by considering every possible split of the data series — i.e., where the approximation error is above some user-defined threshold — and selecting the best position amongst them. The algorithm then recursively continues to split the resulting subseries until they all have approximation errors below the threshold [10].

An often used and quite famous top-down method is the *Douglas-Peucker* (DP) algorithm [12]. It was originally proposed for line simplification, and tries to

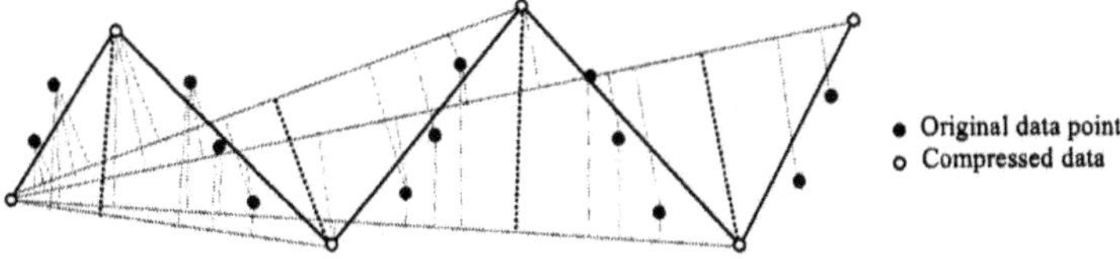

Fig. 1. Top-down Douglas-Peucker algorithm. Original data series of 19 points. In this case, only the first segment was recursively cut at data points 16, 12, 8 and 4.

preserve directional trends in the approximation line using a distance threshold, which may be varied according to the amount of simplification required. McMaster [15] who gives a detailed study of mathematical similarity and discrepancy measures, ranks the DP algorithm as 'mathematically superior'. White [16] performed a study on simplification algorithms on critical points as a psychological feature of curve similarity and showed that the DP algorithm was best at choosing splitting points; he refers to the obtained results as 'overwhelming'.

The algorithm works on the following basis. The first point of the data series is selected as the *anchor point*; the last data point is selected as the *float point*. For all intermediate data points, the (perpendicular) distance to the line connecting anchor and float points is determined. If the maximum of these distances is greater than a pre-defined threshold, the line is cut at the data point that causes that maximum distance. This cut point becomes the new float point for the first segment, and the anchor point for the second segment. The procedure is recursively repeated for both segments. The algorithm is illustrated in Fig. 1.

The DP algorithm clearly is a batch algorithm, as the whole data series is needed at the start; the time complexity of the original algorithm is $O(N^2)$ with N being the number of data points. Due to its simplicity, different implementations have been proposed. One such proposal, which succeeded to reduce the complexity of the method to $(N \log N)$ was Hershberger's proposal [17], who defined the path hull as a basis for their implementation.

2.2 Opening Window Compression Algorithms

Opening window (OW) algorithms anchor the start point of a potential segment, and then attempt to approximate the subsequent data series with increasingly longer segments. It starts by defining a segment between a first data point (the anchor) and the third data point (the float) in the series. As long as all distances of intermediate data points are below the distance threshold, an attempt is made to move the float one point up in the data series. When the threshold is going to be exceeded, two strategies can be applied: either,

- the data point causing the threshold violation (Normal Opening Window, a.k.a. NOPW), or
- the data point just before it (Before Opening Window, a.k.a. BOPW)

becomes the end point of the current segment, and it also becomes the anchor of the next segment. If no threshold excess takes place, the float is moved one up

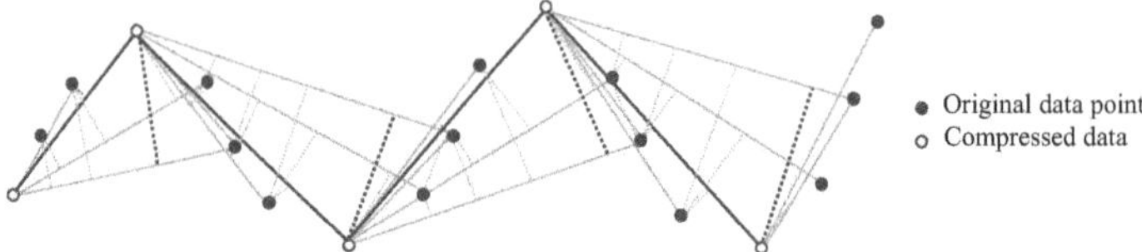

Fig. 2. Data series compression result of NOPW strategy: the threshold excess data point is the break point. The data series was broken at data points 4, 8, 12 and 16.

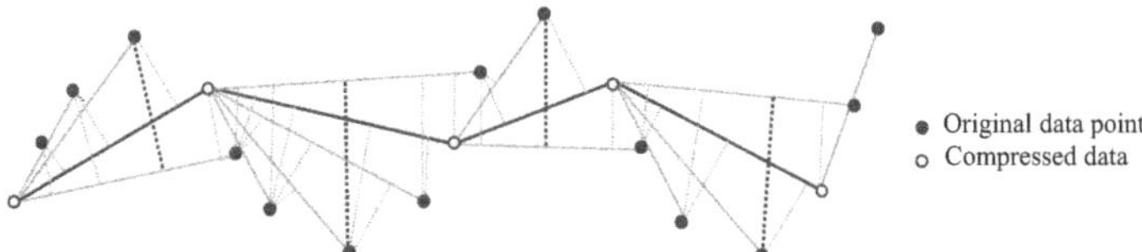

Fig. 3. Data series compression result of BOPW strategy: the data point just before the threshold excess data point is the break point. The first window opened up to point 6 (point 4 causing excess), making point 5 the cut point; second window opened up to point 11 (8 causing excess) with 10 becoming the cut point etc.

the data series — the window opens further — and the method continues, until the entire series has been transformed into a piecewise linear approximation. The results of choosing either strategy are illustrated in Figs. 2 and 3.

An important observation, which can clearly be made from Figs. 2 and 3 is that OW algorithms may lose the last few data points. Countermeasures are required.

Although OW algorithms are computationally expensive, they are popular. This is because they are online algorithms, and because they can work reasonably well in presence of noise but only for relatively short data series. The time complexity of these algorithms is $O(N^2)$.

3 Spatiotemporal Algorithms

3.1 Why Line Generalizations Do Not Quite Apply

We discussed the above algorithms because they are well-known techniques for generalizing line structures. All of them use *perpendicular distance* of data points to a proposed generalized line as the condition to discard or retain that data point. This is the mechanism at work also when we apply these algorithms to our data series, the moving object trajectories, viewed as lines in two-dimensional space.

But our trajectories have this important extra dimension, time. Intrinsically, they are not lines, but historically traced points. As a consequence, the use of perpendicular distance as condition is at least challenged, and we should look at more appropriate conditions.

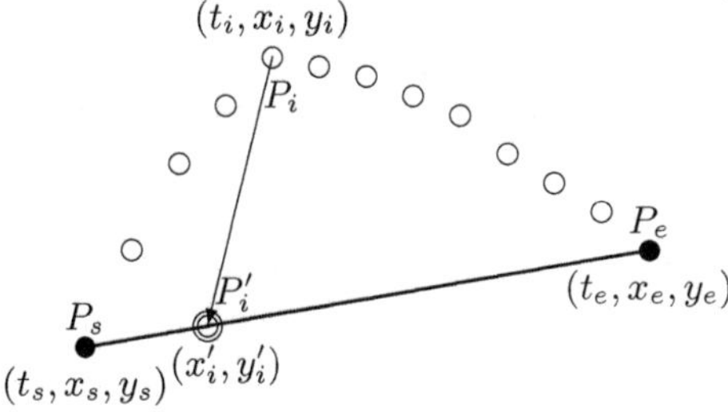

Fig. 4. Original data points (open circles), including P_i, the start and end points P_s and P_e of the approximated trajectory, and P_i's approximated position P'_i.

A trajectory is represented as a time series of positions. Generalizing a trajectory means to replace one time series of positions with another one. Like before, we can measure how effective this generalization is by looking at (a) the compression rate obtained, and (b) the error committed. Unlike before, the error committed is no longer measured through (perpendicular) distances between original data points and the new line, but rather through distances between pairs of temporally synchronized positions, one on the original and one on the new trajectory. This is a fundamental change that does justice to the spatio*temporal* characteristic of a moving point trajectory.

3.2 A Simple Class of Spatiotemporal Algorithms

The computational consequence of the above arguments is that the decision of discarding a data point must be based on its position *and* timestamp, as well as on the approximated position of the object on the new trajectory. This gives a distance not necessarily perpendicular to the new, approximated, trajectory.

The situation is illustrated in Fig. 4, in which the original data point P_i and its approximation P'_i on the new trajectory $P_s - P_e$ are indicated. The coordinates of P'_i are calculated from the simple *ratio* of two time intervals Δe and Δi, indicating respectively travel time from P_s to P_e (along either trajectory) and from P_s to P_i (along the original trajectory), respectively. These travel times are determined from the original data, as timestamp differences. We have

$$\Delta e = t_e - t_s$$

$$\Delta i = t_i - t_s$$

$$x'_i = x_s + \frac{\Delta i}{\Delta e}(x_e - x_s) \quad (1)$$

$$y'_i = y_s + \frac{\Delta i}{\Delta e}(y_e - y_s) \; . \quad (2)$$

After the approximate position P'_i is determined, the next step is to calculate the distance between it and the original P_i, and use that distance as a discarding criterion against a user-defined threshold. This is an important improvement not only because we are using a more accurate distance measure but also because the temporal factor is now included. The continuous nature of moving objects necessitates the inclusion of *temporal* as well as *spatial* properties of moving objects.

The application of the above distance notion for moving object trajectories, in either top-down and opening window algorithms, leads to a class of algorithms that we call here *time ratio algorithms*. We will later see that under an improved error notion, this class gives substantial improvements of performance in compression rate/error trade-offs.

In the sequel, by

- *TD-TR* we denote a top-down time-ratio algorithm, obtained from the DP algorithm through application of the above time-ratio distance measuring technique, and by
- *OPW-TR* we mean a opening-window algorithm applying the same time-ratio distance measurement.

3.3 A More Advanced Class of Spatiotemporal Algorithms

Further improvements can be obtained by exploiting other spatiotemporal information hiding in the time series. Our time-ratio distance measurement was a first step; a second step can be made by analysing the derived speeds at subsequent segments of the trajectory, when these are available. A large difference between the travel speeds of two subsequent segments is another criterion that can be applied to retain the data point in the middle. For this, we will assume a *speed difference threshold* will also have been set, indicating above which speed difference we will always retain the data point.

By integrating the concepts of *speed difference threshold* and the *time-ratio distance* discussed in Sect. 3.2, we obtain a new algorithmic approach, that we call the class of *spatiotemporal algorithms.*

Observe that in principle both these concepts allow application in top-down and opening-window algorithms. We have restricted ourselves here to an opening-window version, applying both criteria. The pseudocode for the algorithm is provided below. The notation used is described in Table 1.

The algorithm sets the anchor point, and then gradually 'opens the window'. In each step, two halting conditions are verified, one on the synchronous distance measure (using the time interval ratio), the other being a difference in speed values between previous and next trajectory segment. These speeds are *not* measured speeds, as we do not assume these to be available; rather, they are speed values derived from timestamps and positions.

procedure $SPT(s, max\_dist\_error, max\_speed\_error)$
if $len(s) \leq 2$
then return s
else $is\_error \leftarrow false$
  $e \leftarrow 2$

Table 1. Overview of data types, variables and functions used in algorithm SPT

$\mathbb{R}, \mathbb{N}$	the real, natural numbers
$\mathbb{T}, \mathbb{L}$	time stamps ($\mathbb{T} \cong \mathbb{R}$), locations ($\mathbb{L} \cong \mathbb{R} \times \mathbb{R}$)
$\mathbb{P}$	trajectories (paths), $\mathbb{P} \cong$ seq ($\mathbb{T} \times \mathbb{L}$)
$(x, y) : \mathbb{L}$	(easting, northing) coordinates
$p : \mathbb{P}$	a trajectory (path) p
$\dfrac{p : \mathbb{P}}{len(p) : \mathbb{N}}$	the number of data points in trajectory p.
$\dfrac{p : \mathbb{P}; 1 \leq i \leq len(p)}{p[i] : \mathbb{T} \times \mathbb{L}}$	the ith data point of p, viewed as a time-stamped location
$\dfrac{p : \mathbb{P}; 1 \leq k \leq m \leq len(p)}{p[k, m] : \mathbb{P}}$	the subseries of p, starting at original index k up to and including index m
$\dfrac{d : \mathbb{T} \times \mathbb{L}}{d_t : \mathbb{T}, d_{loc} : \mathbb{L}}$	time stamp, location of the data point d
$\dfrac{q, r : \mathbb{L}}{dist(q, r) : \mathbb{R}}$	A function that takes two locations q, r and returns the distance between them
$\dfrac{p, s : \mathbb{P}}{p ++ s : \mathbb{P}}$	A function that concatenates two trajectories

while $e \leq len(s)$ **and not** *is_error* **do**
  $i \leftarrow 2$
  while ($i < e$ **and not** *is_error*) **do**
      $\Delta e \leftarrow s[e]_t - s[1]_t$
      $\Delta i \leftarrow s[i]_t - s[1]_t$
      $(x'_i, y'_i) \leftarrow s[1]_{loc} + (s[e]_{loc} - s[1]_{loc})\, \Delta i / \Delta e$
      $v_{i-1} \leftarrow dist(s[i]_{loc}, s[i-1]_{loc}) \,/\, (s[i]_t - s[i-1]_t)$
      $v_i \leftarrow dist(s[i+1]_{loc}, s[i]_{loc}) \,/\, (s[i+1]_t - s[i]_t)$
      if $dist(s[i]_{loc}, (x'_i, y'_i)) > max\_dist\_error$ **or** $\|v_i - v_{i-1}\| > max\_speed\_error$
        then *is_error* $\leftarrow$ *true*
        else $i \leftarrow i + 1$
      end if
    end while
    if *is_error*
      then return $[s[1]] ++ SPT(s[i, len(s)], max\_dist\_error, max\_speed\_error)$
    end if
    $e \leftarrow e + 1$
  end while
  if not *is_error*
    then return $[s[1], s[len(s)]]$
  end if
end if

Table 2. Statistics on the ten moving object trajectories used in our experiments

statistic	*average*	*standard deviation*
duration	00:32:16	00:14:33
speed	40.85 km/h	12.63 km/h
length	19.95 km	12.84 km
displacement	10.58 km	8.97 km
# of data points	200	100.9

4 Comparisons and Results

To assess their appropriateness and relative performance, both spatial and spatiotemporal compression techniques were tested using real moving object trajectory data. In total, we obtained 10 trajectories through a GPS mounted on a car, which travelled different roads in urban and rural areas. The data includes short and lengthy time series; various statistics of our data set are provided in Table 2.

In using lossy compression techniques there is always a trade-off between compression rate achieved and error allowed. In our case, the optimal compression technique should find a subseries of the original time series that has a high enough compression and a low enough error. This error notion is the main tool to evaluate the quality of the compression technique. But the literature has not paid a lot of attention to explicitly measuring error. Mostly, attention has been given to the identification of proper heuristics for discarding data points.

Such heuristics may or may not be proper for compressing moving object trajectories. One of the contributions of this paper is the introduction of an error formula for moving object trajectory compression; it is described below. Since writing up this paper, we have found a similar approach was published by Nanni [18], though in a more general setting, and thus not providing the full details of the formula that we are after.

4.1 Error Notions

The quality of compression techniques is evaluated by using some notion of error. Several mathematical measures have been proposed for this error notion, for instance by [15,19]. Error notions can be based on different principles: length, density, angularity and curvilinearity. Some of these notions have been used to improve the appeal of the approximation (usually a line) in cartographic context.

Distance-based error notions seem less biased towards visual effect. In plain line generalization, perpendicular distance is the error measure of choice. A simple method determines all distances of original data points to the approximation line, and determines their average, but this is sensitive to the actual number of data points. A method least sensitive to this number essentially determines the area between original line and approximation. It effectively assumes there are infinitely many original data points.

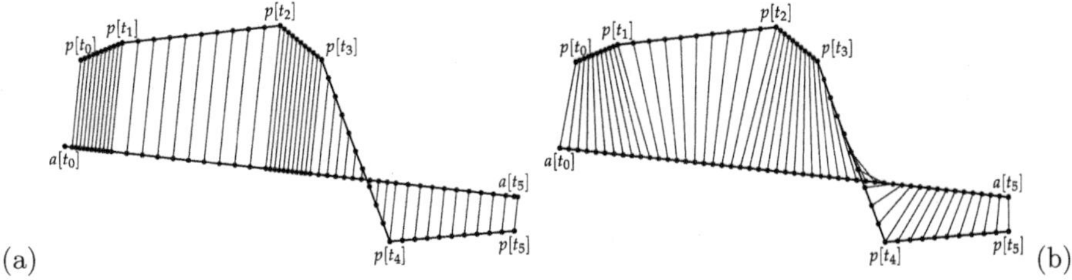

Fig. 5. Two error notions for a trajectory p being approximated by a. (a) error measured at fixed sampling rate as sum of perpendicular distance chords; (b) error measured at fixed sampling rates as sum of time-synchronous distance chords.

How would such an error measure translate to the spatiotemporal case of object movement? Applying still perpendicular distances, insensitivity to the number of data points can be obtained by considering progressively finer sampling rates, as illustrated in Fig. 5a. In this figure, p represents an original trajectory with five segments, a represents its 1-segment approximation. The t_i are equally spaced time instants. On slower segments (like the first and third), distance chords become more condensed. For progressively finer sampling rates, this error notion becomes the sum over segments of weighted areas between original and approximation. The associated formulas are simple and direct.

4.2 A Spatiotemporal Error Notion

Given an original trajectory $(p : \mathbb{P})$ and an approximation trajectory $(a : \mathbb{P})$ of it, we are interested in finding a measure that expresses without bias how well the second approximates the first. The plain intuition we have for this is that the *average distance between the original object and the approximation object*—both *synchronously* travelling along their respective trajectories p and a—during the time interval of their trajectories is the best measure that one can have. In the remainder of this section, we are developing the formulas for that average distance.

We will assume that both trajectories (p and a) are represented as series of time-stamped positions, which we will interpret as piecewise linear paths. Given the classes of compression algorithms that we study, we can also safely assume that the time stamps present in the trajectory a form a subseries of those present in the original p. After all, we have obtained that series by discarding data points in the original, and we never invented new data points, let alone time stamps. Assume that p has data points numbered from 1 to k.

Following from the above, we can define the *average synchronous error* $\alpha(p, a)$ between p and a as a summation of the weighted contributions of all linear segments in p.

$$\alpha(p, a) = \frac{\sum_{i=1}^{k-1} (p[i+1]_{\mathrm{t}} - p[i]_{\mathrm{t}}) \cdot \alpha(p[i : i+1], a)}{\sum_{i=1}^{k-1} p[i+1]_{\mathrm{t}} - p[i]_{\mathrm{t}}} . \tag{3}$$

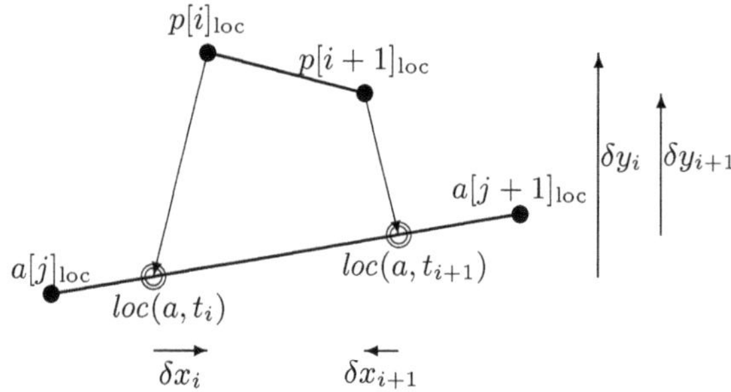

Fig. 6. Definition of $\delta x_i, \delta x_{i+1}, \delta y_i$ and δy_{i+1}. Illustrated is the i-th segment of original path p (at top), between points $p[i]_{\rm loc}$ and $p[i+1]_{\rm loc}$, and its approximation $loc(a, t_i)$–$loc(a, t_{i+1})$ on trajectory a. Observe that this approximation will be part of an a-segment, but that its start and end points may or may not coincide with real data points of a.

We have not defined the function α fully in this way. Equation 3 covers the case that p is a multi-segment trajectory, but not the case that it is a single segment. We will cover that case through (4) below.

Now let us derive the *single segment average synchronous error*. If q is a single segment trajectory, we can define $loc(q, t)$ as the moving object position at time t, in the style of (1) and (2). We generalize this notion of object position for an arbitrary length trajectory p in the obvious way, such that $loc : \mathbb{P} \to (\mathbb{T} \to \mathbb{L})$ is a total function such that for any p, $loc(p)$ is a partial function with domain $[p[1]_{\rm t}, p[len(p)]_{\rm t}]$.

With the single segment average synchronous error $\alpha(p[i : i{+}1], a)$ we express the average distance between original and approximate object during the time interval between indices i and $i+1$, for convenience written as $[t_i, t_{i+1}]$. It can be expressed as

$$\alpha(p[i : i+1], a) = \frac{1}{t_{i+1} - t_i} \int_{t_i}^{t_{i+1}} dist(loc(p, t), loc(a, t))\, dt \ . \quad (4)$$

In our further derivations, differences in coordinate values at time instants t_i and t_{i+1} between p and a (in that order) will be important. We will denote these (four) differences, respectively as $\delta x_i, \delta x_{i+1}, \delta y_i$ and δy_{i+1}. E.g., δy_i equals $loc(p, t_i).y - loc(a, t_i).y$, and so on. Observe that these are constants; they are illustrated in Fig. 6.

Since both p and a during the given time interval are represented as straight segments, the distance formula in (4) can be derived as having a well-known polynomial format:

$$dist(loc(p, t), loc(p, t)) = \frac{1}{c_4}\sqrt{c_1 t^2 + c_2 t + c_3},$$

where

$$c_1 = (\delta x_i - \delta x_{i+1})^2 + (\delta y_i - \delta y_{i+1})^2$$

$c_2 = 2 \cdot ((\delta x_{i+1} t_i - \delta x_i t_{i+1}) \cdot (\delta x_i - \delta x_{i+1}) + (\delta y_{i+1} t_i - \delta y_i t_{i+1}) \cdot (\delta y_i - \delta y_{i+1}))$
$c_3 = (\delta x_{i+1} t_i - \delta x_i t_{i+1})^2 + (\delta y_{i+1} t_i - \delta y_i t_{i+1})^2$ and
$c_4 = t_{i+1} - t_i$.

Using the above results we can rewrite (4) to

$$\alpha(p[i : i+1], a) = \frac{1}{(t_{i+1} - t_i)^2} \int_{t_i}^{t_{i+1}} \sqrt{c_1 t^2 + c_2 t + c_3}\, dt \ . \qquad (5)$$

The solution to (5) depends on the values for the constants c_i. We provide a case analysis, omitting cases that cannot happen due to the structure—expressed in the equations for constants c_i—of the problem.

Case $c_1 = 0$ **:** This happens when $\delta x_i = \delta x_{i+1} \wedge \delta y_i = \delta y_{i+1}$. If so, then also $c_2 = 0$, and the solution to (5) is

$$\alpha(p[i : i+1], a) = \frac{\sqrt{c_3}}{t_{i+1} - t_i} \ .$$

The geometric interpretation of this case is simple: equality of δ's indicates that the approximation of this p segment is a vector-translated version of that segment. The distance is thus constant, and its average over the time interval equals that constant. We have:

$$\boxed{\alpha(p[i : i+1], a) = \sqrt{\delta x_i^2 + \delta y_i^2} \ .}$$

Case $(c_1 > 0)$ **:** This happens when $\delta x_i \neq \delta x_{i+1} \vee \delta y_i \neq \delta y_{i+1}$. The solution to the integral part of (5) is non-trivial, and deserves a case analysis in itself. We have the following cases:

Case $c_2^2 - 4c_1c_3 = 0$ **:** In other words, the determinant of the quadratic subformula of (5) equals 0. This happens only when $\delta x_i \delta y_{i+1} = \delta x_{i+1} \delta y_i$. If so, the solution to (5) is

$$\boxed{\alpha(p[i : i+1], a) = \frac{1}{(t_{i+1} - t_i)^2} \left| \frac{2c_1 t + c_2}{4c_1} \sqrt{c_1 t^2 + c_2 t + c_3} \right|_{t_i}^{t_{i+1}} \ .}$$

The geometric interpretation of this case follows from the δ product equality mentioned above. That equality holds in three different cases. These cases are not mutually exclusive, but where they are not, the formulas coincide value-wise.

Case segments share start point : Consequently, we have $\delta x_i = \delta y_i = 0$. The above formula simplifies to

$$\boxed{\alpha(p[i : i+1], a) = \tfrac{1}{2} \sqrt{\delta x_{i+1}^2 + \delta y_{i+1}^2} \ .}$$

Case segments share end point : Consequently, we have $\delta x_{i+1} = \delta y_{i+1} = 0$. The above formula simplifies to

$$\boxed{\alpha(p[i:i+1],a) = \tfrac{1}{2}\sqrt{\delta x_i^2 + \delta y_i^2}\ .}$$

Case δ ratios respected : It turns out that under this condition, the synchronous distance chords (indicated as grey edges in Figs. 5) all lie parallel to each other, and this simplifies the related formulas.

Case $c_2^2 - 4c_1c_3 < 0$: The determinant of the quadratic subformula of (5) is less than 0. This is the general, non-exceptional case. The resulting formula is:

$$\alpha(p[i:i+1],a) = \frac{1}{(t_{i+1}-t_i)^2}\,|F(t)|_{t_i}^{t_{i+1}} \quad \text{where}$$
$$F(t) = \frac{2c_1t+c_2}{4c_1}\sqrt{c_1t^2+c_2t+c_3} - \frac{c_2^2-4c_1c_3}{8c_1\sqrt{c_1}}\operatorname{arcsinh}\left(\frac{2c_1t+c_2}{\sqrt{4c_1c_3-c_2^2}}\right)\ .$$

4.3 Experimental Results

As mentioned earlier, all the compression techniques were tested on real data as summarized in Table 2; i.e., ten different trajectories, for fifteen different spatial threshold values ranging from 30 to 100 m, and three speed difference threshold values ranging from 5 to 25 m/s. The obtained results for each experiment consist of error produced and compression rate achieved. We used the time synchronous error notion derived in the previous paragraph. It is important to note that the choice of optimal threshold values is difficult and might differ for various applications.

A first experiment concerned the comparison between conventional top-down (Normal) DP (NDP) and our top-down time ratio (TD-TR) algorithm. Fig. 7 shows the results. Clearly, the TD-TR algorithm produces much lower errors, while the compression rate is only slightly lower.

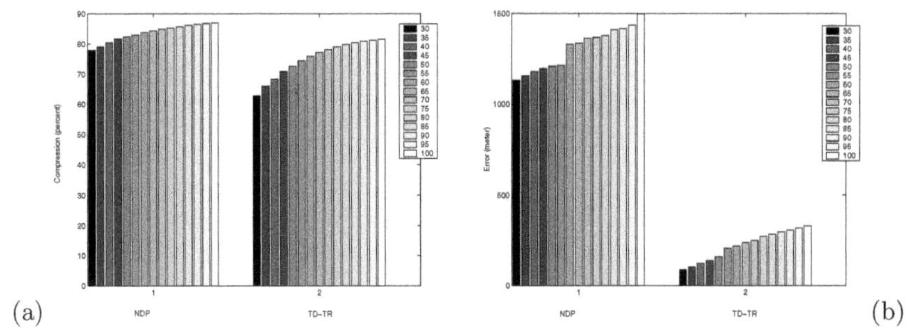

Fig. 7. Comparison between NDP (on left) and TD-TR (on right) algorithms. Colour bars indicate different settings for distance threshold, ranging from 30 to 100 m. (a) Comparison of compression percentages achieved; (b) Comparison of errors committed. Figures given are averages over ten different, real trajectories.

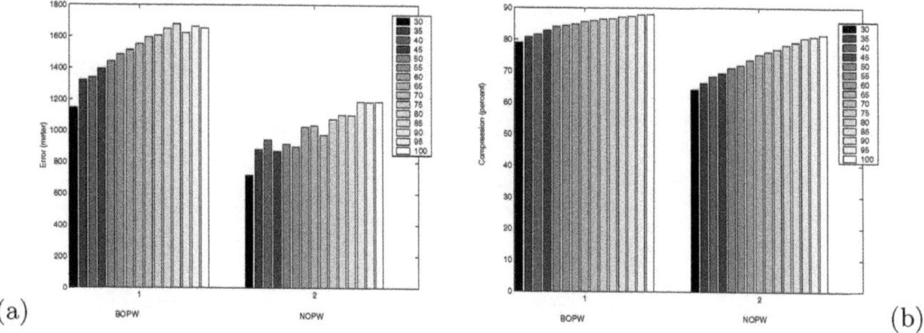

Fig. 8. Comparison between two opening window algorithms, BOPW (on left) and NOPW (on right) algorithms. For other legend information, see Fig. 7.

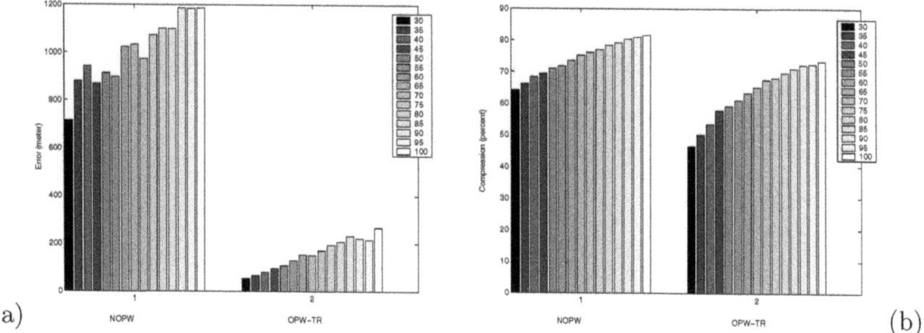

Fig. 9. Comparison between NOPW (on left) and OPW-TR (on right) algorithms. For other legend information, see Fig. 7.

An important observation is that both compression rate and error *monotonically* increase with distance threshold, asymptotically reaching a maximum.

The second experiment concerned the choice of break point in opening window algorithms; i.e., whether to break at the data point causing threshold excess (NOPW) or at the one just before (BOPW). We found that BOPW results in higher compression but worse errors. It can be used in applications where the main concern is compression and one is willing to favour it over error. For most of our application domains, we aim at lower error and high enough compression rate, and will therefore ignore the BOPW method. Results of comparison between BOPW and NOPW algorithms are shown in Fig. 8.

One may observe that error in the case of the NOPW algorithm does not strictly monotonically increase with increasing distance threshold values. We have reason to believe that these effects are systematic; they are likely only an artifact caused by the small set of trajectories in our experiments.

In Fig. 9, we illustrate the findings of a third experiment, comparing our opening window time ratio with a normal opening window algorithm. It demonstrates the superiority of the first (OPW-TR) with respect to the latter (NOPW) algorithm. As can be seen, for OPW-TR a change in threshold value does not dramatically impact error level. Therefore, unlike the NOPW algorithm, in which a choice of threshold is important for the error results, in the OPW-TR algorithm

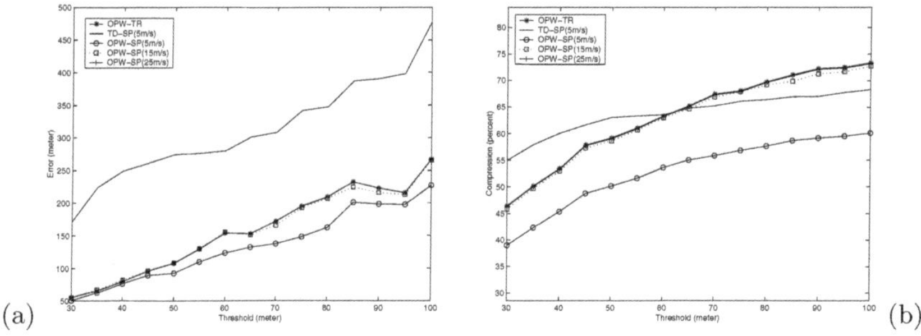

Fig. 10. Comparison between OPW-TR, TD-SP and OPW-SP algorithms. (a) Errors committed; (b) Compression obtained. In both figures, the graph for OPW-TR coincides with that of OPW-SP-25m/s.

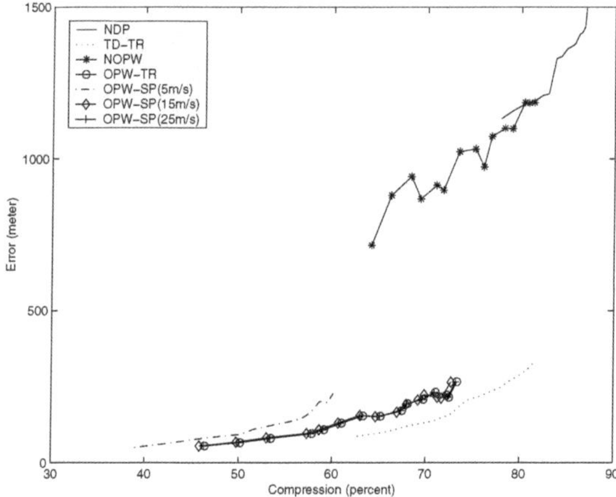

Fig. 11. Error versus Compression in NDP, TD-TR, NOPW, OPW-TR and OPW-SP algorithms. As before, the graph for OPW-TR coincides with that of OPW-SP-25m/s.

this is not the case. This allows choosing a higher threshold value to improve compression while not loosing much on error performance.

Our second spatio-temporal algorithm (SP) was applied in both opening window and top-down fashion. In case of top-down SP (TD-SP), experiments show a high sensitivity towards speed threshold settings, both for error and compression. Among the three speed difference threshold values (5, 15, 25 m/s), only the first value provided reasonable results, and is therefore included in the comparisons. In opening window fashion SP (OPW-SP) changes in threshold value did not lead to dramatic changes in the results. This is an important characteristic of both OPW-TR and OPW-SP algorithms. As can be seen from Fig. 10, the two OPW-SP (15 m/s, 25 m/s) algorithms as well as OPW-TR have very similar behaviour in both compression rate and error. On the other hand, choosing a speed difference threshold of 5 m/s in TD-SP and OPW-SP results in improved compression as well as higher error in TD-SP.

As experiments show reasonably high compression rates as well as low errors for our TD-TR, OPW-TR and OPW-SP algorithms, they effectively fulfill the requirement of *good* compression techniques. A final comparison between these algorithms ranks the TD-TR slightly over their counterparts because of better compression rate. See Fig. 11.

However, two issues should not be forgotten. One is that TD-TR is a batch algorithm, while OPW-TR and OPW-SP are online algorithms. The other issue is that the higher compression rate in TD-TR is accompanied by slightly higher error. Therefore, depending on data availability and error allowed, any of the mentioned algorithms can be used. The results of this final comparison are shown in Fig. 11. It clearly shows that algorithms developed with spatiotemporal characteristics outperform others. Another important observation is that the choice of threshold value for OPW-SP is crucial, as it may rank it higher or lower than OPW-TR.

5 Conclusions and Future Work

Existing compression techniques commonly used for line generalization are not suitable for moving object trajectory applications. Mostly because they operate on the basis of perpendicular distances. Due to the continuous nature of moving objects, both spatial and temporal factors should be taken into account compressing their data.

In this paper, problems of existing compression techniques for moving object application are addressed. Two spatio-temporal techniques are proposed to overcome the mentioned problems. The quality of the methods was tested using a new and advanced error notion. The experiments confirm the superiority of the proposed methods to the existing ones. The proposed algorithms are suitable to be used as both *batch* and *online*.

Obtained results strongly depend on the chosen threshold values. Choosing a proper threshold is not easy and is application-dependent. However, having a clear understanding of moving object behaviour helps in making these choices, and we plan to look into the issue of moving objects of different nature.

Piecewise linear interpolation was used as the approximation technique. Considering that other measurements such as momentaneous speed and direction values are sometimes available, other, more advanced, interpolation techniques and consequently other error notions can be defined. This is an issue that we want to address in the future.

Acknowledgements. We thank the anonymous reviewers for their elaborate and detailed comments that helped us to improve the paper.

References

1. Cooper, M.: Antennas get smart. Scientific American **283** (2003) 48–55
2. Abdelguerfi, M., Givaudan, J., Shaw, K., Ladner, R.: The 2-3TR-tree, a trajectory-oriented index structure for fully evolving valid-time spatio-temporal datasets. In: Proc. 10th ACM-GIS, ACM Press (2002) 29–34

3. Zhu, H., Su, J., Ibarra, O. H.: Trajectory queries and octagons in moving object databases. In: Proc. 11th CIKM, ACM Press (2002) 413–421
4. Güting, R. H., Böhlen, M. H., Erwig, M., Jensen, C. S., Lorentzos, N. A., Schneider, M., Vazirgiannis, M.: A foundation for representing and querying moving objects. ACM TODS **25** (2000) 1–42
5. Šaltenis, S., Jensen, C. S., Leutenegger, S. T., Lopez, M. A.: Indexing the positions of continuously moving objects. In: Proc. ACM SIGMOD, ACM Press (2000) 331–342
6. Agarwal, P. K., Guibas, L. J., Edelsbrunner, H., Erickson, J., Isard, M., Har-Peled, S., Hershberger, J., Jensen, C., Kavraki, L., Koehl, P., Lin, M., Manocha, D., Metaxas, D., Mirtich, B., Mount, D., Muthukrishnan, S., Pai, D., Sacks, E., Snoeyink, J., Suri, S., Wolfson, O.: Algorithmic issues in modeling motion. ACM Computing Surveys **34** (2002) 550–572
7. Meratnia, N., de By, R. A.: A new perspective on trajectory compression techniques. In: Proc. ISPRS DMGIS 2003, October 2–3, 2003, Québec, Canada. (2003) S.p.
8. Foley, J. D., van Dam, A., Feiner, S. K., Hughes, J. F.: Computer Graphics: Principles and Practice. Second edn. Addison-Wesley (1990)
9. Shatkay, H., Zdonik, S. B.: Approximate queries and representations for large data sequences. In Su, S.Y.W., ed.: Proc. 12th ICDE, New Orleans, Louisiana, USA, IEEE Computer Society (1996) 536–545
10. Keogh, E. J., Chu, S., Hart, D., Pazzani, M. J.: An online algorithm for segmenting time series. In: Proc. ICDM'01, Silicon Valley, California, USA, IEEE Computer Society (2001) 289–296
11. Tobler, W. R.: Numerical map generalization. In Nystuen, J.D., ed.: IMaGe Discussion Papers. Michigan Interuniversity Community of Mathematical Geographers. University of Michigan, Ann Arbor, Mi, USA (1966)
12. Douglas, D. H., Peucker, T. K.: Algorithms for the reduction of the number of points required to represent a digitized line or its caricature. The Canadian Cartographer **10** (1973) 112–122
13. Jenks, G. F.: Lines, computers, and human frailties. Annuals of the Association of American Geographers **71** (1981) 1–10
14. Jenks, G. F.: Linear simplification: How far can we go? Paper presented to the Tenth Annual Meeting, Canadian Cartographic Association (1985)
15. McMaster, R. B.: Statistical analysis of mathematical measures of linear simplification. The American Cartographer **13** (1986) 103–116
16. White, E. R.: Assessment of line generalization algorithms using characteristic points. The American Cartographer **12** (1985) 17–27
17. Hershberger, J., Snoeyink, J.: Speeding up the Douglas-Peucker line-simplification algorithm. In: Proc. 5th SDH. Volume 1., Charleston, South Carolina, USA, University of South Carolina (1992) 134–143
18. Nanni, M.: Distances for spatio-temporal clustering. In: Decimo Convegno Nazionale su Sistemi Evoluti per Basi di Dati (SEBD 2002), Portoferraio (Isola d'Elba), Italy. (2002) 135–142
19. Jasinski, M.: The compression of complexity measures for cartographic lines. Technical report 90–1, National Center for Geographic Information and Analysis, Department of Geography. State University of New York at Buffalo, New York, USA (1990)

Non-contiguous Sequence Pattern Queries

Nikos Mamoulis and Man Lung Yiu

Department of Computer Science and Information Systems
University of Hong Kong
Pokfulam Road, Hong Kong
{nikos,mlyiu2}@csis.hku.hk

Abstract. Non-contiguous subsequence pattern queries search for symbol instances in a long sequence that satisfy some soft temporal constraints. In this paper, we propose a methodology that indexes long sequences, in order to efficiently process such queries. The sequence data are decomposed into tables and queries are evaluated as multiway joins between them. We describe non-blocking join operators and provide query preprocessing and optimization techniques that tighten the join predicates and suggest a good join order plan. As opposed to previous approaches, our method can efficiently handle a broader range of queries and can be easily supported by existing DBMS. Its efficiency is evaluated by experimentation on synthetic and real data.

1 Introduction

Time-series and biological database applications require the efficient management of long sequences. A sequence can be defined by a series of *symbol instances* (e.g., events) over a long timeline. Various types of queries are applied by the data analyst to recover interesting patterns and trends from the data. The most common type is referred to as "subsequence matching". Given a long sequence $\mathcal{T}$, a subsequence query q asks for all segments in $\mathcal{T}$ that match q. Unlike other data types (e.g., relational, spatial, etc.), queries on sequence data are usually *approximate*, since (i) it is highly unlikely for exact matching to return results and (ii) relaxed constraints can better represent the user requests.

Previous work on subsequence matching has mainly focused on (exact) retrieval of subsequences in $\mathcal{T}$ that contain or match *all* symbols of a query subsequence q [5,10]. A popular type of approximate retrieval, used mainly by biologists, is based on the *edit* distance [11,8]. In these queries, the user is usually interested in retrieving *contiguous* subsequences that approximately match *contiguous* queries. Recently, the problem of evaluating non-contiguous queries has been addressed [13]; some applications require retrieving a specific ordering of events (with exact or approximate gaps between them), without caring about the events which interleave them in the actual sequence. An example of such a query would be "find all subsequences where event a was transmitted approximately 10 seconds before b, which appeared approximately 20 seconds before c". Here, "approximately" can be expressed by an interval τ of allowed distances (e.g.,

E. Bertino et al. (Eds.): EDBT 2004, LNCS 2992, pp. 783–800, 2004.
© Springer-Verlag Berlin Heidelberg 2004

$\tau_{a,b} = [9, 11]$ seconds), which may be of different length for different query components (e.g., $\tau_{a,b} = [9, 11]$ sec., $\tau_{b,c} = [18, 21]$ sec.). For such queries, traditional distance measures (e.g., Euclidean distance, edit distance) may not be appropriate for search, since they apply on contiguous sequences with fixed distances between consecutive symbols (e.g., strings).

In this paper, we deal with the problem of indexing long sequences in order to efficiently evaluate such non-contiguous pattern queries. In contrast to a previous solution [13], we propose a much simpler organization of the sequence elements, which, paired with query optimization techniques, allows us to solve the problem, using off-the-shelf database technology. In our framework, the sequence is decomposed into multiple tables, one for each symbol that appears in it. A query is then evaluated as a series of *temporal* joins between these tables. We employ temporal inference rules to tighten the constraints in order to speed-up query processing. Moreover, appropriate binary join operators are proposed for this problem. An important feature of these operators is that they are non-blocking; in other words, their results can be consumed at production time and temporary files are avoided during query processing. We provide selectivity and cost models for temporal joins, which are used by the query optimizer to define a good join order for each query.

The rest of the paper is organized as follows. Section 2 formally defines the problem and discusses related work. We present our methodology in Section 3. Section 4 describes a query preprocessing technique and provides selectivity and cost models for temporal joins. The application of our methodology to variants of the problem is discussed in Section 5. Section 6 includes an experimental evaluation of our methods. Finally, Section 7 concludes the paper.

2 Problem Definition and Related Work

2.1 Problem Definition

Definition 1. *Let $\mathcal{S}$ be a set of* **symbols** *(e.g., event types). A* **sequence** *$\mathcal{T}$ is defined by a series of (s, t) pairs, where s is a symbol in $\mathcal{S}$ and t is a real-valued timestamp.*

As an example, consider an application that collects event transmissions from sensors. The set of event types defines $\mathcal{S}$. The sequence $\mathcal{T}$ is the collection of all transmissions over a long time. Figure 1 illustrates such a sequence. Here, $\mathcal{S} = \{a, b, c, d, e, f\}$ and $\mathcal{T} = \langle (a, 1.5), (c, 3), (d, 4.12), \ldots, (b, 32.14) \rangle$. Note that the definition is generic enough to include non-timestamped strings, where the distance between consecutive symbols is fixed. Given a long sequence $\mathcal{T}$, an analyst might want to retrieve the occurrences of interesting temporal patterns:

Definition 2. *Let $\mathcal{T}$ be a sequence defined over a set of symbols $\mathcal{S}$. A* **subsequence query pattern** *is defined by a connected directed graph $Q(V, E)$. Each node $n_i \in V$ is labeled with a symbol $l(n_i)$ from $\mathcal{S}$. Each (directed) edge*

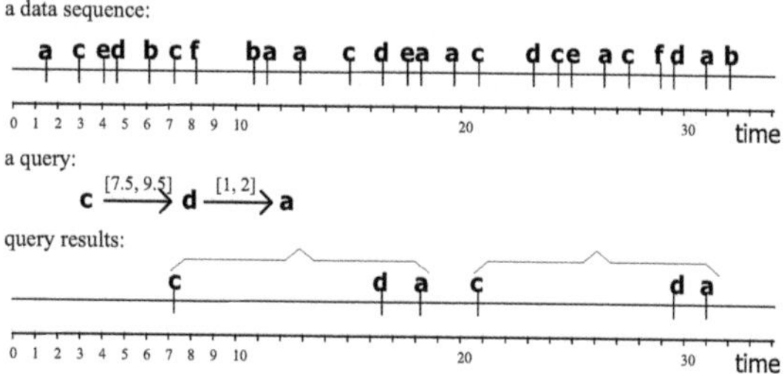

Fig. 1. A data sequence and a query

$\langle n_i \rightarrow n_j \rangle$ in E is labeled by a **temporal constraint** *$\tau_{i,j}$ modeling the allowed temporal distance $t(n_j) - t(n_i)$ between n_i and n_j in a query result. $\tau_{i,j}$ is defined by an interval $[a_{i,j}, b_{i,j}]$ of allowed values for $t(n_j) - t(n_i)$. The* **length** *$|\tau_{i,j}|$ of a temporal constraint $\tau_{i,j}$ is defined by the length of the corresponding temporal interval.*

Notice that a temporal constraint $\tau_{i,j}$ implies an equivalent $\tau_{j,i}$ (with the reverse direction), however, only one is usually defined by the user. A query example, illustrated in Figure 1, is $n_1 \rightarrow n_2 \rightarrow n_3$, $l(n_1) = c$, $l(n_2) = d$, $l(n_2) = a$, $\tau_{1,2} = [7.5, 9.5]$, $\tau_{2,3} = [1, 2]$. The lengths of $\tau_{1,2}$ and $\tau_{2,3}$ are $9.5 - 7.5 = 2$ and $2 - 1 = 1$ respectively.[1] This query asks for instances of c, followed by instances of d with time difference in the range $[7.5, 9.5]$, followed by instances of a with time difference in the range $[1, 2]$. Formally, a query result is defined as follows:

Definition 3. *Given a query $Q(V, E)$ with N vertices and a data sequence $\mathcal{T}$, a* **result** *of Q in $\mathcal{T}$ is defined by an instantiation $\{n_1 \leftarrow (s_1, t_1), n_2 \leftarrow (s_2, t_2), \ldots n_N \leftarrow (s_N, t_N)\}$ such that $\forall 1 \leq i \leq N : (s_i, t_i) \in \mathcal{T} \land l(n_i) = s_i$ and $\forall \langle n_i \rightarrow n_j \rangle \in E : t_j - t_i \in \tau_{i,j}$.*

Figure 1 shows graphically the results of the example query in the data sequence (notice that they include *non-contiguous* event patterns). It is possible (not shown in the current example) that two results share some common events. In other words, an event (or combination of events) may appear in more than one results. The sequence patterns search problem can be formally defined as follows:

Definition 4. (problem definition) *Given a query $Q(V, E)$ and a data sequence $\mathcal{T}$, the* **subsequence pattern retrieval problem** *asks for all results of Q in $\mathcal{T}$.*

Definition 2 is more generic than the corresponding query definition in [13], allowing the specification of binary temporal constraints between any pair of symbol instances. However, the graph should be connected, otherwise multiple queries (one for each connected component) are implied. As we will see in Section

[1] We note here that the length of a constraint $\tau_{i,j} = [a_{i,j}, b_{i,j}]$ in a discrete integer temporal domain is defined by $b_{i,j} - a_{i,j} + 1$.

4.1, additional temporal constraints can be derived for non-existing edges, and the existing ones can be further tightened using a *temporal constraint network minimization* technique. This allows for efficient query processing and optimization.

2.2 Related Work

The subsequence matching problem has been extensively studied in time-series and biological databases, but for contiguous query subsequences [11,5,10]. The common approach is to slide a window of length w along the long sequence and index the subsequence defined by each position of the window. For time-series databases, the subsequences are transformed to high dimensional points in a Euclidean space and indexed by spatial access methods (e.g., R–trees). For biological sequences and string databases, more complex measures, like the *edit distance* are used. These approaches cannot be applied to our problem, since we are interested in non-contiguous patterns. In addition, search in our case is approximate; the distances between symbols in the query are not exact.

Wang et al. [13] were the first to deal with non-contiguous pattern queries. However, the problem definition there is narrower, covering only a subset of the queries defined in the previous section. Specifically, the temporal constraints are always between the first query component and the remaining ones (i.e., arbitrary binary constraints are not defined). In addition, the approximate distances are defined by an exact distance and a tolerance (e.g., a is 20 ± 1 seconds before b), as opposed to our interval-based definition. Although the interval-based and tolerance based definitions are equivalent, we prefer the interval-based one in our model, because inference operations can easily be defined, as we will see later.

[13] slide a temporal window of length ξ along the data sequence $\mathcal{T}$. Each symbol $s_0 \in \mathcal{T}$ defines a window position. The window at s_0 defines a *string* of pairs starting by $(s_0, 0)$ and containing (s, f) pairs, where s is a symbol and f is its distance from the previous symbol. The length of the string at s_0 is controlled by ξ; only symbols s with $t(s) - t(s_0) < \xi$ are included in it. Figure 2a shows an example sequence and the resulting strings after sliding a window of length $\xi = 5$.

The strings are inserted into a prefix tree structure (i.e., trie), which compresses their occurrences of the corresponding subsequences in $\mathcal{T}$. Each leaf of this trie stores a list of the positions in $\mathcal{T}$, where the corresponding subsequence exists; if most of the subsequences occur frequently in $\mathcal{T}$, a lot of space can be saved. The nodes of the trie are then labeled by a preorder traversal; node v is assigned a pair (v_s, v_m), where v_s is the preorder ID and v_m is the maximum preorder ID under the subtree rooted at v. From this trie, a set of *iso-depth lists* (one for each (s, d) pair, where s is a symbol and d is its offset from the beginning of the subsequence) are extracted. Figure 2b shows how the example strings are inserted into the trie and the iso-depth links for pair $(b, 3)$. These links are organized into consecutive arrays, which are used for pattern searching (see Figure 2c). For example, assume that we want to retrieve the results of query $\tau(c, a) = [1, 1]$ and $\tau(c, b) = [3, 3]$. We can use the ISO-Depth index to first

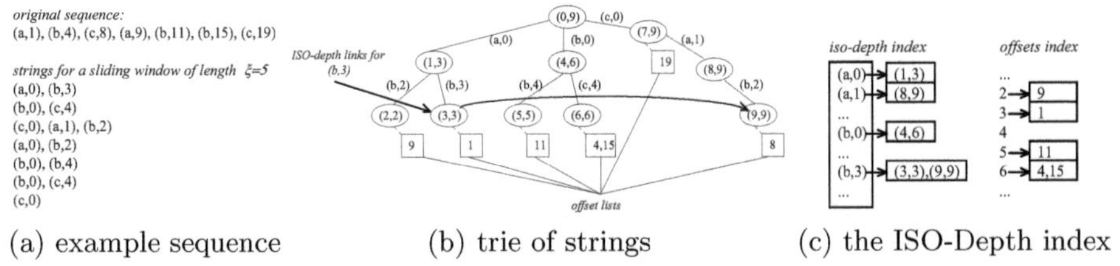

(a) example sequence (b) trie of strings (c) the ISO-Depth index

Fig. 2. Example of the ISO-Depth index [13]

find the ID range of node $(c, 0)$, which is $(7, 9)$. Then, we issue a *containment query* to find the ID ranges of $(a, 1)$ within $(7, 9)$. For each qualifying range, $(8, 9)$ in the example, we issue a second containment query on $(b, 3)$ to retrieve the ID range of the result and the corresponding offset list. In this example, we get $(9, 9)$, which accesses in the right table of Fig. 2c the resulting offset 7. If some temporal constraints are approximate (e.g., $\tau(c, a)$ = [1,2]), in the next list a query is issued for each exact value in the approximate range (assuming a discrete temporal domain).

This complex ISO-Depth index is shown in [13] to perform better than naive, exhaustive-search approaches. It can be adapted to solve our problem, as defined in Section 2.1. However, it has certain limitations. First, it is only suitable for *star* query graphs, where (i) the first symbol is temporally *before* all other symbols in the query and (ii) the only temporal constraints are between the first symbol and all others. Furthermore, there should be a total temporal order between the symbols of the query. For example, constraint $\tau_{a,b} = [-1, 1]$, implies that a can be before or after b in the query result. If we want to process this query using the ISO-Depth index, we need to decompose it to two queries: $\tau_{a,b} = [0, 1]$ and $\tau_{b,a} = [1, 1]$, and process them separately. If there are multiple such constraints, the number of queries that we need to issue may increase significantly. In the worst case, we have to issue $N!$ queries, where N is the number of vertices in the query graph. An additional limitation of the ISO-Depth index is that the temporal domain has to be discrete and coarse for trie compression to be effective. If the time domain is continuous, it is highly unlikely that any subsequence will appear exactly in $\mathcal{T}$ more than once. Finally, the temporal difference between two symbols in a query is restricted by ξ, limiting the use of the index. In this paper, we propose an alternative and much simpler method for storing and indexing long sequences, in order to efficiently process arbitrary non-contiguous subsequence pattern queries.

3 Methodology

In this section, we describe the data decomposition scheme proposed in this paper and a simple indexing scheme for it. We provide a methodology for query

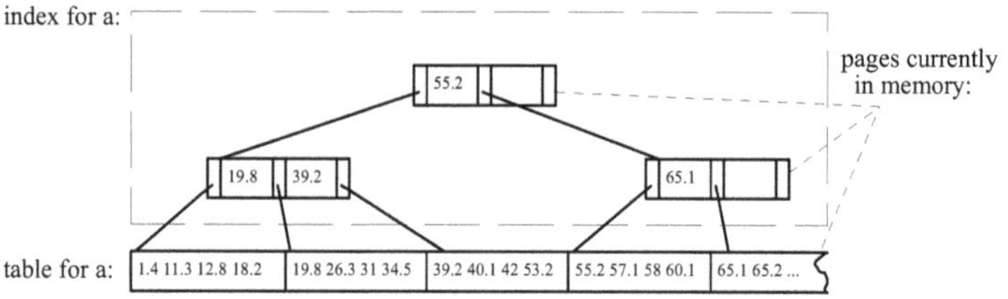

Fig. 3. Construction of the table and index for symbol a

evaluation and describe non-blocking join algorithms, which are used as components in it.

3.1 Storage Organization

Since the queries search for relative positions of symbols in the data sequence $\mathcal{T}$, it is convenient to decompose $\mathcal{T}$ by creating one table T_s for each symbol s. The table stores the (ordered) positions of the symbol in the database. A *sparse* B^+–tree B_s is then built on top of it to accelerate range queries. The construction of the tables and indexes can be performed by scanning $\mathcal{T}$ once. At index construction, for each table T_s we need to allocate (i) one page for the file that stores T_s and (ii) one page for each level of its corresponding index B_s. The construction of T_a and B_a for symbol a can be illustrated in Figure 3 (the rest of the symbols are handled concurrently). While scanning $\mathcal{T}$, we can insert the symbol positions into the table. When a page becomes full, it is written to disk and a new pointer is added to the current page at the B^+–tree leaf page. When a B^+–tree node becomes full, it is flushed to disk and, in turn, a new entry is added at the upper level.

Formally, the memory requirements for decomposing and indexing the data with a single scan of the sequence are $1 + \sum_{\forall s \in \mathcal{S}} (1 + h(B_s))$, where $h(B_s)$ is the height of the tree B_s that indexes T_s. For each symbol s, we only need to keep one page for each level of B_s plus one page of T_s. We also need one buffer page for the input. If the number of symbols is not extremely large, the system memory should be enough for this process. In a different case, the bulk-loading of indexes can be postponed and constructed at a second pass of each T_s.

3.2 Query Evaluation

A pattern query can be easily transformed to a *multiway join query* between the corresponding symbol tables. For instance, to evaluate $\tau_{c,d} = [7.5, 9.5] \wedge \tau_{d,a} = [1, 2]$ we can first join table T_c with T_d using the predicate $\tau_{c,d} = [7.5, 9.5]$ and then the results with T_a using the predicate $\tau_{d,a} = [1, 2]$. This *evaluation plan* can be expressed by a tree $(T_c \bowtie_{\tau_{c,d}} T_d) \bowtie_{\tau_{d,a}} T_a$. Depending on the order and the algorithms used for the binary joins, there might be numerous query evaluation plans [12]. Following the traditional database query optimization approach, we can transform the query to a tree of binary joins, where the intermediate results of each operator are fed to the next one [7]. Therefore, join operators are implemented as iterators that *consume* intermediate results from underlying joins and produce results for the next ones.

Like multiway spatial joins [9], our queries have a common join attribute in all tables (i.e., the temporal positions of the symbols). As we will see in Section 4.1, for each query, temporal constraints are inferred between every pair of nodes in the query graph. In other words, the query graph is *complete*. Therefore, the join operators also validate the temporal constraints that are not part of the binary join, but connect symbols from the left input with ones in the right one. For example, whenever the operator that joins ($T_c \bowtie_{\tau_{c,d}} T_d$) with T_a using $\tau_{d,a}$ computes a result, it also validates constraint $\tau_{c,a}$, so that the result passed to the operator above satisfies all constraints between a,c, and d.

For the binary joins, the optimizer selects between two operators. The first is *index nested loops join* (INLJ). Since B$^+$–trees index the tables, this operator can be applied for all joins, where at least one of the joined inputs is a leaf of the evaluation plan. INLJ scans the left (outer) join input once and for each symbol instance applies a selection (range) query on the index of the right (inner) input according to the temporal constraint. For instance, consider the join $T_c \bowtie T_d$ with $\tau_{c,d} = [7.5, 9.5]$ and the instance $c = 3$. The range query applied on the index of d is $[10.5, 12.5]$. INLJ is most suitable when the left input is significantly smaller than the right one. In this case, many I/Os can be saved by avoiding accessing irrelevant data from the right input. This algorithm is non-blocking; it does not need to have the whole left input until it starts join processing. Therefore, join results can be produced before the whole input is available.

The second operator is *merge join* (MJ). MJ merges two sorted inputs and operates like the merging phase of external merge-sort algorithm [12]. The symbol tables are always sorted, therefore MJ can directly be applied for leaves of the evaluation plan. In our implementation of MJ, the output is produced sorted on the left input. The effect of this is that both INLJ and MJ produce results sorted on the symbol from the left input that is involved in the join predicate. Due to this property, MJ is also applicable for joining intermediate results, subject to memory availability, without blocking. The rationale is that joined inputs, produced by underlying operators, are not completely unsorted on their join symbol. A bound for the difference between consecutive values of their join symbol can be defined by the temporal constraints of the query.

More specifically, assume that MJ performs the join $L \bowtie R$ according to predicate $\tau_{x,y}$, where x is a symbol from the left input L and y is from the right input R. Assume also that L and R are sorted with respect to symbols l_L and l_R, respectively. Let p_L^1 and p_L^2 be two consecutive tuples in L. Due to constraint τ_{x,l_L}, we know that $p_L^2[x] \geq p_L^1[x] - |\tau_{x,l_L}|$, or else the next value of x that appears in L cannot be smaller than the previous one decremented by the length of constraint τ_{x,l_L}. Similarly, the difference between two values of y in R is bounded by $|\tau_{y,l_R}|$. Consider the example query of Figure 1 and assume that INLJ is used to process $T_c \bowtie T_d$. For each instance x_c of c in T_c, a range query

$[x_c + 7.5, x_c + 9.5]$ is applied on T_d to retrieve the qualifying instances of d. The join results (x_c, x_d) will be totally sorted only on x_c. Moreover, once we find a value x_d in the join result, we know that we cannot find any value smaller than $x_d - |\tau_{c,d}|$, next.

We use this bound to implement a non-blocking version of MJ, as follows. The *next*() iterator function to an input of MJ (e.g., L) keeps fetching results from it in a buffer until we know that the smallest value of the join key (e.g., x) currently in memory cannot be found in the next result (i.e., using the bound $|\tau_{x,l_L}|$, described above). Then, this smallest value is considered as the next item to be processed by the merge-join function, since it is guaranteed to be sorted.

If the binary join has low selectivity, or when the inputs have similar size, MJ is typically better than INLJ. Note that, since both INLJ and MJ are non-blocking, temporary results are avoided and the query processing cost is greatly reduced. For our problem, we do not consider hash-join methods (like the partitioned-band join algorithm of [4]), since the join inputs are (partially or totally) sorted, which makes merge-join algorithms superior.

An interesting property of MJ is that it can be extended to a *multiway* merge algorithm that joins all inputs synchronously [9]. The multiway algorithm can produce on-line results by scanning all inputs just once (for high-selective queries), however, it is expected to be slower than a combination of binary algorithms, since it may unnecessarily access parts of some inputs.

4 Query Transformation and Optimization

In order to minimize the cost of a non-contiguous pattern query, we need to consider several factors. The first is how to exploit inference rules of temporal constraints to tighten the join predicates and infer new, potentially useful ones for query optimization. The second is how to find a query evaluation plan that combines the join inputs in an optimal way, using the most appropriate algorithms.

4.1 Query Transformation

A query, as defined in Section 2.1, is a connected graph, which may not be complete. Having a complete graph of temporal constraints between symbol instances can be beneficial for query optimization. Given a query, we can apply *temporal inference* rules to (i) derive implied temporal constraints between nodes of the query graph, (ii) tighten existing constraints, and even (iii) prove that the query cannot have any results, if the set of constraints is *inconistent.*

Inference of temporal constraints is a well-studied subject in Artificial Intelligence. Dechter et. al [3] provide a comprehensive study on solving *temporal constraint satisfaction problems* (TCSPs). Our query definitions 2 and 3 match the definition of a simple TCSP, where the constraints between problem variables (i.e., graph nodes) are simple intervals. In order to transform a user query to a *minimal temporal constraint network*, with no redundant constraints, we use the following operations (from [3]):

- *inversion*: $\overline{\tau_{i,j}} := \tau_{j,i}$. By *symmetry*, the inverse of a constraint $\tau_{i,j}$ is defined by $a_{j,i} = -b_{i,j}$ and $b_{j,i} = -a_{i,j}$.
- *intersection*: $\tau \cap \tau'$. The intersection of two constraints is defined by the values allowed by both of them. For constraints $\tau_{i,j}$ and $\tau'_{i,j}$ on the same edge, intersection $\tau_{i,j} \cap \tau'_{i,j}$ is defined by $[\max\{a_{i,j}, a'_{i,j}\}, \min\{b_{i,j}, b'_{i,j}\}]$.
- *composition*: $\tau \propto \tau'$. The composition of two constraints allows all values w such that there is a value v allowed by τ, a value u allowed by τ' and $v+u = w$. Given two constraints $\tau_{i,j}$ and $\tau_{j,k}$, sharing node n_j, their composition $\tau_{i,j} \propto \tau_{j,k}$ is defined by $[a_{i,j} + a_{j,k}, b_{i,j} + b_{j,k}]$

Inversion is the simplest form of inference. Given a constraint $\tau_{i,j}$, we can immediately infer constraint $\tau_{j,i}$. For example if $\tau_{c,d} = [7.5, 9.5]$, we know that $\tau_{d,c} = [-9.5, -7.5]$. Composition is another form of inference, which exploits *transitivity* to infer constraints between nodes, which are not connected in the original graph. For example, $\tau_{c,d} = [7.5, 9.5] \wedge \tau_{d,a} = [1, 2]$ implies $\tau'_{c,a} = [8.5, 11.5]$. Finally, intersection is used to unify (i.e., *minimize*) the constraints for a given pair of nodes. For example, an original constraint $\tau_{c,a} = [8, 10]$ can be tightened to $[8.5, 10]$, using an inferred constraint $\tau'_{c,a} = [8.5, 11.5]$. After an intersection operation, a constraint $\tau_{i,j}$ can become *inconsistent* if $a_{i,j} > b_{i,j}$.

A temporal constraint network (i.e., a query in our setting) is *minimal* if no constraints can be tightened. It is *inconsistent* if it contains an inconsistent constraint. The goal of the query transformation phase is to either minimize the constraint network or prove it inconsistent. To achieve this goal we can employ an adaptation of Floyd-Warshall's all-pairs-shortest-path algorithm [6] with $O(N^3)$ cost, N being the number of nodes in the query. The pseudocode of this algorithm is shown in Figure 4. First, the constraints are initialized by (i) introducing inverse temporal constraints for existing edges and (ii) assigning "dummy" constraints to non-existing edges. The nested for-loops correspond to Floyd-Warshall's algorithm, which essentially finds for all pairs of nodes the lower constraint bound (i.e., shortest path) and the upper constraint bound (i.e., longest path). If some constraint is found inconsistent, the algorithm terminates and reports it. As shown in [3] and [6], the algorithm of Figure 4 computes the minimal constraint network correctly.

4.2 Query Optimization

In order to find the optimal query evaluation plan, we need accurate join selectivity formulae and cost estimation models for the individual join operators.

The selectivity of a join in our setting can be estimated by applying existing models for spatial joins [9]. We can model the join $L \bowtie R$ as a set of selections on R, one for each symbol in L. If the distribution of the symbol instances in R is uniform, the selectivity of each selection can be easily estimated by dividing the temporal range of the constraint by the temporal range of the data sequence. For non-uniform distributions, we extend techniques based on histograms. Details are omitted due to space constraints.

Estimating the costs of INLJ and MJ is quite straightforward. First, we have to note that a non-leaf input incurs no I/Os, since the operators are non-blocking.

```
boolean Query_Transformation(query Q(V,E))
    for each pair of nodes ⟨n_i, n_j⟩
        if ⟨n_i → n_j⟩ ∈ E then τ_{j,i} := overline(τ_{i,j}); //inversion
        if n_i is not connected to n_j then τ_{i,j} := τ_{j,i} := [−∞, ∞];
    for k := 1 to N
        for i := 1 to N
            for j := i + 1 to N
                τ_{i,j} := τ_{i,j} ∩ (τ_{i,k} ∝ τ_{k,j});
                if a_{i,j} > b_{i,j} then return false; //inconsistent query
                τ_{j,i} := overline(τ_{i,j});
    return true; //consistent query
```

Fig. 4. Query transformation using Floyd-Warshall's algorithm

Therefore, we need only estimate they I/Os by INLJ and MJ for leaf inputs of the evaluation plan. Essentially, MJ reads both inputs once, thus its I/O cost is equal to the size of the leaf inputs. INLJ performs a series of selections on a B^+-tree. If an LRU memory buffer is used for the join, the index pages accessed by a selection query are expected to be in memory with high probability due to the previous query. This, because instances of the left input are expected to be sorted, or at least partially sorted. Therefore, we only need to consider the number of *distinct* pages of R accessed by INLJ.

An important difference between MJ and INLJ is that most accesses by MJ are sequential, whereas INLJ performs mainly random accesses. Our query optimizer takes this under consideration. From its application, it turns out that the best plans are left-deep plans, where the lower operators are MJ and the upper ones INLJ. This is due to the fact that our multiway join cannot benefit from the few intermediate results of bushy plans, since they are not materialized (recall that the operators are non-blocking). The upper operators of a left-deep plan have a small left input, which is best handled by INLJ.

5 Application to Problem Variants

So far, we have assumed that there is only one data sequence $\mathcal{T}$ and that the indexed symbols are relatively few with a significance number of appearances in $\mathcal{T}$. In this section we discuss how to deal with more general cases with respect to these two factors.

5.1 Indexing and Querying Multiple Sequences

If there are multiple small sequences, we can concatenate them to a single long sequence. The difference is that now we treat the beginning time of one sequence as the end of the previous one. In addition, we add a long temporal gap W, corresponding to the maximum sequence length (plus one time unit), between every pair of sequences in order to avoid query results, composed of symbols that belong to different sequences.

For example, consider three sequences: $\mathcal{T}_1 = \langle(b,1),(a,3.5),(d,4.5),(a,6)\rangle$, $\mathcal{T}_2 = \langle(a,0.5),(d,3),(b,9.5)\rangle$, and $\mathcal{T}_3 = \langle(c,2),(a,3.5),(b,4)\rangle$. Since the longest sequence $\mathcal{T}_2$ has length 9, we can convert all of them to a single long sequence $\mathcal{T} = \langle(b,0),(a,2.5),(d,3.5),(a,5),(a,20),(d,22.5),(b,29),(c,40),(a,41.5),(b,42)\rangle$.

Observe that in this conversion, we have (i) computed the maximum sequence length and added a time unit to derive $W = 10$ and (ii) shifted the sequences, so that sequence $\mathcal{T}_i$ begins at $(i-1)*2W$. The differences between events in the same sequence have been retained. Therefore, by setting the maximum possible distance between any pair of symbols to W, we are able to apply the methodology described in the previous sections for this problem. If the maximum sequence length is unknown at index construction time (e.g., when the data are online), we can use a large number for W that reflects the maximum anticipated sequence length.

Alternatively, if someone wants to find patterns, where the symbols appear in *any* data sequence, we can simply merge the events of all sequences treating them as if they belonged to the same one. For example, merging the sequences $\mathcal{T}_1$–$\mathcal{T}_3$ above would result in $\mathcal{T} = \langle(a,0.5),(b,1),(c,2),(d,3),(a,3.5),(a,3.5),(b,4),\ldots\rangle$.

5.2 Handling Infrequent Symbols

If some symbols are not frequent in $\mathcal{T}$, disk pages may be wasted after the decomposition. However, we can treat all decomposed tables as a single one, after determining an ordering of the symbols (e.g., alphabetical order). Then, occurrences of all symbols are recorded in a single table, sorted first by symbol and then by position. This table can be indexed using a B^+–tree in order to facilitate query processing. We can also use a second (header) index on top of the sorted table, that marks the first position of each symbol. This structure resembles the *inverted file* used in Information Retrieval systems [1] to record the occurrences of index terms in documents.

5.3 Indexing and Querying Patterns in DBMS Tables

In [13], non-contiguous sequence pattern queries have been used to assist exploration of DNA Micro-arrays. A DNA micro-array is an expression matrix that stores the expression level of genes (rows) in experimental samples (columns). It is possible to have no result about some gene-sample combinations. Therefore, the micro-array can be considered as a DBMS table with NULL values.

We can consider each row of this table as a sequence, where each non-NULL value v at column s is transformed to a (s,v) pair. After sorting these pairs by v, we derive a sequence which reflects the expression difference between pairs of samples on the same gene. If we concatenate these sequences to a single long one, using the method described in Section 5.1, we can formulate the problem of finding genes with similar differences in their expression levels as a subsequence pattern retrieval problem.

	s_1	s_2	s_3
g_1	50	30	NULL
g_2	190	NULL	120
g_3	15	105	150
...	...	...	...

(a) A DBMS table

g_1	$\langle (s_2, 30), (s_1, 50) \rangle$
g_2	$\langle (s_3, 120), (s_1, 150) \rangle$
g_3	$\langle (s_1, 15), (s_2, 105), (s_3, 150) \rangle$
...	...

(b) Transformed sequences

$(s_2, 0), (s_1, 20),$
$(s_3, 400), (s_1, 430),$
$(s_1, 800), (s_2, 890), (s_3, 935)$
...

(c) Single sequence ($W = 200$)

Fig. 5. Converting a DBMS table, domain=$[0, 200)$

Figure 5 illustrates. The leftmost table corresponds to the original micro-array, with the expression levels of each gene to the various samples. The middle table shows how the rows can be converted to sequences and the sequence of Figure 5c is their concatenation. As an example, consider the query "find all genes, where the level of sample s_1 is lower than that of s_2 at some value between 20 and 30, and in the level of sample s_2 is lower than that of s_3 at some value between 100 and 130". This query would be expressed by the following subsequence query pattern on the transformed data: $\tau_{s_1,s_2} = [20, 30] \wedge \tau_{s_2,s_3} = [100, 130]$.

6 Experimental Evaluation

Our framework, denoted by SeqJoin thereafter, and the ISO-Depth index method were implemented in C++ and tested on a Pentium-4 2.3GHz PC. We set the page (and B^+–tree node) size to 4Kb and used an LRU buffer of 1Mb. To smoothen the effects of randomness in the queries, all experimental results (except from the index creation) were averaged over 50 queries with the same parameters.

For comparison purposes, we generated a number of data sequences $\mathcal{T}$ as follows. The positions of events in $\mathcal{T}$ are integers, generated uniformly along the sequence length; the average difference of consecutive events was controlled by a parameter $\overline{G}$. The symbol that labels each event was chosen among a set of $\mathcal{S}$ symbols according to a Zipf distribution with a parameter θ. Synthetic datasets are labeled by D$|\mathcal{T}|$-G$\overline{G}$-A$|\mathcal{S}|$-Sθ. For instance, label D1M-G100-A10-S1 indicates that the sequence has 1 million events, with 100 average gap between two consecutive ones, 10 different symbols, whose frequencies follow a Zipf distribution with skew parameter $\theta = 1$. Notice that $\theta = 0$ implies that the labels for the events are chosen uniformly at random.

We also tested the performance of the algorithms with real data. Gene expression data can be viewed as a matrix where a row represents a gene and a column represents the condition. From [2], we obtained two gene expression matrices (i) a Yeast expression matrix with 2884 rows and 17 columns, and (ii) a Human expression matrix with 4026 rows and 96 columns. The domains of Yeast and Human datasets are $[0, 595]$ and $[-628, 674]$ respectively. We converted the above data to event sequences as described in Section 5.3 (note that [13] use the same conversion scheme).

The generated queries are star and chain graphs connecting random symbols with soft temporal constraints. Thus, in order to be fair in our comparison with ISO-Depth, we chose to generate only queries that satisfy the restrictions in [13]. Chain graph queries with positive constraint ranges can be converted to star queries, after inferring all the constraints between the first symbol and the remaining ones. On the other hand, it may not be possible to convert random queries to star queries without inducing overlapping, non-negative constraints. Note that these are the best settings for the ISO-Depth index, since otherwise queries have to be transformed to a large number subqueries, one for each possible order of the symbols in the results. The distribution of symbols in a generated query is a Zipfian one with skew parameter $Sskew$. In other words, some symbols have higher probability to appear in the query according to the skew parameter. A generated constraint has average length $\overline{R}$ and ranges from $0.5 \cdot \overline{R}$ to $1.5 \cdot \overline{R}$.

6.1 Size and Construction Cost of the Indexes

In the first set of experiments, we compare the size and construction cost of the data structures used by the two methods (SeqJoin and ISO-Depth) as a function of three parameters; the size of $\mathcal{T}$ (in millions of elements), the average gap $\overline{G}$ between two consecutive symbols in the sequence, and the number $|\mathcal{S}|$ of distinct symbols in the sequence. We used uniform symbol frequencies ($\theta = 0$) in $\mathcal{T}$ and skewed frequencies ($\theta = 1$). Since the size and construction cost of SeqJoin is independent of the skewness of symbols in the sequence, we compare three methods here (i) SeqJoin, (ii) simple ISO-Depth (for uniform symbol frequencies), and (iii) ISO-Depth with reordering [13] (for skewed symbol frequencies).

Figure 6 plots the sizes of the constructed data structures after fixing two parameter values and varying the value of the third one. Observe that ISO-Depth with and without reordering have similar sizes on disk. Moreover, the size of the structures depends mainly on the database size, rather on the other parameters. The size of the ISO-Depth structures is roughly ten times larger than that of the SeqJoin data structures. The SeqJoin structures are smaller than the original sequence (note that one element of $\mathcal{T}$ occupies 8 bytes). A lot of space is saved because the symbol instances are not repeated; only their positions are stored and indexed. On the other hand, the ISO-Depth index stores a lot of redundant information, since a subsequence is defined for each position of the sliding window (note that $\xi = 4 \cdot \overline{G}$ for this experiment). The size difference is insensitive to the values of the various parameters.

Figure 7 plots the construction time for the data structures used by the two methods. The construction cost for ISO-Depth is much higher than that of SeqJoin and further increases when reordering is employed. The costs for both methods increase proportionally to the database size, as expected. However, observe that the cost for SeqJoin is almost insensitive to the average gap between symbols and to the number of distinct symbols in the sequence. On the other hand, there is an obvious cost increase in the cost of ISO-Depth with $\overline{G}$ due to the low compression the trie achieves for large gaps between symbols. There is also an increase with the number of distinct symbols, due to the same reason.

Table 1 shows the corresponding index size and construction cost for the real datasets used in the experiments. Observe that the difference between the two

Table 1. Index size and construction time (real data)

Dataset	Method	Index Size (Mb)	Construction time (s)
Yeast	SeqJoin	0.3	0.4
	ISO-Depth	5.5	4.2
Human	SeqJoin	2.14	3.1
	ISO-Depth	251	416.2

methods is even higher compared to the synthetic data case. The large construction cost is a significant disadvantage of the ISO-Depth index, which adds to the fact that it cannot be dynamically updated. If the data sequence is frequently updated (e.g., consider on-line streaming data from sensor transmissions), the index has to be built from scratch with significant overhead. On the other hand, our symbol tables T_s and B$^+$–trees can be efficiently updated incrementally. The new event instances are just appended to the corresponding tables. Also, in the worst case only the rightmost paths of the indexes are affected by an incremental change (see Section 3.1).

6.2 Experiments with Synthetic Data

In this paragraph, we compare the search performance of the two methods on generated synthetic data. Unless otherwise stated, the dataset used is D2M-G100-A10-S0, the default parameters for queries are $\overline{R} = 50$, $Sskew = 0$, and the number N of nodes in the query graphs is 4.

Figure 9 shows the effect of database size on the performance of the two algorithms in terms of page accesses, memory buffer requests, and overall execution time. For each length of the data sequence we tested the algorithms on both uniform ($Sskew = 0$) and Zipfian ($Sskew = 1$) symbol distributions. Figure 9a shows that SeqJoin outperforms ISO-Depth in terms of I/O in most cases, except for small datasets with skewed distribution of symbols. The reason behind this unstable performance of ISO-Depth, is that the I/O cost of this algorithm is very sensitive to the memory buffer. Skewed queries on small datasets access a small part of the iso-depth lists with high locality and cache congestion is avoided.

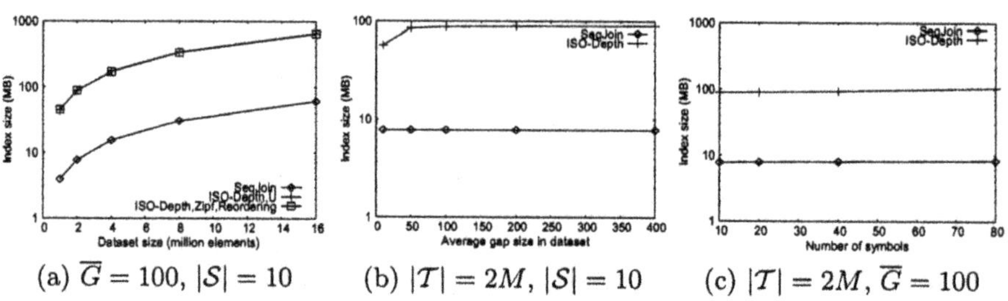

(a) $\overline{G} = 100$, $|S| = 10$ (b) $|T| = 2M$, $|S| = 10$ (c) $|T| = 2M$, $\overline{G} = 100$

Fig. 6. Index size on disk (synthetic data)

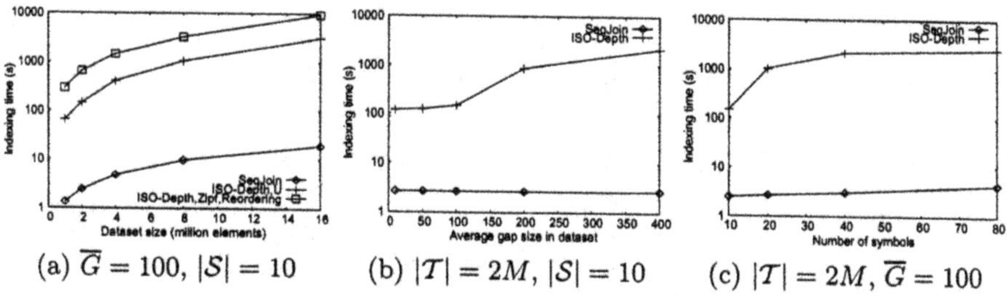

(a) $\overline{G} = 100$, $|S| = 10$ (b) $|T| = 2M$, $|S| = 10$ (c) $|T| = 2M$, $\overline{G} = 100$

Fig. 7. Index construction time (synthetic data)

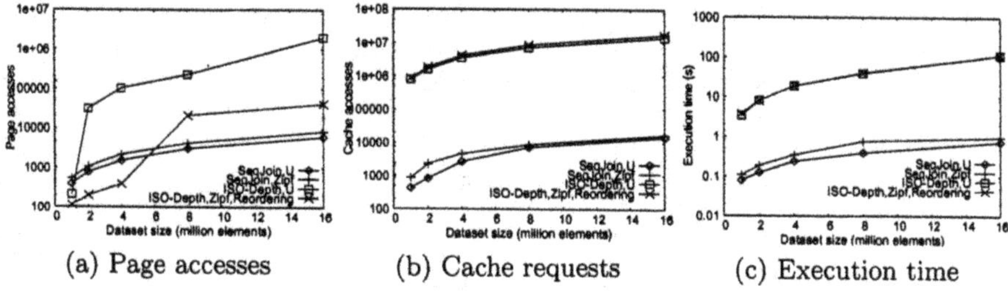

(a) Page accesses (b) Cache requests (c) Execution time

Fig. 8. Performance with respect to the data sequence length

On the other hand, for uniform symbol distributions or large datasets the huge number of cache requests by ISO-Depth (see Figure 9b), incur excessive I/O. Figure 9c plots the overall execution cost of the algorithms; SeqJoin is one to two orders of magnitude faster than ISO-Depth. Due to the relaxed nature of the constraints, ISO-Depth has to perform a huge number of searches.[2]

Figure 9 compares the performance of the two methods with respect to several system, data, and query parameters. Figure 9a shows the effect of cache size (i.e., memory buffer size) on the I/O cost of the two algorithms. Observe that the I/O cost of SeqJoin is almost constant, while the number of page accesses by ISO-Depth drops as the cache size increases. ISO-Depth performs a huge number of searches in the iso-depth lists, with high locality between them. Therefore, it is favored by large memory buffers. On the other hand, SeqJoin is insensitive to the available memory (subject to a non-trivial buffer) because the join algorithms scan the position tables and indexes at most once. Even though ISO-Depth outperforms SeqJoin in terms of I/O for large buffers, its excessive computational cost (which is almost insensitive to memory availability) dominates the overall execution time. Moreover, most of the page accesses of ISO-Depth are random, whereas the algorithm that accesses most of the pages for SeqJoin is MJ (at the lower parts of the evaluation plan), which performs mainly sequential accesses.

[2] In fact, the cost of ISO-Depth for this class of approximate queries is even higher than that of a simple linear scan algorithm, as we have seen in our experiments.

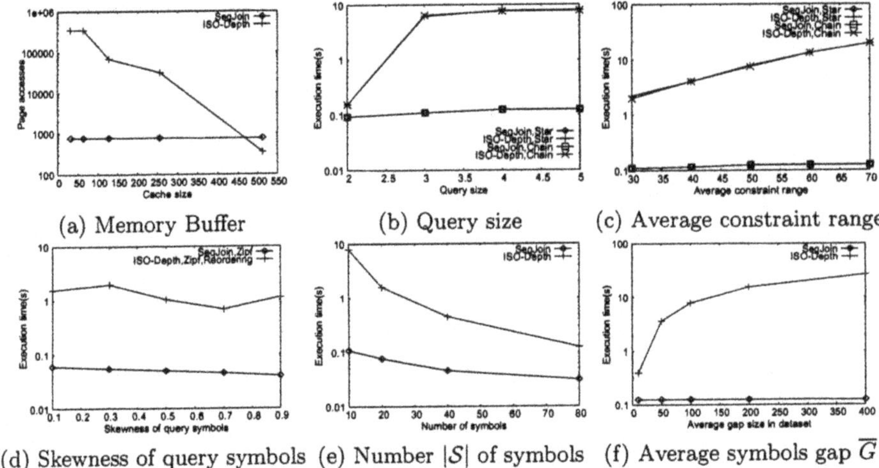

(a) Memory Buffer (b) Query size (c) Average constraint range

(d) Skewness of query symbols (e) Number $|S|$ of symbols (f) Average symbols gap $\overline{G}$

Fig. 9. Performance comparison under various factors

Figure 9b plots the execution cost of SeqJoin and ISO-Depth as a function of the number of symbols in the query. For trivial 2-symbol queries, both methods have similar performance. However, for larger queries the cost of ISO-Depth explodes, due to the excessive number of iso-depth list accesses it has to perform. For an average constraint length $\overline{R}$, the worst-case number of accesses is $\overline{R}^{N-1}$, where N is the number of symbols in the query. Since the selectivity of the queries is high, the majority of the searches for the third query symbol fail, and this is the reason why the cost does not increase much for queries with more than three symbols.

Figure 9c shows how the average constraint length $\overline{R}$ affects the cost of the algorithms. The cost of SeqJoin is almost independent of this factor. However, the cost of ISO-Depth increases superlinearly, since the worst-case number of accesses is $\overline{R}^{N-1}$, as explained above. We note that for this class of queries the cost of ISO-Depth in fact increases quadratically, since most of the searches after the third symbol fail. Figure 9d shows how *Sskew* affects the cost of the two methods, for star queries. The cost difference is maintained for a wide range of symbol frequency distributions. In general, the efficiency of both algorithms increases as the symbol occurrence becomes more skewed for different reasons. SeqJoin manages to find a good join ordering, by joining the smallest symbol tables first. ISO-Depth exploits the symbol frequencies in the trie construction to minimize the potential search paths for a given query, as also shown in [13]. The fluctuations are due to the randomness of the queries. Figure 9e shows the effect of the number of distinct symbols in the data sequence. When the number of symbols increases the selectivity of the query becomes higher and the cost of both methods decreases; ISO-Depth has fewer paths to search and SeqJoin has smaller tables to join. SeqJoin maintains its advantage over ISO-Depth, however, the cost difference decreases slightly.

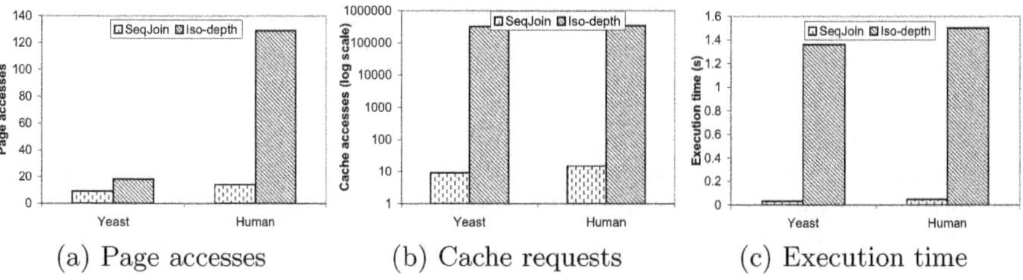

(a) Page accesses (b) Cache requests (c) Execution time

Fig. 10. Random queries against real datasets

Finally, Figure 9f shows the effect of the average gap between consecutive symbol instances in the sequence. In this experiment, we set the average constraint length $\overline{R}$ in the queries equal to $\overline{G}/2$ in order to maintain the same query selectivity for the various values of $\overline{G}$. The cost of SeqJoin is insensitive to this parameter, since the size of the joined tables and the selectivity of the query is maintained with the change of $\overline{G}$. On the other hand, the performance of ISO-Depth varies significantly for two reasons. First, for datasets with small values of $\overline{G}$, ISO-Depth achieves higher compression, as the probability for a given subsequence to appear multiple times in $\mathcal{T}$ increases. Higher compression ratio results in a smaller index and lower execution cost. Second, the number of search paths for ISO-Depth increase significantly with $\overline{G}$, because of the increase of $\overline{R}$ with the same rate. In summary, ISO-Depth can only have competitive performance to SeqJoin for small gaps between symbols and small lengths of the query constraints.

6.3 Experiments with Real Data

Figure 10 shows the performance of SeqJoin and ISO-Depth on real datasets. In both Yeast and Human datasets, SeqJoin has significantly low cost, in terms of I/Os, cache requests, and execution time. For these real datasets, we need to slide a window ξ as long as the largest difference between a pair of values in the same row. In other words, the indexed rows of the expression matrices have an average length of $\frac{|\mathcal{S}|+1}{2}$. Thus, for these real datasets, the ISO-Depth index could not achieve high compression. For instance, the converted weighted sequence from Human dataset only has 360K elements but it has a ISO-Depth index of comparable size as that of synthetic data with 8M elements. In addition, the approximate queries (generated according to the settings of Section 6.2) follow a large number of search paths in the ISO-Depth index.

7 Conclusions and Future Work

In this paper, we presented a methodology of decomposing, indexing and searching long symbol sequences for non-contiguous sequence pattern queries. SeqJoin has significant advantages over ISO-Depth [13], a previously proposed method for this problem, including:

- It can be easily implemented in a DBMS, utilizing many existing modules.
- The tables and indexes are much smaller than the original sequence and they can be incrementally updated.
- It is very appropriate for queries with approximate constraints. On the other hand, the ISO-Depth index generates a large number of search paths, one for each exact query included in the approximation.
- It is more general since (i) it can deal with real-valued timestamped events, (ii) it can handle queries with approximate constraints between any pair of objects, and (iii) the maximum difference between any pair of query symbols is not bounded.

The contributions of this paper also include the modeling of a non-contiguous pattern query as a graph, which can be refined using temporal inference, and the introduction of a non-blocking merge-join algorithm, which can be used by the query processor for this problem. In the future, we plan to study the evaluation of this class of queries on unbounded and continuous event sequences from a stream in a limited memory buffer.

References

1. R. Baeza-Yates and B. Ribeiro-Neto. *Modern Information Retrieval.* ACM and Mc-Graw Hill, 1999.
2. Y. Cheng and G. M. Church. Biclustering of expression data. In *Proc. of International Conference on Intelligent Systems for Molecular Biology*, 2000.
3. R. Dechter, I. Meiri, and J. Pearl. Temporal constraint networks. *Artificial Intelligence*, 49(1–3):61–95, 1991.
4. D. J. DeWitt, J. F. Naughton, and D. A. Schneider. An evaluation of non-equijoin algorithms. In *Proc. of VLDB Conference*, 1991.
5. C. Faloutsos, M. Ranganathan, and Y. Manolopoulos. Fast subsequence matching in time-series databases. In *Proc. of ACM SIGMOD International Conference on Management of Data*, 1994.
6. R. W. Floyd. ACM Algorithm 97: Shortest path. *Communications of the ACM*, 5(6):345, June 1962.
7. G. Graefe. Query evaluation techniques for large databases. *ACM Computing Surveys*, 25(2):73–170, 1993.
8. T. Kahveci and A. K. Singh. Efficient index structures for string databases. In *Proc. of VLDB Conference*, 2001.
9. N. Mamoulis and D. Papadias. Multiway spatial joins. *ACM Transactions on Database Systems (TODS)*, 26(4):424–475, 2001.
10. Y.-S. Moon, K.-Y. Whang, and W.-S. Han. General match: a subsequence matching method in time-series databases based on generalized windows. In *Proc. of ACM SIGMOD International Conference on Management of Data*, 2002.
11. G. Navarro. A guided tour to approximate string matching. *ACM Computing Surveys*, 33(1):31–88, 2001.
12. R. Ramakrishnan and J. Gehrke. *Database Management Systems.* Mc-Graw Hill, third edition, 2003.
13. H. Wang, C.-S. Perng, W. Fan, S. Park, and P. S. Yu. Indexing weighted-sequences in large databases. In *Proc. of Int'l Conf. on Data Engineering (ICDE)*, 2003.

Mining Extremely Skewed Trading Anomalies

Wei Fan, Philip S. Yu, and Haixun Wang

IBM T.J.Watson Research, Hawthorne NY 10532, USA,
{weifan,psyu,haixun}@us.ibm.com

Abstract. Trading surveillance systems screen and detect anomalous trades of equity, bonds, mortgage certificates among others. This is to satisfy federal trading regulations as well as to prevent crimes, such as insider trading and money laundry. Most existing trading surveillance systems are based on hand-coded expert-rules. Such systems are known to result in long developing process and extremely high "false positive" rates. We participate in co-developing a data mining based automatic trading surveillance system for one of the biggest banks in the US. The challenge of this task is to handle very skewed positive classes ($< 0.01\%$) as well as very large volume of data (millions of records and hundreds of features). The combination of very skewed distribution and huge data volume poses new challenge for data mining; previous work addresses these issues separately, and existing solutions are rather complicated and not very straightforward to implement. In this paper, we propose a simple systematic approach to mine "very skewed distribution in very large volume of data".

1 Introduction

Trading surveillance systems screen and detect anomalous trades of equity, bonds, mortgage certificates among others. Suspicious trades are reported to a team of analysts to investigate. Confirmed illegal and irregular trades are blocked. This is to satisfy federal trading regulations as well as to prevent crimes, such as insider trading and money laundry. Most existing trading surveillance systems are based on hand-coded expert-rules. Such systems are known to result in long developing process and extremely high "false positive" rates. Expert rules are usually "yes-no" rules that do not compute a score that correlates with the likelihood that a trade is a true anomaly. We learned from our client most of the predicted anomalies by the system are false positives or normal trades mistakenly predicted as anomalies. Since there are a lot of false positives and there is no score to prioritize their job, many analysts have to spend hours a day to sort through reported anomalies and decide the subset of trades to investigate.

We participate in co-developing a data mining based automatic trading surveillance system for one of the biggest banks in the US. There are several goals to use data mining techniques. i) The developing cycle is automated and will probably be much shorter; ii) The model ideally should output a score, such as, posterior probability, to indicate the likelihood that a trade is truly anomalous; iii) Most importantly, the data mining model should have a much lower

E. Bertino et al. (Eds.): EDBT 2004, LNCS 2992, pp. 801–810, 2004.
© Springer-Verlag Berlin Heidelberg 2004

false positive rate and higher recall rate, which will help the analysts to focus on the "really bad" cases. Besides engineering works to understand the task and data, the real technical challenge is to mine very skewed positive classes (e.g. $< 0.01\%$) in very large volume of data (e.g., millions of records and hundreds of features). The unique combination of very skewed distribution and huge data volume poses new challenges for data mining.

Skewed distribution and very large data volume are two important characteristics of today's data mining task. Skewed distribution refers to the situation where the interesting or positive instances are much less popular than un-interesting or negative instances. For example, the percentage of people in a particular area that donates to one charity is less than 0.1%; the percentage of security trading anomalies is less than 0.01% in the US. Skewed distribution also has unbalanced loss functions. For example, classifying a real insider trading as a normal transaction (false negatives), means millions of dollars of loss and law suit against a bank; while false positives, i.e., normal trades classified as anomaly, is a waste of time for the bank's analysts. One big problem of skewed distribution is that many inductive learners completely or partially ignore the positive examples, or in the worst case, predict every instance as negative. One well cited case in data mining community is the KDDCUP'98 Donation Dataset. Even the positives are around 5% in the training data (not very skewed at all compared with trading anomalies), using C4.5 decision tree, a pruned tree has just one node that says "nobody is a donor"; an unpruned tree predicts as small as 4 household as donors while the actual number of donors are 4873. These kind of models are basically useless. Besides skewed distribution, another difficulty of today's inductive mining is very large data volume. Data volume refers to the number of training records multiplied by the number of features. Most inductive learners have non-linear asymptotic complexity and requires data to be held in main memory. For example, decision tree algorithm has complexity of approximately $O(k \times n \cdot \log(n))$, where k is the number of features and n is the number of data records. However, this estimate is only true if the entire data can be held in main memory. When part of the data is on secondary storage, "trashing" will take place and model construction will take significantly longer period of time.

There has been extensive research in the past decade on both skewed distribution and scalable algorithms. Related work is reviewed in Section 4. However, most of these known solutions are rather complicated and far from being straightforward to implement. On the other hand, skewed distribution and large data volume learning are solved separately; there is no clear way to combine existing approaches easily. In this paper, we propose a simple systematic approach to mine "very skewed distribution in large volumn of data". The basic idea is to train ensemble of classifier (or multiple classifiers) from "biased" samples taken from the large volumn of data. Each classifier in the ensemble outputs posterior probability $P(\ell|\mathbf{x})$ that $\mathbf{x}$ is an instance of class ℓ. The probability estimates from multiple classifiers in the ensemble are averaged to compute the final posterior probability. When the probability is higher than a threshold, the trade will be classified as anomalous. Different thresholds will incur different true positive and false positive rates. The best threshold is dictated by a given loss function in each application. To handle "skewed" positive class distribution, the first step is to generate multiple "biased" samples where the ratio of positive examples are intentionally increased. To find out the optimal ratio for positive examples, we apply a simple "binary" search like procedure. After the sample distribution is determined, multiple biased samples of the same size and distribution are sampled from the very large dataset. An individual classifier is trained from each biased sample. We have applied the proposed approach to a trading surveillance application for one of the biggest banks in the US. The percentage of positives is less than 0.01%, and the data volumn on one business line is 5M records with 144 features.

2 The Framework

The training proceeds in three steps. We first need to find out how much data can be held in main memory at a time. We then apply a binary search algorithm to find out the optimal ratio of positives and negatives to sample from the dataset which gives the highest accuracy. Finally, we generate multiple biased samples from the training data set and compute a classifier from each biased sample. Since our algorithm is built upon concepts of probabilistic modeling and loss functions, we first review its important concepts.

Probabilistic Modeling and Loss Function. For a target function $t = F(\mathbf{x})$, given a training set of size n, $\{(\mathbf{x}_1, t_1), \ldots, (\mathbf{x}_n, t_n))\}$, an inductive learner produces a model $y = f(\mathbf{x})$ to approximate the true function $F(\mathbf{x})$. Usually, there exists $\mathbf{x}$ such that $y \neq t$. In order to compare performance, we introduce a loss function. Given a loss function $L(t, y)$ where t is the true label and y is the predicted label, an optimal model is one that minimizes the average loss $L(t, y)$ for all examples, weighted by their probability. Typical examples of loss functions in data mining are 0-1 loss and cost-sensitive loss. For 0-1 loss, $L(t, y) = 0$ if $t = y$, otherwise $L(t, y) = 1$. In cost-sensitive loss, $L(t, y) = c(\mathbf{x}, t)$ if $t = y$, otherwise $L(t, y) = w(\mathbf{x}, y, t)$. In general, when correctly predicted, $L(t, y)$ is only related to $\mathbf{x}$ and its true label t. When misclassified, $L(t, y)$ is related to the example as well as its true label and the prediction. For many problems, t is nondeterministic, i.e., if $\mathbf{x}$ is sampled repeatedly, different values of t may be given. The optimal decision y_* for $\mathbf{x}$ is the label that minimizes the expected loss $E_t(L(t, y_*))$ for a given example $\mathbf{x}$ when $\mathbf{x}$ is sampled repeatedly and different t's may be given. For 0-1 loss function, the optimal prediction is the most likely label or the label that appears the most often when $\mathbf{x}$ is sampled repeatedly. Put in other words, for a two class problem, assume that $P(\ell|\mathbf{x})$ is the probability that $\mathbf{x}$ is an instance of class ℓ. If $P(\ell|\mathbf{x}) \geq 0.5$, the optimal prediction is class ℓ. When mining skewed problems, positives usually carry a much higher "reward" than negatives when classified correctly. Otherwise, if positives and negatives carry the same reward, it is probably better off to predict "every one is negative". Assume that positives carry a reward of \$100, and negatives carry reward of \$1, we predict

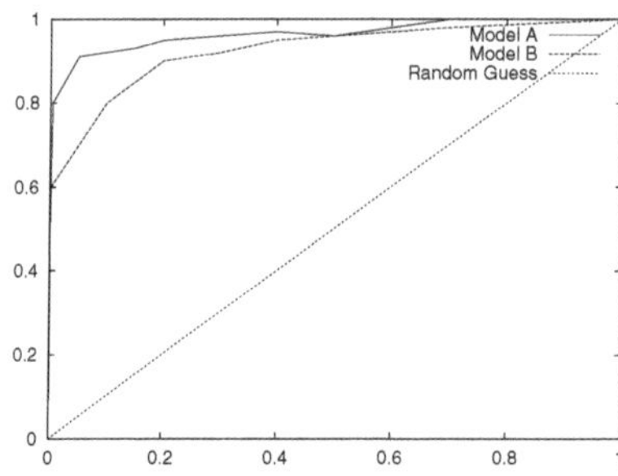

Fig. 1. ROC Example

positives when $P(+|\mathbf{x}) > 0.01$. Comparing with 0.5, the decision threshold of 0.01 is much lower.

For some applications, an exact loss function is hard to define or may change very frequently. When this happens, we employ an ROC-curve (or Receive Operation Characteristics curve) to compare and choose among models. ROC is defined over true positive (TP) and false positive rates (FP). True positive rate is the percentage of actual positives that are correctly classified as positives, and false positive rate is the percentage of negatives mistakenly classified as positives. An example ROC curve is shown in Figure 1. The diagonal line on the ROC is the performance of random guess, which predicts true positives and true negatives to be positive with the same probability. The top left corner (true positive rate is 100% and false positive rate is 0%) is a perfect classifier. Model A is better than model B at a particular false positive rate if its true positive rate is higher than that of B at the false positive rate; visually, the more an ROC curve closer to the top left corner, the better its performance is. For classifiers that output probabilities $P(\ell|\mathbf{x})$, to draw the ROC, we choose a decision threshold t ranging from 0 to 1 at a chosen step (such as 0.1). When $P(\ell|\mathbf{x}) > t$, the model predicts $\mathbf{x}$ to be positive class ℓ. We compute true positive and false positive rates at each chosen threshold value.

The probability estimates by most models are usually not completely continuous. Many inductive models can only output a limited number of different kind of probability estimates. The number of different probability estimates for decision trees is at most the number of leaves of the tree. When this is known, the decision thresholds to try out can only be those probability outputs of the leaves. Any values in between will result the same recall and precision rates as the immediately lower thresholds.

Calculating Probabilities. The calculation of $p(\ell_i|x)$ is straightforward. For decision trees, such as C4.5, suppose that n is the total number of examples and n_i is the number of examples with class ℓ_i in a leaf, then $p(\ell_i|x) = \frac{n_i}{n}$ The probability for decision rules, e.g. RIPPER, can be calculated in a similar way. For naive Bayes classifier, assume that a_j's are the attributes of x, $p(\ell_i)$ is the prior probability or frequency of class ℓ_i in the training data and $p(a_j|\ell_i)$

is the prior probability to observe feature attribute value a_j given class label ℓ_i, then the score $n(\ell_i|x)$ for class label ℓ_i is: $n(\ell_i|x) = p(\ell_i)\prod p(a_j|\ell_i)$ and the probability is calculated on the basis of $n(\ell_i|x)$ as $p(\ell_i|x) = \frac{n(\ell_i|x)}{\sum n(\ell_{i'}|x)}$

Choosing Sample Size. In order to scale, sample size cannot be more than that of available main memory. Assume that data records are fixed in length. To find out approximately how many records can be held in main memory, we simply divide the amount of available main memory by the size (in byte) of each record. To take into account main memory usage of the data structure of the algorithm, we only use 80% of the estimated size as an initial trial and run the chosen inductive learner. We then use "`top`" command to check if any swap space is being used. This estimation can just be approximate, since our earlier work has shown that the significantly different sampling size does not really influence the overall accuracy [1].

Choosing Biased Sampling Ratio. Since positive examples are extremely skewed in the surveillance data set, we choose to use all the positive examples while varying the amount of negative examples to find out the best ratio that results in best precision and recall rates. Finding the exact best ratio is a non-trivial task, but an approximate should be good enough in most cases. It is generally true that when the ratio of negatives decreases (or the ratio of positive increases), both the true positive rate and false positive rate of the trained model are expected to increase. Ideally, true positive rate should increase at a faster rate than false positive rate. In the extreme case, when there are no negatives sampled at all, the model will predict any $\mathbf{x}$ to be positive, resulting in perfect 100% true positive rate but false positive rate is also 100%. Using this heuristic, the simple approach to find out the optimal amount of negatives to sample is to use progressive sampling. In other words, we reduce ratio of negatives progressively by "throwing out" portions of the negatives in the previous sample, such as by half. We compare the overall loss (if a loss function is given) or ROC curves. This process continues until the loss starts to rise. If the loss of the current ratio and previous one is significantly different (the exact significance depends on each application's tolerance), we use a binary search to find the optimal sampling size. We choose the median ratio and computes the loss. In some situations if fewer negatives always result in higher loss, we reduce the ratio of positives while fixing the number of negatives.

Training Ensemble of Classifiers. After an optimal biased sampling distribution is determined, the next step is to generate multiple biased samples and compute multiple models from these samples. In order to make each sample as "uncorrelated" as possible, the negative examples are completely disjoint; in other words, each negative sample is used only once to train one base classifier. Since training multiple models are completely independent procedures, they can be computed either sequentially on the same computer or on multiple machines in parallel. In a previous work [1], we analyze the scalability of averaging ensemble

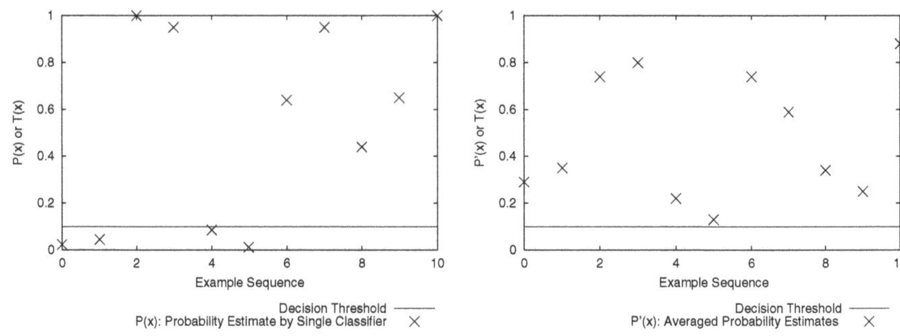

Fig. 2. Decision plots

in general. As a summary, it has both linear *scalability* and *scaled scalability*,the best possible scalability physically achievable.

Predicting via Averaging. When predicting a test example $\mathbf{x}$, each model in the ensemble outputs a probability estimate $P_i(\ell|\mathbf{x})$ that $\mathbf{x}$ is an instance of positive class ℓ. We use simple averaging to combine probability output from K models $P(\ell|\mathbf{x}) = \frac{\sum_i P_i(\ell|\mathbf{x})}{K}$ We then use the techniques discussed previously to make optimal decision.

Desiderata. The obvious advantage of the above averaging ensemble is its scalability. The accuracy is also potentially higher than a single model trained from the entire huge dataset (if this could happen). The base models trained from disjoint data subsets make uncorrelated noisy errors to estimate posterior probability $P(\ell|\mathbf{x})$. It is known and studied that uncorrelated errors are reduced by averaging. Under a given loss function, different probability estimates on the same example may not make a difference to final prediction. If the decision threshold to predict $\mathbf{x}$ to be an instance of the positive class is 0.01, probability estimates 0.1 and 0.99 will make exactly the same final prediction.

The multiple model is very likely more accurate than the single model because of its stronger bias towards predicting skewed examples correctly and skewed examples carry more reward then negative examples. Inductive learners have tendency to over-estimate probabilities. For example, decision tree learners try to build "pure" nodes of a single class. In other words, the leaf nodes tend to have one class of data. In this case, the posterior probability tends to be very close values to 0's and 1's. However, the averaging ensemble has an interesting "smoothing effect" to correct this over-estimation problem. Since each sample is mostly uncorrelated, the chances that all of the trained models predict close values to 0's and 1's are rare. In other words, the averaged probability estimates are smoothed out evenly towards the middle range between 0 and 1. Since the decision threshold to predict positive is less than 0.5 (usually much less than 0.5), it is more likely for true positives to be correctly classified. Since true positives carry much higher rewards the negatives, the overall effect is very likely to result in higher accuracy.

In Figure 2, we have one conjectured example to show the idea. In both plots, each "cross" represents a skewed positive example. Its location on the x-axis is just to separate each example away from each other. However the y-axis is the estimated probability $P(+|\mathbf{x})$ that $\mathbf{x}$ is a positive example. The horizontal line is the value of the decision threshold to predict $\mathbf{x}$ to be a member of positive class, i.e., we predict positive iff $P(+|\mathbf{x}) > t$. The left plot is the results of the single classifier trained from entire data as a whole (on a computer with enormous amount of memory) and the lost plot is the results of the averaging ensemble. As shown in the conjectured plot, all the probability estimates of averaging ensemble tend to move to the middle of the y-aix. This results in its correct prediction of the two examples on the bottom left corner, which were incorrectly classified as negative by the single model.

3 Experiment

The weekly data on one business line has approximately 5M records. We have one week data for training and another week for testing. The original number of features are 144 which include a lot of id's (such as trader id, broker id, entry id, legal entity id among others), time and location information, and so on. Some of these fields cannot be used directly. For example, if a particular combination of id's is an anomaly at a particular time, some inductive learner will pick that as a good rule which is obviously wrong. To avoid coincidences like this, we have encoded all id's as either Y if this field is not empty or N otherwise. All dates are removed from the data; however the differences in days among all dates are computed and added into the original feature set. There are 34 different types of trading anomalies. Their total prior probability is less than 0.01%. Some of these anomalies are more frequent then others. A few of these anomalies are extremely rare; we only have 65 positive instances out 5M for one of the anomalies.

There are three learning tasks requested by the bank. The first task is to predict if a trade is an anomaly without identifying its particular type. The second task is to predict if a trade is a particular type of anomaly, and the same trade can be more than one type of anomaly. The last task is to identify some types of extremely rare anomalies. We were only given the labelled training data to generate the ensemble and *unlabelled* testing data to predict. Only after we sent our predictions to the bank, the true labels of the testing data were provided to us. Results were verified by our client.

We have used C4.5 decision tree algorithm to compute the base level models.

Task 1: Predicting Anomalies. The first task is to predict if a trade is an anomaly (any of the known types). The ratio of anomalies in the data is about 0.01%. It took about 20 mins to find the optimal biased sampling rate. The best ratio is 2% positives. The training took less than 2 hours on a PC running Linux.

The ROC curve of the results is shown in Figure 3. There are three curves in the plot. The random guess is the diagonal line. The curve on the top is "upper bound" of accuracy on the dataset, and the curve below that is the result of

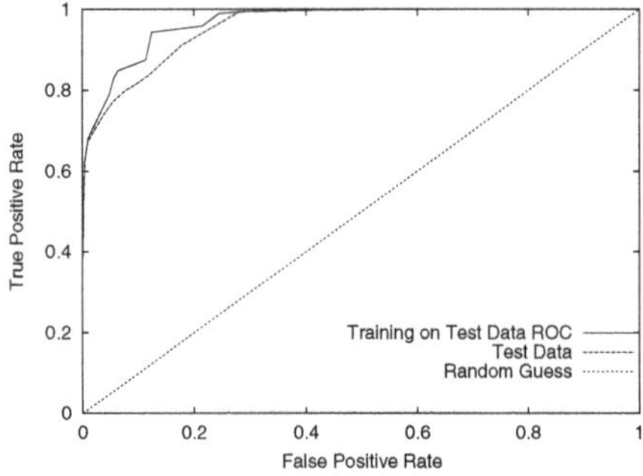

Fig. 3. ROC curve to predict anomalies

Table 1. True Positive Rate (tp) to Predict Anomaly Types

Type	num	tp(%)	Type	num	tp(%)	Type	num	tp(%)	Type	num	tp(%)
183	7027	99.9	101	2543	100.0	125	4028	99.9	129	4973	99.8
157	1645	98.6	108	503	90.7	152	172	100.0	119	272	82.4
110	1095	99.2	124	155	86.5	128	243	64.2	121	79	1.3
114	109	27.5	105	122	96.7	109	62	67.7	113	89	97.8
127	378	87.8	150	139	84.9	137	41	78.0	102	124	20.2
153	347	98.8	118	22	95.5	140	15	0.0	158	10	100.0
161	3	33.3	*112	3	0.0	*116	1	0.0	165	6	0.0
126	2	0.0	139	2	0.0	156	14	0.0	*154	24	0.0
171	1	0.0	166	3	0.0						

our model. Since it is not known how accurate a model can possibly be trained from the feature set, we have plotted the curve of "training error on the same test data". In other words, we trained an additional ensemble on the test data. Obviously, training and testing on exactly the same dataset is very likely to have higher accuracy than training from a different dataset. We use this curve as the upper bound of accuracy. As clearly shown in the figures, the upper bound curve and our model's curve are very close.

Task 2: Predicting Anomaly Types. The second task is to predict the types of anomalies. The data set is exactly the same as the task 1, however the class label is either normal or one of the anomaly types. We used the same sampling ratio as found in Task 1. The training took about 4 hrs on the same computer. The criteria to predict $\mathbf{x}$ as a type of anomaly is if its estimated probability is the highest than the probability to be of normal or any other types. The results are shown in Table 1. We list the types of the anomaly (denoted by a "code" at the request of the bank for confidentiality concerns), the number of instances in the training data and the true positive rate of the learned ensemble. If a particular type of anomaly does not appear in the training data, we put an * in front of the type code. For anomalies that are frequent (at least a few hundred instances), the model has very high true positive rate (at least 80%).

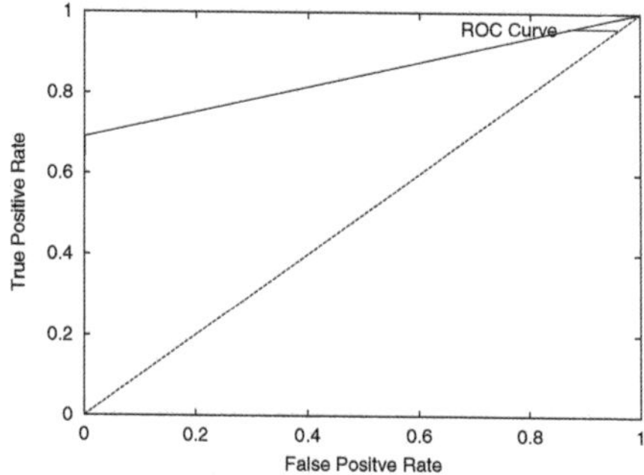

Fig. 4. ROC curve to predict a rare type of anomaly

Task 3: Predicting Extremely Rare Anomaly Types. Since some of the anomaly are extremely rare. For example, there are only 119 cases of anomaly type "114" in the test data. Since there are 34 different types of anomalies in total and some anomalies have thousands of instances in the dataset, those extremely rare anomalies are likely ignored by the learner due to their statistical insignificance. To solve this problem, we train an ensemble that only identifies on particular type of extremely rare anomaly. The bank is interested to predict anomaly type "114" which we only have 65 positive examples in the training data. The ROC curve to predict 114 is shown in Figure 4. The ensemble reaches true positive rate of about 70% with very low false positive rate (less than 0.01%). However, 30% of true anomalies are not able to be detected by the model. Our client conjectures that the feature set we use are not sufficient. We may have to look at multiple records to see a sequence of events.

4 Related Work

To scale up decision tree learning, SPRINT [2] generates multiple sorted attribute files from the original dataset. Decision tree is constructed by scanning and splitting attribute lists, which eliminates the need for large main memory. Since each attribute list is sorted. for a data file with f attributes and N examples, the total cost to produce the sorted lists is $f \cdot O(N \cdot log(N))$. External sort is used to avoid the need for main memory. Each attribute list has three columns- a unique record number, the attribute value and the class label; the total size of attribute lists is approximately three times the size of the original dataset. When a split takes places at a node, SPRINT reads the attribute lists at this node and breaks them into r sets of attribute lists for r child nodes, for a total of f file read and $r \cdot f$ file writes. More recently, BOAT [3] constructs a "coarse" tree from a sample of the dataset that can fit into main memory. The splitting criterion in each node of the tree is tested against multiple decision trees trained from bootstrap samples of the sampled data. It refines the tree later by scanning the complete dataset, resulting in a total of two complete dataset read. Chan proposed meta-learning [4] to scale up inductive learning. He has also applied the data reduction technique, however meta-learning build a tree of classifiers and only combine class label instead of probabilities. It has been shown that the quality of the decision tree is sometimes worse than a single decision tree. Most importantly, meta-learning cannot estimate its predictive accuracy until the model is fully constructed. In addition, meta-learning has sublinear speedup.

Previous research on skewed data mostly casts the problem into a cost-sensitive problem where skewed examples receive a higher weight. Some of previous proposed techniques are effective when both the cost-model is clearly defined and don't change often and the volume of the data is small. When one of these conditions fails, existing approaches are not applicable. Our proposed approach is a effective solution when the volume is too big and/or the cost model cannot be clearly defined.

5 Conclusion

In this paper, we have proposed an ensemble based approach to mine extremely skewed data. We have applied this approach on a very large trading surveillance data (5M with 144 features) with very skewed positives (less than 0.01%) from one of the biggest banks in the US. In three different tasks, the training on a desk top PC running Linux took less than 4 hrs. The ROC curve on unlabelled test data is as good as the best can be possibly obtained on this dataset. When the data volume is huge and positive examples are rare, the proposed ensemble approach provides a satisfactory solution.

References

1. Fan, W., Wang, H., Yu, P.S., Stolfo, S.: A framework for scalable cost-sensitive learning based on combining probabilities and benefits. In: Second SIAM International Conference on Data Mining (SDM2002). (2002)
2. Shafer, J., Agrawl, R., Mehta, M.: SPRINT: A scalable parallel classifier for data mining. In: Proceedings of Twenty-second International Conference on Very Large Databases (VLDB-96), San Francisco, California, Morgan Kaufmann (1996) 544–555
3. Gehrke, J., Ganti, V., Ramakrishnan, R., Loh, W.Y.: BOAT-optimistic decision tree construction. In: Proceedings of ACM SIGMOD International Conference on Management of Data (SIGMOD 1999). (1999)
4. Chan, P.: An Extensible Meta-learning Approach for Scalable and Accurate Inductive Learning. PhD thesis, Columbia University (1996)

Flexible Integration of Molecular-Biological Annotation Data: The GenMapper Approach

Hong-Hai Do[1] and Erhard Rahm[2]

[1] Interdisciplinary Centre for Bioinformatics,
[2] Department of Computer Science
University of Leipzig, Germany
www.izbi.de, dbs.uni-leipzig.de
{hong,rahm}@informatik.uni-leipzig.de

Abstract. Molecular-biological annotation data is continuously being collected, curated and made accessible in numerous public data sources. Integration of this data is a major challenge in bioinformatics. We present the GenMapper system that physically integrates heterogeneous annotation data in a flexible way and supports large-scale analysis on the integrated data. It uses a generic data model to uniformly represent different kinds of annotations originating from different data sources. Existing associations between objects, which represent valuable biological knowledge, are explicitly utilized to drive data integration and combine annotation knowledge from different sources. To serve specific analysis needs, powerful operators are provided to derive tailored annotation views from the generic data representation. GenMapper is operational and has been successfully used for large-scale functional profiling of genes. Interactive access is provided under http://www.izbi.de.

1 Introduction

Over the past few years, genomes of several organisms, especially the human genome, have been completely sequenced. Now the focus of genomic research has shifted to understand how genes and ultimately entire genomes are functioning. The knowledge about molecular-biological objects, such as, genes, proteins, intra- and inter-cellular pathways, etc., is typically encoded by a large variety of data commonly called annotations. Such annotation is are continuously collected, curated, and made available in numerous public data sources. A current survey [14] lists more than 500 such databases. Furthermore, an increasing number of ontologies is maintained, mostly in the form of standardized vocabularies and hierarchical taxonomies. Typically, objects in one source are annotated by information in other sources and ontologies in the form of cross-references (web-links) [8,7,11]. A few sources focus on sequence-based objects and uniformly map them onto the genome of a particular species for the visual comparison and correlation of co-located objects [2,6,17].

Many applications such as gene functional profiling, gene expression analysis, etc., require molecular-biological objects and their annotations to be integrated from different sources and made accessible in a flexible way for varying analysis focus. This integration task is a major problem since annotation data is highly diverse and

E. Bertino et al. (Eds.): EDBT 2004, LNCS 2992, pp. 811–822, 2004.
© Springer-Verlag Berlin Heidelberg 2004

only structured to some extent. Moreover, the number and contents of relevant sources are continuously expanding [26]. The use of web-links or the display of related objects on the genome represent a first step to integrate annotations, which is very useful for interactive navigation. However, these approaches do not support automated large-scale analysis tasks (queries, data mining). While more advanced integration approaches are needed, it is important that the semantic knowledge about relationships between objects, which are typically established by domain experts (curators), is preserved and made available for analysis.

A survey of representative data integration systems in bioinformatics is given in [26]. Current solutions mostly follow a data warehouse (e.g. IGD [30], GIMS [29], DataFoundry [16]) or federation approach (e.g. TAMBIS [21], P/FDM [24]) with a physical or virtual integration of data sources, respectively. These systems are typically built on the notion of an application-specific global schema to consistently represent and access integrated data. However, construction and maintenance of the global schema (schema integration, schema evolution) are highly difficult and thus do not scale well to many sources. DiscoveryLink [22] and Kleisli [31] also follow the federation approach but their schema is simply the union of the local schemas, which have to be transformed to a uniform format, such as relational (DiscoveryLink), or nested relational (Kleisli). A general limitation of these systems is that existing cross-references between sources are not exploited for semantic integration.

SRS [19] and DBGET/LinkDB [20] completely abandon a global schema. In these systems, each source is replicated locally as is, parsed and indexed, resulting in a set of queryable attributes for the corresponding source. While a uniform query interface is provided to access the imported sources, join queries over multiple sources are not possible. Cross-references can be utilized for interactive navigation, but not for the generation and analysis of annotation profiles of objects of interest. Recently, Kementsietsidis et al. [23] established a formal representation of instance-level mappings, which can be obtained from the cross-references between different sources, and proposed an algorithm to infer new mappings from existing ones.

GenMapper (*Gen*etic *Mapper*) represents a new approach to flexibly integrate a large variety of annotation data for large-scale analysis that preserves and utilizes the semantic knowledge represented in cross-references. The key aspects of our approach are the following:

- GenMapper physically integrates all data in a central database to support flexible, high performance analysis across data from many sources.
- In contrast to previous data warehouse approaches, we do not employ an application-specific global database schema (e.g. a star or snowflake schema). Instead, we use a generic data model called GAM (Generic Annotation Management) to uniformly represent object and annotation data from different data sources, including ontologies. The generic data model makes it much easier to integrate new data sources and perform corresponding data transformations, thereby improving scalability to a large number of sources. Moreover, it is robust against changes in the external sources thereby supporting easy maintenance.
- We store existing cross-references (mappings) between sources and associations between objects and annotations during data integration and exploit them by combining annotation knowledge from different sources to enhance analysis tasks.
- To support specific analysis needs and queries, we derive tailored annotation *views* from the generic data representation. This task is supported by a new

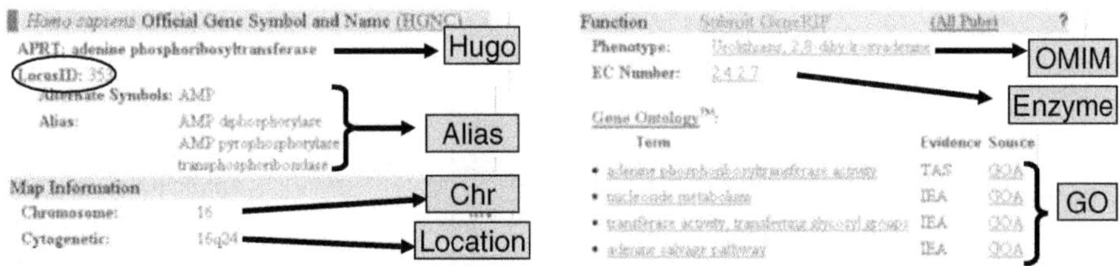

Fig. 1. Sample annotations from LocusLink

approach utilizing a set of high-level operators, e.g. to combine annotations imported from different sources. Results of such operators that are of general interest, e.g. new mappings derived from existing mappings, can be materialized in the central database. The separation of the generic data representation and the provision of application-specific views permits GenMapper and its (imported and derived) data to be used for a large variety of applications.

GenMapper is fully operational and has been successfully used for large-scale functional profiling of genes [25,27]. Major public data sources, including those for gene annotations, such as LocusLink [8] and Unigene [12], and for protein annotations, such as InterPro [7] and SwissProt [11], have been integrated. Furthermore, GenMapper also includes various sub-divisions of NetAffx, a vendor-based data source of annotations for genes used in microarray experiments [1]. Interactive access to GenMapper is provided under http://www.izbi.de.

The paper is organized as follows. In the next section we give an overview of our data integration approach implemented in GenMapper. Section 3 presents the generic data model GAM. Section 4 discusses the data import phase and the generation of annotation views. Section 5 describes additional aspects of the technical implementation as well as an application scenario of GenMapper. Section 6 concludes the paper.

2 Overview of GenMapper

To better understand the problem that GenMapper addresses it is instructive to examine some typical annotation data that is available to the biologist when gathering information about a molecular-biological object of interest. Figure 1 shows annotations for a genetic locus with the source-specific identifier (accession) *353* in the popular public source LocusLink. As indicated in the figure, the locus is annotated by a variety of information from other public sources, e.g., Enzyme [3] for enzyme classification, and OMIM [9] for disease information, and vocabularies and taxonomies such as Hugo [5] for official gene symbols and GeneOntology (GO) [4] for standardized gene functions. GenMapper focuses on combining this kind of inter-related information during data integration and making it directly available for analysis.

Figure 2 shows an overview of the GenMapper integration approach. Integration of source data is performed in two phases: *Data import* and *View generation*. In the first phase, source data is downloaded, parsed and imported into a central relational database following the generic GAM representation. This representation is used for

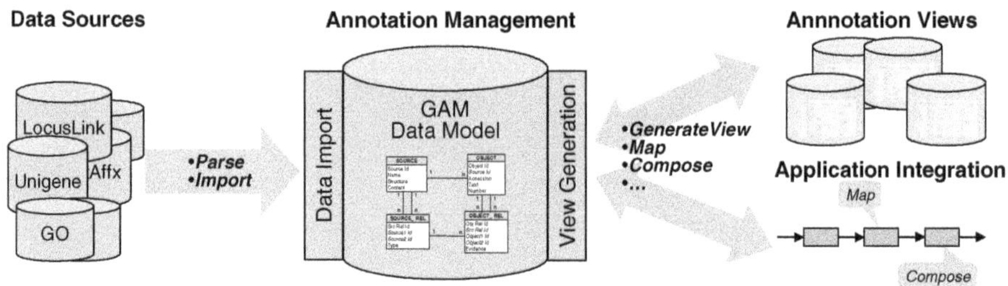

Fig. 2. GenMapper architecture for annotation integration

Annotation view

LOCUSLINK	HUGO	GO	LOCATION	OMIM
10220	GDF11	GO:0008372, GO:0005125, GO:0008083, GO:0040007, GO:0007498, GO:0007399, GO:0001501	12q13.13	603936
2297	FOXD1	GO:0005634, GO:0003700, GO:0006355	5q12-q13	601091
3280	HES1	GO:0005634, GO:0003677, GO:0007399, GO:0006355	3q28-q29	139605
353	APRT	GO:0016757, GO:0003999, GO:0006168, GO:0009116	16q24	102600

Fig. 3. An annotation view for LocusLink genes

objects and their annotations originating from different sources, such as public sources and taxonomies, as well as the different kinds of relationships.

Since directly accessing the GAM representation may result into complex queries, applications and users are typically provided with annotation views tailored to their analysis needs. Figure 3 shows an example of such an annotation view for some Locuslink genes. In such a view, GenMapper can combine information and annotations from different sources for an arbitrary number of objects. Both the objects (the loci from LocusLink in the example) and the kinds of annotations (e.g., Hugo, GO, Location, and OMIM) can be chosen arbitrarily. Such annotation views are very helpful for comparing and inferring functions of the objects, e.g., if they have been detected to show some correlated behavior in experimental processes.

In general, an annotation view is a structured (e.g., tabular) representation of annotations for objects of a particular source. Annotation views are queryable to support high-volume analysis. A view consists of several attributes which are derived from one source or different sources. The choice of attributes is not fixed as in the underlying sources but can be tailored to application needs. Enabling such a flexible generation of annotation views requires the combination of both objects and annotations, i.e. relationships between objects. This is supported by the uniform representation of data from different sources in our approach.

The annotation views can be flexibly constructed by means of various high-level functions which can operate on entire sources and mappings or also a subset of them. Key operators include *Compose* and *GenerateView,* and are specifically defined on the GAM data model. They also represent the means to integrate GenMapper with external applications to provide automatic analysis pipelines with annotation data.

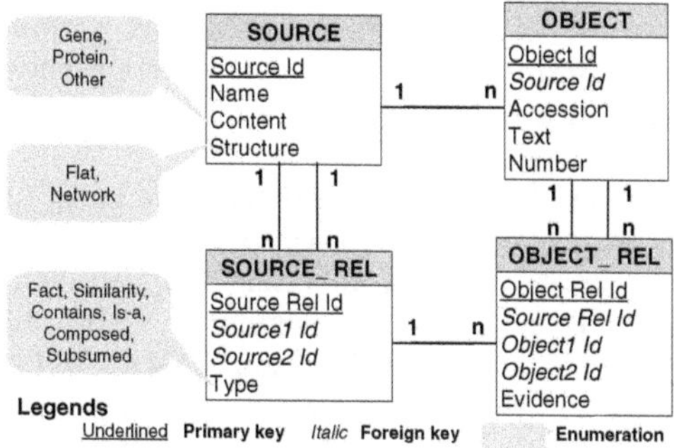

Fig. 4. The GAM data model

3 The Generic Annotation Model (GAM)

Generic data models aim at uniformly representing different data and metadata for easy extensibility, evolution, and efficient storage. Typically, metadata and data are stored together in triples of object-attribute-value (also coined as Entity-Attribute-Value (EAV) [28]). A molecular-biological example of such a triple is (*APRT*, Name, *adenine phosphoribosyltransferase*). This approach has been used in repository systems to maintain database schemas from different data models [15], in e-Commerce to manage electronic catalogs [13], in the medical domain to manage sparse patient data [28], or in the Semantic Web to describe and exchange metadata [10].

In GenMapper, we follow the same idea to achieve a generic representation for molecular-biological annotation data by using a generic data model called GAM (Generic Annotation Model). Figure 4 shows the core elements of GAM in a relational format. In particular, we have enriched the EAV representation with several specific properties. First, to avoid the mix of metadata and data in EAV triples and to support data integration from many sources, we explicitly provide two levels of abstraction, *Source* and *Object*. A source may be any predefined set of objects, e.g. a public collection of genes, an ontology, or a database schema. Second, we allow relationships of different semantics and cardinality to be defined at both the source and object level (*Source_Rel* and *Object_Rel*). Both intra- and inter-source relationships are possible. A relationship at the source level (a mapping) typically consists of many relationships at the object level (associations).

We roughly differentiate between *gene-oriented*, *protein-oriented* and *other* sources according to their content. A source, whose objects are organized in a particular structure, such as a taxonomy or a database schema, is indicated as a *Network* source. Typically, each object has a unique source-specific identifier or accession, which is often accompanied by a textual component, for example to represent the name of the object. Alternatively, an object may also have a numeric representation.

In *Source_Rel*, we distinguish three types of relationships between and within sources. *Structural* and *annotation* relationships are imported from external data sources and represent the internal structure of a source or semantic correspondences between sources, respectively. In addition, GenMapper supports the calculation and storage of *derived* relationships to increase the annotation knowledge and to support frequent queries. We discuss the single types of relationships in the following.

Annotation relationships. Annotations are determined using different computational or manual methods and typically specified by cross-references between sources. These relationships represent the most important and also the largest amount of data to be managed. Currently we group them into *Fact* and *Similarity* mappings. The former indicate relationships which can be taken as facts, for example, the position of a gene on the genome, while the latter contain computed relationships, e.g. determined by sequence comparisons and alignments (homology) between instances or by an attribute matching algorithm. In *Object_Rel*, an *evidence* value can be captured to indicate the computed plausibility of the association between two any objects.

Structural relationships. Source structure is captured using the *Contains* and *IS_A* relationship types. *Contains* denotes containment relationships between a source and its partitions, such as between GO and its sub-taxonomies Biological Process, Molecular Function and Cellular Component [4], while *IS_A* is the typical semantic relationship found between terms within a taxonomy like Biological Process or Enzyme.

Derived relationships. Two forms of derived relationships, *Composed* and *Subsumed*, are supported. Composed relationships combine cross-references across several sources to determine annotations that are not directly available. For example, the new mapping Unigene↔GO can be derived by combining two existing mappings, Unigene↔LocusLink and LocusLink↔GO. Subsumed relationships are automatically derived from the *IS_A* structure of a source and contain the associations of a term in a taxonomy to all subsumed terms in the term hierarchy. This is motivated by the fact that if a gene is annotated with a particular GO term, it is often necessary to consider the subsumed terms for more detailed gene functions.

4 Data Integration in GenMapper

In the following we first discuss the data import process. We then outline the use of high-level operators to generate annotation views from the GAM representation.

4.1 Data Import

The integration of new data sources into the GAM data model is performed in two steps, *Parse* and *Import*. For all sources, the output of the *Parse* step is uniformly stored in a simple EAV format as illustrated by the example shown in Table 1 for the locus *353* from Fig. 1. It represents a straightforward way to capture annotations as provided on the web pages of public data sources, and therefore makes the construction of parsers very simple.

Table 1. Parsed annotation data from LocusLink

Locus	Target	Accession	Text
353	Hugo	APRT	adenine phosphoribosyltransferase
353	Location	16q24	
353	Enzyme	2.4.2.7	
353	GO	GO:0009116	nucleoside metabolism
...	...	...	...

The *Import* step transforms and integrates data from the EAV into the GAM format. During this, it prevents that already existing sources, objects, mappings and associations are inserted again. This duplicate elimination is performed at the object level by comparing object accessions and at the source level by examining source names. Audit information, such as date and release of a source, is also captured allowing to identify and purge abandoned objects from a previous import. Integrating new data requires relating provided associations with existing data. For example, if GO has already been imported into GAM, *Import* simply relates the new objects, e.g. from LocusLink, with the existing GO terms.

The functional split between the *Parse* and *Import* step essentially helps us to limit development effort. *Parse* represents the smallest portion of source-specific code to be implemented, while *Import* realizes a generic EAV-to-GAM transformation and migration module and needs to be implemented just once. This makes the integration of a new source relatively easy, mainly consisting of the effort to write a new parser.

4.2 View Generation

To explore the relationships between molecular-biological objects, scientists often have to ask queries in the form "*Given a set of LocusLink genes, identify those that are located at some given cytogenetic positions (Location),* ***and*** *annotated with some given GO functions,* ***but not*** *associated with some given OMIM diseases*". In particular, it exhibits the following general properties:

- A query involves one or more mappings between a single *source*, e.g. LocusLink, of the objects to be annotated, and one or more *targets* providing the annotations of interest, e.g. Location, GO and OMIM. Both the source and the targets can be confined to respective subsets of only relevant objects.
- The mappings in a query represent logical conditions on the source objects, i.e. whether they have/do not have some associated target objects. Hence, the mappings can be combined using either the AND or OR logical operator and individually negated using the NOT logical operator, like LocusLink↔OMIM.

GenMapper supports the specification of this kind of queries and answers them by means of tailored annotation views, which can be flexibly constructed using a set of GAM-based high-level operations. In the following, we briefly present some simple operations, such as *Map*, *Range*, and *Domain* (see Table 2), and discuss the most important operations to determine annotations views, *Compose* and *GenerateView*, in more detail. Note that the operations are described declaratively and leave room for optimizations in the implementation.

Table 2. Definitions und examples for some simple operations

Operation	Definition	Example
Map(S, T)	Identify associations between S and T	map = *Map*(S, T) = $\{s_1 \leftrightarrow t_1, s_2 \leftrightarrow t_2\}$
Domain(map)	SELECT DISTINCT S FROM map	*Domain*(map) = $\{s_1, s_2\}$
Range(map)	SELECT DISTINCT T FROM map	*Range*(map) = $\{t_1, t_2\}$
RestrictDomain(map, s)	SELECT * FROM map WHERE S in s	*RestrictDomain*(map, $\{s_1\}$) = $\{s_1 \leftrightarrow t_1\}$
RestrictRange(map, t)	SELECT * FROM map WHERE T in t	*RestrictRange*(map, $\{t_2\}$) = $\{s_2 \leftrightarrow t_2\}$

Simple Operations. The *Map* operation takes as input a source S to be annotated and a target T providing annotations. It searches the database for an existing mapping between S and T and returns the corresponding object associations. *Domain* and *Range* identify the source and the target objects, respectively, involved in a mapping. *RestrictDomain* and *RestrictRange* return a subset of a mapping covering a given set of objects from the source and from the target, respectively.

Compose. The *Compose* operation is based on a simple intuition: transitivity of associations to derive new mappings from existing ones. For example, if a locus l in LocusLink is annotated with some GO terms, so are the Unigene entries associated with locus l. *Compose* takes as input a so-called *mapping path* consisting of two or more mappings connecting two sources with each other, for which a direct mapping is required. For example, it can combine map_1: $S_1 \leftrightarrow S_2$ and map_2: $S_2 \leftrightarrow S_3$, which share a common source S_2, and produces as output a mapping between S_1 and S_3.

Compose represents a simple but very effective way to derive new useful mappings. The operation can be used to derive new annotations, which are not directly available in existing sources and their cross-references. However, *Compose* may lead to wrong associations when the transitivity assumption does not hold. This effect can be restricted by allowing *Compose* to be performed with explicit user confirmation on the involved mapping path. The use of mappings containing associations of reduced evidence is a promising subject for future research.

GenerateView. This operation assumes a source S to be annotated and a set of targets T_1, ..., T_m, providing required annotations. The relevant source and target objects are given in the corresponding subsets s and t_1, ..., t_m, respectively, each of which may also cover all existing object of a source. Finally, the operation requires a method for combining the mappings (AND or OR), and a list of targets for which the obtained mappings are to be negated. The result of such a query is a view of m+1 attributes, S, T_1, ..., and T_m, which contains tuples of related objects from the corresponding sources. In particular, *GenerateView* implements the pseudo-code shown in Fig. 5 to build the required annotation view V.

V is first set to the given set s of relevant source objects. For each target T_i, a mapping M_i between S and T_i is to be determined. It may already exist in the database, or in many cases, may be not yet available. In the former case, the required mapping is directly retrieved using the *Map* operation. In the latter case, we try to derive such a mapping from the existing ones using the *Compose* operation. A subset m_i is then extracted from M_i to only cover the relevant source objects s and target objects t_i. If necessary, the negation of m_i is built from the subset $s_{\bar{i}}$ of s containing the objects not involved in m_i. Finally, V is incrementally extended by performing a left outer join (OR) or inner join (AND) operation with the sub-mapping m_i.

```
GenerateView(S, s, T1, t1, ..., Tm, tm, [AND|OR], {negated})
V = s                                         //Start with all given source objects
For i = 1..m
    Determine mapping Mi: S↔Ti                //Using either the Map or Compose operation
    mi = RestrictDomain(Mi, s)                //Consider the given source and target objects
    mi = RestrictRange(mi, ti)
    If negated[Ti]                            //The mapping is specified as negated
        s‡ = s \ Domain(mi)                   //Source objects not involved in the sub-mapping
        m‡ = RestrictDomain(Mi, s‡)           //Find associations for these objects
        mi = m‡ right outer join s‡ on S      //Preserve objects without associations
    End If
    V = V inner join / left outer join mi on S   //AND: inner join, OR: left outer join
End For
```

Fig. 5. The algorithm for *GenerateView*

5 Implementation and Use

GenMapper is implemented in Java. We use the free relational database management system MySQL to host the backend database implementing the GAM data model. It currently contains approx. 2 million objects of over 60 different data sources, and 5 million object associations organized in over 500 different mappings. In the following we present the basic functionalities in the user interface of GenMapper and discuss the use of GenMapper in a large-scale analysis application.

5.1 Interactive Query Interface

The interactive interface of GenMapper allows the user to pose queries and retrieve annotations for a set of given objects from a particular source. First, the relevant source can be selected from a list of available sources automatically determined from the current content of the database. The accessions of the objects of interest can be uploaded from a file or manually copied and pasted. If no file or accessions are specified, the entire source will be considered.

In the next step, the user can then arbitrarily specify the targets from the available sources. GenMapper internally manages a graph of all available sources and mappings. Using a shortest path algorithm, GenMapper is able to automatically determine a mapping path to traverse from the source to any specified target. The user can also search in the graph for specific paths, for example, with a particular intermediate source. With a high degree of inter-connectivity between the sources, many paths may be possible. Hence, GenMapper also allows the user to manually build and save a path customized for specific analysis requirements.

When the relevant paths have been selected or manually constructed, the user can specify the target accessions of interest, the method for combining the mappings, and the negation of the single mappings as shown in the screenshot of GenMapper in Fig. 6a. GenMapper then applies the *GenerateView* operation to construct the annotation view (Fig. 6b). The interesting accessions among the retrieved ones can be selected to start a new query. Alternatively, the user can also retrieve the names and other information of the corresponding objects (Fig. 6c). All results can be saved and downloaded in different formats for further analysis in external tools.

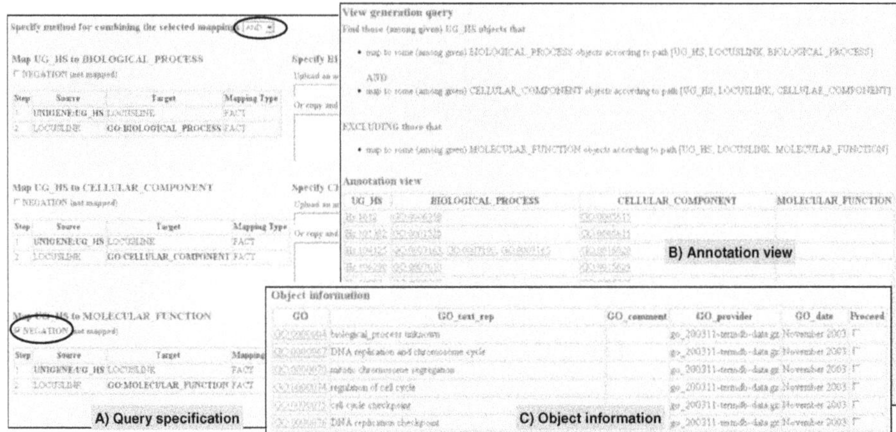

Fig. 6. Query specification and annotation view for Unigene objects

5.2 Large-Scale Automatic Gene Functional Profiling

In an ongoing cooperation project aiming at a comparative analysis between humans and their closest relatives, chimpanzees [18], GenMapper has been successfully integrated within an automated analysis pipeline to perform complex and large-scale functional profiling of genes.

Gene expression measurements have been performed using Affymetrix microarray technology [1]. From a total of approx. 40.000 genes, the expression of around 20.000 genes were detected, from which around 2.500 show a significantly different expression pattern between the species thus representing candidates for further examination [25,27]. Functional profiling of the differently expressed genes was based on the analysis of the annotations about their known functions as specified by GeneOntology (GO) terms. In particular, the genes are classified according to the GO function taxonomy in order to identify the functions, which are conserved or have changed between humans and chimpanzees.

Using the mappings provided by GenMapper, the proprietary genes of Affymetrix microarrays were mapped to the generally accepted gene representation UniGene, for which GO annotations were in turn derived from the mappings provided by LocusLink. Furthermore, using the structure information of the sources, i.e. *IS_A* and *Subsumed* relationships, comprehensive statistical analysis over the entire GO taxonomy was possible to determine significant genes. The adopted analysis methodology is also applicable to other taxonomies, e.g. Enzyme, to gain additional insights.

6 Conclusions

We presented the GenMapper system for flexible integration of heterogeneous annotation data. We use a generic data model called GAM to uniformly represent annotations from different sources. We exploit existing associations between objects to drive data integration and combine annotation knowledge from different sources to enhance analysis tasks. From the generic representation we derive tailored annotation views to serve specific analysis needs and queries. Such views are flexibly constructed using a set of powerful high-level operators, e.g. to combine annotations imported from different sources. GenMapper is fully operational, integrates data from many sources and is currently used by biologists for large-scale functional profiling of genes.

Acknowledgements. We thank Phil Bernstein, Sergey Melnik and Peter Mork and the anonymous reviewers for helpful comments. This work is supported by DFG grant BIZ 6/1-1.

References

1. Affymetrix: http://www.affymetrix.com/
2. Ensembl: http://www.ensembl.org/
3. Enzyme: http://www.expasy.ch/enzyme/
4. GeneOntology: http://www.geneontology.org/
5. Hugo: http://www.gene.ucl.ac.uk/nomenclature/
6. Human Genome Browser: http://genome.ucsc.edu/
7. InterPro: http://www.ebi.ac.uk/interpro/
8. LocusLink: http://www.ncbi.nlm.nih.gov/LocusLink/
9. OMIM: http://www.ncbi.nlm.nih.gov/omim/
10. RDF: http://www.w3.org/RDF/
11. SwissProt: http://www.expasy.ch/sprot/
12. Unigene: http://www.ncbi.nlm.nih.gov/UniGene/
13. Agrawal, R., A. Somani, Y. Xu: Storage and Querying of E-Commerce Data. Proc. VLDB, 2001
14. Baxevanis, A.: The Molecular Biology Database Collection: 2003 Update. Nucleic Acids Research 31(1), 2003
15. Bernstein, P. et al.: The Microsoft Repository. Proc. VLDB, 1997
16. Critchlow, T. et al.: DataFoundry: Information Managemenet for Scientific Data. IEEE Trans. on Information Management in Biomedicine 4(1), 2000
17. Dowell, R.D. et al.: The Distributed Annotation System. BMC Bioinformatics 2(7), 2001
18. Enard, W. et al.: Intra- and Inter-specific Variation in Primate Gene Expression Patterns. Science 296, 2002
19. Etzold, T., A. Ulyanov, P. Argos: SRS – Information Retrieval System for Molecular Biology Data Banks. Methods in Enzymology 266, 1996
20. Fujibuchi, W. et al.: DBGET/LinkDB: An Integrated Database Retrieval System. Proc. PSB, 1997
21. Goble, C. et al.: Transparent Access to Multiple Bioinformatics Information Sources. IBM System Journal 40(2), 2001
22. Haas, L. et al.: DiscoveryLink – A System for Integrated Access to Life Sciences Data Sources, IBM System Journal 40(2), 2001
23. Kementsietsidis, A., M. Arenas, R.J. Miller: Mapping Data in Peer-to-Peer Systems: Semantics and Algorithmic Issues. Proc. SIGMOD, 2003
24. Kemp, G., N. Angelopoulos, P. Gray : A Schema-based Approach to Building Bioinformatics Database Federation. Proc. BIBE, 2000

25. Khaitovich, P., B. Mützel, G. Weiss, H.-H. Do, M. Lachmann, I. Hellmann, W. Enard, T. Arendt, J. Dietzsch, S. Steigele, K. Nieselt-Struwe and S. Pääbo: Evolution of Gene Expression in the human brain. Submitted for publication
26. Lacroix, Z., T. Critchlow (Ed.): Bioinformatics: Managing Scientific Data, Morgan Kaufmann, 2003
27. Mützel, B., H.-H. Do, P. Khaitovich, P., G. Weiß, E. Rahm, S. Pääbo: Functional Profiling of Genes Differently Expressed in the Brains of Humans and Chimpanzees. In preparation
28. Nadkarni, P. et al.: Organization of Heterogeneous Scientific Data Using the EAV/CR Representation. Journal of American Medical Informatics Association 6(6), 1999
29. Paton, N. et al.: Conceptual Modeling of Genomic Information. Bioinformatics 16(6), 2000
30. Ritter, O.: The Integrated Genomic Database (IGD). In Suhai, S. (Ed.): Computational Methods in Genome Research. Plenum Press, 1994
31. Wong, L.: Kleisli, Its Exchange Format, Supporting Tools, and an Application in Protein Interaction Extraction. Proc. BIBE, 2000

Meta-SQL: Towards Practical Meta-querying

Jan Van den Bussche[1], Stijn Vansummeren[1], and Gottfried Vossen[2]

[1] Limburgs Universitair Centrum
[2] University of Münster

Enterprise databases often contain not only ordinary data, but also queries. Examples are view definitions in the system catalog; usage logs or workloads; and stored procedures as in SQL/PSM or Postgres. Unfortunately, these queries are typically stored as long strings, which makes it hard to use standard SQL to express *meta-queries:* queries about queries. Meta-querying is an important activity in situations such as advanced database administration, database usage monitoring, and workload analysis. Here are some examples of meta-queries to a usage log. *(i)* "Which queries in the log do the most joins?" *(ii)* "Which queries in the log return an empty answer on the current instance of the database?" *(iii)* View expansion: "Replace, in each query in the log, each view name by its definition as given in the system catalog." *(iv)* Given a list of new view definitions (under the old names): "Which queries in the log give a different answer on the current instance under the new view definitions?"

We present *Meta-SQL*, a system that allows the expression of meta-queries directly in SQL. Our presentation is extremely condensed; a full paper on the language and our prototype implementation is available.[1]

Storing SQL expressions as syntax trees. Consider a simplified system catalog table, called `Views`, containing view definitions. Traditionally, there is a column `name` of type string, holding the view name, and a column `def`, also of type string, holding the SQL expression defining the view. Because such a flat string representation of an SQL expression makes structured syntactical manipulations difficult, we instead declare `def` to be of type XML, which is an allowed column datatype in Meta-SQL (and in many modern SQL implementations as well). We then store SQL expressions as syntax trees in a convenient XML format. Here is an example:

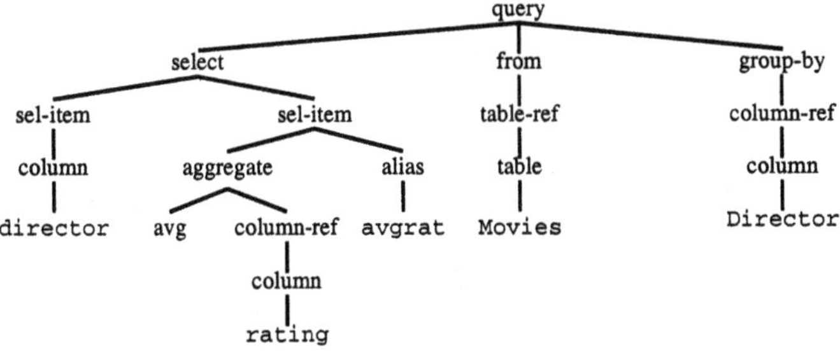

[1] J. Van den Bussche, S. Vansummeren, and G. Vossen. Towards practical meta-querying. http://arxiv.org/abs/cs.DB/0202037.

E. Bertino et al. (Eds.): EDBT 2004, LNCS 2992, pp. 823–825, 2004.
© Springer-Verlag Berlin Heidelberg 2004

Calling XSLT from within SQL. Suppose, in addition to our `Views` table, we are given a list `Removed` of names of tables that are going to be removed, and we want to know which views will become invalid after this removal because they mention one of these table names. To express this meta-query in Meta-SQL, we write a simple auxiliary XSLT program `mentions_table`, which we then call from within SQL:

```
function mentions_table
param tname string
returns string
begin
<xsl:param name="tname"/>
<xsl:template match="/">
<xsl:if
  test="//table[string(.)=$tname]">
true
</xsl:if></xsl:template>
end

select name from Views, Removed
where mentions_table(def,Removed.name)
      = 'true'
```

Indeed, XSLT is a widely used manipulation language for XML data. An XSLT program takes an XML tree as input, and produces as output another XML tree (which could be in degenerate form, holding just a scalar value like a number or a string). We also use the XSLT top-level parameter binding mechanism, by which programs can take additional parameters as input. Our system embraces XSLT because it is the most popular and stable standard general-purpose XML manipulation language to date. When other languages, notably XQuery, will take over this role, it will be an easy matter to substitute XSLT by XQuery in our system.

As a second example, suppose we are given a second view definitions table `Views2`, and for every view name that is listed in both views tables, we want a new definition that equals the union of the first definition and the second definition. To express this meta-query in Meta-SQL, we write:

```
select name, unite(v.def,v2.def)
from Views v, Views2 v2
where v.name=v2.name
```

Here `unite` is an easy XSLT program (omitted) that transforms two trees t_1 and t_2 into the tree

`<union>` t_1 t_2 `</union>`

XML variables. Consider the meta-query "give all pairs (v, t), where v is a view name and t is a table name mentioned in the definition of view v." We express this query in Meta-SQL using an *XML variable*:

```
select v.name, string_value(x)
from Views v, x in v.def[//table]
```

Here, `x` is an XML variable ranging over the `<table>` subelements of `v.def`. XML variables are bound in the from-clause, in a similar way variables are bound in OQL. We can use any XPath expression within the square brackets to delimit the range of nodes.

As another example, suppose we are given a log table `Log` with stored queries (in a column `Q`), and we want to identify "hot spots": subqueries that occur as a subquery in at least ten different queries. To express this meta-query, we write:

```
select s
from Log l, s in l.Q[//query]
group by s
having count(l.Q) >= 10
```

EVAL. So far we have only seen examples of meta-queries that rely on the syntax of the stored SQL queries only. Meta-SQL also allows the expression of meta-queries whose answer depends on the results of dynamically executing stored queries. This is done via the new built-in function EVAL, which takes an SQL query (more correctly, its syntax tree in XML format) as input, and returns the table resulting from executing the query.

As an example, suppose we are given a table `Customer` with two attributes: `custid` of type string, and `query` of type XML. The table holds queries asked by customers to the catalogue of a store. Every query returns a table with attributes `item`, `price`, and possibly others. The following meta-query shows for every customer the maximum price of items he requested:

```
select custid, max(t.price)
from Customer c, EVAL(c.query) t
group by custid
```

There is also a function UEVAL in case we have no information about the output scheme of the stored queries we are evaluating. UEVAL presents the rows resulting from the dynamic evaluation of the query in XML format.

The System. We have developed a prototype Meta-SQL implementation, usable on top of DB2 UDB, and freely available at http://www.luc.ac.be/theocomp. Our implementation takes a cross-compilation approach, and heavily relies on the facility of user-defined functions.

A Framework for Context-Aware Adaptable Web Services

Markus Keidl and Alfons Kemper

Universität Passau, D-94030 Passau, Germany
lastname@db.fmi.uni-passau.de

1 Introduction

The trend towards pervasive computing involves an increasing number of ubiquitous, connected devices. As a consequence, the heterogeneity of client capabilities and the number of methods for accessing information services on the Internet also increases. Nevertheless, consumers expect information services to be accessible from all of these devices in a similar fashion. They also expect that information services are aware of their current environment. Generally, this kind of information is called *context*. More precisely, in our work context constitutes information about consumers and their environment that may be used by Web services to provide consumers a customized and personalized behaviour.

In this paper, we present a context framework that facilitates the development and deployment of context-aware adaptable Web services. We implemented the framework within our ServiceGlobe system [1,2], an open and distributed Web service platform.

2 The Context Framework

In our framework, context information is transmitted (in XML data format) as a SOAP header block within the SOAP messages that Web services receive and send. A context header block contains several *context blocks*. Each context block is associated with one dedicated *context type*, which defines the type of context information a context block is allowed to contain. At most one context block for a specific context type is allowed.

The life-cycle of a Web service's context begins at the client: First, the client application gathers all relevant context information and inserts it into the SOAP header. Then, the request is sent to the Web service. After the request was received, the context is extracted by the context framework and provided to the invoked Web service as its *current context*. During its execution, the Web service can access and modify this current context using the API provided by the framework. When the Web service invokes another service during its execution, its current context is automatically inserted into the outgoing request. The response to such a request may also contain context information. In this case, the Web service can extract the interesting parts of the context data from the

E. Bertino et al. (Eds.): EDBT 2004, LNCS 2992, pp. 826–829, 2004.
© Springer-Verlag Berlin Heidelberg 2004

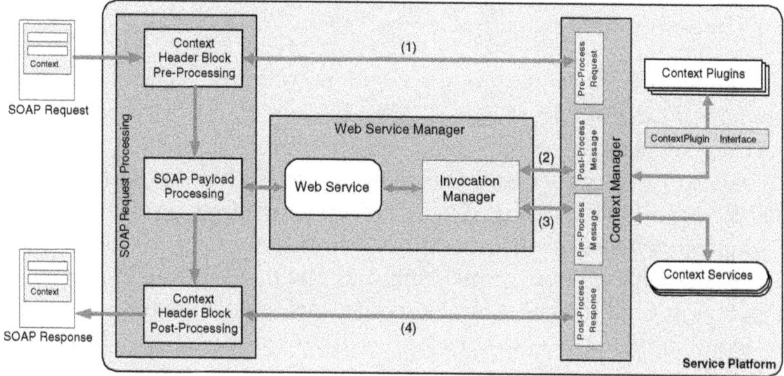

Fig. 1. Components for Context Processing

response and insert them into its current context. After the Web service's termination, its current context is automatically inserted into its response and sent back to the invoker. If the invoker is a client application, it can integrate portions of the returned context into the consumer's persistent local context (for use in future requests).

2.1 Processing Context

There are four components that process context information (see Figure 1): Web services, context plugins, context services, and clients (not shown). Invoked *Web services* themselves can always process any context information. They have full control over how the context information influences their execution and their replies, and they can also modify the context. *Context plugins* are implemented in Java and must be installed locally at a host. Every plugin is associated with one dedicated context type. *Context services* are Web services that implement the `ContextService` interface, which is defined using the WSDL standard. Just as context plugins, every context service is associated with one context type. In contrast to context plugins, context services need not be installed locally, but can be available anywhere on the Internet. The *client application* also processes context information, e.g., it converts price information in a response into the currency at the consumer's current location.

There are four occasions at which context is processed automatically, as shown in Figure 1: First, the incoming SOAP request of an invoked Web service is pre-processed (1), based on the context in the request. Furthermore, whenever the Web service invokes other services, outgoing requests are post-processed before they are actually sent (2). All incoming responses to outgoing requests are pre-processed before they are returned to the Web service (3). Finally, the outgoing response of the invoked Web service is post-processed (4), based on the service's current context.

2.2 Processing Instructions

In our framework, a context block could potentially be processed by several components. Furthermore, it can be processed by all hosts on which the invoked Web service invokes other services. Context processing instructions are used to specify rules of precedence and the components and hosts that should actually be used for context processing. They encompass context service instructions and processing guidelines. With context service instructions, context services that should be used for context processing and their execution order are specified. With processing guidelines, the components that should be used to process a certain context block are specified as well as the hosts at which the context block should be processed.

Context processing instructions can be inserted into the context itself as a self-contained context block. Furthermore, a Web service's UDDI metadata may be annotated with them. Providers or developers of Web services can use this option to specify context services that should be used for processing certain context blocks. Additionally, context services may be published in a UDDI registry, just as ordinary Web services. Our framework then uses the available UDDI metadata to automatically determine available context services for context processing.

2.3 Context Types

Our context framework provides several integrated context types. One of the most important context types for information services is *Location*. It contains information about the consumer's current location, e.g., the consumer's GPS coordinates, country, local time and time zone. It may also include semantic location information, e.g., that the consumer is currently at work. The *Consumer* context type contains information about the consumer invoking the information service, e.g., name, email address, preferences, and so on. *Client* context information is data about a consumer's client, e.g., its hardware (processor type or display resolution) as well as software (Web browser type and version).

3 Description of the Demo

For our demonstration, we use a well-known information service from the Internet as basis, the Amazon Web service. We developed the information service *MyBook* that enhances the Amazon service's query capabilities with context awareness. The MyBook service uses, for example, Client context information to adjust its response to the client's capabilities. If the display of the client device is small (e.g., on PDAs or cell phones), unnecessary data, e.g., customer reviews, is removed from the response. We also present a context service that uses Location context information to convert price information in the service's response into the currency at the consumer's current location.

We implemented several clients for different devices, e.g., Java-based clients for PDAs and cell phones. With them, the usefulness and the advantages of context information are demonstrated, based on the MyBook service. We also implemented a Web-based client that allows the investigation of the influence of various types of context information on information services in more detail.

References

1. M. Keidl, S. Seltzsam, and A. Kemper. Reliable Web Service Execution and Deployment in Dynamic Environments. In *Proc. of the Intl. Workshop on Technologies for E-Services (TES)*, volume 2819 of *Lecture Notes in Computer Science (LNCS)*, pages 104–118, 2003.
2. M. Keidl, S. Seltzsam, K. Stocker, and A. Kemper. ServiceGlobe: Distributing E-Services across the Internet (Demonstration). In *Proc. of the Conf. on Very Large Data Bases (VLDB)*, pages 1047–1050, 2002.

Aggregation of Continuous Monitoring Queries in Wireless Sensor Networking Systems*

Kam-Yiu Lam and Henry C.W. Pang

Department of Computer Science
City University of Hong Kong
83 Tat Chee Avenue, Kowloon, Hong Kong
cskylam@cityu.edu.hk, henry@cs.cityu.edu.hk

Abstract. In this demo paper, we introduce our sensor query aggregation system, *Continuous Monitoring Query Evaluation System (CMQES)*, which is a test-bed for studying the aggregation problems of continuous monitoring queries (CMQ) on sensor data streams in a wireless sensor networking system. A CMQ monitors the data values from sensor nodes distributed in the system environment. The objective of CMQES is to provide a configurable test-bed to study various important issues in aggregation of CMQ. An aggregation scheme, *Sequential Pushing (SeqPush)* has been implemented. Various system settings and parameters can easily be configured with the interface provided in CMQES, and statistics such as the number of messages, complexity in processing and the energy consumption rate at the sensor nodes, are collected.

1 System Setup

The wireless sensor networking system consists of a collection of *mobile sensor processing units (MSPU)* and a *base station (BS)* connected by a low bandwidth wireless network. The MSPUs are distributed in the system environment to capture the real-time status, i.e., temperature, light-intensity and pressure, of its surrounding environment. The base station is responsible for the communication between the MSPUs and the users of the system. Users submit *continuous monitoring queries (CMQ)* into the system to monitor the status of their interested entities in the system environment. During the activation period of the queries, the sensor data values generated from the MSPUs are evaluated continuously and the query results are likewise presented continuously to the users through the base station.

2 Evaluation Problem of CMQ

In CMQES, if the base station receives a query, CMQ_i, it will perform a pre-analysis and decompose it into a set of sub-queries $\{SCMQ_{i,1}, SCMQ_{i,2} \ldots, SCMQ_{i,n}\}$ based on

* The work described in this paper was partially supported by a the Research Grants Council of Hong Kong Special Administration Region, China [Project No. CityU 1076/02E].

E. Bertino et al. (Eds.): EDBT 2004, LNCS 2992, pp. 830–833, 2004.
© Springer-Verlag Berlin Heidelberg 2004

the syntax and distribution of the required sensor data items of CMQ_i. A sub-query, $SCMQ_{i,j}$ is forwarded to a sensor node (a participating node) and stays there until the end time of CMQ_i. One of the participating nodes is assigned as the coordinator node which is responsible for aggregating the sub-query results. Each sub-query may be defined with a *selection condition* to select the data values generated from a sensor node for evaluation. If the selection condition is satisfied, the sub-query result (for this case, it is the sensor data value) will be passed to the coordinator node for processing through the wireless network. When the coordinator node has received all the evaluation results from its participating nodes, a *condition* for aggregation has to be satisfied before the performance of the aggregate operation. Otherwise, *false* result will be generated for that time point to be propagated to successive upper level nodes to the root node. Note that the *aggregate condition* is determined from the accuracy requirement of the query or as an input from the user who initiates the query. Continuously forwarding sub-query results is obviously undesirable due to the limited bandwidth and high data generation rates (especially when the data sampling rate is high). In addition, we need to deal with the problem of disconnection.

3 Sequential Pushing(*SeqPush*)

In CMQES, we have designed sequential aggregation scheme, called *Sequential Pushing* (*SeqPush*) to collect the sub-query results from the participating nodes of a CMQ. The main objectives of *SeqPush* are to: (1) reduce the number of messages for sub-query results aggregation; and (2) distribute the workload for sub-query evaluation to different nodes instead of concentrating the processing at the coordinator node. *SeqPush* considers the evaluation results of individual sub-query to determine the aggregation sequence. In the first step of *SeqPush*, each participating node submits sensor data values to the coordinator node for data aggregation. After completing the first evaluation, the coordinator node sorts the participating nodes according to the number of false results (i.e. sub-query condition dissatisfied) in the message from each the node. The node with the *largest number* of false evaluations is designated as the *triggering node*. For the nodes having the same number of satisfied results, the order is assigned randomly. The node order is broadcast to all the participating nodes and the nodes will record down what is their next node in the sequence. This arrangement ensures that the first node is the one predicted to have the lowest probability to satisfy the condition defined in its sub-query in the next evaluation.

The subsequent aggregation of results from the participating nodes then follows the assigned sequence and is started by the triggering node, which periodically pushes sub-query results to the next node in the sequence. When the next node receives a sub-query result message, it will first check the received results. If all of them are false values or the aggregation condition of the query is dissatisfied, it will stop the pushing of sub-query results and immediately returns a false evaluation message to the coordinator node. Otherwise, the node merges the received sensor data values in the message with the sensor data values returned from its own sub-query for the same time interval to perform a *partial* query aggregation. This procedure will be repeated until all nodes have been traversed in sequence.

Due to the dynamic properties of sensor data, the probability of satisfying the condition in a sub-query at a node may change with time. Therefore the coordinator node needs to reorder the sequence of the participating nodes periodically. The reorder procedure is performed when the following condition is satisfied: the evaluation is stopped at the same node, called the *false node*, consecutively for a pre-defined period of time, and the false node is not the first node. Satisfaction of these conditions suggests that the sensor data values generated at the false node may have a high probability to be false in next evaluation. Hence the coordinator node will reorder the sequence of the nodes using the following procedure:

a. The false node is now the first node in the sequence.
b. All the nodes following the false node will remain in the same relative order to each other.
c. All the nodes in front of the false node remain in their original relative order. They rejoin the node sequence but are now attached after the last node of the original sequence.

4 Implementation

CMQES is implemented with MICA Motes [MM]. In CMQES, one of the MSPUs is connected with the base station through a mote interface board. It is the base station MSPU. CMQES contains two main software components: the sensor program in the MPSU, and the server program in the base station. The sensor program is implemented in NesC, which is a C-like language for TinyOS [TINY], and is responsible for capturing sensor data values, evaluating sub-queries, submitting sub-query results to the coordinator nodes, and collecting performance statistics at each MPSU. We have implemented *SeqPush* in the sensor program. The evaluation results of a CMQ and performance statistics are periodically sent to the base station through the base station MSPU for reporting.

The second program is the server program residing at the base station. This program is implemented in Java, with MS Windows 2000 and MS SQL server chosen respectively as the operating systems and database. The server program is responsible for collecting results and performance statistics. In addition, the following parameters can be set using the server program at the base station for submitting a CMQ and controlling the operations at the MPSUs:

1. The sampling rate of the MSPUs.
2. The number of nodes participating in a CMQ.
3. Aggregation functions to be performed at a node, i.e., calculate the mean, maximum and minimum from the values of sub-queries.
4. Condition for the sub-query of a CMQ at an MPSU.

5 Demonstration and Sample Results

In the demonstration, through the interface at the base station, we can submit CMQs for processing at the MPSUs, as shown in Figure 1. Currently, the MPSU is programmed to capture the light intensity of its surrounding environment periodically, i.e., every 2 sec, as sensor data values, and a message is sent every 30 sec to the coordinator node. The sampling rate and message reporting period can be varied at the base station. The message size for communication in TinyOS is 34 bytes. Five bytes are reserved for the message header and the message contains the results from 10 evaluations with each reading taking up 2 bytes. The remaining 9 bytes are for cycle number, message type and the destination address. Currently, the transmission delay of a single message from a MSPU to another one in the testing environment is between 300ms and 700ms. As TinyOS only provides best effort message delivery service. A lost message will be considered a missed evaluation cycle and logged accordingly by the coordinator node.

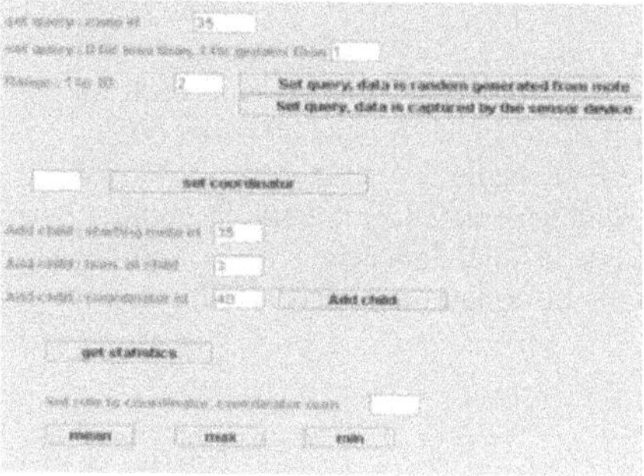

Fig. 1. Program at the base station

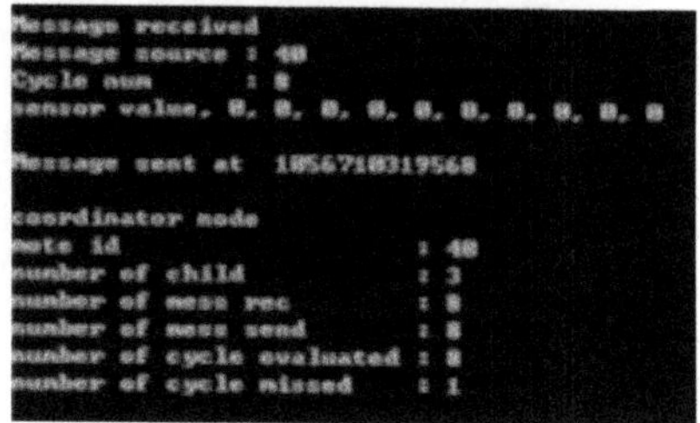

Fig. 2. Real time display of received messages and statistics

Our experiment results show that the number of messages submitted in central aggregation scheme (CAS), i.e. all the participating MSPU submits sub-query result to a central MUPU for data aggregation periodically, is much larger than that in *SeqPush*. Two ammeters are connected to one of the participating nodes and the coordinator node to measure the energy consumption rates of the nodes when different operations are performed at the nodes.

The result captured by the base station is displayed in real time as shown in Fig. 2. The statistics include:

(1) Number of message transmitted, including sending and receiving messages.
(2) Number of successful evaluations and number of missed query results due to loss of messages.
(3) Number of reorder of nodes in *SeqPush*.

References

[MM] www.xbow.com
[TINY] http://today.cs.berkeley.edu/tos/

eVitae: An Event-Based Electronic Chronicle

Bin Wu, Rahul Singh, Punit Gupta, Ramesh Jain

Experiential Systems Group Georgia Institute of Technology
30308 Atlanta, USA
{binwu,rsingh,jain}@ece.gaetch.edu
punit@cc.gatech.edu

Abstract. We present an event based system for storing, managing, and presenting personal multimedia history. At the heart of our approach is information organization using the concept of an event. Events allow modeling of the data in a manner that is independent of media. To store events, a novel database called EventBase is developed which is indexed by events. The unique characteristics of events make multidimensional querying and multiple perspective explorations of personal history information feasible. In this demo we present the major functions of eVitae.

1 Introduction

Personal history systems electronically record important activities from a person's life in the form of photographs, text, video, and audio. Examples of some existing systems such as [3] have shown that there are a number of salient challenges in this domain. *First*, information is fundamentally anchored to space and time and people often exploit them as cues for querying information. *Second*, the data as the carrier of information stays in respective silos. This fragments meaningful information across data. *Third*, to break down these silos, an information model independent of media is required to depict the content of information. *Lastly*, presentation of the information must be dynamically generated according to individual users' preferences.

We have developed a personal eChronicle [1] called eVitae [4]. In eVitae we utilize a novel generative theory based upon the concept of *event* to design an information system [2]. In this paper, we show how eVitae system as an access environment ingests heterogeneous data into meaningful information conveyed by events, aids the user to quickly focus on what is of interest and presents a multidimensional environment for exploration of events with their details stored in appropriate media.

2 Event-Based Data Modeling

The approach we employ to design and implement eVitae is based on the notion of events [6]. An event is an occurrence or happening of significance that can be defined as a region or collection of regions in spatial-temporal-attribute space. Given k events,

E. Bertino et al. (Eds.): EDBT 2004, LNCS 2992, pp. 834–836, 2004.
© Springer-Verlag Berlin Heidelberg 2004

the i_{th} event is formally denoted as $e_i(t, s, a_1^i, ... a_m^i)$ and uniquely identified by eID (event identifier). In this notation t characterizes the event temporally, s denotes the spatial location(s) associated with the event, and $a_1^i, ..., a_m^i$ are the attribute associated with the event. An event is defined by its event models, which includes the mandatory attributes: space, time, transcluded-media, event-name, and event-topic, and a finite set of free attributes.

Events can be grouped together in collections, called event categories. Formally, an event category can be represented as: $\mathbf{C} = \{\mathbf{e}_1, \mathbf{e}_2, ..., \mathbf{e}_k\}$, where $\{\mathbf{e}_1, \mathbf{e}_2, ..., \mathbf{e}_k\}$ is the set of events that comprise the category. Event categories provide a powerful construct to support the multiple ways of organizing information, definition of complex queries and notification, personalized views of information space where the user is interested.

According to the definition of the event, the information layer implemented by events breaks down the data silos. This layer uses an event-based data model to construct a new index that is independent of data type. The organization, indexing, and storage of events conveying potentially changing information are accomplished by parsing the data as it is entered, and storing all events in a database of events called EventBase. The data is parsed by the system and events are produced using the event model. The EventBase also stores links to original data sources, which means the system can only present the appropriate media in the context of a particular event. EventBase is the extension of traditional database. In the implementation of prototype eVitae system, we use MySQL as the database to store and index events.

3 System Architecture

The architecture of eVitae system comprises three modules, namely, *Event Entry*, *EventBase*, and *What-You-See-Is-What-You-Get (WYSIWYG) query and exploration environments*. The key features of the system are briefly discussed as following.

Event Entry. An event may include multifarious data from different sources, such as video, audio, sensors, texts. The Event Entry module of the system is designed to produce events using event models, and record the link between events and related data.

EventBase. EventBase is the backend of eVitae system which stores the Events. The transclusion of media is maintained by storing links between an event and the data it is based upon. EventBase uses the eID attribute of events as the unified index and is supported by MySQL.

WYSIWYG query and exploration environment. This is an integrated interaction environment to explore electronic chronicle of a person, as shown in figure 1. By using temporal and spatial relationship as cues and by defining event categories to organize events, we create an exploratory environment for the user. The event exhibit panel (Fig. 1) presents an overall picture of events. Options for zooming, filtering, extraction, viewing relations, history keeping, and details-on-demand make the environment appealing and powerful.

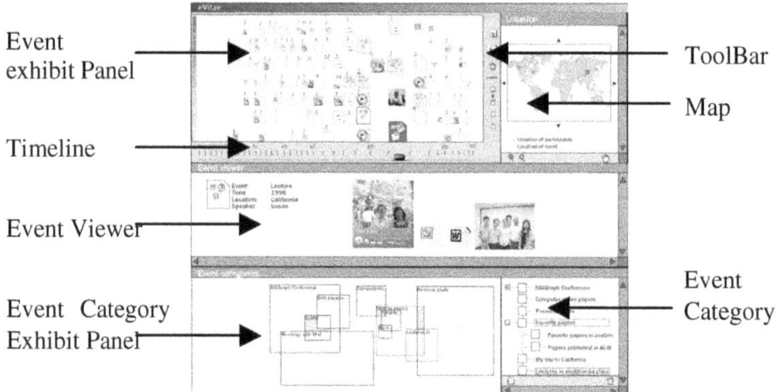

Fig. 1. WYSIWYG Query and Exploration Environment

4 Conclusion

eVitae system demonstrates an event-based approach for organization, storage, management, and querying of personal history information comprising of multifarious data. The system provides an event entry module for importing data from heterogeneous data sources and assimilating them into events. This information is stored in EventBase which is indexed by events. Event-based modeling allows multidimensional querying and exploration of personal history information. Furthermore, flexibility in event definition and organization allows exploration of the data from multiple perspectives. Preliminary results indicate that an event-based system not only offers significant advantages in information organization, but also in exploration and discovery of information from data.

References

1. R. Jain. "Multimedia Electronic Chronicles", IEEE MultiMedia, pp. 102-103, Volume 10, Issue 03, July 2003.
2. R. Jain, "Events in Heterogeneous Data Environments", Proc. International Conference on Data Engineering, Bangalore, March 2003.
3. J. Gemmell, G. Bell, R. Lueder, S. Drucker, and C. Wong. "MyLifeBits: fulfilling the Memex vision", ACM Multimedia, pp. 235-238, ACM, 2002.
4. R. Singh, B. Wu, P. Gupta, R. Jain. "eVitae: Designing Experiential eChronilces", ESG Technical Report Number : GT-ESG-01-10-03, http://www.esg.gatech.edu/report/GT-ESG-01-10-03.pdf

CAT: Correct Answers of Continuous Queries Using Triggers

Goce Trajcevski[1], Peter Scheuermann[1*], Ouri Wolfson[2], and Nimesh Nedungadi[2]

[1] Department of Electrical and Computer Engineering, Northwestern University, Evanston, Il 60208,
{goce,peters}@ece.northwestern.edu
[2] Department of Computer Science, University of Illinois at Chicago, Chicago, Il 60607,
{wolfson,nnedunga}@cs.uic.edu

1 Introduction and Motivation

Consider the query *Q1: Retrieve all the motels which will be no further then 1.5 miles from my route, sometime between 7:00PM and 8:30PM*, which a mobile user posed to the Moving Objects Database (MOD). Processing such queries is of interest to wide range of applications (e.g. tourist information systems and context awareness [1,2]). These queries pertain to the *future* of a dynamic world. Since MOD is only a model of the objects moving in the real world, the accuracy of the representation has to be continuously verified and updated, and the answer-set of *Q1* has to be re-evaluated in every clock-tick[1]. However, the re-evaluation of such queries can be avoided if an update to the MOD does not affect the answer-set.

The motion of the moving object is typically represented as a *trajectory* – a sequence of 3D points $(x_1, y_1, t_1), (x_2, y_2, t_2), \ldots (x_n, y_n, t_n)$, and its projection in the X-Y plane is called a *route*. The details of the construction based on electronic maps and the *speed-profiles* of the city blocks are given in [5]. After a trajectory is constructed, a *traffic abnormality* may occur at a future time-point, due to an accident, road-work, etc..., and once it occurs, we need to: *identify* the trajectories that are affected, and *update* them properly (c.f. [5]). In the sequel, we focus on the impacts of the abnormalities to the continuous queries.

Figure 1 shows three trajectories – Tr_1, Tr_2 and Tr_3 and their respective routes R_1, R_2 and R_3. If a road-work starts at 4:30PM on the segment between A and B which will last 5 hours, slow down the speed between 4:30PM and 9:30PM. Tr_1 enters that segment after 4:30PM, and its future portion will need to be modified. As illustrated by the thicker portion of Tr_1, instead of being at the point B at 4:50, the object will be there at 5:05. A key observation is that if the object, say o_1, whose trajectory is Tr_1, issued the query $Q1$, we have to re-evaluate the answer.

* Research partially supported by NSF grant EIA-000 0536

[1] Hence the name *continuous queries* – formally defined for MOD in [3].

E. Bertino et al. (Eds.): EDBT 2004, LNCS 2992, pp. 837–840, 2004.
© Springer-Verlag Berlin Heidelberg 2004

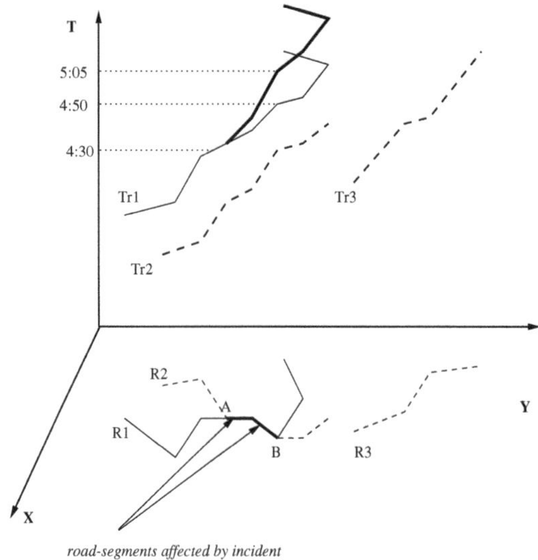

Fig. 1. Trajectories, Routes and Updates

2 System Architecture

Figure 2 illustrates the main components and behavioral aspects of the CAT system:

• There are tables which: store the trajectories (MOT) and landmarks of interest (BUILDINGS); keep track of the queries posed and their answers (PENDING_QUERIES and ANSWERS); and store the information about the traffic abnormalities (TRAFFIC_ABN). The trajectories and the landmarks were obtained using the real maps of Cook County, Chicago.

In the heart of the CAT system is the set of *Triggers*, part of which we illustrate in the context of the example query $Q1$. If $o1$ posed the query $Q1$ at 3:30PM, its answer contains the motels m_1 and m_2 to which $o1$ should be close at 7:55PM and 8:20PM, respectively. When an abnormality is detected, its relevant parameters are inserted in the TRAFFIC_ABN table. This, however, "awakes" $Trigger_1$, whose event is:

ON INSERT TO TRAFFIC_ABN

$Trigger_1$ checks if the abnormality affects some of the trajectories stored in the MOT and, if so, updates their future part. However, the action part of $Trigger_1$ which updates the MOT, in turn, is the event for $Trigger_2$:

ON UPDATE TO MOT

IF HAS_PENDING_QUERIES ...

$Trigger_2$ checks if the corresponding moving object has posed some queries which are still of interest (i.e. their time has not "expired"). The condition of $Trigger_2$ is satisfied by $o1$ and its action part will re-evaluate the query $Q1$, based on the new future-portion of Tr_1. Due to the delay, o_1's trajectory will

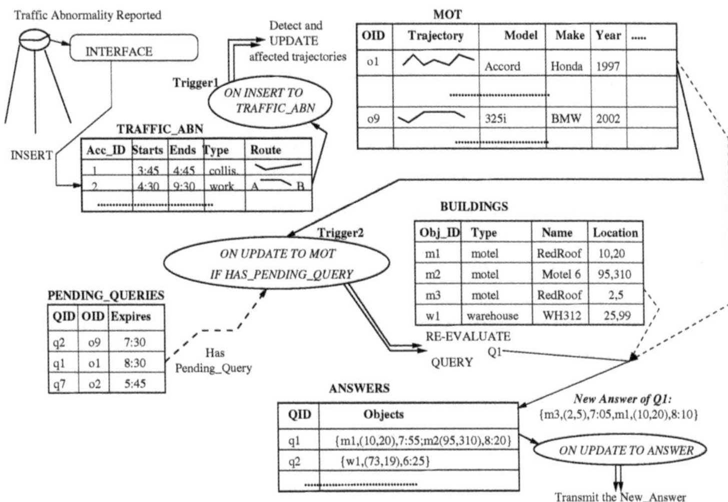

Fig. 2. Behavioral Aspects of the CAT

be near m_2 at 8:35PM, which is a bit too late for the user. On the other hand, o_1 will be near the motel m_3 at 7:05PM. Before the traffic incident $m3$ was not part of the answer, (it would have had the desired proximity at 6:50PM).

3 Demonstration

All the back-end components are implemented using Oracle 9i as a server. We used User-Defined Types (UDT) to model the entities and User-Defined Functions (UDF) to implement the processing, exploiting the Oracle Spatial predicates.

• The front-end client, which is the GUI presented to the end-user, is implemented in Java. The GUI gives the options of specifying the queries (i.e. time of submission; relevant time interval; objects of interest; etc...). Once the user clicks the SUBMIT button, the query is evaluated and its answer is displayed. In the server, the query is assigned an *id* number and it is stored in the PENDING_QUERIES table. Clearly, in a real MOD application, the client will be either a wireless (mobile) user of a web browser-based one, properly interfaced to the server.

• To test the execution of the triggers and the updates of the answer(s) to the continuous queries posed, the GUI offers a window for generating a traffic abnormality. The user enters the beginning and the end times of the incident as well as its "type" (which determines the impact on the speed-profile). He also enters the route segments along which the traffic incident is spread. The moment this information is submitted to the server, the affected trajectories are updated AND the new answer(s) to the posed continuous queries are displayed back to the user.

References

1. A. Hinze and A. Voisard. Location-and time-based information delivery in tourism. In *SSTD*, 2003.
2. A. Pashtan, R. Blatter, A. Heusser, and P. Scheuermann. Catis: A context-aware tourist information system. In *IMC*, 2003.
3. A. P. Sistla, O. Wolfson, S. Chamberlain, and S. Dao. Modeling and querying moving objects. In *ICDE*, 1997.
4. G. Trajcevski and P. Scheuermann. Triggers and continuous queries in moving objects databases. In *MDDS*, 2003.
5. G. Trajcevski, O. Wolfson, B. Xu, and P. Nelson. Real-time traffic updates in moving object databases. In *MDDS*, 2002.

Hippo: A System for Computing Consistent Answers to a Class of SQL Queries

Jan Chomicki[1], Jerzy Marcinkowski[2], and Slawomir Staworko[1]

[1] Dept. Computer Science and Engineering, University at Buffalo
{chomicki,staworko}@cse.buffalo.edu
[2] Instytut Informatyki, Wroclaw Uniwersity, Poland
Jerzy.Marcinkowski@ii.uni.wroc.pl

1 Motivation and Introduction

Integrity constraints express important properties of data, but the task of preserving data consistency is becoming increasingly problematic with new database applications. For example, in the case of integration of several data sources, even if the sources are separately consistent, the integrated data can violate the integrity constraints. The traditional approach, removing the conflicting data, is not a good option because the sources can be autonomous. Another scenario is a long-running activity where consistency can be violated only temporarily and future updates will restore it. Finally, data consistency may be neglected because of efficiency or other reasons.

In [1] Arenas, Bertossi, and Chomicki have proposed a theoretical framework for querying inconsistent databases. *Consistent* query answers are defined to be those query answers that are true in every repair of a given database instance. A *repair* is a consistent database instance obtained by changing the given instance using a minimal set of insertions/deletions. Intuitively, consistent query answers are independent of the way the inconsistencies in the data would be resolved.

Example 1. Assume that an instance of the relation *Student* is as follows:

Name	*Address*
Smith	*Los Angeles*
Smith	*New York*
Jones	*Chicago*

Assume also that the functional dependency $Name \rightarrow Address$ is given. The above instance has two repairs: one obtained by deleting the first tuple, the other - by deleting the second tuple. A query asking for the address of *Jones* returns *Chicago* as a consistent answer because the third tuple is in both repairs. However, the query asking for the address of *Smith* has no consistent answers because the addresses in different repairs are different. On the other hand, the query asking for those people who live in *Los Angeles* or *New York* returns *Smith* as a consistent answer.

This conservative definition of consistent answers has one shortcoming: the number of repairs. Even for a single functional dependency, the number of repairs

E. Bertino et al. (Eds.): EDBT 2004, LNCS 2992, pp. 841–844, 2004.
© Springer-Verlag Berlin Heidelberg 2004

can be exponential in the number of tuples in the database [3]. Nevertheless, several practical mechanisms for the computation of consistent query answers *without computing all repairs* have been developed (see [5] for a survey): query rewriting [1], logic programs [2,4,9], and compact representations of repairs [6, 7]. The first is based on rewriting the input query Q into a query Q' such that the evaluation of Q' returns the set of consistent answers to Q. This method works only for SJD[1] queries in the presence of universal binary constraints. The second approach uses disjunctive logic programs to specify all repairs, and then with the help of a disjunctive LP system [8] finds the consistent answers to a given query. Although this approach is applicable to very general queries in the presence of universal constraints, the complexity of evaluating disjunctive logic programs makes this method impractical for large databases.

2 The System Hippo

The system Hippo is an implementation of the third approach. All information about integrity violations is stored in a *conflict hypergraph.* Every hyperedge connects the tuples violating together an integrity constraint.

Using the conflict hypergraph, we can find if a given tuple belongs to the set of consistent answers without constructing all repairs [6]. Because the conflict hypergraph has polynomial size, this method has polynomial data complexity and allows us to efficiently deal even with large databases [7]. Currently, our application computes consistent answers to SJUD queries in the presence of denial constraints (a class containing functional dependency constraints and exclusion constraints). Allowing union in the query language is crucial for being able to extract indefinite disjunctive information from an inconsistent database (see Example 1).

Future work includes the support for restricted foreign key constraints, universal tuple-generating dependencies and full PSJUD[2] queries. However, because computing consistent query answers for SPJ queries is co-NP-data-complete [3, 6], polynomial data complexity cannot be guaranteed once projection is allowed.

The whole system is implemented in Java as an RDBMS frontend. Hippo works with any RDBMS that can execute SQL queries, and provides a JDBC access interface (we use PostgreSQL). The data stored in the RDBMS needs not be altered.

The flow of data in Hippo is presented on Figure 1. Before processing any input query, the system performs *Conflict Detection* and creates *Conflict Hypergraph* for further usage. We are assuming that the number of conflicts is small enough for the hypergraph to be stored in main memory. The only output of this system is the *Answer Set* consisting of the consistent answers to the input

[1] When describing a query class, P stands for projection, S for selection, U for union, J for cartesian product, and D for difference.

[2] Currently, our application supports only those cases of projection that don't introduce existential quantifiers in the corresponding relational calculus query.

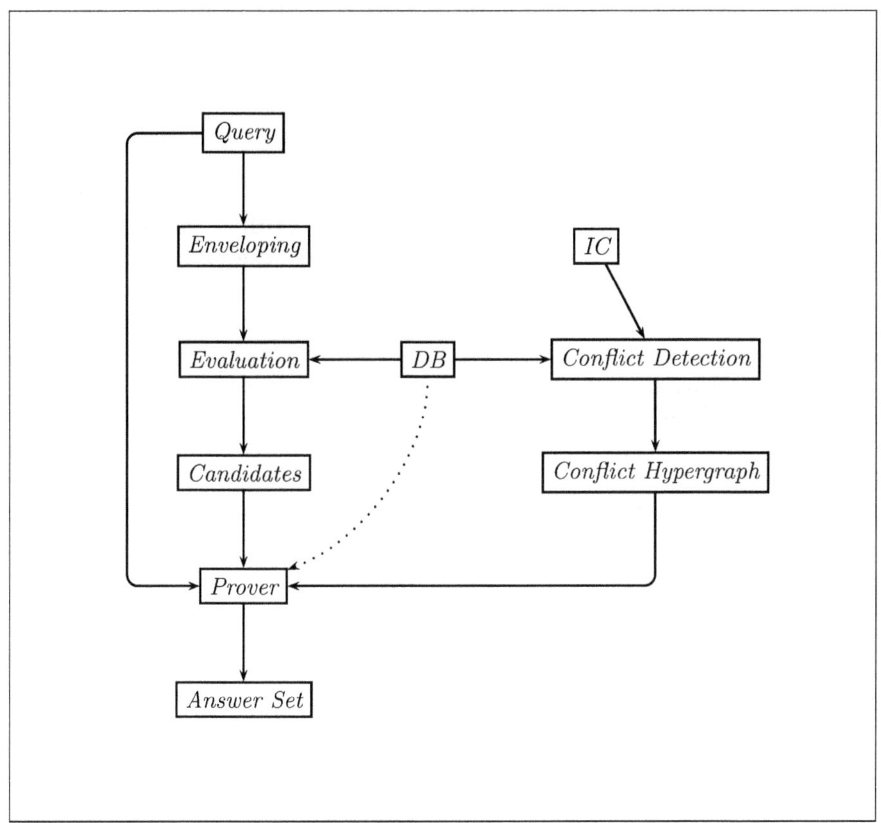

Fig. 1. Data flow in Hippo

Query in the database instance *DB* with respect to a set of integrity constraints *IC*.

The processing of the *Query* starts from *Enveloping*. As a result of this step we get a query defining *Candidates* (candidate consistent query answers). This query subsequently undergoes *Evaluation* by the RDBMS. For every tuple from the set of candidates, the system uses *Prover* to check if the tuple is a consistent answer to the *Query*. Depending on the result of this check, the tuple is either added to the *Answer Set* or not.

For every tuple that *Prover* processes, several membership checks have typically to be performed. In the base version of the system this is done by simply executing the appropriate membership queries on the database. This is a costly procedure and it has a significant influence on the overall time performance of the system. We have introduced several optimizations addressing this problem. In general, by modifying the expression defining the envelope (the set of candidates) the optimizations allow us to answer the required membership checks without executing any queries on the database. Also, using an expression selecting a subset of the set of consistent query answers, we can significantly reduce the number of tuples that have to be processed by *Prover*. A more detailed description of those techniques can be found in [7].

3 Demonstration

The presentation of the Hippo system will consist of three parts. First, we will demonstrate that using consistent query answers we can extract more information from an inconsistent database than in the approach where the input query is evaluated over the database from which the conflicting tuples have been removed. Secondly, we will show the advantages of our method over competing approaches by demonstrating the expressive power of supported queries and integrity constraints. And finally, we will compare the running times of our approach and the query rewriting approach, showing that our approach is more efficient. For every query being tested, we will also measure the execution time of this query by the RDBMS backend (it corresponds to the approach when we ignore the fact that the database is inconsistent). This will allow us to conclude that the time overhead of our approach is acceptable.

References

1. M. Arenas, L. Bertossi, and J. Chomicki. Consistent Query Answers in Inconsistent Databases. In *ACM Symposium on Principles of Database Systems (PODS)*, pages 68–79, 1999.
2. M. Arenas, L. Bertossi, and J. Chomicki. Answer Sets for Consistent Query Answering in Inconsistent Databases. *Theory and Practice of Logic Programming*, 3(4–5):393–424, 2003.
3. M. Arenas, L. Bertossi, J. Chomicki, X. He, V. Raghavan, and J. Spinrad. Scalar Aggregation in Inconsistent Databases. *Theoretical Computer Science*, 296(3):405–434, 2003.
4. P. Barcelo and L. Bertossi. Logic Programs for Querying Inconsistent Databases. In *International Symposium on Practical Aspects of Declarative Languages (PADL)*, pages 208–222. Springer-Verlag, LNCS 2562, 2003.
5. L. Bertossi and J. Chomicki. Query Answering in Inconsistent Databases. In J. Chomicki, R. van der Meyden, and G. Saake, editors, *Logics for Emerging Applications of Databases*. Springer-Verlag, 2003.
6. J. Chomicki and J. Marcinkowski. Minimal-Change Integrity Maintenance Using Tuple Deletions. Technical Report cs.DB/0212004, arXiv.org e-Print archive, December 2002. Under journal submission.
7. J. Chomicki, J. Marcinkowski, and S. Staworko. Computing Consistent Query Answers Using Conflict Hypergraphs. In preparation.
8. T. Eiter, W. Faber, N. Leone, and G. Pfeifer. Declarative Problem-Solving in DLV. In J. Minker, editor, *Logic-Based Artificial Intelligence*, pages 79–103. Kluwer, 2000.
9. G. Greco, S. Greco, and E. Zumpano. A Logical Framework for Querying and Repairing Inconsistent Databases. *IEEE Transactions on Knowledge and Data Engineering*, 15(6):1389–1408, 2003.

An Implementation of P3P Using Database Technology

Rakesh Agrawal, Jerry Kiernan, Ramakrishnan Srikant, and Yirong Xu

IBM Almaden Research Center
650 Harry Road, San Jose, CA 95120, USA
{ragrawal,kiernan,srikant}@almaden.ibm.com, xuyirong@cn.ibm.com
http://www.almaden.ibm.com/software/quest

1 Introduction

The privacy of personal information on the Internet has become a major concern for governments, businesses, media, and the public. Platform for Privacy Preferences (P3P), developed by the World Wide Web Consortium (W3C), is the most significant effort underway to enable web users to gain more control over their private information. P3P provides mechanisms for a web site to encode its data-collection and data-use practices in a standard XML format, known as a P3P policy [3], which can be programmatically checked against a user's privacy preferences.

This demonstration presents an implementation of the server-centric architecture for P3P proposed in [1]. The novel aspect of this implementation is that it makes use of the proven database technology, as opposed to the prevailing client-centric implementation based on specialized policy-preference matching engines. Not only does this implementation have qualitative advantages, our experiments indicate that it performs significantly better (15 - 30 times faster) than the sole public-domain client-centric implementation and that the latency introduced by preference matching is small enough (0.16 second on average) for real-world deployments of P3P [1].

2 Overview of P3P

The P3P protocol has two parts:

1. *Privacy Policies:* An XML format in which a web site can encode its data-collection and data-use practices [3]. For example, an online bookseller can publish a policy which states that it uses a customer's name and home phone number for telemarketing purpose, but that it does not release this information to external parties.
2. *Privacy Preferences:* An XML format for specifying privacy preferences and an algorithm for programmatically matching preferences against policies. The W3C APPEL working draft provides such a format and corresponding policy-preference matching algorithm [2]. For example, a privacy-conscious consumer may define a preference stating that she does not want retailers to use her personal information for telemarketing and product promotion.

E. Bertino et al. (Eds.): EDBT 2004, LNCS 2992, pp. 845–847, 2004.
© Springer-Verlag Berlin Heidelberg 2004

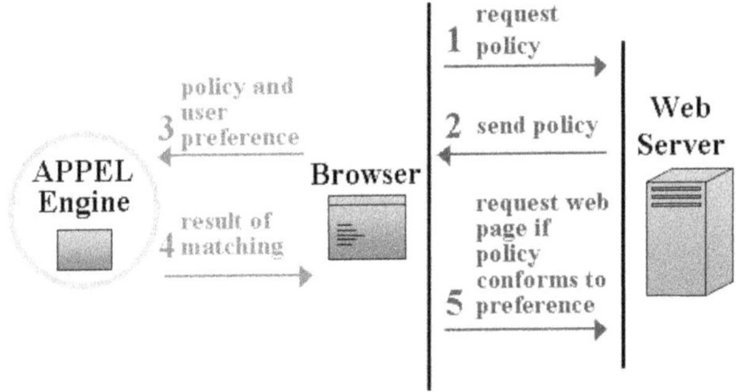

Fig. 1. Client-centric policy-preference matching

2.1 Client-Centric Implementation

A client-centric architecture for implementing P3P has been described in [4]. As a user browses a web site, the site's P3P policy is fetched to the client side. The policy is then checked by a specialized APPEL engine against the user's APPEL preference to see if the policy conforms to the preference (see Figure 1). There are two prominent implementations of this architecture: Microsoft IE6 and AT&T Privacy Bird.

2.2 Server-Centric Implementation

Figure 2 shows the server-centric architecture we have developed. A web site deploying P3P first installs its privacy policy in a database system. Then database querying is used for matching a user's privacy preference against privacy policies. The server-centric implementation has several advantages including: setting up the infrastructure necessary for ensuring that web sites act according to their stated policies, allowing P3P to be deployed in thin, mobile clients that are likely to dominate Internet access in the future, and allowing site owners to refine their policies based on the privacy preferences of their users.

3 Demonstration

Our implementation consists of both client and server components.

3.1 Client Components

We extend Microsoft Internet Explorer to invoke preference checking at the server before a web page is accessed. The IE extension allows a user to specify her privacy preference at different sensitivity levels. It invokes the preference checking by sending the preference to the server.

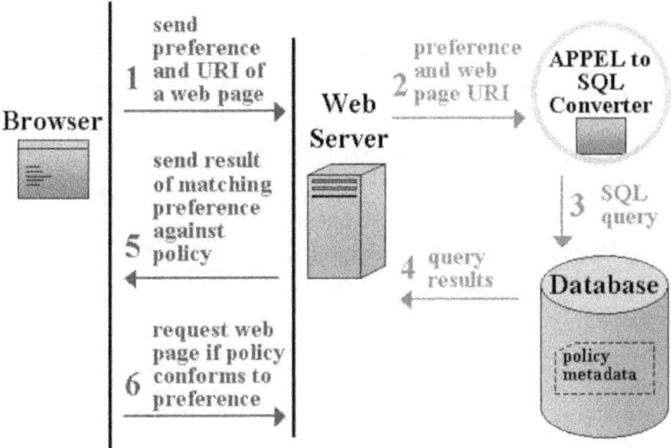

Fig. 2. Server-centric policy-preference matching

3.2 Server Components

We define a schema in DB2 for storing policy data in the relational tables. This schema contains a table for every element defined in the P3P policy. The tables are linked using foreign keys reflecting the XML structure of the policies. We extend IBM Tivoli Privacy Wizard (a web-based GUI tool for web site owners to define P3P policies) with the functionality of parsing and shredding P3P policies as a set of records in the database tables.

When the server receives the APPEL preference from the client, it translates the preference into SQL queries to be run against the policy tables. The SQL queries corresponding to the preference are submitted to the database engine. The result of the query evaluation yields the action to be taken. The evaluation result is sent back to the client. If the policy does not conform to the preference, the IE extension will block the web page and prompt a message to the user. Otherwise, the requested web page is displayed.

References

1. Rakesh Agrawal, Jerry Kiernan, Ramakrishnan Srikant, and Yirong Xu. Implementing P3P using database technology. In *19th Int'l Conference on Data Engineering*, Bangalore, India, March 2003.
2. Lorrie Cranor, Marc Langheinrich, and Massimo Marchiori. *A P3P Preference Exchange Language 1.0 (APPEL1.0).* W3C Working Draft, April 2002.
3. Lorrie Cranor, Marc Langheinrich, Massimo Marchiori, Martin Presler-Marshall, and Joseph Reagle. *The Platform for Privacy Preferences 1.0 (P3P1.0) Specification.* W3C Recommendation, April 2002.
4. The World Wide Web Consortium. *P3P 1.0: A New Standard in Online Privacy.* Available from `http://www.w3.org/P3P/brochure.html`.

XQBE: A Graphical Interface for XQuery Engines

Daniele Braga, Alessandro Campi, and Stefano Ceri

Politecnico di Milano
Piazza Leonardo da Vinci,32 - 20133 Milano, Italy
{braga,campi,ceri}@elet.polimi.it

Abstract. XQuery is increasingly popular among computer scientists with a SQL background, since queries in XQuery and SQL require comparable skills to be formulated. However, the number of these experts is limited, and the availability of easier XQuery "dialects" could be extremely valuable. Something similar happened with QBE, initially proposed as an alternative to SQL, that has then become popular as the user-friendly query language supported by MS Access. We designed and implemented XQBE, a *visual* dialect of XQuery that uses hierarchical structures, coherent with the hierarchical nature of XML, to denote the input and output documents.
Our demo consists of examples of queries in XQBE and shows how our prototype allows to switch between equivalent representations of the same query.

1 Introduction

The diffusion of XML sets a pressing need for providing the capability to query XML data to a wide spectrum of users, typically lacking in computer programming skills. This demonstration presents a user friendly interface, based on an intuitive visual query language (XQBE, *XQ*uery *B*y *E*xample), that we developed for this purpose, inspired by the QBE [2]. QBE showed that a visual interface to a query language is effective in supporting the intuitive formulation of queries when the basic graphical constructs are close to the visual abstraction of the underlying data model. Accordingly, while QBE is a relational query language, based on the representation of tables, XQBE is based on the use of annotated trees, to adhere to the hierarchical nature of XML. XQBE was designed with the objectives of being intuitive and easy to map directly to XQuery. Our interface is capable of generating the visual representation of many XQuery statements that belong to a subset of XQuery, defined by our translation algorithm (sketched later).

XQBE allows for arbitrarily deep nesting of XQuery FLWOR expressions, construction of new XML elements, and restructuring of existing documents. However, the expressive power of XQBE is limited in comparison with XQuery, which is Turing-complete. The particular purpose of XQBE makes *usability* one

E. Bertino et al. (Eds.): EDBT 2004, LNCS 2992, pp. 848–850, 2004.
© Springer-Verlag Berlin Heidelberg 2004

```
<bib>
 <book year="1994"> <title> TCP/IP Illustrated </title>
                    <author> <last> Stevens </last> <first> W. </first> </author>
                    <pub> Addison-Wesley </pub> <price> 65.95 </price> </book>
 <book year="2000"> <title> Data on the Web </title>
                    <author> <last> Abiteboul</last> <first> Serge </first> </author>
                    <author> <last> Buneman </last> <first> Peter </first> </author>
                    <author> <last> Suciu </last> <first> Dan </first> </author>
                    <pub> Morgan Kaufmann Publishers </pub> <price> 39.95 </price> </book>
</bib>
```

Fig. 1. A sample document (bib.xml)

of its critical success factors, and we considered this aspect during the whole design and implementation process. Still from a usability viewpoint, our prototype is a first step towards an integrated environment to support both XQuery and XQBE, where users alternate between the XQBE and XQuery representations.

2 XQuery by Example

XQBE is fully described in [1]. Here we only introduce its basics by means of the query (Q1) "*List books published by Addison-Wesley after 1991, including their year and title*", on the data in Figure 1. Its XQBE version is in Figure 2(a), while its XQuery version is

```
<bib> { for $b in document("bib.xml")/bib/book
        where $b/pub="Addison-Wesley" and $b/@year>1991
        return <book year="{ $b/@year }"> { $b/title } </book> } </bib>
```

A query is formed by a *source* part (on the left) and a *construct* part (on the right). Both parts contain labelled graphs that express properties of XML fragments: the source part describes the XML data to be matched, the construct part specifies which are to be retained. Correspondence between the two parts is expressed by explicit bindings. XML *elements* in the target are represented as labelled rectangles, their *attributes* as black circles (with the *name* on the arc), and their PCDATA as an empty circle. In the construct part, the paths that branch out of a bound node indicate which of its contents are to be retained. In Figure 2(a) the source part matches the `book` elements with a `year` greater than 1991 and a `publisher` equal to "Addison-Wesley". The binding edge between the `book` nodes states that the result shall contain *as many* `book` elements *as* those matched. The trapezoidal `bib` node means that all the generated `books` are to be contained into one `bib` element.

The translation process translates an XQBE query into a sentence of the XQuery subset defined by the grammar in figure 3.

The generated translation of Q1 is:

```
<bib> { for $book in doc("bib.xml")/bib/book
        where ( some $pub in $book/publisher/text() satisfies
                some $year in $book/@year satisfies $year>1991 and $pub="Addison-Wesley" )
        return <book> { $book/@year, $book/title } </book> } </bib>
```

It is also possible to obtain the XQBE version of an XQuery statement. The automatically generated XQBE version of Q1 is shown in Figure 2(b).

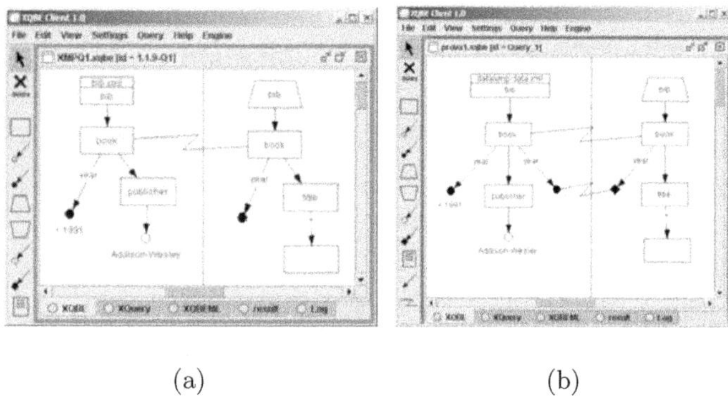

(a) (b)

Fig. 2. The XQBE version of Q1(a) and the automatically generated XQBE for Q1(b).

```
 [1] <query>          ::= <flwor_expr>|<startTag>'{'<query>'}'<endTag>|<emptyTag>|<const>
 [2] <flwor_expr>     ::= <for_clause> <where_clause>? <return_clause> <order_clause>?
 [3] <for_clause>     ::= 'for' <var_binding> ( ',' <var_binding> )*
 [4] <var_binding>    ::= <variable> 'in' <path_expr>
 [5] <where_clause>   ::= 'where' <ex_quantifiers>? '(' <conjunction> ')'
 [6] <ex_quantifier>  ::= 'some' <var_binding> ( ',' <var_binding> )* 'satisfies'
 [7] <conjunction>    ::= <atom_list>  |  <neg_clause>  |  <atom_list> 'and' <neg_clause>
 [8] <atom_list>      ::= <atom> ( 'and' <atom> )*
 [9] <atom>           ::= <pred_term>   |   'exists(' <path_expr> ')'
[10] <pred_term>      ::= <expression> <comparator> <expression>
[11] <expression>     ::= <const> | <variable> | <computation> | <aggregate>
[12] <comparator>     ::= '='  |  '<'  |  '>'  |  '<='  | '>='  |  '!='
[13] <neg_clause>     ::= 'not(' <ex_quantifier>* '(' <atom_list> '))'
[14] <return_clause>  ::= 'return'( <emptyTag> | <variable> | <computation> | <aggregate>) |
                          'return' <startTag> <projection_list> <endTag>
[15] <project_list>   ::= <startTag> <project_list> <endTag> <project_list> |
                          '{'<path_expr>'}'<project_list>|'{'<flwor_expr>'}'<project_list> |
[16] <order_clause>   ::= 'order by (' <name> ( ',' <name> )* ')'
```

Fig. 3. EBNF specification of the XQuery subset expressible with XQBE

3 Conclusions

The contribution of our work is the availability of an environment in which users can query XML data with a GUI, access the generated XQuery statement, and also visualize the XQBE version of a large class of XQuery statements. Moreover they can modify any of the representations and observe the changes in the other representation.

References

1. D. Braga and A. Campi. A graphical environment to query xml data with xquery. In *Proc. of the 4th WISE*, Roma (Italy), December 2003.
2. M. M. Zloof. Query-by-example: A data base language. *IBM Systems Journal*, 1977.

P2P-DIET: One-Time and Continuous Queries in Super-Peer Networks

Stratos Idreos, Manolis Koubarakis, and Christos Tryfonopoulos

Dept. of Electronic and Computer Engineering
Technical University of Crete, GR73100 Chania, Greece
{sidraios,manolis,trifon}@intelligence.tuc.gr

1 Introduction

In peer-to-peer (P2P) systems a very large number of autonomous computing nodes (the *peers*) pool together their resources and rely on each other for *data* and *services*. P2P systems are application level *virtual* or *overlay networks* that have emerged as a natural way to share data and resources. The main application scenario considered in recent P2P data sharing systems is that of *one-time querying*: a user poses a query (e.g., "I want music by Moby") and the system returns a list of pointers to matching files owned by various peers in the network. Then, the user can go ahead and download files of interest. The complementary scenario of *selective dissemination of information (SDI)* or *selective information push* is also very interesting. In an SDI scenario, a user posts a *continuous query* to the system to receive notifications whenever certain *resources* of interest appear in the system (e.g., when a song of Moby becomes available). SDI can be as useful as one-time querying in many target applications of P2P networks ranging from file sharing, to more advanced applications such as alert systems for digital libraries, e-commerce networks etc.

At the Intelligent Systems Laboratory of the Technical University of Crete, we have recently concentrated on the problem of SDI in P2P networks in the context of project DIET (`http://www.dfki.de/diet`). Our work, summarized in [3], has culminated in the implementation of P2P-DIET, a service that unifies one-time and continuous query processing in P2P networks with super-peers. P2P-DIET is a direct descendant of DIAS, a Distributed Information Alert System for digital libraries, that was presented in [4]. P2P-DIET combines one-time querying as found in other super-peer networks and SDI as proposed in DIAS. P2P-DIET has been implemented on top of the open source DIET Agents Platform (`http://diet-agents.sourceforge.net/`) and it is available at `http://www.intelligence.tuc.gr/p2pdiet`.

2 The System P2P-DIET

A high-level view of the P2P-DIET architecture is shown in Figure 1(a) and a layered view in Figure 1(b). There are two kinds of nodes: *super-peers* and *clients*. All super-peers are equal and have the same responsibilities, thus the

E. Bertino et al. (Eds.): EDBT 2004, LNCS 2992, pp. 851–853, 2004.
© Springer-Verlag Berlin Heidelberg 2004

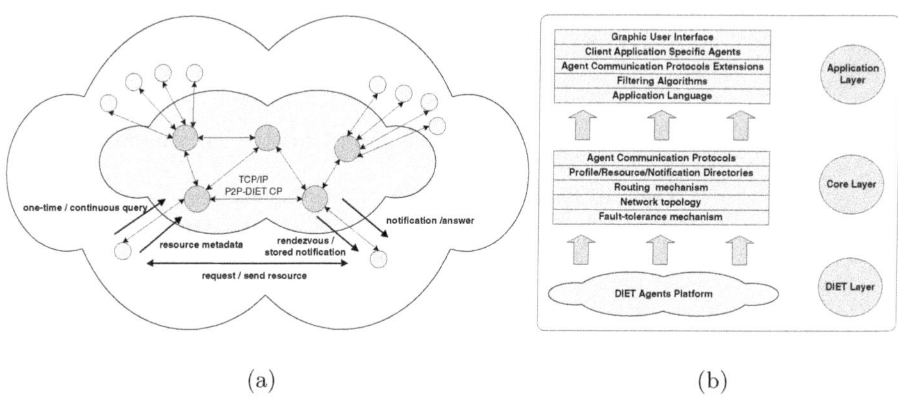

(a) (b)

Fig. 1. The architecture and the layered view of P2P-DIET

super-peer subnetwork is a *pure* P2P network. Each super-peer serves a fraction of the clients and keeps *indices* on the resources of those clients.

Clients can run on user computers. Resources (e.g., files in a file-sharing application) are kept at client nodes, although it is possible in special cases to store resources at super-peer nodes. Clients are equal to each other only in terms of download. Clients download resources directly from the resource owner client. A client is connected to the network through a single super-peer node, which is the *access point* of the client. It is not necessary for a client to be connected to the same access point continuously since *client migration* is supported in P2P-DIET. Clients can connect, disconnect or even leave from the system silently at any time. To enable a higher degree of decentralization and dynamicity, we also allow clients to use *dynamic IP addresses. Routing* of queries (one-time or continuous) is implemented using *minimum weight spanning trees* for the super-peer subnetwork. After connecting to the network, a client may *publish* resources by sending resource metadata to its access point, *post an one-time query* to discover matching resources or *subscribe* with a continuous query to be notified when resources of interest are published in the future. A user may *download* a file at the time that he receives a notification, or save it in his *saved notifications folder* for future use. Additionally a client can download a resource even when he has *migrated* to another access point. The feature of *stored notifications* guarantees that notifications matching disconnected users will be delivered to them upon connection. If a resource owner is disconnected, the interested client may arrange a *rendezvous* with the resource. P2P-DIET also offers the ability to add or remove super-peers. Additionally, it supports a simple fault-tolerance protocol based on *are-you-alive* messages. Finally, P2P-DIET provides message authentication and message encryption. For the detailed protocols see [5].

The current implementation of P2P-DIET to be demonstrated supports the model $\mathcal{AWP}$ [4] and it is currently been extended to support $\mathcal{AWPS}$ [4]. Each super-peer utilises efficient query processing algorithms based on indexing of resource metadata and queries and a hierarchical organisation of queries (poset) that captures query subsumption as in [1]. A sophisticated index that exploits commonalities between continuous queries is maintained at each super-peer, enabling the quick identification of the continuous queries that match incoming resource metadata. In this area, our work extends and improves the indexing algorithms of SIFT [6] and it is reported in [2].

References

1. A. Carzaniga and D.S. Rosenblum and A.L. Wolf. Design and evaluation of a wide-area event notification service. *ACM Transactions on Computer Systems*, 19(3):332–383, August 2001.
2. C. Tryfonopoulos and M. Koubarakis. Selective Dissemination of Information in P2P Networks: Data Models, Query Languages, Algorithms and Computational Complexity. Technical Report TUC-ISL-02-2003, Intelligent Systems Laboratory, Dept. of Electronic and Computer Engineering, Technical University of Crete, July 2003.
3. M. Koubarakis and C. Tryfonopoulos and S. Idreos and Y. Drougas. Selective Information Dissemination in P2P Networks: Problems and Solutions. *ACM SIGMOD Record, Special issue on Peer-to-Peer Data Management, K. Aberer (editor)*, 32(3), September 2003.
4. M. Koubarakis and T. Koutris and C. Tryfonopoulos and P. Raftopoulou . Information Alert in Distributed Digital Libraries: The Models, Languages and Architecture of DIAS. In *Proceedings of the 6th European Conference on Research and Advanced Technology for Digital Libraries (ECDL 2002)*, volume 2458 of *Lecture Notes in Computer Science*, pages 527–542, September 2002.
5. S. Idreos and M. Koubarakis. P2P-DIET: A Query and Notification Service Based on Mobile Agents for Rapid Implementation of P2P Applications. Technical Report TUC-ISL-01-2003, Intelligent Systems Laboratory, Dept. of Electronic and Computer Engineering, Technical University of Crete, June 2003.
6. T.W. Yan and H. Garcia-Molina. Index structures for selective dissemination of information under the boolean model. *ACM Transactions on Database Systems*, 19(2):332–364, 1994.

HEAVEN
A Hierarchical Storage and Archive Environment for Multidimensional Array Database Management Systems

Bernd Reiner and Karl Hahn

FORWISS (Bavarian Research Center for Knowledge Based Systems)
Technical University Munich
Boltzmannstr. 3, D-85747 Garching b. München, Germany
{reiner,hahnk}@forwiss.tu-muenchen.de

Abstract. The intention of this paper is to present HEAVEN, a solution of intelligent management of large-scale datasets held on tertiary storage systems. We introduce the common state of the art technique storage and retrieval of large spatio-temporal array data in the *High Performance Computing* (HPC) area. An identified major bottleneck today is fast and efficient access to and evaluation of high performance computing results. We address the necessity of developing techniques for efficient retrieval of requested subsets of large datasets from mass storage devices. Furthermore, we show the benefit of managing large spatio-temporal data sets, e.g. generated by simulations of climate models, with *Database Management Systems* (DMBS). This means DBMS need a smart connection to tertiary storage systems with optimized access strategies. HEAVEN is based on the multidimensional array DBMS RasDaMan.

1 Introduction

Large-scale scientific experiments often generate large amounts of multidimensional data sets. Data volume may reach hundreds of terabytes (up to petabytes). Typically, these data sets are stored as files permanently in an archival mass storage system on up to thousands of magnetic tapes. The access times and/or transfer times of these kinds of tertiary storage devices, even if robotically controlled, are relatively slow. Nevertheless, tertiary storage systems are currently the common state of the art storing such large volumes of data. Concerning data access in HPC area the main disadvantages are high access latency compared to hard disk devices and to have no direct access. A major bottleneck for scientific application is the missing possibility of accessing specific subsets of data. If only a subset of such a large data set is required, the whole file must be transferred from tertiary storage media. Taking into account the time required to load, search, read, rewind and unload several cartridges, it can take many hours/days to retrieve a subset of interest from a large data set. Entire files must be loaded from the magnetic tape, even if only a subset of the file is needed for a further processing. The processing with data across a multitude of data sets, for example, time slices is hard to support. Evaluation of search criteria requires network transfer of each required data set, implying sometimes a prohibitively immense

E. Bertino et al. (Eds.): EDBT 2004, LNCS 2992, pp. 854–857, 2004.
© Springer-Verlag Berlin Heidelberg 2004

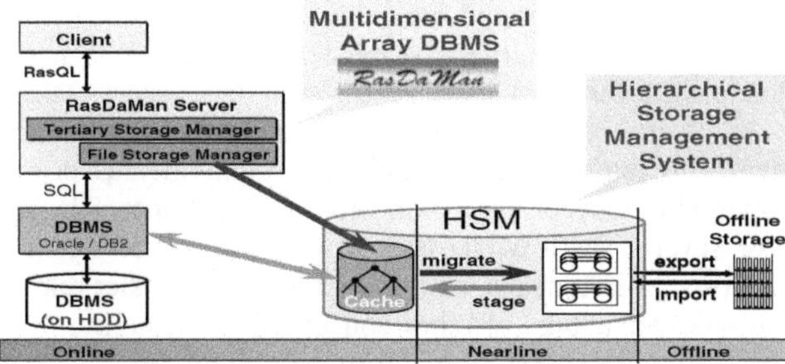

Fig. 1. HEAVEN system architecture

amount of data to be shipped. Hence, many interesting and important evaluations currently are impossible. Another disadvantage is that access to data sets is done on an inadequate semantic level. Applications accessing HPC data have to deal with directories, file names, and data formats instead of accessing multidimensional data in terms of simulation space or time interval. Examples of large-scale HPC data are climate-modeling simulations, cosmological experiments and atmospheric data transmitted by satellites. Such natural phenomena can be modeled as spatio-temporal array data of some specific dimensionality. Their common characteristic is that a huge amount of *Multidimensional Discrete Data* (MDD) has to be stored. For overcoming the above mentioned shortcomings and for providing flexible data management of spatio-temporal data we implemented HEAVEN (*Hierarchical Storage and Archive Environment for Multidimensional Array Database Management Systems*).

2 HEAVEN System Architecture

HEAVEN combines the advantages of storing big amounts of data and the realization of efficient data access and management with DBMS. This means the DBMS must be extended with easy to use functionalities to automatically store and retrieve data to/from tertiary storage systems without user interaction. We implemented such intelligent concepts and integrated it into the kernel of the first commercial multidimensional array DBMS RasDaMan (*Raster Data Management*). RasDaMan is specially designed for generic multidimensional array data of arbitrary size and dimensionality.

Fig. 1 depicts the architecture of the extended RasDaMan system (client/server architecture with the conventional DBMS) with tertiary storage connection. We realize the tertiary storage support by connecting a *Hierarchical Storage Management* (HSM) System with RasDaMan. Such HSM-Systems have been developed to manage tertiary storage archive systems and can handle thousands of tertiary storage media. The virtual file system of HSM-Systems is separated into a limited cache on which the user works (load or store his data) and a tertiary storage system with robot controlled tape libraries. The HSM-System automatically migrates or stages data to or from the tertiary storage media, if necessary. For realizing the retrieval of subsets of large data sets (MDDs) RasDaMan stores MDDs subdivided into sub-arrays (called tiles). Detailed information about tiling can be found in [1, 3, 5]. Tiles are in RasDaMan the smallest unit of data access. The size of tiles (32 KByte to 640 KByte) is optimized for main memory and hard disk access. Those tile sizes are much too small for data sets held on tertiary storage media [2]. It is necessary to choose different granularities for hard disk access and tape access, because they differ significantly in their access characteristics (random vs. sequential access). A promising idea is to introduce additional data granularity as provided by the new developed Super-Tile concept. The main goal of the Super-Tile concept is a smart combination of several small MDD tiles to one Super-Tile for minimizing tertiary storage access costs. Smart means, exploiting the good transfer rate of tertiary storage devices, and to take advantage of other concepts like clustering of data. Super-Tiles are the access (import/export) granularity of MDD on tertiary storage media. Extensive tests have shown that a Super-Tile size of about 150 MByte shows good performance characteristics in most cases. The retrieval of data stored on hard disk or on tertiary storage media is transparent for the user. Only the access time is higher if data stored on tertiary storage media. Three further strategies for reducing tertiary storage access time are clustering, query scheduling and caching. Please find more information in [4].

3 Demonstration

We will demonstrate HEAVEN using the visual front-end RView, to interactively submit RasQL (*RasDaMan query language*) queries and display result sets containing 1-D to 4-D data. For demonstrating tertiary storage access we will use our own developed HSM-System with a connected SCSI DDS-4 tape drive. Demonstration will start by showing sample retrieval, thereby introducing basic RasQL concepts. Queries will encompass both, search and array manipulation operations. We will show typical access cases like retrieval of subsets and data access across a multitude of objects. Furthermore, performance comparison of DBMS cache area access, HSM cache access, HSM tape access and traditional access will be presented. Next, selected queries will serve to demonstrate the effect of several optimization concepts, like inter and intra Super-Tile clustering. Also performance improvements regarding query scheduling and caching algorithms will be shown. This allows discussing, how they contribute to overall performance. Finally, implications of physical data organization within RasDaMan (tiling strategies) and on tertiary storage media (Super-Tile concept) will be presented. Queries such as sub-cube extraction and cuts along different space axes indicate strengths and weaknesses of particular tiling and Super-Tile schemata. Various tiling strategies are offered as a database tuning possibility similar to indexes for optimal query performance.

References

1. Chen L. T., Drach R., Keating M., Louis S., Rotem D., Shoshani A.: Efficient organization and access of multi-dimensional datasets on tertiary storage, Information Systems, vol. 20, no. 2, p. 155-183, 1995
2. Chen L. T., Rotem D., Shoshani A., Drach R.: Optimizing Tertiary Storage Organization and Access for Spatio-Temporal Datasets, NASA Goddard Conf. on MSS, 1995

3. Furtado P. A., Baumann P.: Storage of Multidimensional Arrays Based on Arbitrary Tiling, Proc. of the ICDE, p. 480-489, 1999
4. Reiner B., Hahn K., Höfling G.: Hierarchical Storage Support and Management for Large-Scale Multidimensional Array Database Management Systems, DEXA conference, 2002
5. Sarawagi S., Stonebraker M.: Efficient Organization of Large Multidimensional Arrays, Proc. of Int. Conf. On Data Engineering, volume 10, p. 328-336, 1994

OGSA-DQP: A Service for Distributed Querying on the Grid

M. Nedim Alpdemir[1], Arijit Mukherjee[2], Anastasios Gounaris[1], Norman W. Paton[1], Paul Watson[2], Alvaro A.A. Fernandes[1], and Desmond J. Fitzgerald[1]

[1] Department of Computer Science
University of Manchester
Oxford Road, Manchester M13 9PL
United Kingdom
[2] School of Computing Science
University of Newcastle upon Tyne
Newcastle upon Tyne NE1 7RU
United Kingdom

Abstract. OGSA-DQP is a distributed query processor exposed to users as an Open Grid Services Architecture (OGSA)-compliant Grid service. This service supports the compilation and evaluation of queries that combine data obtained from multiple services on the Grid, including Grid Database Services (GDSs) and computational web services. Not only does OGSA-DQP support integrated access to multiple Grid services, it is itself implemented as a collection of interacting Grid services. OGSA-DQP illustrates how Grid service orchestrations can be used to perform complex, data-intensive parallel computations. The OGSA-DQP prototype is downloadable from www.ogsadai.org.uk/dqp/. This demonstration aims to illustrate the capabilities of OGSA-DQP prototype via a GUI Client over a collection of bioinformatics databases and analysis tools.

1 Distributed Query Processing on the Grid

Both commercial and scientific applications increasingly require access to distributed resources. Grid technologies have been introduced to facilitate efficient sharing of resources in a heterogeneous distributed environment. Service-oriented architectures are perceived to offer a convenient paradigm for resource sharing through resource virtualisation, and the Open Grid Services Architecture/Infrastructure (OGSA/OGSI) [4] is emerging as the standard approach to providing a service-oriented view of Grid computing. Taken together, these developments have highlighted the need for middleware that provides developers of user-level functionalities with a more abstract view of Grid technologies.

From its inception, Grid computing has provided mechanisms for data access that lie at a much lower level than those provided by commercial database technology. However, data in the Grid is likely to be at least as complex as that

E. Bertino et al. (Eds.): EDBT 2004, LNCS 2992, pp. 858–861, 2004.
© Springer-Verlag Berlin Heidelberg 2004

found in current commercial environments. Thus, high-level data access and integration services are needed if applications that have large amounts of data with complex structure and complex semantics are to benefit from the Grid.

2 OGSA-DQP

OGSA-DQP [1] is essentially a high-throughput distributed data-flow engine that relies on a service-oriented abstraction of grid resources and assumes that data sources are accessible through service-based interfaces. OGSA-DQP delivers a framework that

- supports declarative queries over *Grid Database Services* (GDSs) and over other web services available on the Grid, thereby combining data access with analysis;
- adapts techniques from parallel databases to provide implicit parallelism for complex data-intensive requests;
- automates complex, onerous, expert configuration and resource utilisation decisions on behalf of users via query optimisation;
- uses the emerging standard for GDSs to provide consistent access to database metadata and to interact with databases on the Grid; and
- uses the facilities of the OGSA to dynamically obtain the resources necessary for efficient evaluation of a distributed query.

OGSA-DQP uses the reference implementation of OGSA/OGSI, viz., Globus Toolkit 3 (GT3) [3], which implements a service-based architecture over virtualised resources referred to as Grid Services (GSs). OGSA-DQP also builds upon the reference implementation of the GGF Database Access and Integration Services (DAIS) standard, viz., OGSA-DAI [2].

OGSA-DQP provides two services to fulfil its functions: The *Grid Distributed Query Service (GDQS)* and the *Grid Query Evaluation Service (GQES)*. The GDQS provides the primary interaction interfaces for the user, collects the necessary metadata and acts as a coordinator between the underlying query compiler/optimiser engine and the GQES instances. GQES instances are created and scheduled dynamically, to evaluate the partitions of a query constructed by the optimiser of the GDQS.

3 The Demonstration

The demonstration illustrates, using a GUI Client, how OGSA-DQP can be employed to orchestrate distributed services for achieving data retrieval and data analysis in a single framework via a declarative query language. The demonstration set-up consists of three distributed database servers, two of which are located in Manchester, UK, and one of which is located in Newcastle, UK. In addition, a analysis web service is deployed on a server in Manchester. It is, however, possible to extend the set of resources with other available data sources

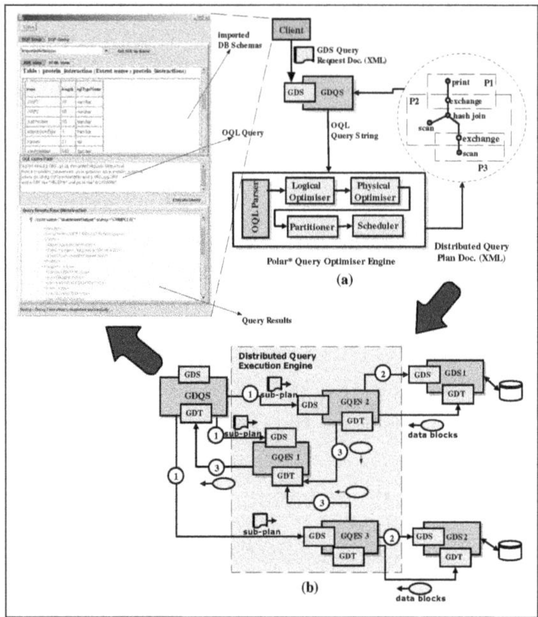

Fig. 1. Execution of a Query

and web services if required. The client is implemented in Java and accesses the GDQS via SOAP.

The demonstration shows that a typical query session using OGSA-DQP starts with a set-up phase where the client submits a list of resources (i.e. data resources and web services) that are anticipated to be required for subsequent OQL queries. The demonstration then illustrates that a query session can continue with multiple query requests to the same GDQS instance. As illustrated in Figure 1 (a), for each request a GDQS instance compiles, optimises, partitions and schedules the query to generate a distributed query plan optimised for specific requirements of the submitted query. It then commands the creation of GQESs as stipulated by the partitioning and scheduling decided on by the compiler (Figure 1 (b), interaction 1), and co-ordinates the GQESs into executing the plan, which effectively constructs a tree-like data flow system with the GDQS instance at the root, GDS instances at the leaf and a collection of GQESs in the middle (Figure 1 (b), interactions 2-3).

Acknowledgements. The work reported in this paper has been supported by the UK e-Science Programme through the OGSA-DAI and DAIT projects, the myGrid project, and by the UK EPSRC grant GR/R51797/01. We are grateful for that support.

References

1. M. Alpdemir, A. Mukherjee, N. W. Paton, P. Watson, A. A. Fernandes, A. Gounaris, and J. Smith. Service-based distributed querying on the grid. In *to appear in the Proceedings of the First International Conference on Service Oriented Computing.* Springer, 2003.
2. A. Anjomshoaa et al. The design and implementation of grid database services in ogsa-dai. In S. J. Cox, editor, *Proceedings of UK e-Science All Hands Meeting Nottingham.* EPSRC, 2–4 September 2003.
3. T. Sandholm and J. Gawor. Globus Toolkit 3 Core - A Grid Service Container Framework. Technical report, 2003. www-unix.globus.org/toolkit/3.0/ogsa/docs/.
4. S. Tuecke et al. Open Grid Service Infrastructure (OGSI). Technical report, OGSI-WG, Global Grid Forum, 2003. Version 1.0.

T-Araneus: Management of Temporal Data-Intensive Web Sites

Paolo Atzeni and Pierluigi Del Nostro

Dipartimento di Informatica e Automazione — Università Roma Tre
{atzeni,pdn}@dia.uniroma3.it

Abstract. T-Araneus is a tool for the generation of Web sites with special attention to temporal aspects. It is based on the use of high-level models throughout the design process, and specifically on a logical model for temporal Web sites, T-ADM, which allows the definition of page-schemes with temporal aspects.

1 Introduction

The effective support to the management of time has received a lot of attention in the database community leading to the notion of temporal database (Jensen and Snodgrass [1]). The need for an analogous support arises also in Web sites, as time is relevant from many points of view: from the history of data in pages to the date of last update of a page, from the access to previous versions of a page to the navigation over a site at a specific past date. Indeed, most current sites do handle very little time-related information, with histories difficult to reconstruct and often past versions not even available.

We believe that the management of time in Web sites can be effectively supported by leveraging on the experiences made in the above mentioned area of temporal databases with the ideas related to model-based development of Web sites. These were developed by various authors, including Atzeni et al. [2, 3], Ceri et al. [4], which both propose logical models in a sort of traditional database sense, so that sites can be described by means of schemes and can be obtained by applying suitable algebraic transformations to data in a database.

Our goal is to extend the experiences in the Araneus project [2,3] in order to propose a tool, called T-Araneus, which supports the development of temporal data-intensive Web sites. We now have a first version referring to temporal aspects of the content and to valid time. Future extensions will consider additional degrees of change as well as the interaction with a Content Management System handling the updates.

2 Backgound: The Araneus Models and Methodology

The Araneus approach [3] is focused on data-intensive web sites and it proposes a design process (with an associated tool) that leads to a completely automatic

E. Bertino et al. (Eds.): EDBT 2004, LNCS 2992, pp. 862–864, 2004.
© Springer-Verlag Berlin Heidelberg 2004

generation of the site extracting data from a database. Models are used to represent the intensional features of the sites from various points of view: (i) the Entity Relationship (ER) model is used to describe the data of interest at the conceptual level, (ii) a "navigational" variant of the ER model (N-ER) is used to describe a conceptual scheme for the site (with major nodes, called macroentities, and navigation paths), and (iii) a logical scheme for the site is defined using the Araneus Data Model (ADM), in terms of page schemes, which represent common features of pages of the same "type" with possibly nested attributes, whose values can be text, numbers, images or links to other pages. The design methodology [2], supported by a tool called Homer, leads to the automatic generation of the actual code for pages with access to a relational database built in a natural way from the ER scheme.

3 Management of Temporal Aspects

The tool we are proposing here handles temporal aspects in each of the models, by means of features that are coherent with the focus of the phase of the development process the model is used in.

Let us start by briefly illustrating the temporal features available in ADM, as this is the main goal of the design process. T-ADM, the temporal extension of ADM, includes the possibility of distinguishing between temporal and non-temporal page schemes, and, for each page scheme, the distinction between temporal and non-temporal attributes; since the model is nested, this distinction is allowed at various levels in nesting. Temporal pages and attributes can have additional pieces of information attached, including the following:

- LAST MODIFIED: the date (at the granularity of interest) of the last change;
- VALIDITY INTERVAL: the interval during which the element is/was valid;
- VERSIONS: a link to a page containing all the versions of the element;
- TIME POINT SELECTOR: a means to access the version valid at a certain instant.

A special page scheme, called VERSION LIST, is also provided to be referred by VERSIONS attributes and to be used to contain links to the various versions.

The other models used in the design process require only higher-level temporal features, following proposals in the literature (Gregersen and Jensen [5]). The temporal ER model allows the designer to specify which are the entities, the relationships, and the attributes to be considered as temporal. Similarly, the temporal N-ER model allows the indication of the temporal macroentities and navigation paths.

4 The T-Araneus Methodology and Tool

The best way to see how our tool supports the designer is to refer to its original, non-temporal version: a "snapshot" site is a special case of a temporal site where all elements are non-temporal. Also, we can see a temporal site as the "extension" or evolution of a snapshot site.

In the conceptual design phase, after the definition of the ER scheme, the temporal features are added, by indicating which are the entities, relationships and attributes for which the temporal evolution is of interest. This (beside being the input to the subsequent phases, to be discussed shortly) causes the generation of a relational database with the needed temporal features.

The hypertext conceptual design phase requires the specification of the temporal features over hypertext nodes (macroentities) and paths. In the N-ER model a macroentity is considered to be temporal if it includes temporal elements from the T-ER model. The main decisions in this phase are related to the facets of interest from the temporal point of view, including the choice among alternatives, such as (i) the last version with a timestamp; (ii) versions at a given granularity; (iii) all versions.

The logical design of the site, with the goal of producing the actual T-ADM scheme, is based on the choices made in the previous phases. The decisions here mainly concern the organization of the temporal attributes for which versioning has been chosen in the previous phase. There are various alternatives:

1. All versions in the same page, each of which with the validity interval.
2. The current value, possibly with a LAST MODIFIED attribute, in the page scheme, with a VERSIONS attribute that points to a VERSION LIST page scheme. A VALIDITY INTERVAL attribute can be attached to each temporal value.
3. A time point selection: the page will show all attribute values where the validity interval include the time point. Constant attributes will always be presented. The validity interval can be shown using the VALIDITY INTERVAL attribute.

At the end of the design process, the tool can be used to generate the actual site, which can be static (plain HTML) or dynamic (JSP); actually, some of the features (such as the time point selector) are allowed only in the dynamic environment.

References

1. Jensen, C., Snodgrass, R.: Temporal data management. IEEE Transactions on Knowledge and Data Engineering **11** (1999) 36–44
2. Atzeni, P., Merialdo, P., Mecca, G.: Data-intensive web sites: Design and maintenance. World Wide Web **4** (2001) 21–47
3. Merialdo, P., Atzeni, P., Mecca, G.: Design and development of data-intensive web sites: The araneus approach. ACM Trans. Inter. Tech. **3** (2003) 49–92
4. Ceri, S., Fraternali, P., Bongio, A., Brambilla, M., Comai, S., Matera, M.: Designing Data-Intensive Web Applications. Morgan Kauffman, Los Altos (2002)
5. Gregersen, H., Jensen, C.: Temporal entity-relationship models—a survey. IEEE Transactions on Knowledge and Data Engineering **11** (1999) 464–497

τ-Synopses: A System for Run-Time Management of Remote Synopses

Yossi Matias and Leon Portman

School of Computer Science, Tel Aviv University
matias@cs.tau.ac.il, leonpo@cs.tau.ac.il

Abstract. τ-Synopses is a system designed to provide a run-time environment for remote execution of various synopses. It enables easy registration of new synopses from remote platforms, after which the system can manage these synopses, including triggering their construction, rebuild and update, and invoking them for approximate query processing. The system captures and analyzes query workloads, enabling its registered synopses to significantly boost their effectiveness (efficiency, accuracy, confidence), by exploiting workload information for synopses construction and update. The system can also serve as a research platform for experimental evaluation and comparison of different synopses.

Data synopses are concise representations of data sets, that enable effective processing of approximate queries to the data sets. Recent increased interest in approximate query processing and in effectively dealing with massive data sets resulted with a proliferation of new synopses addressing new problems as well as proposed alternatives to previously suggested synopses.

For both operational and research purposes, it would be advantageous to have a system that can accommodate *multiple synopses*, and have an easy way to integrate new synopses and manage them. The multiple synopses could be placed in remote locations for various reasons: they may be implemented on different types of platforms, they may be summarizing remote data whose transfer is undesirable or impossible due to performance or security constraints, and it would be beneficial to share the load of operating a large number of synopses using different systems for load balancing and redundancy reasons.

Motivated by the above, the τ-Synopses system was designed to provide a run-time environment for remote execution of various synopses. It enables easy registration of new synopses from remote SOAP-enabled platforms, after which the system can manage these synopses, including triggering their construction, rebuild and update, and invoking them for approximate query processing. The system captures and analyzes query workloads, enabling its registered synopses to significantly boost their effectiveness (efficiency, accuracy, confidence), by exploiting workload information for synopses construction and update. The system can serve as a research platform for experimental evaluation and comparison of different synopses.

The τ-Synopses system is independent, and can work with data sources such as existing relational or other database systems. It supports two types of users:

E. Bertino et al. (Eds.): EDBT 2004, LNCS 2992, pp. 865–867, 2004.
© Springer-Verlag Berlin Heidelberg 2004

synopses providers who register their synopses within the system, and end-users who submit queries to the system. The system administrator defines the available data sources and provides general administration.

When a new synopsis is registered, the relevant data set and the supported queries are defined. A query submitted to the system is executed using the appropriate synopsis, based on the registration and other information. The result is returned to the user or optionally processed by other modules in the system. The system transforms updated data from its original datasource to be consistent with the format known to the synopses, so that synopses are not required to support any data transformation functionality or database connectivity logic. Any relational database or even real-time data providers can be data sources in the system.

Workload information is recorded by the system and becomes available to the registered workload-sensitive synopses.

The τ-Synopses system has the following key features:

- *multiple synopses*: The system can accommodate various types of synopses. New synopses can be added with their defined functionalities.
- *pluggable integration*: For integration purposes, a synopsis has to implement a simple interface, regardless of its internal implementation. By utilizing a light-weight host provided by the system, the synopsis can be executed on any SOAP-enabled platform.
- *remote execution*: Synopses can be transparently executed on remote machines, over TCP/IP or HTTP protocols, within local area networks or over the internet.
- *managed synopses*: The system allocates resources to synopses, triggers their construction and maintenance, selects appropriate synopses for execution, and provides all required data to the various synopses.
- *workload support*: Workload is captured, maintained and analyzed in a centralized location, and made available to the various synopses for construction and maintenance.
- *research platform*: The system provides a single, consistent source of data, training and test workload for experimental comparison and benchmarking, as well as performance measurements. It can therefore serve as an effective research platform for comparing different synopses without re-implementing them.

The core of the τ-Synopses system architecture features the following components, and depicted in Figure 1: Query Execution Engine, Synopses Manager, Updates Logger, and Workload Manager. In addition, the system includes a query-application which is used by end-users, an administration-application used by the administrator and by synopses-providers (not displayed), and a pool of registered synopses.

The Synopses Manager is used for registration and maintenance of the synopses. A new synopsis is added to the system by registering its parameters (including a list of supported queries and data sets) in the Synopses Manager Catalog.

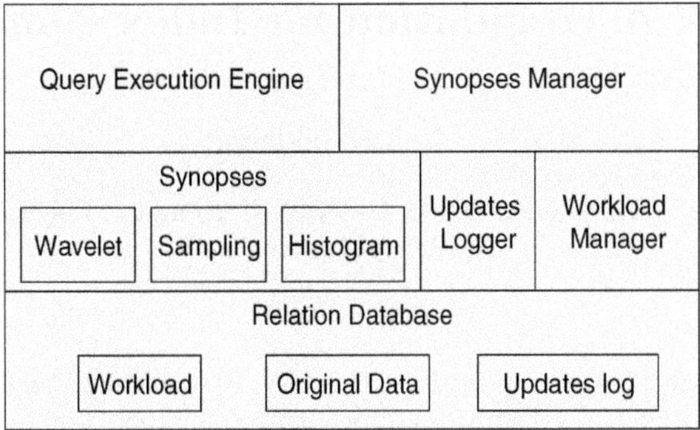

Fig. 1. Synopses Framework Architecture

The Query Execution Engine provides interface for receiving a query request from end-users and invoking the appropriate synopsis (or synopses), as determined by the Synopses Manager in order to process such query.

The Updates Logger provides all data updates to the registered synopses by intercepting data updates information in the data sources.

The Workload Manager captures, maintains and analyzes workload information for building, maintaining and testing synopses.

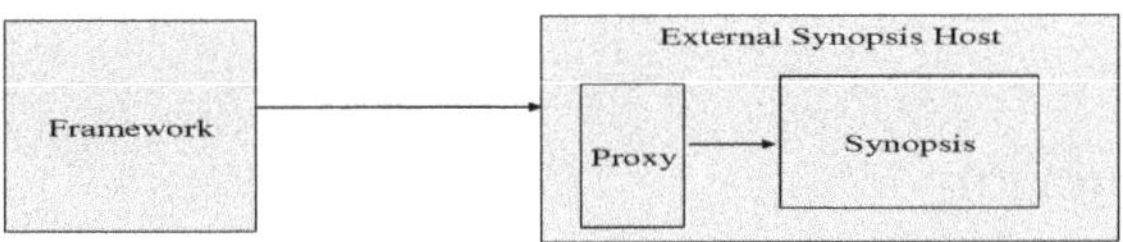

Fig. 2. Synopses Integration

Figure 2 depicts the integration process of a remote synopsis within the framework. The External Synopsis host is responsible for all communication with the system and is transparent to the synopsis. This design enables an unconstraint deployment. A remote synopsis can be integrated into the system by deploying or adapting such host into the remote system, and connecting the synopsis module locally into the host.

The system was tested by having groups of graduate and under-graduate students implement remote synopses as part of their projects, and have these synopses connect to the core system using the simple interfaces. The implemented state of the art synopses include different histograms, sketches, wavelet-synopses, etc.

We now encourage other research groups connect their synopses to the τ-Synopses system. This would allow access to a wide variety of different datasources and workloads, and a fair comparison with other synopses with little effort.

AFFIC: A Foundation for Index Comparisons

Robert Widhopf

FORWISS, Boltzmannstraße 3, D-85747 Garching b. München, Germany
widhopf@in.tum.de

Abstract. Comparing indexes (UB-Tree, R*-Tree, etc.) on a structural and theoretical level provides upper bounds for their worst-case performance, but it does not reflect the performance in real world applications. Measuring just query executions times is not fair either, but differences may be caused just by bad implementations. Thus, a fair comparison has to take into account the algorithms, their implementation, real world data, data management and queries and I/O behavior as well as run time.
Therefore, we need to take care that the implementations of indexes rely on a common foundation and differ just where there are conceptual differences. Furthermore, the foundation should be simple and flexible in order to allow adding new indexes easily while providing full control to all relevant parts. In our demo we present a small and flexible C++ library fulfilling these requirements. We expect to release this library in 2004 and thus provide a UB-Tree implementation to the database community useful for further research.

1 Introduction

Our decision to create a new library was driven by the following reasons:

- Implementing variations [7] of the UB-Tree required full access to the index part of the underlying B-Tree and the buffer manager, but the original prototype of the UB-Tree [10] was built on top of a RDBMS and thus could not provide direct access to them.
- The UB-Tree of Transbase Hypercube (the kernel integration [13]) is restricted by commercial laws and its code is huge and complex.
- For a fair comparisons of the UB-Tree with other indexes (e.g., R*-Tree) a common foundation is required ensuring that only index specific code differs.

Before considering an implementation from scratch we had been inspecting the following existing projects as a starting point for the new UB-Tree implementation: **Commercial DBMSs:** Function-Based B-Trees, Interfaces to extent indexes and **Free DBMS and Code:** GiST, Shore, Predator, PostgreSQL, java.XXL. However, all of them have severe drawbacks and thus we decided to start from scratch and built a new implementation satisfying just our requirements while remaining small and easy to maintain. In the following we discuss the drawbacks of the existing code bases and why they were no option for us.

E. Bertino et al. (Eds.): EDBT 2004, LNCS 2992, pp. 868–871, 2004.
© Springer-Verlag Berlin Heidelberg 2004

Function-Based B-Trees are using a function F to compute the key for tuples. Commercial implementations are: Oracle8i [12], IBM DB2 [6] and MS SQL Server 2000 (computed columns [11]). However, they do not allow for integrating of new split and query algorithms (e.g., UB-Tree range query). Therefore, implementing the UB-Tree with $F =$ Z-value will not lead to the expected performance.

Interfaces to Extent Indexes: Some commercial DBMSs provide enhanced indexing interfaces allowing for arbitrary index structures in external modules: Extensible Indexing API [12] and Datablade API [9]. The user has to provide a set of functions that are used by the database server to access the index either stored inside the database (i.e., mapped to a relation in Oracle) or in external files. However, neglecting the cost of ownership for a commercial DBMS, only non-clustering indexes are supported inside the DBMS and internal kernel code cannot be reused for external files, leading to a significant coding effort for re-implementing required primitives.

The General Search Tree (GiST) approach: GiST [8] provides a single framework for any tree-based index structure with the basic functionality for trees, e.g., insertion, deletion, splitting, search, etc. The individual semantics of the index are provided by the user with a class implementing only some basic functions. The UB-Tree fits into GiST, but an efficient implementation requires more user control for the search algorithm and page splitting as also suggested by [5]. Still, the code does not provide a generic buffer manager, and appropriate tools for managing, inspecting and querying data.

Other Options: Shore [1] has the buffer management we were missing in GiST, but it consists of too much source code. For similar reasons we voted against an integration in PostgreSQL [3], Predator [4] or XXL [2] as these systems were providing functionality (e.g., locking, SQL interface, Client/Server architecture) not relevant for our goal of comparing indexes, but they all have a huge code base, which is too complex to maintain and adapt.

2 Architecture

Based on our observations discussed in the previous section, we decided to implement a new library, being extensible for new indexes while being simple and providing full control on all relevant aspects. It provides a page based buffer manager, relational primitives and indexes as well as query operators.

We implemented basic fixed size data-types (int, float, string), relational primitives (tuple, attribute, relation), a buffer manager for fixed size pages, indexes (heap, B-Tree, UB-Tree, BUB-Tree, UB-Tree with Hilbert-address calculation, R*-Tree, etc.) and query operators (point, range, tree structure, nearest neighbor, skyline, etc.)

Additionally, there are applications for creating databases, loading (bulk and random insertion), inspecting the database/index structure, query processing, data and index visualization. Measurement points are available to track every aspect, i.e., besides time measures there are page counter (physical, logical, du-

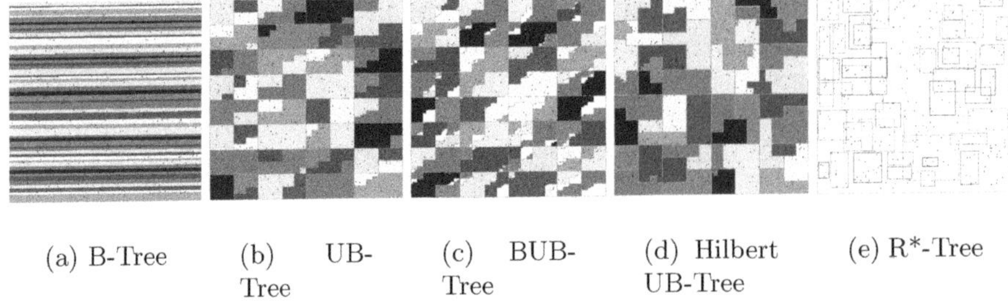

(a) B-Tree (b) UB-Tree (c) BUB-Tree (d) Hilbert UB-Tree (e) R*-Tree

Fig. 1. Partitioning of a two dimensional universe for different indexes

plicates), key comparisons counter and buffer manager statistics. Sophisticated logging and debugging code allows to exactly track runtime behavior.

3 Outline of Demonstration

The demonstration will cover the following topics:

- Code inspection and discussion: In order to gain an overview for the amount of code necessary to implement different indexes and see their complexity we will show and discuss chosen code sections. The R*-Tree code will be inspected as well as B-Tree based indexes like the UB-Tree and BUB-Tree.
- An online comparison of indexes with artificial as well as real world data (data warehousing and GIS data) will be performed for:
  - maintenance operations: bulk loading, random insertion, ...
  - query processing
- Data and index structures will be visualized, e.g., the space partitioning of different indexes for two dimensional uniform distributed data is depicted in Figure 1.

References

1. Shore - a high-performance, scalable, persistent object repository (version 2.0). http://www.cs.wisc.edu/shore/, 2000.
2. java.xxl: extensible and flexible library. http://dbs.mathematik.uni-marburg.de/research/projects/xxl/, 2003.
3. Postgresql version 7.3.4. http://www.postgresql.org/, 2003.
4. Predator - enhanced data type object-relational dbms. http://www.distlab.dk/predator, 2003.
5. Paul M. Aoki. Generalizing "search" in generalized search trees (extended abstract). In *Proc. ICDE*, pages 380–389. IEEE Computer Society, 1998.
6. Weidong Chen et al. High level indexing of user-defined types. in *Proc. VLDB*, pages 554–564. Morgan Kaufmann, 1999.
7. Robert Fenk. The BUB-Tree. In *Proc. VLDB*, 2002. Postersession.
8. Joseph M. Hellerstein et al. Generalized search trees for database systems. In *Proc. VLDB*, pages 562–573. Morgan Kaufmann, 1995.

9. *Informix Dynamic Server with Universal Data Option, Documentation.* 1999.
10. Volker Markl. *Processing Relational Queries using a Multidimensional Access Technique.* PhD thesis, DISDBIS, Band 59, Infix Verlag, 1999.
11. Microsoft. *SQL Server Books Online, Microsoft Foundation.* 2000.
12. Oracle. *Oracle 8i Utilities / Documentation.* 1999.
13. Frank Ramsak, Volker Markl, Robert Fenk, Martin Zirkel, Klaus Elhard, and Rudolf Bayer. Integrating the UB-Tree into a Database System Kernel. In *Proc. VLDB*, 2000.

Spatial Data Server for Mobile Environment

Byoung-Woo Oh, Min-Soo Kim, Mi-Jeong Kim, and Eun-Kyu Lee

Telematics Research Division, Electronics Telecommunication Research Institute,
161 Gajeong-dong, Yuseong-gu, Daejeon, 305-350 South Korea
{bwoh,minsoo,kmj63341,ekyulee}@etri.re.kr

Abstract. In this paper we present a spatial data server which provides not only interoperability but also rapid response for mobile environment with efficient ways, such as use of main memory to eliminate access time from disk on request, management of target data (i.e., GML) in the main memory to eliminate conversion time, spatial index to reduce search time, progressive transmission of spatial data to reduce response time, etc.

1 Introduction

Recently, advances in hardware and communication technology make mobile computing feasible. It is possible to use portable devices at any place with the state of the art mobile computing technology. Because almost mobile applications on the portable devices deal with the user's location, manipulation of spatial data gains importance in mobile environment. Usually in mobile environment, wireless communication is used to access spatial data concerned with the user's location. However, wireless communication is generally slow and expensive. Furthermore, low performance of mobile device requires dedicated spatial data server for mobile environment.

We propose a spatial data server for mobile environment with interoperability and efficient performance. In order to provide interoperability and reusability for the spatial data, we adopt the implementation specifications of Open GIS Consortium, such as Simple Features Specification (SFS) for OLE/COM, Web Feature Service (WFS) Implementation Specification, and Geography Markup Language (GML) Implementation Specification [2, 3, 4]. The SFS is used for access database from disk without consideration of its specific storage format. The WFS provides operations to obtain not only spatial data but also metadata about them. The GML is used for encoding spatial data for the response of the WFS. The target GML data is stored in memory to eliminate disk access time and conversion time.

2 Architecture

Figure 1 shows the architecture of the spatial data server for mobile environment.

E. Bertino et al. (Eds.): EDBT 2004, LNCS 2992, pp. 872–874, 2004.
© Springer-Verlag Berlin Heidelberg 2004

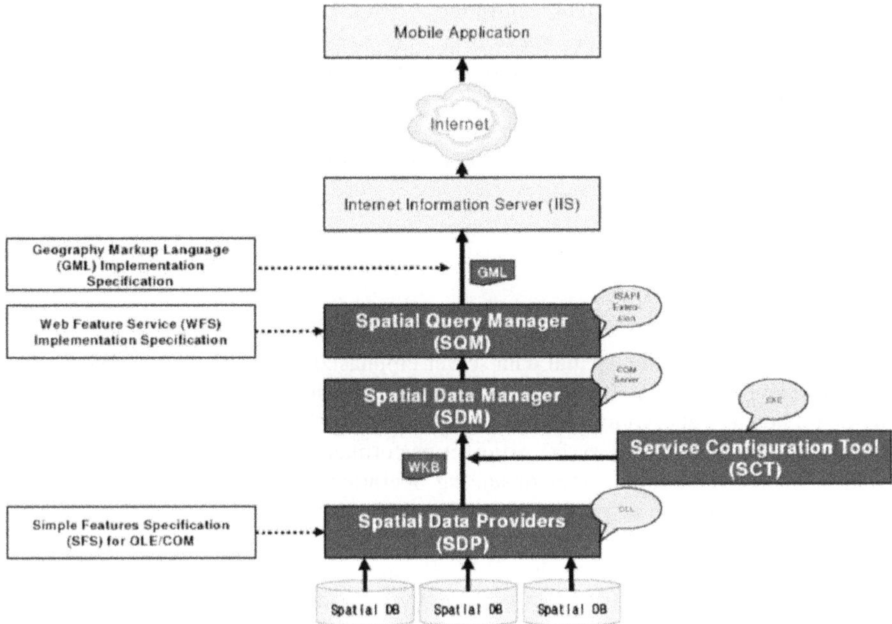

Fig. 1. The architecture of the spatial data server for mobile environment comprises four managers; spatial data provider, spatial data manager, service configuration tool, and spatial query manager. It uses the Microsoft Internet Information Server (IIS) as a web server.

Spatial Data Provider (SDP). Any kinds of spatial databases that have data providers conform to the standard of the simple feature specification for OLE/COM [2] can be used as data sources.

Service Configuration Tool (SCT). The SCT is an executable file who invokes the spatial data management component at the beginning, reads spatial data to be serviced through the SDP from databases or files, and loads them to the allocated main memory using the spatial data management component. An administrator can select SDP and spatial data set which will be served. The SCT can be used to show status and log information of the server.

Spatial Data Management component (SDM). The SDM manages spatial data from the SCT in the main memory and fetches spatial data corresponding to user's query with MBR and a list of type names. The management of spatial data in the main memory gives rapid response by reducing access time from database in disk for each request. The format of spatial data in memory is GML as target data format for reducing conversion time for each request. The spatial data management component is an out-of-process COM server to be shared with other processes, such as the SCT and the SQM. The R*-tree as a spatial index structure is implemented to support efficient access for spatial data.

Spatial Query Management component (SQM). The SQM adopts the WFS specification [3] and invokes methods of the SDM to fetch spatial data. It is an Internet Server Application Programming Interface (ISAPI) extension component which guarantees more efficient service than CGI approach though many clients request the service at the same time. It minimizes overload of the server and enables rapid service without replication of process. The SQM provides basic WFS operations, such as GetCapabilities, DescribeFeatureType, and GetFeature.

3 Demonstration

We will demonstrate the spatial data server emphasizing its advantages. We focus on management of main memory, progressive transmission of spatial data, and compression and encryption. Following are some highlights of the demonstration.

We exploit main memory for efficient performance to manage spatial data which can be served. It reduces time-consuming operations such as reading database from disk, conversion from a specific storage format of spatial data to well-known-binary (WKB) in data provider component for unified access among different formats, and conversion from the WKB to the GML. Because the cost of the main memory has been decreased gradually, content providers who want to support rapid response may willingly increase the main memory for better services. We support up to 64 Gigabytes of physical main memory. The physical main memory supported by the MS-Windows' kernel guarantees that it is never swapped to the disk by operating system for context switching.

The spatial data server processes user request to access spatial data in web environment. We extend it to support progressive transmission for rapid response. The goal of progressive transmission is to reduce latency time by representing only received spatial data. Once, the client draw already transmitted geometry data, the client should merge remainder part of geometry to the previous data and redraw periodically. The progressive transmission is useful when a user request spatial data with mobile device through expensive wireless communications.

The spatial data server supports compression and encryption for efficiency of transmission and security, respectively. The compression is developed using public gzip library The encryption and decryption uses Crypto API which is provided by MS-Windows' kernel for both server and mobile client.

References

1. Oh, B.W., Lee, S.Y., Kim, M.S., and Yang, Y.K.: Spatial Applications Using 4S Technology for Mobile Environment, Proc. of IGARSS 2002 IEEE Int. (2002)
2. Open GIS Consortium: OpenGIS Simple Features Specification for OLE/COM, OGC (1999)
3. Panagiotis A. Vretanos: Web Feature Service Implementation Specification, OGC (2002)
4. Simon Cox, Paul Daisey, Ron Lake, Clemens Portele and Arliss Whiteside: OpenGIS Geography Markup Language Implementation Specification, version 3.0.0, OGC (2003)

Author Index

Lecture Notes in Computer Science

For information about Vols. 1–2846

please contact your bookseller or Springer-Verlag

Vol. 2992: E. Bertino, S. Christodoulakis, D. Plexousakis, V. Christophides, M. Koubarakis, K. Böhm, E. Ferrari (Eds.), Advances in Database Technology - EDBT 2004. XVIII, 877 pages. 2004.

Vol. 2973: Y. Lee, J. Li, K.-Y. Whang, D. Lee (Eds.), Database Systems for Advanced Applications. XXIV, 925 pages. 2004.

Vol. 2970: F. Fernández Rivera, M. Bubak, A. Gómez Tato, R. Doallo (Eds.), Grid Computing. XI, 328 pages. 2004.

Vol. 2964: T. Okamoto (Ed.), Topics in Cryptology – CT-RSA 2004. XI, 387 pages. 2004.

Vol. 2962: S. Bistarelli, Semirings for Soft Constraint Solving and Programming. XII, 279 pages. 2004.

Vol. 2961: P. Eklund (Ed.), Concept Lattices. IX, 411 pages. 2004. (Subseries LNAI).

Vol. 2957: P. Langendoerfer, M. Liu, I. Matta, V. Tsaoussidis (Eds.), Wired/Wireless Internet Communications. XI, 307 pages. 2004.

Vol. 2954: F. Crestani, M. Dunlop, S. Mizzaro (Eds.), Mobile and Ubiquitous Information Access. X, 299 pages. 2004.

Vol. 2953: K. Konrad, Model Generation for Natural Language Interpretation and Analysis. XIII, 166 pages. 2004. (Subseries LNAI).

Vol. 2952: N. Guelfi, E. Astesiano, G. Reggio (Eds.), Scientific Engineering of Distributed Java Applications. X, 157 pages. 2004.

Vol. 2951: M. Naor (Ed.), Theory of Cryptography. XI, 523 pages. 2004.

Vol. 2949: R. De Nicola, G. Ferrari, G. Meredith (Eds.), Coordination Models and Languages. X, 323 pages. 2004.

Vol. 2947: F. Bao, R. Deng, J. Zhou (Eds.), Public Key Cryptography – PKC 2004. XI, 455 pages. 2004.

Vol. 2946: R. Focardi, R. Gorrieri (Eds.), Foundations of Security Analysis and Design II. VII, 267 pages. 2004.

Vol. 2943: J. Chen, J. Reif (Eds.), DNA Computing. X, 225 pages. 2004.

Vol. 2941: M. Wirsing, A. Knapp, S. Balsamo (Eds.), Radical Innovations of Software and Systems Engineering in the Future. X, 359 pages. 2004.

Vol. 2940: C. Lucena, A. Garcia, A. Romanovsky, J. Castro, P.S. Alencar (Eds.), Software Engineering for Multi-Agent Systems II. XII, 279 pages. 2004.

Vol. 2939: T. Kalker, I. Cox, Y.M. Ro (Eds.), Digital Watermarking. XII, 602 pages. 2004.

Vol. 2937: B. Steffen, G. Levi (Eds.), Verification, Model Checking, and Abstract Interpretation. XI, 325 pages. 2004.

Vol. 2934: G. Lindemann, D. Moldt, M. Paolucci (Eds.), Regulated Agent-Based Social Systems. X, 301 pages. 2004. (Subseries LNAI).

Vol. 2930: F. Winkler (Ed.), Automated Deduction in Geometry. VII, 231 pages. 2004. (Subseries LNAI).

Vol. 2923: V. Lifschitz, I. Niemelä (Eds.), Logic Programming and Nonmonotonic Reasoning. IX, 365 pages. 2004. (Subseries LNAI).

Vol. 2917: E. Quintarelli, Model-Checking Based Data Retrieval. XVI, 134 pages. 2004.

Vol. 2916: C. Palamidessi (Ed.), Logic Programming. XII, 520 pages. 2003.

Vol. 2915: A. Camurri, G. Volpe (Eds.), Gesture and Sign Languages in Human-Computer Interaction. XIII, 558 pages. 2004. (Subseries LNAI).

Vol. 2914: P.K. Pandya, J. Radhakrishnan (Eds.), FST TCS 2003: Foundations of Software Technology and Theoretical Computer Science. XIII, 446 pages. 2003.

Vol. 2913: T.M. Pinkston, V.K. Prasanna (Eds.), High Performance Computing - HiPC 2003. XX, 512 pages. 2003. (Subseries LNAI).

Vol. 2911: T.M.T. Sembok, H.B. Zaman, H. Chen, S.R. Urs, S.H. Myaeng (Eds.), Digital Libraries: Technology and Management of Indigenous Knowledge for Global Access. XX, 703 pages. 2003.

Vol. 2910: M.E. Orlowska, S. Weerawarana, M.M.P. Papazoglou, J. Yang (Eds.), Service-Oriented Computing - ICSOC 2003. XIV, 576 pages. 2003.

Vol. 2909: K. Jansen, R. Solis-Oba (Eds.), Approximation and Online Algorithms. VIII, 269 pages. 2004.

Vol. 2909: R. Solis-Oba, K. Jansen (Eds.), Approximation and Online Algorithms. VIII, 269 pages. 2004.

Vol. 2908: K. Chae, M. Yung (Eds.), Information Security Applications. XII, 506 pages. 2004.

Vol. 2907: I. Lirkov, S. Margenov, J. Wasniewski, P. Yalamov (Eds.), Large-Scale Scientific Computing. XI, 490 pages. 2004.

Vol. 2906: T. Ibaraki, N. Katoh, H. Ono (Eds.), Algorithms and Computation. XVII, 748 pages. 2003.

Vol. 2905: A. Sanfeliu, J. Ruiz-Shulcloper (Eds.), Progress in Pattern Recognition, Speech and Image Analysis. XVII, 693 pages. 2003.

Vol. 2904: T. Johansson, S. Maitra (Eds.), Progress in Cryptology - INDOCRYPT 2003. XI, 431 pages. 2003.

Vol. 2903: T.D. Gedeon, L.C.C. Fung (Eds.), AI 2003: Advances in Artificial Intelligence. XVI, 1075 pages. 2003. (Subseries LNAI).

Vol. 2902: F.M. Pires, S.P. Abreu (Eds.), Progress in Artificial Intelligence. XV, 504 pages. 2003. (Subseries LNAI).

Vol. 2901: F. Bry, N. Henze, J. Ma luszyński (Eds.), Principles and Practice of Semantic Web Reasoning. X, 209 pages. 2003.

Vol. 2900: M. Bidoit, P.D. Mosses (Eds.), Casl User Manual. XIII, 240 pages. 2004.

Vol. 2899: G. Ventre, R. Canonico (Eds.), Interactive Multimedia on Next Generation Networks. XIV, 420 pages. 2003.

Vol. 2898: K.G. Paterson (Ed.), Cryptography and Coding. IX, 385 pages. 2003.

Vol. 2897: O. Balet, G. Subsol, P. Torguet (Eds.), Virtual Storytelling. XI, 240 pages. 2003.

Vol. 2896: V.A. Saraswat (Ed.), Advances in Computing Science – ASIAN 2003. VIII, 305 pages. 2003.

Vol. 2895: A. Ohori (Ed.), Programming Languages and Systems. XIII, 427 pages. 2003.

Vol. 2894: C.S. Laih (Ed.), Advances in Cryptology - ASIACRYPT 2003. XIII, 543 pages. 2003.

Vol. 2893: J.-B. Stefani, I. Demeure, D. Hagimont (Eds.), Distributed Applications and Interoperable Systems. XIII, 311 pages. 2003.

Vol. 2892: F. Dau, The Logic System of Concept Graphs with Negation. XI, 213 pages. 2003. (Subseries LNAI).

Vol. 2891: J. Lee, M. Barley (Eds.), Intelligent Agents and Multi-Agent Systems. X, 215 pages. 2003. (Subseries LNAI).

Vol. 2890: M. Broy, A.V. Zamulin (Eds.), Perspectives of System Informatics. XV, 572 pages. 2003.

Vol. 2889: R. Meersman, Z. Tari (Eds.), On The Move to Meaningful Internet Systems 2003: OTM 2003 Workshops. XIX, 1071 pages. 2003.

Vol. 2888: R. Meersman, Z. Tari, D.C. Schmidt (Eds.), On The Move to Meaningful Internet Systems 2003: CoopIS, DOA, and ODBASE. XXI, 1546 pages. 2003.

Vol. 2887: T. Johansson (Ed.), Fast Software Encryption. IX, 397 pages. 2003.

Vol. 2886: I. Nyström, G. Sanniti di Baja, S. Svensson (Eds.), Discrete Geometry for Computer Imagery. XII, 556 pages. 2003.

Vol. 2885: J.S. Dong, J. Woodcock (Eds.), Formal Methods and Software Engineering. XI, 683 pages. 2003.

Vol. 2884: E. Najm, U. Nestmann, P. Stevens (Eds.), Formal Methods for Open Object-Based Distributed Systems. X, 293 pages. 2003.

Vol. 2883: J. Schaeffer, M. Müller, Y. Björnsson (Eds.), Computers and Games. XI, 431 pages. 2003.

Vol. 2882: D. Veit, Matchmaking in Electronic Markets. XV, 180 pages. 2003. (Subseries LNAI).

Vol. 2881: E. Horlait, T. Magedanz, R.H. Glitho (Eds.), Mobile Agents for Telecommunication Applications. IX, 297 pages. 2003.

Vol. 2880: H.L. Bodlaender (Ed.), Graph-Theoretic Concepts in Computer Science. XI, 386 pages. 2003.

Vol. 2879: R.E. Ellis, T.M. Peters (Eds.), Medical Image Computing and Computer-Assisted Intervention - MICCAI 2003. XXXIV, 1003 pages. 2003.

Vol. 2878: R.E. Ellis, T.M. Peters (Eds.), Medical Image Computing and Computer-Assisted Intervention - MICCAI 2003. XXXIII, 819 pages. 2003.

Vol. 2877: T. Böhme, G. Heyer, H. Unger (Eds.), Innovative Internet Community Systems. VIII, 263 pages. 2003.

Vol. 2876: M. Schroeder, G. Wagner (Eds.), Rules and Rule Markup Languages for the Semantic Web. VII, 173 pages. 2003.

Vol. 2875: E. Aarts, R. Collier, E.v. Loenen, B.d. Ruyter (Eds.), Ambient Intelligence. XI, 432 pages. 2003.

Vol. 2874: C. Priami (Ed.), Global Computing. XIX, 255 pages. 2003.

Vol. 2871: N. Zhong, Z.W. Raś, S. Tsumoto, E. Suzuki (Eds.), Foundations of Intelligent Systems. XV, 697 pages. 2003. (Subseries LNAI).

Vol. 2870: D. Fensel, K.P. Sycara, J. Mylopoulos (Eds.), The Semantic Web - ISWC 2003. XV, 931 pages. 2003.

Vol. 2869: A. Yazici, C. Şener (Eds.), Computer and Information Sciences - ISCIS 2003. XIX, 1110 pages. 2003.

Vol. 2868: P. Perner, R. Brause, H.-G. Holzhütter (Eds.), Medical Data Analysis. VIII, 127 pages. 2003.

Vol. 2866: J. Akiyama, M. Kano (Eds.), Discrete and Computational Geometry. VIII, 285 pages. 2003.

Vol. 2865: S. Pierre, M. Barbeau, E. Kranakis (Eds.), Ad-Hoc, Mobile, and Wireless Networks. X, 293 pages. 2003.

Vol. 2864: A.K. Dey, A. Schmidt, J.F. McCarthy (Eds.), UbiComp 2003: Ubiquitous Computing. XVII, 368 pages. 2003.

Vol. 2863: P. Stevens, J. Whittle, G. Booch (Eds.), "UML" 2003 - The Unified Modeling Language. XIV, 415 pages. 2003.

Vol. 2860: D. Geist, E. Tronci (Eds.), Correct Hardware Design and Verification Methods. XII, 426 pages. 2003.

Vol. 2859: B. Apolloni, M. Marinaro, R. Tagliaferri (Eds.), Neural Nets. X, 376 pages. 2003.

Vol. 2857: M.A. Nascimento, E.S. de Moura, A.L. Oliveira (Eds.), String Processing and Information Retrieval. XI, 379 pages. 2003.

Vol. 2856: M. Smirnov (Ed.), Quality of Future Internet Services. IX, 293 pages. 2003.

Vol. 2855: R. Alur, I. Lee (Eds.), Embedded Software. X, 373 pages. 2003.

Vol. 2854: J. Hoffmann, Utilizing Problem Structure in Planing. XIII, 251 pages. 2003. (Subseries LNAI).

Vol. 2853: M. Jeckle, L.-J. Zhang (Eds.), Web Services - ICWS-Europe 2003. VIII, 227 pages. 2003.

Vol. 2852: F.S. de Boer, M.M. Bonsangue, S. Graf, W.-P. de Roever (Eds.), Formal Methods for Components and Objects. VIII, 509 pages. 2003.

Vol. 2851: C. Boyd, W. Mao (Eds.), Information Security. XI, 453 pages. 2003.

Vol. 2849: N. García, L. Salgado, J.M. Martínez (Eds.), Visual Content Processing and Representation. XII, 352 pages. 2003.

Vol. 2848: F.E. Fich (Ed.), Distributed Computing. X, 367 pages. 2003.

Vol. 2847: R.d. Lemos, T.S. Weber, J.B. Camargo Jr. (Eds.), Dependable Computing. XIV, 371 pages. 2003.

GPSR Compliance
The European Union's (EU) General Product Safety Regulation (GPSR) is a set of rules that requires consumer products to be safe and our obligations to ensure this.

If you have any concerns about our products, you can contact us on

ProductSafety@springernature.com

In case Publisher is established outside the EU, the EU authorized representative is:

Springer Nature Customer Service Center GmbH
Europaplatz 3
69115 Heidelberg, Germany

www.ingramcontent.com/pod-product-compliance
Ingram Content Group UK Ltd.
Pitfield, Milton Keynes, MK11 3LW, UK
UKHW021903190726
13853UKWH00003B/1397

* 9 7 8 3 6 6 2 1 8 0 5 1 8 *